The
Harper Dictionary
of Modern Thought

The
Harper Dictionary
of Modern Thought

New and Revised Edition

edited by
ALAN BULLOCK
and
STEPHEN TROMBLEY
assisted by
BRUCE EADIE

1817

HARPER & ROW, PUBLISHERS, New York
Cambridge, Philadelphia, San Francisco, Washington
London,

This book is published in England under the title *The Fontana Dictionary of Modern Thought*.

Library of Congress Cataloging-in-Publication Data

The Harper dictionary of modern thought.

1. Encyclopedias and dictionaries. I. Bullock,
Allan, 1914—   . II. Stallybrass, Oliver.
III. Trombley, Stephen. IV. Title: Dictionary of
modern thought.
AG5.H19 1988   031   87-45604
ISBN 0-06-015869-7

88 89 90 91 92 HC 10 9 8 7 6 5 4 3 2 1

In memory of
Oliver Stallybrass

Preface

When the first edition of this book was published in 1977, Oliver Stallybrass and I wrote in the original preface:

'The idea of a dictionary of modern thought springs from the recognition of two facts. The first is that all of us are ignorant of whole areas of modern thought. In an age of specialization this may be as true of a Nobel Laureate as it is of a college freshman – a point driven home in a letter written to one of the editors by one of the Nobel Laureate contributors to this volume, Sir Peter Medawar: "I am looking forward immensely to the publication of the Dictionary, because there are a whole lot of things I should like to look up myself." The second fact is that most of us never quite give up the attempt, however sporadic, to explore our areas of ignorance. But as soon as we venture outside our own territory we encounter a formidable barrier of language, of unfamiliar terms and concepts and of unexplained allusions that puzzle and frustrate us.

'Where do we go for help? An ordinary dictionary helps a little, but its definitions are necessarily brief and formal, and make no attempt to set the words defined in their intellectual, historical, or cultural context. Also, an ordinary dictionary has to be comprehensive in its coverage, and must therefore include thousands of words familiar to us all. If, on the other hand, we turn to an encyclopedia – which for most of us will mean a visit to the library – we may need to thread our way through a vast amount of irrelevant material. The present volume steers a middle course between an ordinary dictionary and an encyclopedia. It takes key terms from across the whole range of modern thought, sets them within their context and offers short explanatory accounts (anything from ten to a thousand words) written by experts, but in language as simple as can be used without *over*-simplification or distortion. All this is done within a single pair of covers; but the reader who wishes to pursue an enquiry further is enabled to do so, not only by numerous cross-references, but by the carefully selected reading-lists which have been provided in appropriate cases.'

We then discussed two questions. To the first, What is meant by 'Modern'?, we replied: in broad terms, 'twentieth-century', and in the introduction which follows, Stephen Trombley and I elaborate this further.

To the second question, What, in the context of this book, is meant by 'thought'?, Oliver Stallybrass and I replied:

'If "modern" is used in a flexible sense, so, or even more so, is "thought". Does a painter or a composer or a poet "think"? T. S. Eliot's phrase "felt thought" suggests one answer; the same author's DISSOCIATION OF SENSIBILITY suggests another. But, whether or not the artist thinks as he practises his art, he, or more probably the art critic, unquestionably does so the moment either of them starts theorizing about it. Hence the scope of this dictionary includes literature, music and the visual arts as well as, more obviously, PHILOSOPHY, RELIGION, MATHEMATICS, PSYCHOLOGY, and the whole range of HUMANITIES, SOCIAL SCIENCES and NATURAL SCIENCES, together with those aspects of TECHNOLOGY which are of wide general interest. Included, moreover, are terms with a wide variety of relationships to thought: not only IDEAS, CONCEPTS, schools and tools of thought, but – for example – events and phenomena which have *influenced* people's thoughts, inventions which are the *product* of thought (and may in turn affect our thinking), and even terms which might well be regarded as symptoms of *anti-* or *counter*-thought, but which are, for better or worse, part of the intellectual climate of our age.'

The idea for such a dictionary first occurred to me when I was on holiday in Portugal and was reading an article in the *Times Literary Supplement* on anthropology. I came across the word HERMENEUTICS and was irritated to discover that I was uncertain what it meant. This led me on to think how many words there are which are first used in a specialized field of scholarship or science and then come into general usage without many of those who meet them, or even use them, having a clear idea of what they mean. Before I finished my holiday I had made a list of between two and three hundred such words and was convinced there were a lot more. I sent the list and an outline of what I had in mind to my literary agent, Andrew Best, of Curtis Brown Ltd., who fastened on to the idea and found me, first, publishers, and then a partner. I could not have been more fortunate. In Oliver Stallybrass I found the ideal collaborator, with an extraordinary range of interests and of out-of-the-way knowledge; and in Andrew Best, and Helen Fraser and Simon King of Collins/ Fontana, and in Hugh Van Dusen of Harper & Row, friends whose continued interest in the project enabled us to overcome all the difficulties in the way.

The problem, of course, was what to put in and what to leave out. Oliver Stallybrass and I began by scouring every dictionary and encyclopedia, both general and specialized, that we could lay hands on. We then produced lists of terms covering some twenty main areas of 'thought', and submitted these for criticism and suggestions to a small group of distinguished consultants: Sir Isaiah Berlin, Sir Peter Medawar, Professors Daniel Bell, Jerome Bruner and John Ziman, and Mr John Willett. Professors Wilfred Beckerman, Leo Labedz and Robert Lekachman played a similar role a little later. The consultants' help was invaluable not only in establishing the scale of the dictionary and the level of explanation at which we should aim, but also in suggesting contributors. As these were recruited, so the network of consultation grew and the lists were submitted to further extensive discussion. By the time we had finished, the total number of entries had grown to nearly 4,000 and the list of contributors (including several of our own consultants) to 138. We had also added bibliographical references to many of the entries to enable users of the dictionary to follow up an inquiry by further reading.

Quite the hardest task was to keep the dictionary within bounds so that it could be published as a single volume and at a price which would attract the 'common reader' so highly regarded by that great lexicographer, Samuel Johnson. We had to accept two restrictions. For practical reasons, and because we had European and American readers principally in mind, we limited ourselves to modern western thought, except for a handful of entries on the major religions of the world and on systems such as MAOISM or ZEN which had become part of the western cultural scene.

The other restriction was the need to abandon our original intention of including entries not only on the key terms but also on the key figures of modern thought, from Marx and Freud, down to Keynes and Lévi-Strauss. Very reluctantly we had to confine ourselves to making cross-references from individual names to the various headings (such as MARXISM and FREUDIAN) under which they were mentioned. In the new edition, as we explain in the introduction, this feature has been dropped since the *Fontana Dictionary of Modern Thought* now has a biographical companion, *The Fontana Dictionary of Modern Thinkers* (edited by R. B. Woodings and myself) in which we have been able to carry out our original plan in full.

The favourable reception which the dictionary has had, the number of impressions which have been called for, and the fact that there is no other work which seeks to cover, however selectively, the whole range of modern thought, have led us to undertake the full-scale revision which is necessary if it is to be kept up to date. We suffered a tragic loss in the death of Oliver Stallybrass, to whose memory this new edition is dedicated. I have been very fortunate in finding in Stephen Trombley a collaborator who brings special qualities of his own to the work of revision. I have particularly enjoyed the fact that he and I represent the points of view of two widely separated generations. I am sure that the new edition of the dictionary has gained immeasurably from Stephen Trombley's acute sensitivity to the changes which have taken place since the original edition was published, and from his ability to recruit a team of younger consultants and contributors who have been able not only to revise it, but to add more than a thousand new entries.

Alan Bullock

Introduction

'Modern' is a curious term in that it is always receding into the past as we move forward into a future where 'contemporary' ideas become not just pasts, but 'posts' – POSTMODERNISM, POST-INDUSTRIAL SOCIETY, etc. Perhaps one way of qualifying the term 'modern' as used in the title of this book is that it refers to ideas, movements, theories and events which have an impact on today's thought, or which are important to an understanding of it. Hence, Heisenberg's UNCERTAINTY PRINCIPLE, though discovered in 1927, is modern. So, too, is DARWINISM, despite the Victorian birth of the *Origin of Species*.

The first edition contained nearly 4,000 entries. The initial task in revising was to see how many entries could be deleted. To the editors' surprise, something like 80 per cent of the entries had stood the test of time, though more than half required revision. Many have been entirely rewritten.

The task of deciding on new entries to be included posed greater difficulties. The requirement that this should remain an easily used, one-volume work meant that we had to be fairly rigorous in the acceptance or rejection of new terms across all areas of knowledge – a sometimes difficult task when one is blessed with the services of 93 new contributors in addition to the 138 contributors to the first edition. In the event, more than a thousand new entries have been commissioned.

The consultant editors to the new edition gave much thought to the problem of which new entries should be included and which old ones deleted or revised. We owe a debt of thanks to Peter Newmark and Philip Campbell, who advised over a wide range of subjects in the sciences; Anna Grimshaw (ANTHROPOLOGY and women's studies); Krishan Kumar (SOCIOLOGY); Hugh L'Etang (medicine); John Pierson (ECONOMICS); Roger Poole (PHILOSOPHY and critical theories); Roy Porter (history of science); and Steve Reilly (contemporary politics and HISTORY).

The area which, predictably, includes the largest number of new entries is that of contemporary history and politics. Since the first edition, we have entered the eras of THATCHERISM and REAGANISM. We are living through EL SALVADOR, AFGHANISTAN, LEBANON, STAR WARS, and a hundred other future-shaping events. Similarly, economics has been extensively revised in face of the rise of MONETARISM, the growth of mass unemployment and the deregulation of financial institutions.

In the SOCIAL SCIENCES, ANTHROPOLOGY has been revised and expanded to include many important theoretical developments which have occurred over the past fifteen years. In PSYCHO-ANALYSIS and related disciplines, there has been radical revision to take account of the work of Lacan and others.

A significant element of the new edition is the inclusion of many new entries in medicine. In the sciences, particularly in the fields of PHYSICS and BIOLOGY, the book reflects the accelerating pace of revision and discovery in those subjects. In philosophy, a number of entries have been added to pay greater attention to the 'Continental' tradition of thought from Husserl to Derrida. Finally, in the arts, several new areas have been included, especially in contemporary music, dance and architecture where the new entries reflect the proliferation of styles and debates which has marked the last five years in Europe and the United States.

In academic work one often discovers the principles (intuitive impulses might be a better word) of organization and selection after the bulk of a work has been completed, and this work belongs to that noble tradition. A colleague asked, when the second edition was being prepared for press, 'How can you possibly decide what to include or exclude?' Dr Johnson, maker of one of the great dictionaries in the language, was offered as a mentor. His book was characterized by what might be called enlightened prejudice – the world as seen through the eyes of its learned, irascible and rather formidable author. The editors make no claim to Johnsonian greatness. What is offered here is a peculiar variation on the theme of enlightened prejudice in which hundreds of contributors, each of them properly qualified to write in a particular area, present a concise account of the subject from their point of view. We have eschewed any attempt to impose a rigid editorial 'point of view'. We have striven to be 'objective'; no one can ever claim to succeed. We have sought to curb our prejudices even when we believe them to be enlightened. The intention has been to represent modern thought as it is, a process – often apparently messy, occasionally paradoxical, very much open to revision. That being said, every contributor has in mind the interests of the non-expert venturing into unfamiliar territory. Where the reader wishes to inquire further, most entries have bibliographies which should put them on the road to further knowledge.

Alan Bullock
Stephen Trombley

Acknowledgements

The editors wish to thank:

Bruce Eadie, who assisted ably and beyond the call of duty in every aspect of the conception, editing and production of the present edition. His industry, wide-ranging competence and diplomatic skills play a very large part in any success this work may claim.

Andrew Best of Curtis Brown, who is responsible for introducing the editors of the first two editions of this book, and who has continued to take a creative and detailed interest in a book which far exceeds the usual scope of a literary agent.

Our publishers, particularly Helen Fraser and Simon King of Fontana/Collins and Hugh Van Dusen of Harper & Row.

Mrs Pamela Thomas for her helpful administrative support.

Our proofreader, Anne Rieley, for her devotion to a difficult task.

Friends and colleagues too numerous to mention whose suggestions have been invaluable.

Our wives for every conceivable encouragement, and particularly for their virtue of patience.

Most importantly, the contributors who have made a large and potentially daunting job pleasurable.

The editors of *Collins English Dictionary* for permission to quote acronyms from the current edition.

How to use this book

The arrangement of this book should be largely self-explanatory, and the best general rule is: follow your nose. Words and phrases should always, in the first place, be sought directly, not under some more comprehensive term; this is a dictionary rather than an encyclopedia. The term sought *may*, of course, prove to be explained under some other heading; if so, there will always be a cross-reference. Thus, a reader wishing to learn the meaning of 'antigen' will find '**antigen,** see under IMMUNITY'.

Alphabetical arrangement. This is on the word-by-word principle – meaning, for example, that all the phrases beginning with 'art' – ART AUTRE, ART BRUT, ART MUSIC, ART NOUVEAU, ART OF THE REAL, ART SACRÉ – precede ARTHROSCOPY, ARTIFICIAL INSEMINATION and ARTIFICIAL INTELLIGENCE (which on the letter-by-letter principle would come immediately before ART MUSIC). *Hyphenated words* are regarded as two words if each constituent can stand on its own (e.g. ALL-OR-NONE LAW precedes ALLELE), but as one word if the first constituent is merely a prefix (e.g. ANTI-NOVEL follows ANTIMONY). *Sets of initials* (see also below under *Full or abbreviated heading*) are treated as if they were words (e.g. ABC ART comes between ABBEY THEATRE and ABDUCTION).

Phrases. These are mostly given under the first word of the phrase, e.g. ABSTRACT EXPRESSIONISM, AGE-AND-AREA HYPOTHESIS, NUCLEAR PHYSICS, STREAM OF CONSCIOUSNESS, THEATRE OF THE ABSURD. In certain cases, however, the phrase has been inverted, either because the important word is not the first (e.g. SCIENCE, SOCIOLOGY OF, *not* SOCIOLOGY OF SCIENCE), or because a number of terms with the same second element are most easily differentiated by being grouped under it (e.g., under WAR, *catalytic war, conventional war, nuclear war,* and other varieties are distinguished. Cross-references have been inserted wherever they seemed likely to be needed.

Full or abbreviated heading. Entries on *organizations* commonly known by their initials (EEC, EFTA, UNO) will be found *under these initials* (see also *Alphabetical arrangement* above) and not under the full name, which in many cases (KGB, MVD) is known only to specialists. The same applies to certain *other sets of initials*

(ABM, ESP), the widespread use of which may send readers to the dictionary precisely to find out what they stand for. Where, however, few readers seem likely to need this information (e.g. that IQ stands for INTELLIGENCE QUOTIENT), or where the use of the abbreviation without prior explanation is mostly confined to professionals addressing other professionals (AI for ARTIFICIAL INTELLIGENCE), the unabbreviated term has been preferred.

Cross-references. Many entries include an explicit suggestion that the reader should 'see' or 'see also' some other entry on a related topic. In addition, an *implicit* suggestion to this effect is made whenever, in the course of an entry, a word, phrase, or set of *unpunctuated'* initials is picked out in SMALL CAPITALS. (By 'unpunctuated we mean that a reference to UNO implies an entry on that subject, a reference to the U.S.A. or the U.S.S.R. does not.)

In many cases, these implied cross-references are to a slightly different form of the capitalized word or phrase. Thus, singulars and plurals are regarded as interchangeable, as are the terminations -ism and -ist: e.g., a reader following up an allusion to 'MARXIST thought' will find an entry, not on MARXIST but on MARXISM. Care has been taken, however, to avoid capitalizing consecutive words which are the subjects of two or more *separate* entries; *not,* therefore '. . . MARXIST ECONOMICS' (since there is no such heading) but '. . . Marxist economics (see MARXISM; ECONOMICS)'. In the last example the cross-reference to ECONOMICS will only have been included if it seems genuinely relevant; and in general we have refrained from capitalizing if the entries in question have no relevance to the context.

List of contributors

A.B.　　　　Albert Bandura, David Starr Jordan Professor of Social Science in Psychology, Stanford University.

A.B.E.　　　Bruce Eadie, freelance writer.

A.C.　　　　Sir Alec Cairncross, F.B.A., formerly Master of St Peter's College, Oxford; Economic Adviser to the British Government.

A.CL.　　　Angus Clarke, Research Associate in Human Genetics, University of Newcastle upon Tyne.

A.C.G.　　　A. C. Grayling, Lecturer in Philosophy, King's College, University of London.

A.D.M.　　　A. D. Mendelow, Reader and Honorary Consultant Neurosurgeon, Newcastle General Hospital.

A.E.B.　　　A. E. Bender, Emeritus Professor of Nutrition, University of London.

A.F.B.　　　the late Alastair Buchan, formerly Professor of International Relations, University of Oxford, and Director of the Institute of Strategic Studies.

A.G.　　　　Anna Grimshaw, author and editor.

A.H.　　　　Anthony Hopkins, composer, conductor, pianist, and writer and broadcaster on music; formerly Lecturer and Piano Professor, Royal College of Music, London.

A.J.H.R.　　Anthony J. Harding Rains, Editor, *Journal of the Royal Society of Medicine*; formerly Professor of Surgery, Charing Cross Hospital, London, and Assistant Director of the British Post Graduate Medical Federation.

A.J.M.W.　　Andrew Wheatcroft, Department of History, University of Edinburgh.

A.J.W.　　　A. J. Wing, Consultant Physician, St Thomas's Hospital, London.

A.K.　　　　Alexander Knapp, formerly Visiting Lecturer in Music, Goldsmiths' College, London.

A.KU.　　　Annette Kuhn, teacher and cultural critic; writer on feminism and representation, film theory and the history of the cinema.

A.K.S.　　　Amartya Sen, F.B.A., Drummond Professor of Political Economy, University of Oxford.

A.K.W.　　　Angela K. Westwater, art gallery proprietor and director; formerly Managing Editor, *Artforum*.

A.L.　　　　Andrew Lumsden, formerly Associate Editor, *New Statesman*.

A.L.C.B.　　Alan (Lord) Bullock, F.B.A., Fellow and Founding Master of St Catherine's College, Oxford; formerly Vice-Chancellor of the University of Oxford.

A.P.　　　　Andrew Pomiankowski, Research Student, Wellcome Institute for the History of Medicine, London.

C.P.   Chris Philo, Department of Geography, University of Cambridge.

C.S.   the late Christopher Strachey, formerly Professor of Computation, University of Oxford.

D.A.P.   D. A. Pyke, formerly Physician-in-Charge, Diabetic Department, King's College Hospital, London.

D.B.   Daniel Bell, Henry Ford II Professor of Social Sciences, Harvard University.

D.BR.   David Brown, formerly Assistant Keeper, Modern Collection, Tate Gallery, London.

D.C.   David Crystal, Honorary Professor of Linguistics, University College of North Wales.

D.C.M.Y.   D. C. M. Yardley, Chairman, Commission for Local Administration in England.

D.C.W.   Donald Cameron Watt, Stevenson Professor of International History, University of London.

D.D.   David Doyle, Consultant Rheumatologist, Whipps Cross and St Bartholomew's Hospitals, London.

D.E.   Douglas Evans, author and lecturer.

D.E.B.   Donald Broadbent, F.R.S., external staff, Medical Research Council, University of Oxford.

D.H.   David Hartley, formerly Lecturer in Psychology, University of Strathclyde.

D.H.G.   Dennis H. Gath, Clinical Reader in Psychiatry, University of Oxford; and Honorary Consultant Psychiatrist, The Warneford Hospital, Oxford.

D.H.M.W.   the late D. H. M. Woollam, formerly Fellow of Emmanuel College, Cambridge.

D.J.E.   D. J. Enright, poet, novelist, critic, editor and publisher.

D.J.W.   D. J. Wood, Professor of Psychology, University of Nottingham.

D.L.   Darian Leader, Founder of the Cultural Centre for Freudian Studies and Research, London.

D.L.E.   David L. Edwards, Provost of Southwark Cathedral, London.

D.L.W.   Douglas Woolf, Medical Director, Horder Centre for Arthritis; Honorary Consultant Rheumatologist in the Waltham Forest Health Authority.

D.M.   David Morris, Consultant Paediatrician, Emeritus.

D.P.   David Papineau, Lecturer in History and Philosophy of Science, University of Cambridge.

D.PR.   David Priestland, research student, Magdalen College, Oxford.

D.P.M.   Daniel Patrick Moynihan, United States Senator, Washington, D.C.

D.S.   David Souden, writer and producer, Still Waters Ltd; formerly Fellow of Emmanuel College, Cambridge.

D.T.M.   David McLellan, Professor of Political Theory, University of Kent at Canterbury.

D.V.	Deryck Viney, Czechoslovak Programme Organizer, B.B.C. External Services.
D.W.	Don White, President of the London Creative Circle.
D.W.R.	D. W. Ryan, Consultant in Intensive Care, Freeman Hospital, Newcastle upon Tyne.
E.E.	E. Ernst, Haemorheology Research Laboratory, Clinic for Physical Medicine, University of Munich.
E.G.	E. Grebenik, formerly Principal, Civil Service College, and Joint Editor, *Population Studies*.
E.H.	Edward Higginbottom, F.R.C.O., Fellow of New College, Oxford.
E.H.P.B.	Sir Henry Phelps Brown, F.B.A., Professor Emeritus of Economics of Labour, University of London.
E.L.-S.	Erika Lueders-Salmon, formerly Research Officer, Inner London Education Authority.
E.O.W.	Edward O. Wilson, F. B. Baird Professor of Science, Harvard University.
E.R.L.	E. R. Laithwaite, Emeritus Professor of Heavy Electrical Engineering, Imperial College of Science and Technology, London.
G.B.	George Butterworth, Professor of Psychology, University of Stirling.
G.B.R.	George Richardson, Fellow of St John's College, Oxford; Secretary to the Delegates of the Oxford University Press.
G.H.P.	G. H. Peters, Research Professor in Agricultural Economics, University of Oxford.
G.M.	Gordon Mangan, Senior Research Fellow, Department of Psychology, University of Auckland.
G.N.	Garet Newell, Teacher of the Feldenkrais Method.
G.S.	G. Stuvel, Emeritus Fellow of All Souls College, Oxford; formerly University Lecturer in Economic Statistics, University of Oxford.
GE.S.	Geoffrey Smith, writer and lecturer.
GR.S.	Graham Smith, Department of Geography, University of Cambridge.
H.L.	Hope Liebersohn, formerly Lecturer in Linguistics, Hatfield Polytechnic.
H.L'E.	Hugh L'Etang, Editor, *Travel Medicine International*; Consultant Medical Editor, *The Physician*.
H.L.A.H.	Herbert Hart, F.B.A., formerly Principal of Brasenose College, Oxford, and Professor of Jurisprudence, University of Oxford.
H.M.R.	H. M. Rosenberg, Reader in Physics, Clarendon Laboratory, University of Oxford.
H.TA.	the late Henry Tajfel, formerly Professor of Social Psychology, University of Bristol.
H.TH.	Howard Thomas, formerly Director of Decisions Analysis Unit, London Graduate School of Business Studies.
I.M.D.L.	Ian Little, F.B.A., formerly Professor of the Economics of Underdeveloped Countries, University of Oxford, and Special Adviser to the World Bank.

I.M.L.H. Ian M. L. Hunter, Professor Emeritus of Psychology, University of Keele.

J.A.A.S. J. A. A. Stockwin, Nissan Professor of Modern Japanese Studies, University of Oxford.

J.A.G. Jeffrey A. Gray, Professor of Psychology, Institute of Psychiatry, University of London.

J.A.M. J. A. Mirrlees, F.B.A., Professor of Economics, University of Oxford.

J.D. John Davy, Assistant Principal, Emerson College, Forest Row.

J.D.B. John D. Barrow, Lecturer in Astronomy, University of Sussex.

J.D.O. J. D. Oriel, Consultant Physician, Department of Genito-Urinary Medicine, University College Hospital, London.

J.E.S. J. E. Stoy, Fellow of Balliol College, Oxford; University Lecturer in Computation.

J.G. Jean Gottmann, F.B.A., Emeritus Professor of Geography, University of Oxford.

J.G.R. Julian Rushton, formerly Lecturer in Music, University of Cambridge.

J.G.W. John Weightman, Professor Emeritus, University of London.

J.H. Janet Husband, Consultant Radiologist, Royal Marsden Hospital, Surrey.

J.H.G. John H. Goldthorpe, F.B.A., Official Fellow of Nuffield College, Oxford.

J.H.H. J. H. Humphrey, Professor Emeritus of Immunology, University of London.

J.I. John Izbicki, Chief Paris Correspondent, *Daily Telegraph*; formerly Education Editor, *Daily Telegraph*, London.

J.L.M.L. J. L. M. Lambert, freelance writer and part-time academic; formerly Museum Lecturer, Geological Museum, London.

J.L.V. Julian Verbov, Consultant Dermatologist, Liverpool Health Authority; Clinical Lecturer in Dermatology, University of Liverpool.

J.M. James Montaldi, Research Assistant, Mathematics Institute, University of Warwick.

J.M.C. J. M. Cullen, Department of Zoology, Monash University, New Zealand.

J.M.S. J. Maynard Smith, F.R.S., Professor of Biology, University of Sussex.

J.N.B. J. N. Buxton, Professor of Information Technology, King's College, London.

J.N.W. Sir John Walton, Warden of Green College, Oxford; formerly Professor of Neurology, University of Newcastle upon Tyne.

J.P. John Peirson, Lecturer in Economics, University of Kent at Canterbury.

J.R. Jonathan Raban, writer and journalist.

J.R.T. John Torrance, Fellow of Hertford College, Oxford.

J.R.Y. J. R. Yarnold, Consultant in Radiotherapy and Oncology, The Royal Marsden Hospital, London.

J.S.B. Jerome Bruner, George Herbert Mead Professor, New School for Social Research, New York; formerly Watts Professor of Experimental Psychology, University of Oxford.

J.S.F. J. S. Fleming, Economic Adviser to the Governor of the Bank of England.

J.T. James Thorpe, Director, Huntingdon Library, Art Gallery and Botanical Gardens, San Marino, California.

J.V.D. Sir John Dacie, F.R.S., formerly Professor of Haematology, Post-Graduate Medical School, Hammersmith Hospital, London.

J.V.H.K. J. V. Harvey Kemble, Consultant Plastic Surgeon, St Bartholomew's Hospital, London, and North-East Thames Regional Plastic Surgery Centre, St Andrew's Hospital, Billericay, Essex.

J.W. John Willett, formerly Assistant Editor, *Times Literary Supplement*; author of books on Brecht, Expressionism, etc.

J.WI. John Winstanley, Consulting Ophthalmic Surgeon, St Thomas's Hospital, London.

J.Z. John Michael Ziman, F.R.S., Chairman of the Science Policy Support Group; Visiting Professor, Imperial College, London; formerly Professor of Physics, University of Bristol.

K.A. Kingsley Amis, writer.

K.E.H. the late K. E. Hunt, formerly Director, Institute of Agricultural Economics, University of Oxford.

K.H. Keith Hope, Professor of Sociology, Southern Illinois University.

K.K. Krishan Kumar, Professor of Social Thought, University of Kent at Canterbury.

K.M. Kenneth Mellanby, Editor, *Environmental Pollution*; Honorary Professor of Biology, Cardiff University College, University of Wales.

L.A. Liz Aggiss, Senior Lecturer in Dance, Brighton Polytechnic.

L.J.F. Leisa J. Freeman, Honorary Lecturer, Department of Cardiology, Charing Cross Hospital, London.

L.L. Leopold Labedz, Editor, *Survey*; formerly Professor of Politics, Stanford University.

L.M. Lynda Morris, writer on art.

M.A. Michael Anderson, Professor of Drama, University College of North Wales.

M.A.H.D. M. A. H. Dempster, Professor of Mathematics, Dalhousie University, New Brunswick.

M.BA. Michèle Barrett, Senior Lecturer in Sociology, The City University, University of London.

M.BE. Marion Bernstein, District Psychologist, West Lambeth Health Authority, London.

M.BI. Michael Billington, drama critic, *The Guardian*.

M.BR.   Michael Brawne, practising architect; Professor of Architecture, University of Bath.

M.C.   Mary Chamot, formerly Assistant Keeper, Tate Gallery, London.

M.D.B.   Michael D. Biddiss, Professor of History, University of Reading.

M.E.   Maria Enzensberger, freelance writer and translator.

M.E.A.B. the late Marian Bowley, formerly Emeritus Professor of Political Economy, University College London.

M.F.   the late Maurice Freedman, formerly Professor of Social Anthropology, University of Oxford.

M.FG.S. M. FG. Scott, Official Fellow, Nuffield College, Oxford.

M.J.C.   M. J. Crowe, Consultant Psychiatrist, Maudsley Hospital, London.

M.K.   M. Kinsbourne, Associate Professor of Pediatrics and Neurology, Duke University Medical Center.

M.L.   Mary Lambert, geography teacher, Highworth School, Ashford, Kent.

M.LO.   Michelle Lowe, Department of Geography, University of Cambridge.

M.R.   Mark Ridley, Research Fellow, St Catharine's College, Cambridge.

M.S.   Michael Shepherd, Professor of Epidemiological Psychiatry, Institute of Psychiatry, University of London.

M.S.BA. the late M. S. Bartlett, formerly F.R.S., Emeritus Professor of Biomathematics, University of Oxford.

M.S.BR. Malcolm Bradbury, novelist and Professor of American Studies, University of East Anglia.

M.S.P.   Michael Piraino, Executive Assistant to the President and College Council, Allegheny College, Meadville, Pennsylvania.

M.S.-S. Martin Seymour-Smith, lately Visiting Professor of English, University of Wisconsin; author of *Guide to Modern World Literature* (1986).

M.V.B.   Michael V. Berry, F.R.S., Professor of Physics, University of Bristol.

M.V.P.   Michael Posner, formerly Economic Director, National Economic Development Office, London.

M.W.   Michael Walters, postgraduate student in politics, University of Kent at Canterbury.

N.G.   N. Glazer, Graduate School of Education, Harvard University.

N.H.H.   Nigel Harris, Consultant Orthopaedic Surgeon, St Mary's Hospital and Medical School, London.

N.M.   Nicola Miller, formerly at the Latin American Centre, St Anthony's College, Oxford.

N.T.   Niko Tinbergen, F.R.S., Emeritus Professor of Animal Behaviour, University of Oxford; Nobel Laureate in Physiology.

LIST OF CONTRIBUTORS

O.S.	the late Oliver Stallybrass, Joint Editor of the original edition of *The Fontana Dictionary of Modern Thought*.
O.Y.E.	O. Y. Elagab, Lecturer in Law, University of Oxford.
P.B.	Peter Burke, Fellow of Emmanuel College, Cambridge.
P.B.M.	Peter Mandelson, Press Officer, The Labour Party.
P.C.	Patrick Conner, Associate, Martyn Gregory Gallery, London.
P.C.P.	Patrick C. Pietroni, Senior Lecturer in General Practice, St Mary's Hospital Medical School, London.
P.E.B.	Peter Bryant, Watts Professor of Psychology, University of Oxford.
P.G.F.N.	Peter Nixon, Consultant Cardiologist, Charing Cross Hospital, London.
P.H.	Peter Haggett, Professor of Urban and Regional Geography, University of Bristol.
P.J.	Peter Jay, Editor, *Banking World*; broadcaster; formerly British Ambassador to the U.S.A.
P.J.S.	Peter J. Smith, Reader in Earth Sciences, The Open University; Scientific Editor, *Geology Today*.
P. L. H.	Paul L. Harris, Fellow of St John's College, Oxford.
P.M.	the late Sir Peter Medawar, O.M., F.R.S., Member of Scientific Staff, Medical Research Council; Nobel Laureate in Medicine.
P.M.K.	P. M. Kelly, Assistant Director, Climatic Research Unit, University of East Anglia.
P.M.O.	P. M. Oppenheimer, Student of Christ Church, Oxford.
P.N.	Peter Newmark, Deputy Editor, *Nature*.
P.S.L.	Peter S. Leuner, Chairman, Division of Social Sciences, Richmond College, Surrey.
P.W.	Paul Wilkinson, Professor of International Relations, University of Aberdeen.
Q.B.	Quentin Bell, Emeritus Professor of Fine Art, University of Sussex.
R.A.H.	R. A. Hodgkin, formerly Lecturer in Education, University of Oxford.
R.B.	Ronald Butt, political columnist, *The Times*; formerly Assistant Editor, *Sunday Times*.
R.C.	Robert Conquest, writer; author of *The Great Terror* etc.
R.C.C.	Rachel Chaplin, research student, University of Sussex; dancer.
R.C.O.M.	R. C. O. Matthews, F.B.A., Master of Clare College and Professor of Political Economy, University of Cambridge.
R.F.	Ronald Fletcher, Professor Emeritus in Sociology, University of Reading; freelance author.
R.G.	Robin Gandy, Emeritus Reader in Mathematical Logic, University of Oxford.
R.GI.	Raanan Gillon, Director, Imperial College of Health Centre, London; a Deputy Director, Institute of Medical Ethics; Senior Fellow, Centre for Medical Law and Ethics, King's College, University of London.

R.G.T	R. G. Twycross, Consultant Physician-in-Charge, Sir Michael Sobell, House, Churchill Hospital, Oxford; Honorary Clinical Lecturer, Faculty of Clinical Medicine, University of Oxford.
R.H.	the late Sir Roy Harrod, F.B.A., formerly Tutor of Christ Church, Oxford.
R.H.S.	R. H. Salter, Consultant Physician, Cumberland Infirmary, Carlisle.
R.I.T.	R. I. Tricker, Professor of Finance and Accounting, University of Hong Kong.
R.L.	Robert Lekachman, Distinguished Professor of Economics, City University of New York.
R.L.G.	Richard L. Gregory, Professor of Neuropsychology and Head of the Brain and Perception Laboratory, University of Bristol.
R.M.J.	R. M. Jameson, formerly Consultant Urologist, Royal Liverpool Hospital.
R.M.N.	R. M. Needham, F.R.S., Professor of Computer Systems, University of Cambridge; Head of Deparment, University of Cambridge Computer Laboratory.
R.P.	Roy Porter, Senior Lecturer in the Social History of Medicine, Wellcome Institute for the History of Medicine, London.
R.PO.	Roger Poole, Lecturer in English, University of Nottingham.
R.P.-S.	Renée Paton-Saltzberg, Senior Lecturer in Psychology, Oxford Polytechnic.
R.R.	Richard Rosencrance, Professor of International and Comparative Politics, Cornell University.
R.SI.	Robin Sibson, Professor of Statistics, University of Bath.
R.ST.	Sir Richard Stone, F.B.A., P. D. Leake Professor of Finance and Accounting, University of Cambridge.
R.S.C.	Richard Crouch, Research Assistant, Computer Laboratory, University of Cambridge.
R.W.S.	R. W. Sharples, Lecturer in Department of Greek and Latin, University College London.
S.A.	Stanislav Andreski, Professor of Sociology, University of Reading.
S.B.	Shaun Breslin, research student, East Asia Centre, University of Newcastle upon Tyne.
S.BE.	Stafford Beer, Visiting Professor of Cybernetics, University of Manchester; Adjunct Professor of Social Systems Sciences, University of Pennsylvania.
S.BR.	Samuel Brittan, Assistant Editor, *Financial Times*; Visiting Fellow, Nuffield College, Oxford.
S.J.G.	Julius Gould, Professor Emeritus of Sociology, University of Nottingham.
S.J.S.	S. J. Steele, Director of the Academic Unit of Obstetrics and Gynaecology, The Middlesex Hospital Medical School, London.
S.L.	Sutherland Lyall, journalist.

LIST OF CONTRIBUTORS

S.M.	Sonia Mazey, Senior Lecturer in Politics, Polytechnic of North London.
S.R.	Steve Reilly, Lecturer in Politics and Government, University of Kent at Canterbury.
S.T.	Stephen Trombley, author.
T.C.C.M.	Tom Milne, film critic and film historian.
T.M.	Terence Morris, Professor of Social Institutions, University of London.
T.S.	Tim Steel, Chairman, Self Direct Ltd.
T.Z.C.	Thomas Z. Cassel, Faculties of Human Development, Wayne State University and the Merrill-Palmer Institute.
W.A.C.S.	W. A. C. Stewart, formerly Vice-Chancellor and Professor of Education, University of Keele.
W.B.	Wilfred Beckerman, Fellow of Balliol College, Oxford; formerly Professsor of Political Economy, University of London, and Head of Department of Political Economy, University College London.
W.D.M.P.	W. D. M. Paton, F.R.S., Emeritus Professor of Pharmacology, University of Oxford.
W.E.C.G.	Bill Gillham, Senior Lecturer in Psychology, University of Strathclyde.
W.K.	Wilfrid Knapp, Fellow and Tutor in Politics, St Catherine's College, Oxford.
W.R.L.	W. R. Lee, Professor of Occupational Health, University of Manchester.
W.R.T	W. R. Tyldesley, Director of Dental Education, University of Liverpool.
W.Z.	Wendy Zerin, formerly Research Assistant, Department of Experimental Psychology, University of Oxford.

A

Abbaye de Créteil. An early-20th-century experiment in COMMUNITY living, called after the utopian Abbaye de Thélème imagined by Rabelais. In 1906 a group of young French writers, artists, and musicians, of whom Georges Duhamel was to become the most famous, settled in a house at Créteil, near Paris, and tried, while pursuing their artistic vocations, to support themselves by growing their own vegetables and working a printing-press. During this period Jules Romains, an associate member of the group, evolved the short-lived literary theory known as *l'unanimisme*, which tried to draw rather facile humanistic (see HUMANISM) reassurance from the fact that all the individuals in a given social group tend to be interdependent and to react on each other. The experiment ended after 14 months, because of disagreements and lack of money. In 1937 Duhamel gave a rather melancholy transposition of it in his novel *Le Désert de Bièvres*.   J.G.W.

Abbey Theatre. A Dublin theatre, after 1904 the home of the Irish National Theatre Society. Under the leadership of W.B. Yeats and Lady Gregory the Abbey presented plays in verse and prose, whose subject-matter was taken from contemporary Irish life and Celtic myth, with Yeats himself and J.M. Synge as the major dramatists of the movement. From 1923 to 1926 the Abbey again achieved international recognition with the early plays of Sean O'Casey; its refusal in 1928 to stage his play *The Silver Tassie* contributed to a decline in its stature.   M.A.

ABC art, see MINIMAL ART.

abduction. A term popularized by the American pragmatist philosopher C.S. Peirce (1839-1914) as part of an attempt to redefine the relations between facts and theories. Peirce denied the plausibility of INDUCTION, i.e. the doctrine that generalizations emerged almost automatically from the piling up of data. Against this Peirce argued that theorizing was, and should be, a creative process, and that theories should have a validity in their own right, to some degree independent of the data already available which they explained. Not least, he claimed, theories possessed an important predictive function, enabling the formulation of hypotheses which could later be tested experimentally. Good theories should also embody other rational characteristics, such as being simple or readily modified when confronted with counter-factual evidence. Peirce's 'abduction' represents one of many ways in which traditional induction, POSITIVISM and EMPIRICISM began to appear shallow and arid to 20th-century philosophy.   R.P.

Bibl: J. Losee, *An Historical Introduction to the Philosophy of Science* (Oxford, 1980).

Abell clusters, see under GALAXY CLUSTERS.

ABM (anti-ballistic missiles). Nuclear MISSILES designed for defensive purposes, to intercept inter-continental and intermediate-range nuclear ballistic missiles and destroy them in space, either at the apogee of their trajectory or during the descent towards their target. Should they achieve near-absolute effectiveness, the apparent invulnerability they would confer on those using them would effectively alter the balance of mutual DETERRENCE. Their development has, however, proved so costly, and the defence they provide so far from absolute, that their original possessors, the U.S.A. and Russia, have agreed to limit their production and deployment to what is necessary to protect their respective capital cities.   D.C.W.

abnormal psychology. The branch of PSYCHOLOGY concerned with the abnormal behaviour and functioning of organisms. The organisms may be human or infra-human; but the many psychologists investigating the conditions that produce abnormalities of animal behaviour (e.g. by the use of drugs, by surgical methods, by the design of conflict-producing situations) would not naturally be described as working in the field of abnormal psychology unless their studies were also de-

1

signed to throw light on the abnormalities of human functioning. The expression is further restricted to functioning that is abnormal in ways which make life difficult for the people concerned, and which may lead them to require special help. Thus, studies of men who are 6'6" tall, or who have an INTELLIGENCE QUOTIENT of over 140, would not usually and naturally be called studies of abnormal psychology; whereas similar studies of dwarfs, or of people with I.Q.s of under 60, would be so classified (see also MENTAL RETARDATION). The expression is applied, in particular, and most importantly, to phenomena that are abnormal in that they are regarded as 'morbid' in character, i.e. as evidence that the person concerned is in an unhealthy condition. In consequence of the growth, over the last century, of a whole array of therapeutic procedures for the relief of people suffering from mental morbidities, workers in abnormal psychology have also been involved in studying the effectiveness of different methods of therapy.

Because a psychologist working in this field is characteristically concerned with people who are in difficulties or suffering from mental ill-health, he meets them (typically) as patients in a psychiatric and therefore medical context. Whereas the psychiatrist (see PSYCHIATRY) is the medical specialist concerned with the diagnosis and treatment of these patients, the psychologist is solely concerned with the scientific study of their condition, or of the therapy being given them; and he conducts his enquiries with the permission and cooperation (often very active) of the psychiatrist in charge of the patients.

In this century, work in abnormal psychology has contributed to raise standards of precision and caution in the whole field of abnormal mental functioning. It has also uncovered much that was new, e.g. about the constitutional correlates of abnormal functioning, the variables of personality involved (see PERSONALITY TYPES), the environmental conditions that adversely affect the development of personality, and the difficulties of establishing that a therapeutic method is really effective. On the other hand, it is difficult to find any general discovery claim in this field (as with psychology in general) that

can stand up to sceptical scrutiny. This is not surprising, because abnormal psychology is really concerned with the malfunctioning of the machinery of the NERVOUS SYSTEM. Since we do not know yet how this machinery works, we can hardly expect the relatively crude methods of contemporary psychology to give us definitive results about what happens when our nervous machinery goes wrong.
B.A.F.

Bibl: R.W. White and N. F. Watt, *The Abnormal Personality* (New York, 5th ed., 1981).

abortion. The death and expulsion of a fetus or embryo before it is viable. In the U.K. this is legally 28 weeks, though babies born before this time can survive and 24 weeks would be realistic. Spontaneous abortion (often called miscarriage) occurs in at least 15% of pregnancies, frequency decreasing as pregnancy advances. It is most frequently due to abnormality of the fetus or embryo; other causes include infection, uterine abnormality and weakness (incompetence) of the cervix. Abortion may be induced (termination of pregnancy) when the pregnancy is abnormal or there is a threat to the life or health of the woman or of her family. Many countries have laws permitting abortion in defined circumstances but the concept is still unacceptable to many people and certain religions, notably the Roman CATHOLICS and Muslims. Where legal abortion is not permitted illegal abortion is obtained by many women with unwanted pregnancies and the methods used, often by unqualified operators, can lead to death, serious illness or subsequent infertility. The ethical issues are complex; some believe that termination of a pregnancy can never be justified while others believe that it should be entirely the choice of the woman. Others believe it is acceptable in certain situations such as fetal abnormality or risk to the health of the mother or other children.
S.J.S.

abreaction. In PSYCHOTHERAPY, a term used most usefully, and perhaps most frequently, for the actual release of emotion into CONSCIOUSNESS in which the process of CATHARSIS (sense 3) culminates. It is, however, also used synonymously with 'catharsis'.   B.A.F.

absolute, the. In PHILOSOPHY, a term used by post-Kantian metaphysical idealists (see METAPHYSICS; IDEALISM) to denote the totality of what really exists, conceived as a unitary system and as the source or explanation of all the apparent variety of the world. The idea is anticipated in Spinoza's theory that the whole of reality is a single substance, called by him *Deus sive Natura* (God or Nature). For such post-Kantian idealists as Schelling and Hegel reality is spiritual in character and so their Absolute is more God than Nature, although it is a philosophical God, purged of anthropomorphic features. It is not itself a person, although it somehow contains all the persons that there are.
                                                A.Q.

absolute liability, see under STRICT LIABILITY.

absolute space and time. The laws of mechanics finally formulated by Isaac Newton presupposed that uniform motion would continue indefinitely in straight lines unless impeded by other objects or forces. Such a view demanded conceptions of space and time as abstract, infinitely extendible grids within which movement over time could be comprehended. Such concepts of space and time as independent of mundane, transient objects gained plausibility during the Scientific Revolution because the New Astronomy suggested that the universe did indeed extend infinitely, and cosmogony was to open up the prospect of an infinitely old cosmos. Classical PHYSICS flowered after Newton within a concept of the independence of space from time which was to be fundamentally challenged by Minkowski's formulation in 1908 of the notion of SPACE-TIME (i.e. their interdependence as dimensions) and the exploitation by Einstein of this idea in his theory of general RELATIVITY. Many important cultural movements of the 20th century have rejected objective notions of space and time, substituting instead subjective concepts based on human experience. Important in this respect was the philosophy of Bergson.   R.P.

Bibl: S. Toulmin and J. Goodfield, *The Discovery of Time* (London, 1965).

absolute threshold, see under THRESHOLD.

absolute zero. The temperature of $-273.15°C$, which is the lowest possible according to the well-established theories of THERMODYNAMICS and STATISTICAL MECHANICS. At the absolute zero, the random heat motion of the constituents of matter is at a minimum, and structural order is at a maximum. This means that thermal NOISE in measuring instruments is greatly reduced at low temperatures, enabling very weak signals to be detected, e.g. faint radio emissions from distant GALAXIES and stars. Near the absolute zero, two dramatic effects of QUANTUM MECHANICS occur: SUPERCONDUCTIVITY, which is the total vanishing of electrical resistance in some metals, and superfluidity, which is the total vanishing of flow resistance in liquid helium. Temperatures within $1/1000$ of a degree above absolute zero can be attained by modern CRYOGENIC techniques, but the absolute zero itself remains an unattainable limit. See also BROWNIAN MOTION; ZERO POINT ENERGY.   M.V.B.

absorption cost, see under MARGINAL COSTING.

abstract. Not perceivable by the senses. Such things as numbers, ideas, and social climates are said to be abstract, while things that can be perceived by the senses, e.g. buses, blankets, and bottles, are said to be concrete. Concrete things, however, may be described with a greater or lesser degree of *abstractness*, e.g. the same diagram may be described as either (*a*) a square of side half an inch drawn with black ink or (*b*) a polygon. The second description *abstracts* from some of the qualities of the square, and is therefore said to be more abstract, or more of an *abstraction*. The first description is also abstract to the extent that it does not include everything that could be said about the picture, e.g. its location and orientation. See also EQUIVALENCE RELATION.

The process of abstraction is sometimes

3

applied also to descriptions or theories which distort in order to simplify. For instance, economists sometimes describe human beings as if they ('economic man') had a single motive, namely to get as much as possible for themselves. This may make it easier to construct theories of economic processes which are mathematically easy to understand and use, but which do not give accurate descriptions, predictions, or EXPLANATIONS of what actually happens. Similarly, if a physicist treats a gas as if it were composed of perfectly elastic, perfectly small PARTICLES, exerting no forces on one another, this makes his calculations easier, but distorts the facts. Such distortions for the sake of simplicity or elegance are sometimes called abstractions, sometimes idealizations, sometimes schematizations, and sometimes MODELS.

A.S.

abstract art. Paintings and sculpture making no identifiable reference to the visible world. Such works, which must have some claim to exist in their own right if they are to be distinguished from ornament or decoration, are often considered analogous to works of music. They have become increasingly common in Western art (and CULTURES influenced by it) since c. 1910, when a number of scattered experimenters influenced by SYMBOLISM and/or CUBISM began producing art with no recognizable 'subject' in the traditional sense. Among these were the German Adolf Hoelzel, the Russians Wassily Kandinsky, Kasimir Malevich, Michel Larionov, and Sonia Delaunay-Terk, the Lithuanian M.K. Čiurlionis, the Czech František Kupka, and the Dutchman Piet Mondrian. The term itself, whose use only became common after 1918, appears to derive from Wilhelm Worringer's *Abstraktion und Einfühlung* (1907), though Kandinsky's *Über das Geistige in der Kunst* (1912) is the classic exposition from a symbolist, quasi-musical point of view.

The first abstract films, by the DADA artists Hans Richter and Viking Eggeling, were shown in Germany in 1921. The first exhibition of abstract art in Paris, in 1930, led to the formation in 1931 of the Abstraction-Création group, consisting mainly of non-French artists. This became the main stream of the movement during the 1930s when abstract art was condemned in Germany and Russia for (respectively) DEGENERACY and FORMALISM. After World War II this condemnation made it seem an embodiment of Western values, particularly after the emergence in the 1950s of ABSTRACT EXPRESSIONISM in the U.S.A. Hence it has developed into an established, academically respectable form of art, with many overlapping versions, e.g. (1) such early branches as Malevich's SUPREMATISM (1915), Alexander Rodchenko's NON-OBJECTIVISM (c. 1920), and Theo van Doesburg's CONCRETE ART (1930); (2) general sub-categories like 'geometric' and BIOMORPHIC art (two basic divisions often adopted by critics), or, more recently, HARD-EDGE; (3) alternative names for the whole trend, such as 'non-figurative', 'non-representational', or 'non-objective'; (4) genuinely distinct recent branches like KINETIC ART and OP ART; finally (5) critics' and dealers' labels which give a deceptive air of novelty, for instance '*art autre*', MINIMAL ART, and '*réalités nouvelles*'. Other movements more or less involved with abstract art are ORPHISM, CONSTRUCTIVISM, DE STIJL and Larionov's RAYONISM, while even SURREALISM has a link with it in the biomorphic abstractions of Joan Miró and Hans Arp.

J.W.

Bibl: Museum of Modern Art Catalogue, *Cubism and Abstract Art* (New York, 1936): W. Kandinsky, tr. H. Rebay, *On the Spiritual in Art* (New York, 1947).

abstract expressionism. A term first used in 1919, in Germany and Russia, to describe the painting of Wassily Kandinsky, and again in that context in 1929 by Alfred Barr, director of the Museum of Modern Art, New York. It was subsequently applied by the *New Yorker* critic Robert Coates in 1946 to the emerging post-World-War-II American painting, both abstract (see ABSTRACT ART) and figurative. Stylistically, the term implies loose, rapid paint-handling, indistinct shapes, large rhythms, broken colour, uneven saturation of the canvas, and pronounced brushwork, as found in the work of de Kooning, Pollock, Kline, and Gorky; it also includes more reductive painters (e.g. Barnett Newman, Mark

Rothko, and Ad Reinhardt) who focus on single, centralized images expressed in terms of large areas or fields of colour — hence the term *colour field painting* subsequently applied to such painters. The term has been extended to cover several sculptors stylistically related to the painters. See also ACTION PAINTING; COBRA; NEW YORK SCHOOL. A.K.W.

Bibl: I. Sandler, *The Triumph of American Painting* (New York, 1970).

abstraction, see under ABSTRACT.

absurd, theatre of the, see THEATRE OF THE ABSURD.

acceleration. The rate at which the velocity of a body is changing. Since velocity is a VECTOR involving both speed and direction of motion, a change in either of these constitutes acceleration. Thus a car starting up from rest on a straight road, and a car rounding a bend at constant speed, are both accelerating. see also NEWTONIAN MECHANICS. M.V.B.

accelerator.

(1) In PHYSICS, a device for accelerating sub-atomic particles of matter to high energy (see PARTICLE COLLIDER, ELEMENTARY PARTICLES). Particle accelerators collide particles at the highest obtainable energies in order to investigate the internal structure of the colliding particles which disintegrate in the collision process. Most research in elementary particles is carried out by this method at very large purpose-built facilities. These are often funded by international collaboration (as in the case of CERN in Geneva). The acceleration of particles can be achieved by electric fields alone, as in the VAN DE GRAAF GENERATOR and the LINEAR ACCELERATOR, or in conjunction with magnetic fields which deflect particles into space-saving circular paths, as in the *cyclotron, synchrotron, synchrocyclotron* and BEVATRON. Most particle accelerators accelerate charged particles (ELECTRONS, POSITRONS or PROTONS). The most energetic accelerators at present are the UA1 (UA is an acronym for 'underground area') and UA2 devices at the CERN collider in which the W and Z Bosons (see QUANTUM STATISTICS) were recently discovered. J.D.B.

Bibl: R. Wilson, 'The Next Generation of Particle Accelerators', *Scientific American*, January, 1980.

(2) In ECONOMICS, the accelerator principle states that the level of INVESTMENT depends on the expected change in output. For an expected increase in output, it is necessary for investment to increase in order to have sufficient capacity to produce the expected level of output. The expected increase in output refers to a permanent rather than a temporary increase. Sophisticated versions of the principle allow for the depreciation of the capital stock, replacement investment and the impossibility of having negative gross investment. The accelerator and multiplier principles form the basis of simple MODELS of the TRADE CYCLE and ECONOMIC GROWTH. J.P.

Bibl: D. Begg *et al.*, *Economics* (London, 1984).

acceptability. In LINGUISTICS, the adjudged normality of linguistic data, especially of sentences. An acceptable utterance is one whose use is considered permissible or possible in some context by most, or all, native speakers. The CONCEPT is distinguished from the more specific notion of GRAMMATICALITY, which is merely one possible CRITERION of acceptability. An unacceptable (or *deviant*) sentence is generally indicated by a preceding asterisk, e.g. *A cats was asleep.* D.C.

access time. In COMPUTING, the time that elapses between starting a reading operation on the STORE and getting back the result. Different types of store vary widely in their access times and hence in the ways in which they are used, ranging from REGISTER (10-100ns — a nanosecond being the time light takes to travel about a foot) via SCRATCHPAD, core store, DRUM STORE, and moving-head DISC STORE to MAGNETIC TAPE (several minutes). For the last three, most of the time is the *latency* period spent waiting until the information has moved physically to the reading-head; once this has happened, information can be transferred rapidly. For this reason these types of store are generally used for SERIAL ACCESS rather than RANDOM ACCESS. C.S.

accommodation. In DEVELOPMENTAL PSY-CHOLOGY, a PIAGETIAN term for the adjustment of an organized schema of action to fit new situations. More generally, the subordination of activity to the requirements of external reality, as in imitation. Along with ASSIMILATION, it is one of the main organizing concepts of Piaget's PSY-CHOLOGY. P.L.H.

accountability. Ever since the 1960s in Britain when traditional time-tables at schools and colleges started to be supplemented — and sometimes even substituted — by para-educational subjects (peace-studies, multi-racial education, equal opportunities and the like) parents began to clamour for explanations. Schools were expected to account for the public funds that were being spent on the curriculum. Thus, accountability — a word first coined in this context in the U.S. — became a part of the educational vocabulary. J.I.

accretion (as power source). Massive objects in space attract material by the force of GRAVITY. For many objects the rate of capture of extraneous material by the accretion process is negligible. For example the Milky Way GALAXY gains a mass equal to about the mass of the sun each year but its total mass is 100 billion times greater than this. In other astronomical sites the accreted material can be very significant. When two stars are in close orbit, then if one is sufficiently large it can lose its loosely bound outer material to its companion. This material may then orbit the capturing star in a disc-like configuration — an accretion disc. Very large amounts of energy can be radiated by material as it is accreted by a strong gravitational field. This process is believed to be responsible for the energy output from QUASARS and other active galaxies and in these cases it is believed that the accretion is taking place on to a BLACK HOLE. The material in the accretion disc of orbiting material is slowly captured by the central source of gravitational attraction. When a black hole occurs in close orbit around an ordinary star it will very readily accrete material from the outer layers of the star which will fall into an accretion disc and radiate large quantities of x-radiation (see

X-RAY ASTRONOMY). This distinctive combination of large X-ray emission from a binary system, with one member of the system the unseen source of the X-rays, is therefore regarded as the signature of a black hole by astronomers. The strongest candidate for a black hole of this sort is the unseen companion in the binary X-ray source Cygnus X-1. J.D.B.
Bibl: G. Bath, ed., *The State of the Universe* (Oxford, 1980).

accretion disc, see under ACCRETION.

acculturation (U.S. term; in the U.K., *culture contact*). A kind of CULTURE change that emerges from the interaction of two or more societies or groups with different cultural traditions. Acculturation theory was slow to emerge in ANTHROPOLOGY, which was dominated, up to the 1930s, by a historical approach that concentrated on EVOLUTION and diffusion (see DIFFUSION-ISM) of cultural traits. Following the efforts of Malinowski and Fortes in England, and Redfield and Linton in the U.S.A., to formulate a more consciously FUNCTIONALIST approach — which saw culture as a system rather than a collection of disparate traits — culture contact theory became more important as a means of analysing social change. The earlier contact theories tended to assume that the normal outcome of acculturation was cultural fusion or assimilation; the dominant (because of superior TECHNOLOGY or political power) culture became the melting-pot for the weaker one. Later theories have tended to be more pluralist, i.e. to show how new and creative mixtures often result from the interaction of diverse cultural traditions and groups. D.B.

accumulation theory, see under SOLAR SYSTEM.

acephalous. 'Headless'. A term applied to societies without centralized political organization or a recognized head. The term developed by Evans-Pritchard and Fortes (*African Political Systems*, 1940) as part of a typology of political systems. They made a distinction between societies with centralized authority and judicial institutions (primitive states) and those without (stateless, acephalous societies). The question raised by acephalous societies was to understand how order was maintained in the absence of centralized authority. The Nuer of East Africa were cited as the classic example of an acephalous society. The basis of Nuer political organization was the segmentary LINEAGE. Other acephalous societies include HUNTER-GATHERING communities and those organized on the basis of AGE-SET SYSTEMS.

A.G.

Bibl: T.C. Lewellen, *Political Anthropology: An Introduction* (Boston, Mass., 1983); E. Copet-Rougier, '"Le Mal-Court": Visible and Invisible Violence in an Acephalous Society', in D. Riches, ed., *The Anthropology of Violence* (Oxford, 1986).

achievement orientation, see under PATTERN VARIABLES.

acid. A chemical substance which loses a PROTON (hydrogen ION) to a second substance known as a BASE; this definition, which stems from Brønsted and Lowry in 1923, is the most commonly used. Strong acids such as hydrochloric acid in water (the base) lose a proton easily, but for weak acids, e.g. acetic or citric acid, the tendency to donate a proton is feeble and the acid remains largely undissociated (see DISSOCIATION). The term is sometimes used more generally as any SPECIES which accepts a pair of ELECTRONS from a donor (the base).

B.F.

acid rain. Popularly thought to be a new and devastating form of air POLLUTION, which is killing the forests of Europe and the fish in rivers and lakes. In fact all rain (unless neutralized by lime dust near a cement factory) is acid because of being in equilibrium with the carbon dioxide in the air. The purest rain has a pH of 5.6, but in industrial areas it may be much more acid with a pH of 4 or even lower. Even this very acid rain does little direct damage to plants or animals. Much more dangerous is gaseous sulphur dioxide, which in the past in Britain and other industrial countries killed trees and many other plants over wide areas. The dying trees in Eastern Germany are being affected mainly by sulphur dioxide from Czechoslovakia and other Eastern Bloc countries.

In other areas, damage is probably caused by OZONE, produced by the interaction of oxides of nitrogen (largely from car exhausts), hydrocarbons (also from cars) and sunlight. Stonework in buildings is also affected by sulphur dioxide. Conditions in cities have been greatly improved by diverting air pollutants away with high chimneys, when the pollutants are diluted and dispersed. Formerly this was thought to solve the problem. Unfortunately we now know that oxides of sulphur and nitrogen are slowly transformed to sulphuric and nitric acid. These acids are very dilute, and the rain again is not directly harmful. However, the rain contaminated with them accumulates in the soil, and where this contains little lime, the run off water, and so the streams and lakes, become acid. This may kill fish, either directly or by leaching out toxic metals, particularly aluminium, from the soil. So air pollution is still a serious problem, but acid rain itself is only a minor contributor to the damage to the environment.

K.M.

Bibl: Environmental Resources Ltd, *Acid Rain* (London, 1983).

Acmeism (from Greek *acme*: 'zenith, blossoming, ripening'). A movement in Russian poetry which grew out of SYMBOLISM as a reaction against its MYSTICISM and excessive allusiveness. The Acmeists wanted to restore concreteness and immediacy to poetic language, 'to admire a rose because it is beautiful, not because it is a symbol of purity'. Their refined lyrical verse combined poetic archaisms with simple everyday language.

The first Acmeist group, the 'Guild of Poets', was founded in St Petersburg in 1912 by Gumilev, the movement's main theoretician. Acmeism produced three outstanding poets: Gumilev, Anna Akhmatova, and Mandelshtam. Its main publication was *Apollon* (1909-17). It was suppressed in the early 1920s, stamped as 'decadent' and 'individualist'. Gumilev was executed in 1921 for his association with a counter-revolutionary plot, Mandelshtam perished in the purges of the 1930s (see YEZHOVSHCHINA), Akhmatova remained silent. During World War II she published patriotic poetry. In 1946 she was severely criticized (see ZHDANOVSH-

CHINA), but after the thaw she reemerged on the literary scene and published several volumes of poetry. M.E.

Bibl: R. Poggioli, *The Poets of Russia* (Cambridge, Mass., 1960).

acoustics. All activities concerned with the production, transmission, reflection, dispersion, or reception of sound waves, whether in air or some other substance. It includes such things as the design and manufacture of anechoic chambers, where sound waves generated within the chamber are entirely absorbed by the walls of the chamber; acoustic RADAR (sometimes called SONAR) used for depth recording at sea and for the location of shoals of fish, submarines or sunken wrecks; and the design of lecture theatres, sound-reproducing apparatus (HI-FI etc.), hearing aids, and MAGNETOSTRICTION oscillators.
E.R.L.

acquired characteristics, see under LA-MARCKISM.

Action Directe. A French, far-LEFT urban GUERRILLA movement which grew out of the 1968 MAOIST movement and began operations in 1979. There are now two sections of Action Directe: one has close links with similar international movements such as the RED ARMY Faction in West Germany and the Red Brigade in Italy; the other concentrates on less violent protests against French domestic policy. Between 1983 and 1986 Action Directe claimed responsibility for 45 bombings, two political murders and two assassination attempts. S.M.

action painting. A phrase coined by the critic Harold Rosenberg in 1952 to define the abstract (see ABSTRACT ART), GESTURAL painting then prevalent. Rosenberg referred particularly to Willem de Kooning, although later the phrase came to be popularly associated with the name of Jackson Pollock, and with the splashing or squirting of paint on canvas; it has also been used synonymously with ABSTRACT EXPRESSIONISM and with *tachisme*, a French term for much the same thing. According to Rosenberg, the canvas had become 'an arena in which to act', the scene of an encounter between the artist and his materials — an encounter possessing a psychological as well as a physical dimension. The term has been rejected by many artists and critics because of Rosenberg's linkage of the artist's psyche to European EXISTENTIALIST thought, and because of the FORMALIST criticism of, notably, Clement Greenberg. See also NEW YORK SCHOOL. A.K.W.

action potential. The electrical change that accompanies the propagation of an impulse down the length of a nerve or muscle fibre. The change is the result of a redistribution of electrical charge across the membrane of the nerve or muscle fibre and the charge is carried by IONS, such as sodium and potassium, which pass through special holes or channels in membrane PROTEINS. P.M.;P.N.

action systems, see under PARSONIAN.

activation energy. In most CHEMICAL REACTIONS the MOLECULE or molecules involved must acquire a state of higher ENERGY before they can react. The additional energy is described as the activation energy and its requirement is the reason why some thermodynamically feasible reactions do not occur. It also accounts for the increase in the rate of chemical reaction as the temperature is raised. B.F.

active galaxies, see under QUASAR.

activism. Two main senses can be distinguished:

(1) In its German form *Aktivismus*, a term used at the end of World War I to signify the principle of active political engagement by INTELLECTUALS; hence a subdivision of EXPRESSIONISM, whose political wing was strong at that time. It was associated particularly with Kurt Hiller, organizer of the *Neuer Club* of early expressionist poets, and with Franz Pfemfert, whose magazine *Die Aktion*, founded in 1911, was the more politically engaged rival of DER STURM. J.W.

(2) More widely, an especially vigorous attitude towards political action, an attitude resulting in particularly zestful political practice. It implies a special role for *activists* who form the active core of political parties. It is notable in REVOLUTION-

ARY movements and particularly important in radical party politics (see RADICAL-ISM). In its extreme form it is held to justify DIRECT ACTION and/or the use of force for political ends. In LEFT-wing politics *militant* is sometimes used, substantivally, in the same sense as *activist*, but the first refers properly to the degree of radicalism in a person's politics, the second to the degree of his involvement in politics; though usually correlated, the two are clearly distinguishable. Activists of all parties are as a rule more concerned with the purity of the party's creed than are their fellow members; this is particularly true of COMMUNIST Parties, at least before they come to power, after which the role of the APPARAT becomes paramount.

L.L.

Bibl: S.M. Lipset, *Political Man* (London, rev. ed., 1983).

Actors' Studio, see under METHOD, THE.

actuator. The mechanism for causing a particular event (usually a physical movement) to take place at a desired instant in time; e.g. an electromagnet may be supplied with current when it is required to attract an iron armature which in turn pushes an object from a moving conveyor belt at a desired position. Actuators are much used in control systems (see CONTROL ENGINEERING). E.R.L.

acupuncture. An approach to treatment based on the Chinese model of health and disease. The Chinese believe that in addition to a circulatory and nervous system the body possesses an energy system which flows in channels called meridians. This energy, chi, is seen to have two opposing forces, YIN and YANG. Disease occurs when the energy flow for whatever reason is blocked. Needles are placed in different parts of the body along meridians to help 'unblock' energy channels. The placing of needles is only one aspect of acupuncture and a physician trained in traditional Chinese medicine will take a very long time to arrive at his diagnosis and will pay particular attention to diet, emotional and environmental factors. Although western science has been unable accurately to locate the existence of either 'energy flow' or meridians, there is good scientific evidence that acupuncture causes the release of brain chemicals (endorphins) which act as an internal analgesic. In the west acupuncture has largely been used for muscular and arthritic conditions to relieve pain. It has also been used as an anaesthetic and there are several reports of operations being conducted solely with the use of acupuncture. Chinese medicine as practised in China, of which acupuncture is only a part, is practised in this country mostly by non-doctors. They generally accept and treat a much wider range of disorders than conventional medical practitioners. P.C.P.

Ada. A HIGH-LEVEL PROGRAMMING LANGUAGE, the design of which was commissioned, after a competition, by the U.S. Department of Defense as a successor to FORTRAN, PL/I etc. It is a complicated language and the Department of Defense is still exercising rigorous control over its development. J.E.S.

adaptable theatre, see under OPEN STAGE.

adaptation.
(1) In general BIOLOGY, the process by which an organism becomes fitted to its ENVIRONMENT, or the characteristic that renders it fit.
(2) In BACTERIOLOGY, a change in a bacterial population which makes it possible, after a certain interval, for bacteria to use a new foodstuff or avoid the action of a new ANTIBIOTIC.
(3) In sensory PHYSIOLOGY the process by which an end organ ceases to respond to some uniformly applied stimulus — e.g. the adaptation of the nose to a uniform pervasive smell. In vision, adaptations are prevented from occurring by tiny wandering or scanning movements of the eye.
P.M.

adaptive radiation. The exploitation by the members of an animal or plant group of a wide variety of different HABITATS or habits of life to each of which the organisms are appropriately adapted. Thus the higher (placental) mammals show a high degree of adaptive radiation as exemplified by terrestrial carnivores, whales, moles, bats, and chimpanzees. The marsupial mammals have undergone an adaptive radiation of their own curiously similar in many ways to that of the terrestrial higher mammals. In this context the word 'radiation' is of course figurative and refers to a fanning out of evolutionary lines; and adaptive radiation calls for no special explanations that do not apply equally to the remainder of EVOLUTION.

P.M.

additive rhythm. A method of constructing musical rhythm by adding together the smallest rhythmical units (e.g. semiquavers) to produce the note durations, rather than the more normal method of subdividing larger units of time. Whereas the latter produces symmetrical rhythms that are easily comprehended, additive rhythm can produce very complex rhythms that are difficult to understand. Because of the irregularity of additive rhythm it is usually notated with continually changing time signatures.

B.CO.

additive synthesis. In ELECTRONIC MUSIC the technique of constructing complex waveforms by the superimposition of simpler waves (usually sine waves). The converse, *subtractive synthesis*, is where the composer starts with a complex wave (e.g. a square wave) and simplifies it by filtering (see also SYNTHESIZER).

B.CO.

Bibl: D. Ernst, *The Evolution of Electronic Music* (New York, 1977).

additives, food. Substances intentionally added to foods during processing or preparation to add or restore colour and flavour, to preserve the food or otherwise improve it. May be synthetic or extracted from natural sources. Their use is controlled by legislation.

A.E.B.

Bibl: British Nutrition Foundation, *Why Additives?* (London, 1977).

Adelphi, The, see under CRITERION, THE.

adelphic polyandry, see under POLYANDRY.

adequacy. A term used in GENERATIVE GRAMMAR as a CRITERION of the extent to which the goals of linguistic theory have been achieved. Three *levels of adequacy*, or stages of achievement, are recognized.

Observational adequacy is achieved when a grammar gives a correct description of a CORPUS of data, but does not make generalizations based on this. *Descriptive* adequacy is achieved to the extent that a grammar gives a correct account of a speaker's COMPETENCE, his intuitive knowledge of a language. *Explanatory* adequacy is achieved to the extent that a linguistic theory provides principles for determining which of a number of descriptively adequate grammars is the best (see EVALUATION PROCEDURE). Structural LINGUISTICS was criticized by Chomsky as being too preoccupied with observational adequacy. Very little headway has been made in the study of explanatory adequacy.

D.C.

adjustable speed, see VARIABLE SPEED.

Adlerian. Adjective applied to a school of PSYCHOANALYSIS originating in the work of Alfred Adler (Vienna, 1870-1937); also a substantive, meaning a member of that school. In the course of an early, close association with Freud (see FREUDIAN), Adler began to develop his own INDIVIDUAL PSYCHOLOGY, in which he came to reject Freud's LIBIDO theory, together with his views of infantile sexuality and of sexuality as the root source of NEUROSIS; and finally (1912) he severed relations with Freud. Adler's fundamental notion was the helplessness of the infant, with its feelings of inferiority. The infant has an urge to overcome and compensate for all this. The key conditions that determine how he achieves this compensation are the inter-personal relations in the family. The upshot is that the child acquires his own LIFE STYLE, or way of dealing with his situation. Where this fails, the person may retain an uncompensated feeling of inferiority (an INFERIORITY COMPLEX), and this can lead to a neurotic style of behaviour. Adler's influence, though to some extent indirect and unacknowledged, has been considerable, especially in the U.S.A.

B.A.F.

Bibl: A. Adler, tr. P. Radin, *The Practice and Theory of Individual Psychology* (London and New York, 1924).

admass. Term coined by J.B. Priestley in 1955 (*Journey Down a Rainbow*) for an economic, cultural and social order dominated and saturated by the drive reflecting the illusory world of the ADVERTISING copy-writer's 'ad', and obsessively promoted through the mass MEDIA. Admass leads to the creation and purveying of LIFE STYLES in the context of a glittering CONSUMER SOCIETY which, it is claimed, stifles creativity and individuality, and distorts human feelings, needs, and emotions.

P.S.L.

administrative law. In England, the legal rules and principles on which the courts act in controlling the exercise by public authorities of the powers of rule-making and adjudication conferred upon them by law. Administrative law is therefore an important part of official constitutional law designed to secure that the wide powers and discretions conferred upon administrative bodies and regulatory agencies, both to make general rules and to determine the rights of individuals, are exercised fairly and within the limits expressed or implied in the law conferring such powers. In the early years of the century 'administrative law' was sometimes understood as referring to a system of special courts for deciding cases in which government officials were involved and where they might enjoy special privileges and immunities, as in France. Today it is recognized that this understanding was too narrow. H.L.A.H.; D.C.M.Y.

Bibl: H.W.R. Wade, *Administrative Law* (Oxford and New York, 2nd ed., 1982); D.C.M. Yardley, *Principles of Administrative Law* (London, 1986).

ADP. Automatic data processing. Data processing performed by automatic electromechanical devices. C.E.D.

adrenal gland. A composite endocrine gland (see ENDOCRINOLOGY) of dual origin and dual function.

(1) The central core (medulla) secretes *adrenalin (= epinephrine)* and *noradrenalin,* which have some of the effects of general sympathetic nervous stimulation: heart rate increases, the subject turns pale, and hairs prickle as their levator muscles contract. These physical signs are accompanied by the EMOTIONS of which they are usually thought to be the consequence, e.g. fright or extreme disquiet.

(2) The shell (adrenal cortex) produces the secretions which control the traffic of salts through the body and exercise a long-term effect on the activity of the lymphoid TISSUES upon which immunological responses depend (see IMMUNITY). This second function is mediated through hormones related to cortisone. The disease associated with failure of adrenal function, particularly of the cortex, is 'Addison's disease'. P.M.

adsorption. The concentration of one substance very near the surface of another (not *ab*sorption, where one substance is uniformly dispersed through the body of another). Adsorption is involved in all industrial processes relying on surface activity, such as detergent production, spraying, and mineral separation. M.V.B.

adult education. In Britain, spare-time education for adults, often conducted at special evening classes, but also available during the daytime at numerous colleges run and financed by local education authorities. A particularly important part of social life with the growing need for leisure activities. Often these courses are non-vocational but there are exceptions (modern languages, car maintenance, engineering, higher mathematics). More than 100,000 adults attend extra-mural departments of universities and about 90,000 take part in courses run by the Workers' Educational Association. J.I.

adventurism, see under DEVIATIONISM.

advertising. The earliest advertisement extant can be found in the ruins of Ephesus. It is for a brothel. Advertising thinking has not advanced a great deal since then. Prior to World War II, advertising was sloganeering. 'Guinness is good for you', 'Friday night is Amami night'. With the advent of commercial television it became big business. Thinking now originated with marketing directors and brand managers (clients), agency reps and bagcarriers (account executives) assumed a new importance as 'custodians of the brand' with the consumer represented by a curious mixture of researcher and strategy creator (planners). Their findings were passed to the copywriter and art director whose job it became to translate the strategy into a memorable and effective television, press or poster advertisement, the key word being creativity. Creativity, to be noticed by the TV viewer, newspaper or magazine reader, or poster observer, necessarily means instant attention-getting, resulting in a glibness or lateral cleverness, not to be confused with creativity in, say, film, literature or art, and frequently is exposed as a new form of pre-war sloganeering ('Heineken refreshes the parts other beers cannot reach', 'Drinka pinta milka day', 'Hello Tosh gotta Toshiba'). Concern that such creativity has hidden shallows has resulted in a plethora of self-aggrandizing award festivals, locally and internationally, at which 'creatives' award each other glittering prizes to celebrate the quality of their creative thinking.   D.W.

aerobes, see under BACTERIOLOGY.

aerodynamics. The study of the flow of gases (particularly air) past solid bodies (such as ROCKETS or aircraft), and in response to temperature and pressure variations. See also HYDRODYNAMICS. M.V.B.

aerography. A branch of AEROLOGY which seeks to measure and describe the physical and chemical properties of the atmosphere (e.g. temperature, pressure, humidity). An aerograph is any self-recording instrument carried aloft by any means to obtain such data.   M.L.

aerology. Formerly a synonym for METEOROLOGY, but now that subdivision of it which deals with the free atmosphere, removed from the effect of surface conditions, through its vertical extent, as distinguished from studies confined to the atmosphere adjacent to the earth's surface.   M.L.

aeronautics. All activities connected with aerial locomotion, whether powered flight, as in aircraft, or non-powered, as in gliders, or even the flight of birds. The subject embraces aeronautical engineering, i.e. the design, production, and maintenance of aircraft structures, their instru-ments, engines, and control. It also includes the design and control of space vehicles during their passage through the earth's atmosphere and beyond.   E.R.L.

aesthetic distance. In drama and other forms of art, a critic's phrase intended to remind the spectator (reader, etc.) that a work of art is not to be confused with reality, and its conventions must be fully respected: there is little point in warning the hero that the villain is creeping up behind him with a knife. The process whereby the artist seeks to establish the aesthetic distance is known as *distancing*, or in BRECHTIAN parlance ALIENATION (*Verfremdung*). Distancing should not preclude some degree of 'identification' on the spectator's part.   D.J.E.

aestheticism. Either (1) the view that works of art should be judged by strictly aesthetic criteria (see AESTHETICS; CRITERION) and that their value has nothing to do with their moral, political, or religious UTILITY; or (2) the more extreme view that in life and action as a whole aesthetic values should take precedence over values of other kinds. Gautier's slogan 'art for art's sake' expresses the more moderate view. The theory of life expounded in the conclusion to Pater's *Renaissance* and practised by Oscar Wilde is closer to the more extreme one. It has seldom been chosen as a label by those who are held to adhere to it and has a mildly derogatory flavour.   A.Q.
  Bibl: Richard Aldington, *The Religion of Beauty* (London, 1950).

aesthetics. The philosophical study of art, and also of nature to the extent that we take the same attitude to it as we do to art. The notion of an aesthetic attitude is thus of central importance. It is commonly held to be a style of PERCEPTION concerned neither with the factual information to be gained from the things perceived, nor with their practical uses, but rather with the immediate qualities of the contemplative experience itself. Works of art are human productions designed to reward this kind of attention. But it can also be given to natural objects such as scenery, flowers, human bodies. Aesthetics aims to define the CONCEPT of the aesthetic attitude and of the work of art which is its primary object. It asks to what extent works of art should be representative, and to what extent they should express the emotions of their creators. It aims to identify the characteristic value (which few would now call beauty) of aesthetically satisfying objects. It considers the problem of the nature of a work of art's existence (is it a pattern of words or sounds or patches of colour, or is it a physical thing?), and that of the relation between aesthetic and moral value.   A.Q.

Bibl: M.C. Beardsley, *Aesthetics* (New York, 1958); R. Scruton, *Art and Imagination* (London, 1974).

aetiology (or *etiology*), see under EPIDEMIOLOGY.

affective fallacy. Term invented by W.K. Wimsatt and Monroe C. Beardsley to describe the supposed fallacy of reading a work in terms of its 'results in the mind of its audience'. The CONCEPT is useful but limited: part of reading a work is indeed the study of it as an independent STRUCTURE; but it would not, in practical terms, be worth study if it had no emotional effect. In fact, works have an 'effect' on Wimsatt and Beardsley, and whenever they discuss them they too are guilty of their own fallacy, even if in terms which only initially appear to be 'non-affective': these critics prefer one, 'dry', kind of emotion over another 'wet' one, and that is what the critical debate was *really* about. Egregious though the 'affective fallacy' may be in terms of the humanity of literature, however, it has been of stimulative value.   M.S.-S.

Bibl: W.K. Wimsatt, *The Verbal Icon* (Lexington, 1954; London, 1970); D. Newton-de Molina, *On Literary Intention* (Edinburgh, 1976).

affectivity, see under PATTERN VARIABLES.

affine geometry, see under GEOMETRY.

affinity. A term widely used in early chemical literature to express the capacity of a substance for CHEMICAL REACTION. This is now seen to be related to the FREE ENERGY change.   B.F.

affinity chromatography. A technique of CHROMATOGRAPHY in which the stationary PHASE has a strong affinity for a particular MOLECULE in the mobile phase. These molecules alone are removed from the mobile phase as it passes into the stationary phase and are subsequently released from the stationary phase by a separate procedure. A very powerful technique for the separation and concentration of one substance from a complex mixture.   P.N.

affirmative action. Term which describes government policies which give preferential treatment to particular social groups — for instance, in access to education and employment — on the grounds that the accumulated consequences of past discrimination or disadvantage require and justify such a remedy. The idea has been most developed in the U.S. since the early 1970s, and is a continuing source of political conflict. Opponents of affirmative action policies, which they prefer to call 'reverse discrimination' so as to replace the positive connotations of the original phrase, regard them as unjust in that they allegedly discriminate against individuals outside the preferred group, who are themselves not personally responsible for the group's disadvantages. In practice the conflict is along RACIAL lines, although some conflict also turns on affirmative action for women.   S.R.

Bibl: N. Glazer, *Ethnic Dilemmas* (New York, 1983); J.C. Livingstone, *Fair Game? Inequality and Affirmative Action* (San Francisco, 1979).

affluent society. Term made famous by John Kenneth Galbraith with his book *The Affluent Society* (1958), in which the first and still most complete exposition of its popular meaning is given. An affluent society is one where the widespread poverty and want that have been the lot of mankind through the ages have been replaced by sufficient abundance to enable the population as a whole to enjoy conventional notions of a reasonably comfortable standard of living. In such a society the 'conventional wisdom' of economic theory, designed as it is for dealing with the problems of scarcity, is no longer a useful tool of economic analysis. For the priority

13

traditionally given to increasing production in the PRIVATE SECTOR of the economy is no longer rational. It leads to a neglect of the supply of PUBLIC GOODS, e.g. roads and the police force. This situation is aggravated by the artificial stimulation of consumer DEMAND through ADVERTISING, and the excessive expansion of consumer credit provisions. The imbalance between private and public sector output, and other effects of the conventional economic goals, means that although national income may rise, human welfare may decline.   W.B.; J.P.

Bibl: W. Beckerman, *In Defence of Economic Growth* (London, 1974).

Afghanistan. The Soviet invasion of Afghanistan in late December 1979 was the first time Soviet troops had been involved in large-scale military activity outside the Warsaw Pact area since World War II. The Soviet Union justified its action by claiming that it had been invited to help the MARXIST regime of Hafizullah Amin against insurgents from abroad. However, as Amin was killed immediately after the invasion, western analysts have seen the Soviet action as an attempt to replace the unpopular Amin regime with a Marxist government which would be more flexible internally and sympathetic to the Soviet Union. Such a government was established under Babrak Karmal, Amin's rival in the Afghan COMMUNIST Party. The invasion was widely condemned by NATO and non-aligned nations, and has been seen as being instrumental in ending the period of DÉTENTE between eastern Europe and the western bloc. The Soviet Union has found it extremely difficult to control Afghanistan and an estimated 120,000 troops are still fighting the Afghan partisans (Mujahedin). In January 1987, an initiative designed to bring about the withdrawal of Soviet troops was announced, sponsored by the new Soviet leadership under General-Secretary Mikhail Gorbachev. Soviet and Afghan government troops called a cease-fire and the Afghan government agreed to hold talks, with the Pakistanis representing the rebels. However the Mujahedin ignored the cease-fire and the talks had reached an impasse by mid-1987 over the timetable for the withdrawal.   D.PR.

Bibl: J. Steele, *The Limits of Soviet Power* (Harmondsworth, 1983).

African National Congress (ANC). A leading force in the political struggle against APARTHEID, the ANC evolved from the South African Native National Congress and acquired its current name in 1923. Initially a small organization of moderate tenor which espoused constitutional approaches to reform, it developed a more militant character in the 1940s. It was captured by its own radical Congress Youth League, developed links with the South African Communist Party, and in 1949 issued a Programme of Action which produced the 1952 Defiance Campaign of non-violent protest. This drew a great increase in membership from a few thousand to nearly 100,000 and encouraged contact with other political groups, who joined in the adoption in 1955 of the Freedom Charter which still represents the ANC's publicly stated goals. Throughout the 1950s the state was hostile to the ANC and banned it and its splinter group the Pan-African Congress after the Sharpeville episode of April 1960. The movement was forced underground and revised its strategy and methods. In 1961 it formed a military wing, Umkhonto we Sizwe (Spear of the Nation) under the command of Nelson Mandela, who with other ANC leaders was arrested and imprisoned for life.

During the 1960s the ANC developed increasing links with other African liberation movements, the U.S.S.R. and other SOCIALIST states. Its vocabulary became more thoroughly MARXIST and strategy more comprehensive. Despite continued attempts by the state to destroy it, the ANC survived and benefited from the upsurge of black militancy in the 1970s (see BLACK CONSCIOUSNESS). Since then it has pursued a combined strategy of mass mobilization and GUERRILLA actions, generally against state property. As the regime's stability has been increasingly threatened, the ANC has come to be internationally regarded as an organization vital to prospects of a relatively orderly reconstruction of the South African state.   S.R.

Bibl: T. Lodge, *Black Politics in South Africa since 1945* (Harlow, 1984).

14

Afro-Cuban. JAZZ has always been receptive to Latin rhythms, even from its early days: the St Louis Blues, for instance, sported a habanera section. This 'Spanish tinge' came into its own in the 1940s, spearheaded by BEBOP trumpeter Dizzy Gillespie, who hired the conga drummer Chano Pozo to play with his BIG BAND. Pozo's intoxicating pulse and colourful accents set the style for what was dubbed Afro-Cuban, and many bands adopted one or even more Latin percussion players. The exotic fad was less adaptable to small groups and faded somewhat as the big bands declined. Nonetheless, the tinge has remained an effective part of the jazz vocabulary, and has sometimes become a dominant hue of its own, as in the bossa nova craze of the early 1960s and the heady salsa form of the 1980s. GE.S.

after-burning.

(1) In internal combustion engines, the process whereby the burning of the fuel in the cylinder occurs, not instantaneously between the compression period and the working stroke, but partly during the latter. Despite the loss of efficiency involved, after-burning is necessary to prevent excessive (in theory infinite) pressure being created by a very rapid (in theory instantaneous) burning.

(2) In jet engines, the use of special 'after-burners' in the outlet pipe in order to minimize the escape of combustible materials and augment the power of the main jet engine.

(3) The use in exhaust pipes of catalytic or other burners in order to reduce atmospheric POLLUTION. E.R.L.

after-image. In PERCEPTION, the visual after-effect produced by focusing on an object and then looking at a blank surface. It usually appears in a colour complementary to the original and obeys *Emmert's Law* to the effect that its apparent size varies in direct proportion to the apparent distance of the surface against which it is cast. J.S.B.

AFTN. Aeronautical fixed telecommunications network: a worldwide system of radio and cable links for transmitting and recording messages. C.E.D.

age-and-area hypothesis. Anthropological hypothesis that CULTURE traits tend to diffuse from single or multiple centres rather like ripples on a pond after a stone is thrown. Consequently cultures on the periphery may show traits which were characteristic of the centre in an earlier period. There is considerable dispute as to the reliability of the MODEL in reconstructing any given culture history. See also DIFFUSION, SPATIAL. P.H.

Bibl: M.J. Herskovits, *Cultural Anthropology* (New York, 1955), pp. 468 ff.

age-grade, see under AGE-SET SYSTEM.

age-set system. A form of social organization in which males become members of groups through the process of initiation. The system divides males into different groups and ranks them in a hierarchy based upon seniority. Age-set systems are commonly found among societies in East Africa: for example among the Masai, Jie and Turkana. All young men born within a certain number of years are initiated at the same time into an age-set. They remain members of this set throughout their lives, but the members of the set move collectively through a series of age-grades — from junior warriorhood to senior warriorhood to junior elderhood to senior elderhood. An age-set system establishes a series of roles through which individuals pass in an ordered and socially recognized way. It also frequently provides the basis for the exercise of political authority (see ACEPHALOUS, RITES DE PASSAGE). A.G.

Bibl: B. Bernardi, *Age Class Systems* (Cambridge, 1985).

agency shop, see under CLOSED SHOP.

aggiornamento. Italian word meaning 'bringing up to date'; it usually refers to the renewal of Roman CATHOLICISM begun while John XXIII was Pope (1958-63) and in large measure authorized by VATICAN COUNCIL II. The Mass has been made a more corporate act of worship, and the use of Latin has almost ceased (see LITURGICAL MOVEMENT). More responsibility has been attributed to the laity, instead of to the clergy; and to all the bishops, instead of a Papal monopoly of power. There has been more emphasis on the Christian's involvement in the modern world (see PACEM IN TERRIS), sustained by simpler prayer. An intellectually active and free THEOLOGY, in its inspiration BIBLICAL, has begun to emerge. More acknowledgement of other Christian Churches, and more cooperation with them in the ECUMENICAL MOVEMENT, have been encouraged. Some Roman Catholics have reacted conservatively, suspecting MODERNISM. Others have felt that the officially tolerated pace of change has been too slow and have left either the priesthood or the Church. The election of Karol Wojtyla as Pope John Paul II in 1978 ended the period when the Papacy itself had seemed to be involved in this uncertainty. Essentially conservative as befitted a bishop who had experienced the popularity of a conservative Catholicism in Poland, this masterful leader was no blind reactionary. He advocated the renewal of the Church in the form of CONCILIARITY. D.L.E.

Bibl: M. Winter, *What Ever Happened to Vatican II?* (London, 1985); K. Wojtyla, *Sources of Renewal* (London, 1980).

agglutinating (or *agglutinative*). In comparative LINGUISTICS, terms applied to a language (e.g. Turkish) in which words typically consist of long sequences of affixes and roots, each element usually having a clear identity and separate meaning. English shows little tendency to agglutinate: humorous constructs such as *antidisestablishmentarianism* are exceptional. The term is one of three used in the approach to linguistic typology proposed by August von Schlegel (1767-1845), the others being ISOLATING and INFLECTING. D.C.

agglutination. In immunology (see IMMUNITY), the clumping together of CELLS, particularly red blood corpuscles, brought about by the action of a specific antibody. Thus SERUM from someone of BLOOD GROUP B or O will agglutinate the red blood corpuscles from someone of blood group A. The antibodies that bring this about are called *agglutinins*. P.M.

agglutinative, see AGGLUTINATING.

aggregate demand. The value of total planned expenditures on domestically produced output, i.e. public and private consumption and investment, plus exports minus imports. In a one sector KEYNESIAN economic MODEL, aggregate demand depends mainly on the level of NATIONAL INCOME and the exchange rate — the latter affects exports and imports. The EQUILIBRIUM level of national income is that income which is equal to aggregate demand, i.e. income is equal to planned expenditure. Keynesian economic theory proposes that certain markets, particularly the labour market, may fail to move towards equilibrium and involuntarily UNEMPLOYMENT occurs. The demand of the involuntarily unemployed is ineffective, as it is not backed by income. A possible lack of effective demand lies behind the view that national income is the major determinant of effective aggregate demand. In MONETARIST economic theory, it is assumed that all markets adjust towards equilibrium, in which case the interactions of supplies and demands for products and inputs of production would eventually determine an equilibrium in which there is no excess demand or supply for anything and, in particular, there is no involuntary unemployment. In an economic model which has markets for money, labour and a single good, aggregate demand is a relation between the price level and output, which gives equilibrium in the money and the goods markets. In this economic model, AGGREGATE SUPPLY and demand determine total output and employment. J.P.

Bibl: R. Levacic and A. Rebmann, *Macroeconomics* (London, 2nd ed., 1982).

aggregate supply. The total value of output that the economy wishes to supply at each price level. AGGREGATE DEMAND and supply together determine NATIONAL INCOME. See KEYNESIAN and MONETARISM. J.P.

Bibl: R. Levacic and A. Rebmann, *Macroeconomics* (London, 2nd ed., 1982).

aggregation.
(1) In STATISTICS, ECONOMETRICS and ECONOMICS the grouping of similar vari-

ables together, i.e. into aggregates, to simplify the description or modelling of complex phenomena. For example, NATIONAL INCOME is not described by recording the output of each product, but is represented by the sum of the level of each output multiplied by its price; and, in modelling the effects of INFLATION, the increases in prices of different goods may be represented by a single index. Condensation of different variables into a single aggregate involves a loss of information. The cost of this loss should be balanced against the benefits that are gained from conciseness. See INDEX NUMBER.   J.P.

Bibl: M. Desai, *Applied Econometrics* (London, 1976).

(2) In BIOLOGY, a grouping or crowding together of separate organisms. The term is used also to describe the movement of tentacles and tendrils to a point which is stimulated, as for instance in sea anemones. The gregarious habit, producing aggregations of animals, is considered to be a primitive form of social behaviour. It implies a temporary grouping of individuals, usually of the same age and in the same state of development (e.g. caterpillars on a food plant, mosquitoes over a pond). Mating may occur when aggregations exist, but the pairs usually separate soon afterwards.   K.M.

Bibl: J.L. Cloudsley-Thompson, *Animal Behaviour* (Edinburgh, 1960; New York, 1961).

aggression. Animal or human behaviour which is provoked by another individual and which has deterrent or aversive effects on that individual: it leads him to withdraw, either by moving away or by ceasing to dispute some object which is the occasion of the aggression. The charge of a ram in rut, the measured display of two male Siamese fighting fish, and the malicious remark made by a man about a professional colleague may all represent examples of aggression in these SPECIES.

Animal aggression is extremely widespread, and appears to evolve whenever a species needs some kind of deterrent behaviour to secure access to some commodity in short supply. Thus there may be fighting over TERRITORY, food, females, sleeping places, or nesting burrows, or for social precedence as a determinant of access to any of these. The hunting behaviour of predators shares some of the features of aggression but is essentially different in that the goal is to eat the other animal rather than simply to drive it away. It may, however, provoke aggression in the form of defensive reactions. Such reactions against predators and against prey should be distinguished from social aggression directed at members of the same species. In the latter, while there is usually the ultimate sanction of physical violence, more often the fight consists of a graduated series of escalating displays which indicate to each combatant how ready the opponent is to continue the struggle. The fight ends when one combatant either runs away or assumes some special posture of appeasement which tends to ensure safety from attack. If, however, space to flee is restricted, e.g. in captivity, the attack on the defeated animal may continue and it may be killed.

The relation between aggression in animals and in man has been much disputed. This is especially true of the last decade, with the development of the specialized study of SOCIOBIOLOGY, which has reaffirmed the continuity between animal and human behaviour within the DARWINIAN framework of adaptive evolutionism (see EVOLUTION). Postulating some kind of putative genetic (see GENETICS) underpinning, sociobiologists have contended that apparently dysfunctional human attributes (such as mass aggression) may mark not cultural backwardness but necessary survival strategies. A more complex approach argues that socio-cultural requirements and genetic programming have here become out of step. Certainly, however, the view outlined above suggests that the matter should be examined in the light of the life styles and needs of each species. The complexity of human society involves infinitely complex social, psychological, and biological needs, and many of these goals are achieved through aggressive behaviour, often largely verbal. Such behaviour seems to correspond to animal threat signals in that it is designed to gain access to special facilities, and if unsuccessful may lead to more violent forms of aggression. The expression of individual aggression in man can take almost any form and be associated with a great num-

17

ber of motivational factors, frustration of some goal-directed behaviour being a common one. In man too there is WAR, which operates as aggression at the level of society, but in which the motives of the combatants may be very different from the anger of a private dispute.　　　J.M.C.;R.P.

Bibl: K. Lorenz, tr. M. Latzke, *On Aggression* (London and New York, 1966); C. Stern, *Principles of Human Genetics* (San Francisco, 3rd ed., 1973).

agitprop. A term derived from the name of the Department of Agitation and Propaganda, set up in September 1920 as a section of the Central Committee secretariat of the COMMUNIST Party of the Soviet Union. Through all subsequent changes of its name, its function has remained the same: the control of activities concerned with the ideological conditioning of the population. More generally, the term is sometimes used to denote any kind of communication designed explicitly to manipulate ideological beliefs, especially if the intended result includes a raising of enthusiasm or intensity of belief. L.L.;S.R.

agnosia, see under NEUROPSYCHOLOGY.

agnosticism. A word coined by T.H. Huxley (1825-95) to refer to his own conviction that knowledge (Greek *gnosis*) is impossible in many of the matters covered by religious doctrines and by philosophical speculation, so that on these matters, unless science can speak, silence is the only wisdom. A considerable degree of agnosticism about the supernatural has been a mark of almost all thinking people in the 20th century, whether or not these hold that there is TRUTH in THEISM and VALUE in THEOLOGY. In particular it has generally been agreed that religious faith does not provide factual knowledge more authoritative than NATURAL SCIENCE, and that Huxley was therefore right to defend the DARWINIAN discovery of EVOLUTION against Christians who took the biblical COSMOGONY literally. See also ATHEISM; HUMANISM; NON-THEISTIC RELIGION.
　　　　　　　　　　　　　　　　D.L.E.

Bibl: W.M. Dixon, *The Human Situation* (London and New York, 1937).

AGR. Advanced gas-cooled reactor. A NUCLEAR REACTOR using carbon dioxide as the coolant, graphite as the moderator, and ceramic uranium dioxide cased in stainless steel as the fuel.　　　C.E.D.

agrarian history. The history of farming techniques and peasant customs. The term came into general use about 1950, and covers two rather different approaches:

(1) that of economic historians interested in a particular industry, agriculture; this approach is dominant in England (the 'Leicester school') and the Netherlands (the 'Wageningen school', led by B.H. Slicher van Bath);

(2) that of social historians interested in a particular social group, the peasants; this is the French approach, associated in particular with Marc Bloch and Emmanuel Le Roy Ladurie, and perhaps better described as *rural history*.　　　P.B.

Bibl: Joan Thirsk (series ed.), *The Agrarian History of England and Wales* (Cambridge, in progress since 1972).

agribusiness. The sum total of all operations involved in (1) the manufacture and distribution of products used for production purposes on farms; (2) production on farms; and (3) the storage, processing, and distribution of commodities produced on farms and items made from them. For the situation in most developed countries in the mid-20th century the term can be regarded as covering those activities which were carried out on family farms before draught animals were displaced by tractors and before the growth of the artificial fertilizer and specialist animal feeding-stuffs industries and the highly organized processing and distribution industries for food and natural fibres. Interest in the subject usually centres on the means of securing coordination between the various stages.　　　K.E.H.

Bibl: G.L. Cramer and C. W. Jensen, *Agricultural Economics and Agribusiness* (New York, 1982).

agricultural policy. A set of official measures, of widely varying type, used to influence the agricultural sector often with the aim of increasing incomes. In Britain after a long period of laissez-faire through the later 19th century and some intervention in 1914-21, specific instruments (notably the formation of marketing boards and introduction of some deficiency payments) were adopted as a response to the 1930s depression and continued after wartime control under the 1947 Agriculture Act. Prices of products paid to farmers were raised by DEFICIENCY PAYMENTS and imports were subsidized through production grants. This phase ended with accession to the EEC and the gradual adoption of the markedly different frontier protection, intervention purchase and export subsidization characteristic of the CAP. The U.S. also adopted wide-ranging price support measures in the 1930s (the loan rate scheme) and has continued to do so, bolstering their effect with other devices such as land set-aside schemes and deficiency payments. Some attempt to reorientate American agriculture to market forces was made in the 1985 Farm Bill. Centrally planned economies frequently, though not exclusively, base their policy on forms of collectivization. In the THIRD WORLD there is emphasis on promoting development through LAND REFORM, the use of GREEN REVOLUTION technology, and irrigation, though pricing policy is common. The emphasis sometimes switches towards FOOD POLICY.

Influential opinion, best expressed by the WORLD BANK, is that many developed countries have been over-protectionist, thus misallocating resources and forgoing the benefits of increasing trade. The laudable aims of increasing the stability of a sector, notoriously subject to fluctuating prices and sometimes in need of STRUCTURAL reform, have been underemphasized. It is also not uncommon in developing countries for micro- and macroECONOMIC policies to inhibit agriculture (through overvalued EXCHANGE RATES, protection of domestic manufactures providing inputs, and TAXATION of exportable and import competing crops), though this is not universal.   G.H.P.

Bibl: World Bank, *World Development Report* (Oxford, 1986).

agrology, see SOIL SCIENCE.

agronomy. The scientific study of agricultural production processes.   K.E.H.

AID, see under ARTIFICIAL INSEMINATION.

AIDS. Acronym of the acquired immune deficiency syndrome, an end result of infection by the human immunodeficiency virus (HIV, formerly called HTLV3). AIDS is a disease complex of opportunistic infections and malignant disease which occurs because defence mechanisms have been irreparably damaged by the virus, and is invariably fatal. Common manifestations are severe weight loss, intractable diarrhoea, pneumonia and cerebral disease. The incubation period between infection by HIV and the appearance of AIDS may be several years, during which the victim feels well but is infectious to others. The proportion of people infected by HIV who subsequently develop AIDS is not known with certainty, but may be as high as 50%. HIV is sexually transmissible, the greatest risk coming from anal intercourse. It has also been transmitted by the administration of infected blood and blood products (although this can be prevented), and by the sharing of syringes and needles by intravenous drug abusers. Accidental infection is very rare. In Europe and North America the majority of cases of AIDS, and carriers of HIV, are at present male homosexuals, followed by drug abusers. In sub-Saharan Africa, however, most infections are acquired heterosexually, and there are fears that heterosexual transmission may become established in industrialized countries as well. There is neither a cure nor a preventive vaccine for AIDS. The only control possible is by health education to encourage monogamy or, failing that, the general use of condoms. A blood test which detects exposure to HIV (but not AIDS) is available, and voluntary testing to discover whether a person is infected, and therefore liable to infect other people, is to be encouraged.   J.D.O.

Bibl: D. Miller, J. Weber, J. Green, *The Management of AIDS Patients* (London, 1986).

AIH, see under ARTIFICIAL INSEMINATION.

air photography. As an adjunct of ARCHAEOLOGY, the technique of photographing archaeological sites or landscapes from the air. Among the earliest archaeological air photographs were those of Stonehenge (1906). In the 1920s the method was developed by O.G.S. Crawford, Major Allen, Père Poidebard, and Col. Charles Lindberg. Its success depends on choosing the optimum conditions for registering the visibility of the buried remains. Thus in ploughed fields features may show as discolorations in the soil, while, under crop, differential growth may reflect subsoil variations. When slight relief is preserved, low sunlight will throw sharp shadows. Vertical photographs in overlapping pairs are used for stereoscopic scanning and photogrammetric planning; oblique photographs are generally used to demonstrate the buried features more clearly. Experiments with INFRA-RED photography are now under way.   B.C.

Aktion, Die, see under ACTIVISM; EXPRESSIONISM.

Alawites, see under ISLAM.

albinism. A congenital defect, of mutational origin (see MUTATION), in the pigmentary system of human beings and rodents, caused by a biochemical deficiency of pigmentary CELLS and leading to the virtually complete absence of pigmentation in the skin and the retina of the eye (which accordingly looks red). In one form of albinism the deposition of pigment is stimulated by a low skin temperature with the effect that the body generally is white but the 'points' (nose, eartips, paws) are black. This is the so-called 'Himalayan' pattern.   P.M.

alcoholism. Before the 19th century excessive habitual consumption of alcoholic drinks was chiefly seen as a vice or a sin. From the time of Thomas Trotter and Benjamin Rush at the beginning of the 19th century, the weakness was increasingly called a disease by medical men and temperance reformers alike, on the grounds that a biochemically based dependence was created, withdrawal produced illness symptoms, and psychiatric disturbance followed. This MEDICALIZATION of alcoholism reached its high-point with Jellinek's 1960 book, *The Disease Concept of Alcoholism.* The anti-addictive organization, Alcoholics Anonymous, set up in 1935, also subscribed to the disease theory, partly because it reduced stigmatization. Today's therapists are deeply divided as to whether the DISEASE MODEL is either accurate or helpful. BEHAVIOUR THERAPIES have recently found preference over drug and AVERSION THERAPIES, and supportive groups are commonly used. It is nowadays stressed that the motivation and cooperation of the patient are requisite to overcome this increasing social scourge.   R.P.

aleatory (or, less commonly, *aleatoric*). An adjective (derived from Latin *alea*, a game using dice) applied to several of the arts, and indicating that the artist or writer or composer allows some element of chance to be involved.

In art, the deliberate exploitation of the workings of chance can be held to go back to the 'blot drawings' of Alexander Cozens in the late 18th century. In our own century the practice began with the 'found objects' (see OBJET TROUVÉ) of the SURREALISTS and, in the 1940s, the accidental drip technique of Jackson Pollock (see ACTION PAINTING). In KINETIC ART effects are sometimes regarded as aleatory merely in so far as they are achieved with the aid of unpredictable natural forces such as air, water, fire, magnetism, or chemical action. A more mathematical use of random selection can be seen in many forms of COMPUTER art (e.g. COMPUTER GRAPHICS) and in the permutation of symbols in some CONCRETE POETRY.

In literature, the 'cut-out' and 'fold-in' method of William Burroughs involves the random stringing together of sentences (his own and other people's) in whose combination some mystical significance is assumed; other writers (e.g. B.S. Johnson in *Trawl*) allow the reader to assemble pages *ad lib.* Michel Butor and Henri Pousseur's opera, *Votre Faust*, allows the audience to select the ending. Again, the computer is sometimes used to generate random combinations of preselected words or sentences, as by the Italian poet Nanni Balestrini or the German aesthetician (see AESTHETICS) Max Bense. The results can only be made acceptable if it is assumed that repetitiousness and boredom are legitimate elements of art.

In music, an aleatory element is introduced if, e.g., the order in which sections of a composition are performed is decided by the throwing of a dice, or if there is improvisation by the performers, usually on patterns suggested in the score. In its more extreme forms, music commonly but improperly called aleatory (since it is *indeterminate* rather than determined by chance) can be criticized as a dereliction of responsibility by the composer, as when the performer is expected to interpret symbols having no basis in any previously known form of musical notation. Yet, used imaginatively, it has proved a useful addition to the resources of the 20th-century composer.

In HAPPENINGS and other mixed-media exercises, similar random choices are common. The *I Ching* or Book of Change has had a considerable influence on some of the leading practitioners, giving an alleged deep meaningfulness to the abrogation of human choice. Other adjectives used with connotations similar to those of aleatory are *stochastic* and PERMUTATIONAL.   J.W.;P.C.;A.H.

Alexander Technique. A movement awareness technique created by Frederick Matthias Alexander (1869-1945), which focuses on conscious participation, correcting and re-educating habitual movement patterns. Alexander lessons are conducted on a one-to-one basis in which the student is guided through simple everyday actions, e.g. walking, getting up from a chair, writing. The key to postural realignment in Alexander Technique is that of initiating movement from the head in a forward and upward motion concentrating on the process of the action rather than the end product. The application of Alexander Technique can also have a therapeutic value and create a sense of physical and psychological relaxation by preventing habitual overreactions to everyday stimuli. Traditionally the Alexander Technique has been used by musicians and actors to relieve themselves from the tensions and postural problems related to their acts, but is now increasingly studied by a wide range of individuals. Dancers, and particularly those involved in NEW DANCE, often study Alexander Technique alongside other awareness through movement techniques (see FELDENKRAIS METHOD, RELEASE DANCE and CONTACT IMPROVISATION).   L.A.

Bibl: M. Gelb, *Body Learning* (London, 1981); W. Barlow, *The Alexander Principle* (London, 1975).

algebra. The branch of MATHEMATICS traditionally associated with performing arithmetic operations on expressions containing letters (VARIABLES) which stand for unknown or indeterminate NUMBERS. If division, except by an integer, be excluded, then every such expression is a POLYNOMIAL with rational COEFFICIENTS, e.g. $\frac{1}{2}xy^3 + \frac{1}{4}z^2 - 3x + \frac{2}{3}$. An *algebraic equation* (see also EQUATION) is the condition on the variables expressed by setting such a polynomial equal to zero. If there is only one variable then there are finitely many real or COMPLEX numbers which satisfy the equation — its *roots*. An *algebraic number* is a root of some such equation. The theory of these numbers, *Galois theory*, is one of the most satisfying branches of mathematics; it was founded by Évariste Galois (1811-32), who was killed in a duel at the age of 21. He showed that there can be no algebraic formula for solving equations of the 5th degree. His methods also prove that some famous geometrical problems (doubling the cube, trisecting an angle) cannot be solved by ruler and compasses. The theory of algebraic equations in more than one variable is the concern of algebraic GEOMETRY. *Abstract algebra* is concerned with general MATHEMATICAL STRUCTURES which have analogues of the arithmetical operations; see, e.g., BOOLEAN ALGEBRA; GROUPS; MATRICES; QUATERNIONS; VECTORS. Such structures may be characterized by axioms (see AXIOMATIC METHOD); of particular importance are the ASSOCIATIVE LAW and the COMMUTATIVE LAW. Algebraic methods, which reduce the solution of problems to manipulations of symbolic expressions, permeate all branches of mathematics.   R.G.

Bibl: L. Nový, *Origins of Modern Algebra* (Prague, 1973).

algedonic. Pertaining to REGULATION in a non-analytic mode. The word derives

21

from the Greek words for pain and pleasure, and expresses the fact that some regulators operate within a SYSTEM from CRITERIA that exist only in a METASYSTEM. For example, people may be trained to perform a task by explaining the system in which that task plays a part, analysing the 'why' and the 'how' of the job. But they may also be trained algedonically by a series of rewards and punishments which offer no such explanations. The metasystem making these awards constrains the system by regulating outcomes and not by direct intervention. For example, a fail-safe device switches off an entire system because some output of the system has reached a level regarded as dangerous to the whole: it may take days to discover later what actually went wrong. S.BE.

algorithm. A procedure for performing a complicated operation by carrying out a precisely determined sequence of simpler ones — e.g. the digit-by-digit multiplication of large numbers which only uses single-digit multiplication and addition; or the direction 'First left, second right, turn right at the Red Lion, my house is the third on the left'. The same task can often be performed by different algorithms of widely varying COMPLEXITY. The development of algorithms has introduced a hierarchical structure into human thought which has greatly increased its power. They form suitable subjects for computer programs (see COMPUTER; PROGRAM) since they exclude all personal judgement; and part of the importance of computers lies in the way in which they have extended the length and complexity of algorithms which can be used, and hence the range of problems which can be tackled mechanically. VALUE-JUDGEMENTS and many complicated situations are not amenable to algorithmic treatment except in the form of greatly simplified MODELS. See also PROGRAMMING. C.S.

alias transformation, see under TRANSFORMATION.

alienation. For about a century (c. 1840 to 1940) the term was used to denote either the transfer of ownership or title of a piece of property, or a quality of mental derangement or insanity. Then a set of new and different meanings began to appear: a sense of estrangement from society, a feeling of powerlessness to affect social change, or a depersonalization of the individual in a large and bureaucratic (see BUREAUCRACY) society. By the 1950s the new meanings had become widely established and alienation had become a central term of contemporary SOCIOLOGY.

Reasons for these developments included the evident disorientations of the Western world in the upheaval of society following World War II; the expansion of an intelligentsia (see INTELLECTUALS) which found its own ROLE and STATUS problematic; the growing influence of German sociological writers (notably Georg Simmel and Max Weber) who stressed bureaucratization and the helplessness of the individual; the theological writings of Paul Tillich with his emphasis on the depersonalization of the individual in modern society; and — the most direct and important influence — the discovery of some early writings of Marx which had used alienation as a key CONCEPT in the analysis of CAPITALISM. (For another key concept see REIFICATION.) These were the so-called Economic and Philosophical Manuscripts written in 1844, and published only in 1932 in the abortive *Marx-Engels Gesamtausgabe*. They reflect the strong influence on Marx's thinking of Hegel, for whom alienation is the central process in the growing self-consciousness of Man. As Hegel traces the idea in his *Phenomenology of Mind*, CONSCIOUSNESS 'divides' itself into subject and object, and alienation is the process whereby mind 'objectifies' itself in thought — a positive step in the development of self-consciousness. Marx concentrates on the alienation of labour and emphasizes the invidious aspects. He uses three terms, all of which have confusingly been translated as 'alienation': *Vergegenstandlichung*, or objectification, whose English equivalent in the philosophical sense is reification; *Entfremdung* or estrangement (Hegel had used principally *Selbstentfremdung* — 'self-estrangement'); and *Entäusserung* or the sale of one's self as a commodity. In effect, Marx is saying that in the condition of alienation a worker loses control over the *processes* of work, over the *product* of his labour, and becomes a *thing*. Later, as

Marx focused his attention on social organization and CLASS relations, this cluster of terms disappeared from his vocabulary, and was replaced by the specific analytical concept of *Ausbeutung* or exploitation. The resurrection of the term 'alienation' in the late 1940s and 1950s was part of the effort of NEO-MARXISTS to reinstate a broader, more HUMANIST version of Marx's thought.

Within academic sociology, alienation was given a social-psychological emphasis (see SOCIAL PSYCHOLOGY) and, for a time, mingled with the concept of ANOMIE. Social psychologists sought to develop 'scales' of alienation to measure the degree of 'powerlessness', 'normlessness', 'meaninglessness', and 'social isolation' felt by individuals, and further efforts were made to correlate these psychological states with conformity, political apathy, cynicism, suicide, and a host of similar phenomena. Most of these efforts had evaporated by the end of the 1960s. (In the modern theatre the BRECHTIAN *Verfremdungseffekt*, alienation effect, indicates 'distancing' — see AESTHETIC DISTANCE — as opposed to the direct emotional involvement of the spectator in the action on the stage.) Within MARXISM, an onslaught against the concept of alienation as central to Marx was mounted by the French COMMUNIST philosopher Louis Althusser, who contended that Marx had discarded the earlier Hegelian influences and had come to what Althusser calls a STRUCTURALIST interpretation of society. For these reasons, plus the rise of a mood of revolutionary (see REVOLUTION) activism by students in the late 1960s, the concept of alienation had by the close of the decade begun to lose much of its resonance in LEFT-wing thinking.　　　　　　　D.B.

Bibl: D. Bell, 'The Debate on Alienation', in L. Labedz (ed.), *Revisionism* (London and New York, 1962); R. Schacht, *Alienation* (New York, 1970); B. Ollman, *Alienation: Marx's Conception of Man in Capitalist Society* (Cambridge and New York, 1976).

alkali. A hydroxide of lithium, sodium, potassium, rubidium, or caesium; most commonly sodium hydroxide. Solutions of alkalis are strongly basic (see BASE).　B.F.

alkaloid. A member of an arbitrary and ill-defined class of (pharmacologically active) plant extractives, mostly possessing pronounced pharmacological effects, and all tasting very bitter — the property to which they owe their name. They include atropine, morphine, and digitalis. Most of the alkaloids are BASES and form salts with ACIDS.　　　　　　　　　　　　　P.M.

alkathene, see POLYTHENE.

all-or-none law. A law governing the relationships between the excitatory STIMULUS acting upon a nerve fibre (whether by direct stimulation or through a sense organ) and the impulse which it excites. Nothing happens until the excitatory stimulus exceeds a certain 'threshold' value, whereupon the nerve fibre propagates an impulse at a rate which is different for different nerve fibres. As the passage of this impulse is followed by an inexcitable period known as its *absolute refractory state* it follows that the nerve fibre will perform either fully or not at all.

　　　　　　　　　　　　　　　P.M.

all people's state. The formula used in Soviet IDEOLOGY to describe the present nature of the STATE in the Soviet Union. Marx and Lenin considered that once class conflict had ended the state would wither away. Stalin explained the growth of state power under the dictatorship of the proletariat even after SOCIALISM had officially been achieved by citing the need to oppose hostile forces abroad and class enemies within. The concept of the all people's state, first used in the early 1960s and enshrined in the 1977 Constitution, explains why the state is being strengthened now these internal and external threats have diminished. The idea stresses the unity of Soviet society, particularly in the new stage of MATURE or DEVELOPED SOCIALISM, which makes the notion of the state as the instrument of dictatorship by the working class redundant. Instead the state's duty, while still defending its territory, is increasingly directed towards WELFARE provision and the administration of the economy. Because of the increasing complexity of these functions, the responsibilities of the state will necessarily grow rather than wither away.　　　　　D.PR.

23

Bibl: N. Harding, ed., *The State in Socialist Society* (London, 1984).

allele (formerly *allelomorph*). One of the hereditary factors which, in Mendelian (see MENDELISM) HEREDITY, are present in pairs, one factor from each pair deriving from each parent. When the two factors represent a choice of two from a range larger than two, the alleles are referred to as *multiple alleles*.   J.M.S.

allergy. A form of exaggerated immunological reactivity (see IMMUNITY) towards foreign organic substances such as pollen grains or certain industrial chemicals. Such *allergens* are normally harmless in themselves but the reactions they sometimes excite may cause considerable physical distress. The allergies conceived in a wide sense include asthma, hayfever, urticaria, eczemas, local and systemic ANAPHYLAXIS, sensitization to industrial chemicals, and the strong reactivity towards tuberculin that is used in the Mantoux test for exposure to tubercular infection. Allergic reactivity can often be transferred from one individual to another by means of transfusions of blood SERUM containing the appropriate antibody.   P.M.

Alliance for Progress. A U.S. foreign policy initiative towards Latin America launched by the Kennedy Administration in August 1961. The Alliance was largely a response to the 1959 Cuban Revolution and was devised to pre-empt the emergence of further radical governments within Latin America or the Caribbean. It was a two-pronged strategy involving (1) the first U.S. public accession to long-standing Latin American demands for a long-term and substantial transfer of U.S. resources to assist in Latin American development along democratic PLURALIST lines (promoting goals such as sustained ECONOMIC GROWTH, more equitable income distribution, PUBLIC-SECTOR-led INDUSTRIALIZATION, agrarian reform, and improved education and health services) and (2) a sustained drive to equip and train the region's local armies for the implementation of counter-insurgency techniques to defeat incipient guerrilla uprisings. The policy foundered, however, partly on its own inherent contradictions (it was drasti-

cally undermined by the U.S. invasion of the Dominican Republic in 1965) and partly because of the activities of CONSERVATIVE vested interests in Washington. Economic assistance fell far short of projected levels, and by the late 1960s the Alliance was widely recognized to be redundant.   N.M.

Bibl: Julio Cotler and Richard R. Fagen, *Latin America and the United States: the Changing Political Realities* (Stanford, Ca., 1974).

Alliance Party, see under SOCIAL DEMOCRATIC PARTY.

allo-. A prefix used widely in linguistics to refer to any variation in the form of a linguistic unit which does not affect that unit's functional identity in the language. The formal variation is not linguistically distinctive, and results in no change in meaning. For example, different graphic shapes of the letter *A* (a, *a*, etc.) can be said to be *allographs* (i.e. graphic variants) of the same underlying unit. Variations in the phonetic shape of a PHONEME are called allophones (such as different pronunciations of the phoneme /p/ at the beginning and end of the word *pup*). Variations in the form of a MORPHEME are called allomorphs (such as the different forms of the plural ending in *cats*, *dogs*, and *horses*). Several other allo-terms have been invented.   D.C.

Bibl: D. Crystal, *Linguistics* (Harmondsworth, 1985).

allomorph, see under MORPHEME.

allopathy. A term used to describe the conventional medical system of treatment which is contrasted with HOMOEOPATHY. Allopathic treatment is said to be effective as a result of suppressing a symptom. The rise of allopathic medicine is linked to the development of pharmacology and anaesthesia in the late 19th and early 20th centuries. The criticisms levelled against an allopathic approach by the homoeopaths is that the incidence of side effects of the drugs used is high and the body's own defence system against illness and disease is not enhanced and indeed may well be jeopardized. Homoeopaths would add that allopathic treatment focuses on the diseased part and does not address the 'whole patient' and thus cannot bring about a cure. P.C.P.

allophone, see under PHONEME.

allotrope. When an ELEMENT exists in more than one molecular or structural form, each of these is called an allotrope. There are numerous examples: molecular oxygen contains two ATOMS, ozone has three; carbon has graphite and diamond as allotropes. The interconversion of allotropic forms is often brought about by changes in temperature and/or pressure. B.F.

allotypy. A state of affairs first described by the French immunologist (see IMMUNITY) Oudin in which the different individuals of a SPECIES possess antibody MOLECULES (immunoglobulins) belonging to one or another of a small number of distinct and well-defined chemical classes. There has since been some tendency to extend the notion to cover chemical POLYMORPHISM generally. This usage is unusual, however. P.M.

alloy. A mixture of metallic ELEMENTS, e.g. brass (copper and zinc), bronze (copper and tin), stainless steel (iron, with various other elements). B.F.

alpha particle. A very stable association of two PROTONS and two NEUTRONS, which is emitted during RADIOACTIVE decay, and which also constitutes the NUCLEUS of the helium ATOM. See also PARTICLE. M.V.B.

alternation of generations. A state of affairs in which, in the ordinary course of reproduction, vegetatively and sexually reproducing organisms succeed each other alternately. Asexual reproduction by budding or equivalent processes can only give rise to genetic replicas of the parent; sexual reproduction raises the possibility of a genetic intermingling between two different kinds of GENOME, and ultimately the formation of new kinds. Alternation of generations is common in the group of animals to which hydroids and jellyfish belong, and, among plants, in bryophytes and pheridophytes. P.M.

alternative architecture. Omnibus term for a number of architectural ideas of around the end of the 1960s mainly to do with self-build architecture based on earth, geodesic and similar structures. They were made from cheap, often recycled materials — sheet metal, plywood, tin cans, tree trunks, lumber and the like. A mainly American phenomenon, alternative architecture tapped a deep-rooted tradition of self-reliance in American culture. Intellectual support was to be provided by several passages in linguistic STRUCTURALIST literature, then fashionable in architectural theory, which made admiring reference to *bricolage* — the act of creation via ad hoc piecing together of elements which happened to be at hand — rather than deliberate, knowing, engineering design. S.L.

alternative economic strategy. Those policies that were developed by the LEFT wing of the Labour Party and movement, as a SOCIALIST response to the MONETARIST policies of the post-1979 Conservative government of the United Kingdom and, in particular, to the high levels of unemployment and DEINDUSTRIALIZATION that occurred. The term is often used loosely and there are a number of variants of the strategy, though six major elements can be distinguished: (1) A reflationary expansion of the economy, mainly through increased public spending, the purpose of which is to increase investment and employment (see KEYNESIAN). (2) Controls on foreign trade (see PROTECTIONISM) and movements of international capital (see EXCHANGE CONTROLS), the purposes of which are to improve the current and capital accounts of the BALANCE OF PAYMENTS, as the first element of the strategy would otherwise lead to a greater level of imports, and increase investment and employment. (3) Extension of public ownership, particularly of financial institutions (see NATIONALIZATION); this greater public involvement would be used to increase investment and government's control of the economy. (4) A national economic plan and planning agreements at the level of individual firms and industries (see STATE ECONOMIC PLANNING). (5) An increase in the participation of labour in the decision-making of firms. (6) Price controls. INCOMES POLICIES are sometimes included in alternative economic strategies, though in the Labour Party and movement there are great differences in views about their desirability. The major aims of alternative economic strategies are to increase employment, output, move the distribution of income in favour of labour and increase labour's participation in decision-making. Critics of these strategies have argued that they will lead to increased inflation, at best only a temporary increase in output and employment, foreign retaliation to import controls, balance of payment problems, the extension of inefficient public ownership and planning, a restriction on the ability of MANAGEMENT to run private firms, a squeeze on profit margins and a reduction in investment.   J.P.

Bibl: The Conference of Socialist Economists, *The Alternative Economic Strategy* (London, 1981).

alternative medicine, see under COMPLEMENTARY MEDICINE.

alternative society, see under UNDERGROUND.

alternative theatre. The term which is now most commonly applied to theatre presented outside the REPERTORY or regional theatres and the commercial West End, Broadway or BOULEVARD theatres. It has largely replaced such definitions as FRINGE, OFF-BROADWAY, ANTI-THEATRE and even experimental theatre. Although there have been companies devoted to experiment and innovation throughout the 20th century (see THÉÂTRE LIBRE), the contemporary alternative theatre movement blossomed during the intellectual upheavals of the 1960s, when most of the work had a radically political outlook. Nowadays companies are equally likely to be concerned with the exploration of the performers' own creative and technical skills, CELEBRATORY THEATRE, gay and feminist theatre, or the local production of theatre of ethnic and social minorities who are considered culturally deprived. Many alternative theatre companies are short-lived and financially insecure, but others have achieved relatively generous subsidies (see THIRD THEATRE).   M.A.

Bibl: S. Craig (ed.), *Dreams and Deconstructions: Alternative Theatre in Britain* (Ambergate, 1980); T. Shank, *American Alternative Theatre* (London, 1982).

Althusserianism. The distinctive contribution to contemporary MARXISM of the French philosopher and sociologist, Louis Althusser. Althusser has argued — contrary to most recent interpretations — that Marx did not remain under the spell of Hegel for most of his life. There is, from the late 1840s onwards, a distinct 'epistemological break' (*coupure epistémologique*) in Marx's thinking, whereby he shook off the residual IDEALISM of his youth and embarked on a thoroughly materialistic, scientific SOCIOLOGY. From Marx's later writings Althusser has distilled a formal model of the economy and society whose distinctive feature is the absence of the extreme economic determinism which characterizes most Marxist theory.

In particular, Althusser has reformulated the 'base and SUPERSTRUCTURE' relationship central to traditional Marxism. While the economy — the base — is seen as the determinant 'in the last instance' of other areas of social life, such as politics and IDEOLOGY, the economic base itself depends for its functioning on these other areas: they are 'conditions of existence' of the economy. Thus the political system of the ancient world was the condition of existence of the slave economy, just as religion was the condition of existence of the feudal economy of medieval Europe — even though the slave and feudal economies were 'in the last instance' the determinants of the forms of politics and religion. Althusser allows for the 'relative autonomy' of the different levels or realms of society — such as politics or culture — to the point where some feel that the distinctively Marxist emphasis on the economic base is in danger of disappearing altogether. He also suggests a degree of overlapping or *overdetermination* of levels of society which further complicates the simple model of an economic base determining a superstructure. Cultural divisions such as those between town and country, particular national or CLASS traditions, and the precise state of international relations at any one time, can all 'act back' on the economic base, inhibiting or reinforcing the primary conflict of classes that takes place there. All social phenomena, Althusser suggests, are so 'overdetermined': there is no such thing as 'pure' relations of production. The precise form of overdetermination in any society at any time can make all the difference to such matters as the success or failure of REVOLUTION.

The importance Althusser attaches to the superstructure in the operation of the economic base is seen especially in his concept of *Ideological State Apparatuses*. In order to persist over time, he argues, an economic system such as CAPITALISM must continually 'reproduce' its relations of production, that is, the exploitative class relationship arising out of ownership or non-ownership of the means of production. Much of this is done through the work of the Ideological State Apparatuses, which include TRADE UNIONS and political parties, religious and educational institutions, the family, the mass MEDIA, sport, art and literature. All these act to integrate individuals into the existing economic system by subjecting them to the HEGEMONY of a DOMINANT IDEOLOGY, a set of ideas and values which ultimately supports the dominance of the capitalist class. Once again this emphasis on the importance of ideology in the functioning of capitalism has led some Marxists to accuse Althusser of substituting a cultural determinism for the more traditional economic determinism. Certainly there is a nice paradox here, that a thinker who has been the foremost advocate of the 'scientific' character of Marxism should at the same time be the principal opponent of straightforward materialist explanations of social life.

K.K.

Bibl: L. Althusser, *For Marx* (London, 1969); L. Althusser, *Lenin and Philosophy, and Other Essays* (London, 1971).

Amal, see under LEBANON.

amalgam. An ALLOY containing mercury. Amalgams of silver, gold, and tin are used in dentistry.   B.F.

ambient music. Term used by the composer Brian Eno to describe some of his compositions which are designed to form an aural background rather than be the centre of the listener's attention. The music is often very simple, repetitive, even MINIMAL, and played at low volume. This type of music has links with FURNITURE MUSIC and also MUZAK although its artistic rather than commercial purposes would tend to distance it from the latter. B.CO.

ambiguity. The coexistence in a piece of writing of two or more meanings. William Empson introduced his *Seven Types of Ambiguity* (1930; 2nd ed., 1947) by stating: 'I propose to use the word in an extended sense, and shall think relevant to my subject any verbal nuance, however slight, which gives room for alternative reactions to the same piece of language.' This study, directly influenced by I.A. Richards and Robert Graves, was very much a product of a time excited by T.S. Eliot's poetry and criticism, by the revival of the 17th-century Metaphysical poets, and by Freud. If over-ingenious, *Seven Types of Ambiguity* is a complex and sophisticated work (Empson reminds us that 'if an ambiguity is to be unitary there must be "forces" holding its elements together'), but during the 1930s and 40s 'ambiguity' became so fashionable that many versifiers cultivated it, whether usefully or not, while critics hunted it down indiscriminately, thus denigrating those kinds of literature where they could not find it. Ambiguity is a quality of much fine writing, endowing it with richness, subtlety or surprise, but in itself (like rhyme, onomatopoeia, figures of speech, etc.) it is neither good nor bad. See also PLURISIGNATION.   D.J.E.

ambivalence. Term used originally (as *ambivalency*) in ABNORMAL PSYCHOLOGY and PSYCHIATRY, later annexed by literary criticism, to denote the situation in which someone entertains, simultaneously or in alternation, opposed attitudes or feelings or sets of values; the familiar 'love-hate relationship' may be said to exemplify reciprocal ambivalence. Whereas, in general, ambivalence is a potential source of undesirable stress (and in extreme forms is one of the four cardinal symptoms of SCHIZOPHRENIA listed by Eugen Bleuler), in a writer it is widely regarded as a source of strength and desirable TENSION, and in a fictional character as evidence of subtlety in his or her creator.   O.S.; M.J.C.

Amiens, Charter of, see under SYNDICALISM.

amino acids. The molecular elements out of which PROTEINS are compounded. Proteins generally are compounded of some 20 different kinds of amino acid, some of which are essential constituents of the diet — e.g. lysine. Not all proteins contain a full representation of amino acids. Those that contain the essential amino acids are often referred to as 'complete' or 'first-class' proteins; those that lack one or more essential amino acids (e.g. gelatin) are referred to as 'second-class' proteins.   P.M.

amnesia, see under NEUROPSYCHOLOGY.

amorphous materials. Solids in which the constituent ATOMS or MOLECULES are not arranged in a perfectly regular pattern as they are in crystals. The most common example of an amorphous material is ordinary glass. There is usually a tendency for many amorphous materials to revert to a crystalline form with time, especially if they are heated, and they generally have to be made by rapidly cooling the molten material to room temperature. The current interest in these materials comes from the SEMICONDUCTOR industry which up to now has relied on very tiny pieces of crystalline silicon or germanium for the fabrication of devices such as TRANSISTORS, etc. However, the exploitation of the properties of semiconductors to produce electrical power from sunlight (solar CELLS) requires large areas of semiconductor so that as much sunlight as possible is trapped, and since it would be very difficult to make these as perfect crystals, it is in principle much easier and cheaper to make them in the amorphous form. It has proved difficult to make amorphous semiconductors with the same electrical properties that crystals have. Nevertheless, amorphous silicon solar cells are now being used to power small calculators and other devices, but their use as power generators on a large scale is still in the development stage.   H.M.R.

amplidyne. An electrical machine mostly used as a large direct current power source in which the output power level is controlled by means of a very small quantity of electric power. Basically the system is equivalent to a pair of DC generators, each separately excited. The first has its output winding connected to the field circuit of the second machine. The field winding of the first machine carries the very small control current. The system can be identified with a 2-stage electronic amplifier in which the power output is derived from a battery. In the case of the machines the power output is obtained mechanically via the drive shaft from a prime mover. In the amplidyne system the two machines are combined into a single unit by making use of the phenomenon of armature reaction, whereby the passage of armature current produces a field in the cross axis, not linking with the field coil. This current is maximized by short-circuiting the armature, and the cross field is then supplemented by connecting additional coils located in the cross axis in series with the shorted armature. The armature current then acts as field current in the second stage and magnetizes the cross axis. A second pair of brushes orthogonal to the first, collects the power output. Compensating coils on the first field axis are used to prevent armature reaction in the second stage from neutralizing the control field.   E.R.L.

amplitude modulation (AM). A method for the radio transmission of AUDIO FREQUENCY signals, which are made to vary (or MODULATE) the strength of a RADIO FREQUENCY carrier wave. Broadcasts on short, medium, and long wavebands make use of amplitude modulation; this enables more transmissions to be crowded onto each waveband, at the price of some distortion of the signal (see also FREQUENCY MODULATION).   M.V.B.

AMU. Atomic mass unit. A unit of mass used to express atomic and molecular weights that is equal to one-twelfth of the mass of an atom of carbon-12. It is equivalent to 1.66×10^{-27} kg. It is also called a unified atomic mass unit or a dalton (after John Dalton, 1766-1844, the English chemist and physicist who formulated the modern form of the atomic theory). C.E.D.

anabolism, see under METABOLISM.

anaerobes, see under BACTERIOLOGY.

anaesthesia. A loss of sensation produced by an anaesthetic. This may be provided as a general anaesthetic involving a drug administered intravenously or inhaled as a gas or vapour, or by administration of a local anaesthetic to provide regional blockade to a limb. The term also means loss of the sense of pain, touch, movement produced by disease. D.W.R.

anal character, see under PSYCHOSEXUAL DEVELOPMENT.

analgesia. A state of not feeling pain but without loss of consciousness. Achieved by a variety of drugs usually of the opiate (narcotic) group which can be given orally, intramuscularly or intravenously. Inhalation of some anaesthetics and the use of regional nerve blocks with local anaesthetics also achieve this effect. D.W.R.

analogue computer, see under COMPUTER.

analogue-to-digital converter, see under DIGITAL-TO-ANALOGUE CONVERTER.

analogy.
(1) In historical and comparative work in LINGUISTICS, the process of regularization which affects the exceptional forms in the grammar of a language. Irregular forms tend to become regular — a process which can be heard in early child utterance in such forms as *mans*, *mouses*, and *wented*, which are coined on analogy with regular plurals and past tenses. D.C.
Bibl: F. Palmer, *Grammar* (Harmondsworth, 1984).
(2) In PHILOSOPHY, likeness or similarity, usually with the implication that the likeness in question is systematic or structural. To argue by analogy is to infer from the fact that one thing is in some respects similar to another that the two things will also correspond in other, as yet unexamined, respects. In LOGIC, reasoning by analogy is a form of non-demonstrative

(see DEMONSTRATION) argument which, unlike INDUCTION proper, draws conclusions about the nature of a *single* unknown thing from information about a known thing or things which it to some extent resembles. It is a form of reasoning that is peculiarly liable to yield false conclusions from true premises. A.Q.

analogy tests, see under MENTAL TESTING.

analysis.
(1) In MATHEMATICS, the rigorous investigation of limiting processes (see LIMIT; CONVERGENCE). In particular it provides a firm foundation for the infinitesimal CALCULUS. Although Newton realized the importance of limits, so long as VARIABLES were thought of as things in motion it was not possible to pin down the basic CONCEPTS. In the 19th century this obstacle was overcome: the work of Bolzano, Cauchy, and Weierstrass replaced intuitive notions by precise definitions. It became clear that *naive* intuition is a poor guide to the correct handling of limiting processes; e.g. a FUNCTION (or curve) may be continuous (see CONTINUITY) and yet nowhere have a DERIVATIVE (or tangent). The construction of such queer nonintuitive counter-examples (often described by mathematicians as *pathological*) is an essential part of analysis. Through them intuition is refined to the point where correct formulations of definitions and theorems can be found and rigorous proofs given. *Classical analysis* is concerned with functions of *real numbers* (see NUMBERS) and with COMPLEX FUNCTION THEORY. Many of its problems come from mathematical PHYSICS. In this century new branches of analysis have developed (e.g. MEASURE THEORY) and the subject has been enriched by the growth of TOPOLOGY. *Functional analysis* is concerned with operations on functions; it makes great use of (infinite-dimensional) VECTOR space and provides a mathematical foundation for QUANTUM MECHANICS (see also FOURIER ANALYSIS).
Unlike Newton, Leibniz thought in terms of *infinitesimals* — actually existing infinitely small quantities. As rigour developed these were rejected as metaphysical (see METAPHYSICS) and inconsistent.

Recently, with the help of a trick from MATHEMATICAL LOGIC, it has been shown that they can be given a sound interpretation, so that vivid imagery and rigorous proof can go hand in hand in what is called *non-standard analysis*. This has already found applications in mathematical economics (see ECONOMETRICS). R.G.

Bibl: D.H. Fowler, *Introducing Real Analysis* (London, 1973); A. Robinson, *Non-Standard Analysis* (Amsterdam, 1970).

(2) In PHILOSOPHY, the discovery of verbal forms of expression for complex ideas and PROPOSITIONS which make explicit the complexity that is hidden by the more abbreviated character of their usual verbal formulation. As originally conceived by Russell and Moore, it was a kind of defining process, in which the defining terms are more elementary and unproblematic than the terms being defined. Examples are Mill's analysis of 'cause' as 'invariable unconditional antecedent' or the analysis of 'knowledge' as 'justified true belief'. Russell's theory of *descriptions* supplied a technique of analysis that was widely adopted. It showed how sentences with problematic terms in them could be replaced by sentences equivalent in MEANING to them in which the troublesome expressions do not occur. A.Q.

Bibl: A.J. Ayer, *Language, Truth and Logic* (London and New York, 1936); Bertrand Russell, *Our Knowledge of the External World* (London and New York, rev. ed., 1926), ch.8.

analytic.
(1) In PHILOSOPHY, a term introduced by Kant, who defined a statement as analytic if it is either (*a*) one in which the predicate is contained, 'though covertly', in the subject (e.g. 'This square has four sides') or (*b*) one whose denial is self-contradictory. Statements that are not analytic are *synthetic*: their predicates do not repeat part or all of the MEANING of the subject and their denials are CONSISTENT and not self-contradictory (e.g. 'This square is large'). Some recent philosophers have defined analytic statements, perhaps too comprehensively, as those which are true in virtue of their meaning. A connected notion of the analytic statements as those which can be shown to be true by

laws of LOGIC and definitions alone has been widely adopted. It is universally accepted that definitional truisms are analytic (e.g. 'That bachelor is not married'). Many philosophers take the laws of logic and the PROPOSITIONS of pure MATHEMATICS to be analytic and, indeed, maintain that all necessary truths, establishable by reasoning alone, are analytic too. The distinction between analytic and synthetic has been criticized by Quine as resting on an unacceptably obscure and imprecise notion of meaning. A.Q.

Bibl: A. Pap, *Semantics and Necessary Truth* (New Haven, 1958; London, 1966); W.V. Quine, *From a Logical Point of View* (London and Cambridge, Mass., 2nd ed., 1961) ch 2; and see under ANALYSIS (sense 2, item 2).

(2) In comparative LINGUISTICS, adjective applied to a language (e.g. Vietnamese) in which the word forms are invariable, grammatical relations being indicated primarily by word order and the use of particles, not by inflections or compounding (as in INFLECTING and AGGLUTINATING languages respectively). An alternative term is *isolating*. D.C.

analytic philosophy. The most general term for a wide variety of recent philosophical movements, largely in the English-speaking world, which (1) are sceptical of or hostile to constructive METAPHYSICAL speculation, (2) agree that there is a characteristic method of ANALYSIS with which alone philosophy can arrive at secure results, and (3), for the most part, favour the piecemeal tackling of philosophical problems. The EMPIRICISM of Locke, Hume, and Mill was analytical in tendency, seeking to show how the complex IDEAS (e.g. material object, cause, person) with which the mind thinks about the world are composed of simple ideas acquired through the senses. Analytical philosophers of this century have concentrated as a matter of principle, not on ideas in the mind, but on the language in which the mind's thinking is expressed. Bertrand Russell and G.E. Moore inaugurated analytic philosophy in the early years of the century by applying the new LOGIC, to which Russell had so greatly contributed, as an instrument of analysis. Wittgenstein, learning from and influencing Russell,

made the practice systematic and emphasized the linguistic character of its proper subject-matter (see LOGICAL ATOMISM). The LOGICAL POSITIVISM of the VIENNA CIRCLE carried the work further, and the earlier suspicion of metaphysics hardened into principled hostility. Wittgenstein later came to question the adequacy of formal logic as the instrument of analysis, and his school, and that of the ordinary-language philosophers of Oxford (see LINGUISTIC PHILOSOPHY) preferred to carry out the analysis of language informally, acknowledging the multiplicity of its uses and the variety and flexibility of the rules that govern it.   A.Q.
Bibl: J.O. Urmson, *Philosophical Analysis* (Oxford, 1956); L. J. Cohen, *Dialogue of Reason* (Oxford, 1986).

analytic psychology, see under JUNGIAN.

analytical chemistry. The branch of CHEMISTRY concerned with the identification and estimation of ELEMENTS, RADICALS, or compounds. *Qualitative analysis* is concerned with the detection of chemical SPECIES and often makes use of CHEMICAL REACTIONS which give distinctive products (recognized by colour, solubility, etc.), but characteristic physical properties are often directly investigated. For *quantitative determinations* a wide variety of chemical and physical methods have been developed. Chemical procedures include the precipitation and weighing of an insoluble product, the determination of the oxidizing or reducing properties of a solution, and the measurement of the ACID or BASE strength of a solution. Extensive use is made of physical measurements which may be based on spectroscopic or electrical behaviour (see SPECTROSCOPY; ELECTRICITY), the use of radioactive (see RADIOACTIVITY) ISOTOPES, or MASS SPECTROMETRY. CHROMATOGRAPHIC or ION EXCHANGE methods may be employed to effect an initial separation of mixtures.
                                                                B.F.

anaphora. In the field of GRAMMAR, the way in which a linguistic unit refers back to some previously expressed unit of meaning. In the sentence *He did that there*, each word has an 'anaphoric reference', making complete sense only when

some previous sentence (such as *John painted this picture in Bermuda*) is known. Anaphora often contrasts with *cataphora*, where the words refer forward, and with *exophora*, where the words refer directly to the extralinguistic situation.
                                                                D.C.
Bibl: F. Palmer, *Grammar* (Harmondsworth, 1984).

anaphylaxis. Literally, the opposite of PROPHYLAXIS. In practice its use is confined to an acute form of ALLERGY associated with the introduction of an antigen (see IMMUNITY), particularly a soluble antigen, into an organism that has already made antibodies (see IMMUNITY) directed against it. Anaphylaxis may be systemic or local.
(1) *Acute systemic anaphylaxis* occurs (notably in human beings, guinea pigs, and dogs) when an antigenic substance enters the bloodstream of an organism containing specific antibodies against it. In severe cases the anaphylactic shock may be associated with rapid shallow breathing, and in extreme cases with waterlogging of the lungs and heart failure. Since the PHARMACOLOGICAL agent of anaphylactic shock is histamine, some protection can be achieved by antihistaminic drugs.
(2) *Local anaphylaxis* is brought about when an antigen, particularly a soluble antigen, is injected into the skin or other tissues of an immune animal. Human beings, guinea pigs, and rabbits are specially liable to local anaphylaxis, an intense inflammation, confined to the area in which the antigen was injected, but causing in extreme cases TISSUE death.   P.M.

anarchism. A political movement advocating the abolition of the state and the replacement of all forms of governmental authority by free association and voluntary cooperation of groups and individuals. Anarchists disagree about what specific relationships the future society is to be based on, and about how it is to be achieved. Contemporary LIBERTARIAN writers describe themselves as 'anarcho-capitalists' and base their hostility to the STATE on the inviolability of each individual's ownership of himself and his property. Historically, anarchists have been hostile to private property as ordinarily understood. The first English anarchist, William Godwin (1756-1836), was uninterested in political action and wished the 'EUTHANASIA of government' to result from individual moral reformation; more commonly, anarchists have advocated some form of DIRECT ACTION. Their MARXIST critics have complained that this is inimical to good organization and effective tactics. Proudhon (1809-65) and Blanqui (1805-81) divided the allegiances of 19th-century anarchists in France, the former wanting peaceful change, the latter an advocate of spontaneous insurrection. Bakunin led the anarchist wing of the First INTERNATIONAL; his quarrels with Marx and Engels destroyed the organization in 1876. Bakunin's enthusiasm for insurrection and spontaneity degenerated into the romantic and suicidal craze for 'propaganda by the deed' which swept Europe and America at the turn of the century. Johann Moser's obsession with the creative possibilities of dynamite was characteristic of this period, but even Malatesta, Kropotkin and Emma Goldmann were tempted by the thought that assassinating the rich and powerful would lead to a workers' revolt and thence to the anarchist utopia (see UTOPIANISM).

After 1900, anarchism ceased to make much impact on the politics of developed countries. In revolutionary Russia, however, Makhno defied the BOLSHEVIK armies for most of the Civil War, while anarchists held power in Catalonia during the Spanish Civil War. In France, the hold of anarchist ideas on the LEFT has never quite died out; ANARCHO-SYNDICALISM was a powerful force in TRADE UNION circles until after World War I, and in the 'events' of MAY 1968 anarchism rather than orthodox Marxism ruled the day. The TERRORISM which the far left practised during the 1970s was based on an orthodox hatred of CAPITALIST society, but the expectation of insurrection was anarchist. Of much greater intellectual interest has been the continuing revival of INDIVIDUALIST American anarchism associated with writers such as Murray Rothbard and Robert Nozick.   L.L.;A.R.

Bibl: G. Woodcock, *Anarchism* (Cleveland and Harmondsworth, 1963); J. Joll, *The Anarchists* (London and New York,

1964); Murray Rothbard, *For a New Liberty* (New York, 1978); Robert Nozick, *Anarchy, State and Utopia* (New York and Oxford, 1974); David Miller, *Anarchism* (Oxford, 1982).

anarcho-syndicalism. The attempt, which reached its climax at the turn of the century, to unite ANARCHIST and TRADE UNION politics; it began when Bakunin's followers in the Swiss Jura Federation of the First INTERNATIONAL turned away from conspiracy to trade union struggle under the urging of Bakunin's disciple James Guillaume. Trade unions were to provide the spearhead of REVOLUTION as well as a model for economic organization after the revolution. French anarcho-syndicalism developed from the 'revolutionary syndicalism' of Fernand Pelloutier, who had migrated from MARXISM through anarchism to a belief in the revolutionary general strike. Trade unions could abolish CAPITALISM by DIRECT ACTION if they saw the struggle for economic goals as a prelude to the political general strike. Pellloutier's revolutionary syndicalism was emulated elsewhere, but only in Spain did the trade union movement embrace anarchism. In France, the CGT was anarcho-syndicalist before World War I, as was the IWW (see WOBBLIES) in America; the better entrenched union movement in Britain and Germany generally shunned anarchism in favour of less violent and more REFORMIST doctrines. Although it vanished after World War I, it left one notable intellectual achievement in Georges Sorel's *Reflections on Violence*, and a non-violent version of syndicalism is discussed with some sympathy in Bertrand Russell's influential *Roads to Freedom* (1919).   A.R.

Bibl: P.N. Stearns, *Revolutionary Syndicalism and French Labor* (New Brunswick, N.J., 1971).

anatomy. The branch of MORPHOLOGY which deals both generally and in detail with the structure of animals — a sort of bodily geography, as the widely used and self-descriptive terms *regional anatomy* and *surface anatomy* suggest. *Comparative anatomy* is that branch of anatomy which deals with the similarities and differences between cognate structures in related animals — e.g. with the relationship between fins and limbs or the suspensory bones of the jaw on the one hand and the ossicles of the ear which in an evolutionary sense derive from them. In the latter part of the 19th century comparative anatomy played a vitally important part in establishing EVOLUTION theory.   P.M.

ANC, see under AFRICAN NATIONAL CONGRESS.

ancestor worship. Complex of beliefs and practices which focus upon the veneration of dead ancestors. It involves the recognition of an active relationship between the living and the dead. Ancestors or the spirits of the ancestors can intervene in the social order as Fortes demonstrated in his classic work *Oedipus and Job in West African Religion* (new edn., 1983). The ancestors provide the legitimation for structures of authority and they have the power to threaten retribution. Ancestor worship is most commonly found in societies with DESCENT groups and tombs or shrines are an important symbolic focus for the group. Contact may be made with the ancestors at tombs or shrines where offerings and SACRIFICES are made by representatives of the descent group.   A.G.
Bibl: E. Ahern, *The Cult of the Dead in a Chinese Village* (Stanford, 1973); M. Bloch, *From Blessing to Violence* (Cambridge, 1986).

and-gate, see under GATE.

androgyny. From ancient Greek 'andro' (male) and 'gyn' (female). Concept which recognizes both male and female characteristics in human identity. GENDER is not fixed or biologically based, but is fluid. 'Whole' personality is an amalgam of male and female characteristics. Androgyny was a concept developed in the feminist movement (see FEMINISM) particularly by C. Heilbrun (*Towards a Recognition of Androgyny*, 1973) and it represented a movement away from theories of rigid sex-role or gender stereotyping, i.e. the idea that men and women were forced into the acceptance of separate conventional roles. The solution to sexual oppression was sought through the elimination of gender stereotyping. Androgyny implied

that men should develop 'feminine' qualities, women 'masculine' qualities and thereby dissolve the difference, the source of inequalities, between the sexes. Other feminists, however, have criticized the concept of androgyny for failing to deal with the issue of power and for continuing to recognize conventional male/female traits, if uniting rather than separating them. There has also been some unease in situating the question of sexual oppression in PSYCHOLOGY rather than in material or political spheres.   A.G.
Bibl: H. Eisenstein, *Contemporary Feminist Thought* (London, 1984).

Anglicanism. The form of church life characteristic of the Anglican Communion, with about 50 million adherents. This consists of the Church of England (Latin *Ecclesia Anglicana*), which rejected the control of the Pope in the 16th century, and of the Churches outside England which send their bishops to the Lambeth Conference (since 1868 every ten years or so) under the presidency of the Archbishop of Canterbury. In some countries Anglicanism is better known as EPISCOPALIANISM; its branch in the U.S.A. is the Episcopal Church. Because it originated in England's national Church, Anglicanism tries to be comprehensive, reconciling CATHOLICISM with PROTESTANTISM, and also religious LIBERALISM with orthodoxy, in a community united in 'common prayer' and in mutual charity. This example has been an inspiration to the modern ECUMENICAL MOVEMENT. In practice, however, Anglicanism has suffered from the old-fashioned nature of the Church of England, from the declining prestige of England in the world, and from its internal controversies, e.g. those between ANGLO-CATHOLICISM and EVANGELICALISM. Different 'provinces' (groups of dioceses, each with its own bishop) have made different decisions about the ordination of women as priests, a development which has been extensive in North America.   D.L.E.
Bibl: S. Neill, *Anglicanism* (Harmondsworth and Baltimore, 1977); J. Howe, *Highways and Hedges: A Study of Developments in the Anglican Communion 1958-82* (London, 1985).

Anglo-Catholicism. A movement within ANGLICANISM, emphasizing the heritage of CATHOLICISM, in contrast with Bible-based EVANGELICALISM, as well as with modernizing LIBERALISM. D.L.E.

Angry Brigade. A small LEFT-wing group which in the name of the working class mounted sporadic attacks upon various representatives of the ruling class or ESTABLISHMENT. Their claimed successes included the machine-gunning of the U.S. Embassy in London on 20 August 1967 (the first such incident) and the bombing of the Minister of Employment's home on 11 January 1971 during the time when he was preparing the controversial Industrial Relations Bill. Like the American WEATHERMEN, the Italian Red Army Faction and the German Baader-Meinhof gang the activists of the Angry Brigade appeared to be mainly MIDDLE-CLASS ex-students; politically the group appeared to be more ANARCHIST than MARXIST. In 1972 its leaders were tried and imprisoned, and its bombings have been eclipsed by more recent and effective terrorist activities. The Angry Brigade constitutes an early manifestation of European TERRORIST activity from left and right against western state and private LIBERAL institutions which is distinguishable from other sources of terror by its lack of nationalist IDEOLOGY and consequent political weakness. P.S.L.

Bibl: P. Wilkinson, *Terrorism and the Liberal State* (London, 1986).

angry young man. Term indiscriminately applied to a number of British writers in the mid 1950s, some of whom were remarkable for stupidity rather than anger. Writers saddled with the label have included Kingsley Amis, John Osborne, and Colin Wilson. The paradigm of the angry young man is Jimmy Porter, in Osborne's play *Look Back in Anger* (1956): confused in the process of violently rejecting ESTABLISHMENT values, but frustrated by ignorance and the lack of alternative values to which to enslave himself. Invention of the phrase in this connection has been authoritatively attributed to the Irish writer, the late Leslie Paul, whose autobiographical *Angry Young Man* appeared in 1951. But he was then 46; and was over 50 when he wistfully drew attention to his choice of title in a letter to the press. M.S.-S.

Bibl: J.R. Taylor, *Anger and After* (London, 1962; Baltimore, 1963).

Angst. Variously translated as anxiety, anguish, dread. It was first used in an EXISTENTIAL sense by Søren Kierkegaard in *The Concept of Anxiety* (1844), where he describes the terrifying reality of the state of splitness, indecisiveness and responsibility in front of choice. Heidegger in *Sein und Zeit* (1927) freely paraphrases Kierkegaard and does not add anything significant to Kierkegaard's analysis. Sartre, in *Being and Nothingness* (1943) again follows Kierkegaard, but adds an element of determinism by making 'anguish' a state of BAD FAITH in which the conscious subject (see SUBJECTIVITY) tries to renege on his inalienable freedom to choose. R.PO.

anima. JUNGIAN term, derived from its original meaning of life force or soul, and referring to the autonomous ARCHETYPE within a man's COLLECTIVE UNCONSCIOUS which symbolizes the feminine side of his nature. In its most basic form this is an inherited collective image of woman. As with all archetypes, the *anima* is projected onto the world of experience, finding its first incarnation in one's mother; and a similar projection may govern the choice of a wife. The artist's 'muse', with its feminine and creative CONNOTATIONS, is another representation of *anima*. In his later work, Jung introduced the analogous term *animus* to refer to a woman's masculine principle, although the additional functions of *anima* for the male were never fully articulated in his presentation of the female's *animus*. T.Z.C.

animal sonar. A faculty which enables animals to locate objects by means of the high-frequency sound waves reflected from them, and to communicate with each other by emitting such waves. Objects are located by one or both of two methods: the phase relationship between the sound impulses reflected back to each ear (whether in phase or out of phase), or the relative amplitude from sounds reaching the two ears. Animal sonar occurs in water (e.g. whales, dolphins) as well as in air (e.g. bats). P.M.

animism. In ANTHROPOLOGY, a term first used by E.B. Tylor (*Primitive Culture,* 1871) for belief based on the universal human experiences of dreams and visions, in 'spiritual beings', comprising the souls of individual creatures and other spirits. In modern anthropology animism as a theory has been criticized, partly because it is concerned with unknowable origins of belief, and partly because it fails to discriminate adequately between concepts of soul and of spirit. The animism debate was revived by Spiro (*Buddhism and Society,* 1970) in his analysis of Burmese religion. Spiro's approach was to draw a distinction between BUDDHISM (the formal, literate tradition) and animism (popular beliefs and practices). Other anthropologists working in Buddhist societies of south east Asia (e.g., S.J. Tambiah, *Buddhism and the Spirit Cults,* 1970) have addressed this question, but they have disputed the validity of Spiro's concept of animism.

M.F.;A.G.

Bibl: S.J. Tambiah, *The Buddhist Saints of the Forest and the Cult of Amulets* (Cambridge, 1984).

anion, see under ION.

***Annales* school.** A group of historians associated with the journal founded by Lucien Febvre and Marc Bloch in 1929 and now known as *Annales: économies, sociétés, civilisations.* The group stands for a particular style of history. Its members believe that the historian should place less emphasis than is customary on narrative (especially political narrative), on the chronicle of events (*histoire événementielle*), and more emphasis on analysis, on long-term STRUCTURES and trends (*la longue durée*). They also believe that economic, social, cultural, and political history should be integrated into a total history, and that, to do this, historians need to be well acquainted with the SOCIAL SCIENCES. Distinguished living members of the group include Pierre Chaunu, Pierre Goubert, and Emmanuel Le Roy Ladurie. An outstanding example of the *Annales* approach translated into English is Fernand Braudel's *The Mediterranean and the Mediterranean World in the Age of Philip II.* See also CONJUNCTURE; SERIAL HISTORY.

P.B.

Bibl: P. Burke (ed.), *Economy and Society in Early Modern Europe* (London and New York, 1972).

annealing. The process of heating a solid metal or POLYMER to a high temperature, at which it is kept for a time, and then cooling it very slowly to its original temperature. This treatment 'dissolves' DISLOCATIONS and other crystal DEFECTS, thus relieving internal strains. When applied to glasses, annealing relieves stresses introduced during fabrication, thus reducing brittleness. When applied to metals, it has a softening effect which makes it easier to work them.

M.V.B.

anode, see under ELECTRODE.

anodizing. A process designed to give a protective (and often, by the use of pigment, attractive) finish to articles made of aluminium (aluminum) or aluminium alloy. Although the surface of aluminium oxidizes rapidly in contact with air the oxide layer is often too thin to prevent CORROSION, and the process of anodizing involves the deposition of further oxide on the surface.

E.R.L.

anomaly. Literally something which will not fit in with an existing taxonomic order, anomaly can be taken as 'falsifying' accepted theories, and thus, within Karl Popper's view of science (see POPPERIAN), providing the essential trigger to scientific advance. (For Popper science moves on not by establishing truths but by dispelling errors.) Anomaly plays an equally important part in T.S. Kuhn's vision of how the practice of 'normal science' is occasionally interrupted by 'SCIENTIFIC REVOLUTIONS'. According to Kuhn, established theories can tolerate a certain build-up of anomalies (which can be accommodated by *ad hoc* hypotheses); beyond a particular threshold, however, anomalies demand rational interpretation in their own right, leading to new scientific GESTALTS or theories. Paul Feyerabend, by contrast, has emphasized the degree to which orthodox science clings to, or turns a blind eye to, the anomalies it creates (science is conservative rather than critical).

R.P.

Bibl: T.S. Kuhn, *The Structure of Scientific Revolutions* (Chicago, 1970).

anomie. Term, resurrected from the Greek (literally, without law) by the French sociologist Émile Durkheim, to denote that condition of society which results from the disintegration of a commonly accepted NORMATIVE code. For Durkheim, industrial CLASS conflict was a symptom of anomie. More loosely, anomie was used in the 1950s and 1960s as a CONCEPT akin to ALIENATION, to describe a condition where an individual had lost his traditional moorings and was prone to disorientation or psychic disorder. D.B.

Bibl: É. Durkheim, tr. J.A. Spaulding and G. Simpson, *Suicide* (Glencoe, Ill., 1951; London, 1952); S. Lukes, *Emile Durkheim: His Life and Work* (London, 1973).

anonymous Christian. A term used by the Roman CATHOLIC theologian Karl Rahner (1904-84) to describe the non-Christian who, while not being able or willing to accept identification as a Christian by being named as such in Baptism, responds to God's self-revelation and grace, and obeys his moral law, so far as circumstances permit. Such a person is thought to be promised ultimate salvation by the God revealed by Jesus Christ as the merciful Father of all. This was a development of the teaching of VATICAN COUNCIL II. See also REDEMPTOR HOMINIS. D.L.E.

Bibl: H. Vorgrimler, tr. J. Bowden, *Understanding Karl Rahner* (London, 1986).

anorexia nervosa. A term describing a propensity towards excessive dieting, achieved either through refusal of food or its regurgitation (BULIMIA NERVOSA). Often called 'the slimmers' disease', it is primarily associated in our society with teenage girls and young women, though historically it may be linked with the heroic mortifications of the flesh of male and female ascetics within Christianity. Sufferers develop a fear of fatness, and have a self-image as overweight even when undergoing severe weight loss. The association of slimness with desirability in western culture may offer a partial explanation. Commonly the anorexic girl is also in rebellion against her parents (seen as food providers), and is troubled about becoming an adult woman with full sexual char-

acteristics (anorexia commonly curtails menstruation). Medical opinion has been somewhat divided as to whether to treat anorexia mainly as an eating disorder or as a wider psychiatric condition. Occasionally fatal, anorexia is rarely fully cured, and anorexics show a tendency to relapse or to develop other obsessional disorders. R.P.

Bibl: Peter Dally, *Anorexia Nervosa* (London, 1969); A.H. Crisp, *Anorexia Nervosa* (London, 1980).

anthropic principle. Introduced by the British physicist Brandon Carter to describe a collection of ideas associating the structure of the universe, the constants and the laws of nature, with those conditions that are necessary for the evolution and existence of life. The *weak anthropic principle* is a version of Bayes' theorem of statistical sampling. It is stated by Barrow and Tipler as follows: the observed values of all physical and cosmological quantities are not equally probable but take on values restricted by the requirement that there exist sites where carbon-based life can have evolved and by the requirement that the universe be old enough for it to have already done so. Observed physical quantities (for example, the size of the universe) could not be observed to take on any value with equal PROBABILITY because observers could only exist in universes in which their values were within a very restricted range. The expansion of the universe requires that universes old enough (more than ten billion years) for the chemical building blocks of human life to have arisen within stars must also be very large (more than ten billion light years in size). This argument was introduced in 1961 by Robert Dicke in a particular form to explain the existence of coincidences between the values of cosmological quantities of very large magnitude. In 1937 Paul Dirac had argued that these coincidences would be explained if the law of gravitation were changing with time but Dicke pointed out that the observed coincidence was necessary for the existence of chemical life. Our existence places restrictions upon the type of universe we could ever expect to find ourselves observing and investigating. The weak anthropic principle delineates the extent of applicability of the Copernican principle that we do not occupy a special place in the universe. Although we should not expect our position to be special in every way this does not mean it cannot be special in any way because particular conditions must hold for the EVOLUTION of life to be possible.

The *strong anthropic principle* of Carter claims that the universe must have those properties which allow life to develop within it at some stage. This is a speculation that would imply either that the universe was a teleological structure designed with life in view as was believed by natural theologians and scientists in Britain during the 17th to 19th centuries, or that there exists an ensemble of different possible universes and that we inevitably exist in one that contains one of the rare universes whose permutation of physical properties allows life to evolve. The strong anthropic principle suggests in some, as yet unclear way, that observers are necessary to give the universe 'meaning'.

It has been suggested that the role played by the observer in the quantum picture of nature may introduce a more precise version of the strong anthropic principle. According to the COPENHAGEN INTERPRETATION of QUANTUM MECHANICS introduced by Niels Bohr no phenomenon can be said to exist unless it is an 'observed' phenomenon. Observers are necessary to collapse quantum WAVE FUNCTIONS and bring phenomena into being. John A. Wheeler has suggested a *participatory anthropic principle* which interprets the Copenhagen interpretation of quantum mechanics as indicating that observers must exist in order to bring the universe into being. This does not require conscious observers to play any special role but Eugene Wigner has argued that CONSCIOUSNESS may be necessary to collapse wave functions. Alternatively, the MANY WORLDS HYPOTHESIS suggested by Hugh Everett III is an alternative interpretation of quantum mechanics that predicts that quantum wave functions do not collapse. Instead, physical interactions and observations split reality into disjoint universes, one for each possible outcome of the interaction or observation. Hence, in this interpretation we would inevitably find ourselves in a member of the special subset of all possible universes which was structured to allow life to evolve successfully. The strong anthropic principle would be tautologically true. A *final anthropic principle* has been proposed which hypothesizes that information processing can continue indefinitely in the future of the universe.   J.D.B.

Bibl: J. D. Barrow and F. J. Tipler, *The Anthropic Cosmological Principle* (Oxford, 1986); J. A. Wheeler and W. H. Zurek, *Quantum Theory and Measurement* (Princeton, N.J., 1982); P. C. W. Davies, *Accidental Universe* (Cambridge, 1981); W. H. McCrea and M. J. Rees, eds., *The Constants of Nature* (London, 1983).

anthropogeography. The study of the distribution of human COMMUNITIES on the earth in relation to their ENVIRONMENT. Some geographers assume it to be synonymous with *human geography* (see GEOGRAPHY), which is the more commonly used term.   M.L.

anthropological linguistics. A branch of LINGUISTICS which studies language variation and use in relation to the cultural patterns and beliefs of man, e.g. the way in which linguistic features may identify a member of a community with a social, religious, occupational, or kinship group. See also ETHNOLINGUISTICS; SOCIOLINGUISTICS.   D.C.

anthropology. From 'anthropos', the study of man.

(1) *Early phase.* The history of anthropology is part of the history of European thought, but it did not become established as an independent discipline until the late 19th century. It began with the explorers and travellers of earlier centuries (Columbus, Marco Polo) who broadened the area of the known world and increasingly uncovered the diversity of mankind, even if some of their 'discoveries' were not entirely based upon observation. The people they wrote about in their journals (often dog-headed and with tails) interested the Renaissance philosophers (Montaigne and, later, Vico, Rousseau and Montesqieu) in their speculations on the nature of man. 'Primitive' man was established as the 'other' by the philosophers of Europe.

37

He represented either savagery and barbarism in contrast to the civilization of Europe or he represented innocence and childishness in contrast with European depravity.

(2) *Nineteenth-century evolutionists.* Ideas of RACE and EVOLUTION were important in late 19th-century thinking and anthropology developed as a discipline in this intellectual mould. It was also tied to colonial expansion and could provide justification for the 'civilizing' process of colonial peoples. Primitive man was understood by Morgan, McLennan and Maine to be a 'survival', a representation of earlier stages of mankind. The 1898 Torres Straits expedition (members included Haddon, Rivers, Wilkin, Seligman, Myers and McDougall) was an important landmark in the development of anthropology. It was an early exercise in FIELD-WORK and did much to establish anthropology's empirical base. Anthropology at this time, however, was still an amalgam of different subjects (LINGUISTICS, MATERIAL CULTURE, social custom, physiological typologies). By the beginning of the 20th century the various sub-disciplines had begun to develop independently (in particular social, cultural and physical anthropology) and today they are quite separate subjects. *Physical anthropology* is concerned with the physical evolution of the human species and is a matter for geneticists (see GENETICS) and physiologists. *Cultural anthropology* developed in the United States under the influence of Tylor and Boas. It became a very broad subject, concerned with CULTURE, but often broken down into specialist areas: linguistics, culture and personality studies, primitive art, etc. By contrast, anthropologists in Britain concentrated upon social systems and drew on the work of Durkheim and Weber to establish the independent discipline of *social anthropology*.

(3) *The functionalists.* Malinowski transformed social anthropology by his introduction of fieldwork methodology. It was henceforth founded not upon arm-chair speculation and conjecture, but upon first-hand participant observation. Malinowski also broke with evolutionary theories and interpreted his Trobriand material within a FUNCTIONALIST frame-work. STRUCTURAL-FUNCTIONALISM was a later development associated with Radcliffe-Brown. This approach moved away from Malinowski's concern with the individual and his needs to the question of SOCIAL STRUCTURE and its continuity over time. Social anthropology expanded in Britain during the 1930s and 1940s. It had a very strong empirical base and fieldwork was largely carried out in the colonial areas of Africa and south east Asia.

(4) *Structuralism.* In 1949 Lévi-Strauss published *Les Structures élémentaires de la parenté* (Eng. trans., *The Elementary Structures of Kinship*, 1969). It had an enormous impact on social anthropology. Lévi-Strauss's work, the attempt to establish a model of the human mind, emerged from a European tradition, one much more concerned with PHILOSOPHY and theory than with empirical method. In Britain STRUCTURALISM was taken up as a method by Leach, Douglas and Needham, but they adapted and modified it in accordance with the ethnographic tradition in which they worked (E.R. Leach, *Lévi-Strauss*, 1970). The American tradition continued to develop independently and although Margaret Mead and Ruth Benedict gained popular prominence, few anthropologists seriously engaged with their work. One of the important consequences of structuralism was that it drew the different schools in Europe, the U.S., Canada and Britain into a common debate.

(5) *Crisis of the 1970s.* The interest in MARXIST ideas which emerged in the wake of structuralism represented another attempt to provide social anthropology with a coherent theoretical framework. Again the stimulus originated in France, and Marxist concepts were most fully elaborated by Meillassoux, Terray and Godelier. The publication of *Woman, Culture and Society* (R.Z. Rosaldo and L. Lamphere, eds., 1974) opened FEMINIST debate and subsequent work has steadily expanded anthropological discourse. Ethnographic film increasingly developed as a sophisticated and independent medium (M. Eaton, ed., *Anthropology-Reality-Cinema*, 1979). The crisis in anthropology lay not in the realm of ideas or concepts but in ETHNOGRAPHY, in the geographical areas for investigation. By the 1970s the

colonial empires were largely dismantled and anthropologists found that they were no longer welcome in many newly independent countries. Indeed, anthropology was accused from some quarters of being in the service of colonialism (T. Asad, ed., *Anthropology and the Colonial Encounter*, 1973) and the increasing numbers of British and American anthropologists engaged in 'development' work has raised this very question. Other anthropologists have sought out new areas of fieldwork in history, in rural Europe and in the cities of the developed world. This new orientation may have profound consequences for the discipline. There has been a retreat from grand theory and a return to the examination of concepts accepted as cornerstones of social anthropology (e.g., DESCENT, MARRIAGE, DOMESTIC GROUP) but which were developed in the traditional ethnographic areas.   A.G.

Bibl: A. Kuper, *Anthropology and Anthropologists* (London, 1983); M. Augé, *The Anthropological Circle* (Cambridge, 1982); E.R. Leach, *Social Anthropology* (London, 1982); I. Langham, *The Building of British Social Anthropology: W.H.R. Rivers and His Cambridge Disciples in the Development of Kinship Studies 1898-1931* (Dordrecht, 1981).

anthropomorphism. Less an architectural movement of the 1980s than a recognition that the combination of windows and doors and porches in buildings could sometimes be read as faces or parts of the human body. One or two architects actually designed buildings in this form.
                                                    S.L.

anthroposophy. The term (literally 'wisdom about man') adopted by Rudolf Steiner (1861-1925) to denote his teachings and to distinguish them from the THEOSOPHY whose adherents constituted his first audience. These teachings he claimed to derive from 'spiritual research' based on an exact 'scientific' mode of supersensible PERCEPTION. A central thesis of anthroposophy is that the present intellectual capacities of humanity have evolved from an earlier mode of CONSCIOUSNESS which brought a direct experience of the transcendental (see TRANSCENDENCE) realities of which Steiner

spoke. To carry the clarity and objectivity of the intellect now gained into new modes of spiritual perception (which he called Imagination, Inspiration, Intuition) is according to Steiner an essential future task for mankind. Such a 'resurrection' of consciousness has become possible, he held, through the deed of Christ in uniting himself with the destiny of man on earth. Steiner accordingly described one of his earliest books, *The Philosophy of Freedom*, as a 'Pauline theory of knowledge'. His work has given rise to many practical endeavours in education (see STEINER SCHOOLS), farming, medicine, the arts, etc.
                                                    J.D.

Bibl: R. Steiner, tr. G. Metaxa, *Knowledge of the Higher Worlds* (London and New York, 1923) and other works published in London by the Rudolf Steiner Press.

anti-art. A term used for works of the DADA movement, which used the ARTS to attack or deride all established institutions, including the very notion of 'art'. Duchamp's READYMADES were an early manifestation. The term was subsequently used by other AVANT-GARDE movements including Gruppe Zero, FLUXUS, and CONCEPTUAL ART. Other radical movements in modern art, such as POP ART and KINETIC ART, were considered to be anti-art in their initial stages but quickly became accepted as legitimate art forms. This fate has also overtaken the original Dada objects.   L.M.

antibacterial. A member of a heterogeneous class of substances united by the property of being toxic or lethal to bacteria (see BACTERIOLOGY). They include:

(1) ANTISEPTICS, comprising all substances that are antibacterial through physical or chemical action;

(2) natural substances such as (*a*) LYSOZYME, an ENZYME which attacks the CELL walls of some bacterial SPECIES, (*b*) *complement*, which acts in concert with antibodies (see IMMUNITY) to puncture the membranes of bacteria or red cells, and (*c*) *properdin*, a natural blood-borne antibacterial substance of unknown nature and function;

(3) ANTIBIOTICS, which presumably play

some part in the ECOLOGY of the organisms that manufacture them;

(4) substances such as sulphanilamide, sulphathiazole, and sulphapyridine which exercise an antibacterial effect by metabolic means (see METABOLISM); thus sulphanilamide in effect deprives bacteria of the para-aminobenzoic acid which for most of them is an essential food factor — an early example of 'competitive inhibition'. P.M.

anti-ballistic missiles, see ABM.

antibiotic. A substance which impedes the growth or multiplication of microorganisms. Examples are penicillin, streptomycin, terramycin. The *spectrum* of an antibiotic is the range of bacteria (see BACTERIOLOGY) over which it exercises its effect. 'Broad spectrum' antibiotics such as terramycin are particularly useful in medical practice. In general, antibiotics are ineffective against viruses (see VIROLOGY). Naturally occurring ANTIBACTERIAL substances such as INTERFERON and LYSOZYME are not normally classified as antibiotics. P.M.

antibody, see under IMMUNITY.

anti-colonialism, see under IMPERIALISM.

antigen, see under IMMUNITY.

anti-hero. In literature, a figure bearing the same relation to the conventional hero as does the ANTI-NOVEL to the conventional novel. The term was first used in this sense by W.P. Ker in 1897; but the anti-hero as type — foolish, bumbling, boorish, clumsy, immoral — is ancient. He occurs in the Greek 'new comedy', in the picaresque novel, and in the fiction from which the latter originates. The first deliberately devised anti-hero is in Honoré d'Urfé's sensationally successful *Astrée* (1607-27): this is a sentimental romance, but Hylas, with his championship of infidelity, is clearly a satirical foil to the conventional hero, Céladon. In lyrical poetry Edwin Arlington Robinson's Miniver Cheever provides an excellent example, and T.S. Eliot's Prufrock owed much to him. Modern anti-heroes include Hašek's Good Soldier Švejk, Christopher

Isherwood's Christopher Isherwood, Jimmy Porter in John Osborne's *Look Back in Anger,* Jim Dixon in Kingsley Amis's *Lucky Jim,* and numerous spies and go-getters in conventionally structured popular works. By way of contrast, we have the 'positive hero' of Soviet literature. M.S.-S.

anti-imperialism, see under IMPERIALISM.

anti-knock, see under KNOCKING.

anti-literature. The first, it seems, of the 'anti-arts' to be so named in English: by David Gascoyne in 1935. For other (selected) examples of arts, literary genres, etc. that stand previous conventions on their heads, or at least their shoulders, see ANTI-ART; ANTI-HERO; ANTI-NOVEL; ANTI-THEATRE. O.S.

anti-matter. Some ELEMENTARY PARTICLES are the *anti-particles* of others. For example, a POSITRON and an ELECTRON mutually annihilate one another, producing an enormous amount of ENERGY in the form of RADIATION (see MASS-ENERGY EQUATION). Matter made up of the antiparticles of ordinary matter would be *anti-matter.* None has positively been identified in nature, and its existence on a large scale is therefore hypothetical. However, it is possible that some of the intense radiation detected with RADIO TELESCOPES may be the result of collisions between GALAXIES made up of ordinary matter and anti-matter. M.V.B.

anti-naturalism. An approach to PSYCHOLOGY and the SOCIAL SCIENCES which assumes that human beings (and perhaps intelligent animals) are so different from the subject-matter of the NATURAL SCIENCES that quite different approaches are needed for their study. Thus, in studying human beings one can communicate with them, and attempt to understand the meanings of their words and deeds, whereas a physicist cannot in the same way communicate with the physical substances and mechanisms that he studies. A related view is that human behaviour and mental processes cannot be explained in terms of the physical and chemical, or physiological, processes in the human body (see REDUCTION), and that no amount of study of the structure of the human brain and the processes that occur in it can explain the way people think, decide, act, feel, etc. The opposite view is NATURALISM (sense 3). An intermediate position is that, although human social systems have a kind of complexity unmatched by other physical systems, so that quite new theoretical frameworks and experimental methods are required for their study, nevertheless they are a fit topic for an objective scientific study, albeit a study that is unlike PHYSICS. Cognitive science would be such a study (see MENTALISM).

A.S.

Bibl: H.P. Rickman, *Understanding and the Human Studies* (London, 1967; New York, 1968).

antinomianism. The rejection of any element of 'law' (Greek *nomos*) in ETHICS, especially in Christian MORAL THEOLOGY, on the grounds that no detailed code of behaviour has been laid down by God. A PROTESTANT sect arising in Germany in 1535 was so named. In the 20th century, while most Christians have accepted that some rules are needed, most have put first the element usually contrasted with 'law' in this debate: love. Christians are believed to be essentially free to act as they think best in the light of love. See also SITUATION ETHICS.

D.L.E.

antinomy. A contradiction (see CONSISTENCY) between two assertions for each of which there seem to be adequate grounds. It should be distinguished from a *dilemma*, which is a form of argument designed to show that something, usually unpleasant, will follow either if a given assumption is true or if it is false, and also from a PARADOX, which is a single, unacceptable, and often self-contradictory conclusion for which there are seemingly irresistible grounds.

A.Q.

Bibl: W. V. Quine, *The Ways of Paradox* (New York, 1966).

anti-novel. A compendious label for any novel that protests, explicitly or implicitly, against some other novel or novels regarded as unduly popular or influential. Although Charles Sorel described the 1633 edition of his *Le Berger extravagant*

(1627), in part a satire on d'Urfé's *Astrée*, as an *anti-roman*, the first thoroughgoing anti-novel is Cervantes's *Don Quixote* (1605): devised partly as protest against popular chivalric fiction, it grew into a tragic masterpiece. It is a paradigm of the true anti-novel: it revolts against conventional form, on the grounds that the latter lulls the reader into a sense of unreality, into an avoidance of (in contemporary EXISTENTIALIST parlance) his own AUTHENTICITY, and itself jerks the reader, by a series of shocks, into awareness of his own predicament. The first English anti-novel is Sterne's *Tristram Shandy* (1759), which continually confronts the reader with what he does *not* expect from fiction. The anti-novel has been revived in the 20th century (especially in France in the form of the NEW NOVEL), though not always successfully, being often either too self-consciously or too dully and philosophically expressed. The contemporary revival has been much influenced by the PHENOMENOLOGY of Husserl, if only because this is exclusively concerned with subjective experience.

M.S.-S.

Bibl: N. Sarraute, tr. M. Jolas, *Tropisms and The Age of Suspicion* (London, 1963); P. West, *The Modern Novel* (London, 1963).

anti-particles, see under ANTI-MATTER.

antiphoton, see under ELEMENTARY PARTICLES.

anti-psychiatry. A movement in therapeutic practice, associated in Britain above all with R.D. Laing, and in the U.S.A. principally with Thomas S. Szasz, which rejects conventional PSYCHIATRY (in particular, in its public and institutional guises), and argues that the concept of mental illness is both stigmatizing and unscientific. Laing argued in the 1960s that the mentally ill were essentially the victims of intolerable pressures exerted against them by society and in particular the family; and saw the flight into mental illness as at least understandable, and increasingly as a healthy response to sick society. Laing eventually argued that what was conventionally labelled SCHIZOPHRENIA might be regarded as a particularly sane and insightful condition. Consequential upon this diagnosis was an attack upon psychiatric institutions as coercive and conducive to creating rather than relieving mental illness. Drug and mechanical therapies and PSYCHOSURGERY were especially rejected. Above all, Szasz questioned the ontological status of mental illness, contending that the category of 'illness' should apply properly only to physical, somatic conditions. 'Mental illness' was a dangerous metaphor.   R.P.

Bibl: R. Boyers and R. Orrill (eds.), *R.D. Laing and Anti-Psychiatry* (Harmondsworth, 1972).

anti-realism. A label for any theory which is opposed to one or other of the different kinds of REALISM. In general, a theory is anti-realist if it denies that certain entities exist independently of our knowledge, thought, talk or experience of them. Thus IDEALISM is anti-realism concerning material objects; NOMINALISM is anti-realism concerning abstract objects.
                                                              A.C.G.

Bibl: M.A.E. Dummett, *Truth and Other Enigmas* (London, 1978).

antisemitism. The adherence to views or practices directed against the interests, legal rights, religious practices, or lives of Jews; a more or less constant feature of Jewish life since the Diaspora. The term was apparently coined by Ernest Renan in the 1870s, but justification has been couched in terms of the dominant structure of thought of each period, changing, as these changed, from religious to racial, from NATIONALIST to CLASS conflict theories. Since the attempt by the NAZIS in the FINAL SOLUTION physically to eliminate the European Jewry, the burden of guilt and the fear of being associated in any way with the views which led to that catastrophe have been a potent force in European politics, leading in many countries to legislation against the incitement to racial hatred (see RACE) and internationally inclining the countries of Western Europe and the U.S.A. towards the side of Israel. Antisemitism is still a potent force in East European political life and, under the guise of hostility to ZIONISM, in Arab states.   D.C.W.

Bibl: E. Levine, ed., *Diaspora: Exile and the Jewish Condition* (New York, 1983);

M. Gilbert, *The Holocaust* (London, 1986).

antisense RNA. Single-stranded molecules of RNA that are complementary to messenger RNA. The complementary strands attach to one another thus incapacitating the messenger RNA and impeding protein synthesis. Apart from its presence in some bacteria, antisense RNA is not known to occur naturally but is used in MOLECULAR BIOLOGY.   P.N.

antiseptic. A member of a class of compounds of which carbolic acid is historically the most important member, having the property of killing the organisms responsible for wound infection (sepsis) in which bacterial proliferation is accompanied by extensive TISSUE damage and accumulation of pus. Antiseptics have a great variety of important uses in medicine and hygiene (although the attempted sterilization of wounds is no longer one of them). Thus chlorine is used to disinfect domestic water supplies, and formaldehyde vapour (very poisonous) to decontaminate rooms. Unhappily, the very properties that confer upon antiseptics their power to kill micro-organisms make them unsuitable for use in the presence of living tissues and so for attempting to secure surgical sterility; thus phenol and alcoholic solutions of iodine could only cause extensive tissue damage. (The anointment of cuts with tincture of iodine must be regarded as a RITUAL rather than a therapeutic procedure.)

In modern surgery antiseptics have an important place as adjuncts to ASEPSIS. Thus scalpels and carbon steel instruments that would be severely damaged by high-pressure steam are sterilized as a matter of routine by immersion in strong antiseptics which are washed off before the instruments are used. By far the most effective antiseptic procedure is the exposure to steam at temperatures above 100°C and therefore, necessarily, under pressure; steam at 120°C (at a pressure of 102 pounds per square inch) is the usual method of sterilizing the drapes and gowns used in surgical operations. *Antiseptic surgery*, specially associated with the name of Joseph Lister, is the procedure in which an attempt is made to combat infection by direct use of antiseptics (e.g. by conducting an operation in a phenol spray and treating wounds with carbolic acid or other antiseptic solution). It has been wholly supplanted by asepsis.

P.M.

anti-theatre. Imprecise journalistic term generally used to denote any type of theatre that does not conform to the familiar patterns of NATURALISM. Coined in the 1950s at the same time as ANTI-NOVEL (and cf. the cult of the ANTI-HERO), it may cover anything from the plays of Ionesco and Beckett (see THEATRE OF THE ABSURD) to the wildest form of experiment. In general parlance it has now been overtaken by the more neutral term ALTERNATIVE THEATRE.

M.BI.

antithesis, see under SYNTHESIS.

anti-trust (or **monopoly**) **policy.** The name given to legislation and policies designed to protect the consumer against the exploitation of their market power by MONOPOLIES or 'trusts', as they were known in the 19th century. While there may be powerful reasons for the development of a monopoly situation in certain industries, economic theory suggests that under a monopoly prices tend to be higher and output smaller than would otherwise be the case. This restriction of output reduces ECONOMIC EFFICIENCY and may represent a loss in SOCIAL WELFARE. Monopolies may offer ECONOMIES OF SCALE and give rise to greater TECHNICAL PROGRESS. Thus, monopolies may or may not give rise to net losses in social welfare. In the U.K., in order to act against a monopoly or merger, the government has to prove a net economic cost to society of the existence of the monopoly or merger. The underlying assumption in U.S. anti-trust legislation is that monopoly works against the public interest. Federal anti-trust legislation includes the Sherman Anti-Trust Act of 1890 and the Clayton Act of 1914, when the Federal Trade Commission was also established. British landmarks in monopoly policy are the establishment of the Monopolies Commission (1948) and the Monopolies and Mergers Commission (1965) and the Restrictive Trade Practices Act (1956).

D.E.; J.P.

Bibl: M. C. Sawyer, *The Economics of Industries and Firms* (London, 1981).

anti-utopia (or **dystopia**). A variety of thinking developed to counter what is seen as the false and dangerous optimism of UTOPIANISM. It uses the form of utopian fiction to present future society as a nightmare of oppression and sterility. Taking its lead partly from older satires such as Swift's *Gulliver's Travels*, it has been particularly influenced by the fears explored in Mary Shelley's *Frankenstein* (1816) and Feodor Dostoyevsky's 'Legend of the Grand Inquisitor' from *The Brothers Karamazov* (1880). Science and SOCIALISM, the great hopes of the modern utopia, are its principal antagonists and targets. In this century the most influential anti-utopias have been Evgeny Zamyatin's *We* (1924), Aldous Huxley's *Brave New World* (1932) and George Orwell's *Nineteen Eighty-Four* (1949). Since the 1950s, the function of the literary anti-utopia has been largely taken over by science-fiction films spelling out messages of doom and destruction at the hands of atomic weapons, environmental decay, and strange new diseases unleashed by scientific hubris. But some literary anti-utopias have had considerable impact, such as Kurt Vonnegut's *Player Piano* (1952), F. Pohl and C.M. Kornbluth's *The Space Merchants* (1953), Anthony Burgess's *A Clockwork Orange* (1962), and William Burroughs's *Nova Express* (1964). The short stories and novels of the science-fiction writer J.G. Ballard — e.g. *The Terminal Beach* (1964), *The Disaster Area* (1967) — contain some of the most powerful anti-utopian imagery of recent times. Latterly indeed the anti-utopia has abandoned the precise social and political criticism of writers such as Huxley and Orwell. It traffics now in apocalyptic images of doom and disaster on a cosmic scale.

K.K.

Bibl: C. Walsh, *From Utopia to Nightmare* (London, 1962); M.R. Hillegas, *The Future as Nightmare* (New York, 1967).

anxiety. In ABNORMAL PSYCHOLOGY and PSYCHIATRY, a term used to refer both (1) to an emotional state (see EMOTION) and (2) to a trait of character. As (1) it is often used synonymously with 'fear', and, more specifically, of fears whose object is not known, as in the *anxiety state*, a NEUROSIS characterized by feelings of fear for which the patient can give no reason; within learning theory, it refers to the emotional state elicited by signals of impending punishment. As (2) it describes different degrees of susceptibility to fear. According to H.J. Eysenck, this trait is not unitary, but a composite of neuroticism and INTROVERSION, highly anxious people being neurotic introverts. As such, it is more prominent in women than in men, while women are also more prone to psychiatric disturbances involving anxiety in sense (1).   J.A.G.

Bibl: I.M. Marks, *Fears and Phobias* (London and New York, 1969).

ANZUS. Acronym for Australia, New Zealand and the United States, with reference to the security alliance between them.   C.E.D.

apartheid. Afrikaans word meaning literally 'apart-ness'; applied to the system of policies maintaining the domination of South Africa's white majority over the non-white populations. The system built on existing patterns of segregation and was established after the election in 1948 of the National Party. Various euphemisms have been offered by apartheid's apologists, including 'separate development' and recently the yet more disingenuous 'co-operative co-existence'. In reality the system comprehensively institutionalizes the superior status of whites in economic, political and social matters. Among its principal mechanisms is the 'homelands' or *Bantustans* policy, which seeks to divide and restrict blacks to ten 'tribal homelands', themselves anthropological fictions. Its purpose is to maintain the supply of black labour to the South African economy while inhibiting the full development of black communities in white-dominated towns and cities, and ultimately to create an alternative basis of citizenship which will deny South African citizenship to its blacks.

The PASS LAWS were a vital support of this system. The legal requirement that blacks carry a 'pass' or document proving their presence in an area legal has a history almost as long as that of white settlement of the region. It was codified and more rigorously applied after 1948. The laws' function, effect and symbolic power made them a major target for resistance, culminating in pressure (particularly from the South African Congress of Trade Unions) which forced their abandonment in 1986. The replacement system requiring members of all races to carry an identity document did not satisfy many blacks.

The remaining legal structure which sustains apartheid is vast, ranging from measures maintaining the segregated and subordinate status of blacks and other non-whites to restrictions on the civil liberties of all South Africans. Recent reforms such as those embodied in the 1984 constitution have not fundamentally altered the apartheid system, which at the time of writing (1987) is increasingly unstable.   S.R.

Bibl: T. Lodge, *Black Politics in South Africa since 1945* (Marlow, 1985); R. Davies *et al.*, *The Struggle for South Africa* (2 vols., London, 1984).

aphasia, see under NEUROPSYCHOLOGY.

Apocalypse, see NEW APOCALYPSE.

Apollonian and Dionysian cultures. Terms used by Ruth Benedict to distinguish two 'patterns' of CULTURE. Rooted in the school of cultural ANTHROPOLOGY of Franz Boas, she regarded cultures, especially of the simpler societies, as consistent and enduring patterns of behaviour, thought, and action; systems of INSTITUTIONS and psychological orientations with attendant PERSONALITY TYPES. Deriving the terms from Nietzsche (in his discussion of Greek drama) and Oswald Spengler, Benedict used Dionysian to denote a pattern of culture engendering and encouraging emotional abandonment in social responses, and Apollonian to denote one producing order and control. In the burial of the dead, for example, the Zuni Indians (Apollonian) controlled and contained their grief; the Kwakiutl Indians (Dionysian) abandoned themselves in a demonstrative orgy of wailing. Evans-Pritchard called this 'the rustling-of-the-wind-in-the-palm-trees' kind of anthropology. See also FOLK CULTURE; SUBCULTURE.   R.F.

Bibl: R. Benedict, *Patterns of Culture* (Boston and New York, 1934; London, 1935).

Apparat. Term usually applied to the body of full-time officials who staff the COMMUNIST Parties of the Soviet Union and of other countries in the SOCIALIST bloc. These functionaries, the apparatchiki, are responsible for the implementation, at all levels of the Party, of Party policy formulated by the POLITBURO and Central Committee. The Apparat is organized strictly hierarchically, and at its top is the Party's Central Committee and its Secretariat, which is in overall charge of the Apparat. Official information on the size of the Apparat in socialist countries is not usually made available, but estimates of the number of apparatchiki in the Soviet Union have ranged from 100,000 to 500,000, out of a total Party membership of over 18 million. One of the most important tasks of the Apparat is filling nomenklatura posts, those positions in administration to which the Party has the power of appointment, and supervising state organizations. D.PR.
Bibl: G. Hosking, *A History of the Soviet Union* (London, 1985).

appeasement. A term first employed in political contexts in the 1920s, when it meant the removal by mutual agreement of the grievances arising out of the 1919 peace settlement. After the appointment, on 30 January 1933, of Adolf Hitler as Chancellor in Germany, the word was applied to the (unsuccessful) policy pursued by the British and French governments of trying to avoid war with Germany by injudicious, frequently dishonourable, and inevitably unrequited concessions, weakening to those who made them and often made at the expense of third parties. The epitome of the policy of appeasement was the MUNICH agreement of 30 September 1938. D.C.W.
Bibl: A.P. Adamthwaite, *The Making of the Second World War* (London, 2nd ed., 1979).

apperception. The mental state of PERCEPTION when it is self-conscious, when the perceiver is aware of the fact that he is perceiving as well as of the object perceived. The term was introduced into PHILOSOPHY by Leibniz as a means for distinguishing what had hitherto been supposed inseparable: the mind's activities of perception and its awareness of those activities. Leibniz's view was that it is possible for a mind to perceive something without being aware that it is doing so. A persuasive argument he gave for this conclusion is that we can be surprised by the cessation of a noise, such as the ticking of a clock, which we had not been conscious of perceiving during the time before it stopped. A.Q.

applied mathematics. Strictly, all those branches of MATHEMATICS developed to assist deductive reasoning in the physical and NATURAL SCIENCES. In the U.K. the term is often used in a more specialized sense to refer to the mathematical techniques useful in CLASSICAL PHYSICS.
M.V.B.

applied psychology. The examination of specific practical problems of human life, using the methods and criteria of academic PSYCHOLOGY. In contrast to applied physical sciences, this area of activity can only rarely make use of generalizations which are well established by theoretical work and require merely to be related to the problem. Rather, the practical situation may often reveal new and unsuspected aspects of human nature, whose understanding is a gain to general knowledge as well as to the solution of the particular problem. Occasionally the applied psychologist may differ from the intelligent layman by knowledge of some fact, such as the likely effects of line thickness upon the visibility of illuminated signs seen at night. More usually, he differs only by the habit of seeking some specific breakdown of function behind an undesired action; e.g. multiple accidents on high-speed roads lead psychologists to suspect failures of perception of speed and distance, and of anticipation of likely delays in the driver's own response, and these failures in turn can be traced to the particular visual and other information given to the driver.

Some fields of application are now so highly developed that they are usually distinguished under their own name. Thus

45

applications to mental health are normally termed *clinical psychology*; those to learning and adjustment at school, EDUCATIONAL PSYCHOLOGY; those to the well-being and efficiency of people engaged in industry, INDUSTRIAL PSYCHOLOGY. In most fields of application, however, there are related problems, including the construction of methods for assessing the past performance of people, whether schoolchildren, industrial managers, or some other category; the attempt to predict which people will be able to meet some situation adequately in the future, as by aircrew selection tests or clinical prognosis; and the comparison of different detailed systems of presenting information and required action, as in the EVALUATION of TEACHING MACHINES, of different keyboards for telephones, or of different phrasings of public notices of pension entitlement. The physical ENVIRONMENT is also a common problem, as in the effects of airport noise or school lighting; and so is the social or human environment, as in the effects of family background on school performance, or of PARTICIPATION upon the self-respect of an industrial worker.

In many of these areas the applied psychologist has had an influence, which is retrospectively seen to have been salutary, upon general attitudes to human beings. Thus the problems of assessment and prediction forced a respect for individual differences upon academic psychology; the problems of work design in complex semi-automatic systems made it clear that the mind performs highly sophisticated operations upon the STIMULI reaching it, rather than simply associating them; and the problem of the social environment, while complicating response to persuasion on food habits or RACE relations, helped to establish the importance of the cultural matrix of individual behaviour. Thus far, however, the output of applied psychology has consisted of verbal analyses and recommendations, which can be accepted or rejected like any others. More recently, tentative techniques have been explored for changing human behaviour directly: advertising, conditioning techniques (see, for example, BEHAVIOUR THERAPY), or the participation by psychologists in GROUP sessions in a business with the aim of producing an altered organization. These techniques are likely to raise ethical questions amongst practitioners, as well as complaints of manipulation amongst those affected; but if successful they may well provide intellectual and practical gains substantially greater than those of the past.   D.E.B.

appropriate technologies. Methods of production that use resources and inputs that are compatible with those available in the economy — in particular, a developing economy — and produce products which are suited to the economy. The appropriate technology movement originated from the view that the technologies used in developing countries are often inappropriate and should be changed to be more labour-intensive, to make more use of local labour, skills and materials and to produce products that are useful to a low-income country. Appropriate technologies can be established by adapting the technologies existing in developed countries or by improving the traditional technologies used in developing countries. As appropriate technologies make better use of the available resources and labour, they may well be more efficient (see ECONOMIC EFFICIENCY). Through using more labour, they may give a more desirable distribution of income, though statements of the latter type require a VALUE JUDGEMENT.
                                           J.P.

Bibl: F. Stewart, *Technology and Underdevelopment* (London, 2nd ed., 1977).

apraxia, see under NEUROPSYCHOLOGY.

apriorism. In PHILOSOPHY, a more precise term for the opposite of EMPIRICISM than the more commonly used RATIONALISM. An apriorist holds either or both of the following opinions: (1) that the mind is constitutionally endowed with CONCEPTS or IDEAS which it has not derived from experience; (2) that there is knowledge which does not depend for its justification on experience and yet which is still substantially informative and not merely verbal or ANALYTIC in character. The most plausible instances of *a priori* concepts are the formal concepts of LOGIC, e.g. those of negation and implication (see under ENTAILMENT), expressed by the words 'not' and 'if'. More controversial instances are the METAPHYSICAL concepts which Kant called CATEGORIES, in particular those of SUBSTANCE and cause. The most notable alleged instances of substantial, non-analytic, *a priori* knowledge are also metaphysical, for example the PROPOSITIONS (called by Kant 'principles' or, more fully, 'pure principles of the understanding') that there is a fixed amount of substance in the universe (i.e. *ex nihilo nihil fit*) and that every event has a cause. More loosely, an apriorist is one who ascribes large powers for the discovery of new knowledge to pure reasoning, unassisted by experience.   A.Q.

Bibl: W.H. Walsh, *Reason and Experience* (Oxford, 1947); J. Hospers, *An Introduction to Philosophical Analysis* (London and New York, 2nd ed., 1967).

aptitude tests, see under MENTAL TESTING.

AQ. Achievement quotient. A measure of ability derived by dividing an individual's achievement age by his actual age. C.E.D.

aquaplaning. The action which takes place when a solid object moves on the surface of a liquid at such a speed as to create a REYNOLDS WEDGE ACTION, thereby producing a lifting force on the solid object. It is commonly used to describe the reaction between the wheel of a motor car and a wet road. At a sufficiently high speed, and if the tyre on the wheel is unable, by means of its tread, to pump the water from under the wheel sideways, the tyre may begin to slide by aquaplane action, resulting in loss of control from the steering wheel. The expression is also used in relation to certain types of water surface craft where Reynolds wedge action results from viscous effects. See also HYDROFOIL.   E.R.L.

Arab nationalism. A political emotion of shared identity based on a common language, past glory, territory and religion which has acquired much of its strength and rhetoric from opposition to foreign rule. Its origins are found in an Arab renaissance under the Ottomans dating from 1875. In both ideas and action Arab nationalism has fluctuated between loyalty to the Arab nation as a whole (the

umma or Islamic community) and to a part of the nation territorially defined (the *watan*), so that it has found expression in Hashimite nationalism (based on Jordan and Iraq), Syrian and Egyptian nationalism. In general Arab nationalism proved resistant to attempts at alliance by Britain and America but embraced European ideas, including CONSTITUTIONALISM and then SOCIALISM. As imperial influence has declined and the machinery of independent Arab states has entrenched itself, Arab nationalism has transferred its outward hostility to Israel and exists in uneasy alliance with the resurgence of ISLAM.
                                                      W.K.

Bibl: P. Mansfield, *The Arabs* (London, 3rd ed., 1985).

Arbeitsrat für Kunst. German artists' and architects' council, formed after the November 1918 Revolution, with Walter Gropius emerging as chairman, and the BRÜCKE painters as prominent members. It was important chiefly for its influence on the BAUHAUS and on German social-architectural thinking in the 1920s. In December 1919 it merged with the somewhat similar Novembergruppe.   J.W.

Bibl: M. Franciscono, *Walter Gropius and the Creation of the Bauhaus in Weimar* (Urbana, Ill., 1971).

archaebacteria. A recently suggested new group of single-celled PROKARYOTIC organisms, which would include various species previously classified as bacteria. Modern archaebacteria include forms that inhabit high temperature and acidic environments (thermacidophiles), salty environments (halobacteria), and anoxic bogs (methanogenic bacteria). These all differ from other bacteria in various ways, most notably in their characteristic NUCLEIC ACID structure. It has been suggested that the former group 'bacteria' should now be divided into two *kingdoms* (see BIOSYSTEMATICS), archaebacteria and eubacteria; but the classification of the bacteria remains uncertain. The archaebacteria are probably the surviving representatives of the ancestors of the eubacteria. The early environment of the Earth would have been anoxic, and the METABOLISM of archaebacteria is in some respects more primitive than that of other bacteria. M.R.

archaeology. The technique of studying man's past using material remains as a primary source. In *text-free archaeology* material remains are the sole evidence, the study being known as PREHISTORY. When texts are available the term PROTOHISTORY is often used. Specialist branches proliferate: *classical archaeology, medieval archaeology, post-medieval archaeology* and INDUSTRIAL ARCHAEOLOGY are now accepted as individual disciplines, while FIELD ARCHAEOLOGY refers to an approach used by all. *Landscape archaeology* is now used to describe the study of visible traces of the past, usually over large tracts of countryside. *Environmental archaeology* uses recent advances, particularly in prehistory, to emphasize man's dynamic relationship with his ENVIRONMENT. In this way it is possible to study man through his effects on the ECOSYSTEM even when artifacts are absent. Many specialist techniques contribute to archaeology, e.g. LINGUISTICS, PALAEOBOTANY, PALAEOPATHOLOGY, PALAEOSEROLOGY, etc. History can, loosely speaking, be regarded as a technique used to augment the most recent fraction of the time span studied by the archaeologist. B.C.

Bibl: D. Brothwell and E. Higgs (eds.), *Science in Archaeology* (London, 2nd ed., 1969; New York, 1970); J.G. Evans, *An Introduction to Environmental Archaeology* (London, 1978); M. Aston, *Interpreting the Landscape* (London, 1985).

archaeomagnetism. The study of residual or *remanent* (in full, *thermo-remanent*) MAGNETISM, usually in an artifact or structure of baked clay. It is based on the principle that magnetite, an oxide of iron, when heated above a certain point (the *Curie point*), loses its magnetism, taking on the qualities of the earth's magnetic FIELD as it cools. These remain fossilized unless heat is again applied. Thus an *in situ* structure (e.g. a hearth or kiln) retains the magnetic characteristics of its location at the time of its use. For purposes of DATING, the remanent magnetism of the sample is measured for direction (a horizontal component known as *declination* or

D, and a vertical one known as *inclination* or *I* or *dip*) and intensity. These factors are compared with the pattern of known changes in the earth's field. The dating method is not absolute, since before *c*. 1500 A.D. calibration data must be acquired by measuring samples of known date. A wide margin of error is often encountered. B.C.

Bibl: R.M. Cook, 'Archaeomagnetism', in D. Brothwell and E. Higgs (eds.), *Science in Archaeology* (London, 2nd ed., 1969; New York, 1970), pp. 76-87.

archaeometallurgy. The study of metallurgical processes practised by past societies. Archaeologists provide the raw data, metallurgists study it. B.C.

Bibl: R.F. Tylecote, *The Prehistory of Metallurgy in the British Isles* (London, 1986).

archetype. A JUNGIAN term for any of a number of prototypic phenomena (e.g. the wise old man, the great mother) which form the content of the COLLECTIVE UNCONSCIOUS (and therefore of any given individual's unconscious), and which are assumed to reflect universal human thought found in all CULTURES. W.Z.

archigram. A seminal AVANT-GARDE British architectural group of the 1960s which intermittently published an architectural magazine. Archigram's designs were predicated on impermanence, the deployment of leading edge electronic and structural technology plus the general notion that architecture was to do with creating pleasure and entertainment for people.

S.L.

architecture autre. Omnibus term for a range of architectural ideas of the 1960s including BIOMORPHISM, ad hocism, Bowellism. These and a small number of other -isms, were self-consciously architectural. But they sought to create new forms and spaces from unconventional and new HIGH TECHnology materials as various as sprayed CONCRETE, plastic foam, hand crafted timber, glass fibre, plastics and steel. These materials enabled young designers to experiment with easily-built, mouldable three-dimensional forms difficult or impossible to create using orthodox, largely rectilinear building materials. Because of the necessarily idiosyncratic nature of their design, buildings in either group were not readily resellable in the real estate market and the phase remains an interesting side track in the history of architectural experiment.   S.L.

area. As used by geographers, a general, generic term for any portion of the earth's surface. An area may range in size up to the whole surface of the earth and has the dual properties of locational position and environmental content. See also AREA STUDIES; REGION.   P.H.

area studies. Educational term for inter-disciplinary, scholarly studies focusing on the peoples of a definable geographical sector. Although classical studies concerned with the culture of ancient Greece and Rome represent an early form of area studies, the term is commonly reserved for contemporary studies. In England the School of Oriental and African Studies was founded in 1916 as a language training centre but was extended after 1945 to include cultural and social studies. The post-war period has seen rapid growth of other area-focused studies (e.g. Slavonic studies, Latin American studies, African studies) in both Europe and the U.S.A.   P.H.

areal linguistics. In LINGUISTICS, the study of the linguistic forms found in any geographically defined region — their present-day distinctiveness and their historical antecedents. Particular groups of languages would be established in an *areal classification* (such as the Scandinavian languages, or the British dialects influenced by the speech of London).   D.C.

Bibl: P. Trudgill, *On Dialect* (Oxford, 1983).

ARENA (Nationalist Republican Alliance). Ultra right-wing and virulently anti-COMMUNIST political party in EL SALVADOR, which rose to prominence when its highly charismatic leader, Major Roberto D'Aubuisson, won the presidency in U.S.-sponsored elections in 1982. D'Aubuisson, who had political and financial backing from the Salvadoran oligarchy and the support of a significant sector of the peasantry, has proven links with death squad activity and had pledged a campaign of STATE TERROR to 'pacify' El Salvador. The U.S. intervened to secure the inauguration of an alternative president, and in the 1984 elections D'Aubuisson was defeated by Christian Democrat leader José Napoleón Duarte. From 1982-5, however, ARENA led rightist groups in the National Assembly in blocking all attempts at reform, particularly agrarian reform.   N.M.

Bibl: J. Donkerley, *The Long War — Dictatorship and Revolution in El Salvador* (London, 1982).

argument. In MATHEMATICS, a term that denotes what a FUNCTION is a function of; i.e. the independent VARIABLE(S). It is used both generically — as in 'a function of one numerical argument', and specifically — as in 'the value of the function is zero when the argument is zero'.   R.G.

arithmetic, higher, see NUMBER THEORY.

Armory Show. A landmark in the history of modern art in America, this 'International Exhibition of Modern Art' opened in February 1913 in the 69th Regimental Armory in New York and was later shown in Boston and Chicago. It contained over 1,000 works by some 300 artists, from Ingres to Marcel Duchamp. Cézanne, Gauguin, Redon, the FAUVES, and Augustus John were well represented, German EXPRESSIONISM scarcely, and FUTURISM not at all. It attracted the subsequent DADA artist Francis Picabia to the U.S.A., and thus laid the foundation of his and Duchamp's activity there.   J.W.

arms control. Restraint intentionally exercised by one or more powers upon the level, characteristics, deployment, or use of their armaments in order to promote stability, reduce the danger of WAR, limit its consequences, or otherwise minimize the hazards inherent in the existence or future development of modern weapons. The term is a broad one and includes measures of DISARMAMENT, inter-state agreements on mutual restraint, and unilateral policies (normally of the great powers). The term originated in the American strategic literature in the later

1950s, and the CONCEPT derives partly from economic theory, that STATES, like FIRMS, can decide to preclude activities that are mutually injurious without abandoning their general competitive or adversary stance; the term and the policy gained acceptance in the early 1960s as the need to control certain military activities (e.g. the atmospheric testing of NUCLEAR WEAPONS) and to limit the number of nuclear-weapon states became palpable while the prospects of negotiated MULTI-LATERAL disarmament remained unpromising. Recent arms control agreements include that on the non-militarization of Antarctica (1959), the Atmospheric Test Ban Treaty (1963), the Non-PROLIFERATION Treaty (1968), and the Soviet-American agreements of 1972 (SALT 1) on the permanent limitation of anti-ballistic missiles (see ABM) in each country and on a five-year standstill on levels of deployed MISSILES. Measures to control the build-up of strategic nuclear weapons were discussed in the 1976 (SALT 2) talks. An example of a unilateral arms control measure was the decision of the U.S.A. (and other governments) in 1969 to suspend research on biological weapons and to destroy stocks of them. For subsequent developments, see NUCLEAR WEAPONS, LIMITATION AND CONTROL. A.F.B.

Bibl: J.H. Barton, *The Politics of Peace: An Evaluation of Arms Control* (Stanford, Calif., 1981); R. Burt (ed.), *Arms Control and Defence Postures in the 1980s* (London, 1984).

arms race. The continuous accretion of military power by two or more states, based upon the conviction that only by retaining an advantage in such power can they ensure their national security or supremacy. Arms races have a quantitative and a qualitative aspect; but a contemporary distinction has emerged between arms races among minor powers (e.g. Israel and the Arab states), where both aspects are of significance, and among the great (i.e. NU-CLEAR WEAPON) powers where the qualitative aspect — improvements in the explosive power, accuracy, penetration, or invulnerability of long-range weapons — is the more significant. Hence the concentration of modern ARMS CONTROL policy as much on the characteristics of weapons as on their numbers. See also NUCLEAR WEAPONS, LIMITATION AND CONTROL. A.F.B.

Bibl: J. Turner, *The Arms Race* (Cambridge, 1983); D. Carlton and C. Schaerf, eds., *The Arms Race in the 1980s* (London, 1982).

aromatic. Adjective applied to a vast class of cyclic organic compounds where ELEC-TRONS are delocalized over a closed framework of carbon ATOMS (see BENZENE RING). A number of these substances have a pleasant smell; hence the term. The sharing of electrons over several carbon atoms has a characteristic influence on chemical behaviour. Petroleum is the major source of aromatic compounds which form the basis of many POLYMERS, insecticides, DETERGENTS, dyes, etc. B.F.

art autre, see under ABSTRACT ART.

art brut. The casual, often jarring, spontaneous graphic products of non-professionals, whether they be psychotics (see PSYCHOSIS), children, or graffiti-writers; or art which imitates these. *Art brut* ('raw art') was christened, adopted, and promoted by Jean Dubuffet, whose own paintings and assemblages of waste materials (see COLLAGE) owe much to the untutored scrawlings which he regards as truly creative reflections of the UNCON-SCIOUS mind. P.C.

Bibl: *Jean Dubuffet: a Retrospective* (New York, Solomon R. Guggenheim Foundation, 1973).

Art-Language, see under CONCEPTUAL ART.

art music. A term used loosely to categorize a composition defined by the intention and method of its composer. He does not write primarily for money, though he usually insists on being paid, and will gladly compose to a commission. He does not despise popular success, but will not modify or simplify his style to achieve it; nor, probably, will he deny that his audience is an ÉLITE. He uses accepted methods of composition, with a high degree of technical sophistication; according to fashion, this might be academic ingenuity or controlled chaos (see ALEATORY). He writes in conventional notation, unlike the composer-performer of FOLK MUSIC, whose work is perpetuated by oral tradition. Folk music is, however, always heard, whereas art music includes academic exercises doomed to eternal silence.

The passing of time and change of taste can recategorize a composition: Mozart's dance music, for example, is now regarded as art music, whereas a jazzed-up version of his 40th symphony would not be. The label 'art music' does not, in any case, imply high artistic worth, nor does the withholding of the label imply the absence of such worth. To dress up a simple expressive folk tune in the trappings of a symphony is to degrade it; and a JAZZ band may exhibit a vitality and imagination well beyond the capacity of many a composer of string quartets and symphonies. To this extent, the term 'art music' has fallen into disrepute.   B.K.

art nouveau. An artistic movement based on the use of linear flowing forms which emerged in the early 1890s in Europe and the U.S.A. and was probably strongly influenced by the introduction of Japanese art objects to the West. Named after a Paris shop, it was known in Germany as *Jugendstil* (after the satirical paper *Jugend*) and in Italy as *Stile Liberty* (after the London department store). In Austria it became associated with the Vienna SE-ZESSION started in 1897. The sinuous interweaving forms which became current in painting had their first major architectural application in the interior of the Auditorium Building in Chicago (1888) by Louis Sullivan and a house in Brussels (1893) by Victor Horta. These were attempts to define a new, vigorous style free of academicism and capable of unifying the arts. The notion of 'structural and dynamographic ornamentation' was developed largely by the Belgian architect Henry van de Velde, who was prominent in the WERKBUND and directed the Weimar Design School which developed into the BAUHAUS.

Art nouveau had a strong impact on the applied arts and is most visible in architecture where these meet — the furniture and decorations of the Tea Rooms in Glasgow by Charles Rennie Mackintosh, the iron-work outside his Glasgow School of Art, and that of Hector Guimard for the entrances of the Paris Métro. A full, plastic and often polychromatic expression was achieved by Antonio Gaudi in a number of buildings in Barcelona. *Art nouveau* declined soon after 1900 and remained out of favour until the late 1950s, when a search for more varied and richer forms (see, e.g., PSYCHEDELIC ART) appeared to make it relevant. See also ARTS DÉCO; GLASGOW SCHOOL; WIENER WERKSTÄTTE.   M.BR.

Bibl: L.-V. Masini, *Art Nouveau* (London, 1984).

art of the real, see MINIMAL ART.

art sacré, l'. French movement for the renewal of religious art in the light of modern painting and the example of the BEURON school in Germany. It dates from the foundation of the *ateliers d'art sacré* by Desvallières in 1919. In 1935 the magazine *L'Art sacré* was started, and after World War II an annual *salon d'art sacré* in Paris. From about 1950 (completion of the church of Notre-Dame at Assy in Savoie) a number of remarkable individual or collective works were created, quite often by unbelievers, under the influence of this movement, with wide international repercussions (e.g. on the decoration of the new cathedrals at Coventry and Liverpool). In particular, Matisse at Vence and Le Corbusier at Ronchamp produced world-famous masterpieces, while outside the movement proper the ex-FAUVE Georges Rouault devoted much of his life to religious art.   J.W.

arthroscopy. The term refers to a refined technique for the examination of a joint — usually the knee joint — by means of a special instrument. It allows the surgeon to inspect the inside of a joint without the need to make an incision to open the joint. It is used commonly to inspect the inside of the knee joint for a torn semi-lunar cartilage (meniscus). It is possible to perform certain well defined operative procedures through the arthroscope — for example, removal of a torn meniscus.
                N.H.H.

artificial insemination. The insemination of a female (human or animal) by other means than sexual intercourse. Semen is collected from the male — by masturbation or in the case of animals by an artificial vagina — and injected into the cervix (neck of the womb).

In animal breeding, especially cattle breeding, artificial insemination is now widely used. Centres exist for the collection of semen from high-quality males which is then directly injected into the females or cooled, preserved, and despatched to recipient animals anywhere. Since more semen is produced at a single ejaculation than is necessary to inseminate one female, artificial insemination has the advantage that several females can be inseminated from a semen sample of one male.

In humans a distinction is drawn between artificial insemination by the husband (AIH) and by a donor (AID) whose identity is usually unknown to the married couple. AIH is used when, because of difficulty with intercourse or, rarely, anatomical deformity, natural insemination is impossible; AID is used — in an unknown but probably small number of cases — where the husband is sterile and the wife fertile. There has been controversy about AID between those who object on moral, legal, and even GENETIC grounds and those who feel that, provided certain safeguards are observed, it should be available to married couples who prefer it to adoption. See WARNOCK REPORT. D.A.P.

artificial intelligence (AI or *machine intelligence*). A branch of COMPUTING SCIENCE which attempts to create machines exhibiting characteristics associated with human or animal intelligence. In practical terms, AI is not committed to producing machines that do anything more than appear intelligent. However, drawing on MATHEMATICAL LOGIC and theories of COMPUTABILITY, it is often hoped that AI will also serve to shed light on the processes underlying human COGNITION. This has led to the association of AI with *cognitive science* — a synthesis of such subjects as EXPERIMENTAL PSYCHOLOGY, LINGUISTICS, PHILOSOPHY, and LOGIC.

Initial efforts in AI often consisted of attempts at PROBLEM-SOLVING for tightly restricted sets of problems, such as chess playing. This produced (and still does) PROGRAMS that worked well in their own particular area, but which could not be extended to do anything else. The search for the unifying principles in AI necessary for producing machines displaying 'general' intelligence has proved extremely difficult. One central area of investigation is the knowledge representation problem: If computers are to reason intelligently about the world, they must have some knowledge of the world. This knowledge needs to be represented in such a way that it is easy to acquire, retrieve, and manipulate. Candidates for a representational system include logical AXIOMS, HOLISTIC networks of interconnecting CONCEPTS, and *production systems* like those used in EXPERT SYSTEMS. Even if an adequate representational framework were found, the most basic commonsense knowledge would still prove very resistant to analysis and formalization. Many AI systems operate by laboriously trying out a vast range of possible solutions to a problem until one is found that works. This is unlike the way in which people appear to solve many simple problems. A solution to the knowledge representation problem would allow the retrieval of information directly relevant to the task at hand. This would greatly reduce the number of possibilities that must be considered without resorting to more or less arbitrary HEURISTICS.

Other areas of interest in AI include the automatic proof of mathematical and logical theorems, planning tasks like ROBOTS negotiating obstacle courses or running an industrial process, and getting machines to learn from experience. Overlapping with other subjects are such things as machine vision, speech recognition, and *natural language processing* (the understanding of natural languages like English — see COMPUTATIONAL LINGUISTICS). With the exception of certain aspects of natural language processing, these last three attempt to simulate PERCEPTION rather than (conscious) cognition. They are being used to improve the so-called MAN-MACHINE INTERFACE. A recent development is connectionism, which uses interconnecting units similar to NEURONS to build up machines that are supposed to resemble brains. It remains to be seen whether connectionism will prove fruitful.

Some critics of AI argue that a machine could never be truly intelligent. Ultimately, computers perform purely blind, SYNTACTIC operations on strings of digits, and it is suggested that it is only the interpretation of the results of these operations by intelligent people that invests them with any meaning. Less persuasively, GÖDEL'S THEOREM is sometimes cited as evidence that there are certain things that people can know but which (consistent) machines cannot in principle ever know. Whether or not such scepticism is well founded, even moderate success in AI depends on the solution of problems that have stood for hundreds of years. (See also FIFTH-GENERATION COMPUTERS.)   R.S.C.

Bibl: E. Feigenbaum, A. Barr, P. Cohen, *The Handbook of Artificial Intelligence,* vols. I-III (Los Altos, 1981).

arts and crafts movement. A reaction to the Industrial Revolution and its products (especially as seen at the Great Exhibition of 1851) which was given social and intellectual definition in the writings of Ruskin and translated into practical terms by the founding by William Morris in 1861 of Morris, Marshall & Faulkner, Fine Art Workmen in Painting, Carving, Furniture and the Metals. Morris intended to foster an art restoring the dignity of the craftsman and, since 'it is not possible to dissociate art from morality, politics and religion', to establish a form of society that would combine medieval and SOCIALIST features. The movement, and its followers like Walter Crane, though backward-looking and unable to come to terms with machine production, nevertheless exerted a strong influence on the WERKBUND and hence the BAUHAUS.

The fusion of the applied arts of the movement with those in architecture can be seen in the Red House (1859), designed by Philip Webb for Morris. This later influenced Norman Shaw and C.F. Voysey, whose simple, airy houses of the 1890s proved so important to 20th-century architecture, becoming eventually almost a VERNACULAR of much suburban development.   M.BR.

Bibl: N. Pevsner, *Pioneers of Modern Design* (Harmondsworth, rev. ed., 1960).

arts centre. Building or group of buildings devoted to a mixture of cultural activities, such as has been favoured by official and semi-official bodies concerned with public patronage of the arts in England since 1945. It may range from a specially built metropolitan complex (as on London's South Bank) to a local library staging occasional exhibitions and entertainments, but generally it involves public and/or foundation finance. The rather similar French *maisons de la culture* which started in the 1960s are more uniform, centring normally on a theatre and an exhibition space, but various other continental or North American institutions could be brought under this head. Analogous earlier centres were the Belgian *maisons du peuple*, the early Soviet Workers' Clubs, and the Italian FASCIST *dopolavoro.*   J.W.

Bibl: *The Arts Enquiry: The Visual Arts* (London, 1946); A. Schouvaloff (ed.), *Place for the Arts* (Liverpool, 1970).

arts déco. Abridged name of the Exposition des Arts Décoratifs Modernes (Paris, 1925) used, then and now, for the style predominant there: a jazzy application of a second-hand visual vocabulary, derived from CUBISM, FUTURISM, FUNCTIONALISM, and other recent movements, to decorative, fashionable, and commercial ends. The architects Robert Mallet-Stevens and Michel Roux-Spitz were among those prominent in this trend, which coincided with the great period of cinema construction and still continues in, e.g., luxury bookbinding. Following a revival (exhibition at the Paris Musée des Arts Décoratifs, 1966), it has been seen by some as the natural sequel to ART NOUVEAU, whose formal inventiveness and social commitments, however, it fails to share.   J.W.

Bibl: B. Hillier, *Art Déco* (London and New York, 1968).

ASCII (American Standard Code for Information Interchange). An assignment of the upper and lower case letters, digits, punctuation marks and some other symbols to 7-BIT values, to enable text to be processed by a COMPUTER etc. This is the code in most widespread use, though IBM equipment (and its LOOKALIKES) uses a different one (EBCDIC). J.E.S.

ascription, see under PATTERN VARIABLES.

ASEAN (Association of Southeast Asian Nations). An expanded version of The Association of Southeast Asia. ASEAN was established by foreign ministers of its member states on 9 August 1967 in Bangkok. Its aim is to build a framework for regional cooperation amongst the non-COMMUNIST states of southern Asia: Indonesia, Malaysia, Philippines, Singapore, Thailand and Brunei. Caught up in the Sino-Soviet conflict in East Asia (see SINO-VIETNAMESE CONFLICT), it is inevitably concerned with international affairs, but differing responses by member states to the post-Mao policies in China have weakened its force in international politics. Its main concern therefore has been to accelerate ECONOMIC GROWTH in the area through such measures as the introduction of margins of tariff preference in January 1978. Its headquarters are in Djakarta, Indonesia. S.B.
Bibl: P. Lim, *ASEAN, a Bibliography* (Singapore, 1984).

asepsis (or *aseptic* SURGERY). The procedure by which wound infections are so far as possible prevented from occurring in the first place by the use of sterile instruments, drapes, gowns, etc., and by scrupulous attention to hygiene. Asepsis differs from *antisepsis* (or *antiseptic surgery*) in that the latter was an attempt to *kill* microorganisms *in situ*, whereas aseptic surgery aims at *excluding* them from the operation site. Although antiseptic surgery as such is obsolete, ANTISEPTICS have an important part to play in asepsis. Thus the skin into which a surgical incision is to be made is often prepared by repeated applications of iodine in alcoholic solution or by thorough cleansing with cationic DETERGENTS.
The principal cause of wound infection used to be the surgeon himself who before the days of antisepsis or asepsis could propagate infection from one patient to another, and even today it is the microorganisms to be found in hospitals themselves that are the major causes of wound infection — a particularly grave matter inasmuch as so many of the bacterial populations of the hospital ward are resistant to ANTIBIOTICS. P.M.

Ashby's Law, see under VARIETY.

Ashcan School. Term applied to American painting at the beginning of the 20th century characterized by the naturalistic (see NATURALISM) depiction of scenes from everyday life, especially in the city. It has been used misleadingly as a synonym for *The Eight*, a group of independents who revolted against New York academic painting, but it more appropriately describes the painting of Robert Henri, John Sloan, George Luks, and George Bellows. A.K.W.
Bibl: M.S. Young, *The Eight* (New York, 1973).

assemblage. In ARCHAEOLOGY (for its meaning in art see under COLLAGE), a group of artifacts found together in a closed CONTEXT or ASSOCIATION, e.g. in a hoard, a grave, or a single occupation level, in such a way as to imply that they were likely to have been in use at the same time. In palaeolithic studies an assemblage of tool types is usually referred to as an *industry*, while recurring assemblages can constitute a CULTURE. B.C.

assembler. In COMPUTING, a PROGRAM which takes as input any program written in ASSEMBLY LANGUAGE and transforms (translates) it into the corresponding form of machine-code instructions. It may leave these instructions inside the machine to be obeyed immediately, in which case it may be known as an *assembler-loader* or merely a *loader*. C.S.

assembly language. In COMPUTING, a PROGRAMMING LANGUAGE which produces, in general, one machine-code instruction for each line written in it. As a result programs written in assembly language tend to be very long and difficult to read. Despite various improvements the languages remain very close to actual machine code, so that different makes of machine require different assembly languages. See also ASSEMBLER; HIGH-LEVEL PROGRAMMING LANGUAGE.   C.S.

Assessment of Performance Unit (APU). An organization set up by the British Department of Education and Science (DES) in 1975 to 'promote the development of methods of assessing and monitoring the achievement of children and to seek to identify the incidence of underachievement'. A number of subject groups are involved in detecting underachievement at school, including language, mathematics and science. It is run by a coordinating group of teachers, local authority advisers, H.M. Inspectors and teacher trainers who recommend the areas most suitable for investigation.   J.I.

assimilation. In DEVELOPMENTAL PSYCHOLOGY, a PIAGETIAN term for (1) the incorporation of a new situation transformed to fit into an already organized schema of action; (2) more generally, the subordination of the external world to the activity of the self, as in fantasy and play. For a different sense of the word, see under INTEGRATION (sense 2).   P.L.H.

Assisted Places Scheme (APS). A scheme started in Britain by the Conservative government in 1981 to help academically bright children from poorer home backgrounds to attend independent, fee-paying schools. In all, 5,000 places were made available and parents were assisted with the payment of fees according to their income. Thus, some paid nothing while others contributed fees according to their means. About half the children — normally aged 11 to 13 on admission — come from homes whose income falls below the national average. The APS, opposed by the Labour opposition as 'divisive', was introduced as the nearest alternative to the old Direct Grant Schools system which was phased out by a Labour government from September 1976.   J.I.

association.
(1) In COGNITIVE PSYCHOLOGY, the mental connection between two or more IDEAS or SENSE DATA (percepts) or memories, such that the presence of one tends to evoke the other(s). These are presumed to mirror the associations that exist in the external world, so that association provides a mechanism whereby the STRUCTURE of experience reflects 'reality'. The CONCEPT was central to Aristotle's doctrine of mind as well as that of the British EMPIRICISTS.   W.Z.
(2) In ARCHAEOLOGY, when artifacts are found together in a closed CONTEXT they are said to be in *close association*, implying contemporaneity of deposition. The term *loose association* is sometimes used in the case of contexts of broader chronological range. Characteristics may be associated on a single artifact. Juxtaposition is not necessarily association. The term is imprecise and much abused in archaeological literature.   B.C.
(3) In ANTHROPOLOGY, a term used to describe the process by which an IMMIGRANT becomes part of the host society. It is a flattening process, that is assimilation is achieved through the eradication of all distinguishing features (e.g. language and customs) which have been brought by the immigrant to the new country. Assimilation and its desirability were based upon earlier Jewish and Irish settlements which were assumed to have been successfully assimilated or to have 'disappeared' within British society. The question of RACE, however, presented serious problems for this approach. Assimilation was also based on the idea that there was a homogenous host culture. It implied that the host culture was 'pure' and in danger of being overwhelmed or swamped by newcomers. INTEGRATION replaced assimilation as the policy formulated to deal with the consequences of post-war migration to Britain. It has been closely tied to the need for immigration control.   A.G.
Bibl: Centre for Contemporary Cultural Studies, *The Empire Strikes Back* (London, 1982); E. Cashmore and B. Troyna, *An Introduction to Race Relations* (London, 1983).

associationism. The recurring and variously formulated view (in R.S. Woodworth's classification, one of the six main SCHOOLS OF PSYCHOLOGY) that psychological phenomena comprise elements, such as ideas, SENSATIONS, feelings, STIMULI, and responses, which have become associated (see ASSOCIATION) according to some law or laws, such as similarity or frequency of contiguity.

I.M.L.H.

associative law. The law, obeyed in the multiplication of NUMBERS, which states that $a \times (b \times c) = (a \times b) \times c$. Any FUNCTION of two ARGUMENTS which satisfies a similar identity is said to be *associative*; other examples are addition and the composition of functions (since $f.(g.h)(x) = f(g(h(x))) = (f.g).h(x)$). For many MATHEMATICAL STRUCTURES (e.g. GROUPS) the law is taken as an axiom (see AXIOMATIC METHOD).

R.G.

associative store (or *content-addressed store*). In a COMPUTER, a form of STORE in which the location to which access is required is indicated, not by its 'address' (or physical location) as in the usual type of store, but by a key; the location chosen will be one whose contents match the key in some way. Special arrangements are made for the cases in which there are either no locations or more than one location matching the key. An associative store appears expensive, because comparison with the key is carried out for all locations simultaneously and this involves a considerable amount of LOGIC for each location. However, as these circuits are highly repetitive, they are particularly suitable for L.S.I. (see INTEGRATED CIRCUIT), which reduces their cost.

C.S.

asteroid (or *minor planet* or *planetoid*). One of several thousand masses of rock or ice, the largest about 300 miles across, which circle the sun in orbits distributed between those of Mars and Jupiter. They may be the debris of a planet ruptured by collision with another body, or by the gravitational effects (see GRAVITATION) of a close approach to Jupiter; alternatively, they may be the raw material for a planet which never consolidated.

M.V.B.

asthenosphere. The analysis of earthquake waves passing through the earth has led to a simple threefold division of the interior of the earth. The outermost solid shell, the *crust*, is of variable thickness, 30 to 75 km in continental areas but some 5 km under the oceans. The crust is succeeded inwards by the still solid and denser *mantle* which

extends to a depth of 2,900 km below the surface. The very high density and mainly liquid interior of the earth is known as the *core*. In general the strength or, more correctly, the rigidity of the crust and mantle rock material increases with depth. More detailed seismic study has revealed the presence of a relatively weak plastic zone in the upper part of the mantle named the asthenosphere which extends from 100 to 400 km below the surface. The mechanical weakness of the zone is thought to be due to the presence of small quantities of interstitial liquid. The plastic asthenosphere allows the rigid lithosphere above it to move laterally over the surface of the earth (see PLATE TECTONICS).

J.L.M.L.

astronautics. The TECHNOLOGY of travel in space, involving ROCKET propulsion, TELECOMMUNICATION, CELESTIAL MECHANICS, and the design of life-support systems.

M.V.B.

astronomical unit (AU), see under SOLAR SYSTEM.

astronomy. The oldest exact science, in which the heavenly bodies (moon, sun, planets, stars, NEBULAE, GALAXIES, etc.) are studied. By analysing the RADIATION received from space as visible light and, more recently, X-RAYS, radio waves (see RADIO ASTRONOMY), and MICROWAVES, the following picture of the universe has been built up: the nearly-spherical earth is orbited by the moon; together they move in an ORBIT round the sun, as do the planets and their SATELLITES, and the ASTEROIDS, all the bodies so far mentioned constituting the *solar system*. The sun in turn is one star among millions, which together with nebulae and sparse interstellar debris make up the *Milky Way*, which is in turn one galaxy among millions whose mutual recession constitutes the EXPANSION OF THE UNIVERSE.

Distances in astronomy are vividly expressed in light-time, using the fact that light travels 186,000 miles per second. From the earth to the moon is 1.4 light-seconds, from the earth to the sun about 8 light-minutes; the whole solar system is a few light-hours across. The nearest star is 4 light-years away, and the Milky Way is about 100,000 light-years across. The nearest galaxy is about two million light-years away. The distance at which the galaxies are receding from us with the speed of light, which on our present understanding represents the limit of the observable universe, is about ten thousand million light-years.

The study of the motion of the heavenly bodies constitutes CELESTIAL MECHANICS, the investigation of their physical nature ASTROPHYSICS. In COSMOLOGY the universe as a whole is studied, and attempts are made to account for its origin in COSMOGONY. Precise observations of the positions of heavenly bodies were used until recently to establish standards of time measurement (see ATOMIC CLOCK), while for millennia these observations have formed the basis for navigation (recently in the air and outer space as well as on the sea), as well as for astrology.   M.V.B.

Bibl: M. Zeilik, *Astronomy: the Evolving Universe* (New York, 4th ed., 1985); D.B. Herrman, *A History of Astronomy from Herschel to Hertzsprung*, tr. and revised by K. Kriscivnas (Cambridge, 1984).

astrophysics. A branch of theoretical ASTRONOMY: the study of stars, and the gases between them, in which the laws of PHYSICS established on earth are applied to the electromagnetic RADIATION and COSMIC RAYS received from space. See also BLACK HOLE; CARBON CYCLE; PULSAR; QUASAR; RADIO ASTRONOMY; RADIO TELESCOPE; SPECTROSCOPY.   M.V.B.

asymptotic. A FUNCTION f is an asymptotic approximation to the function g if the percentage error $g(x)–f(x)/f(x)$ tends to zero as x tends to infinity.   R.G.

atavism. The unsubstantiated belief that complete ancestral types can reappear as 'throwbacks' among an otherwise normal family. This concept of atavism, though based on a grain of truth — the fact that in Mendelian (see MENDELISM) HEREDITY grandparental or more remotely ancestral characteristics may reappear unexpectedly among offspring — belongs to the folklore of RACISM (see also RACE); cf. the totally unwarranted name 'mongolism' for a congenital affliction (DOWN'S

SYNDROME) caused by an accidental derangement of the CHROMOSOMES.   P.M.

atheism. The opinion that there is no God. The chief grounds on which this is asserted are: the extent of disorder, chance, and evil in the universe as known by science and by honest experience; the impossibility of knowing anything beyond space and time, such as God (see AGNOSTICISM); the failure of believers' (mutually conflicting) attempts to claim that God has been revealed and can be spoken about reasonably (see THEISM); the substitution of religious belief in illusory consolations for activity in the struggle for a better society (see MARXISM). The chief problems confronting atheism are man's wonder at the existence of good (see MYSTICISM), and the need which many people feel for faith and a supernatural consolation in order to endure (see RELIGION). See also HUMANISM; SECULARISM.   D.L.E.

Bibl: J. Monod, *Chance and Necessity* (London and New York, 1972); J. L. Mackie, *The Miracle of Theism* (Oxford, 1982).

Athens Charter, see under CIAM.

atom. The smallest unit of a chemical ELEMENT. The idea that matter, which appears continuous to our gross senses, may in fact consist of tiny discrete PARTICLES which cannot be further subdivided, seems to stem from Democritus (*c.* 400 B.C.). But it was only in the late 19th century that accumulating evidence (e.g. the BROWNIAN MOTION) led to the general acceptance of the *atomic theory* among scientists. The entities which we call atoms today are only one of several 'smallest units' at the microscopic level of nature; MOLECULES are the structural units involved in chemical processes, while atoms themselves have a complicated structure (see ATOMIC PHYSICS) of which the ELEMENTARY PARTICLES represent the fundamental units.   M.V.B.

atomic clock. A device for counting the vibrations of ATOMS. Because of their extreme regularity, these vibrations are used to define the standard for the measurement of time (1 second = 9,192,631,770 cycles of a certain vibration of the

Caesium atom); this is expected to be consistent to about one second in a thousand years (a previous standard, based on the earth's rotation, was accurate only to about one second in one year). M.V.B.

atomic energy. ENERGY obtained from the atomic NUCLEUS during a CHAIN REACTION, which may either be controlled, as in a NUCLEAR REACTOR, or uncontrolled, as in nuclear weapons. See also FISSION; FUSION; MASS-ENERGY EQUATION. M.V.B.

atomic number (of an ELEMENT). The number of PROTONS in the atomic NUCLEUS. It is equal to the number of ELECTRONS in a neutral ATOM, and the ordinal number of the element on a scale of increasing atomic weights. No elements whose atomic number exceeds 92 (uranium) occur naturally; nuclei of the TRANSURANIC ELEMENTS are unstable because the disruptive effect of the ELECTROSTATIC repulsion between the protons outweighs the attraction due to the shorter-ranged STRONG INTERACTION. See also ISOTOPE. M.V.B.

atomic physics. The branch of PHYSICS devoted to studying the structure of ATOMS. The atom is an open structure about a ten-thousand-millionth of a metre across, consisting of a positively charged NUCLEUS about ten thousand times smaller across, whose attraction binds a number of negatively charged orbiting ELECTRONS; this number is equal to the ATOMIC NUMBER if the atom is neutral, but higher or lower if the atom is an ION. It is often helpful to compare the atom with the solar system of sun and planets, but this is not a strict analogy because electrons obey the laws of QUANTUM MECHANICS, not of NEWTONIAN MECHANICS (see WAVE-PARTICLE DUALITY; BOHR THEORY). The weakly bound outer electrons are detached and exchanged during the CHEMICAL REACTIONS which may occur when atoms are close together. Transition of electrons from one ORBIT to another, with a change of QUANTUM NUMBER, involves an emission or absorption of ENERGY in the form of PHOTONS, either of visible light (outer electrons) or X-RAYS (inner electrons). See also ELECTRON SHELL; ENERGY LEVEL; SPECTROSCOPY. M.V.B.

atomic pile, see NUCLEAR REACTOR.

atomic submarine, see NUCLEAR SUBMARINE.

atomic weight. Building upon Lavoisier's pragmatic definition of element (as a substence never yet reduced to any simpler components), John Dalton argued that distinct chemical elements were characterized by being composed of PARTICLES of different (relative) atomic weights. Dalton published his first list of relative weights in 1803, and his idea found widespread acceptance, though it was not until the 1860s that these values were internationally standardized. Belief in a stable, atomic composition of the elements provided the crucial foundations for chemistry's rapid development as a coherent science from the mid-19th century onwards, leading to VALENCY theory, the triumphs of the kinetic theory of gases, and the PERIODIC TABLE of the elements, which predicted the existence of other, not yet discovered, ELEMENTS. Despite 20th-century investigations of the fine structure of particles, the theory of atomic weights remains the basis of practical CHEMISTRY. R.P.

Bibl: A.S. Rocke, *Chemical Atomism in the Nineteenth Century* (Columbus, Ohio, 1984).

atonal music. Music divorced from the concept of *tonality* which dominated Western musical thought for more than three centuries. Traditionally, a composer selected one of the 24 tonal families — 12 major and 12 minor — each of which is spelled out by a *scale* and known as a *key*, one note being the *tonic* towards which the others gravitate. It was common practice for the opening phrase of a work to establish the key unequivocally by stating its essential notes in melodic or harmonic terms; similarly it was virtually an unbroken rule that the final cadence (sequence of chords) should confirm the tonality. In the latter part of the 19th century, however, the increasingly free use, notably by Wagner and Liszt, of chromatic notes (those not belonging to the key of the work) led to a gradual erosion of tonality. The process was continued by Debussy (see IMPRESSIONISM; WHOLE-TONE SCALE), Scriabin, and particularly Schoenberg, and culminated in *atonalism*. Atonalism is the deliberate avoidance of key; *atonality* is the term used to designate a state of atonalism.

The largest problem in atonal music is to overcome the natural tendency of certain basic intervals such as the fifth and the third to establish a tonality of sorts, however temporary. It is for this reason that atonal music is largely dissonant, since only by avoiding traditional consonances can the implications of tonality be avoided; similarly the melodic lines are harder for the average listener to absorb, since they are often characterized by angularity and wide-spaced intervals. Much, but not all, atonal music is composed according to the SERIAL principles evolved around 1920 by Schoenberg. A.H.

attachment. In ETHOLOGY, the initial 'bonding' of mother and infant of various SPECIES, during which many crucial response mechanisms in the growing infant have been found to depend upon an adequate relationship with the mother. See also IMPRINTING. J.S.B.

Bibl: J. Bowlby, *Attachment and Loss* (London and New York, 1969).

AU (astronomical unit), see under SOLAR SYSTEM.

au-dessus de la mêlée ('above the battle'). An expression which became current during the 1914-18 war, as the title of an article in the *Journal de Génève* (15 September 1914), and later of a pamphlet, a collection of articles by the French writer Romain Rolland, author of *Jean-Christophe*, who had strong sympathies with German musical and literary culture. The pamphlet, a plea for peace and reasonableness, offended nationalistic sensibilities — Hermann Hesse was the only writer on either side who immediately welcomed it — and the expression came to signify reprehensible detachment or indifference. J.G.W.

audio frequency. A vibration frequency in the range 20-20,000 Hertz (1 Hertz = 1 complete vibration cycle per second). This is the range over which the human ear responds to sound waves, so that HI-FI consists of the faithful reproduction of audio frequencies. See also ULTRASONICS. M.V.B.

Austinian. Adjective formed from the name of John Austin (1790-1859). Austin's vastly influential *The Province of Jurisprudence Determined* (1832) elaborated a theory of law which insisted that the notion of a command was the key to the understanding of law, and that though there were many empirical connections between law and morals there was no necessary connection between them. Human law is therefore, according to Austin, essentially a command (expressed or tacit) of a sovereign (see SOVEREIGNTY) defined as a person or body of persons in receipt of habitual obedience from the bulk of a given society but not in any such habit of obedience to any other person or body of persons. The word 'Austinian' is most often used to refer to the imperative elements in this theory or its separation of law and morals. H.L.A.H.

autarky. A national policy of economic self-sufficency, for example in food, energy and TECHNOLOGY. Such policies tend to be associated with controls and other interferences with free economic exchange across national frontiers and to be contrasted with such postwar ideals as FREE TRADE, the free exchange of a country's currency for other countries' currencies and multilaterialism (see BILATERALISM). The high period of autarkic policies was between the two world wars, when the U.S.A. inclined to ISOLATIONISM, Britain looked to a system of IMPERIAL PREFERENCE and the STERLING AREA to assure its markets and raw materials, Japan tried to construct its Greater East Asia Co-Prosperity Sphere, and Hitler's Central Bank Governor, Dr Schacht, constructed his notorious Schachtian system of controls designed to insulate Germany from the world DEPRESSION while promoting a massive armaments programme at home. More recent examples of autarkic states have been Albania, Tanzania and China; though the latter two have, since the mid-1970s, become more outward looking. P.J.; J.P.

auteur. Term used analogously to its literary sense of 'author' by the French film critics whose theoretical writing precipitated the *nouvelle vague* (NEW WAVE) to distinguish between a film-maker responsible for the entire conception of his films and one who merely stages scripts written by another artist. These future film-makers believed that a true *auteur* both writes and directs his films; but since they admired above all else Hollywood directors who, like the old-guard French film-makers they were trying to displace, often worked from ready-made scripts imposed by studio chiefs, the critical debate (usually referred to as the *politique des auteurs*) centred on the argument that great film-makers or *auteurs* (e.g. Hitchcock, Hawks) transformed the scripts given to them by imposing, visually, their own preoccupations and continuing themes. Often misunderstood, and sometimes abused to attempt to prove that a director is an *auteur* because his work reveals persistent concerns and mannerisms, or that an *auteur*'s subsequent work must be good because he is an *auteur*, the argument has been adopted by English and American critics as the '*auteur* theory'. T.C.C.M.
Bibl: A. Sarris, 'Notes on the *Auteur* Theory in 1962' (*Film Culture*, Winter 1962); P. Graham (ed.), *The New Wave* (London and Garden City, NY, 1968).

authenticity. In the work of Jean-Paul Sartre, the opposite of BAD FAITH. It is a coincidence of the consciousness of the subject (*pour-soi*) with its own objective reality (*en soi*). If this can be overcome, authenticity is the achieved coincidence of the two. The difficulties in this human enterprise, which are enormous, are sharply presented in Sartre's early novels *La Nausée* (1938) and *L'Âge de raison* (1945). R. PO.
Bibl: J.-P. Sartre, *Being and Nothingness* (London, 1957).

authoritarian personality. A PERSONALITY TYPE characterized by extreme obedience and unquestioning respect for authority. These defining characteristics are usually accompanied by rigidity, conventionality, prejudice, and intolerance of weakness or ambiguity. W.Z.

Bibl: T.W. Adorno *et al., The Authoritarian Personality* (New York, 1964).

authoritarianism. The theory and practice of forms of government in which subjects have few or no rights against their rulers and their rulers' authority is of indefinite scope. Among authoritarian theories of politics one may mention Plato's defence of a philosophical dictatorship, Edmund Burke's defence of tradition and divine right against the French Revolution's appeal to the rights of man, Lenin's appeal to the authority of a 'vanguard' party and Hitler's irrationalist appeal to the 'Fuhrerprinzip' or 'leadership principle'. The concept of authoritarianism has largely been developed to distinguish dictatorial regimes from TOTALITARIAN ones. There is much disagreement over the crucial distinguishing features of each. A.R.
Bibl: J.P. Kirscht and R.C. Dillehay, *Dimensions of Authoritarianism* (Lexington, 1967); Hannah Arendt, *Totalitarianism* (Chicago, 1950).

authority, see under CHARISMA; POWER.

autism. Term derived from the Greek *autos,* self, and used to describe behavioural patterns which suggest to observers that the individual in question is absorbed exclusively in his or her own interior experiences. Early infantile autism is a SYNDROME characterized by Leo Kanner as combining 'extreme self-isolation and the obsessive insistence on the preservation of sameness'. The term is loosely used to describe any non-communicating behaviour, especially in children. C.O.
Bibl: L. Kanner, *Child Psychiatry* (Springfield, Ill., and Oxford, 3rd ed., 1957).

autochthony. Word used by K.C. Wheare in his *Constitutional Structure of the Commonwealth* (1960), and by others since, to designate a characteristic of constitutions to which some countries of the British COMMONWEALTH attached great importance when they achieved independence. They wished not only to have a constitution independent of the Parliament of the U.K., to which they had formerly been subject, but to demonstrate that the status of the new constitution as law was not derived from any legislation of the U.K., and, like the constitution of other independent sovereign states, had a 'home-grown' or autochthonous quality.

H.L.A.H.

auto-destructive. A term used of any artifact designed to damage itself — though generally with a little help from outside. Celebrated examples are the Swiss sculptor Jean Tinguely's machines which dismantled themselves (e.g. 'Study no. 2 for an End of the World', detonated in the Nevada desert), and Gustav Metzger's nylon cloth which he destroyed with hydrochloric acid. Metzger described this as simultaneously 'auto-creative', on the tenuous grounds that the work of art (and not simply the artist) had a measure of 'initiative' in transforming itself. Some auto-destructive art has been intended as a reflection on the built-in obsolescence of CONSUMERS' GOODS, or on the suicidal tendencies of military powers.   P.C.

Bibl: G. Metzger, 'Machine, Auto-creative and Auto-destructive Art', *Ark, 32* (1962), pp. 7-8.

autogestion. Literally, 'self-management'. The term was adopted in the 1960s by the French LEFT-wing *Parti Socialiste Unifié* (led by Michel Rocard) as a means of distinguishing its anti-statist IDEOLOGY and policies from those of traditional SOCIALISM. Autogestion was defined by the PSU in terms of decentralization of responsibility and greater citizen participation in all spheres of life, but especially in the workplace and local government. During the 1970s groups within the French Socialist and COMMUNIST parties also began to advocate autogestion, and it was a central theme of the Socialist Party's 1981 election manifesto.   S.M.

autogolpe, see under GOLPE.

auto-immunity/auto-immune disease. Immunity against foreign substances such as microbes depends upon an adaptive reaction of the body to produce PROTEINS (antibodies) and LYMPHOcytes which can recognize and interact with specific chemical structures characteristic of the foreign substance in question (see IMMUNITY). Auto-immunity is a condition in which antibodies and lymphocytes are present which recognize structures characteristic of one or more constituents of the body itself — i.e. they are potentially self-reactive. Since the protective effects of immunity are due to the ability of antibodies and lymphocytes to neutralize and speed the elimination of harmful foreign substances, it might be expected that auto-immunity would be self-destructive and could not occur. In fact it is an inevitable result of the mechanism whereby cells in the body's population of lymphocytes (of which there are some 2×10^{-12} in an average adult) acquire the ability to recognize virtually any foreign chemical structure. During the development of the lymphocyte population rearrangement occurs in each lymphocyte of a large number of genes which control the formation of RECEPTORS (MOLECULES on their surface) whereby structures on other CELLS or molecules are recognized. This process occurs, at a diminishing rate, throughout life, and the result is an almost limitless variety of lymphocytes with different receptors, including many capable of recognizing 'self' components. By mechanisms which are presently only partly understood, those lymphocytes which have receptors able to recognize 'self' are normally eliminated or rendered inactive shortly after they appear. If these control mechanisms fail or are by-passed auto-immunity results. It is usually confined to reactivity with a very limited range of 'self' components, such as other antibody molecules; nucleoproteins; specialized products of ENDOCRINE glands such as INSULIN or THYROID hormone; red blood cells; lining cells of the stomach; or muscle cells. The consequence is *auto-immune disease*, but the manifestations of such disease depend on what 'self' components are involved, and whether they are confined to a particular tissue or are present in the circulation. Auto-immune diseases include rheumatoid arthritis, thyroiditis, pernicious anaemia, myasthenia gravis, and some forms of diabetes, of haemolytic anaemia, of vasculitis and glomerulonephritis. In some auto-immune diseases there is a hereditary disposition, but virus infections can probably act as triggers. The control mechanisms which prevent auto-immunity tend to fail more often with advancing age.   J.H.H.

61

autological, see under HETEROLOGICAL.

autolysis. Literally self-dissolution. Nearly all living CELLS contain vesicles known as *lysosomes*, which are richly charged with hydrolytic ENZYMES. When a TISSUE is deprived of its blood supply or severed from the body and kept at or near body temperature these vesicles rupture and the tissues undergo a process of self-digestion. In the normal life of the body this makes it possible for many cellular ingredients to be re-utilized and recycled. Autolysis has much to do with the process by which the 'hanging' of game makes it more tender and palatable.   P.M.

automatic pilot. A control system used in aircraft to control the altitude of the aircraft in pitch, roll, and yaw. The system can be set to keep the aircraft in straight and level flight without human intervention. The detectors in the control system usually consist of GYROSCOPES, from which error signals are derived as electrical voltages. Artificial signals may be fed into the system by a human operator to make the aircraft turn, bank, climb, or dive. As early as the 1920s automatic pilots were installed in pilotless aircraft which were used for air-gunnery target practice and these aircraft could be controlled by radio from the ground in all manoeuvres, including take-off and landing. Today's airliners are commonly set on automatic pilot immediately after take-off and remain so for the greater part of the journey. The device corrects automatically for what would otherwise be deviations from the flight path produced by storms, winds, jet streams, etc.   E.R.L.

automatic stabilizers. Mechanisms within the economy which act counter-cyclically (i.e. against the prevailing economic TRADE CYCLE) without specific intervention by the authorities. An example is a progressive income-tax system, i.e. one which takes an increasing share of increasing personal incomes and a decreasing share of decreasing ones, thus acting, respectively, to restrain the growth of AGGREGATE DEMAND or to moderate its decline.   D.E.
    Bibl: D. Begg *et al., Economics* (London, 1984).

automatic translation, see MACHINE TRANSLATION.

automation. A word introduced by Delmar S. Harder in 1948 for the automatic control of the manufacture of a product through a number of successive stages. It is now generally used for the control of machines by machines with human intervention reduced to a minimum; examples are an AUTOMATIC PILOT (George), or a COMPUTER-controlled milling machine or assembly line. Automation is an emotionally charged word since it is frequently used to mean the use of machines to replace human labour. According to some, it merely continues a process of technical change (MECHANIZATION) which is at least as old as the INDUSTRIAL REVOLUTION. In industrialized societies the increase in per capita productivity during the past two centuries is largely the consequence of the increase in quantity and the improvement in quality of the machines and tools with which human workers cooperate. For the alarmists, however, automation is qualitatively different, and threatens vast technological UNEMPLOYMENT as growing numbers of skills are rendered obsolete. Thus far the gradualists have had the better of the argument, but the matter is far from settled.   C.S.; R.L.

automatism. In modern English criminal law, involuntary conduct where, owing to lack of normal control over his bodily movements, a person does an act which would, but for such lack of control, constitute an offence. The chief importance for the law of identifying such cases of automatism is that, even where an offence is one of STRICT LIABILITY, an accused person will not be criminally responsible for the consequences of his uncontrolled bodily movements unless the loss of control arose from his own failure to take reasonable precautions. The forms of uncontrolled conduct which lawyers now describe as automatism were formerly referred to as cases where there was 'no act' or 'no volition' on the part of the accused.   H.L.A.H.

automorphism. A structure-preserving PERMUTATION of the elements of a MATH-

EMATICAL STRUCTURE (see also ISO-MORPHIC).   R.G.

autonomic nervous system, see under NERVOUS SYSTEM.

autopoiesis. In CYBERNETICS, a term coined by Humberto Maturana for a special case of HOMEOSTASIS in which the critical variable of the system that is held constant is that system's own organization.   S.BE.

autopolyploid, see under POLYPLOID.

autoradiograph. The image of a radioactive object (see RADIOACTIVITY) obtained photographically by using the RADIATION emitted during the decay process. The distribution of radioactive material is mapped directly on a photographic plate placed in close contact with the object. Autoradiography is an important technique in PHYSIOLOGY and BIOCHEMISTRY. It can be used to follow the diffusion of a radioactive TRACER and in this way has revealed details of the internal boundaries of metals and the permeability of membranes.   B.F.

autosome. A CHROMOSOME other than a SEX CHROMOSOME.   J.M.S.

auto-suggestion. A therapeutic technique whereby an individual attempts to induce a desired effect by self-instruction and self-encouragement; first made popular by Coué (*Self-Mastery through Conscious Auto-Suggestion*, London, 1922).   w.z.

autotelic writing. An appropriately new term, in the NEW CRITICISM, for the old notion that a work of art exists for and within itself. The modern origins of this idea are found in the writings of the 18th-century Swiss critics J.J. Bodmer and J.J. Breitinger. Bodmer wrote that from the poet the reader should demand 'only poetry; in this we shall be satisfied with the probability and the reason which lies in its coherence with itself'. This led into 'art for art's sake', and declined into romantic preciosity or elegant wit (e.g. Oscar Wilde's dictum that life seeks to imitate art). The idea appears again in the 20th century in two scarcely related forms: in

the work of certain poets (e.g. the 'creationism' of the Chilean Vicente Huidobro and the Frenchman Pierre Revendy) and fiction-writers, notably Borges; and in the New Criticism, where it serves to turn attention away from irrelevancies of neoromantic criticism and towards the text. It is not often seriously suggested that literature has no place in life, but only that it must first be studied as if it had not.
                                M.S.-S.

autotrophic. Term applied to organisms which can build up their body constituents from the simplest ingredients — water, mineral salts, and carbon dioxide, with sunlight as a source of energy. Organisms which have to make use of partially synthesized ingredients from other simpler organisms are described as *heterotrophic*.
                                P.M.

avant-garde. French military term used before 1848 for any politically advanced republican or SOCIALIST group, later for the assumption that 'advanced' art must occupy a similar position of leadership in the fight against the BOURGEOIS, and finally in all countries after about 1910 to denote those cultural innovators, whatever their political associations, who appeared most inaccessible to public understanding. Though still able to fire the less sceptical creative artists, middlemen, and critics with a fruitful sense of minority cohesion, it is now an anachronism, since many kinds of art, music, and literature associated with it are widely accepted and officially supported.   J.W.

Bibl: R. Poggioli, tr. G. Fitzgerald, *The Theory of the Avant-Garde* (Cambridge, Mass., 1968); J.E. Bowlt (ed. and tr.), *Russian Art of the Avant-Garde: Theory and Criticism, 1902-1934* (New York, 1976).

avant-garde dance. Term largely related to the work of Cunningham (see CUNNINGHAM TECHNIQUE) and the subsequent development of the POST-MODERN DANCE movement and JUDSON DANCE THEATER which emerged in the 1960s in the U.S.A.
                                L.A.

avant-garde music. Term frequently used in connection with certain European composers in the fifties (see POST-WEBERN SCHOOL). B.CO.

average. Sometimes used synonymously with MEAN, but also more generally, especially in naive statistics, to mean 'typical'. See also MEASURE OF LOCATION. R.SI.

average deviation; average variation, see MEAN DEVIATION.

aversion therapy, see under BEHAVIOUR THERAPY.

Avogadro number. The number of ATOMS or MOLECULES whose weight in grams is equal to the atomic or molecular weight of the substance. Amedeo Avogadro (1776-1856) was the first to point out, in 1811, that equal volumes of gases should contain the same number of molecules. Though real gases do not quite conform to this rule, recognition of the principle helped to clarify the distinction between an atom and a molecule. B.F.

avoidance behaviour. A behaviour pattern enabling an animal to avoid some noxious stimulus. The behavioural responses may or may not be learned. The unicellular organism *Paramecium*, for example, responds to a bubble of carbon dioxide in its water by reversing the direction of its swimming for a short distance, turning a small angle, and then swimming on; the response, if repeated, will get it past any obstacle. Higher animals can learn that a stimulus has to be avoided. Rats, for example, will initially eat a small sample of almost anything; but if what they eat makes them sick they avoid eating it again. This kind of 'one-trial' learning is important in the life of an animal with so flexible a diet as the rat. Avoidance learning is a major area of study in the PSYCHOLOGY of learning. See BEHAVIOUR THERAPY. M.R.

AWACS. Acronym for airborne warning and control system.

axiology. The philosophical theory of value in general, embracing ETHICS or the philosophical theory of morality, but extending far beyond it to include AES-THETIC, technical, prudential, hedonic, and other forms of value. Any field of human discourse in which the general value-terms 'good' and 'ought' figure falls within the range of axiology, even that of SCIENTIFIC METHOD with its principles about the degree of belief one *ought* to give to a hypothesis in the light of a given body of evidence. See also VALUE-JUDGEMENT. A.Q.

Bibl: G.H. Von Wright, *The Varieties of Goodness* (London and New York, 1963).

axiom. For the use of axioms in MATHEMATICS see AXIOMATIC METHOD; in LOGIC see AXIOMATICS. R.G.

axiom of choice, the (or *multiplicative axiom*). An indispensable assumption for the proof of many intuitively reasonable PROPOSITIONS concerning SETS. Let *C* be a collection of mutually exclusive non-empty sets (for example the parliamentary boroughs, each considered as a set of electors). The axiom asserts that there is a *choice set* for *C* (a parliament) which has exactly one member drawn from each of the sets in the collection. It was first formulated by Zermelo in 1904. If *C* is infinite, there may be no definable property or rule of selection by which one can specify the choice set; hence those who believe that mathematical objects must always be *constructed* doubt its validity. But if sets are viewed as *arbitrary* collections it is wholly plausible, and so is usually included among the AXIOMS of SET THEORY. A.Q.; R.G.

Bibl: W. V. Quine, *Set Theory and Its Logic* (Cambridge, Mass., 1963).

axiomatic method. Before the second half of the 19th century mathematicians studied MATHEMATICAL STRUCTURES which were based on practical experience. Proofs were justified, explicitly or implicitly, by an appeal to intuitions (sometimes quite sophisticated) abstracted from that experience. For GEOMETRY Euclid had attempted, with considerable but not complete success, to codify the intuitions in AXIOMS; the theorems should be deduced from these by purely logical arguments. By 1900 AXIOMATICS had become a flourishing industry. The investigations which led to satisfactory sets of axioms for the familiar structures (natural, real, and complex NUMBERS, Euclidean geometry) provoked interest in those seemingly counter-intuitive structures which can be characterized by modifying the familiar axioms in a more or less arbitrary way (e.g.non-Euclidean geometries and number systems, such as the QUATERNIONS, whose multiplication does not obey the COMMUTATIVE LAW). Nowadays the axiomatic method predominates. Axioms for the objects to be studied are no longer presented as codifying intuitions, but simply as rules of a game; Russell's dictum that in mathematics we do not know what we are talking about, nor care whether what we say is true, is taken literally.

The great advantages of the axiomatic method are that it liberates MATHEMATICS from the study of the traditional structures (Cantor wanted pure mathematics to be called 'free mathematics'), and that it concentrates the attention on what is essential to the proof of a particular theorem, which can then be applied to *any* objects that satisfy the axioms used in the proof (see under BOURBAKI). But it may lead to sterile ingenuity, and — as in much contemporary teaching and textbook writing — to the suppression of qualities (in particular, intuition and the appreciation of significance) that are essential to good mathematics. R.G.

Bibl: R.L. Wilder, *Introduction to the Foundations of Mathematics* (New York and London, 2nd ed., 1965).

axiomatics. The branch of logical investigation (see LOGIC) concerned with axiomatic systems, that is to say, with systems of assertions in which a handful of initial PROPOSITIONS is laid down as true (the AXIOMS) or postulated (hence the phrase *postulational method*), and further propositions (the *theorems*) are then deduced from them by means of specified rules of INFERENCE (sometimes called *transformation-rules*). To be set out completely an axiom system should also contain a *vocabulary*, in which the terms of the system are enumerated, and a SYNTAX or set of *formation-rules*, determining which combinations of terms of the system constitute well-formed, or significant, assertions. The model for all later axiom systems is Euclid's geometry (imitated in PHILOSOPHY, for example, in Spinoza's *Ethics*). The axiomatization of other branches of MATHEMATICS was carried out extensively towards the end of the 19th century. Soon techniques for the logical study of axiom systems were developed: techniques for determining the CONSISTENCY of the members of a SET of axioms with each other, their logical *independence* of each other, and the *completeness* of the set, i.e. its adequacy as a basis for the deduction of all the truths statable in the vocabulary of the system. Modern formal logic, as inaugurated by the great treatises of Frege and of Whitehead and Russell, has mostly been expounded in an axiomatic form. A.Q.

Bibl: R. Blanché, tr. G.B. Keene, *Axiomatics* (London and New York, 1962).

Axis. Term invented by Mussolini in a speech of 1 November 1936 to describe the relationship between Nazi Germany and Fascist Italy, after the conclusion of Italo-German agreements (the Berchtesgaden protocols) on international policies; it has been extended to cover other bilateral relationships in which states agree to follow common policies on specific questions. In practice the appearance of joint action and support which the Axis provided was significantly belied by the realities; but it was of some advantage to its adherents so long as active involvement in crisis or war was not in question. D.C.W.

Bibl: A.P. Adamthwaite, *The Making of the Second World War* (London, 2nd ed., 1979).

B

Ba'ath (Arabic for 'resurgence'). The Ba'ath Arab Socialist Party, the IDEOLOGY of which represents an attempt to synthesize a MARXIST analysis of society with a pan-Arab (see pan-ISLAM), NATIONALIST approach to social, economic, and political problems. Theoretically, it regards the 'regional' parties of the various Arab states as no more than branches of a 'national' all-Arab structure; in practice, the Syrian and Iraqi branches, which are the most active, are entirely separate and often at loggerheads with each other. Founded by Michel Aflaq in 1940-41, the Ba'ath party was instrumental in creating the short-lived (1958-61) union of Syria and Egypt; from 1963 it formed the ruling party in Syria, although political power rested mainly with its control over the regional party and created its own pan-Arab command after 1966. More recently, and especially since 1970, the party has lost prominence in Syria, where power has been increasingly concentrated in the hands of a minority Islamic sect, the Alawites. The Iraqi Ba'ath party has been dominant since 1968 but has served as a cloak for the influence of an officers' junta with a regional and familial power-base.

P.B.M.

Bibl: K.S.A. Jaber, *The Arab Ba'ath Socialist Party* (Syracuse, NY, 1966); I. Rabinovich, *Syria under the Ba'ath, 1963-1966* (Jerusalem, 1972).

Babouvism, see under EGALITARIANISM.

backing store, see under STORE.

bacteriology. The science that deals with the structure, properties, and behaviour of bacteria, particularly as disease-causing agents.

Bacteria are a highly heterogeneous group, and attempts to classify them according to the full nomenclatural hierarchy appropriate to larger organisms have not met with the general sympathy of biologists. Nevertheless a first crude division may be made on the basis of shape and habit of growth. Thus, *cocci* are spherical; *bacilli* are generally rod-shaped; *staphylococci* form clusters like grape bunches; *streptococci* form chains; *vibrios* are rod-shaped with a helical twist. A taxonomic distinction of greater functional significance is between 'gram-positive' and 'gram-negative' bacteria. The distinction is based upon the degree of retentiveness with which the organisms bind the stain crystal violet during their preparation for microscopy. Most bacteria (the leprosy bacteria are a notable exception) can be cultivated in simple media outside the body. Some bacteria ('strict' or 'obligate' *aerobes*) can grow only in the presence of oxygen, others (*anaerobes*) only in its absence.

Bacteria increase their number by fission. After a so-called 'lag phase' multiplication is characteristically of the EXPONENTIAL or compound-interest type, though greater or lesser departures from this norm occur as a result of changes in the growth medium produced by the bacteria themselves, e.g. the using up of nutrients and the accumulation of waste-products. Genetic information in bacteria resides in a nucleic acid system and the processes of coding, transcription, and translation are essentially the same in bacteria as in higher organisms. Indeed, the study of heredity in bacteria, notably *Escherichia coli* (probably the most deeply understood of all organisms), has thrown very great light on the processes of heredity in higher organisms.

Bacteria are highly mutable organisms, as evidenced by the readiness with which they can eventually utilize new substrates (see ENZYMES) or develop resistance towards newly devised ANTIBIOTICS. These examples of adaptation were at one time known under the comprehensive heading of 'training'. This is a misleading description, however, because it obscures the essential point that all such processes of training are strictly GENE-dependent and selective in character. Under conditions unfavourable for continued growth or even for life, many bacteria have the power to form highly resistant spores. Spores normally resist desiccation and many ordinary procedures of disinfection. Bacteria and spores are, however, killed by the use of the *autoclave* in which objects to be sterilized are exposed to steam under high pressure and at temperatures as high as 120-130°C. Bacteria are pathogenic by reason of the direct effects of their multiplication or because they contain or liberate toxic substances (*endotoxins* or *exotoxins* respectively). Bacterial infections are cured through the action of antibodies (see IMMUNITY) or of natural or artificial ANTIBACTERIALS including antibiotics. The formation of antibodies may be excited either by structural constituents of the bacteria themselves or by the toxins they liberate.

Sexual reproduction — essentially a genetic intermixture — has been described in certain bacilli. In addition a number of 'parasexual' processes may lead to genetic interchange. The most famous of these processes is the TRANSFORMATION of *pneumococci* first described in 1928 by F. Griffith. In this process a mixture of dead and living bacteria of different types leads to the acquirement by the living type of some of the properties of the dead bacteria. In Griffith's example the transforming agent was deoxyribonucleic acid (DNA). This observation was the start of all that is now known about the genetic functions of the NUCLEIC ACIDS.   P.M.

Bibl: G.S. Wilson and A.A. Miles, *Topley and Wilson's Principles of Bacteriology and Immunity* (London and Baltimore, 7th ed., 1983).

bad faith (*mauvaise foi*). A condition described in Sartre's *Being and Nothingness* (1943). Bad faith comes about as the result of anguish in front of choice, and represents the subject's attempt to deceive himself about the nature of reality. Bad faith is a direct consequence of the radical and inalienable freedom of the subject to choose himself authentically (see AUTHENTICITY), and of his own attempts to deny, escape or obscure this freedom and duty. Bad faith can take many forms, some of which involve the power of nihilating reality, or of conferring absence upon reality, i.e. the power to conceive, and to insist upon, what is not the case. The worst form of bad faith is that self-deception which allows a subject to believe that he is not free to change things, or that things could not be otherwise.   R.PO.

Bibl: J.-P. Sartre, *Being and Nothingness* (London and New York, 1957).

badlands. A name originally applied to an area of semi-arid climate in South Dakota which was notoriously difficult to cross; today it is a National Park with a spectacular landscape of gullies and sawtoothed ridges cut in many-coloured shales and limestones. The term is now used for any region that has been carved by rainwash, over bare ground, into an almost impassable land surface of innumerable closely spaced, steep-sided ridges and furrows. As a rule it is nearly devoid of vegetation and contrasts strongly with any remaining level plateau surfaces in the vicinity.   M.L.

Bahai. A religious movement, originating in ISLAM and stressing the spiritual unity of mankind under God. It was established by Mirza Husein Ali the *Baha-ullah* ('Glory of God') after the founder, Ali Muhammad the *Bab* ('Door'), had been executed in Persia in 1850 for alleged blasphemy. It has attracted adherents, not very numerous but widely distributed, by its support of modern idealistic movements (such as equality between the sexes), its receptivity towards scientific ideas, and its simple, personal forms of prayer.   D.L.E.

Bibl: W.S. Hatcher and J.D. Martin, *The Bahai Faith* (San Francisco, 1986).

Bakhtinian. An approach to cultural history, and especially literature, in the style of the Russian critic Mikhail Bakhtin (1895-1975), best known for his *Problems of Dostoyevsky's Poetics* (1929) and *Rabelais and his World* (presented as a thesis in 1940 but not published until 1965). His work is most famous for its concern with unofficial and popular elements in the work of great writers, with CARNIVALIZATION as a means of subversion or UNCROWNING, and with the interaction of dialogue between different points of view or languages (HETEROGLOSSIA).   P.B.

Bibl: K. Clark and M. Holquist, *Mikhail Bakhtin* (Cambridge, Mass., 1984).

balance of nature. Term sometimes used for the relationship between the various

BALANCE OF PAYMENTS

parts of the BIOSPHERE which makes this, in the absence of human intervention, a self-renewing system. It is the well-founded fear of many ecologists (see ECOLOGY) that this balance is being upset by INDUSTRIALIZATION and the reckless exploitation of the ENVIRONMENT.   P.M.

balance of payments.

(1) The difference between certain credits and debits in the accounts recording the flow of transactions in a specified period of one nation (sometimes region or group of nations) with others, usually with the rest of the world.

(2) The accounts themselves. The *balance on current account* is the difference between payments and receipts for goods and services, including interest, dividends, and profits, and (usually) transfers, e.g. migrants' remittances and aid. The surplus on the current account represents the country's net acquisition of foreign assets. The *balance of trade* is that part of the current account that relates to goods, i.e. it excludes services. The balance on the capital account is the difference of the sales by domestic residents of real and financial assets to foreigners and the purchase by domestic residents of real and financial assets from foreigners. The sum of the current and capital accounts is the difference of the demand and supply, from traders and investors, for the domestic currency. This difference is accounted for by changes in the official foreign exchange reserves and official borrowing. The change in the latter minus the change in the former is the official financing. By definition, the current account, the capital account and official financing must be seen to be zero. However, errors, omissions and delays in recording transactions mean that it is necessary to include a balancing item to insure this equality. The balancing item and revisions of balance of payment statistics are often sizeable. Balance of payments problems arise when there is a persistent tendency for a deficit (or surplus) to occur on the current plus capital account. Such a problem represents running down (or accumulation) of a country's foreign assets. The problem can be solved by DEVALUATION (or appreciation) of the EXCHANGE RATE, deflation (or reflation), EXCHANGE CONTROLS or an increase (decrease) in the interest rate. These measures may have undesirable effects on INFLATION, ECONOMIC GROWTH and real income.   M.FG.S.;J.P.

Bibl: B. Soldersten, *International Economics* (London, 2nd ed., 1980); M. Parkin and R. Bale, *Modern Macroeconomics* (London, 1982).

balance of power. Described by Martin Wight as the 'political counterpart of Newton's physics' for the period between 1701 and 1914, balance of power is the central 'realist' concept for the preservation of international order. At its height in the 19th-century Concert of Europe, the concept dominated the foreign policies of the great powers, to become discredited after 1914, a view also espoused by LIBERALS and MARXISTS before 1914. Clark defines balance of power as an acceptance of the role of legitimate force to create or maintain equilibrium by states. He also sees nuclear deterrence (see BALANCE OF TERROR) theory as a 'subset of the general balance of power school'. The term generally implies a 'balancer' state which acts as principal guarantor of the system.   A.W.

Bibl: Ian Clark, *Reform and Resistance in the International Order* (Cambridge, 1980).

balance of terror. A rhetorical term describing a state of equilibrium or of mutual DETERRENCE between nuclear powers, based on the possession of weapons which allow either side to deal a mortal blow to the other. Probably coined by Lester Pearson ('the balance of terror has replaced the balance of power') in June 1955, at the 10th anniversary of the signing of the U.N. (see UNO) Charter, and based on Winston Churchill's remark 'it may well be that safety shall be the sturdy child of terror....'.   A.F.B.

balance of trade, see under BALANCE OF PAYMENTS.

balance theory. A view of interpersonal relations that has as its starting-point the situation where the subject's COGNITIVE view of the people he is in contact with accords with his EMOTIONS about them. If either his ideas or his feelings concerning them are altered, the balance is disturbed and stress may be introduced. H.L.

balanced budget, see under FISCAL POLICY.

Balfour Declaration. A British Government statement in the form of a letter, dated 2 November 1917, signed by the Foreign Secretary, A.J. Balfour (1848-1930), and addressed to Lord Rothschild, expressing 'sympathy with Jewish ZIONIST aspirations' and viewing 'with favour the establishment in Palestine of a National Home for the Jewish People'. Palestine was then under Turkish occupation but became a British mandate under the LEAGUE OF NATIONS (1922). Thereafter the British Government wrestled with the intractable problem of reconciling the Balfour Declaration with the proviso, contained in the same letter, that 'nothing shall be done which may prejudice the civil and religious rights of existing non-Jewish communities in Palestine'. From this followed the chain of events leading to the breakdown of Arab-Jewish relations, the establishment of the state of Israel, and the Arab-Israeli wars. A.L.C.B.

Bibl: L. Stein, *The Balfour Declaration* (London and New York, 1961).

ballet, see under CLASSICAL BALLET.

ballistic missiles, see under MISSILES.

ballistics. The application of NEWTONIAN MECHANICS to the calculation of trajectories of MISSILES influenced by GRAVITATION and air resistance. The early development of ballistics in the 17th century marked the beginning of the application of modern science to warfare. M.V.B.

bamboo curtain. Phrase coined by American publicists in the 1950s, by analogy with IRON CURTAIN, to describe the controls imposed by the Chinese COMMUNIST regime on the free movement of ideas and individuals across China's borders.

D.C.W.

Band Aid. A POPULAR CULTURAL response to the western MEDIA coverage of the Ethiopian famine of 1984, initiated primarily by ROCK musician Bob Geldof whose aim was to supplement the existing structures of aid and the established famine relief agencies by mobilizing a massive new constituency of donors in the most affluent nations. The means chosen for this mobilization were those characteristic of rock music — electronic communication, youth oriented, participative and international. The success of Geldof's three successive ventures — Band Aid (an amalgam of musicians brought together in late 1984 to produce the hit single 'Do They Know It's Christmas?'), Live Aid (simultaneous concerts in London, Philadelphia and other venues all drawing on the telephone pledge system, in July 1985) and Sport Aid (sponsored marathon runs in dozens of locations in April 1986) — had significant results in different areas. First, a phenomenal amount of money was raised — £100,000,000. Secondly, the political socialization dimension was important — the values of self-interest, autonomy and pursuit of gain characteristic of the moral agenda of REAGANISM and THATCHERISM were challenged by feelings of compassion, charity and interdependence shared by millions of young people. Thirdly, Band Aid and Geldof responded to the logistical and administrative blockages in delivering supplies to those in need by adopting a new style — publicly chastising politicians and bureaucrats for their temerity and sluggishness, and by organizing land, sea and air delivery systems on an unprecedented scale. Fourthly, the voluntaristic nature of the entire exercise spawned a series of analogous fund raising events in higher cultural forms — Opera Aid, Fashion Aid, etc.

Responding to criticism from both older aid agencies and more radical sources, the Band Aid Trust has modified its short-term emphasis and now stresses the importance of long-term development projects that lead to self-sufficiency. Ironically, the very ESTABLISHMENT that prompted Geldof's ire has now seen fit to reward him for his efforts, and he received an honorary knighthood for services to FAMINE relief in June 1986. P.S.L.

band width. CHANNEL CAPACITY, see under INFORMATION THEORY. J.E.S.

Bandung Conference. The first Afro-Asian conference, meeting in Bandung, Indonesia, from 18 to 24 April 1955, with representatives of 29 states of Asia and Africa (including the People's Republic of China). The main motivation of the conference was dissatisfaction with the domination of international politics by the quarrel between the American and Soviet blocs, and concern at the risk of war between the U.S.A. and China. See also NON-ALIGNMENT. D.C.W.

Bibl: P. Calvocoressi, *World Order and New States* (London and New York, 1962).

bank rate. The rate of interest charged by a central bank on loans it makes to the banking system. Most financial institutions borrow short and lend long. This allows central banking to exert some control over financial matters by acting as a tender of last resort to the commercial banks, which allows the latter to preserve their LIQUIDITY. In the U.K. the bank rate was previously an announced minimum lending rate, which was above that offered on treasury bills or bonds. The present system does not have a formal announced rate, but reflects the Bank of England's desire to affect interest rates. In the U.S. the bank rate is called the discount rate and serves a similar purpose. M.V.P.

Bibl: D. Begg *et al., Economics* (London, 1984).

Bantustan, see under APARTHEID.

Baptist. A member of a PROTESTANT denomination which believes that Baptism should be confined to adults after a personal confession of faith. (Other Christian churches allow the baptism of infants, while asking that these should be the children of Christians and should also be sponsored by godparents.) The first Baptist congregation was founded in 1609; today the denomination is worldwide. Congregations maintain their independence in many matters, and Baptists vary greatly in the conservatism or radicalism of their THEOLOGY and politics. The 'Southern' Baptists in the U.S.A. (mainly in the Southern states), and also the Baptist groups in Europe including Russia, are strongly conservative. D.L.E.

Bibl: R.G. Torbet, *A History of the Baptists* (rev. ed., Valley Forge, Penn., 1963; London, 1966).

Barmen Declaration, see under BARTHIAN.

barrier to entry. An aspect of the structure of a market or industry that makes it difficult for a new firm to enter the industry or imposes an additional cost. Important examples are ECONOMIES OF SCALE, absolute cost advantages held by existing firms, control of the supply of inputs to production, control of retail outlets, preferences of consumers for the goods and services of existing firms and the threat of a price war on the entry of a new firm. They are an important element of STRUCTURE-CONDUCT-PERFORMANCE THEORY, as the firms in industries with high barriers would be expected to make larger than average profits and, because of the lack of competitive (see COMPETITION) pressure, they may not be efficient. J.P.

Bibl: M.C. Sawyer, *The Economics of Industries and Firms* (London, 1981).

Barthian. Adjective applied to a style in Christian THEOLOGY associated with Karl Barth (1886-1968), a PROTESTANT who was a professor at Bonn and Basle. Barth attempted to deduce all his doctrines from the Bible, without going so far as FUNDAMENTALISM in rejecting HIGHER CRITICISM. Disillusioned by World War I, in a commentary on St Paul's Epistle to the Romans (1919) he attacked Protestant LIBERALISM'S belief that man could reach religious understanding by his own reason and develop nobly by his own power. He stressed the corruptions of sin, as did other leaders of CRISIS THEOLOGY. But on this narrower basis he built an elaborate system of DOGMATICS marked by a joyous confidence in the TRANSCENDENCE or majestic 'otherness', and in the graciousness, of the God revealed in Jesus Christ. He extolled Jesus Christ as the 'Risen Lord' and as the one Saviour, and (unlike other CALVINISTS) maintained that God had predestined all to heaven. He took the lead in drawing up the *Barmen Declaration* (1934) against the pseudo-religious claims of NAZISM. The influence of the NEO-ORTHODOXY to which he gave eloquent expression helped many Protestants to regard the Bible as the Word of God powerfully confronting the calamities of the 1930s and 1940s. In the 1950s and 1960s his prestige among Protestant preachers was at a peak, but the influence of his theology declined because it was thought not to be sufficiently in touch with modern AGNOSTICISM. D.L.E.

Bibl: E. Busch, *Karl Barth* (London and Philadelphia, 1976).

Bartolozzi sounds. Term, derived from Bruno Bartolozzi's book *New Sounds for Woodwind* (1967), and frequently applied to new ways of playing woodwind (flute, oboe, clarinet, bassoon) which produce, among other things, chords from these traditionally melodic instruments. J.G.R.

baryon. Member of a class of ELEMENTARY PARTICLES including the NEUTRON and the PROTON, that take part in strong interactions and possess half-integral spin. They are fermions (see QUANTUM STATISTICS). A QUANTUM NUMBER, termed *baryon number*, is assigned to each baryon taking the value $+1$ for baryons and -1 for their antiparticles, all other particles having zero. In all known physical interactions the total of the baryon numbers of the participating particles remains unchanged. This is called baryon conservation or conservation of baryon number. It means that protons are stable particles which do not decay. However, it is not believed that baryon number is conserved at very high energies. Theories incorporating the concept of GRAND UNIFICATION require the existence of processes in which that baryon number is not conserved. Attempts are in progress to detect the decay of protons at the very slow rates predicted. The *baryon asymmetry of the universe* refers to the observational fact that the universe is composed primarily of baryons rather than antibaryons. J.D.B.

Bibl: P. C. W. Davies, *The Forces of Nature* (Cambridge, 1979).

baryon number/baryon asymmetry of the universe, see under BARYON.

basal metabolic rate, see BMR.

base.
(1) In ECONOMICS, see INDEX NUMBER.
(2) A chemical SPECIES which accepts PROTONS or donates a pair of ELECTRONS (see ACID). A compound or solution capable of acting as a base is described as *basic*. B.F.

base component, see under GENERATIVE GRAMMAR.

Basic. In COMPUTING, a very simple but verbose PROGRAMMING LANGUAGE designed for teaching purposes and much used by beginners. It is very popular with users of PERSONAL COMPUTERS but not much employed by serious programmers. C.S.; J.E.S.

basic communities. A translation of the Spanish *comunidades de base*, referring to groups of Christians in Latin America meeting for Bible study and other adult education and discussing their problems and possible action in the light of their faith. Many bishops of the Roman CATHOLIC Church have encouraged this widespread movement, although others are cautious since even when a priest is present in these meetings he is not fully in charge, and even when the main emphasis is on personal spirituality, radical, possibly MARXIST, views on politics and economics tend to be expressed in response to daily experience of a society with enormous disparities between the classes. The success of the movement has been due in part to the shortage of priests in a continent where Catholic faith is still widespread, and in part to the shortage of politicians with the will and the freedom to speak for the poor. The contrast is great with previous movements such as Catholic Action which were closely controlled by the clergy (it was claimed, in order to avoid controversial politics) and which tended to accept middle class values despite the existence of some 'Christian' TRADE UNIONS. These communities have inspired, and been inspired by, LIBERATION THEOLOGY. D.L.E.

Bibl: J. Sobrino, tr. M.J. O'Connell, *The True Church of the Poor* (Mary Knoll, 1984, and London, 1985).

bathysphere (or *barysphere* or *centrosphere* or *bathyscaphe*). A diving apparatus generally spherical in shape and capable of containing men (usually two) and instruments so that the whole can be lowered to great depths in the ocean. It is used in OCEANOGRAPHY for the study of deep-water phenomena, fauna, etc. The main feature of the apparatus is that the outer shell is capable of withstanding huge pressures such as obtain at great depth. The record depth to date is 35,082 feet (deeper than Mount Everest is high) achieved by J. Piccard and D. Walsh in 1960 in the Marianas Trench of the Pacific Ocean, 250 miles S.W. of Guam; the pressure at this depth was 16,883 lbs per square inch (over 1,200 atmospheres).   E.R.L.

battlefield nuclear weapons. Short-range, 'miniaturized' NUCLEAR WEAPONS which are intended to achieve local, tactical superiority. Ideally suited to breaking up large enemy formations, they have come to be seen as the key to any future land-battles in Europe. The theory is that the use of these small weapons (up to 7 kilotons) would not trigger a wider nuclear conflict: the analogy is drawn with nuclear depth charges and air-to-air missiles. However, this is a highly optimistic view, bordering on wishful thinking. Artillery or battlefield tactical missiles (like the U.S. Lance) are the most flexible means of delivery. One way of increasing the effectiveness of these weapons is to fit enhanced RADIATION explosives (see NEUTRON BOMB). These kill tank crews but reduce long-term contamination of the battlefield.   A.J.M.W.
Bibl: I. Clarke, *Limited Nuclear War: Political Theory and War Conventions* (Oxford, 1982).

baud. The unit of CHANNEL CAPACITY; the capacity of a channel capable of transmitting one BIT of information per second.   J.E.S.

Bauhaus. A school of design, art, and architecture based on the ideas of the WERKBUND and founded as a development of the Weimar Applied Art School in 1919. It moved to Dessau in 1925 and remained there for its most fruitful years until 1932. It was dissolved by the Nazis (see NAZISM) in 1933. From 1919 to 1928 it was headed by the architect Walter Gropius, who attempted to implement the demands, voiced in his manifesto of April 1919, for a unity of all the creative arts under the primacy of architecture, and for a reconsideration of the crafts by the artist.

Many major figures of modern art and architecture — Klee, Kandinsky, Moholy-Nagy, Schlemmer, Breuer, Hannes Meyer, Mies van der Rohe — taught at the Bauhaus, though they often disagreed, especially over the relative roles of art, TECHNOLOGY, and politics. Their innovatory notions as regards form, materials, and the need for teamwork became the hallmark of the INTERNATIONAL STYLE in architecture and were evident in the extremely simple geometric forms of Bauhaus-inspired industrial design. These ideas eventually, however, hardened into another academic tradition, not least because they focused too much on a formal vocabulary derived from predilection for pure geometric shapes and too little on problems of use. Something like the Bauhaus *Vorkurs*, an introductory course aimed at creating, through practical work, an awareness of the nature of materials and of simple perceptual relationships, continued to be taught at many schools of architecture and design until well into the 1960s. See also MACHINE AESTHETIC; STIJL, DE.   M.BR.
Bibl: H.M. Wingler, tr. W. Jabs and B. Gilbert, *The Bauhaus* (Cambridge, Mass., 1969); T. Wolfe, *From Bauhaus to Our House* (New York and London, 1982).

Bay of Pigs. A site on the north-east coast of CUBA where on 17 April 1961 approximately 1,400 Cuban exiles, organized and clandestinely supported by the CIA, attempted an invasion with the purpose of overthrowing the revolutionary regime established in 1959 by Fidel Castro. The invaders were crushed and American complicity revealed. President Kennedy's responses were publicly to accept personal responsibility for the affair and covertly to endorse other secret efforts to destabilize the Cuban regime, including plans to assassinate Castro. (See CASTROISM.)   S.R.
Bibl: P. Wyden, *Bay of Pigs* (New York, 1979).

Bayesian statistics. A type of statistical reasoning characterized by two distinct features. First, the experimenter has a degree of belief in each hypothesis in the hypotheses open to him, and this degree of belief is represented by a number. Secondly, the experimenter uses the formula known as *Bayes's rule*, originally given by Thomas Bayes (1702-61) for inverting conditional probabilities, to modify his degree of belief in each hypothesis in the light of experiments.   R.SI.

beam radio. In radio, a system for directing all the output from a transmitter along a narrow beam in order to maximize the proportion of output collected by the receiving aerial, and minimize the picking up of the signal by outside receivers. The system is analogous to the focused light beam from an electric torch, as opposed to an electric light bulb used to illuminate a whole room.   E.R.L.

beam splitter, see under NON-LINEAR OPTICS.

Beat. Term coined by the American novelist Jack Kerouac, in the reported phrase 'this is a beat generation', to denote a certain section of American society that emerged in the late 1940s and more particularly the 1950s. Kerouac, who saw the Beats as saintly beings in a pagan world, later connected the word with 'beatific' or 'beatitude' (a related pun turned the wanderers from New York to San Francisco into *Franciscans*); but others preferred the original connotations of weariness and defeat. *Beatnik* was the slightly pejorative generic term coined by an American columnist to denote the followers and hangers-on of the Beats; in time the two words, and the phrase *beat generation*, became interchangeable. Kerouac and his friends Allen Ginsberg, Neil Cassady, Gregory Corso, and others between them exemplified, in a manner deliberately anti-literary, the various trends: rootlessness, rejection of the AFFLUENT SOCIETY and indeed of all social values, a predilection for modern JAZZ, resort to ill-assimilated oriental religions (e.g. ZEN) and to DRUGS, pseudo-relaxation ('coolness'), and free sexuality. (Ginsberg was later self-critical with regard to his attitude to drugs.) The phe-nomenon represented a sudden coalescence of INTELLECTUAL or sensitive people with the *lumpen* elements that exist in all urban societies. The spiritual fathers of the Beats were Walt Whitman and Henry Miller; mentors and spokesmen included Paul Goodman, Norman Mailer, and Kenneth Rexroth (who later became disillusioned). The chief *beat poets* were Ginsberg, Corso, and Lawrence Ferlinghetti; those influenced include Robert Creeley, Gary Snyder, and Michael Rumaker. Other beat or beat-influenced figures include the writers William Burroughs and Alan Watts, the painter Jackson Pollock, and the jazz musician Thelonius Monk. In so far as beat literature is intelligible at all (it set out to defy intelligibility) it represents self-indulgence as a means of self-knowledge, and a hatred of injustice that was often sincere and passionate, even if its expression was immature and over-extravagant. Politically, the Beats found expression in pacifist and anti-nuclear-bomb movements. In appearance, they were distinguished by the wearing of sandals, black roll-neck sweaters, blue jeans, and a straggly beard or pale make-up, and made the same type of sartorial impression upon the 1950s that was later made by the HIPPIES, who owed them numerous cultural and behavioural debts.
                                        P.S.L.; M.S.-S.

Bibl: J. Kerouac, *On the Road* (London and New York, 1958).

Beatles, the. A quartet (John Lennon d.1980, Paul McCartney, Ringo Starr, George Harrison) of young, mainly working-class Liverpudlians whose joint musical productions enjoyed immense popularity from 1962 until the break-up of the band in 1970. The Beatles established an indigenous ROCK style contrasting with Tin Pan Alley's crassly commercial efforts to ape American POP music. Their impact, however, went far beyond their purely musical significance: they inspired an exuberant, often hysterical, adulation ('Beatlemania') among their teenage fans; their unconventional style in clothes and hair, and their articulate and irreverent repartee were accepted and echoed by their contemporaries of all CLASSES. In many ways they exemplify the quintessential flavour of the mid-1960s, though an

73

unusually daring official seal of approval (they were awarded the MBE in 1965) became an embarrassment when they turned openly to experimentation with DRUGS and MYSTICISM. Their LIFE STYLE, however, continued to be endorsed by millions of young people the world over, though Lennon's murder in 1980 seemed to symbolize the end of innocence for a whole generation. The remaining members of the band are still musically active, though Paul McCartney is most prolific in output.   P.S.L.

Bibl: H. Davies, *The Beatles* (London, 1985).

beatnik, see under BEAT.

beaux arts. In architecture, a term used to describe a form of rigid, highly composed, and usually symmetrical design based on classical architecture and academic in character. It is associated with the teaching of the École des Beaux Arts in Paris, and hence (since that school, founded in 1671, has been in frequent opposition to contemporary trends) often used pejoratively.   M.BR.

bebop. Originally just one of the casual store of JAZZ vocal phrases used onomatopoeically to suggest the character of a melody, by the early 1940s bebop had become a code word (also known as rebop and later shortened to bop) for the revolutionary jazz form that overthrew the kingdom of SWING. Compared to earlier jazz, its rhythms were subtler and more complex, its solo lines longer, its harmonic sequences unprecedentedly challenging. The talent of its leading players — the alto saxophonist Charlie 'Bird' Parker and the trumpeter Dizzy Gillespie were regarded as co-principals — was undeniable, and their new orientation made customary jazz practice *passé* overnight. Older musicians were bemused; some opponents of bebop counter-attacked with the deliberately archaic style known as TRAD. The general public found bop tantalizingly abstruse, and the personal eccentricities of its leading players gave the movement a certain cult status, which subsequently inspired subcultures like the BEAT generation. The music itself has unquestionably

remained the basic language of modern jazz.   GE.S.

behaviour therapy. In PSYCHIATRY, the treatment of behavioural disorders by a group of procedures based mainly on learning theory. The principles derive from the experimental work of PAVLOV, Watson, Hull, Skinner, and other experimental psychologists. The procedures, which are increasingly often used, include *desensitization,* an effective treatment for PHOBIAS, the principle being for the patient to re-enter the feared situation gradually and repeatedly, while ANXIETY is neutralized by relaxation; the contrasted (and less widely used) *aversion therapy,* in which an unpleasant stimulus is repeatedly coupled with an undesired behaviour in order to eliminate the latter; and OPERANT CONDITIONING. Behaviour therapy differs from traditional PSYCHOTHERAPY in not drawing on PSYCHODYNAMIC theory such as Freud's and in putting more emphasis on changing outward behaviour than on subjective factors. The two approaches are, however, not conflicting but complementary.

The term *behaviour modification,* though used in many ways and often loosely, has two main applications. First, it is sometimes used synonymously with behaviour therapy as defined above. Second, it may be applied in a more restricted sense to B.F. Skinner's techniques of treating disorders of behaviour by operant conditioning, in which rewards are made contingent upon the subject's own behaviour. The latter methods are, for example, sometimes used to enhance the social behaviour of withdrawn schizophrenic patients (see SCHIZOPHRENIA) or the mentally handicapped (see MENTAL RETARDATION). Relaxation forms one therapeutic technique. Another is Aversion therapy, based upon the association of an unpleasant stimulus used as a conditioning mechanism. This has been extensively used in dealing with sexual offenders, alcoholics and other difficult cases. In ALCOHOLISM, for example, vomit-inducing drugs such as apomorphine have been injected at the same time as alcohol is taken, in order to produce associations of nausea. Early hopes for aversion therapy have not been fulfilled. When applied to the modification of total social systems this approach is sometimes called SOCIAL BEHAVIOURISM. D.H.G.;R.P.

Bibl: H.R. Beech, *Changing Man's Behaviour* (Harmondsworth and Baltimore, 1969).

behavioural engineering, see under SOCIAL ENGINEERING.

behavioural sciences. Those sciences which study the behaviour of men and animals, e.g. PSYCHOLOGY and the SOCIAL SCIENCES (including social ANTHROPOLOGY). Some practitioners of these sciences believe that it is unscientific to study mental processes and other phenomena which are not directly observable and measurable, and they therefore concentrate on the attempt to describe and explain *outward manifestations* of such phenomena, namely observable behaviour (like pressing buttons, eating, running through mazes, making noises) and the relations of such behaviour to external stimuli. The attempt to study men and animals on the basis that they do not have minds, but only patterns of behaviour, is called the *behavioural approach*, or sometimes BEHAVIOURISM. Behaviourism contrasts with MENTALISM. A.S.

Bibl: N. Chomsky, *Language and Mind* (New York, enl. ed., 1972); B.F. Skinner, *Verbal Behavior* (New York, 1957).

behaviourism.

(1) The SCHOOL OF PSYCHOLOGY (in R.S. Woodworth's classification, one of the six main such) that studies only unambiguously observable, and preferably measurable, behaviour. It leaves out of account CONSCIOUSNESS and INTROSPECTION, and its theoretical frames of reference avoid subjective notions such as 'imaging' or 'focus of attention'. In Russia it was closely identified with PHYSIOLOGY and 'reflexes of the brain' as studied by, notably, Ivan Pavlov (see PAVLOVIAN). In America it was launched in 1913 by J.B. Watson, and was represented at its distinctive best by Clark Hull and B.F. Skinner (see also SOCIAL BEHAVIOURISM and, for an opposed view, MENTALISM). American behaviourism attracted, from the start, psychologists with certain kinds of interests, and the word *behaviouristic* came, by

association, to refer to these interests, notably environmental control of behaviour under laboratory conditions which force the 'subject' into a rather passive role with limited freedom of choice; conditioned-response techniques (see CONDITIONED REFLEX); laboratory learning in animals such as rats and pigeons; elementaristic theory involving stimuli, responses, and their objective interrelations (see OPERANT CONDITIONING). This cluster of interests is typically criticized as an elegant but superficial pursuit of trivial problems couched in arid language and too artificial to have relevance for 'real life' problems of either animals or people. Behaviourists typically counter by pointing to the objectivity of their work and stressing that it is only the start of a vastly ambitious enterprise that promises to yield completely general laws of behaviour. Whatever the eventual verdict of history, the deliberate study of objective behaviour has made great strides, and even the 'behaviouristic' approach has contributed much to mainstream PSYCHOLOGY by way of factual discoveries, new ideas, and new methods of enquiry, as well as techniques in BEHAVIOUR THERAPY. I.M.L.H.

Bibl: J.B. Watson, *Behaviorism* (New York, 2nd ed., 1930; London, 1931); B.F. Skinner, *Beyond Freedom and Dignity* (New York, 1971; London, 1972).

(2) As an application of (1) to PHILOSOPHY, the theory that takes statements about mental events and states to be equivalent in meaning to statements about the behaviour of the embodied persons in whose minds the events or states are said to occur. Many behaviourists in psychology have, in practice, seemed to make philosophical claims about what exists, rather than merely to impose methodological restrictions on what they will allow themselves to count as evidence. Thus J.B. Watson identified mental events with actual, if minimally perceptible, items of behaviour: thought, for example, with small subvocal movements of the larynx. Philosophical behaviourists, on the other hand, have generally identified mental facts with DISPOSITIONS to behaviour: for a man to be angry is for him to be disposed to hit out, swear, etc., by ANALOGY with the way in which for a rubber ball to be elastic is for it to have a disposition to

bounce. Carnap and, most thoroughly and consistently, Ryle have adopted this position, which is a form of reductionism (see REDUCTION). The chief incentive to it is the problem of how one person is to know anything about the inner experiences of another when he cannot share those experiences, but must infer them from their manifestations in behaviour. A sophisticated variant of the doctrine is expounded in the later philosophy of Wittgenstein, summarized in the slogan 'Inner processes stand in need of outward CRITERIA'. A.Q.

Bibl: G. Ryle, *The Concept of Mind* (London and New York, 1949), ch. 2.

Being. The fundamental category of EXISTENTIALIST thought. It was Søren Kierkegaard, in his struggle to defeat Hegelian abstraction, who first existentialized the notion of human Being, giving a full description of its various possible modes. In early 20th-century thought, with Heidegger, Jaspers, Marcel, Unamuno, and later Sartre, Camus and Merleau-Ponty, the concept of Being was given full existential status. It is the fundamental term in Heidegger's *Sein und Zeit* (1927). Being is more original and fundamental than any series of actually existing beings or objects, and is the ontologically guaranteeing condition for these. It precedes its various modes of appearance, and thus takes on a quasi-mystical status. Heidegger's presentation of Being has been enormously influential in PHENOMENOLOGY, PSYCHIATRY and HERMENEUTICS, particularly in the work of Hans-Georg Gadamer. Human Being in Heidegger, called *Dasein*, is subsidiary to Being. In Sartre's *Being and Nothingness* (1943) Being is described phenomenologically in three modes, Being-in-Itself, Being-for-Itself and Being-for-Others. These correspond very roughly to brute material existence, without consciousness; self-consciousness set over against the world of brute material existence, yet divided and split in itself and unable fully to coincide with its Being-in-Itself; and a consciousness in the subject that he takes part in, modifies and partly creates, the lived existential projects of other people. In this shared world of inauthentic complicity (see AUTHENTICITY), Sartre gives many of his famous examples of love and hate, masochism and sadism, in their struggle to establish dominance over the Being-for-Itself of the OTHER. In its Sartrian form, this struggle between CONSCIOUSNESS and world is visibly part of the traditional problematic of Descartes and forms a continuation of it, until the power of the alternative tradition of thought, Hegelian-MARXIST, pulls it under and destroys it.   R.PO.

Bibl: S. Kierkegaard, *Either/Or* (Princeton, N.J., 1944); M. Heidegger, *Being and Time* (London and New York, 1962); J.-P. Sartre, *Being and Nothingness* (New York and London, 1957); G. Steiner, *Heidegger* (London, 1978).

Bell's theorem. A mathematical theorem proved by John Bell in 1964. It places constraints upon the interpretations of quantum mechanical reality (see QUANTUM MECHANICS). It showed that no matter what steps are taken to replace the uncertainty of QUANTUM THEORY by hidden deterministic variables the resulting theory must always contain non-local (that is, non-causal) elements. These non-causal elements cannot be employed for faster than light transmission of information. Bell's theorem applies to all interpretations of quantum mechanics except for the MANY WORLDS HYPOTHESIS. The theorem results in the deduction of a quantity that must be measured positive if a theory of the quantum world is to be local and causal. Quantum mechanics results in a negative value. These results have been demonstrated in a famous series of experiments performed by Alain Aspect and collaborators (see COPENHAGEN INTERPRETATION).   J.D.B.

Bibl: J. A. Wheeler and W. Zurek, eds., *Quantum Theory and Measurement* (Princeton, 1983); N. D. Mermin, 'Is the Moon There When Nobody Looks?', *Physics Today*, April, 1985; N. Herbert, *Quantum Reality: Beyond the New Physics* (London, 1986); E. Squires, *The Mystery of the Quantum World* (Bristol, 1986).

Benesh system, see under CHOREOLOGY.

benzene ring. The UNSATURATED six-membered ring of carbon ATOMS which is the principal unit in benzene compounds. The earliest successful ideas on its structure originated with Kekulé in 1865, but proof that the carbon atoms form a planar hexagon was not provided until the X-RAY DIFFRACTION studies of Kathleen Lonsdale in 1929. The carbon atoms are linked by BONDS which include ELECTRONS delocalized over the whole ring. In the benzene MOLECULE itself one atom of hydrogen is attached to each carbon atom, but in one or more cases the hydrogen atom may be replaced by other chemical SPECIES to generate a whole family of benzenoid compounds.   B.F.

Berlin Wall. A concrete wall built by the East German Government from 12 August 1961 onwards to seal off East Berlin from the Western-occupied part of the city, and so prevent any further mass illegal emigration from East Germany to the West. Many would-be emigrés have subsequently been killed by East German frontier guards while attempting to cross. The economic revival of East Germany, and the ÖSTPOLITIK pursued by the West German Government, would, it has been argued by East German apologists, have been impossible without the Berlin Wall; but this is not a view easily accepted in the West, where the Wall continues to be regarded as a symbol of the denial of human rights by the Soviet and East European regimes.   D.C.W.

Berliner Ensemble. East German state theatre company founded in Berlin in 1949 by Bertolt Brecht and his wife Helene Weigel, noted particularly for its harshly perfectionist 'model' productions of Brecht's plays. With its insistence on clear narration, its use of projections, and its relatively cool style of acting, it could be seen as an example of BRECHTIAN (*q.v.*) EPIC THEATRE, even though Brecht's theories were not deployed there.   J.W.

beta particle. A fast ELECTRON or POSITRON emitted during the RADIOACTIVE decay of a NUCLEUS.   M.V.B.

betatron. A compact type of ACCELERATOR for ELECTRONS.   M.V.B.

béton brut, see under CONCRETE.

Beuron. Influential school of religious painting at the South German Benedictine abbey of that name. It was founded by Didier (Fr. Desiderius) Lenz with the aim of evolving an art comparable with plainsong and based on a canon of sacred measurements inspired by those of ancient Egypt. Its principal work was the decoration, 1877-1910, of the mother abbey at Monte Cassino in Italy. Through Denis and Sérusier of the NABIS, the school helped form French ART SACRÉ, while other mystically inclined artists in touch with it include Émile Bernard of PONT-AVEN, Alexei Jawlensky of the NEUE KÜNSTLERVEREINIGUNG, and the BAUHAUS master Johannes Itten.   J.W.

Bevatron. A kind of ACCELERATOR for PROTONS.   M.V.B.

biased galaxy formation, see under BIASING.

biasing (or *biased galaxy formation*). Name given to the theory that the distribution of luminous galaxies (see GALAXY) in the universe is not representative of mass in the universe (see DARK MATTER). It is sometimes used to describe a mechanism which might give rise to such a state of affairs, most notably the possibility that galaxy formation can only occur in regions of the universe where the density of matter exceeds some critical level. This process could give rise to VOIDS in space.
                                    J.D.B.

Bible Belt. Term coined by the American satirist H.L. Mencken, in 1925, to designate the southern and rural midwestern parts of the U.S. in which FUNDAMENTALISTS who believed in the literal accuracy of the Bible attempted to impose their values on public life (for their modern counterparts see NEW CHRISTIAN RIGHT).
                                D.C.W.;S.R.

biblical theology. The attempt of BARTHIAN and other 20th-century theologians (see THEOLOGY) to develop Christian doctrine afresh by studying the Bible instead of relying on DOGMAS. The movement has produced much enthusiasm among Roman CATHOLICS, and the decrees of VATICAN COUNCIL II appealed to the Bible more than to tradition. Biblical theology is opposed both to FUNDAMENTALISM (because it accepts the HIGHER CRITICISM of the Bible) and to religious LIBERALISM (because it denies the ability of modern man to reach religious truth without learning humbly from God's self-revelation in the events and teachings recorded in the Bible). Because of the desire to understand the Old and New Testaments without importing modern ideas, special attention is paid to the original meaning of biblical words in Hebrew or Greek. The main criticism of this movement has concerned its tendency to exaggerate the unity of the Bible.   D.L.E.

Bibl: J. Barr, *The Bible in the Modern World* (London and New York, 1973) and *Holy Scripture* (Oxford, 1983); G.B. Caird, *The Language and Imagery of the Bible* (London, 1980).

bibliography.

(1) (Sometimes called *enumerative*, or *systematic, bibliography*.) The compilation of lists of works by or about a given author or group of authors, or about a given subject, or related to each other by the circumstances of their printing or publication; such a list (known as a bibliography) may be selective or comprehensive, annotated or otherwise, appended to a book or article or separately published.

(2) From the 18th century onwards, the analysis and description of books as physical objects. Bibliography in this sense originally related to the identification of first or best editions. In the later 19th century it came to include the history of printing, typography, book-collecting, and similar topics. In the 20th century greater (and more nearly exclusive) attention has been given to the technical operation of the printing house with respect to such matters as plate corrections, concealed printings, stints of pressmen, and the like. The study of printing and the physical evidence of the books themselves is called *analytical* (or *critical*) *bibliography*; the detailed, formal description of books based on such analysis is called *descriptive bibliography*; the application of these methods and of the resulting evidence to TEXTUAL CRITICISM is called *textual bibliography* by its practitioners, though others (who consider textual criticism a wider subject) object. Bibliography has become an accepted academic discipline; a large and growing group of bibliographers have made great advances in the technical knowledge of the craft of printing and have taken over much of the responsibility for preparing scholarly editions of literary works.   J.T.

Bibl: I. McIlwaine *et al.*, *Bibliography and Reading* (Metuchen, N.J. and London, 1983); P. Gaskell, *A New Introduction to Bibliography* (Oxford, 1972).

bidialectalism (bidialectism). In SOCIOLINGUISTICS, the ability to use two dialects of a language, and thus any educational policy which recognizes the need to develop this ability in children. The notion emerges most commonly in relation to the teaching of non-standard alongside standard English, especially in relation to the abilities of different ethnic groups.   D.C.

Bibl: P. Trudgill, *Sociolinguistics* (Harmondsworth, 1984).

Biennale. A festival of modern art recurring every two years (e.g. the Venice Biennale, the São Paulo Biennale), generally with State encouragement. A *Triennale* recurs every three years.   P.C.

big band. As standardized during the SWING era, an orchestra of about 15 musicians divided into brass, reed and rhythm sections, playing arranged JAZZ and popular music for dancing. The genre was jazz-inspired, with most groups utilizing the 'call and response' interplay pioneered by black bandleader Fletcher Henderson, in which brass and reeds tossed rhythmic phrases ('riffs') back and forth in an atmosphere of mounting excitement. The bands' actual jazz content varied widely, from the syncopated flavouring of Glenn Miller to the unalloyed masterpieces of Duke Ellington and Count Basie. Though the contrast was not absolute, Ellington and Basie illustrate the poles of big-band jazz, the former favouring sophisticated, polychrome arrangements, the latter loose frameworks for soloists known as 'head arrangements' because they were never written down. Musically their groups made the most enduring contributions in the form, though white bandleaders like Miller, Benny Goodman, Artie Shaw and

Tommy Dorsey claimed the lion's share of popularity.   GE.S.

big-bang hypothesis. A theory of the origin of the universe. About 10 thousand million years ago, a very dense primeval aggregate of matter at a temperature of millions of degrees is supposed to have 'exploded' into expanding matter and RADIATION which evolved into the GALAXIES, observed today to be still receding from one another. This theory is today accepted by most cosmologists. It has superseded the rival STEADY-STATE HYPOTHESIS as a result of the evidence from RADIO ASTRONOMY concerning the distribution of distant galaxies, and the discovery of COSMIC BACKGROUND RADIATION. See also COSMOLOGY; EXPANSION OF THE UNIVERSE; PULSATING UNIVERSE.   M.V.B.

Bibl: P.C.W. Davies, *The Accidental Universe* (Cambridge, 1982); P.C.W. Davies, *God and the New Physics* (London, 1983); W.J. Kaufmann, *Universe* (Oxford, 1985).

Big Brother, see under ORWELLIAN.

bilateral/cognatic descent. Tracing of DESCENT from an ancestor through both male and female lines. An individual is a member of as many groups as ancestors through whom descent is traced. Bilateral descent is most commonly found in western Europe. The formation of the unilineal descent group is impossible in bilateral societies as an individual is a member of several different groups at one time. Bilateral descent groups may be established on the basis of residence, for example, but they are not exclusive and rarely permanent. If tied to property, bilateral descent groups may develop PATRILINEAL features which ensure that property is transmitted through a single line and is not therefore dispersed, or place emphasis upon endogamous marriage (see ENDOCAMY).   A.G.

Bibl: J. Goody, *The Development of the Family and Marriage in Europe* (Cambridge, 1983); A.P. Cohen, *Belonging: Identity and Social Organisation in British Rural Cultures* (Manchester, 1982); M. Bloch, *From Blessing to Violence* (Cambridge, 1986).

bilateralism and multilateralism. (1) A term denoting international trade without discrimination between two countries, though trade with the rest of the world may involve discrimination. It contrasts with multilateralism, which is international trade without discrimination between three or more countries. The *most favoured nation clause* in international trade agreements, which is Article 1 of GATT, requires that any tariff concession made by one member country to another must immediately be given to all other members, and so is essentially multilateral. Multilateralism requires the convertibility of currencies and, thus, a country does not have to balance its payments with each country it trades with (see BALANCE OF PAYMENTS).

(2) The meaning of bilateral has changed over time and now refers to trade between two countries and, in particular, where trade agreements have been negotiated. For example, a number of South East Asian countries often tie the decision to import a good to the supplier's acceptance of the country's exports as payment in kind.

(3) Aid is termed bilateral or multilateral depending on whether it is given by a donor directly to a country or through an international agency.   M.F.G.S.; J.P.

Bibl: B. Sodersten, *International Economics* (London, 2nd ed., 1980).

Bildungsroman. German term, literally 'formation-novel', for the type of novel in which the (generally youthful) hero is seen developing through exposure to life; his story is often accompanied by an account of the forms of contemporary society. Variant terms are *Erziehungsroman* ('education novel') and *Entwicklungsroman* ('development novel'). The genre is held to originate with Goethe's *Wilhelm Meister's Apprenticeship* (1775) and includes Novalis's *Heinrich von Ofterdingen* (1799), Gottfried Keller's *Green Henry* (1855), Hermann Hesse's *Demian* (1919), and Thomas Mann's *The Magic Mountain* (1924). The British are less given to classification but, with varying degrees of appropriateness, Fielding's *Tom Jones* (1749), Jane Austen's *Emma* (1816), Dickens's *David Copperfield* (1849-50), Samuel Butler's *The Way of All Flesh*

(1903) and James Joyce's *A Portrait of the Artist as a Young Man* (1914-15) could be ascribed to this genre, though the Germans would rather consider the last-named a *Künstlerroman* ('artist-novel').

D.J.E.

bill of rights. A formal declaration of civil or NATURAL RIGHTS. A bill of rights may be constitutional, legal, or purely political. In the U.S., the first 10 amendments to the constitution form a bill of rights which is both legal and constitutional. It guarantees such rights as freedom of speech and religion. The 'Bill of Rights' in the U.K., however, is purely legal. It can therefore be amended more readily. Other bills of rights, like the U.N. Declaration of HUMAN RIGHTS, may be purely political if they can not be enforced by judicial proceedings.

M.S.P.

binary nerve gases. Conventional nerve gases, like those developed by German scientists during World War II, are stored in liquid form, which often vaporizes on contact with the atmosphere. Any spillage or accidental discharge is highly toxic. This has meant that the chemical agents are stored under secure conditions, and sometimes far from the battlefront, to minimize the danger of unintentional discharge. Binary gases operate on a different principle. They consist of two chemicals which are inert until mixed. Consequently, they are 'safe' weapons, from the user's point of view. The development of binary weapon has revolutionized the possible uses for nerve gas. They are ideally suited for dispersal by gas shells, bombs, or even mines. Even gas hand grenades are a practical proposition. Indeed, the many potential uses of binary weapons has given impetus to negotiations for the control and possible abolition of biological weapons. However, because each part of a binary weapon can be manufactured in different locations, the problem of verification of any agreement becomes more difficult.

A.J.M.W.

Bibl: Sean Murphy, *The Threat of Chemical and Biological Weapons* (London, 1984).

binary pulsar, see under PULSAR.

binary scale. A method of writing numbers with base 2 (instead of the more familiar base 10). It uses only the digits 0 and 1. Examples of binary numbers (each followed by its decimal equivalent): 10 (2), 1001 (9), 10101011 (171). The binary scale is important in INFORMATION THEORY and in COMPUTERS, being the simplest scale that uses positional notation, i.e. where the value of each digit is multiplied by a power of the base depending on its position.

C.S.

binary star. One of a pair of stars held together by GRAVITATION, and revolving about their common centre of gravity. Such pairs are very common: about one third of all stars occur in binaries. M.V.B.

binding. An approach developed in GENERATIVE GRAMMAR of the late 1970s which focuses on the conditions which formally relate, or 'bind', elements of a sentence together. The binding relationships obtain within certain structures, known as 'governing categories' (such as a noun phrase, or a sentence), and the approach as a whole is thus often referred to as the theory of 'government and binding'.

D.C.

Bibl: A. Radford, *Transformational Syntax* (Cambridge, 1981).

binding energy. The ENERGY which must be added to an atomic NUCLEUS to break the bonds between its component NUCLEONS, analogous to the energy needed to separate two pieces of wood which have previously been glued together. This energy is released during nuclear FUSION.

M.V.B.

biochemistry. The CHEMISTRY of living matter. The older biochemistry was largely compositional in its interests, concerned with the chemical composition of the principal ingredients of the body — PROTEINS, CARBOHYDRATES, and fats — and with the composition of the body's material input and output. The new biochemistry is above all else a chemistry of bodily processes, i.e. the chemistry of METABOLISM at both the bodily and cellular level (see CELL). See also BIOPHYSICS.

P.M.

biochip. A futuristic concept in which the limitations of silicon chips (see INTEGRATED CIRCUIT) will be overcome by the use of biological materials and processes.

P.N.

bioclimatology. The study of the relationships between the climate, life, and health of man. One of its principal objects is to determine the range of climatic conditions most favourable to human habitation and to define the areas where such climates exist.

M.L.

bio-cybernetics, see under CYBERNETICS.

bio-energetics, see under REICHIAN.

bio-engineering. A scientific or paramedical discipline concerned with:
(1) the devising of mechanical substitutes for parts or organs of the body, e.g. the artificial kidney, in which the patient's blood is conducted through thin wall tubing immersed in a blood-like fluid, thus making possible a process of filtration analogous to that which occurs in the kidneys;
(2) the designing of artificial limbs and other such artificial devices;
(3) the analysis of bodily structure and function along engineering or physical lines, whether structurally (as in evaluating the mechanical properties of bone) or functionally (as in thermodynamic calculations relating to the body). See also BIONICS.

P.M.

biofeedback. Therapeutic technique used to provide the patient with some *visual* or auditory feedback to an internal or external physiological process. The patient is usually attached to a machine that will monitor and signal in some way changes in skin resistance, finger temperature, muscle contractility or brain-wave activity. It is used most commonly in the treatment of migraine, where there appears to be an association with peripheral constriction of the blood vessels, affecting skin temperature, and the onset of an attack of migraine. The fingers are attached to a thermometer which is seen by the patient. The patient is taught breathing and relaxation techniques, or some form of autogenic training, which induces a reduction in the constriction of the muscles around the blood vessels. This induced state of relaxation, both of the voluntary and involuntary muscles, has been shown both to prevent and reduce an attack of migraine. Biofeedback has been used for pain-control, reduction of general ANXIETY states and PHOBIAS and HYPERTENSION.

P.C.P.

biogenesis. The law of biogenesis — *omne vivum ex vivo* — states that all living things are descended from previously existing living things, i.e. that no such phenomenon as 'spontaneous generation' occurs. Not only living CELLS, but also some of their constituents like mitochondria (see CYTOLOGY), are biogenetic in character; thus no mitochondrion is formed except from a precursor mitochondrion. Louis Pasteur's famous experiments may be said to have disproved the notion of spontaneous generation by showing that bacterial contamination of a sterilized nutrient fluid would only occur if it was re-exposed to air. Claims made for spontaneous generation are now attributed to an innocent form of self-deception, perhaps especially to the confusion created by 'myelin forms' which sometimes simulate amoeboid movement quite closely.

P.M.

biogenetic. Conforming to the principle of BIOGENESIS.

P.M.

biogeography. The study of the geographical distribution of plants and animals over the earth as related to present-day or recent climatic conditions. It is usually limited to land surfaces but can be extended to describe oceanic distributions. It is divided into PHYTOGEOGRAPHY and ZOOGEOGRAPHY.

M.L.

biolinguistics (or *biological linguistics*). A developing branch of LINGUISTICS which studies the biological preconditions for language development and use in man.

D.C.

Bibl: E.H. Lenneberg, *Biological Foundations of Language* (New York, 1967).

biological control. The control of pests by the deliberate introduction of their natural predators, and by other such natural means.

P.M.

biological linguistics, see BIOLINGUISTICS.

biological rhythm. A periodicity of behaviour associated with a natural subdivision of time such as a day, month, or season. Biological rhythms include exactly or approximately circadian (24-hour) rhythms, oestrus and menstrual cycles, the recurrence of breeding seasons, etc. Many such rhythms are deeply grounded physiologically and are by no means totally obscured when animals are removed to an ENVIRONMENT in which the cycles conducive to rhythmic behaviour — e.g. the manifest alternation of night and day — is no longer present. (See also CHRONOBIOLOGY.)   P.M.

biology. The collective name for the *biological sciences* (or, as they are increasingly called in America, *life sciences*), i.e. those NATURAL SCIENCES which deal with the CLASSIFICATION, STRUCTURE or performance of living beings. By convention, the biological sciences include ZOOLOGY, BOTANY, ANATOMY, PHYSIOLOGY, MICROBIOLOGY, BIOSYSTEMATICS, BIOPHYSICS, BIOCHEMISTRY, and, in general, all sciences whose titles incorporate the prefix 'bio-' or the word 'biology' itself (see, for example, DEVELOPMENTAL BIOLOGY; POPULATION BIOLOGY; SOCIAL BIOLOGY). Present convention allocates ANTHROPOLOGY and PSYCHOLOGY to the SOCIAL SCIENCES, but ETHOLOGY is distinctively a biological science.   P.M.

biomathematics. MATHEMATICS applied in biological situations, including medicine and the human sciences. Mathematical reasoning may be used in relation to individual biological organisms or mechanisms (e.g. theoretical MODELS of how nerve fibres, or circulatory systems, function), or to whole animal or human populations. In the latter case especially, statistical CONCEPTS, such as population size, age distribution, sex ratio, become relevant. This leads to related terms such as *biostatistics* and BIOMETRY.   M.S.BA.

Bibl: M.S. Bartlett and R.W. Hiorns (eds.), *The Mathematical Theory of the Dynamics of Biological Populations* (New York, 1973).

biomechanics. Short-lived doctrine of acrobatic acting preached and practised by the director Vsevolod Meyerhold at the Moscow State Higher Theatre Workshop in the 1920s under the influence of CONSTRUCTIVISM and the time and motion researches of A.K. Gastev's Institute for the Scientific Organization of Work and the Mechanization of Man (see WORK STUDY). The actors had to study the mechanics of the body, combining the movements of a skilled worker or sportsman with a dancer's rhythm and balance, performing in blue overalls with no make-up, and using gymnastic and circus apparatus on the stage. In 1922 two plays were given classic productions along these lines, in Constructivist sets: Crommelynck's *Le Cocu magnifique* and Sukhovo-Kobylin's *Tarelkin's Death* (with Eisenstein as Meyerhold's assistant).   J.W.

Bibl: V. Meyerhold, ed. and tr. E. Braun, *Meyerhold on Theatre* (London and New York, 1969).

biometry (or *biometrics*; see also BIOMATHEMATICS). The use of mensuration, enumeration, STATISTICS, and quantitative methods generally in the study of BIOLOGY. In the post-Darwinian era many botanists and zoologists became preoccupied with qualitative descriptions of organisms which were intended to disclose their evolutionary credentials (see EVOLUTION). In reaction a number of scientists — notably Karl Pearson, W.F.R. Weldon, and D'Arcy Thompson — insisted upon the importance of measurement and numeration in the study of all biological phenomena which include an important quantitative or — as in MENDELISM — random element. Among the striking accomplishments of biometry may be mentioned D'Arcy Thompson's and J.S. Huxley's studies of differential growth, the techniques and usages of small-sample statistics introduced by R.A. Fisher, the whole of POPULATION GENETICS, and so much of modern biology that it is hard to think of any branch in which mensuration and numeration are not extremely important. The equation of biometry with statistical analysis of numerical biological data is a degenerate usage which should be discouraged.   P.M.

Bibl: J. Maynard Smith, *Mathematical*

Ideas in Biology (London and New York, 1968).

biomorphic. Term used in ABSTRACT ART and SURREALISM for non-geometrical forms based on natural shapes, i.e. mainly curves, blobs, and bulges. It is associated primarily with the abstract paintings and sculptures of Hans Arp, who consistently used such forms from 1915 on, and secondarily with the work of such surrealists as Yves Tanguy and Joan Miró. Similar characteristics in the work of Henry Moore are sometimes termed *organic*. Before these labels had come into use, however, much the same approach was applied, with great refinement, in ART NOUVEAU and the designs of William Morris.   J.W.

Bibl: K. Nierendorf (intr.), *Art Forms in Nature* (New York, 1967).

bionics. A portmanteau word (BIOlogical electroNICS) coined by Dr Hans L. Oestreicher of Wright-Patterson Air Force Base, Ohio, and meaning the application of biological processes, especially of control, to TECHNOLOGY. It is the part of CYBERNETICS (hence sometimes called *biocybernetics*) which is concerned with taking over 'design principles' seen in biological organisms, to create novel technological devices. (Another word closely related in meaning is BIO-ENGINEERING.) Current emphasis in bionics has moved away from principles of control, to the question of how novelty or intelligence may be simulated (see SIMULATION) or produced by machines — see ARTIFICIAL INTELLIGENCE.   R.L.G.

bionomics, see ECOLOGY.

biophysics. The scientific discipline concerned with the study of living things by the application of physical methods, e.g. *ultracentrifugation* (see SEDIMENTATION); filtering through ordinary plane filters of different porosities or through gels with more or less closely spaced lattice works (*gel filtration*); ELECTROPHORESIS, in which MOLECULES can be separated by reason of inequalities of electrical charge — a most important technique with such fragile and unstable molecules as those of PROTEINS. University departments of bio-physics are often given the responsibility for (1) supervising the general use of physical methods in BIOLOGY, particularly the use of TRACER techniques using radioactive compounds or other ISOTOPES; (2) ULTRASONICS; and (3) therapeutic or investigative techniques turning upon irradiation. By far the most important part of biophysics is MOLECULAR BIOLOGY, the interpretation of biological structures and performances in molecular terms.   P.M.

biopsy, see under HISTOPATHOLOGY.

biorheology, see HAEMORHEOLOGY.

biosensor. A sensing device that uses a biological detection system, for example an ENZYME that, in acting upon the substance which is to be detected generates some kind of measurable signal.   P.N.

biosphere. A word built on the model of atmosphere and HYDROSPHERE and signifying (1) the realm occupied by living things; hence (2) the living things themselves, considered collectively.   P.M.

biostatistics, see under BIOMATHEMATICS.

biosynthesis. A synthetic process occurring characteristically in a living thing. PROTEINS and viruses (see VIROLOGY) are produced only by biosynthesis; they cannot yet be synthesized in the laboratory.   P.M.

biosystematics. The classification of living things; also known as *taxonomy*. Biosystematics was founded by Linnaeus, who introduced the familiar binomial nomenclature in which each organism is given a generic (e.g. *Homo*) and a specific name (*Homo sapiens*). The most majestic of taxonomic distinctions is into plant and animal *kingdoms* (the subject-matters of BOTANY and ZOOLOGY respectively). Next in order of rank is the PHYLUM, the members of which are united by a basic similarity of ground plan which may only be apparent at a relatively early stage of development.

A phylum comprises a number of *classes*. Members of a class are united by a somewhat closer degree of similarity than the members of a phylum — extending to points of anatomical detail as well as to ground plan. For example, the phylum Arthropoda includes the classes Insecta and Crustacea, the Insecta being united by having three pairs of legs attached to the thoracic region of the body and respiring by means of *tracheae*; while within the Vertebrates (often accorded the rank of a sub-phylum within the phylum Chordata) fishes, reptiles, amphibians, birds, and mammals are all graded as classes.

Next below the class come successively the *order*, the *family*, and the *genus* (plural *genera*). It is not possible to specify the degree of resemblance that unites members of orders, families, or genera in a way that will apply to all animals and plants; it may be noted, however, that among mammals the whales and dolphins, the carnivores, the rodents, and the primates each form an order. Finally, below the genus comes the SPECIES; thus the great cats belong to the genus Panthera, in which *Panthera leo* (the lion) and *Panthera tigris* (the tiger) are species.

Of the larger taxonomic subdivisions it may be said that all phyla, classes, and orders are intended to have the same 'value', i.e. to be of the same rank in the systematic hierarchy. Furthermore, each group within itself is intended to be *monophyletic*, i.e. to be such that the common ancestor of the members of the group is itself a member of the group. (There are exceptions: notoriously, the class Reptilia is polyphyletic in the sense that reptiles are subdivided into two main streams — one leading towards birds and one towards mammals — both of which evolved out of amphibian ancestors.) On the other hand, taxonomic divisions are not intended to be a dossier of evolutionary relationships (see EVOLUTION); the purpose of taxonomy is to *name* reliably and consistently. Nevertheless the fact of the evolutionary relationship imposes a certain pattern upon classification which is not to be avoided.

Taxonomic characteristics, i.e. those upon which a systematic allocation may be made, are wherever possible structural, since physiological and behavioural criteria are of little use to the museum taxonomist who normally has to handle dead specimens. Similar difficulties restrict the use of immunological criteria (see IMMUNOLOGY) in determining blood relationships. They have, however, helped to show that whales are more nearly akin to pigs than to other mammals that have been alleged to be their relations.   P.M.

Bibl: Reader's Digest Association, *The Living World of Animals* (London, 1970).

biotechnology. A term comprehending all applications of biological knowledge (see BIOLOGY) to industry. Examples are: (1) industrial fermentation (including brewing, wine-making, and in some countries the accelerated maturation of wines by the addition of ENZYMES); (2) the preparation of leather and of so-called 'biological DETERGENTS', the active ingredients of which are enzymes extracted from heat-adapted bacteria (see BACTERIOLOGY). Much of the food industry, especially as it relates to pre-prepared foods, rests on biological know-how and comes, therefore, under the heading of biotechnology.   P.M.

bipolarity. An intellectual MODEL of the world powers as divided ('polarized') into two main blocs of powers each led by a 'super-power' (the U.S.A. or U.S.S.R.). As a simplified model of international relations, especially in the field of control of nuclear armaments, it seduced many American policy-advisers during the 1950s by its facile answers to some of their problems. The concept lost its attraction when it became obvious that the leadership of the 'super-powers' was never as absolute as the model required, and that this lack offered many opportunities to Soviet and Western anti-American propagandists. Compare MULTIPOLARITY.

D.C.W.

birth trauma. In PSYCHOANALYSIS, a TRAUMA postulated by Otto Rank (one of Freud's early associates), who argued that being born is a deeply disturbing experience, out of which develops the fundamental human conflict: between the wish to return to the embryonic bliss of the womb and the fear of doing so, because the womb is also associated with the fact of birth. This notion has not been widely accepted, even among psychoanalysts.   B.A.F.

Bibl: O. Rank, *The Trauma of Birth* (London and New York, 1929).

BIS (Bank for International Settlements). 'The central bankers' central bank', set up in 1930 (in the wake of the 1929 crash) by the central banks of Britain, Belgium, Germany, Italy, Japan, and France, with the U.S.A. represented by a commercial bank, and with other European central banks, including most in Eastern Europe, taking shareholdings which they have retained to this day. Membership has since expanded; and the U.S. Federal Reserve Board is invariably represented, although the U.S.A. has never formally taken up the seat on the Board still reserved for it. The Board of Directors includes the central-bank Governors of the main Western European countries ('the Basle Club'), as well as representatives of the private business communities. The Bank acts as the agent for central banks in conducting certain operations in financial and currency markets, most notably over the last two decades in the Euro-money markets. The BIS has responsibility for many of the technical aspects of the operations of the various European financial systems, e.g. the European Monetary System.   P.J.; J.P.

bit. (1) In COMPUTER SCIENCE, reputedly short for 'binary digit', a digit in the scale of 2 which will represent the result of a single yes/no decision. Most computer storage and logical elements are made of two-state devices, each of which can represent one bit. (2) In INFORMATION THEORY, the basic unit of information. A 32-bit (sense 1) unit in a computer may be used to represent anything from 0 to 32 bits of information (sense 2).   R.M.N.

bitonality. In music, the mixing together of two *tonalities* (see under ATONAL MUSIC) by the simultaneous use of, e.g., two lines of melody or two blocks of harmony, each in a different key. The conflict of tonalities produces an arresting effect which is more likely to be immediately comprehensible than random dissonance, since each part in itself is based on traditional concepts of key. Bitonality was much used at the start of the century, notably by Stravinsky, Holst (in the Fugal Concerto), and Bartók, and in the 1920s

by Milhaud. See also PANTONAL MUSIC; POLYTONALITY.   A.H.

bivalence, principle of. In PHILOSOPHY, the principle that every sentence in a given class of sentences is either true or false, with 'truth' and 'falsity' as the only possible alternatives. It is a SEMANTIC principle, that is, it relates to the interpretation (establishing the meaning) of sentences in a language. The logical principle to which it corresponds is the law of excluded middle, which states either *A* or not-*A*. The semantic and logical principles are related in that acceptance of the former usually entails acceptance of the latter, but not vice versa. This is because the law of excluded middle depends upon a reading of 'not' which has it that if *A* is true, not-*A* is false, and vice versa, from which it follows that *not-not-A* is equivalent to *A*. This is called the 'classical' reading of negation. However if one reads 'not' differently, for example as 'not provable', then the law of excluded middle ceases to hold, since in this case *not-not-A* and *A* are not equivalent (to assert 'it is not provable that it is not provable that *A*' is not to assert 'it is provable that *A*'). This is the 'intuitionistic' reading of negation. If one does not accept the principle of bivalence one is thereby rejecting the classical reading of negation and with it the law of excluded middle. However, acceptance of that law does not oblige commitment to bivalence, so the relationship is not symmetrical. The principle of bivalence is associated with REALISM in the philosophy of language. See ANTI-REALISM.   A.C.G.

Bibl: M.A.E. Dummett, *Truth and Other Enigmas* (London, 1978).

bivalent. Two CHROMOSOMES of maternal and paternal origin lying side by side during MEIOSIS; also used as an adjective to describe such a pair.   J.M.S.

black. Term used to make a political statement. It does not strictly refer to physical or racial attributes but generally includes people who identify themselves on the basis of a common political experience. The notion of blackness and its development as a political symbol began with Marcus Garvey and his Back to Africa movement. Black became part of everyday vocabulary in the wake of the American CIVIL RIGHTS and BLACK POWER movement of the 1960s. Black in Britain has become a point of mobilization for postwar migrants (from Asia and the West Indies in particular) and subsequent generations. A.G.

black-body radiation. Electromagnetic RADIATION in EQUILIBRIUM with matter; the radiation would be re-emitted by an ideal 'black body' which absorbs all the radiation incident on it. Black-body radiation is distributed over all wavelengths but its ENERGY is concentrated near a particular wavelength region which depends on the temperature. Examples are the INFRA-RED and visible radiation emitted by a red-hot poker, and the MICROWAVES of the COSMIC BACKGROUND RADIATION. Historically the development of the theory of black-body radiation (by Planck in 1900) was the first step leading to QUANTUM MECHANICS. M.V.B.

black-box theory. A theory that attempts to relate INPUT to output in a SYSTEM by a formal description of the *transformation rules* (see AXIOMATICS) that link the two, but without stating the nature of the process that embodies or gives realization to these rules. N. Chomsky's description of language acquisition and B.F. Skinner's theory of learning may both be considered black-box theories, since they avoid the description of the mechanisms involved. J.S.B.

black comedy (or *dark comedy*). Drama which, although it observes many of the conventions of comedy, either presents a sombre or despairing view of the world or else includes themes traditionally excluded from the genre on account of their painful nature. The use of this style in the modern period relates to the widely held belief that tragedy is an inappropriate genre for an age which has lost religious faith and a sense of the heroic. Although the two terms are to some extent interchangeable, *dark comedy* refers rather to the tragicomic form in which laughter and despair are inextricably mingled, in the style perfected by Anton Chekhov (1860-1904), while *black comedy*, exemplified at its most extreme in the plays of Joe Orton,

seeks to unsettle its audiences by laughing at pain, suffering, or serious emotion (and thus has an affinity with *sick jokes* and the THEATRE OF THE ABSURD). The term 'black comedy' (*comédie noire*) derives from Jean Anouilh, who divided his plays of the 1930s and 1940s into *pièces roses* and *pièces noires,* and perhaps also from *Anthologie de l'humeur noir,* the title of a volume (1940) in which André Breton illustrated the long-standing SURREALIST interest in the humorous treatment of the macabre or the shocking to indicate 'the superior rebellion of the mind'; the term 'dark comedy' was coined by the critic J.L. Styan in 1962. M.A.; J.G.W.

Bibl: J.L. Styan, *The Dark Comedy* (London, 2nd ed., 1968).

black consciousness. A political movement in South Africa which emerged in the late 1960s and early 1970s. The movement contained several organizations and factions; their common features included a rejection of APARTHEID, a stress on the value of black cultural identity, and the goal of a comprehensive transfer of power to the BLACK majority. By the mid-1970s it was increasingly subject to state repression: Steve Biko, a prominent movement figure, died in September 1977 in police detention from injuries sustained under torture, and in October 1977 black consciousness groups were banned. The movement's impact was demonstrated in Soweto on 16 June 1976. This township was the scene of an uprising, the immediate focus of which was black student protest at the use of Afrikaans in schools. More generally it expressed accumulated grievances against the STATE and Apartheid. Violence spread throughout most of the Republic, in which hundreds died. Hundreds more left the country, many to ANC training camps. Although the state reimposed control the episode did much to heighten black political consciousness and to stimulate support for the ANC. Like Sharpeville, a black township where police killed 69 black demonstrators on 21 March 1960 and which also sparked wider protests, Soweto has become a byword and landmark in the struggle against Apartheid. S.R.

Bibl: T. Lodge, *Black Politics in South Africa Since 1945* (Marlow, 1984).

black economy. That part of economic activity that takes place outside the tax system and which is illegal. The illicit nature of the black economy means that it is difficult to estimate its size. The loss of tax revenue from the black economy is of concern to governments and has become a political issue in many countries.   J.P.

Bibl: S. Smith, *Britain's Shadow Economy* (Oxford, 1986).

black hole. A hypothetical astronomical system. When a star near the end of its history contracts under GRAVITATION and becomes smaller than a certain *critical radius* (proportional to the star's mass), then, according to Einstein's theory of RELATIVITY, no RADIATION can escape from it; as far as the rest of the universe is concerned it becomes unobservable — its ESCAPE VELOCITY exceeds the speed of light. Such a black hole would still exert gravitational force, so that its existence could be inferred from the motion of neighbouring bodies; several black holes have been tentatively identified in this way. What happens to the matter falling into a black hole? Does it collapse to a point of infinite density, or is this prevented by QUANTUM MECHANICS, or does the matter re-explode, appearing as a 'white hole' in another universe? These are unsolved problems in theoretical PHYSICS. The sun is in no immediate danger of becoming a black hole within the next few hundred million years, because it is about half a million times larger than its critical radius, which is about 2 miles. See also HERTZSPRUNG-RUSSELL DIAGRAM.   M.V.B.

Black Hundreds. Strong-arm gangs employed by RIGHT-wing organizations in Czarist Russia in the period after the Revolution of 1905 and the summoning of the first Russian parliament, to demoralize their political opponents and harass Russian Jewry.   D.C.W.

Black Mountain. Black Mountain College, a PROGRESSIVE-education institution in North Carolina founded by J.A. Rice in 1933. At first the emphasis was on practical education and painting (the art-teachers included Josef Albers, formerly of the BAUHAUS), but in the early 1950s it became a centre of a new, or newly stated, American POETICS, and a place for poets: the CONNOTATION of Black Mountain is now almost exclusively literary, referring to the Black Mountain school of poets. This is one of two latter-day manifestations of an American revolt against conventional and academic poetics which began with Ezra Pound and William Carlos Williams — the other being the group of poets which crystallized round Robert Bly's more mythologically and surrealistically orientated Fifties/Sixties/Seventies Press. The key to the Black Mountain poetics is to be found in American PRAGMATISM as exemplified by John Dewey, with its accompanying blind optimism. Its mentor was Charles Olson (1910-70), Rector of the College from 1951 until 1956, during which period he was joined by other Black Mountain poets (e.g. Robert Creeley, Robert Duncan), as students and as instructors. Olson's makeshift poetics (or anti-poetics) is expressed, in a mixture of baseball instructor's and jocose professional slang, in *Projective Verse* (1950), which has been widely reprinted. It is unscholarly, bloody minded and derivative (mostly from Williams), and raises a host of unanswered questions. But it is important as a summing-up of the attitudes of a somewhat younger generation of American poets, and as a specifically American pragmatic reaction, arising out of what has been called 'intelligent philistinism', to lifeless academicism. Olson's demands had already been fulfilled more humbly by the OBJECTIVIST minor American poets of the early 1930s, with whom Williams and Pound were briefly associated. His disciples do not really fulfil these demands, which are unfulfillable; but they believe that they are doing so. The poet is to concentrate on his own breathing, on the syllable (see SYLLABICS) rather than on metre or rhyme; he is to perform on the typewriter because this spaces more precisely than writing does; syntax, in as much as it hampers the dynamic energy supplied by breath, is to go. There is much emphasis on public readings. And the prime reason for all this is that the old, 'closed' method, as then allegedly practised by such much-loathed poets as Robert Frost, interposed the 'poet's ego' between himself and his audience. In Black Mountain poetry, the

(Deweyan) sense of *use* is not actually carried beyond the simple act of creation, and neither Olson nor his chief disciple Creeley give the least indication, outside or inside their poetry, of why they do what they do. The magazine *Origin* (1951-6), edited by Cid Corman, first printed many of the Black Mountain poets. *Black Mountain Review* (1954-7), edited by Creeley, is also relevant. The claim made in one reference book that the Black Mountain poets 'have long since become a major part of 20th-century literature' was decidedly over-optimistic. But they remain a minor part of the history of American poetry.   M.S.-S.

Bibl: M.L. Rosenthal, *The New Poets* (New York, 1967).

Black Muslims, see under NATION OF ISLAM

Black Panthers, see under BLACK POWER.

Black Papers. Two issues in 1969 of the *Critical Survey*, a periodical associated with the literary *Critical Quarterly*. Their titles were *Fight for Education* and *The Crisis in Education* and the editors were C.B. Cox and A.E. Dyson, two university teachers of English literature. The contributors emphasized a deterioration, in Western Europe generally and Great Britain in particular, in standards of education and discipline ranging from children's reading to student behaviour. Comprehensive schools, EGALITARIANISM, YOUTH CULTURES, and 'progressivism' in general (see PROGRESSIVE) came under fire on what the editors insisted were educational and not political grounds.   W.A.C.S.

black power. A phrase used by several BLACK political activists in the U.S. in the mid-1960s, but dramatized by Stokely Carmichael of the Student Nonviolent Coordinating Committee. It designates the values and strategic aims of radical blacks, including organizations such as the Black Panthers and NATION OF ISLAM, and members of CIVIL RIGHTS MOVEMENT organizations who rejected its LIBERAL, nonviolent character. These values and aims differed in detail, from variants of SOCIALISM to the call for an independent

black nation. It is questionable whether the term denotes a movement, or rather a series of tendencies, organizations and political styles. However, the shared emphasis on raising black cultural pride and political consciousness, and on threatening the stability of the social and political order, had a major impact — not least in polarizing white opinion on racial issues and drawing the government into both repressive measures and a greater acceptance of more moderate black demands.
                                                    S.R.
Bibl: M. Marable, *Race, Reform and Rebellion* (London, 1984); H. Sitkoff, *The Struggle for Black Equality 1945-80* (New York, 1981).

black sections. The demand by BLACK people for the establishment of their own independent organization within a political party, for example within the Labour Party (see NÉGRITUDE, COLOUR).   A.G.

Black Theatre. A movement dedicated to the creation of a drama reflecting the consciousness of black Americans. Lorraine Hansberry's *A Raisin in the Sun* (1959) was the first major success by a black dramatist; in the 1960s, in plays by James Baldwin, Ed Bullins, and LeRoi Jones, black drama became progressively more radical (see RADICALISM) until, influenced by the militancy of the BLACK POWER movement at the end of the decade, Black Theatre groups sought to sever their connection with the white American theatre and perform solely for black audiences. Outside the U.S.A., theatre groups in Jamaica and England (comprising West Indians and expatriate Americans) have been influenced by the Black Theatre movement; the work of West African dramatists, of whom the most powerful is the Nigerian Wole Soyinka, represents a complex fusion of indigenous and ex-colonial traditions; in the French-speaking world the plays of the Martinique-born poet and dramatist Aimé Césaire have made an important contribution to the expression of black identity (see NÉGRITUDE).   M.A.
Bibl: D.E. Abramson, *Negro Playwrights in the American Theatre, 1925-1959* (London and New York, 1969); *Drama Review,* Black Theatre issue, Dec.

1972, pp. 3-61; M. Banham with C.Wake, *African Theatre Today* (London, 1976).

black theology. A style of doing Christian THEOLOGY which uses insights in pre-Christian traditional religion in Africa, which is also inspired by the experience of Christians with African roots under slavery in the U.S.A. and the Caribbean islands, and which actively promotes the liberation of all black people from their remaining disadvantages or sufferings under oppression, specially in the U.S. and South Africa (see APARTHEID, CIVIL RIGHTS MOVEMENT). In countries where African governments are in power, the emphasis is less political and more on INDIGENOUS THEOLOGY, African customs in worship, etc., with great appreciation of the heritage of communion through dancing, etc. This communion is with the Creator, with lesser divinities and spirits in nature, with other members of the village and tribe, with the EXTENDED FAMILY and with ancestors, specially with the 'living dead' who are personally remembered. A rich source of devotional religion, often quoted in this movement, is the Negro Spiritual, originating in (or modelled on) songs of encouragement in the fields being worked by slaves. D.L.E.
Bibl: James H. Cone, *A Black Theology of Liberation* (New York, 1972) and *God of the Oppressed* (New York, 1975, and London, 1977); A.A. Boesak, *Black Theology and Black Power* (London, 1978).

Blast. The 'review of the Great English Vortex', published in London in two issues, June 1914 and July 1915, under the editorship of Wyndham Lewis. Pre-eminently a VORTICIST manifesto, presenting its attitude to the contemporary scene in a Marinetti-like display of 'Blesses' and 'Blasts', it was the most conspicuous expression of this post-Imagist (see IMAGISM) movement in British literature and the arts. Ezra Pound was active in its compilation; there were contributions by T.S. Eliot, Ford Madox Hueffer, etc. But these typographically exciting documents are primarily fascinating as statements of an important theory about the kinetic potential of the MODERNIST arts, and as a synthetic 'projection of a world art'. M.S.BR.

blastocyst. In EMBRYOLOGY, a very early human development state, after cleavage but before implantation, of the embryo, in which the CELLS into which the ZYGOTE has divided come to be arranged in the form of a sac or cyst containing fluid. The stage is thought to be somewhat analogous to the blastula — a stage which all embryos of animals on the chordate line of descent pass through. P.M.

Blaue Reiter, der ('the Blue Horseman'). A Munich-based almanac edited by Kandinsky and Franz Marc in 1912, whose title was used for a group of artists headed by Kandinsky who broke away from the NEUE KÜNSTLERVEREINIGUNG to hold two exhibitions in the winter 1911-12. It included August Macke, Heinrich Campendonk, the (future ATONAL) composer Arnold Schönberg and, in the second show, Paul Klee. Though its members figured in the second Moscow KNAVE OF DIAMONDS show and in many ensuing STURM exhibitions, it ceased to exhibit as a group after 1913. It was, however, one of the main elements in EXPRESSIONISM and early ABSTRACT ART, bringing to each a SYMBOLIST, mystical, quasi-musical flavour tinged with ANTHROPOSOPHY. It later influenced the BAUHAUS, where from 1924 to 1929 Kandinsky, Klee, Lyonel Feininger, and Alexei Jawlensky formed a related group called 'the Blue Four'. J.W.

blending inheritance. Inheritance by children of characteristics which are a more or less equitable blend between those of their parents or, in respect of quantitative characteristics, midway between them. Although such a blending is a natural enough presumption, the great lesson of MENDELISM is that it does not occur. If it did so, GENETIC variance would be extinguished in a few generations, whereas in point of fact genetic variance tends to be indefinitely conserved. This is because the determinants of heredity maintain their integrity generation by generation. So far from being a blend between their two parents, children display a novel and possibly a unique recombination of the genetic determinants transmitted to them by their parents. See also MENDEL'S LAWS. P.M.

blitzkrieg. A German concept describing a style of, literally, 'lightning war'. It involved the use of armour, and motorized infantry, and was used to great effect in Poland in 1939 and against France in 1940. It depended for its effect on the shock wave produced by a deep offensive, which disrupted an enemy's planned resistence. Crucial additional elements were the use of tactical airpower, and the psychological effect of a seemingly 'irresistible' attack. The attack on Russia in 1941 was not a blitzkrieg in this sense, but a massed, concerted attack over a long front. 'The Blitz' was erroneously used to describe the German air attack on London in 1940. With the coming of NUCLEAR WEAPONS, the concept has seemed impractical, but the strategist P.H. Vigor has suggested that the Soviet Union could use a blitzkrieg to great effect against NATO.
A.J.M.W.
Bibl: P.H. Vigor, *Soviet Blitzkrieg Theory* (London and New York, 1983).

blocking. During the 1940s the establishment of regular balloon soundings through the height of the atmosphere resulted in the first complete picture of the general circulation of the atmosphere, the three-dimensional flow of air round the planet. At height in the atmosphere, the flow takes the form of a series of waves, troughs and ridges, with the dominant airflow being zonal, from west to east, in middle latitudes. At times, the zonal flow becomes disturbed, the amplitude of the waves increases and meridional, north-south airflow becomes more frequent. This is known as a 'blocking' episode. At the Earth's surface, it is generally manifest as a quasi-stationary anticyclone occupying a location where mobile depressions embedded in the westerly flow are normally found. Blocking episodes tend to be persistent, lasting from days to weeks, and are often associated with extreme weather and climate: drought beneath a stable anticyclone; cold weather if the dominant flow is from polar regions; warmth if the flow is from tropical climes. The changing frequency of blocking episodes is often cited as a cause of climatic change. Little is known about the causes of blocking events although ocean-atmosphere interaction may be a factor.
P.M.K.

Bibl: R.G. Barry and R.J. Chorley, *Atmosphere, Weather and Climate* (London, 1968).

blood and soil (*Blut und Boden*). A quasi-mystical NAZI catch-phrase intended to glorify the literature and emotions of the peasant as the embodiment of the two qualities from which the high quality of the German race was supposed to stem, German blood and German soil.
D.C.W.

blood-brain barrier. The cells that form the lining of the blood vessels in the central nervous system of mammals and other higher vertebrates are so tightly packed that little can escape from within the vessels into the fluid that bathes the brain. This blood-brain barrier acts to protect the brain but can also impede treatment of diseases when it hinders the passage of drugs from the bloodstream to the fluid that bathes the brain tissues.
P.N.

blood groups. Many early attempts at blood transfusion from one human being to another failed because of an incompatibility between the recipient's and the donor's blood, the mechanism of which was first elucidated by Karl Landsteiner in 1900. Landsteiner found that the SERUM of some human beings caused AGGLUTINATION of the red blood corpuscles of other human beings, and that human beings could be divided into four groups, A, B, AB, and O, whose members' serum agglutinated the corpuscles of members of other groups as follows.

Since the dangerous process is agglutination of the donor's corpuscles by the recipient's serum (because of the dilution effect the reverse process is of lesser significance) it follows that:

Inheritance of A, B, O blood groups was soon shown to follow straightforward Mendelian rules (see MENDEL'S LAWS). The A, B, O blood-group system is, however, only one among many. So many varieties of blood antigen (see IMMUNITY) are now known that a person's blood group is, if defined precisely enough, practically a personal identification mark. Among the other important blood groups are those of the Rh (Rhesus) system and the M, N, MN system. Some of these — the Rh system in particular — were discovered by indirect methods of blood typing. Thus the antibody distinguishing between Rh+ and Rh– red blood cells was formed by injecting the blood of Rhesus monkeys into rabbits. 'Natural' antibodies (see IMMUNITY) against Rh antigens do not appear, so anti-Rh immunity arises as a result of active immunization — through incompatible blood transfusions, or during the course of pregnancy when a Rh-negative mother bears a number of children by a Rh-positive man.   P.M.

Bibl: A.E. Mourant, *The Distribution of the Human Blood Groups* (Oxford and Springfield, Ill., 1954); R.R. Race and R. Sanger, *Blood Groups in Man* (Oxford and Philadelphia, 5th ed., 1968).

Bloom's taxonomy. This theory from the educationist of that name has been applied to the planning and development of the curriculum. It maintains that education should have three objectives: the cognitive (i.e. knowledge and the application of knowledge), the affective (i.e. dealing with the emotions and with values) and the pyscho-motor (i.e. dealing with physical skills). The late Sir Alec Clegg, who for many years was chief education officer for the West Riding of Yorkshire, divided education into only two objectives and called them 'the loaves and hyacynths': the loaves being the cognitive (the facts needed to know how to, say, dance the Highland Fling), the hyacynths representing the emotions (the verve and passion with which to dance it).   J.I.

Bloomfieldian. Characteristic of, or a follower of, the linguistic approach of Leonard Bloomfield, as exemplified in his book *Language*, published in 1933. *Bloomfieldianism* refers particularly to the school of thought which developed between the mid 1930s and 1950s, especially in America, and which was a formative influence on structural LINGUISTICS. It was especially characterized by its BEHAVIOURISTIC principles for the study of meaning, and its insistence on rigorous DISCOVERY PROCEDURES. A reaction against Bloomfieldian tenets was a powerful force in producing GENERATIVE GRAMMAR. Though Bloomfieldianism is no longer fashionable, some of its methods are still widely used in field studies.   D.C.

Bloomsbury. An area of Central London which includes the British Museum, and whose name is used (1) as a synonym for the BLOOMSBURY GROUP or one of its members ('a Bloomsbury', facetious plural 'bloomsberries'); (2) more loosely, and not currently, as a symbol of the British intelligentsia at large ('Bloomsbury INTELLECTUAL') or any section or aspect of it ('a Bloomsbury voice') towards which hostility is felt.   O.S.

Bloomsbury Group. A circle of friends without formal membership, rules, or common doctrine consisting of Lytton Strachey, Virginia and Leonard Woolf, Clive and Vanessa Bell, Maynard Keynes, Duncan Grant, Saxon Sydney-Turner, and (see also OMEGA WORKSHOPS) Roger Fry. Closely associated with this group were E.M. Forster, Gerald Shove, James and Marjorie Strachey, David Garnett, Francis Birrell, Adrian and Thoby Stephen. The group came into existence in 1905, when Thoby Stephen and his sisters, Virginia and Vanessa, then living in BLOOMSBURY, London, continued friendships begun at Cambridge. Its members were united by a belief in the importance of the arts; they were all sceptical and tolerant, particularly in sexual matters.

Beyond this it would be difficult to find any opinion or attitude shared by all. In so far as the group ever had any kind of corporate existence, it began to decline after the death of Lytton Strachey in 1931 and had ceased to exist by 1940.   Q.B.

Bibl: J.K. Johnstone, *The Bloomsbury Group* (London, 1954; New York, 1963); W. Bell, *Bloomsbury* (London, 1968; New York, 1969); D. Gadd, *The Loving Friends: a Portrait of Bloomsbury* (London, 1974); L. Edel, *Bloomsbury: A House of Lions* (New York and London, 1979).

blue beat, see under REGGAE.

Blue Book. Familiar term for British Government publication of official documents presented to Parliament in sufficient number of pages to warrant being bound in a separate blue cover. They are identifiable by their 'Command numbers' and the date and year of their presentation. Those familiar with these source materials maintain that the degree of frankness observed in their publication has diminished progressively with the increase in the size of the electorate. Blue Books should be distinguished from other Command Papers known as White Papers and Green Papers. The former contain statements of Government policy and may include announcements of Government intentions and proposals on future legislation, while Green Papers are used by the Government to put forward ideas and information which are the basis of open debate and discussion rather than a commitment by the Government to a specific course of action.
                                        D.C.W.

blue notes. One of the purest and oldest features of BLUES and JAZZ, the blue notes are the lowered third and seventh (and sometimes the fifth) degrees of what would otherwise be a major scale. The resulting tension between 'major' and 'minor' — though the blue notes are actually neither — produces the characteristic quality of the blues, a potent mixture of sorrow, defiance and affirmation. Like other jazz elements, the blue notes were incorporated into the vocabulary not only of popular music but classical music as well (see SYMPHONIC JAZZ).   GE.S.

blue shift. A displacement towards the blue of the spectral lines of some stars. The shift arises from the DOPPLER EFFECT, and indicates that these stars are approaching us. Because of the overall EXPANSION OF THE UNIVERSE, blue shifts are rare in comparison with RED SHIFTS.   M.V.B.

blues. A specific musical form and one of the most influential musical genres of the century. To a blues singer or JAZZ musician, the blues at its most basic is a twelve-bar structure (occasionally sixteen) consisting of four bars of the tonic chord, two of the subdominant, two of the tonic and two of the dominant with a return to the tonic for a final two bars. When performed vocally, a classic blues verse divides the twelve bars into three four-bar sections, in each of which a single line is sung, the second of which is a repeat of the first. Despite the form's simplicity, its economy and dramatic power have inspired some of the most memorable performances in jazz. Throughout jazz history, the fundamental importance of the blues has never been in doubt, though its harmonic structure has sometimes been elaborately altered. As a musical genre distinct from jazz, the blues has carried on its own development from the 1920s, primarily though not exclusively as a vocal style, with more emphasis on directness of communication than sophistication. Its various forms, urban and country, group or solo, have at times been lumped together under the heading of RHYTHM AND BLUES to distinguish them from jazz. Under any rubric its special qualities remain and have contributed incalculably to rock and roll (see ROCK MUSIC; also BLUE NOTES).   GE.S.

BMR. Basal metabolic rate. The rate at which heat is produced by the body at rest, 12 to 14 hours after eating, measured in kilocalories per square metre of body surface per hour. Basal metabolism is the amount of energy required by an individual in the resting state, for such functions as breathing and circulation of the blood. See METABOLISM.   C.E.D.

body, history of, see under HISTORY OF THE BODY.

body art, see under CONCEPTUAL ART.

body image. According to Paul Schilder, whose work on the image of the body extended previous psychological and psychiatric work in this area into the domain of PSYCHOANALYSIS, the image of the body and the image of the world, together with a zone of indifference between them, are none of them natural or immediate, but the result of a process of construction dependent on the relations between the individual's perceptual experience, and his emotional and libidinal life (see LIBIDO). The body image is originally incomplete and fragmented, and is only given a definite form by persistent effort. New structure is added to the image by a drive to build up a total libidinous structure, always in conflict with a tendency to the cessation of effort leading to the dissolution of the image. Even objects separate from the body, such as semen, blood, breath, voice, and surrounding space, are seen as part of the body image. Erogenic zones play a central role in its construction, as do the complexes of dismemberment and body-unity, of castration, and the OEDIPUS COMPLEX. Schilder however believes that an emotional unity will be achieved when full OBJECT RELATIONS have been developed. This last claim is contested by Jacques Lacan, whose work on the MIRROR PHASE and the IMAGINARY developed these themes of the relation of body and image.   B.BU.

Bibl: P. Schilder, *The Image and Appearance of the Human Body* (New York, 1935); J. Lacan, *The Ego in Freud's Theory and the Technique of Psychoanalysis* (Cambridge, 1987).

body popping, see under POPULAR DANCE.

Bohr interpretation, see under COPENHAGEN INTERPRETATION.

Bohr theory. An explanation, devised in 1913 by the physicist Niels Bohr, of the radiation emitted by atomic hydrogen. The theory is based on NEWTONIAN MECHANICS, with the addition of simple rules which appeared arbitrary at first but which were later explained by the more fundamental QUANTUM MECHANICS. See also ATOMIC PHYSICS; ENERGY LEVEL; SPECTROSCOPY.   M.V.B.

Bolshevism. The term Bolshevism refers to a political tendency founded by LENIN. It originated at the second congress of the Russian Social Democratic Labour Party where delegates divided into two factions on the question of conditions for party membership. Lenin and his supporters favoured a membership strictly confined to committed activists whereas Martov and his supporters wanted a looser definition which could incorporate TRADE UNIONS. When the party split on this issue Lenin and his followers took the name Bolshevik from the Russian word meaning 'majority' in contrast to the MENSHEVIKS or 'minoritarians'. The name Bolshevik was not used in the party title until April 1917; it ceased to be employed in 1925 when the name was changed to the All-Union COMMUNIST Party (Bolsheviks) and finally in 1952 to the Communist Party of the Soviet Union.

The central principle of Bolshevism is that, in its struggle against oppressive ruling groups, the WORKING CLASS needs to be led by a disciplined party of full-time, committed revolutionaries. This 'vanguard' party would be able to take the initiative in revolutionary strategy and develop a revolutionary theory to which the working class could not attain if left to its own devices. The party's organizational basis is in DEMOCRATIC CENTRALISM whereby members participate in electing leaders and formulating policy but thereafter show absolute loyalty to policies and leadership.

The success of the Bolsheviks in 1917 led to the extension of their organizational principles to the international SOCIALIST movement and the abiding division between social democratic parties (see SOCIAL DEMOCRACY) and the newly founded Communist Parties which were organized on the Bolshevik model. With the ascendancy of STALINISM in the Soviet Union, Bolshevism became closely associated with his policies. As the international communist movement became more diverse, different forms of Bolshevism emerged such as TROTSKYISM and MAOISM. And more recently the suitability of Bolshevik principles in more LIBERAL western societies has been questioned by the Euro-communist tendency.   D.T.M.

Bibl: P. Corrigan *et al.*, *Socialist Construction and Marxist Theory: Bolshevism and its Critique* (London, 1978); F. Claudin, *The Communist Movement: From Comintern to Cominform* (London, 1975); A. Ulam, *Lenin and the Bolsheviks* (London, 1966).

bond, chemical. The forces which hold ATOMS together in a MOLECULE or solid. In some molecules, such as gaseous sodium chloride (or ionic solids), the bond arises mainly because of the electrostatic attraction between IONS of opposite charge. Bonds between atoms where the electrons are shared — covalent bonds (see CO-VALENCY) — are much more difficult to explain, and the modern understanding of bonding in molecules such as hydrogen, water, and benzine represents the most important success for the application of QUANTUM MECHANICS in CHEMISTRY. There are two main theoretical MODELS: the VALENCE bond model which considers interaction between individual atoms, and the now more widely used molecular orbital treatment in which the NUCLEI (or charged atomic cores) form a framework of the molecule, which is enveloped by ELECTRONS in discrete ORBITALS of definite ENERGY. Both theoretical models show how electron density builds up nuclei in the formation of a bond. The orbital picture of a molecule is conceptually attractive but it is still an approximation and, except for very simple molecules, directly calculated energies are not very accurate.   B.F.

boogie-woogie. A style of JAZZ piano characterized by infectious rolling bass patterns, energetically repeated (it was also sometimes known as 'eight-beat'). It evolved from the work of primitive BLUES pianists in the American south and was officially named in Pine Top Smith's 1928 recording, 'Pine Top's Boogie-woogie'. Generally, it retained its blues connections, particularly in the work of its most noted practitioners, Meade Lux Lewis, Albert Ammons and Pete Johnson, who became stars when the genre became a national craze in the late 30s. Though its limitations were obvious, its happy sim-plicity made it appealing, and all over America teenagers hammered out boogie-woogie versions of everything from 'Flight of the Bumblebee' to 'Jingle Bells'.   GE.S.

book, history of, see under HISTORY OF THE BOOK.

Boolean algebra. A method, named after its discoverer George Boole (1815-64), of solving problems in the PROPOSITIONAL CALCULUS and in the LOGIC of *classes* by symbolic manipulations based on certain fundamental operations. For propositions these operations are disjunction, conjunction, and negation; for classes, union, intersection, and complement (see SET). In each case the operations are considered as analogues of addition, multiplication, and subtraction and, like them, satisfy various laws; see, e.g., ASSOCIATIVE LAW; COMMUTATIVE LAW. Another application of Boole's ideas is to the design of switching circuits, in particular as used in COMPUTERS (see GATE). An abstract Boolean algebra is a MATHEMATICAL STRUCTURE satisfying the above-mentioned laws (see AXIOMATIC METHOD).   R.G.

Bibl: H.G. Flegg, *Boolean Algebra and its Application* (London and New York, 1964).

born again. It is reported on the basis of public opinion polls that about a third of the citizens of the US say that they have been 'born again'. The term became most popular in the 1970s during the Presidency of Jimmy Carter, who was one such. It means that a person has made a definite, adult decision to be a Christian, experiencing the forgiveness of sins and release from their power. In the tradition of EVANGELICALISM this experience has often been called 'conversion' and has been seen as the decisive stage in a process which involves both 'justification' (the acquittal by God of the penitent sinner who relies on the merits of Christ the Saviour) and 'sanctification' (the much slower receipt of the holiness which is the 'fruit' of God the Holy Spirit in the Christian's life). Faith makes all this possible. It is therefore essential, although it must be 'worked out' in love. But particularly since the SECULARIZATION of a land which used to be nominally Christian means that Baptism as an infant cannot be relied on to be the real beginning of life as a Christian, other Christian traditions including Roman CATHOLICISM are increasingly stressing the need to be converted as an adult. This emphasis, with some use of the American phrase, is now found throughout worldwide Christianity. D.L.E.

Bibl: M.A. Noll *et al.*, *Christianity in America* (Grand Rapids and London, 1983); J.I. Parker *et al.*, *Here We Stand: Justification by Faith Today* (London, 1986).

Borough Group. A group of artists which was formally constituted in January 1948 at the Borough Polytechnic, London. Its leader and prime influence was David Bomberg; there were nine other founder-members. This association broke up in 1950, to be replaced in 1953 by the 'Borough Bottega'. Their painting was broadly figurative, and sought emotional effect through the use of heavy *impasto* (i.e. paint so heavily applied as to stand out in lumps). P.C.

Bibl: W. Lipke, *David Bomberg* (London, 1967; New York, 1968).

Bose-Einstein statistics. The QUANTUM STATISTICS that applies to PARTICLES for which the QUANTUM NUMBER describing SPIN is an integer. M.V.B.

bosons, see under QUANTUM STATISTICS.

botany. The scientific study of plants. The science was founded by Theophrastus, Aristotle's student, and continues to thrive, although it is often disguised under the more modern-sounding term 'the plant sciences'. Botany consists of all the methods and ideas of BIOLOGY in their application to plants. Botanists seek to understand the structure, physiological functioning, embryological development, EVOLUTION, and classification (BIOSYSTEMATICS) of plants. The subject matter of botany is made up of the approximately 280,000 living species of plants that have been described so far, together with the yet-to-be-described forms. The described species are formally classified into 10 main divisions; but are conveniently grouped into more inclusive, though probably not evolutionary (see CLADISM)

groups. Thus, a grand division separates plants into non-vascular (liverworts and mosses) and vascular forms (all the rest). Vascular plants in turn divide into the seedless (ferns) and those with seeds. Gymnosperms and angiosperms (flowering plants) are the main modern groups of seed-producers. Angiosperms are far the largest group of plants; about 235,000 species have been described. Plants are economically important in horticulture and agriculture. *Applied botanists* contribute here both by studying the factors that control the germination, growth, and form of plants and by breeding improved varieties for cultivation. Botanical discoveries in this way recurrently alter the course of human history in the direction of PROGRESS. M.R.

Bibl: P.H. Raven *et al.*, *Biology of Plants* (New York, 4th ed., 1986).

boulevard comedy (*boulevard theatre,* etc.). Theatrical entertainment of a frankly commercial nature, appealing to middle-class or BOURGEOIS audiences without challenging social or artistic conventions. The term derives from the Parisian boulevards whose theatres dominated this form of entertainment in the 19th and early 20th centuries; 'Broadway' and 'Shaftesbury Avenue' carry similar CONNOTATIONS. For a contrasted type of theatre see FRINGE; OFF-BROADWAY; ALTERNATIVE THEATRE. M.A.

bound form, see under MORPHEME.

boundary, see under TOPOLOGY.

Bourbaki, Nicolas. The pseudonym of a gradually changing group of mathematicians centred in Paris which since 1939 has been producing an encyclopaedic work on the basic MATHEMATICAL STRUCTURES (so far some 20 volumes have appeared). The work has been very influential, both as a paradigm of the AXIOMATIC METHOD, and in its insistence that every important theorem has a correct context which may be different from that in which it was first discovered. R.G.

bourgeois. In the medieval period, a member of a free city or *bourg*, being neither a peasant nor a lord; in the 17th and 18th

95

centuries, the master or employer in relation to the journeyman or worker, or the merchant in relation to the artisan. Thus bourgeois became synonymous with the MIDDLE CLASS.

Since the 19th century, a contradictory and paradoxical set of judgements has been applied to the bourgeoisie. Economically and politically, the bourgeoisie was regarded as open, adventurous, and revolutionary; thus Marx, in the *Communist Manifesto*, writes: 'The bourgeoisie, historically, has played a most revolutionary part.... The bourgeoisie cannot exist without constantly revolutionizing the instruments of production.... and with them the whole relations of society.' The political revolutions effected by the bourgeoisie, particularly the French Revolution, ended privileges based on birth, and stressed individualism and achievement as the criteria of place and position in society. Culturally, however, the bourgeoisie has been regarded, from Molière to Balzac, as mean, avaricious, tasteless, REACTIONARY, and rapacious, having no sense of values other than the acquisition of money and objects.

The two attitudes derive from different historical perspectives. Most economic and political historians (e.g. Werner Sombart) have seen the bourgeois CLASS as tearing up the roots of traditional society and its fixed ways. Cultural historians and moralists, on the other hand, have tended to write from an aristocratic point of view and to decry the breakdown of standards when all culture becomes a commodity. (See ADMASS; MASS CULTURE.) In the late 19th and early 20th centuries a distinction was increasingly made between the *haute* or *grande* bourgeoisie, who had learned to use their wealth for purposes of refinement, and the PETITE (or petty) BOURGEOISIE who were regarded as meanspirited and niggardly. In recent usage, 'bourgeois' has become associated less with monetary acquisitiveness than with conventional attitudes to sexual conduct.
D.B.

Bibl: W. Sombart, tr. M. Epstein, *The Quintessence of Capitalism* (London and New York, 1915); C. Morazé, tr. P. Wait and B. Ferryan, *The Triumph of the Middle Classes* (London and Cleveland,

1966); E.J. Hobsbawm, *The Age of Capital* (London, 1977).

bourgeois hegemony, see under HEGE-MONY.

Bradleyan.
(1) In Shakespearean criticism, adjective used to characterize A.C. Bradley's 'Romantic' tendency (in *Shakespearean Tragedy*, 1904) to treat Shakespeare's characters as if they were real people in real life, thus ignoring stage conventions. The best Shakespearean criticism of the 1930s was formed in reaction against Bradley, taking a cooler and more comprehensive view of the play's ingredients and of conditions in the Elizabethan theatre. Yet Bradley's 'closet' commentary, if sometimes lush, is centrally human and preferable to some later critics' RE-DUCTION of Shakespeare to symbol, MYTH, and pattern.
D.J.E.
Bibl: L.C. Knights, *How Many Children Had Lady Macbeth?* (Cambridge, 1933).
(2) In PHILOSOPHY, adjective applied to the ideas, style, etc. of the IDEALIST philosopher F.H. Bradley (1846-1924).
A.Q.
Bibl: R. Wollheim, *F. H. Bradley* (Harmondsworth, 1959).

brain death. Irreversible cessation of respiration due to irreparable brain damage, even though the heart may continue beating with the aid of a mechanical ventilator: widely considered as the criterion of death.
C.E.D.

brain stimulation. In NEUROPSYCHOLOGY, a technique of direct electrical stimulation of the brain for inducing certain states or responses. It was used initially at the end of the 19th century to evoke motor patterns of a reflex nature to illustrate the organization of the motor cortex. More recently, implanted ELECTRODES have been used on awake, intact animals to produce 'pleasure' (e.g. experiments by J. Olds), alertness (Donald Lindsley), various drive states (Juan Delgado). W.G. Penfield pioneered work on electric stimulation of the human brain, carried out during brain operations on patients under local anaesthetic, and showed that vivid

memories could be evoked by the method.
                                        J.S.B.
Bibl: W.G. Penfield, *The Excitable Cortex in Conscious Man* (Liverpool and Springfield, Mass., 1958).

brainstorming. An American experiment in group PROBLEM-SOLVING that attempts to elicit creative thinking and new ideas through intensive discussion. The atmosphere of these sessions is non-critical, and FREE ASSOCIATION and 'thinking aloud' are encouraged.   H.L.

brainwashing. A proselytizing and interrogation technique that aims at the systematic erosion and reversal of a person's habits or convictions, usually with political motive and by the use of prolonged stress.   H.L.

brand image. Every product, or service, has an image, whether by intention or by default. That image derives from understood, visible and appreciated intrinsic qualities, and the halo that is achieved through association, presentation and environment. The combination of intrinsic and extrinsic perceived values contrives to produce a GESTALT that, properly worked on, should be unique to any particular product or service.   T.S.

brave new world. Originally a phrase used by Shakespeare's Miranda in *The Tempest*: 'O brave new world/That has such people in't'. This is ironic, as some of the people she first sees are in fact scoundrels; but it also affirms her own purity of vision. Aldous Huxley's *Brave New World* (1932) tells of a future state where utopian ideals have turned into nightmare dehumanization; and the contemporary use of the phrase alludes to this rather than to Shakespeare.   M.S.-S.

break dancing, see under POPULAR DANCE.

Brechtian. Drama critics' term for anything recalling the work of the German poet, playwright, and theatrical director Bertolt Brecht, a leading proponent of ALIENATION (see especially last paragraph) and the EPIC THEATRE, and artistic director, 1949-56, of the BERLINER EN-SEMBLE. His main concern was with clear dialectical exposition, intelligible language, and the concentration of every theatrical means on putting over, with humour and elegance, a plebeian point of view, anarchic, cynical, revolutionary, or reflective. The term is, however, most commonly identified with grey colours, drab realistic costumes, brilliant lighting, slow episodic narration interrupted by projected scene titles, and the direct addressing of the audience by interpolated songs.   J.W.
Bibl: J. Willett, *Brecht in Context* (London and New York, 1984).

breeder reactor, see under NUCLEAR REACTOR.

Bretton Woods (New Hampshire, U.S.A.). In 1944, the scene of the final meetings between the Americans, British, and Canadians who set up the *International Monetary Fund* (I.M.F.) and the *International Bank for Reconstruction and Development* (popularly known as the *World Bank*). Those who wish to avoid distinguishing between the twin organizations tend to refer to them and their rules as the Bretton Woods system — though this expression is more often used of the I.M.F. only. Almost all non-Communist countries belonged to both organizations; of the COMMUNIST bloc, only Yugoslavia and Romania have been willing to supply the national economic and financial data which are a condition of I.M.F. membership; they are also the only Communist-bloc members of the World Bank.

The I.M.F.'s original purpose was to provide a basis of monetary and currency stability for post-war prosperity in the form of growing world trade and expanding national economies. Members were expected to declare fixed EXCHANGE RATES (see PARITY) which should only be changed in the event of 'fundamental disequilibrium', thus avoiding the pre-war evil of competitive DEVALUATIONS. To help countries deal with temporary BALANCE OF PAYMENTS problems without exchange-rate adjustment, the Fund was empowered to provide short- to medium-term credits to governments. Following the suspension on 15 August 1971 of the

97

dollar's convertibility into gold, the first devaluation of the dollar in December 1971, and subsequent moves to *floating rates* (see under DEVALUATION) by a number of major currencies, the I.M.F.'s role has been much diminished and the Bretton Woods system has ended. Since the early 1970s the I.M.F. has accepted at least the temporary need for flexible exchange rates. Through negotiations between governments and CENTRAL BANKS it has attempted to prevent the unstable fluctuations that have characterized the movements of certain exchange rates. The I.M.F. has lent to countries with severe balance of payments problems on the condition that they implement deflationary FISCAL POLICIES and MONETARY POLICIES to stabilize the growth in the money supply (see DEBT CRISIS, INTERNATIONAL LIQUIDITY).

The *World Bank* was created with European reconstruction in mind, but this role was overtaken by the MARSHALL PLAN, and it became, with its affiliates the International Finance Corporation (I.F.C.) and the International Development Association (I.D.A.), the world's leading international development-lending and aid agency. Voting is weighted by CAPITAL subscription, so that the Bank is effectively controlled by the rich countries. The Bank group acquires its funds mainly by borrowing, but also from its capital and governmental subscriptions to I.D.A. It lends both on near-commercial terms, and at near-zero interest rates to very poor countries.

R.H.; P.J.; I.M.D.L.; J. P.

Bibl: E.S. Mason and R.E. Asher, *The World Bank since Bretton Woods* (Washington, 1973); World Bank, *World Bank Development Report* (Washington, annual); B. Sodersten, *International Economics* (London, 1980).

Brezhnev doctrine. Term applied by Western commentators to the Soviet justification of their action in 1968 in suppressing the Czechoslovak government headed by Joseph Dubček (see PRAGUE) by armed intervention. This was seen in the West as constituting a new principle in the Soviet doctrine of international law. First propounded by Leonid Brezhnev, First Secretary of the Soviet COMMUNIST Party, in a speech to the Fifth Congress of the Polish Communist Party in Warsaw on 12 November 1968, this 'doctrine' asserted the right of the 'SOCIALIST community as a whole' (i.e. the Soviet Union and its allies) to intervene in the territory of any one of the members of the Socialist community whenever 'internal and external forces.... hostile to socialism try to turn the development' of that country 'towards the restoration of a CAPITALIST regime' and thus threaten 'socialism in that country and the Socialist community as a whole'. Western commentators have regarded this as limiting full SOVEREIGNTY as hitherto recognized by INTERNATIONAL LAW, as the 'doctrine' appears to give the unity of the socialist movement precedence over the sovereignty of individual STATES, a view rejected by Soviet commentators. The doctrine was applied for the first time to a country outside the socialist bloc in 1979 when AFGHANISTAN was invaded. Some also thought that it might be used to justify military intervention in Poland in 1980 to destroy SOLIDARITY, the independent TRADE UNION. D.C.W.;D.PR.

Bibl: R. Edmonds, *Soviet Foreign Policy: The Brezhnev Years* (Oxford, 1983).

bridewealth. A form of MARRIAGE payment. It involves the transmission of property at marriage from the groom's kin to the male kin of the bride. It symbolizes the movement in the opposite direction of rights over the reproductive powers of the bride. If the marriage is dissolved, payments usually have to be repaid and this acts as a pressure against divorce. The transferrence of reproductive rights to the husband's male kin through a bridewealth transaction may give rise to the institution of *levirate*. Levirate is the custom whereby a younger brother of the groom 'inherits' the wife and children of his older brother should he die. The amount of bridewealth paid at marriage varies between societies and it is linked to the extent of the rights transferred from the bride's kin to the groom's kin.

Bridewealth is made up of both perishable and non-perishable goods. Livestock, particularly cattle, is an important part of the payment. The bridewealth received may be used to acquire wives or additional wives (POLYGYNY) by the bride's male kin. Wealth in this way is kept in circulation and is part of a system of exchange.

Bridewealth is found largely in Africa and recent work by Goody (*Production and Reproduction*, 1976) has linked its existence with the general economic features of the continent. He has contrasted it with DOWRY, the form of marriage payment associated with Eurasian societies.

A.G.

Bibl: A. Kuper, *Wives For Cattle* (London, 1982); J.L. Comaroff (ed.), *The Meaning of Marriage Payments* (London, 1980).

brinkmanship. A term coined by Professor T.C. Schelling of Harvard (*The Strategy of Conflict*, 1963), and based on a remark of John Foster Dulles in January 1956 about the art of going 'to the brink' of WAR. 'Brinkmanship is thus the deliberate creation of a recognizable risk of war, a risk that one does not completely control. It is the tactic of deliberately letting the situation get out of hand, just because its being out of hand may be intolerable to the other party and force his accommodation.'

A.F.B.

British Commonwealth, see COMMON-WEALTH.

broker. In ANTHROPOLOGY, an intermediary who links different NETWORKS. A broker functions at the point where networks intersect. Boissevain draws a distinction between patrons (see PATRONAGE) and brokers. Patrons offer access to what has been called 'first order resources' (jobs, land, funds etc.) while brokers deal in second order resources, making strategic contacts between people. The resources of patrons are limited, those of brokers unlimited. Strategic gains resulting from the manipulation of relationships can be converted by brokers into first order resources. Brokerage has been developed as a concept by those using network theory to analyse social data from very different areas (see CLIENT). A.G.

Bibl: J. Boissevain, *Friends of Friends* (Oxford, 1974).

Brownian motion. The ceaseless irregular motion of dust PARTICLES which is ob-

served in liquids and gases (and is an example of a STOCHASTIC PROCESS). It provided the earliest evidence for the random heat motion of the underlying MOLECULES, which occurs on a much finer scale.

M.V.B.

Brücke, die ('the Bridge'). Group of young painters active in Dresden, 1905-11, and Berlin, 1911-13. Influenced by the FAUVES and Edvard Munch, they were led by Erich Heckel, E.L. Kirchner, and Karl Schmidt-Rottluff, and included at various times Max Pechstein, Emil Nolde, and Otto Müller. They formed the nucleus of EXPRESSIONISM in the visual arts, giving it its dominant character of modified CUBIST distortion and great graphic virtuosity, particularly in the woodcut medium.

J.W.

bruitisme. The art of noise, as propounded in a manifesto of 1913 by Luigi Russolo, one of FUTURISM'S two principal musicians, and featured by DADA. J.W.

Brussels Treaty. Signed on 17 March 1948 by representatives of Britain, France, Belgium, the Netherlands, and Luxembourg, the Brussels Treaty set up a military alliance to resist armed attack on Western Europe, with a military command under British generalship. The initial impetus was provided by the Soviet-supported ejection of the Beneš-Masaryk government in Czechoslovakia (February 1948; see PRAGUE), and the Brussels Treaty was a first step, taken on British initiative, towards the formation of NATO. In the crisis created by the failure of the French National Assembly to ratify the treaties setting up EDC the treaty was used to provide a means for the admission of West Germany to NATO. D.C.W.

brut, see under ART BRUT; CONCRETE.

brutalism. A movement in architecture that asserted the primacy of architectural elements — space, STRUCTURE, and materials displayed in their untrammelled form — against the visual enfeeblement of the modern movement which had occurred in the late 1940s. It inched mainstream modern from the abstract to the expressive.

Le Corbusier's Unité d'Habitation in Marseilles (1948-54), which turned the use of bare concrete patterned by its rough timber shuttering (see CONCRETE) into a virtuoso performance, showed the potentialities of the vivid expression of materials suggested by economic necessity. His later Maisons Jaoul at Neuilly (1956) extended the vocabulary and provided an idiom capable of imitation. The first building to be labelled 'new brutalist' was the school at Hunstanton, England, by Peter and Alison Smithson (1949). This had an exposed steel frame, unplastered brickwork, exposed floor beams and service runs, and was designed with an austerity derived from Mies van der Rohe.   M.BR.

Bibl: R. Banham, *The New Brutalism; Ethic or Aesthetic?* (London and New York, 1966).

bubble chamber. A device invented by Glaser in 1952 and used to study NUCLEAR REACTIONS and ELEMENTARY PARTICLES. It is based on the fact that fast charged particles leave a record of their paths, in the form of a trail of bubbles, centred on IONS, when they traverse a liquid kept just above its boiling-point. See also CLOUD CHAMBER.   M.V.B.

Bubnovy Valet, see KNAVE OF DIAMONDS.

Buddhism. The RELIGION, covering much of Asia, which venerates Gautama the Buddha (or 'Enlightened'), who taught in India during the 5th century B.C. Its goal is 'Nirvana' or liberation from 'becoming' things or selves; this has usually been conceived as liberation from an endless cycle of reincarnations or rebirths in different bodies. Its self-discipline is aimed at achieving detachment and an inward peace, and in the end ENLIGHTENMENT. It emphasizes compassion, but mainly in the sense of spreading such peace. It avoids the intellectualism of Christian THEOLOGY, and being a practical offer of enlightenment rather than a system of METAPHYSICS it can be regarded as compatible both with a scientific world view excluding belief in God and with a religious tradition. Indeed, disagreements have grown between the *Theravada* (Little Vehicle) in Ceylon, Burma, Thailand etc., and the *Mahayana* (Great Vehicle) in Japan, Korea, China, Tibet, and Nepal, which is more elaborately developed (and closer to Christianity, although very little influenced by it). The difference between these two types of Buddhism can amount, in Western terms, to the difference between AGNOSTICISM or PANTHEISM and a THEISM based on belief in divine 'grace' and therefore in the value of petitionary prayer. But the attractiveness of Buddhism to many onlookers in the 20th century springs from the hope that its methods of meditation may fill the void left both by materialism and by the Churches. ZEN is specially respected. There is also much interest in Buddhist art. Some Westerners have become Buddhists, but many more have admired, and even envied, Buddhism as a way of life. In traditionally Buddhist countries such as Sri Lanka, Thailand and Burma, everyday life is still profoundly influenced by the teaching and example of the monks. See also TANTRA.
          D.L.E.

Bibl: T.C. Humphreys, *Buddhism* (Harmondsworth, 1951); M. Spiro, *Buddhism and Society* (London and New York, 1980); N.W. Ross, *Buddhism: A Way of Life* (London and New York, 1981).

buffer. In CHEMISTRY, a solution capable of maintaining a nearly constant hydrogen ION concentration. Normally the *pH* (*q.v.*) of a solution is very sensitive to the addition of even small amounts of strong ACID or BASE. This sensitivity can be greatly diminished in the presence of a weak acid and its anion (see ION) in comparable amounts, because the anion accepts added hydrogen ions while hydroxyl ions combine with the hydrogen atoms of the weak acid. Physiological systems are often buffered, and in blood the serum protein (see SERUM; PROTEIN) which contains both acidic and basic groups acts as a buffering agent.   B.F.

buffer state. In political GEOGRAPHY, a small independent STATE lying between two or more larger and potentially hostile states and thus reducing the likelihood of border friction between them. Belgium might be thought to have served as a buffer state in respect of France and Germany.   P.H.

bugging. A slang word for the placing of concealed microphones for the purpose of listening to or recording secret or private discussions. Modern TECHNOLOGY has made it possible to use extremely small detectors, which can be stuck underneath a table, concealed in a vase of flowers, etc., and to pick up signals from them at a sufficient distance for the receiver to remain undetected. This technique has facilitated both political and industrial espionage, and, in the case of surveillance by the police or private detective agencies, has raised the issue of whether privacy is or is not a basic HUMAN RIGHT.   E.R.L.

bulimia nervosa. Excessive morbid appetite which can arise during the course of a slimming régime. The severe restriction of food becomes intolerable and the individual finds an outlet by gorging. The guilt arising from breaking the régime is assuaged by eating more; an attempt is made to avoid the consequential weight gain by inducing vomiting or taking laxatives. See also ANOREXIA NERVOSA.   A.E.B.

Bullock Report. Reports of two separate committees of inquiry set up by the British Government (the first by a Conservative, the second by a Labour government) under the chairmanship of the historian and former Vice-Chancellor of Oxford University, Alan (now Lord) Bullock.

The first, *A Language for Life*, published in 1975, was an inquiry into the teaching of reading and the other uses of English in English schools. Its 333 recommendations for improving these, although largely ignored by Government, have had a major impact on practice in the schools and on the education of teachers.

The second, *Industrial Democracy*, published in 1977, was an inquiry into the best means of achieving a radical extension of industrial democracy in the control of companies by means of employee representation on boards of directors, to the principle of which the Labour Government was committed. The report's recommendations, which proposed the appointment of employee representatives to the boards of all companies with more than 2000 workers, were rejected by the industrialist members of the committee as by management in general, and aroused widespread controversy. After 18 months' discussion, a cabinet committee set up by the Labour prime minister, James Callaghan, produced a modified version of the report's proposals, which were incorporated in the Labour Party's programme for the 1979 election. Labour's defeat, however, and the advent of Mrs Thatcher removed industrial democracy from the political agenda, although both the Labour Party and the SDP-Liberal Alliance are committed to introducing some form of worker PARTICIPATION if returned to power.   A.L.C.B.

Bibl: John Elliott, *Conflict or Cooperation? The Growth of Industrial Democracy* (London, 1978).

Bureau International de Surréalisme Révolutionnaire, see under COBRA.

bureaucracy. 'Power, influence of the heads and staff of government bureaux' (definition of *bureaucratie* in the Dictionary of the French Academy, 1789 supplement). The modern theory of bureaucracy derives largely from the German sociologist Max Weber, who saw it as the formal codification of the idea of rational organization. A bureaucracy is characterized by legal rules, a salaried administrative staff, the specialization of function, the authority of the (non-hereditary) office, not the person, and the keeping of written records and documents. For Weber, the rational bureaucracy was the major element in the rationalization of the modern world.

Yet, from the start, popular writers have seen bureaucracy as an irrational force, dominating the lives of people, while political theorists have seen it as an independent force tending to swallow all of society in its maw. Balzac popularized the word in his 1836 novel, *Les Employés*, calling bureaucracy 'the giant power wielded by pigmies.... a government as fussy and meddlesome.... as a small shopkeeper's wife'. Dickens, in *Little Dorrit* (1857), summarized 'the Whole Science of Government' in his representation of the bureaucracy as 'the Circumlocution Office'. John Stuart Mill, in *On Liberty* (1859) and *Considerations on Representative Government* (1861) contrasted bureaucracy with DEMOCRACY and saw the

101

former as a threat to representative government and to liberty. And Gaetano Mosca, in *The Ruling Class* (English edition, 1939), described the modern state as essentially a bureaucratic state ruled, inevitably, by a minority.

In contemporary theory, interest in bureaucracy focuses on two aspects. Sociological theorists tend to see bureaucracy as one modal type of organization, wherein the formal dimensions of rule and administration are paramount. Political writers have concentrated on the question whether the bureaucracy, in modern society, becomes a 'new CLASS' which takes over political rule — as, according to Milovan Djilas, has happened in the U.S.S.R. Indeed, though Marx paid little attention to this aspect of the question, it has been the central issue regarding the characterization of Soviet society. Thus Trotsky regarded bureaucracy as indicating the betrayal of the REVOLUTIONARY ideals by a new class; while SOCIALIST writers have characterized the U.S.S.R. as a new form of 'bureaucratic COLLECTIVISM'.   D.B.

Bibl: M. Weber, *Economy and Society* (New York, 1968), vol. 3; M. Albrow, *Bureaucracy* (London and New York, 1970); W.J. Mommsen, *The Age of Bureaucracy* (Oxford, 1974).

Burnham Committees. A series of committees founded in 1919 under the chairmanship of Lord Burnham. Their task was to negotiate and agree salary scales for teachers in English primary and secondary schools and in further education and recommend them to the Secretary for Education and Science. In 1986 the then Secretary for Education, Mr Kenneth Baker, started putting the final touches to a plan, already mooted by his predecessor, Sir Keith Joseph, to scrap Burnham which, ever since the late 1960s, had become cumbersome, powerless and argumentative. Secretaries of state began to play an increasingly interventionist role in the negotiations which had previously always been settled by local authority leaders on the one side of the table and teacher union leaders on the other, all under an independent chairman. But the Department of Education and Science, which had two representatives on the committee ever since their presence was made possible under the Remuneration of Teachers Act 1965, wielded a total of 15 votes — enough to veto committee recommendations. In recent years, almost every pay deal has had to go to arbitration.   J.I.

business cycle, see under TRADE CYCLE.

business game. A MANAGEMENT training exercise or game in which teams take on the roles of managing firms which are competing against each other. The real business world is simulated by the teams making management decisions across a number of periods. A MODEL, which is usually programmed on a COMPUTER, is used to work out the consequences of the decisions of the teams. These consequences become part of the information used by teams to make decisions in the following periods of the game. At the end of the game the performance of each team can be assessed and criticized, and a winner can be declared.   R.I.T.; J.P.

business roundtable. An elite INTEREST GROUP formed in the U.S. in November 1972, essentially devoted to curtailing the influence and bargaining power of labour unions. It was enlarged in membership and scope in June 1973, and grew quickly to consist of about 130 chief executive officers of major corporations. The Roundtable may be seen as an organized response to the series of defeats inflicted on big business by environmental, consumer and PUBLIC-INTEREST groups from the late 1960s onwards, and to the more general distrust of corporations amplified by political finance scandals and WATERGATE. The organization attempts to forge some consensus on political issues between different individual and sectoral business interests; to gain high-level access to government; and to encourage members' corporations towards greater political awareness and activity. Its tactics include the orchestration of co-operative campaigns with bodies such as the National Association of Manufacturers and the national Chamber of Commerce, the funding of pro-business think-tanks, and the use of the political 'clout' of its individual members. The influence of the Roundtable is hard to estimate precisely. Observers credit it with a major role in the defeat of liberal (see LIBERALISM) consumer-protection and full-employment legislation, in the attack on unionism since 1974 and in promoting the increasing sophistication of other business lobbying efforts.

S.R.

Bibl: T. Edsall, *The New Politics of Inequality* (New York and London, 1984); M. Useem, *The Inner Circle* (Oxford and New York, 1984).

busing. American term for the transfer by bus of children from their own neighbourhood to school in another. The practice evolved in the attempt in the late 1960s to achieve the DESEGREGATION of schools required, but seldom accomplished, since a major Supreme Court decision in 1954. Busing provoked some vigorous white resistance and slow compliance, and was complicated by successive judicial decisions and changes of government. It nevertheless gained momentum until the late 1970s, after which the Reagan administration brought a substantial reversal of government sympathy for mandatory busing. Debate over the merits of maintaining and extending busing continue. Proponents argue that it improves BLACK educational performance and promotes interracial harmony, thus helping progress from desegregation to INTEGRATION. Conservative critics argue that it does neither to any significant extent, while destroying the valued character of neighbourhood schools. Radical critiques claim that its effects are negligible compared to the deleterious consequences of residential segregation and economic inequality, and are sometimes counterproductive as wealthier white parents react by sending children to private schools.

S.R.

Bibl: A. Yarmolinsky *et al.*, *Race and Schooling in the City* (Cambridge, Mass., 1981).

buto dance. Term originated from the Japanese *ankokubuto* meaning dark soul dance. Buto-Buto-Butôh is a Japanese modern dance movement which developed in the 1950s and 1960s under the leadership of Tatsumi Hijikata (1928-1986) and Kazuo Ohno (1906-). Buto is not a formal technique or academic style but an individual form of expressive movement (or 'fighting form' — Hijikata), appropriate to post-war AVANT-GARDE Japanese theatre. It finds its roots from within Japanese tradition and uses a recognizable restraint to create a paradoxically surrealistic approach to DANCE THEATRE. The Buto dancer wears the white face and body paint traditional to Japanese culture in direct contrast to the physical form of the dance. Today more than 30 Buto companies exist in Japan.

L.A.

Bibl: A. Paszkowska, *Buto-Tanz* (Mosel, nd.).

Butskellism, see under CONSENSUS POLITICS.

BWR. Boiling-water reactor. A NUCLEAR REACTOR using water as coolant and moderator, steam being produced in the reactor itself: enriched uranium oxide cased in zirconium is the fuel.

C.E.D.

byte. A unit of 8 BITS of information. It is capable of representing, for example, an integer between 0 and 255, or an ASCII character.

J.E.S.

C

CACM, see under CENTRAL AMERICAN COMMON MARKET.

cacogenic, see under DYSGENIC.

CAD, see COMPUTER-AIDED DESIGN.

Cahiers du Cinéma, see under NEW WAVE.

calcification. In GEOLOGY, the replacement of organic or inorganic material in rocks by the calcium minerals calcite and dolomite. Grains of quartz in a sandstone can be completely replaced by calcite. Fossil plant debris can be preserved by the complete calcification of the plant tissue so that the original cellular structure is retained in a hard fossil plant. Calcification in the latter example must certainly have occurred soon after deposition.
J.L.M.L.

calculus. Any system of rules for symbolic manipulations, as in LOGICAL CALCULUS and its subdivisions PREDICATE CALCULUS and PROPOSITIONAL CALCULUS. But usually, unless qualified, the term refers to the *infinitesimal calculus.* This comprises the *differential calculus,* which is concerned with calculating the DERIVATIVES (rates of change) of FUNCTIONS, and the *integral calculus,* which is concerned with INTEGRATION. The *fundamental theorem of the calculus* asserts that these are inverse operations. Calculus is concerned with the necessary manipulative rules and their application to more or less specific instances. The general theory of the processes and the investigation of the exact conditions under which the rules may be correctly applied are dignified by the title of (mathematical) ANALYSIS. For the *calculus of finite differences* see NUMERICAL ANALYSIS.
R.G.

Bibl: L. Hogben, *Mathematics for the Million* (London, 4th ed., 1967; New York, 1968).

calculus of finite differences, see under NUMERICAL ANALYSIS.

calligramme. A poem written and printed, in a specific shape. The modern revival of this age-old device was pioneered under the influence of CUBISM by Guillaume Apollinaire, a volume of whose *Calligrammes* appeared in 1918. In their simplest and most light-hearted form these consist of words describing rain, or a motor-car. At their most difficult they seek, as a critic explained, to oblige the reader to understand 'syntheticoideologically' instead of 'analyticodiscursively'. They push experimentation as far as Apollinaire ever pushed it, and influenced CONCRETE POETRY.
M.S.-S.

calorie. A unit of heat. One calorie will raise the temperature of one gram of water by one degree centigrade. In terms of ENERGY, $857,000$ calories $= 1$ kilowatthour. For nutritional and dietary purposes the 'large calorie' (also written kcalorie or Calorie), equal to $1,000$ ordinary calories, is the unit commonly employed to quantify energy intake.
M.V.B.

Calvinism. The Christian tradition founded by John Calvin (1509-64) in Geneva, and flourishing specially in Scotland and in New England. It has developed PROTESTANTISM by rejecting every doctrine not found in the Bible, and by finding in the Bible its own doctrines, notably the 'predestination' by God of the 'elect' to heaven and of the rest to hell. The tradition is still creative theologically (see BARTHIAN). A strict and sometimes intolerant morality is associated (see PROTESTANT ETHIC), as is the PRESBYTERIAN form of church government.
D.L.E.

Bibl: J.T. McNeill, *The History and Character of Calvinism* (London and New York, 1967).

Camden Town Group. A society of artists founded in 1911; in 1913 it merged with the LONDON GROUP. Of the sixteen members those who may best be described as 'Camden Town' (a district of north London) were: Spencer Gore (President), Harold Gilman, Robert Bevan, Malcolm Drummond, and William Ratcliffe, painters who were deeply affected by the opposing influences of Walter Sickert and the POST-IMPRESSIONISTS. Q.B.

Camp David. A U.S. presidential conference centre which permits more informal international negotiation than is readily possible in Washington, giving rise to the 'Camp David spirit' as a sense of DÉTENTE. In Middle East politics Camp David has an added significance since it was the site of negotiations between President Carter, President Sadat and Prime Minister Begin leading to an Egyptian-Israeli treaty together with agreements for the autonomy of the occupied west bank which have not been implemented. Camp David has in consequence been anathematized by other Arabs as a separate peace made by Egypt sacrificing the Palestinians and (among other things) making possible the 1982 Israeli invasion of LEBANON. Correspondingly Camp David has been taken by Begin and his successor Shamir as the only appropriate model for any subsequent peace process. (See also MIDDLE EAST WARS.) W.K.

Campaign for Nuclear Disarmament, see under PEACE MOVEMENT.

cancer. A new growth in any TISSUE or organ that behaves as if it had escaped the surveillance of the growth-controlling processes that operate in the other tissues of the body. Cancers are described as more or less malignant in proportion as they are more or less rapidly growing and invasive. Cancer CELLS may escape from their site of origin and set up daughter colonies (*metastases*) in normal tissues elsewhere. Cancers are crudely subdivided into tumours of epithelial tissues (*carcinomas*) and tumours of cells belonging to the connective tissue and bony families (*sarcomas*).

Some industrial chemicals and food additives are known to be cancer-producing (*oncogenic*). Public-health authorities are acutely aware of these dangers, and the use of such chemicals is under very close surveillance. Many causes of cancer are known — e.g. the polycyclic hydrocarbons that are the active ingredients of coal tar, or viruses (see VIROLOGY) such as the Rous virus in chicks, polyoma virus. Although there is a strong and growing pre-

sumption that viruses are a cause of human cancers, particularly some of those of the cervix and liver, it is only in the case of the rare blood cancer, adult T-cell leukaemia, that the evidence of a viral cause is compelling.

The branch of medical science concerned with cancer is known as ONCOLOGY. Cancer research is devoted to the earliest possible diagnosis of malignant changes, to analysing ever more deeply the properties of the malignant cell itself and to the clinical trial of the theoretically or empirically justifiable curative procedures, notably the use of *antiproliferative* drugs (drugs that suppress cell division, e.g. nitrogen mustards) in the leukaemias, the use of x-irradiation, and, wherever possible, the intensification of the immunological response (see IMMUNITY) which represents the body's natural defence. In addition, hormone-dependent tumours may sometimes be controlled by the artificial administration or deprivation of hormones (see ENDOCRINOLOGY). SURGERY and x-irradiation nevertheless remain the bulwarks of cancer treatment throughout the world.

Analysis of malignant cells has revealed many differences between them and healthy cells but it continues to be difficult to gauge which of the differences are the cause and which the result of malignancy. A current focus of attention is ONCOGENES, GENES which in their normal form are essential for the normal controlled growth of cells but which, if mutated, may result in the uncontrolled growth that is characteristic of malignant cells. There is, however, still no evidence that oncogenes contribute to the cause of the most frequent types of human cancer. P.M.;P.N.

canned music, see under MUZAK.

cantilever. A structural device possible with materials strong both in tension and compression which produces horizontal extensions unsupported on their forward edge. When used in either steel or reinforced concrete STRUCTURES, the cantilever has been able to suggest a series of floating planes with only non-structural, usually glass, infill between them. It was greatly used and praised by Frank Lloyd Wright, and the characteristic view of

Falling Water, the house at Bear Run, Pennsylvania (1936), is largely due to its employment. So is the corner view of the Fagus factory (Gropius and Hannes Meyer, 1910), which created the much-imitated corner glazed window apparently dissolving the solidity of the building enclosure.   M.BR.

CAP, see under COMMON AGRICULTURAL POLICY.

capital. (1) Those assets that are used in the production of goods and services. The assets may belong to producers (e.g. factories and machines), consumers (e.g. houses) or the community (e.g. public buildings and roads). *Capital goods* are those goods used to produce other goods and services. *Working capital* is the MONEY used by a business to conduct its transactions. *Human capital* is the ability, skill and knowledge of individuals which is used to produce goods and services. Capital may be valued at its historic cost, i.e. the past expenditure to purchase it, or at its current cost, which will reflect the DISCOUNTED value of the income it is expected to yield. For most purposes, the latter valuation has the most economic meaning. Capital's ability to produce goods and services declines with age and, in valuing capital, it is important and usual to allow for this depreciation.

(2) The capital of a person, firm, institution, etc. is the money value of real and financial assets. This usage of the term emphasizes the money value of assets rather than their ability to produce goods and services, though the former is usually related to the latter.   J.P.

Bibl: D. Begg *et al., Economics* (London, 1984).

capitalism. In MARXIST usage, a word denoting a historical stage and implying a VALUE-JUDGEMENT. As historical description, Marxists mean by capitalism that set of arrangements in which one CLASS, the capitalists or BOURGEOISIE, owns the factories and other tools of production, while a second class, the workers or PROLETARIANS, possesses only its labour power — its capacity to work. As value-judgement, they mean a set of transitional arrangements (terminating in SOCIALISM) which allows capitalists to exploit workers.

Non-Marxist economists define capitalism in terms of resource use and control, without necessarily explicitly referring to EXPLOITATION. Most generally a capitalist society is one in which most of the instruments of production as well as objects of consumption are privately controlled. Sale occurs for profit in markets (see MARKET ECONOMY), which, while variously organized, are free in the sense that, subject to the constraints of law, entrepreneurs are at liberty to enter or depart, to expand or contract, and purchasers to buy or not to buy. Moreover, the profits from these transactions are the rewards to ENTREPRENEURSHIP and are the property of the owners of the enterprise. As an IDEOLOGY, capitalism contains a doctrine of social justice, an implicit assertion that inequalities of income and wealth measure, however roughly, the economic contributions of the men and women who embark their energies and resources in the productive process.

Capitalism is an exceedingly broad and somewhat vague term, covering societies as variously organized as Sweden, France, Japan, Britain, and the U.S.A., in each of which the mixture of public and private enterprise, the legal rules governing the pursuit of profit, the approved market structure, the permitted accumulation of income and wealth, differs significantly from all the others. Broadly speaking, capitalist societies are distinguished from socialist ones by the ideological preference of the former for private property and of the latter for communal ownership. Even though in practice all advanced societies have found it necessary to accept a substantial degree of STATE intervention, socialist societies celebrate, and capitalist ones deplore, the exigencies which have enlarged the role of the State.   R.L.

Bibl: J.A. Schumpeter, *Capitalism, Socialism and Democracy* (New York, 3rd ed., 1962; London, 4th ed., 1965); J.K. Galbraith, *The New Industrial State* (London and New York, 1968).

capitalist state, the. A concept within contemporary MARXISM that attempts to come to terms with the evident fact of the massive presence of the STATE within 20th-century CAPITALISM. It is meant to suggest a new form of state, replacing the limited 'nightwatchman state' of 19th-century capitalism. In the era of 'managed' or 'monopoly' capitalism, the state is seen as increasingly necessary to the preservation of the capitalist system through the public provision of a complex economic INFRA-STRUCTURE — transport and communications, subsidies and market regulation, cheap and guaranteed supplies of energy and power — as well as a SOCIAL WELFARE system that stabilizes the social order and absorbs costs — e.g. of education and training — that would otherwise have to be borne by private capitalists.

K.K.

Bibl: B. Jessop, *The Capitalist State* (London, 1982).

capitation allowance. Also known as the per capita allowance, or literally the 'per head' allowance given on an annual basis by local education authorities in Britain to schools for the purchase of text books, equipment and other materials. The amount is calculated on the basis of school size and pupil ages. A primary school receives less per capita than a secondary and a sixth form receives most, since it is felt that these pupils require more specialist equipment and advanced books. Not all local authorities spend the same amounts and a number are more generous than others.

J.I.

capitulationism, see under DEVIATION-ISM.

capture theory, see under ECONOMIC REGULATION.

carbohydrates. Compounds of carbon, hydrogen and oxygen found in plants which form the major part of the human DIET. Available carbohydrates, that is those that are utilized in the body as a source of energy, include sugars and starches; unavailable carbohydrates which cannot be digested but serve as bulk or roughage include cellulose, hemi-cellulose, pectins and plant gums. These, together with lignin, are collectively termed *dietary fibre*.

A.E.B.

Bibl: R. Passmore and M.A. Eastwood, *Human Nutrition and Dietetics* (London, 1986).

carbon cycle. In PHYSICS (for its meaning in BIOLOGY see under LIFE CYCLE), a sequence of NUCLEAR REACTIONS thought to occur inside stars, in which a mass of hydrogen NUCLEI at extremely high temperatures is converted into a smaller mass of helium nuclei in the presence of carbon nuclei; the resulting energy leaves the star as RADIATION which is observed by us as starlight or sunshine. See also BINDING ENERGY; MASS-ENERGY EQUATION. M.V.B.

carbon dating, see RADIOCARBON DATING.

carbon fibre. Immensely strong threads of pure graphite which may be incorporated into other materials (e.g. metals) to reinforce their strength. M.V.B.

carcinogen (a preferable if less familiar term is *oncogen*). A substance or procedure that causes the formation of a tumour (see CANCER). Oncogenic substances and treatments include coal tar derivatives, ionizing RADIATIONS and some viruses (see VIROLOGY) or virus-like particles. P.M.

carcinomas, see under CANCER.

cardiac catheterization. An invasive technique whereby hollow catheters are inserted into a peripheral vein and/or artery, most commonly in the leg (at the groin), or arm (at the elbow). The catheters are connected to a fluid filled pressure monitoring system and can be advanced into the right side of the heart from the peripheral vein and into the pulmonary artery and peripheral lung vasculature or advanced into the left side of the heart from a peripheral artery and into the left ventricle. It is possible to outline the cavities of the heart and major vessels on cineradiographic recording equipment; concentrations of oxygen saturation in the blood can be taken to look for shunting of blood from high (arterial) to low (venous) systems. It is usually combined with CORONARY ARTERIOGRAPHY. L.J.F.

cardinal (number). This measures the size of a SET and applies to both finite and INFINITE sets. Two sets are *similar*, or *equinumerous*, if it is possible to pair off each member of either set with exactly one member of the other set. This gives an EQUIVALENCE RELATION between sets; the cardinal of a set is defined as the corresponding abstract concept. The smallest infinite cardinal is the cardinal of the set {0, 1, 2,....} and is called *aleph zero*. It is smaller than the cardinal of the CONTINUUM. Infinite cardinals are not now usually counted as NUMBERS. R.G.

cardiology. The study of diseases of the heart and circulation. This includes congenital heart disease, valvular heart disease, ischaemic heart disease (angina pectoris and myocardial infarction), cardiomyopathies, hypertension, arrhythmias and cardiopulmonary disease. L.J.F.
Bibl: E.N. Silber and L.N. Katz, *Heart Disease* (New York, 1975).

cardiomyopathy. A group of conditions, frequently of unknown aetiology, in which the unifying features are enlargement of the heart (cardiomegaly) and cardiac failure; excluded from this is myocardial dysfunction due to valvular, coronary artery or systemic/pulmonary vascular disease. There are three main clinical patterns. 'Dilated' is the commonest form and the main problem is a decreased contractile force of the ventricles. 'Hypertrophic' is a massive enlargement of the heart muscle of the left ventricle. 'Restrictive' means rigid heart muscle which makes filling of the heart with blood very difficult. L.J.F.

cargo cults. A variety of MILLENARIANISM found in New Guinea. Its adherents believe that the valued material goods of Western civilization (the 'cargo') are about to be delivered by miraculous means, arriving with the spirits of the dead and ushering in the millennium. The cargo is clearly symbolic of a desired change in the social position of those who await it, and the cults are concerned with POWER and STATUS, not merely with the magical acquisition of material things. The term has also been applied more loosely to a number of anti-Western nativistic movements in the Melanesian region. M.F.

Bibl: M. Kilani, *Les cultes de cargo mélanésiens* (Editions d'en bas, Switzerland, 1984); I. C. Jarvis, *Rationality and Relativism* (London, 1984).

Caribbean Basin Initiative (CBI). A U.S. foreign policy package directed towards securing development of the Caribbean (including Central America) along the lines of constitutional democracy and free enterprise. It encompasses both an aid and investment programme and a series of trade concessions, intended to facilitate access for Caribbean products to the U.S. market. Originally launched in 1981, the CBI had a difficult passage through Congress at a time of high U.S. unemployment and the necessary legislation — burdened by congressional amendments which drastically reduced the impact of the free trade facilities initially offered — was not signed until August 1983. Cuba, NICARAGUA and revolutionary Grenada (1979-1983) were excluded. The allocation of a large proportion of the funds to Jamaica (which Washington hopes can be a MODEL for the region), together with the making of disclosure of tax and banking details to the U.S. a condition of investment, has resulted in some disillusionment among Caribbean nations. N.M.

carnivalization. Term coined by the Russian critic Mikhail Bakhtin (see BAKHTINIAN) to describe the penetration of carnival into everyday life and language and into literature. Sociologists and anthropologists of the Durkheimian school suggest that the function of rituals of reversal (in which what is normally low becomes high and what is normally forbidden, compulsory) is to act as a 'safety-valve' for the release of tension and thus to maintain the social and political structure. Bakhtin, in contrast, saw the medieval 'culture of folk humour' and carnival in particular as profoundly subversive of official institutions and hierarchies, and he suggested that Rabelais, Dostoevsky and other writers drew on the grotesque bodily imagery of carnival for this purpose. P.B.
Bibl: M. Bakhtin, *Rabelais and his World* (Moscow, 1965; Cambridge, Mass., 1968); D. La Capra, 'Bakhtin, Marx and the Carnivalesque' in his *Rethinking Intel-*

lectual History (Ithaca, N.Y., and London, 1983).

Carnot cycle. In THERMODYNAMICS, a particular sequence of operations involving the transfer of ENERGY to and from a system. At the end of the cycle the system has returned to its original state. The Carnot cycle is of theoretical importance, since no other cycle can convert heat into work more efficiently. Petrol and diesel engines employ cycles closely related to Carnot's. M.V.B.

cartel. A union of sellers of a good or service who raise the price (or other conditions of sale), and the rewards to its own members, to a higher level than would prevail in a FREE MARKET. In order to control the price, a cartel needs to restrict output and this is usually done by agreeing on quotas for each member's production. If output is not restricted, a fixed price would provide an incentive to existing sellers to sell more output. This would lower the price, reduce the rewards to the members and, perhaps, completely undermine the cartel. Similarly, the interests of the members of a cartel are affected adversely by the entry of new sellers. Thus, cartels are interested in erecting BARRIERS TO ENTRY. Cartels are most easily formed and durable when there are only a few members with similar interests. They are usually regarded as undesirable, because COMPETITION is reduced and there are no offsetting gains. By comparison, MONOPOLIES may be justified by the existence of ECONOMIES OF SCALE. Cartels may actually be formed with the intention of saving the weaker members from destruction (cartels flourished in the Great Depression of the 1930s). Most governments have made cartels and most of their activities illegal. The most important modern cartel is OPEC. S.BR.; J.P.

Bibl: D. Begg *et al.*, *Economics* (London, 1984).

Cartel. An informal but influential alliance of the four leading independent Paris theatre directors between 1926 and World War II; known for its fresh approach to the classics, its support of such moderns as Pirandello, Chekhov, and Giraudoux, and its dislike of NATIONAL-

ISM and commercialism. It was formed to carry on the ideas of Jacques Copeau, director of the Vieux-Colombier 1913-24, and consisted of Charles Dullin (Théâtre de l'Atelier), Louis Jouvet (Comédie des Champs-Elysées, later the Athénée), Gaston Baty (Chimère and Théâtre de Montparnasse), and Georges Pitoeff (no fixed theatre). J.W.

Carter doctrine. This was developed by President Carter in January 1980 in response to the Soviet Union's invasion of AFGHANISTAN, which began in late December 1979. Its main element was an indication that the U.S. would contemplate a military response if the Soviet Union threatened the oil-fields of the Persian Gulf, and it was followed by promises of aid to Afghan resistance. More generally, it represented a shift in policy towards the Soviet Union which included Carter's withdrawal of the SALT 2 Treaty from Congress, embargoes on the export to the U.S.S.R. of American grain and sophisticated electronic equipment, U.S. withdrawal from the 1980 Moscow Olympics, and increases in the defence budget. S.R.

Bibl: R. Barnet, *Real Security* (New York, 1981).

Cartesian coordinates, see under COORDINATE.

cartography. The science and art of map-making, as distinguished from the collection of material to be mapped (e.g. through survey or census-taking). The relationship of the map to the earth's surface through scale reduction was originally developed in ancient Greece though the earliest maps date back over 4,000 years. Cartography in the modern period has been strongly influenced by evolving methods of information collection (e.g. through AIR PHOTOGRAPHY and SATELLITE sensors), by changed data processing methods (e.g. COMPUTER analysis; and see DATA ANALYSIS), and by developments in the printing and reproduction of maps. P.H.

Bibl: A.H. Robinson *et al.*, *Elements of Cartography* (New York, 1984).

cascade diffusion, see under DIFFUSION.

case grammar. An approach to linguistic analysis which sees the basic structure of sentences as consisting of a verb plus one or more noun phrases, which relate to it in defined ways. The syntactic MEANING RELATIONS are called *cases* (a term covering more than in TRADITIONAL GRAMMAR, where it was restricted to describing certain systems of word-endings). For example, in the sentence *John opened the door with the key, John* is 'agentive' case, *the door* 'objective', and *with the key* 'instrumental'. This approach, first formulated by Charles Fillmore in 1968, has since developed variant forms, and has exercised considerable influence in contemporary LINGUISTICS.   D.C.

Bibl: D.J. Fillmore, 'The Case for Case', in E. Bach and R.T. Harns, eds., *Universals in Linguistic Theory* (London and New York, 1968), pp. 1-90.

case method. A distinctive feature of American legal education, developed by Christopher Langdell, dean of the Harvard Law School beginning in 1870. The standard pedagogical technique in most American law schools today, the case method uses a question and answer format and relies on case opinions as its primary source material. By encouraging students to analyse the application of law rather than legal rules in general, the case method reflects the pragmatic, fact-oriented approach of American lawyers generally, and exemplifies the triumph of SOCIOLOGICAL JURISPRUDENCE in the American legal system.   M.S.P.

Casimir effect, see under VIRTUAL PARTICLES.

caste. The name (Portuguese: *casta*) for the traditional hierarchical divisions of HINDU society: (1) A hierarchy of purity, the fourfold *varna* division: Brahmin, Kshatriya, Vaisya, Sudra (priests, warriors/rulers, merchants, servants) which is assumed to embrace the whole of society except the scheduled castes (Untouchables/Harijans). (2) The numerous *jati*, local ENDOGAMOUS groups arranged hierarchically which compose the society of any area of the country.

Caste is a relative concept, that is to discuss caste is to discuss intercaste relationships. Caste is both a form of social organization and a system of values. Ideas of purity and POLLUTION keep different castes apart (L. Dumont, *Homo Hierarchicus*, 1970). Endogamous MARRIAGE is an important mechanism for preserving caste integrity. In reality, however, the situation is much more complex and there are different kinds of cross-caste exchange. For example, various marriage strategies (hypergamy and hypogamy; see DOWRY) reveal the fluidity of caste boundaries. Beyond Hindu society caste is to be found in other societies directly influenced by Hindu culture (e.g., Sri Lanka, Bali and among Muslims in the Indian subcontinent). The question of whether caste may be used generally as a concept to describe a system of SOCIAL STRATIFICATION or is culturally specific (i.e. restricted to Hindu society) has been much debated by anthropologists (E.R. Leach, ed., *Aspects of Caste*, 1960).   M.F.;A.G.

Bibl: J.P. Parry, *Caste and Kinship in Kangra* (London, 1979).

castration anxiety. In psychoanalytic theory (see PSYCHOANALYSIS), the allegedly universal fear of castration felt by boys at a certain stage of their PSYCHOSEXUAL DEVELOPMENT; its origin in the OEDIPUS COMPLEX lies in fear of retaliation by the father for the child's feelings of sexuality towards the mother and of hostility towards the competing father. Girls were also said to suffer castration anxiety originating in the ELECTRA COMPLEX; but this view has been largely abandoned.   J.S.B.

Castroism. This term is used to refer to the versions of MARXISM drawing their inspiration from the Cuban REVOLUTION of 1959, led by Fidel Castro, and further articulated by his colleagues Che Guevara and Regis Debray. These theories emphasize the importance of isolated GUERRILLA foci, or bases, as creating the preconditions for revolution in Central and Latin America. The guerrilla force would be the nucleus of a future political party and not the other way round. This involved the elevation of the military above the political in a manner quite uncharacteristic of mainstream Marxism, and an overestimation of the extent to which the social and political structure of Latin America was ripe for revolution. (See also CUBA.)

D.T.M.

Bibl: R. Debray, *Revolution in the Revolution?* (London, 1967); J. O'Connor, *The Origins of Socialism in Cuba* (Ithaca, N.Y., 1970).

CAT (CT), see under RADIOLOGY.

catabolism, see under METABOLISM.

catachresis. In critical theory, a trope (see TROPISM) in which a sign which already stands for one thing is applied to another thing which has had no expression. *Head of lettuce* is a prosaic example. The importance of catachresis is that because there is no subsitution of a figurative expression for a literal one, it calls into question the claim that METAPHOR arises from a contrast between the literal and the figurative. S.T.

Bibl: J. Culler, *The Pursuit of Signs* (New York and London, 1981).

catalysis. An alteration, usually an increase, in the rate of a CHEMICAL REACTION. The substance causing this increase is a *catalyst*. Chemical SPECIES usually require a certain amount of extra energy, the ACTIVATION ENERGY, before they react. Normally this energy is provided internally by the collision of ATOMS or MOLECULES, with the required excess ENERGY, but the number of such collisions may be small, and the rate of reaction slow. A *heterogeneous* catalyst speeds up the reactions by providing a surface on which the chemical reaction can proceed with lower activation energy. A *homogeneous* catalyst operates in the same phase and accelerates the reaction by participating in reaction intermediates. Catalysts play an important role in many industrial processes; the most effective are ENZYMES, which facilitate physiologically important reactions. B.F.

catalytic war, see under WAR.

catastrophe theory. Any system can be regarded as a BLACK BOX (i.e. a mechanism of whose internal workings we may be totally ignorant) with an input and an output. Generally, if the input is changed by a small amount, then the output changes by a small amount (the output depends continuously on the input). However, there are often certain critical values of the input where a small change produces a very large change in the output — a catastrophe. Catastrophe theory is a mathematical model conceived in the 1960s by René Thom which describes these phenomena. It is principally qualitative and provides a very useful framework for understanding these discontinuities. J.M.

Bibl: R. Thom, *Mathematical Models of Morphogenesis* (Chichester, 1983).

categorical imperative. The supreme principle of morality, according to Kant, by which all such specific moral principles as 'Do not lie' and 'Do not commit suicide' are to be tested. His basic formulation of it is: So act that the maxim of your action can be willed without contradiction as a universal law. Another, loosely connected, formulation enjoins us to treat people always as ends and never merely as means. In everyday terms Kant tells us to ask of any projected action: what would happen if everyone acted like this? A.Q.

Bibl: S. Korner, *Kant* (Harmondsworth, 1955).

category. A term introduced into PHILOSOPHY by Aristotle, in very much its everyday sense of a class or kind, but restricted in its application to LINGUISTIC items, specifically to the descriptive or non-logical words or phrases which figure as the subjects and predicates of PROPOSITIONS. With his classification of terms into ten categories, Aristotle tried to systematize the restrictions on the possibilities of significant combination that exist for the different kinds of term. Thus the substance-word 'George' in 'George is heavy' can be replaced only by another term of the same category, such as 'this stone', if significance (not necessarily TRUTH) is to be preserved. Among modern philosophers, very much this idea is present in the influential theory of categories put forward by Gilbert Ryle (see also CATEGORY-MISTAKE), who regarded the tracing of the categorical properties of terms as the prime business of philosophy,

111

but did not believe it is possible to develop a comprehensive formal theory of categories. Different, although related, is Kant's use of the term to refer to the very general and abstract CONCEPTS, such as SUBSTANCE and cause, with which philosophy has always been centrally concerned; see also APRIORISM.   A.Q.

Bibl: G. Ryle, *Collected Papers* (London, 1971).

category-mistake. A grammatically well-formed but nevertheless logically unacceptable sentence in which terms from uncombinable CATEGORIES are put together. 'The number 7 is green' is an uncontroversial example; numbers, unlike numerals, are not perceivable objects in space and cannot be significantly said to be of any colour. Ryle, who named this idea, applied it chiefly to mind-body DUALISM (see also MIND-BODY PROBLEM) which he held to be a massive category-mistake in taking mental and physical things and events to exist or occur in two different worlds.   A.Q.

category theory. A recent development in MATHEMATICS which concentrates attention not on *particular* MATHEMATICAL STRUCTURES but on the RELATIONS between them. It has had a unifying effect in ALGEBRA and TOPOLOGY. Those who like to work on particular, concrete problems refer to it as 'general abstract nonsense'.   R.G.

Bibl: S. MacLane, *Categories for the Working Mathematician* (New York, 1971).

catharsis (Greek word meaning 'purification', 'purgation').

(1) The 'purging' of undesirable emotions through vicarious experience, especially through seeing them represented on the stage; from its application by Aristotle (*Poetics*, ch. 6) to the postulated effect of tragedy in removing, by the 'pity and fear' it excites, (excesses of) 'such emotions' — rather than simply stimulating them, as Plato had argued. (Aristotle seems to intend purification *from* excessive emotions rather than purification *of* them, but the latter interpretation has also been influential.)   R.W.S.

Bibl: Aristotle, ed. D.W. Lucas, *Poetics*

(Oxford, 1968), Appendix II.

(2) In ABNORMAL PSYCHOLOGY, very commonly, the release of repressed emotion, irrespective of the nature of the process.   B.A.F.

(3) In FREUDIAN theory, the word has a more specific meaning. In 1882 Joseph Breuer hit upon a new method of PSYCHOTHERAPY, which he called 'cathartic'. It consisted in encouraging the patient to speak about the first occasion on which a symptom appeared; whereupon, Breuer claimed, the symptom disappeared. Freud adopted and used this method when he still believed that neurotic states (see NEUROSIS) originated in traumatic episodes (see TRAUMA). Later, however, he modified this view to allow for neurotic states that were the result of conflict; and after he developed the technique of FREE ASSOCIATION the cathartic method was seen to be only one aspect of this. In Freud's PSYCHOLOGY the mind contains charged mental elements, each of which has two aspects, the ideational and the affective (or emotional); and the charged elements are in movement towards CONSCIOUSNESS so as to discharge themselves. During treatment the patient is continually struggling to prevent the emergence of repressed emotion. When he does release it into consciousness, the element is thereby discharged. It is this whole process that is known as catharsis. See also ABREACTION.   B.A.F.

cathexis. In psychoanalytic theory (see PSYCHOANALYSIS), (1) the sexual energy (LIBIDO) which an individual 'invests' in another person or object; (2) more generally, a strong attachment to another.   W.Z.

cathode, see under ELECTRODE.

cathode ray tube. A device used in television receivers and oscilloscopes to display a varying electrical signal as a moving spot on a FLUORESCENT screen. The spot is produced by a narrow beam of ELECTRONS which are deflected by the signal. See also ELECTRON GUN; THERMIONICS.   M.V.B.

Catholic commitment, see under COMMITMENT.

Catholicism. Universality, especially in the Christian Church. This is believed to be safeguarded against personal and local errors by acceptance of the Bible, the Apostles' and Nicene Creeds, the ECUMENICAL Councils, the sacraments of Baptism and Holy Communion, ordered, corporate worship, and a regularly ordained (i.e. set apart) 'ministry' of bishops, priests, and deacons. There has been much disagreement as to the exact nature of these safeguards (see DOGMA), especially about the position of the Pope as the 'vicar' or deputy of Christ entitled to jurisdiction over the whole Church. The Eastern ORTHODOX Churches, rejecting the Papal claims, have been separated from the Western Catholic Church since 1054. During the 16th century the Reformation split the Western Church, although the PROTESTANT Churches organized after this further revolt against the Papacy have all claimed that they remain Catholic in some sense, and ANGLO-CATHOLICISM claims it strongly. In modern usage, the word usually refers to *Roman Catholicism*, which obeys the Pope, although often in the modern spirit of AGGIORNAMENTO. While Christians who are Roman Catholics in one sense or another cannot be counted accurately, they certainly outnumber Christians who are not by many hundreds of millions. See also MODERNISM; ULTRAMONTANISM.   D.L.E.

Bibl: J.L. McKenzie, *The Roman Catholic Church* (London and New York, 1969); K. Rahner, ed., *Encyclopaedia of Theology* (London and New York, 1975); P. Nichols, *The Pope's Divisions* (London and New York, 1981).

causal explanation, see under EXPLANATION.

causality (or *causation*). The relation between two events or states of affairs in which one brings the other about or produces it. Hume took the CONCEPT to be a complex one, its components being the priority in time of cause to effect, their contiguity in space and time and what he problematically described as their *necessary connection*. Although it seems inconceivable that a cause should follow its effect, it seems possible that the two should be simultaneous. The phenomenon of GRAVITATION is an apparent exception to the requirement of contiguity; that of interaction between mind and body, if the mind is taken to be non-spatial, is another (see MIND-BODY PROBLEM). The 'necessary connection', however, seems indispensable. EMPIRICISTS follow Hume in identifying it with constant conjunction: that event is the cause of this one if events like that are regularly succeeded, in circumstances like these, by events like this. It follows from this that every singular-looking causal PROPOSITION is really general, since it implies a universal law, and it can be justified only by INDUCTION, which Hume took to be unjustifiable, although natural to us. There is no one standard alternative to this view. Some take causal laws to be *a priori* truths (see APRIORISM), discoverable by reason without the aid of experience; others that we can somehow perceive or intellectually apprehend the causal relation between a pair of particular events, most plausibly, perhaps, in the case where one's will brings about a movement of one's body. We have a practical interest in knowledge of causes since we can apply it to produce or prevent occurrences through the production or prevention of other, causally related, events that are within our direct control. We have a theoretical interest too: knowledge of causes enables us to explain what has happened and predict what will happen. Many verbs (kill, lift, throw) and many words of other kinds (victim, author, father) are implicity causal.   A.Q.

Bibl: J.L. Mackie, *The Cement of the Universe: a Study of Causation* (Oxford, 1974).

Cavendish Laboratory. The department of PHYSICS at the University of Cambridge, England. Since its foundation in 1871, a series of eminent directors (including Lord Rutherford, Sir John Cockcroft, and Sir Lawrence Bragg) has stimulated the early development of many important areas of present-day science, e.g. NUCLEAR PHYSICS, CRYSTALLOGRAPHY, RADIO ASTRONOMY, and MOLECULAR BIOLOGY.
      M.V.B.

cavitation. In its broadest sense, the formation of cavities within a continuous material. In the case of fluids, cavities are formed behind solid objects moving through a liquid which would normally be in contact with it, e.g. behind the blades of a ship's propeller. In the case of solids, cavities are dug in hard substances by bombarding them with high-frequency sound waves (see ULTRASONICS), generated by such devices as MAGNETOSTRICTION oscillators.

E.R.L.

CBW (chemical and biological warfare), see under WAR.

CDU, see under CHRISTIAN DEMOCRACY.

celebratory theatre. The idea that theatre may be employed, not to interpret reality, dramatize personal conflict, or criticize social conditions, but rather to offer audiences a glimpse, by theatrical means, of some alternative and possibly utopian existence arises from a study of those societies in which drama forms part of the ceremonial or festive life of the community. It is prefigured in J.G. Frazer's account of myth and ritual in *The Golden Bough* (1890-1915). The BAKHTINIAN notion of CARNIVALIZATION and P. Toschi's study of popular dramatic forms in Italy (*Le origini del teatro italiano*, 1955) point to the same conclusion. But most contemporary practitioners of festive or celebratory theatre would probably claim to be more directly influenced by surviving traditions of popular entertainment. Perhaps the most impressive example of contemporary celebratory theatre has been Le Théâtre du Soleil's *1789*, created collectively under the inspiration of Ariane Mnouchkine (b. 1939) in 1970, in which the events of the French Revolution are presented from the viewpoint of the common people. Equally influential was Peter Brook's (b. 1925) Royal Shakespeare Company production of *A Midsummer Night's Dream* (1970), using techniques and imagery drawn from the circus; the Greek director Karolos Koun's productions of Aristophanes in the 1960s should also be mentioned. A different type of celebratory theatre is found in the creation of specially performed pieces to mark particular events or calendar dates: The Welfare State, a British group founded in 1968, has produced many examples.

M.A.

celestial mechanics. The study of the ORBITS, or trajectories, of stars, planets, spacecraft, etc. The form of the orbits arises from the force of GRAVITATION, and calculations are based on NEWTONIAN MECHANICS. Celestial mechanics is characterized by great precision (it is the original 'exact science'); the motion of the moon, for example, can be calculated to within a fraction of a second many years in advance. See also ASTRONAUTICS.

M.V.B.

cell.
(1) The smallest viable functional and structural unit of a TISSUE or organ. The *cell theory*, associated with the name of Theodor Schwann (1810-82), declares that all tissues and organs including the nervous system (see NEURON) are cellular in intimate structure. The process whereby cells multiply is known as *cell division*. See also CELL BIOLOGY; CYTOLOGY.

P.M.

(2) A battery, i.e. a device for converting various forms of ENERGY (usually chemical) into electricity. Types of cell include (*a*) *primary cells*, exemplified by the non-rechargeable dry battery familiar in torches, etc.; (*b*) *secondary cells*, exemplified by the lead-acid accumulator familiar in motor-cars (recharged by adding new fuel); (*c*) the *solar cells*, used to power instruments in spacecraft, by converting the energy of sunlight directly into electrical energy.

M.V.B.

cell biology. A branch of BIOLOGY (to be distinguished from CYTOLOGY) that came to the fore after World War II, and of which the ambition is, wherever appropriate, to interpret physiological performances in terms of the behaviour of individual CELLS. Cell biology has played a specially prominent part in IMMUNOLOGY, in which every endeavour is made to interpret antibody formation and the aggressive actions of lymphocytes (one of the white blood corpuscles) in cellular terms. Indeed, that branch of immunology which deals with cell-mediated immune reactions is to quite a large extent a natural history of lymphocytes.

P.M.

Bibl: L.E.R. Picken, *The Organisation of Cells and Other Organisms* (Oxford, 1960); T.T. Puck, *The Mammalian Cell as a Microorganism* (San Francisco, 1973).

cell theory, see under CELL.

cellular automata. In MATHEMATICS, a technique for constructing or modelling very complicated SYSTEMS or structures from a large number of identical single elements. These elements are allowed to develop according to a set of prescribed rules in which the development of a particular element is controlled by the behaviour of its neighbours. An everyday example is the growth of a snowflake or other crystal. This starts from a small NUCLEUS and its structure extends by the deposition of more water molecules whose position and orientation depend on the precise pattern of molecules which have already been condensed. The ideas of cellular automata have been applied to biological systems, FRACTAL patterns, complex non-linear phenomena (see NON-LINEAR MATHEMATICS/PHYSICS) such as turbulence, as well as to more abstract fields in mathematics, COMPUTATION and formal language theory (see NOTATIONAL).

H.M.R.

censorship, see under PERCEPTUAL DEFENCE.

census/vital registration. The term census encompasses the collection, collation and publication of data on the demographic, economic and social situation of all persons in a territory at a particular time. The process usually involves universal and simultaneous enumeration (or as near as possible), with censuses to be taken at regular intervals, frequently every ten years. The census provides a cross-sectional picture of the population. Vital registration is the registration of all demographic events — births, marriages, and deaths (and occasionally, especially in Scandinavia, migration) — occurring in a population, and is the basic source for investigating the dynamics of that population. Both have importance not only in the collection of demographic data but also for forward social and economic planning. (See also DEMOGRAPHY.)

D.S.

Bibl: H.S. Shryock *et al., The Methods and Materials of Demography* (condensed edition) (New York and London, 1976).

Central American Common Market (CACM). Set up in 1960 as part of a broader movement towards regional integration, the CACM aimed to promote development through import-substitution INDUSTRIALIZATION by expanding the market through the abolition of local PROTECTIONIST measures and taking advantage of ECONOMIES OF SCALE. For several years this strategy produced impressive growth rates, especially in Guatemala and EL SALVADOR. However, these were largely attributable to outside investment, and indigenous manufacturing capacity did not significantly increase. The organization was drastically weakened by the 1969 war between Honduras and El Salvador, after which the two countries refused to trade with each other. Saturation of the small regional market, followed by the 1979 OIL CRISIS and subsequent world recession, plunged the CACM into crisis, and by 1984 intra-regional trade was 40% below 1980 levels.

N.M.

Central American Defence Council (CONDECA). A pact signed by the defence ministers of Guatemala, EL SALVADOR, Honduras and NICARAGUA in 1964, with strong U.S. backing. Costa Rica (where the army was abolished in 1948) was given observer status with an option to join. The objectives were to coordinate actions against internal subversion (Nicaragua — which under Somoza became the backbone of the alliance — and Guatemala both had GUERRILLA movements operating within their borders), to promote general collaboration between the armed forces of the region (including the standardization of training and equipment) and to reduce regional military rivalries. U.S. armed forces personnel and CIA advisers played a key role and ten anti-guerrilla manoeuvres were conducted under the auspices of CONDECA. Although the organization collapsed into near obscurity after a 1969 war between El Salvador and Honduras, CONDECA left a potent legacy of friendship between RIGHT-wing army officers in the region.

N.M.

Bibl: J. Pearce, *Under the Eagle* (London, 1981).

central bank. The national authority that serves as banker to the commercial banks and regulates their activities, and that acts as banker to the government. In these roles, central banks issue notes and coins, exert some influence on the MONEY SUPPLY and interest rates, supervise the domestic financial system, lend and take deposits from commercial banks, fund the government budget deficit and conduct transfers with other central banks and the IMF (see BRETTON WOODS).   J.P.

Bibl: J. Craven, *Introduction to Economics* (Oxford, 1984).

central dogma, see under MOLECULAR BIOLOGY.

central limit theorem, see under PROBABILITY THEORY.

central nervous system, see under NERVOUS SYSTEM.

central place. A geographic term for villages, TOWNS, and cities that provide centralized wholesale, retail, service, and administrative functions for tributary REGIONS. Central-place theory specifies the relationships between SETTLEMENTS serving such central functions, with special emphasis on their number, size, spatial arrangement, and activity structure. The first formal statement of the theory is usually credited to the German geographer, Walter Christaller, who based his work on the study of South German settlements. Modern mathematical work has been concerned with generalizing Christaller's work to accommodate a wide range of regional variations and to introduce dynamic and evolutionary dimensions to central-place theory.   P.H.

Bibl: L.C. King, *Central Place Theory* (Los Angeles, 1984).

central processing unit (CPU), see under PROCESSOR.

centralism, democratic, see DEMOCRATIC CENTRALISM.

centrality, see under CENTRAL PLACE.

centre, the. If there are RIGHT and LEFT wings in politics, it follows that there must be a centre between them unless the politics of the country in question is polarized between extreme positions. The centre is the name for moderate, middle-of-the-road parties and politics, scorned by the doctrinaire and idealist, and more concerned with finding compromises that will enable government to be carried on than with the pursuit of ideas to their logical conclusions.

A similar function is fulfilled by the centre group in many political parties, holding together those of more radical views (see RADICALISM) on the one hand and those with more conservative views (see CONSERVATISM) on the other. The centre provides a convenient point on the political spectrum by which to place politicians and policies as 'left of centre' or 'right of centre'. The term 'party of the extreme centre' was coined to make the point that those who believe in moderation and the virtues of toleration and compromise may have a commitment quite as intense and quite as much based on principle as those who believe in intolerance and violence.   A.L.C.B.

Centre 42. The playwright Arnold Wesker's largely unfulfilled plan for an ARTS CENTRE to be supported by the British TRADE UNIONS and labour movement. It was based on resolution no. 42 of the 1960 Trades Union Congress, by which the meeting 'recognized' the importance of the arts and decided to see how the movement could contribute. In 1962 six local festivals were held, not very successfully, at the invitation of various trades councils. Despite some support from the Wilson government and the acquisition of a potential centre in the Round House in London, funds were unavailable to run this as intended, let alone realize the ultimate aim of free performances.   J.W.

centres dramatiques. Theatres, sometimes with attached drama schools, set up in various French provincial towns and on the outskirts of Paris, from 1945 onwards, in an attempt to decentralize theatrical culture and bring the theatre to WORKING-CLASS and lower-MIDDLE-CLASS audiences. After 1960, in some localities, the *centres dramatiques* were combined with the new *maisons de la culture* introduced by André

Malraux as Minister for Cultural Affairs. Despite conflicts with local authorities (who supply part of the finance) and the upheavals of May 1968 (most of the directors belong to the LEFT), some of the *centres* have achieved notable, if temporary, success, e.g. Grenier de Toulouse, Centre Dramatique de l'Est (now Théâtre National de Strasbourg), Théâtre de la Cité (Villeurbanne) under Roger Planchon, and Comédie de Saint-Étienne under Jean Dasté. J.G.W.

centrifuge. A device for depositing out fine PARTICLES (e.g. biological MOLECULES, organisms, etc.) suspended in a liquid contained in a tube. When the tube is whirled very rapidly about an axis, centrifugal force causes the densest particles to deposit farthest from the axis much faster than they would have settled under GRAVITATION. M.V.B.

centrography. In GEOGRAPHY, the determination and study of the central points of spatial distributions, e.g. changes in the centre of gravity of the United States population. Centrography developed most rapidly during the 1920s and 1930s in the Soviet Union when attempts were made to define optimal centres for REGIONAL PLANNING purposes. P.H.

centrosphere, see BATHYSPHERE.

cephalic index. In physical ANTHROPOLOGY, the index used for recording the shape of the human skull. The index expresses the maximum width as a percentage of the maximum length measured from just above the eyebrow ridges. Where the index is below 75, the skull is described as *dolichocephalic* (long-headed); above 80 as *brachycephalic* (round-headed). A.L.C.B.

cepheid variable. A class of yellow and orange supergiant stars of considerable importance in the determination of astronomical distances. They are named after the prototype, Delta Cephei, discovered in 1784. Polaris (sometimes called the Pole or North Star) is the nearest cepheid to the Earth. They pulsate with regular periods of variation from 1-50 days during which they vary continuously in colour, size and brightness by up to about twenty per cent. There exists a characteristic relationship between the period of pulsation and the variation of light intensity which was first deduced by Henrietta Leavitt during the period 1908-12. It uniquely distinguishes cepheids from other variable stars. In 1917 Harlow Shapley established a systematic relationship between the intrinsic brightness and the period of variation of a cepheid variable. Walter Beade divided cepheids into Populations I and II according to their PERIOD-LUMINOSITY RELATIONS. Type I are usually found in relatively young galactic star clusters while type II are found among old stars in globular star clusters. Distances to nearby star clusters containing cepheids can be obtained by studying the systematic relationship between the colour and the brightness of the stars within the cluster. J.D.B.

Bibl: M. Rowan-Robinson, *The Cosmological Distance Ladder* (San Francisco, 1985).

ceramic. Originally a man-made refractory material based on silicates, e.g. china and porcelain. Now the term is used for any non-metallic solid made up of small crystals. M.V.B.

cerebral dominance, see under NEUROPSYCHOLOGY.

cerebrotonia, see under PERSONALITY TYPES.

Cerenkov radiation. The cone of light or other electromagnetic RADIATION emitted by charged PARTICLES travelling through a transparent material faster than the speed of light in that material. Cerenkov radiation is impossible in empty space because, according to RELATIVITY theory, particles cannot travel faster than light *in vacuo*. It is analogous to the SONIC BOOM and to the water-wave pattern behind ships. M.V.B.

CERN. European Organization for Nuclear Research (formerly Conseil Européen pour la Recherche Nucléaire), set up in 1954. The world's largest centre, situated in Geneva, for the experimental (using ACCELERATORS) and theoretical study of ELEMENTARY PARTICLES. M.V.B.

Certificate of Secondary Education, see under EXAMINATIONS.

CGS units. A system of fundamental scientific units, based on the centimetre, gram, and second for length, MASS, and time. Now superseded by SI UNITS.

M.V.B.

CGT (Confédération Générale du Travail). French TRADE UNION movement established in 1895 at Limoges, brought together with other trades union organizations in 1902 at Montpellier. It operated both on issues of wage, salary, and working conditions and on political issues; in 1906 it was captured by revolutionary SYNDICALISTS who relied on the general strike as their main weapon. The consequent collisions with state power weakened its impetus and in 1921 the revolutionary wing under COMMUNIST leadership set up a separate organization. Reunited under the slogan of the POPULAR FRONT in 1936, it was dissolved in 1940. Reconstituted in 1946, it came under communist control, its non-communist elements seceding in 1947 to form the Confédération Générale du Travail — Force Ouvrière. With a membership of some 1.5 million in 1986 the CGT is the largest of the French trade unions. While its influence in the service and tertiary sectors is weak, it has traditionally dominated crafts and heavy industries. It has a close, albeit often troubled, relationship with the Communist Party; its leadership is dominated by members of the Communist Party hierarchy. D.C.W.; S.M.

chain index, see under INDEX NUMBER.

chain of being, see GREAT CHAIN OF BEING.

chain reaction. Any chemical or nuclear process where each reaction produces PARTICLES which cause a chain of further similar reactions. The process may be unstable, as in explosions (conventional or nuclear), or controlled, as in NUCLEAR REACTORS. See also FISSION; FUSION; NUCLEAR REACTION. M.V.B.

chamber tomb. General term for an artificially constructed burial place designed for use on more than one occasion. Chamber tombs may be cut out of rock (MEGALITHIC) or constructed of drystone work. This type of burial place was common in Western Europe throughout the third millennium B.C., but occurs in many parts of the world at different times. B.C.

Chamberlin-Moulton hypothesis. Popular in the 19th century was the so-called nebular hypothesis, which attributed the origins of the planets to the condensation of the supposedly nebulous material which had once been the sun's atmosphere. This in turn was largely discredited at the end of the 19th century by a theory devised by the American geologist T.C. Chamberlin (1843-1928) and the astronomer F.R. Moulton (1872-1952) which claimed that a close encounter between the sun and a passing star would best account for the genesis of the planets and their orbits. The gravitational pull of the star had drawn material away from the sun, which in time formed into 'planetesimals', which had cooled, and, orbiting the sun, had gathered together into the present planets. The hypothesis enjoyed popularity especially in America, before being discredited in the 1930s as part of a rising general scepticism towards theories of stellar collision and catastrophe. R.P.

Bibl: O. Struve and V. Zerbergs, *Astronomy of the Twentieth Century* (New York, 1962).

chancroid. A SEXUALLY TRANSMITTED DISEASE caused by *Haemophilus ducreyi*, common in developing countries but rare in Europe and North America. Chancroid affected many service personnel in World War II and during the conflicts in Korea and Vietnam. Large painful ulcers appear on the genitals, and the infection may spread to cause abscesses (buboes) in the groin. ANTIBIOTICS are generally effective, although in some parts of the world treatment schedules have had to be revised owing to the development of resistant strains of H. ducreyi. J.D.O.

channels, see under ACTION POTENTIAL.

chaos. In PHYSICS and MATHEMATICS there are phenomena and expressions for which it is not possible to predict how the situation or the calculation is going to develop when the starting conditions only change very slightly. A simple example is the uncertainty in the result of spinning a coin. A more complex problem is the development of turbulence in a fast flowing fluid in which the behaviour depends very critically on the shape of the channel or on how the flow was initiated. In mathematics there are expressions which when evaluated give results which vary in an unpredictable way when the value of one of the initial quantities is changed even by a very small amount. These are all examples of chaotic behaviour. Chaotic processes can be simulated by electronic circuits and these are being used to investigate the behaviour of these complex situations which can be quite unwieldy and time-consuming if they are evaluated with a COMPUTER. H.M.R.

character. A written sign, to indicate a sound, a meaning, or part of a word (a letter); this meaning dates from 1665. In COMPUTING, the use is extended to marks, holes in data-tape, or magnetic or other signals, 'recognized' and 'read' by machines, for information-processing or storing. Except in picture languages such as Egyptian hieroglyphics, it is now rare for a single mark or picture to stand for a meaning except in mathematical or logical notation. The numbers 1 and 2 are characters, but even here we soon get combinations, such as 12, which have a different meaning. R.L.G.

characterology. A pseudo-science of diagnosing personality traits from such evidence as GRAPHOLOGY or the study of handwriting, formulated and practised by the Munich philosopher Ludwig Klages (1872-1956), and sometimes denounced (e.g. by Georg Lukács) for its contribution to the IDEOLOGY of NAZISM. It became pertinent once more after World War II with the rise of quasi-calligraphic painting and with ABSTRACT EXPRESSIONISM'S concern with GESTURAL significance. It also relates to Rorschach's system of PSYCHODIAGNOSTICS. J.W.

charisma. A term derived from New Testament Greek (meaning the gift of grace) and introduced into SOCIOLOGY by Max Weber to denote an 'extraordinary quality' possessed by persons or objects, which is thought to give them a unique, magical quality. Weber distinguished between *individual* charisma, which arises out of the personal qualities of the individual, and the charisma of *office*, which derives from the sacred nature of the position.

Weber carried the CONCEPT over into a general theory of *authority*, in which he distinguished between three types of legitimacy — traditional, charismatic, and LEGAL-RATIONAL — and into a rudimentary theory of social change. For, where religions or societies are hidebound, or ruled by customs sanctified by the past, the only way such authority can usually be challenged is by some *charismatic* leader whose legitimacy resides in his personal qualities. To that extent, charisma is a great revolutionary force. But once the charismatic leader has achieved his aim, he has to set about creating rational, administrative rules; secondary individuals have to be endowed with the authority of the leader, SYMBOLS replace the person, and there ensues the 'routinization of charisma'.

Among English-speaking sociologists, the concept has been seen primarily in political terms, and has been applied to men like Nkrumah in Ghana, Sukarno in Indonesia, Nehru in India, whose personal appeals were the source of authority in these new nations. It has also been applied, by journalists and others, to all kinds of individuals and phenomena that seemed to have a special, magical ability to evoke an immediate, personal assent from the masses. D.B.

Bibl: H.H. Gerth and C.W. Mills, eds., *From Max Weber: Essays in Sociology* (London, 1984).

charismatic movement, see under PENTECOSTALISM.

Charter 77. The movement established in Czechoslovakia in 1977 to campaign for the observance of HUMAN RIGHTS by the government. Named after a charter initially signed by 243 people, it urged the authorities to abide by the country's existing laws and international declarations agreed to by the government, such as the HELSINKI Final Act. It demanded freedoms of expression and religious belief and the observance of the right to education, irrespective of political affiliation. It stressed that it was not forming an opposition and it had no political programme, claiming that it operated within the constitution. It hoped to engage in dialogue with the government, but was accused of being a subversive organization and many of its members were arrested and punished or forced to emigrate. Its membership consisted mainly of intellectuals of diverse political backgrounds, ranging from the former reformist COMMUNIST Jiri Hajek, to the non-communist playwright Vaclav Havel. The organization still operates underground producing much (SAMIZDAT) material.   D.PR.

Bibl: H. Gordon Skilling, *Charter 77 and Human Rights in Czechoslovakia* (London, 1981).

chauvinism. Excessive and unreasonable NATIONALISM mingled with XENOPHOBIA. The word is derived from the name of Nicolas Chauvin, a Napoleonic soldier famous for his simple-minded devotion to Napoleon, and applied by analogy to all extreme intellectual positions held by defenders of a particular set of interests, e.g. 'male chauvinism' (see SEXISM).   D.C.W.

chelate. Term, derived from the Greek word for claw, which describes a chemical SPECIES with more than one ATOM capable of bonding (see BOND) to a central metal atom or ION. Chelating agents, more usually referred to as *polydentate ligands*, frequently form more stable complexes with a metal atom than similar monodentate groups. They find considerable use in industrial and ANALYTICAL CHEMISTRY — particularly in extraction processes. Metal ions in biological systems are often bound to chelates.   B.F.

chemical and biological warfare, see under WAR.

chemical bond, see BOND, CHEMICAL.

chemical equation. A representation in symbols of a chemical reaction. Since the 19th century when Dalton restated early atomic theories in quantitative form it has been common practice to use such equations, which describe the change in atomic combinations and demonstrate that ATOMS are conserved in the process. Each atomic SPECIES is represented by an appropriate letter or letters; thus the production of water, which involves the overall reaction of two hydrogen MOLECULES with one molecule of oxygen to give two water molecules, is given as $2H_2 + O_2 = 2H_2O$. The subscript figures indicate the number of atoms of that particular element in the molecule; e.g., the hydrogen molecule, H_2, is diatomic. Equations are sometimes presented in diagrammatic form so as to give an elementary description of bonding (see BOND) and STEREOCHEMISTRY.   B.F.

chemical equilibrium, see under EQUILIBRIUM.

chemical physics, see under PHYSICAL CHEMISTRY.

chemical reaction. The process by which chemical compounds transform one another into different compounds. Nearly every substance has the ability to take part in a variety of chemical reactions and such reactions are a feature of normal life: the burning of oil, the discharge of a battery, the rusting of iron, the production of carbon dioxide from baking powder, etc. In addition a great many chemical reactions are involved in plant growth, the assimilation of food and oxygen by animals, and other biological activities.   B.F.

chemical warfare, see under WAR.

chemiosmosis. The mechanism by which energy is harnessed by MITOCHONDRIA, chloroplasts and bacteria. In the process, high-energy ELECTRONS, which are either present in foodstuffs or generated by PHOTOSYNTHESIS, are used to set up a gradient of PROTONS across a biological membrane. The energy generated by the gradient is harnessed in a variety of ways.   P.N.

chemistry. The scientific discipline concerned with the investigation and rationalization of the properties of the many thousands of substances which exist in nature or can be made artificially (see SYNTHETIC CHEMISTRY). Traditionally it is subdivided into PHYSICAL CHEMISTRY, which is concerned with the physical laws governing chemical behaviour and includes the specialized branches ELECTROCHEMISTRY, PHOTOCHEMISTRY, and STEREOCHEMISTRY as well as studies involving SPECTROSCOPY and THERMODYNAMICS (including THERMOCHEMISTRY); ORGANIC CHEMISTRY, which involves the study of substances containing carbon; and INORGANIC CHEMISTRY, which deals with substances containing the remaining elements. THEORETICAL CHEMISTRY is concerned particularly with the applications of QUANTUM MECHANICS and STATISTICAL MECHANICS to chemistry. The detection and estimation of chemical SPECIES is the sphere of ANALYTICAL CHEMISTRY and (where minute amounts are involved) MICROCHEMISTRY. The distribution of elements in the earth's crust and atmosphere constitutes the study of GEOCHEMISTRY. A good deal of modern chemistry involves interdisciplinary study, especially in conjunction with PHYSICS, BIOCHEMISTRY, and METALLURGY. B.F.

Bibl: J.B. Ifft and J.E. Hearst (intr.), *General Chemistry: Readings from Scientific American* (San Francisco, 1973); G.D. Schaumberg, *Concerning Chemistry* (London and New York, 1974).

chemotaxis, see under TROPISM.

chemotherapy. The treatment of diseases by chemicals whose composition is known. Chemotherapy is usually attributed to Ehrlich's use of salvarsan for syphilis in 1910 after Schaudinn described the spirochete in 1905. Previously diseases, whose causes were generally unknown, were treated by a variety of non-specific remedies of varying and obscure composition. With the clearer definition of diseases in the last century, and the recognition of the microbial origin (see MICROBE) of many of them, it became possible to develop more rational treatment. The two greatest recent advances in chemotherapy have been the discovery in the 1930s of the sulphonamide group of drugs, and the introduction about 10 years later of penicillin and other ANTIBIOTICS — although, strictly speaking, penicillin treatment was not chemotherapy since penicillin, an extract from a mould, was not then a compound of known chemical composition. D.A.P.

chemotropism, see under TROPISM.

Chernobyl. The Ukrainian town where the world's most serious accident involving a NUCLEAR REACTOR occurred on 25 April 1986. The nuclear fall-out produced contamination throughout Europe and the disaster led to increased opposition to the use of nuclear power all over the world. The accident appears to have been caused by human error rather than through any design fault. The Soviet government was subjected to considerable criticism by those nations affected by the fall-out, first for refusing to make the accident public until RADIOACTIVITY was discovered in Sweden and then failing to provide adequate information on its extent. It was alleged that the Soviet leadership's newly declared policy of greater 'openness' in making information available to the public was not being implemented. However, since the immediate aftermath of the nuclear leak, the Soviet Union has been more willing to allow international experts to examine the circumstances of the disaster. D.PR.

Chicago. JAZZ'S second city, following chronologically after NEW ORLEANS. It attracted great New Orleans musicians like King Oliver (soon joined by the young Louis Armstrong) and Jelly Roll Morton, and the teenage white Chicagoans who crowded to hear them were soon imitating and experimenting. Influenced as well by white bands like the New Orleans Rhythm Kings, the resulting Chicago style was rough and enthusiastic, featuring solos more than the New Orleans players did, and also unlike them, employing ensemble passages worked out in advance. The Chicagoans thus laid some of the groundwork for the BIG BAND formulas of the SWING era; correspondingly, Chicago players like Dave Tough, Bud Freeman and, above all, Benny Goodman went on to become its stars. GE.S.

Chicago school.
(1) In SOCIOLOGY, the first graduate department to be established in the world,

and for many years the greatest. Founded in 1892 by Albion Small (who in 1895 founded the *American Journal of Sociology*), it was centrally important in the development of sociology. Robert Park and E.W. Burgess developed basic research on 'the city' within a wide conception of sociological analysis and theory. C.H. Cooley, G.H. Mead, and W. I. Thomas developed (each with slightly different emphases) a distinctive analysis of the 'self' in 'society': perhaps the most fruitful exploration of the field of SOCIAL PSYCHOLOGY yet achieved. This 'school' in particular — now represented by 'symbolic interactionism' (see SYMBOLIC INTERACTION) and the work of Erving Goffman (see ROLE) — is referred to as the Chicago school.   R.F.

Bibl: R.C. and G.J. Hinkle, *The Development of Modern Sociology* (New York, 1954), pp. 28-43.

(2) An architectural movement rooted in the rapid development of Chicago following the Great Fire of 1871 and continuing up to about 1925. It had two facets: the erection of mainly commercial buildings in the business district of the Loop in the form of SKYSCRAPERS, and the development of freely planned single- or two-storey houses in the suburbs by Frank Lloyd Wright, Louis Sullivan, and their followers. It is the evolution of the skyscraper which is most frequently associated with the achievements of the Chicago school. Both aspects were neglected by historians, and it was not until the publication of Giedion's *Bauen in Frankreich* (1926) and its English-language sequel, *Space, Time and Architecture* (1941) that international interest was revived. This was reinforced by Mies van der Rohe, who had gone to Chicago in 1938 and who demonstrated the validity of its tradition; technical innovation and pure form could even in commercial buildings create architecture of a high order.   M.BR.

Bibl: C.W. Condit, *The Chicago School of Architecture* (London and Chicago, rev. ed., 1964).

Chicago strategy. The economic policies implemented in Chile from 1974-1983 under the Pinochet dictatorship by a group of economists who had trained at the University of Chicago under Milton Friedman and Arnold Harberger. The 'Chicago Boys' argued (1) that the unrestricted operation of private enterprise — seen as the most efficient form of economic organization — was essential for ECONOMIC DEVELOPMENT; (2) that prices should be determined purely by market forces, and (3) that INFLATION should be eradicated at any cost, by means of controlling the MONEY SUPPLY. Application of these policies in Chile resulted in high UNEMPLOYMENT, a regressive trend in income distribution and drastic cuts in the living standards of the majority. Failure of the Chicago Strategy to secure its major objective of controlling inflation, together with economic crisis from 1981 onwards as Chile felt the effects of world recession particularly acutely, has recently resulted in a modification of economic policy by the Pinochet regime.   N.M.

Bibl: P. O'Brien and J. Roddick, *Chile: The Pinochet Decade — The Rise and Fall of the Chicago Boys* (London, 1983).

child-centred education. Education based on the interests, needs, and developmental growth of the child and on a knowledge of child development, as contrasted with an education that emphasizes academic features, the curriculum content, standards of achievement, and teaching methods. Originating in a psychological approach, child-centred education has acquired what is sometimes called a philosophy, and is associated with PROGRESSIVE education, and with such names as Rousseau, Froebel, Pestalozzi, Montessori, and A.S. Neil (see FROEBEL METHOD; PESTALOZZI METHODS; MONTESSORI METHOD).   W.A.C.S.

Bibl: W.B. Curry, *The School and a Changing Civilisation* (London, 1934).

child psychiatry, see under PSYCHIATRY.

child psychology, see under DEVELOPMENTAL PSYCHOLOGY.

childbirth techniques. There has recently been a strong lobby in favour of *natural childbirth*, the delivery of the child by maternal effort in the position and way the mother chooses, without medical interference and sometimes away from medical care altogether. This is a reaction against

the increased use of TECHNOLOGY and what is seen as a lack of care and sensitivity by obstetricians and midwives. Grantly Dick Read in 1933 advocated education about labour and childbirth to reduce fear, anxiety and tension which may adversely affect labour. Techniques for teaching relaxation to be practised during labour including controlled breathing (*psychoprophylaxis*) were developed and, perhaps by competition, reduced the comprehension of pain. Other methods of pain relief include ACUPUNCTURE, HYPNOSIS, transcutaneous nerve stimulation, the use of analgesics such as pethidine and anaesthetics such as nitrous oxide and epidural nerve block. Frederick Leboyer, a French obstetrician, became convinced in the 1960s that birth needed to be much gentler in the interests of mother and particularly of the baby, and he advocated quiet and low lit surroundings with very gentle handling of the baby and contact with its mother. Since then Michel Odent, another Frenchman, has developed other techniques designed to increase maternal enjoyment of the birth and the chances of normal delivery. The active birth movement is an even more recent approach. There is widespread acceptance of the need to consider the emotional wellbeing of the parents (for too long the father was excluded from the delivery) and to establish the true place of technology in OBSTETRICS. A balance is required between the desire of a woman to choose how and where she delivers and the reality that labour and delivery are unpredictable and serious complications can occur without warning.   S.J.S.
Bibl: F. Leboyer, *Birth Without Violence* (London, 1975).

childhood, history of, see under HISTORY OF CHILDHOOD.

children, value of, see under VALUE OF CHILDREN.

chiliastic, see under MILLENARIANISM.

chiropody. Chiropody consists of a maintenance of the feet in a healthy condition and the treatment of their disabilities by recognized methods in which the practitioner has been trained. A chiropodist is a specialist capable of palliation of established deformities and disfunctions, curative foot care and preventive services. The therapeutic techniques used include minor surgical techniques, usually performed under local anaesthetic; an example is the management of ingrowing toe nails. Also included are the prescription and provision of specialized appliances.   N.H.H.

chlamydia. *Chlamydia trachomatis* is a bacterium which causes many human diseases. Some strains cause trachoma, a severe and potentially blinding eye disease very common in the Middle East and North Africa. Other strains are SEXUALLY TRANSMITTED and cause genital infections. In men, the commonest is NON-GONOCOCCAL URETHRITIS which can be complicated by epididymitis, a painful swelling of the testicles which may lead to INFERTILITY. In women, C. trachomatis infects the cervix (neck of the womb), and may then spread to cause inflammation of the fallopian tubes (SALPINGITIS) and subsequent infertility. During delivery, the infection may be transmitted from a mother to her baby, and cause conjunctivitis, middle ear disease and pneumonia. In industrialized societies genital chlamydial infection and its complications have reached epidemic proportions. Reliable diagnostic tests are available, and treatment with the tetracycline antibiotics is curative. Control of these infections will require a major effort to examine sex partners of infected individuals, together with screening of high risk groups.   J.D.O.
Bibl: J.D. Oriel and G.L. Ridgway, *Genital Chlamydial Infection* (London, 1982).

chlorophyll. Any of a number of green pigments which occur in plants and a few animals and are the cause of the greenness of grass, of the leaves of trees, and of the countryside generally. Chlorophyll plays an essential part in PHOTOSYNTHESIS. These pigments have also been said to act as deodorants and have been included in toothpaste, though they are probably useless against halitosis.   K.M.

chloroplasts, see under PHOTOSYNTHESIS.

choice, axiom of, see AXIOM OF CHOICE.

Chomskyan. Characteristic of, or a follower of, the linguistic principles of Avram Noam Chomsky (*b.* 1928), Professor of Modern Languages and Linguistics at the Massachusetts Institute of Technology. His book *Syntactic Structures* (The Hague, 1957) was the first to outline and justify a GENERATIVE conception of language, currently the most widely held view. Apart from his technical contributions within LINGUISTICS, he has written at length on the philosophical and psychological implications of a generative theory of language, in particular developing a view of the integral relationship between language and the human mind, and it is this which has made such an impact on disciplines outside linguistics (see, e.g., INNATENESS HYPOTHESIS.) He has also made a powerful impression on the American and, to a lesser extent, the British public through his extensive critical writings on United States policy in VIETNAM.   D.C.
    Bibl: A.N. Chomsky, *Knowledge of Language* (New York and London, 1986); J. Lyons, *Chomsky* (London, 2nd ed., 1977).

chordate, see under ZOOLOGY.

choreography. Although originally meaning the writing down of dance steps, with the developments in DANCE NOTATION and CHOREOLOGY, the word has now come to mean the art of composing all forms of dance from CLASSICAL BALLET and MODERN DANCE to show dancing. The choreographer is the author of the choreography and arranges material using an individual process to present an end product for performance. Choreographers are responsible for the total visual imagery and expect to negotiate with musicians, costume, set and lighting designers.   L.A.
    Bibl: P. Van Praagh and P. Brinson, *The Choreographic Art* (London and New York, 1963).

choreology. Term coined by Rudolph and Joan Benesh to mean the study of dance forms using notation. In 1962 they founded the Institute of Choreology in London, where choreologists are trained to analyse scores and develop DANCE NOTATION skills (in particular the *Benesh system*), and formed a library of choreographic scores from folk dance to ballet. Choreologists are employed largely by CLASSICAL BALLET companies to record and reconstruct ballets.   L.A.
    Bibl: R. and J. Benesh, *An Introduction to Benesh Notation* (London, 1956); J. McGuinness-Scott, *Movement Study and Benesh Movement Notation* (New York, 1983).

chosism. Term imported from France ('thingism') for the occurrence, in the writers associated with the NEW NOVEL, and especially in Alain Robbe-Grillet, of obsessively detailed descriptions of trivial objects (cigar boxes, tomatoes, etc.). Some critics consider it 'arid' and ultimately pointless; others regard it as an important means of drawing attention to the tragically anthropomorphic attitude of human beings towards an indifferent ENVIRONMENT. The craze for *choses* quickly passed and they returned to what they used to be.
                                                   M.S.-S.

Christian democracy. Political IDEOLOGY associated with political parties allied with the Christian Churches, usually the Catholic Church. In the 19th century such parties were usually anti-CAPITALIST, anti-SOCIALIST, and often ANTISEMITIC. Their — sometimes troubled — relations with the Vatican turn on the Papacy of Leo XIII, when the movement began to assume a social character which betrayed some parties (as in Austria) into a COLLECTIVIST, cooperativist view, labelled CLERICO-FASCISM by their opponents. Since 1945, Christian Democratic parties, having broken out of these traditions, have played a major role in West European politics notably in West Germany, Italy, France (in the Fourth Republic), Belgium, Austria, Switzerland and the Netherlands. The three basic principles of Christian democratic ideology are: commitment to liberal democracy (reinforced by anti-COMMUNISM and anti-FASCISM); belief in the SOCIAL MARKET economy; commitment to integration in the dual sense of CLASS reconciliation (through 'non-ideological', mass parties) and transnational integration (manifested through strong support for European integration). The West German Christlich-Demokratische Union/Christlich-Soziale Union (CDU/CSU) in government between 1949-69, returned to power in 1983 and was re-elected in January 1987. The Italian Democrazia Cristiana (DC) has won a plurality of votes cast at every post-war election and formed the backbone of every government. Less RIGHT-wing than its West German counterpart (which in practice now resembles a CONSERVATIVE party), the DC formed an HISTORIC COMPROMISE with the Italian Communist Party between 1976 and 1979. At the European level, the Christian Democrats established a transnational European People's Party in 1976 which constitutes the second largest group in the European Parliament.   D.C.W.;S.M.

Bibl: R.E.M. Irving, *The Christian Democratic Parties of Western Europe* (London, 1979).

Christian existentialism (or *existential theology*). A style of THEOLOGY inspired by Søren Kierkegaard (1813-55) which tests every doctrine by its derivation from human experience and by its power to illuminate human existence. It rejects metaphysical speculation about eternal ESSENCES, even when this is hallowed in traditional DOGMA, and it attempts to DEMYTHOLOGIZE the Bible. In 1950 it was condemned by Pope Pius XII's ENCYCLICAL *Humani Generis*. It is also criticized as being insufficiently concerned with nature and history, and as being too pessimistic about man's reasoning powers. But its mood of urgency and of honesty has made it a possible variety of the CRISIS THEOLOGY which has attracted many Christians in the 20th century.   D.L.E.

Bibl: D.E. Roberts, ed. R. Hazelton, *Existentialism and Religious Belief* (London and New York, 1957).

Christian name politics, see COMMUNITY POLITICS.

Christian Science. The name adopted by a religious body founded by Mrs Mary Baker Eddy (1821-1910), whose *Science and Health* has run into many editions in and since 1875. Its headquarters are in Boston, Mass., where the First Church of Christ, Scientist (the 'Mother Church') was reorganized on a permanent basis in the 1890s, and it is active throughout the English-speaking world. Its principal interest is in increasing health and curing disease by a faith which affirms that matter, the source of sin and suffering, is not a God-created substance, but a mode of human perception. Cure comes from a yielding of the self to God. The low estimate of matter in this doctrine is usually condemned both by the Churches and by AGNOSTICS, but a daily newspaper is widely respected, the *Christian Science Monitor*. Much of the religious and ethical teaching of the movement is shared in common with the Churches, although the unique deity of Christ is denied.   D.L.E.

Bibl: R. Peel, *Mary Baker Eddy*, 3 vols (New York, 1966-77); S. Gottschalk, *The Emergence of Christian Science in American Religious Life* (Berkeley, Ca., 1973).

Christian socialism. Term for a variety of movements which combine the ethical precepts of CHRISTIANITY with the COLLECTIVIST precepts of SOCIALISM. Originating in Britain, and strongest in the 19th century when F.D. Maurice and Edward Carpenter were well-known propagandists for the cause, it has experienced various 20th-century revivals when undoctrinal socialists have attempted to enlist Christ in the service of socialism. Such movements have been prominent in the Protestant churches of France, Germany, Switzerland, Scandinavia and the United States. Distinguished adherents of Christian socialism have included Paul Tillich, Reinhold Niebuhr and R.H. Tawney. Very different, though spurred by the same impulse, has been the movement of 'LIBERATION THEOLOGY' which has been influential in Latin America, though frowned on by the Vatican.   D.C.W.;A.R.

Bibl: E. Heimann, *Reason and Faith in Modern Society: Liberalism, Marxism and Democracy* (Middletown, Conn., 1961; Edinburgh and London, 1962); C. Rowland, *Radical Christianity* (Oxford, 1987).

Christianity. The RELIGION based on the work and teaching of Jesus, who lived *c.* 4 B.C.-A.D. 30. He was regarded by his followers as the 'Anointed King' (Hebrew

Messiah, Greek *Christos*). 'It was in Antioch that the disciples first got the name of Christians' (Acts 11:26). The life of Jesus has been much investigated and debated in the 19th and 20th centuries (see ESCHATOLOGY; MODERNISM). The main modern forms of this religion are CATHOLICISM; ORTHODOXY, EASTERN; and PROTESTANTISM. See also THEOLOGY. D.L.E.

Christology. That part of THEOLOGY which is concerned with doctrines about the person and work of Jesus Christ. See also DOGMA. D.L.E.

Bibl: W. Kasper, *The God of Jesus Christ* (London and New York, 1982); J.P. Mackey, *The Christian Experience of God as Trinity* (London and New York, 1983).

chromatography. A family of chemical separation techniques. The original method, described by Tsvett in 1903, referred to the separation of coloured substances (hence the name), but this is not an essential requirement. All chromatographic methods involve a stationary PHASE (a liquid or solid) and a mobile phase (liquid or gas). Separation depends on individual components of the mixture having different distributions between the two phases, so that they move at varying rates in the mobile phase. Closely similar SPECIES can be separated (e.g. ISOTOPES and ISOMERS), and the detection of very small quantities is possible. See also AFFINITY CHROMATOGRAPHY; GAS CHROMATOGRAPHY; ION EXCHANGE; PAPER CHROMATOGRAPHY. B.F.

chromosomes. Thread-like structures present in the NUCLEI of all CELLS; they are the carriers of the hereditary factors known as GENES. See also CROSSING OVER; GENETICS. J.M.S.

chronobiology. The study of how biological processes are controlled through time. Chronobiology is particularly concerned with periodic biological processes. Processes, such as movement, migration, feeding, sleeping, and breeding, often occur periodically, at intervals of years, months, days or minutes. The periodicity may depend on environmental cues, but in some cases it will persist if the cue is experimen-

tally removed. The periodicity must then be due to the animal's internal clock (see BIOLOGICAL RHYTHM); the physiological mechanisms of internal clocks are little understood. M.R.

chunking. In INFORMATION THEORY, a process of re-CODING information which reduces the number of independent symbols in a message while increasing the number of kinds of symbol. For example 011001001110110 can be recoded (by grouping the digits in threes and converting to the scale of 8: 000=0; 001=1; 010=2; 011=3; etc.) as 31166. The octal version is easier to remember, being shorter, and the fact that there are now 8 different symbols instead of 2 does not matter. The word was first used in this sense by G.A. Miller, who suggested that an analogous process is employed by people to make the best use of the limited number (about 7) of mental or perceptual 'slots' which we seem to have for items for immediate attention. J.S.B.

Church's thesis, see under RECURSIVE FUNCTION THEORY.

CIA (Central Intelligence Agency). The official American intelligence organization established in 1947 by the National Security Act to coordinate the total intelligence effort of the U.S.A. It has persistently combined intelligence-gathering and political warfare with a more extensive role as executor of covert U.S. policy, including active subversion, GUERRILLA warfare and sabotage. Such activities have been directed against COMMUNIST countries, their allies, and other regimes and movements unsuited to America's pursuit of its interests. The lengthy catalogue of involvement includes the overthrow of the Arben government in Guatemala and the Musadegh government in Iran in 1954; the BAY OF PIGS incident in 1961; the destruction of the Allende government in Chile in 1973. In the aftermath of the WATERGATE affair the CIA was briefly challenged by Congressional attempts to scrutinize more closely its actions. Since the later 1970s changing political priorities have restored much of its complex (and at times barely detectable) role — e.g. in efforts to destabilize the government of

NICARAGUA and in preparing the way for the U.S. invasion of Grenada in 1983.

S.R.

Bibl: W. Blum, *The CIA: A Forgotten History* (London and Atlantic Highlands, N.J., 1986).

CIAM (Congrès Internationaux d'Architecture Moderne). A series of attempts, from 1928 onwards, to solve collectively some of the dominant problems of modern architecture which were at first seen as moral rather than stylistic: CIAM's first manifesto emphasized the need to put 'architecture back on its real plane, the economic and sociological plane'. Most of the great figures of the modern movement attended its meetings and Le Corbusier dominated several of these. A number of national sub-groups were formed, that in Britain being known as MARS (Modern Architectural Research Society). CIAM's most widely known document, the *Athens Charter*, stemmed from its 4th Congress in 1933 and dealt with what were considered the four primary functions of the city: dwelling, recreation, work, and transportation. The 10th and last congress, held in Dubrovnik in 1956, saw the introduction of the notion of CLUSTER PLANNING.

M.BR.

Bibl: J.L. Sert, *Can Our Cities Survive?* (Cambridge, Mass., 1944).

cinema, classical Hollywood, see under CLASSICAL HOLLYWOOD CINEMA.

cinema, subjectivity in, see under SUBJECTIVITY IN CINEMA.

cinéma vérité (sometimes known as *cinéma-direct*, from direct, as opposed to post-synchronized, sound recording). Term derived from the Russian slogan *kino-pravda* applied by Dziga Vertov to his own work in the Soviet silent cinema, and used by Jean Rouch to describe the DOCUMENTARY movement in the early 1960s which in part revived Dziga Vertov's kino-eye principles (the camera sees truth; the film-maker should not intervene except in his MONTAGE of what the camera records). It is associated chiefly with the work of Richard Leacock and the Maysles brothers, who attempted to present an objective record of actuality (recon-structed or otherwise), but relegated montage to a subordinate role because new technical developments (lightweight cameras and recording equipment) enabled them to film their subjects unobtrusively and uninterruptedly. Rouch himself subsequently argued that the selectivity of the film-maker's eye negated the supposed objectivity of the camera, and turned increasingly to fiction as a basis for his films, though retaining the element of fact through his approach and his use of non-actors.

T.C.C.M.

Bibl: G.R. Levin (ed.), *Documentary Explorations* (New York, 1971).

CinemaScope. A wide-screen process involving an anamorphic lens (*L'Hypergonar*), demonstrated by Professor Henri Chrétien in 1927 and used by Claude Autant-Lara in an experimental short film, *Construire du Feu*, in 1928, but not developed commercially until bought and copyrighted as CinemaScope by Twentieth Century-Fox in 1952 in an attempt to combat the threat of television by producing bigger images. The first CinemaScope film was *The Robe*, 1953. The standard screen, in use since the earliest days of cinema, is a 4×3 rectangle; CinemaScope, using the anamorphic lens in filming to compress the image onto a standard 35mm frame, with a complementary lens to expand it again during projection, offered a 2.5×1 rectangle. Other Hollywood and foreign film companies followed suit after the success of CinemaScope with variations on this wide-screen process known as Warnerscope, Superscope, VistaVision, Dyaliscope, Tohoscope, Technirama, etc.

Analogous attempts to extend the cinema screen include *Cinerama*, a development of the triple screen used by Abel Gance in his *Napoléon* in 1927: marketed in 1952, Cinerama originally employed three separate projectors on a curved screen, but later used only one. Subsequent processes (Todd-AO, Panavision 70) dispensed with the anamorphic lens by using 70mm film, double the width of the standard 35mm frame. 70mm film had been used for a few films in the early days of sound cinema, the first being *The Big Trail* and *Billy the Kid* (both 1930).

T.C.C.M.

cinémathèque. French term coined (on the analogy of *bibliothèque,* library) to describe a film museum or library. The Cinémathèque de la Ville de Paris, founded in 1919, preserved only films which were considered important as historical documents or for teaching purposes. The Cinémathèque Française, founded by Henri Langlois, Georges Franju, and Jean Mitry in 1936 (three years after the British Film Institute, its sister organization in London which incorporates the National Film Archive), considers film as an end in itself rather than as a means to education: it collects, preserves, and displays not only entertainment films as well as DOCUMENTARIES, but film stills, designs, scripts, models, costumes, and optical toys.

T.C.C.M.

cinematic address. A concept in film theory to refer to the specific qualities of enunciation in cinema. In the context of structural linguistics, the term enunciation describes the aspect of an utterance, or SPEECH ACT, which addresses and positions its recipients. Enunciation operates in two registers, *discours* and *histoire:* the former inscribing both a speaker (e.g. 'I') and an addressee (e.g. 'you'); the latter being a mode of address — characteristic of narrations of past events — in which no addresser/addressee is implied. Christian Metz has argued that cinematic address operates largely within the register of *histoire.* Cinematic enunciation does not, he suggests, normally identify itself as proceeding from any particular source: a film seems simply to be 'there', unfolding itself before the spectator's eyes. To this extent, cinematic language conceals the marks of its own enunciation, constructing an omniscient, impersonal 'narrating instance'.

A.KU.

Bibl: C. Metz, *Psychoanalysis and Cinema: The Imaginary Signifier* (London, 1982).

cinematic apparatus. A concept used in psychoanalytically informed film theory to refer to the conditions under which meaning is produced through the interaction of film text and spectator (see SUBJECTIVITY IN CINEMA). The cinematic apparatus is comprised of the context in which films are consumed — darkened auditorium, projection system, shadows on the screen — together with the spectator's psychic positioning within this context. It has been suggested that this apparatus structures the spectator's subjectivity in ways identical to the developmental processes in which the human subject is formed. Such arguments tend to stress the UNCONSCIOUS element of spectator-text relations in cinema: cinematic 'speech', for example, is regarded as analogous to the rhetoric of unconscious language; while the 'cinematic state' or the 'filmic condition' is held to be like the dream-state, or in some other sense evocative of regressive, pre-linguistic, states of subjectivity. It is useful for its suggestion that the moment of reception is crucial to meaning production in cinema.

A.KU.

Bibl: Jean-Louis Baudry, 'The apparatus', *Camera Obscura,* no.1 (1976), pp. 104-26.

Cinerama, see under CINEMASCOPE.

circadian rhythm. A BIOLOGICAL RHYTHM with a period of exactly or approximately 24 hours.

P.M.

circulation of élites, see under ÉLITE.

citric acid cycle, see KREBS CYCLE.

City, the. The name given to the square mile of London which has traditionally housed one of the world's major financial centres. A residue of Britain's era of commercial and industrial supremacy, it has proved itself more adaptable to changing world conditions than most other parts of the British economy. Among its leading financial institutions are the Stock Exchange, the money markets, the insurance institutions (including Lloyds), commercial and merchant banks, and the various commodity exchanges. It is a major source of Britain's overseas earnings and has become progressively and proportionately more important to Britain's BALANCE OF PAYMENTS. Nevertheless its channelling of British INVESTMENT overseas rather than into British industry became a contentious domestic issue in Britain in the 1970s. As an international financial centre its only major rivals are WALL STREET and Tokyo. In the 1980s, the City has been affected by a number of financial scandals. These, and the need to compete with other financial centres, have led to changes in the ECONOMIC REGULATION of the different parts of the City. For example, fixed commissions on dealings in shares have been abolished; and the institutional distinction between those firms buying and selling shares, and those firms advising clients on dealings in shares has been abolished.

D.E.; J.P.

Bibl: M. J. Artis, ed., *The UK Economy* (London, 1986).

civil disobedience. The strategy of securing political goals by non-violent refusal to cooperate with the agents of the government. Most famously, the strategy which Mahatma Gandhi persuaded the Indian National Congress to adopt in April 1930, which envisaged the disruption of British government in India by the mass ceremonial performance of illegal actions. The aim of such mass action is to overload the police and the courts and so to impair the CREDIBILITY of the government. In insisting so strongly on NON-VIOLENCE, the strategy makes great demands on the self-control and patience of its adherents. This was one of its merits in Gandhi's eyes. Interest in civil disobedience has been revived both by those who advocate a non-violent defence strategy as an alternative to nuclear DETERRENCE and by those who adopted civil disobedience in the attempt to alter American policy towards and military involvement in VIETNAM.   A.R.

Bibl: G. Sharp, *The Politics of Non-Violent Action* (Boston, 1974); M.K. Gandhi, *Non-Violent Resistance* (New York, 1961).

civil rights movement. (1) The campaign for legal enforcement of rights guaranteed to American BLACKS as citizens under the U.S. constitution. It developed in the late 1950s as earlier efforts by groups such as the National Association for the Advancement of Colored People (founded 1910) and the National Urban League (1911) became increasingly regarded as too gradualist and unsuited to overcome southern white resistance to change. The movement was a coalition of organizations including the Southern Christian Leadership Conference led by Dr Martin Luther King Jr,

the Student Non-Violent Coordinating Committee and the Congress on Racial Equality. Its tactics included various forms of DIRECT ACTION, such as boycotts, sit-ins and marches; in the face of great provocation it tried to adhere to NON-VIOLENCE and the principles of CIVIL DISOBEDIENCE, and to incorporate the support of white liberals. The movement achieved some successes such as the Civil Rights Act of 1964 and Voting Rights Act of 1965; it became increasingly disunited as some elements extended their claims from liberal demands for formal civil rights and electoral participation, to a more radical prospectus for economic equality both within and outside the South. The fracturing of the movement's identity and the growth of more militant BLACK POWER organizations occurred in 1965-6.

Bibl: H. Sitkoff, *The Struggle for Black Equality 1945-80* (New York, 1981); M. Marable, *Race, Reform and Rebellion* (London, 1984).

(2) The officially non-sectarian but essentially Catholic campaign to achieve equality of status between Catholic minority and Protestant majority in Northern Ireland. It was led by the Civil Rights Association which was formed in January 1967 and had a diverse base, including the SOCIALIST faction, 'People's Democracy'. The movement's tactics of marches and demonstrations were countered by Protestant marches, violence and a mixture of police aggression and proscription. The escalating conflict led to the introduction of British troops in mid-1969, and to the splintering of the Civil Rights Movement as the issue became recast in Nationalist terms.   S.R.

Bibl: K. Boyle *et al., Ten Years on in Northern Ireland* (London, 1980).

cladding. The use of lightweight building materials as an enclosure where the load-bearing function of the wall is taken by some other element of the STRUCTURE. This first occurred in greenhouses, railway stations, exhibition pavilions and factories of the 19th century, and the buildings of the CHICAGO SCHOOL. A highly developed form of cladding in which MODULAR factory-made units of glazing and opaque panels are fixed to a framework held by the floor structure and referred to as a *curtain wall* has become ubiquitous and has affected the appearance of most towns. See also PREFABRICATION.　　　　　M.BR.

Bibl: M. Rostron, *Light Cladding of Buildings* (London, 1964).

cladism. Method of classification in BIOLOGY (see BIOSYSTEMATICS) in which SPECIES are classified together strictly according to the order of their EVOLUTIONARY branching. (Cladism comes from the Greek *klados*, branch.) Alternatively, species might be grouped according to their similarity of appearance; which is called phenetic classification. Generally, cladistic and phenetic classifications are similar, but not always. For example, crocodiles are more similar in appearance to lizards than either are to birds, and in phenetic classification crocodiles and lizards are grouped together as reptiles, separate from birds. However, crocodiles share a more recent common ancestor with birds than with lizards, and the cladist therefore classifies crocodiles with birds and the group 'Reptilia' ceases to exist in formal classification. Cladism was particularly advocated by the German entomologist Willi Hennig. Cladism can be preferred to phenetic classification on the grounds that evolutionary relations (once known) are unambiguous whereas phenetic similarity is an ambiguous criterion which depends on the taxonomists' points of view. Cladism may be criticized on the grounds that it produces strange novelties (such as the abolition of reptiles) and is unnecessary.　　　　　M.R.

Bibl: M. Ridley, *Evolution and Classification* (London, 1986).

clairvoyance, see under ESP.

clan. Groups recruited on the basis of common DESCENT but the ties with an ancestor are assumed rather than demonstrated. If descent is claimed through the male line, the group is known as a *patri-clan*, through the female line, a *matri-clan*. Clans are larger and looser groupings than descent groups. However, even if members are widely dispersed and lack a corporate structure, MARRIAGE for clan members is usually EXOGAMOUS, that is marriage outside the clan.　　　　　A.G.

Bibl: J. Goody, *The Development of the Family and Marriage in Europe* (Cambridge, 1983).

class.
(1) In MATHEMATICS and LOGIC, a synonym for SET.

(2) In SOCIOLOGY, a CONCEPT which denotes different social strata in society. Many sociologists, such as Ralf Dahrendorf, distinguish between the 'estate' systems of feudal and pre-industrial society — in which distinctions were primarily of *rank*, resting on tradition and an intricate system of age-old, often codified rights and duties — and the true class system which emerged when CAPITALISM and the INDUSTRIAL REVOLUTION substituted for these criteria the external criterion of material possessions. In the *Communist Manifesto* Marx identified classes in relation to the means of production, and thus generalized the concept of class to all societies where such distinctions could be made. (See also SOCIAL STRATIFICATION.)

Economic class. For Marx, the criterion of class was economic. However, he never specifically defined 'economic', and at various points in his writings he laid down several quite different criteria for the identification of classes. Moreover, it is difficult to find a single unambiguous criterion, whether it be OCCUPATION or a common standing in the processes of production, that does not encounter logical difficulties in classification. (If, for example, one takes the production process as the criterion, how does one classify those who stand outside production?)

For Max Weber, class is an analytical term which identifies individuals who have similar 'life chances' in the opportunities for gaining income; market assets include skill as well as property. He sees the major historical class struggle as being between creditors and debtors, with the conflict under capitalism between employers and workers as merely a special case.

Social class. For Marx, this was determined by, and coterminous with, economic class. Other sociologists see social class as a more complex variable which includes STATUS, prestige, family lineage, and other criteria. In the U.S.A., W. Lloyd Warner and his students sought to establish a six-grade ranking system defined simply by a dichotomous division within the upper, middle, and lower classes.

Class conflict. Marx predicted, under capitalism, an increasing POLARIZATION of society, increased exploitation of the worker, and ever sharper conflict between the two classes, leading ultimately to the social REVOLUTION. Social development for the West has belied that prediction. Real wages of the WORKING CLASS have risen, the working class has gained increasing social and political rights, and class conflict, though not eliminated, has become regulated (i.e. subject to legal rules) and institutionally isolated (i.e. there is little carry-over from industrial conflicts into other areas of life). In many industrial societies, moreover, other forms of conflict cut across class lines and divide, say, Irish Protestant from Irish Catholic workers rather than workers from bosses.

Class consciousness. Marx assumed that such consciousness would develop in class struggle created by the crises of the capitalist system. Lenin, however, regarded the working class, unaided, as able to develop only 'TRADE-UNION consciousness'; and to this extent the creation of 'socialist consciousness' is the task of the INTELLECTUALS. In that case the MARXIST notion that 'existence determines consciousness', and the relation between social position and IDEOLOGY, cannot easily be maintained. This is a conundrum from which Marxist theory has not yet extricated itself. D.B.

Bibl: R. Dahrendorf, *Class and Class Conflict in Industrial Society* (London and Stanford, 1959); S. Ossowski, tr. S. Patterson, *Class Structure in the Social Consciousness* (London and New York, 1963); P. Calvert, *The Concept of Class* (London, 1982).

classical ballet. Term derived from the Italian *ballare* meaning to dance. Classical ballet strictly means theatre entertainment employing a codified academic dance form called the *danse d'école* (classical school). With the cross-fertilization of dance techniques, the term ballet is often applied to choreographic works performed by MODERN DANCE companies. Classical ballet is based on the fundamental 5 positions laid down by Pierre Beauchamps in 1650 and built on the principle of outwardness or turnout (i.e. the rotation of the legs in the hip socket) and the codified romantic classical ballet vocabulary established by Carlo Blasis in 1820. The technique aims to produce virtuosity from seemingly effortless execution through disciplined training in body alignment. The classical ballet aesthetic strives for nobility rather than serviceability; the ballerina representing the graceful, ethereal, unattainable romantic female ideal, further enhancing beauty of line and expression by wearing pointed shoes, and the male assuming a steadfast, vital and vigorous authority. Classical ballet is built on a hierarchical system in direct contrast to modern dance, from the prima ballerina down to the corps de ballet. The historical development ranges from a diversion for the nobility in the 17th century, to the romantic era of the 19th century, through Diaghilev's revitalization in the early 20th century to its worldwide popularity today. L.A.

Bibl: S.J. Cohen, ed., *Dance as a Theatre Art* (London, 1974); R. Copeland and M. Cohen, eds., *What Is Dance?* (New York, 1983).

classical conditioning (also known as PAVLOVIAN or *respondent* conditioning). A form of CONDITIONED REFLEX; after an arbitrary stimulus has been repeatedly paired with the eliciting stimulus of a reflex, the previously neutral stimulus comes to elicit the reflex response even in the absence of the characteristic elicitor. The traditional example is the Russian physiologist I.P. Pavlov's experiment (1906), in which, after the ringing of a bell (the *conditioned stimulus*) had repeatedly been accompanied by the provision of meat (the *unconditioned stimulus*), it was found that the ringing of the bell caused dogs to salivate (the *conditioned response*) even if no meat was produced. Interest in the objective and precise Russian studies was a major influence on the BEHAVIOURIST revolution in America. However, many modern psychologists believe that classical conditioning is merely a special case of OPERANT CONDITIONING: since the conditioned response prepares the organism for the appearance of the unconditioned stimulus, it seems more parsimonious to view the unconditioned stimulus as an operant reinforcer than to regard classical conditioning as an independent kind of learning. Procedures developed from classical-conditioning paradigms, especially *aversion therapy* and *desensitization*, are described under BEHAVIOUR THERAPY.   D.H.

classical economic theory. The system of economic theory which was included in Adam Smith's *Wealth of Nations* (1776) and developed during the period ending about 1870. It was based on the assumption that the individual was usually the best judge of his own interests. The conclusion that under a freely competitive economic system the individual pursuit of economic self-interest would result in the economic benefit of the community depended on the analysis of the functioning of the PRICE MECHANISM in allocating resources in response to the supplies and demands for goods and services. When combined with the analysis of the role of the DIVISION OF LABOUR and the INVESTMENT of CAPITAL in promoting ECONOMIC GROWTH, this led to the further conclusion of the desirability of freedom in international trade and freedom of economic activity, generally, from government intervention. The classical economists generally accepted the QUANTITY THEORY OF MONEY.

There were, however, numerous differences of view among writers of this school, particularly with respect to the theories of VALUE, wages, rent, population, underconsumption, banking policy, and the functions of government. One of the best-known and for a short time most influential MODELS based on classical economic theory is the *Ricardian*. This incorporated the Malthusian (see MALTHUSIANISM) theory of population, the Ricardian theory of rent based on the law of DIMINISHING RETURNS to land, and Ricardo's variant of the LABOUR THEORY OF VALUE. An important conclusion derived from this model was that economic growth was doomed to come to an end owing to the increasing difficulty of producing sufficient food as population increases. See NEO-CLASSICAL ECONOMIC THEORY.

M.E.A.B.

Bibl: M. Blaug, *Economic Theory in Retrospect* (London, 1985).

classical Hollywood cinema. In general, the products of the Hollywood film studio system in its heyday between the late 1920s and early 1950s. In recent usage in film theory, the term refers more particularly to a set of stylistic and formal conventions characteristic not only of Hollywood but — given the worldwide cultural dominance of American cinema — also to a large extent of fiction films produced elsewhere. In the classic narrative, events are organized around a structure of enigma and resolution, proceed from beginning to end according to a cause-effect logic, and hinge upon the actions of fictional characters presented as psychologically-rounded individuals. The verisimilitude of this narrative logic is reinforced by the cinematic rendering of the fictional world through conventions of MISE-EN-SCÈNE and editing which map out the space of the narrative in a coherent manner, and organize narrative time accordingly.   A.KU.

Bibl: David Bordwell *et al.*, *The Classical Hollywood Cinema: Film Style and Mode of Production to 1960* (London, 1985).

classical physics. Those areas of PHYSICS which were formulated before the 20th-century developments of RELATIVITY and QUANTUM MECHANICS. Classical physics is built on the four great theories of NEWTONIAN MECHANICS, ELECTROMAGNETISM, THERMODYNAMICS, and STATISTICAL MECHANICS. Two points must be stressed: first, these theories have not been proved wrong by modern discoveries; instead they are revealed as approximately valid under fairly clearly-defined circumstances (e.g. relativity only supersedes Newtonian mechanics for PARTICLES moving almost as fast as light). Second, both in the study of its conceptual foundations and in the development of its applications, classical physics remains a living, growing subject.   M.V.B.

classification. In ordinary language, either the *construction* of a classification ('How do you classify architectural styles?') or the *identification* of an individual specimen ('How would you classify the architecture of Salisbury Cathedral?') In STATISTICS and DATA ANALYSIS the word is used for the former of these activities, the latter being called 'identification' or 'diagnosis'. The problems of classifying bacteria led to the development during the 1950s of numerical methods of constructing various types of classification from descriptive data about the objects to be classified, and such methods now form an important part of data analysis. See also BIOSYSTEMATICS.   R.SI.

clathrate. A compound in which one molecular component (see MOLECULE) is imprisoned in the cage structure of the other. The first clathrate, a compound of hydrogen sulphide and hydroquinone, was made in 1849, and clathrates have since aroused some curiosity because their behaviour is intermediate between that of normal compounds and that of simple mixtures. B.F.

cleavage, see under EMBRYOLOGY.

client. In ANTHROPOLOGY, an individual in a relationship with a patron (see PATRONAGE) through whom he gains access to resources. In return a client may pledge his support, vote or solidarity to his patron. Patrons often compete for clients and try to enhance their standing by extending NETWORKS of influence. Clients themselves, however, can exercise checks on the power of patrons either through the invocation of quasi-KINSHIP or personal obligations or by threatening to leave one patron for another.

The status of patron—client is frequently a relative one since relationships are part of an extended chain: a client at one level may be a patron to individuals at other levels.   A.G.

Bibl: S.N. Eisenstadt and L. Roniger, *Patrons, Clients and Friends* (Cambridge, 1984); Caroline White, *Patrons and Partisans* (Cambridge, 1980).

climatology. The study of average temperature, rainfall, humidity, and sunshine in different localities over long periods of time (at least 30 years), as contrasted with METEOROLOGY, which studies short-term changes. It is hoped that long-term climatic changes such as ice ages (as revealed by fossil vegetation, for example) may be explained by changes in the composition of the atmosphere.   M.V.B.

climax. In ECOLOGY, a final or culminating state of an undisturbed vegetational COMMUNITY. A distinction is usually drawn between an EQUILIBRIUM achieved with respect to climate (*climatic climax*) and to soil (*edaphic climax*).   P.H.

clinical linguistics. The application of the theories, methods, and descriptive findings of LINGUISTICS to the analysis of spoken or written language handicap, such as APHASIA, language delay, or pronunciation disorders.   D.C.

Bibl: D. Crystal, *Clinical Linguistics* (Vienna, 1981).

clinical psychology, see under APPLIED PSYCHOLOGY.

cliometrics, see under ECONOMIC HISTORY.

clock paradox. The prediction of Einstein's theory of RELATIVITY that clocks and other temporal processes run more slowly as seen by an observer moving relatively to them than similar clocks and processes in his own FRAME OF REFERENCE. This effect (which is only appreciable when the moving clock travels almost as fast as light) does not violate the principle of CAUSALITY or the rules of LOGIC. Indeed it has been confirmed experimentally by the discovery that swiftly-moving MESONS in the atmosphere are observed by us to live much longer before decaying than slower-moving mesons produced in the laboratory; the meson decays according to its internal 'clock', which runs slow as seen by us.

Despite this, the clock paradox has occasioned lively controversy for over 50 years, particularly in the sharpened form of the *twin paradox*, in which a traveller is imagined to leave the earth at high speed and then, after some years, to turn round and come back; his twin, who has stayed behind, will have aged, while the traveller (whose clocks have run slow relative to those on earth) will still be young. The paradox is this: since each twin has been moving relative to the other, might one not equally well look at the situation from the traveller's point of view, in which case the twins' roles and ageing processes will be reversed? It is resolved by the fact that the twins are not in symmetrical situations: when turning around, the traveller must accelerate, and accelerating frames of reference are not dealt with in special relativity; a full analysis requires the general theory of relativity. Einstein's position has been vindicated by the recent experiments of J.C. Hafele and R.E. Keating, who measured small differences, compatible with the predictions of relativity theory, between the times indicated by clocks that had been flown round the world and clocks that had remained in the laboratory.   M.V.B.

Bibl: L. Marder, *Time and the Space Traveller* (London, 1971).

cloisonnisme, see under SYNTHETISM.

clone, see CLONING.

cloning. (1) GENE or DNA cloning is the production of many identical copies of a gene or piece of DNA, usually to provide sufficient quantities for analysis or for use in GENETIC ENGINEERING. Typically, the gene is inserted into a *plasmid,* which is a small circular piece of DNA extracted from a bacterium. Upon reintroduction into a bacterium and stimulation of bacterial growth, the original bacterium produces numerous progeny in a short time and the plasmid independently multiplies many times in each bacterial cell. As a result numerous clones of the original gene or piece of DNA are produced. (2) Similarly, CELL cloning is the production of large numbers of identical cells, as for example in the production of MONO-CLONAL ANTIBODIES. (3) It is much less easy to clone whole plants or animals than their genes or cells. Nonetheless, certain plant tissue can be induced to sprout many plantlets, each of which will develop into an identical plant. With the partial exception of some amphibians, there has been little success in cloning animals and the cloning of humans remains a remote and repugnant possibility.   P.N.

closed class, see under WORD CLASS.

closed shop. The restriction of employment in a workplace to members of a particular TRADE UNION, or unions. In the *pre-entry closed shop* only those who are already union members can be engaged. In the *union shop* (U.S.A.) or *agency shop* (U.K.) non-members may be engaged, but can keep their jobs only if they become members (or alternatively, in the U.K., contribute the amount of union dues) within a reasonable time. All forms of closed shop meet the feeling of unionists that no one working alongside them should benefit from the activity of their union without paying dues to it. The authority of the union over dissidents is greatly increased when those who leave the union or are deprived of membership are thereby deprived of their jobs too. Some employers have found the closed shop advantageous in this last respect, and many have had no alternative but to accept it; but for an employer to dismiss a satisfactory worker only because he has fallen out with the union is embarrassing, and may be actionable as unfair dismissal. To have to maintain union membership under penalty of losing his job restricts the worker's freedom. In the U.S.A. the Taft-Hartley Act, 1947, made it unlawful for employers and unions to enforce the closed shop, but not the union shop. In the U.K., since 1971, there have been several Acts of Parliament which have altered the rules governing the operation of the closed shop. In 1987 the closed shop was still legal, although the CONSERVATIVE government issued a green paper (a paper containing proposals to be discussed by Parliament) in that year with the proposal that the closed shop should be made illegal.   A.B.E.;E.H.P.B.

Bibl: M. J. Artis, ed., *The UK Economy* (London, 1986).

closure. The completion of incomplete forms, e.g. the perception of continuity in an outline drawing which is composed of dots. In GESTALT psychology 'tendency toward closure' refers to the way in which perceiving, remembering, or thinking strive toward patterned wholes that are as coherent and stable as circumstances will allow.   I.M.L.H.

cloud chamber. A device, invented by C.T.R. Wilson in 1911, and used to study

NUCLEAR REACTIONS and ELEMENTARY PARTICLES. It is based on the fact that a fast charged PARTICLE leaves a record of its path, in the form of a trail of droplets, centred on IONS, when it traverses a vapour kept just below its condensation temperature. See also BUBBLE CHAMBER.

M.V.B.

Club of Rome, see under LIMITS TO GROWTH.

cluster (in music), see TONE-CLUSTER.

cluster analysis. A form of FACTOR ANALYSIS in which multivariate measurements or observations on a number of individual entities are statistically analysed, usually with the aid of a COMPUTER, to try to identify internal structure, e.g. the chronological ordering of archaeological objects, or the grouping of a set of manuscripts by authorship.

M.S.BA.

cluster planning. A town-planning CONCEPT, introduced at the 10th congress of CIAM (1956), which attempts to create a complex and closely knit aggregation with a comprehensible structure; it defines an attitude rather than a specific built form. The attitude stems from a dissatisfaction both with the dispersed forms of the GARDEN CITY and with the simplistic concept of an overall organization for the whole city; the cluster suggests a way of planning by the gradual accumulation of elements, each viable, to produce a town or building complex, and is thus perhaps closer to traditional town building.

M.BR.

Bibl: A. and P. Smithson, *Urban Structuring* (London and New York, 1967).

CMEA, see under COMECON.

CND, see under PEACE MOVEMENT.

cobol. A HIGH-LEVEL PROGRAMMING LANGUAGE for commercial data-processing (see COMPUTING).

C.S.

COBRA. A group of artists that flourished between 1948 and 1951. Its name combines the initial letters of the capital cities where the founder-members worked: Copenhagen, Brussels, Amsterdam. The association inherited the ideas (and many of the members) of three groups, the Dutch *Experimentele Groep,* the Danish *Spiralen* group, and the Belgian *Bureau International de Surréalisme Révolutionnaire.* Its leading figures were Asger Jorn, Karel Appel, Christian Dotremont, Pierre Alechinsky, Constant Nieuwenhuys, and Cornelis van Beverloo Corneille. In their exhibitions and publications they sought to express, spontaneously and/or unconsciously, profound psychic forces, and their images are often primitive, violent, and fantastic. COBRA may be seen as a European variant of ACTION PAINTING and ABSTRACT EXPRESSIONISM.

P.C.

Bibl: É. Langui, 'Expressionism since 1945 and the Cobra Movement', in J.P. Hodin *et al., Figurative Art since 1945* (London, 1971).

cobweb theory (or *model*).

(1) In international relations, a theory developed by J.W. Burton as an alternative to the state-centric approach. Some American scholars were simultaneously applying SYSTEMS concepts and theories, and elaborating the WORLD SOCIETY concept. Burton's model sees society as comprising millions of 'cobwebs', each representing a system, not as a distinct territorial unit, but as a set of dynamic social relations, constantly growing in complexity as a result of increased functional interdependence and channelling values and expectations of communities and individuals. Critics have attacked the MODEL for failing to allow sufficiently for the roles of STATES and their foreign policies and interactions, and for being so diffuse and unmanageable that it is of negligible value in developing a general theory of international relations.

P.W.

Bibl: J.W. Burton, *World Society* (Cambridge, 1972).

(2) In ECONOMICS, a model of how a market may behave when production of a good takes a period of time. The decision about how much to produce must be based on the expectation (see RATIONAL EXPECTATIONS) of the price at the time the output is supplied to the market. In this model, the lag between production and supply is taken as one period and producers assume that the next period's price will be equal to the present price. This

135

means that the present price determines the level of current production and thus how much is supplied to the market in the next period. In the next period, price adjusts to ensure that all that is supplied is demanded. If demand at the expected price is not equal to the amount supplied, i.e. the market is not in EQUILIBRIUM, future prices and production will vary.

J.P.

Bibl: R.G. Lipsey, *An Introduction to Positive Economics* (London, 6th ed., 1983).

code. In SOCIOLINGUISTICS, a term loosely applied to the language system of a community or to a particular *variety* within a language, e.g. Bernstein's characterization of the different linguistic capabilities of middle- and working-class children in terms of elaborated and restricted codes.

D.C.

code-switching. In SOCIOLINGUISTICS, the way bilingual or BIDIALECTAL speakers change from the use of one language or dialect to another, depending on who they are talking to, where they are, and other contextual factors. The amount of code-switching which takes place in everyday conversation between bilinguals has been much underestimated, and is often misinterpreted as illustrating uncertainty or confusion on the part of the speakers. The current view is that the alternations reflect systematically the social and psychological factors involved in the interaction.

D.C.

Bibl: P. Trudgill, *Sociolinguistics* (Harmondsworth, 1984).

co-determination, see under PARTICIPATION.

coding.
(1) In INFORMATION THEORY, the representation of data for transmission or storage. Coding theory concerns itself with such questions as 'Is this the shortest representation of the data?'; 'How likely is this datum to be confused with other data if the representation is corrupted?' and with the measurement of REDUNDANCY. It is the basis of the design of ENCODERS and DECODERS.

R.M.N.

(2) In COMPUTING, the final stage in preparing a problem for a COMPUTER (the others being SYSTEMS ANALYSIS and PROGRAMMING). It involves writing exhaustive instructions to make a computer carry out the tasks which have been specified in the previous stages. Typically, coders write their instructions in ASSEMBLY LANGUAGE — a very lengthy and largely mechanical process in which they are prone to error. It is difficult for anyone who has not experienced it to realize the degree of detail required in coding. This is similar to that required in a knitting pattern (English, not continental, style), and coding corresponds to constructing such a detailed pattern, given the dimensions of the garment and the basic stitch pattern. Coding can be eliminated by the use of an appropriate HIGH-LEVEL PROGRAMMING LANGUAGE.

C.S.

codomain (in MATHEMATICS), see under FUNCTION.

coefficient. In MATHEMATICS and its applications, a term more or less synonymous with PARAMETER (2), but most frequently used with reference to some specified class of FUNCTIONS. For a mathematical example see ALGEBRA; a typical example from PHYSICS is the coefficient of thermal expansion.

R.G.

coercion. Although all commentators agree that the bank clerk reluctantly handing money to the armed robber is a victim of coercion, there is little agreement on the boundaries between what is and what is not a coercive relationship. Some claim that apparently 'free' bargains are in fact coercive; the employer who offers a starving man a badly paid job may be said to be forcing him to work rather than merely offering him a free choice between working and not working. MARXISTS, who hold that relations between capitalists and workers are coercive rather than a matter of freely reached agreement, point to the origins of CAPITALISM in the forced expropriation of small farmers and the like. Others point to the implausibility of describing bargains struck between participants of very unequal bargaining power as 'free' bargains. Others point to the difference between relationships in which both parties expect to benefit and those in which one party extracts a disproportionate share of the benefits of agreement by his ability to impose worse terms on the other party in the event of their proving recalcitrant — the bank clerk would rather not hand over the money demanded by the robber, but the robber can impose the option of death or injury. Whether this is definitive of coercion or only a symptom of it is another question, and one to which no answer is entirely persuasive.   A.R.

Bibl: Robert Nozick, 'Coercion' in *Philosophy, Politics and Society*, IV (Oxford, 1972).

coexistence, peaceful. A phrase originally coined, in a slightly different form as 'peaceful cohabitation' (*mirnoe sozhitelstvo*) between peoples, by Leon Trotsky on 22 November 1917, and used with varying connotations by successive Soviet leaders until December 1927 when the present term (*mirnoe sosushchestvovanie*), which has a slightly less active sense, of passive existence rather than active cohabitation, officially replaced it. Descriptive of the pacific relations between the SOCIALIST Soviet Union and its CAPITALIST rivals, the concept was designed to mobilize opinion in the latter against actively anti-Soviet policies, delaying war by 'buying off' the capitalists, in the words of Josef Stalin. In the aftermath of Stalin's death the risk of mutual destruction by NUCLEAR WEAPONS was felt by his successor, Khrushchev, to rule out open WAR between the Soviet and non-Soviet worlds. He nevertheless made it clear that competition between states with different social systems would continue in all other fields until COMMUNISM proved itself superior and presided over the burial of capitalism. In practice it has also become evident that avoidance of a major war between the nuclear powers does not rule out support and intervention by both sides in wars of 'national liberation'.
                                        D.C.W.

cognatic descent, see under BILATERAL/COGNATIC DESCENT.

cognition. A collective term for the psychological processes involved in the acquisition, organization, and use of knowledge. Originally, the word distin-

guished the rational from the emotional (see EMOTION) and impulsive aspect of mental life. It passed out of currency, to be revived with the advent of COMPUTER SIMULATION of thought processes (see ARTIFICIAL INTELLIGENCE). The term is now used in COGNITIVE PSYCHOLOGY to refer to all the information-processing activities of the brain, ranging from the analysis of immediate STIMULI to the organization of subjective experience. In contemporary terminology, cognition includes such processes and phenomena as PERCEPTION, memory, attention, PROBLEM-SOLVING, language, thinking, and imagery.   G.B.

Bibl: J.R. Anderson, *Cognitive Psychology and its Implications* (San Francisco, 1980).

cognitive. Adjective applied to those aspects of mental life connected with the acquisition of knowledge or the formation of beliefs (which fail, through falsehood or lack of justification, to qualify as items of knowledge). It is applied to distinguish the kind of MEANING possessed by statements, true or false, from that possessed by such utterances as commands or exclamations which, although plainly meaningful, cannot be assessed as true or false. EMOTIVISM in ETHICS maintains that the meaning of VALUE-JUDGEMENTS is either wholly ('that is wrong') or partly ('that is theft') non-cognitive.   A.Q.

Bibl: I. Goldman, *Epistemology and Cognition* (Boston, 1986).

cognitive consonance and **cognitive dissonance.** *Cognitive consonance* is a consistency between the knowledge, ideas, and beliefs which make up a COGNITIVE SYSTEM so that the system is harmonious and without internal contradictions; *cognitive dissonance* is the absence of such consistency. The latter term is also applied to a perceived incongruity between a person's attitudes and his behaviour. There is evidence that people tend to reduce such dissonance by making appropriate changes in their attitudes and beliefs; thus a heavy drinker rationalizes his drinking behaviour by doubting the integrity of those reporting research on the evil effects of alcohol.   A.L.C.B.; J.S.B.

Bibl: L. Festinger, *A Theory of Cogni-*

tive Dissonance (London and Stanford, 1962).

cognitive psychology. A branch of PSY-CHOLOGY defined partly by its subject-matter, i.e. COGNITION, partly by its point of view. With respect to point of view, its main PRESUPPOSITION is that any interaction between an organism and its EN-VIRONMENT changes not only its overt behaviour or physiological condition, but also its knowledge of or information about the environment, and that this latter change may affect not only present response but also future orientation to the environment. Historically speaking, cognitive psychology arose out of a combination of Enlightenment psychological SEN-SATIONALISM and associationist (see AS-SOCIATIONISM) EPISTEMOLOGY, grounded in individual and social learning theories and philosophies of educability and CON-DITIONING. E.C. Tolman, characterizing the difference between the BEHAVIOURIST theory of *stimulus* and *response* and cognitive approaches to the study of learning, applied to the former the image of a telephone switchboard in which incoming stimuli came by practice to be connected to responses, and to the latter that of a map-room where the incoming stimuli were put together into 'cognitive maps' by the use of which responses were constructed to achieve intended outcomes. Whilst the distinction is no longer so clear, thanks to the greater sophistication of the modern CONNECTIONIST'S view of 'switchboards', Tolman's distinction highlights the emphasis of cognitive psychology on those mediating 'knowledge processes' that affect the complex relation between INPUT in the form of stimulation and OUT-PUT in the form of response. Within the last generation, the metaphorical MODELS of cognitive psychology have been transformed by the rise of ARTIFICIAL INTELLI-GENCE and computer-based concepts of learning systems. How far COMPUTERS themselves can be understood within the categories of cognitive psychology now forms an important philosophical and practical debate.

Perhaps the main contribution of cognitive studies to the great debates in psychology has been to redress the imbalance created by the radical behaviourism intro-duced in the 1920s. The new emphasis was undoubtedly given great support by new approaches to information processing in CYBERNETICS, INFORMATION THEORY, and COMPUTING.   J.S.B.;R.P.

Bibl: U. Neisser, *Cognitive Psychology* (New York, 1967).

cognitive system. A collection of inter-related items of knowledge or belief held by an individual about a person, group, event, class of objects, or any subject, either concrete or abstract. Every human individual establishes a number of such cognitive systems. The degree to which they are interrelated varies greatly; one of the characteristics of an IDEOLOGY is the high degree of interconnection between the most important cognitive systems. For the degree of consistency *within* a cognitive system see COGNITIVE CONSONANCE AND COGNITIVE DISSONANCE.   A.L.C.B.

cohabitation. A term coined to describe the new constitutional situation which emerged in France after the legislative elections in March 1986. The French constitution divides executive power ambiguously between a president (Head of State) who is directly elected for a seven-year period and a prime minister who is directly elected every five years. Hitherto, the president and prime minister have always held similar political outlooks and the former has exercised a powerful influence over the activities of the premier. Following the victory of the RIGHT-wing coalition parties in the 1986 legislative elections, the SOCIALIST François Mitterrand became the first president of the Fifth Republic to face a hostile parliamentary majority. He must therefore 'cohabit' with the Gaullist prime minister, Jacques Chirac, who does not share his objectives and who has declared his intention to assert fully his authority as prime minister.   S.M.

coherence. In PHYSICS (for its more general meaning see under TRUTH), a property of a beam of RADIATION, which is coherent if all its component waves have the same PHASE. A LASER emits COHERENT LIGHT, but an ordinary electric light (where the ATOMS vibrate independently) emits incoherent light.   M.V.B.

coherent light. When light is emitted from a surface the waves that emanate from the different ATOMS in the surface are generally out of PHASE with each other in random fashion. But it is possible to generate light waves in such a way that the same phase of wave is emitted from all parts of the source. The reinforcement of each wave on each of the others produces light with very different properties from that of ordinary light. For example a beam of coherent light has the power to cut through thick steel plate. The RADIATION has great powers of penetration and persistence and can be bounced off very distant objects such as the moon. It is invaluable as a phase reference in the process known as HOLOGRAPHY. One method of generating coherent light is by passing ordinary light through a hole in an opaque sheet, the hole being so small that only one PHOTON of light can pass through at a time. But the light scrambles itself again within a few millimetres distance. The first persistent source of coherent light was obtained by irradiating a ruby crystal. Later it was found possible to stimulate a rarefied gas in such a way as to cause it to emit coherent light. Medically it is now used to seal internal haemorrhages, to fix detached eye retinas and perform other similar beneficial functions.   E.R.L.

cohesion. The bonding together (see BOND) of ATOMS or MOLECULES in a solid.   B.F.

cohort analysis/period analysis. In DEMOGRAPHY, a cohort is defined as a group of persons who experience a significant event during the same period of time, e.g. the cohort of women born 1946-50, the cohort of all men marrying in 1980. Cohort analysis traces the subsequent vital history of such cohorts (e.g. of the cohort of children born in 1966), with the study of each cohort over many years or the lifetime. Period analysis is concerned with demographic events observed in a particular period, often a year (e.g. the number of births in 1987) and so cuts across many cohorts. Cohort analysis has been used particularly in the study of FERTILITY: the number of children born to members of a cohort at different periods of their lives is an important measurement. But the method has many applications in other fields, e.g. educational and morbidity studies.   E.G.;D.S.

Bibl: J. Hobcraft *et al.,* 'Age, period and cohort effects in demography: a review', *Population Index,* 48 (1982), pp. 4-43; H.S. Shryock *et al., The Methods and Materials of Demography* (condensed edition) (New York and London, 1976).

coincidence counter. Any device for counting events which simultaneously trigger two separate detectors. For example, two GEIGER COUNTERS placed one above the other will both register a COSMIC RAY arriving vertically, whereas only one will signal the arrival of a PARTICLE from the side. The two Geiger counters constitute a coincidence counter.   M.V.B.

cold, see under HOT AND COLD.

cold war. A phrase coined by journalist Herbert Bayer Swope, used by financier and government official Bernard Baruch in a speech on 16 April 1947, and given wide currency by journalist Walter Lippman. It describes the state of extreme hostility which developed after World War II between the U.S.S.R and the U.S. and its western allies. The term denotes a conflict which stops short of a 'hot war' and so while avoiding direct armed engagement seems to increase its likelihood. A cold war is conducted through political, economic, propaganda and subversive activity; is marked by a heightened mobilization for real WAR and by a reduction of diplomatic and cooperative contacts. It also includes support for 'hot wars' involving allies or clients in the THIRD WORLD. The term is variously applied to cover the period 1945-55; the years from 1945 to the 1963 U.S.-U.S.S.R. agreement to restrict the testing of nuclear MISSILES; the entire post-war period except the years of DÉTENTE between the two states in 1969-79.
                S.R.

Bibl: W. LaFeber, *America, Russia and the Cold War* (New York, 4th ed., 1980); T. Paterson, *On Every Front* (New York, 1979).

cold-worked. Metal that has been deformed at a temperature too low for ANNEALING to occur. Wire-drawing and bending, and panel-beating in motor-cars, are processes depending on cold-working.

M.V.B.

collage. Internationally current French term for the sticking together of disparate elements to make a picture. The modern use of this technique, now an artistic and educational commonplace, stems from (*a*) the traditional scrapbook, (*b*) *trompe l'oeil* effects in painting, and (*c*) such house-painter's techniques as marbling and graining. In 1912 the CUBISTS began incorporating scraps of wallpaper, print, etc. in their pictures; a year later Picasso applied similar principles to the construction of three-dimensional reliefs; and thereafter such methods became adopted by FUTURISM (Soffici and Carrà), DADA (Grosz), Russian CUBO-FUTURISM (Tatlin's reliefs), MERZ with its use of rubbish, and, in the mid-1920s, SURREALISM with its incongruous cutting-up of old engravings.

New terms emerged during the collage boom of the 1950s and early 1960s, which accompanied the Dada revival and the rise of POP ART: *combine-painting* (Robert Rauschenberg's use of three-dimensional components), *tableau-piège* (Daniel Spoerri's ditto) and *assemblage* (embracing both these), while DÉCOLLAGE came to signify the reverse process. Examples of collage also occurred in other arts, e.g. the 'cut-ups' of the novelist William Burroughs. The real extension of this concept, however, lay in the MONTAGE practised in the 1920s, a much wider artistic principle subsuming photomontage and all other forms of collage.

J.W.

Bibl: H. Janis and R. Blesh, *Collage* (Philadelphia and New York, 1962).

collective bargaining. The central job undertaken by a TRADE UNION is to undertake collective bargaining on behalf of its members. Members decide what they wish to claim from a MANAGEMENT, or what response they might take to a management initiative, the union bargains on their behalf, given that decision. The collective nature of the bargaining is needed because it is realized that an individual is at a disadvantage when confronting a corporate entity. Collective bargaining is an attempt to equalize the advantages which accrue to either side of the bargaining table. In the last resort the right of management to hire and fire is matched by the ability of each employee to remove his or her own labour, along with colleagues. If this sanction is known by an employer to be totally absent then employees bargain from a moral position only. Free collective bargaining is a euphemism for a lack of central government controls over pay bargaining, generally expressed as an INCOMES POLICY. This is rapidly becoming more unrealistic as the percentage of workers paid directly and indirectly by central government grows. Many European countries use highly centralized wage bargaining. West Germany, Sweden and Italy all have large sector bargaining. Holland and Belgium include the government. In the U.K. collective bargaining is only national at a time of incomes policy, but then pay bargaining is suspended. Collective bargaining is no longer just about pay. Redundancies, technological and job changes have become as important. Other non-basic wage elements of the terms and conditions of employment have come to the fore in collective bargaining in recent years. Mortgages, productivity payments, pensions, health care, cars, allowances of all descriptions, equal pay, profit sharing, holidays, shorter hours, leisure provisions and health and safety matters are now collectively bargained. In Germany and Holland unions bargain on the running of the enterprise (see PARTICIPATION). B.D.S.

Bibl: H.A. Clegg, *Trade Unionism under Collective Bargaining* (Oxford, 1976); C. Jenkins and B. Sherman, *Collective Bargaining* (London, 1977).

collective choice, see under SOCIAL CHOICE.

collective consciousness. A term used by Durkheim (in *The Rules of Sociological Method*) when trying to clarify his conception of SOCIAL (or associational) FACTS. It denotes, not the mere sum total of given elements in all the individual consciousnesses in a society, but the engendering, through associative activities within the constraints of specific collective conditions, of new elements of human experience, knowledge, value, will, and behaviour. These elements are termed by Durkheim 'collective REPRESENTATIONS': distinguishable sentiments and values (e.g. the British sense of 'justice and fair play') associated with shared cultural SYMBOLS (e.g., in this instance, the perpetuated traditions of the legal profession, courts, schools, games, and patterns of education and upbringing). In their totality, these 'collective representations' make up the 'social heritage', the framework of the distinctive collective life of a community. See also CULTURE; FOLKWAYS; SOCIAL FACT; SOCIAL STRUCTURE; STRUCTURE; SUB-CULTURE.   R.F.

collective farm, see under COLLECTIVIZATION.

collective leadership. The principle, enunciated in the rules of the COMMUNIST Party of the Soviet Union, that the power to make decisions should be shared by the leadership rather than concentrated in the hands of one person. According to these rules, collective leadership should operate at all levels of the Party. However, the principle is normally applied to the relationship between the general secretary of the Party and other members of the POLIT-BURO. After Stalin's death in 1953, his successors emphasized the idea of collective leadership, opposing it to the PERSONALITY CULT and the dictatorial methods of STALINISM. A collective leadership actually existed after 1953, but it was marked by serious rivalries between the leaders and after N. Khrushchev had defeated his colleagues, G. Malenkov and L. Beria, he became supreme leader in 1956. Khrushchev was in his turn accused of establishing a cult of the individual, and collective leadership was restored by L. Brezhnev, elected general secretary of the Party, and A. Kosygin, elected Chairman of the Council of Ministers after Khrushchev's resignation in 1964.   D.PR.

Bibl: D. Lane, *State and Politics in the Soviet Union* (Oxford, 1985).

collective security. The principle of maintaining international peace by the concerted efforts of the nations, especially by the efforts of international organizations such as the LEAGUE OF NATIONS and UNO. The concept was introduced into the Covenant of the League of Nations on British initiative and embodied the ancient Anglo-Saxon idea of a crime against civil peace being answered by the 'hue and cry' against the transgressor to which all citizens were bound to respond. During the 1930s, however, many people in the U.K. deceived themselves and others into believing that by support for the slogan of collective security (with little consideration of how it was to be enforced) they could avoid the hard choices of national foreign and defence policy. It was left to Japan, Italy, and German to show how little substance was in collective security when put to the test. Great efforts were made after World War II to embody these lessons in the machinery of UNO, whose action in calling on its members to contribute forces for the KOREAN WAR in 1950 was the first example of collective security involving military SANCTIONS. The split between the great powers, however, and the rival alliance systems (NATO, Warsaw Pact) have reduced UNO to a marginal role in preserving peace.

A.L.C.B.

collective unconscious. JUNGIAN term for the past experience of the human species, which has been built into the inherited brain structure, and which manifests itself in the recurrent phenomena of the ARCHETYPES. Jung argued that an individual's functioning is the product of this collective unconscious as well as of a *personal unconscious* whose contents are forgotten, repressed, subliminally perceived, thought, and felt matter of every kind, and which, therefore, is not to be equated with the UNCONSCIOUS of FREUDIAN theory.

B.A.F.

collectivism. A politico-economic theory advocating that the means of production and/or distribution should be collectively owned or controlled, or both, and not left to the actions of individuals pursuing their self-interest; also a system based on such collective control. SOCIALISM, COMMUNISM, and other collectivist IDEOLOGIES proclaim the desirability of such control through public ownership in the interest of the community as a whole. Forms of collective ownership range from State property to a variety of COOPERATIVE institutions, with varying degrees of control by members over decisions affecting their lives. Collectivism has a different significance in the context of an Israeli KIBBUTZ, a Soviet *kolkhoz*, and a Chinese COMMUNE. State ownership in itself does not signify collective control. The question of who controls the State and the collective institutions existing in it has been raised by many critics of collectivism as well as by some of its advocates, who have tried to tackle such problems by advocating forms of collectivism which would provide for workers' PARTICIPATION in economic decision-making, e.g. GUILD SOCIALISM and various forms of workers' control.   L.L.

collectivization. A conversion, usually compulsory, of individually owned agricultural holdings into large collective farms; the system of agriculture which predominates in most COMMUNIST states, with the exception of Poland and Yugoslavia, and which, with certain local variations, derives from the system set up in the U.S.S.R. in the early 1930s. In the U.S.S.R. collectivization was imposed in 1930 by draconian methods which met bitter peasant resistance: millions of them starved or were arrested and deported. Collectivization in the East European Communist countries has not been so brutally enforced, and in Poland and Yugoslavia was stopped, the peasants being allowed to adhere or revert to individual farming.

In the U.S.S.R. the *kolkhoz*, the collective farm, is to be distinguished from the *sovkhoz*, the State farm, in which the peasants are employees of the State. The *kolkhozy* are, legally speaking, the joint property of their members, who receive payment in accordance with the particular farm's profits. The original 'COMMUNE' form of *kolkhoz* was early abandoned, for the most part in favour of the less rigorous *artel*, in which the peasant is permitted a small private plot and the odd cow or two. One of the reasons for this change was the decline in agricultural output: the peasants show a much higher level of productivity in cultivating their own plots. Soviet agricultural productivity still lags greatly behind that of most other comparable countries, and new types of economic incentive and forms of work are now being tried out in the U.S.S.R. in the hope of raising productivity on the collective farms.   L.L.; R.C.

Bibl: N. Jasny, *The Socialized Agriculture of the USSR* (Stanford, 1949); M. Lewin, tr. I. Nove, *Russian Peasants and Soviet Power* (London and Evanston, Ill., 1968); R. Conquest, *The Harvest of Sorrow* (London and New York, 1986).

collocation. In LINGUISTICS, a term, primarily FIRTHIAN, applied to the regular occurrence together of lexical items in a language, e.g. *bar* is said to collocate with such items as *steel, soap, harbour, public*. See also LEXICON.   D.C.

colloid. A dispersion of small PARTICLES of one substance (usually electrically charged) throughout the body of another. Colloids are neither true solutions (where the dispersed particles are single MOLECULES) nor suspensions (where the particles are large enough to tend to concentrate as a sediment under the action of GRAVITATION). Typical colloids are albumen and starch.   M.V.B.

colonialism, see under IMPERIALISM.

colour/coloured. (1) Pejorative term used to describe BLACKS in the U.S. and migrants from Britain's former colonies, particularly those from the Asian subcontinent and the Caribbean. It is a category which groups together very different peoples on the basis of a crude racial generalization (see RACE). Black has largely replaced coloured in everyday vocabulary, but the latter continues to be used as a term of abuse.

(2) Official terminology employed by the South African government to classify persons of mixed race, concentrated mainly in the Cape Province.   A.G.;S.T.

colour field painting, see under ABSTRACT EXPRESSIONISM.

combinatorial mathematics. A branch of MATHEMATICS concerned with the computation of the number of different ways certain operations can be performed. A traditional example, which shows its use in calculating probabilities (see PROBABILITY THEORY), is to compute the number of hands of a certain sort that may be dealt in a card game. It is not a unified subject, but deals with a wide range of problems and techniques. Some of the latter (e.g. GRAPH theory) have developed into distinct mathematical disciplines.　　R.G.

combine-painting, see under COLLAGE.

COMECON (or CMEA: Council for Mutual Economic Assistance). A Soviet-sponsored economic organization, set up in January 1949 in reply to the successful working of the MARSHALL PLAN. Originally only comprising states of the SOCIALIST bloc in Eastern Europe it now has ten members, including VIETNAM, CUBA and Mongolia. Initially there was little attempt to use the organization to integrate the member economies, but in the early 1960s Khrushchev attempted to force members into economic specialization, pressure which was largely resisted. The Soviet Union is still encouraging Eastern European countries to accept further bloc integration, but despite the adoption of the 'comprehensive programme' by the CMEA in 1971 it has largely failed and the organization remains one mainly concerned with trade between member nations.　　D.C.W.;D.PR.
　　Bibl: M. Kaser, *Comecon* (London and New York, 2nd ed., 1967); G. Schiavone, *The Institutions of Comecon* (London, 1981).

comédie noire, see BLACK COMEDY.

comedy of menace. A dramatic style which emerged in the British theatre of the late 1950s, in which the reaction of one or more characters to some terrifying and often obscure threat to their security is treated as a subject for comedy. The term was first used by David Campton as a subtitle to his four playlets *The Lunatic View* (1957), but was soon applied more widely by critics, in particular to the early work of Harold Pinter. See also BLACK COMEDY; THEATRE OF THE ABSURD.　　M.A.

Cominform. Abbreviation for the COMMU-NIST Information Bureau, established on Stalin's instruction in September 1947 at a meeting in Poland. The participants included representatives of the Communist Parties of Bulgaria, Czechoslovakia,

France, Hungary, Italy, Poland, Romania, the U.S.S.R., and Yugoslavia. Stressing that the world is divided into SOCIALIST and CAPITALIST camps, the Soviet delegate, Andrei Zhdanov, called for an irreconcilable hostility towards the latter. The new hard Communist line soon led to the tightening of controls in Eastern Europe and to a world-wide Communist offensive.
　　It was originally planned that the offices of the Cominform should be established in Belgrade, but following the Stalin-Tito break they were set up in Bucharest, and in June 1948 the Yugoslav leaders were denounced as traitors to the Communist cause. The political coordination of the Party line internationally was largely effected through the Cominform journal, *For a Lasting Peace, For People's Democracy.* The Cominform never achieved the importance of its predecessor, the COMINTERN, and after Khrushchev's attempt at reconciliation with Tito it was dissolved in April 1956. (See also TITOISM).　　L.L.

Comintern. Abbreviation for the Communist (see COMMUNISM) INTERNATIONAL, established in March 1919 at a meeting in Moscow. As an association of revolutionary MARXIST parties of the world rejecting REFORMISM, it was to replace the SOCIALIST International. From the outset its policies were dominated by the Russian Bolsheviks (see BOLSHEVISM), who imposed on it their own LENINIST principles of organization through the *21 Conditions of Admission* (which included the subordination of the member parties to the authority of the Executive Committee of the Comintern). This meant in effect the subordination of the national sections (i.e. parties) to Soviet control of their policies.
　　At the 2nd Congress of the Comintern in the summer of 1920, when the Bolshevik leaders thought that Europe was on the verge of a PROLETARIAN revolution, they promoted an intransigent revolutionary strategy; they repudiated 'bourgeois democracy' (see BOURGEOIS; DEMOCRACY), and denounced both moderate and radical (see RADICALISM) socialist leaders. When Bolshevik hopes of the imminent REVOLUTION in Europe collapsed, the Comintern leaders proclaimed a 'temporary stabilization of CAPITALISM' and devel-

oped various forms of UNITED FRONT tactics.

Beginning with the 5th Congress in 1924 the Comintern reflected the internal factional struggles in the Soviet Communist Party: the elimination from it of Trotsky, Zinoviev, Bukharin, and their followers led to corresponding purges in the leadership and the national sections of the Comintern. Its 6th Congress in 1928 inaugurated the 'CLASS against class' policy aimed at the 'radicalization of the masses'. But the disastrous result of Communist policy in Germany (where Stalin's denunciation of socialists as 'social FAS-CISTS' facilitated Hitler's victory in 1933) led to the adoption of POPULAR FRONT tactics at the 7th Congress of the Comintern in 1935. Soon after, most of the leaders of the Comintern, Russian and foreign, were liquidated during the Great Purge (1936-8; see YEZHOVSHCHINA).

Stalin transformed the Comintern into an obedient instrument of Soviet foreign policy. When he concluded the pact with Hitler in August 1939, Comintern propaganda which for years had inveighed against the Nazi menace was peremptorily switched to an anti-Western line. It changed again after Hitler's attack on the Soviet Union in 1941. In 1943 the Comintern was dissolved, presumably as a gesture to the Western allies. It was, however, temporarily resurrected as the COMIN-FORM.   L.L.

Bibl: F. Borkenau, *The Communist International* (London, 1938); J. Degras (ed.), *The Communist International, 1919-1943: Documents,* vols. 1 and 2 (London and New York, 1956 and 1960); F. Claudin, *The Communist Movement from Comintern to Cominform* (London and New York, 1975).

commensalism, see under SYMBIOSIS.

commitment. A term the widespread use of which (as of ENGAGÉ, committed) in recent years derives from the position of Jean-Paul Sartre, most succinctly presented in *L'Existentialisme est un humanisme* (1946). Sartre affirms his ATHEISM and his belief in free will; concedes that he cannot be confident in 'human goodness' or in the socially just outcome of the Russian Revolution, which he none the less admires because 'the PRO-LETARIAT plays a part in Russia which it has attained in no other nation'. 'Does that,' he asks, 'mean that I should abandon myself to Quietism?' The answer is: 'No....one need not hope in order to undertake one's work....people reproach us with....the sternness of our optimism... What counts is total commitment (*engagement*), and it is not by a particular case or....action that you are committed altogether.' 'Commitment' *tout court* is usually assumed to be LEFT-wing, usually quasi-MARXIST; other brands are usually given a specific label, e.g. *Catholic commitment* ('eternal vigilance').   M.S.-S.

commodity economy. Since 1978 China has moved away from the typical command economy of COMMUNIST party states and adopted a commodity economy. The allocation of goods and resources is no longer dependent on central planning, but responds to the effects of market forces. However, this does not mean that central planning and commands no longer exist, merely that more notice is paid of forces of supply and demand in the formulation of economic policy (see DENGISM; FOUR MODERNIZATIONS).   S.B.

Bibl: M. Chossudovsky, *Towards Capitalist Restoration* (London, 1986).

commodity fetishism. Term used (with sardonic reference to FETISHISM) by Marx in *Das Kapital* in maintaining that though commodities appear to be simple *objects*, they are, in fact, bundles of social relationships, transcendentals, with a life of their own once they enter the sphere of market exchange and values. According to Marx, the apparent 'object' (a table, for example) 'abounds in metaphysical and theological niceties'. In defining the treatment of commodities in CAPITALIST production and exchange, we must therefore, he adds, 'have recourse to the mist-enveloped regions of the religious world'.   R.F.

Common Agricultural Policy (CAP). Policy of the European Economic Community (see EEC). The theoretical aims of the policy are to increase agricultural productivity in the Community, stabilize agricultural commodity prices, and ensure that enough food is available to consumers at reasonable prices. Agricultural market organization is now extremely complex; for the wide range of commodities covered, common prices are established in terms of the EUROPEAN CURRENCY UNIT (ECU) which are translated into national currencies using 'representative rates' of exchange (the term 'green pound' is often used to describe the exchange rate appropriate in the case of the U.K.). Depending on the commodity covered (i.e. on the commodity regime) the broad aim is to fix a target price (nomenclature varies widely between regimes) for the region of greatest Community deficit (frequently taken as the Ruhr), and to maintain that price either by a levy on imports designed to raise entry prices from third countries when world prices are higher than those in the Community, or by support buying (the common term is 'intervention') which involves purchasing and removing from the Community market produce such as cereals, beef, sugar, olive oil and milk products when market prices fall. It was initially envisaged that the main mechanism for price support, and at the same time for market stabilization, would be the levy system which would concurrently be a source of TAX revenue accruing to the Community budget and available either for financing structural change in agriculture or for general purposes. In the event, and particularly in the 1980s, improvements in agricultural productivity and a rise in output partly stimulated by high internal prices have resulted in large increases in the costs of intervention purchases and creation of 'food mountains' of produce removed from the market. It has also become common for surplus food to be sold in world markets, with the aid of export subsidies, which are both a further charge on the Community budget and a source of potential trade disputes with major agricultural exporting countries. Though some action has been taken to reduce output and hence budgetary cost (milk production, for example, was subjected to quota control in 1984 and co-responsibility levies on internal prices have been introduced for important commodities), major 'reform' of the system, which is little more than a euphemism for introduction of tighter controls and lower prices with a switch of funding to struc-

tural adjustment, has proved elusive largely for political reasons.

There is also considerable dispute about the way in which the costs and benefits of the policy impinge on member nations through the principle of common financing. Because of adjustments in exchange rate values it has also proved difficult to form a truly common market in farm products since the representative rates of currency conversion can diverge from market exchange rates requiring a complex system of agro-monetary adjustments.   G.H.P.

Bibl: A. Birchwell *et al., Costs of the Common Agricultural Policy* (London, 1982); S. Harris *et al., The Farm and Food Policies of the European Community* (Chichester, 1983).

common law. Term used in three different and distinct ways. (1) Originally the rules developed by the ordinary courts of England from the middle ages as opposed to those applied by the Lord Chancellor's Court of Chancery, which were called equity and which formed a supplement to or gloss on the common law, especially in the field of property. (2) Later came to be used as description for all law, even including equity, derived from decisions of courts and not laid down by Acts of Parliament as an Act can override or alter any previous law (see SOVEREIGNTY), and as Parliament in modern times has enacted a great volume of legislation, the areas still covered by pure common law in this sense have progressively shrunk. Today statute regulates most law, or provides for its enactment by means of STATUTORY INSTRUMENTS, but the courts must still apply law in individual cases and in doing so exercise considerable authority over the development of the law by way of interpretation of statutes and statutory instruments: and the common law still covers much of the area of private relations, e.g. CONTRACT, TORTS, and some parts of criminal law. (3) More generally common law is used to mean a court-based system of law on the English model in contrast with continental code-based systems. In this sense common law covers not only the whole of English law, including equity and statute law, but also the laws of

145

most other COMMONWEALTH countries and of the U.S.A. D.C.M.Y.

Bibl: W. Geldart, *Introduction to English Law* (Oxford and New York, 9th ed., 1984).

Common Market, see under CUSTOMS UNION; EEC.

common sense. The source or system of those very general beliefs about the world which are universally and unquestioningly taken to be true in everyday life but with which the findings of philosophers seem frequently to conflict. Examples are the beliefs that there is a material world which exists whether I am perceiving it or not, that there exist other people besides myself, that the material world and its human inhabitants have existed for a long time and will continue to do so, that what has happened often and without exception in the past will happen again in the future. Much, perhaps most, PHILOSOPHY begins from sceptical doubts: about the material world, other minds, the past, the lawfulness of nature. In the face of such conflict some philosophers, e.g. Russell, conclude that it is so much the worse for common sense; others, e.g. Thomas Reid and G.E. Moore, regard the acceptance of commonsense beliefs almost as a criterion of sanity. In this spirit many LINGUISTIC PHILOSOPHERS have sought to unmask countercommonsensical philosophical theses by revealing the seductive misuses of language on which they take the reasoning behind them to rest. A.Q.

Bibl: G.E. Moore, *Philosophical Papers* (London and New York, 1959); A.J. Ayer, *Metaphysics and Common Sense* (London, 1969).

Commonwealth. The loose and flexible association of independent countries most of which have at an earlier period been within the now defunct British Empire. Originally the Empire was governed by the United Kingdom, but from the latter part of the 19th century onwards the British Parliament gradually conferred self-government and then full independence upon the great majority of its overseas territories. In the early 20th century these countries, at first called Dominions, shared a common allegiance to the British Crown, and their citizens had the same nationality as those of the United Kingdom. Now however many are republics, e.g. India, Cyprus, Nigeria, and some have their own monarchs, e.g. Tonga, Malaysia, Swaziland, though all recognize the British Queen as Head of the Commonwealth; and all have their own citizenship laws and separate nationalities. There are no overt rules governing the Commonwealth, and its existence seems to depend on mutual interest and cooperation, and not law. Some countries have renounced membership, e.g. Republic of Ireland, South Africa, Pakistan, while others have been admitted from areas not formerly colonized, e.g. Brunei, Western Samoa. In 1986 there were 49 full members of the Commonwealth. There remain a few dependent territories, mostly of the United Kingdom, largely because they would not be viable international entities on their own, e.g. St Helena, Pitcairn, or because of difficult international complications, e.g. Gibraltar. The most heavily populated, Hong Kong, will revert to China in 1997 under a 1948 agreement providing for a 50-year transitional period. Some territories have a large measure of self-government, but for external purposes are represented by the United Kingdom, e.g. the Isle of Man, the Channel Islands. D.C.M.Y.

Bibl: D.C.M. Yardley, *Introduction to British Constitutional Law* (London, 6th ed., 1984).

Commonwealth preference, see IMPERIAL PREFERENCE.

commune. The form of organization of life and work in a collective (see COLLECTIVISM) in which the members hold no private property, share equally the results of their labour, and usually make joint decisions by democratic means which attach little importance to leaders or hierarchies but stress each member's equal right to PARTICIPATION. Early communes were founded under the influence of utopian socialists (see UTOPIANISM, SOCIALISM) such as Proudhon, Fourier, Owen and Cabet, but soon disintegrated. The Paris Commune of 1871 also included elements of JACOBIN thought and was celebrated by Marx. During the period of War COMMU-

NISM (1917-21) in the U.S.S.R. agricultural communes were formed, but were dissolved by the New Economic Policy (see NEP) or transformed by the COLLECTIVIZATION of Soviet agriculture. During the GREAT LEAP FORWARD in China (1958-61) large rural communes were organized; political pressure and propaganda replaced economic incentives and the strategy was unsuccessfully promoted as a short cut to the full-scale communist society. Since the renewed diversification of left-wing thought, the rise of the COUNTERCULTURE and the spread of critiques of industrial CAPITALISM and political centralization in the 1960s, communes of various idiosyncratic kinds have enjoyed a modest revival. They have only a marginal impact in societies fundamentally wedded to large-scale, highly interdependent economic units and elaborate, bureaucratized political arrangements.   L.L.;S.R.

communication, ethnography of. Phrase coined by the American social anthropologist Dell Hymes to refer to the extension to other media of an approach which he calls 'the ETHNOGRAPHY of speaking' and others 'the SOCIOLOGY of language', SOCIOLINGUISTICS or ETHNOLINGUISTICS. Imagery, RITUAL, gesture and even silence (particularly eloquent in the case of the American Indians studied by Hymes) are analysed as forms of language with their own rules. A key concept in the ethnography of communication is that of CODE or REGISTER, in other words the variety of language used by a particular speaker (more generally, 'sender'), to communicate with particular listeners ('receivers'), in particular situations or about particular subjects ('domains'). It has been pointed out, for example, that in a number of cultures women are more careful to obey the rules of grammar than men are, and that when a conversation turns to religion, the code is 'switched' from a lower or more colloquial variety of language to a 'higher' or more literary one.   P.B.

Bibl: M. Saville-Troike, *The Ethnography of Communication* (Oxford, 1982).

communication, fallacy of. Allen Tate's term, in the context of the NEW CRITICISM, for what he regards as the false belief that literature can communicate non-poetic

(e.g. political) ideas. Contrast COMMITMENT.   M.S.-S.

communication, heresy of. Cleanth Brooks's term, occasionally employed in the NEW CRITICISM, for what he regards as the mistaken belief that a poem consists of two components which are separable: an 'idea' and a 'form' which ornaments it. To any new critic, a successful poem is an organic whole.   M.S.-S.

Bibl: C. Brooks, *The Well-Wrought Urn* (New York, 1947; London, 1949).

communication, theories of. In SOCIOLOGY, theories which seek to expound the origins of the meanings (especially the symbolic meanings) that constitute human CULTURE, to map the channels through which those meanings are diffused (see DIFFUSION), and to trace the consequence for social groups of their dependence upon such meanings and their capacity to create them. Most sociologists would accept as an initial assumption that communication via language is in some sense a prerequisite for 'society' — though they find a place, too, for the discussion of NON-VERBAL COMMUNICATION. The nature of communication systems is a matter for empirical study — prior to the formulation of any theories about them.   S.J.G.

Bibl: H.D. Duncan, *Communication and the Social Order* (Oxford, 1968); J. Habermas, *Communication and the Evolution of Society* (London, 1979).

communication theory, see INFORMATION THEORY; and preceding entry.

communications. A term used in GEOGRAPHY to cover all means of transport, for example by sea, road, rail, air, canal, or mule, by which people can make contact and trade with others.   M.L.

communicative competence. In LINGUISTICS, the speaker's awareness of the way language use is appropriate to social situations (identified in terms of formality, class background, occupation, and so on). The notion contrasts with the original sense of COMPETENCE, as introduced in GENERATIVE GRAMMAR, where it was seen as a purely formal notion, referring to the

147

speaker's awareness of the grammatical system of a language.   D.C.

Bibl: D. Hymes, *Foundations in Sociolinguistics* (London, 1977).

communism. A term denoting:

(1) A set of ideas and the ideological tradition (see IDEOLOGY) connected with them. Historically the point of reference for communist ideas is the principle of communal ownership of all property. Thus primitive communism refers to non-literate societies, in which basic economic resources (such as land, boats, etc.) belong to the community as a whole and not to individuals or families. Religious groups (such as early Christians or medieval monasteries) based on communal sharing of property are referred to as examples of communist organization; so are historical societies, such as Sparta, the Münster Anabaptists, or the Jesuit Paraguay republic, as well as theoretical schemes for ideal societies, such as Plato's *Republic*, Sir Thomas More's *Utopia*, or Campanella's *City of the Sun*.

Modern communism is specifically linked with the ideas of Karl Marx and the concept of a classless society (see CLASS) based on common ownership of the means of production. Such a society should, according to Marx and his followers, emerge after the transitional period of the DICTATORSHIP OF THE PROLETARIAT and the preparatory stage of SOCIALISM. In a full communist society the State will 'wither away', differences between manual and intellectual labour and between urban and rural life will disappear, there will be no limits to the development of individual human potentialities and of productive forces, and social relations will be regulated by the principle 'from each according to his ability, to each according to his needs'.

(2) Movements, parties, and governments deriving their support and legitimation from the claim that they are implementing such ideas. See BOLSHEVISM; CASTROISM; COMINFORM; COMINTERN; LENINISM; MAOISM; MARXISM; MARXISM-LENINISM; NEO-MARXISM; POLYCENTRISM; REVISIONISM; STALINISM; TITOISM; TROTSKYISM.

(3) Distinctive methods used by such movements, parties, and governments,

and institutions emerging historically as a result of their actions. See AGITPROP; APPARAT; COLLECTIVIZATION; COMMUNE; CULTURAL REVOLUTION; DEMOCRATIC CENTRALISM; FORCED LABOUR; FRONT ORGANIZATION; KGB; KULAK; LYSENKOISM; MVD; POLITBURO; POPULAR FRONT; REVOLUTION; SAMIZDAT; SHOW TRIALS; SOVIET; STAKHANOVISM; UNITED FRONT; YEZHOVSHCHINA; ZHDANOVSHCHINA.   L.L.

Bibl: V. Lenin, *The State and Revolution* (Eng. tr. London, 1969); R.V. Daniels, *A Documentary History of Communism* (New York, 1960); L. Holmes, *Politics in the Communist World* (Oxford, 1986); A. Westoby, *The Evolution of Communism* (Oxford, 1987).

community. In ECOLOGY, a term used (e.g. 'plant community') to define a unit of vegetation or group of plants sharing the same HABITAT, having distinct recognizable features which distinguish it from others. In human GEOGRAPHY the term is also used to define a group of people living in the same village, TOWN, or suburb in a sympathetic association.   M.L.

community architecture. An approach to architectural practice advocated by socially aware architects especially in the U.K. Its intention is to provide architectural skills and services to poor and run-down communities, often providing development and finance-finding skills as well. It is predicated on the active consent and participation of the community whose buildings are to be rehabilitated — which may be as small as a section of a street or as large as a local area. Community architects set up their drawing boards in the locality and many live there while the regeneration programme is in progress. It is practised both in the PUBLIC and PRIVATE sectors. In the latter case architects sometimes also operate as builders and developers taking small fees — and options on property whose value increases dramatically when the local improvements are completed. Community architects effectively ignore the traditional stylistic and ideological preoccupations of architecture.   S.L.

community arts. An English term, coined about 1970, for the activities of groups of (primarily visual) artists attempting to work largely with and for local authorities, schools, remedial institutions, and other communal bodies rather than for the art market. Among media commonly used are mime, costume, movement, games, live and recorded music, and the use of INFLATABLES. J.W.

community politics. A term which found widespread currency in Britain during the revival of Liberal Party fortunes after 1972. It first denoted a tactical stress on local issues and grievances as the material for party growth in urban and suburban constituencies. It has acquired a more elaborate meaning; it connotes a distrust of central government and national ELITES, and an emphasis on reform initiatives from the 'grass roots'. The approach has been criticized as suited only to an opposition party which profits from the airing of grievances and exposure of government failings. S.R.
Bibl: P. Hain, *The Democratic Alternative* (Harmondsworth, 1984).

community psychiatry, see under PSYCHIATRY.

commutative law. In MATHEMATICS, the law that is obeyed when the result of a binary operation (e.g. addition, multiplication) is the same regardless of the order in which the operands are taken; thus $a + b = b + a$, $a \times b = b \times a$. Operations that satisfy this law are called *commutative*. For abstract MATHEMATICAL STRUCTURES the law may be taken as an AXIOM. Examples of *non*-commutative operations are *exponentiation* (e.g. $2^3 \neq 3^2$) and the multiplication of QUATERNIONS and MATRICES. R.G.

commuting (or *commutation*). Term referring primarily to the daily movement of employed people between their residence and work. This definition is sometimes extended to include other less regular components such as the journey to school or to shops. Since commuter movements make up over half of all vehicular movements in many modern urban areas and are usually concentrated into two peak periods each day, they contribute the major share to contemporary urban transport problems. P.H.

compact disc technology. A process whereby digitally ENCODED information is etched onto the surface of a small plastic disc, whence it may be read by reflecting a carefully controlled beam of LASER light from the surface as it spins and analysing the resulting MODULATION of the laser beam. Dust and other imperfections in the surface inevitably introduce NOISE, so considerable REDUNDANCY (including extensive use of ERROR-CORRECTING CODES) is necessary to allow the original information to be accurately reconstructed. Compact discs can be used explicitly as a high-capacity STORE for COMPUTERS, but at present their most widespread use is as a medium for high-quality recorded sound. In this case, after the digital information is reconstructed (using, if all else fails, INTERPOLATION) it is fed through a DIGITAL-TO-ANALOGUE CONVERTER and thence to an amplifier and loudspeaker. The sound (in each STEREO channel) is encoded at the rate of some 44,000 samples per second; the processing of this information at the required speed and tolerable cost would be impossible without modern MICROCOMPUTERS. J.E.S.

comparatist. A follower of the COMPARATIVE METHOD in LINGUISTICS or literature. Comparative philology began in the 18th century; it involved the hypothetical reconstruction of parent languages (e.g. 'Indo-European'), based on a multiplicity of examples from known languages. The work of Ferdinand de Saussure (see SAUSSURIAN) in linguistics grew out of his involvement with comparative philology, as did his view of language 'as a system of mutually defining entities'. This has had a crucial influence on later developments. Comparative methods in literature embrace such things as the habit (exemplified by Sacheverell Sitwell) of comparing literary works with paintings, architecture, and music, as well as the comparison of different literatures. Comparative literature is far more widely taught in the U.S.A. than in Britain. M.S.-S.
Bibl: R. Wellek and A. Warren, *Theory of Literature* (3rd ed., New York, 1956; London, 1966).

comparative education. The branch of educational theory concerned with analysing and interpreting policies and practices in different countries. Despite problems of METHODOLOGY, factors like language, SOCIAL STRUCTURE, political system, IDEOLOGY, geography (e.g. mountains or jungles producing isolated communities), all provide differences which can be studied comparatively, in addition to administrative structures and economic factors.

W.A.C.S.

Bibl: G.Z.F. Bereday, *Comparative Method in Education* (London and New York, 1964); N.A. Hans, *Comparative Education* (London, 3rd ed., 1967).

comparative history. Although the ambitious studies of Spengler and Toynbee are both comparative and historical, the term is not normally used to refer to that kind of book. It refers to more modest attempts to compare two or three societies, often neighbours but sometimes as remote from one another as France and Japan. The comparative historian is usually interested in a specific problem, such as the nature of FEUDALISM or of absolute monarchy; tends to emphasize the differences as well as the parallels between the societies he studies; and resorts to comparison not to produce general laws but to understand particular situations. P.B.

Bibl: Marc Bloch, tr. J.E. Anderson, 'Towards a comparative history of European societies', in his *Land and Work in Medieval Europe* (London and Berkeley, 1967).

comparative law. A misleading but established name for the systematic comparison of laws of different systems. It is a method of legal study and research, and not as the name suggests a distinct branch of the law or body of legal rules. Many studies in comparative law have been inspired by various practical aims, such as the establishment of uniformity in commercial law and in private international law. H.L.A.H.

Bibl: H.C. Gutteridge, *Comparative Law* (Cambridge, 2nd ed., 1949).

comparative linguistics, see under LINGUISTICS.

comparative method. Frequently used in the simple sense of comparing one set of facts with another (for examples, see other headings beginning with COMPARATIVE). In SOCIOLOGY the term is of central importance as referring to sociology's only alternative to *controlled experiment.* It is the sociological method *par excellence* for the formulation of definitive theories, including the specification of conditions for the *crucial testing* of hypotheses. What experiment is in the NATURAL SCIENCES, the comparative method is in the SOCIAL SCIENCES. (See also SOCIAL THEORY.)

At least four distinct conceptions have been employed: (1) that of classifying societies according to some criterion (e.g. the nature of the 'social bond'), thus forming a clear framework for amassing and arranging factual information and uncovering connections between social INSTITUTIONS (Spencer, Hobhouse, etc.); (2) that of constructing a TYPOLOGY on the basis of some hypothesis (e.g. Comte's 'Law of the Three States', Spencer's 'military-industrial' polarity, Tönnies's contrast between GEMEINSCHAFT AND GESELLSCHAFT, and Marx's distinctive stages of 'productive forces') and then comparing it with actual historical societies, to see how far it illuminates them, and to test its reliability; (3) that of comparing specific sets of SOCIAL FACTS (e.g. the rate of suicide and the degree of integration within specific groups — familial, religious, etc.) in order to test theories about their 'constant concomitance'; (4) that of constructing a MODEL in order to understand one particular 'cultural configuration' (e.g. of the rise of industrial CAPITALISM in Western Europe) and comparing other similar configurations with it, in order to test the correctness and sufficiency of the interpretation (Weber). R.F.

Bibl: H. Spencer, *The Principles of Sociology*, vol. 1 (London, 3rd ed., 1885); E. Durkheim, tr. S.A. Solovay and J.H. Mueller, *The Rules of Sociological Method* (London and New York, 8th ed., 1964); Max Weber, tr. A.M. Henderson and T. Parsons, *The Theory of Social and Economic Organization* (Glencoe, Ill., 1947; 2nd ed., New York and London, 1964); I. Vallier (ed.), *Comparative Methods in Sociology* (Berkeley, 1971).

comparative psychology. The rapidly developing branch of PSYCHOLOGY whose focus of interest is the similarities and differences between animal SPECIES, including man, especially where these can be understood in relation to the species' BIOLOGY and way of life or to their phylogenetic relationships (see PHYLOGENY). The comparative psychologist — who often prefers to call himself a psychologist *tout court*, or an ethologist (see ETHOLOGY), or just a student of animal behaviour — may study animals because they are simpler than man in their behaviour or brain structure and therefore easier to investigate; or because they represent in some sense an earlier evolutionary stage in man's history, with the implication that the behaviour of a fish or a monkey may tell us something of the fish or monkey stage of man's EVOLUTION. It is, of course, questionable whether the behaviour of such ancestors bore much resemblance to that of the fishes and monkeys alive today; and in any case the various monkey species today show substantial differences in behaviour, so that it is difficult to generalize about *the* monkey. Despite these difficulties it has been possible to investigate some of the animal precursors of human abilities such as INTELLIGENCE, learning skills and language.

Although comparative psychology's interest in animals is by tradition anthropocentric, problems in animals' PERCEPTION or learning or motivation or development are also studied for their own sake. Field studies of animals in their natural environments, by zoologists and psychologists, have given a great impetus to such work, and have shown how the particular psychological and behavioural characteristics of each species are often closely adapted to their everyday needs. The emergence of SOCIOBIOLOGY in the 1970s has added a new dimension and a new controversial edge to the field. Hard-line advocates of the new discipline have argued for the comprehensive interpretation of patterns of human social behaviour and culture in terms of adaptive evolutionary processes designed to enhance survival prospects. Such facets of human behaviour as aggression or GENDER inequality, which mirror patterns in the animal world, have been newly argued to be not culturally contingent, the product of nurture, but 'natural' and genetically transmitted. The degree to which extrapolation of animal ethology to human society is legitimate remains deeply unclear and contentious.   J.M.C.;R.P.

Bibl: K. Lorenz, tr. R. Martin, *Studies in Animal and Human Behaviour*, 2 vols. (London and Cambridge, Mass., 1970-1971); W.H. Thorpe, *Animal Nature and Human Nature* (London, 1974); E. O. Wilson, *Sociobiology: The New Synthesis* (Cambridge, Mass., 1975).

comparative religion. The attempt to compare the RELIGIONS of the world objectively. The extent and variety of the faiths held by mankind were not generally known before the 19th century, and then much of the information was conveyed to the West by Christian missionaries and colonists. During the 20th century a much more sympathetic attitude has been adopted by many Westerners with a Christian background towards BUDDHISM, HINDUISM, ISLAM, JUDAISM, and other, more local, religions; indeed, each of these faiths has attracted converts from CHRISTIANITY. In many universities the comparative study of religion, rather than Christian THEOLOGY, has flourished. A dialogue has begun between the leaders of the religions, although with great caution due to ignorance, prejudice, and the more reasonable fear of a syncretism that would deny the differences.   D.L.E.

Bibl: R.C. Zaehner (ed.), *The Concise Encyclopaedia of Living Faiths* (London, rev. ed., 1971); N. Smart, *The Religious Experience of Mankind* (New York, 1969; London, 1971) and *Beyond Ideology* (London and New York, 1981); J. Hick, *God Has Many Names* (London and New York, 1982).

compatibilism. The philosophical theory stating that although human beings are subject to causal laws (see DETERMINISM) they have free will and are morally responsible for their actions. The compatibility of freedom with causal determinism is defended by Hume and others, who argue that it is not causal determinism but constraint or compulsion which is the antithesis of freedom.   A.C.G.

compensatory education. A phrase used in Britain following the PLOWDEN REPORT, to denote additional educational provision in educational priority areas in order to 'compensate' socially disadvantaged children. In 1967 the Schools Council supported a research project to screen and identify children in infants' schools in need of compensatory education and to devise teaching programmes to help those whose early experience has been stunted and distorted. Educational priority areas have been set up in Liverpool, in London, and elsewhere.   W.A.C.S.

Bibl: Schools Council, *Children at Risk* (Swansea, 1969).

competence (in BIOLOGY), see under ORGANIZER.

competence and **performance.** A distinction which is central to GENERATIVE GRAMMAR, and has become widely used in LINGUISTICS as a whole. Competence refers to a person's knowledge of his language, the system of rules which he has mastered so that he is able to produce and understand an indefinite number of sentences, and to recognize grammatical mistakes and ambiguities. Performance refers to specific utterances, containing features foreign to the basic rule system (e.g. hesitations, unfinished sentences). According to Chomsky, linguistics before generative grammar had been preoccupied with performance in a CORPUS, instead of with the underlying competence involved (see ADEQUACY, sense 1). The validity of the distinction has, however, been questioned (e.g. are INTONATION, STYLISTICS, DISCOURSE matters of competence or performance?). See also LANGUE.   D.C.

Bibl: D. Crystal, *Linguistics* (Harmondsworth, 1985).

competition. In ECONOMICS, firms compete when they attempt to gain profits at the expense of other firms (by comparison, see CARTEL). Competition will, in certain circumstances, efficiently coordinate the demand and supply for goods, services and inputs (see PERFECT COMPETITION). More generally, competition is regarded as a means of making markets operate more efficiently. The Austrian school emphasizes that competition takes place in price, the characteristics of the product, ADVERTISING, research, etc. Successful firms acquire (temporary) MONOPOLY positions and the associated level of profits are a necessary reward and incentive. This view is one of dynamic FREE MARKETS, as compared to the NEOCLASSICAL ECONOMIC THEORY notion of competition as a static EQUILIBRIUM and the possibility of MARKET FAILURES. The MARXIST view of competition emphasizes the deliberate attempt to acquire and maintain a monopoly position through collusion, growth and takeover. The modern corporate view of competition is that the notion is largely redundant, as large interdependent firms have replaced the competitive market and they can only be analysed in the context of their technological, social and political environment (see FIRM, THEORIES OF).   J.P.

Bibl: M. Waterson, *The Economic Theory of the Industry* (Cambridge, 1984).

competitive equilibria. An equilibrium of the economy in which, given prices, wages and the initial distribution of resources, no firm or consumer can improve their position. It is an important theoretical concept in ECONOMICS (see EQUILIBRIUM, CORE and PERFECT COMPETITION).   J.P.

Bibl: E.R. Weintraub, *General Equilibrium* (London, 1975).

compiler. In COMPUTING, a PROGRAM which reads a program written in a HIGH-LEVEL PROGRAMMING LANGUAGE and translates it into machine code, i.e. a form suitable for a COMPUTER. This translation process can be quite elaborate, and a compiler is an expensive piece of SOFTWARE needed in the development of any computing system. *Load-go* compilers leave the machine codes inside the computer to be run immediately; other compilers output (or store) the code in a form suitable for use by an ASSEMBLER.   C.S.

complement, see under SEROLOGY.

complementarity principle. A principle in QUANTUM MECHANICS (enunciated by Niels Bohr in 1927) by which an experiment on one aspect of a system of atomic dimensions is supposed to destroy the possibility of learning about a 'complementary' aspect of the same system. See also UNCERTAINTY PRINCIPLE: WAVE-PARTICLE DUALITY.   M.V.B.

complementary distribution, see under DISTRIBUTION (sense 2).

complementary filiation, see under DESCENT.

complementary medicine. Term used to describe approaches to health-care not normally taught at conventional medical schools. The term encompasses (1) *Systems of healing,* e.g. HOMOEOPATHY, ACUPUNCTURE, osteopathy, chiropractic and herbal medicine. (2) *Diagnostic practices,* e.g. hair analysis, muscle testing, iridology, Kirlian photography. (3) *Therapeutic skills,* e.g. massage, reflexology, HYPNOSIS. (4) *Self-help skills,* e.g. relaxation techniques, meditation, autogenic training. Many of these therapies and practices stem from cultures and philosophies which challenge the Cartesian notion of duality of mind and body. Many posit the notion that man has an 'energetic' base to his being and function; they thus link back to the notion of VITALISM. A further common element lies in their ability to catalyse the self-healing potential present in all humans. They thus lay emphasis on the notion of both internal and external homoeostasis. There is great variety in the education and training offered to complementary practitioners and as yet no unified system of registration or code of ethics exists. Research into the effectiveness of complementary medicine is sparse but there is growing interest among the public and the scientific community.   P.C.P.

complementation. In GENETICS, the process whereby the effects of a defective GENE inherited from one parent can be masked by a functional gene from the other. If the two genes in an individual concerned with a particular function are both defective, they cannot complement one another, even if the defects are in different parts of the gene; this fact can be used to decide whether defective MUTATIONS are situated in the same functional unit.   J.M.S.

complex. In psychoanalytic theory (see PSYCHOANALYSIS), a word with no single precise meaning; most often, a nexus of repressed ideas (see REPRESSION) and related EMOTION that plays a distinct role in human development and in the genesis of neurotic disorders (see NEUROSIS). Examples are the OEDIPUS COMPLEX, the ELECTRA COMPLEX, and the INFERIORITY COMPLEX. In popular usage, the term is loosely used as a synonym for OBSESSION, also in a popular sense.   B.A.F.

complex function theory (or simply *function theory*). The branch of MATHEMATICS dealing with those FUNCTIONS which have COMPLEX NUMBERS both as ARGUMENTS and values and which have a well-defined DERIVATIVE in a neighbourhood of each 'point' of their domain. Such a function f is necessarily rather smooth and well-behaved. Calculations involving such functions (in particular INTEGRATION) can often be reduced to simple algebraic manipulations. Since many of the functions which occur in mathematical PHYSICS and in NUMBER THEORY can be extended to complex functions, the theory provides a powerful and indispensable tool for their study. Further, the beauty of the subject and its connections with TOPOLOGY and algebraic GEOMETRY give it a central place in mathematics.   R.G.

complex number. An extension of the notion of real NUMBER which was made so as to ensure that every algebraic equation (see ALGEBRA) has a solution. Each complex number can be written in the form $a + ib$ where a and b are real numbers and i is treated like an unknown which satisfies $i \times i = -1$; this suffices to determine the laws of addition, multiplication, and division for such numbers, e.g. $(0+i) \times (0+i) = (i \times i) = -1$. Formerly complex numbers were also called *imaginary* numbers; now this term is applied only when a (the—*real* part of $a + ib$) is zero. Though once regarded as mysterious, they now seem a relatively concrete example of an abstract MATHEMATICAL STRUCTURE. Besides their use in algebra they are important because of the power of COMPLEX FUNCTION THEORY, and because the equation $e^{i\theta} = \cos \theta + i \sin \theta$ allows problems concerning PERIODIC FUNCTIONS to be solved by

153

simple algebraic manipulations and waves. Because of the WAVE-PARTICLE DUALITY, complex numbers are essential to any mathematical description of the physical universe.   R.G.

complexity. In the theory of ALGORITHMS, the study of the resources, most commonly of time and STORE, required by an algorithm, expressed as a function of the size of one of the input PARAMETERS.
                                          J.E.S.

complexity theory. (1) The study of how complex an ALGORITHM is, which reflects how long it takes to run, and thus how expensive. (2) The complexity of a sequence of symbols is closely related to the amount of information it contains. It can be defined as the length of (= number of symbols used in) the shortest algorithm which will produce that sequence. For example, a random sequence can only be produced by an algorithm which is essentially as long as the sequence itself, so it has a very high complexity. At the other extreme, a sequence consisting of only one symbol repeated many times can be specified by a much shorter algorithm (whose length is approximately the logarithm of the length of the sequence, at least for long sequences), and so has a very low complexity.   J.M.

componential analysis. In SEMANTICS, a method of specifying word-meanings by establishing common components of sense, e.g. *man, woman, child, bull, cow, calf* can be distinguished semantically by setting up the components *human/ animal, male/female,* and *adult/young* — the sense of *man* being a combination of the notions *humans, male* and *adult.* Theoretical discussion continues over the psychological reality of the semantic components, and over the extent to which words in different languages can be analysed into the same components.

The term should be distinguished from the general term 'component', referring to a section of a GENERATIVE GRAMMAR.
                                          D.C.

composite particle approach, see under ELEMENTARY PARTICLES.

composition (in MATHEMATICS), see under FUNCTION.

comprehensive test ban treaty. The attempt to ban all testing of NUCLEAR WEAPONS. This began with the Nuclear Test Ban Treaty of 1963, which prohibited nuclear testing in the atmosphere. This did not attempt to control underground or undersea testing, both of which have been used extensively since that time. The pressure for a comprehensive ban has, at times, been resisted by all the nuclear powers. Frequently, it is advanced as a political move by those STATES with a complete test programme. A comprehensive treaty would now need to control tests in space as well as those on earth, although this would not become a major area for testing. A test ban treaty is a useful device in reducing tension, because it does not upset the present nuclear balance. In that sense, with other CONFIDENCE BUILDING MEASURES of arms reduction, it can be an approach to breaking the upward spiral of increasing armaments. A comprehensive test ban treaty could also be a move to a *nuclear freeze.* This would freeze the level of nuclear weapons at a set point. It would permit only the replacement of existing systems, but not their extension or enhancement. Such an agreement would affect the replacement of the Polaris weapon by the improved TRIDENT. See also NUCLEAR WEAPONS, LIMITATION AND CONTROL.   A.J.M.W.

Bibl: Stockholm Institute for Peace Research, *The Arms Race and Arms Control* (London, 1982).

compulsion. In ABNORMAL PSYCHOLOGY and PSYCHIATRY, a force or drive or impulse within the individual to do or think or say something or other, a force which he finds difficult to resist. It is a prominent feature in obsessional disorders (see OBSESSION).   B.A.F.

computability, see under RECURSIVE FUNCTION THEORY.

computation, see COMPUTING.

computational linguistics. A branch of LINGUISTICS which studies COMPUTER SIMULATION of human linguistic behaviour, especially such applications as MACHINE TRANSLATION and SPEECH SYNTHESIS. D.C.

computed tomography, see under RADIOLOGY.

computer. A mechanical or electrical device for processing information. Originally used only for numerical calculations, computers were used secretly during the 1939-45 war for cryptography and by the 1950s for commercial data processing; by now their non-numerical uses (for example, as WORD PROCESSORS) are at least as important as their numerical ones. Nowadays the word 'computer' refers almost always to the digital computer rather than the analogue computer.

In *analogue computers,* which are almost entirely confined to the numerical solution of physical problems, each physical quantity that occurs in the problem is represented by a mechanical displacement or by an electric voltage or current. The various parts of the computer are connected up in such a way that these displacements are related to one another in the same way as the corresponding quantities in the real system. The computer thus behaves as a mechanical or electrical analogue of the physical problem. The accuracy of analogue computers is limited, and the time required to set them up for a problem is usually long: as general purpose devices they are therefore practically obsolete, though the technique is sometimes employed in devices dedicated to a particular task (such as navigation systems, or automatic transmission systems).

Digital computers operate arithmetically, or according to other logical rules, on strings of digits, generally on the BINARY SCALE. (There are also *hybrid computers,* which are partly analogue and partly digital.) As they work by manipulating symbols and not by direct analogues of the quantities represented, their accuracy in numerical work is limited only by the size of their STORE and the nature of the ALGORITHM used, and they are equally capable of operation on non-numerical information such as text.

The importance of modern digital computers is their ability to carry out computations involving many steps (often over a million) at high speed and without human intervention. They do this by storing the instructions (or PROGRAMS) as well as the data being manipulated. What they do *not* do is to perform those specifically human operations (thinking, proving, etc.) sometimes attributed to them by anthropomorphizers — often people who know nothing about computers, or computing enthusiasts who know little else. In the first place, computers are *aids* to thought, proof, etc., not substitutes for them: all they can do is carry out a sequence of instructions which a human programmer, or team of programmers, has judged will be adequate for the particular task. In the second place, claims that 'computers have shown....' are almost always doubly false, because they are almost always made about precisely those problems which, because they involve VALUE-JUDGEMENTS and other complicated situations (and most human problems *are* complicated by computer standards), are the least possible to represent by a completely accurate MODEL. The computer can do no more than work out the consequences of the assumptions which underlie the model, and which are therefore built into its program. If the assumptions are seriously wrong, the model will be seriously inaccurate, and its behaviour as shown on the computer will bear only a tenuous resemblance to that of the real world. See also PROCESSOR; INPUT/OUTPUT; INTERFACE; LOGIC. C.S.

Bibl: M.L. Dertouzos and J. Moses, eds., *The Computer Age: A 20-Year View* (Cambridge, Mass. and London, 1979).

computer-aided design. The use of a COMPUTER, typically associated with a VISUAL DISPLAY, in such a way that a designer can see his design immediately and the consequences of changing it, while remaining free to exercise the unprogrammable qualities of taste and judgement. This might involve showing a perspective view of a complicated 3-dimensional object; often the point of view can be moved, giving the impression that the object is being rotated. More sophisticated systems allow for binocular vision, and the designer may even get the impression of walking about inside his proposed design. The technique makes heavy demands on computing power, and has therefore only recently become widespread; it is now an important part of engineering practice in many areas, including architecture, automobile design and electronics.　　C.S.; J.E.S.

computer architecture. The study of the various ways in which the components of a COMPUTER (PROCESSOR, STORE, etc.) might be interconnected. The most common form is that of the VON NEUMANN COMPUTER, but other forms can better exploit the PARALLELISM of the HARDWARE.　　J.E.S.

computer-assisted instruction, see under PROGRAMMED INSTRUCTION.

computer graphics. Designs drawn by means of a COMPUTER. Their principal use is at present to produce output in the form of graphs, histograms, etc., in many application areas, and COMPUTER-AIDED DESIGN. They have also been used for purely artistic purposes. In this instance the designs may be recognizable transformations of existing works of art or photographs; or the operator may supply the initial image himself (often with the aid of a mechanical plotter, or a LIGHT PEN applied to a CATHODE RAY TUBE display); or the computer may be programmed to act unpredictably, and in many respects 'creatively'.

The term is also used, in the COMPUTING world, to cover the HARDWARE and SOFTWARE required to make it possible to present and manipulate the designs. For instance, if the screen shows a perspective view of a three-dimensional object, a PROGRAM of considerable sophistication is required to allow the viewer to change the point of view so that the object appears to rotate. A TERMINAL with graphics capability is one on which it is possible to draw lines and curves.　　P.C.; C.S.; J.E.S.

Bibl: J. Reichardt (ed.), *Cybernetics, Art and Ideas* (London and Greenwich, Conn., 1971); W.M. Newman and R.F. Sproull, *Principles of Interactive Computer Graphics* (London and New York, 1981).

computer music. COMPUTERS have been used in connection with music in many different ways: to compose or aid in the composition of music, to generate sounds, to control analogue SYNTHESIZERS and in the notation of music. After being programmed with relevant stylistic details and processes a computer can be made to compose music. An important early example of this is the Illiac Suite by Lejaren Hiller where the computer produced sections of music that were later performed by a string quartet. At the present level of development in ARTIFICIAL INTELLIGENCE, however, computers are probably more useful as aids to composition, especially when the composition of the music involves mathematical calculations, e.g. the works of Iannis Xenakis (see STOCHASTIC MUSIC). Computers have also been used as sound generators (see also ADDITIVE SYNTHESIS, ELECTRONIC MUSIC, SOUND SAMPLING, DIGITAL MUSIC) where, after being programmed with the different characteristics of the sound required, the computer creates the sound waveform digitally and this is then processed through a DIGITAL TO ANALOGUE CONVERTER and recorded on tape. Early experiments were conducted at the Bell Labs in New Jersey by Max Mathews, eventually leading to the important computer program Music IV in the 1960s. New ways of producing complex waveforms were discovered by John Chowning using FREQUENCY MODULATION, which enabled computers to produce sounds rivalling natural sounds in interest and complexity. The early experiments in computer synthesis usually required great amounts of expensive computer time to produce single sounds, but by the seventies computers could process quickly enough to produce REAL TIME music, and this progress in TECHNOLOGY has led to the development of very sophisticated computer instruments such as the Fairlight CMI and the Synclavier.

Computers have also been linked to analogue synthesizers where they can remember and reproduce complex sound settings (patches) and thus enable the synthesizer to produce instantaneously large ranges of different sounds. Computers can also play synthesizers acting as SEQUENCERS, often using MIDI as an interface. Computer systems are now being developed that can read, write and print music; i.e. the musical equivalents of WORD PROCESSORS.　　B.CO.

Bibl: R. Hammond, *The Musician and*

the Micro (Blandford, 1983); M. Mathews, *The Technology of Computer Music* (Cambridge, Mass., 1969).

computer science, see COMPUTING SCIENCE.

computer simulation. The construction and use of a computer program (see COMPUTER; PROGRAM) to act as a MODEL for a SYSTEM in the real world and so to aid in its experimental study. Two main areas of effort can be distinguished: the *continuous* and *discrete* areas. One range of problems, including population studies, economic systems, and real-time control (see COMPUTING), covers areas where a system lends itself to expression by sets of DIFFERENTIAL EQUATIONS. These have been studied by *analogue computation*, but studies are now more often carried out by *continuous simulation* techniques on *digital computers*, using incremental INTEGRATION of the sets of equations. Another substantial range of problems, often STOCHASTIC in nature, arises in industrial MANAGEMENT or control. Where the problem is beyond the scope of LINEAR PROGRAMMING or QUEUEING THEORY one may build a computer program as a model, experiment on the model to improve its behaviour, and then transfer the results to the real thing. Such models are usually called *discrete simulations*.

The term is also used in PSYCHOLOGY and ARTIFICIAL INTELLIGENCE work to describe programs which embody hypotheses about how people play games, solve problems (see PROBLEM-SOLVING), or understand messages. A measure of 'realistic' behaviour on the part of the program may be taken as evidence for the plausibility of the hypotheses.

Simulation programs are frequently large and complex. In both the discrete and continuous areas, special-purpose HIGH-LEVEL PROGRAMMING LANGUAGES have been produced and have achieved some popularity. The importance of an adequate model needs to be stressed, as do the dangers inherent in accepting the predictions of an inadequate one. With this proviso, there are areas, e.g. heavy industry and government, in which computer simulation is important, useful, and, though expensive, cheaper than experimentation on the real world — which indeed may be impractical or even disastrous. J.N.B.

computing (also known as *data-processing; electronic data-processing* or *EDP; information-processing*). The use of a digital COMPUTER. (The use of an analogue computer is generally called *analogue computing.*) In outline the steps required for presenting a problem to a computer are: (1) analysing the problem and preparing a suitable PROGRAM; (2) verifying or DEBUGGING the program on a computer; (3) running the program on the computer with the appropriate sets of data. The first stage is carried out essentially by people, the second partly and the third very largely by computer. Computers are nowadays so fast that the time taken by individual jobs, particularly in the debugging phase, is so short that human operators are unable to keep pace with the computer. Various modes of operation have been introduced in order to get round this mis-match of speeds; all are implemented by an OPERATING SYSTEM which largely takes the place of a human operator. For PERSONAL COMPUTERS, however, the mis-match may be of no consequence; then the operating system's job is merely to provide a repertoire of useful facilities to the user, to save him the chore of writing programs for them himself.

In *batch processing* the jobs are run to completion in sequence; the input (of program and data) and output (of results) takes place generally via an intermediate *backing* STORE, often MAGNETIC TAPE. The operators load the program and data on to this *off-line* — e.g. using a small auxiliary computer while the main machine is engaged in some lengthy job. When a whole batch of jobs has been loaded, the main machine will process them all in sequence, putting the output into a similar backing store or tape. When the batch is finished the results are printed off-line by the auxiliary machine. Batch processing, though relatively simple, suffers from the fact that the *turnround time* (the time between presenting a job to the operators and receiving the printed results) is much greater than the running time in the computer, being typically from

157

an hour to a day or more and virtually independent of the running time; it is still useful, however, for machines intended for the regular running of a few long jobs.

Modes of operation which get round this difficulty all involve *time-sharing*, in which the computer appears to do several jobs simultaneously; actually it works on each job for only a short time before moving on to another. In *multi-programming*, time-sharing is used to allow several batch-processing queues in the computer at the same time. By separating the large from the small jobs the turnround time for the latter can be improved. A further step is to allow *on-line computing* from a TERMINAL in place of one or more of these queues; in this mode of operation the user is in direct contact with the main computer without the intermediary of an auxiliary machine or backing store. This reduces still further the turnround for the programs from the data station while allowing a *background job* in a batch-processing queue to use any time which would otherwise be wasted in waiting for the operator at the data station.

An extension of this is to replace the data station by a number of consoles. The terminals, which may be hundreds of miles from the computer, are situated for the convenience of the user. A system which is principally run from terminals in this way is often called a time-sharing or *multiterminal* system. Terminal systems can be *dedicated* — i.e. confined to a few special programs, such as airline bookings or banking — or *general-purpose*, with no foreknowledge of the programs which will be run, so that stringent precautions have to be taken to prevent one program from interfering with another, whether accidentally or by malice.

In *real-time computing* and PROCESS CONTROL there is the additional requirement that the computer complete its response to any input within a certain *critical time* which is determined by the application. This poses additional problems, particularly in situations where the computer is heavily loaded. Real-time systems are always dedicated and often need extraordinary precautions to guard against possible breakdown of the computer. C.S.

computing science. The study of the use and sometimes construction of digital COMPUTERS. (Analogue computers are generally excluded.) It is a fashionable, interesting, difficult, and perhaps useful activity. Unfortunately, in spite of appearing to be a mathematical or physical science, it has so far only a fairly small body of generally accepted fundamental laws or principles which are likely to remain valid even for the next 20 years; there is also a large amount of almost entirely ephemeral 'state of the art' information. A more appropriate title for this latter part would probably be 'computer technology'. See also SOFTWARE ENGINEERING; COMPLEXITY.   C.S.; J.E.S.

concentration. In urban GEOGRAPHY, a term used in the description of the population pattern of an urban area. The *density gradient*, i.e. rate of change of density per unit distance measured from the centre to the edge, is used as a measure of the concentration of a town's population. In contrast to this its *central density*, i.e. number of people per unit area, is used as a measure of its *congestion*. See also DENSITY.   M.L.

concentration camps. A term originally used to describe internment centres set up in the Cuban rebellion of 1895 by the Spanish military and in the Boer War (1901-2) by the British military in an attempt to pacify rebels by depriving them of civilian support in their areas of operation.

Since the 1930s, however, the term has been used to describe the prison camps characteristic of TOTALITARIAN states, notably NAZI Germany and the Soviet Union (see FORCED LABOUR) staffed by the secret police (the SS in Germany; the NKVD/ KGB in Russia) and used for the imprisonment, torture and frequently execution of those whom the regime regards as opponents or sets out to eliminate on the grounds of RACE or CLASS.

The first German concentration camps were established in 1933 and used mainly for the 'protective custody' of political prisoners (COMMUNISTS and Social Democrats); the number of such prisoners was reduced to around 7,500 in winter 1936-7. With the territorial expansion of Germany in 1938 (Austria; Sudetenland) the numbers of camps and prisoners began to grow under the overall control of Himmler as *Reichsführer SS*. The number of Germans imprisoned, other than German Jews, fell and the great majority of the prisoners, in addition to Jews, were nationals of occupied territories suspected of resistance. From 1941-2 the camps were increasingly used to provide forced labour for the German war-effort. In a mass expansion, millions of Poles, Russians, Jews and other East and Central European nationals were rounded up under appalling conditions in which an average of 60% of the inmates were literally worked to death. The most notorious of all were the extermination or death camps (Auschwitz, Maidanek and Treblinka in Poland, Buchenwald in Germany) in which the mass slaughter of Jews and others was systematically organized, by shooting, medical experimentation and (the largest number) by the use of gas chambers. The number of Jews known to have perished is between 5 and 6 millions; the total number of those who were killed or died from ill-treatment in Nazi concentration camps (including the Jews) has been estimated as at least 10-12 million, possibly as high as 20 million. See also FINAL SOLUTION.

A.L.C.B.

Bibl: E. Kogon, *The Theory and Practice of Hell* (Eng. tr. London, 1950); H. Krausnick, H. Buchheim, M. Broszat, H.A. Jacobsen, *Anatomy of the SS State* (Eng. tr. London, 1968).

concept. The MEANING of a term and thus the smallest unit of thought, just as a term is the smallest unit of DISCOURSE. As terms combine to form sentences, so concepts combine to form PROPOSITIONS or complete thoughts. To acquire a concept is primarily to know the meaning of some term that expresses it (only primarily, since the capacity to recognize instances of a concept sometimes precedes the possession of a word to express it). In recent times philosophers have tended to agree that a concept should not be thought of as a kind of object, such as a mental image. People can share concepts (indeed they must do so if they are to communicate), but the items of their mental furniture are distinct and proprietary to each of them.

To possess a concept, then, is not to own some easily identifiable article but to be able to *do* something, specifically to recognize instances of the concept in question and to construct, and draw INFERENCES from, sentences in which some word that expresses the concept occurs. The analysis of concepts, which some would take to be the chief or even the whole business of PHILOSOPHY, is a matter of finding more perspicuous and complexity-revealing words in which to express something commonly expressed by a single term. A.Q.

Bibl: H. H. Price, *Thinking and Experience* (London, 2nd ed., 1969).

conceptual architecture. An attempt in the early 1970s to establish an architectural parallel with CONCEPTUAL ART. Some sort of authority existed in a passage in the writings of the Renaissance architect Alberti, itself loosely based on the PLATONIC theory of Forms. And in the designs of French pre-Revolutionary architects based loosely on the Platonic or Phileban solids which symbolized the four elements. The co-existing architectural interest in STRUCTURALISM seemed to offer the possibility of establishing ultimate architecture Forms. Of necessity no conceptual architecture was ever built. S.L.

conceptual art. A deviant movement in the visual arts which employs unprepared, eccentric materials (e.g. earth, fat, refuse) and everyday media (e.g. snapshots, typescripts, video, human and animal bodies) in serial or ALEATORY 'installations', 'environments', performances, lists of instructions, and documentary displays, for the deliberately banal or paradoxical presentation of concepts drawn from PHILOSOPHY, LINGUISTICS, art-criticism, and ordinary life. Legitimized by exhibition in museums and galleries and reproduction in the art press, yet radically violating traditional canons of artistic production, form and (to a lesser extent) content, conceptual works hold the spectator's normal modes of interpretation and appreciation at bay. Highly self-referential, they seek thus to stimulate scepticism about conventional aesthetic communication, and above all to open out or explode the concept 'art' and its cognates, which are perceived as tainted by elitism, commodifica-

159

tion and materialism inherent in the art world. Deriving from DADA, Duchamp and Magritte, and with more recent analogies in the 1950s neo-Dada of Piero Manzoni and Yves Klein, conceptualism (as it is alternatively called) arose by reaction out of MINIMAL ART in the early 1960s (the term 'concept art' being first published by Henry Flynt in 1961) and flourished till the late 1970s. International, loose-knit and diverse, the movement still has many adherents (including Joseph Beuys, Sol Lewitt and Richard Long) who frequently reject the label 'conceptual'. Though accepted by sections of the commercial and official art establishment, its works cause continuing puzzlement and unease. Hence conceptual art has been both dismissed as aesthetic NIHILISM producing a meretricious ANTI-ART, and hailed as the heroic vanguard of an alternative aesthetic.　　　　　　B.M-H.

Bibl: L.R. Lippard, *Six Years: The Dematerialization of the Art Object from 1966 to 1972* (London and New York, 1973); T. McEvilley, 'I Think Therefore I Art', *Artforum*, Summer 1985.

conceptual scheme. In PHILOSOPHY, the beliefs, assumptions, science, morality, traditions and general outlook of some community, taken together as a loosely knit inclusive theory in terms of which the community's members explain and interpret their empirical and/or moral experience. By 'community' may be meant a particular society or sub-group in society, or all humans, or even all intelligent beings (including gods and Martians, if any exist); but usually either of the two last. On the grounds that thought (possession and manipulation of CONCEPTS) is not possible above a rudimentary level without language, conceptual schemes are sometimes identified with languages or sets of intertranslatable languages. On this view, to learn language is to acquire the conceptual scheme it embodies. It has been said that one task of philosophy is to investigate the structure of such schemes, tracing connections within them, identifying the most fundamental concepts, and investigating the inconsistencies which, given their amorphous and historically cumulative character, they may be expected to contain. A major question concerning them is whether there is only one possible conceptual scheme, or many; if the latter, the problem of RELATIVISM arises.　　　　　　A.C.G.

Bibl: D. Davidson, *Truth and Interpretation* (Oxford, 1984).

conceptualism.

(1) A philosophic theory of UNIVERSALS which takes them to be CONCEPTS in the minds of those who understand the general word (whether verb, adjective, or common noun) whose MEANING the universal is. To the extent that a concept is defined as the meaning common to all of a set of synonymous words, this theory is a truism, since whatever else a universal may be it is the meaning of a general word. What is controversial is the contention that a concept is something mental and proprietary to a particular mind: for if I am to understand what you say I must attach the same meaning to your words as you do. A variant form of conceptualism takes a universal or concept to be a mental image. Here the difficulty is to see how one could have an image of economic inflation or negative electric charge or the conscience. Furthermore a specific, particular image is ambiguously representative: a mental picture of a particular dog could represent retriever, dog, left-hand surface of an animal, loyalty, chestnut colour, life, or hair.　　　　　　A.Q.

Bibl: H.H. Price, *Thinking and Experience* (London, 2nd ed., 1969).

(2) A vice of legal reasoning, attributed to some lawyers and legal theorists, which consists in treating the general terms and CATEGORIES used in the formulation of legal rules as having an invariant and completely determinate meaning, so that their application to particular cases is regarded as a simple exercise in syllogistic reasoning. On such a view, which has been stigmatized as *mechanical jurisprudence* or the *jurisprudence of concepts*, it would be possible, simply by consulting the definition or analysis of general terms and categories, to determine whether any real or imaginary case fell within the scope of a legal rule. Legal conceptualism has been regarded as an obstacle to the judicial adaptation of the law to social change and sometimes as a cause of unreasonable or even unjust decisions.　　　　　　H.L.A.H.

Bibl: R. Pound, *Interpretations of Legal History* (Cambridge, 1923); J. Stone, *Social Dimensions of Law and Justice* (London and Sydney, 1966).

conciliarity. A term used in CATHOLICISM to express the belief, strengthened by the experience and teaching of VATICAN COUNCIL II, that there should be harmony after consultation between the Pope and the bishops; between the bishops of the world-wide Church and of a nation; and between the bishop, clergy and laity in a diocese. See AGGIORNAMENTO. This belief has encouraged hopes in the ECUMENICAL MOVEMENT that the way to greater Christian unity may be found through such meetings involving Christians who are not Roman Catholics, rather than through submission to an 'hierarchical' authority able to dictate. Such hopes have been strengthened by the experience of the World Council of Churches, formed in 1948 and including representatives of ORTHODOXY (EASTERN) although not of Roman Catholicism. But the extent to which the actual power exercised by the Pope or the bishop should be sacrificed remains a matter of uncertainty. See also INFALLIBILITY. D.L.E.

concrete.
(1) A material used in construction either (*a*) as *mass concrete*, a mixture of cement, sand, and aggregate with water, where only compressive strength is required; or (*b*), more usually, as *reinforced concrete*, i.e. combined with steel in the form of bars or wires to create a material able to take both tensile and compressive forces. While the material is setting it is held in place, and its ultimate shape and surface texture determined, by *shuttering*, which may be timber boarding, plywood, steel sheeting, or moulded plastic; this process can occur either *in situ* or during *precasting* on special beds.

A patent for reinforced concrete was taken out by Coignet in 1855, and Hennebique showed a highly developed system of columns, beams, and floors in 1892. Reinforced concrete has since been used and highly refined by engineers such as Maillart in various spectacular bridges in Switzerland, by Nervi in exhibition halls and sports palaces, and Freyssinet in bridges and hangars, and by such architects as, e.g., Auguste Perret. A new plasticity was given to the material by Le Corbusier, who also pioneered *béton brut*, the use of unplaned timber shuttering to create a rough boarded finish often seen in BRUTALIST architecture. A method of inducing compressive forces in the concrete by stressing the reinforcement before it has to take its normal loads was developed by Freyssinet from *c.* 1926 and is now known as *prestressing*.

Many of the characteristic shapes of civil engineering (curved dams, elevated motorways) and of modern architecture (thin slab floors on columns, curved shells) owe their forms to the use of reinforced concrete, commonplace in all but the smallest buildings. See also CANTILEVER; PREFABRICATION; STRUCTURES.
M.BR.
Bibl: S. Giedion, tr. E. Matthews, *Space, Time and Architecture* (London and Cambridge, Mass., 3rd ed., 1954); P. Collins, *Concrete* (London and New York, 1959).

(2) In the ARTS, a term used to emphasize materiality and specificity, i.e. concrete as opposed to what philosophers mean by ABSTRACT. See CONCRETE ART; CONCRETE MUSIC; CONCRETE POETRY. J.W.

concrete art. Term used in the Abstraction-Création group from *c.* 1930 when Hans Arp was calling his sculptures 'concretions' and Van Doesburg of De STIJL began editing the short-lived *Art Concret*. Associated above all with Max Bill, the Swiss BAUHAUS-trained artist whose strongly geometrical art is based on mathematical reasoning, it signifies the materialization of an intellectual CONCEPT. In 1944 Bill organized an International Exhibition of Concrete Art at Basel, and thereafter the movement spread to Argentina, Italy, and Brazil. The work of Joseph Albers in the U.S.A. also relates. J.W.

concrete music. A form of music, first developed by the Frenchman Pierre Schaeffer in 1948, involving sounds of all types (musical, natural, human, mechanical, etc.) which, recorded on tape, are filtered or manipulated so as to disguise their origin. The music so produced is

161

sometimes powerful and evocative, though often needing a balletic or theatrical interpretation to make its full effect. Maurice Béjart has used *musique concrète* in a number of ballets. The composition of concrete music, though slow and laborious, has attracted composers of the stature of Boulez, Messiaen, and Sauguet in France, the Greek Xenakis, and the veteran Franco-American Varèse. See also BRUITISME; COMPUTER MUSIC; ELECTRONIC MUSIC; FUTURISM. A.H.

concrete operation. In DEVELOPMENTAL PSYCHOLOGY, a PIAGETIAN term for a mental operation involved in the classification, seriation, and enumeration of objects. The notion is applied to the mental operations governing the organization of real (concrete) objects but not the organization of imagined possibilities. Such operations are mastered by children in the middle stage of intellectual development. P.L.H.

concrete poetry. A CONCEPT formulated under the influence of Max Bill and Eugen Gomringer, and launched at the São Paulo exhibition of CONCRETE ART in 1956 by a group of Brazilian poets and designers. According to the 'Pilot Plan' in their review *Noigandres* 4 (1958), the concrete poem is an object 'in and by itself', consciously using graphic space in its structure along lines foreshadowed by Mallarmé and Guillaume Apollinaire. Subdivisions of their movement, as it spread across the world in the 1960s, were *semiotic poetry* using symbols, *emergent poetry* exploiting quasi-cryptographic juggling of letters, the related KINETIC poetry with its serial methods and PERMUTATIONS, the *logograms* of the Brazilian Pedro Xisto, and *phonetic* or sound poetry. This last was not in the 'Pilot Plan' but shares its concern with what Max Bense calls 'materiality, verbal, visual, or vocal', though deriving more from the *Lautgedichte* of MERZ and the noises made by FUTURISM and DADA. With this one exception concrete poetry is essentially visual or typographic, and thus emerges in a much larger (and older) confluence of the verbal, visual, and printer's arts to which LETTRISM, spatialism (see SPACE), and POP ART contribute also. J.W.

Bibl: E. Williams (ed.), *An Anthology of Concrete Poetry* (New York, 1967).

concrete universal.
(1) In PHILOSOPHY, a term used by absolute IDEALISTS to describe individual things of a more substantial kind (see SUBSTANCE); 'concrete' aims to emphasize the thing's individuality, 'universal' the rationally systematic coherence which such philosophers take to be the hallmark of the true individual. The only wholly genuine individual for these philosophers is the ABSOLUTE, or Spirit, or the totality of what there really is. But its preeminently substantial individuality is approximated to by finite minds or personalities and by such articulated systems of persons or persistent social groups as nations, professions, and classes. A.Q.
(2) In literature, an abstraction developed by W.K. Wimsatt in *The Verbal Icon* (1954) and much used in the NEW CRITICISM. Wimsatt over-optimistically sought, on HEGELIAN lines, to erect a holistic (see HOLISM) POETICS in which the 'particulars' of a 'successful' poem would coalesce into a totality that is its 'own' universal. Another New Critic, John Crowe Ransom, accepted the term — but on condition that it should be understood in a 'Kantian' rather than in a Hegelian sense. He felt that Wimsatt left no room for Kantian 'natural beauty': man needs a 'double vision', so that he may see both the rose itself, *and* (then) its 'idea'. M.S.-S.
Bibl: J.C. Ransom, *Poems and Essays* (New York, 1955).

CONDECA, see under CENTRAL AMERICAN DEFENCE COUNCIL.

condensation. In Freud's analysis of the dream-work, condensation and DISPLACEMENT are two of the means by which the 'dream-thoughts' or 'latent content' are transformed into the 'manifest content' of the dream. The much richer, longer and more complex text of the dream-thoughts is 'condensed' as it is filtered through the dream-work, and the dream as remembered may be 'brief, meagre and laconic'. Not only that, but the work of displacement will also have contributed to the 'scrambling' of the dream-thoughts in their passage to the text of the dream.

Condensation and displacement then, are two rhetorical transformations which the repressing 'censor' will have imposed on the dream in its passage from latent to manifest form, and the task of the PSYCHO-ANALYST will be to interpret these transformations in an attempt to find the deeper or earlier 'text'. The essay by Roman Jakobson on METAPHOR and METONYMY threw a different light on not only Saussure's but also Freud's theories. Metaphor, it seems, is like condensation in its activity, while metonymy is like displacement. Freud's discovery has been interpreted, in the light of Jakobson's distinction, to great effect in the work of Lévi-Strauss, Lacan (see LACANIAN), Barthes and most STRUCTURALIST and post-structuralist literary theory.   R.PO.

Bibl: S. Freud, *The Interpretation of Dreams* (1899; Eng. tr. London, 1954).

conditioned reflex. The customary translation (more accurately, 'conditional reflex') of the Russian term for a connection established by a CLASSICAL CONDITIONING procedure between an arbitrary stimulus and a reflex response. Pavlov's work (see PAVLOVIAN) suggested to early BEHAVIOURISTS an analysis of all behaviour in terms of involuntary stimulus-response bonds, thus removing the necessity for mental CONSTRUCTS such as 'will', 'motive', and 'intention'. However, conditional reflexes in the Pavlovian paradigm can be clearly established only in physiological systems served by the autonomic NERVOUS SYSTEM; the conditioning of voluntary behaviour seems to require reward (*reinforcement*). So, although learned emotional reactions may be analysed as conditioned reflexes, most voluntary behaviour must be conditioned by operant rather than classical procedures (see OPERANT CONDITIONING).   D.H.

conditioning. The deliberate and systematic attempt to control some aspect of human or animal behaviour, either, in CLASSICAL CONDITIONING (also known as PAVLOVIAN or *respondent* conditioning), by establishing a CONDITIONED REFLEX, or, in OPERANT CONDITIONING (also known as *instrumental* conditioning), by controlling the consequences of behaviour.   D.H.

confidence building measures (CBM). Term first used in the Conference on Security and Co-operation in Europe (CSCE) in HELSINKI in 1975 to refer to measures designed to reduce tension by increasing the flow of information and increasing the possibility for each side to verify the military intentions and activities of the other. CBMs include the notification of military manoeuvres and the presence of observers at such manoeuvres. Fairly wide-ranging measures were agreed at the 1985 Stockholm CSCE. See also COMPREHENSIVE TEST BAN TREATY.   A.WI.

Bibl: W. G. Baudissin, ed., *From Distrust to Confidence* (Baden-Baden, 1983).

confidence interval, see under INTERVAL ESTIMATION.

configuration. An English alternative to the German word GESTALT.   I.M.L.H.

confirmation. The support given to a hypothesis by evidence: the fundamental relation between premise and conclusion in INDUCTION. The fact that every known A is B confirms the hypothesis that every A whatever is B, but does not establish it conclusively, since it is possible that some as yet undiscovered A is not B, and thus that the unrestricted generalization is false. If evidence confirms a hypothesis, then it confers some probability on it. Some broad principles of confirmation are intuitively acceptable, i.e. those which hold it to increase with the bulk and variety of the evidence. Attempts have been made, most elaborately by Carnap, to develop comprehensive formal theories of confirmation on the basis of such principles. See also FREQUENCY THEORY. A.Q.

Bibl: R. Swinburne, *An Introduction to Confirmation Theory* (London, 1973).

conflict theory. A term loosely applied to the work of a number of sociological theorists who have mounted critiques of STRUCTURAL-FUNCTIONAL THEORY on the grounds that it neglects the empirical fact that conflicts of value and interest are inherent in all forms of human society; or, at best, treats conflict as a phenomenon of only secondary interest by taking the very existence of an ongoing society as in itself evidence that some fundamental consensus must prevail. Consequently, it is held, exponents of structural-functional theory underestimate the degree to which the coordination of social activities and the stability of societies derive from the direct or indirect COERCION of less powerful by more powerful groups. Some versions of conflict theory are of a MARXIST character; others, however, reflect a political philosophy of PLURALISM.   J.H.G.

Bibl: J. Rex, *Social Conflict: a Conceptual and Theoretical Analysis* (London, 1981).

confounding, see under VARIANCE, ANALYSIS OF.

confrontation. Term employed, originally by Indonesian President Sukarno in the 1960s against Malaysia, to describe a conflict in which a direct attack or declaration of war is avoided, and techniques of subversion, propaganda, and GUERRILLA raids are employed as well as playing upon the fears of international conflict entertained by the allies and associates of the opposing power in order to cause them to intervene and bring diplomatic pressure to bear. More loosely, any conflict in the stage before a declaration of war or outbreak of general hostilities.   D.C.W.

Confucianism. The main RELIGION of the Chinese, so named after Kung the Master (Chinese Kung Fu-tzu, Latin Confucius) whose traditional dates are 551-479 B.C. The *Analects* of Confucius present a religion of self-control and duty. They advocate gentlemanly conduct and conformity to the 'way of heaven'. They neither deny THEISM nor are very keen on it. The term 'Confucianism' was invented by 19th-century Christians under the mistaken impression that such a powerful religion must, like CHRISTIANITY, have had one extraordinary founder. The enduring influence of Confucius was thought a worthy target for a hostile campaign mounted by China's COMMUNIST rulers in the 1970s. Since the failure of that GREAT PROLETARIAN CULTURAL REVOLUTION the strict morality of everyday Chinese life seems to be a continuing witness to Confucian influence.   D.L.E.

Bibl: H.G. Creel, *Confucius* (New York, 1949; London, 1951).

congestion, see under CONCENTRATION.

conglomerate. A firm operating in more than one distinct industry; its activities are said to be diversified. Such firms may obtain ECONOMIES OF SCALE in the actual production of each good and service and, more importantly, they may obtain economies across the range of their activities, e.g. raising finance, planning investment, RESEARCH AND DEVELOPMENT and MARKETING. A more vague and common justification for their existence is that it allows a superior MANAGEMENT to operate across a wider range of activities. However, the size of conglomerates and their ability to cross-subsidize their products may be used to reduce COMPETITION in each of the industries it operates in. The growth of conglomerates, particularly through mergers, may represent a managerial desire for growth (see FIRM, THEORIES OF) rather than an activity that is of benefit to society. The political, economic and social power of conglomerates has also been of concern.   J.P.

Bibl: D.A. Hay and D.J. Morris, *Industrial Economics: Theory and Evidence* (Oxford, 1979).

Congrès Internationaux d'Architecture Moderne, see CIAM.

conjugation. In BIOLOGY, the coming together of two whole MICRO-ORGANISMS followed by the exchange of genetic material. Such a process occurs among some PROTOZOA and (see BACTERIOLOGY) some bacilli. Conjugation is thus a pregametic (see GAMETE) sexual process. P.M.

conjuncture. A term derived from the French *conjoncture* (German *Konjunktur*), meaning 'the state of the economy' or 'the way the economic situation is developing'. Economists making short-term economic forecasts (see FORECASTING) use the word as shorthand for 'the complex trends in employment, output, prices, the BALANCE OF PAYMENTS, and other key economic variables'. Analysis of the conjuncture is closely related to the theory of economic fluctuations and business cycles (see TRADE CYCLE). A.C.

connectionism. Edward Thorndike's term for his analysis of psychological phenomena in terms of ASSOCIATION between, not ideas, but situations and responses. 'Learning,' he wrote in 1931, 'is connecting. The mind is man's connection system.' I.M.L.H.

Bibl: E.L. Thorndike, *Selected Writings from a Connectionist's Psychology* (New York, 1949).

connotation and **denotation.** Two aspects of the MEANING of expressions: the *connotation* being, roughly, the meaning proper of an expression, the *denotation* the actual thing or things to which it refers or applies or of which it is true. The distinction, thus put forward by John Stuart Mill, largely corresponds to that between the *sense* and *reference* of expressions (Frege) and that between their *intension* and *extension* (Carnap); it is quite different from the distinction between the everyday senses of the words, in which denotation is what a term really means, while connotation is what is associated with or suggested by a term. Two terms with the same connotation (e.g. 'man' and 'rational animal') are synonymous; the replacement of one by the other yields a sentence that is a proper translation of the original. Two terms with the same denotation (e.g. 'man' and 'featherless biped') will not generally preserve identity of meaning under substitution, but the TRUTH-VALUE of the two statements will be the same. The distinction can be extended to cover sentences as a whole, as well as the terms of which they are composed. The connotation or sense of a sentence is a PROPOSITION; its denotation is a truth-value (Frege) or, a little less provocatively, reality if it is true, nothing if it is false. The two aspects are intimately and reciprocally related: each, in a sense, determines the other. If the connotation is determined, the things to which it refers or applies are fixed. On the other hand, we learn the meaning of some terms by being made acquainted with what they denote or, where the terms are general, with representative instances of it. A.Q.

Bibl: J. S. Mill, *A System of Logic* (London, 1843); C.I. Lewis, *Analysis of*

Knowledge and Valuation (La Salle, Ill., 1946).

consciousness. The state of an individual when his faculties of seeing, hearing, feeling, thinking, etc., are functioning normally. It contrasts (1) with his state when he goes into a coma, or dead faint, or is deeply hypnotized (see HYPNOSIS), or is asleep dreamlessly; and (2) with his state when, e.g., instead of feeling a pin prick as he would normally do, he is unconscious of it — either because he has been locally anaesthetized, or because, unconsciously, he does not wish to feel it, or because AUTO-SUGGESTION has successfully enabled him to avoid feeling it, or because he has been mildly hypnotized, or for some other reason. In these latter cases, the content of his STREAM OF CONSCIOUSNESS is somewhat restricted in character. In the case of a man blind from birth, the content is greatly and permanently restricted, since he lacks one of our normal faculties.

At present we do not know what constitutes the full set of necessary and sufficient neuro-physiological conditions (see NECESSARY AND SUFFICIENT CONDITIONS) for the normal functioning of any one of our perceptual and COGNITIVE faculties. *A fortiori* we do not know what constitutes this set of conditions for our conscious functioning in general. Moreover, although consciousness is under constant and widespread investigation under the guise, in particular, of studies in PERCEPTION and COGNITION, there are deep conceptual conflicts about the CONCEPT of consciousness embedded in our CULTURE, including the SUBCULTURE of scientists. Thus, how far down the phylogenetic scale (see PHYLOGENY) is it correct to ascribe conscious functioning? We would probably all agree to ascribe it to a monkey reaching for a banana, or a dog running to greet its master. But what about a rat learning a new maze? If we say 'yes' here, then we will also be obliged to ascribe it to an earthworm learning a maze, and we resist this ascription. If we say 'no' to the rat, our refusal and doubts at once spread upwards to embrace the dog and the monkey. Our scepticism is strengthened by current attempts in PSYCHOLOGY to explain the behaviour of the rat without postulating conscious functioning. It is all too evident, therefore, that we are really quite unclear what we are saying when we ascribe consciousness to an animal or to ourselves.

One solution has been to suggest that our conscious functioning consists in a complex and continuous process of conceptualizing input from within and without the organism. This suggestion is promising and its HEURISTIC value has not yet been fully tapped, let alone exhausted. However, it will probably turn out to have the consequence of restricting conscious functioning to ourselves and to the higher animals for parts of their daily waking lives. This, in turn, has the logical consequence that the lower animals cannot feel pain. Equally serious, this solution by itself leaves unresolved the central problem of consciousness. If we say, e.g., that, when the clamour of the church bells strikes my ears, all I do (relevantly) is to conceptualize input, then (it has been argued) we leave out of account the sensuous and phenomenal features of my auditory experience and consciousness at the time. This, in turn, suggests that there are constituents or aspects of our consciousness that cannot be brought within the order of natural events and the scope of science. So our concept of consciousness seems to commit us to a DUALISM (see also MIND-BODY PROBLEM).

There have been various attempts to remove this dualism, or make it more palatable; e.g. it has been argued that, when I hear the clamour of the bells, the bodily processes and events involved are contingently identical with those that are my hearing the bells. Though this proposal may remove the dualism of events, it leaves us with a dualism of properties, or qualities, that is just as baffling. Again, it can be argued, that, in the sense that matters, it is a mistake to claim that there is any sensuous and phenomenal manifold over and above the conceptualizing I perform in hearing the bells. This is a profound contention stemming in part from Wittgenstein. But it is also a very difficult one to grasp, and it has not been as widely appreciated as, perhaps, it deserves to be. One of the reasons for this may be that Wittgenstein's solution appears to commit us to changing our concept of consciousness (and cognate ones) in such a way that

it is no longer correct and tempting for us to speak of a sensuous and phenomenal manifold over and above our conceptualizing activity. If this conceptual change were to occur, then the traditional dualism of consciousness would disappear. One of the factors helping to bring this change about is the development of science. The more psychology, and related disciplines, can show how our conscious functioning consists in conceptualizing activity, the weaker will be our resistance to the conceptual changes that will remove the problem, and so bring the phenomena of consciousness fully within the order of nature.

B.A.F.

Bibl: C. McGinn, *The Character of Mind* (Oxford, 1982).

consciousness-raising. Means for making women more aware of their situation, the objective conditions of sexual oppression or PATRIARCHY and their experiences within it. Consciousness-raising groups emerged as an important element in the women's movement of the 1960s. They were usually small (6-12 members), women only and they were not hierarchically organized or focused on a group leader. Within these groups women could express and explore themselves with other women. Not only did women learn more about the objective state of male dominance, but they also became aware of the more subtle, hidden, unconscious (often repressed) elements of sexual oppression. Consciousness-raising groups validated women's knowledge and experience, and linked the personal to the political. Male consciousness-raising groups are now appearing. These have been established to enable men to reflect upon the politics of their own personal relationships and their place within a patriarchal society. (See also FEMINISM.)

A.G.

Bibl: H. Eisenstein, *Contemporary Feminist Thought* (London, 1984); A.K. Shulman, 'Sex and Power', *Signs*, 5, no.4.

Conseil Européen pour la Recherche Nucléaire, see CERN.

consensus politics. A term popularized in the 1960s and since used with increasing imprecision to characterize the alleged character of successive Labour and Conservative governments in Britain from 1951 to 1979. It denotes, with some exaggeration, the extent to which they shared a commitment to similar policies which commanded broad popular support across party lines. These included an economy of mixed public and private ownership, limited and selective economic intervention by government, and the maintenance of an extended WELFARE STATE. The approach depended on both parties subduing their more radical elements and on levels of national prosperity which were increasingly hard to achieve. The phrase disguises the extent to which governments of this era preferred ELITE to popular opinion on other issues such as immigration, law and order, and questions of morality. The term was a development of 'Butskellism', coined from the names of the moderate Conservative and Labour Chancellors of the Exchequer, R.A. Butler and Hugh Gaitskell. It was notably disdained by Margaret Thatcher, who on becoming Prime Minister in 1979 declared herself to be a 'conviction politician'.   S.R.

Bibl: K. Middlemas, *Politics in an Industrial Society* (London, 1979).

consequentialism, see TELEOLOGY.

conservation.
(1) In ECOLOGY, the use of natural RESOURCES (hence often, explicitly, *resource conservation*) in a manner such as to prevent their unnecessary waste or spoliation. Conservation implies use (as distinct from preservation), but for the benefit of mankind on a long-term rather than a short-term basis; in the words of Gifford Pinchot, first head of the U.S. Forest Service, 'conservation means the greatest good for the greatest numbers and that for the longest time'. It may be achieved by positive steps through change in TECHNOLOGY (e.g. stubble-mulching to conserve soil from wind erosion) or ownership (e.g. creation of National Parks for conserving areas of outstanding natural beauty), or by negative steps such as legislation to arrest wasteful practices (e.g. limitations on the size of fish catches). See also RECYCLING.   P.H.

(2) In DEVELOPMENTAL PSYCHOLOGY, a PIAGETIAN term for the principle that quantity does not vary across transformations in its embodiment. Thus a given number of objects remains constant whatever their grouping, and the volume of liquid remains constant whatever the shape of the vessel in which it is contained. The child is said by Piaget to lack this principle as a conceptual formulation until approximately seven years of age.   P.L.H.

conservation laws. Principles of great generality and power in PHYSICS, which state that the values of certain quantities characterizing an isolated system do not alter as the system evolves. Thus, in a power station, chemical ENERGY in coal is changed into an equal amount of electrical energy plus heat energy, and in a NUCLEAR REACTION the various colliding PARTICLES may change their electric charge but the total charge is the same before and after. Many more recondite 'conserved quantities' exist, such as the PARITY of the WAVE FUNCTION in QUANTUM MECHANICS during STRONG INTERACTIONS. At a deeper level, some conservation laws follow from SYMMETRY or homogeneity principles involving space and time. Thus the deeply-rooted view that space is homogeneous — that 'one place is as good as another', so that an isolated system will behave identically in different places — leads to the conservation of MOMENTUM, and the homogeneity of time leads to energy conservation. Conserved quantities are often called *invariants*. See also MASS-ENERGY EQUATION; TRANSFORMATION.   M.V.B.

conservatism/conservative. Conservatism has two distinct senses today. As the doctrine of Conservative parties in Britain, Europe and North America, it combines an enthusiasm for CAPITALISM and the free enterprise economy which is best described as 'NEO-LIBERAL' with an appeal to the patriotic sentiments of the electorate and an emphasis on social order and moral discipline which is more in tune with traditional conservative values. As a philosophical doctrine, conservatism emphasizes 'the politics of imperfection'. Philosophical conservatism emphasizes tradition, authority, law and order, and the impossibility of achieving anything resembling the UTOPIAS which radicals have longed for. Human nature, in the eyes of most conservatives, is too imperfect to allow society to dispense with the guidance of tradition and the government of firm authority. Mankind is too short-sighted and too passionate to agree on one answer to the question how best to order our social and political affairs, let alone to do everything that it would demand. It is better to emphasize known duties, to accommodate individual diversity by letting individuals use their own property in the ways they see fit, to preserve the authority of the STATE by limiting its role to national defence and the policing of the market place, and to strengthen institutions such as the family, schools and churches as a means of securing a sound public morality. Many conservatives have objected to attempts to elicit a 'philosophy' of conservatism on the ground that conservatism is not a creed but a disposition, and that the conservative differs from radicals and INTELLECTUALS precisely because he is willing to change his mind and abandon any particular doctrine or any particular goal for the sake of conserving the vital interests of his society. Whether or not this is true, some distinguished philosophers have written in defence of conservatism during the past two decades.   A.R.

Bibl: A.M. Quinton, *The Politics of Imperfection* (London and New York, 1975); Roger Scruton, *The Meaning of Conservatism* (London, 1984).

consistency. The relationship between PROPOSITIONS which obtains if it is logically possible that they should both be true. Two propositions are inconsistent if from the truth of either it follows that the other is false: e.g. 'All men are fools' is inconsistent with 'No men are fools'. In this example, it does not follow from the falsity of either that the other is true: they cannot both be true but may be, and presumably are, both false. An inconsistency in which it *does* follow from the falsity of one that the other is true is known as a *contradiction*, e.g. 'This man is a fool' and 'This man is not a fool', one of which *must* be true. The notion of inconsistency can also be applied to groups of propositions larger than two, e.g. a triad any two of which, taken together, imply the falsity of the third.   A.Q.

consociation. The action or fact of associating together. In the 17th and 18th centuries it was widely used to denote an association of churches. In international relations it covers a whole spectrum of associations between states, ranging from the vaguest alliance to the full-scale confederation. It stops short of full-scale federation because consociation implies entirely voluntary participation. More recently the term has been adopted in the study of domestic politics. A. Lijphart, in a seminal article (1968), outlined his influential model of 'Consociational Democracy' in which ethnic, religious and CLASS conflicts are managed, and stability maintained, through a process of mutual adjustment and concession. But this method requires a rare degree of political will and capacity for compromise among all parties to the conflict if it is to succeed.   P.W.

Bibl: A. Lijphart, 'Consociational Democracy', *World Politics*, 21, 1968, pp. 207-25.

consonance, cognitive, see under COGNITIVE CONSONANCE.

conspicuous consumption. A term heavily used by Thorstein Veblen in his *Theory of the Leisure Class* (1899) for the extravagant use of expensive goods or services in order to demonstrate STATUS (sense 2) and wealth. Such ostentatious displays of purchasing power have led in many countries to the situation where a large proportion of economic resources is allocated to the production of luxury goods and so-called CONSUMER DURABLES which need periodic replacement. Consumption patterns which are used to reinforce or emphasize one's resources and status form one of the essential features of ADMASS.   P.S.L.

constancy phenomenon. In PERCEPTION, the process whereby an object maintains an apparent size, shape, or colour that conforms to its 'real' properties rather than to its retinal projection. Thus a circle held obliquely to the line of regard looks 'more circular' than warranted by its oval retinal projection shape, and white paper standing in shadow looks whiter than a piece of black coal in sunlight, though the latter is reflecting more light to the eye. When objects are isolated from their surroundings, as when viewed through a pinhole, constancy is destroyed. J.S.B.

Bibl: M.D. Vernon, *Visual Perception* (Cambridge and New York, 1937).

constants of nature, see under FUNDAMENTAL CONSTANTS.

constituent analysis. In LINGUISTICS, the analysis of a sentence into its *constituents*, i.e. identifiable elements. Any complex constituent may itself be analysed into other constituents; and sentences thus come to be viewed as consisting of 'layers' of constituents. Thus the sentence *The boys are sleeping* consists of two main constituents. *The boys* and *are sleeping*; each of these has two constituents, *the* and *boys, are* and *sleeping*; and of these, two may be split further: *boy* + *s* (the marker of plurality), and *sleep* + *ing* (the marker of continuity). Brackets are often used to indicate constituent structure, e.g. {[The ((boy)s)] [are ((sleep)ing)]}. Such sentence analysis is generally referred to, following Bloomfield, as *immediate constituent* (IC) analysis, and the 'immediate' constituents in which the analysis results are distinguished from the residual, unanalysable *ultimate constituents* (UCs). D.C.

constitutional government. A system of limited government according to clearly articulated principles. These principles are usually set out in a written constitution (as in the U.S.) and occasionally in an 'unwritten' constitution (as in the U.K.). Examples of written constitutions include the U.S. Constitution and its Bill of Rights, and the French Declaration of the Rights of Man and of the Citizen. Constitutions set out the powers of the various organs of government and the standards for determining the legality of their actions. The success of constitutional government depends on its adaptibility. Constitutional change usually results from JUDICIAL REVIEW, and less frequently by amendment of the original document. Constitutional law is therefore found only partly in the written constitution; most American constitutional law, for example, is found in judicial decisions. M.S.P.

constitutionalism. The doctrine that governments must act within the constraints of a known constitution, whether this is written or in part a matter of unwritten convention. The doctrine dates from the 17th-century conflicts between kings asserting their absolute authority, usually by divine right, and parliaments and the judiciary asserting the ultimate authority of a system of law stemming from something other than royal decree. In the 20th century, constitutionalists have seen the rule of law as a bulwark against extreme LEFT-wing governments inclined to substitute the divine right of the people or the party for that of the monarch or the czar, but reformers in the U.S. have advanced the cause of BLACK Americans, women, and the poor by appealing to the constitutional protection of the equal rights of all citizens, too. See also EQUAL PROTECTION and EQUAL RIGHTS AMENDMENT. A.R.

Bibl: G.M. Marshall, *Constitutional Theory* (Oxford, 1983).

construct (or *logical construct,* or *logical construction,* or *hypothetical construct*). Names given to a term or CONCEPT to which it is thought that there is nothing corresponding in reality, so that it is merely a useful fiction. It may be useful for summarizing masses of detailed facts, or formulating explanatory theories. Thus, if a historian or social scientist talks about 'the mood of a nation', this is a construct summarizing, and perhaps slightly distorting, the attitudes and behaviour of millions of people. Some would argue that the theoretical terms of science (e.g. ELECTRON, GRAVITATION, FIELD, GENE, MOTIVATION, SUPEREGO) are all constructs. Others would argue that even familiar terms of everyday language (e.g. table, tree, house) are constructs. Usually the alleged construct is contrasted with something else which 'really' exists, as opposed to being a useful fiction. However, it is very difficult to formulate and defend any precise analysis of the distinction between real existents and useful fictions. See also ABSTRACTION; ONTOLOGY; REDUCTION; SOCIAL CONSTRUCT. A.S.

Bibl: Bertrand Russell, *The Problems of Philosophy* (London, 1911; New York, 1912); R. Harré, *Theories and Things* (London and New York, 1961).

constructivism. Internationally influential Soviet art movement of the 1920s based on the elimination of easel painting. It applied a three-dimensional CUBIST vision, inspired by the sculptor Alexander Archipenko and by Picasso's reliefs of 1912-14, first to wholly ABSTRACT non-objective 'constructions' with a KINETIC element (1914-20) and thereafter to the new social demands and industrial tasks of the time. It was thus made up of two threads: (1) the concern with space and rhythm expressed in Anton Pevsner's and Naum Gabo's *Realist Manifesto* (1920), and (2) a tussle within the Education Commissariat between such supporters of 'pure' art and a more socially-oriented group headed by Alexei Gan, Alexander Rodchenko, and his wife Varvara Stepanova who wanted this art to be absorbed in industrial production. Though all these people shared much the same constructivist vision, as did Vladimir Tatlin whose model rotating tower for the Third INTERNATIONAL was its classic realization, there was a split when Pevsner and Gabo emigrated in 1922, leaving the newly christened movement to develop on socially UTILITARIAN lines. As the *productivist* majority went into typography, photography, industrial and theatre design (see BIOMECHANICS) it gained the support of the PROLETKULT and of the 'Left Front' of art in Vladimir Mayakovsky's magazine *Lef* (1923-8), becoming also a dominant influence in the modern Soviet architectural group O.S.A. Through El Lissitzky's contacts with DADA, De STIJL, MERZ, and the Hungarian László Moholy-Nagy the movement spread after 1922 to the BAUHAUS, thence to be carried everywhere as part of that school's ever widening influence in design and basic art education.

In its 'pure' form it was later assimilated in the Abstraction-Création wing of international ABSTRACT ART, making a particular impression on such English artists as Ben Nicholson, Barbara Hepworth, and, after 1950, Victor Pasmore. In Russia, meanwhile, both sides of the movement alike became identified with FORMALISM, leading to its virtual suppression between the early 1930s and the *thaw* of the mid-1950s, after which there was a tentative REHABILITATION of the productivist branch and its contributions to architecture and book design.   J.W.

Bibl: N. Gabo, *Constructions, Sculpture, Paintings, Drawings, Engravings* (London and Cambridge, Mass., 1957); C. Lodder, *Russian Constructivism* (Yale, 1983).

consumer durables. CONSUMERS' GOODS that are also multiple-use assets, i.e. assets which, when used, are not used up at once but rather gradually over a period of time. Obvious examples are houses, cars, washing-machines, dish-washers, refrigerators, vacuum cleaners, furniture, clothes, etc. It is not so much the fact that they are durable instead of perishable that distinguishes consumer durables from other consumers' goods but rather their multiple-use character as against the single-use character of the other consumers' goods; e.g. tinned fish is durable and it is a consumers' good, but it is not a consumer durable. In the case of particularly long-lasting and expensive items of consumer durables it is advisable to count the services they render rather than these goods themselves as entering into consumption. This in fact is the treatment that in the NATIONAL ACCOUNTS is applied to owner-occupied houses.   G.S.

Bibl: G. Stuvel, 'The Production Boundary in National Accounting', *Development and Change*, vol. 4, 1972-3, no.2.

consumer price index.
(1) In the U.K., an index comparing the current cost of all goods and services purchased by all consumers with the cost of the same commodities if they could have been bought at the prices prevailing in the base year. This current-weighted price index is implied in and can readily be obtained from NATIONAL ACCOUNTS estimates of consumers' expenditure at current prices and the corresponding estimates at constant (i.e. base-year) prices.
(2) In the U.S., what in the U.K. is called COST OF LIVING INDEX.   G.S.

consumer society. A society that sets an inordinate value on CONSUMERS' GOODS, which it tends to regard not merely as 'the ultimate aim of all economic activity' but as the ultimate good. See also ADMASS; CONSPICUOUS CONSUMPTION.   O.S.

consumerism. Manipulation of the behaviour of consumers, through every aspect of MARKETING communication, from pricing to PACKAGING, and point of sale presentation to ADVERTISING, has led to increasing concern about its economic effect and its morality. There has, therefore, been a rise in consumerist resistance. The American, Ralph Nader, has been credited with achieving the greatest early influence in this movement, with his criticism of, particularly, the American motor industry. But most countries now embody consumer protection legislation within their legal framework. Most people accept, however, that the law can only marginally influence the behaviour of marketing companies and the strength of consumer response to them. Ultimately, as any marketing textbook will claim, the consumer is sovereign (so long as he can organize himself in sufficient strength to ensure that his feelings are understood and appreciated). In an age when multi-national corporations have assets as large as some of the twenty most powerful nations on earth, and derive their strength from manipulation of their consumers, but derive their MANAGEMENT control from a self-electing oligarchy who carefully divide and manage their shareholders, the strength of consumerism may be felt to be inadequate.   T.S.

consumers' goods. The ultimate aim of all economic activity is the satisfaction of human wants by means of the consumption of goods and services. It is these goods and services that are referred to as consumers' goods. All goods at earlier stages in the production process, that is before they pass into the hands of consumers, are called *producers' goods*.   G.S.

contact improvisation. A dance form created by Steve Paxton in 1972 during GRAND UNION residencies in America. It combines elements of the martial arts (particularly Tai Chi, Aikido, Capoeira), gymnastics and RELEASE DANCE techniques. Contact improvisation is an organic and continuous process between partners involving touch, balance and taking weight. Trust, spontaneity and wordless communication signal the structure of the dance, while detail is left to improvisation. In performance the presentation is casual, clothing is functional and the content unedited.   L.A.

Contadora. A DIPLOMATIC initiative launched in January 1983 by the presidents of Mexico, Venezuela, Colombia and Panama aimed at resolving the Central American crises. It seeks to achieve a negotiated settlement among conflicting parties by formulating agreements and regulations on issues of regional security. The September 1983 Contadora Document of Objectives tried to promote a regional arms freeze, a prohibition against the installation of foreign military bases and a reduction in foreign military advisers. Contadora was motivated by fears of U.S. military intervention in EL SALVADOR or NICARAGUA and is remarkable for its shift away from traditional Latin American acquiescence in U.S. foreign policy. In 1985 a Contadora Support Group was formed in Lima by Peru, Uruguay, Argentina and Brazil. However, the inherent limitations of the Contadora initiative were revealed in September 1984 when Nicaragua accepted all Contadora's terms, only for the U.S. to find fault with the treaty's verification procedures. N.M.
    Bibl: G. Di Palma and L. Whitehead, *The Central American Impasse* (London, 1986).

contagious diffusion, see under DIFFUSION (sense 3).

containment. In politics (for its sense in PHYSICS see under MAGNETOHYDRODYNAMICS), a policy towards the Soviet Union originally advocated by the U.S. diplomatist and head of the State Department's policy planning staff, George Kennan, writing under the pseudonym 'X' in the American quarterly magazine *Foreign Affairs*, July 1947, on 'The Sources of Soviet Conduct'. The policy assumed the current antagonism displayed by the leadership of the Soviet Union towards the Western democracies to be inherent in the internal system of power in the Soviet Union, and called for a 'long-term, patient but firm and vigilant containment of

Russian expansionist tendencies'. Kennan's recommendations became thereafter the basis of American policy towards the Soviet Union, a policy aimed at accommodation, not war, and expressed in economic and technical aid to non-Communist countries as well as through diplomacy. Kennan himself, however, subsequently maintained that the policy of ringing the Soviet Union's frontiers with collective security organizations (NATO, CENTO, SEATO) and bilateral military agreements misconceived the nature of the containment for which he had called.

D.C.W.

Bibl: G. Kennan, *Memoirs 1925-1950* (Boston, 1967; London, 1968).

contemporary dance. See MODERN DANCE. Contemporary dance is a term most associated with modern dance in Britain, i.e. London Contemporary Dance Theatre.

L.A.

contemporary history. Like the serious academic study of the subject, the term goes back to about 1950. It is usually employed to refer to the history of the last 70 years or so, though in France it may refer to history since 1789. The validity of the subject is still challenged by some historians, on the grounds that it is impossible to obtain crucial documents and impossible to see recent events in perspective. It is more reasonable to regard it as a valid field of historical study with its own problems and its own methods; as one useful way, among others, of approaching the events and trends of the contemporary world. See also ORAL TRADITION. P.B.

Bibl: G. Barraclough, *An Introduction to Contemporary History* (London, 1964; New York, 1965).

content-addressed store, see ASSOCIATIVE STORE.

content analysis. The systematic, and usually COMPUTER-aided, study of speeches, newspaper reports, novels, and other writings for the purpose of producing some new description or CLASSIFICATION of the content which is both objectively testable and useful for purposes of scientific research or political decision-making. For instance, analysis of subtle changes in the style of speeches made by a politician (usually one's opponent) may reveal important changes in his attitudes or aims or expectations. A.S.

content word, see under WORD CLASS.

context. In ARCHAEOLOGY, a term frequently employed to define the exact location of an artifact or structure. A *closed context* is one in which the ASSOCIATION of artifacts is not likely to have been disturbed. A statement of the context of an object or feature involves an assessment of the STRATIGRAPHY of the site. See also PROVENANCE. B.C.

context-free and **context-sensitive** (or *context-dependent* or *context-restricted*). In GENERATIVE GRAMMAR, terms used to distinguish between rules which apply regardless of the grammatical context, and rules specifying grammatical conditions which limit their applicability. Grammars containing context-sensitive rules are called *context-sensitive grammars*. It is claimed that they provide more accurate and economical descriptions of sentence structure than do *context-free grammars*. D.C.

context of situation. In LINGUISTICS, a term applied by FIRTHIAN linguists to the non-linguistic environment of utterances. Meaning is seen as a complex of relations operating between linguistic features of utterances (e.g. sounds, words) and features of the social situation in which utterances occur (e.g. the occupation of the speaker, the number of listeners present). Contexts of situation are a means of specifying and classifying those situational features that are necessary in order to understand the full meaning of utterances. Firth, and the anthropologist Malinowski, made various suggestions for the analysis of relevant contextual categories, but there have been few detailed studies. (See PHATIC LANGUAGE.)

The term is also used, with a similar meaning, outside Firthian linguistics, though *situational context*, or just *context*, is more common. D.C.

context-sensitive, see under CONTEXT-FREE.

contextual definition. In general, a means of defining words or phrases by showing how they are used; definition by giving an example of use in context. This method is employed as a supplement or alternative to other kinds of definition; for example, it is often used when standard *lexical definitions* (providing synonymous or near-synonymous words or phrases) are inadequate or unavailable. In particular, the method is used to define the functional expressions of LOGIC. Contextual definition is sometimes called *implicit definition*.   A.C.G.

contextualism. A somewhat pompous architectural term developed in the 1980s to describe a well developed and widely agreed belief that buildings and building developments should be in context with their settings. Contextualism goes beyond the small scale visual arguments of TOWN-SCAPE and seeks to embrace the cultural, social and historical context of a work of architecture. Because of the many possibilities of interpretation of existing contexts most claims for contextualism in individual designs have a rather post hoc ring.   S.L.

contextuality. Whereas most social theories and SOCIAL SCIENCES seek to establish *logical* relationships between structural categories — such as person, CLASS, economy, politics and STATE — plucked somewhat arbitrarily from the hat of all possible categories, a number of voices are now beginning to argue that this compositional approach should be supplemented by a *contextual* approach sensitive to the essentially contingent relationships binding together diverse structural categories in specific times and specific places. This argument is perhaps best developed in GEOGRAPHY, a discipline that has always been centrally concerned with the ways in which all manner of natural and human phenomena interact to produce the unique 'character' of particular localities and RE-GIONS — the hallmark of *regional geography* — and a discipline that is currently striving to produce a more theoretically-informed account of why this project is so important. A wide variety of theoretical and substantive materials are being mobilized in the process, but of especial note is the difficult but illuminating fusion of what has become known as 'time-geography' with the complex 'structuration theory' developed by the sociologist, Anthony Giddens. Although some commentators fear that this development is returning geography to a 'non-scientific' concern with uniqueness, and is thereby denying the claims of geography as SPATIAL SCIENCE, this is to miss the way in which a 'reconstructed' regional geography is deliberately seeking to synthesize long-standing geographical traditions with newer ideas — chiefly those introduced into the discipline by HUMANISTIC GEOGRAPHY and RADICAL GEOGRAPHY — that explicitly attack spatial science for employing a model of 'science' incapable of dealing adequately with either creative human agency or overarching economic and social structures, and incapable of dealing with the intricate interweaving of these different realities in particular temporal and spatial contexts.   C.P.

Bibl: N. Thrift, 'On the determination of social action in time and space', *Environment and Planning D: Society and Space*, 1, 1983, pp.23-57.

continental drift. A theory originally suggested in the 17th century but only comprehensively stated by A. Wegener in 1911. Wegener based his theory very largely on the remarkably similar shape of the facing coastlines of Africa and South America and on close geological similarities between the two continents. He extended this evidence to propose that the earth, until some 200 million years ago, consisted of a single huge continent, which he called Pangea, surrounded by ocean. The present distribution of the continents had resulted from the breaking up of Pangea followed by a drifting apart of the continental masses. The theory required the continental segments of the crust to move freely through the mantle and oceanic crust. However, geophysical evidence indicated that the mantle and oceanic crust were stronger (more rigid) than the continental crust, and since there were no known forces of sufficient magnitude to move continents the theory lost support. Recently evidence of sea-floor spreading indicates that the continents have moved relative to one other as part of the thicker LITHOSPHERIC plates. Horizontally directed CONVECTION currents in the ASTHENOSPHERE dragging mantle material against the base of the plates are a plausible driving force. See also PLATE TECTONICS.   J.L.M.L.

continentalism, see under ISOLATIONISM.

contingency.
(1) In PHILOSOPHY, the property of PROPOSITIONS or states of affairs which neither have to be true or obtain nor have to be false or not obtain. A contingent proposition may be true and may equally be false; the matter is contingent on factors external to the proposition itself. Likewise a contingent state of affairs may obtain but may equally not obtain. That there are four apples in this bowl is *contingent*; that there are four apples in a bowl containing two pairs of apples is *necessary*.   A.Q.
(2) In THEOLOGY, the state of affairs in which each and every existing person or thing might not have existed, all creation being contingent or dependent on the will of the Creator.   D.L.E.

contingency planning, see under FORECASTING.

continuing professional development (CPD). Term used to describe the in-service continuing education of professionals. In the U.K., CPD has been a particularly controversial issue for the surveying and architectural professions. Since the mid-1980s, CPD has been compulsory for members of the Royal Institution of Civil Engineers (RICE). The council of the Royal Institute of British Architects (RIBA) debated the issue many times in this period, but has had difficulty in implementing a mandatory scheme.
                                            S.T.

continuity. Precise mathematical characterization of this fundamental CONCEPT is one of the initial tasks of TOPOLOGY. If one draws a line without lifting the pencil from the paper then, intuitively, the line is continuous. On the one hand this says something about the line as a *completed product* — it has no holes or gaps; this is expressed mathematically by saying that the line is a CONTINUUM, that is a topological space having certain well-defined properties. On the other hand, the drawing of the line is a *continuous process*, one which does not make sudden jumps. Mathematically, the line is a FUNCTION f from one topological 'space' (the interval of time during which it is drawn) to another (the plane of the paper). The continuity of f is defined as follows; if P is any point on the line and d is any distance, however small, then there is an interval of time during which the point of the pencil remains within distance d from P. In other words, an arbitrarily small change in the value is produced by *all* sufficiently small changes in the ARGUMENT. This gives a *general* definition applicable whenever the notions 'arbitrarily small' and 'sufficiently small' are well defined. Continuous is often contrasted with discrete. If instead of drawing a line one merely makes a mark every half inch, the set of marks is discrete. Digital COMPUTERS operate on discrete symbols, analogue computers on continuous quantities, like voltage.
                                      R.G.; A.S.

continuous assessment. A mode of replacing formal EXAMINATIONS at the end of a year or a course by a running check on achievement throughout the course. This cumulative testing is seen as part of the current work, a cross-check and not a ritual ordeal; thus the distorting effect of examinations is thought to be removed from the curriculum and the student relieved of much anxiety. Critics of continuous assessment point to the element of strain present in perpetual judgement, and to the lack of an incentive which a final examination provides to sum up and reflect on the course as a whole. This criticism would not apply to a combination of continuous assessment and terminal examination.   W.A.C.S.

continuous creation, see STEADY-STATE HYPOTHESIS.

continuum.
(1) In PHYSICS, the SET of values of a QUANTITY which can vary continuously. Thus, the points on a line form a one-dimensional continuum, and the points on a surface form a two-dimensional con-

tinuum. By contrast, the points on a crystal LATTICE, whose atomic positions vary discontinuously, do not form a continuum. M.V.B.

(2) In MATHEMATICS, *the* continuum is the set of real NUMBERS; other sorts of continuum have been characterized in TOPOLOGY. Cantor's *continuum hypothesis* is that the CARDINAL of the continuum is the least cardinal greater than aleph zero. This remains an open problem of SET THEORY; it can neither be proved nor disproved from the standard axioms. R.G.

contraception. The limitation of FERTILITY by a range of methods. One of the oldest methods of contraception, which also provides protection from SEXUALLY TRANSMITTED DISEASES, is the condom, a rubber sheath worn on the penis which prevents sperm from entering the vagina. The 'Dutch' cap was advocated by early pioneers of contraception such as Marie Stopes and Margaret Sanger. This is a rubber device worn by the woman which covers the entrance to the womb and prevents sperm from entering. This is often used in conjunction with a spermicidal cream. More recent developments have been the intra-uterine device (or IUD), which is semi-permanently implanted in the womb. Use of this form of contraception has declined following research which associates its use with a range of unpleasant side-effects, including cervical CANCER. From the late 1960s, a popular choice of contraceptive device was 'the pill' — steroid hormones which inhibit ovulation. These too have recently fallen out of favour with many women as their use has been shown to be associated with unwanted side-effects.

Less reliable 'natural' methods of contraception include the 'rhythm method', advocated by the Catholic Church (which forbids the use of any other form of contraception), in which intercourse is restricted to a 'safe' period during the menstrual cycle when no ovum is present to be fertilized. *Coitus interruptus*, in which the male withdraws prior to ejaculation, is an ancient but unreliable method.

In the 1970s and 1980s Depo-Provera (DMPA), an injectable progestogen, began to be employed by FAMILY PLANNING agencies in THIRD WORLD countries, despite the fact that most first world doctors reject it because of its unpleasant side effects. One of the most widely practised forms of contraception worldwide is STERILIZATION — the ultimate contraceptive. But sterilization is often coercive, and is especially pressed upon multiparous nonwhite women in the U.S. (see EUGENICS). S.T.

Bibl: G. Greer, *Sex and Destiny* (London and New York, 1984).

contract. The basis of enforceable legal relations in England between those who make a bargain (see TORTS). Essential elements are an offer by one party, unequivocally accepted by the offeree, the mutual intention to enter into legal relations, and the provision by each of some valuable consideration, i.e. an act or forbearance, or the promise of some act or forbearance, in return for the other party's promise. Thus, in a sale of goods, the supply of the goods or the promise to supply them will be consideration for the promise to pay; and the promise to pay or actual payment is consideration for the promise to supply them. Alternatively a contract will be binding if made by way of deed under seal, even if there is no consideration. Mistakes or misrepresentations may vitiate a contract, as does fraud. Any failure to perform what is promised is a breach of contract which gives the injured party the right to bring legal proceedings for the recovery of damages, i.e. a financial award by the court based upon the loss suffered, or exceptionally for specific performance of the contract. D.C.M.Y.

Bibl: H. S. Fifoot and M. P. Furmston, *The Law of Contract* (London, 11th ed., 1986); G. H. Treitel, *An Outline of the Law of Contract* (London, 3rd ed., 1984).

contract theory. The SOCIAL CONTRACT was used by innumerable political theorists of the 17th and 18th centuries to explain the origins of government and to justify the doctrine that governments had limited powers over their subjects. But Hobbes, Locke and Rousseau were accused by their critics of trying to explain the origins of government and its authority over us by a contract which nobody had ever signed, and which, anyway,

175

would have bound nobody except its original signatories. A contract which was simultaneously non-existent and inadequate to its purpose naturally fell into philosophical disfavour. However, in recent years contract theory has seen a striking revival. In John Rawls's masterpiece, *A Theory of Justice*, the political and economic principles appropriate to a modern democratic state are derived from a 'hypothetical contract', that is to say, from reflection on the principles which rational, moderately self-interested individuals facing an uncertain future would have agreed to as the principles best suited to frame their political and economic affairs if they had made that agreement under conditions which prevented them from taking advantage of each other. Such an agreement would yield a government constrained by CONSTITUTIONALIST principles about the rule of law and individual civil rights, and an economic order devoted to the achievement of social justice.　　A.R.

Bibl: John Rawls, *A Theory of Justice* (Cambridge, Mass and Oxford, 1971); M. Lessnoff, *Social Contract* (London, 1986).

contraction hypothesis. A long-standing theory which attempts to explain the formation of major structures of the earth, such as mountain chains, by crustal shortening. A major prop for the theory is the observation that the earth is losing heat and may therefore be cooling and contracting overall. The most rapid rate of cooling and contraction is assumed to be in a zone a few hundred kilometres below the surface. The outer crust, which is assumed not to be cooling nor contracting to any extent, has therefore crumpled and thickened to fit a smaller surface area. The simplest picture of the crust in this condition would be the skin on a dried apple. Apart from the fact that it is not known whether the earth is cooling down or heating up (radiogenic heat is probably the principal source of heat within the earth), crustal shortening does not explain vertical displacement of rocks nor the major lateral movements of the crust (as part of the LITHOSPHERE) implied in PLATE TECTONICS theory.　　J.L.M.L.

contradiction, see under CONSISTENCY.

Contras. Since 1981 NICARAGUA has been subject to attacks by the Contras, armed groups whose aim is to overthrow the Sandinista National Liberation Front (FSLN) government and who pursue it by GUERRILLA warfare tactics of hit-and-run raids on civilian and services targets. Brutality is a feature of these attacks, which are carried out from within Honduras into Nicaragua's economically crucial northern coffee-growing regions, or from Costa Rica. The majority of the Contras — particularly within the command structure — are ex-Somocista National Guards, who were renowned for HUMAN RIGHTS abuses. Disaffected Miskito Indians from Nicaragua's north Atlantic coast have joined up, as have exiled businessmen and foreign mercenaries. Originally a force of 500 men, the Contras were recruited by the CIA and have grown in size (an estimated 15,000 in 1985) and effectiveness in direct proportion to increases in funding — both official and unofficial — from the U.S. Although they have at times maintained a significant presence within Nicaragua itself, the Contras have failed to spark off an uprising against the FSLN and their very limited popular support is confined to poor and isolated peasants in the north. They have proved militarily unable to penetrate to major targets.　　N.M.

Bibl: George Black, *Triumph of the People: The Sandinista Revolution in Nicaragua* (London, 1981); David Nolan, *The Ideology of the Sandinistas and the Nicaraguan Revolution* (Miami, 1984).

control, command, communications, intelligence. Usually known by the equation C^3I, this concept is the key to modern technological warfare. Much modern military equipment is automatic or semiautomatic in operation, controlled by COMPUTERS which depend on huge quantities of intelligence and data. Command decisions at all levels are now taken on the basis of highly stratified and filtered information. There is concern that countermeasures which will corrupt the data, attack which could destroy or divert the vital surveillance satellites, and even the electromagnetic pulse produced by NU-

CLEAR WEAPONS, which will destroy all unprotected electronic equipment, could invalidate the whole operation of the 'computerized battlefield'. The attraction of C³I is that it allows battlefield control to be retained at a higher level: the rear echelon commander can dictate the detailed action on the battlefield. Such control is imperative as powerful BATTLEFIELD NUCLEAR WEAPONS and BINARY NERVE GASES are deployed. In general terms, the most technically sophisticated U.S. forces rely heavily on C³I, while the Soviet armies are much less reliant on this developed technology.   A.J.M.W.

control engineering. The branch of ENGINEERING that deals with the adjustment of apparatus and SYSTEMS, whether or not a human operator is involved. It therefore embraces the subject of AUTOMATION and is concerned with closed-loop systems of control. The detection of an error, and the use of this information to correct the error, is often termed a FEEDBACK system. It involves the use of measuring instruments (detectors), amplifiers and power units. Control engineering, which began experimentally, developed fairly rapidly into a mathematical discipline whose theoretical aspects are closely allied to those of COMPUTING.   E.R.L.

Bibl: R.C. Dorf, *Modern Control Systems* (Reading, Mass., 1967); O.I. Elgerd, *Control Systems Theory* (London and New York, 1967).

control group. In EXPERIMENTAL PSYCHOLOGY, a group of subjects matched as evenly as possible with a second group (the *experimental group*), and submitted to the same test but without prior exposure to the factor — practice, fatigue, DRUGS, or whatever — whose effects are under investigation. If the groups perform differently, the difference (the *dependent variable*) is presumed to be due to that factor (the *independent variable*). Ideally, those conducting the test and analysing the results should be unaware of which subjects are in which group.   J.S.B.

control theory, see under CONTROL ENGINEERING; CYBERNETICS.

conurbation. In GEOGRAPHY, a single, continuous urban region formed by the coalescence of two or more previously separate urban centres. A conurbation normally extends across several administrative divisions. The term was first used by Patrick Geddes and C.B. Fawcett in the first quarter of this century in describing English city regions, and officially incorporated into the British census in 1951.   P.H.

convection. The rising of hot portions of a liquid or gas, and the sinking of cold parts, which occurs because of the smaller force of GRAVITATION on the less dense hot portions. Convection is the principal agent of heat transfer in the atmosphere and oceans.   M.V.B.

conventional war, see under WAR.

conventionalism.
(1) In philosophy of science (see SCIENCE, PHILOSOPHY OF), a doctrine advanced principally by Henri Poincaré, which holds that scientific theories are not summaries of passively received experience but are free creations of the mind for the simplest and most convenient interpretation of nature. Two degrees of conventionality in scientific theories need to be distinguished. The Newtonian formula that force is the product of MASS and ACCELERATION is a pure convention of language; it registers a decision, although not an arbitrary one, about the use of the word 'force' within PHYSICS. On the other hand, the element of convention in the choice between the Ptolemaic and Copernican accounts of the solar system is less fundamental. Both accounts agree with experience, although inconsistent with each other. Convenience dictates that Copernicus's should be preferred since it is the simpler of the two.

Bibl: P. Alexander, *Sensationalism and the Philosophy of Science* (London, 1963).

(2) The theory that, since the meaning of linguistic expressions is assigned to them by convention, analytic propositions (see ANALYTIC; PROPOSITIONS) owe their TRUTH to the conventions of language.   A.Q.

177

convergence.

(1) Consider the infinite sequence ½, ¾, ⅞, ¹⁵/₁₆, ...; intuitively this *converges* (or *tends*) to the LIMIT 1. This is made precise by saying that however large the number k there can be found a corresponding number m such that all members of the sequence beyond the mth differ from 1 by less than $1/k$. A sequence *converges* if there is some number to which it tends. Otherwise it may *oscillate* (e.g. 1,0,1,0,1,0, ...) or may *diverge* (tend to infinity) (e.g. 1,2,3,4, ...). Corresponding definitions apply to infinite SERIES, the series $½ + ¼ + ⅛ + ¹/₁₆ + ..., 1 - 1 + 1 - 1 + ..., 1 + 1 + 1 + 1 + ...$ are associated in an obvious way with the above three sequences. Infinite series are a valuable tool in the CALCULUS and in the computation of mathematical tables. R.G.

(2) The view, developed especially by several western sociologists in the 1950s and 1960s, that whatever their origins, IDEOLOGIES, or historical traditions, all industrial societies will eventually converge on a common pattern of political, economic, and cultural institutions. The 'logic of industrialism', it is held, compels all modern societies to adopt certain 'core' practices as functional requirements of an industrial system. These include the specialized DIVISION OF LABOUR, industrial work discipline, co-ordinated planning and MANAGEMENT, relatively free labour mobility, and relatively high levels of education and WELFARE. Although largely based on western experience, convergence theories predict important developments in both CAPITALIST and COMMUNIST countries. Capitalist societies will increasingly be marked by significant areas of STATE enterprise and planning, while for their part communist societies will be increasingly forced to relax state direction and to allow in particular a significant degree of managerial autonomy in the industrial sector. In this fine disregard for formal ideological differences, and in their emphasis on the technical requirements of industrial societies, the original convergence theorists were evidently in tune with those who proclaimed 'the end of ideology'. While both groups were somewhat disconcerted by developments in the later 1960s and 1970s, they have made something of a come-back under the banner of POST-INDUSTRIAL theory. K.K.

Bibl: C. Kerr *et al.*, *Industrialism and Industrial Man* (Harmondsworth, 1973).

convergers and **divergers.** Two contrasted PERSONALITY TYPES postulated by Liam Hudson, who had observed two distinct patterns of intellectual style within a group of ably working children. *Convergers* are those who do better at conventional intelligence tests; *divergers* are those who do better at open-ended tests, without fixed limits or single correct responses. The distinction is a measure of bias, not of level of ability. Hudson suggests that students of the physical sciences are on the whole convergers, while students of ARTS subjects are divergers. See also INTELLIGENCE; VERTICAL AND LATERAL THINKING. M.BE.

Bibl: L. Hudson, *Contrary Imaginations* (London and New York, 1966).

conversation analysis. In LINGUISTICS and associated fields, a method of studying the structure and coherence of conversations, usually employing the techniques of ETHNOMETHODOLOGY. The approach studies recordings of real conversations, to establish what properties are used in a systematic way when people interact using language. It is basically an empirical, inductive study, which is often seen in contrast with the deductive procedures characteristic of DISCOURSE analysis. D.C.

Bibl: S. Levinson, *Pragmatics* (Cambridge, 1983).

conversion. In psychoanalytic theory (see PSYCHOANALYSIS), the translation of repressed material into overt symptomatic behaviour, frequently in the form of *conversion hysteria*, a nervous disorder characterized by memory lapse, hallucination, and loss of control of various sensory and motor processes. W.Z.

converter (in COMPUTING), see under DIGITAL-TO-ANALOGUE CONVERTER.

convertibility, see under BILATERALISM AND MULTILATERALISM.

cool. In JAZZ, both a code of behaviour and a musical style that appeared in the late 1940s. The style was specifically launched with records made by a band led by Miles Davis, which featured a controlled, aloof, rather pastel sound instead of the daring impetuosity of BEBOP or the hearty extroversion of SWING and the earlier styles. As a mode of personal and musical conduct, cool superseded HOT as the attitude most appropriate to jazz, signifying artistic *savoir-faire* and a certain ironic detachment instead of old-fashioned attempts to engage the public. The forefather of cool might well be considered to be Lester Young, whose light, lithe tenor saxophone sound and arch, slightly otherworldly demeanour were imitated by scores of musicians. This was especially true on the West Coast of America, which became synonymous with cool jazz in the early 1950s, while bebop smouldered in the East.　　　GE.S.

cooperative principle. In LINGUISTICS, a notion, derived from the philosopher H.P. Grice, which is often used as part of the study of the structure of conversation. The principle states that speakers try to co-operate with each other when communicating — more specifically, that they will attempt to be informative, truthful, relevant, and clear (see MAXIMS OF CONVERSATION). Listeners will normally assume that a speaker is following these criteria. It is of course possible to break these maxims (in lying, sarcasm, etc.), but conversation proceeds on the assumption that speakers do not generally do so.
　　　D.C.
Bibl: S. Levinson, *Pragmatics* (Cambridge, 1983).

cooperatives. Voluntary associations created for mutual economic assistance. They are owned and run by their members, who are workers and/or customers, rather than investors. In most cooperatives, the members receive a share of the net earnings. The cooperative movement grew from the 19th-century ideas of Robert Owen in Britain and Charles Fourier in France. Cooperatives have been set up all over the world and include farming cooperatives (for selling, MARKETING,*processing and purchasing), wholesale cooperatives, mutual insurance companies,

credit and banking cooperatives, shops and health schemes.　　　D.E.; J.P.
Bibl: A. Clayre, *The Political Economy of Cooperatives and Participation* (Oxford, 1980).

coordinate. A mathematical device by which a geometrical or physical configuration can be represented in numerical terms. Thus the *Cartesian coordinates* (x,y) of a point P in the plane are the signed parallel projections of OP onto a chosen pair of (not necessarily perpendicular) rectilinear axes OX, OY measured in terms of a chosen unit of length. The *polar* coordinates of P (with respect to the original O and the axis OX) are the distance OP and the angle XOP. A curve can then be described by an EQUATION involving the coordinates of P which is satisfied if, and only if, P lies on the curve. See also TENSOR; TRANSFORMATION; VECTOR.　　　R.G.

co-partnership, see under PROFIT-SHARING.

Copenhagen interpretation. An interpretation of the theory of QUANTUM MECHANICS developed by the Danish physicist Niels Bohr in the 1920s. Sometimes called the Bohr interpretation. It arises from the fact that quantum mechanical experiments contradict the expectations of naive REALISM. It ascribes reality only to observed phenomena and these phenomena are viewed as being partially created by the act of measurement. Crucial to this view is Bohr's notion of COMPLEMENTARITY. Complementary variables cannot be measured simultaneously with complete accuracy. Position and momentum are complementary variables as are time and ENERGY. Bohr argued that quantum mechanical uncertainty is not just a failure to be able to measure complementary quantities with high accuracy. The complementary aspects cannot exist simultaneously in the quantum world except as an approximation. The Copenhagen interpretation maintains that QUANTUM THEORY does not describe the measurement process. The measurement process is described by an instantaneous collapse of the quantum WAVE FUNCTION. This is the

interpretation of quantum mechanics usually adopted by applied scientists.
J.D.B.

Bibl: J. A. Wheeler and W. Zurek, eds., *Quantum Theory and Measurement* (Princeton, 1983).

core (of an economy). A concept referring to the production of goods and services and their allocation to members of the economy. A particular organization of the economy is in the core, if there is no coalition consisting of some members of the economy who trade among themselves and which improves the economic position of each member of the coalition. It has been shown that if consumers and producers cannot influence prices and under certain other conditions, as the number of producers and consumers increases, the core only contains COMPETITIVE EQUILIBRIA. Thus, there is no coalition whose members would prefer its outcome to a competitive equilibrium. As competitive equilibria can be obtained by the operation of perfect FREE MARKETS, it has been suggested that economies will naturally tend to organize themselves into free markets. This assertion is dubious, as there are many possible MARKET FAILURES and the concept of coalitions does not allow for the agreements, threats, institutions and production possibilities that occur in actual economies, e.g. MONOPOLIES, ECONOMIES OF SCALE and CARTELS. As it is possible for an economy not to have even one competitive equilibrium, it is possible that the core is empty. The concept of the core was first used in GAME THEORY. J.A.M.; J.P.

Bibl: E.R. Weintraub, *General Equilibrium* (London, 1975).

core (of the earth), see under ASTHENOSPHERE.

core curriculum. The subjects that form or should form the most essential part of a pupil's learning. At school, such a core might well comprise mother tongue, a foreign language, MATHEMATICS, a science and the HUMANITIES. Clearly, there are permutations, and successive British governments have tried to lay down clearer definitions of a core. Thus, at primary level, the Three Rs and a science might form such a core, while more advanced syllabuses could be laid down at secondary level. Teachers, who have jealously guarded their autonomy for years, now fear that any directive from the centre on what should be taught will erode that freedom. In fact, the only two subjects on an English school's time-table by law are religious education and physical education. J.I.

core grammar. In recent GENERATIVE GRAMMAR, the set of principles which characterize all the basic trends in grammatical structure found in the world's languages. D.C.

Bibl: A. Radford, *Transformational Syntax* (Cambridge, 1981).

core values, see under PARSONIAN.

corona. A luminous halo of tenuous gas surrounding the sun. Normally it is invisible in the glare from the main body of the sun; during a total eclipse it stands out dramatically. M.V.B.

coronary arteriography. Selective catheterization of the right and left coronary arteries which arise from the sinus of Valsalva, just above the aortic valve. The Judkins technique advances a catheter from the leg; these are specifically preformed so that the torque within the catheter aids selective catheterization of either the left or right coronary arteries. The Sones technique advances a preformed looped catheter from the arm which can be manipulated by the operator to canulate either of the arteries. Radioopaque dye is then injected in order to outline the arteries. Originally introduced in the 1950s, it is now regarded as the 'gold standard' in the assessment of ischaemic heart disease. It is a mandatory prerequisite before coronary artery bypass SURGERY. L.J.F.

coronary artery bypass grafting. An operation in which the narrowed segments of the coronary artery are bypassed by a vessel running from the aorta proximally to the normal calibra native vessel distally. Usually a vein from the leg is taken (long saphenous), but sometimes an artery in the chest is used (internal mammary). The sternum is split open and the heart stopped during the operation. The vital functions of the body are maintained by the heart-lung machine. Grafts may, as necessary, be inserted into all major arteries and their larger branches. Angina is abolished in 50% of cases and greatly improved in a further 30-40%. The mortality of the operation is less than 2%.

L.J.F.

corporal punishment. Physical punishment usually inflicted by a cane, a slipper, a tawse (Scotland) or a paddle (U.S.). In 1986 the U.K. became the last country in Europe (and one of the last in the world) to outlaw corporal punishment from schools thanks to a decision by the House of Lords to amend a Conservative government's Education Bill to this effect. A ruling in the EUROPEAN COURT a year earlier had implied that parents ought to have the choice of whether their child should or should not be physically punished. This was considered highly confusing since schools would need to differentiate between the two kinds of children. It was at one stage considered giving pupils labels of the 'you may — or may not — cane me' variety. Until the change in law (which does not affect independent schools) the teacher, who is considered *in loco parentis*, was able to administer corporal punishment of the kind that a caring parent might also give. Each punishment had to be entered in a book, kept by the head teacher or school secretary, containing the name of the child concerned, reason and date of punishment and the number of strokes applied.

J.I.

corporate communications. Every human structure requires organization to achieve an optimum effect. And no aspect of organization is more important than communication. Corporate communications have, therefore, become a highly developed specialization with the communications world. Unlike public communications, it is pointless to attempt to hide or distort. Someone, somewhere, will know the truth, and recognize the attempt to mislead. And they will, accordingly, react against the attempt. In Japanese companies, apart from information sheets, bulletins and reports and the common usage of newspapers, television and video are extensively utilized. In the U.S. and Europe videos are used, but print is more relied upon. There are those who believe that this might reflect not only on the greater Far Eastern commitment to staff involvement, but on generally greater levels of staff motivation.

T.S.

corporate state. A STATE based on the theory that the political community is composed of numerous economic and other functional groups whose importance in the life of the state and the individual is so overwhelming that they, rather than localities or individual suffrage, should form the basis of political representation. Theoretically, the doctrine looks back to medieval 'estates' and 'guilds' for a model of corporate representation. In practice the doctrine of the corporate state has been tainted by its association with FASCISM, although fascist practice rendered all institutions powerless in the process of transferring all power to the party and its leader. For all that, many writers have claimed that the modern industrial state must *de facto* be a corporate state to govern effectively; a state which fails to incorporate business organizations and organized labour is doomed to impotence because it will be unable to manage the modern economy without acceptance of its policies on pay, prices, investment and public services by these groups. Those who remain hostile to corporatism point out that corporate representation leaves the unincorporated unrepresented, and that these characteristically include the weakest and most vulnerable members of society.

D.C.W.;A.R.

Bibl: R.H. Bowen, *German Theories of the Corporate State* (London and New York, 1947); J.K. Galbraith, *The New Industrial State* (Boston and London, 1968); Keith Middlemas, *Politics in an Industrial Society* (London, 1979).

corporate strategy. The statement of the long-term objectives of a company and the plans which allow these objectives to be achieved. The development of corporate strategies involves the identification of these objectives and the evaluation of alternative strategies. Corporate strategies emphasize the overall objectives of the

181

company, though this necessarily involves consideration of all of the activities of the organization, e.g. production, finance, sales and research. R.I.T.; J.P.

Bibl: G.A. Cole, *Management Theory and Practice* (Eastleigh, 1982).

corporatism (or *neo-corporatism*). A revival of the theory of the CORPORATE STATE, popular in the 1920s and 1930s. Developments in the 1960s and 1970s in all western societies suggested that public decision-making was increasingly becoming a tripartite affair of bargaining between the STATE, employers' associations, and TRADE UNIONS. Corporate bodies, representing functional interests, were being incorporated in the machinery of state, complementing and to some extent replacing formally representative bodies such as parliament. In return for a share in the making of political decisions, the non-state organizations were expected to be able to discipline their members and to 'deliver' them in support of the agreed policies.

During the 1970s, British governments of different parties set great store by the SOCIAL CONTRACT with the trade unions. The evident failure of such a strategy, due largely to the inability of the Trades Union Council to control its member unions — and of individual unions to control their own members — led to its rejection by most parties by the end of the decade. But corporatism has continued to be pursued with considerable success in the Scandinavian countries, notably Sweden, and is still strong in Germany and Austria. Some thinkers believe it is the natural form of political rule in complex INDUSTRIAL SOCIETIES, given the insufficiency of the system of representative DEMOCRACY especially where technical matters of economic management are concerned. They believe that, despite set-backs, corporatism must sooner or later be fully institutionalized. K.K.

Bibl: T. Smith, *The Politics of the Corporate Economy* (London, 1979); K. Middlemas, *Politics in an Industrial Society* (London, 1979).

corpus (plural *corpora*). In LINGUISTICS, a collection of recorded spoken or written utterances, used to suggest or verify hypotheses about linguistic structure (see, e.g., ADEQUACY). D.C.

corpuscular theory. A theory in OPTICS, in which light is treated as a stream of PARTICLES. Because of the great authority of Newton, the corpuscular theory survived until 1820, even though it could not account for wave effects such as DIFFRACTION. In the present century the theory has been partially revived because of the discovery that light is emitted and absorbed in discrete PHOTONS. See also WAVE-PARTICLE DUALITY. M.V.B.

corrasion. In GEOLOGY, a process of erosion in which the principal action is abrasion. Rock particles carried along by running water, wind, or glaciers are rubbed against adjacent bedrock, and in doing so are themselves broken down into smaller particles. They are thus more easily carried away. The bed of a river is partly worn away by corrasive action, and potholes are developed in the solid rock of the bed by pebbles and boulders swirling around in eddy currents. The sea erodes the shore and cliffs of the coast in part by this process: waves pick up pebbles and sand from the beach, batter the cliffs, and wash backwards and forwards across the shore. J.L.M.L.

correlation. In STATISTICS it is common to make two or more observations simultaneously, e.g. to measure both a man's height and his weight. If neither of these observations gives any information about the other they are *independent*. If (as with height and weight) they tend to increase or decrease together, they are *positively correlated*; if the tendency is for one to decrease as the other increases, they are *negatively correlated*. If changes in one variable are proportional (whether positively or negatively) to changes in the other (as with the lengths and breadths of leaves from a tree), the correlation is *linear*; otherwise (as with the leaves' lengths and areas) it is *non-linear*. The usual type of correlation coefficient measures linear correlation, and is often misused in circumstances where the dependence is nonlinear. R.SI.

correspondence, see under TRUTH.

correspondence principle. Correspondence theory was formulated by Niels Bohr (1885-1962) to cope with a fundamental problem area within the PHILOSOPHY OF SCIENCE, revealed by the development of quantum physics. The correspondence principle postulated that, within problematic areas of science such as those addressed by QUANTUM THEORY, the behaviour of micro-particles (e.g., atoms) should be seen as that predicted by the laws of classical PHYSICS, in so far as that was intelligible. In other words, wherever possible, the explanations offered by new scientific theories (such as quantum theory) should be congruent with the expectations of traditional theories (e.g. NEWTONIAN MECHANICS). The principle thus stressed the relative continuities of a sequence of scientific theories (contrast Kuhn's later notion that science advances by a succession of 'revolutions'), and also provided *ad hoc* support for quantum theory, by allowing it to explain a particular range of phenomena, while invoking classical mechanics to account for others.

R.P.

Bibl: M. Jammer, *The Conceptual Development of Quantum Mechanics* (New York, 1966).

corrosion. The chemical processes which progressively destroy a metal. Corrosion is often caused by oxygen in the air and moisture, e.g. the rusting of iron, but it may arise from the attack of other gases, ACIDS, or ALKALIS. Dissolution of the metal may occur, but OXIDATION generally takes place and the reactions are frequently ELECTROCHEMICAL, although the details of many corrosion processes are still obscure.

B.F.

cosmic background radiation. On the BIG-BANG HYPOTHESIS, the first ten-thousandth of the universe's history was dominated by RADIATION. Because of the EXPANSION OF THE UNIVERSE, this primordial BLACK-BODY RADIATION should by now have cooled to a pale remnant, in the form of MICROWAVES, with a temperature a few degrees above ABSOLUTE ZERO. Its observation in 1965 by A.A. Penzias and R.W. Wilson has, more than anything else, contributed to the wide acceptance of the big-bang hypothesis among cosmologists.

M.V.B.

cosmic radio waves, see under INVISIBLE ASTRONOMY.

cosmic rays. Very fast PARTICLES (mainly PROTONS) arriving from space from largely unknown sources. Collisions between particles and ATOMS in the upper atmosphere produce cosmic ray showers made up of a variety of ELEMENTARY PARTICLES, which are detected at ground level by devices such as GEIGER COUNTERS.

M.V.B.

cosmogony. Any scientific theory, religious doctrine, or MYTH about the origins of the universe (particularly the heavenly bodies). In the West the most famous cosmogony is that presented in *Genesis* at the beginning of the Old Testament, but this is generally regarded even by religious believers as needing to be DEMYTHOLOGIZED. Currently, the BIG-BANG HYPOTHESIS, based on the discovery of the COSMIC BACKGROUND RADIATION, is widely accepted. See also COSMOLOGY; THEISM.

D.L.E.; M.V.B.

Bibl: M. Eliade, *Cosmos and History* (New York, 1959) and *Myth and Reality* (New York, 1963); A. Peacocke, *Creation and the World of Science* (Oxford, 1979).

cosmological constant. A new constant of nature introduced by Einstein in 1916 in order to obtain a MODEL of the universe which was static rather than in a state of expansion or contraction. Einstein later referred to its introduction as the 'biggest blunder of my life'. Subsequently it was found that there existed expanding universe models with a cosmological constant included. The effect of the cosmological constant upon the Newtonian inverse-square law of GRAVITATION is to add to it another force directly proportional to distance.

Of all the physical quantities that can be measured or constrained by measurement none is restricted to be so close to zero as the cosmological constant. For this reason many cosmologists believe that it is probably exactly equal to zero for some fundamental but as yet unknown reason. The

ANTHROPIC PRINCIPLE requires that its value be very small. Since 1981 interest in the cosmological constant has grown with the discovery that in the first moments following the Big Bang (see BIG-BANG HYPOTHESIS) it is possible for matter and RADIATION to behave under the influence of gravity so as to cause the universe to expand for a brief period in the way that it would if there existed a cosmological constant. This type of induced temporary effect is termed an *effective cosmological constant* and would be responsible for the period of accelerated expansion INFLATION which has been suggested as a resolution of a variety of problems concerning the structure of the universe. In recent years it has become conventional to interpret the cosmological constant as a form of matter with a particular relation between pressure and density rather than as a new constant of gravitation. (The ratio of the pressure and the density of this matter field is equal to minus the square of the velocity of light.) The stress exerted by this type of matter has the unique property of looking the same to all observers no matter how they are in relevant motion. For this reason the cosmological constant has been interpreted as representing the lowest energy state, or vacuum state/energy, of the universe. J.D.B.

Bibl: J. D. North, *The Measure of the Universe* (Oxford, 1950); M. Rowan-Robinson, *Cosmology* (Oxford, 2nd ed., 1980); E. R. Harrison, *Cosmology* (New York, 1981); J. D. Barrow and J. Silk, *The Left Hand of Creation: The Origin and Evolution of the Expanding Universe* (New York, 1983).

cosmology. The study of the physical universe as a whole, in which the theories of PHYSICS, especially RELATIVITY, are invoked to explain the observed distribution and motion of the stars and GALAXIES. See also BIG-BANG HYPOTHESIS; COSMIC BACKGROUND RADIATION; EXPANSION OF THE UNIVERSE; PULSATING UNIVERSE; RADIO TELESCOPE; STEADY-STATE HYPOTHESIS. M.V.B.

Bibl: J.E. Charon, tr. P. Moore, *Cosmology: Theories of the Universe* (London, 1970); D. Sciama, *Modern Cosmology* (London, 1971).

cosmopolitanism. Soviet term first used by *Pravda* in 1949 in denigration of a few pro-Western theatre critics and extended during the Zhdanovshchina to mean any reflection of Western influences in, or application of international standards in criticism of, the Soviet arts. Regarded, like FORMALISM, as an offence against the official SOCIALIST REALIST canon, cosmopolitanism became difficult to disentangle from its overtones of ANTISEMITISM. J.W.

Bibl: H. Swayze, *Political Control of Literature in the USSR, 1949-1959* (Cambridge, Mass., 1962).

cost benefit analysis (CBA). A means of setting out the social costs and benefits of an investment project and evaluating whether or not the project should be undertaken. The analysis first quantifies the inputs used in the project and the effects of the project; in many cases, this is a difficult task. For example, a new motorway will require resources to build it, will have effects on the ENVIRONMENT, alter travelling times and will have an effect on the pattern of the economy. Secondly, the different aspects of the project have to be valued in a common unit: MONEY. It is often very difficult, if not impossible, to value certain effects, e.g. loss of life. These valuations can sometimes be obtained from markets, e.g. how much people are willing to pay to reduce the probability of death. These monetary values are then discounted appropriately (see DISCOUNTING). Finally, the difference of the suitably discounted social benefits and costs of the project, i.e. the NET PRESENT VALUE, is calculated. That set of INVESTMENTS which gives the highest total net present value should be proceeded with. This implies that certain investments with positive and high net present values may not be recommended. This can occur because such investments preclude other investments with a higher net present value or because investment funds may be limited. Cost benefit analysis is rarely used as the sole basis on which to make a decision. Political considerations are not included in the analysis and it is difficult to allow for changes in the distribution of income. The valuations of the social costs and benefits are often only poor estimates and the net present values may vary crucially with different valuations, in particular, when different discount rates are used.

Cost benefit analysis differs from financial appraisal, as social cost and benefits are estimated, rather than the costs and benefits affecting an individual firm or person. It differs from cost-effectiveness in that the latter considers the most efficient means of achieving a particular objective.

J.P.

Bibl: R. Sugden and A. Williams, *The Principles of Practical Cost Benefit Analysis* (Oxford, 1978).

cost-of-living index (U.K. term; in the U.S.A., *consumer price index*). A price index designed to show periodically, usually month by month, the percentage increase in the cost of maintaining unchanged the standard of living among WORKING-CLASS households in a given base period. In the U.K. the original cost-of-living index, which goes back to 1914, has been superseded by the general index of retail prices. The latter is a chain index (see INDEX NUMBER); the weights are revised annually on the basis of information derived from the Family Expenditure Surveys for the three preceding years. It is also more widely based, since it relates to the purchases of the great majority of households, excluding only the very rich and the very poor. G.S.

cost-push, see under INFLATION.

Council for Mutual Economic Assistance, see under COMECON.

Council of Europe. An organization set up on 5 May 1949 by a statute signed by representatives of Britain, France, Belgium, the Netherlands, Luxembourg, Denmark, Eire, Italy, Norway, and Sweden. Six other states (including West Germany) joined later. The Council consists of (1) a Committee of Ministers and (2) a Consultative Assembly, with a permanent secretariat meeting at Strasbourg. To these was added a EUROPEAN COURT OF HUMAN RIGHTS. Opposition on the part of governments, notably the British, drastically limited the powers of the Council, but the meetings of the Assembly have provided a forum for public discussion of matters of common interest. The Council

is organizationally separate from the institutions of the EEC. D.C.W.

countable. A SET is *countable* if it is finite or has the same CARDINAL NUMBER as the set $\{0,1,2,3....\}$. Countably infinite sets are also called *denumerable*; examples are the sets of rational and algebraic NUMBERS. The CONTINUUM (sense 2) is not countable.

R.G.

counter-culture, see under UNDERGROUND.

counterfactual (or *counterfactual statement* or *counterfactual proposition*). A statement concerned with a hypothetical event, process, or state of affairs that runs counter to the facts, i.e. has not occurred or does not exist. A *counterfactual conditional* (statement) says what would have happened if something *had been* the case, e.g. 'If the American Civil War had been averted, the South would have abolished Negro slavery in an orderly fashion within one generation'. A *counterfactual question* asks what would have happened in some state of affairs known not to exist, e.g. 'If the American Civil War had not occurred, would slavery have persisted for the rest of the century?'. There are considerable difficulties in clarifying the procedures appropriate for testing such assertions or answering such questions, especially when the counterfactual assumptions depart far from reality, or when the connection between the assumptions and the question or alleged consequent is remote, as in 'If people had wings all nations would be more prosperous'. Counterfactuals are widely employed by practitioners of econometric history (see under ECONOMIC HISTORY). Opponents of the method claim that counterfactuals are not history and cannot be verified (see VERIFICATION). Supporters reply that all historical judgements involve implicit counterfactuals and that they can be tested indirectly. A.S.; P.B.

counter-force capability, see under STRATEGIC CAPABILITY.

countervailing power. A term used to describe the forces which generally arise in MIXED ECONOMIES to counterbalance the bargaining power of large buyers and sellers. The classical example of countervailing power in the U.S. economy, for instance, is the large labour unions which, by their influence on the wages that the great corporations must pay, partially counterbalance the monopolistic power (see MONOPOLY) of big business. Similarly, the large retail chains, by their influence on purchasing policies of major manufacturing companies, partly dictate the price the manufacturer receives. Critics of the theory claim its influence on OLIGOPOLIES is marginal. D.E.

Bibl: J.K. Galbraith, *American Capitalism: the Concept of Countervailing Power* (London and Boston, 1952).

Coup de Prague, see under PRAGUE (2).

course credits. The units in a system of higher education which divides the academic programme into a number of self-contained courses, allots credits (so many marks) to each individual course unit, and allows the student to choose whichever combination of courses he wishes. The total programme may require three or four years for completion and may be modular in kind, each unit contributing so much towards a required minimum aggregate of credits. In particular there are usually requirements within which a choice has to be made — e.g. a minimum of so many semester hours required in the arts, in social science, and in science. This elective system was found at Harvard between 1882 and 1910 and in a modified form has since spread all over the U.S.A. It is now well known in the U.K. also, e.g. through its adoption by the OPEN UNIVERSITY. W.A.C.S.

Court of Justice of the European Communities. Set up under Article 4 of the Treaty of Rome establishing the EUROPEAN ECONOMIC COMMUNITY in 1957. It has assumed all the functions of the Court of Justice of the European Coal and Steel Community which had existed since 1952. The court, which sits in Luxembourg, serves all three European Communities (the European Coal and Steel Community, the European Economic Community, and the European Atomic Energy Community).

The court consists of 10 judges appointed for terms of 6 years by member STATES acting in common agreement. The court has several types of competence regarding the interpretation and application of the treaties establishing the three communities. First, it may hear appeals for annulment of decisions taken by the executive organs of the communities. The right to challenge the legality of those decisions is open to the member states, to the executive organs of each community and, to some extent, to natural or artificial persons. Secondly, the court has general jurisdiction to hear appeals against sanctions and penalties ordered by the executive organs. In such cases the aggrieved state or individual could petition the court for a JUDICIAL REVIEW of the order in question. In addition to this, proceedings may be initiated with a view to enforcing the contractual and non-contractual liability of the community. Thirdly, the court has administrative jurisdiction to hear appeals by staff members against decisions of the administration of the three communities. Fourthly, the competence of the court extends to preliminary questions raised before municipal tribunals. Fifthly, appeals may be lodged against a member state by an organ of the community or by other member states when breach of obligations is alleged. Although there is no effective means of enforcing judgments of the courts against states, judgments against natural or artificial persons are enforceable by the municipal courts through their normal judicial processes.

O.Y.E.

Bibl: P. Mathijsen, *A Guide to European Community Law* (London, 1985).

Court Theatre, see ROYAL COURT THEATRE.

covalency. Chemical bonding (see BOND) through the sharing of ELECTRONS by two ATOMS. B.F.

covering law theory. A theory about the logical character (see LOGIC) of the EXPLANATION of singular events or states of affairs. It holds that in order to explain an event (e.g. the breaking of a string) the statement reporting it must be deduced from a description of the *initial conditions* ('this string was loaded with a 10-lb weight') together with a PROPOSITION or law ('the breaking-point of this type of string is 6lb'). Although it is widely regarded as an adequate account of explanation in the NATURAL SCIENCES, its application to HISTORY has been much contested. Its opponents argue that there are no universal historical laws, that human actions are explained by reference to motives, and that these are not causes; they insist (to use the language of the entry on EXPLANATION) that *purposive explanation* is not a special case of *deductive explanation* in the way that *causal explanation* is commonly held to be.   A.Q.

CPD, see CONTINUING PROFESSIONAL DEVELOPMENT.

CPU (central processing unit), see under PROCESSOR.

cracking. The process by which paraffin hydrocarbons are heated under pressure to give olefins, lower-boiling-point paraffins, and hydrogen. Originally devised as a means of obtaining petrol from oils with a high boiling-point, it is now the principal method by which the chemical industry obtains the basic materials — ethylene, propylene, and butylene — for the manufacture of PLASTICS and artificial rubber products.   B.F.

creation/creationism.
(1) The word may be held to imply the more or less literal acceptance of the stories of the origins of the world and of mankind recorded in the first two chapters of Genesis in the Hebrew scriptures inherited also by Christians. 'Creationism' of this kind remains fairly strong in the U.S. But the term is more commonly used by believers in God who reject FUNDAMENTALISM. It is often held that the really fundamental religious attitude is that God is the source, ground and goal of all that exists or is possible in the universe — which can now be truly described by modern sciences. Some support is lent to this degree of LIBERALISM in theology by the facts that two stories, of different origins and incompatible in some details, are given in Genesis, while other ancient Hebrew creation MYTHS are referred to in the

Psalms and the Book of Job. Most scholars agree that Genesis was never intended as an account to rival scientific or other knowledge of nature. The term, being traditional, is also used as an alternative to 'nature' by people whose religious beliefs incline to AGNOSTICISM or ATHEISM.

                    D.L.E.

Bibl: A.R. Peacocke, *Creation and the World of Science* (Oxford, 1979); H. Montefiore, *The Probability of God* (London, 1985).

(2) Creationism is the theory that living species have separate origins, rather than having evolved from a common ancestor (see EVOLUTION). Creationism can take on secular forms, but always has religious inspiration; its source is the biblical book of Genesis, according to which the different species of living things were separately created by God. Scientific evidence points against the separate creation of species, but creationism is rejected by scientists more because it contradicts the scientific world-view, as it introduces a supernatural agency, than because of any evidence. Creationism is particularly promulgated by southern fundamentalists in the U.S. who have made various legal attempts to enforce the teaching of creationism alongside evolution in BIOLOGY lessons. It is thus as much a social movement as a 'scientific' theory.   M.R.

credentialism. The tendency in modern society to demand educational qualifications for every type and manner of work, whether or not the gaining of the qualification actually fits one for the work in question. A cognate term is 'the diploma disease'. Not only does this distort the educational system by forcing it to appear to have mainly a training function, it also disguises the extent to which the system, especially at the level of higher education, is a screen for perpetuating the privileges of the wealthier classes, who tend to possess the necessary CULTURAL CAPITAL for succeeding in the system. The educational system can then appear as a means for restricting access to the more highly paid and respected occupations, such as the professions.   K.K.

Bibl: R.P. Dore, *The Diploma Disease* (London, 1976).

credibility. The degree to which factors associated with an undertaing create in the minds of others the expectation that it will be carried out if the contingency to which it is addressed should arise; failure to create such an expectation is sometimes known as a *credibility gap*. The term originated in American strategic analysis in the 1950s as a component of an effective strategy of DETERRENCE vis-à-vis the U.S.S.R. and China in relation to the security of the territorial U.S.A. and to the American alliance commitments in Europe and Asia. It is accepted as having (*a*) a *quantitative* aspect — enough long-range nuclear weapons to inflict unacceptable damage upon a potential adversary; (*b*) a *technological* aspect — weapons accurate and dependable enough to achieve this purpose and invulnerable enough to prevent an adversary's first strike being a wholly disarming one; (*c*) a *political and social* aspect — the decision-making structure and the demonstrable national will to engage in a strategic conflict. To this was added another element as Soviet long-striking power grew in the 1950s and early 1960s, namely (*d*) *local defences*, especially in Europe, adequate to deter minor pressure or blackmail for which the U.S.A. (or any other guarantor power) was palpably unprepared to risk nuclear WAR.

The concept of credibility is of particular relevance to the stance of allies who do not themselves possess NUCLEAR WEAPONS. Hence the saying that 'it takes only 5% of American nuclear weapons to deter the Russians, and the other 95% to reassure the NATO allies'. The term is now used increasingly widely to assess political promises or undertakings of any kind.

A.F.B.

Bibl: H. Kahn, *On Thermonuclear War* (Princeton, 1960); T.C. Schelling, *Arms and Influence* (New Haven, 1966).

credit creation, see under MONEY CREATION.

creep. In PHYSICS, the slow 'flow' of a solid acted on by forces. Thus, stone lintels and tombstones sag under GRAVITATION after many years, metal bolts in hot parts of machines slowly stretch (requiring the nuts to be periodically re-tightened), and lead flows slowly down church roofs. It is thought that the flow takes place by the movement of DISLOCATIONS. See also RHEOLOGY.

M.V.B.

creole. In SOCIOLINGUISTICS, a PIDGIN language which has become the mother-tongue of a speech community, as in the case of Jamaica, Haiti, and many other parts of the world. The process of development, in which the structural and stylistic range of the pidgin is expanded, is known as *creolization*.

D.C.

Bibl: P. Trudgill, *Sociolinguistics* (Harmondsworth, 1984).

Cretaceous-Tertiary boundary. The point in time and in the rock record at which the Cretaceous Period of the earth's geological history ended and the Tertiary Period began, about 65 million years ago (see GEOLOGICAL TIME CHART). The Cretaceous-Tertiary boundary is no different in principle from the boundary between any two other geological periods, but it has become the focus of considerable attention in recent years because it coincides in time with the demise of the dinosaurs and numerous other species (see EXTRATERRESTRIAL CATASTROPHISM), a MASS EXTINCTION event for which a revolutionary hypothesis has been proposed. In 1980 L. W. Alvarez and colleagues at the University of California suggested that the extinctions were the result of an impact upon the earth of an asteroid with a diameter of about 10 km. There is no question of the asteroid having hit the organisms directly on their collective heads; rather, the impacting body would have disintegrated and thrown up masses of dust, cutting out sunlight, impeding PHOTOSYNTHESIS, and producing breaks in vital FOOD CHAINS. The chief evidence for the impact comes from the abnormally high concentrations of the elements iridium and osmium in sediments at the Cretaceous-Tertiary boundary, a phenomenon that has since been confirmed at scores of sites around the world. The concentrations are significantly higher than those found generally in the earth's crust but are not uncharacteristic of meteorites, from which comparison Alvarez and his co-workers concluded that the extra iridium/osmium must indeed have come from extraterres-

trial sources. However, there has since appeared a rival hypothesis that attributes the high levels of iridium/osmium to a particularly intense episode of explosive volcanism (see VOLCANOLOGY), possibly in India. Volcanoes raise material from the earth's mantle where the levels of iridium/osmium could well be as high as in extra-terrestrial bodies. This issue will take some time to resolve, if indeed it is ever resolved.
P.J.S.

criminology. The scientific study of criminal behaviour. Cesare Lombroso (1835-1909) is often considered the 'father' of criminology since his theories relating criminal behaviour to the physical characteristics of criminals were the earliest systematic attempts to explain crime in other than moral or social terms. The popularity of what may be broadly termed biological theories of criminality persisted well into the present century in studies of mental defects, the relationship between personality and constitutional factors, and the genetic characteristics of offenders such as the extra CHROMOSOME. The study of criminology includes the study of *criminal statistics*, the *psychology of criminal behaviour*, and the study of offences of a particular character such as *white-collar crime* (business frauds and trust violations) and what are commonly termed *crimes without victims* (DRUG offences, ABORTION, and certain sexual offences). Contemporary criminologists have tended to emphasize approaches derived from their own disciplines, e.g. SOCIOLOGY, PSYCHOLOGY, PSYCHIATRY, STATISTICS, GENETICS, etc. The general subject-matter of criminology is also said by some to include what is more specifically defined as PENOLOGY.
T.M.
Bibl: A.K. Bottomley, *Criminology in Focus* (London, 1979); H. Mannheim, *Comparative Criminology*, 2 vols. (London and Boston, 1965).

crisis management. Phrase coined after the Cuban missile crisis (see CUBA; MISSILES) of November 1962, by Robert McNamara, then U.S. Secretary of Defense, who remarked: 'There is no longer any such thing as strategy, only crisis management.' The term implies a somewhat mechanistic view of the relations between states as a system which needs to be managed by its chief members so that crises in their relations with one another may be prevented from turning into courses which could only lead to mutual destruction.
D.C.W.
Bibl: C. Bell, *The Conventions of Crisis* (London and New York, 1971).

crisis theology. A movement arising among German and Swiss PROTESTANT theologians but also influential elsewhere, attempting to restate CHRISTIANITY in response to the crises of the two world wars, the grim years between, and the aftermath of Europe's ruin in 1945. This social crisis was seen as a reminder of the perpetual crisis of sinful humanity under the judgement of God (see ESCHATOLOGY). The most famous exponent was Karl Barth (see BARTHIAN), but other theologians of the period responded to the crisis by CHRISTIAN EXISTENTIALISM. The movement was also known as *dialectical theology*, since it attempted (more strongly than EMPIRICAL THEOLOGY) to preserve the otherness of God while acknowledging that the limitations of human speech prevented DOGMAS about God from being entirely satisfactory. This term is traditional in THEOLOGY, recognizing that every statement about God involves a DIALECTIC between two others each of which is more or less unsatisfactory; e.g. to assert 'God's love' means also asserting both 'God's mercy' and 'God's holy wrath'. But the term 'dialectical' was used for these 'crisis' theologians for a wider reason: to them, every theological statement involved a dialectic between God and man.
D.L.E.
Bibl: K. Barth, tr. G. Foley, *Evangelical Theology* (London and New York, 1963); W. Nicholls, *Systematic and Philosophical Theology* (Harmondsworth and Baltimore, 1969).

criterion.
(1) Most generally, any standard by which somebody or something is judged.
(2) More specifically, a ground for judging that something is the case which is not a logically NECESSARY AND SUFFICIENT CONDITION of the truth of the judgement but is rather a thoroughly reliable contingent indication (see CONTINGENCY) of its truth; e.g. the height of the mercury in a

thermometer is a criterion of the temperature of the environment. Criterion in this sense is contrasted with the defining characteristics which are, as a matter of LOGIC, the severally necessary and jointly sufficient conditions of its presence. Thus *coherence* has been said to be a criterion, but not a definition, of TRUTH.

(3) More specifically still, in the later PHILOSOPHY of Wittgenstein, a special sense is given to the term, according to which the connection between the criterion and what it indicates is logical but nevertheless incomplete, in that its satisfaction does not ENTAIL, nor its nonsatisfaction logically preclude, the presence of what it indicates. In regarding *behaviour* as the criterion of inward feeling, Wittgenstein's interpreters take him to say that behaviour is, as a matter of logic, not-wholly-conclusive evidence for the judgement that the behaver is in a certain mental state. Wittgenstein's view is that sentences about mental events could have a publicly intelligible significance only if logically linked to what can be publicly observed. What differentiates his position from straightforward BEHAVIOURISM is that the logical linkage in question is one of CONFIRMATION, not entailment.   A.Q.
Bibl: J. Pollock, *Knowledge and Justification* (Princeton, 1974).

Criterion, The. A quarterly — for a brief period, monthly — review of art and letters edited from London by T.S. Eliot between 1922 and 1939. Its international importance is suggested by the fact that Volume 1 contained Eliot's 'The Waste Land', cantos by Pound, Valéry Larbaud on *Ulysses*, and contributions by Virginia Woolf, Paul Valéry, W.B. Yeats, and E.M. Forster. Concerned with 'the autonomy and disinterestedness of literature', it carried such writers as Joyce, Lawrence, Proust, Gertrude Stein, Archibald MacLeish, Hart Crane, and, in the 1930s, Auden, Spender, MacNeice, Empson, Allen Tate, and Dylan Thomas. It maintained a 'classicist', and later a religious, NEO-THOMIST, position against the 'ROMANTICISM' of Middleton Murry's *Adelphi.*   M.S.BR.

criterion function, see under OPTIMIZATION THEORY.

criterion referenced test (CRT). Test that measures the ability of a candidate against that of another. In other words, it enables the examiner to see whether the pupil/student has reached a required criterion. This differs from the principle often adopted in EXAMINATIONS, where the result reflects not so much the candidate's knowledge as his/her placing in a league table of grades. Thus, if, for argument's sake, all candidates manage to score over 90% in an examination, those getting 90 to 92% might well be placed in the 'fail' category while only those with more than 98%, say, will receive a Grade A. This would be known as a *norm referenced test* (NRT). With a CRT all the candidates would be considered of Grade A standard since they are highly likely to have reached (and surpassed) the given criterion. See also PSYCHOMETRICS.   J.I.

critical mass. The minimum quantity of RADIOACTIVE material which will enable a CHAIN REACTION to proceed by means of nuclear FISSION. Although the critical mass for the atomic bomb is not hard to estimate, its value was one of the 'secrets' of the COLD WAR.   M.V.B.

critical path analysis. A NETWORK ANALYSIS technique whose main application is to provide optimally efficient scheduling of different phases of some complicated task. Suppose, for example, that a house is to be built by conventional methods. Certain phases — constructing foundations, building walls, fitting roof timbers, tiling — have a natural sequence, and the next cannot be started until the last is complete. Other phases — making joinery, inserting piping and wiring — fit into this scheme more flexibly, although not with complete freedom. It is usually not difficult to work out the time each phase will take, which phases must precede it, and which must follow it. Critical path analysis then provides a technique for scheduling the phases so as to complete the job as quickly as possible. When this scheduling is done it is found that some phases have the property that a small delay in them will cause changes in the schedule as a whole — these phases form the *critical path.* Other phases have a certain amount of slack, and it may be

possible to take longer over them, e.g. by using a smaller work-force, without delaying completion of the job as a whole.
R.SI.

critical period. In ETHOLOGY, a short period in the early life of organisms when they are susceptible to IMPRINTING or ATTACHMENT to another organism.　　J.S.B.

critical realism, see REALISM, CRITICAL.

critical sociology. A form of contemporary social theory inspired largely by the FRANKFURT SCHOOL. It opposes much traditional sociological theory, such as FUNCTIONALISM and PLURALISM, on the grounds that this is largely an apologia for existing institutions and practices in CAPITALIST societies. By contrast critical SOCIOLOGY sees its task largely as one of 'unmasking' — showing in particular the discrepancy between the formal values and goals of contemporary institutions and their actual practices. Thus the market is formally 'free', bureaucracy formally 'rational', and the political system formally 'democratic'. But in no case do any of these institutions truly live up to the promise of their formal principles. Critical sociology shares with MARXISM a concern for social change. But it does not pin its hopes on any particular agency, such as the PROLETARIAT. It retains rather a HEGELIAN belief in the critical power of thought *per se*. By constantly subverting society's self-regarding IDEOLOGIES, and repeatedly confronting it with the unpleasant truth about itself, it hopes to stimulate a critical awareness that might lead to the desire for change.　　K.K.
Bibl: P. Connerton, ed., *Critical Sociology* (Harmondsworth, 1976).

critical temperature. The highest temperature at which a liquid and its vapour can coexist. The critical phenomenon was first observed in 1869 by Andrews, from whose experiments it is possible to show that above the critical temperature there is no clear distinction between a liquid and its vapour. Similar critical behaviour is sometimes shown by solid or liquid solutions.　　B.F.

critical theory, see under FRANKFURT SCHOOL; CRITICAL SOCIOLOGY.

critical time, see under COMPUTING.

cross-cultural study. An investigation comparing performance in some psychological function (PERCEPTION, memory, INTELLIGENCE, motivation) in two or more different CULTURES in order to determine whether and in what manner it might be affected by differences between the cultures studied. The cultural differences usually investigated are patterns of child-rearing, patterns of motivation (notably achievement motivation), and differences in linguistic structure (cf. the WHORFIAN hypothesis). Earlier emphasis on the cultural RELATIVISM of mental functioning has, in recent years, been replaced by increasing evidence of certain basic universals in functioning that differ principally, between one culture and another, in emphasis and form of realization. See also ETHNOPSYCHOLOGY; PATTERN VARIABLES.
J.S.B.
Bibl: P.E. Vernon, *Intelligence and Cultural Environment* (London and New York, 1969); B. Lloyd, *Perception and Cognition* (Harmondsworth and Baltimore, 1972).

cross-over value, see under CROSSING OVER.

cross-section. The effective area that a target presents to an incident projectile; if the area is large, the probability is high that a collision will occur. The concept originated in NUCLEAR PHYSICS as a means of specifying the strength of interaction between colliding NUCLEI or ELEMENTARY PARTICLES.　　M.V.B.

cross-sectional methods, see under LONGITUDINAL.

crossing over. The process whereby GENES on the same CHROMOSOME (i.e. linked genes; see LINKAGE) can be recombined. Crossing over is important in EVOLUTION because it increases the number of genetically different individuals that can arise in a population. It occurs during MEIOSIS, probably by a process of breakage of two chromosomes and reunion after an exchange of parts. The frequency with which two characteristics recombine, known as their *cross-over value,* is an increasing function of the physical distance between the corresponding genes on the chromosome; this fact is used in 'mapping' the genes on a chromosome.   J.M.S.

CRT, see under CRITERION REFERENCED TEST.

cruelty, theatre of, see THEATRE OF CRUELTY.

cruise missiles. The principle of the cruise missile is roughly that of the V.1 'flying bomb' of World War II. They are cheap, slow-flying bomb carriers, with their own internal guidance systems. But for all their apparent similarities, the cruise missile is a product of new TECHNOLOGY, and one of the most dramatic new variables in strategic warfare. Three new developments have made cruise MISSILES possible. Small, economical turbo-fan engines have been produced which allow the missile to 'cruise' over great distances at subsonic speeds. Bomb design has advanced so that a powerful warhead can now be made both light and compact. Finally, advances in computer mapping and inertial guidance have made it possible to create a missile which flies below all land-based RADAR screens, often at less than 100 feet above the ground. Cruise missiles are programmed to fly around known obstacles, even weaving their way through city buildings to deliver their warhead with unparalleled precision. The missiles can be launched on land or from ships at sea; alternatively, submarines and aircraft make ideal launch platforms. And since the weapons are so cheap to manufacture, it would be possible to swamp any possible defence by sheer numbers. The detractors of cruise missiles consider them to be politically destabilizing, and easy for countries too poor to afford a strategic missile technology to imitate. For while a high-grade cruise missile demands sophisticated equipment to give it accuracy, and the capacity to survive enemy attack, a crude version would still stand a good chance of penetrating existing defences. But many strategists are sceptical about the claims made for cruise technology.

None of the tests to date have proved that the cruise principle will work reliably in practice, especially since it depends on matching the terrain it passes over to its inbuilt programme. Even quite minor changes were enough to confuse the early systems. As cruise technology has advanced, so have defensive techniques, especially since likely cruise flight paths are well-known. But, on balance, cruise seems likely to retain the advantage for the offensive over defensive. There is no known defence to a mass-attack by these missiles, even though it may take them three hours or longer to reach their targets.

One unforeseen effect of the deployment of the new systems in NATO countries has been as a focus for antinuclear agitation. To be effective, land-based cruise missiles must be mobile. Unlike earlier weapons systems which are located in military bases away from public scrutiny, cruise missiles come out, in convoys, into the community. As such they are a highly visible symbol of the new dimensions in nuclear warfare. However, such stereotyping masks the principal quality of sophisticated cruise technology, which would be just as effective using conventional or chemical warheads. See also NUCLEAR WEAPONS.   A.J.M.W.

Bibl: R.K. Betts, ed., *Cruise Missiles: Technology, Strategy and Politics* (Washington D.C., 1981); C. Bertram, ed., *Strategic Deterrence in a Changing Environment* (London, 1981).

cryogenics. The branch of PHYSICS which studies the behaviour of matter at abnormally low temperatures. Within the atomistic physics which became dominant during the 17th century, heat was widely regarded as a function of the motion of particles. Cold therefore became associated with their immobilization. Practically, study of the responses of substances at extremely low temperatures was impossible before the development of powerful artificial cooling techniques in the late 19th century. From the 1870s refrigerators were constructed which worked on the principle of the expansion of ammonia, and these proved capable of liquefying air by cooling it below 180°K on the absolute temperature scale. Later oxygen was liquefied at 170°K, hydrogen at 20.4°K and lastly helium at 4.2°K. Such successes permitted experimentation upon the behaviour of extremely cold objects. One finding which has proved of major practical application was that below a certain critical temperature, the electrical resistance of many metals (including tin and lead) drops to almost zero. This SUPERCONDUCTIVITY facilitates the construction of highly powerful ELECTRO-MAGNETS using very little current. See also ABSOLUTE ZERO; THERMODYNAMICS.   R.P.

Bibl: K. Mendelssohn, *The Quest for Absolute Zero* (London, 2nd ed., 1977).

crystallography. The study of the external forms of crystals and the arrangement of ATOMS within them, using X-RAY DIFFRACTION and ELECTRON DIFFRACTION. See also LATTICE; SOLID STATE PHYSICS. M.V.B.

CS gas. The most important tear gas. It is a derivative of benzene-chlorobenzalmalonitrile first synthesized in 1928 by the American chemists, Corson and Stroughton. An almost colourless solid with a pungent peppery smell, it is dispersed either by thermal volatilization or as a dust. The gas has been used for civilian riot control as well as militarily. Very low levels, about 50 micrograms per cubic metre, can be detected, and the lethal dose for a human is probably about 0.2 g.   B.F.

CSE, see under EXAMINATIONS.

CT (CAT), see under RADIOLOGY.

Cuba. Shorthand expression for (1) the COMMUNIST regime in Cuba established by Fidel Castro after overthrowing the repressive government of General Batista on 1 January 1959 (see CASTROISM); (2) the Cuban MISSILE crisis of 1962 in which the U.S.A. under Kennedy's leadership forced the Soviet Union to dismantle the ROCKET sites it was building in Cuba. This unsuccessful adventure is believed to have been a decisive factor in Khrushchev's fall from power.   A.L.C.B.

Bibl: H. Thomas, *Cuba* (London and New York, 1971); H.S. Dinerstein, *The Making of a Missile Crisis* (Baltimore, 1976).

Cubism. An artistic movement often regarded as the most revolutionary and influential of the 20th century. Led by Picasso and Braque, the Cubists, while attempting to represent what the eye sees, aimed to render objects more essential and tangible by means of stylized forms and symbols.

Three phases are commonly distinguished. The first may be dated from the completion early in 1907 of Picasso's *Les Demoiselles d'Avignon*, whose angular, distorted shapes reflected the growing interest in PRIMITIVE sculpture and the work of Cézanne. In the next two years Picasso and Braque depicted familiar objects by means of interlocked geometrical figures, abandoning traditional perspective and chiaroscuro.

The second, 'analytical' phase (1910-12) is notable for the development of the techniques of presenting different facets of an object simultaneously, superimposed or side by side. Guitars, bottles, pipes, and written words appear regularly in the paintings of Picasso and Braque at this time. Other artists associated with Cubism included Gris, Léger, Delaunay, Metzinger, and Gleizes; the latter two published a theoretical work, *Du Cubisme* (1912), though their own painting tended merely to 'cubify' their subject-matter in harmonious designs, without any radical restructuring.

In May 1912 Picasso included a piece of printed cloth, representing a chair seat, in a painting — a significant moment in the history of COLLAGE; in September of that year Braque incorporated strips of wallpaper in his work, and he, Picasso and Gris soon developed the new medium of *papier collé*, which (they felt) introduced a fresh element of 'reality' into their art. This concern with textures led them to experiment with sculpture: Cubist sculpture, again pioneered by Picasso, was to reach its peak during World War I in the work of Archipenko, Laurens, and Lipchitz (forerunners of CONSTRUCTIVISM).

In the final, 'synthetic' phase (1913-14), Cubist painting tended to become more complicated and colourful, employing multiple repetitions of forms and a language of visual signs. But by this time it was less easy to discern a single Cubist school; moreover, the influence of Cubism

193

had spread abroad, affecting EXPRESSIONISM, FUTURISM, DADA, VORTICISM, ORPHISM, SUPREMATISM, De STIJL, etc. The ARMORY SHOW (New York, 1913) included a Cubist contingent. The PURISTS, on the other hand, presently joined by Léger himself, reacted against Cubism in returning to undissected shapes and a severe machine-like precision.

Cubism had affinities with the new European interest in JAZZ; and in 1923 Léger designed Cubist sets for Milhaud's negro jazz ballet *La Création du Monde*. Indeed, works of art in several other fields have been called 'Cubist', either because they were directly inspired by Cubist painting (as was some of the poetry of Apollinaire and Cendrars) or because of their fragmented, multiple-image structure (Stravinsky's *Petrushka* of 1911, Satie's *Parade* of 1916, Joyce's *Ulysses* of 1922).   P.C.

Bibl: M. Raynal, *Picasso* (Paris, 1922); R. Rosenblum, *Cubism and Twentieth-Century Art* (London and New York, 1961); J. Golding, *Cubism* (London and Boston, 2nd ed., 1968); D. Cooper, *The Cubist Epoch* (London and New York, 1971).

Cubo-Futurism. Russian name for the modern poetry and art movement of *c.* 1912-18, as imported from France and Italy and identified with the early days of the BOLSHEVIK revolution. Its component elements were (*a*) the CUBISM of painters and sculptors — Kasimir Malevich, Nadezhda Udaltsova, Liubov Popova, and Ivan Puni (Jean Pougny) — who had studied in Paris; (*b*) the FUTURIST-influenced RAYONISM of Larionov and Goncharova; and (*c*) the impact, reflected most strongly in ZAUM and the poetry of Mayakovsky, of Italian Futurism, whose leader Marinetti visited Russia in 1914. It played some part in Soviet aesthetic discussions, but by then had been largely absorbed in SUPREMATISM and CONSTRUCTIVISM.   J.W.

Bibl: V. Markov, *Russian Futurism* (Berkeley, 1968; London, 1969); V.D. Barooshian, *Russian Cubo-Futurism 1910-30* (The Hague, 1975).

cult. Organization founded upon the veneration of deity, spirits or a religious or political figure. A cult is a complex of beliefs and practices and members display a high degree of commitment to the organization. It is usually a localized group, but recruitment may be ascribed on the basis of KINSHIP ties (e.g. ANCESTOR WORSHIP) or voluntary (e.g., CARGO CULTS). A cult may emerge spontaneously in opposition to a centre of established authority. These cults have elements of MILLENARIANISM: religious fervour and an anticipation of salvation and deliverance for cult members. The focus of such a cult is a *charismatic* leader and members are drawn from the dispossessed (in a political rather than an economic sense). In the early stages of development cults are unstable, EGALITARIAN groups perceived to be a threat to social and legitimate order. As time passes, however, a cult becomes 'routinized' and established, and in turn its members view the rise of new cults as potentially subversive.   A.G.

Bibl: E.R. Leach, 'Melchisedech and the Emperor' in E.R. Leach and A. Laycock, *Structuralist Interpretations of Biblical Myth* (Cambridge, 1983); S.J. Tambiah, *The Buddhist Saints of the Forest and the Cult of Amulets* (Cambridge, 1984).

cultural capital. A concept largely developed by the French sociologist Pierre Bourdieu. Bourdieu argues that the BOURGEOIS class in modern society no longer maintains its position by transmitting material property to its children, but more through its transmission of 'cultural capital' to them. By providing a home environment which encourages reading and stimulates an interest in the arts, through foreign travel and study, and by the general inculcation of the values of the educational system, bourgeois parents ensure that their children will perform well in the system, and so acquire the qualifications necessary to secure the best jobs in society. The concept has value in being applicable not just to western CAPITALIST societies, but also to the COMMUNIST societies of eastern Europe, whose ELITES can similarly ensure that their privileges are transmitted to their own children, despite the absence of private property.   K.K.

Bibl: P. Bourdieu and J.-C. Passeron, *Reproduction in Education, Society and*

Culture (London and Beverly Hills, 1977).

cultural history. Defined by one of its greatest exponents, Johan Huizinga, as the study of 'themes, SYMBOLS, CONCEPTS, IDEALS, styles, and sentiments', it overlaps with INTELLECTUAL HISTORY but is also concerned with the HISTORY OF MATERIAL CULTURE and with RITUAL. It is sometimes referred to as *Geistesgeschichte* by those who believe that the art and literature, science and religion of an age are all expressions of the same spirit, that an age is a whole (see HISTORICISM). For those who believe that the 'spirit of an age' (see ZEITGEIST) is an unnecessary entity, cultural history is in danger of fragmenting into such parts as art history and history of science. Cultural history is to be distinguished from *culture history*, a synonym for ETHNOHISTORY.   P.B.

Bibl: J. Huizinga, 'The task of cultural history', in his *Men and Ideas* (New York, 1959; London, 1960).

cultural imperialism, see under IMPERIALISM.

cultural lag. Term coined by W.F. Ogburn (*Social Change*, 1922) for 'the strain that exists between two correlated parts of CULTURE that change at unequal rates of speed' (W.F. Ogburn and M.F. Nimkoff, *A Handbook of Sociology*, 1947). An example is the disjunction that occurs when the organization of the family is considered to be lagging behind other changes in society. The term names an important fact of social life, but does not help to account for it. See also FUNCTIONALISM.
                                                   M.F.

cultural relativism, see RELATIVISM, CULTURAL.

Cultural Revolution, see under GREAT PROLETARIAN CULTURAL REVOLUTION.

culture. The subject of a book by T.S. Eliot entitled, with extreme caution, *Notes towards the Definition of Culture* (1948), of one by George Steiner entitled *In Bluebeard's Castle: Notes towards the Redefinition of Culture* (1971), and of *Culture: A Critical Review of Concepts and Defini-*tions (Papers of the Peabody Museum of American Archaeology and Ethnology, vol. 47, I, 1952), this elusive and emotive word ('When I hear the word culture I reach for my gun', declared the poet Heinz Johst — not Goering as is generally believed) cannot be comprehensively treated in a work such as this. The following definitions are by an archaeologist and a sociologist respectively. For an anthropologist's use of the word see ANTHROPOLOGY; for an example of its biological meaning see TISSUE CULTURE.   O.S.

In general archaeological usage, that aspect of social behaviour which can be recognized in the archaeological record. More often it is the material culture that is defined. The assumption has often been made that culture closely reflects social groupings; such a view is now treated with reserve. More precisely, culture has been defined as the consistent recurrence of an ASSEMBLAGE limited in time and space. Here again the assumption is that a culture, thus defined, reflects contemporary social distinctions. The concept was first given prominence by V.G. Childe in 1929 and was of considerable value in the simple ordering of the basic archaeological data; in recent years, however, its limitations have been recognized, and the precise definition is now rapidly declining in use.   B.C.

The 'social heritage' of a community: the total body of material artifacts (tools, weapons, houses, places of work, worship, government, recreation, works of art, etc.), of collective mental and spiritual 'artifacts' (systems of SYMBOLS, IDEAS, beliefs, aesthetic perceptions, values, etc.), and of distinctive forms of behaviour (INSTITUTIONS, groupings, RITUALS, modes of organization, etc.) created by a people (sometimes deliberately, sometimes through unforeseen interconnections and consequences) in their ongoing activities within their particular life-conditions, and (though undergoing kinds and degrees of change) transmitted from generation to generation. See also FOLK CULTURE; SUBCULTURE.   R.F.

culture area. Geographical term for a region within which a single CULTURE or similar cultures are found; originally used (*Kulturprovinz*) by the German geogra-

195

pher, Ratzel, in the last century and given prominence by the American anthropologist, A.L. Kroeber, in his studies of North American Indians. Thus the Great Plains formed a clearly defined geographical area associated with distinctive Plains Indian MATERIAL CULTURE, economy, and social values.   P.H.

culture contact, see ACCULTURATION.

culture history, see ETHNOHISTORY.

culture of narcissism. Phrase used as title and denoting the main thesis of an influential critical analysis of American CULTURE and society by Christopher Lasch. He argued that the U.S. suffered from the increasingly degenerate form of individualism whose characteristics are those of the NARCISSISTIC personality writ large across society. The thesis represents an elaborate attempt to account for a national temper which was widely seen in the 1970s as disturbing and dysfunctional. The alleged trend towards preoccupation with self, a decay of public values and related traits was described by journalist Tom Wolfe as that of the 'Me Decade'.   S.R.
   Bibl: C. Lasch, *The Culture of Narcissism* (New York, 1979).

culture shock. The TRAUMA of bewilderment and ANXIETY supposedly experienced, most often by those who, whether voluntarily (e.g. as missionaries) or involuntarily (as refugees), find themselves isolated in an alien CULTURE, but also in certain circumstances (e.g. under IMPERIALISM) by their 'hosts'. Although the phrase is perhaps used more by journalists than by anthropologists (the best of whom are doubtless largely immune), the phenomenon it describes is well attested, with symptoms ranging from overt XENOPHOBIA to (more commonly) apathy, withdrawal, and such behavioural disorders as OBSESSIONAL hand-washing.   O.S.

Cunningham technique. A teaching method and movement style based on the work of Merce Cunningham, who is considered to be one of the foremost influences of change in MODERN DANCE stimulating the POST-MODERN DANCE rebellion (see AVANT-GARDE DANCE). Since his early

collaborations with John Cage in 1952 at Black Mountain College and his experiments with aleatoric form, Merce Cunningham evolved an innovative choreographic process. A former member of the Graham company (see GRAHAM TECHNIQUE), Cunningham rebelled to establish his own choreographic needs and technical demands. Cunningham maintains that dance be its own subject matter, rejects literary, psychological preoccupations and thematic development, insists on decentralizing space, ignoring stage hierarchies and works independently from musical accompaniment and visual design while retaining co-existence with them. Despite such radical changes, Cunningham has never dispensed with dance technique still maintaining a traditional appearance to dance while denying its expressive possibilities. However, the content works to destroy logical kinetic phrasing, ignores predetermined positions and preparations and has no floorwork and set combinations. Collaborations with contemporary artists are an important element of the final CHOREOGRAPHY, e.g. Rauschenberg, Warhol, Johns, Stella, Duchamp, Cage, Tudor and La Monte Young.   L.A.
   Bibl: J. Lesschaeve, *The Dancer and the Dance* (New York, 1985).

current fertility, see under FERTILITY.

curtain wall, see under CLADDING.

custom. Expected forms of behaviour which derive legitimacy by reference to tradition. Members of a particular society recognize implicit rules or conventions and are bound by them. Customs introduce elements of regularity, predictability and conformity into social relationships. To break a custom may be TABOO, it may invoke mystical SANCTIONS. This raises the question of the coercive nature of custom. Malinowski (*Crime and Custom in Savage Society*, 1926) took up this issue and examined the binding qualities of custom in societies lacking formal legal machinery. This theme was later explored by anthropologists concerned with political organization and the maintenance of order (particularly Radcliffe Brown and Gluckman). Leach (*Custom, Law and Terrorist Violence*, 1977) broadened the area of analysis beyond small scale societies and explored the ambiguities and contradictions embodied in the concept of custom.

A.G.

Bibl: G. Lewis, *Day of Shining Red* (Cambridge, 1980); E. Leach, *Social Anthropology* (London, 1982).

customs union. A group of nations between whom trade is free and which apply the same duties and other regulations to trade with non-members. This second provision distinguishes the union from a *free trade area*, whose members can apply different duties and other regulations to trade with non-members. While this later freedom to differ has its advantages, it may divert imports so that they enter the area through low-duty members and in this and other ways undermine the import-duty structures of the others, an undermining which can be prevented only at some administrative cost. Although they infringe the principle of nondiscrimination, both systems are permitted by the GATT. There have been many attempts to form them, but outside Europe few really successful examples exist. A *common market* goes beyond a customs union in permitting free movement of labour, CAPITAL and enterprise, as well as goods. See also EEC, EFTA and FREE TRADE. M.FG.S.

cut-ups, see under COLLAGE.

cybernetics. A subject which dates from 1942 and was named in 1947 by Norbert Wiener and Arturo Rosenbleuth, distinguished mathematician and physician respectively. It was then defined as 'the science of control and communication in the animal and the machine'. This definition indicated (1) that a state of 'in control' depends upon a flow of information, and (2) that the laws governing control are universal, i.e. do not depend on the classical dichotomy between organic and inorganic systems. The name cybernetics derives from the Greek word meaning 'steersman', and was chosen to show that adaptive control is more like steersmanship than DICTATORSHIP. Today, a more general definition of cybernetics might be preferred: *the science of effective organization.*

Always an interdisciplinary subject, cybernetics was seen by its founding fathers moreover as *trans*disciplinary. This perception was followed by the original U.S. workers, and by cyberneticians in the U.K., who looked to the science as linking organizational notions in every field, and as specifying quite general principles. Elsewhere in the U.S.A., and in some other countries, notably France, early discoveries about the importance of FEEDBACK and the role of ENTROPY focused the subject on its ENGINEERING aspects, at the expense of its BIOLOGY, its ECONOMICS, its ECOLOGY, and so on. In the U.S.S.R., cybernetics was officially treated as an 'imperialist device' until the mid-1950s. At this time, Soviet work in the field, heavily dependent on MATHEMATICS, achieved such importance internationally that the Soviet authorities admitted the science officially.

There remains disagreement about its generality, especially in relation to General Systems Theory (see GST), which has objectives identical with those expressed by the founders of cybernetics. Thus, for some, cybernetics and GST are coextensive, while those could be found who regard either one as a branch of the other. In their origins, at least, they express the same intentions.

Thanks to the academic forces that will always seek to classify in a REDUCTIONIST way, one may hear of *engineering cybernetics* (as mentioned above), of *neurocybernetics* (which deals especially with the brain), of *biocybernetics* (also called BIONICS), of COMPUTER cybernetics, of MANAGEMENT cybernetics, and so on. A clear perception of cybernetics must accept these distinctions by areas of application, but will not take them as undermining the transdisciplinary unity of cybernetics itself. S.BE.

Bibl: F. H. George, *The Foundations of Cybernetics* (London, 1977).

cyclogenesis, see under FRONTAL THEORY.

cyclone, see under DEPRESSION (sense 1).

cyclotron. A type of ACCELERATOR. The PARTICLES travel in circular ORBITS under the action of a magnetic FIELD inside two hollow D-shaped ELECTRODES with their straight sides adjacent. Twice during each revolution, when the particles cross the narrow space between the D's, they are accelerated by an oscillating voltage. When the beam emerges after several thousand revolutions, its ENERGY may reach extremely high levels.   M.V.B.

cytogenetics. A term sometimes used in place of GENETICS by those who overestimate the contribution made by CYTOLOGY to our understanding of heredity. It refers especially to the cellular structures and events associated with the hereditary process.   J.M.S.

cytology. The biological science which deals with the properties that CELLS enjoy in common. It is usually contrasted with HISTOLOGY, which deals rather with the properties distinctive of each individual TISSUE and the modifications of cells associated with them, and is to be distinguished also from CELL BIOLOGY. An important branch of cytology (*karyology*) deals especially with the properties and behaviour of the cell NUCLEUS and the CHROMOSOMES contained within it. The 'generalized' animal cell as envisaged in cytology comprises a nucleus which is the seat of genetic information (see GENETIC CODE), and a greater or lesser quantity of CYTOPLASM bounded externally by a plasma membrane. In addition to the plasma membrane, the cells of plants and of bacteria have more or less structurally rigid cell walls. The cytoplasm houses a number of minute structural features known as *organelles* which serve specific cellular functions, e.g. the *mitochondria* which are the seat of oxidative processes, the *ribosomes* (see NUCLEIC ACID) which are the seat of PROTEIN synthesis, the *lysosomes* (see AUTOLYSIS), and a number of adventitious fluid-filled spaces or *vacuoles*. There is evidence that mitochondria represent the contemporary evidence of some deeply ancestral SYMBIOSIS between animal cells and bacteria.   P.M.

cytoplasm. The sap of the CELL, excluding the NUCLEUS.   P.M.

cytoskeleton. A CONCEPT introduced by the biochemist R.A. Peters to account for the orderly progression of biochemical processes in the CELL and the fact that they need not be disastrously impeded by the stratification of the contents of the cell in the ultracentrifuge (see SEDIMENTATION). The cytoskeleton consists of filaments of PROTEIN arranged in a complex network in the CYTOPLASM of the cell but with attachments to the NUCLEUS, plasma membrane and organelles (see CYTOLOGY). Cell shape, movement and internal organization depend on the cytoskeleton.   P.M.;P.N.

Czech Reform Movement. The movement, within the Czech COMMUNIST Party and outside, which from the early 1960s until 1968 attempted to make the political system more LIBERAL and democratic and the economic system more flexible. In December 1967, the reformers within the Communist Party were powerful enough to compel the leader, A. Novotný, to resign and replaced him with Alexander Dubček. In the period before the Soviet invasion, several measures were introduced which provided for DEMOCRACY within the party, relaxed censorship and allowed associations to be established independent of the party which could make political demands. Although Czechoslovakia remained a member of the Warsaw Pact, the Soviet Union and other socialist bloc countries considered that the leading role of the party was being weakened, and in August 1968 Warsaw Pact troops invaded to put an end to the reforms. The intervention was justified in what has been called the BREZHNEV DOCTRINE, in which one socialist country can intervene in another if SOCIALISM is being threatened.   D.PR.

Bibl: G. Golan, *Reform Rule in Czechoslovakia* (Cambridge, 1971).

C³I, see under CONTROL, COMMAND, COMMUNICATIONS, INTELLIGENCE.

D

DAC (Development Assistance Committee), see under OECD.

Dada (-ism, -ists). International movement in the arts originating in Zurich in 1916 from a sense of total disillusionment with the art-loving public, the role of the creative artist, and, finally, with art as such; famous consequently more for its spirit of artistic flippancy, BOURGEOIS-baiting, and NIHILISM than for its purely formal methods, most of which were borrowed from CUBISM and FUTURISM. Its name was 'found in a lexicon — it means nothing. This is the meaningful nothing, where nothing has any meaning'. Its founders were mainly German — the theatre director Hugo Ball, the artist Hans Arp, and the poet Richard Hülsenbeck — plus the Romanian Tristan Tzara, while its adherents at one time or another over the next few years included Georg Grosz and John Heartfield (both in Berlin), Max Ernst (Cologne), and Kurt Schwitters (Hanover; see MERZ); the Cuban Francis Picabia and the Frenchman Marcel Duchamp (both of whom had previously experimented in a comparable nihilism in New York; see READYMADES); and finally a literary group centred around André Breton's Paris review *Littérature* (1919-24).

By 1924 the various groups had either stagnated, transferred loyalties, or merged into CONSTRUCTIVISM or SURREALISM; after which the movement's characteristic methods — phonetic poetry (see CONCRETE POETRY), BRUITISME, COLLAGE, and nonsense dialogue, as well as its two original contributions, the PHOTOGRAM and photo-MONTAGE — were hardly again recognized as such till the publication in New York in 1951 of Robert Motherwell's *The Dada Painters and Poets*, the consequent FLUXUS revival, and the rise of POP ART. In this new context Dada, like its Futurist precursors, became relevant above all for its basic, if unformulated, conception of art as HAPPENING or manifestation, and an exercise in public relations.   J.W.

dance notation. The method of recording movement and dance using symbols. Earliest forms of dance notation range from abbreviations, figure illustration, track drawings, stick figures, to current forms of notation practised today, i.e. the analysis of movement based on spatial, anatomical and dynamic principles called *Labanotation*, Eshkol and Wachmann's accurate mathematical description and Benesh notation based on 3-dimensional representation linked to the musical score. Of these systems Benesh and Labanotation are the most widely used. Labanotation or *kinetography Laban* is appropriate to all forms of movement from ANTHROPOLOGY to PHYSIOTHERAPY as it can record all movement inflections, spatial orientation, movement motivation and dynamics. *Motif writing* is a simpler form of dance notation and was also developed by Laban as a freer more general indication of basic movement concepts. Labanotation is linked to Laban's work on MODERN EDUCATIONAL DANCE while the Benesh system tends to be used by choreologists (see CHOREOLOGY) employed by CLASSICAL BALLET companies.   L.A.
Bibl: A. Hutchinson, *Labanotation* (London, 1954).

dance theatre. A synthesis of dance and theatre which aims to present a new form of dance performance with its own language. The term emerged in 1928 in Germany from radical discussion led by Kurt Jooss which denied that dance was an absolute art but part of theatre and capable of dramatizing social and political issues.   L.A.

dark comedy, see under BLACK COMEDY.

dark matter (or *missing matter*). Observations of the motions of stars and GALAXIES in the universe show that only about one-tenth of the total density of the universe exists in luminous forms. The remainder, termed dark matter or missing matter/mass, and revealed by its gravitational field strength, resides in undetected forms of non-luminous material and the question

199

of its identity is called the dark matter or missing mass or missing light problem.

There are three parts to the dark matter problem. First, it has been argued, on the basis of the observed motions of stars, since it was first suggested by Jan Oort in 1934, that about 50% of the mass in the disk of the Milky Way in the vicinity of the sun must be in non-luminous form. This dark matter is expected to reside in very faint stars or planetary-sized bodies similar to the planet Jupiter (and hence often referred to collectively as 'Jupiters'). The second dark matter problem is found in spiral galaxies. Measurements of the velocities of stars moving in orbits at different distances (called rotation curves) from the centre in the disks of spiral galaxies reveal that there must exist about 10 times more mass within these galaxies than exists in the form of visible stars and that the extent of this underlying mass is about 10 times larger than that of the visible galaxy. This unseen material within which the visible parts of spiral galaxies reside is called massive haloes/dark haloes/galaxy haloes. Third, the motions of galaxies within clusters of galaxies have an average speed about eight times larger than that needed to escape the gravitational attraction exerted by all the luminous material within the cluster. It is concluded therefore that there must exist large amounts of non-luminous material within the clusters which contributes additional gravitational attraction. This problem, which first gave rise to the term *missing mass problem*, was first pointed out by the Swiss astronomer Fritz Zwicky in the 1930s. The amount of material necessary to resolve the first dark matter problem associated with the disk of our galaxy falls well short of the amount necessary to resolve the second and third dark matter problems. The dark matter within galaxies and galaxy clusters could also consist of faint stars and 'Jupiters' or BLACK HOLES but this possibility is strongly constrained by the effect upon the primordial NUCLEOSYNTHESIS of light elements of introducing additional BARYONIC matter into the universe. The observed abundances of deuterium, helium and lithium in the universe are in perfect agreement with what would be produced in the Big Bang (see BIG-BANG HYPOTHESIS) if the only baryonic material in the

universe was that observed in luminous forms. Because of this it is widely believed that the dark matter in galaxies and clusters consists of weakly interacting massive ELEMENTARY PARTICLES (acronym WIMPS) — for example, NEUTRINOS possessing a small rest mass (about thirty ELECTRON volts) or particles predicted to exist if Nature is supersymmetric (see SUPERSYMMETRY). Plans are in progress in several countries to detect these particles using ground-based detectors if they comprise the halo of our own galaxy, the Milky Way.

The total amount of non-luminous material that must be found in order to resolve the three dark matter problems (as they are currently understood) is about five times smaller than that required to ensure that the universe ceases to expand and subsequently recollapses to a high temperature fate similar to the big bang from which it originated.   J.D.B.

Bibl: M. Disney, *The Hidden Universe* (London, 1985); J. D. Barrow, P. J. Peebles and D. W. Sciama, *The Material Content of the Universe* (London, 1986).

Darwinism. The theory of how EVOLUTION might have come about which constitutes the great contribution to science made by Charles Darwin (1809-82). Darwin saw the evolutionary process as a series of adaptations: plants and animals differ one from another in their hereditary endowments, and those variants which equip an organism specially well to cope with the exigencies of the ENVIRONMENT will be preserved in the 'struggle for existence' and will thus become the prevailing type. Darwin used the term NATURAL SELECTION for this process of discrimination, mainly to avoid the lengthy periphrases that would be necessary to avoid its animistic overtones (see ANIMISM), of which he was fully aware. At the turn of the century Darwinism was seriously faulted for its explanatory glibness: 'the natural selection of favourable variations' was a formula that fitted all phenomena too well. In due course Darwinism had to be reformulated in the new language of Mendelian (see MENDELISM) GENETICS, and this revised doctrine, the prevailing one today, is called *neo-Darwinism*.

Neo-Darwinism is still solidly Darwinian in principle. Inheritable variation (no other kind is relevant) is provided for by the recombinations and reassortments of GENETIC factors which Mendelian heredity allows for, and natural selection becomes now the overall name for inequalities of survival or of reproductive rate, or more generally for inequalities in the contributions made by different organisms to the ancestry of future generations. Those hereditary endowments which increase their representation generation by generation are said to confer *fitness*, and the organisms that possess them to be 'fitter' than those that do not. Thus evolution by natural selection could be represented as the *survival of the fittest*. It is to be noted that although the Mendelian process of shuffling and reshuffling GENES provides the variants upon which natural selection works, yet new genes, i.e. new genetic information (see GENETIC CODE), can arise only by the totally random and unpredictable process of MUTATION. Critics of Darwinism regard this as a deeply objectionable and irreverent element in the process; it is, however, the case. With its emphasis on human and animal inequality and on qualities that are already present because inborn, Darwinism is naturally repugnant to LEFT-wing thought; hence the support lent by a number of British scientists and others, for purely political reasons, to the doctrine known as LYSENKOISM.   P.M.

Dasein. In Heidegger's *Sein und Zeit* (1927) Dasein is the recognizably human element in the doctrine of BEING. Being itself precedes all beings but many of the modes in which Being appears are modified by being sunk in a human and socialized world. Dasein, literally *Being-There*, is itself a socializing consciousness and exists very much in the condition of *Being-With* and *Being-Towards*. Since *Sein und Zeit* is at once phenomenological and existential, Dasein is described in a series of strikingly original and poetic categories, whose mundanity is unmistakable, such as *Idle Talk, Curiosity, Ambiguity, Falling* and *Thrownness*. But Dasein can also involve the individual in lonely existential exposure to such asocial realities as *Care, Conscience* and *Guilt*, and ultimately to the realities of *Being-Towards-Death*. Heidegger's descriptions of the experience of a recognizably 20th-century sensibility under the hold-all term of Dasein have had an immense influence. EXISTENTIALISM, HERMENEUTICS and much DECONSTRUCTIVE literary theory are marked by the peculiarly plangent quality of Heidegger's categorization of Dasein sunk, in a complicit yet helpless way, in the environing absoluteness of being.   R.PO.

Bibl: M. Heidegger, *Being and Time* (London, 1962); G. Steiner, *Heidegger* (London, 1978).

dash-pot. Any device where motion resulting from impact is damped out by friction in a viscous fluid. Buffers on railway rolling stock provide a familiar example.

M.V.B.

data analysis. The process of extracting information from complicated data. It is sometimes taken to include classical STATISTICS and sometimes to be complementary to it. The main methods of data analysis (other than statistics) include CLASSIFICATION, SCALING, the use of representational techniques such as HISTOGRAMS, FACTOR ANALYSIS, and SPLINE FUNCTIONS, and numerous techniques for transforming data so as to display more clearly the features under investigation.

R.SI.

data bank. An alternative name for a DATA BASE more generally used if the information is not held in a COMPUTER.   C.S.

data base. A large and systematically organized body of homogeneous information, often stored inside a COMPUTER. Examples are: information relating to the policies of an insurance company; the forward bookings of an airline; the fingerprints and records of criminals known to the police. Data bases are interesting technically because they nearly always have to be constructed before all the uses to which they will be put are known. Their internal structure has therefore to be designed with great care.

The layman is generally more concerned with their possible unethical uses. These dangers are often attributed to the use of computers, but are in fact a consequence of the increasing centralization of society. This tendency may have been assisted by the use of computers, but certainly exists without them; and one of the most objectionable types of data base, that of credit ratings, was for long not computer-based. In many countries legislation has been introduced to regulate the use of data bases. See also INFORMATION STORAGE AND RETRIEVAL. C.S.

data-processing, see COMPUTING.

data retrieval, see under INFORMATION STORAGE AND RETRIEVAL.

data station. A collection of equipment, usually removed from the main machine, whence a COMPUTER can be used. Often this function may be fulfilled by a TERMINAL. Sometimes powerful devices (e.g. line-printers and card-readers) are used. In the latter case, a small *satellite* computer may be used at the station to allow certain simple jobs to be carried out there. C.S.; J.E.S.

dating. The establishing of dates for structures, events, and artifacts. The need for dating is paramount in such disciplines as GEOLOGY, GEOMORPHOLOGY, and ARCHAEOLOGY. In archaeology, until recently, traditional methods such as STRATIGRAPHY and TYPOLOGY were employed to provide a sequence which was then related by various means to historical dates (e.g. the Egyptian King lists). The cross-dating links were often tenuous and the resulting dated sequences were, at best, imprecise. Techniques introduced from the NATURAL SCIENCES began to be used in the 1930s, e.g. DENDROCHRONOLOGY and *varve dating* (the use of sediment sequences formed by melting ice). More recently the techniques of PHYSICS and CHEMISTRY have been employed to provide a wide range of dating methods including ARCHAEOMAGNETISM, THERMOLUMINESCENCE, and *obsidian dating* which involves measurement of the rate of surface hydration. All these are *relative* methods requiring calibration. Other methods are based on measuring the rate of radioactive decay (see RADIOACTIVITY), e.g. RADIOCARBON DATING, *fission track dating*, and *potassium-argon dating*. These, theoretically, are capable of

providing *absolute dates*. Frequently several techniques are brought to bear on a single problem, thus providing cross-checks. B.C.

Bibl: J.W. Michels, *Dating Methods in Archaeology* (London and New York, 1973).

DDT. A powerful and probably the best known insecticide. A chlorinated hydrocarbon, dichloro-diphenyl-trichloro-ethane, it acts on most insects, though resistant forms may develop. It plays the major role in anti-malarial spraying but its toxicity has led to restrictions in its use. As far as is known, DDT is harmless to man; the prime case against its widespread use is that it upsets the ecological balance (see ECOLOGY; BALANCE OF NATURE) among insects. But chemical degradation is very slow so that it becomes more concentrated in successive stages of the FOOD CHAIN with, in some cases, demonstrably harmful effects on animal life. B.F.

Dead Sea scrolls. An unprecedented find of ancient manuscripts discovered in 1947-56 in caves in and around Qumran, close to the north-west shores of the Dead Sea in Israel. In all there are some 500 manuscripts, some only fragments, but ten of them perfectly preserved, thanks to their storage in clay jars with lids. Dating from the 1st centuries BC and AD, they include all the books of the Old Testament except Esther, plus the Apocrypha, and have enabled scholars to push back the date of a stabilized Hebrew Bible to no later than AD 70 as well as to clarify the relationship between early CHRISTIANITY and Jewish religious traditions. The manuscript of Isaiah, a thousand years older than any previously known text, has been placed on display in the specially built Shrine of the Book in Jerusalem.

Other scrolls reflect the life of a devout community, consisting of (or connected with) the Jewish sect known as the Essenes, ending with the Roman suppression of the Jewish revolt in AD 70. Hidden in the wilderness, this community purified itself and prayed in preparation for the coming 'Day of the Lord'. These scrolls are, very roughly, contemporary with the Christian gospels. At some points (e.g. this monastic community's contempt for sinful laymen and for normal daily life) they are very different. They throw more light on John the Baptist than on Jesus.

D.L.E.; A.L.C.B.

dealignment, see under REALIGNMENT.

death instinct. In psychoanalytic theory (see PSYCHOANALYSIS), the impulses within a person to bring about his own destruction and death. Most FREUDIANS have not accepted this CONCEPT, and when they have used it they have transformed it into innate AGGRESSION and destructiveness. The death instinct is contrasted with the LIFE INSTINCT. B.A.F.

death of God theology. A movement which flourished in the U.S.A. during the 1960s and essentially did not die, being continued in a different form through the influence of, e.g., Don Cupitt's books and broadcasts in England in the 1980s. It attempted to preserve much of CHRISTIANITY (especially its ETHICS and its sense of the tragedy of life) while admitting the validity of ATHEISM or at least of AGNOSTICISM. The phrase 'death of God' became famous through the *Joyous Wisdom* of Friedrich Wilhelm Nietzsche (1844-1900), whose philosophy attempted to reconstruct man's understanding of life and good on the basis of a consistent atheism. The exploration of this idea by some writers holding theological posts has been courageous, but scarcely a THEOLOGY. In the background is an old and widespread non-Christian tradition of NON-THEISTIC RELIGION. D.L.E.

Bibl: D. Cupitt, *Taking Leave of God* (London and New York, 1980) and *The Sea of Faith* (London and New York, 1984) and *Only Human* (London and New York, 1985).

death squads, see under STATE TERROR.

de Broglie wavelength. The distance between successive crests of the wave which, according to QUANTUM MECHANICS, is associated with every moving PARTICLE. Its value is given by the EQUATION, put forward by Louis de Broglie in 1924, *wavelength* = PLANCK'S CONSTANT ÷ MOMENTUM *of particle*. The motion of the particle may be described by NEWTONIAN MECH-

ANICS to a good approximation only if the wavelength is small in comparison with the range of the forces acting on it; this is true for all systems larger than MOLECULES. See also ELECTRON MICROSCOPE; WAVE-PARTICLE DUALITY. M.V.B.

debt crisis. Since the mid-1970s, the high level of foreign borrowing by many developing countries has led to a debt crisis. Foreign borrowing is a useful source of finance for ECONOMIC DEVELOPMENT. The burden of foreign debt is the need to pay the interest and principal in foreign exchange that is obtained from export earnings or by reducing imports. The OIL CRISIS of 1974 led many developing countries to increase their foreign borrowing to pay for their imports of oil. This borrowing was largely achieved through a recycling of the oil revenue of OPEC countries through EUROCURRENCY markets. The second oil crisis of 1979 was more difficult to cope with as interest rates had increased, the prices of many of the primary exports of developing countries had fallen, growth in the world economy and trade was sluggish and many existing loans were coming to maturity. Many countries were unwilling to deflate their economies, in order to reduce imports and free foreign exchange to pay for the servicing of debts and the greater cost of oil imports. By 1983, many countries were in a very insecure financial position and began to attempt to renegotiate with private international banks the structure and terms of their debts. These banks, concerned about these countries and their own financially insecure position, formed consortia and insisted that the debtor countries first apply to the IMF for further funds and accept the IMF's conditions on the future conduct of economic policy. The world financial system has managed to cope with most of the short term problems of the debt crisis. Whether it can continue to do so and whether the long term problems of the debt crisis and world economic system can be solved is a matter of importance and speculation. J.P.

Bibl: M.P. Todaro, *Economic Development in the Third World* (London, 3rd ed., 1985).

debugging.
(1) The final testing or commissioning of a piece of technological apparatus — an expression that arose in Britain during the 1939-45 war, when unexplained faults in Royal Air Force equipment were blamed on 'gremlins' or 'bugs'.

(2) More recently, the process of finding and removing errors from a COMPUTER program. Detailed and sustained accuracy of the kind required to program correctly is not within the normal range of human achievement except, perhaps, by the use of more rigorously mathematical techniques than are yet common. It has therefore been necessary to work on the assumption that all PROGRAMS have errors and to develop techniques for finding and correcting them. These techniques are still very imperfect, time-consuming, and costly.

(3) The removal of secret sound-detecting devices (see BUGGING).

E.R.L.; C.S.; J.E.S.

decadence. In literature, an aspect and offshoot of the 19th-century SYMBOLIST and aesthetic (Art for Art's Sake) movements. Arising from the bohemian protest against BOURGEOIS society in France from the 1840s onward, decadence took and emphasized the febrile, neurasthenic, and world-weary element in the Symbolist presumption about the poet, and also dramatized its belief in the essential amoralism of art. As in much Symbolism, it was a subject-matter and an imaginative response enacted as a LIFE STYLE. Owing much to Flaubert and Rimbaud, the motto of its exponents (known as *the decadents*) was Rimbaud's: 'The poet makes himself a seer by a long, intensive, and reasoned disordering of all the senses.' Intensified by a sense of cultural ANOMIE, a high-style dandyism, and a *fin de siècle* despair, it has particular associations with the 1880s and 1890s, e.g. Huysmans's *À Rebours* (1884) and in England Swinburne, Wilde, Aubrey Beardsley (artistic editor of *The Yellow Book*), Ernest Dowson, and Lionel Johnson. With the Wilde-Queensberry trial in 1895 the public display of decadence suffered a setback. However, as a poetic sensibility it has remained important in modern writing. In popular usage, signifying a decline from established artistic and moral standards, decadence is equivalent to DEGENERACY, a CONCEPT first popularized around the same time. See also AESTHETICISM. M.S.BR.

Bibl: Holbrook Jackson, *The Eighteen-Nineties* (London and New York, 1913); A.E. Carter, *The Idea of Decadence in French Literature, 1830-1900* (Toronto, 1958); E. Moers, *The Dandy* (London and New York, 1960); L.C. Dowling (ed.), *Aestheticism and Decadence: a Selective Annotated Bibliography* (New York and London, 1978).

décalage ('uncoupling, temporal displacement'). In DEVELOPMENTAL PSYCHOLOGY, a PIAGETIAN term for either (*horizontal décalage*) discrepancy in the age or level of intellectual development at which a person can deal with different versions of a problem that are identical when regarded in terms of their formal logical structure; or (*vertical décalage*) a time-gap in his mastery of problems that are different when so regarded. Vertical *décalage* is thus a logical corollary of any theory that posits STAGES OF DEVELOPMENT in the *form* of intellectual functioning, whereas horizontal *décalage* is in the nature of an anomaly. I.M.L.H.

decarceration. A term popularized by the historical sociologist Andrew Scull to depict the move since World War II to remove people (the mentally ill, criminals etc.) from exclusive institutional confinement, and to reinstate them within society at large (e.g., within 'community care'). Scull (who has particularly investigated the case of the mentally ill) has put the motivation of this seemingly-liberal trend under scrutiny. Alongside the obviously idealistic grounds for this policy, Scull has contended that, in the U.S.A. in particular, decarceration represents both a new INDIVIDUALISM of the political RIGHT (the belief that it is not the function of the state to play a paternalistic role) and a financial crisis of WELFARE capitalism. In Britain, policy aims are to reduce institutional confinement for the mentally sick to a minimum, replacing it with community care in various forms (day centres, hospitals, acute units, outpatient clinics and the like). Extensive use of psychotropic (mood-influencing) drugs from the 1950s has guaranteed the safety of such 'deinstitutionalization'. R.P.

Bibl: A. Scull, *Decarceration* (Oxford, 1984).

decentration.

(1) In PERCEPTION and thinking, successive shifts of attention which take account of various aspects of a situation and synthesize therefrom a more representative view or interpretation of it than is obtained by centring attention on one aspect only.

(2) PIAGETIAN term for the progress of the child away from an exclusively egocentric view of the world. I.M.L.H.

decibel (db). A unit used to specify power by comparing it with a reference level. Decibels are commonly encountered in the measurement of sound intensity levels (e.g. with noise meters), and the usual reference is a barely audible sound at the threshold of hearing. The following are approximate levels: a quiet room, 20 db; light traffic, 50 db; a nearby aero engine, 120 db; the pain THRESHOLD, 130 db.
M.V.B.

decision procedure. In LOGIC, a technique for determining whether a PROPOSITION is logically true, i.e. for providing it with a proof or DEMONSTRATION. The oldest method of this kind is the axiomatic procedure (see AXIOMATICS) in which a proposition is deduced from others given as logically true. An attractively mechanical decision procedure is that of *truth-tables*, but it is applicable only to the PROPOSITIONAL CALCULUS and a part of the PREDICATE CALCULUS. Algebraic and diagrammatic techniques are available for some parts of logic. The method of natural deduction, in which only the validity of certain rules of INFERENCE is assumed, allows for the demonstration of logical TRUTHS as those which follow from any arbitrary assumption whatever. Demonstration proper (indirect proof by *reductio ad absurdum*) is a *prima facie* convincing decision procedure but has been rejected by mathematical INTUITIONISTS. A.Q.

decision theory. The context in which the theory of STATISTICS is usually constructed nowadays. The experimenter is faced with a number of possible courses of action and a number of possible states of the real world; in decision theory a cost is associated with each combination of response and reality, and, loosely speaking, the decision on which course of action to adopt is taken so as to minimize the cost. Since the state of the world is usually only known in terms of relative probabilities of different states, a genuine minimal-cost policy is not usually available, and normally policies — *decision procedures* — are constructed so as to minimize the maximum possible cost or the expected cost. The type of policy sought will depend on the experimenter's trade-off between expected cost and cost VARIANCE — a classic economic problem. Most statistical reasoning, whether orthodox or BAYESIAN, can be fitted into the framework of decision theory. Decision theory is often used in the context of MANAGEMENT SCIENCE, notably in the form of RISK ANALYSIS. R.SI.

Bibl: H. McDaniel, *An Introduction to Decision Logic Tables* (New York, 1968); H. Raiffa, *Decision Analysis* (London and Reading, Mass., 1968).

decision tree, see under RISK ANALYSIS.

decoder. In INFORMATION THEORY, a device or PROGRAM which takes the output of an ENCODER after transmission or storage and reconstitutes the original data. If the encoder has produced REDUNDANCY in its output, the decoder usually exploits this to correct corruptions or to detect them. R.M.N.

décollage. A technique developed notably by the German graphic artist Wolf Vostell in the late 1950s, by which strips are torn off a COLLAGE to suggest a peeling poster. As these works often involve fragments of words and letters they bear some relation to LETTRISM, as well as to the FLUXUS movement of which Vostell formed part. J.W.

decolonization, see under IMPERIALISM.

deconstruction. A technique associated with Jacques Derrida, who in 1967 inaugurated the Poststructural movement with his book *Of Grammatology*. In a series of astute readings of major philo-

205

sophical and literary texts, Derrida showed that, by taking the unspoken or unformulated propositions of a text literally, by showing the gaps and *supplements*, the subtle internal self-contradictions, the text can be shown to be saying something quite other than what it appears to be saying. In fact, in a certain sense, the text can be shown not to be 'saying something' at all, but many different things, some of which subtly subvert the conscious intentions of the writer. By throwing into relief the self-betrayal of the text, the effects of the supplement and of *différence*, of *trace* and of *dissemination*, Derrida shows that the text is telling its own story, quite a different story from what the writer imagines he is creating. A new text thus gradually begins to emerge, but this text is too subtly at variance with itself, and the deconstruction continues in what could be an infinite regress of dialectical readings. The main effect of Derrida's deconstructive teaching has been to destroy the naive assumption that a text has 'a' MEANING, which industry, application and attentive good faith will eventually winnow out — the basic assumption of the old NEW CRITICISM of the 1940s and 1950s. Meaning is not encased or contained in language, but is co-extensive with the play of language itself. Derrida shows that the meanings of a text are 'disseminated' across its entire surface, but are and remain purely linguistic surface features: there is no one guaranteeing 'meaning' which inhabits a text and which constitutes its 'presence'. The link between text and meaning is cut. Authorial intention dissolves in the play of signifiers; the text is seen to subvert its own apparent meaning; and there is no reference from the language of the text to some mystical interior of the text, in which some non-linguistic essence ('meaning') would or could ultimately be found.

Derrida's technique, continued through a series of applied studies of texts, has had an enormous influence, particularly in literary theory in the U.S. The YALE SCHOOL, comprising Paul de Man, Harold Bloom, J. Hillis Miller and Geoffrey Hartman, dominated American criticism in the 1970s with its deconstructive talent and panache. Deconstruction reached the limits of its enterprise in the early 1980s, and is now in a fallow period, seeking a new theoretical foothold. A recent contribution by Derrida to a volume edited by Geoffrey Hartman on *Midrash* shows one possible way deconstruction may go now.

R.PO.

Bibl: C. Norris, *Deconstruction* (London, 1982).

découpage. Signifying 'cutting up' or 'cutting out' in common French usage, *découpage* has a specific meaning in film terms equivalent to the English 'shooting script': the breakdown, before filming begins, of dialogue and action into shots, scenes of sequences dependent on camera placement, movement of actors, or change of location. By extension, however, *découpage* may be used as a structural concept (as 'shooting script' cannot) referring to the underlying rhythm of a film in terms of spatial and temporal movement. English critical terminology, lacking an equivalent, sometimes borrows *découpage* in this secondary sense.

T.C.C.M.

deduction, see under DEMONSTRATION.

deductive explanation, see under EXPLANATION.

deductivism, see under POPPERIAN.

deep strike. The extension of a battlefront (usually by airpower or MISSILE attack) deep into an enemy's rear. The strategic concept of any war in Europe assumes a Soviet attack which will replace losses by an inexaustible supply of reserves from behind the 'front line'. The success of any such attack depends on the efficiency of reinforcement, so keeping up the momentum of the assault. If this re-supply, both of troops and equipment, could be halted, then NATO would stand a fighting chance of defeating an attack without resort to nuclear weapons. The theory of a Follow on Forces Attack (FOFA) depends on being able to pinpoint the choke points where the stream of reinforcements can be halted. In turn, these attacks depend on superb intelligence and complete command of the airspace. If the concept is not new (the German army pioneered it in 1941 on the Eastern Front), it has profound implications for NATO, whose Supreme Commander, General Bernard Rogers, has listed the conditions whereby NATO could implement a deep strike policy (the Rogers Plan). It requires a considerable investment in CONTROL, COMMAND, COMMUNICATIONS, INTELLIGENCE : C³I, plus the highly accurate and selective bombs and missiles needed to implement it. The plan turns on the perception that the Soviet Union could launch a BLITZKRIEG sudden attack, which would sidestep all NATO's plans to counter a traditional mass attack. So the 'new' concepts have a role in seeking to uncouple NATO from an exclusively nuclear response to a Soviet attack; it also carries the implication of a successful counterattack deep into the Soviet Union, which is also thought to make WAR less likely. Behind the complex of issues involved — political, tactical, and financial — lies the belief that NATO's strategic doctrine has been left behind by new developments. Deep strike seeks to recapture the initiative. A.J.M.W.

deep structure and **surface structure.** A central theoretical distinction in GENERATIVE GRAMMAR. The surface structure of a sentence is the string of sounds/words that we articulate and hear. Analysing the surface structure of a sentence through CONSTITUENT ANALYSIS is a universal procedure which indicates many important facts about linguistic structure; but it by no means indicates everything, e.g. it cannot explain how we recognize ambiguous sentences which have different surface forms but the same basic meaning (e.g. *cats chase mice* and *mice are chased by cats*). For such reasons, linguists in the late 1950s postulated a deep or 'underlying' structure for sentences — a LEVEL of structural organization in which all the factors determining structural interpretation are defined and interrelated. The main current view is that a grammar operates by generating a set of abstract deep structures in its phrase-structure rules, subsequently converting these underlying representations into surface structures by applying a set of TRANSFORMATIONAL rules. This two-level conception of grammatical structure has been questioned, but is still the most widely held. D.C.

defamiliarization (*ostranenie*). The central concern of the Russian FORMALISTS was to identify and define what distinguishes a literary work from any other kind of written expression, to define what constitutes LITERARINESS. They settled for *ostranenie*, 'making strange'. Far from reflecting reality in some direct way as 19th-century fiction pretends to do, the literary work tends to upset and disorient readerly expectations, so as to throw into relief the sheerly constructed, arbitrary, written nature of the work of art. AVANT-GARDE literary technique, in particular, by parody, distortion, irreverence, tends to throw into relief the merely conventional nature of precursor works in the same genre. By parodying or undermining previous work in the same genre, the operative assumptions of a genre are 'defamiliarized' and the work's inherence in mere 'literariness' is made self-evident. R.PO.

Bibl: T. Bennett, *Formalism and Marxism* (London, 1979).

defeasibility and **incorrigibility.** In PHILOSOPHY, a belief or statement is said to be defeasible when it is vulnerable to refutation by further or future evidence. For example, any of our everyday beliefs, assumptions and expectations may turn out to be wrong and is thus defeasible. The opposite of defeasibility is *incorrigibility*. Beliefs or statements are incorrigible when it is impossible for them to be wrong or for one to be mistaken about them, as for example when they are directly self-verifying. Thus Descartes' 'I exist' is an incorrigible statement since one cannot be mistaken about its truth whenever one utters it. Beliefs and statements about the contents of one's private psychological states, including one's sensory experiences, are said to be incorrigible likewise; their being so is not affected by the fact that they may trivially be misdescribed, as when someone, owing to a slip of the tongue or ignorance, says 'this seems to me red' when to observe convention correctly he should not have used 'red' but 'blue'.

There is a narrower sense of 'defeasibility' in which something, say, a CONCEPT or a legal provision, is said to have this property if it only applies when not prevented from doing so by any defeating or obstructing conditions. This is the original legal meaning of the term from which its philosophical use has been adapted.

A.C.G.

defect (crystal). Any break in the regularity of the crystalline arrangement of ATOMS in a solid. The defect may be localized at a single point on the LATTICE, as in the case of vacancies or substituted 'foreign' atoms, or it may be centred on a line, as in the case of a DISLOCATION. The term 'defect' carries no pejorative implication.

M.V.B.

defence mechanism. In psychoanalytic theory (see PSYCHOANALYSIS), a FREUDIAN term for any number of unconscious techniques or devices used by the EGO to avoid danger (which is signalled by ANXIETY). There is no single agreed list of defence mechanisms, but these techniques would usually be said to include IDENTIFICATION (sense 2), PROJECTION, RATIONALIZATION, and REGRESSION (sense 2). Most of them are unsuccessful defences, i.e. they do not succeed in getting rid of the dangerous impulse. The two best-known successful defences are the destruction of the repressed impulse in the ID, and SUBLIMATION.

B.A.F.

defibrillator. A piece of equipment designed to give an electric shock (direct current) to the heart in order to restore normal rhythm. It is usually given in an emergency situation when ventricular fibrillation is present. An electrical discharge of 200 Joules may be used. It is sometimes used in a planned situation to 'cardiovert' a patient from a supraventricular irregularity (e.g. atrial fibrillation) to normal rhythm. In these cases the shock is regulated to occur only at set times of the heart beat ('synchronous').

L.J.F.

deficiency payments. Payments from general exchequer funds to supplement market prices received by farmers with the aim of raising them to some predetermined level. Migration from farming to other occupations over a period tends to reduce the disparity in incomes with those in other sectors of the economy but not enough to prevent governments from coming under pressure to make farming more prosperous (see AGRICULTURAL POLICY). In consequence, they have introduced a variety of measures, many of them directed towards increasing the prices for farm products above the normal market price. Some of these arrangements raise the level of prices at all stages of the distribution process, e.g. the COMMON AGRICULTURAL POLICY (CAP) of the EEC. Others, e.g. the deficiency payments scheme, introduced first in the U.K. in the early 1930s, allow the market to operate freely. Typically, a guaranteed price is set in advance, the average actual market price is calculated, and the difference between the two paid direct to the farmer as a deficiency payment. For another method of assisting uneconomic parts of an agricultural industry see STRUCTURAL REFORM.

K.E.H.

Bibl: A. E. Buckwell *et al.*, *Costs of the Common Agricultural Policy* (London, 1982).

deficit finance, see under FISCAL POLICY.

deficit spending, see under FISCAL POLICY.

defining, see under ESSENCE.

deflation, see under INFLATION.

degaussing. The process of neutralizing the magnetization of ferromagnetic objects (see FERROMAGNETISM) by encircling them with a coil system carrying electric current. It is commonly applied to ships in wartime, for protection against magnetic mines, and to all objects near apparatus where sensitive magnetometers are being used.

E.R.L.

degeneracy. The German term *Entartung* (departure from the *Art* or 'breed'), as applied to MODERNISM in the arts, derives from a book (1893) of that name by Max Nordau, a doctor and a founder of ZIONISM, who argued that much of the CULTURE of his time was pathologically degenerate. Already potentially racialist (see RACE), this expression became frankly so in the 1920s with the writings of Hans Günther (*Rasse und Stil*, 1926) and the architect Paul Schultze-Naumburg

(*Kunst und Rasse*, 1928), to emerge after 1933 as the principal slogan in NAZISM'S campaign against modern art. During 1937 the German museums were systematically purged of 'degenerate art', of which a great derisive exhibition was held in Munich; a Degenerate Music show in Düsseldorf followed in 1938. Movements condemned included CUBISM, FAUVISM, EXPRESSIONISM, DADA, CONSTRUCTIVISM, and SURREALISM, most of IMPRESSIONISM, and all but the MAGIC REALIST wing of NEUE SACHLICHKEIT (Italian FUTURISM was exempted on political grounds); and in music the twelve-note school (see SERIAL MUSIC), GEBRAUCHSMUSIK, and JAZZ. Many artists were banned from working or exhibiting; many emigrated, including all the principal teachers of the BAUHAUS. Ironically, degeneracy was largely identified with *Kunstbolschewismus* or 'Art BOLSHEVISM' though actually fulfilling much the same role as did FORMALISM in the similar purge conducted simultaneously in the U.S.S.R.   J.W.

Bibl: H. Lehmann-Haupt, *Art under a Dictatorship* (New York, 1954).

degenerationism. Ideas that mankind has declined and decayed from some former Golden Age or Paradisical state have pervaded culture, literature and science ever since Biblical and Greek times. Modern scientific ideas of degenerationism take their intellectual ancestry from these roots. But they assumed a new synthesis and power from the mid-19th century. Central to modern degenerationism were medical notions of the progressive manifestation of inherited physical and mental defect, advanced in particular by the French psychiatrist B.A. Morel (syphilis and ALCOHOLISM proved influential models). Such views were supported, perhaps paradoxically, by evolutionary theory (unless society weeded out, rather than protecting, the unfit, mankind would become a declining rather than a progressive species). THERMODYNAMICS also lent a cosmic dimension, with its notions of ENTROPY and the eventual HEAT DEATH OF THE UNIVERSE. Literary bohemianism and the philosophies of Schopenhauer and Nietzsche popularized and even sensationalized *fin de siècle* world-weariness, and the sense of the enervation of liberal and Romantic CULTURE. It remains hotly contested how much 20th-century IRRATIONALIST cults and TOTALITARIAN political movements owe to degenerationist theories (overtly of course FASCISM denounced such decadence). At the scientific level, mainstream currents in 20th-century PSYCHIATRY and evolutionary BIOLOGY have rejected degenerationism as speculative and biased.   R.P.

Bibl: J. E. Chamberlin and Sander L. Gilman, eds., *Degeneration* (New York, 1985).

dehumanization. The restriction or denial of free play to those qualities, thoughts, and activities which are characteristically human. Dehumanization is self-alienation rather than ALIENATION from an external STRUCTURE or system, although Marx saw it (*Entmenschung*) as an inseparable element of the general alienation of labour in a social system where the worker is obliged to work in order to survive rather than to manifest and develop his individual personality or sensibility. Today the term is widely used in connection with those mechanical, repetitive, assembly line tasks which reduce the performers to the level of components in a machine.   P.S.L.

deindustrialization. The decline in the absolute or relative size of the manufacturing sector, where size is measured by output. Correspondingly, the relative sizes of other sectors increase. This decline must be viewed in the context of the characteristic of ECONOMIC DEVELOPMENT that in mature economies the relative level of employment in the manufacturing sector declines. Deindustrialization is important as: (1) the manufacturing sector represents a large proportion of total employment and output, and it may be difficult to switch unemployed resources and labour, in the manufacturing sector, to other sectors; (2) in developed economies, the manufacturing sector has grown rapidly in terms of output and productivity; (3) if manufacturing and other exports are not able to support the FULL EMPLOYMENT level of imports, NATIONAL INCOME and employment may have to be reduced to balance the current account of the BALANCE OF PAYMENTS.

There are three hypotheses concerning

209

the causes of deindustrialization. (1) The increased share of resources taken by the public sector has crowded out the manufacturing sector (see MONETARISM). (2) The output of the manufacturing sector is particularly affected by a country's and its competitors' abilities to export manufactured goods. Decline in a country's export performance may be caused by an overvalued EXCHANGE RATE, production of types of manufactured goods for which the world demand is only increasing slowly, not producing new types of manufactured goods for which the world demand is increasing rapidly, lack of technical progress and poor MARKETING. (3) This is really a special case of (2); it is commonly referred to as *Dutch-disease*. Countries that begin to export substantial quantities of oil may experience surpluses on the current account of the balance of payments that lead to the exchange rate rising. This reduces the exports of other tradeable goods, particularly manufactures. This can have serious consequences on UNEMPLOYMENT, as, by comparison with oil production, manufacturing is labour intensive. J.P.

Bibl: F. Blackaby, *Deindustrialization* (London, 1979).

deism. The belief that God exists but has not revealed himself except in the normal courses of nature and history. Deists have been very cautious about describing God or offering any hope that he will save men from disaster or death. Deism flourished in England, France, and the U.S.A. in the 18th century, but more recently people so suspicious of personal RELIGION have usually described themselves as AGNOSTICS, particularly since modern studies have sharply raised the question whether God can be known in nature or history. See also THEISM. D.L.E.

Bibl: R. Sullivan, *John Toland and the Deist Controversy* (Cambridge, 1982); M. Wiles, *God's Action in the World* (London, 1986).

deixis (deictic). In LINGUISTICS, features of language which relate directly to the personal, temporal, or locational characteristics of the situation in which an utterance takes place, and whose meaning is thus relative to that situation. Examples include *here/there, now/then, I/you, this/that.* The notion is analogous to that of 'indexical expression' in PHILOSOPHY.
D.C.

Bibl: S. Levinson, *Pragmatics* (Cambridge, 1983).

déja-vu ('already seen'). The phenomenon whereby a person feels, contrary to reason, that he has previously experienced or lived through some presently-occurring event or situation. I.M.L.H.

delinquency. A fault, misdeed, or transgression (Latin *delictum*; *in flagrante delicto* = red-handed) against some written or unwritten law; also the state of being, or tendency to be, a transgressor. In the literature of CRIMINOLOGY the word, whether explicitly or implicitly qualified as *juvenile*, is used with particular reference to children and young offenders, and is almost synonymous with *juvenile crime*, although *juvenile delinquency* is perhaps more likely to imply a theory of the subject. Such theories have been derived from studies of PEER GROUPS (especially in the urban context), while psychiatrists and psychoanalysts maintain that the key to the problem lies in early childhood experiences. Whatever the causes of delinquency, there is today general agreement that juvenile delinquents are less responsible than older offenders, and require special handling in the form of juvenile courts, training institutions, etc. T.M.

Bibl: A. Platt, *The Child Savers* (London and Chicago, 2nd ed., 1969); D.J. West, *Delinquency* (London, 1982).

demand. In ECONOMICS, the demand for a commodity is the quantity which potential purchasers would like to buy and depends on their preferences, their incomes, the price of other products, and the price of the product in question. When allowance has been made for the other three factors the dependence of demand on the product's own price is often illustrated by a *demand curve* which shows demand falling as the price rises. Together with supply, demand determines prices in markets (see also SUPPLY AND DEMAND). The total of demands of different people for different products is very important in determining (NATIONAL) INCOME. See also AGGREGATE DEMAND; PRICE MECHANISM.

J.S.F.

Bibl: J. Craven, *Introduction to Economics* (Oxford, 1986).

demand-pull, see under INFLATION.

dematerialization. A word used by Lucy Lippard and John Chandler in 1968 to describe a shift in interest from art as object or product to art as idea, to art based on the thinking process prior to its physical execution. Drawing on Sol Lewitt's term and articulation of CONCEPTUAL ART, they noted the rise of '....an ultra-Conceptual art that emphasizes the thinking process almost exclusively' and the disintegration of traditional visual processes of art-making. A.K.W.

Bibl: L. Lippard, *Six Years: the Dematerialization of the Art Object from 1966 to 1972* (London and New York, 1973).

deme. Originally denoting a township in ancient Attica, and then a COMMUNE in modern Greece, the word has also been used, though not very widely, since 1883 by some biologists to denote an assemblage or AGGREGATION particularly of single-CELL organisms or even of subcellular bodies such as plastids. Occasionally the term was applied to higher plants and animals, which explains its adoption by some experimental taxonomists (see BIOSYSTEMATICS) from 1939 onwards as a root, to be used with an appropriate prefix, to denote a group of individuals belonging to a specific taxon or SPECIES, e.g. *gamodeme* (a deme of individuals which can interbreed), *ecodeme* (a deme occurring in a specified HABITAT), *topodeme* (a deme occurring in a specified area), *genodeme* (a deme differing from others genotypically; see GENOTYPE). These uses have, however, only been generally accepted by those associated with the Cambridge (England) school of experimental taxonomy. K.M.

dementia, see under NEUROPSYCHOLOGY.

democracy.

(1) A word originating in the classical Greek city states, and meaning the rule of the *demos*, the citizen body: the right of all to decide what are matters of general concern. The size of modern nation states has meant that (apart from those which include provision for a referendum in their constitutions) democracy is no longer direct but indirect, i.e. through the election of representatives; hence the term *representative democracy*. The CRITERIA of democracy are therefore: (*a*) whether such elections are free: i.e. whether they are held frequently and periodically, whether every citizen has the right to vote, whether candidates and parties are free to campaign in opposition to the government of the day, and whether the voter is protected against intimidation by the secrecy of the ballot; (*b*) whether such elections provide an effective choice: i.e. whether the choice of the electors is not limited to a single party, and whether a majority vote against the government in power leads to a change of government; (*c*) whether the elected body of representatives — variously known as parliament, congress, national assembly — has the right of legislation, the right to vote taxes and control the budget (deciding such matters by majority vote), and the right publicly to question, discuss, criticize, and oppose government measures without being subject to threats of interference or arrest.

Democracy is based on a belief in the value of the individual human being, and a further criterion is therefore the extent to which certain basic rights are guaranteed (in practice, not just on paper) to every citizen. These are: security against arbitrary arrest and imprisonment; freedom of speech, of the press, and of assembly (i.e. the right to hold public meetings); freedom of petition and of association (i.e. the right to form parties, TRADE UNIONS, and other societies); freedom of movement; freedom of RELIGION and of teaching. As a corollary, democracy is held to require the establishment of an independent judiciary and courts to which everyone can have access.

Critics of democracy fall into two groups. The first is opposed to democracy, root and branch, on the grounds that it is the least efficient form of government and one in which the stability of the State is threatened by faction, complex issues are distorted by popular discussion, difficult decisions evaded or put off, and matters of judgement reduced to the lowest common denominator acceptable to a majority of the voters. (See TOTALITARIANISM; FASCISM.) The second, in favour of the *principles* of democracy, argues that these are inadequately realized unless carried further, e.g. by extending equal rights for all citizens from the political and legal to the economic sphere, without which (so it is argued; see SOCIALISM; COMMUNISM) democracy remains at best incomplete, at worst a sham (*formal democracy*) disguising the reality of CLASS rule.

A variant of this type of criticism argues that, with the growth of BUREAUCRACY and the power of governments, decisions are no longer effectively influenced by the view of the government or the elected representatives; hence the demand for greater PARTICIPATION at all levels of decision-making and the problem of how to reconcile this demand with the need for prompt and effective decision on complex and controversial issues.

(2) The same principles of representative democracy can be applied to other organizations besides the State, e.g. local government councils, trade unions, political parties, Protestant churches, etc. One of the demands of the radical movement of protest in many Western countries since the 1960s has been for democracy to be made more effective in such organizations, as well as in government, by greater participation of the rank-and-file membership in decision-making, and for the extension of democratic procedures to other types of organization, e.g. factories (*industrial democracy*), universities (*student democracy*).

(3) Judged by the criteria set out in (1) above, no single-party Communist state, at least on the Russian pattern, can be regarded as democratic since it offers no freedom of choice and little, if any, freedom of expression to its citizens. The Communists, however, have refused to give up the appeal of the word 'democratic' and assert that they have established an alternative form with a better claim to the title — see PEOPLE'S DEMOCRACY; COMMUNISM; DEMOCRATIC CENTRALISM. See also SOCIAL DEMOCRACY.

A.L.C.B.

Bibl: S.I. Benn and R.S. Peters, *Social Principle and the Democratic State* (London, 1959); J.A. Schumpeter, *Capitalism, Socialism, and Democracy* (New York, 3rd ed., 1962); K.R. Popper, *The Open Society and its Enemies* (London and Princeton, 5th ed., 1966); J.P. Plamenatz, *Democracy and Illusion* (London, 1973).

democratic centralism. A basic tenet of LENINISM used as the organizational principle in all COMMUNIST parties. It is supposed to combine free political discussion in the Party and free election of its leaders with strict hierarchical discipline in the execution of decisions reached by democratic methods (see DEMOCRACY). Historical evidence suggests that the first part of the formula has nowhere been operative for any length of time and that it has consistently been subordinated to the second. In effect, 'democratic centralism' came to signify the method of autocratic or oligarchic control of the Party through its central APPARAT. This was made clear in the *21 Conditions of Admission* to the COMINTERN, which declared that 'the Communist Party will be able to fulfil its duty only if its organization is as centralized as possible, if iron discipline prevails, and if the Party centre, upheld by the confidence of the Party membership, has strength and authority and is equipped with the most comprehensive powers'.

L.L.

Bibl: L. Schapiro, *The Communist Party of the Soviet Union* (London and New York, 1970); M. Waller, *Democratic Centralism: An Historical Commentary* (Manchester, 1981).

demographic transition. General statements of the shift from high FERTILITY and high MORTALITY in traditional societies to low fertility and mortality in modern, developed societies. The transition has been identified as occurring through western Europe in the later 19th and early 20th centuries, and subsequently in eastern Europe and other developed nations, and to be associated with INDUSTRIALIZATION and modernization. The classic idea of the demographic transition included not only this past description and explanation, but also a future prescription for other, developing parts of the world. With few exceptions, control of fertility within marriage was not apparent until the mid and late

19th century; in the classical view, the trigger mechanism for the transition was improvement in mortality together with a new urban industrial society which broke traditional profertility values. The expectation has been that as other nations join the process of modernization so fertility falls would automatically follow. Closer investigation has undermined the general theory. In the developing world, big mortality falls in some countries have not been accompanied by rapidly declining fertility, while in some countries (e.g. Thailand, Sri Lanka) major fertility falls have been accompanied by little ECONOMIC DEVELOPMENT. Although the theory stands as a general statement of what occurred, investigations of countries in the 19th and 20th centuries have not shown a simple or consistent relationship between socioeconomic development and demographic change, have demonstrated the variability of pre-transition demographic regimes, and have shown cultural values, of religion and language, as being of particular local significance in effecting the transition.   D.S.

Bibl: A.J. Coale and S.C. Watkins (eds.), *The Decline of Fertility in Europe* (Princeton, 1986).

demography. The study of human populations through the interaction of births, deaths, and migration. The term was first used by Achille Guillard in 1855, although the study itself is of greater age. Formal (or pure) demography deals with the properties and dynamics of human populations, the relationship between age structure and vital rates, in abstraction from their association with other phenomena. Population studies embraces wider relationships with social and economic factors.   E.G.; D.S.

Bibl: H.S. Shryock *et al.*, *The Methods and Materials of Demography* (condensed edition) (New York and London, 1976); R. Pressat, ed. C. Wilson, *The Dictionary of Demography* (Oxford, 1985).

demography, historical, see HISTORICAL DEMOGRAPHY.

demonstration. In LOGIC, an INFERENCE which seeks to show that its conclusion must be true. It commonly proceeds by *reductio ad absurdum*, in other words by first assuming that the conclusion in question is false and then deducing a *contradiction* (see CONSISTENCY) from this assumption. It must be distinguished from *derivation* (or, more simply, *deduction*) in which a conclusion is validly inferred from some premises, and must be true if they are, but may not be true, and has not been shown to be true, if they are not.   A.Q.

demonstratives. In PHILOSOPHY, interest is shown in the demonstrative pronouns 'this' and 'that' because they are guaranteed a reference whenever they occur as the subjects of propositions, for example 'this is red', 'that costs forty pounds', for in every such case there is something at which the speaker might literally point his finger. Therefore no problems arise as they do when use is made of a name or phrase which may fail to refer to anything. For example: there is at present no King of France. If one said 'the present King of France is wise' would one have said something true, or false? If one says 'false', does this imply the truth of 'the present King of France is unwise'? Clearly not. The problem here does not concern whether someone is wise or unwise, but the fact that in this case there is no 'someone' of whom wisdom or its opposite can be asserted: the proposition's subject term, namely 'the present King of France', does not refer to anything. In the course of a famous piece of logical analysis concerning this problem (the *Theory of Descriptions*) Bertrand Russell argued that 'this' and 'that', and their plurals, are the only expressions of ordinary language which are logically acceptable subject-terms in propositions, and that all other expressions which may occupy subject place in the sentences of ordinary language can be 'analysed out' when one inspects their underlying logical structure. Such analysis, he said, shows that whereas the expressions in question may occupy grammatical subject place in sentences, they do not, unlike the demonstratives, also occupy logical subject place in the propositions expressed by those sentences. See ANALYSIS.   A.C.G.

Bibl: B. Russell, *Logic and Knowledge* (London, 1956).

demythologize. To confess disbelief in the legends and mythological ideas present in the Bible, while translating the Bible's message into a religious understanding compatible with modern science and philosophy. Thus the vivid picture-language of biblical ESCHATOLOGY is held to amount to a summons to choose a more 'authentic' way of human existence relying on faith in God. The necessity of such a ruthless translation was advocated by the German Protestant theologian, Rudolf Bultmann (1884-1976). Controversy resulted, particularly since Bultmann preferred CHRISTIAN EXISTENTIALISM to a literal acceptance of the Bible. To BARTHIAN and other conservatives, the transcendent, living, active God as well as the time-honoured myths had been sacrificed to a passing philosophy; to AGNOSTIC critics, too much of the Bible's message about God remained. Bultmann's intention was to respond to the spiritual crisis (see CRISIS THEOLOGY) with the Christian Gospel but without causing needless offence by the use of imagery natural to the 1st century A.D. but not to the 20th. This wish is now shared by most Christian thinkers, but there is no general agreement about how much of the Bible should be demythologized. D.L.E.

Bibl: J. Macquarrie, *The Scope of Demythologizing* (London, 1960; New York, 1961).

denatured, see under PROTEIN.

dendrochronology. In PALAEOBOTANY, DATING by means of counting the annual growth rings observed in a cross-section through a tree. These rings are affected by climate during the growing season, giving rise to distinctive patterns reflecting local climatic variations. By comparing the tree-ring patterns of isolated timber samples from archaeological CONTEXTS it is possible to construct a sequence in which any ring can be dated relative to any other. It the sequences can be linked to a growing tree or a sample felled at a known time, the floating chronology can be converted into an absolute chronology. The best results are obtained in areas of extreme climatic variation. The classic study was carried out by A.E. Douglass in 1929, using timbers from Pueblo villages in the south-west U.S.A. More recently, extremely long counts covering 6,500 years have been constructed, using the bristlecone pine which grows at high altitudes in California. These sequences have proved an invaluable check to RADIOCARBON age assessments. B.C.

Bibl: D. Eckstein, *Dendrochronological Dating* (Strasbourg, 1984).

Dengism. A phrase usually taken to mean the policies adopted in China after Deng Xiaoping consolidated his power at the 3rd plenum of the 11th CCP Central Committee, September 1978. Economically, this led to a radical move away from central planning to a greater role for market forces, and the decentralization of decision-making powers to production level units; a move towards CAPITALISM that the Chinese prefer to refer to as 'Socialism with Chinese Characteristics'. There has also been a relaxation of controls over literature and freedom of speech, although the arrest of Wei Jingshan for advocating that DEMOCRACY should be the 5th Modernization (see FOUR MODERNIZATIONS), and the banning of certain plays, such as *WM* in 1985, show that the party's control over society has only been curtailed, not removed. Although Dengism is usually used in reference to the post-1978 period, it is important to note that Deng's policies have varied greatly over time, and an overview of his political career shows that Deng's political philosophy is heavily based on PRAGMATISM. S.B.

Bibl: D.S.G. Goodman *et al.*, *The China Challenge* (London, 1986).

Denishawn. A school established by Ruth St Denis and Ted Shawn from which most American MODERN DANCE originates. Denishawn provided a technical training in all forms of dance including Oriental, Primitive and CLASSICAL BALLET. Students of Denishawn included Martha Graham (see GRAHAM TECHNIQUE), Doris Humphrey and Charles Weidman. Denishawn presented serious concert dance often on the vaudeville stage from 1914-1930, appealing to a wide range of audiences across America, Europe and the Orient. Costume, lighting and make-up played a significant role in the glamorous and exotic performances. Denishawn's special interests were religious and philosophical texts, dance tradition and values of other cultures. Ted Shawn's contribution to modern dance lies in his inspiration to introduce men into dance and to equalize male/female ratios. Graham, Humphrey and Weidman emerged from Denishawn as major choreographic talents who unlike Denishawn wished to use dance to communicate change in social and intellectual order and indicate dissatisfaction with the changed IDEOLOGY of the inter-war years.   L.A.

Bibl: J. Sherman. *The Drama of Denishawn* (Middleton, Conn., 1979).

denotation, see under CONNOTATION.

density. A CONCEPT borrowed from CHEMISTRY and used to express a quantitative relationship between land and the people inhabiting it. Population density is usually expressed in numbers of persons per unit of area. Density is increasingly used to measure the CONCENTRATION of a variety of human activities (traffic, buildings, etc.).

The formation of thick densities of sedentary populations in ancient times has been held a cause of innovations such as law, government, urban society, the DIVISION OF LABOUR, and the keeping of records. High density is now considered undesirable as it leads to crowding and problems of congestion; present planning calls for the lowering of densities whenever possible, although low densities are often recognized as costly, land-consuming, and possibly inefficient. Statisticians have endeavoured to calculate 'optimum' densities for certain situations.   J.G.

dentistry. An art and craft concerned with the repair or replacement of damaged or missing teeth. Only recently has it become accepted as part of the wide field of medicine. The present day practice of dentistry requires a high degree of manipulative skill which must be taught to the student almost from the beginning of training. Together with this technical skill the dentist is expected to have a background knowledge of general medicine which will enable the recognition of disease processes which might be of great significance in the diagnosis or treatment of patients. The dentist must also be aware of the scientific basis of the profession — particularly in terms of such subjects as the pharmacology of drugs in general use and the science of dental materials. There are a number of specialities which are dentally based (oral and maxillofacial SURGERY) which deal with abnormalities and trauma around about the mouth, face and jaws. The general practice of dentistry, which for most of the first half of the 20th century was devoted to the repair of decay, the removal of teeth and their artificial replacements, is now much more oriented to the prevention of dental disease.   W.R.T.

denudation. A term that embraces all the processes involved in the wearing away and lowering of the land surface. *Weathering*, normally the initial stage in denudation, involves physical and chemical breakdown of the bedrock by various agents, principally ground water, but without any substantial removal of weathered material from the site. All the processes in which a transporting agent, including gravity operating on slopes, is involved are described as *erosion*. Fluvial, glacial, and wind erosion each impose a characteristic form on a denuded landscape. See also SOIL EROSION.   J.L.M.L.

denumerable, see under COUNTABLE.

deontic logic. The branch of LOGIC in which a systematic study of the relations between propositions expressing *obligation* and permission are studied. It is sometimes called 'the logic of obligation' and it is of particular relevance to ETHICS, in which among other things questions arise as to what one *ought* to do and of what one's duties and *obligations* are. Among the principles which deontic logicians seek to clarify and express are 'nothing can be both obligatory and forbidden at once', 'anything obligatory is permissible', and so on. There are close connections between deontic and MODAL LOGIC; the former may be treated as a special case of the latter.   A.C.G.

Bibl: G.H. von Wright, *An Essay in Modal Logic* (London, 1951).

deontology. Strictly, and as the title of a book allegedly by Bentham, the branch of ETHICS which inquires into the nature of moral duty and the rightness of actions; as currently used, the particular ethical theory that takes principles of duty or obligation, those that lay down what men morally ought to do, to be self-evident or self-substantiating and neither to need, nor to be susceptible of, derivation (see DEMONSTRATION) from any supposedly more fundamental moral truths, in particular from propositions or principles about the goodness of the consequences of action. The opposed view, that the rightness or wrongness of actions is determined by the goodness or badness of their consequences (whether actual, predictable, or intended) is called TELEOLOGY or consequentialism. 'Let justice be done though the heavens fall' is a deontological slogan. Kant seeks to establish deontology at the outset of his chief ethical treatise by proving that the rightness of an action is unaffected by its having, in a particular case, unfortunate consequences.   A.Q.

Bibl: B. Blanshard, *Reason and Goodness* (London and New York, 1961), ch. 4.

dependence or **dependencia theory.** A NEO-MARXIST theory of international relations formulated in the 1960s and 1970s. Although it makes extensive use of the concepts of DIALECTICAL MATERIALISM and CLASS *conflict*, it differs from classical MARXISM in its major assumptions: (1) that a system of world CAPITALISM already exists and is exploiting the colonial and post-colonial countries; and (2) that as the industrialized 'core' of world capitalism develops ever greater wealth and power, so the exploited 'periphery' becomes relatively more underdeveloped.

Dependencia theorists argue that foreign economic penetration and heavy external dependence cause major distortions in the economies of less developed countries (LDCs), leading to stagnation and the outward flow of surplus capital and expertise from the LDCs to the 'core' countries. This process widens the gulf between the powerful and technologically innovative rich world and the poor THIRD WORLD which becomes ever more vulnerable to exploitation. They draw very pessi-mistic political conclusions from this analysis, suggesting that 'the development of UNDERDEVELOPMENT' gives rise to more severe state repression in the LDCs as their regimes attempt to protect the interests of the wealthy ELITES who, as the 'clients' of the capitalist 'core', do well out of the system. Any chance of real progress towards popular democracy is thus denied. Critics of dependence theory contest both its underlying neo-Marxist assumptions and the flaws that emerge from attempts to apply it to specific cases. Nevertheless, it does offer one of the most interesting alternatives to the power politics PARADIGM of international relations. It has already considerably influenced political perceptions, especially in the third world, and the movement for a NEW INTERNATIONAL ECONOMIC ORDER.   P.W.

Bibl: A.G. Frank, 'The development of underdevelopment' in J. Cockroft, A.G. Frank and D.L. Johnson (eds.), *Dependence and Underdevelopment* (New York, 1972).

dependency grammar. In LINGUISTICS, a type of formal grammar, developed in the 1950s (especially by the French linguist Lucien Tesnière (1893-1954), which established types of dependencies between the elements of a construction as a means of explaining grammatical relationships. Syntactic structure is represented as 'dependency trees' — sets of nodes whose interconnections specify structural relations.

Bibl: P. Matthews, *Syntax* (Cambridge, 1981).

dependency ratio, see under VALUE OF CHILDREN.

depersonalization. In ABNORMAL PSYCHOLOGY and PSYCHIATRY, a pathological state characterized by loss of the sense of reality of the physical or psychological self.   W.Z.

depreciation, see under DEVALUATION.

depression. A term whose many meanings include the following:

(1) In METEOROLOGY, an area of low atmospheric pressure with associated weather phenomena. It is formed by a

system of air rotating anticlockwise in the northern hemisphere and clockwise in the southern. In the middle latitudes depressions are associated with most of the precipitation and high winds recorded in these areas. The term *cyclone* is sometimes used synonymously with mid-latitude depressions but is usually restricted to severe tropical storms or hurricanes. P.H.

(2) In PSYCHIATRY, a state of malaise (formerly known as *melancholia*) accompanied by lowered mental and physical responsiveness to external stimuli. It may be symptomatic of a serious mental disorder (e.g. MANIC-DEPRESSIVE PSYCHOSIS), but normal depression is also known to be widespread. W.Z.

Bibl: A.T. Beck, *Depression* (New York, 1967; London, 1969).

(3) In ECONOMICS, the period of the TRADE CYCLE when the rate of increase in economic activity is below that which is potentially obtainable over a long period of time. It is usually accompanied by high UNEMPLOYMENT. Economic stabilization policies attempt to flatten out the fluctuations between economic booms and slumps, and maintain a more uniform rate of increase in output (see STOP-GO, KEYNESIAN, MONETARISM). A recession has a similar definition, but its duration is shorter. J.P.

Bibl: M. Parkin and R. Bade, *Modern Macroeconomics* (Oxford, 1982).

depth psychology. The FREUDIAN and other SCHOOLS OF PSYCHOLOGY that place major emphasis on the UNCONSCIOUS aspects of mental functioning and their effects on behaviour. W.Z.

de-rehabilitation, see under REHABILITATION (sense 2).

derivation, see under DEMONSTRATION.

derivative (or *differential coefficient*). Let x be a quantity which varies smoothly with respect to some other quantity t, so that x is a FUNCTION of t; $x = f(t)$. The *derivative* of f denoted by $f'(t)$ or df/dt or dx/dt is the instantaneous rate of change of x with respect to t; it is itself a function of t. For example if t denotes time and x the distance travelled by an object moving

in a straight line then $f'(t)$ is the speed at time t. The operation can be repeated to give *higher order derivatives*; in the example the second derivative $f''(t)$ or d^2x/dt^2 is the ACCELERATION at time t. Approximations to a function can be calculated in terms of its derivatives. Using first-order derivatives f can be approximated by a LINEAR function, using second-order derivatives by a quadratic function and so on. Differential CALCULUS is concerned with calculating and manipulating derivatives, ANALYSIS with the rigorous justification of these manipulations. R.G.

dermatology. The science of the skin, the largest organ of the body. The skin consists of a stratified cellular epidermis and an underlying connective tissue dermis. Below the dermis is subcutaneous fat. Human skin may be hairy, possessing hair follicles and sebaceous glands but lacking encapsulated sense organs, or glabrous (hairless), as on palms and soles possessing such sense organs within the dermis. Signs and symptoms related to the skin may indicate local disease or, less commonly, systemic disease. The work of the dermatologist embraces all aspects of the nature and function of the skin both in health and disease, and includes management of its disorders. Such disorders are common and many present problems particularly to the non-specialist.

Apart from the biology of the skin, its physical and chemical properties are subject to much current research. Research into the causation of atopic dermatitis (atopy indicates an inherited tendency to develop one or more of a related group of conditions including asthma, atopic dermatitis and hay fever) and psoriasis involves many experts and knowledge is increasing in many areas such as wound healing, melanogenesis (production and structure of melanin), inflammation and IMMUNOLOGY. The synthetic retinoids (analogues of Vitamin A used in the treatment of severe forms of acne, psoriasis and some congenital disorders) and the antiviral drug acyclovir (an effective treatment for HERPES simplex infections) represent important therapeutic advances. J.L.V.

Bibl: A.J. Rook *et al., Textbook of Der-*

matology, 3 vols. (Oxford, 4th ed., 1986).

desacralization, see under SACRIFICE.

desalination. The process of removing dissolved salts from water (usually sea water). The simplest method is by distillation, but this involves the supply of a large amount of heat ENERGY. Recent developments include the use of ION EXCHANGE solids (a similar process to that used in water-softeners) and a membrane process which could be described as the reverse of OSMOSIS, in which the water is squeezed through a membrane under pressure. The latter process is useful where the density of salt is of the order of 3 to 5 parts per million but difficult to apply to sea water, which has about 35 parts salt per million.

E.R.L.

descent. In ANTHROPOLOGY a relationship based on the tracing of a continuous line between an individual and an ancestor. Kin ties based on descent may govern relations between people concerning the inheritance of property and succession to office. Descent may also form the basis for a social group (descent group), the members of which are descended or claim descent from an ancestor (real or mythic). Descent may be traced through a single line, unilineal descent, or through two lines, BILATERAL or COGNATIC DESCENT. Unilineal descent can be further divided into PATRILINEAL (tracing descent exclusively through the male line, also known as agnatic) and MATRILINEAL (tracing descent exclusively through the female line, also known as uterine).

The operation of the principle of unilineal descent allocated individuals to discrete and mutually exclusive units. Societies recognizing the principle of *double unilineal descent* or *double descent* are rare. The Yako of Nigeria is one such example: the inheritance of *moveable property* is organized on matrilineal lines, *immoveable property* on patrilineal lines. Individuals in this system are still allocated to discrete, exclusive units — members of one patrilineage and of one matrilineage. The case of bilateral or cognatic descent is different. An individual traces common ancestry through both male and female lines. He becomes a member of all the cognatic lineages of his lineal ancestors: 2 in his parents' generation, 4 in his grandparents' generation, 8 in his great grandparents' generation and so on. In contrast to the unilineal case, the cognatic system allocates an individual to several, often overlapping units. Although in theory different societies may be distinguished according to whether they are patrilineal, matrilineal or bilateral, in practice the picture is much less clear cut. All societies have features of the different systems, but one principle is more dominant.

The concept of descent dominated anthropological debate in Britain during the 1950s and 1960s and exercised a profound influence on KINSHIP studies. It was developed particularly by those working in African societies and received its greatest theoretical elaboration in the work of Meyer Fortes. Central to Fortes's work was the idea of descent as a jural institution. Descent groups were identified as corporations, distinct from other groups and existing in perpetuity. They were understood as part of the politico-jural domain and as such one of the fundamental units of social structure. To balance the descent principle, Fortes developed the concept of *complementary filiation*, that is the relationship between an individual and the side of his family through which descent is not traced. Problems in analysis arose when the concept of descent was transferred to other societies, particularly those outside Africa. It also became clear that a distinction had to be made between the *idea* of descent and what it actually meant in practice.

A.G.

Bibl: A. Barnard and A. Good, *Research Practices in the Study of Kinship* (London, 1984).

de-schooling. A view of schooling and education associated with the names of Ivan Illich, Paul Goodman, and Paulo Freire. Illich and Freire speak from experience of the impoverished THIRD WORLD of Latin America, Goodman (who died in 1972) from urban U.S.A. All three men reject CAPITALIST, materialist society and see the school as at present a perpetuator of exploitation, and a destroyer of education, which ought to be lifelong;

education must be separated from the institution of school and operate through 'educational webs', by which is meant the pupil's life experience rather than a curriculum constructed by his teachers. The de-schooling view is partly political and NEO-MARXIST, partly religious, partly ANARCHISTIC, wholly radical-reformist (see RADICALISM). W.A.C.S.

Bibl: P. Goodman, *Growing Up Absurd* (New York, 1960; London, 1961); I. Illich, *Deschooling Society* (London and New York, 1971).

descriptions, see under ANALYSIS (sense 2).

descriptions, theory of, see under ANALYSIS (sense 2) and DEMONSTRATIVES.

desegregation. The process of ending the provision of separate (i.e. inferior) facilities for recognizably distinct racial or social groups, commonly the American blacks. The term was first used in the context of legal action brought by members of the American CIVIL RIGHTS MOVEMENT to end the provision of separate schools and higher education for BLACKS and non-blacks in the southern states of the U.S.A., an action pronounced on by the Supreme Court in 1954. As a result orders were issued to the schools and colleges concerned to 'desegregate' and admit blacks to their classes. It is a term which is occasionally employed in discussions relating to APARTHEID in South Africa, particularly in the abolition of petty apartheid (mixed race public transport, for instance). D.C.W.; S.T.

desensitization, see under BEHAVIOUR THERAPY.

designator, rigid. In PHILOSOPHY a name or any expression with a naming function is said to designate its bearer. A name does so *rigidly* when it designates the same individual in every situation (in every POSSIBLE WORLD) in which that individual exists. Thus '2×2' rigidly designates 4, but 'the most famous student of Plato' does not rigidly designate Aristotle since Aristotle could have studied with someone else. The concept of rigid designation is chiefly associated with the work of Saul Kripke who, with others, argues that names do not have sense (colloquially, connotation or 'meaning') but only the function of referring to their bearers, a point upon which he insists in opposition to those philosophers who have held that the sense of a name is what a user of it has to know in order to be able to apply it correctly. A.C.G.

Bibl: S. Kripke, 'Identity and Necessity' in M. Munitz, *Identity and Individuation* (London, 1971).

desire. The French term 'desire', as it is used in LACANIAN psychoanalysis, takes on a more specific connotation than the English word 'wish'. Whereas in Freud, UNCONSCIOUS wishes could be fulfilled, even though only in a distorted way in dreams or in the symptom, through a chain of DISPLACEMENTS and CONDENSATIONS which keeps them repressed, desire is intrinsically unfulfillable, because it is desire for something else which is always missing in us. It is desire for the OTHER (mother, for example) who will never fill our own lack of being, however hard she might try, but it is also desire of the Other, as all we find in this Other is his or her desire, by which we are captured. Unlike need or demand, which can be partially satisfied by a particular object, the only object of desire is an originally lost object, which Lacan calls OBJECT (a). B.BE.

de-skilling. The loss of skill, creativity, and control in the work process of industrial societies. Most official occupational censuses suggest the opposite. They show a general rise over time in the skill requirements of jobs in industry, as marked by the higher levels of training and education formally demanded for their performance. Taking its lead from these censuses, POST-INDUSTRIAL theory looks forward to a future in which the majority of workers are 'knowledge workers'. De-skilling proponents suggest that the impression of increased skill and knowledge in most jobs is a statistical illusion, created by the tendency to inflate job descriptions, and by the increasing reliance on formal educational qualifications in the allocation of jobs, irrespective of their relevance to the actual work tasks involved (CREDENTIALISM). The actual skill content of most jobs has in fact been declining, as a result of the steady increase in the DIVISION OF LABOUR and the application of the techniques of SCIENTIFIC MANAGEMENT. K.K.

Bibl: H. Braverman, *Labor and Monopoly Capital: The Degradation of Work in the Twentieth Century* (New York, 1974).

détente. The extensive reduction of tensions between formerly hostile STATES, and consequent reduction of the risk of war. The term is most commonly applied to a phase in U.S.-U.S.S.R. relations from 1971 to an uncertain point in the late 1970s. The period of détente was marked by both states' asymmetrical and fluctuating interest in establishing a more harmonious relationship. The methods used included attempts at ARMS CONTROL; an increased tolerance of the other state's social and political systems; a less aggressively competitive approach to THIRD WORLD states and to western Europe; the rebuilding or creation of stronger diplomatic, economic and cultural ties. The decay of détente is explained variously as due to the undermining of U.S. policy by divisions in elite and popular opinion and by WATERGATE; the impossibility of genuine accommodation being offered by the U.S.S.R.; the change in U.S. priorities produced by the election of President Carter in 1976; the overambitious attempt to link too many issues, some of which were intractable. S.R.

Bibl: S. Hoffmann, *Primacy or World Order* (New York, 1978); R.D. Schulzinger, *American Diplomacy in the Twentieth Century* (New York and Oxford, 1984).

determinant, see under MATRIX.

determination, see under MORPHOGENESIS.

determinism. The theory that the world, or nature, is everywhere subject to causal law (see CAUSALITY), that every event in it has a cause. If it is true, then every event that actually happens has to happen; since it logically follows from a description of the conditions of its occurrence, together with the relevant laws of nature, that it occurs. Likewise any event that does not

happen could not have happened. Sometimes the principle of determinism is taken (as by Hume and J.S. Mill) to be the most general and comprehensive of all the laws of nature, and is held to be confirmed by the way in which knowledge of causal laws so often follows the close investigation of a particular field. Sometimes, however, it is held to be a necessary TRUTH: by some because they regard it as self-evident, by others (e.g. Hobbes and Locke) because it seems easy to DEMONSTRATE, by others again (particularly Kant) because its truth is held to be a NECESSARY CONDITION of the possibility of organized and coherent experience. Its necessity would appear to be impugned by the view of the dominant school of QUANTUM physicists that the ultimate laws of nature are not causally deterministic but assert only the statistical PROBABILITY of occurrences at the SUB-ATOMIC level. If human actions are included in the deterministic system it follows that no one could ever have acted otherwise than he did, and therefore — though Hume and others have disputed this — that no one is morally responsible for his actions. A.Q.

Bibl: S. Hook (ed.), *Determinism and Freedom in the Age of Science* (New York, 1958); K. Popper, *The Open Universe* (London, 1982).

deterministic problems, see under DYNAMIC PROGRAMMING.

deterrence. The concept of deterrence, a word whose implications are more accurately conveyed by its French equivalent, *dissuasion*, acquired a largely strategic connotation from the 1930s onwards, by reason of the development of increasingly powerful and long-range means of mass destruction which gradually rendered obsolete older strategies of territorial or maritime defence. Though NUCLEAR WEAPONS are often called 'the deterrent', deterrence essentially involves all acts of STATE policy intended to discourage, by arousing fears of effective counter-action, hostile action by another state. It is thus applicable to general military, economic, and political as well as strategic relationships.

In its strategic context different forms of deterrence are distinguished. Thus, by a posture of *active deterrence* (British term) or *extended deterrence* (American term) a state implies that its deterrent power extends to attacks or provocative acts not only against its own territory and nationals, but against those of its allies. Conversely, a policy of *minimum* or *finite deterrence* is intended only to protect the state that exercises it (normally by having only sufficient weapons to destroy the adversary's cities, of which there are a finite number, rather than his forces and bases). By a strategy of *graduated deterrence* a state demonstrates its ability and intention to punish a whole range of hostile actions in proportion to their seriousness, while a situation of *mutual deterrence* is one in which two powers are deterred from attacking each other because of the unacceptable damage that would result from the victim's retaliation.   A.F.B.

Bibl: C. Bertram, ed., *Strategic Deterrence in a Changing Environment* (London, 1981); R. Speed, *Strategic Deterrence in the 1980s* (London, 1979); B. Brodie, *War and Politics* (New York, 1973; London, 1974).

deuterium. The ISOTOPE of hydrogen whose NUCLEUS consists of a NEUTRON as well as the usual PROTON. About 0.01% of natural hydrogen occurs as deuterium. See also HEAVY WATER.   M.V.B.

Deutsches Theater. Berlin theatre associated for three decades with Max Reinhardt, an eclectic perfectionist whose handling of new stage devices (e.g. spotlights, the revolving stage) and power over his actors were decisive in the history of modern theatre and film. Founded in 1893 by Adolf L'Arronge, the theatre was taken over in 1903 by Otto Brahm, whose FREIE BÜHNE society of 1889 had been constituted to perform the new NATURALIST drama, and who presented numerous plays by Ibsen, Hauptmann, Sudermann, Schnitzler, and others. In 1905 Reinhardt followed with a programme of naturalist and SYMBOLIST works (notably by Strindberg, whose chief interpreter he became) interspersed with revitalized classics, especially Shakespeare; to EXPRESSIONISM he was less sympathetic. During the 1920s, when Reinhardt increasingly left the Deutsches Theater to be managed by his

aides, new staff members included the playwrights Carl Zuckmayer and, in 1924-5, Bertolt Brecht (see BRECHTIAN). In 1933 the NAZIS took it over; in 1945 it became the main theatre of the Soviet sector of Berlin, under Wolfgang Langhoff's direction, with Brecht's BERLINER ENSEMBLE as an offshoot.   J.W.

devaluation (or *depreciation*). An increase in the number of units of domestic currency required to purchase a unit of foreign currency, i.e. the EXCHANGE RATE is reduced. Devaluation is often suggested as a means of improving the current account of the BALANCE OF PAYMENTS. It reduces the price of exports in terms of foreign currency and increases the prices of imports in terms of the domestic currency. The producers of exports may increase their prices in terms of the domestic currency, but not so far as to increase their prices in terms of the foreign currency. As the price of exports in terms of the foreign currency falls, the demand increases and as the price of exports in terms of the domestic currency stays the same or increases, the revenue from exports increases (in terms of the domestic currency). Producers of imports may bear some, but not all, of the increase in the price of imports, in terms of the domestic currency. In this case, the demand for imports falls and the revenue, in terms of the domestic currency, increases or decreases, depending on the net effect of the changes in prices and demands. The net effect of a devaluation on the balance-of-payments current account depends on the sum of the beneficial effect on export revenue and the, possibly harmful, effect on import revenues. Initially, a devaluation may worsen a deficit on the current account of the balance of payments, as the domestic expenditure on imports increases and the changes in demands for exports and imports only take place slowly. This effect is known as the J-CURVE. In the long run, the changes in demands may improve the current account. A devaluation implies a worsening of the TERMS OF TRADE and a consequent reduction in the real NATIONAL INCOME of the country. For the current account to improve, there must be unemployed resources in the economy, which can be used to produce more exports and more substitutes for imports. The use of these unemployed resources will raise the real income of the country and, possibly, offset the effect of the decline in the terms of trade on real income. An improvement in the current account of the balance of payments resulting from a devaluation may be offset by the increase in import prices leading to INFLATION, which reverses the beneficial price effects of the devaluation. The fear of devaluation leads to a flight of CAPITAL, as it will reduce the foreign currency value of domestic holdings of capital. Devaluation may increase the confidence in a currency and improve the capital account of the balance of payments, though, if the devaluation is thought to be small, capital may still be moved out of the country. The level of the exchange rate is often linked to national prestige and governments have often been reluctant to devalue.　　　　　J.P.

Bibl: B. Sodersten, *International Economics* (London, 2nd ed., 1980).

development area. An area designated for special economic assistance, usually because of an above average level of UNEMPLOYMENT. The assistance can take various forms: financial incentives to firms locating in the area; relaxation of the controls on firms within or moving into the area; and stricter control on expansion of firms outside the area. It has been suggested that the past use of these instruments of REGIONAL PLANNING may not be justified in that the estimated resulting benefits, usually greater employment, are low relative to the costs.　　　　　J.P.

Bibl: H. Armstrong and J. Taylor, *Regional Economic Policy and its Analysis* (Oxford, 1978).

Development Assistance Committee (DAC), see under OECD.

development economics. This in a broad sense comprises all work on the growth of incomes per head, including that of the CLASSICAL ECONOMIC THEORISTS from Smith to Mill. However, many post-KEYNESIAN models of growth have in mind developed economies; and these models may be excluded. Development economics embraces the whole transition from poor primitive to modern industrial

societies. It includes such economic theorizing as seeks to explain the co-existence of rich and poor nations; less certainly it can be held to include grand theories of historical development, or the rise and fall of civilizations, which (except for MARXIST theory in its strictly economic interpretation of history) draw their explanations of economic change predominantly from politics, PSYCHOLOGY, and SOCIOLOGY; taken perhaps too widely it can include any economic HISTORIOGRAPHY with some theoretical content. By convention, however, development economics seems increasingly to mean simply the study of the characteristics, problems, and policies of the less developed economies as they are today: a subject in which there has been a tremendous upsurge of interest since 1945. Some economists take the view that the concepts and analytical tools developed in the West are inappropriate to this study, and have demanded a new ECONOMICS. The majority, probably, believe that the concepts are so elastic, and the tools so adaptable, that this demand makes little sense. The facts and the problems are to some extent characteristically different, and different assumptions are appropriate; but these differences give rise to special theoretical offshoots rather than to new principles. (See also ECONOMIC DEVELOPMENT.)　　　　　I.M.D.L.

Bibl: G.M. Meier, *Leading Issues in Economic Development* (London and New York, 2nd ed., 1970).

developmental biology. The study of all aspects of the development of organisms, from the molecular events underlying the differentiation of CELLS to the patterns of multiplication, growth, and movement of masses of cells that create TISSUES and entire organisms.　　　　　E.O.W.

developmental cycle. Concept developed by Meyer Fortes (*The Developmental Cycle in Domestic Groups*, 1958) to understand the changes which take place within the DOMESTIC GROUP. It provided as a concept the link between the individual and society. Fortes analysed the domestic group as the focus of social reproduction, where members move through a cycle of recognized ROLES at different stages of their lives. The cycle is expressed in spatial or residential arrangements. Fortes identified three phases in the developmental cycle. (1) Expansion, the period of marriage, birth and rearing of children. (2) Fission, marriage of children, departure from the domestic group and the establishment of a new conjugal unit. (3) Replacement, death of parents and birth of children to second generation. Relations between individuals within the domestic group may be reflected in its different stages of development. For example, the tension between father and son over succession may be lessened through the establishment of separate residence.　　　A.G.

Bibl: A. Barnard and A. Good, *Research Practices in the Study of Kinship* (London, 1984); J.P. Parry, *Caste and Kinship in Kangra* (London, 1979); R. Netting *et al.*, eds., *Comparative and Historical Studies of the Domestic Group* (Berkeley, 1984).

developmental linguistics. A branch of LINGUISTICS which studies the acquisition of language in children; also sometimes known as *developmental psycholinguistics*. The subject involves the application of linguistic theories and techniques of analysis to child language data, in order to provide a precise description of patterns of development, and an explanation of norms and variations encountered, both within individual languages and universally.　　　D.C.

Bibl: P. Fletcher and M. Garman (eds.), *Language Acquisition* (Cambridge, 1986).

developmental psychology. The study of the changes in behaviour which typically take place with age, together with an analysis of their causes. Until now it has been mainly concerned with the behaviour of children as they grow older (and hence is widely known as *child psychology*); recently, however, there have been suggestions that psychologists should concern themselves with 'life-span developmental psychology', i.e. with changes in behaviour occurring in adulthood as well as in childhood. Broadly speaking, there have been three main approaches to the study of development: observational, psychometric, and experimental.

(1) The first significant studies of chil-

dren's behaviour were *observational*; particularly notable were studies based on the observation of infants, and those by Dietrich Tiedemann, Charles Darwin, and Jean Piaget still provide some of the basic data on the emotional responses and the changes in SENSORY-MOTOR coordination which typically occur in the first few years of life. In the second quarter of this century, however, enthusiasm for the observational approach began to wane, and it remained low until comparatively recently when two events led to a notable revival. The first was the remarkable reawakening of interest in the acquisition of language (a subject well suited to observational study) which stemmed from developments in LINGUISTIC and PSYCHOLINGUISTIC theory. The second was the success of ETHOLOGY, with its observational studies of animals in their natural HABITATS.

(2) the PSYCHOMETRIC approach also had an early place in the history of developmental psychology. It provides extremely convenient measuring instruments for comparing one child's present abilities and future prospects with another's, but makes very little theoretical contribution to the understanding of development.

(3) In the *experimental* method (see also EXPERIMENTAL PSYCHOLOGY) the aim is to study different aspects of behaviour, e.g. babies' understanding of the permanence of objects which disappear from their view, or young children's understanding of the concept of number, or the extent to which children imitate AGGRESSION. This approach has proved its ability to provoke and to test some interesting hypotheses about development, such as the PIAGETIAN claim that children only gradually acquire the most basic of logical abilities, or the suggestion put forward at different times by L.S. Vigotsky and by J.S. Bruner that the acquisition of language transforms the child's understanding of his environment. Sometimes, however, the experimental situations are so artificial that the behaviour which takes place in them may be quite unrelated to behaviour in ordinary life. The solution to this problem is perhaps to combine as far as possible observation and experiment.

See also EDUCATION; PSYCHOSEXUAL DEVELOPMENT.　　　P.E.B.

developmental theory. Developmental theory owes its greatest debt to the work of Karl Abraham on the development of the LIBIDO. Although there are many relevant passages in Freud which could be interpreted as asserting the usefulness of such a theory, the bases of the theory were developed by Abraham. The central idea that organizes most varieties of developmental theory is that there is a linear development of successive phases whereby at each phase one particular erotogenic zone dominates the libidinal life of the child, the first two phases being the oral phase and the anal phase. Pathologies can thus be accounted for in terms of a FIXATION at one particular phase of development, or a REGRESSION to such a phase, such that any progression to the supposedly healthy genital stage is blocked, and instead of this, one particular DRIVE seems to freeze the subject at the phase in question. Abraham also stressed how SADISM gets attached to the developmental phases, in such a way that we can view each phase as having two or more substages. Lacan's work, however, has shown the implausibility of the developmental MODEL, particularly in its stress on a linear development, since any serious consideration of what Freud called 'deferred action', the process by which present events give a meaning to past events, would show that the phases in question would take on their values not just synchronically, but at later times in the supposed development of the child. On a more general level, since PSYCHOANALYSIS in the LACANIAN orientation is concerned with structure, it is less concerned with the development of the child, than with the structural relations between the SUBJECT, the OBJECT(a) and the signifying chain.   D.L.

Bibl: K. Abraham, *A Short Study of the Development of the Libido, viewed in the light of Mental Disorders* (London, 1924).

deviance (or *deviancy*). In SOCIOLOGY (for deviance in LINGUISTICS see under ACCEPTABILITY), social behaviour that is subjected to social sanctions, including legal sanctions. Deviant behaviour is thus defined in terms of social attitudes rather than intrinsic quality, and includes, as defined at present, not only crime but such things as HOMOSEXUALITY, mental illness, and even deviance from GROUP NORMS that may themselves be deviant from more widely accepted NORMS. The *sociology of deviance* has developed, as a discipline, partly as a reaction (especially in the U.S.A.) against traditional CRIMINOLOGY, with its emphasis on positivistic multicausal theories of crime, and partly against consensus theories of social order.   T.M.

Bibl: I. Taylor, P. Walton, and J. Young, *The New Criminology* (London and New York, 1973); S. Box, *Deviance, Reality and Society* (London and New York, 1981); D. Downes and P. Rock, *Understanding Deviance* (Oxford, 1982).

deviationism. A tendency within COMMUNIST parties to stray from the official Party line. Such tendencies are branded either as RIGHT or LEFT deviationism, depending on whether they advocate a 'harder' or 'softer' policy. In the former case, it is sometimes branded as *adventurism*; in the latter, as *capitulationism*. In doctrinal terms, deviationists are also often described as displaying *dogmatism* (i.e. sticking to the letter of MARXISM) or REVISIONISM (i.e. violating the spirit of REVOLUTIONARY theory). The adherence to one world-wide Party line was possible only as long as communism was a unitary movement. With the emergence of communist POLYCENTRISM, deviationism has remained a political offence leading to factionalism. It is therefore prohibited in accordance with the LENINIST principle of DEMOCRATIC CENTRALISM. Intra-Party polemics have gone beyond the charges of deviationism and in many cases (particularly in the Sino-Soviet dispute) have produced mutual charges of the betrayal of Marxism.   L.L.

diachronic. Term coined about 1913 by Ferdinand de Saussure (see SAUSSURIAN) to refer to the study of LINGUISTIC change or evolution, as opposed to *synchronic* which covers 'everything that relates to the static side of our science'. The terms were borrowed by sociologists and anthropologists to distinguish two different approaches in their own fields. Compare the distinction between 'process' and STRUCTURE made by American sociologists, and that between *conjoncture* and *structure* made by French historians. P.B.

dialect geography, see DIALECTOLOGY.

dialectic. A theory of the nature of LOGIC which is also a theory of the STRUCTURE and development of the world. It was devised by the post-Kantian IDEALISTS, starting with Fichte and reaching a culmination in the philosophy of Hegel. It was taken over from Hegel by Marx and put to rather different uses. Kant had distinguished two aspects within logic: (1) analytic, or the logic of understanding, which, applied to the data of sensation, yields knowledge of the natural, phenomenal world; and (2) dialectic, or the logic of reasoning, which operates independently of experience and purports, erroneously, to give knowledge of the TRANSCENDENT order of *noumena* (or 'things-in-themselves'). Hegel interpreted the dialectic operations of reason, not as concerned with the transcendent, but with reality as a whole, rather than its abstracted, mutilated parts, and thus as giving truer and deeper knowledge than the analytic understanding, which he saw as adequate for NATURAL SCIENCE and the practical concerns of everyday life but not for PHILOSOPHY. Furthermore, taking reality to be of the nature of the mind or spirit, he supposed its activities and development to be of an essentially rational or logical kind. Standard or analytic logic, on this view, is rigid and abstract, a matter of fixed connections and exclusive oppositions. Dialectical logic sees contradictions as fruitful collisions of ideas from which a higher truth may be reached by way of SYNTHESIS. Marx took over the view that dialectical thinking is necessary if true knowledge is to be obtained, and held the process of history to be a dialectical development in which mankind progresses through the clashes of contradictory social systems. A.Q.

Bibl: K.R. Popper, *Conjectures and Refutations* (New York, 2nd ed., 1968; London, 3rd ed., 1969).

dialectical materialism. A term which came into prominence in the generation after Marx's death to describe the philosophy of MARXISM as opposed to its historical or political aspects. Marx had applied the DIALECTIC to social and historical processes; it was Engels, in such widely popular works as *Anti-Dühring*, who extended the scope of the dialectic to the natural world and proclaimed a series of completely general scientific laws which governed nature and society alike. These fundamental laws were: the transformation of quantity into quality whereby gradual quantitative change culminated in a revolutionary change of quality; the interpenetration of opposites whereby any entity is constituted by an unstable unity of contradictions; and the negation of the negation whereby any negative force is in its turn negated in a process of historical development which conserves something of the negated elements.

The term dialectical materialism was not itself used by Marx or Engels. It was popularized by Lenin's teacher Plekhanov and became the official philosophy of the Soviet Union. Although it appeared to endow Marxist social and economic theories with the growing prestige of natural science, many have thought the assimilation of the methods of natural and social science implied in dialectical materialism to be untrue to the Hegelian and HUMANIST aspects of Marx's thought. D.T.M.

Bibl: Z. Jordan, *The Evolution of Dialectical Materialism* (London, 1967); R. Norman and S. Sayers, *Hegel, Marx and Dialectic* (Brighton, 1980); G. Wetter, *Dialectical Materialism* (London, 1958).

dialectical theatre, see EPIC THEATRE.

dialectical theology, see CRISIS THEOLOGY.

dialectology (or *dialect geography*). A branch of LINGUISTICS which studies local linguistic variation within a language. Dialects are normally defined in geographical terms (*regional* dialects), but the concept has been extended to cover socioeconomic variation (CLASS dialects) and occasionally other types of linguistic VARIETY (e.g. *occupational* dialect). There is therefore some overlap with SOCIOLINGUISTICS. Within dialectology, a distinction is often made between *rural* and *urban* studies. There is also a distinction between the *traditional* dialectology of the early language atlases, with its emphasis on ISOGLOSSES, and more recent studies of systems of dialect contrast, using techniques of structural linguistics, and known as *structural* dialectology.   D.C.

Bibl: P. Trudgill, *On Dialect* (Oxford, 1983).

dialysis, see under HAEMODIALYSIS.

dianetics. A mechanistic technique of therapy developed in 1948 by L. Ron Hubbard. It is based upon the belief that memories reach back before the moment of conception to previous lives or existences even in non-human forms or on planets elsewhere in the universe, and that if these memories can be recalled without pain or emotion an individual will be freed to develop his personality and 'beingness'. Dianetics later developed into SCIENTOLOGY.   M.BE.

diathermy. Local heating from high-frequency current used (1) in treatment of soft-TISSUE disorders ('muscular rheumatism'), when short-wave diathermy may bring relief of symptoms even when their cause is not fully understood; (2) for chronic deep-seated infections, when the rise of temperature is thought to accelerate healing — since the advent of ANTIBIOTICS this has become a less important method of treatment, but is still valuable, particularly in pelvic infections in women; (3) instead of ligatures, for coagulation of smaller blood vessels in surgical operations.   D.A.P.

dictatorship. Originally an office, created in times of emergency by the classical Roman republic, which conferred on a single individual complete authority over the State and the armed forces for a limited period — usually six months. By transfer, the rule of any individual other than a king who enjoys complete authority, unchecked by constitutional limits, over a state. In recent history, dictatorships can be divided into personal tyrannies, usually backed by the armed forces (e.g. in Latin American and Arab countries), and TOTALITARIAN regimes, where the dictator is the charismatic leader (see CHARISMA) of a totalitarian movement.
D.C.W.

Bibl: M. Latey, *Tyranny* (London, 1969); B. Moore Jr, *Social Origins of Democracy and Dictatorship* (New York, 1966; London, 1984).

dictatorship of the proletariat. A MARXIST concept used to refer to the transitional period between the successful proletarian revolution and the advent of a COMMUNIST society. Marx himself mentioned the term only rarely but seems to have thought (at least at the time) that the Paris Commune of 1871 was an example of such a dictatorship in which direct DEMOCRACY could be ensured by the election, revocability and mandating of all officials whether legislative, executive or judiciary. It should be noted that Marx's notion of dictatorship did not have the contemporary connotation of arbitrary tyranny, but harked back to the classical Roman concept of *dictatura* which was both republican and constitutional. The idea of the DICTATORSHIP of the PROLETARIAT as implementing direct participatory democracy was taken up in Lenin's *State and Revolution*. But circumstances surrounding the birth of the Soviet Union meant that, in practice, the dictatorship of the proletariat came to mean little more than the use of repression by the state over the whole of society in the name of the proletariat. Because of the embarrassing connotations thus acquired, several communist parties in CAPITALIST countries have recently dropped mention of the dictatorship of the proletariat from their programmes.   D.T.M.

Bibl: E. Balibar, *On the Dictatorship of the Proletariat* (London, 1977); H. Draper, *Karl Marx's Theory of Revolution*, vol. 2 (New York, 1977); B. Wolfe, *Marxism: 100 Years in the Life of a Doctrine* (London, 1965).

didactic play, see LEHRSTÜCK.

diet. Strictly, whatever we eat is our diet; more generally the term refers to modified diets, e.g. low-sugar (for diabetics), slimming diets and diets modified for various physiological reasons. Diets may also be modified for religious or moral reasons. *Vegetarians* (who do eat eggs and milk, i.e. ovo-lacto-vegetarians) and *vegans* (who eat no animal products) may do so for moral reasons, or because they believe that animal products are harmful to health, or because the production of animal foods is much less efficient than plant foods so they assist world food supplies. There is no evidence that these diets in general are better or worse than a mixed diet although on the benefit side it is currently considered preferable to consume more fruits and vegetables and less saturated fat, while on the risk side there have been deaths reported among vegans due to a deficiency of vitamin B12 (found in animal foods). There are diets linked to religion, such as the avoidance of pork, or meat, or of all foods grown below the ground (Jains). There are fad diets without any basis such as those involving the consumption of only raw foods or white foods or fruits — which can be harmful if they restrict nutrient intake. Some diets are based on philosophies such as the ZEN MACROBIOTIC diet, which is an American version of what is claimed to be eastern mysticism. This divides all foods, and all aspects of life, into *yin* and *yang* which must be balanced; deeper involvement in the philosophy limits the foods that may be eaten and has resulted in severe MALNUTRITION.   A.E.B.

dietary fibre, see CARBOHYDRATES.

dietary goals. Public health objective widely agreed as conducive to improved health, particularly in relation to coronary heart disease. The goals include reducing the consumption of fats and sugar, and increasing that of starchy foods, dietary fibre, fruits and vegetables.   A.E.B.

dietary supplements. Partly purified or synthetic concentrates of dietary essentials — VITAMINS, minerals, AMINO ACIDS, PROTEINS.   A.E.B.

differential calculus, see under CALCULUS; DERIVATIVE.

differential coefficient, see DERIVATIVE.

differential equation. In MATHEMATICS, a RELATION, expressed as an EQUATION between the value of a FUNCTION f at a given ARGUMENT or arguments, the argument(s), and one or more of the DERIVATIVES. A *solution* of the equation is function which satisfies the relation for all arguments within some given interval; in general such a solution is only uniquely determined if certain *boundary conditions* on the behaviour of f at the ends of the interval are also specified. The fundamental laws of many branches of PHYSICS (e.g. DYNAMICS, ELECTROMAGNETISM, general RELATIVITY) can be concisely expressed by differential equations.   R.G.

differential psychology. The branch of PSYCHOLOGY, pioneered by Francis Galton (1822-1911) and greatly developed in this century, that studies differences between the psychological characteristics of one person and another, especially by PSYCHOMETRIC techniques designed to yield quantitative measures of such differences.   I.M.L.H.

Bibl: A. Anastasi, *Differential Psychology* (London and New York, 3rd ed., 1958) and *Psychological Testing* (London and New York, 1982).

differential threshold, see under THRESHOLD.

differentiation. In EMBRYOLOGY, the process in the course of which the CELLS derived by MITOSIS from the fertilized egg turn into the various different cells of the body. Differentiation is always a realization of the genetic potentialities of the cells that undergo it. Its detailed mechanism is not yet known.   P.M.

diffraction. In PHYSICS, the spreading of waves into the shadows behind objects or into apertures placed in their path, which occurs because of the interference between waves from different parts of the unobstructed region. In the case of sound waves, for example, diffraction enables us to hear round corners, and causes the sound from wind instruments to radiate in all directions instead of in a narrow beam directed forwards. With light, diffraction causes the pattern observed when a street lamp is viewed through the fine mesh of an umbrella. In the case of the waves associated with matter according to QUANTUM MECHANICS (see WAVE-PARTICLE DUALITY), diffraction is the basis of Heisenberg's UNCERTAINTY PRINCIPLE. See also

227

DIFFUSENESS

ELECTRON DIFFRACTION; OPTICS; X-RAY DIFFRACTION. M.V.B.

diffuseness, see under PATTERN VARIABLES.

diffusion.

(1) In CHEMISTRY, an atomic process by which substances may mix or spread. Thus in gases the MOLECULES move almost independently and diffusive motion is hindered only by random collisions between different molecules. In a solid or liquid, diffusion can only occur when an ATOM or molecule acquires sufficient ENERGY to jump into a nearby position, and eventually these atomic movements can lead to a change in form of the solid (as in SINTERING) or to a blurring of the interface between two solids or two liquids. In liquids and even gases, mixing may be produced much more efficiently in practice by stirring or CONVECTION than by diffusion. B.F.

(2) In archaeology, the spread of some aspect (whether material or non-material) of a CULTURE from its place of origin into a new area. In the early years of this century *diffusionism* was taken to ludicrous extremes, particularly by W. Perry and Elliot Smith in their support for the belief that all ideas were developed in the East and diffused to the rest of the world. Before the development of RADIOCARBON DATING the validity of diffusionist thought could not easily be tested, but with the appearance of large numbers of absolute dates it is now clear that independent invention was more common in the ancient world than was hitherto thought possible. There is at present a tendency to over-react against diffusion as an explanation for culture change. B.C.

(3) In ANTHROPOLOGY, the idea that cultural features have their origins in a single source. At the beginning of the 20th century *diffusionism* was an important theory for understanding cultural diversity. Diversity was understood to have resulted from the diffusion of traits from a centre and this movement was traced in a manner akin to the way ripples may be traced from a stone being dropped into a pool of water. W. H. R. Rivers, a member of the 1898 Torres Straits expedition, was a leading diffusionist. He had fallen under the influence of the ideas of Perry and Elliot Smith and asserted that ancient Egypt was the original source of civilization. Later anthropologists believe that Rivers's increasing insistence upon the idea of diffusion obscured his much more important and original work in KINSHIP.

A.G.

Bibl: Ian Langham, *W. H. R. Rivers and His Cambridge Disciples in the Development of Kinship Studies 1898-1931* (Dordrecht, 1981).

(4) Geographers use the word (often qualified by the adjective *spatial*) in much the same sense as (2). They have shown special interest in identifying the centres of innovation, the channels of spread, and the barriers to transmission. Theoretical MODELS have been built which allow limited prediction of future patterns of spatial diffusion. Applied studies are designed to help to determine and limit unwanted spread (e.g. of an epidemic disease) and to encourage desirable innovations (e.g. adoption by farmers of improved strains of corn). A distinction is commonly drawn between *contagious diffusion*, in which the spatial pattern of spread is continuous, and *cascade diffusion*, in which the transmission is via a network of discrete points (e.g. villages, towns, and cities). P.H.

Bibl: T. Hägerstrand, tr. A. Pred, *Innovation Diffusion as a Spatial Process* (Chicago, 1967).

digital computer, see under COMPUTER.

digital music. Music consists of waveforms which can be broken down by an ANALOGUE TO DIGITAL CONVERTER into a series of numbers representing the successive dynamics of the soundwave. The number of times the waveform is analysed per second is the sampling rate. The series of numbers can then be stored and then reproduced and converted back into sound (see COMPACT DISC) or manipulated in various ways by computer processors, e.g. to simulate reverberation (see SOUND SAMPLING). B.CO.

digital-to-analogue converter. In COMPUTING, a device which changes the representation of a numerical value from a digital ENCODING (in which it might be manipulated by a digital COMPUTER for example) to a particular value of some variable physical quantity (usually an electrical potential), as used in analogue computers or to interact with other physical processes (e.g. by regulating part of an industrial plant, or driving a loudspeaker). There are *analogue-to-digital converters*, too. J.E.S.

diglossia. In SOCIOLINGUISTICS, a situation in which two very different varieties of a language co-occur throughout a speech community, each with a distinct range of social functions. Both varieties are standardized to some degree, and have usually been given special names by native speakers. Sociolinguists generally refer to one variety as 'high', the other as 'low', the distinction broadly corresponding to a difference in formality. Diglossic situations can be found in Greek (high: Katharevousa; low: Dhimotiki), Arabic (high: Classical; low: Colloquial), and Swiss German (high: Hochdeutsch; low: Schweizerdeutsch). D.C.
Bibl: P. Trudgill, *Sociolinguistics* (Harmondsworth, 1984).

dilemma, see under ANTINOMY.

dilution of labour. The assignment to other workers of parts of the work customarily performed only by skilled workers, or the employment on skilled work of persons who have not passed through the course of training, usually apprenticeship, customarily required for admission to that work; more generally, the assignment to other workers of work previously reserved by custom to a particular category of workers. The issue arose in the U.K. during World War I, when the shortage of craftsmen relative to the demand in engineering and shipbuilding prompted management to concentrate the time of craftsmen on those parts of their customary work that they alone could perform, and to advance semi-skilled persons to do skilled work. In both world wars it was provided for that the customary lines of demarcation should be restored after the war. In PRODUCTIVITY BARGAINING dilution of labour occurs as tasks are reallocated across customary lines of demarcation. E.H.P.B.; J.P.

dimension. Roughly speaking, if a situation can be mathematically described by specifying *n* NUMBERS independently, then the totality of possible situations has *n dimensions* and the situation has *n degrees of freedom*. In RELATIVITY theory, for example, an 'event' is specified by 3 space COORDINATES and one time coordinate, so that SPACE-TIME is 4-dimensional. Various elaborations of the concept occur in GEOMETRY, TOPOLOGY, and the theory of VECTOR spaces. R.G.
Bibl: G.A. Gamow, *1,2,3,....x* (New York, 1955; London, 1962).

diminished responsibility. In English law, a mental condition which, since the Homicide Act of 1957, can be pleaded by any person charged with murder, and which in murder cases has largely replaced the old plea of insanity. The Act provides that a person charged with murder can be convicted only of manslaughter if he was 'suffering from such abnormality of mind as substantially impaired his mental responsibility'. This means that he may be considered only for manslaughter although he both knew that he had killed another person and that his act was illegal, if his capacity to act in accordance with rational judgement was substantially impaired. H.L.A.H.

diminishing productivity of a factor; diminishing returns... In ECONOMICS, the circumstances in which equal increases in the use of one FACTOR OF PRODUCTION successively smaller increases in output — the use of all other factors is held constant. This phenomenon is identical to the concept of a declining marginal product of a factor. It is important because, in NEOCLASSICAL ECONOMIC THEORY it forms the basis of the MARGINAL PRODUCTIVITY THEORY OF WAGES. It has been enshrined in an ECONOMIC LAW: the law of diminishing returns of a factor. J.P.
Bibl: D. Begg *et al.*, *Economics* (London, 1984).

Dinge-an-sich, see NOUMENA.

Dionysian cultures, see APOLLONIAN AND DIONYSIAN CULTURES.

diophantine equations, see under NUMBER THEORY.

diploid (noun or adjective). A CELL containing two sets of CHROMOSOMES, one set inherited from each parent. The body cells of man and of most higher plants and animals are diploid. Contrasted on the one hand with HAPLOID, on the other with POLYPLOID.   J.M.S.

diplomacy. Has been variously defined as the 'application of intelligence and tact to the conduct of relations between nations' (Satow) and the 'management of international relations by negotiation' (*OED* and Nicolson). It is carried out generally by diplomats up to ambassadorial level through foreign ministries and guided by a code of protocol since the Vienna Congress of 1815. Major elements of diplomacy are communication and negotiation, leading to Sir Henry Wotton (1568-1639) describing the diplomat as 'an honest man sent abroad to lie for his country', a remark which cost him his position. Styles of diplomacy vary, with Nicolson dividing diplomats into 'shopkeepers' and 'warriors'. Since 1918 there has been a certain opening up of diplomacy in what was termed the 'new diplomacy' and which sees its major expression in multilateral parliamentary diplomacy in the UNO. Much of diplomacy is still bilateral however, and often on economic issues. The diplomat has lost much of his autonomy with the growth of rapid communications and the complexity of much technical negotiation. 'Shuttle' diplomacy, as by Haig in the FALKLANDS WAR, and SUMMIT DIPLOMACY are now often tried to settle particularly difficult and sensitive political issues by leaders themselves.   A.W.
  Bibl: H. Nicolson, *Diplomacy* (London, 1939); A. Eban, *The New Diplomacy* (New York, 1983).

dipole. Any pair of small objects close together, some of whose properties may be described by quantities having opposite signs. Examples: (1) a MOLECULE where the positive and negative charges are separated (e.g. water); (2) a radio aerial consisting of two antennae radiating out of PHASE; (3) a HYDRODYNAMIC system made up of a source and a neighbouring 'sink' of fluid; (4) a small magnet with its north and south poles (see MAGNETISM).   M.V.B.

direct action. ANARCHISTS have always advocated unconventional, unconstitutional and non-parliamentary political action of one sort or another. The political general strike of ANARCHO-SYNDICALIST theory was one such form. Non-violent direct action or *satyagraha* was a feature of Gandhi's campaigns of CIVIL DISOBEDIENCE; the same insistence on non-violence marked the American CIVIL RIGHTS campaigns of the 1950s and 60s, whose techniques of 'sit-downs' and 'sit-ins' were adopted by protesters against the VIETNAM War in later years. NON-VIOLENT direct action is likely to be successful only against authorities who are easily embarrassed by having to resort to force or legal suppression, as the British were in India. This limitation may explain why so many radicals who begin with a commitment to non-violent direct action either drift back into conventional politics or move further towards insurrectionary politics instead.
                                A.R.
  Bibl: A. Carter, *Direct Action and Liberal Democracy* (London, 1973).

direct marketing. TECHNOLOGY now permits the gathering of a great deal of relevant information, from a large number of diverse sources, about every individual. While this raises the issue of individual rights to privacy, for the MARKETING man, the opportunity is a welcome one and, potentially, a cost effective one for the consumer. By profiling customers, and seeking like characteristics elsewhere, it is now possible to target sales prospects far more efficiently. Responsive television, radio and press ADVERTISING, together with piggy-bank mailings, inserts and direct mailing, are all being increasingly utilized in the process of eliminating the middle-man, and affording closer contact with customers.   T.S.

direct realism, see REALISM, NAIVE.

direct rule. A term which in its commonest application refers to the suspension of the provincial Stormont-based government of Northern Ireland in March 1972, and the imposition of greater control by the central government of the United Kingdom. The move was stimulated by the escalation of violence between members of the province's Catholic and Protestant communities, and by the Catholic perception of the Stormont government as illegitimate and discriminatory. Direct rule was intended to reintroduce order and to demonstrate fairness in policies regarding jobs, housing etc. Direct rule has been accused of being no more than extended CRISIS MANAGEMENT; the charge is too crude, but since 1972 moves to restore a greater degree of autonomy have made little progress.   S.R.

Bibl: K. Boyle and T. Hadden, *Ireland: A Positive Proposal* (Harmondsworth and New York, 1985).

dirigisme. A policy of STATE intervention in economic affairs. As it does not necessarily imply direct control, it can coexist with CAPITALIST, SOCIALIST, and many other systems of property ownership. *Dirigisme,* a term originally used to characterize French interventionist policy in the 17th century, has to some extent continued to guide French official economic thinking — and has strongly clashed with the German neo-liberal (see ECONOMIC LIBERALISM) post-war approach.   S.BR.

disappeared, the, see under STATE TERROR.

disarmament. A form of ARMS CONTROL, which may be unilateral, but which normally implies the promotion of international security by the MULTILATERAL reduction of existing military forces and weapons to some agreed minimum with provision for inspection and enforcement of the agreement. Proposals for what has become known as 'G.C.D.', i.e. disarmament that would be *general* (applying to all countries) and *comprehensive* (applying to all categories of forces and weapons) were discussed desultorily, first by the LEAGUE OF NATIONS between 1927 and 1934, and then by UNO in the decade up to 1962; neither was able to solve the problems of defining equivalence of force reductions or the subsequent issues of inspection and enforcement. Examples of *multilateral* but *partial* disarmament are the Washington Naval Treaties of 1922

and 1930. Examples of *unilateral* disarmament are the rapid demobilization of the American and other armed forces after both world wars, and the gradual reduction of the Soviet forces after the death of Stalin.   A.F.B.

Bibl: B.H. Weston (ed.), *Towards Nuclear Disarmament and Global Security: A Search for Alternatives* (London, 1984); J.A. Joyce, *The War Machine: The Case Against the Arms Race* (London, 1980).

disc store. A form of computer STORE in which the information is stored on rotating discs with magnetic surfaces with read/write heads on arms which can move across them. A disc store is a form of backing store with an enormous capacity but a relatively long ACCESS TIME. *Floppy discs* are made of flexible plastic and are enclosed in a protective cardboard case. They are extremely cheap and portable, and are therefore extensively used with PERSONAL COMPUTERS and for transferring information between machines (e.g. for the sale of SOFTWARE). They have, however, lower speed, capacity and reliability than other kinds of disc. *RAM discs* are not discs at all, but large SEMICONDUCTOR STORES. They are organized, however, so that the user, and sometimes even the OPERATING SYSTEM, can treat them exactly as though they were disc stores (except that they work much faster), because to do so, though more restricting, is cheaper than altering all the PROGRAMS concerned to use the new store directly.   C.S.; J.E.S.

discipline history. In the history of science, 'discipline history' draws attention to the fact that knowledge advances not simply through a sequence of abstract, intellectual theories, but through the successive formation and reformation of demarcated bodies of knowledge — that is, the different sciences, such as PHYSICS, CHEMISTRY, and more narrowly, BIOCHEMISTRY or MOLECULAR BIOLOGY. Far from these disciplines being 'timeless', they have their own history. Thus coherent and organized sciences of 'BIOLOGY' and 'GEOLOGY' date only from the beginning of the 19th century. Before then their subject matters were either comprehended within other disciplinary frameworks (e.g. natural history) or were considered scientifically unimportant. Molecular biology arose as a distinct science only after World War II; GENETIC ENGINEERING is essentially a development of the last decade. Recognition of the importance of disciplinary boundaries as stimuli to scientific development (and, perhaps more frequently, as hindrances to cross-fertilization) involves attention to the structure as much as to the content of science. It requires a grasp both of the wider philosophical allegiances of science and of its socio-economic dimensions.

R.P.

Bibl: B. Barnes, *Interests and the Growth of Knowledge* (London, 1977).

discontinuity. The opposite of CONTINUITY.

R.G.

discount rate, see under BANK RATE.

discounted cash flow. A method used to assist the MANAGEMENT decision-maker in the evaluation of capital investment projects (see CAPITAL; INVESTMENT). Investment opportunities involve the flow of funds: capital payments out and net receipts from the venture in return. Simple comparison between the two gives a rate of return on the investment; but the earlier the return of funds the better. The DCF method takes the timing of funds-flow into account, by calculating the discount rate that is inherent in the expected funds-flow. The *net-present-value* method also takes the timing of the funds-flow into account, but calculates a present value of expected flows, at a standard DISCOUNTING rate, for assessing projects.

R.I.T.

Bibl: A.J. Merrett and A. Sykes, *The Finance and Analysis of Capital Projects* (London and New York, 1963).

discounting. In ECONOMICS, the procedure that values future costs and benefits. As it is usually assumed that individuals and society prefer a unit of consumption in the present, rather than in the future, a benefit or cost in the present is of greater value than if it occurs at a future date. From the viewpoint of the present, it is necessary to adjust, i.e. discount, future costs and benefits; the adjustment depending on when they occur. In order to value these costs

and benefits it is necessary to have a common measure: MONEY. The rate of discount that is most frequently used is the interest rate, after it is corrected for the effect of INFLATION. The difference of the suitably discounted benefits and costs is the *net present value*. Net present values are used as a criterion for judging between different investments, e.g. in COST-BENEFIT ANALYSIS. The choice of discount rate can make a large difference to net present values and the ranking of investment projects (see INTERNAL RATE OF RETURN).

J.P.

Bibl: R. Sugden and A. Williams, *The Principles of Practical Cost Benefit Analysis* (Oxford, 1978).

discourse.

(1) In LINGUISTICS, a stretch of language larger than the sentence. The term *discourse analysis* is often applied to the study of those linguistic effects — semantic, stylistic, syntactic — whose description needs to take into account sentence sequences as well as sentence structure.

D.C.

(2) The term has also become prominent in the work of recent French theorists such as Roland Barthes, Gérard Genette and especially Michel Foucault, whose *The Order of Things* (1966) focused not on texts or authors but on 'fields' such as economics or natural history and the conventions according to which they were classified and represented in particular periods. Major shifts in these conventions were to be excavated by Foucault by his method of 'intellectual archaeology'. The later Foucault placed more stress on relations between discourse and other social practices.

P.B.

discourse of power. A phrase associated with the work of Michel Foucault. In a number of brilliantly documented studies after 1961, Foucault analysed the ways in which apparently objective and natural structures in society, which privilege some and punish others for non-conformity, are in fact 'discourses of power'. Studies like *Madness and Civilisation* (1961), *The Order of Things* (1966), *The Birth of the Clinic* (1973), and above all *Discipline and Punish* (1975) elicit the various modes in which the subject is objectified according to the ruling interests of his or her society. Objectification of the subject can take various forms, perhaps the most dramatic being what Foucault calls 'dividing practices', the example he gives in 1961 being the isolation of the 'mad' in the very asylums which once housed the lepers; or the way that the criminal, who was tortured to death as a public entertainment in the 18th century, was numbed into conformity by solitary confinement and moral opprobrium in the 19th century, to become at last the object of medical and PSYCHIATRIC and PSYCHOANALYTIC expertise in the 20th century, when all guilt has been internalized and the patient is imprisoned in himself. A second mode of objectifying the subject comes about through the classifications and reifications of science and scientific discourse (*Words and Things,* 1966). Finally, in his recent work on *The History of Sexuality,* for instance, Foucault studies the way the subject, in an attempt to come to terms with the dominant POWER structures in his society, attempts to create a meaningful identity for himself. In all this, Foucault's main attention is not so much on the historical facts and contours themselves (though these are impressively vast) but on the discourse which Foucault detects as the real power behind the actual forms of domination. In an interview of 1977, Foucault admitted that he had not, at the time of writing *Madness and Civilisation,* or *Birth of the Clinic,* realized that he was writing about power as such: that was a realization made possible by the MAY EVENTS of 1968. Although it is difficult to 'place' Foucault's academic work, his major effect on philosophy, and on the social and human sciences, has been at the point where the 'objectivity' of a discipline was most proudly vaunted, or where the hidden nature of its participation in the discourse of power was suddenly made apparent. His brilliant debut in 1961 was an inspiration to EXISTENTIAL PSYCHIATRY in the 1960s and 1970s, when the controlling power of psychiatry as an institution was suddenly seen to be a part of the enforcement machinery of HEGEMONIC rationality. *The Birth of the Clinic,* too, threw into relief the extent to which the patient is turned into an object by the 'medical gaze', and deprived of his SUBJECTIVITY. In his later

work, Foucault emphasizes again and again that it is only by consistent vigilance and hard intellectual work in examining the hegemonic assumptions of our society that we can come to understand, and to control, our own discourse of power.

R.PO.

Bibl: A. Sheridan, *Michel Foucault, The Will to Truth* (London, 1980).

discovery procedure. In LINGUISTICS, a set of techniques which enable an investigator to derive the rules of a grammar from a CORPUS of utterances, with as little reference to INTUITION as possible. Chomsky has criticized BLOOMFIELDIAN linguistics for its preoccupation with discovery procedures at the expense of theoretical questions.

D.C.

disease, environmental causes of, see ENVIRONMENTAL CAUSES OF DISEASE.

disease model. A term widely used to depict a particular conception of illness widely held nowadays, particularly among the medical profession. It postulates that sickness is caused by particular pathogenic agents (germs, bacteria, viruses), typically regarded as invading the body from outside. Particular physical organs are attacked and somatic functions impaired. Health in turn is restored largely by physical intervention from outside (e.g. by surgery or drug therapies). The disease model thus regards sickness as essentially a mechanical defect of the body, largely independent of the 'MIND' or 'personality' of the sufferer. As such it is to be distinguished from HOLISTIC or PSYCHOSOMATIC models of health and sickness, which commonly regard illness as involving an expression of the mental state of the sufferer, as registering a malaise of the whole organism, and as dependent, to some degree, upon the cooperation of the sick person to overcome. The disease model was largely vindicated by the success of scientific medicine in overcoming infectious diseases through drugs such as antibiotics. Controversy still rages as to how far it is the proper way to conceptualize intractable diseases such as cancer. R.P.

Bibl: O. Temkin, 'Health and Disease', in *The Double Face of Janus* (Baltimore, 1977).

disengagement. A form of ARMS CONTROL, much discussed in the 1950s by European politicians and strategic writers (e.g. Anthony Eden, Hugh Gaitskell, Adam Rapacki, and the German Social Democratic Party) for reducing international tension in Europe by drawing back all non-indigenous forces or those equipped with NUCLEAR WEAPONS (Soviet, American, British, Canadian) from Central Europe while permitting the indigenous states of the area a controlled level of non-nuclear armament.   A.F.B.

Bibl: E. Hinterhoff, *Disengagement* (London, 1959).

disinflation, see under INFLATION.

disinhibition theory, see under DISPLACEMENT ACTIVITIES.

disintegration. The breaking-up of an atomic NUCLEUS during RADIOACTIVE decay or during a NUCLEAR REACTION.
M.V.B.

dislocation. A crystal DEFECT centred on a line. The two main types are the *edge dislocation*, where an extra plane of ATOMS has been inserted part-way into the crystal, and the *screw dislocation*, about which the planes of atoms are distributed like the steps of a spiral staircase. The mode of growth of crystals, and many of the mechanical properties of solids (such as CREEP), are determined by dislocations; because of this, they have been intensively studied in recent years, principally with the ELECTRON MICROSCOPE.   M.V.B.

displacement.

(1) In ETHOLOGY, the elicitation of an instinctive response by an inappropriate object or event or animal, consequent upon arousal of the INSTINCT to a degree that broadens the range of objects capable of releasing it (see RELEASER); see also DISPLACEMENT ACTIVITIES.

Bibl: I. Eibl-Eibesfeldt, tr. E. Klinghammer, *Ethology* (London and New York, 1970).

(2) In PSYCHOANALYSIS, the implication is of more 'purposeful' displacement, as when feelings of AGGRESSION are aroused by a powerful figure and expressed toward one less powerful in order to avoid retaliation — however unconscious the displacement may be. See also CONDENSATION.

(3) In literary theory, see CONDENSATION.   J.S.B.

displacement activities.

(1) In ETHOLOGY, a term applied to animals' movements which, to the observer who knows their primary function and causation, appear 'out of context'. Thus starlings preen their plumage under two specific and distinct sets of circumstances: (*a*) when it is wet or out of order, and (*b*) — the displacement activity — when their aggressive behaviour and withdrawal are elicited at the same time, and neither is shown in full. Displacement activities seem to occur most frequently either (*a*) when two wholly or partly incompatible behaviour systems are simultaneously elicited (as in the example of the starling), or (*b*) when a behaviour system is elicited, but is prevented from running its full course, by the absence of indispensable stimuli for the later phases or by physical prevention. Human instances of displacement activities include, in certain circumstances, scratching, lighting a cigarette, yawning, pacing up and down.

About the causation of displacement activities there are various theories, not necessarily incompatible. One, the *disinhibition theory*, is based on the fact that when one behaviour system (see INSTINCT) is strongly elicited it suppresses other systems; the theory posits that when two such systems are elicited simultaneously they suppress each other, including the suppressing effect that each normally exerts on third systems, and so allow such a system 'free rein'. Another theory, applicable to movements which belong to the rest-and-sleep systems, argues that the central NERVOUS SYSTEM compensates for the hyperexcitation caused by conflicting motivations by activating the sleep system with all its subsidiary movements.   N.T.

(2) The current popular application of the term to human activities which are 'out of context' merely in the sense that they are undertaken as an escape (conscious or otherwise) from some more urgently needed activity is not quite in line with ethological usage.   O.S.

displacement theory. An obsolete term for the theory of CONTINENTAL DRIFT.   M.L.

disposition. The property or state of a thing in which, if certain conditions are satisfied, certain predictable results will ensue. Elasticity, solubility, inflammability are PARADIGM CASES of dispositions in natural objects. For a thing to possess a certain disposition is, minimally, for some hypothetical PROPOSITION to be true of it. Philosophical BEHAVIOURISTS, notably Ryle, have held that the mental states and events we are aware of in ourselves and other people are really dispositions to behave in certain ways.   A.Q.

Bibl: G. Ryle, *The Concept of Mind* (London, 1949; New York, 1950), ch. 2.

dissociation. The spontaneous break-up of a chemical compound in EQUILIBRIUM conditions of temperature and pressure, or in solution. Normally dissociation occurs with an increase in temperature, for example when a gaseous MOLECULE dissociates to give two or more molecules or FREE RADICALS, but it also describes the process by which a neutral molecule forms IONS in solution.   B.F.

dissociation of sensibility. A phrase from T.S. Eliot's essay, 'The Metaphysical Poets' (1921). Having described the unity of feeling and thought in the poetry of the Metaphysicals ('A thought to Donne was an experience; it modified his sensibility'), Eliot suggests that after the 17th century 'a dissociation of sensibility set in, from which we have never recovered'. This 'dissociation', aggravated by the powerful examples of Milton and Dryden, manifested itself in a split between 'thinking' and 'feeling' whereby poets 'thought and felt by bits, unbalanced'. The theory defines well the special achievement of the Metaphysicals in their best poems, but should not be regarded as an event as real as the INDUSTRIAL REVOLUTION and as precise in its effects as a lobotomy. The truth is that 'dissociation of sensibility' has always been with us, and that 'unification of sensibility' is a rare phenomenon, not always possible and perhaps not always called for.   D.J.E.

dissonance, cognitive, see under COGNITIVE CONSONANCE.

distinctive feature, see under PHONEME.

distributed computing. The use of several COMPUTERS (physically close, or widely separated and communicating over a NETWORK) co-operating on a single task. The low cost of small computers (such as the TRANSPUTER) has increased the importance of this area. Its difficulties are caused because computers run at different speeds, and there are extra delays (and perhaps unreliabilities) in the communication; the PROGRAMS are therefore essentially NONDETERMINISTIC. Elaborate precautions are necessary to ensure that the co-operation is harmonious. For example, if several computers are together providing an airline reservation system, it is essential that no machine allocates a seat until it has established that none of the others is trying to do so too, and to resolve any such conflicts without everlasting deadlock.   J.E.S.

distribution.

(1) In STATISTICS and PROBABILITY THEORY, the set of values taken by a RANDOM VARIABLE, together with the associated probabilities. Thus, the experiment 'toss a fair coin twice' and the random variable 'number of heads' generate a distribution in which the values 0 and 2 each have probability (chance of occurring) equal to $1/4$ and the value 1 has the probability equal to $1/2$. The *distribution function* is the FUNCTION F such that if x is a value, then $F(x)$ is the probability that the random variable does not exceed x. The *probability density* is the derivative (slope) of F if this exists. Distributions arising empirically are often described roughly by a MEASURE OF LOCATION and possibly a measure of dispersion such as the VARIANCE. The *skewness* of a distribution is a measure of its asymmetry. Its *range* is the separation of its upper and lower extreme values (if meaningful) and the *mid-range* is the mid-point of this interval. The distribution given above is symmetrical about the value 1 and so has zero skewness, and its range is the interval whose endpoints are 0 and 2. Among the most important theoretical distributions are the NORMAL

235

(*Gaussian*) and POISSON distributions. See also EXPECTATION; MODE. R.SI.

(2) In LINGUISTICS, the range of contexts in which a linguistic unit (e.g. a WORD CLASS or PHONEME) can occur. Units which occur in the same set of contexts are said to have an *equivalent* distribution (e.g. the phenomes /h/ and /w/, which in English words occur only initially and medially); units which have no contexts in common are in *complementary* distribution (e.g. prefixes and suffixes). D.C.

Bibl: D. Crystal, *Linguistics* (Harmondsworth, 1985).

distribution map. In ARCHAEOLOGY, a map showing the spatial distribution (or DIFFUSION) of a CULTURE trait, e.g. a distinctive type of axe. It serves as a visual statement of a class of data for which an explanation is then sought. The more valuable distribution maps record both the presence and absence of the trait at every examined location. It has been said that distribution maps often reflect the distribution of field archaeologists. B.C.

distributive justice. A specific form of justice distinguished by Aristotle, which required the burdens and benefits of social life to be distributed among individuals proportionately according to merit and the strength of other prior claims. The expression is now frequently used for standards of fair distribution (not necessarily based on merit or prior claims) which should determine the extent of individual liberties, political rights, opportunities, and ownership of property. Various alternative philosophical bases, some of which, but not all, are utilitarian, have been proposed by social theorists for the principles of distributive justice. H.L.A.H.

Bibl: N. Rescher, *Distributive Justice* (Indianapolis, 1966); J. Rawls, *A Theory of Justice* (Cambridge, Mass., 1971; London, 1972).

divergence, see under CONVERGENCE (sense 1).

divergers, see under CONVERGERS.

divination. Procedure to discover information about the past, present and future or the means to ascertain the cause of illness and misfortune. It is carried out by an individual specially appointed or trained: an oracle, diviner or medium. Divination may involve communication with the gods and spirits, usually through possession (see SPIRIT POSSESSION). It may concern the ordering of forces that operate in the world (geomancy or horoscope). Divination is usually a RITUAL occasion and in the case of sickness or misfortune it often involves the manipulation of certain objects to discover the cause: the use of oracles, the throwing of dice, the dissection of a chicken. A.G.

Bibl: E.M. Ahern, *Chinese Ritual and Politics* (Cambridge, 1981).

division of labour. A concept, akin to specialization, first developed in ECONOMICS and then more generally applied in SOCIOLOGY.

(1) Adam Smith, in the *Wealth of Nations* (1776), demonstrated how the productivity of labour could be enormously improved if tasks previously carried out by a single worker were subdivided into simple, repetitive operations each carried out by separate workers. A man on his own might produce one pin a day; with pin-making divided into 8 distinct operations, each performed by 'distinct hands', each pin worker could be reckoned as producing upwards of 4,800 pins a day. Smith, like Charles Babbage after him, pointed out that not only would such specialization allow the employer to dispense with more skilled, and more expensive, workers, but it would also lead to greater mechanization of production. The division of labour thus carried within it the seeds of a progressive DE-SKILLING of work, leading eventually to total AUTOMATION.

This form of the division of labour is sometimes called the technical or *detailed* division of labour. Understood in the sense that it fragments work and reduces the worker to the status of an appendage of the machine, it was taken over by Karl Marx as a central element of his theory of ALIENATION.

(2) In sociology, the concept is associated especially with Herbert Spencer and Emile Durkheim, and is used to refer to the growth in the social division of labour corresponding to the process of social dif-

ferentiation. As societies progress, they become more complex and achieve an increasing specialization of ROLES and tasks. The 'social organism' here follows the path of the individual organism, as it develops from the simple undifferentiated embryonic form to the complex set of specialized and interdependent structures of the adult organism. For Durkheim, this process was leading to a new principle of the social and moral order in modern societies. The 'mechanical solidarity' of traditional societies, based on unquestioning and automatic obedience to moral and religious norms, was in modern societies replaced by 'organic solidarity', where social integration was achieved by the awareness of the mutual interdependence of specialized parts. In this way, Durkheim thought, modern societies could dispense altogether with the requirements of NORMATIVE consensus. Durkheim later came to think that this was too optimistic a view, and sought increasingly for some secular or 'civil religion' as a substitute for the binding and integrating force of traditional religion.

(3) In more recent use, the concept has come to be applied to the *sexual* division of labour: the division of tasks and roles between men and women.   K.K.

Bibl: E. Durkheim, *The Division of Labor in Society* (1893; Eng. trans., Glencoe, Ill., 1964); A. Giddens, *Capitalism and Modern Social Theory* (Cambridge, 1971).

divisionism, see under NEO-IMPRESSIONISM.

Dixieland. At best, a misleading popular term for all forms of traditional JAZZ. It owes its origin to the Original Dixieland Jazz Band, a white group who brought the music to New York in 1917, when they also made the first jazz recordings. It came to be associated particularly with the white exponents of CHICAGO style to distinguish them from the older generation of NEW ORLEANS players. Nowadays, however, it can mean anything, and usually conjures up an inoffensively jolly, thoroughly derivative jazz, dispensed by an ingratiating band in straw hats and striped blazers.   GE.S.

DNA (deoxyribonucleic acid), see under NUCLEIC ACID.

DNA library. For the CLONING of the DNA of, say, liver tissue, the DNA has first to be fragmented by RESTRICTION ENZYMES into pieces small enough for cloning techniques. Since the fragmentation is a random process, the total liver DNA will be represented by numerous cloned fragments. This collection of fragments is known as a liver DNA library or *gene library*. HYBRIDIZATION with specific DNA or RNA reagents can be used to withdraw particular pieces of DNA from a library if they are present.   P.N.

document retrieval, see under INFORMATION STORAGE.

Documenta. A series of major art exhibitions held in Kassel, Germany, at roughly four-year intervals from 1955 on, and strongly orientated towards the latest movements.   L.M.

documentary. Adjective applied to novels, plays, films, and radio and television programmes with a high factual content, especially if this takes the form of quotations from actual documents, newspapers, live camera shots of real-life material, etc. The use of documentary elements in novels is associated with literary NATURALISM and has been common since Zola's Rougon-Macquart series of novels (1871-93); other examples are John Dos Passos's *U.S.A.* (1938) and Truman Capote's self-styled 'non-fiction novel', *In Cold Blood* (1966). But the use of the term in this sense has only become widespread since the advent of the *documentary film* (or *documentary* used as a noun). First used by John Grierson in 1926 when reviewing Flaherty's *Moana* (though the concept goes back to Eisenstein and Dziga Vertov, and indeed to Lenin's idea of film), it gained currency during the early 1930s in relation to the sociologically orientated, State- or industry-sponsored work of the British documentary school headed by Grierson.

The techniques of *documentary theatre* — historical, political, social drama incorporating authentic material in the form of quotations, projected photographs, newsreels, etc. — were developed in the work of Erwin Piscator (see EPIC THEATRE) and the LIVING NEWSPAPER tradition; in the 1960s plays by Heinar Kipphardt and Rolf Hochhuth gave wider currency to the term. In England a documentary style developed by Peter Cheeseman at the Victoria Theatre, Stoke-on-Trent, has been influenced by THEATRE WORKSHOP's *Oh What a Lovely War!* and the ballad documentaries created for B.B.C. radio by Charles Parker in the 1960s. In writing there is now a form vaguely referred to as 'faction', but this has so far been frivolous and has not attracted serious attention.

M.S.-S.; T.C.C.M.; M.A.

Bibl: F. Hardy (ed.), *Grierson on Documentary* (London, 1946); P. Rotha, *Documentary Film* (London and New York, 3rd ed., 1963).

dodecaphonic music, see under SERIAL MUSIC.

dogma. A term in Christian THEOLOGY, meaning a doctrine claiming authority over any private opinion or hesitation in a believer's mind. It is held to be a religious truth established by divine revelation and defined by the Church. If the believer rejects it, he becomes to that extent a heretic. The term is applied specially to the decrees, mainly about CHRISTOLOGY, of the ECUMENICAL Councils of the Church (325-787). Roman Catholics accept 14 subsequent Councils. It is also believed that the Pope's *ex cathedra* (solemnly very official) teaching is free of error, according to a dogma defined in 1870 (see INFALLIBILITY). Protestants give greater emphasis to the authority of the Bible (see DOGMATICS). In RELIGION as in other fields, the term is today mostly used pejoratively, to mean an opinion held on grounds, and propagated by methods, which are unreasonable. D.L.E.

Bibl: G. O'Collins, *Has Dogma a Future?* (London, 1975).

dogmatics (or *systematic theology*). In Christian THEOLOGY, the systematic presentation of doctrines so as to form a coherent whole. Although the word DOGMA is usually associated with CATHOLICISM, 'dogmatics' is most familiar in connection with the BARTHIAN attempt to cover the whole theological field afresh in the light of a new understanding of the Bible. Publication of Karl Barth's major work *Die Kirchliche Dogmatik* (*Church Dogmatics*) was begun in 1932 but left incomplete on his death in 1968. D.L.E.

dogmatism (in COMMUNIST politics), see under DEVIATIONISM.

dollar imperialism, see under IMPERIALISM.

domain (in MATHEMATICS), see under FUNCTION.

domain walls, see under STRINGS.

domestic group. In ANTHROPOLOGY, a general term to describe residential, reproductive and economic units. In rural societies these three units are often coterminous, but in industrial societies they are usually distinct. Domestic group as a concept was developed by anthropologists to replace family, a value-laden term which raised many problems in analysis. External factors, for example demographic and economic, affect the size and composition of domestic groups, but all groups move through phases of expansion and contraction in the DEVELOPMENTAL CYCLE. KINSHIP systems also influence the composition of a domestic group. In MATRILINEAL societies it is usually focused on a woman, her children and brothers. In PATRILINEAL societies it is focused upon a man, his wives and their children. A.G.

Bibl: C. Hugh-Jones, *From The Milk River* (Cambridge, 1979); R. Netting *et al.* (eds.), *Households: Comparative and Historical Studies of the Domestic Group* (Berkeley, 1984).

dominance. The behaviour pattern by which, in social animals, individuals establish the *hierarchy* of the group. In some birds, including domestic fowls, a *pecking order* develops, with one bird dominant to all the rest, and the remainder occupying more or less fixed positions in the chain. Rats and some other mammals behave similarly. Dominance is maintained by aggressive or threatening behaviour on the part of an animal, and by submission on the part of its inferior. In most cases, particularly in the wild, this aggressive behaviour becomes ritualized and ceases when the threatened individual is seen to submit, so violent combat is rare. However, some species (e.g. wild cattle, certain deer) fight to the death for the position of the leader of the group. Extrapolation from animal studies to human behaviour may be misleading, though attempts to dominate others by both men and women are made through ostentation, cunning, and personal sartorial elegance or eccentricity of appearance. In BOTANY, dominance in a plant community is also described (e.g. beech trees in a beech wood, heather on moorland). Here the term is applied to the species which is tallest and most obvious. K.M.

Bibl: N. Tinbergen, *Social Behaviour in Animals* (London and New York, 2nd ed., 1965); R. Ardrey, *The Territorial Imperative* (New York, 1966; London, 1967).

dominant, see under GENE.

dominant ideology. 'The ideas of the ruling class', Karl Marx had said in *The German Ideology* (1845), 'are in any age the ruling ideas'. Building on this, certain MARXIST theorists such as Antonio Gramsci (see HEGEMONY) and Louis Althusser have elaborated the notion that the principal mechanism whereby subordinate classes are kept in subjection in society at large of a particular set of attitudes, beliefs and values which validate the rule of a particular CLASS, and which together constitute a dominant IDEOLOGY. In traditional societies, religion usually supplies the dominant ideology, acting to reconcile the lower classes to their fate on this earth with the promise of better things to come in the hereafter (cf. Marx: 'religion is the opium of the people.'). In modern societies, the dominant ideology is less easy to identify, but is generally thought to include, in the west, the principles of liberal CONSTITUTIONALISM, together with an attachment to the institution of private property, and a widely diffused belief in the beneficence of ECONOMIC GROWTH. COMMUNIST societies share this belief in the virtues of economic growth, but justify both its costs and benefits in terms of a dominant ideology that stresses the advantages of collective ownership and pro-

claims the end of the kind of class rule that is held to disfigure ECONOMIC DEVELOPMENT in the west. Needless to say, the point of regarding all such beliefs as ideologies is to indicate the discrepancy between the propagated ideals and the actual realities in both east and west. K.K.

Bibl: N. Abercombie, S. Hill, and B.S. Turner, *The Dominant Ideology Thesis* (London, 1980).

domino theory. Phrase coined by President Eisenhower in 1954 to describe the belief of successive American administrations since 1947 that the fall of one nation to a COMMUNIST régime would surely lead to the fall of its neighbours. Used by presidents Kennedy (in 1963) and Nixon (as vice-president, in 1965) to justify American involvement in VIETNAM, and by other American leaders to justify intervention in Latin America. Subsequent to the U.S. withdrawal from S.E. Asia the concept has been somewhat devalued by inter-communist disputes (SINO-VIETNAMESE CONFLICT and civil war in Cambodia) and the resistance of other states in the region to communist takeover. D.C.W.;A.W.

Donkey's Tail.

(1) Title of an art exhibition in Moscow, 1912, organized by the painter Michel Larionov. In contrast to the KNAVE OF DIAMONDS it contained works in the neo-PRIMITIVE style, influenced by Russian icons, FOLK ART, and the East. The provocative title, suggested by a prank in Paris (when brushes were tied to a donkey's tail and the resulting smear exhibited at the Salon des Indépendants), led to the removal of Goncharova's religious works by the police. Other painters taking part included Malevich, Chagall, and Tatlin.

(2) An almanack entitled *Donkey's Tail and Target* (Moscow, 1913) contained FUTURIST poetry and the manifesto of RAYONISM. M.C.

Bibl: see under KNAVE OF DIAMONDS.

Doomwatch. A word popularized through a B.B.C. television series of the early 1970s about a semi-official watchdog agency which monitored developments in all fields of scientific research and acted

239

whenever it felt that human values or social responsibility were being ignored or flouted. It is, therefore, a popular term for social control of the 'mad scientist'. Less sensationally, it can embrace such organizations as the CLUB OF ROME and the Pugwash conferences which periodically extrapolate trends of growth or consumption in order to forecast scarcities of resources, and attempt to avoid potential disasters and irresponsible research. See also TECHNOPOLIS.   P.S.L.

doping. The introduction of controlled and usually small amounts of a foreign ATOM to a pure compound, often in the form of a crystal, in order to modify its properties. The addition of dopants is important in determining the electrical characteristics of SEMI-CONDUCTORS and in the preparation of LASER materials.   B.F.

dopolavoro, see under ARTS CENTRE.

Doppler effect (named after the Austrian physicist Christian Johann Doppler, who discovered it in 1842). The change in the perceived frequency of a wave which results when the observer moves relatively to the source. The frequency is raised when the source and observer are approaching, and lowered when they are receding. For sound waves the Doppler effect causes the drop in pitch of the whistle of a passing train, and the SONIC BOOM. For light waves, the RED SHIFT in the spectrum of distant GALAXIES is a Doppler effect (see EXPANSION OF THE UNIVERSE). Finally, police RADAR traps are based on the change in frequency of a MICROWAVE signal reflected from a moving vehicle.   M.V.B.

double articulation, see DUALITY OF STRUCTURE.

double descent, see under DESCENT.

double entrenchment, see under ENTRENCHED CLAUSES.

double helix, the. The name given to the crystalline structure of deoxyribonucleic acid (DNA) — see NUCLEIC ACID. Also the title of a well-known book by J.D. Watson describing his discovery of this

structure in 1953 in collaboration with F.H.C. Crick.   P.M.
Bibl: J. Monod, *Chance and Necessity* (New York, 1971; London, 1972).

doublethink, see under ORWELLIAN.

double-track systems, see under RECIDIVISM.

double unilineal descent, see under DESCENT.

doves and **hawks.** Figures of speech used by the American and, by adoption, European press to distinguish those U.S. politicians who prefer DIPLOMACY and caution (doves) from those who prefer to stress American military strength (hawks) to solve international problems. The terms have a long history, acquired a wide currency during the presidencies of Kennedy and Johnson, and continue to be overworked.   S.R.

Down's syndrome. A form of congenital idiocy first adequately described by J.L.H. Down (1828-96) in 1866. In this SYNDROME, as he described it, the face is flat and broad, and the eyes rather narrow and set obliquely in the face, their inner angles being abnormally far apart. Down believed quite mistakenly that his syndrome was a sign of DEGENERACY (see ATAVISM) — hence the vulgar names mongolism, Mongolian idiocy. It is in fact caused by an accidental derangement of the CHROMOSOMES. Some forms of Down's syndrome increase in frequency with the age of the mother at childbirth; others do not.   P.M.
Bibl: G.E.W. Wolstenholm and R. Porter (eds.), *Mongolism* (London, 1967).

dowry. The transfer of property from parents to daughters at MARRIAGE. The property the bride receives in this way remains in her name and she retains control over it within the marriage. Dowry does not pass to her husband or his kin (as in BRIDEWEALTH). It is a vertical property transmission, that is between generations rather than a horizontal redistribution of wealth which characterizes bridewealth transactions. This has implications for the kind of marriage associated with dowry, usually MONOGAMY. There is usually control over a daughter's marriage if she is property bearing. Dowry may be used as part of a marriage strategy, to make a good match. Tambiah showed in India that limited caste mobility is possible through *hypergamy* (a woman marries a man in a higher caste group and the children produced take their father's status) and the role of dowry here is crucial.

Dowry is used to establish a conjugal or familial fund. This will be eventually passed on to the children produced by the marriage. A conjugal fund represents the pooling, but not the merging, of a husband's and wife's resources. If the marriage is dissolved the wife reclaims her dowry portion.

Moveable goods, jewellery, money and household items most commonly make up a woman's dowry. It is found particularly in association with marriage in Europe and Asia. It occurs in societies where the principle of BILATERAL inheritance is recognized (both sons and daughters inherit from parents). It is, however, a premortem property settlement: once a dowry has been paid, the daughter can make no further claims on the parental estate. Work by Goody (*Production and Reproduction*, 1976) has linked the institution of dowry to certain economic conditions and systems of production in Eurasia. A.G.

Bibl: J.P. Parry, *Caste and Kinship in Kangra* (London, 1979); Ursula Sharma, *Women, Work and Property in North West India* (London, 1980).

Dreyfus case. In 1894 Captain Alfred Dreyfus, a French general staff officer of Jewish origins, was condemned to life imprisonment on Devil's Island for betraying secrets to Germany. The evidence was flimsy, and a campaign, in which Clemenceau and Zola played a leading part, was launched to secure a re-trial. Fearing the effect of an acquittal on the Army's position as the embodiment of France's national will, senior officers withheld or forged evidence and secured Dreyfus's conviction at a re-trial in 1899. President Loubet immediately pardoned him. In 1906 the Court of Appeal quashed the 1894 verdict and Dreyfus was reinstated. For more than a decade *l'affaire Dreyfus*

bitterly divided France and dominated French politics: it became a trial of strength between anti-clerical radicals (*Dreyfusards*, including such people as Anatole France, Marcel Proust, Daniel Halévy, and Léon Blum) on the one hand and ANTISEMITIC, Catholic, conservative defenders of the French officer corps (*anti-Dreyfusards*) on the other. A.L.C.B.

Bibl: G. Chapman, *The Dreyfus Case* (London and New York, 1955); D. Johnson, *France and the Dreyfus Affair* (London, 1966; New York, 1967).

drive. In PSYCHOANALYSIS, the drive is not to be confused with INSTINCT, the latter a biological function tied to external stimuli, and not constantly present, since a need can be satisfied. Freud argued that a drive involved internal stimuli, and a constant force, thus distinguishing drives and instincts. Freud's whole discussion of drives involves grammatical and linguistic considerations, and it is this SYMBOLIC aspect that forms a main part of Lacan's theory of drives. The other central aspect for Lacan is the REAL side to the drive, in the form of the lost or fallen object (see OBJECT (a)). We can say that the drive is a movement or drift of signifiers which turns around this object, itself unable to be taken up into the signifying chain. The body orifices which Freud refers to come into play to the extent that a correspondence is established between the lack in the OTHER, that is, a signifying lack, and the anatomical edges that concern the real. It is these edges that localize JOUISSANCE for the neurotic. D.L.

Bibl: S. Freud, *Instincts and Their Vicissitudes* (London, 1915).

drop-out. Literally one who drops out of, or eschews, the generally accepted behaviour patterns of the society to which s/he belongs. While society has always had drop-outs in the form of vagrants, hermits, etc., the contemporary drop-out phenomenon was closely associated with DRUGS and with the emergence of HIPPIES and the UNDERGROUND. Dropping out in this context involves a deliberate decision to discontinue some conventionally approved course of action (e.g. higher education, or the use of previously acquired specialist qualifications, or even the earning of a

DRUGS

high wage on the assembly line) and to turn elsewhere for fulfilment. Popular choices in the 1960s and 1970s included agriculture (subsistence farming), craft and artisan work, etc., which can be seen as offering an element of individualism against the MASS SOCIETY backdrop, and as a reaction to DEHUMANIZATION. How many of the people who followed Dr Timothy Leary's advice to 'turn on, tune in and drop out' remain engaged in alternative economic activity is a matter for conjecture. Dropping out is not only often a transient activity for individuals but has become a less viable option in an age where high levels of youth unemployment have made vocational training highly desirable.   P.S.L.

drugs.

(1) The substances which form the subject-matter of PHARMACOLOGY; see also PSYCHOPHARMACOLOGY.

(2) More narrowly, in colloquial use, those chemical substances which, when taken orally, nasally, by inhalation, hypodermically, or intravenously, alter CONSCIOUSNESS, PERCEPTION, or mood. There are four groups: (*a*) *Anaesthetics and sedatives*, such as alcohol, barbiturates, tranquillizers, and 'glues' (which are sniffed); these blunt psychic and physical pain; TOLERANCE develops, and with high doses withdrawal causes convulsions or delirium. They have the virtue of not being smoked, but barbiturate injection is particularly damaging; alcohol, fortunately, is often taken for taste or diluted with food. (*b*) *Opiates*, natural and synthetic, include morphine and heroin; these are important in medicine for relief of pain, and may produce tolerance and withdrawal symptoms. Of the latter, despite the popular literature, prolonged insomnia may be hardest to deal with. (*c*) *Stimulants* such as cocaine and amphetamines; cocaine, though possibly the most addictive, generates little tolerance, and only DEPRESSION on withdrawal; but an extraordinary degree of tolerance can arise to amphetamines. (*d*) *Hallucinogens* such as mescaline, LSD, and cannabis; tolerance develops rapidly to LSD, more slowly to cannabis. Cannabis is unique in its cumulative effect and the resultant slow onset of its full action and of recovery from it. Its

chemical structure was only recently discovered, as also its effects on sex hormones (see ENDOCRINOLOGY) and CELL development, and on MEMORY and MOTIVATION.

Illicit trade in drugs, and drug addiction, was a significant international problem in the late 1960s and early 1970s. With the growing wealth of the YUPPIE generation in the 1980s, cocaine abuse became rife among a new MIDDLE-CLASS audience, to the extent that the authorities in the U.S.A. have encouraged many companies to test employees for traces of drugs and to offer counselling. The emergence of 'crack', a cheap and extremely addictive mixture of cocaine and baking soda, has proved a major social problem among the young in the U.S.A. In Britain, heroin addiction, which had been a feature of youth SUBCULTURE (see YOUTH CULTURE) in the 1960s, increased during the late 1970s and 1980s, with mass UNEMPLOYMENT and ready availability of cheap supplies cited as contributory causes.

There are probably as many reasons for taking drugs as there are individuals; recurrent themes are availability, curiosity, PEER pressure, depression, the avoidance of a problem, and boredom. Multiple drug use is now common. The great danger is *continued* use, which is why the many psychological, social, and physical factors involved in drug dependence and progression to other drugs are important. The death rate for a heroin addict is about 30 times that normal for his or her age, largely from self-neglect or overdose.

S.T.; W.D.M.P.

Bibl: M. Gossop, *Living with Drugs* (London, 2nd ed., 1987).

drum store. A form of computer STORE similar to a DISC STORE but with the information stored on the surface of a rotating magnetized drum and with stationary read/write heads. Drum stores have a smaller capacity and a shorter ACCESS TIME than disc stores.   C.S.

Druze, see under ISLAM; LEBANON.

dual organization, see under MOIETIES.

dualism. Any theory which holds that there is, either in the universe at large or in some significant part of it, an ultimate and irreducible distinction of nature between two different kinds of thing. Examples are (1) Plato's *dualism of eternal objects* (forms or UNIVERSALS), of which we can have true knowledge, and temporal objects, which are accessible to the senses, and of which we can at best have opinions; (2) Descartes's *mind-body dualism*, i.e. of mind, as conscious, and of body, as occupying space, the former always infallibly, the latter never more than fallibly, knowable (see also MIND-BODY PROBLEM); (3) *ethical dualism*, which holds, in conformity with the doctrine of the NATURALISTIC FALLACY, that there is an irreducible difference between statements of fact and VALUE-JUDGEMENTS; (4) *explanatory dualism*, which holds that, while natural events, including mere bodily movements, have causes, human actions do not but must be explained by reference to motives or reasons; (5) sometimes called *epistemological dualism* (see also EPISTEMOLOGY), the theory that a distinction must be drawn between the immediate object of PERCEPTION (i.e. the appearance or SENSE-DATA) and the inferred, public, material objects.   A.Q.

Bibl: J.A. Passmore, *Philosophical Reasoning* (New York, 1961; London, 2nd ed., 1970).

duality of structure (sometimes referred to as *double articulation*). In LINGUISTICS, a major defining characteristic of human language, which is seen as containing two fundamental LEVELS of structure: (1) a phonological level, at which sounds, themselves meaningless, are organized into (meaningful) combinations (see PHONETICS; PHONOLOGY); (2) a syntactic level, at which the properties of the meaningful expression are studied (in terms of SYNTAX, LEXICON, SEMANTICS).   D.C.

due process. A rule of American law, found in the 5th and 14th amendments to the U.S. constitution, that no person may be deprived of 'life, liberty or property, without due process of law'. Originally intended as a guarantee of fair procedure, the meaning of the phrase was greatly expanded in the late 19th century, and came to encompass guarantees of substantive rights as well. Substantive due process became similar to the idea of natural law, allowing American courts to assess the reasonableness of federal and state laws. Together with the EQUAL PROTECTION clause, due process is the foundation of much modern American constitutional law.   M.S.P.

Dumbarton Oaks. Name of the private estate in Washington D.C., at which in August and September 1944 British, American, Soviet, and Chinese representatives met to draft a charter for the postwar international security organization to be named the United Nations (see UNO). The draft proposed four principal organs, a Security Council, a General Assembly, an INTERNATIONAL COURT OF JUSTICE, and an international secretariat.   D.C.W.

Bibl: R.N. Gardner, *Sterling-Dollar Diplomacy* (New York, 2nd ed., 1980).

dumping. Selling in a foreign market at a price below that prevailing in the exporter's home market, or below his cost of production. In comparing prices or costs in the two markets, allowance must be made for differences in terms and conditions of sale and in taxation. The conditions under which dumping is injurious or beneficial to the importing country have been long discussed. The GATT permits countries to levy anti-dumping duties if their industries are or might be injured.
          M.FG.S.

dust-bowl. In GEOGRAPHY, a type of man-made desert. It is a region subject to low rainfall and occasional severe drought in which arable farming is a hazardous practice. The top soil of the dust-bowl has been removed by wind erosion, usually because of excessive grazing or ploughing and cultivation of land without the necessary precautions against wind EROSION, and a broad hollow is imposed on the land. The term was originally applied to areas in the western U.S.A., i.e. in western Kansas, Oklahoma, and Texas, extending into south-eastern Colorado and eastern New Mexico, and is still used mainly in this context.   M.L.

dwarf star. A small, faint, hot star of extremely high density. It is possible that dwarf stars are what is left after the explosion of SUPERNOVAE, and therefore represent a late stage in the evolution of stars. See also BLACK HOLE; HERTZSPRUNG-RUSSELL DIAGRAM.   M.V.B.

dwarf wheat, see under GREEN REVOLUTION.

dymaxion. A term used by the American engineer Buckminster Fuller (*b*. 1895) to describe his CONCEPT of the maximum net performance per gross ENERGY input. It has been applied by him to a factory-produced house (a hexagonal space suspended from a central mast), a bathroom, and a map projection, and is most in evidence in the construction of his *geodesic domes*. These lightweight enclosures are parts of spheres subdivided along lines following Great Circle routes across their surface. Such domes have been airlifted by the U.S. Marine Corps, have housed RADAR equipment in arctic conditions, travelled as exhibition pavilions, and, most notably, housed the U.S. Pavilion at the Montreal Expo in 1967. M.BR.
Bibl: J. Meller (ed.), *The Buckminster Fuller Reader* (London, 1970).

dynamic labyrinth, see under ENVIRONMENT (sense 2).

dynamic programming. A technique for attacking OPTIMIZATION problems by choosing the values of the variables sequentially rather than simultaneously. It tends to be particularly appropriate for problems involving time-dependence, such as control problems. The method is expected to provide an *optimal policy*, i.e. a rule for choosing the values of the variables so as to optimize the *criterion function*. Three broad classes of dynamic-programming problems may be distinguished:
(1) In *deterministic problems* all desired information is available at all times and the criterion function can be calculated to discover the effects of any given policy. Many control problems are of this type, e.g. the problem of selecting the minimal-time or minimal-fuel flight-path for an aircraft.
(2) *Learning problems* are deterministic, but the relation between control and effect is *a priori* unknown to the optimizer, who thus has to learn about the behaviour of the criterion function while trying to optimize it. Search procedures (e.g. the classic problem of identifying the broken wire in an unlabelled multi-core cable) are usually of this type.
(3) *Stochastic problems* have the additional feature that the future behaviour of the system is not fully determined by the past and present, knowledge of which merely makes the various future possibilities more or less probable; the best that the optimizer can hope to find is a policy which will maximize the expected value of the criterion function. Among the most important problems in this last class are correction problems for systems without inherent stability, where the policy has to make the best choice between the costs of using an incorrectly set mechanism and the costs of correcting it.   R.SI.

dynamic psychology. (1) A SCHOOL OF PSYCHOLOGY that emphasizes the role of MOTIVATION. (2) More narrowly, the ideas of Freud and other psychoanalytically oriented psychologists (see FREUDIAN; PSYCHOANALYSIS) who, indeed, lay paramount stress on motivation.   I.M.L.H.

dynamics. One of the two branches of MECHANICS.   M.V.B.

dysfunctional. The opposite of one of the many meanings of *functional*. In this sense, a process or mechanism within an organism or social system is functional if it serves the interests, needs, aims, or purposes of that organism or system, dysfunctional if it interferes with them.   A.S.

dysgenic. Term coined in 1915 by Dean W.R. Inge, meaning that which tends to exert a detrimental influence over the GENETIC quality of the human race — or indeed over smaller units, such as nations or CLASSES. It means the opposite of EUGENIC. For obvious reasons there has been no concerted effort to promote dysgenic policies and therefore no science of dysgenics exists. In 1917 Inge coined a second term, *cacogenic*, which has the same meaning as dysgenic.   A.B.E.

dyslexia. The condition of those who experience a difficulty in learning to read which cannot be accounted for by limited ability or by emotional or extraneous factors. The term is not susceptible of precise operational definition.   A.L.C.B.

Bibl: P. Young and C. Tyre, *Dyslexia or Illiteracy?* (London, 1983).

dystopia, see under ANTI-UTOPIA.

E

earth art, see under CONCEPTUAL ART.

earth sciences. In the widest sense, the complete range of the sciences of the solid earth, the oceans and the atmosphere. The origin and motions of the earth as a component of the SOLAR SYSTEM form part of ASTRONOMY; GEOPHYSICS and GEOCHEMISTRY deal, respectively, with the physical and chemical characteristics of the earth and its environs; PALAEONTOLOGY is concerned with the origin and evolution of life on earth; GEOMORPHOLOGY involves the study of surface landforms; OCEANOGRAPHY is the study of the ocean waters and the basins that contain them; METEOROLOGY and CLIMATOLOGY cover, respectively, the short-term (weather) and long-term (climate) behaviour of the atmosphere; and GEOLOGY is the study of the nature of earth materials and processes with particular reference to the way in which they have interacted through time to generate the earth's existing features. There is also a host of subsidiary names. SEISMOLOGY deals with earthquakes and seismic waves, VOLCANOLOGY with volcanoes, GEOMAGNETISM with the earth's magnetic field, STRATIGRAPHY with rock strata, and so on.

The boundaries between these disciplines and subdisciplines are highly blurred. Moreover, some words may be used in more than one sense. Geology, for example, is sometimes used in the limited sense above but at other times as a more general term to cover all the sciences of the solid earth (geophysics, geochemistry, palaeontology, etc.). In the latter usage it is synonymous with geological sciences and the solid-earth sciences. Earth sciences, too, is more often than not used in a restricted sense that excludes astronomy, water and air, making it also synonymous with geological sciences and the general form of geology.

An interesting recent development concerns the names given to the study of the moon and planets. Research into the solid bodies of the moon and planets — made possible by satellites, space probes, manned and unmanned lunar missions, and the placing of instrument packages on planetary surfaces — is now considered part of the earth sciences, geological sciences and geology (general). But while no one would ever refer to, say, 'the earth science of Mars' or 'the geological science of Mercury', scientists are quite happy to speak of 'the geology of Venus' even though to do so is etymological nonsense (geo = earth). Terms such as marsology, uranology and (for the moon) selenology are sometimes used, albeit very infrequently, and in any case imply coverage of more than just the solid parts of the relevant bodies. The general term *planetology*, which also covers more than the solid, is rather more common.   P.J.S.

earth shelters. Buildings which are dug into the ground and covered with a layer of earth and turf. The interiors are thus very heavily insulated. Insulated windows and doors add to the energy efficiency of this kind of structure. Popular as an idea in the 1960s and early 1970s, particularly in the U.S.A., earth shelters have many real life models in VERNACULAR architecture around the world. Translating those models into a western real estate culture has not necessarily been easy to achieve.   S.L.

Eastern Orthodoxy, see ORTHODOXY, EASTERN.

EBCDIC. Extended Binary-Coded Decimal Interchange Code, see under ASCII.

ECA, see under MARSHALL PLAN.

ecclesiology. That part of Christian THEOLOGY which is concerned with the Church. The modern debate about the Church's essential nature and changing tasks has been stimulated by the ECUMENICAL MOVEMENT and, in CATHOLICISM, by the AGGIORNAMENTO. Sometimes the word refers only to the architecture and furnishings of church buildings.   D.L.E.

echocardiography. The use of ULTRASOUND as a method of investigating the heart non-invasively. The basic principle was derived from the SONAR systems for ship navigation and remote detection of submarines developed during World War II. The echoes from all structures of the heart can be identified from a single ultrasound beam and recorded on photographic strip chart recorders. This is called 'M-Mode' recording. In 1972, Bom and co-workers introduced real time sector scanning of the heart which allows correct anatomic representation of an entire cardiac cross section ('cross-sectional' or '2D'). It is a simple and painless method for investigation of heart function. It is especially useful for assessment of abnormalities of the valves and pericardium as well as ventricular performance. New developments include the use of DOPPLER sound recordings, which are particularly helpful in quantifying the degree of valvular regurgitation and stenosis.   L.J.F.

echo sounding, see SONAR.

ecliptic. When we consider the earth as a planet, the *celestial sphere* is that imaginary sphere surrounding the earth infinitely far away on which the earth's equator and poles are projected. The plane of the earth's orbit round the sun is thus a plane passing through the centre of the celestial sphere. Its intersection with the celestial sphere will be a great circle — the ecliptic. The *plane of the ecliptic* is therefore the plane of the earth's orbit round the sun. Since it does not change, the great circle of the ecliptic on the celestial sphere will remain in a fixed position relative to other points (e.g. stars) projected on it. The earth's axis has an inclination from the vertical with respect to the plane of the ecliptic of about $23^1/_2^\circ$ (more accurately $23^\circ 27'$). Thus the plane of the ecliptic makes the same angle with the plane of the equator.   M.L.

ecodeme, see under DEME.

École de Paris. An expression used confusingly with three overlapping meanings, all relating to the fine arts as practised in Paris during the present century:

(1) Immediately after World War I it referred to a number of artists of non-French origin and predominantly Jewish background: notably the Russians Chagall and Soutine, the Bulgar Jules Pascin, the Czech Coubine, the Japanese Foujita, the Poles Kisling and Zak, and the Italian Modigliani. Sometimes distinguished (first, second École) according to whether they arrived in Paris before or after the war, they formed a distinctive school of FIGURATIVE, easily sentimentalized, more or less EXPRESSIONIST painting which emerged as the main new movement between CUBISM and the extension of SURREALISM to the visual arts.

(2) Later it was extended to include Picasso, Juan Gris, and even, by association, Maurice Utrillo and his mother Suzanne Valadon.

(3) Finally, as in the Royal Academy's exhibition in 1951 and the annual shows at the Galérie Charpentier from 1955, it was used for virtually the whole modern art movement centring on Paris.   J.W.

ecology (also known as *bionomics*).

(1) A term (Greek *oikos*, household or living-place) first used by Ernst Haeckel in 1873 for that branch of BIOLOGY which deals with the interrelationships between organisms and their ENVIRONMENT (sense 1). During the first half of the 20th century the concept spread rapidly, and ecology became an increasingly important part of many university courses. Studies of botanical ecology generally advanced more rapidly than those involving animals, but the subject played an important part in bringing together zoologists and botanists. Within the scientific community there is some division between those who place the greatest emphasis on field observations (the 'muddy-boot ecologists') and those who are more concerned with SYSTEMS analysis, modelling (see MODEL), and COMPUTER SIMULATION of ecological processes (the 'theoretical ecologists'). Ecology is sometimes divided into various subdivisions, i.e. population ecology, evolutionary ecology, community ecology, physiological ecology, and behavioural ecology. Usually these divisions have little validity except to indicate that, possibly in some defined HABITAT, the interrelations of several species are being studied from the point of view of population dynamics, EVOLUTION, and so on.   K.M.

(2) The word is also used in a more popular sense to denote concern for the

protection of the environment from a wide range of pollutants. Growing awareness of environmental problems during the 1960s and 1970s led to the formation of activist groups, particularly in the U.S.A. and western Europe, with the result that governments increasingly introduced legislation to control the release of toxic substances into the environment. Major environmental disasters, such as the release of deadly gas from the Union Carbide plant at Bhopal in India on 3 December 1984 (2,500 dead) and the CHERNOBYL nuclear reactor disaster on 26 April 1986 (36 died immediately; 231 suffered acute radiation sickness; estimates suggest that as many as 34,000 could die over the next 40 years), have placed ecological issues firmly on the political agenda of most countries. In 1987, the 'Green' party (see GREEN MOVEMENT) held ten seats in the West German Bundestag (parliament).

S.T.

ecology, human. An extension of zoological and botanical ECOLOGY to include man. The growth of human ecology is usually associated with sociological writing in the U.S.A. in the 1920s; it has since been widely adopted in a number of other SOCIAL SCIENCES. For each discipline, the distinctive character of ecological studies is the attempt to link the structure and organization of a human community to interactions with its localized ENVIRONMENT.

P.H.

Bibl: A.H. Hawley, *Human Ecology* (New York, 1950); S.R. Eyre and G.R.J. Jones (eds.), *Geography as Human Ecology: Methodology by Example* (London, 1966).

econometric history, see under ECONOMIC HISTORY.

econometrics. The investigation of economic relationships using mathematical and statistical techniques. The econometric method is to develop a mathematical MODEL that has a basis in economic theory. Using economic data, the strengths of the relationships proposed by the model are estimated and the model is tested statistically. The methods of statistical INFERENCE are used to determine whether the model is an adequate representation of reality. Thus, econometrics in its broadest sense is concerned with the development and testing of economic models and theories. It is also used to construct quantitative models, which are used to forecast the economy. Econometrics suffers from a number of problems. Most economic models are, at best, only approximations to very complex phenomena and are unlikely to be valid in all possible circumstances. The data with which models are tested is rarely measured exactly and does not always directly correspond to the VARIABLES used in the model. The development of models is usually a compromise between what is acceptable in terms of economic theory, the available data and what is computationally possible. There is little possibility of conducting meaningful economic experiments. The economy is made up of complex interacting systems which are difficult to separate out, model and test statistically; this leads to the problem of IDENTIFICATION. The actual forecasts of economic models may affect the economy, e.g. a forecast of increasing INFLATION may lead to expectations of higher rates of inflation that are self-fulfilling. In economic models, it is usual to assume that non-economic factors are constant. In many cases, this is an unrealistic assumption (e.g. the actions of OPEC). In spite of these problems, the quantitative investigation of the economy is necessary in order to test economic theories and to develop economic policies that are based on valid assumptions, models and forecasts of the economy.

R.ST.; J.P.

Bibl: M. Desai, *Applied Econometrics* (London, 1976).

economic anthropology. The study of production, distribution and consumption in non-industrialized societies. For many years the central debate in economic anthropology concerned the value of a formal as opposed to a substantivist approach. On the one hand the formalists (e.g., Firth, *Primitive Polynesian Economy*, 1939) advocated the universal applicability of concepts (such as profit, credit, CAPITAL) derived from NEOCLASSICAL ECONOMICS. The substantivists, on the other hand, argued that these concepts were value-laden and proposed the use of indigenous concepts in the analysis of economic activity in a particular society. A fresh impetus during the 1970s came from MARXISM. The work of certain French anthropologists, particularly Meillassoux, Terray and Godelier, stimulated and initiated new debates in economic anthropology. Particularly important was the identification of the coexistence within a society of different MODES OF PRODUCTION. Hitherto anthropologists had presented particular 'tribal' or 'peasant' economies as self-contained and had neglected to consider their place within a much wider social formation, specifically as a part of a colonial system.   A.G.

Bibl: S. Ortiz (ed.), *Economic Anthropology* (Lanham, Md, 1983); C.A. Gregory, *Gifts and Commodities* (London, 1982).

economic development. Economic development is the process of ECONOMIC GROWTH and transformation of poor societies. Economic development is desired as it allows various objectives to be pursued. Until recently, economic development was seen in terms of growth in income per head and the alteration of the structure of production, in which the share of agriculture declines and the shares of the manufacturing and service industries increase. During the 1950s and 1960s, many developing countries experienced rapid growth in income per head, but the results of this economic growth were not considered to be particularly satisfactory. In the 1970s, economic development began to be defined in terms of the elimination or reduction of poverty, inequality and UNEMPLOYMENT. This definition views economic development as a means of meeting the basic needs, i.e. food, shelter, water supply, sanitation, health, education and protection of individuals and social groups. This view was quickly broadened from life-sustenance to include the concept of individuals and societies gaining self-esteem through their own or national prosperity and the freedom from economic servitude and DEPENDENCE on others. Since 1945, there has been a tremendous increase in interest in the study of economic development. Of particular interest has been the large differences in the economic growth of different coun-

tries, e.g. the rapid growth of the NEWLY INDUSTRIALIZING COUNTRIES and the dependence between developing and developed countries. There has been considerable dispute about the appropriateness of the concepts and analytical tools of NEO-CLASSICAL ECONOMIC THEORY to the study of developing economies. See also DEVELOPMENT ECONOMICS.   J.P.

Bibl: M.P. Todaro, *Economic Development in the Third World* (London, 3rd ed., 1985).

economic efficiency. This concept is considered in three parts. Firstly, an economy is efficient in production, at a moment in time, if there is no means of using the available inputs to increase the production of one or more goods without reducing the production of one or more other goods. This is sometimes referred to as *X-efficiency*. Secondly, an economy is efficient in exchange, if it is not possible to revise the distribution of a set amount of goods and services between people so as to leave one or more persons better off and no person worse off. Finally, there must be efficiency between exchange and production. This exists when, for all possible pairs of goods and services, consumers' willingness to substitute one good for the other is just equal to the economy's ability to switch production from this good or service to the other (see SUBSTITUTION).

Economic efficiency necessarily requires efficiency in investment in TECHNICAL PROGRESS. As the results of such investment are by their very nature uncertain, it is difficult to analyse whether an economy at one moment of time is economically efficient. UNCERTAINTY reduces the usefulness of the concept of economic efficiency. WELFARE ECONOMICS has mainly been concerned with the conditions necessary for economic efficiency. With certain assumptions, both PERFECT COMPETITION and STATE ECONOMIC PLANNING are economically efficient. In evaluating an economy, weight must be given to both its efficiency and distribution of income. The concept of economic efficiency is often applied to the analysis of MARKET FAILURE, e.g. MONOPOLIES, TRADE UNIONS and EXTERNALITIES, and is also used in the theory of COST-BENEFIT ANALYSIS.   J.P.

Bibl: D. Begg *et al.*, *Economics* (London, 1984).

economic growth. Increase over time in real NATIONAL INCOME or in real national income per head; usage is not uniform between these two alternatives, either in statistical or in theoretical writings, but the second is the more usual. The concept refers to growth sustained over a substantial length of time, not to movements within TRADE CYCLES or shorter periods. Economic growth is most usually measured in annual percentage terms. In most industrial countries the long-run rate of growth of real national income per head has been between 1 and 2% a year. The rate has been higher than this in most industrial countries since World War II, but there has been a general slowing down since 1973. In some countries (notably Japan and Sweden) it has been higher than this over a long period. Economic growth at these rates is a distinctive feature of the past 150 or so years. It did not occur in earlier periods and it has not generally occurred in UNDERDEVELOPED countries (but see NEWLY INDUSTRIALIZING COUNTRIES). The exact definition and measurement of economic growth depends on the definition of national income and is subject to the same limitations. If the conventional definition of national income were replaced by a wider one that allowed more adequately for non-market activities, leisure time, environmental conditions, and so on, some differences would result in measured rates of growth; but it is unlikely that the broad conclusions would be altered. R.C.O.M.

Bibl: S. Kuznets, *Modern Economic Growth* (London and New Haven, 1966).

economic history. The history of economies in the past. The history of agriculture, trade, and industry was already flourishing, especially in Germany, in the 19th century, but economic history was recognized as a separate discipline in universities only in the 20th. 'Business history' split off from it in the U.S.A. in the 1920s. Since about 1950 economic historians have made greater use of quantitative methods and taken more interest in the MODELS and theories of economists.

This *new economic history* (*econometric history* and *cliometrics* are other terms often used) differs from traditional economic history in METHODOLOGY. Instead of building up generalizations gradually as a result of accumulating a large number of facts and reflecting on specific historical cases, very much as any historian might, the exponents of the new method start by framing a hypothesis, and collect data with a view to establishing its validity, very much as an applied economist would. Econometric historians also make considerable use of *counterfactual propositions* (see COUNTERFACTUAL; PROPOSITION). The new methods have made it possible to supplement traditional microeconomic history (the history of specific industries and firms) with macroeconomic history (the measurement of GROSS NATIONAL PRODUCT and ECONOMIC GROWTH in the past). P.B.

economic imperialism, see under IMPERIALISM.

economic law. A proposition in ECONOMICS which is supposed to be of general validity (e.g. GRESHAM'S and SAY'S LAWS). The empirical testing of laws of economics is often less well-founded than the testing of laws in the NATURAL SCIENCES (see ECONOMETRICS). For this reason, the laws of economics as propositions of general validity may be less secure. The term is often avoided by modern economists who are more conscious, perhaps, of the differences between reality and their economic MODELS. R.ST.;J.P.

economic liberalism. The application to ECONOMICS of the doctrines of classical LIBERALISM. It is a preference for competitive markets (see MARKET ECONOMY) and for the use of the PRICE MECHANISM rather than more direct intervention in the economy, e.g. STATE ECONOMIC PLANNING. Economic liberalism is usually considered to differ from LAISSEZ FAIRE, as, in the former, it is accepted that there is a need for government intervention to deal with EXTERNALITIES, MONOPOLIES and to provide PUBLIC GOODS. Many, but not all, economic liberals favour redistribution of income, preferably in the form of taxes and cash transfer payments, rather than through provision by goods in kind or the regulation of wages and prices. Economic liberals are not necessarily committed to any particular form of property ownership; for example, COOPERATIVES are compatible with this economic doctrine. If government intervention is necessary, economic liberalism suggests that it should be implemented through general impersonal rules and not on a piecemeal basis, which allows politicians and officials to make decisions reflecting their own objectives and prejudices.   S.BR.; J.P.

Bibl: A.K. Dasgupta, *Epochs of Economic Theory* (Oxford, 1985).

economic regulation. The STATE may intervene in markets and industries. Intervention can take the form of legislation, administration, TAXATION and subsidization. There are three theories that attempt to explain the existence and forms of regulation. (1) The *public interest theory* argues that regulation is an attempt to correct for MARKET FAILURES, such as MONOPOLY, EXTERNALITIES and lack of information. For example, the prices of a natural monopoly may be limited so as to restrict profits and increase output, safety measures may be enforced on airlines and doctors may be licensed to prevent charlatans from treating patients. (2) This theory suggests that there is a market for regulation. Consumers and producers compete in a political and economic market for regulation. For example, the regulation of airline safety, routes and prices may be in the interest of the airlines, as BARRIERS TO ENTRY are imposed and COMPETITION is reduced. Regulation is regarded as serving the interests of those who are willing to offer the most for the regulation. In this theory, regulation can be purchased through offering political influence and help, and direct financial contributions. Regulation may be regarded as a PUBLIC GOOD, to which the consumer is expected to contribute. The benefit to the individual consumer of an increase in personal expenditure on securing favourable regulation is likely to be small. Thus, though the aggregate benefit to consumers of favourable regulation may be high, as individuals they may not be willing to contribute to the cost of obtaining the regulation. The costs of acquiring information about regu-

lation are also likely to be high. As producers are a smaller group and individual producers stand to gain more from favourable regulation, producers will have more incentive to try and obtain favourable regulation. (3) *Capture theory* has some similarities to the previous theory, in that it is suggested that producers capture regulatory agencies and control them in their own interests. Capture may occur through regulations being enforced by persons previously employed in the industry, or who hope to be, and holding the same perceptions as the industry. The latter two theories suggest that regulation is made or implemented in the interests of producers rather than the public interest. Thus, it may be in the PUBLIC INTEREST to remove regulations and allow increased competition to reduce costs and prices, and improve the quality of goods and services supplied. This view lies behind the market orientated policies that have deregulated airlines in Australia and America, and bus and financial services in the U.K. Self-regulation is where the industry regulates itself. The advantages of self-regulation are that use is made of the industry's knowledge, the often discretionary nature of the regulations, lower costs of implementation of regulation, and the fact that it often does not require the passing of legislation and recourse to the legal system. The disadvantages are that the regulations may be formed or implemented in favour of the industry rather than the public interest. See PRIVATIZATION and NATIONALIZATION.   J.P.

Bibl: R. Posner, 'Theories of economic regulation', *Bell Journal of Economics*, Autumn 1971.

economic rent. The income of a FACTOR OF PRODUCTION (e.g. land, labour or CAPITAL) may be greater than the amount needed to induce the factor to offer its services. The difference between the former and the latter amounts is the economic rent. The large sums paid to film stars and the best professional footballers are mostly economic rents reflecting the shortage of supply of such persons. In the long run, economic rents provide an incentive for a greater supply of the factor to be provided. Thus, a shortage of land for building houses may lead to higher land prices and a switch of land from other uses. The economic rent rations the limited supply to those most willing to pay for the factor.   J.P.

Bibl: J. Craven, *Introduction to Economics* (Oxford, 1984).

economic theory of imperialism, see under IMPERIALISM.

economic warfare. The disorganization of an enemy's economy so as to prevent him from carrying on war, especially by the denial to him of imports, interference with his exports, and destruction by bombing or sabotage of his industrial centres of production, storage, and distribution. In its widest sense (and in official American usage), the term includes all measures against economic activities which directly or indirectly further a belligerent's war effort. In British usage, it only covers measures against an enemy.   D.C.W.

economics. The study of methods of allocating scarce resources in production, the distribution of the resulting output and the effects of this allocation and distribution. This definition differs from the widely quoted and accepted definition of Robbins that 'economics is concerned with that aspect of behaviour which arises from the scarcity of means to achieve a given end (and) economics is not concerned with ends as such'. This latter definition considers 'ends' to be the problem of other subjects and economics to be the study of how best to achieve given ends. The attempt to limit economics to VALUE-FREE investigation represented a major move from its progenitor, POLITICAL ECONOMY, and, in its pure form, has few present-day adherents. *Positive economics* is concerned with verifiable propositions, e.g. the level of INVESTMENT is positively related to the interest rate (see MODEL). Normative economics is concerned with what should be done and necessarily involves the use of a VALUE-JUDGEMENT and often uses a positive model, e.g. UNEMPLOYMENT should be reduced by forcing the interest rate down to increase investment and employment. *Microeconomics* is the study of the decisions of individual economic agents, e.g. consumers and FIRMS. It is often associated with the economics of prices and SUPPLY AND DEMAND, though it is much broader in scope, e.g. it includes the economics of UNCERTAINTY and large parts of MARXIST economics. *Macroeconomics* is the study of the aggregate effects of microeconomic decisions, e.g. NATIONAL INCOME, UNEMPLOYMENT, BALANCE OF PAYMENTS. As such, macroeconomic theory is based upon microeconomic theory.

Marxist economics is, in the words of Oskar Lange, 'the social laws governing the production and distribution of the material means of satisfying human needs'. Marxist economics places more emphasis on historical, political and sociological analysis than micro- and macroeconomics. However, Marxist economics can use, and be analysed in terms of, conventional micro- and macroeconomics. Social laws are the product of historical evolution and of the conflict between CLASSES which is the motive force of historical change. The central element of Marxist economics is that labour is the only source of value (see LABOUR THEORY OF VALUE).   R.L.; J. P.

Bibl: J. Craven, *Introduction to Economics* (Oxford, 1984); D. Begg *et al.*, *Economics* (London, 1984); M. Blaug, *Economic Theory in Retrospect* (London, 1985).

economies of scale. Circumstances that cause the proportionate increase in the total cost of supplying a good or service to be less than the proportionate increase in the amount produced. Economies of scale are usually interpreted as increasing RETURNS TO SCALE with the prices of FACTORS OF PRODUCTION held constant. They are divided into internal economies, which occur as the size of the firm increases, and external economies, which occur as the size of the industry or group of firms increases. Economies occur in the production process (e.g. a more efficient organization of production may be possible at higher levels of output), transport (e.g. it may be relatively cheaper to deliver goods in a geographical area, the greater the volume of goods transported), MARKETING, RESEARCH AND DEVELOPMENT (e.g. in the case of the latter three, the associated fixed costs can be spread across a greater level of output). Economies can also be of a dynamic type, e.g. longer production runs and LEARNING BY DOING. Economies can be real, i.e. they represent a saving in society's use of resources, or pecuniary, in that they are offset by money losses to other firms (e.g. discounts that are extracted by large buyers who threaten to take their business elsewhere), or a mixture of both.   J.P.

Bibl: M. C. Sawyer, *The Economics of Industries and Firms* (London, 1981).

ecosystem. The system formed by the interaction of all living organisms, plants, animals, bacteria, etc. with the physical and chemical factors of their ENVIRON-MENT. The variety of meanings attached to the word by different ecologists (some of whom now doubt its usefulness as a precise term with a rigid definition) reflects the variety of boundaries drawn for 'the environment'. Thus foresters speak of a 'woodland ecosystem' meaning the whole tree-covered area, while an entomologist working in the same wood will restrict the term to a fallen log with its insect fauna and the fungi living on the dead material; such restricted uses have their practical value in helping scientists to define their problem. However, since an ecosystem is usually thought of as occurring within a self-contained and restricted area, and since complete isolation of most areas is impossible, it can be argued that the Earth itself is the only real ecosystem. See also ECOLOGY.   K.M.

écriture. Writing. A term thrown into prominence by Roland Barthes in his *Writing Degree Zero* (1953). With his play upon this central term, which makes the act of writing itself distinct both from the writer and from what is written, Barthes ushers in the STRUCTURALIST movement in literary criticism. *Ecriture classique*, the convention of writing practised in France from the 17th to the 19th century, relied for its effectiveness upon the unquestionable truths of a social order which it mirrors. But from 1848 each writer has to create his own *écriture*, his own style within style, which enters into the inherited language and literature in order to set itself against these in new 'engaged' hostility to received opinion and literary custom. *Ecriture* is thus not only a con-

vention of writing, it is a refusal to go along with what there is, the 'natural', the obvious, the received. *Ecriture* is put at the service of demystifying and demythologizing the BOURGEOIS conviction that whatever is, is natural.   R.PO.

Bibl: J. Culler, *Structuralist Poetics* (London, 1975).

ECSC (European Coal and Steel Community). An organization originating in a proposal (the Schuman Plan, 5 May 1950) by Robert Schuman, then French Foreign Minister, for the creation of a FREE MARKET in coal and steel under a supranational authority. The scheme was seen by the French as the only remaining means of preventing a NATIONALIST revival of West German heavy industry after the establishment the previous year of the West German state. The U.K. was invited to join, but refused. Signed on 18 April 1951 by representatives of France, West Germany, Italy, the Netherlands, Belgium, and Luxembourg, the Charter of the ECSC established a 9-member High Authority with powers to set prices, draw up plans, ensure free COMPETITION, prevent MONOPOLY, and look after the welfare of employees; a common assembly as a watchdog over the Authority; a Council of Ministers and a High Court; all but the Assembly being located in Luxembourg. The ECSC served as a model for the later EEC into which it was incorporated.

D.C.W.

Bibl: D.W. Urwin, *Western Europe since 1945* (New York and London, 3rd ed., 1981).

ECT, see ELECTRO-CONVULSIVE THERAPY.

ectomorph, see under PERSONALITY TYPES.

ecumenical movement. 'Ecumenical' (from Greek *oikoumenikos*, 'of the inhabited world') is still sometimes used to refer to the whole of mankind. But its usual usage is Christian, and refers to the Councils of the undivided Church which laid down orthodox CHRISTOLOGY and defined other DOGMAS; to the Ecumenical Patriarch in Constantinople (see ORTHODOXY, EASTERN); or to the modern movement for Christian reunion. This movement began with the World Missionary Conference at Edinburgh in 1910. The formation of the International Missionary Council was accompanied by other world conferences on problems of 'Life and Work' and of 'Faith and Order'. These three streams united in the World Council of Churches, constituted at Amsterdam in 1948. The Roman CATHOLIC Church is the only major Christian denomination which is not a member of the W.C.C., though it participates in many of the latter's activities, and warmer relations with other Christians form an important part of this Church's AGGIOR-NAMENTO. Discussion about the reunion of the Churches has been active in many countries, and some mergers have been achieved. However, progress in the Churches towards unity has been disappointingly slow, and towards the end of the 1960s a new mood began to grow among Christians, largely ignoring the Churches' problems and hesitations, and concentrating instead on a more informal and radical witness and service in the modern world. This mood restored to the word 'ecumenical' much of its original connection with humanity. D.L.E.

Bibl: G. Wainwright, *The Ecumenical Movement* (Grand Rapids, Mich. and London, 1983); A.J. van der Bent, *Vital Ecumenical Concerns* (Geneva, 1986).

edaphology, see under SOIL SCIENCE.

EDC (European Defence Community). A scheme originating in a proposal (24 October 1950) by the French Prime Minister, René Pleven, in reply to American proposals, inspired by the KOREA war, for the participation of West German armed forces in 'an integrated force for the defence of Western Europe'. Despite Britain's refusal to participate, the proposals led to the signature in Paris of the EDC treaty of 27 May 1952. American pressure failed, however, to secure the treaty's ratification by the French National Assembly, and after its rejection (30 August 1954) the rearmament of West Germany was secured within the less restricted framework of the Western European Union, and later of NATO. D.C.W.

Bibl: D.W. Urwin, *Western Europe since 1945* (New York and London, 3rd ed., 1981).

eddy currents. Term originally applied to the irregular flow of fluids past an obstacle or series of obstacles and, as such, generally associated with a swirling motion in liquids. Since the flow of electric current is often likened to fluid flow, the term became associated with electric currents flowing in large sheets or volumes of conductor (as opposed to thin wires), especially when those currents are produced by electromagnetic induction (see INDUCTION MOTOR). E.R.L.

Bibl: J. Lammeraner and M. Štafl, *Eddy Currents* (London and Cleveland, 1966).

EDP (electronic data processing), see COMPUTING.

education. A word susceptible of various definitions according to the stance of the user; e.g. (1) education is a passing on of a cultural heritage; (2) it is the initiation of the young into worthwhile ways of thinking and doing; (3) it is a fostering of the individual's growth. Many of the controversies in educational thought arise from the tension between these three attitudes. At one end of the spectrum the prime agent is seen as *the teacher*, marked with the appropriate signs of authority; at the other it is *the student*, whose unfolding gifts may perhaps be speeded up by a teacher's insight and care. In the middle ground is the view of education as a joint process, of teachers managing and arranging curriculum resources and of children acquiring the sensibilities and skills necessary to explore and to create the small world of playground and school. All three views are valid for different circumstances and are complementary. R.A.H.

Education Acts. Basically the famous 1944 Education Act — the 'Butler Act' — still remains the foundation stone of British education. There have been a number of supplementary Acts, particularly in the 1980s. For instance, school government has been changed radically, with fewer politicians being appointed and more representatives of the parent and teachers' bodies now elected. Each school must have its own governing body instead of, as in the past, one person (usually a local councillor) being a governor of several schools. Parents have been given more power in schools and more choice of their children's education. Local authorities, local business and the school staffs are now evenly represented. CORPORAL PUNISHMENT is no longer permitted and sex education must be taught with teachers stressing the need for moral standards and the responsibility of the family.　　J.I.

educational linguistics. In LINGUISTICS, the application of linguistic theories, methods, and descriptive findings to the study of mother-tongue teaching or learning in schools or other educational settings. The subject deals with both spoken and written language (including the development of literacy), and also the range of linguistic varieties (accents, dialects, etc.) available in the community.　　D.C.

Bibl: P. Gannon and P. Czerniewska, *Using Linguistics: An Educational Focus* (London, 1980).

educational psychology. A branch of APPLIED PSYCHOLOGY concerned with several kinds of activity. The first is with studies of learning and associated forms of PROBLEM-SOLVING as these are revealed in the learning of bodies of knowledge. Closely connected are applications of DEVELOPMENTAL PSYCHOLOGY to the organization of learning and of curricula. More recently, educational psychology has also dealt with the inter-personal and social aspects of classrooms and other less formal learning situations, particularly with the manner in which these affect attitudes as well as the acquisition of knowledge; and moral education has become increasingly a matter of concern in an age of change in cultural NORMS.

A second large area of activity is in testing and EVALUATION, both of INTELLIGENCE and of special abilities such as mathematics, music, spatial capacities (i.e. ability to decipher representational pictures or diagrams of spatial arrays), etc. A principal contribution to this work (notably by Charles Spearman, L.L. Thurstone, and Sir Charles Burt) has been the partitioning of intelligence into component abilities and investigation of the extent to which those component abilities are found by FACTOR ANALYSIS to be dependent upon general intelligence — as measured by the common CORRELATION of the components.

Educational psychology has also had an active part in the organizing of school curricula, both in analysing the special problems of learning certain subject-matters, and developing theories of how subjects are learned. An example is the work of J.S. Bruner indicating that central structural CONCEPTS within a field, once learned, aid considerably in mastery of detailed information when such material is shown to be derivable from general principles. Ideas about the structuring of the curriculum have recently been embodied in PROGRAMMED INSTRUCTION.

Finally, educational psychology concerns itself with problems of the SPECIAL EDUCATION, of the culturally underprivileged, the mentally retarded (see MENTAL RETARDATION), and those with physical handicaps like deafness and blindness.
　　J.S.B.

Bibl: J.C. Quiche, *The Cautious Expert: a Social Analysis of Developments in the Practice of Educational Psychology* (Milton Keynes, 1982); M. Donaldson, *Children's Minds* (London, 1978).

educational tests, see under MENTAL TESTING.

educationally subnormal (ESN). Term used of children who, through limited ability (usually an INTELLIGENCE QUOTIENT of under 75) or severe but maybe temporary MENTAL RETARDATION, require SPECIAL EDUCATION. It is estimated that about 1% of the British school population requires such treatment, which is given in special schools or units. These figures do not include the much larger number of 'slow learners' for whom provision is made by special teaching arrangements in ordinary schools.　　W.A.C.S.

EEC (European Economic Community). The leading example of a *common market* (see CUSTOMS UNION). Conceived by pro-Europeans as a re-launching of the European Movement after the failure of EDC, it originated in the Messina conference of June 1955 between the member states of ECSC, and was formally established by the Rome Treaty (March 1957), with France, West Germany, Italy, the Netherlands,

Belgium, and Luxembourg ('the Six') as members. Belated British attempts to join were rebuffed by French opposition in 1963 and 1967, but in January 1972 agreement was reached that Britain, Denmark, and Eire should be admitted to membership. The Community was further enlarged by the admission of Greece in 1981 and Spain and Portugal in 1984. Movements of CAPITAL have not yet been completely freed, but in other respects the EEC goes beyond a common market in providing for common or harmonized policies in, e.g., agriculture, transport, energy, indirect TAXATION, MONOPOLIES, regional problems, and *macro-economic* affairs (see ECONOMICS). It thus approaches a full *economic union*, although it seems unlikely that it will complete the journey (with, e.g., a common currency) without a *political union* as well.   D.C.W.

Bibl: L. Tsoukalis (ed.), *The European Community: Past, Present and Future* (Oxford, 1983); G. George, *Politics and Policy in the European Community* (Oxford, 1985).

EEG, see ELECTROENCEPHALOGRAPH.

effective cosmological constant, see under COSMOLOGICAL CONSTANT.

EFTA (European Free Trade Association). An association of countries whose main objectives are to bring about FREE TRADE between members and with the EEC. Members have chosen not to join the EEC as it involves a certain loss of SOVEREIGNTY (see CUSTOMS UNION). Thus free trade agreements between EFTA and the EEC have allowed the creation of a larger free trade area than would have occurred if only membership of the EEC had been available. Austria, Britain, Denmark, Portugal, Sweden and Switzerland formed the association in 1959. For industrial products, free trade was established between members by 1966 and with the EEC by 1977. Britain (1973), Denmark (1973) and Portugal (1984) left EFTA to join the EEC. Finland (1961) has associate membership and Iceland (1970) has also joined. Members are small countries, vary in economic structure and are distributed across Europe. However, they have high average per capita incomes and are generally regarded to have benefited from the free trade area that EFTA helped create.   J.P.

Bibl: European Free Trade Association, *The European Free Trade Association* (Geneva, 1980).

egalitarianism. A belief in the high value of EQUALITY among human beings and the desirability of removing inequalities. Such a belief forms part of many religious, political, and social movements. In the French Revolution, with its famous slogan of Liberty, Equality, and Fraternity, the second term of the revolutionary trinity took an extreme form in Babeuf's *Conspiracy of Equals* (1796), which bequeathed its legacy to a host of secret organizations in the early 19th century espousing the idea of the universal equality of incomes. 'Babouvism' provided the ground for the emergence of SOCIALIST and COMMUNIST ideas.

Marx (see MARXISM), however, stressed the paramount importance of CLASS divisions as against individual inequalities and recognized that unequal individual capacities and work will be differentially remunerated in the first stage of building communism. Stalin (see STALINISM) seized this point in his attack on the egalitarian wage structure prevailing in the U.S.S.R. until 1930 and replaced it by a system of unequal rewards to provide incentives for industrial development. In contrast, Mao Tse-tung (see MAOISM) favoured a more egalitarian economic policy.

The problems of the egalitarian distribution of goods in society have acquired a new perspective in the 20th century, because historical experience has shown that removal of one kind of inequality can be accompanied by the sharpening of other kinds. While income differences may diminish, differences in POWER within society may increase, since economic, social, and political differences do not necessarily change together. Another awkward question is raised by 'equality of opportunity'. Egalitarianism has found it difficult to accept the idea of MERITOCRACY. It also has to face the possibility that 'unequal individual endowment' may be more resilient to social change, because of GENETIC factors, than the ENVIRONMENTALIST beliefs of earlier egalitarians allowed for (see NATURE VERSUS NURTURE). Nonetheless egalitarianism remains one of the most powerful ideas in modern history.   L.L.

Bibl: R.H. Tawney, *Equality* (London, rev. ed., 1952); J. Rees, *Equality* (London and New York, 1971); J. Rawls, *A Theory of Justice* (Cambridge, Mass., 1971; Oxford, 1972).

ego. The ego is the system of PERCEPTION, which is presented in PSYCHOANALYSIS as a psychic function whose operations govern the construction of reality. In Freud's early work two phenomena — of negative hallucination in HYPNOSIS, where the subject devises a gloss of explanations for his actions in a situation where he is unable consciously to perceive certain objects; and of the compulsive establishment of 'false connection' in HYSTERIA — are claimed by Freud to be not entirely pathological, but general characteristics of ego functioning. It follows from this that the REALITY PRINCIPLE, which is delegated its tasks by the ego's basic orientation towards the avoidance of pain, is subject to typical forms of misrepresentation and illusion. The epistemological problems arising from this have been treated by Jacques Lacan (see LACANIAN).

In Freud's later work the ego is constructed as a precipitate of IDENTIFICATIONS, where the conflict between these internalizations plays a determining role in the functioning of the reality principle. However, since an identification is a misunderstanding of who one is, the same problems of misrecognition and illusion appear. Lacan distinguished SYMBOLIC identification (see EGO-IDEAL) from specular identification (see IDEAL EGO), neither type escaping from the systems of illusion and lure characteristic of the ego (see IMAGINARY). Lacan's original formulations of this problem are to be found in his early work on the MIRROR PHASE.

Lacan's claim is that the relations existing between the SUBJECT and the ego allow a study of psychic conflict and structure that can avoid subordination to the captivating misunderstandings that rule the domain of the ego.   B.BU.

Bibl: J. Lacan, *The Ego in Freud's Theory and in Psychoanalytic Technique* (Cambridge, 1987).

ego-ideal. A key concept in Lacan's version of PSYCHOANALYSIS. The ideal-functions of the EGO are based on two types of identification: SYMBOLIC and IMAGINARY. The ego-ideal, on the one hand, is based on an attempt to subordinate the psyche to the authority perceived to be operative in the Oedipal triangle, and is constructed through symbolic identification. On the other hand, the IDEAL EGO is an attempt to regain the omnipotence threatened by these Oedipal dynamics, and is based on imaginary identification. The relation of these two forms of identification was worked on by Jacques Lacan in the 1960s, extending his earlier work on the MIRROR PHASE, and developing his theory of the dialectics of DESIRE. The ego-ideal represents an internalized plan of the law; but the conscience thus generated, being based on identification, represents a misunderstanding of the law. Lacan's variables seek to establish that desire, and the conflict that it enters into, establishes the real structure of the law, which is beyond the scope of the functions of the ego. The ego-ideal works in conjunction with the SUPEREGO, which uses the ego-ideal as a template in the imposition of its morality.   B.BU.

Bibl: J. Lacan, *Ecrits* (London, 1977); *The Ego in Freud's Theory and the Technique of Psychoanalysis* (Cambridge, 1987).

ego-psychology. A school within PSYCHOANALYSIS that originally developed its theses in the 1930s as an attempt to formulate how the problems and theories of psychoanalysis could be developed as a science. Where Freud, and even analysts in some respects fairly close to the ego-psychologists, such as Nunberg, had taken the EGO (see EGO-IDEAL, IDEAL EGO) to be structured by psychical conflict, the leaders of this school (following Heinz Hartmann) postulated the existence of a conflict-free sphere of the ego, a zone whose autonomy was seen as extending to a range of functions including PERCEPTION, thinking, and the operations of language. In taking the functioning of the ego as the base where they hoped to establish sufficient cognitive autonomy to be able to construct laws of the mind, their programme flew in the face of Freud's constantly repeated claim that the ego is the locus of illusion and misrecognition. The theories of science, and the associated theories of reality assumed by the ego-psychologists, have been criticized by Jacques Lacan. In terms of analytical practice, ego-psychology aims to orientate the technique of psychoanalysis around the rationality available to the analyst's autonomous ego. By the end of the 1950s this school had come to dominate the main body of psychoanalysis in the U.S.

B.BU.

Bibl: H. Hartmann, *Ego Psychology and the Problem of Adaptation* (London, 1958).

egoism.
(1) In ETHICS, the view that the foundation of morality is, or ought to be, individual self-interest;
(2) the behaviour of one who abides by this view. W.Z.

Egoist, The. Title from 1914 until its demise in 1919 of a London fortnightly review, the exemplary 'little magazine' of this crucial period and central organ for Anglo-American MODERNISM. Originally the feminist *New Freewoman*, sponsored by Harriet Shaw Weaver, the paper changed title and content after Ezra Pound became literary editor. It included major work, creative and critical, by Pound himself, his editorial successors Richard Aldington, H.D. (Hilda Doolittle), and T.S. Eliot, and such writers as Rémy de Gourmont, James Joyce (including extracts from *Ulysses*), Ford Madox Hueffer (Ford), and F.S. Flint. In particular it introduced IMAGISM in England and was the main English outlet for new American poets, including Amy Lowell, Marianne Moore, William Carlos Williams, and Robert Frost. M.S.BR.

eidetic image. A vividly clear, detailed mental image of what has previously been seen. It is lifelike, i.e. seen as located outside rather than in the head, and often contains a surprising amount of accurate detail. I.M.L.H.

eidetic reduction. In Edmund Husserl's PHENOMENOLOGY, this is the second of six 'reductions' that are carried out in an effort to purify the APPERCEPTION of a mental phenomenon. Firstly, the entire world of fact, history and nature is eliminated by the famous phenomenological 'bracket' (*epoche*). No reference is to be had to any empirical science. Then, after the 'naturalistic thesis' has been bracketed out, the 'reductions' begin. The first is the 'psychological reduction' which eliminates the idiosyncrasies of the perceiver or analyst himself. Secondly there is the 'eidetic reduction', which sets up the phenomenon as a perceived essence. After the fifth or sixth 'reduction' there is nothing left but the 'pure transcendental EGO', whose apperceptions, just because they have been refined through so many sieves of SUBJECTIVITY, are now purely objective. The 'reductions' are not only very difficult to understand, they also involve a high degree of paradox, which critics of all traditions have not been slow to point out. Nevertheless, it is clear that Husserl was aiming at a breakthrough of some sort with his 'reductions', a freeing of philosophy both from EMPIRICISM and from scientific POSITIVISM. By 'bracketing' the entire world of historical and empirical reality, Husserl believed that acts of INTENTIONALITY could be directed solely and exclusively towards the 'essence' of the bracketed phenomenon in question. He sought for direct access to 'essential' content, an apperception of the essence of a phenomenon which is necessary, complete, objective and unquestionably veridical. Following the work of Hans-Georg Gadamer, Paul Ricoeur has recently queried the usefulness of the initial 'bracketing' out of the real world, and the reality of the ensuing 'reductions', on the grounds that all understanding is necessarily historical, and that HERMENEUTICS has 'ruined' the particularly IDEALISTIC interpretation of phenomenology which Husserl gives, though it may well have left other, later, kinds intact. R.PO.

Bibl: Q. Lauer, *Phenomenology: Its Genesis and Prospect* (New York, 1965); P. Ricoeur, *Hermeneutics and the Human Sciences* (Cambridge, 1981).

Einstellung ('attitude', 'set'). German term for a habitual procedure for dealing with repeatedly encountered problems of similar type. See also PROBLEM-SOLVING.

I.M.L.H.

ekistics. Term coined by the Greek planner, C.A. Doxiadis, for the study of human SETTLEMENTS and their problems by bringing together in an interdisciplinary and international approach experts from such subjects as ECONOMICS, GEOGRAPHY, SOCIOLOGY. A.L.C.B.

Bibl: C.A. Doxiadis, *Ekistics* (London and New York, 1968).

élan vital, see under VITALISM.

elastic rebound theory. This theory explaining the origin of earthquakes was developed by H.F. Reid after he had studied the effects of the disastrous San Francisco earthquake of 1906. In essence Reid's theory postulates as the immediate cause of earthquakes the sudden movement of rocks of the crust and mantle (see LITHOSPHERE) either side of a pre-existing fracture or fault. This rapid phase is, however, only the culmination of a slow and increasing elastic distortion of the rocks over tens of years. The situation is analogous to pushing one rubber eraser over another. Both will be distorted elastically but only while the frictional resistance of their contacting surfaces is not exceeded. The rubbers 'grip' each other. When the frictional resistance is exceeded each rubber will rebound to its original shape but it will be displaced. Similarly the rocks either side of the potential fault suffer increasing distortion until the frictional resistance of the fault is exceeded. Suddenly, over a period of a few seconds the fault slips, allowing the distorted rocks to rebound to their original shape. Measured displacements along earthquake faults at the surface range from a few centimetres to several metres. J.L.M.L.

elasticity. In ECONOMICS, a measure of the response of a VARIABLE, e.g. DEMAND or SUPPLY, to a change in a determining variable, e.g. price. The measure is the ratio of the relative change in the variable to the relative change in the determining variable. A low elasticity represents a situation in which a moderate relative change in the determining variable gives only a small relative change in the other variable. Elas-

ticities are known to vary between different time periods, prices, incomes, etc. Elasticities depend on the time period over which the changes are considered. Thus, the price elasticity of demand for oil is low in the short run, as people, firms, etc. will not immediately replace oil-burning equipment if the price of oil increases, but they may reduce their consumption slightly. In the long run, the equipment will be replaced and the associated change in the demand for oil will be greater. Though a simple concept, ECONOMETRIC studies of the same elasticity in similar economic circumstances often give quite different estimates. J.P.

Bibl: J. Craven, *Introduction to Economics* (Oxford, 1984).

Electra complex. In psychoanalytic theory (see PSYCHOANALYSIS), a normal emotional crisis in females resulting, at an early stage of PSYCHOSEXUAL DEVELOPMENT, from sexual impulses towards the father and jealousy of the mother. It is the female counterpart of the OEDIPUS COMPLEX. W.Z.

electrocardiogram. A recording of the heart's electrical activity by means of ELECTRODES attached to the skin of the extremities and by six further electrodes positioned across the sternum and left side of the chest. Deviation from the normal pattern can be identified in disease states.

L.J.F.

electrochemistry. The oldest branch of PHYSICAL CHEMISTRY, electrochemistry is the study of solutions of ELECTROLYTES and of the processes occurring at ELECTRODES. It involves investigation of the structure of electrolytes, which are usually (but not necessarily) aqueous, the measurement and formulation of theories of ionic transport, and the kinetics of CHEMICAL REACTIONS between IONS. Electrode processes relate to the measurement of THERMODYNAMIC and KINETIC properties of reactions taking place at electrodes, to POLAROGRAPHY, and to ionic EQUILIBRIA involving membranes. B.F.

Bibl: J. Koryta, J. Dvořák, and V. Boháčková, *Electrochemistry* (London, 1970).

electro-convulsive therapy (ECT). A technique in PSYCHOSURGERY through which artificial convulsions are induced by means of electric shock, to treat particular mental disorders such as DEPRESSION. At least from the 18th century onwards, shock therapy was used on a purely empirical basis for the relief of melancholy and similar disorders. Its modern application stems largely from the experiments of Ugo Cerletti in Rome in the 1930s, who proceeded from dogs to men, refined his techniques (in terms of the precise quantity of current flowing) and claimed success in relieving epileptics (see EPILEPSY) and gross schizophrenics (see SCHIZO-PHRENIA) from 1938 onwards. ECT came to be widely used, though to this day it remains unclear as to precisely how it produces its effects, or indeed as to whether it is truly effective. Most believe that there are temporary gains in excitation but little long term benefit. Many patients complain of short term memory loss as an unpleasant side effect of ECT.

R.P.

Bibl: W.L. Jones, *Ministering to Minds Diseased* (London, 1983).

electrode. An emitter (*cathode*) or receiver (*anode*) of ELECTRONS, as in an ELECTRON GUN (emitter) or a THERMIONIC valve (receiver).

M.V.B.

electrodynamics. The common ground between MECHANICS and ELECTROMAGNET-ISM which deals with the motion of charged PARTICLES in an ELECTROMAG-NETIC FIELD. Typical electrodynamic effects are VAN ALLEN BELTS and focusing in an ELECTRON MICROSCOPE. For *quantum electrodynamics* see FIELD THEORY; OP-TICS.

M.V.B.

electroencephalograph (EEG). In NEURO-PSYCHOLOGY, (1) an instrument used for recording changes of electric potentials originating in the brain, by means of ELEC-TRODES applied to the scalp or implanted within the tissues of the brain; (2) the print-out of these electric currents, i.e. records of brain waves.

W.Z.

electroencephalography. The technique of recording and interpreting the electrical activity of the brain on a series of channels (8 or 16 in each hemisphere via ELEC-TRODES glued to the skin of the scalp) is useful in diagnosing the presence of EPI-LEPSY. It has now been superseded by modern imaging techniques which more accurately demonstrate the brain's structure (computed tomography and nuclear magnetic resonance: see RADIOLOGY) and function (positron emission tomography). New COMPUTER-assisted electroencephalographic techniques allow more accurate localization of abnormalities. The combination of electroencephalographic recording with visual, auditory and cutaneous stimulation (*evoked potential recordings*) is more useful than simple electroencephalographic recordings. Intraoperative electroencephalographic and evoked potential recordings give early warning of impending damage to the central NERVOUS SYSTEM structures of patients undergoing operations while under general ANAES-THESIA.

A.D.M.

electrolysis. A CHEMICAL REACTION occurring as the result of the passage of an electric current. Commercially important electrolytic processes include the extraction of metals from their ores, particularly aluminium, and the production of hydrogen and chlorine from brine.

B.F.

electrolyte. A substance which gives rise to IONS in solution. A strong electrolyte is a substance which is largely dissociated (see DISSOCIATION) into its ions in solution.

B.F.

electromagnetic field. The FIELD whose sources are charges, currents, and magnets. Combinations of electric and magnetic fields whose strengths vary with time constitute RADIATION; they may travel great distances from their sources. The existence of an electromagnetic field in a region is indicated by forces exerted on test charges, currents, and magnets. See also ELECTROMAGNETISM; ELECTRO-STATICS; MAGNETISM.

M.V.B.

electromagnetism (or *electromagnetic theory*). One of the main branches of PHYSICS, linking the phenomena of ELECTRO-STATICS, electric currents, MAGNETISM, and OPTICS into a single conceptual framework. The final form of the theory was devised by Maxwell and is one of the triumphs of 19th-century science. One of Maxwell's earliest predictions was the existence of radio waves, and his EQUATIONS are fundamental throughout modern TELECOMMUNICATIONS. See also RADAR; RADIATION. M.V.B.

electromyography, see MYOPATHY.

electron. The first ELEMENTARY PARTICLE to be discovered (in the late 19th century). The electron is negatively charged, stable, and about 2,000 times lighter than the hydrogen ATOM. Its importance for science as a whole stems largely from its occurrence as a relatively mobile constituent of atoms; thus it participates in the emission of light (see ATOMIC PHYSICS) and in electric conduction (see SOLID-STATE PHYSICS). M.V.B.

electron diffraction. The DIFFRACTION of a beam of ELECTRONS by matter in the form of a crystal LATTICE. The successful observation of electron diffraction led to the general acceptance of the WAVE-PARTICLE DUALITY. See also CRYSTALLOGRAPHY. M.V.B.

electron gun. An arrangement for producing a beam of ELECTRONS which may be focused and deflected at will, for use in, e.g., CATHODE RAY TUBES. See also ELECTRODE; THERMIONIC. M.V.B.

electron microscope. An instrument invented in 1931 for studying small material structures, such as crystals, microorganisms, and TISSUES. It is analogous to an ordinary optical microscope with the specimen illuminated by an ELECTRON beam (accelerated by a high voltage) instead of a light beam, and focused by combined electric and magnetic FIELDS instead of glass lenses. The image is displayed on a FLUORESCENT screen instead of being viewed directly. Because of DIFFRACTION, it is impossible in any microscope to resolve objects smaller than the wavelength of the RADIATION used; the very short DE BROGLIE WAVELENGTH of high-voltage electrons (see QUANTUM MECHANICS) has enabled single ATOMS to be discerned — more than a thousand times smaller than can be resolved op-

tically. BIOLOGY has been revolutionized by *electron microscopy*: it has opened up the ultrastructural world of CYTOLOGY and has revealed the anatomical structure of infective PARTICLES such as viruses (see VIROLOGY). M.V.B.; P.M.

electron shell. ELECTRONS in ATOMS can be assigned to different ORBITALS so that, according to the EXCLUSION PRINCIPLE, each has a unique set of QUANTUM NUMBERS. Electrons with the same principal quantum number comprise members of a particular shell; the K shell is closest to the NUCLEUS and has 2 electrons, the next shell (L) has 8 electrons, and so on. Each atom has a characteristic shell structure, but the ENERGIES of electrons in the higher shells overlap and in these cases only electrons in the same sub-shell — i.e. with identical principal and azimuthal quantum numbers — have similar energies. The CHEMISTRY of the ELEMENTS is strongly influenced by the nature and number of electrons in the outer sub-shells. B.F.

electron spin resonance. The application of MAGNETIC RESONANCE to the SPINS of ELECTRONS. M.V.B.

electronegativity. A measure of the ability of an ATOM to attract an ELECTRON. There have been several attempts to produce a scale of electronegativity, but the concept cannot be put in a uniquely quantitative way. Pauling devised a method based on BOND energies (see ENERGY) which makes fluorine the most electronegative element, followed by oxygen, nitrogen, and chlorine. B.F.

electronic music. This term can be applied to any music which uses electronic musical instruments. It is however more normally used to describe music in which sound sources are manipulated or new sounds are created electronically. Early experiments were made with unusual ways of playing records (speed changing, playing backwards, altering the record grooves, etc.). There was no simple way of recording these experiments until the general availability of the tape recorder after World War II. As well as giving a means to record sound experiments the tape recorder provided a whole new series of ways to treat sound (editing, multilayering etc.). Among the first composers to make substantial use of the tape recorder were those involved with *musique concrète* who manipulated naturally occurring sounds. Initially this was seen as distinct from the more purist form of electronic music which eschewed natural sounds and constructed its own new sounds from simple electronic test equipment such as sine wave generators, white noise generators, filters, amplifiers etc. (see ADDITIVE SYNTHESIS). In practice, however, the distinction was quickly lost and most early electronic music combined the advantages of both methods (the flexibility of pure electronic sound and the diversity of natural sound). Studios were set up in Cologne, Princeton, Milan and elsewhere in the 1950s to produce electronic music, which at this time required months of painstaking work to construct. Experiments were carried out combining live performance (see MUSIC NOTATION) with taped electronic music (e.g. Stockhausen's 'Kontakte') and also treating live instrumental or vocal performances by amplifying, filtering, RING MODULATING them etc. (see also SPATIAL MUSIC).

In the 1960s a new era of electronic music was brought in by the widespread introduction of the SYNTHESIZER which was capable of manipulating sound in REAL TIME. Other important developments included COMPUTER MUSIC and more recently, SOUND SAMPLING. The practice of electronic music is now firmly established as an essential branch of musical development and nearly all universities and colleges have facilities for its study.
B.CO.

Bibl: T.B. Holmes, *Electronic and Experimental Music* (New York, 1985).

electronics. The design of electric circuits (for use in radio receivers, COMPUTERS, amplifiers, etc.) incorporating devices such as TRANSISTORS and THERMIONIC valves, whose operation depends on the behaviour of ELECTRONS. M.V.B.

electrophoresis. The movement of a charged colloidal (see COLLOID) PARTICLE under the influence of an electrical FIELD. The effect is similar to the migration of IONS in solution. Because different colloids do not have the same velocity, electrophoresis is widely used in clinical medicine to separate colloids, either as aid in preparation or prior to chemical analysis.
B.F.

electrostatics. The branch of ELECTROMAGNETISM dealing with bodies with an excess of (positive or negative) electric charge. The operation of condensers in alternating-current circuits, and the frictional charging of clouds and aeroplanes, are electrostatic effects. M.V.B.

element. A substance which cannot be broken down into simpler constituents by chemical means, because all its ATOMS have the same ATOMIC NUMBER. The naturally-occurring elements range from hydrogen (No. 1) to uranium (No. 92), and about a dozen TRANSURANIC ELEMENTS have been produced artificially. M.V.B.

elementarism. The SCHOOL OF PSYCHOLOGY which holds that experience or behaviour is to be studied by analysing it into its component elements and then discovering how these elements associate together to produce the complex experience or behaviour. For the opposite approach see ORGANISMIC PSYCHOLOGY.
I.M.L.H.

elementary particles. The smallest constituents of matter. At present the most elementary constituents of matter are believed to be QUARKS and LEPTONS (the ELECTRON, MUON, tauon and their associated NEUTRINOS and ANTIPARTICLES), the PHOTON, GLUONS, the W and Z bosons, the GRAVITON and, it is predicted by GRAND UNIFIED THEORIES, a number of very heavy X and Y bosons. These particles are believed to have zero spatial extent and behave as points in scattering experiments. This belief has some experimental support. The electron is known to be at least smaller than $10^{1\ 5}$ centimetres in diameter.

Protons and NEUTRONS, MESONS and other HADRONS are not truly elementary particles. They are known to possess internal constituents (quarks). These constituents reveal themselves in scattering experiments. There exist theories which endow quarks and leptons with internal constituents called prequarks, preons or rishons but there exists no experimental evidence for the existence of these more elementary constituents of quarks particles as yet.

Elementary particles possess a variety of properties: MASS, electric charge, lifetimes, SPIN, QUANTUM NUMBERS. These individual properties cannot yet be explained by theories of elementary particles and must be determined by observation. Particles with finite lifetimes are called unstable, the others are denoted stable.

There exist theories which accurately describe the behaviour of different classes of elementary particles (see QUANTUM CHROMODYNAMICS and QUANTUM ELECTRODYNAMICS). Until recently these theories governed the behaviour of disjoint classes of elementary particles but progress has been made in merging them together within the framework of an all-embracing theory which gives a unified description of all the different forces and elementary particles of nature. These are called 'grand unified' theories.

Until very recently mathematical theories of elementary particles were invariably quantum FIELD THEORIES but current interest has moved towards the study of SUPERSTRING theories in which the basic elements are linear strings rather than points. Different elementary particles are envisaged to be the different vibrational excitations of a string of energy.

All elementary particles are believed to possess antiparticles of identical mass and lifetime, but opposite values of all additive quantum numbers like electric charge. In some cases the particle and the antiparticle are identical because the relevant additive quantum numbers are zero (for example, the photon and the antiphoton are identical).

Many physicists believe that there exist a finite number of truly elementary particles from which all the other SUBATOMIC PARTICLES are built up. This is called the *composite particle approach*. Another recurrent idea is that there exists an infinite number of particles of increasing mass and every particle is composed of every other particle. These theories are called *bootstrap* theories and predict that there exists a maximum temperature in nature.

This maximum temperature is sometimes called the *Hagedorn temperature*. They are not currently consistent with experimental evidence unless that maximum temperature is far higher than any yet attained in accelerator experiments.

All successful theories of elementary particles are gauge theories. These theories are built upon particular mathematical symmetries which predict which particles do and do not exist and which other particles they will interact with. *Group theory* is used to impose these mathematical symmetries upon theories of elementary particles. The resulting theories are called gauge theories or gauge invariants. Every symmetry of the theory corresponds to a CONSERVATION LAW of nature.

The study of elementary particles is the most extensive area of theoretical PHYSICS and the most expensive area of experimental science. It is carried out using PARTICLE COLLIDERS and ACCELERATORS which collide subatomic particles together at high speed and monitor the debris of the collisions using sensitive particle tracking devices and computers to identify the constituents revealed in the collision. The most successful accelerators are those at CERN in Geneva, administered by a collective of European nations, and Fermi-Lab in Chicago respectively. The experimental teams involved in the search for a new elementary particle using one of these devices now number many hundreds of individuals.   J.D.B.

Bibl: S. Weinberg, *The Discovery of Subatomic Particles* (San Francisco, 1984); P. Davies, *The Forces of Nature* (Cambridge, 1979); A. Pais, *Inward Bound* (Oxford, 1986).

élite. Collective noun for those who occupy a position (or positions) of superiority within a society or group by virtue of qualities (actual, claimed, or presumed) of excellence or distinction. The term's history owes much to the use made of it by V. Pareto and the observations made by him with regard to (1) the élite as distinguished from the non-élite groups within a social order and (2) the divisions within the élite as between a governing élite and a non-governing élite. Pareto's work and that of others (such as G. Mosca and R. Michels) has generated much debate, e.g.

263

concerning the functions and social supports of *political élites*, the types of such élites as found in different societies, their cohesiveness, and their relation to *ruling classes*. Pareto himself sought to establish the psychological basis of élite status, authority, and continuity. Within his special conceptual framework and his theory of history as 'the graveyard of aristocracies' he took shifts in that basis as explaining the *circulation of élites* — a cyclical process of élite replacement over a period of time. See also ÉLITISM; POWER ÉLITES. S.J.G.

Bibl: V. Pareto, ed. S.E. Finer, tr. D. Mirfin, *Sociological Writings* (London and New York, 1966); G. Parry, *Political Élites* (New York, 1970).

élitism. A term of abuse for an educational system in which children of above-average ability are segregated (in, e.g., British PUBLIC SCHOOLS) and educated to above-average levels; some theorists extend the term, and their disapproval, to any form of educational selection, e.g. streaming or university entrance requirements. The purely educational arguments for and against selection tend to be overshadowed by socio-political considerations, e.g. the tendency of the educational system to reflect and reinforce the existing SOCIAL STRATIFICATION. W.A.C.S.

Bibl: J. Floud, A.H. Halsey, and F.M. Martin, *Social Class and Educational Opportunity* (London, 1956).

El Salvador. The smallest country on the American continental mainland, El Salvador is racially and culturally homogeneous but has a very high population density (4.4 million in 8,259 square miles) which creates enormous pressure on land resources in an economy still largely dependent on primary export crops (coffee, cotton and sugar). A strongly oligarchical society, El Salvador has mostly been ruled by the military, but towards the end of the 1970s the power of this alliance was challenged by the emergence of a GUERRILLA movement, the Farabundo Martí National Liberation Front (FMLN), named after a 1932 COMMUNIST martyr, and its political organization, the Democratic Revolutionary Front (FDR). Since then the country has been plunged into civil war, with some

parts of the country — mostly in the north — declared 'liberated zones' which are effectively beyond the control of government forces. By 1983 a military stalemate had emerged between the U.S.-aided, -trained and -equipped Salvadoran army and the FMLN, which has evolved into a highly effective rural guerrilla army with substantial support amongst the peasantry. The U.S. has taken a strong interest in Salvadoran affairs, particularly since the 1979 victory of the Nicaraguan revolution (see NICARAGUA). However its attempts to promote a centrist solution through the Christian Democrat Party have proved problematic in an atmosphere of extreme polarization between LEFT and RIGHT (see ARENA). Following 1984 presidential and 1985 congressional elections the Christian Democrats are in government in El Salvador, but the war continues unabated. N.M.

Bibl: James Dunkerley, *The Long War — Dictatorship and Revolution in El Salvador* (London, 1982).

embodiment. A concept fundamental to contemporary PHENOMENOLOGY. That PERCEPTION and understanding of the world are partly a function of the fact that CONSCIOUSNESS is not 'pure', but exists within a membrane of flesh and blood, has led to a situation in which many of the problems seen as otiose by Descartes have been re-introduced as vital to the understanding of how human beings do in fact perceive or *constitute* their world. In his early work, Edmund Husserl touched on the problem of embodiment in his effort to distinguish *marks* from signs in human communication, but in his revulsion towards all forms of PSYCHOLOGISM he did not allow himself to take up the human body itself into the problem of perception. In fact, he tried more and more strenuously to exclude all human or 'relativistic' factors from his philosophy. However, by the time of *Ideas 2* and *Cartesian Mediations* (1931), Husserl came to see that human embodiment might well be important in the matter of interpreting both one's own perceptions and the perceptions of the OTHER. It was only in the work of the French existentializing phenomenologists, however (e.g. Sartre and Merleau-Ponty), that the fact that the body actually 'lives' a world, and thus projects 'its' values over a world by INTENTIONALITY was taken serious account of. Sartre (1943) has many famous descriptions of how embodiment in its various kinds of BAD FAITH projects its meanings over the world of the Other. Merleau-Ponty's 1945 essay, *The Phenomenology of Perception*, examines embodiment as the fundamental problem in philosophy, the manner in which the world appears to the embodied consciousness and the way in which the world is changed by the projections of embodied consciousness. In 1960, R.D. Laing's *The Divided Self* used the clue of embodiment to take account, as conventional PSYCHIATRY does not, of the subjective or lived quality of the patient's experience. Embodiment, then, represents the subject's own view of his or her body as it has to be lived with subjectively. It represents the exact opposite of one's body as perceived by others in the objective outer world. Sometimes the inner perception of embodiment can be at variance with public perception in a significant and possibly painful way: ANOREXIA NERVOSA is a striking example of this variance, as are many forms of what is lightly called SCHIZOPHRENIA, when the patient's own view of his own embodiment is systematically left out of account. In *The Leaves of Spring* (1970) Aaron Esterson showed how the facts of embodiment can render socially intelligible the behaviour of a whole family, and in particular, the apparently 'incomprehensible' activities of one member of it. The phenomenological accent on the importance of embodiment as a clue in understanding has enriched EXISTENTIAL PSYCHOTHERAPY in the work of Peter Lomas and David Smail.

Literary theory has also profited from the insight, allowing a new recognition of the importance of a writer's embodiment in the textual DISPLACEMENTS of his or her own literary constructions. The work of Roger Poole, Stephen Trombley and Mark Hussey on Virginia Woolf has shown that no text is innocent of its embodied origins. The fact that the subject's own view of his or her embodiment is just as 'true' for him or for her as the public or outer perception of the body has led to a new questioning of the received understanding of 'objectivity' itself.   R.PO.

Bibl: M. Merleau-Ponty, *Phenomenology of Perception* (London, 1962).

embourgeoisement. An explanation, popular with MARXISTS since first invented by Friedrich Engels, of the failure of the western WORKING CLASS to support radical political parties and movements, specifically those committed to full-blooded SOCIALISM. A newfound affluence, it is said, has led workers to adopt middle-class (BOURGEOIS) attitudes and values, so cutting their traditional attachment to working-class institutions and causing a significant minority to transfer their allegiance to political parties of the CENTRE and RIGHT (see also INCORPORATION).

                                                         K.K.
Bibl: J.H. Goldthorpe *et al.*, *The Affluent Worker in the Class Structure* (Cambridge, 1969).

embryology. The branch of ZOOLOGY that deals with the history and theory of development — in particular the development that begins with a ZYGOTE. (1) In chordate animals development begins with the subdivision (*cleavage* — sometimes called *segmentation*) of the zygote into a number of separate daughter CELLS which rearrange themselves to form a hollow vesicle (*blastula*) or something equivalent to it (e.g. BLASTOCYST). (2) The next major manoeuvre is *gastrulation*, the conversion of this hollow sac into a three-layered larva — the *gastrula*. Then (3) all chordate animals go through a stage called the *neurula* — a slightly elongated embryo with a bulky head and a tapering tail with the elementary NERVOUS SYSTEM in the form of a hollow tube running from end to end, and under that the notochord or skeletal rod to which the chordates owe their name, both tube and rod being flanked on either side by *somites*, i.e. by muscle blocks arranged segmentally down the length of the body, reminding us that vertebrates are in their origin segmented animals. In chordates the principal body cavity is a *perivisceral coelom*, i.e. a cavity which holds the guts and viscera generally. The kidneys originate in all vertebrates from the narrow connections between the cavities of the segmental muscle blocks and the perivisceral coelom. The eyes of vertebrate animals are formed through the conjunction of an outgrowth from the brain which becomes the retina with a thickening of the ectoderm which becomes the lens. A transverse section through a neurula at this stage looks very much the same in all vertebrates, and only an experienced embryologist can identify the class of vertebrate animal to which a given neurula belongs. It is this fact, that the embryos of related animals resemble each other far more closely than the adults into which they develop (*von Baer's principle*), which contains the germ of truth in the doctrine of RECAPITULATION. In its simplest form this doctrine declares that in development an animal 'climbs up its own family tree'. In the heyday of recapitulation theory it was contended that the gastrula larva represents recapitulation of a very early stage in the EVOLUTION of many-celled animals, namely that stage seen today in hydroids and jellyfish, which are in essentials also simple invaginated two-layered sacs the single aperture of which serves both as mouth and anus. Embryonic development is guided by instructions contained within the DNA (see NUCLEIC ACID) of the CHROMOSOMES of the zygote. It is only in this sense that the old PREFORMATIONIST theory is true. The instructions are preformed, but their carrying out is 'epigenetic', i.e. dependent upon the right sequence of STIMULI from the ENVIRONMENT and from the cells into which the embryo itself develops.   P.M.

Bibl: L. Hamilton, *From Egg to Adolescent* (London and New York, 1976).

emergence. In hierarchically organized systems, especially in BIOLOGY, the appearance at some tier of the hierarchy of a novelty which is not obviously predictable or foreseeable in terms of anything that has preceded it. Thus consciousness or cerebration has been said to have 'emerged' in the EVOLUTION of higher primates. Much earnest and confused thought surrounds the notion that emergence is a kind of evolutionary stratagem which explains the appearance of novelties.   P.M.

emergent poetry, see under CONCRETE POETRY.

emergent property. A property of some complex whole which cannot be explained in terms of the properties of the parts. Some think the mind is an emergent property of the brain. See also REDUCTION.

A.S.

emergent technology. The doctrine that TECHNOLOGY will create a new style and pattern of battle. It depends on a belief that warfare can be systematized and controlled by ARTIFICIAL INTELLIGENCE, reducing dependence both on large reserves of manpower and crude NUCLEAR WEAPONS. Surveillance by satellite over a huge range of military and economic data will provide a WAR plan which extends the battlefront deep into the enemy's base areas (see DEEP STRIKE). It is a visionary view of warfare produced as much by the political circumstances of NATO as any realistic assessment of likely developments. The case for emergent technology was advanced in a scheme called 'Battlefield 2000', which resolved all NATO's major problems within a single concept. Its admitted disadvantage was the enormous cost of such a programme. Critics claimed that the 'electromagnetic pulse' emitted by a nuclear explosion high in space would destroy the communications links on which this theory depends. Like the STRATEGIC DEFENCE INITIATIVE, another aspect of emergent technology, its claims remain unproven.   A.J.M.W.

emic and etic. In LINGUISTICS, terms derived from the contrast between phonemics (see PHONOLOGY) and PHONETICS, and used to characterize opposed approaches to the study of linguistic data. An *etic* approach is one where the physical patterns of language are described with a minimum of reference to their function within the language system, whereas an emic approach takes full account of functional relationships, setting up minimal contrastive units as the basis of a description. Thus an etic approach to INTONATION would describe an utterance's pitch movement as minutely as possible, whereas an emic approach would describe only those features of the pitch pattern which are used to signal meanings.   D.C.

Emmert's Law, see under AFTER-IMAGE.

emotion. A word used in ordinary language to refer principally to subjective experience. The Platonic tradition regarded emotion as the enemy of reason, and hence of judgement, truth and morality. From Hume in the mid-18th century onwards, the necessary emotional basis of right conduct and moral philosophy has been repeatedly insisted upon; and many influential 20th-century figures, such as D. H. Lawrence, have elevated the morality of the heart and the healthiness of feeling over the dictates of reason. Such experience is of its nature outside the reach of EXPERIMENTAL PSYCHOLOGY, whose subject-matter, like that of any objective empirical science, must contain specifiable experimental operations, empirical observations, and theories formulated to account for such relationships; whereas 'emotion' refers neither to operations nor to observations, and can find a home in the language of experimental psychology only as a theory-word. However, the high tide of BEHAVIOURISM in the 1920s left psychologists reluctant to talk theory at all, preferring instead STIMULI (the psychologist's comprehensive term for experimental operations) and 'responses' (i.e. observations). None the less, the feeling persisted that the layman's term 'emotion' in some way specified a class of behaviour in a specific class of situations. To satisfy this feeling, and yet eschew the dangers of MENTALISM, the vogue arose for studying 'emotional stimuli' and 'emotional responses or behaviour'. In the absence of a theory of emotion, however, such terms are totally undefined, so it is not surprising that they have caused much confusion. One reaction has been to say that there is *no* unitary class of behaviour which can be distinguished as 'emotional', and that the word should be dropped altogether.

A more useful reaction is to construct an explicit theory of emotion, rather than hiding behind the implicit theory embodied in the stimulus-response formulation. 'Emotion' being a layman's term, one might perhaps begin by attempting to illumine the intuitions behind our ordinary language. This, properly speaking, is the business of the philosopher of language (see LINGUISTIC PHILOSOPHY) but to date PSYCHOLOGY has not drawn much on such work. None the less, at least one current philosophic view of 'emotion' (see EMOTIVISM) — that emotion-words have to do with the appraisal as 'good' or 'bad' of the objects which give rise to emotional states — finds a satisfying echo in recent developments in the psychology of emotion. These developments spring in the main from the theory of learning; in particular, that part which concerns the way subjects (including animals; see also ETHOLOGY) respond to and learn about rewards and punishments. These (the two major forms of *reinforcement*; see OPERANT CONDITIONING) are defined operationally by the changes they produce in the behaviour on which they are contingent. A reward is a stimulus which, when made contingent upon a response, increases the latter's probability of recurrence; a punishment is a stimulus which decreases this probability.

With this in mind, we can define emotion as consisting in the set of states of the organism produced by reinforcing events or by *conditioned stimuli* (see CLASSICAL CONDITIONING) that have in the subject's previous experience been followed by reinforcing events. Put less technically, an emotional state consists in a DISPOSITION to act in particular ways, produced by exposure to stimuli which the subject wants to experience or to avoid, or by exposure to signals which predict the imminent occurrence of such stimuli. Such states are, of course, accompanied by changes in neural and hormonal processes, and these have been extensively studied. Signals of the subject's emotional state are also of biological significance for other members of the subject's SPECIES (its *conspecifics*). The study of the way in which one animal communicates to another its current emotional state, thus enabling its conspecifics to predict its likely future behaviour, was first given scientific prominence by Darwin in 1872. Recently, there have been a number of important attempts to apply to the study of emotional expression in man the techniques previously used with animals.

The MODELS proposed by psychologists for an understanding of emotion posit only a few emotional states. Yet in ordinary language there are hundreds of different names of apparently separate emotions. A simple resolution of this discrepancy is to hand. It is clear from experimental work in SOCIAL PSYCHOLOGY that, in ascribing a name to one's current emotional state, one takes into account not only its nature but also the specific circumstances that gave rise to it, and that a multiplicity of names may reflect a multiplicity, not of states but only of types of situation giving rise to a single state. For example, the tension felt by someone anticipating a specific painful experience or danger is commonly called 'fear'; the same state is often called 'ANXIETY' when the feared event is unknown or diffuse; and there is experimental evidence that it is this same state which is produced by signals of omission of reward, when one might be described as anticipating 'frustration' or 'disappointment'. J.A.G.;R.P.

Bibl: C. Darwin, *The Expression of the Emotions in Man and Animals* (London, 1872; New York, 1873; Chicago and London, 1965; New York, 1969); R.A. Hinde (ed.), *Non-Verbal Communication* (London, 1972); Roger Poole, *Towards Deep Subjectivity* (New York and London, 1972).

emotive and referential language. A distinction between two kinds of language popularized by C.K. Ogden and I.A. Richards (*The Meaning of Meaning*, 1923); sometimes expressed as a distinction between CONNOTATION AND DENOTATION. Richards, throughout his earlier career, advocated the rights of a complex, organized emotional language — affecting attitudes — against those of the referential language of science, LOGIC, or MATHEMATICS. Poetry was 'the supreme form of emotive language'. The distinction, which crystallized with the advent of ROMANTICISM, is a necessary one; but it requires considerable and subtle refinement, if only because no serious critic could assert that there is an actual split between the emotive and the referential. The NEW CRITICISM is full of such attempted refinements.

M.S.-S.

emotivism. In ETHICS, the theory that VALUE-JUDGEMENTS, particularly moral judgements, are expressions of the speaker's emotions about the action, person, or situation to which they refer and not, as they grammatically appear to be, statements of fact, true or false. Emotivists emphasize the distinction between utterances that *express* feeling, such as ejaculations or expletives, and utterances that *state* that a certain feeling is being experienced. It is to the former that they assimilate judgements of value. Hinted at by C.K. Ogden and I.A. Richards in the 1920s, emotivism was set out as an explicit theory by A.J. Ayer in the following decade and was developed with great detail and thoroughness in the *Ethics and Language* (1944) of C.L. Stevenson. Its immediate foundation is the apparent irresolubility of much moral disagreement. Indirectly it supplies a need created by the improved version of the doctrine of the NATURALISTIC FALLACY, which holds that value-judgements are quite different in nature from statements of fact. Emotivism's exponents tended to agree, on reflection, that the distinctive feature of value-judgements was that their acceptance by someone committed him to *acting* in a certain way, whereas the acceptance of a statement of fact committed him only to the adoption of the corresponding *belief*. If this is correct, value-judgements are more like imperatives than merely expressive utterances. As a result emotivism, notably in the influential works of R.M. Hare, has largely given way to *imperativism* or *prescriptivism*. A.Q.

Bibl: R.M. Hare, *The Language of Morals* (Oxford, 1952; New York, 1964); J.O. Urmson, *The Emotive Theory of Ethics* (London, 1968).

empathy. Projection (not necessarily voluntary) of the self into the feelings of others or, anthropomorphically, into the 'being' of objects or sets of objects; it implies psychological involvement, at once Keats's pain and joy. The word itself was coined by Vernon Lee in 1904, and then employed by the psychologist E.B. Titchener in 1909 as a translation of the German *Einfühlung* ('feeling-into'), the notion of which had been developed in Germany by R.H. Lotze in *Mikrokosmos* (1856-64; tr. 1886); it largely provoked the ALIENATION theories of Brecht in reaction to it. M.S.-S.

empirical theology. Challenged by the general acceptance among educated people of the inductive scientific method (see INDUCTION; see also, however, POPPERIAN) as the only means of knowing anything, Christian THEOLOGY has in this century reviewed its own METHODOLOGY. Apart from DEATH OF GOD THEOLOGY, three main responses have appeared. One is the defiant reaffirmation of DOGMA. The second is the insistence in CRISIS THEOLOGY that God is not an object to be known scientifically but is nevertheless the great self-revealing reality, to be encountered and obeyed. The third is the argument that God can be known rationally or at least intuitively like any other object (or, as many would prefer, subject) in human experience, while he is also greater. D.C. Macintosh, in *Theology as an Empirical Science* (1919), exemplified this effort to fit THEISM into the scientific worldview. Other LIBERAL theologians of this school included Shailer Mathews and H.N. Wieman, both of the University of Chicago. Although this mainly American movement was largely defeated by the emphasis in crisis theology on the otherness and mystery of God, the challenge which it had taken up remained, and was not entirely met by CHRISTIAN EXISTENTIALISM's derivation of doctrines from a more specifically religious experience. In the 1960s and later, Christian philosophers, mainly in England, returned to the task with a more modest programme discussing the nature and scope of religious statements, specially about God, in comparison with science and in the light of LINGUISTIC analysis. Questions asked included these: Is any religious statement necessarily nonsense? If not, what is its meaning, or at least its use? Is it verifiable, or even falsifiable, by experience — in this world or in eternity? If it is based on a disclosure of the divine presence, what sort of situation contains this disclosure, and what sort of attempt to describe it, or to draw a conclusion from it, is valid? How odd do normal words become when used in a religious context? Thus about every doctrine it is asked: what is its empirical value?   D.L.E.

Bibl: K. Cauthen, *The Impact of American Religious Liberalism* (New York, 1962); I.T. Ramsey, *Religious Lan-*guage (London, 1957; New York, 1963); A.G.N. Flew and A. MacIntyre, *New Essays in Philosophical Theology* (London, 1955; New York, 1964); I.G. Barbour, *Issues in Science and Religion* (London and Englewood Cliffs, N.J., 1966).

empiricism. The theory (1) that all CONCEPTS are derived from experience, i.e. that a linguistic expression can be significant only if it is associated by rule with something that can be experienced, and (2) that all statements claiming to express knowledge depend for their justification on experience. The two aspects of the theory are not inseparable. Many empiricists, moreover, allow some exceptions under both heads. The formal concepts of LOGIC, e.g. those expressed by the words 'not', 'and', and 'all', are widely regarded as being purely syntactical and as having no connection with experience. As for knowledge, empiricists generally agree that there is a class of purely conceptual or analytic propositions (see ANALYTIC; PROPOSITIONS) which are necessarily true in virtue of the meanings of the words that express them, even if they stigmatize these propositions as 'trifling' (Locke) or 'merely verbal' (J.S. Mill). The opposite of empiricism is RATIONALISM or, more precisely, APRIORISM. The principle of VERIFICATION is a modern formulation of empiricism. Any statement of the empiricist theory, to be consistent (see CONSISTENCY) with itself, must be empirical or, if not, analytic. An empirical basis for the theory is provided by elementary facts about the way in which the meaning of words is learned.   A.Q.

Bibl: W.H. Walsh, *Reason and Experience* (Oxford, 1947); H.H. Price, *Thinking and Experience* (London, 1969).

emporiatrics. The science of travellers' health. The term is derived from the Greek *emporos* (a ship's passenger) and *iatriké* (medicine). The new speciality can be justified since travellers are exposed to changes in ENVIRONMENT, altitude, and temperature, to the effects of bodily (CIRCADIAN) rhythms being out of phase in a different time zone and to infectious or exotic diseases in tropical countries. Emporiatrics applies not only to business travellers and tourists, but also to the crews of aeroplanes, ships, and land vehicles as well as to immigrants, refugees and migrant labourers. Dr Myron G. Schultz, formerly of the U.S. Department of Health and Human Services, has observed that the new science of emporiatrics could aid the development of policies which would prevent avoidable suffering in travellers and help trade and tourism.

H.L'E.

emulsion.

(1) A system where one liquid is dispersed in droplet form throughout another with which it does not mix (e.g. mayonnaise, which consists of oil droplets in a mixture of vinegar and egg yolk).

(2) The suspension containing silver bromide which forms the light-sensitive coating on photographic plates. M.V.B.

enclaves and **exclaves.** Complementary geographical terms for a non-contiguous TERRITORY of a STATE embedded within the territory of another state; thus West Berlin forms an *enclave* from the viewpoint of East Germany, the state within which the outlier is located, but forms an *exclave* from the viewpoint of West Germany, the state to which the outlier belongs. Such outliers are now less common than in the past (e.g. Prussia before 1866 consisted of more than 270 disconnected segments of territory) but retain an important irritant role (e.g. Gibraltar) or economic role (e.g. Hong Kong) out of proportion to their size. P.H.

encoder. In INFORMATION THEORY, a device or PROGRAM which alters the representation of data to some desired form, usually in order to transmit the data or store them. If the transmission or storage medium is imperfect, an encoder is frequently designed to produce REDUNDANCY in its output. See also DECODER.

R.M.N.

Encounter. Monthly review of 'literature, art, politics', founded in London in 1953 by Stephen Spender and Irving Kristol; among subsequent editors have been Melvin Lasky, Frank Kermode, Nigel Dennis, D. J. Enright, and Anthony Thwaite. Sponsored by the Congress of Cultural Freedom, which probably had CIA funding, the magazine was one of an international, U.S.-financed stable (*Der Monat* in Germany was another), which exchanged articles and had contributors in common; it was a symptom both of the Americanization of Europe and of the close alliance of European and American INTELLECTUALS during the COLD WAR phase. *Encounter* none the less was the main British literary-intellectual journal of the period, and pursued an independent critical line. The intellectual alliance was and remains productive; *Encounter* has published some of the most interesting figures of the time (e.g. Arthur Koestler, Michael Polanyi, Sir Karl Popper), as well as admirable poetry, criticism, and, to a lesser extent, fiction. M.S.BR.

encounter group. In GROUP THERAPY, any therapeutic group in which body contact and emotional expression is encouraged rather than the traditional purely verbal interaction. The aim of encounter groups is to increase sensitivity to others, including both physical and emotional awareness. They may take many different forms, including marathon sessions (24 to 48 hours without sleep), meeting in warm baths (the *Esalen* group), and the use of special techniques such as soliloquy, ROLE-playing, PSYCHODRAMA, etc. It has been shown that encounter groups, apart from their positive effects, may also cause breakdowns in vulnerable participants.

M.J.C.

Bibl: I.D. Yalom, *The Theory and Practice of Group Psychotherapy* (New York, 1970).

enculturation. A term coined by M.J. Herskovits (1948) for the process by which individuals are brought up to be members of their CULTURE or society, i.e., how they are made, by EDUCATION in the broadest possible sense, to have the culture appropriate to them. The CONCEPT is thus very close to that of SOCIALIZATION, much used in SOCIOLOGY and DEVELOPMENTAL PSYCHOLOGY. M.F.

encyclical. An official statement by a Pope, known from its opening words (in Latin), e.g. PACEM IN TERRIS, QUADRAGESIMO ANNO, RERUM NOVARUM, RE-

DEMPTOR HOMINIS. INFALLIBILITY is not claimed for encyclicals.　　　D.L.E.

end stage, see under OPEN STAGE.

endocrinology. The branch of medical BI-OLOGY that deals with the nature and manner of action of endocrine glands and their SECRETIONS. Whereas most glands in the body (*exocrine glands*) communicate through ducts with the regions of the body in which their secretions (e.g. digestive ENZYMES) are to act, the *endocrine glands* are ductless and liberate their secretions (*hormones*) directly into the lymph vessels or the blood stream. The chief endocrine glands are: the various elements of the PITUITARY gland, the THYROID, the islet tissue of the pancreas, the thymus, the ADRENAL GLAND, and the sex glands of both sexes.

The anterior pituitary gland holds a key position in the endocrine regulation of the body, because its secretions control the activities of the adrenal cortex, the sex glands, and other endocrine organs. Its hormones belong to the PROTEIN family and are indeed *polypeptides* (see PEP-TIDES); the same is true of INSULIN, secreted in the pancreas. The sex hormones and the secretions of the adrenal cortex are all STEROIDS. Many hormones can now be manufactured synthetically.　　　P.M.

endogamy. Term developed by McLennan (*Primitive Marriage*, 1865) to describe a set of rules relating to MARRIAGE. They specify in-marriage, the unit within which an individual must marry. Marriages between first cousins are a common type of endogamous marriage.

Endogamy is a central feature of the Indian CASTE system: marriages should take place within and not between caste groups. In practice, however, Tambiah has shown that this system is more complicated and various strategies, particularly hypergamy, blur caste boundaries (*From Varna to Caste Through Mixed Unions*, 1973). Endogamy is also commonly found in association with wealth and property. Marrying within the group pools and preserves resources, protects status and acts against the dispersal of wealth (see EXOGAMY).　　　A.G.

Bibl: A. Barnard and A. Good, *Re-search Practices in the Study of Kinship* (London, 1984); M. Bloch, *From Blessing to Violence* (Cambridge, 1986).

endomorph, see under PERSONALITY TYPES.

endorphins. A family of PEPTIDES that regulate pain and other senses in the body. The first members of the family were the *enkephalins*. The RECEPTORS for endorphins also act as receptors for morphine and chemically related pain killers.　　　P.N.

endoscopy, see under UROLOGY.

endotoxins, see under BACTERIOLOGY.

endovascular prosthesis. An artificial heart valve sewn onto the inner lining of the heart (endocardium). These may be made from metal, plastic, sterilized tissue from another person (homograft) or animal (xenograft). They are frequently used to replace stenotic or leaking aortic and mitral valves.　　　L.J.F.

ENEA. European Nuclear Energy Agency. The European body responsible for the development of nuclear generated electric power.　　　C.E.D.

energy. The capacity of a physical system for doing mechanical work — i.e. for moving objects against forces. Energy exists in various forms, the most fundamental according to current theory being KINETIC ENERGY, matter (see MASS-ENERGY EQUA-TION) and the POTENTIAL ENERGIES due to GRAVITATION, ELECTROMAGNETIC FIELDS, and forces between ELEMENTARY PAR-TICLES (e.g. STRONG INTERACTIONS, WEAK INTERACTIONS). Other kinds of energy arise from these in complicated systems; thus, chemical energy is due to electromagnetic forces between ELECTRONS and NUCLEI in ATOMS, and heat energy is the total kinetic energy of random atomic motion. All these energies may be interconverted without loss because of a CONSER-VATION LAW whose apparent universality makes energy one of the most important CONCEPTS in PHYSICS. The basic unit of energy is the *joule* — roughly equal to the work done when an apple is lifted through one yard. One kilowatt-hour is 3.6 million joules. See also CALORIE.   M.V.B.

energy crisis. The view that the world's finite reserves of fossil fuels are being consumed too quickly and that the resulting scarcity will raise energy prices. The OIL CRISIS of the 1970s and the consequent large increases in the prices of all sources of energy provided dramatic evidence for this widely held point of view. The actual level of world reserves of fossil fuels is a matter of dispute and has led certain energy specialists to argue that there will be no energy crisis, only the possibility of a lack of effort in exploring for new reserves. Since the mid-1970s, most countries have become more efficient in their use of energy. Governments and firms have invested in research investigating energy efficiency and energy sources that are alternatives to fossil fuels. Oil-importing developing countries have suffered particularly from past increases in energy prices and there is concern about how future scarcities of fuel wood and fossil fuels would affect them (see DEBT CRISIS).   J.P.
   Bibl: P.C. Chapman, *Fuel's Paradise* (London, 1975); P.R. Odell, *Oil and World Power* (London, 8th ed., 1986).

energy level. In microscopic systems such as ATOMS the ENERGY is constrained to take only certain discrete values. The lowest level is called the *ground state* of the system, and higher levels are *excited states*. Transitions from a higher to a lower level must involve a loss of energy, which is usually emitted as PHOTONS of light or other electromagnetic RADIATION, while transitions to higher levels occur by absorption of light. These energy levels may be predicted more or less directly by QUANTUM MECHANICS whereas in the earlier BOHR THEORY they were the result of apparently arbitrary rules restricting the application of NEWTONIAN MECHANICS (in which the energy normally varies continuously). See also ATOMIC PHYSICS; SPECTROSCOPY.   M.V.B.

engineering. The utilization of (1) raw materials, (2) metals and other products from raw materials, (3) natural sources of ENERGY, and (4) the SCIENTIFIC METHOD in order to build machines and structures intended to serve a specific purpose. This purpose is most often utilitarian — transport, communication, water-supply — but may also (e.g. in the building of a RADIO TELESCOPE) subserve the ends of the NATURAL SCIENCES, i.e. enhance understanding of the physical world. It is in the use of the scientific method that engineering transcends (though it may incorporate) the traditional manufacturing crafts, and is aligned with TECHNOLOGY, of which indeed it is an important part.
   Engineering has been traditionally divided into civil engineering ('civil', as in 'civil service', implying public functions such as are served by roads, bridges, harbours, waterways, etc.) and mechanical engineering (dealing with machines). During the 19th century, however, electrical engineering emerged as a distinct discipline demanding its own training and qualifications; the advent of aircraft brought with it aeronautical engineering; and an ever-growing list of special branches now includes municipal, electronic, radio, gas, mining, production, structural, chemical, fuel, marine, and railway engineering.   E.R.L.

English Stage Company, see under ROYAL COURT THEATRE.

enkephalins, see under ENDORPHINS.

Enlightenment. There could rarely be a greater contrast between the use of this word to describe the European and North American movement, flourishing in the 18th century, which stressed tolerance, reasonableness, common sense and the encouragement of science and TECHNOLOGY, and the spread in the 20th century of the same term to refer to the goal of Asian religious MYSTICISM, particularly in the still vigorous traditions of HINDUISM and BUDDHISM. But the ability of many Japanese to combine a technical efficiency with a self-disciplined spirituality may indicate that the two Enlightenments are ultimately compatible. What is already appreciated by many who wish to retain a modern scientific outlook is that accusations of escapism and irrationality do not do complete justice to the mysticism. The aim is to control and eliminate wandering, materialistic, lustful and selfish thoughts;

then to overcome the sense that one thing or self is fundamentally divided from another; and finally to enter in ecstasy the nothingness of the divine or ultimate reality, thus experiencing a bliss which transcends all other joys. Such meditation may still be criticized as attempting the impossible, either because 'God' cannot be known or reached or because he has already been revealed by his own 'grace'. But at least parts of this spiritual quest are widely respected by those familiar with the emotional problems of the industrial nations. D.L.E.

Bibl: W. Johnston, *Silent Music: the Science of Meditation* (London and New York, 1974); B. Griffiths, *Return to the Centre* (London and New York, 1976).

Enosis. Greek word for union or unification, used in various political contexts, originally by Greek NATIONALISTS intent on the realization of a Greek empire over those areas outside mainland Greece which had been under Greek rule in classical and Byzantine times and still had substantial Greek-speaking populations, a dream known as the *Megale Idea*. From 1930 the word was more particularly invoked by Cypriot Greeks in their long campaign to obtain independence from British rule, a campaign opposed bitterly by the Turkish minority on the island. The achievement of independence in 1960 led to an equally bitter conflict between the advocates of union with Greece and the Cypriot government of Archbishop Makarios. The death in January 1974 of the movement's leader, General Grivas, led to a marked if temporary decline in its activities. In July 1974, however, the military regime in Greece used its forces in Cyprus to support a coup against the Makarios government by pro-Enosis forces. Their action led to communal strife between Greek and Turkish Cypriot communities and to the invasion of Cyprus by Turkish forces. These seized part of the island, into which the Turkish community was evacuated, while Greek Cypriots took refuge in the unoccupied areas. Relations between Greece and Turkey deteriorated so badly that international mediation was unable to secure any agreement. Despite the overthrow of the military regime in Greece, the emotional support there for Enosis ran far too strong for the democratic government which succeeded it to accept the truth that the massacres of Greek and Turkish Cypriots during the period of communal strife precluded any restoration of the *status quo ante*. D.C.W.

entailment and **implication.** In LOGIC, *entailment* is the converse of the relation of logical consequence: for *p* to entail *q* is for *q* to follow logically from *p*. *Implication* is a more generic notion. One PROPOSITION implies another if the conditional statement that has the former as antecedent and the latter as consequent is true. 'It is cloudy' implies 'It will rain', provided that 'If it is cloudy it will rain' is true. Entailment is thus a species of implication, entailments being those implications that are guaranteed by logic or the MEANINGS of the terms involved. In modern formal logic there is a type of formula, called by Russell *material implication*, which partially corresponds, but is not strictly equivalent in meaning, to ordinary conditional statements of the form 'if *p* then *q*'. It is defined to mean the same as 'not both *p* and not-*q*' and, although statements of this form follow from the corresponding conditionals, the converse is not true. Because of this difference of sense C.I. Lewis introduced the notion of *strict implication*, defined as 'It is not possible that *p* and not-*q*', the object being a juster representation of the ordinary conditional. The systems of strict implication are the basis of contemporary MODAL LOGIC.

A.Q.

Bibl: W.V. Quine, *Methods of Logic* part 1 (London and New York, 3rd ed., 1972).

entelechy. (1) In Aristotelian PHILOSOPHY, the endowment that realizes or gives expression to some potential. (2) For its special use in BIOLOGY see VITALISM.

P.M.

entomology. The scientific study of insects; it is a division of ZOOLOGY. Entomology consists of all the methods and theories of BIOLOGY in their application to insects. Because about 80% of living species are insects, entomology is deservedly recognized as a major part of biology. Entomologists seek to understand the structure, physiological functioning, embryological development, EVOLUTION, and classification (see BIOSYSTEMATICS) of insects. Insects are divided into two great groups according to the manner of their development. The Exopterygota include among other groups the dragonflies, crickets, and bugs (including aphids); in them the wings develop as external wing buds that grow larger with each succeeding moult until the adult stage. In the Endopterygota the wings initially develop internally and only appear externally in their final form in the adult stage, after a major metamorphosis (such as the chrysalis stage of butterflies). Beetles, wasps, flies, and moths are all Endopterygote insects. The Exopterygota and Endopterygota are further subdivided into about 26 *orders*. Many insects are agricultural pests or spread disease; applied entomology seeks to understand the life cycles of these insects and to invent techniques to prevent their destructive habits.

M.R.

Bibl: O.W. Richards and R.G. Davies, *Imms General Textbook of Entomology* (London, 1977).

entrenched clauses. Those clauses of a constitution for the repeal or amendment of which a special legislative process is required in order to protect them from hasty or too frequent alteration. Such protection may take various forms: it may consist of a requirement that legislation amending or repealing the protected clause must be passed by a larger majority than that required for ordinary legislation, or that it must be passed by a majority of two chambers of a legislature (which normally sit separately) sitting together, or that it must be confirmed by a referendum. To give the fullest measure of protection the special procedure must be made applicable not only to the clauses of the constitution which are to be specially protected, but also, by a provision known as *double entrenchment*, to the clauses providing for such special protection. A much debated question is whether or not it is open to the British Parliament to entrench legislation (e.g. guaranteeing individual liberties) so as to preclude its repeal by the ordinary process of legislation.

H.L.A.H.

Bibl: G. Marshall, *Parliamentary Sovereignty in the Commonwealth* (Oxford and New York, 1957).

entrenchment. An idea developed in modern philosophy of knowledge by Nelson Goodman (1906-), arising out of the long-standing problems of INDUCTION. We might, empirically, derive CONCEPTS or theories on the basis of the facts available (e.g. we might call it a law of nature that the sun rises every day, because it has been observed to do so regularly in the past). But, argued Hume and later critics of induction, that affords no sufficient reason for believing that such events will continue to occur, unless, by a leap of faith, we smuggle in a metaphysical principle such as the uniformity of nature. Doing this, however, compounded rather than resolved the problem. Goodman spelt out the subtle implications of this dilemma. He stressed that the schemes of words and concepts we use to describe our sense experiences have no special validity. They are merely the ones which, through historical accident, we habitually use: they are, in other words, entrenched. What is commonly seen as privileged rationality is merely habitual entrenchment.

R.P.

Bibl: L. Losee, *An Historical Introduction to the Philosophy of Science* (Oxford, 1980).

entrepreneur. The individual who perceives the profitability of production of a good or service and organizes its production. The production of a good or service could be achieved by individuals trading their particular parts of the production process in the market. However, market transactions are not costless and it may well be efficient for the entrepreneur to bring together the different parts of production into one FIRM. The entrepreneur directs the operation of the firm and is usually, but not always, considered to be the owner. The reward to the entrepreneur is profit, i.e. the residual after all other FACTORS OF PRODUCTION have been paid out of the firm's revenue. The concept of a single entrepreneur owning and running a firm is a theoretical abstraction and in many cases is not an adequate description of reality, but it may provide accurate predictions of actual behaviour.

In many companies, ownership and MAN-AGEMENT are distinct. Ownership is usually spread across many individuals and institutions. This is achieved through the holding of transferable shares, which do not imply liability for the debt of the firm. These characteristics are important and ignored by the hypothetical construct of the entrepreneur. J.P.

Bibl: M. Blaug, *Economic Theory in Retrospect* (London, 5th ed., 1985).

entropy.
(1) In THERMODYNAMICS, a QUANTITY forming (along with ENERGY, tempera-ture, pressure, etc.) part of the specifi-cation of the thermal state of a SYSTEM; a typical system is the steam in a boiler. Entropy may be calculated from the heat which must be added to the system to bring it via intermediate states to the state being considered. It is found that the en-tropy of any closed system never de-creases. This is one formulation of the *second law of thermodynamics*, which can be explained by STATISTICAL MECHANICS, where entropy is interpreted as a measure of the *disorder* among the ATOMS making up the system, since an initially ordered state is virtually certain to randomize as time proceeds. See also HEAT DEATH OF UNIVERSE. M.V.B.

(2) In CYBERNETICS, entropy is general-ized to measure the tendency of any closed system to move from a less to a more probable state, using the same mathemat-ical apparatus as in (1). If, however, the system is open to information, then this tendency may be arrested. This is because, mathematically speaking, information can be defined precisely as negative entropy (or *negentropy*). S.BE.

Entwicklungsroman, see BILDUNGS-ROMAN.

environment.
(1) In ECOLOGY, the sum total of the biological, chemical, and physical factors in some circumscribed area, usually an area associated with a particular living organism. Essentially an environment only exists because it is inhabited by this organism. Thus a field is the environment for a cow, a cow-dung pat is the environ-ment for a dung-beetle, and the exoskele-ton of the dung-beetle is the environment of a parasitic mite. Therefore the field comprises an infinity of overlapping en-vironments. 'Environment' is also used in the sense of HABITAT or ECOSYSTEM.

K.M.

(2) In architecture, theatre, and the vis-ual arts, the current use of this term, dating from the late 1950s, seems confined to the English language; there is no French or German equivalent. It com-bines three main concepts: (*a*) the notion of the all-embracing three-dimensional work of art as evolved by the American Allan Kaprow in 1958 and featured in the '*Dylaby*' (dynamic labyrinth) show (Am-sterdam, 1962) by Rauschenberg, Jean Tinguely, and others, with Schwitters's Hanover MERzbau of the 1920s as its fore-runner; (*b*) the HAPPENING, which devel-oped from Kaprow's and Claes Olden-burg's work in that direction; (*c*) the use of such works and events, together with more orthodox and less autonomous as-pects of visual art, to shape, enliven, em-bellish, and improve our surroundings. Hence such new notions as 'environmental art', 'environmental design' (covering any-thing from landscape gardening to the colour of bus shelters), ENVIRONMENTAL CONTROL, POLLUTION of the environment, and finally in 1970, as one of the Heath government's innovations, a Ministry of the Environment to deal with town-planning and CONSERVATION. J.W.

environmental archaeology, see under AR-CHAEOLOGY.

environmental areas, see under TRANS-PORT PLANNING.

environmental causes of disease. In the 19th century, physicians divided the causes of disease into two groups, 'nature' and 'nurture'. Nowadays, that is expressed by grouping causative agents as either a GENETIC effect or some influence of the ENVIRONMENT. The two are not mutually exclusive. For example, a person geneti-cally programmed to produce certain im-munoglobulins and subject to hay fever or asthma may thereby show increased sen-sitivity to certain environmental contami-nants such as dusts or pollens. The human environment comprises four components;

275

chemical, physical, MICROBIOLOGICAL and psychosocial. In recent years, particularly with regard to the chemical and physical environments, there has been a tendency toward subdivision into the macroenvironment, over which the individual generally has little control (air pollution is an example) and the microenvironment (the environment which immediately surrounds the individual and over which he may exert greater control, such as cigarette smoking). Microbiological diseases such as tuberculosis or cholera are now no longer 'acts of God' but regarded as controllable as we learn to regulate our environment and the way we behave in it. Time will show whether AIDS comes to be regarded in the same light although control will involve influencing the psychosocial environment. Similarly, cancer of the female cervix is now believed to be due to an infection received from male partners. The chances of infection increase both with the number and promiscuity of such partners. Should the disease be regarded, therefore, as environmental? Current interest in stress in the inner cities, and at work, and the stresses of poverty, acknowledges the influence of the psychosocial environment. It is the physical and chemical factors of the environment which are frequently in mind when talk is of environmental causes of disease. The physical causes include such diverse factors as cigarette and chimney smoke, noise, heat and cold, increased barometric pressure (deep diving), reduced atmospheric pressure (high altitude flying), ionizing radiation (see RADIATION BIOLOGY and RADIATION GENETICS), non-ionizing radiation (such as LASERS and microwaves). Dusts which may cause disease (asbestos and silica) are included among the physical hazards. From antiquity, many chemicals, of which lead is a well known example, have been known to cause disease. Newer processes may release newer chemicals into the workplace or the general environment either in well publicized accidental releases or continuously in smaller quantities. ACID RAIN and mercury compounds provide examples of the latter. The control of environmental hazards depends on whether the exposure of a population is voluntary or involuntary. For the latter, exposure may be regulated by legislation and inspection such as clean air acts, radiation protection and the provision of wholesome drinking water. When exposure is voluntary, such as smoking, alcohol, inappropriate DIETS or sexual behaviour, then we find increasing emphasis on programmes of health education which attempt to influence the individual to reduce his or her own exposure.

W.R.L.

environmental control. The regulation of the air's temperature, humidity, rate of movement, and particle content within a building by mechanical means, together with the use of artificial lighting. There has been an increasing reliance on these mechanical services as building plans have become larger, and especially deeper, and external conditions in cities less and less tolerable. Services rather than STRUCTURE have as a result become one of the dominant controlling elements in architectural design.

M.BR.

Bibl: R. Banham, *The Architecture of the Well-Tempered Environment* (London and Chicago, 1969).

environmental determinism, see under ENVIRONMENTALISM.

environmental studies. Term used to cover almost all activities in schools, colleges, and universities which are aimed at making pupils more aware of, and critical of, the conditions in the world in which they live, and of the interrelationships between man, his CULTURE, and his living and non-living surroundings. Environmental studies includes, at different levels, natural history, ECOLOGY, POLLUTION, METEOROLOGY, architecture, and much that is normally included in GEOGRAPHY. Environmental education is intended to give these topics more coherence.

K.M.

environmentalism. Geographical term for the philosophical doctrine that stresses the influence of the ENVIRONMENT on man's activities. (Environment is here usually defined in terms of the physical factors, e.g. climatic conditions.) In its more extreme form it is termed *environmental determinism* or *geographical determinism*. The doctrine was enunciated by Hippocrates in the 5th century B.C. and reached its peak in the mid 19th century. Modern workers tend to acknowledge the importance of the natural environment but see it operating through a complex network of psychological, social, and economic channels which may dampen or accentuate different properties of the environment for different groups, or for the same group at different points in time.

P.H.

enzymes. Complex organic catalysts which mediate nearly all material TRANS-FORMATIONS in the body. The substance an enzyme acts upon is known as its *substrate*, and in biochemical terminology an enzyme is named by adding the suffix -ase to the (truncated) name of the substrate; thus *proteases* are PROTEIN-splitting enzymes, etc. Compounds like proteins which are formed by the 'condensation' of their smaller structural units accompanied by the elimination of the elements of water are broken down by the opposite process of *hydrolysis*, involving the release of water. Thus most digestive enzymes are hydrolytic — among them pepsin formed in the walls of the stomach and liberated into the stomach cavity, trypsin formed in the pancreas and working in the duodenum, the carbohydrase ptyalin, a starch-splitting enzyme present in the saliva.

P.M.

epic theatre. Originally a German expression, used in contrast to 'dramatic' theatre. 'Epic' in this sense means essentially narrative, defying the Aristotelian unities: i.e. presenting a story step-by-step (as in *Antony and Cleopatra*) rather than tying it together in a self-contained 'plot' (as in *The Tempest*). Its current use, originating in the NEUE SACHLICHKEIT phase in Berlin, is due particularly to Erwin Piscator and Bertolt Brecht.

Starting with the production of Alfons Paquet's *Fahnen* (1924), a 'dramatic novel' subtitled 'epic', Piscator developed the use of projected texts, film, the treadmill stage, and other devices, to make a new kind of DOCUMENTARY drama, revivified after his return to Berlin in 1962. Brecht took up this concept in 1926 (before coming to work with Piscator), summarized it in his *Mahagonny* notes (1930), and made it for some twenty years

the keystone of his thinking. Though he also (see BRECHTIAN) saw it as an aid to tackling new social and economic themes in the theatre, and as subsuming the new technical devices, the essential, for him, lay rather in linear narration ('each scene for itself'), stimulating the audience's reason as against its EMPATHY, and presenting the events as if quoting something already seen and heard. Though he came to call this kind of theatre 'non-Aristotelian', fusing it with his later formula of ALIENATION, he decided in the 1950s that 'epic' was too formal a concept, and thought of replacing it by the more MARXIST-sounding phrase *dialectical theatre*, meaning in effect epic theatre in a changed society.

J.W.

Bibl: B. Brecht, tr. and ed. J. Willett, *Brecht on Theatre* (London and New York, 1964); J. Willett, *The Theatre of Erwin Piscator* (London and New York, 1978).

epidemiology. The study of infectious and other diseases which appear in groups or communities. Epidemiologists try to discover the ways in which diseases develop and spread, linking their occurrence with environmental factors and with the demographic characteristics — race, age, sex, occupation — of populations affected. In the past, epidemiology was mostly concerned with infectious diseases: a classical example was John Snow's identification of the Broad Street pump as the source of a virulent outbreak of cholera in 1854. Today, epidemiological method is also applied to non-infectious diseases, for example the relation of DIET and exercise to cardiovascular disease and of smoking to lung CANCER. Epidemiology plays a crucial role in the study of the *etiology* (the study of the causes of disease) and control of many diseases; there are academic departments in the subject at many universities.

J.D.O.

epigenesis, see under PREFORMATION.

epigraphy. The study of inscriptions carved or otherwise written on durable material, such as stone or metal, and placed on buildings, tombs, etc. to indicate their name or purpose. Epigraphy provides one of the main sources for our knowledge of the ancient world.   A.L.C.B.

epilepsy. Known to the Greeks as the 'sacred disease', epilepsy has often been associated with notions of the divine or transcendental nature of sickness, and of special powers possessed by sufferers (Dostoievsky for example was a victim). In the middle ages, epileptics were often shunned, and during the 19th century they were frequently confined in lunatic asylums (without it necessarily being believed that epilepsy was a 'mental disease'). Modern scientific research into epilepsy effectively dates from the latter part of the 19th century, with the work of Charles Edward Brown-Sequard, John Hughlings-Jackson and Paul Broca, who conducted experimentation upon the localization of functions in the brain and pioneered brain SURGERY. In a celebrated innovative operation in 1884, Victor Horsley removed a brain tumour and relieved focal epilepsy. In the present century attention has shifted to drug treatments. Replacing 19th-century bromides, phenobarbitol was introduced in 1912 as an effective suppressant; it has been supplemented by dilantin and primidone. No complete cure has yet been found.   R.P.
Bibl: Owsei Temkin, *The Falling Sickness* (Baltimore, 1971).

epinephrine, see under ADRENAL GLAND.

epiphany. In the Christian religion the Epiphany, celebrated on 6 January, commemorates Christ's first manifestation to the Gentiles, in the form of the Magi. James Joyce was responsible for its introduction as a critical term: Stephen Hero (*Stephen Hero*, ed. 1944) is passing through Eccles Street when he overhears a colloquy: a 'triviality' that makes him 'think of collecting many such moments together in a book of epiphanies'. By epiphany he means 'sudden spiritual manifestation[s]', 'the most delicate and evanescent of such [memorable,] focusing moments'. Joyce was concerned to recapture, from the commonplace, the 'radiance', the 'whatness' — as Stephen puts it to Lynch in his conversation with him in *Portrait of the Artist as a Young Man* (1916) — the 'enchantment of the heart'.

He was anticipated, e.g. by Pater's phrase 'exquisite pauses in time'. It is now often used to mean, less precisely, 'sudden, precious insight'.   M.S.-S.

epiphenomenalism. A theory about the nature of the causal relations between mental and bodily events (see MIND-BODY PROBLEM), where these are understood, in accordance with DUALISM, as radically different in nature. It holds that mental events are the effects of physical happenings in the organism, particularly in the brain and NERVOUS SYSTEM, but that they do not themselves exert any causal influence on the body. In T.H. Huxley's phrase epiphenomenalism conceives mental life as 'the steam above the factory'. Epiphenomenalism follows from the assumptions that mental and bodily events are, though distinct in nature, regularly correlated and that all bodily events are fully explainable as parts of the inclusive DETERMINISTIC system of physical nature, which leaves no room for causal intrusion from the domain of the mental.   A.Q.
Bibl: T.H. Huxley, *Lectures and Essays* (London and New York, 1903); K. Campbell, *Body and Mind* (New York, 1970; London, 1971).

episcopalism. The belief that episcopacy, i.e. the government of the Church by bishops (Greek *episkopos*, overseer), is best, or essential to CATHOLICISM, especially in ANGLICANISM. Those who hold this belief are *episcopalians*.   D.L.E.

episome. A GENE or group of genes which can reproduce independently of CHROMOSOME reproduction, but which can also be incorporated into and reproduced with the chromosome. Known only from bacteria (see BACTERIOLOGY). See also PLASMA-GENE.   J.M.S.

epistasis. The phenomenon whereby the effects of GENES at one LOCUS are altered or masked by those at another. Thus the genes in a mouse which determine whether its hair pigment will be black or brown have no effect if the mouse is a genetic albino (see ALBINISM) because of a defect at another gene locus.   J.M.S.

epistemics. Word coined at Edinburgh University in 1969 with the foundation of the School of Epistemics. It signifies the scientific study of knowledge, as opposed to the philosophical theory of knowledge, which is known as EPISTEMOLOGY. A more extended definition of epistemics is 'the construction of formal MODELS of the processes — perceptual, intellectual, and linguistic — by which knowledge and understanding are achieved and communicated'. C.L.-H.

epistemological realism, see under REALISM.

epistemology. The philosophical theory of knowledge, which seeks to define it, distinguish its principal varieties, identify its sources, and establish its limits. On the topic of *definition*, it has been recognized since the time of Plato that knowledge involves true belief but goes beyond it. The specification of this residual element is still a matter of controversy. One view is that what distinguishes genuine knowledge from a lucky guess is justification; another is that it is the causation of the belief by the fact that verifies it. One way of distinguishing *kinds* of knowledge is into practical knowledge-how, propositional knowledge-that, and knowledge-of (cf. French *connaître* and German *kennen*). However, the various sorts of knowledge-of seem reducible either to knowledge-how (e.g. knowing Italian) or to knowing-that (e.g. knowing the date of the battle of Waterloo). Within knowledge-that, the prime concern of epistemologists, empirical and *a priori* knowledge (see EMPIRICISM; APRIORISM) are distinguished and, within each of these realms, the basic or intuitive items of knowledge are distinguished from the derived or inferred ones. *A priori* knowledge is derived from its self-evident axiomatic bases (see AXIOMATICS) by *deduction*; empirical knowledge from uninferred observation-statements by INDUCTION. The usually acknowledged *sources* of empirical knowledge are sense-perception (see PERCEPTION; SENSEDATUM) and INTROSPECTION, while *a priori* knowledge is said to come from reason. The determination of the *limits* of knowledge is a matter of continuing controversy, particularly about the inclusion within the realm of the knowable of morality (see ETHICS), THEOLOGY, and METAPHYSICS. A.Q.

Bibl: A.J. Ayer, *The Problem of Knowledge* (London and New York, 1956); J. Dancy, *Introduction to Contemporary Epistemology* (London, 1976).

epitrochoidal engine, see WANKEL ENGINE.

epoche, see under EIDETIC REDUCTION.

equal protection. Principle of American constitutional law which provides that people in similar circumstances must be treated in a similar way. It has been one of the most important ideas in the U.S. for the protection of civil liberties, and has been applied in a variety of settings, including housing, transportation, employment, education, and voting rights. The doctrine is now applied primarily to racial matters, where it has had far-reaching effects. Its best known application was in the 1954 school DESEGREGATION case, *Brown v. Board of Education of Topeka*. M.S.P.

Equal Rights Amendment (ERA). A proposed amendment to the constitution of the U.S. which in its most important modern version sought to enshrine the principle that 'Equality of rights under the law shall not be denied or abridged by the United States or by any State on account of sex', and thus assist in the reduction of economic and other forms of discrimination against women. A similar amendment was first produced in the early 1920s by women's organizations which had recently succeeded in winning female suffrage. The issue was revived in the 1940s and raised sporadically and unsuccessfully until it profited from the modern growth in support for FEMINIST causes. The ERA was passed by Congress in March 1972; after a spectacular rate of ratification by some 30 states within a year, it made inadequate headway in the others until the available period ended on 30 June 1982. Its failure was in part due to the successful organization of opposing groups, in part to tactical and organizational weaknesses of pro-ERA groups. S.R.

Bibl: J.J. Mansbridge, *Why We Lost the E.R.A.* (Chicago and London, 1986).

equality, principle of. An assertion made most commonly in this conditional form: that in public matters all persons should be treated identically, except in contexts where sufficient reasons exist for treating particular individuals or groups differently. Such prescriptions for treating men equally (a matter as much of equity as of equality) have, however, been too readily assimilated with assertions that all men *are* equal — assertions which ignore important measurable discrepancies between individuals, e.g. in mental or physical ability. EGALITARIAN assumptions are, indeed, no more self-evidently 'natural' than inegalitarian ones; and utterances of the kind 'All men are born equal' are best viewed as moral exhortations — pleas to allow, at the very least, that by virtue of their shared humanity men should enjoy equal satisfaction of certain basic common rights and needs.

All this leaves vast room for disagreement, especially about the extent of basic rights and needs, and about the criteria for assessing whether a particular instance of differential treatment is justified. Further difficulties arise not only over conflicts between equality and other possible social goals, such as maximal freedom of action for the individual, but even over the relationship between various kinds of equality itself: equal political rights do not necessarily imply identical shares in wealth, and equality of opportunity scarcely ends inequality of condition.

For at least 300 years much of Western political debate has focused on equality, and the drive to implement various interpretations of it has been a major force of the 20th century. Despite conceptual muddle over its positive content, the principle of equality has been negatively of great value in placing the onus of justification firmly on its opponents.   M.D.B.

Bibl: J. Rees, *Equality* (London and New York, 1971); J. Rawls, *A Theory of Justice* (Cambridge, Mass., 1971; Oxford, 1972).

equation. An assertion that two mathematical expressions have the same value. An equation may represent a particular fact ($2 + 2 = 4$), a general law ($x + y = y + x$); a definition ($y^2 = y \times y$), or a condition on the VARIABLES occurring in it ($x^2 + 2x + 1 = 0$). For *diophantine equations* see NUMBER THEORY; see also ALGEBRA; DIFFERENTIAL EQUATION.   R.G.

equilibrium.
(1) In general, a state of affairs that has no inherent tendency to change while circumstances remain the same. The idea is used in many different sciences, e.g. PHYSICS, CHEMISTRY, ECONOMICS (see also below), PSYCHOLOGY, ECOLOGY. The equilibrium may be *static* or *dynamic*. In *static equilibrium* there is no change occurring (of interest to the science in question); e.g. the equilibrium of balanced scales. In *dynamic equilibrium* something is changing in a steady way (e.g. planets moving in a fixed orbit; a chemical reaction in a closed system proceeding as fast in one direction as the other, so that the concentrations of the reactants remain constant; or incomes rising at a fixed rate), but there are forces tending to change some aspect of the process (e.g. GRAVITATION tending to draw a planet nearer the sun, or advertisements creating increased consumption and therefore increasing wage claims), and other opposing forces which tend to produce the opposite effect and so prevent the disturbance from occurring. Other categories of equilibrium are as follows. In *unstable equilibrium*, the slightest external disturbance will alter the state radically (e.g. a pencil balanced on its point). In *metastable equilibrium* a state may persist for a long time before changing radically (e.g. a RADIOACTIVE nucleus before its decay, or the liquid in a BUBBLE CHAMBER). In *neutral equilibrium* the state may be altered gradually by external influences (e.g. a car at rest with its brakes off on a level road). In *stable equilibrium* the system responds to small influences by returning to its original state (e.g. a cone resting on its base, or an ATOM in its lowest ENERGY LEVEL).   A.S.; M.V.B.

(2) In ECONOMICS, a state of the economy in which for every good and service (other than goods whose price is zero), total demand and supply are exactly equal. Equilibrium is usually considered to be a hypothetical state, but the economy may be thought of as moving towards an

equilibrium or moving towards different equilibria. The concept of equilibrium is complicated by the KEYNESIAN distinction between effective and notional DEMAND. The most commonly used concept of equilibrium is that of COMPETITIVE EQUILIBRIUM. The existence and uniqueness of an equilibrium are important considerations. The behaviour of economies out of equilibrium may not always be movement in the direction of equilibrium and is complicated to analyse. The actual behaviour of an economy out of equilibrium may affect the demand and supply functions, e.g. the incomes of consumers may change and this effects demand, and also the long run equilibrium. The economic study of equilibrium has investigated such effects, the role of expectations, costs of market transactions, the use of cost of information, RISK and GAME THEORY.   J.P.

Bibl: E. R. Weintraub, *General Equilibrium* (London, 1975).

equity capital. The class of CAPITAL in a company that represents the basic ownership of the company. The remuneration it receives is that income left after deducting, from total revenue, all the costs of production, payments of interest and the principal of outstanding debt, the dividends to preferred shares, taxes and retained profits. If a company is wound up, the value of equity is determined by what is left after all costs, debts, taxes and other forms of capital have been paid. Equity capital in a company is exposed to a greater risk than other forms of capital, but there is the possibility of greater returns.   J.P.

Bibl: J. Craven, *Introduction to Economics* (Oxford, 1984).

equivalence relation. '*A* is the same as *B*' is often used to mean not that *A* and *B* are identical, but that they are the same in all respects which are relevant in the given context. This RELATION is reflexive, symmetric, and transitive. Any relation satisfying these conditions is an *equivalence relation*. It divides objects up into non-overlapping *equivalence classes* (or SETS); all the objects in each class are the 'same' as each other, and not the same as objects in any other class. The *principle of (mathematical) abstraction* consists in associating with each class an abstract property,

notion, or object (e.g. the class itself) which stands for what the things in the class have in common. Thus, in deciphering an unknown script one first decides on a relation of sameness between marks, and then associates with each mark an abstract object — the letter which the mark is an instance of. In MATHEMATICS the principle is of great importance; for examples see CARDINAL NUMBER; ORDINAL NUMBER; VECTOR.   R.G.

ERA, see under EQUAL RIGHTS AMENDMENT.

Erastianism. The belief, named after Thomas Erastus (1524-83), that the State ought to have control over the Church even in ecclesiastical matters.   D.L.E.

ergonomics. The study of physical relationships between machines and the users of machines, with the object of reducing strain, discomfort, and fatigue in the former and improving overall efficiency. Applications include the layout of controls on a machine tool, the design of a suitable driving seat, and the positioning of dials in an aircraft.   R.I.T.

eros, see LIFE INSTINCT.

erosion, see under DENUDATION; SOIL EROSION.

error analysis.

(1) In applied LINGUISTICS, a technique for identifying, classifying, and systematically interpreting the unacceptable forms produced by someone learning a language. Errors are assumed to reflect, in a systematic way, the level of COMPETENCE achieved by a learner.   D.C.

Bibl: S.P. Corder, *Introducing Applied Linguistics* (Harmondsworth, 1973).

(2) In STATISTICS, especially in REGRESSION analysis, it is often assumed that an observed value is a combination of a determinate true value together with an *error term* which is randomly distributed, e.g. has a normal DISTRIBUTION. *Error analysis* is a name often applied to simple ESTIMATION techniques which make assumptions of this type, especially in the experimental sciences.   R.SI.

281

error-correcting code. A method of encoding (see ENCODER) digital information using REDUNDANCY, so that errors in transmission may be not only detected but perhaps corrected. For example, it might allow an error in any one BIT of an encoded word to be corrected, while an error in any two bits would be detectable. See INFORMATION THEORY. J.E.S.

Erziehungsroman, see under BILDUNGSRO-MAN.

escalation. The process whereby each side in turn increases the scope of an international crisis or the violence of an international conflict, in the hope that its adversary's self-imposed limits will be reached before its own. Escalation is thus an aspect of DETERRENCE and of CRISIS MANAGEMENT. (See also BRINKMANSHIP.) President Kennedy's decision in the Cuban MISSILE crisis of 1962 to impose a naval blockade on the incoming Soviet missile-carrying ships deliberately escalated the crisis to a point where any further escalation was judged, correctly, to be above the self-imposed limits of the Soviet Union. The Kennedy administration also developed an explicit doctrine of controlled escalation to give CREDIBILITY to its posture of extended deterrence in Western Europe, by making clear that a Soviet attack on the European NATO powers would incur, as it grew heavier, an increasing level of first tactical and then strategic nuclear riposte. Soviet strategic doctrine now embraces a broadly similar concept in relation to a Nato attack on the Warsaw Pact states.

Like other STRATEGIC terms, escalation is increasingly used in general political contexts, and has conceptual affinities with bargaining theory. A.F.B.

Bibl: H. Kahn, *On Escalation* (London and New York, 1965).

escape velocity. The speed with which an object must be projected upwards from the surface of a heavenly body in order to escape, without further propulsion, from the GRAVITATIONAL field of the body. For the earth, the escape velocity is about 25,000 m.p.h.; for the moon, the escape velocity is only about 5,000 m.p.h., which explains the lack of any lunar atmosphere:

any gas MOLECULES would tend to leak away, since their random heat motion is faster than the escape velocity. M.V.B.

eschatology. A word coined in 1844 to cover the discussion of doctrines about the end of the world, or of this age in the world's history. The discussion has been prominent in modern Christian THEOLOGY, for two reasons. First, the dramatic impact of Albert Schweitzer's study *The Quest of the Historical Jesus* (1906, Eng. tr. 1910), in which, reviewing previous German scholars' lives of Jesus, he drew attention to the expectation of the imminent end of the world found in the gospels' accounts of the teaching of Jesus. Second, this consistently eschatological message, which would have seemed bizarre in more secure times, has been thought relevant, particularly to the disasters overwhelming Europe (see CRISIS THEOLOGY). Schweitzer made Jesus out to be one of the many 'Apocalyptic' visionaries of the first century who claimed that the dooms and glories of the future had been revealed to them, but later biblical scholars have stressed that the original message of Jesus, if it is recoverable from the gospels, proclaimed a 'realized' or at least an 'inaugurated' as well as a 'final' eschatology: the Kingdom of God was not only to come finally at the end of that age but was also present, already real at least in its beginnings, in the victories of Jesus himself. It has also been pointed out that Jesus disclaimed knowledge about the 'hour' or the exact manner of the final arrival of God's Kingdom. But the eschatological nature of the Christian Gospel has now generally been acknowledged, and the problem for modern theologians has been one of interpretation. Should the Christian claim that the Kingdom of God exists on earth in the Church, or is coming in the general life of society, whether through progress or revolution, as in the THEOLOGY OF HOPE? Or should the message, stripped of its old images, be entirely a call to personal decision (see DEMYTHOLOGIZE)? While such questions have been debated, many FUNDAMENTALIST Christians have continued to await the 'Second Coming' or 'Advent' of Jesus, on the basis of a literal interpretation of the biblical prophecies. Others have continued to con-

sider only the 'four last things' of traditional CATHOLICISM: death, judgement,
heaven, and hell.   D.L.E.

Bibl: J. Hick, *Evil and the God of Love*
(London and New York, 1966); N. Perrin,
*The Kingdom of God in the Teaching of
Jesus* (London and New York, 1963); B.
Hebblethwaite, *The Christian Hope*
(London, 1984).

ESN, see EDUCATIONALLY SUBNORMAL.

ESP (extra-sensory perception). In PARA-
PSYCHOLOGY, PERCEPTION or knowledge
of something achieved without using
sense-organs or sensory information. In
clairvoyance, that something is an object
or event; in *telepathy*, another person's
thoughts; and when clairvoyance or
telepathy concerns something in the future it constitutes PRECOGNITION. The
main question is: does ESP exist? Anec-
dotal instances are open to the criticism of
biased selection; e.g. premonitions of
disaster are remembered when a disaster
follows but forgotten when it doesn't. To
avoid this bias, experiments have been
done asking people to guess at an event or
thought about which they could have no
possible sensory information. Some experiments have seemed to validate ESP
but others have been criticized on the
ground of either trickery or failure to
eliminate subtle but helpful clues of which
neither experimenter nor 'subject' need be
consciously aware. The history of these
experiments demonstrates that, at best,
ESP is not robustly producible under the
conditions of scientific experiment.

Another important consideration arises
from the logic of scientific enquiry (see
METHODOLOGY). It is held in science that
a negative hypothesis can never be proved
conclusively true; yet ESP is, by definition, a negative hypothesis, since it can be
proved true only if all possible alternative
assumptions are disproved. Thus the alleged phenomena of ESP pose both practical and logical difficulties for scientific
study. At present, the conclusion is that
ESP is, from a scientific viewpoint, not
proven.   I.M.L.H.

Bibl: C.E.M. Hansel, *ESP* (London,
1966); H.L. Edge *et al.*, *Foundations of
Parapsychology* (London, 1986).

ESS, see EVOLUTIONARY STABLE STRAT-
EGY.

essence. The set of properties of a thing or
of instances of a kind of thing which that
thing or those instances *must* possess if it
is to be that particular thing or they are to
be instances of that particular kind. The
essence can also be said to be the *defining
properties* of a thing or a kind. It is, thus,
part of the essence of a ship that it is
designed to float on water; but its having
sails rather than an engine or carrying
cargo rather than passengers is accidental
or *contingent* (see CONTINGENCY). Any
consistent set of properties defines an essence, but it is always a further question as
to whether the kind has any instances,
whether anything with just that set of
properties exists. The ONTOLOGICAL proof
of God's existence holds that in his case
alone existence is included in essence.
Critics of the proof argue that existence,
not being a genuine property, cannot be
part of any essence.   A.Q.

essential contestability. The doctrine that
many morally and politically important
concepts are not susceptible of 'neutral'
definition or explication but are 'contest-
able' in the sense that rival definitions
embody different and undecidable social
and political allegiances. So it is held that
what morality *is* cannot be agreed outside
some agreement on what sort of society is
morally acceptable; SOCIALIST and LIB-
ERAL definitions of morality are so deeply
involved in socialist and liberal theories of
social and political organization that only
by agreeing on the whole theoretical position can we expect to agree on the particular concept of morality. Similarly, it
has been said that POWER and FREEDOM
are essentially contested concepts. Our
view that one actor has exercised power
over another or that a man or a people is
free implies an extended theory of society
and human nature so that two observers
who hold different views about these will
be unable to agree on the application of
these narrower concepts too.   A.R.

Bibl: W.E. Connolly, *Concepts in Political Theory* (Cambridge, 1980); S.M.
Lukes, *Power* (London, 1974).

essentialism. Most generally, the theory that there are ESSENCES. More specifically it is applied to the following, quite distinct, beliefs:

(1) that particular things have essences which serve to identify them as the particular things that they are;

(2) that abstract entities or UNIVERSALS exist as well as the instances or exemplifications of them that we meet with in space and time, i.e. Platonic REALISM;

(3) a thesis (sketched by Locke) in the philosophy of science (see SCIENCE, PHILOSOPHY OF) that objects have real essences which are distinct from, but capable of explaining, their observable properties, and that discovery of these real essences is the ultimate goal of scientific investigation.　　　　　　　　　　　　A.Q.

Bibl: S. Kripke, *Naming and Necessity* (Oxford, 1980).

Establishment, the. A term, usually pejorative, for an ill-defined amalgam of those INSTITUTIONS, social CLASSES, and forces which represent authority, legitimacy, tradition, and the status quo. The term was popularized by Henry Fairlie in a 1955 *Spectator* article, and in Britain the phenomenon is regarded, with varying degrees of consensus and justice, as comprising the Monarchy, Parliament, the Civil Service (and the Foreign Office *par excellence*), the Church of England, the Armed Forces, the Law, the professions generally, the CITY, the B.B.C., certain newspapers, Oxford and Cambridge universities, the PUBLIC SCHOOLS, the landed gentry, and public opinion and individual behaviour patterns as moulded by these. (An oft-cited element in the American 'Establishment' is WASPS.) Its precise composition, however, tends to reflect the nature and extent of the changes desired, and the sources of opposition or hostility encountered or expected, by the person using the term. It is thus likely to mean very different things on the lips of, say, a self-made millionaire, a radical (see RADICALISM) politician, a HIPPIE, and a member of the ANGRY BRIGADE. At its least precise it may merely mean everyone richer or more powerful than the speaker.　　　　　　　O.S.

estates, see under CORPORATE STATE.

esthetics, see AESTHETICS.

estimate. In STATISTICS the experimenter may be faced with the task of using his observed data to guess the value of some PARAMETER in the MODEL he is using. Such a guess is called an estimate (or *point estimate*), and the rule for calculating the estimate from the data is called an *estimator*. The observed frequency of heads in a given number of tosses of a coin is an estimator for the probability that the coin will land heads; the actual value of this on some particular occasion is an estimate. An estimate may be good (if it is close to the true value) or bad, but since it is dependent on data whose values are random and is therefore subject to random errors it can seldom be meaningfully analysed; there is, however, an extensive theory of estimators, and much is known about how to design them so as to give consistently good estimates. See also INTERVAL ESTIMATION.　　　　　　　R.SI.

eternal sentence. A sentence free of *indexicals*, that is, expressions like 'now', 'here', 'you'. Indexicals relativize sentences to particular times, places, persons or things, so that in order to determine whether or not a given sentence containing indexicals is true one has to know which time, place, etc. is meant. For example, the sentence 'I had a headache yesterday' is dependent for its truth or falsity on when it is said and by whom: it may be true if I say it now but not if you do; it may be true for me today but not tomorrow. By contrast, an indexical-free or eternal sentence is completely explicit in all its temporal, spatial and other references, for example 'Elizabeth I of England died in 1603', and therefore does not change its TRUTH-VALUE according to when, where, or by whom it is asserted.　　　　　　　A.C.G.

ether. Because light is known to consist of waves, it used to be thought that an underlying, all-pervasive medium must exist to support the undulations, by analogy with air (which supports sound waves) and water (sea waves). This hypothetical medium was called the ether, and its properties provoked much speculation among 19th-century physicists. However, the MICHELSON-MORLEY EXPERIMENT (which led to the theory of RELATIVITY) showed that if the ether existed it could not be observed; furthermore, other kinds of wave (matter waves — see WAVE-PARTICLE DUALITY) are now known which do not have 'ethers' associated with them.

M.V.B.

ethical neutrality, see VALUE-FREEDOM.

ethics. The branch of PHILOSOPHY that investigates morality and, in particular, the varieties of thinking by which human conduct is guided and may be appraised. Its special concern is with the MEANING and justification of utterances about the rightness and wrongness of actions, the virtue or vice of the motives which prompt them, the praiseworthiness or blameworthiness of the agents who perform them, and the goodness or badness of the consequences to which they give rise. A fundamental problem is whether moral utterances are really the statements of fact, true or false, that they grammatically appear to be. If they are not statements of fact, as adherents of the doctrine of the NATURAL- ISTIC FALLACY and, in particular, EMOTIV- ISTS, believe, how should moral utterances be interpreted: as exclamations or commands? If they are statements of fact, are they empirical statements about such observable characteristics as conduciveness to the general happiness, as ethical NATU- RALISTS maintain, or are they *a priori* the position of ethical rationalists (see APRIOR- ISM)? A further range of problems concerns the relation of moral CONCEPTS to each other. Is the rightness of actions inferable from the goodness of their consequences? Is the virtuousness of a motive to be inferred from the rightness of the actions that it typically prompts? Next, there is the problem of distinguishing moral value from values of other kinds (see AXI- OLOGY). Is the distinguishing mark the factual nature of the ends by reference to which moral injunctions are justified, such as the happiness of mankind in general, or is it the formal character of the injunctions themselves? Finally there is the problem of the conditions under which moral judgements are properly applicable to conduct. To be morally responsible, to be liable to the sanctions of blame and punishment, must an agent be free in the sense that his actions are uncaused, or is it enough that what he did was not wholly caused by factors that sanctions cannot influence?

A.Q.

Bibl: J. Hospers, *Human Conduct* (New York, 1961; London, 1963); W.K. Frank- ena, *Ethics* (New York, 1963).

ethnicity. A relatively new CONCEPT of group association (the term first appears in the 1972 *Supplement* of the *Oxford English Dictionary*) which can refer to a whole range (and frequently a combination) of communal characteristics: lingual, ancestral, regional, religious, etc., which are seen to be the basis of distinctive identity. Ethnicity appears to be a new phenomenon as well as a newly recognized one. Especially in nations formed by immigration (e.g. the U.S., Brazil, Australia) ethnic characteristics were at first seen as survivals from preceding generations which would more or less quickly disappear, or else persist as sentimental associations of no substantive content. Thus the IDEOLOGY of the 'melting pot', which at least in the U.S. was seized upon as a form of reassurance that the CULTURE of the old immigrants would not be overwhelmed.

In the *Communist Manifesto*, Marx and Engels forecast that all preindustrial distinctions of an ethnic character would disappear with the emergence of a world-wide industrial PROLETARIAT united by a perceived common condition and shared interest. The Workers of the World belief, central to MARXISM, is increasingly presented as central to the falsification of Marxist prediction. (In 1907 the socialist Otto Bauer depicted the nationalist conflicts in the Austro-Hungarian empire as a form of class conflict. Marxism could not readily account for this.)

Twentieth-century nations frequently display a mixture of ethnic and social CLASS stratification, often with the one serving as a surrogate for the other. Ethnicity, combining interest with affect (D. Bell) recurrently proves the stronger attachment and the most volatile source of domestic violence. This tendency appears to intensify as modern communications bring dispersed groups in contact with one another, and inform one and all of victories, defeats and especially of atrocities.

Ethnic conflict within the Soviet empire is likely to prove a major element in 21st-century world politics. In the meantime Walker Connor estimates that nearly half of the independent countries of the world have in recent years experienced some degree of 'ethnically inspired dissonance'.

N.G.; D.P.M.

Bibl: N. Glazer and D.P. Moynihan, *Ethnicity, Theory and Practice* (Cambridge, 1975); W. Connor, *The National Question in Marxist-Leninist Theory and Strategy* (Princeton, 1984); D. Horowitz, *Ethnic Groups in Conflict* (Berkeley, 1985).

ethnoarchaeology. Archaeological techniques used to study past communities but within constraints imposed by anthropological concepts. Usually used to study peoples whose direct ancestors are still alive. Thus the true interface between AR-CHAEOLOGY and ANTHROPOLOGY. Not to be confused with the sport, popular with some archaeologists, of using ethnographic analogy to 'explain' archaeological observation.

B.C.

Bibl: C. Kramer (ed.), *Ethnoarchaeology* (Columbia, 1979).

ethnocentrism. Term coined by W.G. Sumner (*Folkways*, 1906) and nearly always used perjoratively, for the attitudes which uncritically presuppose the superiority of one's own group or CULTURE. Such attitudes may be found not only among the members of a tribe or nation who despise other tribes or nations about them, but among anthropologists (sociologists, etc.) if they evaluate the culture or behaviour of members of another society by the light of their own culture. The question of ethnocentrism in ANTHRO-POLOGY cannot be avoided. It is inherent in many of the debates concerning the interpretation of beliefs and practices found in other societies. Investigations of European witchcraft have also revealed that ethnocentrism is a problem in historical understanding as much as in contemporary study.

M.F.; A.G.

Bibl: J. Overing (ed.), *Reason and Morality* (London, 1985); C. Larner, *Witchcraft and Religion* (Oxford, 1984).

ethnography and **ethnology.** In some languages the word corresponding to *ethnography* is the name for social or cultural ANTHROPOLOGY. In the English-speaking countries the term is usually confined to the *descriptive* activities and results of social/cultural anthropology. But it is not to be supposed that ethnography and the non-descriptive parts of anthropology are largely separable: to describe, one needs CRITERIA of relevance; to theorize, one needs facts. *Ethnology* as a name for social or cultural anthropology is still sometimes used in the U.S.A. in that sense. But in Britain it has come, at least since the 1930s, to mean the history of peoples, HISTORIOGRAPHY thus being contrasted with the analysis of and generalization about society. See also FIELD WORK. M.F.

Bibl: A. Kuper, *Anthropology and Anthropologists* (London, 1983); C. Hugh-Jones, *From the Milk River* (Cambridge, 1979).

ethnography of communication, see under ETHNOLINGUISTICS; COMMUNICATION, ETHNOGRAPHY OF.

ethnohistory. A term which came into use in the 1940s to describe the history of non-literate peoples, a subject which had been neglected both by anthropologists (because it was concerned with the past) and by historians (because written documents were lacking). Ethnohistorians need to combine the skills of the archaeologist, the social anthropologist (to interpret ORAL TRADITION), and the conventional historian (to deal with documents produced by conquerors and missionaries). Their results are likely to be more reliable when they reconstruct CULTURAL HISTORY and SOCIAL HISTORY than when the attempt is made to produce a narrative of events. P.B.

Bibl: K.C. Wylie, 'The uses and misuses of ethnohistory' (*Journal of Interdisciplinary History*, 3, 1973, pp. 707-20).

ethnolinguistics. A branch of LINGUISTICS which studies language in relation to the investigation of ethnic types and behaviour. It often overlaps with ANTHROPO-LOGICAL LINGUISTICS and SOCIOLINGUIS-TICS, and recently the phrase ETHNOGRA-PHY OF COMMUNICATION has been applied by sociolinguists to the study of language in relation to the entire range of extra-linguistic variables.   D.C.

Bibl: J.J. Gumperz and D. Hymes (eds.), *Directions in Sociolinguistics: the Ethnography of Communication* (London and New York, 1972).

ethnology, see under ETHNOGRAPHY.

ethnomethodology. A term coined, misleadingly (since the first element bears no relation to its usual meaning), by Harold Garfinkel for an activity which he inaugurated: the sociological study of everyday activities, however trivial, concentrating on the methods used by individuals to report their COMMON SENSE practical actions to others in acceptable rational terms. This process of imposing a *rational* scheme onto what are essentially *practical* activities is referred to in the shorthand terminology of the ethnomethodological language as 'practical reasoning'. Ethnomethodology, with its interest in how the individual experiences and makes sense of social interation, is directly and controversially opposed to sociological theories (e.g. those of Marx, Weber, and Durkheim) that concentrate on the larger questions of SOCIAL STRUCTURE. It is therefore nearer to SOCIAL PSYCHOLOGY than sociological theory proper, as is also true of the two previous theories from which it has derived the most — G.H. Mead's SYMBOLIC INTERACTION theory and, more importantly, Alfred Schutz's PHENOMENOLOGY. Its critics insist that a preoccupation with trivialities is not a virtue, and that trivial exchanges like 'Hi'-'Hi' are neither illuminated nor rendered less trivial by such pronouncements as (an actual example from the first book listed below) 'A basic rule of adjacency pair operation is: given the recognizable production of a first pair part, on its first possible completion its speaker should stop and a next speaker should start and produce a second pair part from the pair type the first is recognizably a member of'.   M.BA.

Bibl: R. Turner (ed.), *Ethnomethodology* (Harmondsworth, 1974); D. Benson and J. A. Hughes, *The Perspective of Ethnomethodology* (London, 1983).

ethnomusicology. The study of all categories of music (including FOLK MUSIC) other than Western ART MUSIC. Although the English word dates only from 1950, the subject, under its earlier name of 'comparative MUSICOLOGY', evolved at the beginning of the 20th century, in Germany, where a predominantly musicological approach was favoured, and later in the U.S.A., where anthropological methods were preferred. The two traditions were to some extent amalgamated with the foundation in 1955 of the international Society for Ethnomusicology, whose activities focus attention upon (1) the collection of data from (*a*) tangible materials (e.g. excavated instruments, early manuscripts) and (*b*) oral traditions (e.g. songs and dances); (2) transcription from tape-recordings, structural analysis (aided by mechanical and electronic devices) of *what* is performed, and detailed description of *how* it is performed; (3) collation of findings with general cultural phenomena. British universities have been conspicuously cautious in extending to the subject the recognition it has gained elsewhere.   A.K.

Bibl: B. Nettl, *Theory and Method in Ethnomusicology* (London and New York, 1964); A.P. Merriam, *The Anthropology of Music* (Evanston, Ill., 1964).

ethnopsychology. The branch of PSYCHOLOGY that studies the psychological characteristics of people considered as members of cultural, social, religious, or national groups. See also CROSS-CULTURAL STUDY; RELATIVISM; CULTURE.   I.M.L.H.

ethology. The name now generally accepted for a type of behavioural study that began as a branch of ZOOLOGY, and attained prominence in the early 1930s with the work of Konrad Lorenz of Vienna. Emphasis was laid on the need to observe and describe the behaviour of as many SPECIES as possible, and there was a tendency to interpret behaviour as the result of EVOLUTION moulded by NATURAL SELECTION. Historical circumstances, e.g. the over-emphasis in PSYCHOLOGY on learning, made ethologists emphasize the non-learned aspects of animal, and even of human behaviour; much work was also concentrated (mainly under the influence of Heinroth in Germany and J.S. Huxley

287

in Britain) on vertebrates, especially birds. Ethology was at first ignored, later severely (and in part justifiably) criticized, by psychologists and physiologists, while ecologists were on the whole receptive. Since the war ethology, psychology, and NEUROPHYSIOLOGY have come closer together, and there are signs that a more unified, more biologically oriented science of behaviour is emerging.

The importance of ethology for the understanding of human behaviour is beginning to be recognized, and the works of Lorenz and Desmond Morris have aroused worldwide interest, though many students of human behaviour (psychologists, psychopathologists, anthropologists) have found them over-assertive. There is a growing consensus that, although facts and conclusions about animal behaviour cannot be generalized and applied to human behaviour, certain methods are equally suitable to the study of either. The fact that human behaviour is the result of accumulative non-GENETIC transfer or individually acquired modifications from one generation to the next can no longer be denied. This 'cultural' or 'psychosocial' evolution, however, must not be allowed to obscure the effects of the genetic evolution which preceded it, and which still determines the direction, and the limitations, of human behaviour.

N.T.

Bibl: R.A. Hinde, *Ethology* (London, 1982); D.J. McFarland, *Oxford Companion to Animal Behaviour* (Oxford, 1981).

etic, see under EMIC.

etiology (or *aetiology*), see under EPIDEMIOLOGY.

etymological fallacy. The view, criticized in LINGUISTICS, that an earlier (or the oldest) meaning of a word is the correct one, e.g. that *history* 'really' means 'investigation', because this was the meaning the word had in Classical Greek. Linguists, by contrast, emphasize that the meaning of a word can be determined only by an analysis of its current use. D.C.

Bibl: D. Crystal, *Linguistics* (Harmondsworth, 1985).

Eucharistic theology. The discussion of doctrines about the Eucharist (from the Greek for 'thanksgiving') or Holy Communion, the most ancient and important act of Christian worship. The modern LITURGICAL MOVEMENT has stimulated both rethinking and fresh agreement about the meaning of the Eucharist.

D.L.E.

Bibl: E.L. Mascall, *Corpus Christi* (London, 2nd ed., 1965).

Euclidean geometry, see under GEOMETRY.

eugenics. Term coined in 1883 by Francis Galton (1822-1911), Charles Darwin's cousin, meaning literally 'well-born' but used to describe the science of improving humankind through selective breeding. Eugenic ideas go back at least as far as Plato, but only received systematic elucidation after Darwin's *Origin of Species* (1859) (see DARWINISM) located humankind in the context of a natural process of EVOLUTION. Eugenics is often divided into a positive and negative variety. *Positive eugenics* encourages the reproduction of allegedly superior human beings (e.g. by means of financial incentives to potential parents), while *negative eugenics* attempts to prevent procreation by those with allegedly undesirable traits (e.g. by means of sexual STERILIZATION or segregation from society). Those who advocate eugenics see it as a science based on GENETICS, but the element of objective scientific thinking behind eugenics typically is small. This spurious appeal to 'science' has been used to legitimize a variety of social prejudices, especially those of RACE and CLASS. In fairness, some eugenic decisions can be unprejudiced, when taken voluntarily and concerning conditions with a known hereditary mechanism (e.g. an individual with a family history of Huntington's chorea may decide not to procreate). But more typically eugenicists attempt to coerce or force others to reproduce (or not), while they confuse cultural-'inheritance' (see CULTURE) with genetic-inheritance, and mistakenly ascribe a variety of social characteristics to genetic factors (see GENETICISM).

Eugenics first became a popular social movement in Britain. It was largely a professional MIDDLE-CLASS preoccupation, stimulated by the fear that Britain's slow progress in the Boer War was the consequence of the degeneration of the Imperial race. By 1906 eugenics was considered one of the four main branches of SOCIOLOGY in Britain. British eugenic writings spawned popular eugenic movements and centres for eugenic study in the U.S., in Russia and in many European countries. In the U.S., unlike Britain, negative eugenic laws were enacted. By 1943, 30 states in the U.S. allowed the sterilization of individuals deemed genetically 'unfit' — particularly the inmates of mental institutions. Most of these laws permitted compulsion when necessary.

As a consequence of Nazi (see NAZISM) involvement in eugenics, it has been viewed with suspicion since World War II. But eugenic ideas survive in all but name and influence attitudes to immigration, the right of the mentally ill and handicapped to procreate, etc. Nazi espousal of eugenic ideas has also obscured the fact that eugenics was and is as much a LEFT-wing preoccupation as that of the RIGHT. Indeed some of the most enthusiastic early eugenicists were the Fabians (see FABIANISM) in Britain and PROGRESSIVE states like California in the U.S. Today eugenics tends not to be institutionalized, but influences the decisions of individual bureaucrats and doctors. A notable exception is the Singapore of Lee Kuan Yew, where positive eugenic thinking still shapes government social policy. See also EUTHENICS; DYSGENIC.   A.B.E.

Bibl: D.J. Kevles, *In the Name of Eugenics* (New York, 1985); S. Trombley, *The Right to Reproduce* (London, 1988).

eukaryote. A fundamental division of living things, made up of organisms whose CELLS contain a separate nucleus. All living things are either eukaryotes or PROKARYOTES, according to their cellular structure. In eukaryotes, cells have greater internal distinction than in prokaryotes. Eukaryotic cells have a separate nucleus, which contains the cell's DNA, surrounded by a nuclear membrane; they also have other internal organelles, such as MITO-CHONDRIA. Fungi, plants, and animals are all eukaryotes; bacteria are prokaryotes.

Eukaryotes probably evolved from prokaryotic ancestors, some time between one and two thousand million years ago. It is a matter of controversy whether eukaryotes evolved by the internal DIFFERENTIATION of the prokaryotic cell, or by the symbiotic union of several kinds of prokaryote (see SYMBIOSIS).   M.R.

eurocurrency, see under EURODOLLARS.

eurodollars. Deposits held in U.S. dollars at banks located outside the U.S., though not necessarily in Europe, e.g. there are 'eurodollar markets' in South-East Asia. Other *eurocurrency* markets exist, but the eurodollar market has been and is the most important. The holders of eurodollars may be of any nationality. The deposits and corresponding loans are usually short-term. The eurodollar market exists because of the official restrictions on U.S. banks that allow Euro-banks to offer better rates to lenders and borrowers. In its search for preferred interest rates and currencies, CAPITAL has become internationally mobile and eurodollar markets have greatly increased this mobility. This mobility has reduced U.S. control over its interest rates and monetary system and, it has been suggested, affected the U.S. BALANCE OF PAYMENTS. It also has had important effects on INTERNATIONAL LIQUIDITY and the world money supply. In the mid-1970s, the eurocurrency markets recycled to oil importers a considerable portion of OPEC's surplus oil revenues and so prevented a larger shock to the world economic system. These markets were put under great strain to find short-term borrowers to match the often very short-term nature of these new deposits (see DEBT CRISIS).   J.P.

Bibl: R.B. Johnston, *Economics of the Euro-Market* (London, 1983).

European. For organizations beginning with this word see EDC; EEC; EFTA; ENEA; and next entry.

European Court of Human Rights. This court, which sits in Strasbourg, was established on 3 September 1958 in accordance with the provisions of the European Convention for the Protection of Human Rights and Fundamental Freedoms of

1950 (The Convention). It is stipulated there that the court shall consist of 'a number of judges equal to that of the Members of the Council of Europe'. The members of the court are elected by the Consultative Assembly for a period of 9 years. Article 48 of the Convention provides that the following may bring a case before the court: (a) the Commission; (b) a high contracting party whose national is alleged to be a victim; (c) a high contracting party which referred the case to the Commission; and (d) a high contracting party against which the complaint has been lodged. The conclusion to be inferred from this provision is that an individual who has petitioned the Commission for an alleged violation of the Convention can never bring his case before the court himself. As to the position of respondents, proceedings may be commenced before the court only against a contracting STATE which has either signed the declaration of recognition provided for in Article 46 of the Convention or has consented to reference being made to the court in a particular matter. Once a case has been brought before the court, the latter must decide whether or not there has been a violation of the Convention. If it is satisfied that a violation of the Convention by a contracting state has taken place, its decision may afford just satisfaction to the injured party. The decision of the court which is binding on the parties to the case is final. Its execution is supervised by the Committee of Ministers of the Council of Europe. See also HUMAN RIGHTS.   O.Y.E.

Bibl: J.E.S. Fawcett, *The Application of the European Convention on Human Rights* (Oxford, 1969).

European Currency Unit, see under IN-TERNATIONAL LIQUIDITY.

eurythmics (or *eurhythmics*). The art of interpreting music through body movements; specifically, the system of rhythmical gymnastics taught by the Swiss composer and educationist Émile Jacques-Dalcroze (1865-1950) in order to develop his students' physical, intellectual, and aesthetic sense of musical forms and rhythms; to increase their capacity to analyse musical structure; to give them musi-cal 'experience' rather than musical 'knowledge'.   B.L.B.

eurythmy (or *eurhythmy*). An art form evolved by Rudolf Steiner (1861-1925), the founder of ANTHROPOSOPHY. It aims to make visible certain qualities of movement, feeling, and character which are held to be inherent in the sounds of speech or music. Stage performances present interpretations of music, poetry, and prose by groups or soloists. It is also used educationally for adults and children (notably in STEINER SCHOOLS), and therapeutically, as *curative eurythmy*, under the direction of anthroposophical doctors.   J.D.

Euston Road Group. A group of painters associated with The School of Drawing and Painting which was established in 1937, at first in Charlotte Street, then, from 1938 to 1939, at 314-316 Euston Road, London; more particularly, Graham Bell, William Coldstream, Lawrence Gowing, Victor Pasmore, and Claude Rogers. The work of these painters was at that time marked by an insistence upon objective drawing, tonality, and realistic subject-matter.   Q.B.

euthanasia. Literally, death without suffering. Used to describe the 'mercy killing' by a medical practitioner of an incurably ill patient. In the adult, this implies the administration of a drug (or drugs) deliberately and specifically to precipitate or accelerate death. Theoretically, euthanasia can be either voluntary or involuntary (compulsory). In no country is either form legal, though there is *de facto* acceptance of voluntary euthanasia in Holland. *Voluntary* euthanasia, requested by the sufferer, has also been described as assisted suicide or homicide by request. *Involuntary* euthanasia implies a decision by society (or by an individual) to end the life of a sufferer who cannot signify volition, for example, the severely handicapped infant or the demented. Discussion relating to euthanasia has been complicated by the use of the term '*passive* euthanasia'. This is defined as withholding treatment that might lengthen the lives of the incurably sick. However, as it does not involve the deliberate administration of a drug to accelerate death, it should not be described as euthanasia. The use of the term derives from a failure to distinguish between acute and terminal illness. The two are distinct biological entities, and what is appropriate for one may be inappropriate for the other. For example, intravenous infusions, ANTIBIOTICS, respirators and cardiac resuscitation are all supportive measures for use in acute or recurrent illnesses to assist a patient through a critical period towards recovery. Generally, to use these measures in the terminally ill, with no expectation of a return to health, is inappropriate and, therefore, bad medicine. A doctor clearly has a duty to sustain life where life is sustainable; he has no duty — legal or ethical — to prolong the distress of a dying patient. The term '*indirect* euthanasia' has been used to describe the administration of morphine to cancer patients in pain. This is incorrect; giving a drug to lessen pain cannot be equated with giving an overdose deliberately to end life. Should life be marginally shortened by the use of morphine or related drugs, this is an acceptable risk in the circumstances. Correctly used, however, such drugs are much safer than commonly supposed. There is circumstantial evidence that those whose pain is relieved may outlive those whose nutrition and rest continue to be disturbed by persistent pain.   R.G.T

Bibl: J. Rachels, *The End of Life: Euthanasia and Morality* (Oxford, 1986).

euthenics. From the Greek to thrive or flourish, euthenics is the art or science of improving the well-being of humankind through the betterment of the conditions of life. Euthenics is totally at odds with EUGENICS in that it seeks to improve 'nurture' (e.g. by the provision of better housing, sanitation, education, etc.). Eugenicists see these efforts as at best ephemeral and argue for policies to improve 'nature' (e.g. through the sexual STERILIZATION of individuals who are, allegedly, of genetically (see GENETICS) inferior stock). The term euthenics, unlike eugenics, is little used today. But the debate continues between those who see nature and those who see nurture, as pre-eminent in determining the quality of society and the abilities of individuals. See also NATURE VERSUS NURTURE.   A.B.E.

evaluation. In education, the process of obtaining information, usually for administrators and teachers, about the effects and values of educational activities. As a systematic pursuit, evaluation is typically associated with programmes of educational reform, particularly with the Anglo-American curriculum development movement (see NUFFIELD APPROACH) of the 1960s and 1970s. The initial theoretical framework (R.W. Tyler, *Constructing Achievement Tests*, 1934) stressed the PSYCHOMETRIC assessment of learning objectives, but during the 1960s the SOCIAL ENGINEERING assumptions of this MODEL were challenged, and the field is currently characterized by a proliferation of theory. A major conventional division is that of M. Scriven (1967) between *formative* evaluation, designed to improve a programme, and *summative* evaluation, designed to judge its worth.

Evaluations are typically commissioned by executive branches of central government, both as a CYBERNETIC aid to interventionist management and as a form of public reassurance that central initiatives are subject to disinterested assessment. Much of the diversity evident in the theory and practice of evaluation can be explained in terms of their underlying potential LOGIC. The crucial issue in such an analysis is the impact of evaluation on the distribution of POWER, particularly where, as is now increasingly the norm, government-backed programmes embody technocratic values. Especially in England, attempts to democratize the process of evaluation have led its practitioners to take risks with both bureaucratic convenience and scientific respectability in order to stimulate and inform a broader public discourse about educational change. Given that sponsored independence is a sine qua non of such developments, and that more docile and technicist alternatives are readily available, the future of evaluation is likely to reflect government definitions of the need and the right to know.   B.M.

Bibl: E.R. House, *Evaluating With Validity* (Beverly Hills, Ca., 1980).

evaluation procedure. In LINGUISTICS, a set of techniques which enable a linguist to judge which of two GRAMMARS is the bet-

291

ter account of a language. The importance of this notion was first pointed out by Chomsky, and there has since been considerable discussion of evaluation CRITERIA (e.g. the economy of a description) for particular areas of language, especially PHONOLOGY.   D.C.

evaluative, see under NORMATIVE.

Evangelical. A term sometimes used as another word for PROTESTANT. It is applied, e.g., to LUTHERANISM or to BARTHIAN theology. But its most common use in the English-speaking world has been in the description of Protestants who take a conservative view of the authority of the Bible; of the necessity and sufficiency of acceptance by faith of the salvation won by the sacrifice of Christ on the cross; and of the indispensable importance of miracles including Christ's virgin birth, physical resurrection and (in the future) visible return to earth in glory. The decision to accept Christ as Saviour in this sense can be described as being 'born again'. This movement reacts against LIBERALISM in THEOLOGY and has often been identified with FUNDAMENTALISM. But in the 20th century there has been much debate within it about the character of the truth or trustworthiness of the Bible. While probably most Evangelicals still accept the Bible's INFALLIBILITY or 'inerrancy' with few qualifications or none, some have argued that the Bible is the Word of God in what it teaches when taken as a whole, not in everything in poetry, history or science which it touches, and there has been a cautious acceptance of Biblical criticism and HERMENEUTICS. Similarly there has been greater sophistication in handling what the Bible affirms in relation to modern questions in ETHICS and other fields. In the 1970s it became clear that this movement, for all its internal tensions, was the most lively feature of religion in the U.S. (see BORN AGAIN) and was gaining influence wherever in the world the style of evangelists from the U.S. (the most famous being Billy Graham) was an acceptable model. See also NEW CHRISTIAN RIGHT.   D.L.E.

Bibl: C. Catherwood, *Five Evangelical Leaders* (London, 1984); J. Stott, *The Cross of Christ* (Leicester, 1986).

events, see HAPPENINGS AND EVENTS.

Everett or Everett-Wheeler interpretation, see under MANY WORLDS HYPOTHESIS.

everyday, the. A kind of crossroads of new approaches in SOCIOLOGY, ANTHROPOLOGY, PHILOSOPHY, and in HISTORY. The MARXISTS are naturally concerned with the everyday as they are with ordinary people, a concern visible in the attempt to write HISTORY FROM BELOW by Edward Thompson and others as in the work of the philosophers Henri Lefebvre and Agnes Heller. More or less simultaneously, the phenomenologist (see PHENOMENOLOGY) Alfred Schutz was pursuing his study of what he called the principles of 'commonsense knowledge'. In sociology and anthropology the so-called 'ethnomethodologists' (see ETHNOMETHODOLOGY) such as Harold Garfinkel (who acknowledges a debt to Schutz), Pierre Bourdieu (in his work on 'theoretical practice') and Erving Goffman (author of *The Presentation of Self in Everyday Life*) have all been concerned to make the commonplace problematic, or more exactly, to show that what is taken for granted in one society is perceived as obviously false or foolish in another. In their different ways, Michel Foucault and the feminists (see FEMINISM) have directed attention to what is sometimes called the 'politics of the everyday', the power relations concealed or revealed in everyday transactions at home, at work, in school and so on. These theorists are now having some impact on the practice of social historians (see SOCIAL HISTORY), transforming a few of them into historical anthropologists (see HISTORICAL ANTHROPOLOGY). The pursuit of the everyday has challenged a good many traditional assumptions. It has alerted us to what might be called the importance of the trivial in the understanding of society. Nevertheless, the central concept is more elusive than it may seem. The everyday refers at once to attitudes (or MENTALITIES), to actions (especially to routine), and to MATERIAL CULTURE. The everyday is sometimes opposed to RITUAL (which marks special occasions) yet daily life may be described as a kind of ritual. The idea of everyday knowledge is linked to the notion of cultural rules, but the concept of 'rule' is itself in need of further clarification. P.B.

Bibl: M. Douglas (ed.), *Rules and Meanings: the Anthropology of Everyday Knowledge* (Harmondsworth, 1973).

evolution. The theory that the existing varieties of plant and animal, so far from having existed more or less unmodified from the beginning of biological time, have come into being through a progressive diversification that has accompanied their BIOGENETIC descent from their ancestors. Although the theory had been adumbrated very many times before the publication in 1859 of Darwin's *The Origin of Species*, it was Darwin's ability to propound an acceptable theory (DARWINISM) of how evolution might have come about that brought the subject into public discussion and intensive enquiry. It is naïve to suppose that the acceptance of evolution theory depends upon the evidence of a number of so-called 'proofs'; it depends rather upon the fact that the evolutionary theory permeates and supports every branch of biological science, much as the notion of the roundness of the earth underlies all GEODESY and all cosmological theories on which the shape of the earth has a bearing. Thus anti-evolutionism is of the same stature as flat-earthism. Biologists therefore do not argue about whether evolution has taken place, but many details of how evolution proceeds are still matters of controversy. See LAMARCKISM; MASS EXTINCTION; MOLECULAR CLOCK; PUNCTUATED EQUILIBRIUM; CLADISM. P.M.; M.R.

evolution, social and cultural. Although ideas of the regular development of human CULTURE and society antedate Darwin, the second half of the 19th century was the great period of evolutionary theory in the SOCIAL SCIENCES. It depended on the assumption, now abandoned, that surviving PRIMITIVE peoples represent earlier stages in the development of modern society. In one form, evolutionary theory keeps close to BIOLOGY in speaking of increasing complexity and differentiation; in another, a series of phases or stages of development is posited, although not all societies are expected to go through all of them. Evolutionary thinking is now of secondary importance in Anglo-American and Western European social and cultural ANTHROPOLOGY, but plays a central role in countries adhering to MARXISM, although not under the name of evolution. See also DIFFUSION; EVOLUTION; STRUCTURALISM.

M.F.

Bibl: E. Gellner (ed.), *Soviet and Western Anthropology* (London, 1980); M. Augé, *The Anthropological Circle* (Cambridge, 1982).

evolutionarily stable strategy. In DARWINISM, a strategy which is stable against invasion by any other specified strategy. A 'strategy' here generally refers to a behaviour pattern of an animal, but the theory applies to anything that can evolve by NATURAL SELECTION. Biologists seeking to understand why animals behave in the way they do ask whether the behaviour pattern could be bettered by any alternative behaviour pattern (strategy). If it could not, it is an evolutionarily stable strategy (ESS). Natural selection should give rise to animals that behave according to an ESS. The idea is an application of GAME THEORY to BIOLOGY. The term was coined, and the theory largely developed, by John Maynard Smith. M.R.

evolutionary humanism. A sort of secular RELIGION or religion surrogate founded upon the deeply held conviction that EVOLUTION is the fundamental modality of all change in the universe, so that all agencies that provoke change and all that retard it can be described as 'good' or 'bad' respectively. Sometimes evolutionary humanism is taken for the belief that the human moral sense is itself a product of evolutionary change as opposed to a faculty indwelling in man through the mediation of some supernatural agency. In none of these forms has evolutionary humanism (though its exponents have included T.H. Huxley and Sir Julian Huxley) found for itself a significant following from moralists or theologians. P.M.

evolutionism. A doctrine especially associated with the names of Herbert Spencer (1820-1903) and Teilhard de Chardin (1881-1955) according to which evolution is the fundamental mode of change, both organic and inorganic, in the universe. Evolutionism is normally associated with a belief in the inevitability of progress. In the writings of Teilhard de Chardin (see NOOSPHERE) this assumes an extravagant metaphysical form.   P.M.

examinations. Tests, written and oral, set at schools/colleges in order to assess the pupil/student's progress. There have been a number of newcomers to the field, the most important of them in Britain being (1) the *General Certificate of Secondary Education* (GCSE); launched after much controversy and birthpangs in September 1986, the first papers are to be set in the summer of 1988. It replaces the old O-level and *Certificate of Secondary Education* (CSE) and is meant to be a single system of examining suitable for all ability groups. It is designed to test far more practical knowledge than theoretical and involves oral as well as written work, projects and teacher-assessed exercises; (2) *A/S Level* (Advanced Supplementary) also introduced to widen the horizons of young students and to allow those wishing to stay on at school sixth forms without being capable of sitting the fully-fledged A-levels a chance to succeed in an examination which is worth half a full A-level. Universities have agreed to accept two A/S levels instead of one A — though many would prefer to see the qualification used as a supplement rather than a substitute.   J.I.

exchange. Relationships established between individuals in which goods and services are exchanged. NETWORKS of relationships are based on the notion of indebtedness and they are sustained by the debts not being fully discharged. If a debt between two people is paid off, the relationship is terminated. The theory of GIFT exchange was developed by Marcel Mauss and his *Essai sur le Don* (1924) has become one of the central texts of *social* ANTHROPOLOGY. Mauss drew on Malinowski's work on the KULA of the Trobriand Islands and material collected by Boas relating to the POTLATCH of the Kwatiutl Indians. He understood gift exchange in terms of the social relations it established between people and the binding nature of the principle of reciprocity. Exchange was more than an economic transaction and particularly in nonmonetary societies it formed the basis for social solidarity.

Mauss's work exercised an important influence upon Lévi-Strauss. The theory of exchange became central to Lévi-Strauss's work (*The Elementary Structures of Kinship*, 1949), but in this case it was not founded on the exchange of gifts, rather the exchange of women through systems of marriage. Lévi-Strauss distinguished between complex (found in European type societies) and elementary (found in non-European societies) exchange. He further divided the elementary system into generalized and restricted exchange. Exchange has continued to be an important concept for anthropologists. Attention has focused on the distinctions between gift and commodity exchange and it has become clear that they are rarely absolute distinctions. The designation of goods and transformations in their status highlights the complex system of social classification.   A.G.

Bibl: J.W. Leach and E. Leach (eds.), *The Kula: New Perspectives on Massim Exchange* (Cambridge, 1983); C.A. Gregory, *Gifts and Commodities* (London, 1982).

exchange control. Restriction on the right of a citizen of one country to make a payment to a person not resident in the country. The main purpose of exchange control is to limit the ability to convert home assets into foreign assets, though sometimes they are used to reduce the inflow of unwanted financial assets from abroad. The possibility of adverse movements in the EXCHANGE RATE may lead to holders of home assets converting them into assets denominated in a currency whose value is likely to be maintained or increase. Individuals or firms may wish to acquire foreign financial or physical assets, and hence need to obtain foreign currency with which to make the foreign INVESTMENT. In both these cases, the foreign exchange reserves of the home country are reduced (see BALANCE OF PAYMENTS) and downward pressure is put on the exchange rate. Exchange controls can be used to control the outflow of foreign exchange. With freely floating exchange rates, the demand for and supply of foreign exchange should be balanced, which implies that exchange controls are unnecessary. However, it has been argued that exchange controls can be used to force MULTINATIONAL COMPANIES to invest their profits within the country they were made in. Similarly, exchange controls may be used to make overseas investment more expensive or difficult and, thus, provide a relative incentive for investment within the country. In October 1979, the United Kingdom abolished exchange controls. M.V.P.; J.P.

exchange energy. A stabilizing ENERGY ascribed in QUANTUM MECHANICS terms to ELECTRONS with the same SPIN in an ATOM or MOLECULE. In order not to violate the EXCLUSION PRINCIPLE the electrons must be present in different ORBITALS, and the energy can be thought of as arising from the indistinguishability of electrons with identical spin. The exchange energy is not predominant in chemical bondings (see BOND) but it has some influence on chemical reactivity (see CHEMICAL REACTION), and there are important consequences in SPECTROSCOPY and for the magnetic properties of compounds. B.F.

exchange models. In SOCIOLOGY, MODELS, associated with George Homans and Peter Blau, that concentrate on elementary social processes in which human groups are seen as formed and held together by exchanges of rewards, satisfactions, esteem, and the creation of common sentiments. Whereas the STRUCTURAL-FUNCTIONAL THEORY deals with whole societies (*macrostructures*), exchange theory tends to concentrate on small groups (*microstructures*). D.B.

exchange particle, see under GLUON.

exchange rate. The British definition is the foreign currency price of one unit of the domestic currency. The American definition is the domestic currency price of one unit of the foreign currency, i.e. both America and Britain quote the dollar price of sterling as the exchange rate. The exchange rate determines the domestic prices of a country's imports. It is import-ant in determining the demand for a country's exports and its demand for imports. The current account of the BALANCE OF PAYMENTS depends on the exchange rate. A change in the exchange rate alters the foreign currency value of a domestic asset. Expectations of changes in the exchange rate will affect the flows of CAPITAL into and out of a country, i.e. the capital account of the balance of payments. A net surplus/deficit on the combined current and capital account implies an excess demand/supply for the domestic currency. This will put pressure on the exchange rate to rise/fall, unless the CENTRAL BANK acts to alleviate this pressure. The central bank can buy and sell foreign exchange and alter interest rates. From the BRETTON WOODS conference in 1944 to late 1971, nearly all countries had fixed exchange rates. Since 1973, many countries, including the U.K., have adopted a policy of a managed float. This policy allows the exchange rate to be determined by the demand and supply for the domestic currency, but the government may intervene on occasions to influence the level and speed of adjustment of the exchange rate. Most member countries of the EEC have followed a different policy in the European Monetary System, in which they have agreed to maintain the same exchange rates against each other, within certain bounds. These bounds can be changed and the member countries have access to funds which can be used to defend the set exchange rate. All these policies are a reaction to the rapid and unstable movements in exchange rates that have occurred since the early 1970s. This instability in the movements of exchange rates has mainly been caused by increases in the international mobility of capital and the majority of foreign exchange transactions being for speculative purposes. However, in the long term, countries' exchange rates are likely to be determined by their relative performance in foreign trade. In the short and medium term, the international mobility of capital poses serious problems for ECONOMIC DEVELOPMENT and GROWTH. It may be necessary to maintain very high interest rates to induce internationally mobile capital to remain in a country whose exchange rate is expected to fall, because of high rates of domestic INFLATION and a poor foreign trade performance (see DEVALUATION and DEBT CRISIS). J.P.

Bibl: R.E. Caves and R.W. Jones, *World Trade and Payments* (Boston, 4th ed., 1985).

excited states (in PHYSICS), see under ENERGY LEVEL.

exclaves, see under ENCLAVES.

excluded middle, law of the, see under INTUITIONISM.

exclusion principle (or *Pauli principle*). A principle in QUANTUM MECHANICS, postulated in 1925 by the Austrian physicist Wolfgang Pauli, according to which no two ELECTRONS can exist in an ATOM in the same state, i.e. they cannot share the same set of QUANTUM NUMBERS. See also QUANTUM STATISTICS. M.V.B.

exclusive economic zones, see under LAW OF THE SEA.

existential psychiatry. A psychiatric movement which took inspiration from existential philosophy. The Swiss psychiatrist L. Binswanger's existential analysis (*Daseinsanalyse*) represented a synthesis of psychoanalytical, PHENOMENOLOGICAL and existential concepts applied to his new clinical approach: a reconstruction of the inner world of experience of his patients, a construction of an 'authentic science of persons' based on Heidegger's work on the structure of human existence. He was critical of some mechanical aspects of Freud's descriptions of the human mind (see FREUDIAN) and favoured the technique of the 'encounter' rather than of TRANSFERENCE. The Scottish psychiatrist R.D. Laing (see ANTI-PSYCHIATRY) also refuses to view the patient as a kind of mechanism, and emphasizes the existential concept of 'ontological insecurity' (see ONTOLOGY) of the human state which he describes through the pathological disorders of the 'divided self'. The American psychoanalyst Rollo May's endeavour is to establish a working science of man by uniting science and ontology, and thereby to go beyond the traditional distinction between subject and object: man is under-

stood as experiencing the world in a uniquely human way. In this perspective, May denounces the dehumanizing tendencies in traditional psychotherapeutic approaches, and in the industrial system as a whole. The Viennese psychiatrist Viktor E. Frankl adds a stress on meaning to his existential clinical approach which he calls 'logotherapy'. The American psychiatrist and psychoanalyst T.S. Szasz gives a further development to the theoretical and clinical framework of the existential approach, by connecting it both to his own socio-historical insights, and to Goffman's ROLE THEORIES. B.BE.

Bibl: T.S. Szasz, *The Myth of Mental Illness* (New York, 1961); R.D. Laing, *The Divided Self* (Harmondsworth, 1965); V.E. Frankl, *The Doctor and the Soul* (Harmondsworth, 1973); R. May, *Love and Will* (New York, 1969; London, 1970).

existential psychology. A SCHOOL OF PSYCHOLOGY which emphasizes that each individual is constantly making choices, great and small, which cumulatively determine the kind of person he becomes. Represented by Rollo May, Abraham Maslow (associated also with HUMANISTIC PSYCHOLOGY), and Carl Rogers, it is concerned with the individual's attempts to discover a satisfying sense of his personal identity and to give meaning to his life.
I.M.L.H.

Bibl: R. May, *Love and Will* (New York, 1969; London, 1970); C.S. Hall and G. Lindzey, *Theories of Personality* (New York, 1978).

existential theology, see CHRISTIAN EXISTENTIALISM.

existentialism. A body of philosophical doctrine that dramatically emphasizes the contrast between human existence and the kind of existence possessed by natural objects. Men, endowed with will and consciousness, find themselves in an alien world of objects which have neither. Existentialism was inaugurated by Kierkegaard in a violent reaction against the all-encompassing absolute IDEALISM of Hegel. For Hegel, God is the impersonal ABSOLUTE; finite human personalities are insubstantial fragments of this engulfing spiritual unity, and everything that happens, including human actions, can be rationally explained as a necessary element in the total scheme of things. Kierkegaard insisted on the utter distinctness of God and Man and on the inexplicability (or 'absurdity') of the relations between them, and of their actions. As developed in this century by Heidegger and Sartre, and by contrast with CHRISTIAN EXISTENTIALISM, existentialism is atheistic (see ATHEISM) and draws on the PHENOMENOLOGY of Husserl as a method for investigating the peculiarities of the human situation. Man, these later existentialists contend, is a self-creating being who is not initially endowed with a character and goals but must choose them by acts of pure decision, existential 'leaps' analogous to that seen by Kierkegaard in the reason-transcending decision to believe in God. For Heidegger, man is a temporal being, conscious, through his will, of a future whose only certainty is his own death. To live authentically is to live in the light of this bleak and unrationalizable fact, in full awareness of le NÉANT both as one's own ultimate destiny and as one's own nature until one has chosen a character for oneself. Sartre's particular interest is in what he sees as the paradoxical relations between one human existence and another.　　　　　　　　A.Q.

Bibl: W. Barrett, *Irrational Man* (New York, 1958; London, 1961); W. Kaufmann (ed.), *Existentialism from Dostoevsky to Sartre* (New York, 1956; London, 1957).

exobiology. The branch of BIOLOGY that deals with the search for extraterrestrial life (see PANSPERMIA and SEARCH FOR EXTRATERRESTRIAL INTELLIGENCE).　P.N.

exocrine glands, see under ENDOCRINOLOGY.

exogamy. Term developed by McLennan (*Primitive Marriage*, 1865) to describe a set of rules relating to MARRIAGE. They specify out-marriage. Exogamy regulates marriage and is distinct from INCEST prohibitions, regulations concerning sex. Exogamy prohibits marriage within a group; an individual must marry out. Corporate groups, for example DESCENT groups, are usually exogamous and rules relating to marriage establish links or alliances between different groups. The role of exogamy and the establishment of marriage alliances have been central to Lévi-Strauss's work in kinship (*The Elementary Structures of Kinship*, 1949). In societies without descent groups, for example BILATERAL societies, rules of exogamy are EGO-focused: an individual is prohibited from marrying within a certain range of kin related to him. (See ENDOGAMY; also KINSHIP.)　　A.G.

Bibl: J. Goody, *The Development of the Family and Marriage in Europe* (Cambridge, 1983).

exon, see under SPLIT GENE.

exotoxins, see under BACTERIOLOGY.

expansion of the universe. A theory formulated by Hubble in 1923. It is observed that the light from faint (and therefore presumably distant) GALAXIES is reddened. This RED SHIFT is interpreted as a DOPPLER EFFECT, so that the galaxies are believed to be receding from us, and from each other, like spots on the surface of a balloon as it is blown up; the farther the galaxy, the greater is its speed of recession. This is measured by *Hubble's constant*, defined as the ratio *distance of galaxy ÷ speed of recession*; its value is about 10 thousand million years. The expansion of the universe is a basic phenomenon which any theory of COSMOLOGY (e.g. the BIG-BANG HYPOTHESIS or the STEADY-STATE HYPOTHESIS) must explain. Galaxies 10 thousand million light-years away are receding from us at the speed of light. More distant objects are receding faster than this so that their light can never reach us. Thus the *observable* universe accessible to ASTRONOMY seems to be finite in extent. See also COSMIC BACKGROUND RADIATION.　　　M.V.B.

expectation. In STATISTICS, the weighted arithmetic MEAN of the values taken in a DISTRIBUTION, the weights being the probabilities attached to the values.　R.SI.

expected utility theory. A theory of how decisions that are subject to RISK are or should be made. The decision-maker is *assumed* to consider each course of action and weight the UTILITY of each possible outcome by the associated probability. The sum of the weighted utility values gives the expected utility of the course of action. After an exhaustive consideration of all possible courses of action, that action giving the highest expected utility is chosen. This theory has been considered and widely used in ECONOMICS, ENGINEERING, MANAGEMENT SCIENCE, PSYCHOLOGY and PHILOSOPHY. However, the evidence of empirical tests systematically contradicts the predictions of the theory. Unfortunately, no alternative model of decision-making subject to risk has yet been offered which is both theoretically and empirically satisfactory.   J.P.

Bibl: J. Hey, *Uncertainty in Economics* (Oxford, 1979).

experimental group, see under CONTROL GROUP.

experimental music. Used mostly in connection with a type of music which became prominent in America in the 1950s and which broke with musical traditions in a more fundamental way than the contemporary European development of AVANT-GARDE MUSIC. In this music John Cage and others sought to weaken the composer-dominated hierarchy of classical music and give more freedom to the performer, the audience and in a way to sound itself (see ALEATORY; INDETERMINACY; MOBILE FORM; TIME NOTATION).
                                          B.CO.

Bibl: M. Nyman, *Experimental Music: Cage and Beyond* (London, 1974).

experimental psychology. The branch of PSYCHOLOGY that is based on the use of experimental methods. The psychologist's fundamental interest lies in the description, CLASSIFICATION, prediction, and EXPLANATION of the behaviour of living organisms. He gains access to this behaviour by a variety of techniques. Sometimes he makes his observations in the 'natural' setting, as when the animal psychologist studies the wild animal in its natural ENVIRONMENT (see ETHOLOGY) and the industrial psychologist observes 'man at work' on the factory floor (see INDUSTRIAL PSYCHOLOGY). Increasingly, however, psychological phenomena (e.g. the effect of sleep deprivation on vigilance) have been brought under scrutiny in carefully controlled experimental situations where, ideally, one is able to identify all the significant factors and uncover correlational and cause-effect relationships. The experimental approach to psychological problems was first adopted principally to investigate 'sensory' phenomena (e.g. PERCEPTION), and a whole range of elegant methods was invented to tackle such questions as just how sensitive the human being is to changes in level of sound, light, and pressure. As a result a number of principles were formulated that expressed relationships — universal under certain limited conditions — between measurable levels of stimulation and of human sensation. The use of experimental methods is continually expanding, and the 'higher mental processes' listed under COGNITIVE PSYCHOLOGY have come increasingly under experimental scrutiny.

The experimental psychologist's ideal, like that of any other experimental investigator, is to control all the factors that might affect the phenomenon under study. Usually, one or a small number of factors (the *independent variables*) is systematically varied, and aspects (the *dependent variables*) of the subject's performance in response to these variables are tabulated. These dependent variables may be relatively simple and observable responses such as a verbal reply to a question, or they may be much more complex and covert, as with many physiological responses (e.g. changes in brain-waves) to different conditions of stimulation. The ideal of complete control is seldom if ever achieved, however, because of the numerous extraneous and uncontrolled factors — the temperature of the room, time of day, the subject's idea of the experiment, etc. — that may affect the dependent variable; a familiar device for overcoming this problem is the use of a CONTROL GROUP. To assess the significance of the results of any test, the experimental psychologist also needs a sound understanding of STATISTICS. Although the experimental approach has its critics, there seems little doubt that it will continue to play an increasingly vital role in psychological enquiry.   D.J.W.

Bibl: P. Harris, *Designing and Reporting Experiments* (Milton Keynes, 1986).

Experimentele Groep, see under COBRA.

expert system. An ARTIFICIAL INTELLIGENCE computer PROGRAM for performing tasks requiring expertise but no great insight or originality. The focus of much commercial interest, expert systems are particularly suited to problems where many possibilities must be considered at once. Some of the domains handled by expert systems include: analysing oil drilling information, offering financial planning advice, and assisting in medical diagnosis. It is a prime example of an *intelligent knowledge-based system* (IKBS).

Most expert systems do not deal with problems that can be reduced to one ALGORITHM, but rather ones where different bodies of information need to be applied in a flexible way. The major difficulty in constructing an expert system is *eliciting* knowledge from a human expert and recording it in a knowledge base in a form suitable for use by the COMPUTER. The expert's knowledge is rarely fully articulated, and it is not yet known how knowledge is best represented to a computer. The knowledge base often consists of rules of the form 'If [conditions] Then [do, or conclude something]'. The expert system works as a *production system* matching information it has against the conditions of these rules, which causes the system to request for or infer further information which may match the conditions of further rules. HEURISTIC rules may determine which rules are most likely to prove helpful in certain circumstances. (See also PROBLEM-SOLVING.) R.S.C.

explanation. The process or end-product of explaining something. The word and its meaning are, of course, perfectly familiar; less so, perhaps, are some related terms and the varieties of explanation that have been distinguished in philosophical analyses of scientific explanations. The thing to be explained is often called the *explanandum* or *conclusion*, henceforth called *C*. *C* may be a fact about some particular event, e.g. 'This apple fell from the tree', or a generalization or law, e.g. 'Unsupported apples fall'. When *C* is explained by means of a set of statements, they are said to constitute the *explanans* or the *premises* of the explanation. Some of the statements in the explanans may themselves express laws, generalizations, or regularities, e.g. 'All bodies attract one another', and the SET of such statements will henceforth be called *L*. Other statements in the explanans, e.g. 'A wind was blowing', 'The branch was rotten', may refer to particular events or states of affairs. These are said to specify *initial conditions*, and the set of such statements will henceforth be called *I*. *I* or *L* may, in special cases, be empty, i.e. there may be no such statements. The types of explanation that can be distinguished include the following; they are illustrated with some oversimplified examples.

(1) *Deductive explanations.* In these the truth of the conclusion *C* follows logically, or deductively, from *I* and *L* together, e.g. 'The apple fell because (*I*) it was unsupported and (*L*) unsupported objects fall'. A major dispute in PHILOSOPHY concerns whether deductive (sometimes called deductive nomological) explanations are the only truly adequate scientific explanations, and whether all other kinds are really disguised versions of this kind.

(2) *Probabilistic* or *statistical explanations.* In these, the truth of the conclusion cannot be inferred logically from *I* and *L*: at most one can infer that it is more *probable* that *C* is true than that it is false, e.g. 'Tom has cancer because (*I*) Tom smokes, and (*L*) 90% of those who smoke get cancer'. Here *L* and *I* together only make Tom's having cancer *highly probable*; it does not follow logically from them that he *will* have cancer. Many explanations in PSYCHOLOGY and in SOCIAL SCIENCES have this structure.

(3) *Causal explanations.* Here *C* describes some event, and the statements in *I* describe *causes* of the event, e.g. 'The butter melted because (*I*) the temperature rose'. But what does it mean to say that one thing causes another? One answer is that there is some law (e.g. of PHYSICS, CHEMISTRY, or other branches of science) which provides a basis for inferring that, if the first thing occurs or had occurred, the second will or would have. On this analysis, causal explanations are simply a special case of deductive explanations,

possibly with the relevant laws (L) left out, either because they are too well known, or else because it is not yet known what they are.

(4) *Functional explanations.* These — which some prefer to regard as descriptions — answer questions of the form 'What is such-and-such for?' They should not be treated as an explanation of why the such-and-such exists. Thus to say that animals have stomachs because the stomach plays a certain role in keeping the animal alive and well does not explain how it came about that animals have stomachs, unless the explanation is enlarged to include some additional hypotheses about an EVOLUTIONARY mechanism which ensures that organisms evolve what they need. Functional explanations are often confused with *purposive explanations.*

(5) *Purposive explanations.* These answer questions about why an agent (which may be a person, an animal, or a corporate body such as a committee) performed some action or took some decision, by describing the agent's intention, motive, purpose, aims, likes, fears, etc., and relating them to what the agent thought would be the consequences of the various alternatives open, e.g. 'He stole the money because he wanted to buy food'. Purposive explanations are common in everyday life and law courts, but also in some of the social sciences and psychology, though some scientists regard them as unscientific, e.g. because the explanations refer to mental events or states.

(6) *Teleological explanations.* This is simply a blanket term used to cover both functional and purposive explanations since these are often not clearly distinguishable.

(7) *Genetic explanations.* These consist of more-or-less lengthy accounts of a sequence of events leading up to the occurrence or existence of the fact to be explained. They are common in HISTORY, GEOLOGY, BIOLOGY, and novels. The account generally mentions only a series of particular facts, so that I (the initial conditions) may be a large set of statements, whereas L may be empty, if no laws are explicitly mentioned. Often such an explanation simply amounts to a sequence of causal and purposive explanations. It is sometimes argued that a genetic explanation is always an abbreviated and sketchy version of a sequence of deductive or probabilistic explanations, where the laws are not stated explicitly because they are sufficiently well known to be taken for granted.   A.S.

exploitation. The payment to the owner of a FACTOR OF PRODUCTION of a sum less than the value of its product. In NEO-CLASSICAL ECONOMIC THEORY, exploitation occurs if the owner of a factor of production is paid less than the value of the marginal product of the factor (see MARGINAL PRODUCTIVITY THEORY OF WAGES). The marginal product of a factor is the extra output produced by using one more unit of the factor, while keeping the use of all other factors constant (see MARGINAL ANALYSIS). The value of the marginal product is the price of output multiplied by the marginal product. Only in PERFECT COMPETITION will a factor be paid the value of its marginal product. If it is assumed that an employer attempts to maximize profits, it can be shown that exploitation occurs if the employer has the market power to influence the price of the factor or product, through variation in the quantity of the factor demanded or output supplied. In MARXIST economics, labour is assumed to be the only source of value, as land and other natural resources are taken as free gifts and CAPITAL is the product of past labour. Ownership of capital, land and natural resources is regarded as appropriation of the product of past labour and free gifts. This appropriation allows the owners of these factors, i.e. the CAPITALISTS and resource owners, to receive part of the output produced by labour. Thus, labour is exploited because their work is the only source of value and they do not receive the full value of their production (see VALUE, THEORY OF and LABOUR THEORY OF VALUE).   J.P.

Bibl: J. Craven, *Introduction to Economics* (Oxford, 1984); R.L. Meek, *Smith, Marx and After* (London, 1977).

exploitation movie. Initially a derogatory term applied to films whose purpose was to titillate through sex, violence or nudity, in particular the cheap programme-fillers turned out by independent producers during the 1950s when the major Hollywood studios, in an attempt to combat the threat of television, elected to devote their resources to long, costly widescreen epics. Aimed primarily at teenage audiences and the drive-in cinema market, exploitation movies often revealed an unusual vitality in their devotion to the principle of fast-moving action, while the work of a talented director like Roger Corman demonstrated that such films could also incorporate skill and intelligence. As an independent producer willing to take risks because of the relatively low costs involved, Corman has effectively turned the exploitation movie into a forcing ground for new talent. Among the now noted film-makers who received their first chance to direct in exploitation movies produced by Corman are Francis Ford Coppola, Martin Scorsese, Peter Bogdanovich, John Milius and Jonathan Kaplan.　　　　　　　　　　T.C.C.M.

explosive nucleosynthesis, see under NUCLEOSYNTHESIS.

exponential smoothing. In MANAGEMENT, an adaptive method of FORECASTING that is ideally suited to COMPUTER operation. The basis of the method is that in obtaining a forecast more weight is given to the most recent information. The weights (see INDEX NUMBER) which are assigned die away exponentially; hence the name by which the method is usually known.
　　　　　　　　　　H.TH.

exponential time. An ALGORITHM will apply to a collection of similar problems but of differing size, N. For example, the 'salesman problem' where a salesman has to visit N towns, the problem being to find the shortest route. Of course, the larger N is the longer the algorithm takes. An algorithm takes exponential time, if the time taken increases as an exponential function of N. This is to be contrasted with polynomial time, where the time taken only increases as a power of N (which, at least for large values of N, is much quicker). The only known algorithms for the salesman problem are all exponential (see COMPLEXITY THEORY).　　　　J.M.

Expressionism. Widely applicable term used since 1910 of all the ARTS, in three main senses:

(1) A quality of expressive emphasis or distortion, to be found in works of any period, country, or medium, e.g. in Dostoevsky's novels, Strindberg's plays, and El Greco's or van Gogh's paintings.

(2) Virtually the whole modern movement in the arts in Germany and Austro-Hungary between 1910 and about 1924, subsuming all local manifestations of FAUVISM, CUBISM, and FUTURISM, and constituting the origins of DADA and NEUE SACHLICHKEIT. Though subsequently extended backwards to cover, e.g., the paintings of the Norwegian Edvard Munch or the early work of the BRÜCKE, the formula 'Expressionism' entered Germany from France in 1910 and thereafter became used to describe the German movements first in art, then in literature, the theatre (from 1918), music, architecture, and the cinema. Its hallmarks accordingly were theirs: distortion, fragmentation, and the communication of violent or overstressed emotion.

With *Der* STURM and *Die Aktion* as its organs, it embraced (*a*) in painting, the Brücke and the BLAUE REITER; (*b*) in literature, the poetry of Georg Heym, Georg Trakl, and Franz Werfel, and the prose of Alfred Döblin and Franz Kafka; (*c*) in the theatre, the plays of Georg Kaiser and Ernst Toller; (*d*) in music, the early works of Arnold Schönberg and Alban Berg; (*e*) in architecture, Erich Mendelsohn's Einstein Tower and the utopian projects of Bruno Taut; (*f*) in the cinema, Robert Wiene's *The Cabinet of Dr Caligari* (1920).

German Expressionism's predominantly PACIFIST and SOCIALIST political aims, crystallizing in the wartime movement of ACTIVISM, were frustrated by such post-war developments as the suppression of the SPARTACISTS and the Munich SOVIET; and it was superseded by the more pragmatic Neue Sachlichkeit — on which, as on the BAUHAUS, it left a distinctive mark. Though NAZISM suppressed all three movements as DEGENERATE, it was again influential in the revival of the arts in Germany after 1945.

(3) 20th-century works of art in other countries or continents which reflect the

influence of German Expressionism or show similar characteristics, e.g. the Flemish Expressionism foreshadowed by Laethem-Saint-Martin, certain works of the ÉCOLE DE PARIS, and the ABSTRACT EXPRESSIONISM of such New York artists as Pollock and de Kooning in the 1950s.

J.W.

Bibl: J. Willett, *Expressionism* (London and New York, 1971); T. Benton *et al.* (eds.), *Expressionism* (Milton Keynes, 1975); British Museum, *The Print in Germany, 1880-1933* (London, 1984).

expressive form, fallacy of. A prescriptive term, adopted by R.P. Blackmur from Yvor Winters, for the 'dogma that once material becomes words it is its own best form'. Winters called this the 'heresy of expressive form'. He was referring to the belief, in his view mistaken, that disintegration (of belief, of civilization) could most effectively be expressed in a chaotic form. He saw Joyce's *Ulysses* as 'disintegrated': it should have been 'disciplined'. But he was answered by critics who pointed out that *Ulysses*, or the poetry of T.S. Eliot, was not really 'chaotic': it only *looked* as though it were. Winters was attacking, essentially, Coleridge's idea of organic form. Blackmur used the notion to try — unsuccessfully — to dispose of the poetry of D.H. Lawrence and Carl Sandburg, but was not dedicated to it as a theory. M.S.-S.

Bibl: S.E. Hyman, *The Armed Vision* (New York, 1947).

expressive movement. Meaningful action that is peculiar to the individual and can, therefore, be used in identifying individuals and differentiating one from another. Examples of such movements are gesture, posture, characteristic actions, or speech habits. See also NON-VERBAL COMMUNICATION. H.L.

Bibl: G.W. Allport and P.E. Vernon, *Studies in Expressive Movement* (London and New York, 1967).

extended family, see under NUCLEAR FAMILY.

extended standard theory. The name given to a model of GENERATIVE GRAMMAR which developed in the 1970s out of that expounded by Noam Chomsky (see CHOMSKYAN) in his *Aspects of the Theory of Syntax* (1965), which was known as the standard theory. The 'extension' was primarily due to the way in which additional factors (other than the traditional notion of DEEP STRUCTURE) were introduced to account for the way in which a sentence's meaning was to be analysed. Further developments of the approach in the mid-1970s became known as the *revised extended standard theory*. D.C.

Bibl: A. Radford, *Transformational Syntax* (Cambridge, 1981).

extension, see under CONNOTATION.

extensionality and **intensionality.** Properties of compound PROPOSITIONS, defined by the relation between the compounds as wholes and the elementary propositions of which they are composed. A compound is *extensional* if its TRUTH or falsity is unequivocally determined by the truth or falsity of its components; it is *intensional* if it is not. Thus 'it is cold and it is wet' is extensional since it is true if both components are true and false in the other three possible cases. 'I believe that it is Thursday' is, however, intensional since the whole belief-statement can be true or false whether it is Thursday or not. The two leading kinds of intensional compound are (1) those in which the main verb refers to a 'propositional attitude' such as belief, knowledge, hope, fear, etc. and (2) modal statements of the form 'It is necessary that p' or 'It is possible that p'. Standard modern LOGIC is resolutely extensional and uses an extensional notion of material IMPLICATION which differs in MEANING from the intensional connection asserted in the conditional statements of ordinary language. LOGICAL POSITIVISTS and LOGICAL EMPIRICISTS have attempted to find ANALYSES in extensional terms of apparently intensional statements about propositional attitudes or involving modal concepts. Thus 'A believes that p' is analysed into 'There is some sentence "s" which means the same as "p" to which A is disposed to assent'. 'It is possible that it is raining' becomes 'The sentence "it is raining" is CONTINGENT'. A.Q.

externalities. In ECONOMICS, the effects of consumers' or producers' actions on others that do not occur through the operation of an economic market. External economies are those that benefit other consumers or producers, e.g. the construction of a beautiful house or an invention. External diseconomies are harmful to other consumers or producers, e.g. pollution and congestion. It is often argued that there is insufficient incentive for the generation of external economies and insufficient discouragement of external diseconomies. If the benefits and costs can be roughly measured, it is usually suggested that external economies should be subsidized and external diseconomies taxed. If the externalities are unspecified and unquantified, care should be taken over calls for subsidization and TAXATION. Externalities are an important, but not the only, reason why the prices of goods, services and inputs differ from the social benefits and costs of their consumption and use (see COST-BENEFIT ANALYSIS). J.P.

Bibl: D. Begg *et al.*, *Economics* (London, 1984).

extinction, see under REINFORCEMENT.

extrapolation and **interpolation.** In STATISTICS (and more generally), extrapolation is the estimation of a function value outside the range in which its values are known; interpolation is the estimation of it within the range but at a point at which it is not known. Thus, censuses are carried out in England in..., 1931, 1941, 1951, 1961, 1971,.... The use of population sizes recorded at these dates to estimate the population size in the year 2000 is extrapolation; their use to estimate the population size in 1956 is interpolation. *Prediction theory*, REGRESSION, and *time series analysis* are names given to deeper analytic techniques similar in spirit to simple extrapolation and interpolation. R.SI.

extra-sensory perception, see ESP.

extraterrestrial catastrophism. The impact of extraterrestrial bodies (e.g. comets, asteroids and meteorites) on the earth, and the effects of such impacts on the life and GEOLOGY of the planet. For more than 150 years, catastrophism was practically a taboo subject in the EARTH SCIENCES, a long-standing reaction against the use prior to the early 19th century of divine intervention (or 'extraordinary agents', as Sir Charles Lyell put it) as an ad hoc explanation for certain geological phenomena. In 1980, however, L. W. Alvarez and colleagues at the University of California proposed, with scientific evidence, that the impact of a large asteroid had resulted indirectly in the extinction of the dinosaurs and other organisms about 65 million years ago (see CRETACEOUS-TERTIARY BOUNDARY). This triggered a controversy that is still raging as some geologists seek to examine the idea of extraterrestrial catastrophism scientifically while others see the vogue as 'science gone mad'. The basic issue at stake is that of the cause(s) of biological extinctions. Virtually all plant and animal species that have ever existed are now extinct, and palaeontologists recognize five major episodes of extinction and numerous lesser ones over the past 600 million years. There are scores of non-catastrophist hypotheses (e.g. climatic change) to explain such extinctions, but none capable of proof. Ironically, although many traditional palaeontologists have no sympathy with the idea of impacts, the recent usurper hypothesis may turn out to be the one capable of proof (or disproof). D. M. Raup and J. Sepkoski of the University of Chicago have claimed to detect in the pattern of MASS EXTINCTIONS a 26-million-year periodicity. This, too, is controversial, because it is by no means clear that the scientific sampling of the record of past life is good enough to support such a precise conclusion. If substantiated, however, such regularity would strongly implicate extraterrestrial phenomena because it could have no conceivable earth-based cause. One of several extraterrestrial possibilities already proposed is that the earth is subjected to bombardment by comets as the SOLAR SYSTEM passes through a spiral arm of the GALAXY at regular intervals. P.J.S.

extraterrestrial intelligence, search for, see under SEARCH FOR EXTRATERRESTRIAL INTELLIGENCE.

extraterrestrial radio waves, see under INVISIBLE ASTRONOMY.

extroversion. A term current in PSY-CHOLOGY that was used by Jung (see JUNG-IAN) to denote a process whereby a person who has experienced pain or conflict through being sensitive to his own feelings invests his attention and concern in others; his rapidity ('Hail, fellow, well met') in establishing inter-personal relations tends to be matched by the superficiality of such relations. This process was later reified (see REIFICATION) and generalized to refer to a PERSONALITY TYPE, the *extrovert*, much of whose life seemed to be charac-terized by these processes and behaviours. Although this usage makes the extrovert and the introvert seem to stand for op-posed personality types, the oft-drawn contrast between extroversion and INTRO-VERSION is entirely superficial, their underlying causes and mechanisms being divergent but in no sense opposites, and frequently united in one personality.

T.Z.C.

F

Fabianism. An approach to the problems of implementing SOCIALIST ideas developed by the Fabian Society (established in London in 1884). Its members put their hopes in the 'permeation' of the existing INSTITUTIONS and the 'inevitability of gradualness' — hence the name, taken from the Roman general Fabius Cunctator who won his campaigns by avoiding pitched battles and instead wearing the enemy down. Fabian ideas were eclectic rather than synthetic. They concentrated on practical detailed reforms ('gas and water socialism') and shunned grandiose theoretical speculations. They rejected the doctrine of economic LAISSEZ FAIRE and stressed the need for State action to ensure greater equality (see EGALITARIANISM) and the elimination of poverty. By accepting a constitutional approach they helped to make socialist ideas respectable in Britain. Prominent members, such as Sydney and Beatrice Webb, H.G. Wells, George Bernard Shaw, and Graham Wallas are remembered through their individual achievements, rather than through their activities in the Fabian Society. Its direct influence was not very great (its membership was 640 in 1893 and under 3,000 in 1914), but it established a mode of approach to social questions, based on socialist ideas and a study of social problems, which has had a lasting impact on politics in Great Britain. L.L.

Bibl: B. Pimlott (ed.), *Fabian Essays in Social Thought* (London, 1984).

fabula. *Fabula* (story) was distinguished from *sjuzhet* (plot, telling technique, narrative style, authorial intention), in the work of the Russian FORMALISTS. Any theory of narrative requires that a distinction be made between the mere narrative, the story, and the way that narrative or story is told. 'Yes — oh dear yes — the novel tells a story', said E.M. Forster, pointing up precisely this difference. Various substitute terms for this pair of terms are to be found through STRUCTURALIST theory, but the distinction remains the same. The formalist category of LITERARI-NESS covers or includes the inter-relation of these two aspects in any literary work. R.PO.

Bibl: J. Culler, *The Pursuit of Signs* (London, 1981).

facilitation. The establishment of a preferred reflex pathway in the central NERVOUS SYSTEM by the repetition of the stimulus that excites the reflex response. The process is no longer thought to be of paramount importance in learning. P.M.

factor analysis. The statistical analysis of a MULTIVARIATE set of observations (e.g. the scores of a group of persons in tests of various kinds) in terms of a set of hypothetical components or factors. Historically, the first such analysis was by the psychologist Charles Spearman, who claimed in 1904 to express test scores in terms of a single common factor, which was identified as general ability, and residual specific factors peculiar to each kind of test. Later, it was found necessary to employ a wider *multi-factor analysis* involving more than one common group factor (e.g. the recognition of a speed factor in test performances). It is now recognized that factor analysis can be used as a general statistical technique in other than the psychological domain (see also CLUSTER ANALYSIS). REIFICATION of any group factors emerging from such an analysis should, however, be treated with caution. M.S.BA.

factors of production. Those inputs used in production, e.g. different types of labour, CAPITAL, land, energy and raw materials. J.P.

factory farming. Systems of livestock production in which farm animals are kept throughout the greater part of their lives indoors under conditions in which movement is severely restricted. Pigs, laying hens, chickens for meat production ('broilers'), and calves for veal production are the animals most commonly kept under this type of intensive production. Particularly for pigs and poultry the systems are closely standardized, making possible large-scale production, with high density of animals per unit area. Many people believe, however, that such systems are unacceptable on humane grounds.

K.E.H.

faculty psychology. The attempt to list classes of things done by the mind, e.g. remembering, willing. Although descriptively useful, such classifications have sometimes led to the incorrect assumption that to each faculty there must correspond one distinct mental operation. The resulting confusion is well illustrated by PHRENOLOGY.

I.M.L.H.

Falange. Spanish FASCIST party founded in 1933 by José Antonio Primo de Rivera, son of the former Spanish dictator, to capture the Spanish WORKING CLASS for an AUTHORITARIAN, socially radical NATIONALISM, and to overcome individualism and SOCIALISM as forces divisive of the nation. The Falange's failure to capture the working class confined its main strength to university students, though other RIGHT-wing forces were alarmed into supporting it by the victory of the POPULAR FRONT in the elections of February 1936. In 1937 the Spanish military leader, General Franco, took over the Falange, disciplined its leadership, and established his brother-in-law, Ramon Serrano Suñer, at its head. It was to remain firmly under Franco's control thereafter, its social RADICALISM a matter solely of rhetoric.

D.C.W.

Bibl: H. Thomas, *The Spanish Civil War* (London and New York, 1977).

Falklands war. The Falklands (Malvinas) are a small group of islands off the southeast coast of Argentina with an economy devoted almost exclusively to sheep-farming, SOVEREIGNTY over which is disputed by Argentina and Great Britain. British settlers have been in continuous occupation since 1833, but the islands are named in a series of earlier treaties between England and Spain involving maritime access to the area which leave the issue unresolved in INTERNATIONAL LAW. In 1964 Argentina formally reasserted its claim to the islands before the United Nations (UNO), and the following year the General Assembly adopted a resolution inviting Britain and Argentina to enter into negotiations. Britain has consistently refused to discuss the issue of sovereignty, maintaining that the wishes of the islanders (who overwhelmingly want to remain under British jurisdiction) were paramount. Negotiations from 1968-1977 concentrated on the possibility of securing Argentine economic cooperation in the islands, and in 1972 Argentina started a weekly air service for essential supplies. In 1980 a British government initiative consulting the islanders about their future resulted in the unilateral announcement of a 25-year freeze on sovereignty negotiations. Subsidiary discussions continued, but were broken off in March 1982 in an atmosphere of great tension.

The armed conflict between Argentina and the United Kingdom was precipitated by the Argentine military government's need for a popular victory, its sense that the United Kingdom attached little importance to the islands, and by the U.K. government's determination, once challenged, to defend its interests. The war began with the Argentinian invasion of the islands on April 2, 1982; the U.K. responded by dispatching an armed 'Task Force' which, while diplomatic efforts to find a peaceful settlement failed, repossessed the islands. The Argentinian surrender took place at Port Stanley on June 14, 1982. The war hastened the demise of the Argentinian Junta, and had a markedly beneficial effect on the popularity of the British government and the Prime Minister, Margaret Thatcher.

N.M.;S.R.

Bibl: M. Hastings and S. Jenkins, *The Battle for the Falklands* (London, 1983).

fallacy.

(1) Any widespread false belief. (For examples of fallacies, as regarded at least by those who named them, see AFFECTIVE FALLACY; COMMUNICATION, FALLACY OF; EXPRESSIVE FORM, FALLACY OF; INTENTIONAL FALLACY; NATURALISTIC FALLACY.) Such a belief may result from:

(2) In LOGIC, an invalid pattern of argument that is frequently mistaken for a valid one. Among the most common formal fallacies are those which involve reversing the direction of an *implication* (see ENTAILMENT). Thus, to infer 'This is *B*' from 'This is *A*' and 'All *B* are *A*' is a

fallacy (called 'affirming the consequent'); whereas if the second premise is reversed (becoming 'All *A* are *B*') the resulting inference is valid. Another common fallacy (that of 'denying the antecedent') is to infer 'This is not *B*' from 'This is not *A*' and 'All *A* are *B*'.   A.Q.

Bibl: C.L. Hamblin, *Fallacies* (London and New York, 1970).

fallibilism. In EPISTEMOLOGY, the view that it is not necessary in science or in everyday life for the factual beliefs that compose the one and guide the other to be established as certain beyond the possibility of doubt. On this view it is sufficient, and perhaps all that is possible, for our beliefs to be reasonably well supported or justified. Fallibilism, of which C.S. Peirce (1839-1914) was the first thoroughgoing exponent, can be seen as a reasonable compromise between scepticism and dogmatism (or, in one of its senses, INTUITIONISM).   A.Q.

Bibl: A. Quinton, *The Nature of Things* (London, 1973).

fallout. RADIOACTIVE material falling from the atmosphere as a result of artificial nuclear explosions or accidents in NUCLEAR REACTORS.   M.V.B.

falsifiability, see under POPPERIAN.

family, extended, see NUCLEAR FAMILY.

family, history of the, see HISTORY OF THE FAMILY.

family, nuclear, see NUCLEAR FAMILY.

family law. The legal principles governing the relations between married persons, the rights of parents, guardians and children (including the unborn). It covers the law of marriage and the legal consequences of certain types of cohabitation; also nullity and divorce, property rights, trusts, wills and intestacy, legitimacy and illegitimacy.   D.C.M.Y.

Bibl: P.M. Bromley, *Family Law* (6th ed., London, 1981); S.M. Cretney, *Principles of Family Law* (4th ed., London, 1984).

family planning. The use of CONTRACEPTION to limit fertility. In the first world, family planning is often a course of action chosen to determine the arrival of children in order to coincide with career moves, personal ambitions and other factors.

Family planning also refers to a movement, largely the result of the campaigns for contraception led in the early years of the 20th century by Marie Stopes and Margaret Sanger. As a movement, family planning, particularly as developed in the U.S. by MULTINATIONAL drug companies and charitable foundations (like the Rockefeller Foundation) has turned its attention to the so-called population explosion in THIRD WORLD countries. Critics of family planning (e.g. Germaine Greer) argue that first world family planning policies are a particularly manipulative form of colonialism in which third world populations are controlled in order to serve first world interests. One danger in the exporting of family planning ideals is that coercion can occur, as happened in India during the 1970s when millions of men were vasectomized, often against their will, or as a result of inducements.   S.T.

Bibl: G. Greer, *Sex and Destiny* (London and New York, 1984); S. Trombley, *The Right to Reproduce: A History of Coercive Sterilization* (London and New York, 1988).

family reconstitution. A method developed by Louis Henry and used in HISTORICAL DEMOGRAPHY. Like genealogy, it consists of collecting information about the births, marriages, and deaths of all known members of a given family. Unlike the genealogist, the demographer reconstitutes families not for their own sake but in order to calculate age at first marriage, birth intervals, infant mortality, and other demographic measures (see DEMOGRAPHY). The main source for family reconstitution is the parish register. Where a long series of such registers have survived and some families have not moved out of the parish for centuries, striking results may be obtained by this method.   P.B.

Bibl: E.A. Wrigley, 'Family reconstitution' in E.A. Wrigley (ed.), *An Introduction to English Historical Demography*

(London and New York, 1966), pp. 96-159.

family responsibility system, see under HOUSEHOLD RESPONSIBILITY SYSTEM.

family therapy. A form of treatment for PSYCHIATRIC or inter-personal problems arising in a family setting (e.g. behaviour disorders and NEUROSIS in children, PSYCHOSIS in the adolescent son of a depressed mother). The technique was pioneered by J. Bowlby (in England) and J.E. Bell (in the U.S.A.), and involves interviews of the whole family together. Similar conjoint interview techniques are used for couples with marital and sexual problems. Family therapists' theoretical roots are in PSYCHOANALYSIS, SYSTEMS theory, or BEHAVIOURISM, and there is a wide variation from short-term, active approaches to long-term, interpretative, and insight-giving ones. There is some evidence of efficacy, at least for the behavioural and systems-based approaches.   M.J.C.

famine; malnutrition. Famine involves an extreme and general lack of food within a population, accompanied often by widespread MORTALITY; malnutrition a general lack of nourishment below the accepted levels for maintaining health, which may apply to a whole population or to part of it. Both are potential outcomes from acute POPULATION PRESSURE, and famine is one of the MALTHUSIAN positive checks on population. Historically, famine has hit many societies, especially outside western Europe, and famine conditions have affected many Asian and African present day societies. There is considerable debate about the actual links between famine and MALNUTRITION conditions, and FERTILITY or mortality. The common assumption that lack of food in itself causes widespread mortality is not borne out by close investigation. Rather, deaths commonly occur more from consuming bad or poisonous food or from the action of epidemic disease. There is evidence that, especially among infants and children in modern developing nations, malnourishment and infectious disease work 'synergistically', that is, interact to produce sustained sickness and death. What is clear is that human populations can continue despite considerable diminution in nutritional levels as metabolic rates re-adjust. Evidence is also accumulating that, for similar reasons, fertility is affected by famine and malnutrition only in the most extreme conditions.   D.S.

Bibl: A. Sen, *Poverty and Famines: an Essay in Entitlement Deprivation* (Oxford, 1981).

FAO (Food and Agriculture Organization). A specialized agency of UNO set up by an international conference meeting at Quebec in October 1945. FAO, with its headquarters at Rome, had forerunners in the international Institute of Agriculture established in Paris in 1905 and took its own origin from the American-sponsored conference held at Hot Springs, Virginia, in 1943. Its original responsibility was seen as the feeding of the population of countries whose economies had been disturbed by the war of 1939-45, but it soon passed to handling the basic problems of world distribution of food between areas of crop surplus and areas of endemic food deficiency.   D.C.W.

Fascism.

(1) Specifically, the Fascist Movement formed in 1919 which Mussolini led to power in Italy (1922-45). The Italian word, *fascismo*, is derived from the fasces, the bundle of rods with a projecting axe which was carried before the consuls as the insignia of state authority in ancient Rome.

(2) Generically, similar AUTHORITARIAN movements in other countries, such as NAZISM in Germany, the FALANGE in Franco's Spain, the Iron Guard in Romania, and Sir Oswald Mosley's British Union of Fascists. Fascism was a product of the deep-seated social and economic crisis in Europe which followed World War I. It produced no coherent system of ideas comparable with MARXISM, and the various Fascist movements reflected the very different national backgrounds of the countries in which they developed. None the less there were a number of common traits. All were strongly NATIONALIST, violently anti-COMMUNIST, and anti-Marxist; all hated LIBERALISM, DEMOCRACY, and parliamentary parties, which they sought to replace by a new authori-

tarian state in which there would be only one party, their own, with a monopoly of power, and a single leader with charismatic qualities (see CHARISMA) and dictatorial powers. Although strongly opposed to democracy, the Fascists, unlike traditional right-wing parties, aimed to mobilize the masses with a populist appeal, as a prelude to the seizure of power. In their political campaigns they relied heavily on propaganda and TERRORISM; where they attained power they liquidated their rivals without regard to the law. All shared a cult of violence and action, exalted war, and with their uniforms, ranks, salutes and rallies, gave their parties a paramilitary character.

RACISM and ANTISEMITISM were strongly marked features of some Fascist movements (e.g. the German) but not all (e.g. the Italian). Fascist movements made a strong appeal to many ex-officers and N.C.O.s resentful of the results of World War I and unwilling to return to civilian life (the 'front' generation); to various groups in the middle and lower MIDDLE CLASSES who felt their position in society threatened by INFLATION, economic DEPRESSION, the organized WORKING-CLASS movements, and the spectre of REVOLUTION; and to youth attracted by the cult of action and the denunciation of 'the system'. Their nationalism and anti-Marxism won them sympathy and sometimes support from the traditional parties of the RIGHT and the Army. Originally radical in many of their demands, they shed most of these when they came to power, though they represented a new ÉLITE drawn from social groups very different from the old ruling classes.

(3) The product of World War I and the social upheaval and economic depression which followed the war, Fascism was discredited by the total defeat of the Fascist states in World War II. A number of NEO-FASCIST parties have appeared in Europe since the war (see also MSI), though without achieving any real success. This has been underlined by the failure of the Falange and the Spanish Right to prevent the replacement of Franco's regime by a democratic constitutional monarchy. Regimes with features borrowed from Fascism have appeared in other continents, e.g. PERONISM in Argen-

tina, but in circumstances better understood in the context of their own national histories than in those of inter-war Europe.

(4) Apart from its historical use, the term 'Fascist' has been kept alive by the Communists who, both before and after World War II, have used it as a label to discredit their opponents, whether genuinely Fascist, CONSERVATIVES, or SOCIAL DEMOCRATS, and to promote their tactics of building up anti-Fascist coalitions under Communist leadership.   A.L.C.B.

Bibl: D. Mack Smith, *Mussolini* (London, 1981); A. Lyttelton, *The Seizure of Power: Fascism in Italy 1919-1929* (London, 1973); S.J. Woolf (ed.), *The Nature of Fascism* (London, 1968); Walter Laqueur (ed.), *Fascism* (New York, 1976; London, 1979).

Fatah, al, see under PALESTINE LIBERATION ORGANIZATION.

fatalism. The theory that every future event is already necessarily determined and inevitable. It seems to be a necessary consequence of DETERMINISM, but, in its usual form, where it asserts not merely that what will happen will happen in conformity with an all-inclusive system of laws of nature, but that what will happen will happen *whatever anybody does*, it is not. Determinism is fully compatible with the view that human action is causally effective and that in its absence events will occur which otherwise would not have occurred. But it does imply that every human action is fully determined by the laws of nature together with the conditions of its occurrence (which will include the character and desires of the agent).   A.Q.

Bibl: G. Ryle, *Dilemmas* (London and New York, 1954); A.J. Ayer, *Philosophical Essays* (London and New York, 1954).

Fauves. A loosely-knit group of French figurative painters distinguished by their use of strong, simple colour and energetic execution. In 1905 the organizer of the Salon d'Automne chose to hang the most violently coloured works in the same room: the painters concerned were Derain, Manguin, Marquet, Matisse, Puy,

Valtat, and Vlaminck, whom the critic Louis Vauxcelles termed *les fauves* (the wild beasts) — referring probably to their rejection of orthodox notions of draughtsmanship, perspective, and light effects, but possibly also to Matisse's hairy overcoat. Gauguin and van Gogh were among their heroes; the IMPRESSIONISTS were not, although many of the Fauves (among whom one may also include Camoin, Rouault, and van Dongen) had themselves been through an Impressionist phase.

Typically *fauve* painting consisted of flat patterns of familiar forms, simply and freely outlined and unpredictably coloured; supposedly 'background' colours were often as vivid as 'foreground'. But by 1908 the Fauves' colour-schemes were generally more subdued. Braque, after a brief *fauve* phase, had turned to CUBISM, Friesz and Vlaminck to Cézanne and Derain to something between the two. Dufy entered a short period of geometrical severity, and then returned to lively colouring, but in a witty, idiosyncratic style; of the leading figures, only Matisse continued to paint in a recognizably *fauve* idiom.

In Dresden the BRÜCKE painters shared with the French group an admiration for Gauguin, van Gogh, Negro sculpture, and spectacular unorthodoxy. Many Brücke canvases of 1910-12 are comparable in colouring and outline to the French *fauve* works of the preceding years. The Russian artists Kandinsky and Jawlensky also underwent *fauve* periods after visiting France. The academy organized by Matisse from 1907 to 1911 was attended by an international group of painters who spread Matisse's principles in Scandinavia, North America, Eastern Europe, and even (in the case of Matthew Smith) in England. P.C.

Bibl: J.P. Crespelle, tr. A. Brookner, *The Fauves* (London, 1963); J.E. Muller, tr. S.E. Jones, *Fauvism* (London and New York, 1967).

FDR, see under EL SALVADOR.

fecundity, see under FERTILITY.

Federal Arts Project, see under WPA.

Federal Reserve System. The CENTRAL BANK of the U.S.A., as established in 1913. There are 12 Regional Federal Reserve Banks, covering the whole of the U.S.A.; and a Board of Governors of the whole system, whose Chairman is essentially the managing director the Central Bank. The U.S. President appoints all members of the Board of Governors. The Federal Reserve System operates in the open market through the New York Federal Reserve Bank, and controls the banking system through open-market operations, variations in its discount rates, and changes in the legal reserve ratios of the member banks. These member banks (about 6,000) are the main banking houses in the U.S.A. M.V.P.

Federal Theater Project, see under WPA.

Federal Writers Project, see under WPA.

federalism. A system of government in which central and regional authorities are linked in an interdependent political relationship, in which powers and functions are distributed with the aim of maintaining a substantial degree of autonomy and integrity in the regional units. In theory, a federal system seeks to maintain a balance such that neither level of government becomes sufficiently dominant as to dictate the decisions of the other. The system is likely to be characterized by a written constitution which entrenches this aim, and in its democratic form will offer citizens the right to vote for representatives at all levels of government which affect them.

The origins of federalism may be remotely discerned in FEUDALISM; more clearly in such systems as the defence leagues of medieval commercial cities, in the Swiss confederation and the United Provinces of the Netherlands. They may be most clearly discerned in 18th-century thought and the formation of the U.S. The American experience, as that of the Federal Republic of Germany, Canada, Australia and other federal states, shows that political practice may depart substantially from theory and that interdependence rather than true separation of functions characterizes federalism in action. The concept should be distinguished from that of *confederation*, which tends to describe a political system in which a central authority is created for limited purposes with the consent of diverse peoples, without disturbing their primary ties to constituent governments — as, for example, in some visions of European development.   S.R.

Bibl: K.C. Wheare, *Federal Government* (Oxford and New York, 1964); D.B. Walker, *Toward a Functioning Federalism* (Cambridge, Mass., 1981).

feedback. The return of part of a SYSTEM'S output to change its INPUT. *Positive feedback* increases the input, *negative feedback* decreases it. Hence, if feedback is used (as it is in all regulatory systems) in comparing output with some standard to be approached, negative feedback is inherently stabilizing (because it decreases the error) while positive feedback is inherently destabilizing (and the error gains explosively in magnitude). The classic example of negative feedback is the Watt steam governor, in which a pair of weights attached to the engine shaft fly outward (by centrifugal force) if the engine tends to race, which movement operates a valve to reduce the supply of fuel. An example of positive feedback is a 'growth economy' in which increased profitability is ploughed back further to increase profitability, a process which indeed becomes destabilizing in the limit. The casual use of 'feedback' to mean 'response to a stimulus' is incorrect.   S.BE.

FEKS, see FEX.

Feldenkrais Method. An 'awareness through movement' re-education programme which proposes that students voluntarily change their unconscious and habitual movement patterns through recognition and observation. The method was pioneered by Moshe Feldenkrais in the 1940s, and involves re-learning through simple and gentle movements in a non-competitive and non-stressful environment. This method of facilitating movement potential involves understanding how to: achieve and maintain correct alignment, eliminate effort and unnecessary muscular stress, control movement and balance and link an uninterrupted breathing pattern to movement. Through

re-educating counter-productive movement patterns, students of the Feldenkrais Method find increased neuromuscular coordination, improvement in body posture, ability to achieve relaxation and extend the range of movements in the joints. Thus the Feldenkrais Method benefits a wide range of individuals including singers, actors and musicians as well as people with neuromuscular disturbances. Dancers and particularly those involved in NEW DANCE, often study awareness through movement techniques such as Feldenkrais Method, RELEASE DANCE and ALEXANDER TECHNIQUE, in order to become more in touch with the body centre and senses which can lead to a more organic and exploratory approach to movement (see CONTACT IMPROVISATION).   G.N.;L.A.

Bibl: M. Feldenkrais, *Awareness through Movement* (Harmondsworth, 1972).

felicific calculus. A method, devised by Bentham, for the quantitative comparison of the amounts of pleasure and pain which will occur as the consequences of alternative courses of action. Some such technique is needed by any utilitarian ethical theory (see ETHICS; UTILITARIANISM) that defines the rightness and wrongness of alternative possible actions in terms of the amounts of pleasure and pain that they produce. Bentham enumerated a number of 'dimensions' of pleasure and pain; intensity, duration, certainty, propinquity, purity, fecundity, and extent. Most of these factors should be taken into account in any appraisal of the consequences of action that aims to be rational and thorough. But Bentham's idea that a fixed amount of intensity is equal in value to a fixed amount of duration rests on a false ANALOGY with spatial measurement, where an inch is the same length in every dimension.   A.Q.

Bibl: J. P. Griffin, *Wellbeing* (Oxford, 1986).

felicity conditions. In LINGUISTICS, a term used in the theory of SPEECH ACTS to refer to the criteria which must be satisfied if the speech act is to achieve its purpose. For example, before a person is entitled to perform the speech act of baptizing, certain 'preparatory conditions' must be present (the person must be invested with the appropriate authority). Or, at a more everyday level, the utterance of a request would be 'infelicitous' if the speaker knew that circumstances would not permit the request being carried out (e.g. asking for a window to be opened in a room with no windows). D.C.

Bibl: S. Levinson, *Pragmatics* (Cambridge, 1983).

fellow-traveller. Originally a Russian term ('poputchik') coined by Trotsky to depict the vacillating intellectual supporters of the young Soviet regime. When STALINISM established a firmer grip on the expression of opinion, the term disappeared in the U.S.S.R. It was adopted in the west to describe strong sympathizers with the Soviet Union who stopped short of COMMUNIST Party membership.

L.L./S.R.

feminine sexuality. One of the most debated and obscure topics in psychoanalytical theory, as well as in FEMINIST thought. The debate can broadly be described by two opposed theoretical tendencies. First, an ESSENTIALIST theory, which postulates an innate factor as the essence of femininity. Even though this classical conception has been overtaken by a new constructionalist view of femininity, as being socially and historically determined, some contemporary women psychoanalysts, such as L. Irigaray and J. Kristeva, have revived the idea of a feminine essence, but as repressed and oppressed by the phallic order of contemporary culture. This approach has appealed to those feminists who do not wish to reassess male values, but seek to reveal what has been hidden and deformed about an original feminine essence. This ambiguity between femininity as an essence and femininity as a deformation has been stressed since Freud; he discovered the original bisexuality in all human beings, men and women, but he also claimed that the sexual energy, that is the LIBIDO, is only masculine. It was the task of other analysts after Freud, such as Deutsch, Jones, and Horney, to make up for this inconsistency. They all claim that as there is only one masculine libido, feminine sexuality must be a deviation from this source, that is, femininity is explained

mainly as a PERVERSION in as much as it characterizes the detour of feminine MASOCHISM. According to these authors, this detour is natural, as it obeys an anatomical and biological reality: the female situation of being castrated, copulated with, and giving birth. This sexual destiny is never easily accepted by women, and results in an underlying UNCONSCIOUS penis-envy. Like the boy, the little girl establishes her sexual identity at the OEDIPUS stage, taking father as her love object, and other men as his future substitutes, from whom she expects to receive the Phallus, that is, the representative of paternal authority, in the form of the penis, and babies. An attempt to overcome this dichotomy between anatomical and psychical realities was carried out by the French psychoanalyst J. Lacan (see LACANIAN) who dismissed both the idea of a feminine essence, and the idea of woman as socially constructed: Lacan considered her as symbolically differentiated in relation to the Phallus. This means that the sexual difference would be neither a natural one, nor a made-up one, but rather positional, that is, relative to the place one is given in the Oedipal structure, whether or not in concomitance with one's own anatomical sex. This entails that the value we attribute to sexual difference is not anatomical, but SYMBOLIC, and women have always shown their regret for the subordinate position that the symbolic order assigns to them (PENIS-ENVY, HYSTERIA, LESBIANISM, FEMINISM). But if the woman because of her position is deprived of phallic enjoyment (see JOUISSANCE), she does nevertheless achieve another kind of enjoyment because of this very position. This jouissance is not phallic in quality but, on the contrary, arises from the possible abandonment of ego-boundaries, and the pleasure of surrendering rather than mastering; that is why it has been compared in its quality to mystical states of ecstasy.

B.BE.

feminism. Broad meaning, advocacy of the rights of women. There is no single accepted definition and feminism encompasses agitation for political and legal rights, equal opportunities, sexual autonomy, and the right of self-determination (ABORTION, CONTRACEPTION). The feminist movement stemmed from the recognition of the subordination of women, from the existence of discrimination and inequality based on sex. Feminism is a set of ideas linked to a social movement for change. The relationship between the ideas and the movement is shifting. Feminism has never been a single unified movement, but it has been made up of different elements which may unite behind a single campaign (e.g. women's suffrage, see SUFFRAGETTE). Its history is one of fission and fusion. Different phases of the feminist movement have gone under different labels: suffragette, women's emancipation, women's liberation, women's movement, feminism, social feminism, radical feminism.

The tension which has run throughout feminism has concerned the advocacy of the rights of women on the basis of similarity (i.e. women are human beings like men and therefore ought to be granted equal rights) or on the basis of difference (i.e. women are different from men and therefore ought to be granted the right to represent themselves).

The origins of the feminism cannot be traced to a single source but are located in a number of traditions. In medieval Europe there were early defenders of women's 'nature': Jean de Meung (C13), Christine de Pisan (C14), Marie de Gournay, Aphra Behn and Mary Astell (C17). 1790-1860 marks the beginning of the feminist movement. This period was dominated by Enlightenment ideas: the rights of man, reason, natural law and equal rights. Both the French and American revolutions raised issues relevant to women's rights and in this atmosphere Mary Wollstonecraft wrote an important feminist document *A Vindication of the Rights of Women* (1792). In both the U.S. and Britain early activists (e.g. Elizabeth Cady Stanton, Margaret Fuller, Lucretia Mott, the Langham Place group) were concerned with securing legal rights for women (in marriage, education and employment). Feminism was also associated with the 19th-century anti-slavery and evangelical movements (e.g. temperance) and was an important element in Unitarian and Quaker traditions. In contrast to this BOURGEOIS or INDIVIDUALIST feminism was the growing importance of SOCIALIST feminism. It drew its ideas from the early socialist or communitarian movement (of Saint-Simon, Fourier and Robert Owen).

The suffragette movement (1860-1930) united women of very different backgrounds. In the context of the struggle for votes, feminism developed with great speed. The campaign for female suffrage was an important landmark: women realized that they could not rely on political parties or the organized labour movement for support and that they would have to fight themselves for equality and justice.

Until Freud, debates concerning the rights of women were conducted in terms of fixed, biologically based categories of male and female. Freud opened up a new area: one of process. His discovery of the UNCONSCIOUS shifted and expanded the discussion of sexuality from surface appearance to what lay beneath. Freud strove to understand the formation of the human subject, the complex process involved in the construction of sexuality. He did not seek to understand what a woman is, but how she comes into being. His discussion of sexuality raised fundamental questions about the foundations of civilization, and more specifically women's oppression under PATRIARCHY. Freud's ideas have been subject to much criticism by feminists but continue to be influential in France. (See FREUDIAN.)

The women's liberation movement of the 1960s grew out of widespread radical protest by students, workers, blacks and women, especially in France and the U.S. Women responded to their relegation to a secondary role in protest activity by establishing their own (often women-only) groups, CONSCIOUSNESS-RAISING groups. The motivating force was an idea of sisterhood, women united with little recognition of RACE or CLASS difference. Feminist activity was also stimulated by the work of MIDDLE-CLASS writers, particularly Simone de Beauvoir (*Le Deuxième Sexe*, 1949, Eng. trans. 1953), Betty Friedan (*The Feminine Mystique*, 1963), Kate Millett (*Sexual Politics*, 1969) and Germaine Greer (*The Female Eunuch*, 1970). For the first time a vast range of issues was debated by women: from experiences at work to those in the marriage bed. The personal became the political.

313

Radical feminism and reaction. The 1970s and 1980s were the decades of the DECONSTRUCTION of woman, expressed in the fission of the feminist movement. Fragmentation into different groups resulted from the recognition of the complexity of women's experience. The universalist claims of the 1960s were increasingly challenged by WORKING-CLASS, THIRD WORLD and black women. In the Anglo-American feminist tradition there has been a growth of *radicalesbianism* ('radical' distinguished from 'LIBERAL' or 'SOCIALIST' feminist in seeing sexual oppression as primary and fundamental). This strand of feminism has advocated separatism, but the problem of sexuality and power has returned in the form of debate over lesbian SADO-MASOCHISM. The SEPARATIST movement has some parallels with the French *féministes révolutionnaires*. In France, however, important feminist ideas have emerged from work in PSYCHOANALYSIS associated with Lacan, Kristeva, Cixous and the *groupe politique et psychoanalyse*. The French tradition has explored questions of language, the construction of sexuality, the articulation of sex and DESIRE in the text. It has opposed the notion of a coherent subject, central to the work of bourgeois or HUMANIST feminism.

A disillusionment with the rate and direction of change has seen a retreat from sexual politics by two of the early influential writers: Friedan (*The Second Stages*, 1981) and Greer (*Sex and Destiny*, 1984). This retreat has been held as representative of the 'post-feminist' era. The centre of gravity in feminism may have shifted, its ideas and forms developed beyond the horizons of the sixties, but the movement is far from dead (see GENDER; FEMINIST CRITICISM). A.G.

Bibl: J. Mitchell and A. Oakley (eds.), *What is Feminism?* (Oxford, 1986); H. Eisenstein, *Contemporary Feminist Thought* (London, 1984); E. Marks and I. de Courtivron (eds.), *New French Feminisms* (Brighton, 1981); O. Banks, *Faces of Feminism* (Oxford, 1986); J. Rendall, *The Origins of Modern Feminism* (London, 1985).

feminist criticism. Criticism concerned with both women as writers and women as readers (of male and female texts). It is an activity which raises questions of AESTHETICS and politics, and the relationship of women to language. Feminist criticism (see FEMINISM) has recovered lost or neglected writers and highlighted the obstacles facing women as authors (the pertinence of Woolf's essay *A Room of One's Own*, 1929). It has also established the importance for women of having their own space in which to speak and express themselves freely. The feminist movement of the 1960s resulted in an explosion of magazines by and for women (e.g. *Ms*, Spare Rib, *Questions féministes*, *Le torchon brûle*, *Signs*) and the foundation of feminist publishing houses (Virago, Women's Press, Des femmes). Women as readers or feminist reading can be divided into Anglo-American (author-centred) and French (text-centred) traditions. In the case of the former, Millett's *Sexual Politics* (1969) was an early challenge to the authority of the author: it questioned, it represented a 'reading against the grain'. Other Anglo-American critics have been uneasy with theory (a male discourse). They have sought to establish the authenticity of the female writer's voice (e.g. Showalter on Virginia Woolf in *A Literature of Their Own*, 1977) and to expose the sexual IDEOLOGY in the work of male and female authors. The French tradition, in contrast, has always been more theoretical and influenced by PSYCHOANALYSIS, STRUCTURALISM and DECONSTRUCTION. It has situated the text (rather than the author) at the heart of critical practice. French feminist criticism (e.g. the work of Cixous, Irigaray and Kristeva) has explored the construction of sexuality through the text and questioned the very existence of a fixed (male or female) human subject. A.G.

Bibl: E. Marks and I. de Courtivron (eds.), *New French Feminisms* (Brighton, 1981); T. Moi, *Sexual Textual Politics* (London, 1985).

feminist history (herstory). An integral part of the feminist movement (see FEMINISM) which grew out of a need to develop an historical perspective which could inform contemporary debate. Feminist history charted the development of the women's movement and the direction in which it was unfolding. It has recovered the lives of women from obscurity, not just the early writers and activists, but ordinary women's lives — those hitherto 'hidden from history' (S. Rowbotham, 1973). Feminist history has revealed the complexity of the category 'woman'. Black women's history (particularly in the U.S.) is a developed strand, exploring the ORAL TRADITION to link the present to the past. Feminist history has not only provided new information about women, but also about men, the family, marriage, production, reproduction, and the articulation of private and public domains. In this way it has overlapped with social or labour history and has contributed to the expansion of historical discourse as a whole. By recovering herstory, the feminist movement has challenged history as formal, official and literally his-story, a male narrative.   A.G.

Bibl: A. Walker, *In Search of Our Mothers' Gardens* (London, 1984); S. Rowbotham, *Dreams and Dilemmas* (London, 1983).

feminist theology. A style of Christian THEOLOGY, mainly written or appreciated by women in the English-speaking world and N. Europe, which seeks to liberate the Churches from male dominance by showing that women are favourably mentioned in the Old Testament, were prominent in the circle around Jesus, were much more active in the early years of the Church than has commonly been thought, and should not be treated as mere assistants or devotees in the 20th century. A practical consequence has been a campaign for the ordination of women to the priesthood (still officially thought impossible in Roman CATHOLICISM and in Eastern ORTHODOXY, but spreading in ANGLICANISM). The movement, if expressed moderately, has been generally accepted where LIBERALISM is acceptable in PROTESTANTISM but has been resisted by many conservatives on the ground that the Bible teaches that the equality of women and men is only spiritual, the divine law being that women should be subordinated for many practical purposes, especially in marriage and in church life. Many Christians who accept many of the points made by FEMINISM are cautious, both because

they feel that their societies or Churches are not yet ready for full EQUALITY and because they fear that valuable traditions may be lost, chiefly the thought of God as 'Father' and the emphasis on distinctively feminine holiness symbolized by the Blessed Virgin Mary.   D.L.E.

Bibl: R.R. Ruether, *Sexism and God-Talk* (London and New York, 1983); E. Moltmann-Wendel, tr. J. Bowden, *A Land Flowing with Milk and Honey* (London, 1986).

Fermat's last theorem. This states that for $n2$ the EQUATION $x^n + y^n = z^n$ cannot be satisfied by positive integers x,y,z. Pierre de Fermat (1601-65) claimed in an annotation to have discovered a proof 'but this margin is too small to contain it'. The result is known to hold for a great many values of n, but no proof of the general statement has yet been found, so that the 'theorem' remains a great challenge in NUMBER THEORY. Efforts to prove it in the 19th century led to important developments in *algebraic number theory* (see ALGEBRA). In 1983 it was shown that for any n greater than 2 the equation can only have finitely many variations.   R.G.

Fermat's principle of least time, see under LEAST-ACTION PRINCIPLE.

Fermi-Dirac statistics. The QUANTUM STATISTICS that applies to PARTICLES for which the QUANTUM NUMBER describing SPIN is a half-integer.   M.V.B.

Fermi paradox. Named after the Italian physicist Enrico Fermi (1901-54) (see SEARCH FOR EXTRATERRESTRIAL INTELLIGENCE).

fermions, see under QUANTUM STATISTICS; SUPERSYMMETRY.

ferrimagnetism. A relatively weak type of MAGNETISM often found in CERAMICS, in which successive elementary atomic magnets (see SPIN) point in opposite directions. The phenomenon is useful in TELECOMMUNICATIONS because most 'ferrites' are electrical insulators and make sensitive aerials for TRANSISTOR sets.   M.V.B.

ferromagnetism. The strong MAGNETISM which can be produced in the metals iron, cobalt, and nickel, where it is possible to align all the elementary atomic magnets (see SPIN) in the same direction. Ferromagnetism often occurs naturally, induced by the magnetic field of the earth. Most common horseshoe and bar magnets are ferromagnetic.   M.V.B.

fertility. A term with specialized meaning in DEMOGRAPHY, where it is restricted to mean actual demographic performance. Thus, a fertile woman has produced at least one live-born child. In medical and everyday language fertility is often used to denote the potential capacity to reproduce, but demographers refer to this capacity as *fecundity*. A distinction is made between *current fertility*, measured on a period basis as the births of a particular year, and COHORT fertility, the total number of children born to a cohort through their reproductive lives. No known human population has attained the theoretical maximum biological fertility. That is a different concept from natural fertility, matrial fertility where couples do not alter their reproductive behaviour according to the number of children they already have (and in practice, the fertility of non-contracepting populations).   E.G.; D.S.

Bibl: H. Leridon, *Human Fertility: the Basic Components* (Chicago, 1977); H.S. Shryock *et al.*, *The Methods and Materials of Demography* (condensed edition) (New York and London, 1976).

festive theatre, see under CELEBRATORY THEATRE.

fetish; fetishism. E.B. Tylor (*Primitive Culture*, 1871) adopted into ANTHROPOLOGY the word fetish, long current in English, to mean an object in which a spirit is embodied, to which it is attached, or through which it conveys magical influence; he applied the term fetishism to the worship, shading into idolatry, of such an object. Influenced by Marx's ideas (*Capital* vol.1, 1867) anthropologists have taken up the idea of the fetishism of commodities. It has become an important concept in the discussion of the nature of goods and the qualities or facets they develop in different contexts. The meaning of goods lies beyond the narrow economic sphere and is situated in a much wider social context. Tambiah has recently expanded the debate in anthropology by considering the Weberian concept of CHARISMA in relation to goods and the fetishism of goods.   E.G.;A.G.

Bibl: S.J. Tambiah, *The Buddhist Saints of the Forest and the Cult of Amulets* (Cambridge, 1984).

feud. State of dispute or latent hostility between two parties over an offence, insult or injury. Feud is a private matter, but it follows established rules and conventions. If an individual commits theft or homocide, a group mobilizes around the victim to demand reparation or compensation from the offender's group. Recruitment to feuding groups is usually on the basis of KINSHIP ties. Feud is often not just an isolated incident, but it may be a long term state of affairs between different groups. Feud is essentially a relationship between groups and implies a roughly equal distribution of POWER and STATUS in society. It is a common feature of EGALITARIAN communities without centralized political organization (for example the Nuer of East Africa) and it is also found in areas of the Mediterranean and Middle East (among the Bedo of Cyrenaica).   A.G.

Bibl: J. Black-Michaud, *Cohesive Force: Feud in the Mediterranean and Middle East* (Oxford, 1975); Pino Arlacchi, *Mafia, Peasants and Great Estates* (Cambridge, 1973).

feudal; feudalism. Terms used since the 18th century to describe the social and military organization prevalent in Europe during the Middle Ages, and also other social systems with similar features in, e.g., China and Japan where it continued down to the 19th century. There have been many varieties of feudalism but it commonly involved a social hierarchy based on the tenure of land, jurisdiction by landlords over their tenants, and the granting of land and offices in return for a vassal's loyalty and services, particularly military service, to the king or lord from whom the land or office was held.

More generally the word 'feudal' is used to characterize (1) any social system in which great landowners or hereditary overlords exact revenue from the land, and exercise the functions of government in their domains (e.g. the Prussian Junker class east of the Elbe); and (2) any society or social group which the writer wishes to condemn as anachronistic and which is based upon inequality and the privileged position of a social, political, or economic dynasty (e.g. the phrase *industrial feudalism* often used in histories of 19th-century America). A.L.C.B.

Bibl: M. Bloch, *Feudal Society* (London, 1961).

FEX. The 'Factory of the Eccentric Actor', initially a theatre, then a film studio, organized in Petrograd in 1921 by the young directors Kozintsev and Trauberg ('the FEXes'). They sought to revolutionize the theatre on principles of 'eccentricity' imported from the circus and vaudeville, and to replace its obsolete methods by the more dynamic 'lower' genres: street shows, slapstick comedy, and sport. In the cinema the FEXes extolled American comedies and gangster films. Their early films tried to convey revolutionary propaganda through grotesque and fantastic imagery, shocking juxtapositions, and circus tricks. In later years their style changed considerably under the influence of Eisenstein and German EXPRESSIONIST cinema. The 'eccentric' tendency gradually gave way to more realistic themes and methods.

The Kozintsev-Trauberg collaboration ended in 1946. Their best-known films were the trilogy *The Youth of Maxim* (1935), *The Return of Maxim* (1937), and *The Vyborg Side* (1939). Kozintsev subsequently reached Western audiences with his *Hamlet* (1964) and *King Lear* (1971). M.E.

Bibl: J. Leyda, *Kino* (London and New York, 2nd ed., 1973).

fibre optics. Ordinary glass is not a particularly good transmitter of light, a few centimetres being sufficient to absorb over 50% of any incident light. This is entirely due to the impurities in the glass. When such impurities have been dissolved away chemically and the spaces which are left are filled with pure glass, the whole can then be heated and drawn out into long thin fibres which are capable of transmitting light, virtually without loss of intensity over very long distances (several kilometres). Fibre optics have many applications. In medicine, for example, they are used to illuminate and make optically examinable, interior parts of the body without the use of SURGERY. By a similar technique but using coherent RADIATION (see COHERENCE) from a LASER they can seal haemorrhages in the stomach and other internal organs. They are used in TELECOMMUNICATIONS to replace wires and hundreds of 'light messages' can be transmitted simultaneously down a single fibre. They also feature in decorative displays for advertising and in the home. E.R.L.

field.

(1) A MATHEMATICAL STRUCTURE which admits analogues of addition, subtraction, multiplication, and division satisfying the familiar laws. Fields are important in ALGEBRA. R.G.

(2) The systems considered in PHYSICS often consist of PARTICLES moving under the action of their mutual forces of attraction or repulsion, according to the laws of NEWTONIAN MECHANICS or QUANTUM MECHANICS. It frequently simplifies the analysis of such systems if some of the particles are considered as the sources of an influence — a *field* — which exists throughout space even when the other particles are not there to feel it. A field is thus basically a matter of conceptual convenience, the carrier of interactions between particles, avoiding the intuitively awkward notion of 'action at a distance' (but see FIELD THEORY). For example: the ELECTRONS constituting the current in the transmitting aerial of a TELECOMMUNICATIONS system produce an ELECTROMAGNETIC FIELD spreading out in space, which then exerts forces on the electrons in any receiving aerial within range; it would be needlessly complicated to consider the electron-electron interactions between transmitter and each separate receiver.

More generally, any physical quantity varying continuously in space and time is referred to as a field (e.g. the temperature in an aircraft wing, or the pressure in a sound wave). M.V.B.

317

field archaeology. That aspect of ARCHAE-OLOGY which deals with the recognition and planning of ancient landscapes. The techniques used include AIR PHOTOGRA-PHY, RESISTIVITY SURVEYING, surface searching ('field walking'), and survey; some archaeologists would include excavation. The importance of field archaeology was emphasized and demonstrated by O.G.S. Crawford during his employment by the Ordnance Survey.   B.C.

Bibl: Ordnance Survey, *Field Archaeology* (London, 4th ed., 1966); J. Coles, *Field Archaeology in Britain* (London, 1972); M. Aston, *Interpreting the Landscape* (London, 1985).

field painting, see under ABSTRACT EX-PRESSIONISM.

field theory. The attempt to unify the basic laws of PHYSICS by deriving them from the interactions between FIELDS. These fields would become the basic entities of physics, and ELEMENTARY PAR-TICLES would, hopefully, appear as a result of applying the laws of QUANTUM MECH-ANICS. This programme is in its infancy, the most successful field theories being the general theory of RELATIVITY (incorporating GRAVITATION into MECHANICS) and *quantum electrodynamics* (incorporating ELECTROMAGNETISM into quantum mechanics).   M.V.B.

fieldwork. Method of obtaining information about a particular society through first hand intensive observation or participant observation. It has become the central and distinguishing feature of social ANTHROPOLOGY. Fieldwork for anthropologists is their RITE DE PASSAGE into the discipline. Expeditions at the end of the 19th century, particularly the famous 1898 Torres Straits expedition, represented a movement away from the armchair speculations of James Frazer and others. Face-to-face contact with the people being studied was established.

It was Malinowski, however, who developed the method of fieldwork which was to distinguish anthropology. Between 1915-18 he lived among the Trobriand Islanders of New Guinea. He participated in their social activity, he learned the local language and kept a detailed record of the daily minutiae of their lives.

For many years anthropologists presented the material they gathered in the form of objective monographs. The relationship between the observer and the observed was rarely, if ever, discussed. Anthropology was pursued as a science and elaborate methods of collection and classification of data were developed by those working in the field (E.R. Leach, *Rethinking Anthropology*, 1961). The question of the objectivity of social anthropology is now much debated. The posthumous publication of the very personal diary kept by Malinowski while he was in the Trobriand Islands (*A Diary in the Strict Sense of the Term*, 1967) did much to open this debate. Subsequent anthropologists have been more willing to recognize themselves as part of the material collected, but they have continued to publish what they regard as scholarly and personal aspects of fieldwork as separate accounts (e.g., N. Barley, *The Innocent Anthropologist*, 1983).   A.G.

Bibl: M. Gardiner, *Footprints on Malekula* (Edinburgh, 1984); G.W. Stocking Jr, *Observers Observed* (Madison, Wisc., 1983).

fifth column. A term coined in October 1936 during the Spanish Civil War by a Nationalist General, Emilio Mola, to denote the underground supporters who, he claimed, were ready to rise within Madrid as four Nationalist columns converged on the city. The term was adopted during World War II to describe secret sympathizers of NAZISM in unoccupied parts of Western Europe, then extended to denote any hidden group of enemies within a state, society or organization.

S.R.

fifth-generation computers, see under GENERATION.

figurative. Adjective applied (as distinct from 'non-figurative' or ABSTRACT) to works of visual art involving the portrayal, however allusive or distorted, of elements of the visible world. Hence also 'figuration'.   J.W.

figure-ground phenomenon. The characteristic organization of PERCEPTION into a figure that 'stands out' against an undifferentiated background, e.g. a printed word against a background page. What is figural at any one moment depends on patterns of sensory stimulation and on the momentary interests of the perceiver. See also GESTALT.   I.M.L.H.

film noir. Generic term originally applied by French critics to a group of markedly pessimistic American films (c.1944-54) reflecting a darkening national mood as World War II drew to a close with chords of uncertainty struck by the death of President Roosevelt, the dropping of the first atomic bombs, the problematic social reintegration of returning servicemen, the formation of the House Un-American Activities Committee, and — by no means least importantly because closest to Hollywood and home — the series of violent labour disputes which had been simmering during the war years within the enormously wealthy film industry. Channelled into plots frequently drawn from pulp writers of the hardboiled Dashiell Hammett school, often directed by émigré filmmakers like Fritz Lang, Billy Wilder, Robert Siodmak and John Brahm who had been schooled in the expressionist ANGST of the German cinema of the 1920s, these doubts and fears emerged transformed into a series of dark, despairing thrillers, redolent of perversity, violence, betrayal, obsession and persecution and haunted by an indefinable sense of menace. *Film noir* was coined by analogy with *La Série Noire*, a French paperback series which specialized in hardboiled thrillers, often translated from Dashiell Hammett, James M. Cain, Raymond Chandler, David Goodis, Cornell Woolrich, Dorothy B. Hughes and other writers regularly adapted as *films noirs*. The term is often now used more loosely to describe a film of any period meeting the requirements of mood.
                                        T.C.C.M.

Bibl: A. Silver and E. Ward, *Film Noir* (London, 1980).

filtration, see under BIOPHYSICS.

final anthropic principle, see under ANTHROPIC PRINCIPLE.

Final Solution (*Endlösung*). A NAZI-German euphemism for the physical extermination of European Jewry — the final solution to 'the Jewish problem'. Implementation of such a policy was first discussed at a conference of Nazi-German ministerial representatives at Wannsee in January 1942. The means were extermination camps using mass gas chambers and mass assassination squads. In all, between four and a half and six million victims perished in what Jewish historians term the *holocaust*. At the NUREMBERG TRIALS various survivors of the Nazi regime were convicted of GENOCIDE.   D.C.W.

Bibl: M. Gilbert, *Holocaust* (London, 1986).

finitism, see under INTUITIONISM (3).

Finlandization. The indirect but total control of a small country by a large and powerful neighbour. It is drawn from the supposed relationship between Finland and the Soviet Union, and has become a term of political abuse in the west. While such arrangements do exist between large and small states, it does not accurately describe the position of Finland. Finland, which until 1917 was a province of Imperial Russia, has learned how to co-exist with her large, dictatorial neighbour. The Finns have demonstrated their capacity to fight against the Russians three times in this century. At the end of World War II, Finland was not annexed like those other former provinces, Latvia, Lithuania and Estonia, but allowed to remain independent. The arrangement has persisted because it is advantageous to both sides. It provides the Soviet Union with a point of contact with the outside world, while the Finns have learned those matters over which it is unwise to provoke the Soviet Union. The consequence has been a nation with a very high standard of living, a continuing sense of Finnish nationality, and a high degree of practical, if limited, freedom. One proposal is that AFGHANISTAN might be 'Finlandized' as a solution to the Soviet Union's direct intervention in that country.   A.J.M.W.

Bibl: G. Ginsburg and A.Z. Rubenstein (eds.), *Soviet Foreign Policy Towards Western Europe* (New York and London, 1978).

firm, theories of. The economic activities of production, transportation, MARKETING, research, development and decision-making are all included in the theory of the firm. The first theories assumed that firms operated purely in the interests of their owners and attempted to maximize profits. Firms may be forced to maximize profits by the owner-managers pursuing their own interests, managers being concerned about their performance being monitored by shareholders, and by the fear of take-overs and MERGERS. The assumption of profit maximization is a convenient analytical tool and has led to many predictions and theories (see STRUCTURE-CONDUCT-PERFORMANCE THEORY). However, the recognition of an increasing separation between MANAGEMENT and ownership of firms led to the development of managerial theories that propose that managers are capable of maximizing their own objectives such as growth, security, salaries and discretionary non-productive expenditure, e.g. luxurious offices. The predictions of managerial theories sometimes differ from those of profit-maximizing theories. For example, managerial theories predict that there will be more mergers and take-overs than can be justified by gains in future efficiency or profitability; these acquisitions are a consequence of managers' desire for growth and security from being taken-over themselves. If firms operate in an environment characterized by UNCERTAINTY, it is not clear that it is possible to maximize any objective. An alternative theory is based on the suggestion that firms are composed of groups and individuals pursuing different objectives. The firm reconciles the different interests and aspirations by negotiation and setting of targets. The firm sets targets by using rules that have given satisfactory results in the past — this behaviour is called *satisficing*. If the targets cannot be met, they are either reassessed or greater efforts are made to achieve them. These theories have variously been termed *behavioural, bargaining, coalition* and satisficing models. They have been criticized for being mere descriptions of actual behaviour and not providing scope for analysis and prediction. The different theories of the firm are not necessarily competing models, as they can be of analytical, descriptive and prescriptive use for different types of problems. J.P.

Bibl: M.C. Sawyer, *Theories of the Firm* (London, 1979).

firmware. In COMPUTERS, a PROGRAM kept in read-only STORE (normally ROM, but sometimes implemented by fixed wiring); it is thus permanently part of the machine, and may hence be considered half-way between HARDWARE and SOFTWARE. It may be used to implement a MICROCODE, and also for the primitive programs which read the software into the machine when it is first switched on or restarted. J.E.S.

first-strike capability, see under STRATEGIC CAPABILITY.

Firthian. Characteristic of, or a follower of, the linguistic principles of J.R. Firth (1890-1960), Professor of General Linguistics in the University of London (1944-56), and the formative influence on the development of LINGUISTICS in Great Britain. A central notion is *polysystemicism*, an approach to linguistic analysis based on the view that language patterns cannot be accounted for in terms of a single system of analytic principles and categories (*monosystemic* linguistics), but that different systems may need to be set up at different places within a description; for other features see COLLOCATION, CONTEXT OF SITUATION, and PROSODIC FEATURE. Relatively little of Firth's teaching was published, but many of his ideas have been developed by a *neo-Firthian* group of scholars, whose main theoretician is M.A.K. Halliday, Professor of General Linguistics at University College London from 1965 to 1970 (see SCALE AND CATEGORY GRAMMAR; SYSTEMIC GRAMMAR).
D.C.

Bibl: J.R. Firth, *Papers in Linguistics 1934-1951* (London, 1957).

fiscal drag. The deflationary impulse (see INFLATION) generated through the budget when rising money incomes cause government revenues to expand (at unchanged rates of tax) while public expenditure lags behind. This withdrawal of purchasing power may arise because of the increase in real output and incomes which overflows into additional tax revenue and acts as a drag on further growth unless offsetting action is taken to increase government expenditure or reduce TAXATION. A similar effect may be produced by inflation if, for example, rising money incomes are tapped by progressive taxation so that tax revenues expand faster than government expenditures.   A.C.

Bibl: D. Begg *et al., Economics* (London, 1984).

fiscal policy. The policy of a government in controlling its own expenditure and TAXATION, which together make up its budget. The term usually refers to transactions of the central government, but, depending partly on a country's political structure, may also extend to other parts of the PUBLIC SECTOR, namely state or local governments and public enterprise.

Fiscal policy has several functions. One is to regulate, together with MONETARY POLICY and *exchange rate policy*, the level of economic activity, the price level, and the BALANCE OF PAYMENTS. Another is to determine the allocation of productive resources between the public and PRIVATE SECTORS, and among the different parts of the public sector. A third is to influence the distribution of income and wealth, both through taxation and through social expenditures. The size of the public sector and the distribution of wealth are also affected by moves to extend or restrict public ownership, but this is not part of fiscal policy as such.

The government budget in a particular year is said to be in surplus, balance, or deficit according as tax receipts exceed, equal, or fall short of expenditure. Spending in excess of tax receipts is called *deficit spending*. This term is sometimes applied more narrowly to an excess of government spending on current account alone — rather than of total spending, which includes capital items — over total tax receipts. The budget position is of key importance in connection with the regulation of economic activity and prices. This function of fiscal policy is closely related to KEYNESIAN economic theory, but the MONETARIST view suggests that fiscal policy has little, or perhaps even a harmful, effect on economic activity. An increase in the budget deficit (or reduction in the surplus)

boosts AGGREGATE DEMAND; a narrowing of the deficit restricts it. The budget position is affected not only by government decisions to alter taxation or expenditure, but also by fluctuations in economic activity itself. In the upswing, as employment and incomes rise, the budget is strengthened by accelerated tax receipts and a slowdown of social security outlays; in the downswing the movement is reversed. Since a tighter budget helps to curb the boom and an easier budget to limit the recession, the fiscal mechanism thus provides some degree of AUTOMATIC STABILIZATION to the economy. The fiscal stance of a government is measured by the FULL EMPLOYMENT SURPLUS.

Deficit finance is the finance for deficit spending, and is normally provided by borrowing against the issue of government securities (bonds or Treasury bills), thus adding to the NATIONAL DEBT. A budget deficit may also be financed directly by MONEY CREATION. Conversely, a budget surplus may be used to redeem debt and reduce the money supply. Fiscal policy and national-debt management have important implications for monetary policy. Newly issued government debt, which is used to finance a deficit, may be taken up by (*a*) the banking system, (*b*) other domestic residents, or (*c*) foreign residents. In (*a*) the quantity of money expands, unless bank credit to the private sector is simultaneously reduced. In (*b*) the money stock is unchanged; a rise in interest rates may be necessary to induce the public to buy the new debt. In (*c*) the money stock again remains unchanged if the government's overseas borrowing serves to finance a balance of payments deficit; otherwise it increases, as the central bank creates domestic currency in exchange for the foreign currency which foreigners sell in order to acquire the government debt in question.
                                              P.M.O.; J.P.

Bibl: J. Craven, *Introduction to Economics* (Oxford, 1984); R. A. Musgrave and P. B. Musgrave, *Public Finance in Theory and Practice* (London, 1980).

fission (in ANTHROPOLOGY), see under LINEAGE.

fission. The splitting of an atomic NUCLEUS, usually by free NEUTRONS during a

CHAIN REACTION. For heavy elements the total mass of the fission fragments is less than that of the original nucleus + neutrons, so that large amounts of ENERGY are released (see MASS-ENERGY EQUATION). The atomic bomb, and NUCLEAR REACTORS, derive their energy from fission. See also MODERATOR; QUANTUM MECHANICS; THERMAL NEUTRON.   M.V.B.

fission (in anthropology), see under LINEAGE.

fission track dating, see under DATING.

fitness, see under DARWINISM.

Five Year Plan, see under GOSPLAN.

fixation. In psychoanalytic theory (see PSYCHOANALYSIS), a NEUROSIS consisting of the arrestation of PSYCHOSEXUAL DEVELOPMENT in one of its immature stages (e.g. anal, phallic).   W.Z.

flash point. The temperature at which spontaneous combustion occurs.   B.F.

flat characters and **round characters.** Terms coined by E.M. Forster (*Aspects of the Novel*, 1927), and used in criticism of novels, plays, and films to distinguish between, at one extreme, characters 'constructed round a single idea or quality' and at the other, highly complex characters 'capable of surprising in a convincing way'. Flat characters, though usually 'best when they are comic', are not necessarily the product of lesser artistry than round ones: Dickens's characters, for example, are mostly flat.   O.S.

flexible response. A STRATEGY based on the ability to react across the entire spectrum of possible military challenges to a state from subversion to strategic nuclear WAR. It is similar to graduated DETERRENCE and is contrasted with MASSIVE RETALIATION. In NATO planning it has acquired a more specialized meaning, namely that the alliance should maintain sufficient conventional land, sea, and air power to enable a Soviet incursion or a Nato–Warsaw Pact crisis to be contained at the lowest possible level of conflict or at least below the nuclear threshold until its

size or seriousness could be accurately assessed and the process of negotiation initiated. But it could also mean the use of NUCLEAR WEAPONS in a controlled fashion, if conflict should escalate, in order to minimize destruction and hasten negotiations. This latter meaning may have become otiose with the loss, in the later 1960s, of a marked American strategic superiority over the Soviet Union. This position may change again at the end of the 1980s with the development of the STRATEGIC DEFENCE INITIATIVE.
                                        A.F.B.;A.J.M.W.
      Bibl: W. Kaufmann, *The McNamara Strategy* (New York, 1964); H. Kissinger, *The Troubled Partnership* (London and New York, 1965).

floppy disc, see under DISC STORE.

flotation process. The process which brings to the surface fine PARTICLES dispersed in a liquid, usually water. A SURFACTANT absorbed in the surface of the particle makes it water-repellent, thus encouraging the particle to remain at the air-water interface. Mainly used for the enrichment of ores, surfactants are used to effect a differential separation of the suspended mixture of particles.   B.F.

flow chart.
(1) In general, any sequential diagrammatic representation of the movements of materials or people.
(2) In COMPUTING, an informal method of representing an ALGORITHM or a computer PROGRAM. It is not suitable for all types of program and is most often used in commercial data-processing. It is intended for use by human beings, and the amount of detail included can vary widely. Even the most detailed flow chart has ultimately to be expressed in a formal PROGRAMMING LANGUAGE — a process known as CODING.
                                        C.S.

fluidics. The TECHNOLOGY of small fluid devices, e.g. pipes, joints, elbows in pipes, etc., used as substitutes for ELECTRONIC circuits. Thus, a Y-shaped junction behaves as a 2-state device analogous to an electronic flip-flop circuit: the supply fluid entering by the vertical member is directed into one or other of the branches by means of a small pilot jet or vane. For some control systems (see CONTROL ENGINEERING; SYSTEMS) fluidic devices are cheaper and more robust than their electronic counterparts. E.R.L.

fluidized bed. A bed of solid particles, e.g. sand, which is given the properties of a liquid by blowing air through the particles. The principle can be applied to the improvement of coal combustion where powdered coal is 'fluidized' by air within the combustion chamber. E.R.L.

fluorescence. The absorption of light at one wavelength and its subsequent emission at a different wavelength, as when the coating of the tube in a fluorescent lamp absorbs ultraviolet light produced by mercury vapour in the tube, and emits visible light. See also RADIATION.
M.V.B.

fluoridation. The addition of minute quantities of fluoride IONS to drinking water to reduce the incidence of dental caries. The mechanism is obscure but the fluoride ions probably exchange with some of the hydroxyl ions in the bone mineral apatite, which forms part of the hard tissues of the teeth. The medical profession is united in recommending fluoridation as a public-health measure, but action is often blocked politically by minority groups in the name of freedom, pure water, etc. B.F.

Fluxus. Latin word for 'flux' applied by George Maciunas in 1962 to an iconoclastic group of artists, primarily American and West German, of which he was the chief spokesman and organizer. A form of DADA revival, this short-lived movement manifested itself in HAPPENINGS (beginning with a performance in Wiesbaden in 1962) and publications. Associated with Fluxus were Wolf Vostell, Allan Kaprow, and the publisher Dick Higgins, while a major influence was the composer John Cage. See also ALEATORY. A.K.W.
Bibl: A. Kaprow, *Assemblage, Environments and Happenings* (New York, 1966).

flying pickets, see under PICKETING.

FM, see FREQUENCY MODULATION.

FMLN, see under EL SALVADOR.

folded plates, see under STRUCTURE (sense 2).

folk. An age-old and familiar word which in comparatively recent years has become the first element in an ever-growing list (see, for example, the Supplement to the *Oxford English Dictionary*) of compound nouns and phrases, a few of which are treated separately below. The common element in all these terms is that the phenomenon in question is regarded as springing from, or intimately associated with, the 'folk' in the sense of the common people, the PRIMITIVE or less educated elements of society. 'Folk' in this sense (as against POP) carries connotations of traditionalism, collective wisdom, anonymity, spontaneity, simplicity, and sincerity, and is something of a rallying cry with those people (within a wide spectrum of political views) who value such qualities, particularly in opposition to sophistication, flamboyant INDIVIDUALISM, commercialism, MODERNISM, COSMOPOLITANISM, and DECADENCE. The adjective *folksy*, on the other hand, is used mostly in a pejorative sense, by those who feel that there is a lack of discrimination, and in some cases an element of selfconsciousness, among 'folk' enthusiasts. O.S.

folk art. A category of art that acquired distinctive status (unsophisticated or PRIMITIVE art has always existed) during the latter half of the 19th century, thanks (a) to the development of ANTHROPOLOGY; (b) to the early writings on popular imagery etc. by, most notably, Champfleury, and (c) to the drive for popular awareness of the arts which followed the institution of compulsory education and the writings of William Morris, Tolstoy, and others. Today the concept has been somewhat tarnished by its abuse in NAZI and Soviet art policy and by its association elsewhere with nostalgia for a pre-industrial society. POP art is another matter. J.W.

folk culture. The social heritage — the INSTITUTIONS, CUSTOMS, conventions, values, skills, arts, modes of living — of a group of people feeling themselves members of a closely bound COMMUNITY, and sharing a deep-rooted attachment and allegiance to it. A folk culture is distinguished from more complex CULTURES in that it is predominantly *non-literate*, and so closely knit as to be transmitted from generation to generation by oral means and by RITUAL and behavioural habituation. See also SUBCULTURE.   R.F.

Bibl: R. Redfield, *Peasant Society and Culture* (Chicago, 1956).

folk literature. Term loosely applied to oral-traditional works of literary value (in the sense that they have invigorated and even been the prime inspiration of literary works, e.g. Homer) that entertain or have entertained, and, to an (arguable) extent originate from, 'the FOLK'. The origins of folk literature (which embraces folk-song, folk-tales, ballads, riddles, proverbs, and folk-drama) are mysterious, as are those of PRIMITIVE art, and they approximate in important respects to the untrained, unsophisticated, NAIVE component in all literature. Thus the greatest writers — Dante, Cervantes, Shakespeare, Goethe — all incorporate much folk material in their work. Important examples of folk literature are: the early epics (the Elder Edda, the East Karelian narrative folk-songs from which Lonnrot compiled the *Kalevala*, etc.), the ballads, the folk-songs, the folk-drama (for example, the dramatic treatment of traditional themes, usually at religious festivals, from which the ancient Greek drama developed), the earlier layers of Homeric epic, and the fairy tales.
M.S.-S.

folk model, see under LINEAGE.

folk music. Songs, instrumental music, and dances reflecting the everyday *mores* and inner psyche of a national group. Basic themes are domestic, social, patriotic, and religious. Melodies spun out by musical individuals are absorbed into their community's living tradition, and are communally moulded to suit the prevailing climate during the process of oral transmission from generation to generation, thus ensuring a genuine folk character. Two broad cultural categories emerge: (1) 'PRIMITIVE', i.e. non-literate, societies,

whose musical style includes irregular rhythmic patterns, vigorous bodily movements, and distortion of the voice; (2) 'civilized', i.e. literate, societies, whose folk music influences, and is influenced by, such features of ART MUSIC as strophic forms, sophisticated metres, modality, TONALITY. Though this intercourse raises the question of 'authenticity' (see ACCULTURATION), European composers have for centuries utilized common folk idioms (especially during periods of political NATIONALISM), thus preserving melodies which might otherwise have been lost through the limited powers of memory and lack of technique among untrained musicians. The serious attention paid by scholars to the traditional music of the poorer classes coincides with the increasing respect for manifestations such as JAZZ and Flamenco among the rich and educated. See also ETHNOMUSICOLOGY.   A.K.

Bibl: C. Sachs, *The Rise of Music in the Ancient World, East and West* (New York, 1943; London, 1944); C.M. Bowra, *Primitive Song* (London, 1962; New York, 1963); D. Johnson, *Music and Society in Lowland Scotland in the Eighteenth Century* (London, 1972), pp. 3-19.

folklore. A word coined by W.J. Thoms in 1846 for a central part of FOLK CULTURE: the collective 'wisdom' or 'learning' of the 'FOLK', as embodied in customs, beliefs, RITUALS, games, dances, songs, legends, MYTHS, tales, proverbs, 'sayings' etc. (see FOLK LITERATURE; FOLK MUSIC), all passed on by word of mouth. The term, and the collection by numerous folklore societies and by scholars like Max Müller, Andrew Lang, and G.L. Gomme of stories, poems, and songs not yet committed to paper, originated in the 19th century. In current popular usage it often means merely a corpus of erroneous but widely held beliefs.   R.F.

Bibl: R.M. Dorson, *The British Folklorists* (London and Chicago, 1968).

folkways. Term used by W.G. Sumner for all those ways of doing things (from technical tasks to religious observances) which, within a COMMUNITY whose members share the same 'life-conditions', gradually come to be not only established, but also sanctioned and obligatory. Sumner believed that in every society an initial body of such folkways underlay all subsequent developments of doctrines, *mores*, law, and reflective morality. They were the distinguishing foundation of all human societies; the bedrock on which all else came to be erected. R.F.

Bibl: W.G. Sumner, *Folkways* (Boston, 1907).

food chain. A series of organisms which eat those lower in the chain, and are eaten by those higher up. A simple food chain is grass—bullock—man. Simple food chains are rare, and the term *food web* is preferable, as this recognizes that most plants are eaten by many different herbivores (e.g. caterpillars, slugs, voles, and cattle all eat grass), and that most predators consume a variety of prey. The concept of the food web also includes the breakdown, partly by bacterial decomposition, of dead animals and plants, the incorporation of the nutrients from their TISSUES into the soil, and the subsequent take-up of the same nutrients by a new generation of plants.

A food chain usually takes the form of a pyramid. The broad base, e.g. grass, contains a great deal of material, in which a smaller mass of herbivores subsist. Higher up come the carnivores, less numerous and containing less materials. The pyramidal structure reflects the inefficiency with which the nutrient elements are used. As well as nutrients, toxic substances (e.g. DDT) pass up food chains from prey to predator, and may be retained in the greatest concentration by the organism highest in the chain. K.M.

food policy. A commonly used phrase to describe a set of policy measures, mainly in a THIRD WORLD context, to improve production and distribution of food, to provide early warning of FAMINE and to secure international assistance. Though necessarily closely related to AGRICULTURAL POLICY the emphasis is switched from the farm sector *per se* to the total population with the aim of promoting food security. International action is promoted by a number of agencies such as FAO, the 1980 Food Aid Convention, and the IMF through its food facility established in 1981 as an extension of the compensatory finance facility. Following the problems in Africa in the 1980s the adequacy of the measures available is strongly debated. G.H.P.

Bibl: A. Valdez, *Food Security for Developing Countries* (Boulder, Co., 1981).

force, see under POWER.

force de frappe. Literally, 'striking force'. This is the popular term for the French independent Strategic Nuclear Force (SNF) developed in the 1960s. The *force de frappe* was a central plank of Gaullist defence policy which was NATIONALIST and anti-Atlanticist in character. Maintenance and development of the SNF is supported by all major political parties in France. S.M.

force ouvrière, see under CGT.

forced labour.

(1) During the NAZIS' wartime domination of Europe millions of workers were forcibly deported from the defeated and occupied countries to provide forced labour for German factories and farms. In many cases they were treated as no more than slaves, and recruiting and employing forced labour was one of the WAR CRIMES with which the defendants at the NUREMBERG TRIALS were charged. See also CONCENTRATION CAMPS.

(2) Forced labour camps were established in the U.S.S.R. as early as 1918 as penal colonies to which millions of Soviet citizens who were regarded with suspicion by the authorities were sent for 'correction', and where most of them died. A great expansion took place during Stalin's campaign, 1928-32, to collectivize Russian agriculture and destroy the resistance of the peasants. The total of those arrested in the period 1930-37 who died in camps is estimated at 3.5 million (in addition to the 11 million peasants estimated to have died in the countryside, the great majority from famine). The Stalinist purges of 1936-38 produced further waves of arrests and imprisonment to which must be added those incarcerated after the Soviet occupation of Poland and the Baltic states, German POWs, and Russian POWs returning to the U.S.S.R. after the war.

The total number at any given time has

never been disclosed but has been estimated as reaching a peak of 12-15 million. The huge complex of camps, estimated at the end of the Stalin era (1950) at around 200 scattered throughout Siberia, the Arctic, and the Far East, was placed under the Central Camps Administration (see GULAG), a subdivision of the KGB, which exercised an economic as well as a political function by providing forced labour for lumbering, mining, and the construction of such major projects as the White Sea—Baltic canal, particularly in areas with harsh climatic conditions.

Taking the whole period of the Stalin regime, 1930-53, it has been estimated that the number of those who died from hunger, cold and maltreatment, or were executed, exceeded 20 million and may have been considerably higher. The inhuman regime in the camps improved somewhat after 1950, but it was only after Stalin's death, when a series of strikes and revolts took place, that the government began to reduce their population. Some camps were dismantled, others were transformed into milder 'corrective labour colonies'. However, a number of labour camps with an especially harsh regime were retained.

L.L.;A.L.C.B.

Bibl: E.L Homze, *Foreign Labor in Nazi Germany* (Princeton, 1967); R. Conquest, *The Harvest of Sorrow: Soviet Collectivization and the Terror-Famine* (London, 1986); *The Great Terror* (London, 1971); Alexander Solzhenitsyn, *One Day in the Life of Ivan Denisovich* (London and New York, 1963); *The Gulag Archipelago* (New York, 1973; London, 1974).

forecasting. In ECONOMICS (but see also TECHOLOGNICAL FORECASTING), the prediction of the future using analytical methods and techniques. Forecasts are required for the development of plans and for evaluating the effects of different policies. Forecasting requires a MODEL of how certain VARIABLES are determined by other variables. These variables are termed endogenous and exogenous respectively. The model has to be tested in some manner and validated as an adequate representation of reality. In order to use the model in forecasting, it is necessary to make forecasts of the exogenous variables. In many cases,

this may be merely a case of shifting the problem of forecasting. As the future is uncertain, it is appropriate to prepare a range of forecasts and test plans and policies for different contingencies. This requires some indication of the PROBABILITIES of the different futures occurring. However, this is a very difficult task due to the nature of UNCERTAINTY. There are many different forecasting techniques (see ECONOMETRICS and SCENARIO ANALYSIS).

J.P.

Bibl: S. Makridakis and S.C. Wheelwright, *Forecasting Methods and Applications* (Chichester, 1978).

foreclosure. In PSYCHOANALYSIS, a term (*Verwerfung*) to which Freud makes a small number of references. In Lacan's work this concept is elaborated, and given an important place within the psychoanalytic theory of the PSYCHOSES. REPRESSION, for both Freud and Lacan, was an operation on a signifier, something that one was only aware of through its return in the signifying chain in, for example, a slip of the tongue, or a joke. What is foreclosed, however, does not return in the signifying chain, but returns in the real, in the form of, for example, visual and auditory hallucinations. It thus testifies to an impairment of the standard neurotic structure of repression, that is, signifying substitution, and Lacan saw it as involving, more precisely, the foreclosure of the NAME OF THE FATHER, that is, the operator which allows the SUBJECT to symbolize and localize JOUISSANCE in the phallic function. In its absence then, the subject is left open to the invasions of jouissance which characterize psychotic states. D.L.

foregrounding. In STYLISTICS, and associated fields, any deviation from a linguistic or socially accepted norm. The analogy is of a figure seen against a background. A 'foregrounded' feature in English poetry would be the use of alliteration or rhyme.

D.C.

Bibl: G. Leech, *A Linguistic Guide to English Poetry* (London, 1969).

foreign-body reaction, see under TRAUMA.

forensic medicine. Also called 'legal medicine' or 'medical jurisprudence'. The interface between medicine and the law. There are a number of specialist aspects, the best known being forensic PATHOLOGY, where post-mortem examinations of obscure, suspicious or criminal deaths assist the law enforcement agencies and the courts in the investigation of crime. The forensic pathologist often visits the scene of death to attempt to determine the time of death and the identity of the deceased where necessary, then performs an autopsy (post-mortem) to discover the cause of death and the extent of injuries or natural disease. His expertise can interpret such matters as the range and direction of gunshot wounds, the type of head injuries, the nature of stab wounds and many other factors. As well as assisting in criminal cases, the forensic pathologist contributes to the knowledge of fatal traffic, domestic and industrial accidents and thus to their prevention; for example, motor-cycle crash-helmets and car seat-belts were developed as a result of forensic recommendations. Poisoning, environmental hazards, cot deaths and many natural diseases causing sudden unexpected death are also the province of the forensic pathologist. Other forensic specialists include the forensic odontologist (who applies dental techniques to legal problems), forensic physicians (who carry out legal examinations on living persons, such as drunken drivers, rape victims, abused children and persons in custody); forensic serologists (who deal with blood groups as well as being concerned with blood-stained weapons and clothing); and forensic psychiatrists (who deal with the mental state of accused and convicted persons, mainly in relation to criminal responsibility). See also DENTISTRY; SEROLOGY; PSYCHIATRY.

B.H.K.

form. In LINGUISTICS, a term used in a variety of technical senses, of which the most important are:

(1) any linguistic element, or combination of elements, especially when studied without reference to their syntactic function;

(2) a variant of a linguistic element in a given context (e.g. the forms of a noun),

(3) the phonetic/phonological/grammatical (see PHONETICS; PHONOLOGY; GRAMMAR) characteristic of a linguistic element or unit, as opposed to its MEANING (e.g. the active form of a sentence). See also MORPHEME; UNIVERSAL; WORD CLASS.

D.C.

Bibl: D. Crystal, *A Dictionary of Linguistics and Phonetics* (Oxford, 1985).

form class, see under WORD CLASS.

form criticism, see under HIGHER CRITICISM.

form word, see under WORD CLASS.

formal (in LINGUISTICS), see under NOTIONAL.

formal operation. In DEVELOPMENTAL PSYCHOLOGY, a PIAGETIAN term for a mental operation involving the manipulation of PROPOSITIONS. For example, given the statements: X is taller than Z; X is shorter than Y, the subject can infer who is the tallest. According to Piaget such INFERENCES about propositions (as opposed to concrete objects) emerge during adolescence and characterize the final stage of intellectual development. P.L.H.

formalism. Any school or doctrine that emphasizes, any emphasis on or preoccupation with, form or forms or formal elements in any sphere: of thought, conduct, religion, art, literature, drama, music, etc. Specific uses include the following: O.S.

(1) The view of MATHEMATICS, developed by Hilbert, that treats mathematical theories as pure deductive systems, no meaning being ascribed to the expressions of the system other than that implicitly assigned to them by its *formation-rules*, which regulate the possibilities of their combination in well-formed formulae (see AXIOMATICS). Russell objected that formalism takes no adequate account of the application of mathematics to the world (most elementarily in the use of arithmetic for counting), and other opponents have described it as 'a game with meaningless marks'. A.Q.

Bibl: R.L. Wilder, *Introduction to the Foundations of Mathematics* (London and New York, 1952).

(2) A school of literary theory which

327

flourished in the decade after 1917 in Russia. Its members included Viktor Schlovsky, Roman Jakobson, Boris Eichenbaum, Osip Brik, Jurii Tynyanov and Boris Tomashevsky. These theorists were concerned with what distinguishes a literary work from any other kind of written expression, and took as their object of study the purely formal, artificial and technical aspects of literature. One of their main contentions was that LITERARINESS is mainly achieved through the effect of DEFAMILIARIZATION. R.PO.

Bibl: T. Bennett, *Formalism and Marxism* (London, 1979).

(3) In music, the use of traditional forms such as the pavane, passacaglia, or gavotte to give formal structure to ATONAL MUSIC, as in Berg's opera *Wozzeck*. A.H.

Fortran. The earliest HIGH-LEVEL PROGRAMMING LANGUAGE to achieve general acceptance, and still by far the most widely used for scientific applications. It is now technically obsolescent (at least) and survives by virtue of the intellectual capital invested in existing PROGRAMS and continued support from COMPUTER manufacturers. C.S.

Fortress America. A term used loosely and widely to characterize an American withdrawal from complex international involvements to an ISOLATIONIST position in which it would rely on its military strength and (mythical) economic independence to resist attacks on its national territory. America's global commitments are so intricate that the phrase should be laid to rest. S.R.

foundationalism. In philosophical discussions of knowledge and belief (see EPISTEMOLOGY) the theory that our beliefs form an edifice resting upon a set of basic or *foundational* beliefs which provide the ultimate source of justification for the rest of the belief system. Any belief other than a basic one will, if it is justified, be so because it is immediately supported by a foundational belief or can be inferred from other beliefs so supported. Foundational beliefs themselves are required to be self-justifying, self-evident, or in some other way not themselves in need of justification. A theory which expressly rejects

foundationalism is the coherence theory, which states that the justification of beliefs arises from relations of mutual support between them, no belief counting as any more 'basic' than any other. A.C.G.

Bibl: K. Lehrer, *Knowledge* (Oxford, 1974).

four-colour conjecture. A mathematical hypothesis stating that if a plane be divided into regions (countries) then it is possible to colour them with at most four colours so that no two countries with a common frontier have the same colour. A fallacious proof (by A.B. Kempe in 1879) was accepted as correct for a decade. Despite intensive research and the development of special techniques (see GRAPH) no counter-example was found. Finally, in July 1976 two mathematicians at Urbana, Illinois, claimed to have proved the conjecture by breaking it down into many thousands of cases and using a COMPUTER to check each one. The proof is nearly 1,000 pages long and has now been generally accepted as correct. R.G.

Bibl: W.W. Rouse Ball, rev. H.S.M. Coxeter, *Mathematical Recreations and Essays* (London, 11th ed., 1939).

Four Modernizations. A term used in China to refer to the modernization of Industry, Agriculture, Science and Technology and National Defence. Although the term has come to be associated with the economic policies pursued by Deng Xiaoping since 1978 (see DENGISM), the term originated with Mao Zedong and was first proclaimed by Zhou Enlai in 1964, and the same four strategic areas for modernization were outlined by Lin Biao in his introduction to the *Quotations of Chairman Mao* (The Little Red Book). Deng took great pains to emphasize these precedents in a speech immediately prior to his establishment as leader of the party at the 3rd Plenum of the 11th Central Committee of the CCP. The term is thus used to grant historical legitimacy to Deng's actions, and as a MILLENARIAN slogan to the masses who see achieving the Four Modernizations as the path to economic wellbeing and personal wealth. S.B.

Bibl: J. Prybyla, *The Chinese Economy* (New York, 1978).

Fourier analysis/series. Let f be a PERI-ODIC FUNCTION of time t with period T. Rather weak conditions on f ensure that, for all times t, f can be expressed by its *Fourier series:*

$f(t) = a_0 + \Sigma_{n=1}^{\infty} (a_n \cos(2\pi nt/T) + b_n \sin(2\pi nt/T))$

Thus f can be analysed as the sum of (a constant term and) a series of simple harmonic FUNCTIONS having periods $T, T/2, T/3,...$ The first of these functions ($a_1\cos(2\pi t/T) + b_1\sin(2\pi t/T)$) is known as the *fundamental*, the subsequent ones as the *harmonics* or *overtones*. Even discontinuous functions (e.g. the 'square waves' and 'sawtooth waves' which occur in television circuitry) can be analysed in this way, and the series can then be used to calculate the effect of applying f as an INPUT to some mechanical or electronic device. If the series is replaced by an integral (see INTEGRATION), non-periodic functions can also be analysed into simple harmonic components; these constitute the *spectrum* of the function. This mathematical analysis corresponds to the physical action of a spectroscope (see SPECTROSCOPY), since an absolutely pure colour represents a single simple harmonic ELECTROMAGNETIC oscillation. Since the time of J. Fourier (1768-1830) many other ways of analysing a function into simpler component functions have been considered; the general theory is part of functional ANALYSIS.

R.G.

Bibl: M.L. Boas, *Mathematical Models in the Physical Sciences* (London and New York, 1966).

Fourteen Points. These were contained in an address by President Woodrow Wilson to the U.S. Congress on 8 January 1918. Despite objections from Britain and France, who had not been consulted, they became the basis of the Armistice with Germany of 11 November 1918, as a result of the Germans invoking them as the basis for an armistice in a note to President Wilson of 4 October 1918. They included: (1) 'Open covenants of peace openly arrived at' instead of secret diplomacy; (2) 'absolute freedom of navigation upon the seas...alike in peace and war'; (3) the removal of all trade barriers; (4) general disarmament; (5) impartial settlement of all colonial claims; (6, 7, 8) evacuation and

restoration of territory in Russia, Belgium, and France (including the return of Alsace-Lorraine); (9) readjustment of Italian frontiers; (10, 12) self-determination for peoples of the Habsburg and Ottoman empires; (11) restoration of territory of Romania, Montenegro, and Serbia; (13) creation of an independent Poland with access to the Baltic; (14) establishment of a LEAGUE OF NATIONS. D.C.W.

fourth dimension. When locating an event, it is not sufficient to specify its position in ordinary three-dimensional space. The *time* at which the event occurred must also be known, and the term 'fourth dimension' emphasizes this property of time. See also SPACE-TIME. M.V.B.

fractals. In PHYSICS, MATHEMATICS and in nature there are shapes and structures which although they appear to be irregular and random, nevertheless have a special pattern of regularity in their 'randomness'. This regularity, called *self-similarity*, derives from the fact that at whatever magnification these systems are viewed they still look much the same. An example, given by the inventor of the term fractal — Benoit Mandelbrot — is the shape of a coastline of a country with its inlets, bays, peninsulas, etc. This looks much the same from a high flying aircraft, from the top of a cliff or close to the sea shore and, unless there was a person or a building in the picture to give some idea of size, it would not be possible to deduce the scale. If we draw a triangle and on each of its sides we draw a smaller triangle and on each side of these we draw a still smaller one — and so on — we have a figure which exhibits self-similarity and hence is a fractal. There are certain mathematical FUNCTIONS which when plotted out never produce smooth curves even over a very small range and these, too, are fractal. It has been suggested that the arrangement of molecules in some AMORPHOUS MATERIALS is fractal and this has led to the development of new mathematical techniques for treating systems with irregular structures. The concept of fractals is now being applied to many other areas where there is a pattern of irregularity — in fields as widely different as GEOLOGY, electrical

NOISE, music and chaotic behaviour (see CHAOS). H.M.R.

fractionation. The separation of chemical substances by a repetitive process. For example, boiling gives a vapour enriched in the more volatile constituent, and successive condensations and reboiling in a specially designed column can effect complete separation. Fractional distillation is widely used in laboratories and industry to separate volatile liquids, and fractional crystallization to separate compounds in solution. B.F.

frame, see under STRUCTURE.

frame of reference. The context, viewpoint, or set of PRESUPPOSITIONS or of evaluative CRITERIA within which a person's PERCEPTION and thinking seem always to occur, and which constrains selectively the course and outcome of these activities. I.M.L.H.

Frankfurt School. The persons and ideas associated with the Institute for Social Research, founded and affiliated to the University of Frankfurt in 1923 under the direction of Carl Grünberg. Exiled to New York during the era of NAZISM, the Institute returned home in 1949. Leading figures have included Max Horkheimer (Director, 1931-58), Walter Benjamin, Theodor Adorno, and Herbert Marcuse. The school agreed on the necessity of providing a *critical theory* of MARXISM. This opposed all forms of POSITIVISM (especially those stressing the possibility of VALUE-FREEDOM in SOCIAL SCIENCE) and all interpretations of Marxism afflicted, like Stalin's, with crude MATERIALISM and immutable dogma. In the school's view, only an open-ended and continuously self-critical approach could avoid paralysis in the theory, and therefore also in the practice, of social transformation. Reinvigoration depended on greater appreciation of Marx's early writings, which became generally available only in the 1930s; they encouraged study particularly of Marxism's debt to certain features of Hegel, whose IDEALIST concern with consciousness as moulder of the world had been undervalued by the economic determinism of later orthodoxy (see HISTORICAL MATERIALISM). Consequently the school devoted more attention to areas that had become regarded as merely SUPERSTRUCTURAL and, especially through its treatment of the AESTHETICS of a MASS SOCIETY, sought to rescue Marxist cultural criticism from sterility. The school's leading contemporary figure, Jürgen Habermas, is notable particularly for his efforts to relate the conditions of rationality to the SOCIAL STRUCTURE of language use.

Though its writings have been more invoked than read, the Frankfurt School has made an important contribution to rehabilitating the LIBERTARIAN aspect of Marx's thought. It has influenced such radical (see RADICALISM) movements as the NEW LEFT, which have been attracted by its rejection of modern technocratic society (see TECHNOCRACY) whether CAPITALIST or Soviet, and by its conviction that some satisfactory clear alternative can emerge only during the actual practice of REVOLUTION. For many opponents this latter point exemplifies most clearly an evasiveness which is deemed to reflect certain irrational inconsistencies in the school's whole approach to the CRITERIA of TRUTH. M.D.B.

Bibl: M. Jay, *The Dialectical Imagination* (London and Boston, 1973); A. Arato and E. Gebhardt (eds.), *The Essential Frankfurt School Reader* (Oxford, 1978); P. Connerton, *The Tragedy of Enlightenment: An Essay on the Frankfurt School* (Cambridge, 1980).

fraternal polyandry, see under POLYANDRY.

free association.
(1) In PSYCHOTHERAPY, a technique which requires the patient to say at once, and to go on saying at once, whatever comes to mind. The chief idea behind free association is that, by using it in the benign and supportive situation of psychotherapy, the patient will be able slowly to approach and face the ANXIETY-producing UNCONSCIOUS material that he cannot face at the beginning, and which is at the centre of his personal difficulties. B.A.F.
(2) In literature, a comparable process whereby one word or image derives spontaneously from another by association of ideas or sounds. The dangers of the

method are suggested by L.A.G. Strong, who wrote of James Joyce's *Finnegans Wake*: 'The two processes, from association to object, from object to association, seldom harmonize, and often create serious confusion.' In art, spontaneity is no guarantee of profundity or even of interesting sense, and T.S. Eliot's remark on FREE VERSE could be adapted to read 'No association is free for the man who wants to do a good job'. D.J.E.

free economy, see MARKET ECONOMY.

free energy. A THERMODYNAMIC property which represents the maximum amount of work obtainable from a mechanical or chemical process. The *Helmholtz free energy* and the *Gibbs free energy* differ only in that the latter includes work done against surrounding atmosphere. The free energy is related to the internal ENERGY or heat content and the ENTROPY of the substance. Each chemical substance under particular conditions has an associated free energy, but when CHEMICAL REACTIONS occur spontaneously there is always a decrease in total free energy. For a chemical reaction in EQUILIBRIUM the driving forces associated with the changes in heat content and entropy are balanced and no change in free energy is possible. B.F.

free enterprise, see MARKET ECONOMY.

free form, see under MORPHEME.

free jazz. Despite the exceptional case of TRAD, the direction of JAZZ has customarily been forward and further out, with soloists striving to free themselves from old formulas and expand their expressive language. BEBOP took jazz to a new height of complexity, and, in the late 1960s, with free jazz, the music seemingly went as far out as it could go. Fired by the modal experiments of John Coltrane and the idiosyncratic style of Ornette Coleman, young musicians rejected artificial notions like harmony and rhythm, subscribing wholeheartedly to Coleman's basic creed of 'expressing our minds and our emotions'. Structural principles were minimal; intensity was supposed to generate its own coherence. In fact, to many

listeners the results were simple anarchy. The larger result was an identity crisis in jazz, exacerbated by the new, vast popularity of ROCK MUSIC which absorbed the audience alienated by jazz's experimental frenzy. Retrenchment began in the 1970s and continues today, with young jazz players re-examining the roots of older jazz for inspiration, seeking direction by going in rather than out (see FUSION). GE.S.

free market. A market which is not impeded by any form of government intervention. If there are many firms in the free market, it may approximate to PERFECT COMPETITION. The resulting operation of the PRICE MECHANISM is often regarded as beneficial since, in certain circumstances, it will result in ECONOMIC EFFICIENCY. However, free markets may not give a socially desirable distribution of income; they cannot cope with the existence of EXTERNALITIES; they may fail to supply PUBLIC GOODS and they may not be particularly close to the ideal of perfect competition. J.P.

Bibl: J. Craven, *Introduction to Economics* (Oxford, 1984).

free port. An area to which goods can be imported, processed and exported without payment of any customs duties. The economic benefits from additional trade and economic activity can offset the loss of revenue from customs duties. Singapore is an important example of the economic benefits that can come from being a free port. J.P.

free radical. An uncharged RADICAL of abnormal VALENCE, which can have an independent existence. The first free radical (triphenylmethane), discovered in 1900, has trivalent instead of the usual tetravalent carbon. Since then numerous free radicals have been studied, including ATOMS of hydrogen and chlorine. Although they usually have only a transient existence free radicals play an important role in propagating CHEMICAL REACTIONS. Living organisms have evolved systems of inactivating free radicals before they cause damage. B.F.;P.N.

free trade, see under PROTECTIONISM and TRADE THEORY.

free variation. In LINGUISTICS, the relationship between linguistic units having the same DISTRIBUTION which are different in FORM (sense 3) but not thereby different in meaning, i.e. the units do not contrast. The concept is most widely used in PHONOLOGY, referring to variant pronunciations of a word; but it may be used in GRAMMAR, and also in SEMANTICS (where it is called *synonymy*). D.C.

free verse (or *vers libre*). Verse that lacks regular metre, rhyme, and other formal devices, relying in its search for 'organic form' on rhythms natural to speech which should also be 'natural' to the theme and feeling of the poem. Though by no means a modern invention, free verse became prominent with the advent of MODERNISM, and constituted a revolt against the set forms of 19th-century poetry. The easiest verse to write badly, free verse is possibly the most difficult to write well, since no external shaping aids are available. As T.S. Eliot remarked, 'no verse is free for the man who wants to do a good job' ('Reflections on *Vers Libre*', 1917). D.J.E.

Freie Bühne. A play-producing organization founded in Berlin by Otto Brahm in 1889 to pioneer the new naturalistic drama (see NATURALISM). It had no permanent ensemble or theatre and played only at Sunday matinées. But it gave high-quality private performances of work banned by the German censors, including Ibsen's *Ghosts*, Zola's *Thérèse Raquin*, and Hauptmann's *Die Weber*. And although in 1894 it was affiliated to the more established DEUTSCHES THEATER it was largely responsible for introducing many key modern works into the regular German repertoire. M.BI.
Bibl: J.L. Styan, *Modern Drama in Theory and Practice*, Vol. 1 (Cambridge, 1981).

French Community; French Union. The *French Union* set up in 1946 united the French Republic with its overseas territories in a union whose citizens were all citizens of France and had representation in the French National Assembly. The defection in 1954 of the various states of Indo-China, Tunisia, and Morocco and the loss of Algeria led President de Gaulle, as part of the process of substituting a Fifth Republic for the Fourth, to set up on 5 October 1958 a *French Community*, membership of which was based on self-determination by the inhabitants of the states concerned on a basis of universal suffrage. Membership of the Community was extended to the former French African colonies together with the Malagasy Republic (Guinea chose independence). It united them in a free-franc zone, largely dependent on France for trade (75% of both imports and exports), investment (over one thousand million dollars' worth, two-thirds from official sources), enterprise, and military aid. All the members were associated with the EEC under the Yaoundé Convention of 1962. D.C.W.

frequency, see under STATISTICAL REGULARITY.

frequency modulation (FM).
(1) A technique in radio transmission whereby AUDIO FREQUENCY signals are made to vary or modulate (see MODULATION) the frequency of a carrier wave of RADIO FREQUENCY. Broadcasts on the radio v.h.f. band employ frequency modulation, which ensures almost total freedom from interference and distortion, at the price of using a greater frequency range for each transmission. M.V.B
(2) In music, a method of producing complex sound waves by allowing the frequency of a simpler wave (e.g. a sine wave) to be modulated by another waveform. This technique was developed by John Chowning (see COMPUTER MUSIC) as a simple way of producing musical tones with a complexity approaching that of real musical instruments and is the basis of several new types of SYNTHESIZER. B.CO.

frequency theory. A system whereby the probability (see PROBABILITY THEORY) of a single event is assigned a numerical value, between 0 and 1, according to the inductively established (see INDUCTION) proportion of situations like that of the event in question in which events of that kind occur. Thus the probability that John will survive until he is 70 will be $1/2$ if 50% of men like John have been found to do so. A problem arises about specifying the relevant situation (or *reference class*): should John be regarded as a man, as an Englishman, as an English postman, as a cigarette-smoking English postman, or what? Usually the STATISTICS will differ as between such alternatives. If all John's characteristics are taken into consideration he may turn out to be the sole instance of the class or SET, so that no statistics are available at all. The requirements of a closely fitting reference class and of copious and thus more reliable statistical evidence pull in opposite directions, and judgement has to be used in reconciling them, a judgement that can be assisted by the theory of statistical significance. It is generally held that not all probability is frequency, although the identification of the two has been attempted. The crucial point is that the statements of the statistical evidence from which frequency-judgements are derived are *inductive* and thus only *confirmed* (see CONFIRMATION) as probable, and not certified, by the grounds on which they rest.   A.Q.

Bibl: A. Pap, *An Introduction to the Philosophy of Science* (New York, 1962; London, 1963).

Freudian. In strict usage, an adjective referring to a tradition or school of psychoanalytic thought and practice, namely the one connected with the work of Sigmund Freud (1856-1939); the word can also be used as a substantive, meaning a member of this school. More loosely, the adjective refers to any view popularly associated with the name of Freud, especially any view that picks on the sexual origins and character of thought, motives, feelings, or conduct.

Freudian PSYCHOANALYSIS has three aspects: it is a general theory of PSYCHOLOGY, a therapy, and a method of enquiry or research. The psychology looks on the mind of the adult individual as a system of elements, each carrying a charge of energy. Any one element (e.g. Smith's love for his father) may be capable of entering CONSCIOUSNESS; but, where entry into consciousness is liable to raise the excitation of the system beyond the limits of what it can tolerate (as might happen with the element of Smith's hatred of his

father), energy is redistributed in such a way that the threatening element cannot enter consciousness and remains UNCONSCIOUS. The energy of the system takes two fundamental forms. In the early version of the theory, the energy was either sexual or self-preservative in character (see LIFE INSTINCT); in the later version it took either a loving or an aggressive and destructive form (see DEATH INSTINCT).

An overriding aim, therefore, of the system is to preserve its psychic equilibrium in the face of the energy distribution, and of threats generated from within and from without. It achieves this aim, in general, by taking defensive action (see DEFENCE MECHANISM) of one sort or another; e.g. RATIONALIZATION, SUBLIMATION, PROJECTION, REGRESSION. To enable it to do this, the mental system of the infant and child develops an internal structure: the ID (the source of energy supply), the EGO (the part of the system that enables it to face reality), and the SUPEREGO (the part that embodies the self-controls of conscience). The child also goes through certain stages in its development to maturity, e.g. the Oedipal period (see OEDIPUS COMPLEX). If this development has been unsatisfactory (such that energy remains tied up, or bound, at some early stage or STAGES OF DEVELOPMENT), then the adult person will be disposed to exhibit pathological conduct (see ABNORMAL PSYCHOLOGY) and to experience difficulties of related sorts. When the defences which were erected early in life to keep the dangerous elements at bay break down, then neurotic conflict ensues, and his pathology becomes manifest (see NEUROSIS; PSYCHOSIS).

As a therapy, Freudian psychoanalysis is based on the rule of FREE ASSOCIATION for the patient, and on rules for the analyst that make him play the role of an anonymous figure who cannot be faulted by the patient. One important consequence of these rules is to produce a special relationship between patient and analyst, which encourages the rapid growth of a subtle emotional involvement with the analyst known as TRANSFERENCE. Freudian analysis relies heavily on this emotional involvement.

It was the use of Freudian analysis, in particular, that has led many analysts, psychiatrists, and others to speak of 'Freud's great discoveries'. But to speak like this presupposes that Freudian psychoanalysis is a valid method of enquiry or research: one which, consequently, uncovers the truth about human nature. This PRESUPPOSITION is so beset by difficulties that it is hardly acceptable:

(1) It can be argued that Freudian practice not merely 'uncovers the facts', but helps to manufacture them, and in ways that go to confirm the Freudian theory used in the practice. In short, it is to some degree a self-confirmatory procedure.

(2) When we try to pinpoint Freud's great discoveries, it is difficult to do so in a way that is generally acceptable, even to analysts in the Freudian tradition.

(3) When we do look at some likely candidate, e.g. the Freudian generalization about the stages of libidinal development (see PSYCHOSEXUAL DEVELOPMENT), it is far from clear what we would have to do to falsify it. (For the principle of falsifiability see POPPERIAN.) For LIBIDO is a theoretical notion, whose observable manifestations are not clear.

(4) When we examine the general psychology that Freudian analysis has erected upon the material produced by the practice, it is evident that it does not embody a 'scientific' theory, in the dominant current sense of this adjective. Its logical relations to science are uncertain, and its whole status controversial.

Unlike Darwin, therefore, Freud's theoretical contribution has not yet been incorporated into science. Nevertheless, his work has revolutionized the popular view of human nature in the West (rather as Marx has changed our view of society); and it has penetrated into almost every nook and cranny of our CULTURE. It is this fact, perhaps, that has led many people to rank Freud as a figure of towering genius. Whether, however, he really turns out to be a Darwin of the human mind, or only someone who, like a Ptolemy or a Mesmer, has led us up an interesting and important dead end, is a matter which the future of science will have to decide.

For a modification of Freudian theory see NEO-FREUDIAN.   B.A.F.

Bibl: B.A. Farrell, *The Standing of Psychoanalysis* (Oxford, 1981).

For the development of Freud's theories

within the school of Jacques Lacan, see LACANIAN. For other research developments within the Freudian tradition see SEARCHING INSTINCT; BODY IMAGE.   B.BU.

Freudian slip. In psychoanalytic theory (see FREUDIAN; PSYCHOANALYSIS), a momentary and transient breakdown in the defensive position of the person, as a result of which he gives unintended expression in speech to repressed (see REPRESSION) thoughts and feelings.   W.Z.

fringe benefits. The elements of an employee's remuneration provided at the employer's expense under the contract of employment, other than the rate of pay per unit of time or output. They commonly comprise such items as holidays with pay, pension plans, life insurance, stock purchase plans, and payment for absence during family emergencies. They are to be distinguished from *ex gratia* payments, and from the provision of general amenities such as canteens and sports grounds. In the U.K. they are usually taken to exclude employers' statutory contributions to national insurance on the employee's behalf, but in the U.S.A., where state schemes have been relatively restricted, trade union members have obtained or supplemented many forms of social insurance by negotiation with employers, and such statutory payments as the employers also make are commonly included with fringe benefits. In common usage, the distinction between fringe benefits and other employee rewards is often unclear. The extent of fringe benefits has increased as the rise in employees' real incomes has made the benefits concerned more attractive relatively to a further increase in the pay packet, though some are taxable, and fringe benefits have been used to ease the pressure on executives of high marginal rates of taxation.   E.H.P.B.

Bibl: L. C. Hunter and D. J. Robertson, *Economics of Wages and Labour* (London, 1978).

Fringe, the. British term (the U.S. equivalent being OFF-BROADWAY) for activities, almost exclusively theatrical — notably of SURREALIST, unconventional, unorthodox, anti-ESTABLISHMENT, obscene, AVANT-GARDE, or pseudo-*avant-garde* type —

that take place away from the main popular centres of entertainment. First used in the late 1950s of events that took place on the periphery of the Edinburgh Festival, it now embraces the highly conventionalized products of the mediocre and ageing, as well as the genuinely zestful activities of students and other young artists.   M.S.-S.

Froebel method. An educational method associated with Friedrich Froebel (1782-1852), who sought to adapt the CHILD-CENTRED principles of Rousseau and Pestalozzi (see PESTALOZZI METHOD) to infant education in Germany. He founded the Kindergarten where children could grow through play, using nature work, games, toys, handicraft, music, stories, drawing, and geometrical shapes (cubes, spheres) which he called 'gifts' — the kind of approach now common in most infant schools. Froebel had an obvious influence on Montessori (see MONTESSORI METHOD), Cizek, and the whole nursery and infant school movement.   W.A.C.S.

Bibl: F. Froebel, ed. I.M. Lilley, *Friedrich Froebel* (London, 1967).

front. In METEOROLOGY, a sharp boundary zone in the atmosphere between air masses of different temperatures and humidities. A *warm front* is a warmer air mass impinging on a colder one, and is characterized by a wide cloud band and rain extending well in advance of the surface position of the front. A *cold front* is colder air advancing on warmer, with associated rain showers and thunderstorms usually developing along the line of the advancing front. See also OCCLUSION.   P.H.

front organization. An organization that serves as cover for aims and activities other than its professed ones; in particular, an ostensibly non-COMMUNIST organization with liberal, religious, or other public men of goodwill as the leading figures, but in fact controlled by the Communists. Front organizations in the latter sense were devised in the 1930s by the COMINTERN'S propaganda genius, Willi Münzenberg, with aims such as supporting the Spanish Republic, justifying the MOSCOW TRIALS, and (in England in 1940) advocating peace with Germany.   R.C.

frontal theory. Air masses are bodies of air with constant physical properties such as temperature and humidity usually formed in characteristic locations such as polar or tropical regions. The realization that marked changes in the weather often occurred on the boundaries between air masses led to many of the major developments of 20th-century weather forecasting. A group of Norwegian meteorologists working during World War I proposed the term 'front' for these zones of conflict between air masses of different origin. Fronts are often characterized by pronounced temperature gradients, strong vertical motion and rainfall. The term *frontogenesis* is used to describe the formation of frontal zones. This tends to occur in well-defined regions where air masses tend to clash. As a result of instabilities, waves often form on air mass boundaries and these can rapidly develop into depressions (cyclones). This process is known as *cyclogenesis*. It is these weather systems, depressions and the fronts associated with them, that are responsible for much of the character of the weather in middle latitudes. Frontal systems also occur in the tropics but they are weaker and less well-defined.   P.M.K.

Bibl: R.G. Barry and R.J. Chorley, *Atmosphere, Weather and Climate* (London, 1968).

frontier. The boundary line or zone delimiting two contiguous but different countries or cultural domains. The specialists have long debated whether the frontier is a line or a zone of transition. In American usage the latter meaning predominates; the historian Frederick Jackson Turner stressed the role of the westward march of the frontier in American history, but recognized that, in the sense of the zone of transition to another civilization, the American frontier shifted after 1910 to the large cities. Metaphorical usages in which frontier means 'new opportunities' include President John F. Kennedy's characterization, in 1960-63, of his political programmes as 'the new frontier', and such phrases as 'the frontiers of science'.   J.G.

Bibl: J.R.V. Prescott, *The Geography of Frontiers and Boundaries* (London and Chicago, 1965); O. Lattimore, *Studies in*

Frontier History (London and New York, 1962).

frontogenesis, see under FRONTAL THEORY.

FSLN, see under NICARAGUA; SANDINISTA; CONTRAS.

fuel cell. A chemical CELL in which two fuel substances (such as hydrogen and oxygen) react to produce electrical ENERGY *directly*. The process is the exact opposite to the decomposition of water by ELECTROLYSIS, for hydrogen is fed to cover one platinum ELECTRODE whilst oxygen is fed to the other. No gas escapes, water is continually produced, and an electric current can be driven through an external circuit connected to the electrodes. Invented by Grove in 1840, the fuel cell received little attention until recently; today much research is being stimulated by the possible advantages of cells which may compete with other sources of energy without polluting the atmosphere (see POLLUTION). E.R.L.

fuel element. That part of a NUCLEAR REACTOR core which contains fissionable material (see FISSION). E.R.L.

Führerprinzip. NAZI German term for the principle of leadership, i.e. the establishment of a national leader and the devolution of sovereign authority and power, by decision of the leader, to a recognized hierarchy of subordinates; the entrustment of governmental powers to such leadership rather than to decision by majority in parliament. Hitler's definition was 'unrestricted authority downwards, unrestricted responsibility upwards'. D.C.W.

full employment. Employment of a country's available MANPOWER to the fullest extent likely to be sustainable. Since it is not possible to manage the economy so that there is an exact match between job opportunities and the number of those who want jobs, full employment is consistent with some residual UNEMPLOYMENT. Published figures of unemployment are not, however, a completely reliable indicator of the margin of available manpower.

They usually exclude housewives and others who would be willing to take paid employment but do not register for it. The figures may change their significance over time, e.g. because of new regulations as to unemployment benefits. There is also room for debate as to the precise level of employment that can be sustained, since the more closely full employment is approached the harder it becomes to reconcile it with other economic objectives such as the avoidance of INFLATION and a deficit in the BALANCE OF PAYMENTS. A.C.

full employment surplus. The hypothetical surplus (or deficit) on the budget, if, with unchanged government policies, employment rose to the FULL EMPLOYMENT level. Such an increase in employment would affect both tax revenues and government expenditure. Changes in the full employment surplus are a more reliable measure of the development of a government's fiscal stance (see FISCAL POLICY) than movements in the realized budget surplus, since the latter are affected by the actual level of UNEMPLOYMENT and output. J.P.
Bibl: D. Begg *et al.*, *Economics* (London, 1984).

full recovery cost, see under MARGINAL COSTING.

function. A fundamental CONCEPT of MATHEMATICS used whenever some quantity (the *value*) is regarded as depending on, or determined by, other quantities (the ARGUMENT(S); see also VARIABLE). A function f of one argument has a specified SET, say X (e.g. instants of time), as its *domain* and a set, say Y (e.g. positions in space), as its *codomain*. It assigns to each argument x in X a unique value y in Y; this is expressed by writing $y = f(x)$. The set of values taken by f (a subset of Y) is called its *range*. If the values of f for distinct arguments are themselves distinct, then f is said to be *one-to-one* or *injective*. If, further, every element of Y is a value of f (so that range and codomain coincide), then f is said to be a *bijection* between X and Y; in this case the *inverse* of f is a function from Y to X.

Before the 19th century it was assumed that the assignment of values was made according to some definite mathematical or natural law (e.g. $v = x^2$). But in contemporary mathematics no such assumption is made; the assignment may be arbitrary or random. Sometimes, especially in the older literature, the term is restricted to functions whose arguments and values are real NUMBERS. The GRAPH of such a function f is obtained by plotting points in the plane whose COORDINATES are $(x, f(x))$. Two functions f and g may be combined by *composition* to give a new function $f.g$ which is defined by $f.g(x) = f(g(x))$. All the above considerations can be extended to functions of more than one argument.

Functions in ALGEBRA and TOPOLOGY are often called *maps* or *mappings*. Functions whose arguments are themselves functions are called *functionals* or *operators*. See also ANALYSIS; COMPLEX FUNCTION THEORY. R.G.

Bibl: see under MATHEMATICS.

function theory, see COMPLEX FUNCTION THEORY.

function word, see under WORD CLASS.

functional analysis, see under ANALYSIS.

functional explanation, see under EXPLANATION.

functional fixedness, see under PROBLEM-SOLVING.

functional grammar. In LINGUISTICS, an approach to grammatical analysis which is based on the pragmatic rules which govern social interaction, the formal rules of PHONOLOGY, SYNTAX, and SEMANTICS being seen as secondary. Functional approaches, in various models, developed in the 1970s as an alternative to the abstract, formalized view of language presented by transformational grammar. D.C.

Bibl: P. Matthews, *Syntax* (Cambridge, 1981).

functional sentence perspective (FSP). In LINGUISTICS, a theory associated with the modern exponents of the PRAGUE SCHOOL. It refers to an analysis of utterances or texts in terms of the information they contain, the role of each utterance element being evaluated for its semantic contribution to the whole. The different levels of contribution involved results in the notion of the 'communicative dynamism' of an utterance. The main structural elements of this theory are known as 'rheme' (the element in an utterance which adds new meaning to what has been communicated already) and 'theme' (the element which adds little or no new meaning). D.C.

Bibl: G.C. Lepschy, *A Survey of Structural Linguistics* (Oxford, 1982).

functionalism.

(1) In PHILOSOPHY, specifically in the philosophy of mind (see MIND, PHILOSOPHY OF and MIND-BODY PROBLEM), the theory that the nature of mental attributes can be specified by means of a description of the causal role or function of those attributes in the mental life and general behaviour of the subject. It states further that mental attributes are 'supervenient' upon brain states, that is, a subject's brain states and activity determine what mental states he is in. A given brain state corresponds to a given mental state just when the causal role played by both is identical. Functionalism counts among those theories whose premise is that mind has a physical basis. A.C.G.

(2) In ANTHROPOLOGY, a group of theories associated above all with the names of B. Malinowski (1884-1942) and A.R. Radcliffe-Brown (1881-1955), although they are perhaps more appropriately, if less agreeably, described as structural-functionalist. In one version, great store is set by the putative human needs, both biological and social, that every society must satisfy. In another (see STRUCTURAL-FUNCTIONAL THEORY), a CULTURE or society is seen as an entity all the parts of which function to maintain one another and the totality, the disruption of one part provoking readjustment among others. Many anthropologists still describe themselves as functionalists in some sense, but none would accept the common criticism that his functionalism precludes an interest in social change and the study of SYSTEMS over time. See also EVOLUTION, SOCIAL AND CULTURAL; STRUCTURALISM. M.F.

Bibl: E. R. Leach, *Social Anthropology* (London, 1982); M. Augé, *The Anthropological Circle* (Cambridge, 1982).

(3) In PSYCHOLOGY, a point of view (one

337

of the six main SCHOOLS OF PSYCHOLOGY as classified by R.S. Woodworth) that sees mental phenomena as activities rather than as states or STRUCTURES. It assumes that function produces structure (as in ANATOMY, where the shape of an organ system reflects the demands of its function), and attempts to explain the nature of phenomena completely in terms of the use they fulfil. In American psychology, the notion that no response occurs without implicit or explicit *reinforcement* (see OPERANT CONDITIONING) exemplifies a kind of utilitarian functionalism. Efforts to understand PERCEPTION in terms of function performed, as in E. Brunswik's 'probabilistic functionalism' where perception is given a predictive role, are still current.

J.S.B.

Bibl: R.S. Woodworth, *Contemporary Schools of Psychology* (New York, 3rd ed., 1964; London, 9th ed., 1965).

(4) In architecture, the theory embodied in Louis Sullivan's dictum 'form follows function', i.e. that the form of a building can be derived from a full knowledge of the purposes it is to serve. It derives from such 19th-century architectural writers as Viollet-le-Duc demanding the expression of each of the elements of a building and especially its structure. The theory had a further extension in the 1920s and 1930s in the view that the form which most closely follows function, as apparent in ships or aeroplanes, is also the most beautiful. See also INTERNATIONAL STYLE; MACHINE AESTHETIC; NEUE SACHLICHKEIT.

M.BR.

fundamental constants. Quantities appearing in laws of nature as proportionality constants which determine the intrinsic strengths of the fundamental forces of nature, the MASSES of the most ELEMENTARY PARTICLES and various other of their intrinsic properties. They are chosen because they should not vary in space or time and are found to be constant in this way to high precision. As yet these quantities can only be determined by measurement. Current GRAND UNIFIED THEORIES and theories of SUPERSTRINGS aim to calculate these quantities numerically or show that they are interrelated. The principal goal of fundamental PHYSICS is to arrive at an understanding of why these constants have the numerical values they do. A number of coincidences between values of combinations of fundamental constants led to the formulation of the ANTHROPIC PRINCIPLES. Precise measurements of these constants are also employed to define the standard units of mass, length and time. They are also termed 'Constants of Nature'.

J.D.B.

fundamental particle, see ELEMENTARY PARTICLE.

fundamental school. American term for a school at which basic education is stressed — i.e. at primary level, the Three Rs; at secondary, subjects taught formally. A large number of these schools were set up in the mid-1970s to counteract the more liberal, and so-called PROGRESSIVE schools of the 1960s.

J.I.

fundamentalism. The belief that the Bible possesses complete INFALLIBILITY because every word in it is the Word of God. The term is derived from a series of tracts, *The Fundamentals*, published in the U.S.A. in 1909. Other doctrines defended (on the basis of this literal acceptance of passages in the Bible) include the interpretation of the death of Jesus as a 'substitutionary' sacrifice to the just wrath of God on mankind's sins; the virgin birth, physical resurrection, and 'Second Coming' of Jesus; and eternal punishment in hell. Fundamentalism is strongest among some American PROTESTANTS, and is usually accompanied by the condemnation both of the Roman CATHOLIC Church and of modern thought. See also under ISLAM. D.L.E.

Bibl: J.I. Packer, *'Fundamentalism' and the Word of God* (London, 1958) and *Knowing God* (London and New York, 1973); J. Barr, *Escaping from Fundamentalism* (London and New York, 1984).

furniture music (*musique d'ameublement*). A type of music envisaged by the composer Erik Satie that would not draw attention to itself but by its presence simply make the environment more pleasant. This concept of music as some form of aural background, rather like musical wallpaper, is an important precursor of both MUZAK and AMBIENT MUSIC. B.CO.

Bibl: J. Harding, *Erik Satie* (London, 1975).

fusion.
(1) In PHYSICS, the production of an atomic NUCLEUS by the union of two lighter nuclei in a NUCLEAR REACTION. Being positively charged, the two original nuclei repel one another, and considerable KINETIC ENERGY (i.e. a high operating temperature) is necessary to get the reaction to proceed. But the amount of ENERGY released can be much greater, because the resulting nucleus is often less massive than its constituents (see MASS-ENERGY EQUATION), and a CHAIN REACTION may occur. The power of the hydrogen bomb, and the warmth and light of sunshine, are derived from fusion. M.V.B.
(2) In music, a prime product of the musical and social turbulence of the 1960s, fusion attempted to marry the genres of ROCK and JAZZ. The most famous convert to fusion (or jazz rock or crossover, as it was variously called) was Miles Davis, whose *Bitches Brew* album in 1970 defined the mode. The highly praised young trumpeter Wynton Marsalis regards jazz as a superior art and has declared 'there is no such thing as fusion'. GE.S.
(3) In ANTHROPOLOGY, see under LINEAGE.

fusional (in LINGUISTICS), see under INFLECTING.

future shock. A phrase coined, on the analogy of CULTURE SHOCK, by Alvin Toffler to describe 'a new and profoundly upsetting psychological disease' caused in Western POST-INDUSTRIAL SOCIETY by 'a rising rate of change that makes reality seem, sometimes, like a kaleidoscope run wild. Change is avalanching upon our heads and most people are grotesquely unprepared to cope with it.' O.S.
Bibl: A. Toffler, *Future Shock* (London and New York, 1970).

Futurism. Italian movement in the arts, originating as a purely literary doctrine with F.T. Marinetti's 'Futurist Manifesto' in *Le Figaro*, Paris, 20 February 1909; subsequently extended to the other arts, then after 1922 partly assimilated in the official IDEOLOGY of FASCISM, to peter out in the mid-1930s. Its principles, asserted in a forceful succession of manifestos, were dynamism, the cult of speed and the machine, rejection of the past, and the glorification of patriotism and war. Techniques put forward and practised to these ends included (1) in literature, FREE VERSE, PHONETIC POETRY, and a telegraphic language without adjectives or adverbs or much syntax ('words in liberty'); (2) in the visual arts, NEO-IMPRESSIONISM, pictorial dynamism ('lines of force'), simultaneity, and the interpenetration of planes; (3) in music, a BRUITISME evolved by Francesco Pratella and Luigi Russolo, and based on the noises of the modern industrialized world; instruments were also to be made which would divide the octave into 50 equal MICROTONES.

These largely new methods were demonstrated and tested by, e.g., the painter-sculptor Umberto Boccioni, the painter Ardengo Soffici, and the architect Antonio Sant'Elia (notably in his 1914 series of architectural drawings, *Città Nuova*), while the movement's shows and lecture-demonstrations from 1912 to 1914 had some influence in France (on Apollinaire, Léger, and Delaunay), England (VORTICISM), and the U.S.A., making a real contribution in Russia (RAYONISM, Ego-Futurism, and CUBO-FUTURISM) and affecting German EXPRESSIONISM via *Der STURM*. Its impact on DADA from 1916 on was even more profound, not only through the new techniques, but still more by Futurism's blurring of the frontiers between different arts, and its conscious exploitation of the mass MEDIA'S power to publicize any adroitly staged piece of cultural provocation. It thus paved the way both for such artistic developments as CONCRETE POETRY, CONCRETE MUSIC, and KINETIC ART, and for the concept of art as a more or less sensational event. J.W.; A.H.
Bibl: M.W. Martin, *Futurist Art and Theory, 1909-1915* (Oxford, 1968).

futurology. A term coined by the German historian Ossip K. Flechtheim in 1949 to designate a 'new science' of prognosis. It has been applied to various efforts, beginning in 1965, to carry out long-range FORECASTING in a wide range of political, sociological, economic, ecological, and other fields. Most practitioners reject the idea of a 'new science' and cavil even at the word futurology. Three terms are often distinguished: a *conjecture* or intellectually disciplined speculation; a *forecast*, which is based either on a continuing trend or on some defined probabilities of occurrences; and a *prediction*, which is a prognosis of a specific event. Most practitioners agree that one cannot formalize rules for prediction but argue that the compilation of fuller data and the use of new methods (e.g. COMPUTER SIMULATION, STOCHASTIC techniques) will allow them to do better forecasting. D.B.

Bibl: O.K. Flechtheim, *History and Futurology* (Meisenheim am Glan, 1965); B. de Jouvenel, tr. N. Lary, *The Art of Conjecture* (London and New York, 1967); H. Kahn and A.J. Wiener, *The Year 2000* (New York, 1967; London, 1969).

G

Gaia hypothesis. The Gaia hypothesis originated with James E. Lovelock whose studies of the possibility of life on Mars led him to question the basis of life on Earth. The Gaia hypothesis suggests that all living things on the planet should be considered as part of a single living being which can alter the planetary ENVIRONMENT as necessary in order to survive. More a way of thinking than a strict scientific hypothesis, Gaia focuses attention on the FEEDBACK systems, often biological in nature, which regulate and control the environment maintaining the conditions that support life. For example, the composition of the atmosphere has stayed stable over much of geological time, ensuring — and as a result of — the EVOLUTION of life. Carbon dioxide (see GREENHOUSE EFFECT) levels have been maintained by a delicate balance between the BIOSPHERE, the oceans and the atmosphere over much of the current interglacial. Gaia also highlights the dangers that lie in perturbing the system and the responsibility that humanity must accept for the state of the global environment. The carbon dioxide cycle is being profoundly disturbed by the destruction of the world's forests and the combustion of fossil fuels. Humankind may have to take a more active role in rational management of the planetary environment if large-scale climatic change results.   P.M.K.

Bibl: N. Myers (ed.), *Gaia: An Atlas of Planet Management* (New York and London, 1984).

galactic clusters (or *open clusters*). Collections of as few as about 10 or as many as a 1000 stars. More than 1000 such aggregates of stars are known and several, for example the Pleiades, are visible to the naked eye. They lie close to the plane of the Milky Way and consist of relatively young stars, the brightest of which are blue or RED GIANTS. They are only loosely held together as aggregates by the gravitational attraction of their components and are gradually dispersed by the effect of external perturbations. Galactic clusters should not be confused with GALAXY CLUSTERS.   J.D.B.

Bibl: B.J. Bok and P.F. Bok, *The Milky Way* (Cambridge, Mass., 1974).

galactic rotation. Since the 18th century a fundamental problem of ASTRONOMY has been the nature of our GALAXY. Once the Milky Way had been resolved into myriads of individual stars (the sun being one of them) apparently related to each other, 18th- and 19th-century astronomy set about the task of mapping the galaxy, assessing its extent and judging its motion. One obvious possibility was that our galaxy might be similar to the spiral nebulae visible through telescopes. How precisely the sun related to other stars in the galaxy remained equally controversial. A major breakthrough came with J.C. Kapteyn's (1851-1922) theory of galactic rotation. Rejecting the traditional view that stars moved essentially randomly through the heavens, Kapteyn claimed that they move systematically in two main directions (star streams). Why this should be remained unclear until Bertil Lindblad (1895-1965) argued that the galaxy was best considered as made up of a number of sub-systems, each with a different speed of rotation around a common rotational axis. Lindblad's hypothesis was verified by J.H. Oort (b.1900) by observational techniques.   R.P.

Bibl: R.W. Smith, *The Expanding Universe* (Cambridge, 1982).

galaxy. One of the collections of stars and gas into which the matter of the universe has been condensed by GRAVITATION. Galaxies usually rotate, resulting in a discusshaped structure with spiral arms. The earth and sun are situated about halfway out from the centre of our own galaxy, the Milky Way, which is about 30,000 PARSECS across. See also EXPANSION OF THE UNIVERSE.   M.V.B.

galaxy clusters. Aggregates of galaxies, containing as few as about 20 members as in the case of the local group of galaxies to which the Milky Way belongs, to as many as several thousand member galaxies. The nearest large galaxy cluster to us is the Virgo Cluster. The larger clusters, containing the densest concentration of galaxies, are usually of spherical appearance and predominantly consist of elliptical (rather than spiral) galaxies. Irregularly shaped clusters lack a central concentration of galaxies and contain all types of galaxy. The most prominent and richly populated clusters are called *rich clusters* or *Abell clusters* and several thousand were catalogued by George Abell. Extensive catalogues of galaxies and galaxy clusters have been compiled, most notably the Zwicky, Shane-Wirtanen and Harvard Center for Astrophysics surveys. (See NGC.)

In recent years there has arisen observational evidence that galaxy clustering occurs in filamentary chains which overlap to create a cobweb network in the universe. One characteristic of this picture is the expectation that there exist large VOID regions in which there exist no visible galaxies.

DARK MATTER is known to exist in large quantities within galaxy clusters. The brightest member galaxies of rich clusters have very similar luminosities and are usually very powerful radio sources. Large amounts of hot gas, at temperatures of several million degrees Kelvin at which X-rays are emitted, have also been found to exist in between galaxies in rich clusters. Galaxy clusters are themselves often found to be aggregated into *superclusters* of irregular shape. These are believed to be the largest structures in the universe.

The existence of galaxy clusters is believed to be an inevitable consequence of the attractive nature of gravity which tends to make a slightly non-uniform distribution of MASS become distributed in a progressively non-uniform fashion. J.D.B.

Bibl: F. Shu, *The Physical Universe* (Mill Valley, Ca., 1982); A. Sandage, M. Sandage and J. Kristian (eds.), *Galaxies and the Universe* (Chicago, 1975).

Galilean moons. The moons (sometimes termed 'satellites', following Kepler) Callisto, Europa, Ganymede and Io orbiting the planet Jupiter which were discovered by the Italian scientist Galileo Galilei (1564-1642) in 1610 using the first astronomical telescope which he had invented in 1609. Their orbits lie close to the plane through the equator of Jupiter. They were first photographed by the Pioneer space missions in 1973 and 1974 and were spectacularly filmed by the Voyager space probes in 1979. Io was found to have volcanic activity on its surface; the surfaces of Ganymede and Callisto were found to be heavily cratered by impacts of small bodies; Ganymede is known to possess an atmosphere probably of ammonia and methane gases. J.D.B.

Galois theory, see under ALGEBRA.

galvanic skin response (GSR). A change in the electrical resistance of the skin occurring in moments of strong EMOTION; measurements of this change are used in lie detector tests. Galvanic skin response is also called psychogalvanic response (PGR). C.E.D.

game theory. The theory of rational behaviour of two or more people in circumstances where their interests are, at least in part, conflicting. As the interests of players conflict, in selecting a STRATEGY a player should take account of the reaction of rivals to the strategy. The theory was first developed by von Neumann and Morgenstern for the case of two-person *zero-sum games* (i.e. the gain of one participant is the loss of the other). They proposed a concept of EQUILIBRIUM known as the *maximin* in which each person chooses a strategy that maximizes the minimum gain the other player can impose on him (or minimizes the maximum loss — *minimax*). A solution to this problem must exist if the player can choose mixed strategies (i.e. strategies in which the player chooses his action at random with PROBABILITIES assigned to the possible actions). The concept of mixed strategies has been criticized as they implicitly assume that a player moves from a maximin strategy that only considers the worst possible outcome of each action, to making a probabilistic choice in which the utility of different outcomes is considered. Mixed strategies may be rather unrealistic, but they could be used to confuse rivals. In n-person *non-zero-sum games*, it may be in the interests of the participants to cooperate and form coalitions. Such games are of more general interest as they reflect the circumstances of, for example, NUCLEAR

WAR OLIGOPOLY and bargaining. The most famous example of a non-zero-sum game is the *prisoner's dilemma*, which concerns two persons suspected of committing a crime together and who are interviewed simultaneously, but separately. If both prisoners admit guilt they both receive sentences of, say, ten years. If one admits guilt and the other remains silent, they receive sentences of one and twenty years respectively. If they both remain silent, they both receive sentences of two years for being present at the scene of the crime. The action of admitting guilt is the best choice of action whatever the action of the other prisoner. However, both suspects would receive short prison sentences if they cooperated and remained silent. The trust necessary for such co-operation may evolve through repetition of the dilemma and punitive behaviour towards cheating. The willingness of players to retaliate, threats and stubbornness are all important aspects of the theory and playing of games. ECONOMICS and other SOCIAL SCIENCES paid little attention to many of the concepts and ideas of game theory until recently. Though game theory has suggested many interesting ideas and concepts concerning cooperation and rivalrous behaviour, it has provided few categorical and general solutions to the problems encountered in this subject. J.P.

Bibl: W.J. Baumol, *Economic Theory and Operations Analysis* (London, 4th ed., 1977); E.R. Weintraub, *Conflict and Cooperation in Economics* (London, 1975).

gamete (or *germ cell*). In sexual reproduction, the reproductive CELLS, comprising spermatozoa and ova, the former generally mobile, the latter stationary. Gametes are distinguished from ordinary somatic cells by having only half the adult number of CHROMOSOMES. The regular DIPLOID number is restored when the gametes unite to form a ZYGOTE. See also MEIOSIS; MENDEL'S LAWS. P.M.

gamma rays. Electromagnetic RADIATION emitted in the form of PHOTONS during RADIOACTIVE decay. The wavelength is about the same as the size of an atomic NUCLEUS (see ATOMIC PHYSICS) or smaller. M.V.B.

gamodeme, see under DEME.

Gang of Four. A group in Chinese politics comprising of Yao Wenyuan, Zhang Chunqiao, Wang Hongwen, and Jiang Qing. Originally all from Shanghai, they rapidly rose to positions of power during the CULTURAL REVOLUTION, largely due to the influence that one-time actress Jiang Qing exerted over her husband, Chairman Mao. After Mao's death, a power struggle emerged between the Jiang Qing clique and the self-proclaimed successor to Chairman Mao, Hua Guofeng, which culminated in Hua teaming up with army factions opposed to the policies of the Cultural Revolution, and the subsequent arrest of the Gang of Four on 6 October 1976. From November 1980 to January 1981, the four were tried along with six members of the so-called 'Lin Biao Clique' for crimes committed under the cover of the Cultural Revolution; death sentences passed on Jiang and Zhang were later commuted to life imprisonment, with Wang also facing a life term, and Yao being sentenced to 20 years. By blaming the Gang of Four for the destructive excesses of the mobs, and the deaths of prominent figures during the period of 'Politics in Command', the new leadership could repudiate the policies of the Cultural Revolution without directly attacking Mao himself. S.B.

Bibl: J. Gardner, *Chinese Politics and the Succession to Mao* (London, 1982).

garden cities. Towns built originally as part of a late-19th-century reformist movement derived from the UTOPIAN IDEAL in planning. They were to be places of work and residence on land of low value, and to combat the social, economic, and ENVIRONMENTAL evils of the industrial city. Though there are earlier examples at Bournville and Port Sunlight, the idea was first comprehensively outlined by Ebenezer Howard in 1898 in *Tomorrow: A Peaceful Path to Real Reform*, later renamed *Garden Cities of Tomorrow*. The first garden city designed as such was built at Letchworth, from 1903 onwards, in the form of English cottages within an arcadian setting of trees and winding roads. This visual motif was later transferred to

343

the design of garden suburbs in many parts of the world. See also SUBURBIA.

M.BR.

Bibl: W.L. Creese, *The Search for Environment* (London and New Haven, 1966).

gas bearing. A simple bearing in which a cylindrical shaft rotates in a cylindrical hole of slightly larger diameter. The space between shaft and cylinder is filled with gas at high pressure whose viscosity is such that when rotating at speed there is no metal-to-metal contact between shaft and cylinder. The frictional drag in such bearings is very much less than in, say, a ball race. See also REYNOLDS WEDGE ACTION.

E.R.L.

gas chromatography. A CHROMATOGRAPHIC method of chemical separation in which a gas or vapour is passed through a stationary PHASE, usually in a heated column, of high surface area. The technique employs either solids or more commonly a liquid phase, e.g. a high-boiling-poing hydrocarbon on a solid support. Extensively used since the early 1950s, its main application is in the separation and analysis of mixtures of volatile organic compounds. Quantities less than 10^{-10} grams may often be detected.

B.F.

gastroenterology. The sub-speciality of medicine devoted to the study of diseases of the gastrointestinal system. Included are conditions affecting the oesophagus, stomach, duodenum, liver, gall bladder, pancreas, small intestine, colon, rectum and anal canal. The term embraces all aspects of disease, i.e. causation (aetiology), diagnosis and treatment and incorporates the study of such common disorders as peptic ulcer, CANCER of the stomach and colon, gall stones, diverticular disease, colitis and bowel infections. Disorders of the gastrointestinal system are common and account for approximately ten per cent of morbidity in the population generally. The cause of many gastrointestinal disorders remains unknown but dietary and other environmental factors are assuming a more important role than was hitherto given credence. The diagnosis of gastrointestinal diseases depends particularly on careful symptom analysis and patient examination with confirmatory special investigations frequently being required. Imaging the various parts of the gastrointestinal tract is the province of the RADIOLOGY and medical physics departments. Hollow organs such as the stomach and colon are demonstrated by the use of radio-opaque contrast media (usually barium), whereas solid organs such as the liver are studied by various scanning techniques, for example *ultrasound*, radioactive isotopes, *CT scanning*. With the advent of FIBRE OPTICS, instruments are now available which allow direct inspection of the lumen of the oesophagus, stomach and duodenum (upper gastrointestinal endoscopy) and colon (sigmoidoscopy; colonoscopy). In consequence it is not only possible to establish whether or not disease is present but specimens of tissue can be taken (biopsy) for microscopical examination (HISTOLOGY). Various treatment procedures can now also be carried out using fibre-optic instruments. Solid organs such as the liver can also be biopsied through the skin using special needles. Despite modern diagnostic methods, the cause of a patient's symptoms (particularly pain) may still not be established and an exploratory operation advised for this purpose (laparotomy). In addition to establishing a diagnosis, the necessary procedure to cure or alleviate the patient's complaint can be carried out at the same time. This may involve removal of various parts of the gastrointestinal tract, for example stomach (gastrectomy), gall bladder (cholecystectomy) or colon (colectomy). Removal of the latter sometimes requires the opening of the large bowel on to the wall of the abdomen (colostomy) as a temporary or permanent procedure. Also the end of the small intestine may be opened on to the abdominal wall (ileostomy) for various reasons. Although SURGERY remains an important diagnostic and therapeutic option, many gastrointestinal disorders can now be controlled if not cured by modern drug therapy. Hopefully, with a better understanding of the causation of disease, the spectrum of gastrointestinal disorders amenable to drug therapy will increase and the need for patients to be submitted to excision of various parts of the gastrointestinal tract gradually reduced.   R.H.S.

gastrulation, see under EMBRYOLOGY.

gate. The basic circuit element in a COMPUTER. There are three main types of gate, each having several INPUTS and a single output. All inputs and outputs can be stable at one of two voltages representing 0 and 1. An *and-gate* gives 1 on its output only if all its inputs are 1's; an *or-gate* gives 1 on its output if any of its inputs are 1's; a *nand-gate* gives 1 on its output unless all of its inputs are 1's. A large computer can contain many millions of gates in its LOGIC circuits.   C.S.

Gate Theatre. (1) A London theatre devoted to the performance of new and experimental drama from 1925 until its closure in 1940. Under Peter Godfrey, later under Norman Marshall, the Gate introduced English audiences to the work of Toller, Cocteau, Eugene O'Neill, Elmer Rice, and Maxwell Anderson, evading the restrictions of censorship by operating as a club theatre; Godfrey was the first English director to be influenced by EXPRESSIONISM. In its later years the Gate became famous for a series of intimate revues. (2) A Dublin theatre founded in 1928 by Hilton Edwards and Micheál Mac Liammóir, devoted to the performance of world classics as well as contemporary Irish drama.   M.A.
  Bibl: (1) N. Marshall, *The Other Theatre* (London, 1947).

GATT (General Agreement on Tariffs and Trade). An international agreement, between countries accounting for over 80% of world trade, covering levels of tariffs (i.e. import duties) and a code of behaviour for governments in international trade. The GATT secretariat is in Geneva. As a result of seven rounds of multilateral negotiations (see BILATERALISM AND MULTILATERALISM), starting in 1947 and ending in 1967, tariffs on manufactures imported by the developed countries have been very substantially reduced. There has been less success in freeing trade in agricultural products, and various *non-tariff barriers* in trade, in general outlawed by the GATT, are attracting more attention.

Developing countries (see UNDERDEVELOPMENT) are absolved from making reciprocal concessions, and many impose severe restrictions on trade.   M.FG.S.
  Bibl: B. Sodersten, *International Trade* (London, 1980).

gauge invariant, see under ELEMENTARY PARTICLES.

Gaullism. A major political movement and IDEOLOGY in France directly associated with the personality and political ideas of General Charles de Gaulle, President of France between 1958 and 1969. The central tenets of Gaullism may be summarized as follows: the primacy of national unity and a denial of the MARXIST notion of CLASS war; the need for order and authority in all branches of public life; the defence of a powerful state and strong executive authority; the creation (supported by the state) of a modern industrial economy; and the assertion of national independence in foreign and European affairs (see FORCE DE FRAPPE).
  In 1976 the Gaullist party changed its name to the *Rassemblement pour la République* (RPR) and elected Jacques Chirac to the presidency of the party. The party organization was also strengthened and the statutes altered to increase the authority of the party leader. These changes marked the beginning of a steady — albeit rather slow — revival of the party's fortunes; following the 1986 legislative elections the RPR became the dominant partner in the right-wing coalition government and Chirac was appointed Prime Minister. Between 1981 and 1986 the dominant ideology of the Gaullist party underwent a significant change from the doctrines associated with General de Gaulle. The *Gaullisme Chiraquien* is POPULIST, NEO-LIBERAL and NATIONALIST in outlook. Since coming to power in March 1986 the Gaullist government has pursued neo-liberal socio-economic policies which contrast sharply with the statist policies of previous Gaullist regimes. (See PRESIDENTIALISM.   S.M.
  Bibl: V. Wright, *The Government and Politics of France* (London, 1983).

Gaussian distribution, see NORMAL DISTRIBUTION.

gay, see under HOMOSEXUALITY.

gay politics. A theoretical analysis and/or ACTIVIST practice intended to correct perceived injustices in historical and current attitudes towards homosexual acts and HOMOSEXUALS. Used loosely, the phrase should be understood to refer both to lesbian politics and to gay men's politics. These are far from identical in their concerns and priorities, though there is overlap both in shared ideas and in co-operative work in post-1969 'gay movement' creations such as information switchboards staffed by volunteers (e.g. London Lesbian and Gay Switchboard, which is the world's largest, taking a quarter of a million calls a year), newspapers and periodicals (though gay men's greater purchasing power has tended to prohibit 50/50 editorial coverage); AIDS counselling and information services (e.g. Gay Men's Health Crisis, in New York; Terrence Higgins Trust and Scottish Aids Monitor, in the U.K.) and non-commercial social venues (e.g. London Lesbian and Gay Centre, originally funded 1985-6 by the Greater London Council, 42% of membership being women). Though rooted in 19th-century western European and American speculations *about* homosexuals and self-description and speculation by homosexuals, gay politics is for historical purposes considered to have its start in the Gay Liberation Front (GLF) which emerged after the 'Stonewall Riots' in New York in the days immediately following 27 June 1969. Patrons of a gay bar named the Stonewall had fought back against a routine raid by police. A movement without membership, GLF spread rapidly to Australasia, through the West generally, and in some degree in the Eastern bloc. As a specific political movement and/or organization, GLF largely disappeared by about 1972. It is most notable as having expressed vociferously and publicly (hence, almost unprecedented) anger by homosexuals of both sexes at the stigmas of 'illness', 'PERVERSION' and 'criminality' imposed by medicine, PSYCHIATRY, RELIGION, statute law, and in the general CULTURE and MEDIA. Rebelliousness against generally contemptuous attitudes within earlier liberation movements of the 1960s such as the black CIVIL RIGHTS and women's organizations — in which homosexuals had played significant but at the time unacknowledged roles — also played a vital part in the emergence of gay politics. From c.1982, initially in the U.S., gay politics globally has overwhelmingly had to concentrate on a response to the vulnerability of gay men to the AIDS virus, and to the homosexual role in its transmission — pioneering, for instance, the concept of 'safer sex' now encouraged among all sectors of the population and addressing revived religious condemnation of any sexual conduct outside marriage.   A.L.

Bibl: J. Weeks, *Coming Out* (London, 1977); D. Altman, *Aids and the New Puritanism* (London and Sydney, 1986).

GCD (general and comprehensive disarmament), see under DISARMAMENT.

GCSE, see under EXAMINATIONS.

Gdansk Agreement. Signed on 31 August 1980 by Lech Walesa, the leader of the newly established independent trade union SOLIDARITY and representatives of the Polish government, the Gdansk Agreement stipulated that the government should implement a wide range of political and economic reforms. It recognized the need to create new TRADE UNIONS free of control by official institutions and it forced the government to accept the right to strike. A wage increase for all workers and the introduction of a five day week were also agreed. Other economic provisions were EGALITARIAN in character and included a number of improvements in welfare and an economic reform which involved self-management and workers' democracy. Management and other administrative personnel were to be appointed on merit rather than because of loyalty to the COMMUNIST Party, a measure which the Party subsequently saw as challenging its leading role in society. In addition political reforms were proposed in the agreement, such as a restriction of censorship and of police activities. The agreement was never fully implemented by the government and it was revoked after the suppression of Solidarity in 1981.   D.PR.

Bibl: N. Ascherson, *The Polish August* (Harmondsworth, 1981).

GDP (gross domestic product). The output produced within an economy during a specified time period. GDP measures the contribution to ECONOMIC WELFARE made by private and public supply of goods and services for consumption, and INVESTMENT, which is needed in order to maintain or improve the future supply of goods and services. As it is a 'gross' figure, the depreciation of the CAPITAL stock is excluded. *Net domestic product* is GDP adjusted for depreciation of the capital stock. GDP can be measured in three different ways, all of which, in principle, give the same result. (1) The expenditure method measures the value of the expenditure necessary to purchase output. (2) The income method measures the incomes generated in producing the output. (3) The value-added method measures and adds together the value of the net addition to output made at every stage of production. In all these methods, in theory, there is no double counting of the production of intermediate products that are used as the inputs of other products. The output of many publicly supplied goods and services has to be valued at their cost, rather than their value, as they are not sold in a market. Among economists there are some, but not major, differences of opinion about what constitutes GDP and NATIONAL ACCOUNTING conventions sometimes differ between countries. (See GNP.)
J.P.
Bibl: D. Begg *et al.*, *Economics* (London, 1984).

gearing ratio. In ECONOMICS, the ratio of a firm's borrowing to the total value of money raised by the firm from shares and borrowing. As interest has to be paid on debt when the rate of return on CAPITAL is less than the interest rate, shareholders of firms with higher gearing ratios receive lower returns on their EQUITY and such firms are more likely to become bankrupt. However, when the return on capital is greater than the interest rate, the shareholders of firms with higher gearing ratios will receive a greater return on their equity.
J.P.

Bibl: J. Craven, *Introduction to Economics* (Oxford, 1984).

Gebrauchs- (utility...). One aspect of FUNCTIONALISM in Germany, associated particularly with the NEUE SACHLICHKEIT period, was the development of a 'utility music' and 'utility poetry', or *Gebrauchsmusik* and *Gebrauchslyrik*, on the analogy of *Gebrauchsgrafik* or commercial art, whose development in the late 1920s at the BAUHAUS and the Reimann School in Berlin stemmed from the same social-aesthetic ethos. Musical functionalism of this kind was associated particularly with Hindemith and typified in his opera *Neues vom Tage* (1929). Its poetic counterpart was christened in an article of 1928 by Kurt Tucholsky and developed most notably by Erich Kästner in light but sharply satirical rhymed verse.
J.W.

geiger counter. A device for measuring levels of RADIOACTIVITY. RADIATION from a decaying atomic NUCLEUS produces a burst of IONS in a gas. These are attracted to ELECTRODES, thus producing a pulse of electric current which can be amplified and fed into a counter.
M.V.B.

Geistesgeschichte, see CULTURAL HISTORY.

Geisteswissenschaften (literally, 'sciences of the spirit'). The disciplines that investigate man, society, and history; broadly speaking, HISTORY, PSYCHOLOGY, and the SOCIAL SCIENCES (SOCIOLOGY, ANTHROPOLOGY, POLITICAL SCIENCE, ECONOMICS). The great development of the human and social sciences in the 19th century had been speculatively reflected in Hegel's philosophy of Spirit, which treated human nature, social INSTITUTIONS, and the aspects of high CULTURE (art, RELIGION, and PHILOSOPHY) as constituting an autonomous realm, superior to, as well as distinct from, that of the material world. By the end of the century the idea was widely held that quite different methods of enquiry were appropriate to the domains of nature and spirit. Nature is to be *explained*, positivistically (see POSITIVISM), by the subsumption of its events under universal laws, inductively arrived at (see INDUCTION); spirit, the field of the *Geistes-*

347

wissenschaften, requires *understanding*, i.e. the sympathetic apprehension of the unique individuality of the persons, institutions, and events of which it is composed. The METHODOLOGICAL distinctness between the NATURAL SCIENCES and the human and social sciences is still an issue of vigorous controversy.   A.Q.

Bibl: G.H. von Wright, *Explanation and Understanding* (London and New York, 1971).

gel filtration, see under BIOPHYSICS.

Gemeinschaft and ***Gesellschaft.*** Two common German words ('community' and 'society') which were used by the sociologist Ferdinand Tönnies in 1887 to contrast a social relationship of solidarity between individuals based on affection, KINSHIP, or membership of a COMMUNITY such as a family or group of friends (*Gemeinschaft*) with one based upon the DIVISION OF LABOUR and contractual relations between isolated individuals consulting only their own self-interest (*Gesellschaft*). Both terms are used as mental CONSTRUCTS or IDEAL TYPES which, though they do not correspond to any existing society, together provide a pair of contrasting hypotheses that can be used in investigating any system of social relationship.   A.L.C.B.

Bibl: F. Tönnies, tr. and ed. C.P. Loomis, *Community and Association* (London, 1955); as *Community and Society* (New York, 1963); and, for a modern version, C.P. Loomis and J.A. Beagle, *Rural Sociology* (Englewood Cliffs, N.J., rev. ed., 1957).

gender. Social construction of male/female identity which is distinguished from sex, the biologically-based distinction between men and women. Gender is an integral part of the process of social classification and organization. It is both a set of ideas (a way of thinking about relations, of influencing behaviour, a set of symbols) and a principle of social organization (allocation to ROLES, DIVISION OF LABOUR). Gender is also an idiom for talking about the relationship between nature and CULTURE. Gender has to be understood within a social context. Although the characteristics associated with male-ness (masculinity: active/rational) and female-ness (femininity: passive/emotional) give the impression of being 'natural' or biologically founded, they are in fact culturally constructed and variable as early work in ANTHROPOLOGY indicated (M. Mead, *Sex and Temperament in Three Primitive Societies*, 1935). The working of the concept of gender has been important in FEMINIST analyses of patriarchal societies (see PATRIARCHY). In particular, gender has been examined as an ideological mechanism in the subordination of women (i.e. the association of women with 'natural' activities like childbearing which confine them as homemakers to private/domestic space). The family has been understood as an important site for the inculcation of gender roles.   A.G.

Bibl: C. MacCormack and M. Strathern (eds.), *Nature, Culture and Gender* (Cambridge, 1980).

gene. Originally (Johannsen, 1909), the atom or unit of heredity, corresponding to Mendel's factors; today, the functional unit is known to be made of NUCLEIC ACID and to specify, via the GENETIC CODE, a single gene product that is a PROTEIN. Generally there is a single primary gene product, as in the hypothesis 'one gene — one ENZYME', or 'one gene — one antigen' (see IMMUNITY), but gene SPLICING can result in alternative products. For each primary function it is typically the case that an individual receives one gene from each parent, each situated at a particular place or LOCUS on the corresponding CHROMOSOMES. The two genes at a locus may differ, in which case they are said to be different ALLELES (or *allelomorphs*). An individual with two identical genes at a locus is a *homozygote*; one with two different alleles is a *heterozygote*. In a heterozygote, it is often the case that only one of the two alleles produces an observed effect. In such cases the allele which produces an effect is said to be *dominant*, the other *recessive*. The recessive allele produces an observed effect only in a homozygote. The superior fitness (see DARWINISM) of a heterozygote to a homozygote is known as *heterosis*, and is important as a cause of variability in natural populations, and of the decline in vigour caused by inbreeding. See also GENET-ICS. J.M.S.;P.N.

Bibl: Bruce Alberts *et al.*, *Molecular Biology of the Cell* (New York, 1983); Benjamin Lewin, *Genes II* (Bristol, 1985).

gene bank. (1) A collection of genetic material, such as seeds or sperm. (2) A synonym for gene library (see DNA LIBRARY). P.N.

gene library, see under DNA LIBRARY.

gene splicing. The production of recombinant DNA (see SPLICING; GENETIC ENGINEERING). P.N.

gene therapy. The concept of curing a genetic disease by providing the sufferer with a good copy of the defective GENE that is the cause of the disease. Ideally, the good copy would replace the defective gene but in practice that is neither possible nor necessary. Diseases of the bone marrow will be the first to be treated because the marrow is readily accessible and amenable to gene therapy. Any embryo obtained by in vitro fertilization (see INFERTILITY) and found to be genetically defective could also be a target for gene therapy but until the techniques are perfected it might be preferable not to implant a defective embryo rather than to try and correct its defect. P.N.

Bibl: D.J. Weatherall, *The New Genetics and Clinical Practice* (Oxford, 2nd ed., 1986).

genealogical method, see under KINSHIP.

General Agreement on Tariffs and Trade, see GATT.

General Certificate of Secondary Education, see under EXAMINATIONS.

general systems theory (GST). A movement in scientific theory which originated from developments in the 1940s and 1950s. It has influenced almost every scientific discipline, including the SOCIAL SCIENCES, and was a reaction against the atomistic and fragmented acquisition of knowledge resulting from excessive specialization. One major source of im-

petus towards a more holistic approach arose in the biological sciences. In studying living organisms' interactions with their ENVIRONMENT it was found rewarding to study the whole ecological system (see ECOLOGY) as a single unit, and the processes by which living organisms maintain homeostasis or metabolic EQUILIBRIUM while adapting to changes in their environment. Other important influences were the growth of CYBERNETICS and information science, particularly such aspects as FEEDBACK, automatic control and ARTIFICIAL INTELLIGENCE. The General Systems Theory movement went much further than simply seeking to avoid REDUCTIONISM and analysing complex interactions. It sought to discover general patterns, trends and structural characteristics in all types of system — natural, social and technological — and on this basis to develop a unifying General Systems Theory of universal applicability. As the extreme difficulty of this ambitious task became clear in the 1960s and 1970s, the confidence of this movement has faltered, even in the biological and applied sciences. Its application to the social sciences was extremely problematic from the outset. For example, the anarchical and decentralized character of international relations and the weaknesses and irrationalities of decision-making by STATES make them particularly intractable for the scientific systems theorist. It is hence not surprising to find that many of the GST regional and global models are impoverished by serious neglect or inadequacy of the political dimensions, national and international. The only major area of international relations in which systems analysis has been of major practical value has been in the field of defence policy-making, where it is a proven tool for weapons evaluation, procurement, and logistical planning. P.W.

Bibl: L. von Bertalanffy, *General Systems Theory* (New York, 1969).

generalized phrase structure grammar (GPSG). In LINGUISTICS, a theory developed in the late 1970s as an alternative to accounts of language which rely on the notion of syntactic transformations (see TRANSFORMATIONAL GRAMMAR). In GPSG there are no transformations at all, and the syntactic structure of a sentence is represented by a single TREE DIAGRAM of its phrase structure.   D.C.

Bibl: G. Gazdar *et al.*, *Generalized Phrase Structure Grammar* (Oxford, 1985).

generation (of COMPUTERS). A TAXONOMY of computers according to the kind of TECHNOLOGY employed. First generation computers used THERMIONIC valves; the second generation used discrete TRANSISTORS; the third and subsequent generations use INTEGRATED CIRCUITS. The fourth generation is characterized by its use of PROBLEM-ORIENTED LANGUAGES, particularly for commercial applications; the fifth by its use of novel forms of COMPUTER ARCHITECTURE, which it is hoped will result in machines of such enormous power that they will be able to tackle hitherto impossible applications, such as the interpretation of complicated spoken instructions. The fifth generation is the subject of much international competition.   J.E.S.

generative grammar. A CONCEPT developed by Noam Chomsky in *Syntactic Structures* (The Hague, 1957), which makes it possible, by the application of a finite number of *rewrite rules*, to predict ('generate') the infinite number of sentences in a language and to specify their structure. Of several possible MODELS of generative grammar he discusses three:

(1) *Finite-state* grammars generate by working through a sentence 'from left to right'; an initial element is selected, and thereafter the possibilities of occurrence of all other elements are wholly determined by the nature of the elements preceding them; Chomsky shows how this extremely simple kind of GRAMMAR is incapable of accounting for many important processes of sentence formation.

(2) *Phrase-structure* grammars contain ordered rules which are capable not only of generating strings of linguistic elements, but also of providing a CONSTITUENT ANALYSIS of these strings, and hence more information about sentence formation.

(3) *Transformational* grammars are in Chomsky's view the most powerful of all, in that very many sentence types can be economically derived by supplementing the constituent analysis rules of phrase-structure grammars with rules for transforming one sentence into another. Thus a rule for 'passivization' would take an active sentence and re-order its elements so as to produce a passive sentence — a procedure both simpler and intuitively more satisfactory than generating active and passive sentences separately in the same grammar. In recent years the role of transformations has been questioned, and alternative approaches devised (e.g. GENERALIZED PHASE STRUCTURE GRAMMAR). In the so-called 'standard' theory of the 1960s, a transformational-generative grammar consists of (*a*) a *syntactic component*, comprising a basic set of phrase-structure rules (sometimes called the *base component*) which provide the DEEP STRUCTURE information about the sentences of a language, and a set of transformational rules for generating *surface structures*; (*b*) a *phonological component*, which provides for converting strings of syntactic elements into pronounceable utterance; and (*c*) a *semantic component*, which provides information about the meaning of the lexical items to be used in sentences (see LEXICON). Later developments (in the 1970s) became known as the EXTENDED STANDARD THEORY and the revised extended standard theory. See BINDING.   D.C.

Bibl: see under CHOMSKYAN; GRAMMAR.

genetic assimilation. Term coined by C.H. Waddington, 1953, for a process which mimics Lamarckian inheritance (see LAMARCKISM) without involving directed MUTATION. If those members of a population which respond to an environmental STIMULUS in a particular way are selected, naturally or artificially, this will result in the accumulation of GENES which favour the response, until the response appears without the environmental stimulus.

     J.M.S.

genetic code. The 'dictionary' relating the sequence of nucleotides in a DNA MOLECULE (see NUCLEIC ACID) with the AMINO ACIDS whose nature and order of assembly into a PROTEIN they specify. An amino acid is specified not by a single nucleotide but by a triplet of nucleotides; thus uracil-

uracil-uracil specifies the amino acid phenylalanine. Some triplets are either nonsensical, in the sense that they do not specify or code for any amino acid, or are 'punctuation marks' marking the beginning or the end of a certain stretch of genetic information. A consensus of scientists considers that the complex of discoveries comprising the discovery of the genetic functions of DNA, the genetic code, and the mechanism of *transcription* and *translation* constitute the greatest intellectual achievement of modern science.

P.M.;J.M.S.;P.N.

Bibl: J.D. Watson, *Molecular Biology of the Gene* (New York, 3rd ed., 1976).

genetic counselling, see under MEDICAL GENETICS.

genetic drift. Changes occurring in GENE frequency in a population as a result of random processes rather than selection, MUTATION or migration. Drift becomes important only when population size is small, so that SAMPLING error occurs when genes are transmitted from one generation to the next. This happens if a population is small and remains so (e.g. on an island), if the population size fluctuates markedly (e.g. varying with a seasonal food supply), or if a new population is founded by a small group leaving an established population.

A.CL.

Bibl: J.S. Gale, *Population Genetics* (London, 1980).

genetic engineering. Deliberate alteration of a piece of DNA (see NUCLEIC ACID), often a GENE. The alteration can consist of removing part of the DNA, adding extra DNA or substituting one piece of DNA for another. Gene CLONING is used to obtain sufficient DNA for the experimental procedures employed, which involve cutting pieces of DNA with RESTRICTION ENZYMES and then recombining the required pieces. The resulting recombinant DNA is most likely to have been constructed either for some experimental test of the function of the engineered DNA or for use in BIOTECHNOLOGY. A typical example of the latter is the engineering of the human gene for insulin into the GENOME of a bacterium or yeast so that upon culture large quantities of the hormone are pro-

duced by the micro-organism. Fears that such 'tinkering' with nature and unnatural mixing of the genes of remote species would be hazardous have so far proved groundless. GENE THERAPY is a form of genetic engineering.

P.N.

Bibl: S. Prentis, *Biotechnology: A New Industrial Revolution* (London, 1985).

genetic epistemology. In DEVELOPMENTAL PSYCHOLOGY, a somewhat idiosyncratic PIAGETIAN coinage which appears to serve as an umbrella term for the theoretical ideas informing his own work on the development of knowledge and understanding in the growing child — a development which he regards, to a considerable extent, as being genetically pre-programmed.

C.L.-H.

Bibl: J.H. Flavell, *The Developmental Psychology of Jean Piaget* (London and Princeton, 1963); Jean Piaget, *Psychology and Epistemology* (Harmondsworth, 1972).

genetic explanation, see under EXPLANATION.

genetic linkage. The tendency for different characteristics to be inherited together. Gregor Mendel's experiments had led him to propose that such characteristics are inherited independently of each other, but William Bateson and others reported in 1905 that certain traits of the sweet pea flower appeared in the parental combinations more often than expected when different strains were crossed. These traits were coupled, or linked. A linkage group consists of all the traits in an organism that tend to be coinherited with any other member of the group: the physical basis of such a group is the CHROMOSOME. The closer that any two GENES are located on a chromosome, the less often will they be separated by recombination events at which genetic information is exchanged between members of a chromosome pair. Thus, the more tightly will the genes be linked. Of great importance is the determination of an organism's sex by its chromosomal constitution; traits inherited on a sex chromosome will be transmitted unequally to offspring of the two sexes.

A.CL.

Bibl: H.L.K. Whitehouse, *Towards an*

Understanding of the Mechanism of Heredity (London, 3rd ed., 1973).

genetic memory. A phrase sometimes employed by nature-philosophers, e.g. Ewald Hering, for the endowment by which, for example, a frog's egg 'remembers' to grow up into a frog. There is, however, no property of genetic memory that is not explicable in terms of ordinary GENETICS and heredity. Genetic memory therefore belongs to the strange philosophical museum that also contains racial memory, *élan vital* (see VITALISM), and ENTELECHY.

P.M.

genetic method. Not so much a precise method as an approach, marked by interest in origins and evolution, which dominated historical studies in the 19th century. More recently historians have been turning away from the 'idol of origins' (as Marc Bloch called it), the tendency to explain recent events in terms of the remote past. The genetic approach has been most successful in biography, and most dangerous, perhaps, when applied to the history of INSTITUTIONS. See also HISTORICISM.

P.B.

genetic psychology. A term used in the 1930s and 1940s to cover COMPARATIVE PSYCHOLOGY and DEVELOPMENTAL PSYCHOLOGY. It meant the phylogenetic and ontogenetic development (see PHYLOGENY; ONTOGENY) of human adult behaviour. This general approach persists and is still a valid one. The term itself, however, seems to have been dropped, probably to avoid confusion with behavioural GENETICS.

P.E.B.

genetic screening. The preliminary testing of large groups for inherited disorders. Newborn infants are regularly screened for phenylketonuria and congenital hypothyroidism by a blood spot taken at one week; pregnant women may be screened for fetal malformation by blood test and by ultrasound scan (see RADIOLOGY). Specific population groups may be screened for additional disorders, e.g. haemoglobin and other red blood cell disorders in Asian, African and Mediterranean groups. Carriers of rare metabolic diseases may be searched for amongst groups where the incidence is high. Screening procedures are recommended where a disorder causes severe illness or handicap, can be detected reliably and cheaply, and where early diagnosis improves the outcome.

A.CL.

genetic system. (1) The reproductive and hereditary processes of a population; (2) more generally, the totality of factors that control the flow of genetic information from one generation to the next.

J.M.S.

geneticism. A word coined in 1959 by P.B. Medawar on the model of EVOLUTIONISM, SCIENTISM, and HISTORICISM to refer to a scheme of thought which extravagantly overestimates the explanatory power of genetical ideas. The pretended explanation on genetic lines of every aspect of human character and every nuance of personality, and the interpretation of the rise and fall of nations along genetic lines, may all be said to belong to geneticism, which has the ill effect of bringing GENETICS into undeserved discredit.

P.M.

genetics. Word coined by William Bateson in 1905 for the science of *heredity*, i.e. the tendency of like to beget like. Its methods are the study of the numbers and kinds of progeny from sexual crosses, supplemented by a microscopic and chemical study (CYTOGENETICS) of the materials actually transmitted by parents to their offspring. Modern genetics originated with the work of Mendel on peas, published in 1865. Mendel used the ratios in which different characteristics appear among the offspring of sexual crosses to develop an atomic theory of heredity. The atoms of heredity, today called GENES, are present in two complete sets in the fertilized egg or ZYGOTE, one set being derived from each parent. (See also MENDELISM.)

Mendel's work was not appreciated at the time. With the rediscovery of his laws in 1900, it was soon recognized that genes are parts of CHROMOSOMES, which are visible at the time of division in the NUCLEI of all CELLS. The chromosome theory of heredity was in the main worked out by T.H. Morgan and his colleagues in the period 1914-28.

The original importance of genetics was that it provided a law of heredity which was the missing element in Darwin's theory of EVOLUTION by NATURAL SELECTION. (See also DARWINISM.) Today genetics can claim to be the central discipline of BIOLOGY. The discovery of the chemical constitution of genes by Watson, Crick, and Wilkins in 1952 revealed in its essentials the process whereby like begets like. This property of heredity, together with the properties of multiplication and variation, provides the necessary conditions for evolution by natural selection, and is therefore the most important property differentiating living from non-living things.

Biochemical (or *molecular*) *genetics* studies the chemical constitution of genes and their immediate products. *Physiological* (or *developmental*) *genetics* is concerned with the control of gene action and the role of genes in development. POPULATION GENETICS is concerned with the frequency of genes in populations, and the mechanism of evolution. *Behavioural genetics* is concerned with the hereditary basis of behaviour in man and in other animal species. Genetics has applications in medicine and in animal and plant breeding.

J.M.S.

Bibl: M. Szekely, *From DNA to Protein: the Transfer of Genetic Information* (London, 1980); R.A. Raff and T.C. Kaufman, *Embryos, Genes and Evolution* (London, 1983); A.C. Pai, *Foundations of Genetics: a Science for Society* (London, 1985).

genito-urinary medicine. The study of SEXUALLY TRANSMITTED DISEASES. In the U.K. this is a hospital-based speciality, formerly called venereology. This is partly to escape the stigma of the older name, and partly because many people attend the clinics for advice on genital conditions which are not strictly sexually transmitted. In other countries it is part of the public health service; in Europe and elsewhere it is usually linked with DERMATOLOGY — dermatovenereology.

J.D.O.

genocide. Term coined by American jurist Raphael Lemkin in 1944 to denote the physical destruction of a national, racial or ethnic population. The term was included in the indictment at NUREMBERG of German war criminals accused of involvement in Nazi attempts to exterminate the Jewish population of Europe. It acquired still wider currency in a United Nations Resolution of 11 December 1946 and UN Convention of 9 December 1948 which sought to make genocide a crime under INTERNATIONAL LAW. Details of the UN definition of the term are contested, for example by radical critics of COLONIALISM who view as genocide the destruction of the social fabric of a colonized people, but it remains the most widely accepted definition.

S.R.

Bibl: L. Kuper, *Genocide* (Harmondsworth and New York, 1981).

genodeme, see under DEME.

genome. The GENETIC apparatus of an organism considered as a whole and as characteristic of it, e.g. 'the human genome' referring to the chromosomal make-up (see CHROMOSOMES) characteristic of human beings and to the sum total of the genetic information which it embodies and imparts.

P.M.

genotype. The genetic constitution of an individual, as deduced from ancestry or breeding performance, in contrast to its *phenotype*, the characteristics which are manifested in the individual. The distinction is important because it is the genotype, not the phenotype, which is reproduced and can be transmitted to future generations.

J.M.S.

gentrification, see under URBAN RENEWAL.

gentry controversy. A controversy which began in 1941 when R.H. Tawney published an article on 'The Rise of the Gentry', arguing that the English Revolution of the mid 17th century resulted from the rise of a group of entrepreneur landlords between 1540 and 1640, and that political power followed economic. He was violently attacked by H.R. Trevor-Roper, who suggested that during that period the gentry were in fact in economic decline. Many historians joined in, finer distinctions were drawn, and both literary and statistical evidence received more careful scrutiny than they had first been given. In

353

the course of this 20-year controversy, English SOCIAL HISTORY came of age.

P.B.

Bibl: J.H. Hexter, 'Storm over the Gentry', in his *Reappraisals in History* (London, 1961; New York, 1963).

geochemistry. The description of the CHEMISTRY of the earth. Traditionally it involves the study of the abundance and distribution of ELEMENTS and their ISO-TOPES, mainly in the LITHOSPHERE, but also in the seas and the earth's atmosphere. Modern geochemistry is increasingly concerned with understanding the way in which the earth and SOLAR SYSTEM have evolved by means of a combined chemical and geological (see GEOLOGY) approach. B.F.

Bibl: W.S. Fyfe, *Geochemistry* (Oxford, 1974).

geochronology. Term used in ARCHAE-OLOGY to cover all DATING methods which are based on measurable changes in natural substances. They include ARCHAEO-MAGNETISM, DENDROCHRONOLOGY, RADIOCARBON DATING, THERMOLUMIN-ESCENCE, varve dating, and other techniques based on PHYSICS and CHEMISTRY.

B.C.

geodesic domes, see under DYMAXION.

geodesy. The observation and measurement of the size and external shape of the earth and the variations in terrestrial GRAVITY. Geodetic surveys based on geometric methods are only considered to be accurate for relatively small areas. Local surveys are referred to a world-wide reference surface, the *geoid*, which coincides with the mean-sea-level surface and its theoretical extension into the continental areas. The shape of the geoid, like the surface of the oceans, is determined by the gravitational attraction of the earth's mass. Since the earth is inhomogeneous, with an irregular distribution of mass (see ISOSTASY), the geoid is also an irregular surface. The precise tracking of artificial satellites has enabled this surface to be more accurately contoured. J.L.M.L.

geographical determinism, see under EN-VIRONMENTALISM.

geography. A body of knowledge organized around a number of broad themes: the relationship between natural and human worlds; the differences — both natural and humanly created — between different parts of the world; the spatial distributions exhibited by all manner of natural and human phenomena; the determinants of such distributions; and the particular environmental and locational associations peculiar to different sorts of phenomena. Furthermore, one feature common to almost all geographical studies has been their use of the *map* as a device for classifying, ordering, describing and explaining (or suggesting factors that might be important in explaining) certain aspects of phenomena under investigation. Behind these broad themes and features, however, there has been a plethora of diverse and often competing theoretical, METHODOLOGICAL and substantive orientations, and this diversity has led the discipline into recurrent crises of identity and self-doubt. And yet, in practice much of the work conducted by geographers has succeeded in being imaginative, bold in scope, sensitive to the very real problems faced by particular people, PLACES and environments, and — on a more methodological note — consistently open to both the ideas of other disciplines and the wider intellectual debates of philosophers and social theorists.

Despite the efforts of many geographers to tackle the intersection of natural and human worlds — efforts which include both older studies of the physical controls on human activity (see ENVIRONMENTAL-ISM) and more recent studies of such vital environmental issues as POLLUTION, the depletion of energy sources and desertification — it remains the case that the discipline straddles two very different bodies of knowledge: *physical geography* and *human geography* (and consider in this connection the differences between NATURAL SCIENCE and SOCIAL SCIENCE). In physical geography there has been a general shift in emphasis over the last 30 or so years from examining — often in a very descriptive fashion — regional landscape complexes and their long-term historical development ('DENUDATION chronology'), to employing much more analytic and quantitative techniques to study the sometimes quite small-scale and short-term physical *processes* that actively shape the landscape. In developing this new approach, physical geographers have drawn upon — and have themselves contributed to — such specialisms as CLIMATOLOGY, GEOPHYSICS, HYDROLOGY and SOIL SCIENCE, and much of the research now undertaken by these researchers is referred to as GEOMORPHOLOGY (the study of topographical forms and the processes that shape them).

In human geography a not dissimilar shift in emphasis has occurred, in that an older concern for the uniqueness of particular peoples and places — the hallmark of *regional geography* (see REGION; REGIONALISM) — was replaced in the late 1950s (but only in certain academic centres) by a SPATIAL SCIENCE concerned to discover the *universal laws* supposedly governing the *spatial organization* and *spatial behaviour* of human beings and their many productions. This manoeuvre called for a more rigorous theorization of the processes that shape the LOCATION of such phenomena as towns, factories, shops, transport routes and political boundaries (see LOCATIONAL ANALYSIS), and one upshot of researchers focusing their attention upon the patterns traced out by these different human productions was the splintering of human geography into various systematic branches: urban geography; industrial geography; retailing geography; transport geography; political geography. (Note, though, that terms such as 'urban geography' were in use before the advent of geography as spatial science, and note too that these terms are still employed as convenient short-hands by current researchers who in many cases would wish to distance themselves from spatial science.) Whilst this reformulation of geographical inquiry generated some important findings, it has itself been criticized on numerous counts, but notably by proponents of HUMANISTIC GEOGRAPHY — who stress the ways in which individual human agents both experience and creatively transform their geographical surroundings (see also PLACE) — and by proponents of RADICAL GEOGRAPHY — who stress the ways in which geographical distributions (and particularly geographically uneven distributions of wealth, WEL-FARE and resources) are embedded within the workings of complex economic, social and political structures. In consequence, whilst spatial science has continued to be an important part of the discipline (and has turned to ever more sophisticated mathematical modelling procedures), both the humanistic and radical approaches have gained ground over the last 15 or so years; the result being a new division within human geography involving much philosophic and social theoretic debate over what some commentators term the 'spatiality' of the world. At the same time researchers have displayed an increasing appreciation of both HISTORY (see HISTORICAL GEOGRAPHY) and issues such as CLASS, RACE and GENDER (see GEOGRAPHY OF GENDER).

In both physical and human geography, however, it might be argued that in recent years there has been a gradual 'rediscovery' and restatement of the unique nature of particular places and regions. In physical geography it is increasingly realized that, although geomorphological processes must ultimately obey the invariant laws of physics and chemistry, it is impossible to predict from these laws the precise manner in which the components of a particular drainage basin, glacial valley, saltmarsh or whatever are put together. Similarly, in human geography it is increasingly supposed that, whilst it may be possible to identify general tendencies present in the workings of advanced capitalist, socialist and developing societies, these tendencies are always played out in very different ways in different places, seemingly in reflection of the quite specific fashion in which local economies, social structures and political systems are constituted. A number of geographers have begun to draw upon philosophic and social theoretic materials to capture the importance of how both natural and human processes come together in specific ways in specific places, and in so doing they have discussed the tensions between the 'immanent' and the 'configurational' and between the 'compositional' and the 'contextual' (see CONTEXTUALITY).   C.P.

Bibl: R. Hartshorne, *Perspective on the Nature of Geography* (Chicago and London, 1959); R.J. Chorley and P. Haggett (eds.), *Models in Geography*

(London, 1967); P. Haggett, *Geography: a Modern Synthesis* (London and New York, 3rd ed., 1983); M. Clark, K.J. Gregory and A. Gurnell (eds.), *Horizons in Physical Geography* (London, 1987); D. Gregory and R. Walford (eds.), *Horizons in Human Geography* (London, 1987); R. Peet and J. Thrift (eds.), *New Models in Geography* (Boston and London, 1987).

geography of gender. Traditionally women have been 'hidden from geography', as is evident from the discipline's conventional concentration upon issues such as 'man's habitat' and 'man and environment'. This omission has been compounded by an emphasis on broad-brush research methodologies focusing on the sphere of production (the 'public') and on classical MARXIST class inequalities (see RADICAL GEOGRAPHY), rather than on the spheres of consumption and reproduction (the 'private'), which have been ideologically constructed as 'women's place'. There has recently been some attempt to redress the balance, especially from the 'Women and Geography' Study Group of the Institute of British Geographers. For example, it has been noted that urban spatial form has differential implications for women concerning their access to public facilities, employment, transport, retailing and so on. Women have, in addition, made up a large proportion of the workforce, and in recent years CAPITALISM has been able to 'take advantage' of the socially-constructed separations between men and women and between public and private (see above). The concentration of women in low-skilled, dull, repetitive jobs is a result of the social construction of GENDER (as differences between males and females) rather than any biologically-determined sex differences, and it is for this reason that a geography of gender — rather than of sex — is preferable. Gender, it must be stressed, includes men, and a study of the unequal POWER relations between men and women (PATRIARCHY) is essential to an understanding of geography and gender.　　　　M.LO.

Bibl: Institute of British Geographers, Women in Geography Study Group, *Geography and Gender: An Introduction to Feminist Geography* (London, 1984).

geoid, see under GEODESY.

geological time chart. The chronological arrangement of the geological events which are recorded in the most complete succession of rocks exposed on the earth's surface. A purely relative chronology of geological age has been constructed and is usually presented in the form of a stratigraphic column in which the fossiliferous rocks formed since the beginning of the Cambrian period (i.e. from about 600 million years ago) are arranged in vertical succession upwards. Radiometric methods (see RADIOCARBON DATING) give a reasonably accurate DATING, usually recorded in millions of years, of rocks, so that the time chart will also indicate the duration of the periods of known geological age. This method has been applied to the metamorphic rocks of pre-Cambrian age which are almost entirely devoid of fossils. The oldest rock of the continents has been dated by this method as 3,500 million years old.　　　　J.L.M.L.

geology. The scientific study of the earth and of other bodies in the SOLAR SYSTEM (e.g. the moon) which may provide evidence relating to its origin and evolution. The main activities of geology have been to map and classify the rocks exposed on the earth's surface and those accessible underground, and to explain their origin and distribution. The most important economic applications of geology are concerned with the discovery and exploitation of ore deposits, fossil fuels, construction materials and underground water.

　　　　J.L.M.L.

geomagnetism, see under MAGNETISM.

geometric art, see under ABSTRACT ART.

geometry. A branch of MATHEMATICS which arose from practical problems of mensuration. Euclidean space (of 2 or 3 dimensions) is an idealization of perceived space (see SPACE PERCEPTION) which can be characterized either algebraically (see below) or axiomatically. *Euclidean geometry* is the study of those properties of figures in Euclidean space which are invariant under the following TRANSFORMA-TIONS: (1) parallel displacements, (2) rotations, (3) reflections, (4) uniform dilations. The least evident of the AXIOMS for Euclidean space is the *fifth postulate* or *parallel axiom*, which, in 2 dimensions, asserts. 2 lines intersect if and only if they do not have the same direction. Unlike the other axioms, it presupposes that space is infinite in extent. Efforts (mostly 1750-1830) to derive it from the other axioms, or to find a more intuitively acceptable equivalent, led to the conception of *non-Euclidean geometry*. In *hyperbolic geometry*, for example, all the lines through a point P which make angles less than θ with a line l fail to intersect l; θ depends on the distance of P from l. In elliptic geometry any 2 lines intersect (and space is bounded — e.g. 'space' is the surface of a sphere and 'lines' are great circles). The transformations (1)-(4) no longer apply, in particular, uniform dilations do not exist. The historical importance of the discovery of non-Euclidean geometry is twofold: it disproved Kant's thesis that our intuitions of space are *a priori* and it encouraged the growth of the AXIOMATIC METHOD.

Projective geometry studies those properties of figures which are not only invariant under the transformations (1)-(4) but also (for 2 dimensions) under the transformation of projecting one plane from a point onto another plane; such projections were first introduced to study the conic sections. A point or line may be 'sent to infinity' by such a projection, so that the *projective plane* is got by adding a *line at infinity* to the Euclidean plane. Angles and distances are not projective concepts. *Affine geometry* is intermediate between Euclidean and projective geometry.

By introducing a system of COORDINATES, geometric objects and PROPOSITIONS may be expressed in algebraic terms. *Analytic geometry* is the study of this reduction for the particular case when the coordinates are obtained from a rectilinear system of axes. For example, in the plane, a straight line consists of all those points whose coordinates (x, y) satisfy an EQUATION of the form $ax+by+c=0$; a, b, c are the PARAMETERS of the line. In practice 'analytic geometry' usually refers to the more elementary investigations. *Algebraic geometry* is used for the more advanced studies where the figures are given by algebraic equations (see ALGEBRA).

From the algebraic point of view there is no reason to use exactly 3 coordinates; one generalizes to n dimension. Another generalization replaces real coordinates by COMPLEX NUMBERS or by elements of other appropriate MATHEMATICAL STRUCTURES. This is what recent work (since 1945) is mostly concerned with. The methods and concepts are wholly algebraic; applications are to NUMBER THEORY rather than to geometry in its original sense.

Analytic methods may be used even when a uniform system of coordinates is not available. For instance, on the surface of the earth the poles do not have a well-defined longitude. This is an example of a *manifold*; one can introduce coordinates locally and define geometric notions (e.g. distance) in terms of them. *Differential geometry* studies the way in which such local geometry may vary from point to point. In particular, *Riemannian geometry* studies (n-dimensional) manifolds in which a metric (i.e. a notion of distance) is given at each point. According to the *general theory* of RELATIVITY space-time constitutes a 4-dimensional manifold with a metric which determines the motion (under gravity) at each point, and which is determined by the distribution of matter.

R.G.

Bibl: D. Hilbert and S. Cohn-Vossen, tr. P. Nemenyi, *Geometry and the Imagination* (New York, 1952).

geomorphology. The study of the nature and evolution of the surface features of the earth, particularly those landscapes produced by sub-aerial erosion. All landscapes owe their form to a balance between constructional processes — such as volcanic eruption and mountain-building, and destructional processes — erosion by the agents water, ice, and wind. Geomorphological research has made it possible to identify distinctive landforms resulting from the predominating action of one of the agents of erosion, even when it has ceased to operate. The present landscape of northern Europe and North America, for example, retains the essential features of the glaciated landscape formed during the Pleistocene epoch, even though the glaciers retreated some 15,000 years ago.

J.L.M.L.

geophysics. An interdisciplinary science where the theories and techniques of PHYS-ICS are applied to the atmosphere, surface, and interior of the earth. In recent decades the study of earthquake waves and rock magnetism has led to the abandonment of the notion of a rigid earth ('*terra firma*'), and its replacement by theories involving the slow flow of rocks over geological time. See also CONTINENTAL DRIFT; PLATE TECTONICS; SEISMOLOGY.   M.V.B.

Bibl: R. Fraser, *Understanding the Earth* (Harmondsworth and Baltimore, 1967); T.F. Gaskell, *Physics of the Earth* (London and New York, 1970); N. Calder, *Restless Earth* (London and New York, 1972).

geopolitics. A long-established area of geographical inquiry which considers SPACE to be important in making sense of the world political order. Its scholarly usage should not be confused with *Geopolitik*, a German school of thought which, in developing DARWINIAN notions such as Lebensraum ('living space'), provided spurious intellectual justification for national 'paranoia', territorial claims and geopolitical objectives in Germany during the 1930s. *Geopolitik* saw STATES as highly individual organisms engaged in perpetual struggle one with another, and in which and through which all nationals are bound spiritually into one organic 'oneness'. In contrast, the intellectual origins of geopolitics can be traced back to the early 20th-century works of Halford Mackinder. In his 1904 'heartland thesis', which is one of the most widely-read and influential of geopolitical expositions, Mackinder interpreted European history as a record of struggle to achieve and prevent control over the pivotal area of the Eurasian land mass, and this thesis was to provide inspiration for much post-war U.S. foreign policy thinking, particularly in the shape of Spykman's 'rimland' theory (the attempt to create a 'buffer zone' around the U.S.S.R. with a string of neutral states). Recent geopolitical approaches focus on (a) the hierarchical and regional structuring of state power; (b) the role of the geographical imagination in forming state IDEOLOGIES which justify specific territorial actions; and (c) the POLITICAL ECONOMY of state behaviour, in which the links between the processes of CAPITAL accumulation, resource competition and foreign policies are analysed as part of a singular and interdependent global system.   G.R.S.

Bibl: D. Pepper and A. Jenkins (eds.), *The Geography of Peace and War* (Oxford, 1985).

geotaxis, see under TROPISM.

geotropism, see under TROPISM.

geriatrics. The branch of medicine that deals with the special medical problems of the aged. As the diseases of youth and middle age yield to medical treatment, so the diseases of the elderly become relatively more important. Geriatrics bears the same relationship to GERONTOLOGY as PSYCHIATRY bears to PSYCHOLOGY.   P.M.

germ cell, see GAMETE.

germ plasm. Term used by August Weismann (1834-1914) for the reproductive CELLS and TISSUES of the body as contrasted with the 'ordinary' parts of the body — the SOMA. Weismann's *germ plasm theory* is the theory that the cells destined to become reproductive cells are segregated very early in development and are thus untouched by influences from the ENVIRONMENT or from elsewhere in the body. This theory, even if it is not in all cases literally true, is now admitted to be effectively true, because the GENETIC information contained in the germ cells is indeed totally unaffected by what goes on around them in the body or in the environment.   P.M.

gerontology. The branch of BIOLOGY that deals with the nature of ageing. Its central problem is whether the ageing process is an epiphenomenon of life or whether it is innate or genetically programmed in the sense that it will occur irrespective of the vicissitudes to which the organism is exposed in the course of its ordinary lifetime. There is nothing paradoxical about the idea of a genetically programmed ageing process, because the post-reproductive period of life is beyond the direct reach of the forces of NATURAL SELECTION. Among the epiphenomenal theories of ageing is

Mechnikov's conjecture, now discredited, that ageing is caused by a progressive auto-intoxication through the assimilation of toxins liberated by an unsatisfactory bacterial population of the gut. Another is Orgel's theory according to which ageing is the consequence of a series of accumulated errors of transcription in the processes by which the genetic information residing in the germinal DNA (see NUCLEIC ACID) is mapped into specific structural PROTEINS or ENZYMES. Experimental evidence lends some support to the latter view. If it is true, the ageing process could not be remedied by any form of physical intervention since it would be largely random in origin.   P.M.

Gesamtkunstwerk (German for 'complete-art-work'). The concept, most closely associated with Richard Wagner, of a total integration of music, drama, and spectacle in which the arts involved are so interdependent that none shall dominate to the detriment of the others. Theoretically, since music, text, and theatrical concept should all emanate from the same mind, a perfect balance should be achieved; in practice, this is rarely so, since the chance of one person possessing equally imaginative gifts in three spheres is remote. After Wagner, musical landmarks in the welding of different artistic media into a synaesthetic experience (see SYNAESTHESIA) include Schoenberg's *Die Glückliche Hand* and Scriabin's *Prometheus*. In recent times, the new resources of ELECTRONIC MUSIC, coupled with immense advances in lighting techniques, back-projection, amplification, and the like, have made the concept of *Gesamtkunstwerk* more likely to be achieved, though the ultimate gain in artistic terms may be less than Wagner predicted. A.H.

Gesellschaft, see under GEMEINSCHAFT.

Gestalt. Imported German word for a configuration, pattern, or organized whole with qualities different from those of its components separately considered; e.g. a melody, since its quality does not inhere in any particular notes as such. Such whole-qualities have always been recognized and commented upon, but their explicit experimental study came into prominence in Germany when, in 1910, the self-styled *Gestalt psychologists* began studying the PHI-PHENOMENON. Here was a perceived movement corresponding neither to actual physical movement nor to elementary STIMULUS events but to several stimulus events in interaction. The founders of Gestalt psychology (in R.S. Woodworth's classification, one of the six main SCHOOLS OF PSYCHOLOGY) were Max Wertheimer, Kurt Koffka and Wolfgang Köhler. Their key argument was that the nature of the parts is determined by, and secondary to, the whole. They saw this argument as applying to every field of PSYCHOLOGY and, indeed, of PHILOSOPHY, science, and art. They insisted that enquiry proceed from-above-down rather than from-below-up, i.e. one must not start with supposed elements and try to synthesize these into wholes, but rather examine the whole to discover what its natural parts are. The three founders, who migrated to the U.S.A. in the 1930s, applied their approach fruitfully to the concrete understanding of a wide range of phenomena in PERCEPTION, learning, and thinking processes, and inspired others to undertake Gestalt-flavoured studies of personality, SOCIAL PSYCHOLOGY, and AESTHETICS. In its early years Gestalt psychology seemed revolutionary and aroused much controversy, but by mid century it had ceased to represent a self-conscious school. While many of its fundamental problems about organized complexities remained unsolved, its main lessons and factual discoveries were absorbed profitably into the mainstream of psychology.   I.M.L.H.

Bibl: W. Köhler, *The Mentality of Apes* (London and New York, 1925); K. Koffka, *Principles of Gestalt Psychology* (London and New York, 1935); M. Wertheimer, *Productive Thinking* (New York, 1959; London, enl. ed., 1961).

gestalt therapy. A form of PSYCHO-THERAPY predicated upon a holistic concept of mind/body, owing much to the philosophical influence of Klaus Conrad and Karl Jaspers. As popularized in the U.S.A. from the 1960s, gestalt therapy stressed the value of immediate, authentic experience (as distinct from the FREUDIAN emphasis upon recovering fundamentally formative repressed childhood experiences). The individual components of emotional response and behaviour are analysed, with particular stress upon appearance and body presentation (the meaning of breathing, of gesture and suchlike). GROUP THERAPY has been developed, especially under Fritz Perls, and the figure of the 'guru' is valued. Overall, the stress in gestalt therapy is upon the value of feeling over thinking.   R.P.

Bibl: Anthony Clare, *Let's Talk About Me* (London, 1981).

Gestapo. German acronym for *Geheime Staatspolizei*, Secret State Police. The term was originally applied to the Prussian plain-clothes political police force evolved during the troubled times preceding the appointment of Adolf Hitler as Chancellor of Germany, but was extended under his chancellorship to the whole machinery of terror and informants untrammelled by any legal constraint which was used by the NAZI state against anyone suspected of political deviation or opposition. It is now freely applied as an adjective of an opprobrious kind — 'Gestapo tactics' — to all police operations, whether open or covert, extra-legal or not, directed to the restraint of illegal actions for which political motives can be adduced. D.C.W.

Bibl: K. Bracher, *The German Dictatorship* (Harmondsworth, 1973).

gestural. In art criticism, an adjective suggesting conspicuous brushwork, and movement of the body in the painting process. It is particularly relevant to ACTION PAINTING.   A.K.W.

Gestus. A German term used by Lessing in his dramatic notes of 1767 to mean something distinct from 'gesture', and adopted in BRECHTIAN parlance around 1930 to convey much the same as the old English 'gest' (bearing, carriage, mien), i.e. a mixture of gesture and gist, attitude and point. In Brecht's view there was a 'basic gest' to any play or scene, while everything in it was to be conveyed by a succession of gests, each dictating its own expression in terms of language, music, grouping, etc. For such expression to be 'gestic' it must communicate not merely the meaning but also the speaker's attitude

to his listeners and to what he is saying.   J.W.

ghetto. Originally applied to the Jewish quarters of medieval Italian cities, the term came to be used of the Jewish quarters of all European cities, especially those of central and eastern Europe. Since World War II, it has achieved a wider sociological currency to refer to any urban area which is inhabited by a group segregated on the basis of ETHNICITY, COLOUR, or RELIGION. So the 'black ghettos' of American cities, the 'CATHOLIC ghettos' of Ulster towns, the 'Asian ghettos' of London and Bradford. While ghettos are often deprived areas, the term does not, unlike concepts such as INTERNAL COLONIALISM, necessarily imply a condition of EXPLOITATION or struggle with other groups; it rather suggests a degree of permanency and co-existence.   K.K.

giant planets, see under OUTER PLANETS.

gift. In anthropological usage, largely based upon M. Mauss's pioneer study, 'Essai sur le don' (*Année Sociologique*, 1923-4), a gift is above all something given in the expectation of reciprocation. Gift-giving in all societies is interested: by means of gifts people and groups create, vary, and maintain relationships among themselves, while, in societies lacking markets and a system of MONEY, gift-giving is likely to be a chief mechanism by which EXCHANGES are affected.   M.F.

Bibl: M. Mauss, tr. I. Cunnison, *The Gift* (London and Glencoe, Ill., 1954); R. Firth (ed.), *Themes in Economic Anthropology* (London, 1967).

GIFT, see under INFERTILITY.

gift exchange, see under EXCHANGE.

glaciology. The study of all forms of natural ice including the study of glaciers, snow, the ice cover of water and subterranean ice, and the interaction of these forms with the atmosphere, HYDROSPHERE, and LITHOSPHERE. To the geologist the principal branch of glaciology is that which deals with the behaviour of ice (principally in the form of ice-sheets and glaciers) on the earth's surface, since this

provides information which can be applied to the study of ancient glaciations.
J.L.M.L.

Glasgow School. A group of painters with an international outlook in the 1880s and 1890s who often referred to themselves as 'the Glasgow boys'. Among the earliest were W. Y. MacGregor, James Guthrie, James Paterson, E. A. Walton and Joseph Crawhall and later James Lavery. Their painting combined vigorous brush work and a lack of narrative content, often rural subjects painted in a style influenced by Bastien Lepage, succeeded in some of the artists by a feeling for the technique and decorative qualities of paintings by Whistler.
D.BR.

glasnost. A Russian term, literally meaning 'openness', which refers to the Soviet policy of promoting public debate on subjects previously considered too sensitive to discuss. It particularly aims to widen the area of permitted criticism of Soviet society and its administration. It also involves a greater responsiveness to public opinion and the airing of a greater diversity of views before the population, both in the MEDIA and in literature and the arts. The concept is not a new one, but the need for *glasnost* has been stressed by the leadership of Mikhail Gorbachev, elected General Secretary of the COMMUNIST party in 1985, and its scope has been increased. Since his election, more attention has been given in the media to problems within Soviet society and failures have been reported more candidly: prominent examples are the nuclear accident at CHERNOBYL, which after initial secrecy was widely publicized, and the NATIONALIST disturbances in Kazakhstan in December 1986. The aim of *glasnost* is not to introduce complete freedom of information and criticism. Instead the leadership hopes that it will lead to the correction of faults in policy and its implementation by making them public, and that it will encourage widespread involvement in the political and economic reforms which have been introduced between 1985 and 1987. It is difficult to assess how far-reaching the implications of the *glasnost* policy will be, because there is some conservative opposition to increasing critical discussion, and the extent of future reforms is uncertain.
D.PR.

glaucoma, see under LASER SURGERY; INTRAOCULAR PRESSURE.

glia, see under NEURON.

global gauge field theory, see under SUPERSYMMETRY.

glossematics. An approach to language adopted primarily by Louis Hjelmslev and associates at the Linguistic Circle of Copenhagen in the mid 1930s. The circle aimed to develop a theory applicable, not just to language, but to the HUMANITIES in general. Language, in this view, was seen as merely one kind of symbolic system, the distinctive features of which would be clarified only when it was compared with other, non-linguistic symbolic systems (e.g. LOGIC, dancing). The study of LINGUISTICS would lead on to the more general study of SEMIOTICS.
D.C.
Bibl: L. Hjelmslev, tr. F.J. Whitfield, *Prolegomena to a Theory of Language* (Madison, Wis., rev. ed., 1961).

glossolalia. In LINGUISTICS, the term used to refer to the religious phenomenon of 'speaking in tongues'.
D.C.
Bibl: W. Samarin, *Tongues of Men and Angels* (New York and London, 1972).

glottochronology. In LINGUISTICS, the QUANTIFICATION of the extent to which languages have diverged from a common source. Using a technique known as *lexicostatistics*, one studies the extent to which the hypothetically related languages share certain basic words (*cognates*) and deduces from this the distance in time since the languages separated. The theory and methods involved are not widely used, and are highly controversial.
D.C.

gluino, see under SUPERSYMMETRY.

gluon. An ELEMENTARY PARTICLE possessing one unit of quantum mechanical spin (see QUANTUM MECHANICS) which is responsible for mediating the strong interaction between QUARKS. There are eight varieties of gluon in the standard theory of quantum chromodynamics. They are sometimes therefore called exchange particles. This interaction is also termed the colour force because it occurs between particles (quarks and gluons) which carry the attribute of 'colour' (see QUANTUM CHROMODYNAMICS). Gluons are massive particles and do not possess electric charge. Their collective name refers to the fact that they bind quarks together to create the observed HADRONS like the PROTON and NEUTRON. J.D.B.

Bibl: H. Pagels, *Perfect Symmetry* (New York, 1985); F. Close, *The Cosmic Onion* (London, 1984).

Gnostics. In the early centuries of CHRISTIANITY, until about AD 300, various Gnostic sects were the chief religious rivals to orthodox Christianity. Their doctrines were very varied, but in essence taught that men and women had a divine spark in them but had fallen into the material world ruled by fate, birth and death. The divine element in humanity could, however, be reawakened through esoteric knowledge (for which *gnosis* is the Greek word) enabling those who achieved mastery of it to be reunited with the realm of the spirit. Denounced by the Church fathers as heretics, the Gnostics' importance in the development of Christianity was in forcing the early Church to settle the canon of the scriptures; to establish a theological creed, and to set up an episcopal organization in defence of orthodox beliefs.

In the modern world considerable interest in Gnostic ideas has been shown by the JUNGIAN school of PSYCHOANALYSIS with its interest in mythology and theory of ARCHETYPES. FEMINIST writers have also been attracted, e.g. by the feminine figure of Sophia, the goddess repressed by the PATRIARCHAL Judaeo-Christian tradition.
A.L.C.B.

Bibl: H. Jones, *The Gnostic Religion* (Boston, 2nd ed., 1958); E. Pagels, *The Gnostic Gospels* (New York and London, 1979); C.G. Jung, *Answer to Job* (Eng. tr. by R.F.C. Hull, London, 1954; New York, 1960).

GNP (gross national product). The output produced by the residents of a country. It differs from GDP by the addition of net wages, interest, profit and dividends earned from abroad. Thus, GNP represents the total income accruing to residents of a country from economic activity within and outside the country. The *net national product* (NNP) is GNP adjusted for the depreciation of the capital stock held by the residents of the country. J.P.

Gödel's theorem (1931) states that in any formal system which contains the arithmetic of natural NUMBERS there is a formula which, if the system is consistent, can neither be proved nor disproved, neither it nor its negation being deducible from the AXIOMS. It follows from this that it is impossible to prove the consistency of a formal system of this kind within the system itself. A generally accepted consequence of this startling discovery is that the ambition of Frege and Russell to create a unitary deductive system in which all mathematical truths could be deduced from a handful of axioms (see LOGICISM) cannot be realized. Gödel's results are comparably destructive of Hilbert's programme of demonstrating the consistency of all mathematical theories using no more than the resources of elementary LOGIC (see FORMALISM). Much more speculative is the INFERENCE of the falsity of any theory which takes the human mind to be a mechanical, deterministic system. A.Q.

Bibl: E. Nagel and J.R. Newman, *Gödel's Proof* (New York, 1958; London, 1959).

gold standard. A state of affairs in which citizens hold their MONEY in the form of gold coins or in the form of bank deposits or notes that are convertible by their banks into gold on demand. A *gold exchange standard* is a state of affairs in which citizens cannot obtain gold on demand in exchange for their deposits etc., but can obtain on demand the currency of some other country which is on a full gold standard. The classical example of a gold standard country before 1914 was the United Kingdom; that of a gold exchange standard country was India. R.H.

Bibl: D. Begg *et al., Economics* (London, 1984).

Goldbach's conjecture, see under NUMBER THEORY.

golpe. Spanish equivalent of coup d'état, i.e. the seizure of power, by force, by an organized group within the polity (in Latin America the term usually, but not invariably, refers to action by the military). A wave of military golpes overtook the Southern Cone countries in recent years, all of which have had far-reaching implications for political and ECONOMIC DEVELOPMENT. The most important took place in Brazil in 1964 (instigating over two decades of military rule), in Uruguay in 1973, in Chile in 1973 (overthrowing the Popular Unity attempt to build a 'peaceful road to SOCIALISM' and bringing General Pinochet to power) and in Argentina in 1976, which paved the way for the anti-COMMUNIST 'dirty war' and its associated disappearances (see STATE TERROR).
N.M.

gonads. The collective name for the male and female reproductive organs — in mammals the testes and ovaries respectively. The gonads contain two elements: a part which manufactures spermatozoa or ova, i.e. the GAMETES, and another part which is responsible for those internal secretions of the sex organs (see ENDOCRINOLOGY) upon which the development of secondary sexual characteristics depends.
P.M.

gonorrhoea. A common SEXUALLY TRANSMITTED DISEASE caused by *Neisseria gonorrhoeae* (the gonococcus). In men, infection of the urethra usually causes a discharge and may spread to the testicle and cause epididymitis, an acute infection which can cause sterility. Other sites infected by the gonococcus are the throat and rectum in homosexual men; these infections are usually symptomless. In women the cervix, urethra and rectum are first infected, often without symptoms, but the microbes may spread and infect the fallopian tubes, causing SALPINGITIS. Gonorrhoea can readily be transmitted to a baby's eyes during delivery and cause a severe and potentially blinding disease. For many years gonorrhoea was cured by penicillin. Penicillin-resistant gonococci are now widespread, particularly in developing countries, but there are good alternative antibiotics. Efforts to control gonorrhoea by energetic treatment and contact tracing have had some success in Europe and the U.S.A.
J.D.O.
Bibl: Y.M. Felman (ed,) *Sexually Transmitted Diseases* (London, 1986).

Gosplan. The STATE planning committee of the Soviet Union. Founded by Lenin in 1921, it became much more powerful after the centralization of the economy by Stalin after 1928. As virtually all of the means of production in the U.S.S.R. are owned by the state, Gosplan is charged with planning and coordinating most of the Soviet economy. Once the POLITBURO has decided on priorities in the economy, Gosplan incorporates these policies into a large number of long- and short-term plans which should, in theory, all be mutually and internally consistent. Levels of wages, profits, sales, productivity and investment are all dealt with in the plans. The most comprehensive of the plans is the Five Year Plan which establishes growth targets and calculates the allocation of resources necessary for their fulfilment for each sector of the economy and each individual enterprise over a five year period. Yearly and quarterly breakdowns are also provided. Gosplan, while officially subordinate to the chairman of the Council of Ministers, is to a large extent autonomous, although it must take into account Politburo policy and consult with the economic ministries when planning for individual sectors of industry. It also frequently finds itself having to reconcile the contradictory interests of different economic sectors, particularly over the distribution of resources.
D.PR.
Bibl: A. Nove, *The Soviet Economic System* (London, 1977).

GPS (General Problem Solver), see under PROBLEM-SOLVING.

GPSG, see under GENERALIZED PHASE STRUCTURE GRAMMAR.

GPU, see under KGB.

gradient methods. OPTIMIZATION methods which represent the mathematical equivalent of climbing a hill by always following the steepest path up it. The simplest form of gradient method for maximizing a function causes the search process to take a step in the direction of steepest slope, then compare the direction of steepest slope at the new point with that at the old; comparison provides guidance for the choice of the next step-length. A carefully designed process of this kind works fast and efficiently except at the very last stages of the search for the optimum. More sophisticated methods allow the step-length to be chosen in the light of the rate-of-change of the gradient, and may also suggest a step-direction not exactly along the line of steepest slope; the *Newton-Raphson method* is of this type. Such methods are more laborious per step but usually need fewer steps than the more naive methods. The methods most widely used in current practice are the *variable-metric methods* developed in the 1960s and based on the work of Davidon, Fletcher, and Powell.

R.SI.

gradualism. In evolutionary BIOLOGY, (1) the uncontroversial doctrine that complex organs (such as the vertebrate eye) must have evolved in many small stages rather than by a single mutation; (2) the controversial (see PUNCTUATED EQUILIBRIUM; MOLECULAR CLOCK) theory that evolutionary change proceeds at a relatively constant rate.

M.R.

Bibl: R. Dawkins, *The Blind Watchmaker* (London, 1986).

Graham technique. A teaching method and movement style based on the work of Martha Graham, who as a founder of MODERN DANCE in the U.S.A and a former member of DENISHAWN, rebelled to explore a more serious social message and dramatic form of dance while striving for intellectual respectability. 'Lamentation' (1930), a solo piece, was a landmark in defining Graham's new personal approach to modern dance which has developed into a recognizable technique worldwide. The technique retains traditional lines and the five positions of CLASSICAL BALLET, but is innovative as all movement emanates from the lower back or solar plexus. The technique is dramatic, uniquely expressive and has its own clear identity in the floorwork. Characteristics of Graham CHOREOGRA-

PHY are dramatic female roles, percussive earthbound dynamics, an episodic choreographic content which intersperses group dynamics with the solo form, distinctive use of full costume and collaboration with artists. Graham is most associated with the rise of CONTEMPORARY DANCE in Britain.

L.A.

Bibl: D. McDonagh, *Martha Graham: A Biography* (New York, 1973); M. Graham, *The Notebooks of Martha Graham* (New York, 1973).

grammar. A central CONCEPT in contemporary LINGUISTICS, traditionally referring to an independent LEVEL of linguistic organization in which words, or their component parts (MORPHEMES), are brought together in the formation of sentences or DISCOURSES. (See MORPHOLOGY; SYNTAX.) In GENERATIVE GRAMMAR, however, and increasingly in other linguistic theories, the word means, more broadly, the entire system of structural relationships in a language, viewed as a set of rules for the generation of sentences. In this sense, the study of grammar subsumes PHONOLOGY and SEMANTICS, traditionally regarded as separate levels. A systematic account of a language's grammar (in either of the above senses) is known as 'a grammar'. See also CASE GRAMMAR; SCALE-AND-CATEGORY GRAMMAR; SYSTEMIC GRAMMAR; TAGMEMIC GRAMMAR; TRADITIONAL GRAMMAR; CORE GRAMMAR; DEPENDENCY GRAMMAR; FUNCTIONAL GRAMMAR; GENERALIZED PHASE STRUCTURE GRAMMAR; LEXICAL FUNCTION GRAMMAR; METAGRAMMAR; MONTAGUE GRAMMAR; NETWORK GRAMMAR; REALISTIC GRAMMAR; RELATIONAL GRAMMAR; TRANSFORMATIONAL GRAMMAR.

D.C.

Bibl: F. Palmer, *Grammar* (Harmondsworth, 1984).

grammatical word, see under WORD CLASS.

grammaticality. In LINGUISTICS, the conformity of a sentence (or part of a sentence) to the rules defined by a specific GRAMMAR of a language. A preceding asterisk (see STARRED FORM) is commonly used to indicate that a sentence is ungrammatical, i.e. incapable of being generated by the rules of a grammar. See also AC-CEPTABILITY.   D.C.

grand unification/grand unified theories.
Also known by the acronym GUTS. Refers to a class of theories of ELEMENTARY PARTICLES which aims to unify the different theories of the weak, strong and electromagnetic forces. This unification can occur at very high energies (10^{15} GeV) and predicts that BARYON number is not conserved in Nature and that PROTON is unstable with an average lifetime of 10^{31} years. This slow decay is detectable and a number of experiments have searched for it with no unanimity that it has been found as yet. The unification of the weak and electromagnetic interaction is well-established and tested by experiment. This theory is known as the Weinberg-Salam theory. When the strong interaction is added to the unification the theories are called 'grand unified' theories. None includes the gravitational interaction and there are at present many candidate theories built upon different symmetries. Grand unified theories have been extended to incorporate SUPERSYMMETRY. Such extensions are known by the acronym SUSY GUTS. These theories have many important cosmological consequences and give a natural explanation for the observed preponderance of matter over ANTIMATTER in the universe (see COSMOLOGY).   J.D.B.

Bibl: G. Ross, *Grand Unified Theories* (New York, 1985); J. D. Barrow and J. Silk, *The Left Hand of Creation* (New York, 1983); H. Pagels, *Perfect Symmetry* (New York, 1985).

Grand Union. An anarchistic collective of dancers/CHOREOGRAPHERS emerging from JUDSON DANCE THEATER in the 1970s in America, in which improvisation and investigation played a significant role. Initiated by Yvonne Rainer, members included Steve Paxton, Trisha Brown, David Gordon and others. During Grand Union residencies in 1972, Paxton began to explore duet improvisation with student athletes and CONTACT IMPROVISATION emerged as a new dance form. Grand Union disbanded in 1976.   L.A.

Bibl: S. Banes, *Terpsichore in Sneakers* (Boston, 1980).

graph. (1) A geometric representation of a FUNCTION. (2) A MATHEMATICAL STRUCTURE consisting of a set of objects (called *points*) some of which are connected to each other by *edges*, thus setting up a binary RELATION between the points. For example, a railway route map represents the relation 'is an adjacent station to'. Graph theory arose from the FOUR-COLOUR CONJECTURE and is of great use in COMBINATORIAL MATHEMATICS.   R.G.

Bibl: A. Kaufmann, *Points and Arrows* (London, 1972).

graphic design. Design intended for printing, generally with a commercial purpose. As well as creating images and patterns, the graphic designer may be responsible for the layout, titling, scale, and colouring of magazines, books, posters, and film and television programmes. Graphic design plays an increasingly influential part in societies dominated by mass MEDIA and susceptible to skilful packaging. Pioneers of 20th-century graphic design include William Morris, El Lissitsky, and the BAUHAUS; today any of a variety of media may be employed, including relief, intaglio and surface printing, screen printing, photographic processes, and COMPUTER GRAPHICS.   P.C.

graphic score. A musical score which uses pictures and graphic symbols instead of or as well as conventional MUSICAL NOTATION. In some works (e.g. György Ligeti's 'Volumina') graphic scores are used to give an element of performance freedom to the music (see INDETERMINACY). In some cases, such as some works of Sylvano Bussotti, the elements of conventional notation virtually disappear and the music becomes very ambiguous. Many graphic scores have an intrinsic visual beauty independent of their musical value.   B.CO.

Bibl: R. Smith Brindle, *The New Music* (London, 1975).

graphology. (1) The study of handwriting as a means of making inferences about the psychological characteristics of the writer. (2) A term applied by some linguists to a branch of LINGUISTICS that describes the properties of a language's orthographic system (spelling, punctuation). Graphology in this sense is analogous to PHONOLOGY in the spoken medium.

I.M.L.H.; D.C.

gravitation (or *gravity*). The force of attraction between PARTICLES which arises from their MASS. Gravity is responsible for the fall of objects towards the centre of the earth, the ORBITS of the moon round the earth and the planets round the sun, and the condensation of the matter in the universe into stars and GALAXIES. The importance of gravitation diminishes as the scale of phenomena is reduced: the life of small insects is dominated by the intermolecular forces of viscosity and surface tension, while in ATOMIC PHYSICS and NUCLEAR PHYSICS gravity is completely overwhelmed by the vastly more powerful ELECTOMAGNETIC FIELDS, STRONG INTERACTIONS, and WEAK INTERACTIONS.

Gravity is in fact the weakest force known in PHYSICS, but it is also the only force which is both (1) long-range in its effects (unlike, e.g., molecular and nuclear forces, which are only appreciable very near their sources) and (2) always attractive (unlike, e.g., electric forces, which may also be repulsive, so that for large masses, where there are generally equal numbers of positive and negative charges, their effects add up to zero). Thus gravity dominates the behaviour of large systems, and is of central importance in COSMOLOGY.

In NEWTONIAN MECHANICS gravitation had the status of an ordinary force, in the same class as, say, MAGNETISM or friction, but in Einstein's general theory of RELATIVITY it is incorporated into the basic structure of MECHANICS from the start (see also MACH'S PRINCIPLE). M.V.B.

gravitational lens. The presence of a massive body between ourselves and a distant astronomical object can create two identical images of the distant object. The massive object is said to behave as a gravitational lens because it deflects the paths of light rays from the source to create two images of it. The process is called 'gravitational lensing' or 'lensing'. A number of cases are known in which duplicate images of distant QUASARS have been observed close to each other. The intervening object has not been seen and may be a very massive BLACK HOLE. The existence of lensing allows limits to be placed on the amount of some types of DARK MATTER in space.

The possibility that the gravitational pull of very massive objects can make them behave as lens by bending the light rays to produce multiple images was predicted by Albert Einstein. J.D.B.

gravitino, see under SUPERSYMMETRY.

graviton. A hypothetical PARTICLE which is predicted to be associated with the FIELD of GRAVITATION in the same way as a PHOTON is associated with the ELECTROMAGNETIC FIELD. See also under SUPERSYMMETRY. M.V.B.

gravity, see GRAVITATION.

Great Chain of Being. All world views and scientific theories require major classificatory systems to map experience. One of the most potent of these ordering devices, handed down from antiquity and integrated into modern thought, was the Great Chain of Being. This postulated that all natural or created things could be arranged into a single vertical line or chain, with each ascending link progressively one degree superior in its attributes to the former. In gross terms, objects in the mineral kingdom possessed only the attribute of existence. Plants had life in addition; animals possessed the qualities of will and mobility; human beings had powers of reason and CONSCIOUSNESS; above men, spiritual beings such as angels were not even encumbered by gross fleshly bodies. Within CHRISTIANITY, God lay at the head of the ladder of being, as its creator. The theory of the chain was capable of infinite sophistication and inflection. Although formally exploded as a scientific scheme as a consequence of Linnaeus's taxonomy, its ghost continues to underpin the evolutionary vision that all living beings are fundamentally connected, forming an ultimate unity. The chain was also used to justify the Romantic notion that every being gloried in its own individuality, as well as later being evoked to support 'racist' forms of ANTHROPOLOGY, which argued for a natural hierarchy of the different races of man, negroes at the bottom being adjacent to the other higher primates.   R.P.

Bibl: A.O. Lovejoy, *The Great Chain of Being* (New York, 1960).

Great Leap Forward. The period in China between 1958 and 1960 when the orthodox Soviet method of organization and production was abandoned in an attempt to dramatically increase output, and move the social REVOLUTION forward. A decentralization of industry took place as Mao tried to decrease the stultifying power of the party and STATE bureaucracy in an attempt to surpass Britain's industrial and agricultural output within 15 years. Political mobilization was seen as the key to solving economic problems, with the political and ideological fervour so intense that targets were repeatedly adjusted in an attempt to speed up the movement; for example, it took just two months to create 24,000 Rural People's Communes as the deadlines for the radical COLLECTIVIZATION of the rural population became shorter and shorter. Although there were spectacular increases in production in the short run, the need to satisfy unrealistic production quotas led to a sacrificing of quality to the extent that much of the steel produced in new 'back yard furnaces' was totally useless. By 1960 the economy had seriously overstretched itself, and the appalling harvests of 1959-61 led to the Great Leap being reined in by Chen Yun and a loss of face and power for the architect of the Great Leap, Mao Zedong. (See also MAOISM.)   S.B.

Bibl: S.R. Schram, *Authority, Participation, and Cultural Revolution in China* (Cambridge, 1973).

Great Proletarian Cultural Revolution. In 1966 with Mao's *de facto* control of Chinese politics eroded by the control of the party and STATE system passing into the hands of Liu Shaoqi and Deng Xiaoping after the disasters of the GREAT LEAP FORWARD, Mao launched a movement aimed at attacking BOURGEOIS influence and CAPITALIST roaders in the party. Mao bypassed the party system to appeal directly to the masses to attack BUREAUCRATIC rightist tendencies within the party in order to restore revolutionary ideals into the system. What followed was

a three year period of mob rule and violence, as teams of RED GUARDS set about attacking anything that was deemed to be 'rightist'. With the party and state system under attack, society became uncontrollable, and Mao had to call in the Red Guard leaders to halt the near civil war, and ordered the Army to step in to restore order in the provinces. By April 1969, the destructive phase of the Cultural Revolution was over, but the term is often used to describe the whole period up to the death of Mao in 1976.   S.B.

Bibl: T. Saich, *China: Politics and Government* (London, 1981).

Great Purge, see YEZHOVSHCHINA.

Great Society. A phrase provided by speechwriter Richard Goodwin and first used on April 23, 1964 by U.S. President Lyndon B. Johnson. It became the slogan characterizing a rapid, multifaceted burst of LIBERAL, REFORMIST policies from 1964-1967. These were an extension of the WELFARE STATE principles of the NEW DEAL, with a new emphasis on the economic and political condition of BLACK Americans, and on the deterioration of inner cities.

The programmes of the Great Society have been condemned from the left as attempts to disguise deep-rooted problems with cosmetic measures, and attacked from the RIGHT as costly, ill-conceived and as at once excessively bureaucratic yet designed to radicalize blacks and the poor. More accurately, the Great Society may be seen as an attempt to offer greater EQUALITY of opportunity to the disadvantaged (through programmes such as the 'Head Start' education policy), and to extend the 'safety-net' of WELFARE rights. There was no serious attempt at major redistribution of wealth, for which legislative or popular support would not have existed. The Great Society suffered from the hasty construction of policies, from Congressional tendencies to mistranslate governmental intentions, and above all from the impact of the VIETNAM War, which accelerated inflation and consumed governmental resources and the energies of the Johnson administration.   S.R.

Bibl: A. Matusow, *The Unraveling of America* (New York, 1984); E. Ginzberg and R.M. Solow, *The Great Society: Lessons for the Future* (New York, 1974).

green belt, see under NEW TOWNS.

Green Movement. A broad political movement in many industrial DEMOCRACIES produced by the growing attention to environmental and ecological questions in the 1960s and 1970s. It expresses alarm at the unprecedented assault on the natural environment by world industrialism: its concerns include the depletion of irreplaceable resources (e.g. fossil fuels), the extinction of species, the effects of POLLUTION by industrial processes, the use of nuclear power and the testing of NUCLEAR WEAPONS. The Green Movement contains some international organizations such as Friends of the Earth and Greenpeace; the latter particularly favours vivid DIRECT ACTION to attract MEDIA attention. Several countries possess 'green' political parties and groups: *die Grunen* (the Greens) in West Germany have been the most visible in Europe, while coalitions of groups in the U.S. made a discernible impact on public consciousness and government policy in the 1970s.   S.R.
    Bibl: J. Porritt, *Seeing Green* (Oxford, 1985); R. Bahro, *Building the Green Movement* (London, 1986).

green pound, see under COMMON AGRICULTURAL POLICY.

green revolution. A dramatic change in grain crop farming in certain developing countries (e.g. Pakistan and India) resulting from the introduction of new high-yielding varieties grown by methods specifically suited to them. Wheat and rice are the crops principally concerned. New varieties, many of dwarf type, were developed during the 1960s, with the potential to produce yields nearly double those of the varieties in common use in many developing countries. To realize their potential, controlled irrigation water, heavy dressings of chemical fertilizer, and pesticides were required. In a number of countries arrangements were made for farmers to have these essential materials available as a 'package'.   K.E.H.
    Bibl: K. Griffin, *The Green Revolution* (London, 1979).

Greenham Common, see under PEACE MOVEMENT.

greenhouse effect. Mankind is radically altering the composition of the atmosphere through POLLUTION and changing land use, in particular, deforestation. Increasing levels of carbon dioxide and other 'greenhouse' gases threaten to produce a change in climate unrivalled in scale since the shift from ice age to interglacial conditions some 10,000 years ago. Carbon dioxide levels have risen by about 25% since the late 19th century. Carbon dioxide and certain other gases insulate the Earth by trapping outgoing heat and energy while letting incoming energy from the sun pass unhindered. This is known as the 'greenhouse effect'. The Swedish scientist Svante Arrhenius, writing in the late 19th century, warned that the combustion of the world's coal reserves would enhance the greenhouse effect and produce large-scale warming. The global warming of about 0.5 degrees Celsius that has occurred since the INDUSTRIAL REVOLUTION is consistent with predictions of the scale of greenhouse warming over this period although a firm link cannot yet be established. If the theory is correct, we face what Roger Revelle, the eminent oceanographer, has termed a 'great geophysical experiment'. Current estimates suggest that temperatures may rise by a further 1 to 4 degrees Celsius (Centigrade), way beyond the range of natural climate variability, by about the middle of the 21st century. Inevitably, the transition will be a time of societal stress. While some regions and activities may benefit, the global impact is likely to be adverse. Many crop varieties, for example, were developed for maximum production under present-day conditions and any departure from normal will reduce yields significantly. Action may have to be taken to reduce the scale of the resulting climatic change and to avert or counter its worst consequences. This may involve controls on the use of fossil fuels, greater emphasis on energy conservation and efficiency, and planned adaptation to the new ENVIRONMENT.   P.M.K.
    Bibl: W.W. Kellogg and R. Schware, *Climatic Change and Society*: *Consequences of Increasing Atmospheric Carbon Dioxide* (Boulder, 1981).

Greenwich Village. An area of New York City whose name reflects its early origins, and which has traditionally had bohemian and literary connections. More recently it has become the backdrop to the BEAT and UNDERGROUND movements. The coffeehouses were meeting-places where creative artists, writers, and singers could present their work to a small but influential public. Henry James, Kerouac, Ginsberg, Jackson Pollock, and Bob Dylan were amongst the artists who lived and worked in the Village. In the 1960s it extended further east, to the Lower East Side which was one of the powerhouses of the Alternative Society, the East Coast equivalent to San Francisco. In the aftermath of the experimentation of the 1960s the Village suffered from a high crime rate and widespread drug abuse, though under the combined pressures of URBAN RENEWAL and profitable nostalgia its status has risen again.   P.S.L.

Gresham's Law. Term in ECONOMICS. A coin whose face value is less than its value as a metal will be taken out of circulation and melted down, leaving coins whose face values are greater than their metal values. This effect has been described by the law: *bad money drives out good money from circulation*. Artificial currencies such as EUROPEAN CURRENCY UNITS (ECU) and SPECIAL DRAWING RIGHTS (SDR) have shown the limitations of this law as individuals, firms and governments prefer to be paid in more readily acceptable forms of money, e.g. in ECUs rather than in SDRs. This could be interpreted as good money driving out bad money. J.P.

grid-group analysis. A major contribution to the SOCIOLOGY OF KNOWLEDGE derived from ANTHROPOLOGY which attempts to demonstrate how knowledge is shaped and ordered by particular kinds of SOCIAL STRUCTURE. 'Grid' is taken as an internal measure of differentiation within a STRUCTURE, relating to matters of STATUS, ROLE, rank, etc. 'Group' is a term defining degrees of differentiation between one body of people and another, and relating to their boundaries. An EGALITARIAN society would be 'low group', a GHETTO 'high group'; an army or BUREAUCRACY would be 'high grid', market relations 'low grid'.

The combination of grid and group factors determine a person's or a body of people's social position. This in turn is said to correlate with the shaping of CONSCIOUSNESS. Grid-group analysis has mainly been applied to the structure of religious beliefs, but could be applicable to any field of consciousness in which questions of openness and closedness, of boundaries and bridges, of inclusion and exclusion, were to the fore.   R.P.
Bibl: M. Douglas, *Cultural Bias* (London, 1978).

gross domestic/national product, see under GDP; GNP.

ground state (in PHYSICS); see under ENERGY LEVEL.

group.
(1) In MATHEMATICS, a SET G of TRANSFORMATIONS forms a *transformation group* if: (1) G is closed under composition; and (2) G contains the identity transformation; and (3) G contains the inverse of each of its elements. Examples: (*a*) the 6 possible permutations of 3 objects; (*b*) the set of all rotations of a body about a fixed point; (*c*) the set of 24 rotations of a cube about its centre which leave it 'looking the same'. Example (*c*) is a *group of symmetry*. In general a situation or figure is *symmetrical* if there are transformations of it besides the identity which leave all (relevant) aspects of it unaltered. The set of all such transformations will form a group, the study of which may elucidate the nature of the symmetry. In PHYSICS, group theory is important for classification in CRYSTALLOGRAPHY, for QUANTUM MECHANICS, and in particular for the classification of the ELEMENTARY PARTICLES. In abstract mathematics the AUTOMORPHISMS of a MATHEMATICAL STRUCTURE may be viewed as its group of symmetry.
An *abstract group* is a set G of elements equipped with a binary operation (usually called 'composition' or 'multiplication') which satisfies abstract versions of (1)-(3) above and in addition the ASSOCIATIVE LAW $(xy)z = x(yz)$. (This is automatically satisfied by transformations.) G is *Abelian* if multiplication is required to satisfy the COMMUTATIVE LAW $xy = yx$. Examples: (*d*)

the integers with the operation of addition; (e) the non-zero rational, real or complex NUMBERS with the operation of multiplication. A group may be finite ((a), (c)), or infinite ((b), (d), (e)); the examples (b) and (c) have in addition a natural topological structure (see TOPOLOGY). Any abstract group may be *represented* in various ways as a group of transformations.   R.G.

Bibl: H. Weyl, *Symmetry* (Oxford and Princeton, 1952); F.J. Budden, *The Fascination of Groups* (Cambridge, 1972).

(2) In Sartre's *Critique de la Raison dialectique* (1960) the group is the achieved socialized community of CON-SCIOUSNESS which is enforced after the condition of self-interested SERIALITY has been annulled. The group sees to it that the aim of each selfish individual is transformed into the aim of all. Individuals are subject to an 'oath' of allegiance, which allows no criticism of its policies and decisions, nor any departure from them. The oath is enforced by terror and, ultimately, 'lynching'. This ferocious social ideal of Sartre's, which has been called a 'humanism of terror' by Raymond Aron, shows the ultimate impossibility of trying to unify MARXISM and EXISTENTIALISM.

R.PO.

Bibl: M. Warnock, *The Philosophy of Sartre* (London, 1965); M. Greene, *Sartre* (New York, 1973).

Group, the. A not yet quite forgotten attempt, in London in the late 1950s, to organize a conservative movement in poetry, by means of weekly meetings at which poets read and discussed their work. The Group, initiated by Edward Lucie-Smith, included for a time Ted Hughes and Peter Redgrove, whose similar groups at the University of Cambridge inspired the notion in the first place. The quality of its work may be judged by Lucie-Smith's and Philip Hobsbaum's *A Group Anthology* (1963). Later the Group, by now a spent force, fell into the hands of amateurs, and became known as *Poetry Workshop.*   M.S.-S.

Bibl: M.L. Rosenthal, *The New Poets* (London, 1967).

group dynamics, see under GROUP PSYCHOLOGY.

group norms. The formation of NORMS within a group of people — a phenomenon widely confirmed by observation as occurring in both natural and experimental groups. Such norms, whether they comprise agreement about mode of dress (teenage groups; see also YOUTH CULTURE), saluting (military groups), mealtimes (family groups), opinions (political groups), or perceptions (experimental groups), tend to act as a cohesive influence in the group, and to increase the number of things the group can take for granted, thus improving its efficiency in task performance. Newcomers to a group which they value may begin by merely complying with its norms, but later they may 'internalize' them. Individual members may reject the norms, either through incompatible external norms, through strong personality needs, through original thinking, or simply through a wish to challenge the leader. Such rejection, or DEVIANCE, is dealt with by the leader, or by more conformist group members, through frowns or other non-verbal signals, through verbal explanation ('not the done thing' etc.), or through punishment and, in the last resort, rejection. There is characteristically more conformity to group norms in public than in private acts; and particularly high degrees of conformity on the part of subjects with an AUTHORITARIAN PERSONALITY, and towards REFERENCE GROUPS with which the subject feels an important need to identify.

M.J.C.

Bibl: M. Argyle, *Social Interaction* (London and New York, 1969).

group psychology. The branch of SOCIAL PSYCHOLOGY concerned with the behaviour of an individual when exposed to the influence of a group of which he is a member, and with the means (the *group process*) by which the group seeks to overcome any resistance to this influence. The subject is also known as *group dynamics*, though this term is more frequently used for the forces of interaction studied than for the study of them. Particularly focused on are the changing patterns of intragroup tensions, conflicts, adjustment and cohesion, and the shifts in these relationships within a group and between one group and another. See also GROUP NORMS.   M.BE.

Bibl: M. Shaw, *Group Dynamics* (New York, 1983).

Group Theatre.
(1) A proselytizing New York theatre company, lasting from 1931 to 1941, that aimed to reflect the social conditions of the time as accurately as possible and to prove that all theatrical technique has to be founded on 'life values'. Run by a fractious triumvirate of Lee Strasberg, Harold Clurman, and Cheryl Crawford, it produced some notable plays including Clifford Odets's *Waiting for Lefty* (1935), Robert Ardrey's *Thunder Rock* (1939), and William Saroyan's *My Heart's in the Highlands* (1939). It also nurtured such impressive actors as Lee J. Cobb and Franchot Tone. Ultimately it collapsed through shortage of funds and division of purpose. But it represented a major attempt to counteract the commercialism of Broadway and to provide America with the kind of ensemble spirit familiar in Europe; and its influence can still be seen in the realistic tradition of modern American drama and in the teaching work of Lee Strasberg at the New York Actors' Studio (see METHOD, THE).

(2) A private play-producing society founded in 1932 at the Westminster Theatre, London. Its policy was never clearly defined but its chief importance lay in persuading major contemporary poets to write for it: Auden and Isherwood's *The Dog Beneath the Skin* (1936), *The Ascent of F6* (1937), and *On the Frontier* (1939), T.S. Eliot's *Sweeney Agonistes* (1935), and Stephen Spender's *Trial of a Judge* (1938) were its major productions. Its bare-stage style of presentation also gave writers a valuable geographical freedom and anticipated the scenic austerity of later years. But when it was wound up in 1953 it had long ceased to be an active or influential body.   M.BI.

Bibl: (1) H. Clurman, *The Fervent Years* (New York, 2nd ed., 1957); (2) M. Sidnell, *Dances of Death: The Group Theatre of London in the Thirties* (London, 1984).

group theory, see under ELEMENTARY PARTICLES.

group therapy. Classically, a form of PSYCHOTHERAPY in which clients, preferably strangers to each other, meet as a group with a trained therapist or therapists. Some therapists see the only advantage over individual therapy as being one of relative cheapness for the client, whereas others believe that a group process takes place which brings additional benefits. Groups can be used with hospitalized patients, although here the more disturbed patients need a more supportive kind of therapy. Recent advances in group techniques include ENCOUNTER GROUPS, PSYCHODRAMA, *sensitivity training, social competence training,* etc., with a wide variety of techniques and of training for the therapists. Some of these group techniques are also used in non-therapeutic contexts (see, e.g., ORGANIZATION THEORY).   M.J.C.

Bibl: H. Walton (ed.), *Small Group Psychotherapy* (Harmondsworth, 1971).

groupthink theory. Term coined by Irving Janis at Yale University and used as the title of a book on foreign policy 'decisions and fiascoes' (1972, 1982 second ed.). Janis drew on psychological, historical and political studies of the BAY OF PIGS invasion, Pearl Harbor and the VIETNAM war to show the dangers of group conformity. 'Deviant' individuals, i.e. those who disagree with (unwise) group decisions, are excluded for 'violating GROUP NORMS'. Opponents of 'appeasement' in the 1930s and the French belittling of the importance of the German Schlieffen Plan in 1914 are taken as good examples of detrimental groupthink. The management of the Cuban missile crisis (see CUBA) and the MARSHALL PLAN by the U.S. are taken as 'counterpoint' examples of how to avoid it.   A.W.

Bibl: Irving L. Janis, *Groupthink: Psychological Studies of Policy Decisions and Fiascoes* (Boston, 1982).

Gruppe 47. Informal group of mainly LEFT-wing German writers meeting annually in West Germany for readings and mutual criticism between 1947 and 1967. Their prize, awarded only when a work was felt to need publicizing, was won by (among others) Heinrich Böll in 1951, Günter Grass in 1958, and Johannes Bobrowski in 1962. Others associated with what soon became the most serious and influential movement in post-World War II German literature included Paul Celan, Uwe Johnson, H.M. Enzensberger, Erich Fried, the critics Walter Jens and Hans Mayer, and the group's founder Hans Werner Richter.   J.W.

GSR, see under GALVANIC SKIN RESPONSE.

GST, see under GENERAL SYSTEMS THEORY.

Guam Doctrine, see under NIXON DOCTRINE.

Guanxi. A Chinese word which directly translated means 'relations' or 'relationship' but is used in a political context to describe the strong personal ties between people who attended the same educational establishment, were brought up in the same place or who share some similar common background. Guanxi places firm, unbreakable and mutual obligations on people who share the special relationship, which traditionally overrides all other imperatives and directives in the decision-making process. Accordingly, Deng Xiaoping's relationship with Liu Shaoqi would be said to be based not on shared aims or philosophies, but on their mutual background as students in France.   S.B.
    Bibl: L. Pye, *The Dynamics of Chinese Politics* (Cambridge, Mass., 1981).

guerrilla. Spanish word for irregular warfare (see WAR) by independent or autonomous units; as used in English, a member of such a unit. Guerrilla warfare is age-old, but only in the 20th century did it come to be seen not just as an auxiliary method but as a road to the victory of REVOLUTION. Its theory was developed by its major practitioners: Mao Tse-tung (see MAOISM), the Vietnamese general Vo Nguyen Giap (see VIETCONG), and Che Guevara (see CASTROISM), all of whom considered it as part of the doctrine of 'people's war'. This doctrine was an extension of LENINIST ideas about 'colonial revolutions' and the 'anti-Imperialist struggle' (see IMPERIALISM). COMMUNISTS in economically backward countries (see

UNDERDEVELOPMENT) found that their revolutionary chances depended on the successful exploitation of local NATIONALISM and peasant grievances. Guerrillas could operate effectively only in favourable surroundings (like 'fish in water') and this provided the perspective for the wars of 'national liberation'. In such 'people's wars', Mao concluded, 'the seizure of power by armed force, the settlement of the issue by war, is the central task and the highest form of revolution'.
    The military implications of this doctrine — and even more of the Chinese revolutionary experience — were elaborated further by General Giap, who not only postulated the transformation of guerrilla warfare into a regular war, but also introduced a psychological element designed to shorten Mao's 'protracted war' in a single stroke — like Dien Bien Phu or the Tet offensive — making the enemy lose his will and give up the struggle. Other adherents of guerrilla revolution went even further beyond Lenin's 'objective' conditions for a 'revolutionary situation'. Che Guevara, Régis Debray, and Carlos Marighella addressed themselves to the question of how to conduct guerrilla warfare in places where Mao's 'support of the people' was lacking. Guevara concluded that 'it is not necessary to wait until all conditions for making revolution exist; the insurrection can create them'. Debray elaborated this by stressing the ideas of *foco insurrecional* and of the guerrilla force as the political vanguard, 'the Party in embryo'. The Brazilian revolutionary Carlos Marighella (killed in 1969) advocated guerrilla action in the cities. Latin American *urban guerrillas* have engaged in TERRORISM, political kidnapping, and hijacking, but with no more success in 'arousing the masses' than ANARCHISTS in the past with their 'propaganda by deed'.
    The experience of revolutionary guerrilla struggles — rural or urban — suggests that it is the political and not the military side of their strategy that is paramount. Initially they hope to elicit indiscriminate repressions, which will 'alienate the masses' and assure their increasing support, thus creating revolutionary conditions which did not exist before. However, the fulfilment or otherwise of this

hope does not depend on guerrillas alone. In Latin America guerrilla activities have so far only led to the proliferation of military *coups d'état*.　　　　　　L.L.

Bibl: R. Moss, *Urban Guerrillas: the New Face of Political Violence* (London, 1972); R.B. Asprey, *War in the Shadows: the Guerrilla in History* (New York, 1975; London, 1976); W. Laqueur, *Guerrilla* (Boston, 1976; London, 1977).

Guild Socialism. A movement within the British labour movement between 1906 and 1923 advocating the achievement of SOCIALISM through the transformation of the TRADE UNIONS into monopolistic producers' guilds controlling and administering their branches of industry. A parallel movement to SYNDICALISM in France, it was less militant and tried to make a synthesis of socialist and syndicalist ideas. Guild Socialist ideas were formulated by A.J. Penty in his *Restoration of the Guild System* (1906), by R.A. Orage, editor of *New Age*, and by S.G. Hobson, author of *National Guilds*. Guild Socialists were antagonistic both to parliamentary politics and to the State, the proper role of which was seen as that of an arbiter in case of conflict rather than of an administrative instrument. In contrast to the Fabians (see FABIANISM), Guild Socialism was hostile to state BUREAUCRACY.

After an unsuccessful attempt to capture the Fabian Society, Guild Socialists established their own National Guilds League. This split after the Bolshevik Revolution, and many members (e.g. R. Page Arnot, R. Palme Dutt, William Gallagher, and Maurice Dobb) joined the newly founded COMMUNIST Party of Great Britain. In 1923 the N.G.L. broke up and its organ, the *Guild Socialist*, ceased publication.　　　　　　L.L.

Bibl: A.W. Wright and G.D.H. Cole, *Socialist Democracy* (Oxford, 1979).

guilt culture, see under SHAME CULTURE.

GULAG. Russian acronym for the Main Administration of Corrective Labour Camps — the department of the Soviet Secret Police responsible for administering the FORCED LABOUR system. Alexander Solzhenitsyn's *The Gulag Archipelago* — publication of which abroad was the

immediate occasion of his expulsion in February 1974 — is a metaphorical expression for the huge scattered 'islands' of Gulag territory existing throughout the Soviet Union.　　　　　　R.C.

Gulf War. Originated with an Iraqi attack on Iran in September 1980 and has proved a debilitating phase of a secular ideological, political and territorial conflict between Persians and Arabs. Iraqi motives were defensive, to counter the expansion of the Iranian revolution, and offensive, aiming to recover the Shatt al-Arab frontier ceded to Iran in 1975 and to achieve paramountcy in the Gulf region. Expectations of a quick victory over Iranian forces divided by the revolution and attacked in the rear by the Arab populations of Khuzistan, proved illusory. The war became a stalemate, confirmed by the failure of a massive Iranian offensive in 1984, with Iraq ready to settle for a return to the status quo but Iran, for whom the war was an essential part of the revolutionary ideal, insisting that the 'godless' Iraqi BA'ATH regime change. The war was sometimes represented as advantageous to all but the combatants since it neutralized the two main rivals for Gulf supremacy and reduced the supply of oil to a glutted market. But the heavy loss of life and resources, the Iraqi use of gas and anxieties lest the war spread down the Gulf came to outweigh the more optimistic calculations of REALPOLITIK.　　　　　　W.K.

Guomindang, see under KUOMINTANG.

guru. A spiritual master in HINDUISM, such as every spiritually ambitious disciple is thought to need. The term is also applied to a Western teacher of the spiritual life, or even, ironically, to any mentor held in what is felt to be excessive reverence. See also SWAMI.　　　　　　D.L.E.

GUTS, see under GRAND UNIFICATION/ GRAND UNIFIED THEORIES.

gynaecology. Literally means diseases peculiar to women as opposed to men. Modern gynaecology has a broader concept for the medical and surgical care of women and children including physical and psychological health, health education, FAMILY PLANNING, screening for disease and psycho-sexual problems as well as those disorders traditionally the responsibility of the gynaecologist. Further changes have resulted from greater knowledge of reproductive ENDOCRINOLOGY, use of hormones and other therapeutic substances affecting endocrine function and the control of FERTILITY. The breasts, genital and urinary tracts are the usual sites of gynaecological disease which may be present at any age. Disorders include developmental abnormalities, menstrual problems such as amenorrhoea, heavy and irregular periods, infections and tumours of the genital tract, abnormal bladder function and leakage of urine, prolapse of the genital tract and many abnormalities due to endocrine disturbance. Preventative medicine and screening for disease for asymptomatic women include examination of breasts, pelvic examination and the taking of cervical smears to detect dysplasia which may be a precursor of carcinoma (see CANCER). Hormone replacement therapy is a term used for the treatment of woman who are suffering or may suffer later from lack of oestrogen due to ovarian failure at the menopause, to absence or removal of the ovaries or to inactive ovaries. Symptoms which affect one woman in four include hot flushes, sweating and vaginal dryness and are usually relieved by oestrogens. Unless the uterus has been removed progestogen should also be taken as oestrogen alone may rarely induce uterine (endometrial) carcinoma. Some women are prone to bone loss in old age and hormone therapy may prevent or reduce this.   S.J.S.

Bibl: S.J. Steele, *Gynaecology, Obstetrics and the Neonate* (London, 1985).

gynandromorphism, see under INTERSEX.

gyroscope (or *gyro*). A rotating wheel so mounted on a shaft that either or both of its basic properties can be used to advantage. The first of these properties is that the wheel tends to maintain the direction of its axis of spin in space, not being influenced by the earth or by any other object in the universe, so far as is known. The second property is that, if a twisting force (torque) is applied to the shaft so as to try to rotate the shaft about an axis perpendicular to the shaft, the resulting motion will be a rotation of the shaft about an axis which is at right angles both to the shaft and to the axis of the torque. Such motion is known as *precession*.

Gyroscopic properties are of great importance in the design of vehicles, including the bicycle, on account of the torques applied to the wheels during cornering. Gyroscopes are used in navigational instruments for ships, aircraft, and spacecraft; also in conjunction with a magnetic compass, for direction-finding and for the control of AUTOMATIC PILOTS. Large gyros have been used to assist the stabilization of ships in rough seas.

A gyroscope may also consist of a vibrating mass rather than a spinning wheel, and in this form it is common in living creatures such as the common crane fly ('daddy-long-legs').   E.R.L.

H

Habimah (Hebrew for 'stage'). A theatre company founded in Moscow in 1917 to perform plays in Hebrew. Stanislavsky arranged for the actors, mostly from Polish theatres, to be trained by Yevgeny Vaktangov; the first performances were immensely successful, and the company visited America and Palestine (1928). Resident in Palestine since 1931, Habimah became Israel's official National Theatre (with a dramatic school and library) in 1953.   M.S.-S.

habitat. In GEOGRAPHY, a term used to denote the natural ENVIRONMENT of a plant or animal. It may be expressed as one of the main natural REGIONS which are recognized in the subject, such as tropical rain forests or temperate grasslands, or as one of their subdivisions, such as chalk grassland or beech woodland.   M.L.

habituation. In CONDITIONING, the process of adjustment to a frequent or constant STIMULUS, whereby a minimal response is produced, or none at all.   H.L.

hadron. Any ELEMENTARY PARTICLE that reacts or decays with STRONG INTERACTIONS (e.g. the PROTON, the NEUTRON).
                                              M.V.B.

haematology. Literally the science of the blood — its formation, composition, function and diseases. In the U.K. most hospitals now have a department of haematology staffed by pathologists, physicians and laboratory technicians. Their function is to provide a diagnostic service, to advance knowledge of their speciality and to be responsible for the care of patients with blood diseases. The department will also be responsible for the hospital's blood transfusion service. In recent years many universities have established professorships of haematology.

Blood comprises a fluid called plasma in which are suspended three types of CELLS. (1) Red cells: they contain the red pigment haemoglobin which picks up oxygen in the lungs and liberates it when the blood passes through the small vessels in the tissues. (2) White cells: they provide an important defence against infection. (3) Platelets: these help to control bleeding. All three cell types are formed in postnatal life in the bone marrow. The number of each type in the blood is relatively constant in health: in disease, their numbers may be markedly altered. Counting blood cells is an important laboratory function; at one time a laborious task, this can nowadays be carried out quickly and accurately by automated equipment. (The term anaemia describes a deficiency in the number of red cells or in the haemoglobin they contain.)

Abnormal counts can result from diseases not primarily connected with the blood cells or bone marrow, as in infections such as pneumonia, or as the result of haemorrhage. More important causes of abnormal counts are the primary blood and bone marrow diseases; there are many hereditary (GENETIC) and acquired types. Hereditary anaemias result from defects of the red cells or of their haemoglobin. Best known and particularly important because of their frequency are thalassaemia (Mediterranean anaemia) and sickle-cell disease (an abnormal haemoglobin disorder). Hereditary disorders of the white cells and platelets are known but are uncommon. The bleeding disorder haemophilia is caused by a hereditary deficiency of a clotting factor present in plasma. Acquired anaemias include pernicious anaemia (easily treatable despite its name) and iron-deficiency anaemia. Rarely, the patient forms antibodies against his own red cells and destroys them: this is AUTO-IMMUNE haemolytic anaemia. Haemolytic disease of the newborn also has an immune basis. Leukaemias are acquired diseases of the white cells — equivalent in nature to CANCERS of organs such as the lung and breast. Acquired diseases of the platelets lead to purpura, i.e., bleeding into the skin or from internal organs. Aplastic anaemia is a rare disease in which there is a failure to produce all three types of blood cells.

Treatment of blood diseases depends upon understanding their cause. Deficiencies of NUTRIENTS necessary for the development of blood cells, such as iron, vitamin B^{12} and folic acid, can be easily remedied. When there is failure of blood cell formation, blood transfusion can be life-saving. However, donated blood has only a limited life-span, up to 3-4 months at the most for red cells and only a matter of days for white cells and platelets. (The blood groups of the donor and recipient have to be compatible.) Leukaemias are difficult to treat although much progress has been made. Powerful drugs are available (chemotherapy); a limitation in their use is their effect on normal blood cells and other tissues as well as on leukaemic cells. The same applies to irradiation. Bone marrow transplantation is valuable in some cases. The donated marrow has to be as compatible as possible with the recipient's tissues. In practice, transplantation is usually restricted to between identical twins (rarely possible) or siblings (brothers and sisters). The procedure is easily carried out: marrow cells are aspirated from the hip bones of the donor and given in suspension into one of the recipient's veins. The marrow cells then 'home' to the recipient's marrow. In exchange transfusion large volumes of the patient's blood are replaced by normal blood. It has been used with particular benefit in infants with haemolytic disease of the newborn. Plasmapheresis involves bleeding a donor of a large volume of blood and returning to him/her the red cells while retaining the plasma. The technique is used when the plasma of the donor is the blood component required rather than the red cells.

J.V.D.

haemodialysis. The use of diffusion across a semi-permeable membrane to remove water and crystalloids from blood. The term dialysis was coined by Graham in 1861 to describe the application to chemical analysis of liquid diffusion across vegetable parchment. Abel and his colleagues applied the principle to the purification of the blood of nephrectomized dogs in 1913 using celloidin tubes as membrane and hirudin (from leeches) as anticoagulant, and they called the apparatus an artificial kidney. In the 1920s Haas in Germany performed the first haemodialysis on uraemic patients. The development of cellophane membranes and purification of heparin anticoagulant set the stage for the present era of haemodialysis which was initiated by Kolff in Holland in 1943, and most importantly advanced when the vascular shunt (1960) and fistula (1967) were described. In any treatment session there are two components to the removal of nitrogenous waste products: diffusive and convective transport across the membrane. If highly permeable membrane is used or the transmembrane pressure gradient is large then ultrafiltration is increased and convective transport plays a larger part. In haemofiltration the blood is ultrafiltered without dialysis fluid (a salt solution) on the other side of the membrane and substitution fluid is added to the bloodstream either before or after the dialyser, thus mimicking physiological renal function. In haemodialfiltration the principles are combined and in sequential ultrafiltration haemodialysis the processes of ultrafiltration and dialysis are performed in sequence. In haemoperfusion blood is passed over coated charcoal particles with particular absorbent qualities.

A.J.W.

haemorheology. This term was coined by A.L. Copley in 1951, as 'a branch of biomedical sciences, concerned with deformation and flow properties of cellular and plasmatic components of blood in macroscopic, microscopic and submicroscopic dimensions, and with the rheological properties of vessel structures, with which blood comes into direct contact'. Blood is an anomalous liquid, a complex suspension of cells and plasma showing extreme variation of flow properties related to flow conditions (shear stresses and geometry of flow system), and determined by blood composition (cellocrits, cell deformabilities and aggregabilities). In addition, important complex phenomena occur at interfaces contacted with blood, including cell adhesion and blood coagulation. Theoretical and experimental haemorheology study the complex behaviour of blood (or components thereof) in 'in vitro' systems, such as whole blood and plasma viscosity, viscoelasticity, blood cell deformability and aggregation, blood flow and distribution in narrow channels or branches, etc. Clinical haemorheology deals with medical aspects studying the role of blood RHEOLOGY in haematological (polcythaemia in adults and neonates, leu-kaemias, red cell dyscrasias, para-proteinaemias) and ischemic (peripheral, myocardial, cerebral) diseases. Its other important aspect is the therapeutical correction of pathological flow properties, as by haemodilution (lowering haematocrit), defibrinogenation, plasmapheresis (exchanging plasma with another fluid), and drug therapy. Haemorheology is an established branch of *biorheology* affiliated with the International Society of Biorheology, and national societies of clinical haemorheology.   E.E.

Bibl: S. Chien *et al., Clinical Hemorheology* (Boston, 1986).

Hagana, see under IRGUN ZVAI LEUMI.

Hagedorn temperature, see under ELEMENTARY PARTICLES.

half-life. In RADIOACTIVITY, the average time which must elapse for half the NUCLEI in a large sample to decay (and which also gives the *probability* of decay in any time interval). More generally, an average time characterizing processes in any large population, e.g. the time taken to sell half the items in a given consignment of goods (the 'shelf-life').   M.V.B.

Hall effect. Discovered by E.H. Hall in 1880, is observed when an electric current is passed along a conductor which itself is in a magnetic field at right angles to the direction of the current. The magnetic field deflects the current so that some of the current carriers (e.g. ELECTRONS) strike the side of the conductor. The build-up of charge thus produced gives rise to a voltage, the Hall voltage, across the conductor in a direction which is perpendicular to the applied magnetic field. Measurements of the Hall effect are very useful because the size of the Hall voltage is a measure of the concentration of the charge carriers in the sample. This is very important in SEMICONDUCTOR technology where the number of charge carriers is very sensitive to small traces of impurity (DOPING) and this can materially affect the operation of a device such as a TRANSISTOR. (See also QUANTUM HALL EFFECT.) H.M.R.

Hall voltage, see under HALL EFFECT.

haploid (noun or adjective). (A CELL) containing only a single set of CHROMOSOMES. Contrasted with DIPLOID; POLYPLOID.
                                                              J.M.S.

happenings and **events.** Performances juxtaposing a variety of aural and visual material in a non-representational manner, with the aim of moving the spectator at an unconscious rather than a rational level. The genre owes its origin to the pieces combining music with other MEDIA developed by John Cage at BLACK MOUNTAIN College in the 1950s; the term 'happening' was first used by the painter Allan Kaprow (1959). In the work of Kaprow and Claes Oldenburg in New York happenings were associated with the POP ART movement of the early 1960s, particularly in the construction of ENVIRONMENTS. Throughout the 1960s the term was applied to pieces presented in Europe (see also WIENER-GRUPPE) and the U.S.A. by artists (e.g. the German graphic artist Wolf Vostell) as well as theatre and dance groups, drawing eclectically upon a variety of traditions from FUTURISM and DADA to the THEATRE OF CRUELTY. In formal terms a happening contains several actions presented sequentially, while an event contains one action (which may be repeated).   M.A.

Bibl: M. Kirby (ed.), *Happenings: an Illustrated Anthology* (New York, 1965); A. Henri, *Environments and Happenings* (London, 1974).

hard-edge. A phrase coined by the Los Angeles critic Jules Lansner in 1958 to describe the painting of several local ABSTRACT artists, including John McLaughlin, characterized by (*a*) flat forms rimmed by hard, clean edges presented in uniform colours, and (*b*) an overall unity in which colour and shape (or form) are one and the same entity. His term appeared in an introduction to the exhibition 'Four Abstract Classicists', but when in 1960 the show travelled to the Institute of Contemporary Arts in London it was re-titled 'West Coast Hard-Edge'. The term has been loosely used since to describe any art that tended towards the geometric.
                                                              A.K.W.

Bibl: J. Coplans, 'John McLaughlin, Hard Edge and American Painting' (*Artforum*, Jan. 1964).

hard X-rays, see under X-RAY ASTRONOMY.

hardware. In COMPUTING, the actual COMPUTER as opposed to the PROGRAMS or SOFTWARE. C.S.

hawks, see DOVES AND HAWKS.

Hawthorne effect. In INDUSTRIAL PSYCHOLOGY, a result extrapolated from experiments conducted in the Hawthorne works of the Western Electric Company, near Chicago, between 1924 and 1936. It was found that increased productivity depended not so much on any particular incentives as on workers interpreting any change as provisional evidence of MANAGEMENT'S interest and goodwill. A Hawthorne effect, then, is initial improvement in performance following a newly introduced change. H.L.
Bibl: F.J. Roethlisberger, *Management and the Worker* (Cambridge, Mass., 1939).

health foods. An undefined group of materials which include a range of VITAMINS, mineral salts and AMINO ACIDS as well as supplements of doubtful value such as kelp, lecithin, cider vinegar, bees' royal jelly, and RNA (see NUCLEIC ACID), and also free range eggs and foods grown without the use of agricultural chemicals. A.E.B.
Bibl: A.E. Bender, *Health or Hoax?* (Goring-on-Thames, 1985).

heartland. Geographical term for the central part of the Eurasian land mass. It was first used by Sir Halford Mackinder (1861-1947) to describe those parts of Eurasia not accessible from the sea and therefore presumed to be immune from attack by a maritime power. P.H.

heat death of universe. The hypothetical situation when the disordering tendency expressed by the second law of THERMODYNAMICS, acting over aeons of future time, results in the absence anywhere in the universe of ENERGY in a form which can be converted into work by organisms or machines of a type familiar to us. The second law may not, however, apply to the universe as a whole, perhaps because of the long-range ordering influence of GRAVITATION. See also STATISTICAL MECHANICS. M.V.B.

heat exchanger. Apparatus for the transfer of heat to a substance which can be used directly in a piece of equipment requiring heat, from one which cannot do so for reasons inherent in the system which generated the heat. Thus, the heat energy in RADIOACTIVE fluid from a NUCLEAR REACTOR can be used, after passing through a heat exchanger incorporating a radioactive shield, to heat water in another vessel which can then be fed to a steam TURBINE. E.R.L.

heat pump. A system for pumping heat 'uphill', i.e. from a place of lower temperature to one of higher. A common example is the domestic refrigerator in which heat is ejected from the inside to the atmosphere outside. The reverse process is to be seen if a building is heated by cooling the air around it. The second law of THERMODYNAMICS demands that work is needed to perform such a task. One method in common use is to compress a gas (in the example of the refrigerator this is done *outside* the vessel). The gas liquefies, releasing in the process large quantities of heat, which is dissipated mostly by convection. The liquefied gas is then passed through a pipe system to the inside of the refrigerator where it is allowed to evaporate, i.e. to reverse the process and *take in* heat from the air inside the refrigerator. The gas is led outside again and the process repeated as many times as are necessary to maintain the required difference between internal and external temperature. E.R.L.

heavy water. Water in which one or both of the normal hydrogen atoms in each MOLECULE is replaced by DEUTERIUM. It is similar to ordinary water except for its ability to slow down NEUTRONS without reacting with them, and for this reason heavy water is used in NUCLEAR REACTORS as a MODERATOR. M.V.B.

hedonism. The theory that pleasure is the only thing that is intrinsically good, pain the only thing intrinsically bad. Other things, for the hedonist, are good or bad only instrumentally, to the extent that they are productive of pleasure or pain. What distinguishes hedonism as a philosophical theory from what is colloquially understood by the same name is that it works with a much more inclusive conception of pleasure and pain. It takes pleasure to be, not just immediate bodily gratification, but the satisfaction of any desire whatever, enjoyment or gratification of any kind; pain, similarly, is not just bodily anguish, but any form of suffering or distress. The usual form of hedonist ETHICS, UTILITARIANISM, takes the pleasure and pain of everyone affected by it to be the CRITERION of an action's rightness, and is associated with a psychological version of hedonism which holds that human actions are motivated (see MOTIVATION) primarily by a search for pleasure and the avoidance of pain. A.Q.

Bibl: R.B. Brandt, *Ethical Theory* (Englewood Cliffs, N.J., 1959); J. Gosling, *Pleasure and Desire* (Oxford, 1969).

Hegelianism. In PHILOSOPHY, the idealistic (see IDEALISM) system of G.W.F. Hegel (1770-1831) in which the method of DIALECTIC is used to systematize and complete all aspects of knowledge and experience and weld them into an inclusive whole. Philosophy, for Hegel, is the highest, or absolute, form of human knowledge, and all other forms must submit to its critical modifications. Hegel concludes that reality as a whole, or the ABSOLUTE, is of the nature of a mind, and that it presents itself to reflection first as a system of CONCEPTS, then as nature, and last, and most satisfactorily, as mind. A.Q.

Bibl: R. Plant, *Hegel* (London and Bloomington, 1973).

hegemony (from Greek *hegemon*, meaning leader or ruler).

(1) Since the 19th century it has been used especially to describe the predominance of one state over others, e.g. the French hegemony over Europe in the time of Napoleon. By extension, *hegemonism* is used to describe 'great power' policies aimed at establishing such a preponder-ance, a use close to one of the meanings of IMPERIALISM.

(2) In the writings of some 20th-century MARXISTS (especially the Italian Gramsci) it is used to denote the predominance of one social CLASS over others, e.g. in the term *bourgeois hegemony*. The feature which this usage stresses is not only the political and economic control exercised by a dominant class but its success in projecting its own particular way of seeing the world, human and social relationships, so that this is accepted as 'COMMON SENSE' and part of the natural order by those who are in fact subordinated to it. From this it follows that REVOLUTION is seen not only as the transfer of political and economic POWER but as the creation of an alternative hegemony through new forms of experience and CONSCIOUSNESS. This is different from the more familiar Marxist view that change in the economic base is what matters and that change in the SUPERSTRUC-TURE is a reflection of this; instead, the struggle for hegemony is seen as a primary and even decisive factor in radical change, including change in the economic base itself. A.L.C.B.

Heisenberg's uncertainty principle, see under UNCERTAINTY PRINCIPLE.

helix, double, see DOUBLE HELIX.

helminthology. The branch of ZOOLOGY concerned with the *helminthes*, i.e. parasitic worms. The word is, however, now generally confined to the study of those internally parasitic flat worms (*platyhelminthes*) which include the flukes and such dangerous human parasites as *schistosoma* (or *bilharzia*). Schistosomiasis is one of the gravest and most intractable diseases of tropical Africa. The intermediate host is a water-snail, and most attempts at eradication or control are concentrated upon it. P.M.

Helsinki 1975. The name given to the Conference on Security and Cooperation in Europe at Helsinki on 1 August 1975, attended by 35 nations both NON-ALIGNED and neutral and belonging to the Warsaw Pact and NATO. In the Final Act of the Conference the NATO countries agreed to the Soviet demand that the Western powers officially recognize the de facto borders established after World War II and the consequent division of Europe. In return for this concession the Soviet Union accepted a declaration on the observance of HUMAN RIGHTS in its sphere of influence, and on a freer flow of information and freer travel between the two halves of Europe. Subsequently the Soviet Union has been embarrassed by this declaration, as groups were set up throughout Eastern Europe to monitor the implementation of the Helsinki agreements (see CHARTER 77; SOVIET DISSENT). It has also been criticized by Western nations at the conferences held to review the execution of the Helsinki accords for ignoring provisions on human rights. However the conference did help to engender a spirit of cooperation and marked the high point of DÉTENTE between the Eastern and Western blocs. Greater contacts between East and West Germany were permitted and a large number of Jews were allowed to emigrate as a result of the treaty.　D.PR.

Bibl: R. Edmonds, *Soviet Foreign Policy: The Brezhnev Years* (Oxford, 1983).

hemispheres of the brain, see TWO HEMISPHERES.

Herbartian psychology. The SCHOOL OF PSYCHOLOGY based on the ideas of Johann Herbart (1776-1841), German philosopher, psychologist, and educationist. He viewed mind as an organized, unitary, and dynamic interplay of ideas which actively attracted and repelled each other and struggled for a place in CONSCIOUSNESS.
　I.M.L.H.

heredity, see under GENETICS.

heresy. In Christian (see CHRISTIANITY) THEOLOGY, the attitude which makes a personal choice (Greek *hairesis*) rather than accepting the doctrines of CATHOLICISM. To a large extent modern thought rests on independent thinking, so that in modern times the term is seldom used pejoratively.　D.L.E.

heritability. That part of the variability of a population which arises from GENETIC rather than environmental causes.　J.M.S.

hermaphrodite, see under INTERSEX.

hermeneutics.
(1) That part of Christian THEOLOGY which is concerned with finding and interpreting (Greek *hermeneus*, an interpreter) the spiritual truth in the Bible, so that the Gospel is understood as addressed to each generation. Many of the issues involved were raised afresh by Rudolf Bultmann's proposal to DEMYTHOLOGIZE the New Testament.　D.L.E.
(2) More generally, the art, skill, or theory of interpretation, of understanding the significance of human actions, utterances, products, and INSTITUTIONS. In this sense the term was brought into PHILOSOPHY from theology by Dilthey in the late 19th century to refer to the fundamental discipline that is concerned with the special methods of the human studies or GEISTESWISSENSCHAFTEN, which do not merely order the raw deliverances of sensation but must seek an understanding (VERSTEHEN) of their essentially meaningful subject-matter. The term has since been more broadly applied by Heidegger to emphasize the general metaphysical purport (see METAPHYSICS) of his investigations into the nature of human existence.　A.Q.

hermetic. Adjective derived from the name of the Greek god Hermes Trismegistus (identified by the Greeks with the Egyptian Thoth, supposed author of mystical works and inventor of a magically airtight container). In literary contexts, it is applied, generally, to poetry of a Platonic, esoteric, recondite, or occult kind; or, more specifically, to a movement in contemporary Italian poetry: *poesia ermetica*. The term was coined, and its subject-matter traced, defined, and criticized, by Francesco Flora in *La poesia ermetica* (1936). The theoretical pioneer was Arturo Onofri, who carried over DECADENT and SYMBOLIST notions of 'pure poetry' from French to Italian, and who was influenced by Rudolf Steiner's ANTHROPOSOPHY. Onofri advocated (1925) a 'naked poetry', from which all logical elements would be eliminated and which would concentrate on the magic of the single word, on silences and (on the page) blankness. His programme was meanwhile being fulfilled by Giuseppe Ungaretti (1888-1970). Ungaretti sought to purge his poetry of rhetoric, and to restore the 'pristine' meanings to words by approaching them with the utmost simplicity: 'All the emphasis was on the word itself, each word, its sound, meaning, resonance, and the space it could be made to fill.' Ungaretti's successors, Eugenio Montale and Salvatore Quasimodo, were of very different temperament, and neither had been through a period of enthusiasm for Mussolini, as Ungaretti had. Since it was necessary for genuine poets to write 'over the heads' of the FASCIST censors, the motives for writing 'hermetically' were enhanced. But both Montale and Quasimodo sought to rid poetry of rhetorical embellishment. Montale added to hermetic poetry a musicality, Quasimodo a Greek purity of diction. Both achieved an underlying HUMANISM at odds with fascism. This simplicity of approach involved a subjectivity which some critics found excessively difficult; but *poesia ermetica* is now seen as a pioneering phase in Italian poetry. Other poets classed as hermetic include Mario Luzi, Alfonso Gatto, and Vittorio Sereni. The inclination still exists in Italian poetry.   M.S.-S.

heroic materialism, see under ZEITGEIST.

herpes. Herpes simplex virus has two types. Type 1 most often affects the mouth, causing 'cold sores', which are usually contracted in childhood. Type 2 usually affects the genitals, is SEXUALLY TRANSMITTED and is commonest in young adults. Shallow painful ulcers appear on the penis, vulva, cervix or anus, which heal in 1-2 weeks. After a first attack of genital herpes the virus disappears from the skin but becomes latent in adjacent nerve ganglia. Reactivation leads to further attacks of herpes at variable intervals, a sequence which persists indefinitely. During an attack, a person with genital herpes can transmit it sexually to others. It is possible for a woman who has an attack of herpes during labour to infect her baby, but this can be avoided by caesarian section. There is no permanent cure for genital herpes, but antiviral drugs can shorten and mitigate the attacks. Immunization may be possible in the future, but no safe and effective VACCINE is currently available.   J.D.O.

Bibl: J.K. Oates, *Herpes* (London, 1983).

herstory, see under FEMINIST HISTORY.

Hertzsprung-Russell diagram. An important GRAPH in ASTROPHYSICS, where the total ENERGY radiated by a star (its 'brightness') is plotted against wavelength (i.e. colour). The positions of the majority of stars on this graph lie near a diagonal line, along which, it is believed, typical 'main-sequence' stars progress in the course of their evolution from blue-bright (hot) to red-dim (cool). See also BLACK HOLE; NOVA; RED GIANT; SUPERNOVA.   M.V.B.

Hessen thesis. The HISTORICAL MATERIALIST theory of the determination of CONSCIOUSNESS by social being, has always found science difficult to place. In the 1930s, official Soviet MARXISM seemingly stated categorically that the Scientific Revolution, as it had developed from the 17th century, was an expression of BOURGEOIS ideology, responding to the needs of CAPITALIST society. In 1931, Boris Hessen argued that Isaac Newton's *Mathematical Principles of Natural Philosophy* (1687) could best be explained as formulated to resolve crucial bottlenecks encountered by industry and TECHNOLOGY in a commercial society. For example, its ASTRONOMY would lead to the advance in navigation required by transoceanic trade. Additionally, Hessen argued that, as an ideologue of the ruling order, Newton chose to retain a place for God in the natural system, rejecting the MATERIALISM which had been espoused by radicals in the Civil War. Though few of Hessen's specific interpretations seem well supported, his analysis of scientific theory as hidden IDEOLOGY has been fruitfully deployed.   R.P.

Bibl: Boris Hessen, 'The Social and Economic Roots of Newton's Principia', in P.G. Werskey (ed.), *Science at the Crossroads* (London, 1971; first published 1931).

heteroglossia (*raznorecie*). A term coined (like 'polyphony') by the Russian critic Mikhail Bakhtin (see BAKHTINIAN) to de-

scribe the diversity of languages or 'social voices' in literature and more especially in the novel. He contrasted the epic, well-defined and official, with the novel, 'one of the most fluid of genres' associated with unofficial ideas, with parody, diversity, and the propensity for dialogue and the confrontation of different views of the world. These possibilities, which he regarded as in some sense built into the genre, were, according to Bakhtin, most fully realized in two of his favourite authors, Rabelais and Dostoyevsky, whose work presents not the viewpoint of the author but the dialogue between different characters, such as Pantagruel and Panurge, or even as in the case of Golyadkin in Dostoyevsky's *The Double*, the 'internal dialogue' of a single character.
P.B.

Bibl: M. Bakhtin, *Problems of Dostoevsky's Poetics* (Leningrad, 1929; Manchester, 1984).

heterokaryote, see under NUCLEUS.

heterological. In LOGIC, a term applied to a word that is not truly predicable of itself, e.g. the word 'long' (which is not long) or the word 'French' (which is not French). Conversely, the words 'short' and 'English' are said to be *autological*. A.Q.

heterosexism, see under HOMOSEXUALITY.

heterosis, see under GENE.

heterostructure, see under SUPERLATTICE.

heterotrophic, see under AUTOTROPHIC.

heterozygote, see under GENE; MENDEL'S LAWS.

heuristic.
(1) (adjective) Concerned with ways of finding things out or solving problems. Also (noun) a contraction of *heuristic method*: a procedure for searching out an *unknown* goal by incremental exploration, according to some guiding principle which reduces the amount of searching required (e.g. to reach the top of an unfamiliar hill in fog, a useful heuristic would be to make

every step an upward one rather than trying steps in all directions). An important concept in CYBERNETICS and ARTIFICIAL INTELLIGENCE. S.BE.

(2) In SOCIAL SCIENCE, the term is used especially to characterize conceptual devices such as IDEAL TYPES, MODELS, and working hypotheses which are not intended to describe or explain the facts, but to suggest possible explanations or eliminate others. J.R.T.

Bibl: G. Polya, *How to Solve It* (Princeton, 2nd ed., 1971); S. Beer, *Brain of the Firm* (London and New York, 1972).

hidden curriculum. Subjects that are not on a school timetable but are nevertheless taught as part of the total syllabus: social awareness and racial tolerance are examples. J.I.

hidden economy, see under BLACK ECONOMY.

hidden variables. An important philosophical idea arising in context of the development of QUANTUM THEORY. Unlike classical PHYSICS, quantum theory involved 'indeterminism', i.e., the admission that certain occurrences in physics could not be predicted with the cast-iron certainty of traditional cause and effect. Predictions would be at best statistical. The idea of hidden variables was put forward as the notion of a set of purely hypothetical physical realities, knowledge of which would enable scientists to make more precise predictions than quantum theory seemed to make possible. Of course, orthodox quantum theorists disbelieved in the reality of such hidden variables, whereas critics of quantum theory set out to discover them. The issue has bedevilled quantum theory for almost half a century. It would seem that the idea of such hidden variables is philosophically interesting, but contains little relevant to the physicist studying quantum phenomena. So far, quantum theory has withstood the test of experiments. R.P.

Bibl: M. Jammer, *The Conceptual Development of Quantum Mechanics* (New York, 1966).

hi-fi. Abbreviation of 'high fidelity', a term applied to ELECTRONIC apparatus designed to reproduce music, the human voice, or other sounds with minimal distortion. Although such reproduction requires the same high quality in the recording microphone, the amplifiers, the transmission or storage unit, and the loudspeakers, the term is most often used colloquially to describe the output side of the apparatus, i.e. the amplifier and its loudspeaker.   E.R.L.

Higgsino, see under SUPERSYMMETRY.

high culture, see under MASS CULTURE.

high-level programming language. In COMPUTING, a PROGRAMMING LANGUAGE designed with the convenience of its human users in mind rather than the peculiarities of any particular machine. Its chief merit is that it allows the programmer to leave many of the routine details of PROGRAM organization to the COMPUTER itself. It requires a COMPILER to translate the program into MACHINE CODE and typically produces 10 or more machine instructions for each statement written in it. Surprisingly, perhaps, it increases the productivity of programmers by about the same factor. A program written in a high-level language, unlike one written in an ASSEMBLY LANGUAGE, is nearly independent of the computer on which it is run.   C.S.

high tech. A distinctive current architectural style which places high visual valuation on the deployment of industrial forms and imagery both outside and inside. It derives from one of the Modern Movement's architectural beliefs that buildings should frankly express the materials from which they are constructed, the way in which they are constructed, and express in some way the new machine culture of the 20th century. It was not until the 1970s that this was realized in any startling way in the form of buildings such as the Centre Pompidou in Paris. Like BRUTALISM, high tech architecture makes aesthetic capital of the building's functional elements — especially mechanical equipment such as air conditioning ducts, window cleaning apparatus and dramatic structures. Unlike brutalism the preferred materials of high tech are lightweight, reinforcing another strand in

high tech to do with the idea of buildings as essentially temporary, flexible structures. Materials include glass, plain sheet materials, especially sheet metal, often highly polished or coloured and often perforated or profiled. Steel is the preferred structural material, often wire braced and in dramatic configurations which in engineering terms are frequently redundant.
                                              S.L.

higher arithmetic, see NUMBER THEORY.

higher criticism. The objective and exact study of the sources and methods used by the authors of the Bible. The pioneers of this scientific approach were almost all 19th-century scholars in German universities. In a book of 1881, by W. R. Smith, who was one of the British pioneers, the attempt to get behind the text to the actual history was contrasted with 'lower' criticism, i.e. with the study of manuscripts and other evidence in order to get at the text as originally written (see also TEXTUAL CRITICISM). In the 20th century, literary *source criticism* has been supplemented by *form criticism* (i.e. the attempt to discern the form taken by a story or teaching in order to make it more easily memorable, or more impressive, as it was passed on in ORAL TRADITION), and also by *redaction criticism* (i.e. the attempt to recover the theological motive of those redactors or editors who gathered these stories or teachings into the books we have).   D.L.E.
  Bibl: M. Black and H.H. Rowley (eds.), *Peak's Commentary on the Bible* (London, rev. ed., 1962); O. Eissfeldt, *The Old Testament: an Introduction* (Oxford, 1965); W.G. Kümmel, *The New Testament: the History of the Investigation of its Problems* (London, 1973) and *Introduction to the New Testament* (London, rev. ed., 1975).

Hilbert space. A CONCEPT introduced by David Hilbert (1862-1943) in his investigation of integral EQUATIONS. The characteristic feature of it and its generalizations is the application of geometric terminology and of methods which had been developed in the study of finite-dimensional (see DIMENSION) VECTOR SPACES to 'spaces' of FUNCTIONS which are infinite-dimensional (e.g. by the use of FOURIER SERIES). It is a fundamental concept of functional ANALYSIS and of QUANTUM MECHANICS. R.G.

Hinduism. The RELIGION of most Indians. It has a rich variety, ranging from popular worship of gods in temples and homes, with petitions and celebrations, through devotional THEISM which sees these gods merely as expressions of the One God (e.g. as incarnations of Vishnu), to an austere MYSTICISM which suspects all religious images and seeks the absorption of the individual in the impersonal World-Spirit (the *Brahman*) through ENLIGHTENMENT. This religion has been spread by Indians in many countries and has impressed many disillusioned or bored Christians by its tolerance, its profusion of religious emotion, its imaginative philosophy, its methods of self-mastery (especially in YOGA), and its power to give stability to a vast nation. Special admiration has been felt for the *Upanishads* (probably *c.* 800 B.C.) or ancient meditations on the position of man in a universe he did not make, and for the more warmly personal religion expressed in a later scripture, the *Bhagavad Gita* (probably *c.* 300 B.C.). The best-known Hindu of this century was Mahatma Gandhi (1869-1948), a saintly lawyer and political leader especially notable for the success of his advocacy of NON-VIOLENT RESISTANCE in ending British imperial rule. But it is difficult for those not born Indians to enter Hinduism's heritage. It is also difficult to reconcile some of its doctrines (e.g. the belief in the reincarnation of the self in successive bodies better or worse according to one's merits) with modern thought; and some of its traditional practices (e.g. the division of the population into 'CASTES' or strictly hereditary classes) with modern convictions about human EQUALITY. In India, which is officially a secular state (see SECULARIZATION), Hinduism is slowly adjusting itself to such challenges. D.L.E.

Bibl: S. Radhakrishnan, *The Hindu View of Life* (London and New York, 1927); *The Principal Upanishads* (London and New York, 1953) and *Religion in a Changing World* (London and New York, 1967); R.C. Zaehner, *Hinduism* (London and New York, 2nd ed., 1966); L. Du-

mont, *Homo Hierarchicus* (London and New York, 1972).

hinterland. The German word *Hinterland* or 'back country' originally referred to the inland territory beyond the occupied coastal districts over which a colonial power claimed jurisdiction; thus it was applied in the late 19th century to parts of Africa. The word has been adapted by geographers to mean the land which lies behind a seaport and supplies the bulk of its exports, and in which most of its imports are distributed. In urban GEOGRAPHY the term is also used with reference to other centres of population, e.g. market towns. M.L.

hip hop, see under POPULAR DANCE.

hippies. Term coined in California in 1966-7 to denote the mainly young people participating in the birth of the UNDERGROUND. As with their precursors the BEATS, the hippies' etymology is contentious; the most plausible derivation is from the Negro slang word 'hep' or 'hip' meaning to be knowledgeable, to have experience. Hippiedom in this first instance involved a 'philosophy' of Peace and Love together with a rejection of things material, a devotion to marijuana and lysergic acid (LSD) as instruments of enlightenment and pleasure, a propensity for communal LIFE-STYLES and LIBERTARIAN sexual behaviour, and a style of dress which included beads, bells, and long hair. This original conception of the hippie did not last in its pure form for longer than two years, the originators themselves staging a 'Death of Hippie' parade in San Francisco in 1968. The era of 'love-ins', 'flower-power', and 'beautiful vibes' soon degenerated, largely by over-exposure in the mass MEDIA, into commercialism, violence and widespread DRUG abuse. Over the intervening period the term hippie was widely, if incorrectly, used to denote any young, long-haired person suspected of unconventional standards. Youthful nonconformity to social conventions, however, has changed in style so that hippies have become a cultural anachronism in the changed economic and socio-political circumstances of the late 20th century. (See also DROP-OUT.) P.S.L.

Hiroshima. The Japanese city selected as target for the first atomic bomb dropped by the U.S. Air Force, on 6 August 1945. Over 78,000 were killed, a further 70,000 badly injured, and two-thirds of the city destroyed. Most of the surviving population suffered long-term consequences of radiation. On 9 August a second bomb was dropped on Nagasaki; their combined effect was the surrender of Japan. The decision to use the bomb was primarily governed by the wish to avoid a full-scale invasion of Japan and the consequent heavy losses to the U.S. It has also been suggested that America wished to end the war quickly to prevent the U.S.S.R. pressing claims on China or participating in the invasion and occupation of Japan.   S.R.

Bibl: M.J. Sherwin, *A World Destroyed: The Atomic Bomb in the Grand Alliance 1941-45* (New York, 1975); J. Schell, *The Fate of the Earth* (New York, 1982).

histochemistry. The branch of HISTOLOGY in which an attempt is made to use differential colour reactions in order to identify the different chemical components of a TISSUE, e.g. PROTEINS, CARBOHYDRATES, and ENZYMES. All microscopical staining actions are in essence histochemical, e.g. the bringing of NUCLEI into prominence by staining with basic dyes such as methylene blue. Histochemistry has been most widely used in the identification of specific enzymes such as phosphatases. It is gradually being supplanted by orthodox biochemical methods of investigation which often turn upon the physical separation of the various elements of the CELL such as the nuclei, MITOCHONDRIA, and cell sap (see CYTOLOGY).   P.M.

histogram. In STATISTICS, a simple representational technique for giving an idea of the shape of an empirical DISTRIBUTION. The range of values of the random variable is divided into (usually equal) intervals and a block is drawn on each interval whose area is proportional to the number of observations falling in that interval, or to the proportion of the distribution lying in it. A typical example of the use of a histogram would be to represent the distribution of heights in a SAMPLE of adult men on a centimetre-by-centimetre basis — the

size of the block on the interval between, say, 175 cm and 176 cm would be proportional to the number of men of height at least 175 cm but less than 176 cm.   R.SI.

histoire du livre, see HISTORY OF THE BOOK.

histoire événementielle, see under ANNALES SCHOOL.

histology. The branch of microscopy (i.e. investigation with the microscope) that deals with the structures and properties distinctive of individual TISSUES — e.g. nervous, muscular, glandular, or connective tissue. Histology is usually contrasted with CYTOLOGY.   P.M.

histopathology. A subject bearing the same relation to PATHOLOGY as do HISTOLOGY and CYTOLOGY to gross ANATOMY. In the interpretation of disease states it often happens that the evidence of gross pathological anatomy is not sufficiently specific or revealing, and the diseased TISSUE is therefore examined microscopically, using the resources of histology and HISTOCHEMISTRY. Histopathology plays a crucially important part in the diagnosis of malignant diseases (see CANCER). It may be carried out on tissues removed from the living subject (such removal and examination being known as a *biopsy*) or upon material obtained at post-mortem examination, in which case allowance must be made for the deterioration of the tissues following death.   P.M.

historic compromise (Italy). The eurocommunist strategy of the Italian Communist Party (PCI) developed by the party leader, Enrico Berlinguer, during the 1960s aimed to establish an historic compromise with other major political parties. Given the dominance of the CHRISTIAN DEMOCRATIC Party (DC) the PCI's aim was to introduce gradually elements of SOCIALISM into government policies through PCI support for Christian Democratic governments. Following the legislative elections in August 1976 the PCI gave parliamentary support to the DC government which, in turn, consulted the PCI (which did not participate directly in the government) over policy. The historic

385

compromise lasted for three years from August 1976 until the elections in June 1979. The strategy was subsequently criticized by many PCI supporters who felt that its strategy had achieved few if any of the Party's objectives. (See ITALIANIZATION.)   S.M.

historical anthropology. A term used to describe the work of those historians (Emmanuel Le Roy Ladurie, for example) who, despite the necessary differences in sources and methods between the two disciplines, share the anthropologists' concern with interpreting the NORMS and categories of other CULTURES, and their view of space, time, GENDER, illness, and other basic concepts as social 'constructions' which vary from period to period as well as from one region to another. These historians believe that 'the past is a foreign country'. This belief informs much current historical work on the EVERYDAY.
                                          P.B.

historical demography. The statistical study of populations in the past, concerned in particular with measuring the rates of birth, marriage, and death at different periods. The subject grew up about 1950. Demographers began to study the period before 1800 (when reliable national statistics begin) and historians began to interest themselves in population movements. At first their emphasis was on the idea of a demographic 'old regime' in pre-industrial Europe, with regular crises as population pressed on the means of subsistence. More recently the stress has been on the regional variations in birth-, marriage-, and death-rates. See also FAMILY RECONSTITUTION; DEMOGRAPHY.
                                          P.B.
Bibl: E.A. Wrigley, *Population and History* (London and New York, 1969).

historical geography. A subfield of human GEOGRAPHY concerned to reconstruct, account for and explain the significance of past geographical distributions. Historical geographers have considered all manner of phenomena — deserted medieval villages, field systems, town plans and urban problems, the diffusion of agricultural and industrial innovations, the formation and struggle of social CLASSES, ways of seeing

and representing nature — and in consequence they are united, not so much by their subject-matter or by the METHODOLOGY of their inquiries, as by a common belief that conventional studies in SOCIAL and ECONOMIC HISTORY neglect the non-accidental association of most historical phenomena with specific places, ENVIRONMENTS and landscapes. Not surprisingly, however, historical geography has periodically experienced definitional disputes as its practitioners have sought either to separate or to reconcile HISTORY and temporal modes of explanation with geography and spatial modes of explanation. In recent years the growing realization that today's geographical distributions cannot be understood without reference to past distributions — or without reference to the dynamic *restructuring* processes binding the former to the latter — is beginning to render such definitional disputes unnecessary.   C.P.
Bibl: A.R.H. Baker and D. Gregory (eds.), *Explorations in Historical Geography* (Cambridge, 1985).

historical materialism. A shorthand term for the MATERIALIST view of history, the cornerstone of Marx's theory of history. He expressed it most concisely in his preface to *A Contribution to the Critique of Political Economy* (1859): 'The MODE OF PRODUCTION in material life determines the general character of the social, political, and spiritual processes of life. It is not the CONSCIOUSNESS of men that determines their existence, but on the contrary, it is their social existence which determines their consciousness.... In the social production which men carry on they enter into definite relations which are indispensable and independent of their will..... The sum total of these relations of production constitutes the economic structure of society — the real basis, on which rises a legal and political SUPERSTRUCTURE and to which correspond definite forms of social consciousness. The mode of production determines the social, political, and intellectual life processes in general.'
This theory (and the concepts used in it) has been subject to a myriad different interpretations, ranging from those which present the materialist conception of history as a monistic (see MONISM) *economic*

(or technological) *determination* to those emphasizing the interaction between the 'economic basis' and the 'political superstructure'.

Engels, like Marx, repeatedly affirmed that their theory 'explains all historical events and ideas, all politics, philosophy, and religion, from the material, economic conditions of life of the historical period in question'. But towards the end of his life he shifted the emphasis and stressed (in a letter to J. Bloch, 21 September 1890) that neither he nor Marx ever subscribed to an unqualified economic determinism which would reduce all historical development to economic causes alone. He wrote that they assert themselves historically only 'in the last resort': 'The economic situation is the basis, but the various elements of superstructure...also exercise their influence upon the course of the historical struggle and in many cases preponderate in determining their form. There is an interaction of all these elements....'

However, as Eduard Bernstein (see RE-VISIONISM) noticed, once historical necessity is made dependent on economic causation only 'in the final analysis', there is no way of predicting the historical development of concrete societies, and SOCIALISM ceases to be 'scientific' in the sense attributed to it by Engels. With the MARXIST-LENINIST stress on political VOLUNTARISM, the original theoretical substance of historical materialism has fallen into disregard, and the MAOIST interpretation of it, for instance, goes so far as to include a condemnation of 'the reactionary theory of productive forces...[which] describes social development as a natural outcome of the development of productive forces only, especially the development of the tools of production'.　　L.L.

Bibl: N.I. Bukharin, *Historical Materialism* (New York, 1925; London, 1926); G.P. Plekhanov, *The Materialist Conception of History* (London, 1940); G. Cohen, *Karl Marx's Theory of History: A Defence* (Oxford, 1978); M. Rader, *Marx's Interpretation of History* (New York, 1979).

historicism
(1) (or *historism*: from German *Historismus*). A word which at different times has been applied to two diametrically opposed approaches to history: (*a*) Originally, in the late 19th century, it meant an approach which emphasized the uniqueness of all historical phenomena and maintained that each age should be interpreted in terms of its own ideas and principles, or, negatively, that the actions of men in the past should not be explained by reference to the beliefs, motives, and valuations of the historian's own epoch. Particularly popular in Germany, this approach went with an emphasis on the function of VERSTEHEN in historical method, and with a rejection of the SOCIAL SCIENCES. (*b*) The term has more recently been used by K.R. Popper in an entirely different sense, which is now at least as commonly intended as the original one. To Popper historicism is the belief in large-scale laws of historical development of the kind to be found in speculative systems of history, whether linear or cyclic, such as those of Hegel, Marx, Comte, Spengler, and Toynbee. Hostile to them as being the intellectual foundations of totalitarian IDEOLOGIES, he argues that the course of history is radically affected by the growth of knowledge and that future acquisitions of knowledge cannot be predicted. Historicism, in this sense, however, is not associated exclusively with TOTALITARIANISM; most liberals (see LIBERALISM) in the 18th and 19th centuries believed in a law of inevitable progress.　　P.B.; A.Q.

Bibl: F. Meinecke, tr. J.E. Anderson, *Historism* (London, 1972); K.R. Popper, *The Poverty of Historicism* (London, 1957; New York, 1960).

(2) In architecture, a term of mild abuse for contemporary architecture which deliberately imitates the modes and styles of architecture of the past. Distinguished from the various 'historical' Post-modern styles by its deadly seriousness of intention and its attempt to reproduce exactly the forms and detailing of its original models. See also POST-MODERN CLASSICISM.　　S.L.

historiography. The history of historical writing. At least as old as La Popelinière's *L'Histoire des histoires* (1599), historiography has become a popular subject of research only in the last 30 years. This awakening of interest in history's own past goes with an increased self-consciousness on the part of historians, and a rejection of the idea that they can produce an 'objective' description, uncontaminated by their own attitudes and values, of what actually happened. P.B.

Bibl: E. Breisach, *Historiography: Ancient, Medieval and Modern* (Chicago, 1983).

historism, see HISTORICISM (1).

history. History in the sense of writing about the past has traditionally been divided by *period* into ancient, medieval, and modern, and also into different *kinds* of history, e.g. political history, ecclesiastical history, art history, which hardly require explanation. This conventional subject-matter has widened enormously in the last few years: CONTEMPORARY HISTORY has been added to the list of periods; ECONOMIC HISTORY, LOCAL HISTORY, and SOCIAL HISTORY have become serious subjects of academic study and have proliferated into HISTORICAL DEMOGRAPHY, AGRARIAN HISTORY, and URBAN HISTORY. Art history has been joined by the history of science, CULTURAL HISTORY, HISTORIOGRAPHY, HISTORY OF IDEAS, and HISTORY OF MENTALITIES. These enlargements, together with the impact of the SOCIAL SCIENCES, have necessitated changes in historical method, signalled by the coining of such terms as COMPARATIVE HISTORY, ETHNOHISTORY, ICONOGRAPHY, PROSOPOGRAPHY, PSYCHOHISTORY, QUANTITATIVE HISTORY, and SERIAL HISTORY. P.B.

history from below. A phrase coined by those who believe that historians have for too long been content to present the past from the perspective of the ruling classes, and that ordinary people also have a point of view and a CULTURE of their own, 'POPULAR CULTURE'. In Britain, E.P. Thompson's *Making of the English Working Class* (1963) did much to launch the movement, but the most important single influence on it has probably been that of Antonio Gramsci. As research has progressed, the difficulties inherent in the notion of 'people' have become ever more apparent. Are the people the poor? The powerless? The 'uneducated'? What is the relationship between the attitudes of ordinary men and women, or between the people and the ELITE? P.B.

Bibl: R. Samuel, 'People's History', in *Village Life and Labour*, ed. Samuel (London, 1975), xiii-xxi; R. Chartier, 'Culture as Appropriation', in *Understanding Popular Culture*, ed. S. Kaplan (Berlin, 1984).

history of childhood. Systematic interest in the subject goes back to the publication in 1960 of a study by the French 'Sunday historian' Philippe Ariès, which argued that before the 17th century the 'sense of childhood' did not exist, in other words that children — as we see them — were viewed either as animals or as miniature adults. Since then the literature on the subject has been increasing at an almost exponential rate, and the methods as well as the conclusions of Ariès have been challenged by many scholars. On the other hand, the idea that 'childhood' is a cultural construct with a history has become widely accepted. P.B.

Bibl: P. Ariès, *Centuries of Childhood* (1960, English trans., London, 1962).

history of ideas. A term popularized, and a discipline founded, by Arthur Lovejoy in the U.S.A. in the 1920s. Lovejoy opposed the fragmentation of the historical study of ideas into the histories of philosophy, literature, science, etc., and suggested an interdisciplinary approach which focused on individual concepts like 'nature' and 'primitivism' and on the changes in their meaning and associations. The focus on individual ideas was a reaction against German *Geistesgeschichte* (see CULTURAL HISTORY), with its emphasis on the unity of systems of thought. Lovejoy's approach ran the risk of personifying ideas. Hence some of his successors use the term *intellectual history*, and place more emphasis on thinking men. A more recent German approach, *Begriffsgeschichte*, is concerned with language and its changing uses in different social situations. See also HISTORY OF MENTALITIES. P.B.

Bibl: A.O. Lovejoy, *Essays in the History of Ideas* (Baltimore, 1948); R. Korelleck, *Futures Past* (Cambridge, 1985).

history of language. Intellectual and social historians have been taking an increasing interest in language. Some historians of political thought, such as J.G.A. Pocock, regard their subject as the history of the changing language (or as followers of Foucault would say, the DISCOURSE) of politics. Some SOCIAL HISTORIANS, inspired by SOCIOLINGUISTS and ETHNOGRAPHERS OF COMMUNICATION, are paying attention to the different 'speech codes' of different social groups (from aristocrats to beggars), and the different ways in which an individual speaks or writes in different social situations or 'speech domains'. There is greater awareness than there used to be of the influence of linguistic conventions on the historians' 'sources'.　P.B.

Bibl: J.G.A. Pocock, *Politics, Language and Time* (London, 1972); P. Burke and R. Porter (eds.,) *The Social History of Language* (Cambridge, 1987).

history of material culture. The history of material objects, from cathedrals to washbasins, from forks to tanks, including the analysis of their various uses in a given society. An expanding area of study on which art historians (no longer confined to 'works of art'), and archaeologists (no longer satisfied with 'PREHISTORY'), as well as ECONOMIC and SOCIAL HISTORIANS are converging. The Marxists entered the field early (the Polish *Quarterly for the History of Material Culture* goes back to 1952). Fernand Braudel produced a brilliant, provocative synthesis in 1967, concentrating on food, clothing and shelter in the early modern world as examples of *civilisation matérielle*. Since then, social historians have learned from social anthropologists and art historians alike to pay more attention to symbolism than Braudel did, noting, for example, that the preference for white rather than brown bread in early modern Europe symbolized the STATUS (or even the purity) of those who could afford to eat it, or that a particular choice of clothing or housing expressed or helped to create a particular social identity.　P.B.

Bibl: F. Braudel, *The Structures of Everyday Life* (1967; revised Eng. trans., London, 1981); H. Medick, 'Plebeian Culture in the Transition to Capitalism' in *Culture, Ideology and Politics*, eds. R. Samuel and G. Stedman Jones (London, 1983), pp. 84-108.

history of mentalities (*mentalités collectives*). An approach to what American scholars call the HISTORY OF IDEAS and PSYCHOHISTORY, developed in France in the 1930s, notably by Lucien Febvre and Georges Lefebvre. It is concerned with everyone's ideas, with peasants' as well as philosophers'; with sensibility as well as with concepts; and, in particular, with basic mental STRUCTURES. Thus Febvre, writing about 16th-century France, suggested that men had an imprecise sense of time and space; lacked any sense of the impossible; and perceived the world more through the ear than through the eye. His conclusions are still debated, but French historians continue to use his methods. See also ANNALES SCHOOL.　P.B.

Bibl: P. Burke, 'Strengths and Weaknesses of the History of Mentalities', *History of European Ideas*, Vol. 7, 1986.

history of the body. A new phrase for a fairly new kind of history, at the point of convergence between the history of medicine (itself a rapidly expanding field), food, GENDER, hygiene, and sexuality, an approach probably influenced as much by movements for GAY and women's liberation as by aspirations towards a 'total history'. The most important contribution so far to the history of the body is surely Michel Foucault's *Discipline and Punish*, concerned with the relationship between POWER and the body and more especially with the idea of bodily 'discipline' in prisons, armies, schools, factories and elsewhere. Historians and others cultivating this field also owe considerable debts to Mikhail Bakhtin (see BAKHTINIAN) on grotesque images of the body and to Norbert Elias on the place of bodily control in the 'civilizing process'.　P.B.

Bibl: M. Foucault, *Discipline and Punish* (1975; English trans., New York, 1978).

history of the book. A growing area of research between bibliographers and socio-cultural historians and first developed in France (hence the continued popularity of the French term *histoire du livre*). The interests of historians of the book include the organization of libraries; the technology of printing and the production of manuscripts; methods of information retrieval; the economics of the book trade; and the attempts by religious and political authorities to control what was published. Their central concern, however, is with the place of the book in social life. Inventories of private libraries are studied, numbers of editions are counted, and marginalia in individual copies of books are scrutinized in order to discover who read what where and when, and how they interpreted or were influenced by what they read. P.B.

Bibl: R. Chartier and D. Roche, 'The Book' in *Constructing the Past*, eds. J. Le Goff and P. Nora (Cambridge, 1985).

history of the family. Specialization in SOCIAL HISTORY concern the with family relations and family forms, which grew out of interest in HISTORICAL DEMOGRAPHY and SOCIAL STRUCTURE. (Family history is usually a synonym for genealogy.) Much of the initial enthusiasm in the 1960s derived from the work of Peter Laslett on household and family structures, especially the NUCLEAR FAMILY, and from the work of the ANNALES SCHOOL. While much of that early research was quantitative and concerned with the size and structure of families and households, subsequent investigations have tended either to be more interested in economic relationships within and between families, or to be more qualitative and concerned with the content and meaning of family relations. As with allied interests such as the HISTORY OF CHILDHOOD there has been considerable debate about the nature and direction of historical change in family forms and relationships. D.S.

Bibl: M. Anderson, *Approaches to the History of the Western Family, 1500-1914* (London, 1980).

HIV, see AIDS.

Hizbollahis, see under LEBANON.

Hohfeldian. Adjective formed from the name of the American jurist W.N. Hohfeld (1879-1918), whose study *Some Fundamental Legal Conceptions as Applied in Judicial Reasoning* (first version, 1917) represents a major clarification of the concept of a legal right. Hohfeld distinguished

four basic elements for each of which the expression a 'legal right' had been losely used by lawyers and others, sometimes without an appreciation of the difference between them. Hohfeld used in a special technical sense the four expressions: *claim-right, liberty* (or *privilege*), *power*, and *immunity* to distinguish these four elements. The distinctions drawn in this Hohfeldian analytical scheme have served to clarify not only the concept of a legal right, but also more complex notions such as that of ownership. H.L.A.H.

Bibl: W.N. Hohfeld, ed. W.W. Cook, *Fundamental Legal Conceptions as Applied in Judicial Reasoning* (London and New Haven, 1974).

holism. The thesis that wholes, or some wholes, are more than the sums of their parts in the sense that the wholes in question have characteristics that cannot be explained in terms of the properties and RELATIONS to one another of their constituents. ORGANICISM is a particular version of holism, which is founded on the analogy of complex systems in general with what are literally organisms, whose parts lose their nature, function, significance, and even existence when removed from their organic interconnection with the rest of the organism. Holism is central to IDEALIST theories of the STATE and other social INSTITUTIONS, to many accounts of the special unity and integrity of works of art, and to the theory of science advanced by Quine, according to which science is not an assemblage of isolable bits of belief but an interconnected system which is adjusted as a whole to the deliverances of experience. Holism is hostile to the philosophical technique of ANALYSIS, which it conceives to be a falsifying mutilation of what it is applied to. See also METHODOLOGICAL INDIVIDUALISM AND METHODOLOGICAL HOLISM. A.Q.

Bibl: E. Nagel, *The Structure of Science*, (London and New York, 1961).

holistic medicine. Term used to describe an approach to health-care which spans both the conventional medical model and COMPLEMENTARY (alternative) MEDICINE. The word *holos* stems from the Greek meaning whole, complete — the 'w' is a late 14th-century addition to the spelling.

The word *holism* was first used by Smuts (1928) in his book *Holism and Evolution*. He used it to describe the philosophical systems that looked on whole systems rather than parts (REDUCTIONISM). The following basic principles govern the approach to holistic practice. (1) *The whole is greater than the sum of its parts.* It is necessary when examining a part, e.g. heart, to be aware of how the whole person (EMOTIONS, thoughts, aspirations, breathing patterns, DIET and exercise practices, family, social CLASS, CULTURE, ENVIRONMENT) impinges on the function of that part. Holism challenges the notion of linear cause and effect and draws on SYSTEMS THEORY for its explanations. (2) *The use of a wide range of interventions*. This may include conventional medical therapies (drugs, SURGERY, RADIOTHERAPY), alternative therapies (ACUPUNCTURE, HOMOEOPATHY), self-help skills (relaxation techniques, meditation). (3) *Involving the patient/client in his care.* There is an emphasis in holistic practice on encouraging and facilitating the patient to take some responsibility for his own recovery process. (4) *'Physician heal thyself'*. An holistic approach suggests that the health (physical, psychological, spiritual) of the practitioner is an important component in the outcome of the inter-action between doctor and patient, therapist and client.

P.C.P.

holocaust, see under FINAL SOLUTION.

holography. A type of photography producing three-dimensional images, which was developed by the engineer-physicist Dennis Gabor in 1947. In conventional photography based on lenses etc. only the straight-line propagation of light is utilized (see OPTICS) and wave effects constitute a nuisance. Holography, however, relies essentially on wave properties: the PHASE of the wave reflected from an object is revealed by interference resulting from the addition of a 'reference wave', the pattern produced by the combination of the two waves being recorded on an ordinary photographic film negative. When this *hologram* is illuminated by the reference wave alone, there results an image of the original object which is fully three-dimensional (i.e. it shows perspective etc.).

Since the light sources must have a high degree of COHERENCE, LASERS are almost universally used.

M.V.B.

Holy Rollers. A nickname given to an American group in the PENTECOSTALIST movement, because its adherents may roll on the floor in religious ecstasy. Sometimes used more widely, in order to attribute to others an enthusiasm for a primitive kind of religion (see PRIMITIVISM) combined with a lack of self-discipline, rationality, or social STATUS.

D.L.E.

homoeomorphism, see under TOPOLOGY.

homoeomorphy, see under PHYLUM.

homoeopathy. A system of therapeutics (treatment) using 'remedies' rather than pharmacologically active drugs. It was developed and established by Hahnemann, a 19th-century German physician. The fundamental principle of homoeopathy is that 'like cures like'. By this is meant that instead of suppressing a symptom of killing bacteria (as modern drugs do), cure is achieved by stimulating the body's own healing powers. This is done by giving a 'remedy' which in much greater doses would *produce* the symptoms the patient is complaining about. These remedies contain minute levels of extracts which have no chemical effect on the body. In homoeopathy it is believed the more dilute the extract or remedy the more potent is its effect. Homoeopathy has a long and traditional history in Britain, having been the preferred approach to treatment among many members of the Royal family. The majority of homoeopaths are doctors who have gone on to receive further training. It is the one branch of COMPLEMENTARY MEDICINE that is available on the National Health Service in Britain. Conventional doctors are still unconvinced that it has a part to play in the treatment of disease but there is little doubt that homoeopathy is a safe method of treatment and that in several conditions it appears to have a dramatic effect.

P.C.P.

homoeostasis.
(1) The widespread DISPOSITION of living beings, including people, to maintain a

state of EQUILIBRIUM in the face of changing conditions, whether physical, chemical, or psychological. This disposition is often used as an explanatory principle in BIOLOGY and PSYCHOLOGY. See also ADAPTATION.   I.M.L.H.

Bibl: W.B. Cannon, *The Wisdom of the Body* (London, 1932; rev. ed., New York, 1939).

(2) In CYBERNETICS, this disposition is generalized mathematically to include all (not only biological) systems that maintain critical variables within limits acceptable to their own structure in the face of unexpected disturbance. See also AUTOPOIESIS; ULTRASTABILITY.   S.BE.

Bibl: W.R. Ashby, *Design for a Brain* (London and New York, 2nd ed., 1960).

homoerotic. Arousing a HOMOSEXUAL response; or — of activities, or works of literature, art or POPULAR CULTURE — believed to be expressive of or derived from homosexual affections. A compound term created from the Greek *homo* (same) and *eros* (sexual love). It has been found useful for critical reappraisals of paintings and novels or poetry whose subject matter and/or authors may or may not have been overtly homosexual. For example, the homoerotic content and well-springs of Michelangelo and Leonardo da Vinci's work have been extensively analysed, as has the tradition of homoerotic ICONOGRAPHY from classical times into the Renaissance to which they and other painters referred, viz. in successive painterly uses of the 'Ganymede myth' of the youth abducted to heaven by Zeus. Social organizations such as the military, single-sex boarding schools and religious orders are sometimes analysed as resulting from or leading to homoerotic 'bonding', without any necessary presumption of homosexual acts. The term is applicable to either sex.   A.L.

homology. A CONCEPT easier to exemplify than to define. The pectoral fins of fish, the wings of birds, and the forelimbs of mammals are homologous; in spite of their differences of function and of detailed ANATOMY, they occupy morphologically equivalent positions in the body and are genetically cognate in the sense that forelimbs evolved out of fins, and wings out of forelimbs. One of the most striking achievements of MOLECULAR BIOLOGY is to have put the concept of homology upon a molecular basis. It is clear, for example, that all vertebrate haemoglobins are homologous — and that the relationship between them can now be interpreted first in terms of the nature and order of their respective AMINO ACID sequences and thus indirectly in terms of the DNA nucleotide chains (see NUCLEIC ACID) that specify the order of these sequences.   P.M.

homology theory, see under TOPOLOGY.

homosexuality. The state or practice of desire between members of the same sex. Term invented in 1869 by Hungarian writer Benkert as compound of Greek *homo* (same) and Latin *sexus* (sex); to be distinguished from *hetero* (other) sexuality, the state or practice of desire between members of different sexes; and *bi*(two)sexuality, desire for either sex. Entered universal as distinct from specialist usage from late 19th/early 20th century. The word and concept homosexuality (hence homosexual, adjectivally and as a noun) marked a break with a western tradition commonly called Judaeo-Christian which defined homosexual acts as optional 'wilful' departures from a (God-given) heterosexual nature common to all. The notion that people can 'be' homosexual rather than 'be' heterosexual, regardless of whether they engage in any homosexual acts — which may be fiercely disapproved of — at present commands general acceptance including from the churches and among the medical and psychiatric professions. Enquiry into causation, however, has not yielded any results commanding general assent: neither GENETIC inheritance of a homosexual disposition (like blue eyes) nor unconscious environmental influence ('strong' or 'weak' father or mother, depending on gender of child) has been proved. Originally designed to refer equally to women or men, homosexual (as noun) has largely been co-opted to refer to men. Accordingly, homosexual women have increasingly preferred to be referred to as lesbians, from Lesbos (Mytilene), home of 6th century B.C. poet Sappho. From c.1969, beginning in the U.S., homosexual men (and, loosely, homosexual women) have preferred the self-description *gay*, asserting an intention of being guilt-free (having self-respect) and open (declining self-concealment) — hence glad to be gay and *out*. A further term evolved from Benkert's original innovation is heterosexism (entered usage c.1980), intended to describe words or acts of overt heterosexual hostility towards lesbians or gays, i.e. homosexuals of either sex.　　　A.L.

homotopy theory, see under TOPOLOGY.

homozygote, see under GENE.

honour. Prestige found as the basis for SOCIAL STRATIFICATION in societies of the Mediterranean. In the broadest sense it refers to the worth or integrity of a person. In a narrow sense it refers to the sexual virtue of a woman. Competition for honour is usually between families and it is very intense. Groups are engaged in attempts to discredit each other through gossip or innuendo.

The male members of a family are expected to display 'manliness' which protects the honour of their women against insult or violation. The women are expected to have shame or modesty, if they are not to bring dishonour on the men. It is unusual for a family to lose honour completely. It is a relative value (X has more honour than Y) and the balance is constantly changing between groups. It has been argued that the competition for honour acts to unite potentially fissiparous tendencies within groups or families.　　　A.G.

Bibl: John Davis, *People of the Mediterranean* (London, 1977); Julian Pitt Rivers, *The Fate of Shechem or the Politics of Sex* (Cambridge, 1977); G. Marvin, 'Honour, Integrity and the Problem of Violence in the Spanish Bullfight' in D. Riches (ed.), *The Anthropology of Violence* (Oxford, 1986).

horizon.
(1) In ECOLOGY, a distinctive stratum, assumed to have been originally horizontal, which extends over a wide area and can be used to establish a regional stratigraphy (see STRATIFICATION).
(2) In PEDOLOGY, an important morphological character exhibited by a soil when inspected in a vertical section known as the *soil profile*. The soil horizons, which occur in layers roughly parallel to the surface, can be distinguished from each other, and from parent rock material at the base of the profile, on the basis of properties such as colour, texture, and amount of organic matter. A number of processes interact to produce soil horizons: the addition and decomposition of organic material, weathering of the parent rock material, and the movement of soluble and suspended constituents by the movement of soil water. The study of the soil profile is basic to the scientific study of soil since it provides a means of identification and classification, and also data relating to soil evolution.　　　J.L.M.L.

(3) 'Horizon' and 'merging of horizons' are terms important in the HERMENEUTICS of Hans-Georg Gadamer. Gadamer borrows the term 'horizon' from Husserl in order to give a figure for our historical situatedness and limitation in our world. We inherit our cultural and personal horizons and have to seek for meaning in terms of them. Gadamer insists that the only understanding one can have of one's world, and of the texts which make up its literature, is a historically aware understanding. Grasping the necessity of this involves *effective-historical consciousness* (*Wirkungs-geschichtliches Bewusstsein*). The 'effective-historical' is the recognition of the modifying power of the horizons we inherit. Understanding is a function of the language that one speaks, the history of that language, and the historical-philosophical situatedness in which the hermeneut finds himself. Understanding is achieved when one's own personal horizon 'fuses' or 'merges' with the historical horizon (*Horizontverschmelzung*). Hans Robert Jauss, a leading member of the RECEPTION-THEORY school at Konstanz, has used the figure of the 'horizon of expectations' within which any given literary work is actually read or understood. Opposed to Gadamer's is the position of Jurgen Habermas. Habermas insists that understanding not only can be, but also ought to be, in some sense trans-historical and can belong in some way to universal reason, however inflected that must be by the influence of local political-economic

393

'interests'. The debate between Gadamer and Habermas in the late 1960s and early 1970s was intense and influential. It is being continued in the 1980s as the POST-MODERNISM of Lyotard and such American relativists as Richard Rorty struggles with the 'legitimization' demands of Habermas' thought. Christopher Norris's *The Contest of Faculties* (1984) has recently tried to propose a satisfactory position on this issue. R.PO.

Bibl: M. Mueller-Vollmer, *The Hermeneutics Reader* (Oxford, 1986).

Horizon. A monthly review of literature and art edited by Cyril Connolly and Peter Watson from London, 1940-50, and displaying a remarkable, eclectic range of talents. Early numbers drew heavily on such writers of the 1930s as MacNeice, Day Lewis, Spender, Auden and Geoffrey Grigson. But it also maintained close contacts with France, and in the post-war period with the U.S.A., printing Malraux, Sartre, Camus, Lionel Trilling, Marianne Moore, Wallace Stevens, e. e. cummings, etc. in addition to such British writers as Evelyn Waugh (whose *Unconditional Surrender*, 1961, includes some satirical remarks about *Horizon*), George Orwell, and Angus Wilson (whom it 'discovered'). It also, in Connolly's view, marked the end of the Modern Movement in literature, and ended in 1950 in some desperation as Connolly noted a decline in the aesthetic, AVANT-GARDE impulse he favoured. M.S.BR.

hormic psychology. William McDougall's term for his form of purposive psychology (see PURPOSIVISM). Human action is governed, in this view, not by a rational search for hedonistic ends, but by primitive urges that have been largely neglected by students of man's social life. I.M.L.H.

Bibl: W. McDougall, *An Introduction to Social Psychology* (Boston, rev. ed., 1926; London, 23rd ed., 1936).

hormone, see under ENDOCRINOLOGY.

hot. One of the earliest figurative descriptions of JAZZ, as when King Oliver declared his CHICAGO band of 1922 was 'hotter than a .45!' It is particularly appropriate for the music's first incarnation, with its extrovert appeal, emphasis on lively syncopation and broad, exciting effects. In the 1940s, however, as jazz became more complex after BEBOP, a more thoughtful, intellectual quality appeared and the up-to-date attitude became COOL. However, it could be said that any jazz is impossible without a distinct degree of emotional pressure, so that coolness is very much a relative concept, and hotness, however banked the fires, will always be present. GE.S.

hot and cold. Terms drawn from JAZZ idiom (see HOT) by Marshall McLuhan (*The Gutenberg Galaxy*, 1962), in the course of establishing his thesis that the spoken word is the fullest means of human communication, since its context (intonation, facial expression, gesture, etc.) offers the most reliable means of transmitting a mental state. On this basis, hearing is 'hotter' than seeing or feeling or tasting. The television image, however, is (from a technical standpoint) poorly defined, and is therefore 'cold' (the poor definition demands — McLuhan claims — an effort from the viewer, thus *involving* him). Before the invention of printing, man was 'aural', 'hot', more 'tribal' than subsequently: his emotions lay near the surface of his personality. 'Hot' is not a precise term; Jonathan Miller's definition 'intrinsically richer' (i.e. involving more of the 'plural and voluminous' nature of human experience) is perhaps as near as it is possible to get. Since McLuhan's death, the terms have fallen into disuse. M.S.-S.

household responsibility system. Term used in connection with changes in the Chinese agricultural system dating from 1978 in which communal operation gave way to increased scope for farming by individual households on a contract basis. Some communal activity is retained (e.g. in provision of irrigation facilities) but land can be leased to households under strict conditions to allow for development of increasing initiative. The change is widely believed to have provoked considerable improvement in total output. Further changes in 1985 removed some state control over agricultural prices. (See also DENGISM.) G.H.P.

hovercraft. A vehicle whose weight is supported a short distance above the ground or above water by the pressure from an air cushion trapped by air blown around its periphery from within the vehicle itself. Hovercraft are usually propelled by one or more conventional airscrews and in this respect they represent a form of low-flying aircraft. Their ability to cross water on a foggy day when no aircraft could fly has made them especially suitable for ferry services, as well as for travelling over difficult country, e.g. swamps.

Hovercraft belong to the broader class of hovering vehicles known as 'ground effect vehicles' (G.E.V.) which include magnetically and electromagnetically suspended vehicles using the system known as Maglev.   E.R.L.

HRT. Hormone replacement therapy: used in the treatment of menopausal symptoms.   C.E.D.

Hubble's constant, see under EXPANSION OF THE UNIVERSE.

human capital, see under CAPITAL.

human function curve. A model that provides a SYSTEMS APPROACH to medical problems by relating the condition of health to arousal and performance. The condition of health is seen as a continuum ranging from healthy function through fatigue, exhaustion and ill-health to breakdown. This continuum is drawn as an inverted 'U' on a graph starting with healthy function and healthy fatigue on the upslope, exhaustion and the subsequent degradation of human function on the downslope. The horizontal axis represents arousal, the general 'drive' state of the individual determined by his efforts of coping, adapting to change and handling information from both the external environment and the internal milieu. The vertical axis is performance, the accomplishment of action and work and the discharge of one's functions. The representation of healthy function by an upslope indicates that the individual can call upon reserves of energy and information for the enhancement of performance up to a point, beyond which exhaustion sets in and the curve turns downwards. Further effort is self-defeating. Maladaptive behaviour patterns are adopted. Sleep is disturbed, and the METABOLISM shifts from an anabolic to a catabolic mode when energy and information-handling ability are no longer adequate for the maintenance of a stable and orderly internal milieu. Habituation is impaired and entropy increased. The consequent degradation of the internal milieu presents as ill-health or breakdown from dysfunction of major systems, e.g. HYPERTENSION, coronary heart disease, diabetes mellitus and gout (neuro-endocrine system); increased vulnerability to infection and neoplasm, and distortion of immune function (neuro-immune system); and loss of stamina and dominance associated with sexual and reproductive morbidity (PITUITARY — sex steroid system). The model enables medical problems to be examined not only in a reductionist or mechanistic fashion (Is there a disease? What is it?), but also in relation to the individual's coping and adapting ability, behavioural patterns and psychosocial burdens, needs for energy and information, and the integrity of his homoeostatic mechanisms (the HOLISTIC or biopsychosocial approach). It enables the therapist to integrate modern technology with information, education and communication, in order to serve the patient and enable him to make the best possible use of his resources for self-organization and self-regulation (HOMOEOSTASIS) in recovering from illness and adapting to handicap.
                                    P.G.F.N.
Bibl: P.G.F. Nixon, 'The Human Function Curve', *Practitioner 217* (1976), pp.765-9 and pp.935-44.

human relations, see under MANAGEMENT.

human rights. That there are human rights is a contemporary form of the doctrine of natural rights, first clearly formulated by Locke and later expressed in terms of the rights of man. Natural or human rights are those which men are conceived to have in virtue of their humanity and not in virtue of human fiat or law or convention. Such rights have therefore been frequently invoked in the criticism of laws and social arrangements. In 1948 the General Assembly of UNO adopted a Universal Declaration of Human Rights, which formulated in detail a number of rights, economic and cultural, as well as political, to form a standard of human rights. This is not a legally binding instrument, but it was followed by a number of international covenants and conventions, including the European Convention for the Protection of Human Rights and Fundamental Freedoms, which have influenced national legislation and provided some machinery for international enforcement.   H.L.A.H.

Bibl: I. Brownlie (ed.), *Basic Documents on Human Rights* (Oxford, 1971); J.J. Waldron (ed.), *Theories of Rights* (Oxford, 1984).

human rights policy. The term applied to a foreign policy initiative of U.S. President Carter which was taken at the start of his administration in 1977 and survived with increasing ambiguities until 1979. Carter, influenced by the VIETNAM experience, the contemporary emphasis on north-south issues, theories of INTERDEPENDENCE and critiques of American support of undemocratic client states, proclaimed a commitment to 'world order politics'. This appeared to mean an emphasis on American moral leadership rather than military HEGEMONY; a 'NORTH-SOUTH DIALOGUE' on economic issues; the search for major ARMS CONTROL agreements; and an attempt to urge allied and client states towards the protection of HUMAN RIGHTS. The State Department acquired a Bureau of Human Rights; the U.S. government tried to exert influence on states such as Chile, Brazil, Argentina, South Korea and the Philippines via cuts in economic aid and via institutions such as the World Bank and I.M.F. (see BRETTON WOODS). The initiative struggled under the conflicting pressures of other foreign policy imperatives — as in continuing support for the Shah of Iran and King Hassan II of Morocco. Its declining coherence and importance reflected the Carter administration's general drift back towards a more conventional U.S. vision of foreign policy.
                                                      S.R.

Bibl: C. Vance, *Hard Choices* (New York, 1983); R. Barnet, *Real Security* (New York, 1981).

humani generis, see under CHRISTIAN EXISTENTIALISM.

humanism.

(1) A term invented by a German eductionalist, F.J. Niethammer, in 1808 to describe the study of the Greek and Latin classics, *literae humaniores*, 'humane letters', the revival of which had been one of the distinguishing features of the Italian Renaissance, later spreading to the rest of Europe as 'the New Learning'. Part of the attraction of classical studies was the fact that they are Man- rather than God-centred (as Cicero said, Socrates brought philosophy down from heaven to earth), studying the works and thought of Man as revealed in history, literature and art (the 'HUMANITIES').

(2) Subsequently the use of the term has been widened to signify theories or doctrines, however varied their conclusions, which take human experience as the starting point for man's knowledge of himself and the work of God and Nature. Thus the critical, rational methods of scientific enquiry, which Newton had applied so successfully to the natural order and which the *philosophes* of the Enlightenment sought to extend to the systematic study of man and society, produced a *secular humanism*, directed from the time of Voltaire (1694-1778) and Hume (1711-76), against the dogmatic claims of orthodox CHRISTIANITY. This was powerfully reinforced by the advancement of science at the expense of revealed religion in the 19th century and the growing SECULARIZATION of Western society. See AGNOSTICISM, a term invented by T.H. Huxley, the champion of Darwin's views on EVOLUTION. See also POSITIVISM and SCIENTISM as expressions of the belief, frequently known as *scientific humanism*, that the SCIENTIFIC METHOD is the sole source of knowledge and that the NATURAL and human SCIENCES alone can (and in time, will) provide a comprehensive, rational explanation of the universe and human life, replacing the incomplete and misleading earlier accounts offered by MYTH and RELIGION.

(3) Human experience, however, is varied; William James, for example, wrote a classic study of the *Varieties of Religious Experience* (1902). In the 20th century,

which no longer shares the robust confidence of the 19th in the identification of science and progress, there has been a reaction against the claim (sometimes made by both secularists and their FUNDAMENTALIST opponents) that the term humanism can be identified with the secular, scientific version of it — any more than religion can be monopolized by fundamentalism.

On this view, humanism is to be viewed as a broad tendency, a dimension of thought and belief within which are found very different views, held together not by a unified structure but by certain shared assumptions. The two most important of these are: (i) The belief that human beings have a potential value in themselves, and that it is respect for this which is the source of all other human values and rights. This value is based upon the possibility, which human beings possess to a unique extent, to create and communicate (language, human relations, the arts, science, institutions) — latent powers which, once liberated (e.g. by education), enable men and women to exercise a degree of freedom of choice and action in shaping their lives. (ii) The rejection of any system of thought which (a) despairs of Man and denies any meaning to human life (see NIHILISM) or (b) treats him as a depraved, worthless creature who can only be saved by divine grace (see CALVINISM) or (c) is DETERMINIST or REDUCTIONIST in its view of human CONSCIOUSNESS (see MATERIALISM; BEHAVIOURISM) or (d) regards men and women as having no value as anything more than expendable raw material for use or exploitation by political or economic systems (see TOTALITARIANISM; ALIENATION).

See also LIBERALISM (1) and (2); EXISTENTIALISM; CHRISTIAN EXISTENTIALISM; PROCESS THEOLOGY; SECULAR CHRISTIANITY; NEO-MARXISM; POST-MODERNISM.

A.L.C.B.

Bibl: E. Cassirer, *An Essay on Man* (New Haven, 1944); A. Bullock, *The Humanist Tradition in the West* (London and New York, 1985).

humanism, evolutionary, see EVOLUTIONARY HUMANISM.

humanistic geography. A perspective which insists that the world's human GEOGRAPHY can only be properly understood by placing the human being explicitly at the centre of geographical inquiry. Whereas the tendency of geography as SPATIAL SCIENCE during the 1960s was to reduce people to little more than automata rushing around geometric landscapes in response to iron laws of spatial behaviour, in recent years the inherent BEHAVIOURISM of this tendency has been criticized — and in part replaced — by studies concerned to elucidate the subjectively-held emotions, meanings and values through which people strive to interpret and act upon their surrounding PLACES, ENVIRONMENTS and landscapes. In attempting to counter the philosophy of POSITIVISM underlying much spatial science, these humanistic studies have drawn inspiration from philosophies as diverse as PHENOMENOLOGY, EXISTENTIALISM, IDEALISM and PRAGMATISM, although this has sometimes led to a mismatch between formal philosophical claims and the more immediate objectives of research in progress. Influential and revealing as this perspective has been, however, it has itself been criticized — notably by proponents of a RADICAL GEOGRAPHY — for slipping into a VOLUNTARISM blind to economic, social and political realities that can both constitute and seriously constrain human thoughts and actions. See also HUMANISM and SUBJECTIVISM.

C.P.

Bibl: D. Ley and M.S. Samuels (eds.), *Humanistic Geography: Prospects and Problems* (London, 1978).

humanistic psychology. A recent SCHOOL OF PSYCHOLOGY founded mainly by Abraham Maslow. It seeks to increase the relevance of PSYCHOLOGY to the lives of individual people, regarded from an EXISTENTIAL viewpoint. It is critical of researches that seem trivial, ahuman, and even dehumanizing because of a preoccupation with STATISTICS, elegant experimentation, white rats, COMPUTERS, and other 'side-issues' of human psychology proper.

I.M.L.H.

Bibl: F.T. Severin (ed.), *Humanistic Viewpoints in Psychology* (New York, 1965); C.S. Hall and G. Lindzey, *Theories of Personality* (New York, 1978).

humanities. A term used in Europe and the U.S.A. to distinguish literature, languages, PHILOSOPHY, HISTORY, art, THEOLOGY, and music from the SOCIAL SCIENCES and the NATURAL SCIENCES. The term originated in Renaissance times, when *litterae humaniores* (a name still in use at Oxford) signified the more humane 'letters' of the revived Latin and Greek authors in contrast to the theological 'letters' of the medieval schoolmen.   W.A.C.S.

Bibl: L. Stenhouse, 'The Humanities Curriculum Project' (*Journal of Curriculum Studies,* no. 1, 1969).

Hundred Flowers. Campaign of intellectual liberalization launched by Mao Zedong in Communist China in 1956. Based on the ancient adage, 'let a hundred flowers bloom and a thousand schools of thought contend', Mao tried to win the support of the INTELLECTUALS by encouraging their comments and criticisms. Mao firmly believed that the party would not be attacked, but the campaign soon got out of hand as existing policies and personalities were bitterly criticized. The party's response was to brand all those who had expressed criticism as 'rightists', and launch an anti-rightist RECTIFICATION campaign. The term Hundred Flowers was supposed to be a by-word for liberalization, but it became tainted by (and was often used to refer to) the anti-rightist movement that it spurred, although the original meaning of the term has emerged in the post-Mao era.   D.C.W.;S.B.

Bibl: R. McFarquhar (ed.), *The Hundred Flowers* (London and New York, 1960).

Hungary 1956. Term referring to the crisis of October 1956 when Soviet troops invaded Hungary to suppress a popular uprising. Soviet forces in the country fired on demonstrations in Budapest which followed the overthrow of the STALINIST government in Poland. Revolutionary Councils were set up throughout Hungary and a national government was established under Imre Nagy, a moderate COMMUNIST. It announced radical political reforms, such as the introduction of a multiparty system and the withdrawal of Hungary from the Warsaw Pact, demanding its recognition as a neutral country. The Soviet Union responded by sending troops, which had withdrawn to the borders during the first phase of the fighting, back into the country in greater numbers. After serious fighting during which about 25,000 were killed, the revolutionary forces were defeated. Subsequently Nagy and others were tried in secret and then executed. This episode led to a significant weakening of support for the Soviet Union outside Russia, particularly among the LEFT in western Europe.   D.C.W.;D.PR.

Bibl: M. Molnár, *Budapest 1956: A History of the Hungarian Revolution* (London, 1971).

hunter-gatherers. Foraging societies which are characterized by extreme technological simplicity, mobility and a distinctive EGALITARIAN structure. There is usually considerable flexibility in membership with individuals moving at will between different hunter-gatherer groups. The recognition of individuality is combined, however, with a high degree of co-operation between members within a particular group. The mobility and adaptability of hunter-gatherers are preserved through a lack of emphasis upon accumulation. Production is geared largely to immediate consumption.   A.G.

Bibl: E Leacock and R. Lee (eds.), *Politics and History in Band Societies* (Cambridge, 1982).

hybridization. (1) In the BIOLOGY of whole organisms, it is the breeding together of two SPECIES. Different species normally do not inter-breed, but they can in some cases be forced to under unnatural conditions. The mule, for example, is the hybrid of a he-ass and a mare; mules are sterile, which suggests why NATURAL SELECTION prevents hybridization in nature. Hybridization is important in BOTANY, because many plant species have originated in the hybridization by accident of two other species. Many horticultural and agricultural species have been artificially produced by the hybridization of species.

(2) In MOLECULAR BIOLOGY, it is the joining together of separate MOLECULES of DNA (or of RNA and DNA: see NUCLEIC ACID). DNA molecules, under appropriate experimental conditions, will join together at a rate proportional to the similarity of

sequence of the two molecules. Hybridized DNA and non-hybridized DNA can be distinguished by *ultracentrifugation* (see SEDIMENTATION). Hybridization can be used to measure how similar different DNA molecules (for instance, from different species) are. It can also be used to 'map' GENES. If the DNA (or RNA) of a particular gene has been isolated, it can be put with the whole GENOME of the organism and the isolated gene will then hybridize at that place in the genome where the gene is normally located. Such hybridization, usually with RNA molecules, is the first step in isolating a gene for CLONING.　　M.R.

hydraulic civilizations. Karl Wittfogel's term for urban or rural SETTLEMENTS based on the establishment of large productive water-works for irrigation, flood control, and hydro-electric power. The type of economy on which they rely is termed by Wittfogel *hydraulic agriculture* to distinguish it from traditional rainfall farming.　　M.L.

Bibl: W.L. Thomas (ed.), *Man's Role in Changing the Face of the Earth* (Chicago, 1956).

hydraulics. The scientific study of the movement of water and other liquids through artificial channels, open or closed, and the engineering applications of hydraulic forces.　　M.L.

hydrobiology, see LIMNOLOGY.

hydrodynamics. The study of the flow of liquids. Fine detail on the atomic scale (see ATOM) is ignored, so that a continuum model (see CONTINUUM; MODEL) is employed. The motion of each small volume in the liquid is analysed by NEWTONIAN MECHANICS, taking account of the pressure and viscous resistance of the surrounding liquid. Typical hydrodynamic phenomena are water waves, turbulent and streamline flow in pipes, oil lubrication, and flow in rivers. See also MAGNETO-HYDRODYNAMICS.　　M.V.B.

hydrofoil. A river- or sea-going craft in which the whole of the hull is maintained completely *above* the water surface. The weight of the vessel is supported by sub-merged foils whose action is precisely analogous to that of the aerofoil section of an aircraft wing, the only difference being that water replaces air as the medium providing the lift. The action depends on MOMENTUM, whereas that of an AQUAPLANE depends on viscosity.　　E.R.L.

hydrogen bond. In some situations hydrogen forms BONDS with two ATOMS instead of one as predicted by classical VALENCE theory. The extra bond — the hydrogen bond — which is found with the more electronegative (see ELECTRONEGATIVITY) ELEMENTS (usually bound in a MOLECULE), though relatively weak, has far-reaching consequences. It is responsible for the fact that water is a liquid under normal conditions, and it determines the configuration of many biological molecules, e.g. DNA (see NUCLEIC ACID).　　B.F.

hydrogenation. The incorporation of hydrogen by organic compounds either by the addition of, or reduction with, molecular (see MOLECULE) hydrogen. Alcohols and amines may be produced, but the most important commercial process is the formation of SATURATED hydrocarbons (alkanes) from UNSATURATED alkenes. A variety of catalysts (see CATALYSIS) are used.　　B.F.

hydrography. The science concerned with the physical aspects of all bodies of water on the earth's surface; in particular, the preparation of navigational charts.　　J.L.M.L.

hydrology. The study of continental water in its normal form as a liquid (for the study of natural ice see GLACIOLOGY), its properties, distribution, and circulation in the HYDROSPHERE and the atmosphere. In a less restricted sense hydrology is concerned with the *hydrologic cycle*, i.e. with the interchanges of water, as a vapour, liquid, or solid between the atmosphere, ocean, and land.　　J.L.M.L.

hydrolysis, see under ENZYMES.

hydroponics. The cultivation of plants without soil, using instead water containing a balanced mixture of salts (see NUTRITION) and a supporting substratum such as

399

sand or plastic granules. Very heavy crops can be produced in a small area, and the world's food production, needed to feed the growing population, might be substantially increased by the wider use of this technique. At present high costs make the method unsuitable except for luxury products such as cut flowers.　　　　K.M.

hydrosphere. The three major realms of the earth are the LITHOSPHERE, the hydrosphere, and the atmosphere, respectively solid, liquid, and gaseous. The hydrosphere includes all the surface waters of the earth, liquid or solid, in the oceans, and on the continents, together with soil and ground water.　　　　J.L.M.L.

hydrothermal vent. A fissure in the floor of the axial zone of an OCEANIC RIDGE from which mineral-laden fluids emerge. Because the axial valleys of oceanic ridges are sites at which molten rock is being forced up from the earth's interior, they are very hot and highly fractured. Seawater enters the fractures, circulates within the molten rock, becomes heated (sometimes above 350°C), dissolves minerals from the rock and finally emerges from fissures which thus become known as hydrothermal (i.e. hot-water) vents. When the hot water pours out into the cold, the mixing produces dense black or white plumes ('black smokers' or 'white smokers') depending upon the precise mineral content; and metals such as manganese, zinc, cobalt, copper, iron, lead and silver are deposited, often as sulphides or oxides. The minerals form crusts on the surrounding rocks and, if present in sufficient profusion, build columns ('chimneys') up to 30 m high. The existence of hydrothermal vents, discovered only during the 1970s, has profoundly altered understanding of the ocean waters. Previously it had been thought that all the minerals dissolved in the oceans had been washed down from the land by rivers. But it is now clear that the entire volume of the oceans circulates through the crust at ridge axes once every 10 million years and thus acquires dissolved minerals in a major way not before envisaged. The first scientists to visit hydrothermal vents (in submersibles) also discovered life forms not before envisaged. Where they never expected to find life at all, they came across previously unknown species of tube worms, clams and bacteria that evidently thrive on sulphides.　　　　P.J.S.

hyperbolic geometry, see under GEOMETRY.

hypergamy, see under DOWRY.

hypergraphy, see under LETTRISM.

hyperinflation, see under INFLATION.

hypersonic, see under MACH NUMBER.

hypertension. Taken to be elevation of the systolic (>160mmHg) and diastolic blood pressure (>95mmHg). There is a wide variation in normal blood pressure within and between individuals, so that absolute levels are difficult to define. It is determined by the cardiac output and peripheral resistance and measured by sphygmomanometer. It predisposes to left ventricular hypertrophy and failure (hypertensive heart disease).　　　　L.J.F.

hypnosis. The induction of a trance-like state by one person in another. The characteristics of the state come under three main heads. (1) The subject suffers a loss of initiative. He will submit to the hypnotist's authority, and he often shows inertia and extreme reluctance to perform complex tasks of which he is perfectly capable. His attention is subject to redistribution, in particular to increased selectivity resulting from the hypnotist's demands. (2) The subject may achieve extremely vivid recall of fantasies and past memories; even to the point when he believes he is actually reliving his past. Because of the hypnotist's inducement of calm and detachment, he is often less persistent in verifying his experience than he would normally be, and he will accept gross and continued distortions of reality. In addition, posthypnotic amnesia frequently occurs: he 'wakes' completely forgetful of what has taken place in the trance. The hypnotist, however, is usually capable of restoring the subject's memory by means of a simple command or gesture. (3) The subject may lose his inhibitions, and lend himself enthusiastically to the acting out of ROLES unusual for him, an aspect exploited for entertainment.

The most important factor in hypnosis is suggestibility, and degree of suggestibility determines the subject's suitability for hypnosis. It is a poorly understood trait. Post-hypnotic suggestion, the carrying out of the hypnotist's commands after the session, has both the most promising (for PSYCHIATRY) and the most sinister implications because it constitutes control of a person's normal waking perceptions, behaviour, and beliefs without his knowledge. This control, however, is not absolute even after the deepest trance, and not even the most suggestible hypnotic subjects will respond to post-hypnotic suggestion that runs very strongly counter to their beliefs and inhibitions.   H.L.

Bibl: E.R. Hilgard, *Hypnotic Susceptibility* (New York, 1965).

hypostatization. The attribution of real existence to abstractions (see ABSTRACT), i.e. to entities which have no definite, or at least continuous, location in space and time. Platonic REALISM, according to its critics, hypostatizes UNIVERSALS (properties, RELATIONS, numbers). HOLISM, likewise, is criticized for hypostatizing social INSTITUTIONS, such as nations or CLASSES, social movements and forces, and large-scale historical events (e.g. ROMANTICISM, INDUSTRIALIZATION, the Renaissance). Resolute NOMINALISTS regard as hypostatization all attributions of substantial existence (see SUBSTANCE) to things other than definitely and continuously located spatio-temporal objects, including human beings. Philosophical ANALYSIS is typically used to unmask hypostatizations.   A.Q.

hypothalamus. In mammals generally the lowermost, i.e. most ventral part of the 'between brain' or thalamus. The hypothalamus may be thought of as the brain of the autonomic NERVOUS SYSTEM and it is known that the excitation of different specific areas will give rise to rage, sleep, pleasure, hunger, or fear. Apart from these neurological functions the hypothalamus is also the seat of neurosecretory CELLS which produce many of the hormones (see ENDOCRINOLOGY) formerly associated with the posterior part of the PITUITARY gland. It is also now thought that the hypothalamus produces so-called 'releasing factors' which cause the liberation of hormones from the anterior part of the pituitary gland. Such hormones include growth hormone and the GONAD-stimulating hormones. Thus the hypothalamus is in general a meeting point or overlapping area of the neurological and endocrinological controls of behaviour.

P.M.

hypothetico-deductive method, see under POPPERIAN; SCIENCE, PHILOSOPHY OF.

hysteresis. The lag of an effect behind its cause in physical systems undergoing cyclic change. For example, an elastic solid will stretch when pulled, but it will frequently not return to quite its original length when the pulling force is reduced back to zero; similar behaviour occurs in the magnetization of FERROMAGNETS.

M.V.B.

hysteria, see under NEUROSIS.

I

I Ching, see under ALEATORY.

iatrogenesis. A term popularized in the analysis of modern medicine developed by Ivan Illich. Taken from Greek roots meaning 'doctor originated', iatrogenesis describes the (allegedly increasing) phenomenon of disease caused by medicine and the medical profession. Illich, a critic of modern medicine (which he condemns for allegedly 'expropriating' the people's health) diagnosed three modes of iatrogenesis. (1) Clinical, the tendency of malpractice and incompetence amongst surgeons and the pharmaceutical industry to cause disease in individuals. (2) Social, the process by which organized professional medicine has taken charge of the nation's health, more for its own than for the public benefit. (3) Cultural. Here Illich refers to raised expectations about the prolongation of life and health, put about by the medical profession and widely accepted, leading to doctor-induced medical dependence and a consequent inability to face pain and death. Illich argues that, despite all its promises, scientific medicine has done little to promote health. Though the evidence has been much contested, these notions have been influential in the critique of modern medicine. R.P.
Bibl: I. Illich, *Limits to Medicine* (London, 1976).

IBM (International Business Machines). By far the largest COMPUTER manufacturer. Their almost overwhelming influence on all aspects of COMPUTING, on both the HARDWARE and the SOFTWARE sides, is not regarded by all as an unmixed blessing. C.S.

IBRD. International Bank for Reconstruction and Development, the official name for the World Bank (see BRETTON WOODS). C.E.D.

IC (immediate constituent), see under CONSTITUENT ANALYSIS.

ICBM (inter-continental ballistic missiles), see under MISSILES.

iconography. Term used in art history for the study of the meaning of images, a visual HERMENEUTICS. An iconographical school of art historians grew up *c.* 1900 in reaction against the stress, in the art criticism of the later 19th century, on form as opposed to content. Pioneers of the new approach were Émile Mâle and Aby Warburg. Some art historians, notably Erwin Panofsky, distinguish iconography from *iconology*, defining the latter as the study through art of 'the basic attitude' of a nation, a period, a class, a religious or philosophical persuasion', i.e. the HISTORY OF MENTALITIES from visual sources. A reaction against the speculations of some iconographers and their emphasis on the content of paintings is now manifesting itself. P.B.
Bibl: E. Panofsky, *Meaning in the Visual Arts* (New York, 1955; Harmondsworth, 1970), ch. 1.

id. In psychoanalytic theory (see PSYCHOANALYSIS), a FREUDIAN term for the UNCONSCIOUS system of personality that acts to reduce pain and enhance pleasure, by giving free rein to primitive impulses. Its PLEASURE PRINCIPLE is assumed to collide with the REALITY PRINCIPLE of the EGO, and with the censorious demands of the SUPEREGO, thus setting the stage for inner conflict. W.Z.

IDA. International Development Association. An organization set up in 1960 to provide low-interest loans to developing countries. It is part of the World Bank Group (see BRETTON WOODS). C.E.D.

idea. The smallest unit of thought or MEANING, the elementary constituent of beliefs or assertions. In contemporary PHILOSOPHY the word CONCEPT is widely preferred because (1) in traditional EMPIRICISM 'idea' was used both in the sense given above and at the same time to mean the same as 'image', since the empiricists took thought to be a matter of operating with images; (2) Locke and Berkeley also used 'idea' to mean sense-impression or SENSE-DATUM, using it to refer to the items of immediate experience of which images are copies; (3) in the philosophy of Plato, an Idea is a UNIVERSAL, conceived, in the manner of REALISM, as existing substantially in a world of timeless ESSENCES.

A.Q.

ideal ego. In contradistinction to the EGO-PSYCHOLOGY school of PSYCHOANALYSIS, that looked for naturalistic explanations of psychic functioning, the French school of analysts sought to define the subject's experience of the world in terms of the variables of PHANTASY, ideal, and DESIRE. They were thus led to take seriously the distinction between ideal ego and EGO-IDEAL, first stressed by Nunberg in 1932. Freud had in various ways distinguished these notions between 1914-1933: the basic problem is that of separating narcissistic types of IDENTIFICATION from what Lacan would later formulate as SYMBOLIC identification. Thus the ideal ego seeks to model itself on omnipotence; it rejects everything which displeases, and accepts everything that pleases; it represents an IMAGINARY mode of identification that ascribes to the ego heroic qualities and glamorous attributes. However sharply this distinguishes it from the ego-ideal, some authors equate the two notions.

B.BU.

ideal types. Term used by Max Weber to denote entities (including, e.g., types of 'action', society, or INSTITUTION) as constructed 'hypothetically' by an investigator from component elements with a view to making comparisons and to developing theoretical EXPLANATIONS; the components out of which a 'type' is constructed being empirically observable or historically recognized. Thus Max Weber used ideal types in his studies of types of action, of religion, economy, and authority — distinguishing, for example, between ideal types of *traditional, rational-legal,* and *charismatic* (see CHARISMA) authority. The word 'ideal' does not carry with it any NORMATIVE load — it relates rather to what Morris Ginsberg (*On the Diversity of Morals,* London, 1956, p.206) called 'HEURISTIC constructions...not definitions and averages...' that emphasize 'certain characteristics of a group of occurrences, and by linking up with others...' are 'so

combined by us as to form a coherent or unitary whole'.

S.J.G.

Bibl: *Max Weber on the Methodology of the Social Sciences,* tr. and ed. E. Shils and H.A. Finch (New York, 1949); W.G. Runciman, *A Critique of Max Weber's Philosophy of Social Science* (London, 1972).

idealism. The philosophical theory that the only things that really exist are minds or mental states or both. (The distinction between the two is rejected by those, like Hume, who take a mind to be no more than a related series of mental states and also by those, like Berkeley, who hold that a mental state is inconceivable except as part of the history of some mind.) Berkeley's philosophy is perhaps the simplest version of idealism. For him the world consists of the infinite mind of God, the finite minds that he has created, and, dependently on them, the ideas possessed or experienced by these minds. For Berkeley there are no material things that exist independently of minds: common objects are collections of ideas, in finite minds to the extent that they are observed by them, in the mind of God to the extent that they are not.

Berkeley's brand of idealism, misnamed *subjective idealism* by adherents of Hegel's *objective idealism,* is in fact as objective as the latter. It is not a form of SOLIPSISM, for it acknowledges that much exists over and above my mind and its ideas, namely the minds and ideas of other people and of God. Where Hegel's idealism differs from Berkeley's is in holding that there is only one true mind, the ABSOLUTE, or Spirit, of which finite minds are dependent fragments, not, as in Berkeley, entities created by the infinite mind with a separate existence of their own. Some idealists of HEGELIAN inspiration hold that in this respect Hegel went too far; see PERSONALISM.

A third type of idealism is found in the philosophy of Plato, in which only IDEAS, in his special sense of the term, are objects of knowledge, and therefore they alone truly exist. Of the changing particulars met with in space and time we can have only opinions, and he infers that these have only a secondary brand of existence.

A.Q.

ideas, history of, see HISTORY OF IDEAS.

identification.

(1) In ECONOMETRICS, it is often only possible to measure and estimate MODELS of the actual consequences of underlying economic relationships. An econometric model is identified if it is possible to estimate the relationships underlying the model. The conditions permitting identification are complicated. It is usually assumed that the underlying economic relationships can be represented by linear EQUATIONS. If it is possible to distinguish a linear equation from any linear combination of the remaining linear equations of the model, then the equation is identified and it is possible to estimate its parameters. A linear equation representing an economic relationship is *underidentified*, or not identifiable, when it is not possible to distinguish it from a linear combination of the remaining linear equations. In this case it is impossible to estimate the parameters of this linear equation. O*veridentification* of an equation occurs when all the linear combinations of other equations always contain more explanatory VARIABLES than the original equation.

R.ST.;J.P.

Bibl: M. Desai, *Applied Econometrics* (Oxford, 1976).

(2) In SOCIAL PSYCHOLOGY, the process of associating oneself closely with other individuals of REFERENCE GROUPS to the extent that one comes to adopt their goals and values and to share vicariously in their experiences. See also PEER GROUP. W.Z.

(3) In PSYCHOANALYSIS Freud sets out three forms of identification: primitive, oral identification of the father; regressive identification with an object, whereby identification appears instead of object choice; and hysterical identification, whereby the spring of the identification is the DESIRE to assume someone else's desire. These distinctions have been taken up and elaborated by Lacan, who clarifies the FREUDIAN account by introducing the category of the signifier. If the child is born into the world of language, it must take on certain signifiers to be represented, and this process is more specifically an identification with a signifier. The consequence of such an identification, given that the signifier only takes on its value in relation to another signifier (see SYMBOLIC) is an ALIENATION of the subject, specified by Lacan as a 'want to be' in the signifying chain. This latter expression indicates both a wish to be, in the sense of being self-identical, identical with just one signifier, and a lack to be, in the sense that the wish to be can never be accomplished owing precisely to the structure of the signifier. Identification, then, is exactly what makes identity, in the sense of self-identity, impossible. D.L.

identity crisis. A crisis that occurs when the integrity of a person's SELF-IMAGE is threatened, disrupted, or destroyed, usually in a conflict of loyalties or aspirations. It is said to be characteristic of adolescence and early adulthood. H.L.

Bibl: E.H. Erikson, *Childhood and Society* (New York, 1951).

identity theory. The view that the apparently private (see PRIVACY) mental states that each person is conscious of (see INTROSPECTION) are literally identical with certain states of the brain and NERVOUS SYSTEM that are accessible in principle to public, scientific observation. The identity in question is held to be *contingent* (see CONTINGENCY) or *empirical*, as is that of a visible flash of lightning and an electrical discharge at the same place and time, and not a matter of logical necessity, i.e. of the MEANING of the terms used to report observations of the two kinds in question. If true, it provides a more satisfactory account of the mind and conscious mental life from the point of view of MATERIALISM, since it neither denies self-consciousness nor asserts an entirely implausible synonymy of mental and neural terms. A.Q.

Bibl: D.M. Armstrong, *A Materialist Theory of the Mind*, vol. 1 (London and New York, 1968).

Ideological State Apparatus, see under ALTHUSSERIANISM.

ideology. A word coined by the French philosopher Destutt de Tracy (*Éléments d'idéologie,* 1801-5) to denote the 'science of ideas' which would reveal to men the source of their biases and prejudices. De Tracy believed only in trusting sense impressions and was thus akin to the impulses of English EMPIRICISM. After a period of disuse the word was revived with the publication in 1927 of Marx's previously unpublished *The German Ideology*, and in 1929 (translated 1936) of Karl Mannheim's *Ideology and Utopia*, which brought the sociology of KNOWLEDGE into contemporary concerns.

The word has been variously used to characterize IDEAS, ideals, beliefs, passions, values, WELTANSCHAUUNGEN, religions, political philosophies, moral justifications; it is, as John Plamenatz puts it, a 'family of CONCEPTS'. (Lionel Trilling, in *The Liberal Imagination*, 1950, defined it as 'the habit or the ritual of showing respect for certain formulas to which, for various reasons having to do with emotional safety, we have very strong ties of whose meaning and consequences in actuality we have no clear understanding'.) It may be employed, as Marx employed it in *The German Ideology*, to deride the PROPOSITION that ideas are autonomous or the belief in the power of ideas to shape or determine reality; or to argue that all ideas are socially determined. Ideologies may be seen as justifications which mask some specific set of interests. Or — a widely held viewpoint — they may be regarded as 'social formulas', as belief systems which can be used to mobilize people for actions; it is in this sense that the COMMUNIST nations talk of 'ideological combat' or 'ideological competition'.

Within contemporary SOCIOLOGY, Mannheim identifies ideologies as different 'styles of thought' and distinguishes between 'particular' ideologies (the self-interests of specific groups, such as the 'ideology of a small businessman') and 'total' ideologies (*Weltanschauungen* or complete commitments to a way of life). In the 1950s and 1960s a group of sociologists, notably Raymond Aron, Edward Shils, Daniel Bell, and S.M. Lipset, applied this concept of ideology as a 'secular religion' to the judgement of an 'end of ideology', or the decline of apocalyptic beliefs in the Western industrial societies.

Talcott Parsons defines ideology as an interpretative scheme used by social groups to make the world more intelligible to themselves (see also COGNITIVE SYS-TEM). Both the MARXISTS and the central sociological tradition see ideology as a 'distortion' of reality, the Marxist contrasting ideology with 'true consciousness', the sociologist with SOCIAL SCIENCE. A later group of writers, notably the anthropologist Clifford Geertz, see ideology in more neutral terms as one kind of SYMBOL system among other cultural symbol systems such as the religious, the aesthetic, or the scientific.   D.B.

Bibl: G. Lichtheim, *The Concept of Ideology and Other Essays* (New York, 1967); K. Thompson, *Beliefs and Ideology* (London and New York, 1986); D. McClellan, *Ideology* (Milton Keynes, 1986).

idiographic and **nomothetic.** Adjectives applied to contrasted types of study: *idiographic* to study of particular cases (e.g. persons, social groups, works of art), *nomothetic* to the search for general laws or theories which will cover whole classes of cases. Thus HISTORY and GEOGRAPHY, in so far as they are concerned with the study of particular events, persons, and PLACES, are idiographic subjects, whereas some economists would claim that, since they formulate ECONOMIC LAWS, ECONOMICS is a nomothetic science. The word *idiographic* is not to be confused with *ideographic*, which is the adjective formed from *ideogram*.   A.S.

idiolect. In LINGUISTICS, the speech habits constituting the language system of an individual.   D.C.

idiotype. An antibody to an antigen which is new to the body (see IMMUNITY) is itself a PROTEIN new to the body and as such is capable of arousing an immune response. The property of the antibody that distinguishes it from antibodies to other antigens, and which confers its antigenicity upon it, is known as its idiotype. Anti-idiotype antibodies and antibodies to these antibodies in turn are now thought to play an important part in regulating the intensity and the duration of the immunological response. The theory which attributes immunological control to the action of anti-antibodies and anti-anti-antibodies is sometimes called *network theory*.   P.M.

IFC. International Finance Corporation. An organization that invests directly in private companies and makes or guarantees loans to private investors. It is affiliated to the World Bank (see BRETTON WOODS) and is part of the World Bank Group. C.E.D.

illocutionary. In LINGUISTICS, used in the theory of SPEECH ACTS to refer to an act which is performed by the speaker once an utterance has been produced. Examples of *illocutionary* acts include promising, commanding, requesting, baptizing, etc. The term is contrasted with *locutionary* acts (the act of 'saying') and *perlocutionary* acts (where the act is defined by reference to the effect it has on the hearer). D.C.

Bibl: S. Levison, *Pragmatics* (Cambridge, 1983).

illusion, argument from. The most common and persuasive argument for the conclusion, drawn by the majority of philosophers until very recent times, that material objects cannot be perceived immediately or directly but must somehow be inferred from the SENSE-DATA, or impressions, or appearances, which alone are directly perceived. The argument is that there is, or need be, no directly perceivable difference between the character of my experience when I am actually perceiving a material thing and its character when, in a dream or hallucination, I falsely believe myself to be doing so. The ground is thus prepared for the traditional problem of PERCEPTION: how is the belief that there exists a material world, independent of my mind, to be justified if all I directly perceive is the private impressions that alone are immediately present to it? Critics see as the fatal flaw in the argument implied by this question what they take to be an equivocation in the use of the phrase 'directly perceive': in the premises of the argument it means 'acquire by perception absolutely certain knowledge of', while in the conclusion it means 'acquire, by perception and without inference, justified belief in'. The indubitable fact that our perception of material objects is *fallible* does not (such critics argue) entail that it is inferential (see INFERENCE). A.Q.

Bibl: A.J. Ayer, *The Foundations of Empirical Knowledge* (London, 1940);

D.M. Armstrong, *Perception and the Physical World* (London and New York, 1961).

ILO (International Labour Organization). A body set up in 1919 by the Treaty of Versailles (in 1946 it became an agency of UNO) with the object of promoting social justice by associating not only the governments but also the TRADE UNIONS and employers' organizations of member states in an endeavour to establish and raise common standards in the employment of labour. These standards it has embodied in conventions dealing with such matters as the limitation of child labour, the provision of social insurance, minimum wage-rates for unorganized workers, freedom of association, and equal pay. Member governments, which now number over one hundred, are invited to ratify these conventions. The annual conferences of the ILO provide a forum for the discussion of labour questions by delegates from each country's government, trade unions, and employers. The office at Geneva, besides its administrative functions, conducts many enquiries — e.g. into the MANPOWER and employment problems of developing countries — on which it issues reports. Since 1945 the ILO has developed technical assistance to the developing countries to form a major part of its work. Its continuous activity since 1919 testifies to its independence and its usefulness in the eyes of its members, especially to the developing countries among them, in raising whose standards of labour law and administration it has probably made its main contribution. E.H.P.B.

imaginary. Lacan's term, like all his other contributions to psychoanalytic theory, is subject to a continual reformulation throughout his work. Initially, it indicates the subject's relation to an image exterior to him, for instance, the visual image in a mirror, or a counterpart. By assuming such an image of wholeness, the child is able to master, to an extent, his motor functions, but such an IDENTIFICATION has a number of consequences. Firstly, the register of aggressiveness is set into motion, since if the child identifies with his counterpart, the introduction of some object will produce a situation of rivalry.

Likewise, the assumption of an exterior form will alienate the child — he will always be somewhere else. It is this structure which constitutes the EGO for Lacan, and gives the matrix of images of wholeness and completeness which, we could say, characterize traditional geometry. In 1955, Lacan extended this theorization of the imaginary to include the idea of signification, thus demonstrating that the imaginary is at play in language, and not simply in the specular register. We could point out a continuity in the fact that both the specular image and the category of signification are, strictly speaking, lures, to the extent that they trap the subject in an illusory ideal of completeness: for the former the completeness of the image, for the latter, the completeness of communication. (See also LACANIAN.)   D.L.

Bibl: B. Benvenuto and R. Kennedy, *The Works of Jacques Lacan* (London, 1986).

imaginary museum (*musée imaginaire*; also translated 'museum without walls'). A phrase coined by André Malraux in the first volume of his *La Psychologie de l'art* (1947) to convey the vast and increasing repertoire of more or less faithful photographic reproductions which now makes it possible to discuss works of art without having been to the actual museums containing them. The implications of this were pointed out much earlier by W. Martin Conway in *The Domain of Art* (1901).
                                    J.W.

imaginary number, see under COMPLEX NUMBER.

Imagism. A brief, central episode in the development of English-language poetry that represented the latter's clearest point of transition into MODERNISM. As a movement it dates from 1912, when Ezra Pound collaborated with F.S. Flint on a manifesto and a list of poetic prescriptions printed in POETRY (CHICAGO) and reprinted in the English *New Freewoman* (later the EGOIST). In 1914 came the first Imagist anthology, *Des Imagistes* containing H.D. (Hilda Doolittle), Richard Aldington, William Carlos Williams, Ford Madox Hueffer, James Joyce, and Amy Lowell, who was to take over the an-

thology side of the movement. It was Pound who enunciated the three primary principles ('direct treatment of the "thing", whether subjective or objective...to use absolutely no word that did not contribute to the presentation...as regarding rhythm, to compose in the sequence of the musical phrase') and defined the idea of the image as 'a verbal concentration generating energy'. Many of these principles were derivations, especially from the activities of a poetic group centred round T.E. Hulme which met at the Eiffel Tower Restaurant, London, around 1909. There was also a derivation from SYMBOLISM, though Imagism is distinguished by its concentration on the hard, verbally created image rather than the translucent symbol. Much subsequent poetry in England, and even more in the U.S.A., was influenced by Imagist lore and practice (e.g. Williams, Stevens). Imagism was not merely an aesthetic, but a campaign in the politics of poetry. It transformed an entire climate and, though its concentration was on the short poem, Eliot's *Waste Land*, Pound's *Cantos*, Williams's *Paterson*, and much other modern poetry is inconceivable without it. Pound moved on from Imagism to VORTICISM, which emphasized a harder, more kinetic view of the image; Amy Lowell took over the popularization of a rather impressionist form of Imagism in the U.S.A., where it was long especially influential.   M.S.BR.

Bibl: S.K. Coffman, *Imagism* (Norman, Okla., 1951); C.K. Stead, *The New Poetic* (London, 1964; New York, 1966); J.B. Harmer, *Victory in Limbo: Imagism 1907-1917* (London, 1975).

imago. In psychoanalytic theory (see PSYCHOANALYSIS), an idealized or fantasized figure from childhood, often a parent, whose standards the individual incorporates and uses as a model for his own behaviour in later life.   W.Z.

IMF (International Monetary Fund), see under BRETTON WOODS.

immanence, see under TRANSCENDENCE.

immediate constituent, see under CONSTITUENT ANALYSIS.

immersion course. A system tried successfully in California and Canada, where English-, Spanish- or French-speaking pupils are 'immersed' in a language other than their mother tongue. In California, English-speaking children would attend lessons given entirely in Spanish and gradually become bilingual. Spanish children would attend lessons totally in English with the same results.   J.I.

immigrant. An individual who moves from his or her homeland to a new country. In a narrow sense the term refers to an individual who migrates in search of work, usually from a rural background to an urban context. The move is voluntary, unlike that of the *refugee*, for whom movement is forced. Immigrant or guest worker indicate the status of the individual in the host country and are used to distinguish him or her from the indigenous population. These terms imply temporary residence. Immigrant has increasingly developed a pejorative meaning, that is, it identifies someone as an 'outsider', as 'not belonging' or as having only limited rights (see COLOUR; BLACK; INTEGRATION). A.G.
Bibl: J. Berger, *A Seventh Man* (London, 1975).

immobilized enzyme. An ENZYME that is held in place, usually by chemical attachment to a solid, so as to improve, for the purposes of BIOTECHNOLOGY, the efficiency with which it converts its substrate to its product.   P.N.

immoveable property, see under DESCENT.

immunity.
(1) In its original and narrower sense, a state of resistance or refractoriness to infection by micro-organisms that might otherwise cause infectious illness. Immunity in this sense can be acquired either 'actively' by direct exposure of the subject to an infectious organism, or 'passively' by the infusion of body fluids containing the protective substances or other agents responsible for the immune state — e.g. that of newborn mammals and chicks, which is passively acquired from the mother via the placenta or the yolk as the case may be.
(2) In the wider sense now universally adopted, any state of resistance or refractoriness caused by an adaptive reaction of the body to invasion by foreign substances including pollen grains, foreign organic matter, and grafts from different members of the same SPECIES. Examples include: ALLERGY towards pollen grains or fur; the rejection of a foreign graft; dermatitis excited by industrial chemicals; anaphylactic shock (see ANAPHYLAXIS); hypersensitivity to drugs such as penicillin. Haemolytic disease of the newborn is an immunological disease caused by accidental leakage of *rhesus positive* (see below) blood (see BLOOD GROUPS) from an unborn child into a *rhesus negative* mother.

Substances that excite immunological reactions and thus lead to states of immunity of one sort or another are called *antigens*. The chief offending antigen in haemolytic disease of the newborn is antigen *D* of the rhesus series. The rhesus antigens owe their name to the fact that they were first discovered by injecting the blood of rhesus monkeys into rabbits, a process leading to the formation of antibodies which will react upon the red blood corpuscles of approximately 85% of human beings.

Immunity reactions are put in effect by, or mediated through, (*a*) *antibodies,* or (*b*) *lymphocytes.* (*a*) *Antibodies* are PROTEIN constituents of the blood, are formed in response to an antigenic stimulus, and have the power to agglutinate, precipitate, disrupt, or otherwise destroy or sequester the offending antigen or the vehicle that carries the antigen, often a living CELL. (*b*) *Lymphocytes* are a species of white blood corpuscle, and it is the action of sensitized lymphocytes that brings about the rejection of foreign grafts and the reactions that manifest themselves as bacterial allergies and drug allergies; see also CELL BIOLOGY.

An important and almost a defining characteristic of immunity reactions is their specificity, i.e. the very exact one-to-one matching of antigen and antibody or antigen and particular immunological response. Thus the immunological reaction excited by antigen *A* is visited upon *A* alone, and has no effect at all upon antigens *B, C,* and *D.*   P.M.
Bibl: J.H. Humphrey and R.G. White, *Immunology for Students of Medicine* (Oxford and Philadelphia, 3rd ed., 1970);

W.W.C. Topley, G.S. Wilson, and A.A. Miles (eds.), *Principles of Bacteriology and Immunity* (London and Baltimore, 7th ed., 1984).

immunoassay. A method of measuring the quantity of a substance, using an ANTI-BODY against the substance to capture it. Immunoassays are frequently used to measure the quantity of a HORMONE in the blood and are the basis of many pregnancy tests that rely on measurements of hormones in the urine.   P.N.

immunology. The science of IMMUNITY.
                                                      P.M.

immunotoxin. A combination of an ANTI-BODY and a toxin, of potential use in CANCER therapy. The toxin kills CELLS but indiscriminately; the antibody is supposed to recognize MOLECULES that are concentrated on, or even unique to, the cancer cells. Therefore the antibody part of an immunotoxin should ensure that the toxin part is delivered largely, or only, to cancer cells. Immunotoxins have also found a use in the removal from bone marrow of the cells that are most prone to cause rejection of the transplant (see SURGERY).   P.N.

imperativism, see under EMOTIVISM.

imperfect competition. The state of affairs in which the conditions required for PER-FECT COMPETITION are not met and, in particular, when FIRMS cannot sell as much as they wish at the market price. COMPETITION is in this technical sense generally imperfect but may be intensive and effective nevertheless.   G.B.R.
  Bibl: D. Begg *et al., Economics* (London, 1984).

imperial preference. The system under which lower (often zero) import duties were charged on goods imported from one member of the British Empire by another than on similar goods imported from elsewhere. The preferences were not always reciprocal, and took other forms besides tariffs. They existed in the 17th and 18th centuries, but those granted by the U.K. were abolished in the latter half of the 19th century as being incompatible with FREE TRADE. Some were reintroduced by the U.K. in 1919 and in the 1920s, and, most importantly, in 1932 at the Ottawa Conference. Since World War II their title has been changed to *Commonwealth preference* and their importance has gradually diminished. Similar relations have existed in the trade between, e.g., Belgium, France, and the U.S.A. and their dependent territories. Since Britain's accession to the EEC in 1973, most Commonwealth preferences have disappeared. The few that do remain (e.g. for New Zealand dairy products) have to be arranged by *special provision* with the EEC.   A.B.E.;J.P.;M.FG.S.
  Bibl: R.S. Russell, *Imperial Preference* (London, 1947).

imperial presidency. The name given to the U.S. presidency in the early 1970s by commentators who believed that the powers of the office had expanded so much, and the standards of their use had fallen so far, that the nation's constitutional system was threatened. The argument was put at greatest length by Arthur Schlesinger Jr, who attributed the phenomenon mainly to presidential abuse of war-making and foreign policy powers, and to excessive secrecy resting on false claims which identified self-interest with national security interests. Other critics stressed such features as the forces in domestic politics since the NEW DEAL which expanded the role of the presidency, and the temperaments of its recent incumbents Johnson and Nixon. The WATER-GATE crisis of 1973-4 and resignation of Nixon, followed by attempts to control presidential power and restore congressional influence and oversight, saw the term fall into disuse.   S.R.
  Bibl: G. Hodgson, *All Things To All Men* (Harmondsworth and New York, 1984).

imperialism.
  (1) In general, the extension of the power of a state through the acquisition, usually by conquest, of other TERRITORIES; the subjugation of their inhabitants to an alien rule imposed on them by force, and their economic and financial exploitation by the imperial power. Imperialism in this general sense of 'empire' is as old as history.
  (2) More specifically, as a development

409

from the older term 'empire', the word 'imperialism' was adopted in England in the 1890s by the advocates of a major effort (led by Joseph Chamberlain) to develop and extend the British Empire in opposition to the policy of concentrating on home development, the supporters of which the imperialists contemptuously dismissed as 'Little Englanders'. The word was rapidly taken into other languages to describe the contest between rival European powers to secure colonies and spheres of influence in Africa and elsewhere, a contest which dominated international politics from the 1880s to 1914 and caused this period to be named the Age of Imperialism. Both British and continental imperialists justified their policies by claiming that they were extending the benefits of 'civilization', based upon the racial, material, and cultural superiority of the white races, to the inferior peoples of backward lands (see SOCIAL DARWINISM). After World War I their ideas were incorporated into the IDEOLOGIES of FASCISM and NAZISM.

The first systematic critique of modern imperialism was provided by the English radical J.A. Hobson, whose *Imperialism* (1902) gave it a primarily economic interpretation. Taken up and developed by Lenin in *Imperialism as the Highest Stage of Capitalism* (1915), this became the *economic theory of imperialism*. According to Lenin the natural tendency of CAPITAL to accumulate leads to falling profits, and this in turn to the growth of MONOPOLIES as a self-protective device to keep the profit rate up. But this is only a palliative, and the monopoly capitalists are driven to search for profits by INVESTMENT abroad, using the control which they have acquired over government to direct foreign policy towards the acquisition of empire with a view to securing markets, raw materials, and above all opportunities for investing their surplus capital. This, however, is the last stage of CAPITALISM, for competing imperialisms lead to WAR, war brings REVOLUTION, and revolution will finally overthrow capitalism and imperialism together. Besides providing an explanation of imperialism, Lenin's theory, it will be noticed, also traced the origin of war, or at least of 'imperialist' wars, to the

inexorable workings of the capitalist system.

No one today would question that economic factors played a large part in modern imperialism; but critics of the MARXIST-LENINIST theory have not found it difficult to show that it provides an oversimplified account even of the economic facts, and that it ignores a whole range of non-economic motives — NATIONALISM, racism (see RACE), the pursuit of national power — which, as in the case of Fascism and Nazism, combine with but are not reducible to the pursuit of economic advantage. The economic interpretation of imperialism, however, as expounded by Lenin, remains one of the most important elements in contemporary MARXIST theory, with the advantage, for propaganda purposes, that by definition only non-COMMUNIST states can be accused of imperialism and Communists can always claim to be on the side of anti-imperialist and anti-colonial movements (for which see below, final paragraph).

Colonialism is a form of imperialism based on maintaining a sharp and fundamental distinction (expressed often in law as well as in fact) between the ruling nation and the subordinate (colonial) populations. Such an arrangement arises most naturally in consequence of a conquest of a remote territory with a population of a conspicuously different physique and CULTURE. These, however, are not necessary conditions — witness Nazi colonialism in Eastern Europe, bolstered up by a pseudo-racialism based on fictitious racial differences. Colonialism always entails unequal rights. The British and the Dutch empires of the last century provide the purest examples: LIBERALISM, DEMOCRACY, and the attrition of CLASS barriers in the metropolitan country, bureaucratic (see BUREAUCRACY) AUTHORITARIANISM and the colour bar in the colonies. Another fundamental feature of colonialism has been the policy of perpetuating the economic differentiation between the colonies and the METROPOLIS, with the former supplying the raw materials while the latter remains the chief source of manufactures.

Decolonization is the process whereby a metropolitan country gives up its authority over its dependent territories and grants them the status of sovereign states. It can be seen most clearly in the development following World War II of the former British Empire into the COMMON-WEALTH of independent states, or the French Empire into the Communauté Française. This represented a triumph for the nationalist movements which had agitated for independence and took over power when the colonial powers withdrew. In many cases, however, the achievement of national SOVEREIGNTY and admission to UNO have been followed by controversy over whether decolonization has led to real independence or only to *neo-colonialism*. This term describes a formal juridical independence accompanied by a *de facto* domination and exploitation by foreign nationals, together with the retention of many features of the traditional colonial situation, e.g. narrow economic specialization, cultural and educational inferiority.

Neo-imperialism, of which neo-colonialism is a form, describes a situation in which an independent country suffers from and resents intervention and control by a foreign government and its nationals, but not necessarily as the result of a previous colonial relationship. In some parts of the world (e.g. Latin America) the synonymous term *economic imperialism* (or, more specifically, *dollar imperialism*) is often preferred. The use of such terms is, of course, coloured by the user's political views: what is 'economic imperialism' to one man is 'aid' to another.

Cultural imperialism may be defined as the use of political and economic power to exalt and spread the values and habits of a foreign culture at the expense of a native culture. A familiar example from an earlier period is the export of American films. Although cultural imperialism may be pursued for its own sake it frequently operates as an auxiliary of economic imperialism — as when American films create a demand for American products.

Anti-colonialism and *anti-imperialism* appear to be self-explanatory. The former is rightly used to describe any movement (e.g. the various African national movements) aimed at ending the subordination of a people to colonial rule. The latter means, more broadly, opposition to any form of imperialism anywhere. Anti-imperialism, however, like anti-Fascism, is a term frequently twisted for propaganda purposes and selectively applied. If it was used with any regard for objectivity or logical consistency, opposition to the Soviet control of Eastern Europe or the Chinese conquest of Tibet or the Nigerian subjugation of Biafra would be called anti-imperialist. In current usage, however, the term is commonly restricted to groups hostile to the U.S.A. or the countries of Western Europe.   S.A.; A.L.C.B.

Bibl: W.J. Mommsen, *Theories of Imperialism* (London, 1980); G. Lichtheim, *Imperialism* (London and New York, 1971).

implication, see under ENTAILMENT.

implicature. In LINGUISTICS, a term derived from the philosopher H.P. Grice and now used as part of the study of conversational structure. *Conversational implicatures* refer to the implications which can be deduced from the form of an utterance on the basis of our general understanding about the efficiency and acceptability of conversations. For example, in a school classroom, the sentence spoken by the teacher *There's some chalk on the floor* would imply that someone should pick the chalk up.   D.C.

Bibl: S. Levinson, *Pragmatics* (Cambridge, 1983).

impossibility theorem. This theorem, discovered by Kenneth Arrow, considers the possibility of using the preferences of individuals, to produce a social ranking that could be used as a representation of society's preferences for alternative organizations of society. The theorem states that it is not possible to use individual preferences for these alternatives to generate social ranking of the alternatives, where the social ranking and individual preferences satisfy five acceptable conditions: (1) the preferences of individuals for the different alternatives may take any form; (2) if the social ranking gives alternative A as preferred to alternative B and, then, the individual preferences change in favour of alternative A relative to B, the social ranking still gives alternative A as being at least as desirable as B; (3) the relative positions of two alternatives in the social ranking is unaffected by the introduction of additional alternatives; (4) there exist a set of individual preferences over the alternatives A and B, such that the social ranking gives alternative A as being preferred to B; (5) the social ranking does not correspond exactly to the preferences of one individual. The major implications of this theorem are the difficulty of constructing a ranking to represent society's preferences (see SOCIAL WELFARE), the possibility of concentration of political power within certain groups or individuals and the problem of society's choices yielding paradoxes (e.g. society may vote in favour of X rather than Y, Y rather than Z and Z rather than X). J.P.

Bibl: E.R. Weintraub, *Conflict and Co-operation in Economics* (London, 1975).

Impressionism.

(1) Movement in French painting originating in the 1860s and so called after the first exhibition, in 1874, of a group including Edgar Degas, Claude Monet, Berthe Morisot, Auguste Renoir, Camille Pissarro, Alfred Sisley, Paul Cézanne, and Armand Guillaumin. One of Monet's pictures there, *Impression — soleil levant* (now in the Musée Marmottan, Paris), suggested the name to the critics, though Léon Lagrange ten years earlier had already heard 'Impression roaring at the gates, with Realism joining in the chorus'. Anticipated in the work of Boudin, Chintreuil, Corot, and Turner, the movement was characterized above all by its concern with fleeting effects of light and motion, its disregard of outlines and distaste for sombre colours, its original angles of vision, and its general aura of delicate yet mundane gaiety. In its subject-matter and attitude it was at the same time a product of the REALISM of Courbet and Manet and of the open-air landscape of the Barbizon school; Degas actually conceived of its exhibitions, which continued for twelve years, as a 'realist Salon'.

Virtually every major development in 20th-century art is traceable to the Impressionists. Thus it was at their 1880 exhibition that Gauguin began showing, in his pre-SYNTHETIST vein, while the eighth and last exhibition in 1886 saw the début of the NEO-IMPRESSIONIST Georges Seurat. Through van Gogh the movement influenced EXPRESSIONISM, through Cézanne the CUBISTS. Meanwhile Monet, whose late works were to be important for ABSTRACT EXPRESSIONISM in the 1950s, continued till his death in 1926 as the prototypical Impressionist, while the movement began to spread across the globe, affecting for instance the NEW ENGLISH ART CLUB and the Berlin SEZESSION, captivating the wealthier collectors everywhere, and selling in millions of colour reproductions. J.W.

Bibl: J. Rewald, *The History of Impressionism* (New York, 1949); P. Pool, *Impressionism* (London and New York, 1967).

(2) In music, by analogy, a style of composition in which the composer evokes a scene in a manner which is undramatic; hence, although there is nearly always a title, the music is descriptive rather than programmatic (see PROGRAMME MUSIC). Its greatest exponent was Debussy, whose *Prélude à l'après-midi d'un faune* (1892) first dramatically established the style. It is marked by a tendency to use sound as colour, to employ shapes of a deliberately nebulous character, to avoid clear-cut rhythm or harmony, and to eschew the dramatic dynamism shown by, e.g., Beethoven. Debussy, Ravel, Delius, Bax, Albéniz, and Respighi are typical examples. The SYMBOLIST poets Verlaine, Baudelaire, and especially Mallarmé were as potent an influence as the Impressionist painters, and that influence has extended in recent years to Boulez, making him seem in certain ways a follower of Debussy, although his music is more consciously directed by the intellect than by emotion. A.H.

(3) In literature, impressionism means, in the most general sense, subjectivism: the work attempts to convey the author's own impression (mood, state of mind) rather than an objective description. STREAM OF CONSCIOUSNESS writing is impressionistic — provided that it avoids the deliberate distortions of Expressionism.

M.S.-S.

imprinting. In ETHOLOGY, a learning process which leads to an extremely rapid CONDITIONING, and consequent narrowing-down of the situation that elicits a response. The best-known and extreme examples are found in goslings and ducklings, which are normally led by the parents from the nest to the feeding-grounds, almost immediately after hatching and drying. When hatched in an incubator, and shown any moving object, even a matchbox or a large balloon, they will follow this, and will later continue to do so even when offered a choice between this object and their own parents. Although the phenomenon had been reported earlier by Spalding and Heinroth, it was Lorenz who first emphasized its peculiar nature, and compared it with INDUCTION (as then known) in EMBRYOLOGY. It seems likely that imprinting is an extreme case of conditioning linked by intermediate phenomena to CLASSICAL CONDITIONING. See also ATTACHMENT; CRITICAL PERIOD.   N.T.

Bibl: N. Tinbergen, *The Study of Instinct* (Oxford, 1951).

improvisation. The art of making music spontaneously without some form of written notation was not used to much extent in Western serious music in the first half of the century although it plays a fundamental part in JAZZ. More recent developments in 20th-century music have often tended to give the performers greater freedom sometimes to the extent of improvisation (see ALEATORY; GRAPHIC SCORE; TEXT SCORE; INDETERMINACY).   B.CO.

impurity, see under POLLUTION (2).

inborn errors of metabolism. GENETIC defects due to the absence of an ENZYME. About 400 of these are known, some being extremely rare, some having insignificant effects on the individuals, while at other extremes some inborn errors are lethal. Some are amenable to dietary treatment.   A.E.B.

Bibl: A.E. Bender and D.A. Bender, *Nutrition for Medical Students* (Bristol, 1982).

incest. Illicit sexual relations among persons closely related by KINSHIP or MARRIAGE. Each society defines that range of sexually forbidden kinsmen and affines for itself, and societies differ greatly among themselves in the SANCTIONS they apply to offenders. The 'horror of incest' is not in fact universal, although there is probably no society which would tolerate sexual relations between a woman and her son. So great are the variations from society to society that some anthropologists deny the existence of a single universal phenomenon which can be called 'incest'. Incest rules and rules of EXOGAMY are related, not identical.   M.F.

Bibl: Jean Renvoize, *Incest: A Family Pattern* (London, 1982); D. Willner, 'Definition and Violence', *Man*, Vol. 18, No. 1, 1983.

incomes policy. A policy which is intended to restrict incomes (i.e. wages, salaries, dividends and rents) in order to reduce INFLATION, particularly through its effects on cost-inflation and inflationary expectations. Many different governments and countries have used incomes policies. After World War II, incomes policies were regarded as necessary because of the declared objective of governments to achieve FULL EMPLOYMENT. This, it was thought, would encourage all forms of labour to bargain for increases in incomes greater than the rate of increase in productivity and, thus, cause inflation. Incomes policies can be mere exhortations or, more commonly, they are backed up by legislation. Incomes policies are usually accompanied by price controls. The control of wages and prices represents attempts to interfere with the PRICE MECHANISM and reduces its effectiveness. Restrictions on incomes may result in evasion and, thus, eventual collapse of incomes policies. Inflation is caused by various economic problems and incomes policies may not solve these problems. For these reasons, certain economists have argued that, in the long run, incomes policies are harmful and ineffective. A recent suggestion is for a tax-based incomes policy, where firms awarding pay rises above a certain amount are taxed. This would reduce the incentive to award pay increases, but would still allow, to a certain extent, the price mechanism to work. This policy has yet to be tried out. Incomes policies may also have a redistributional effect, e.g. the policies of the U.K. Labour government of the 1970s which were designed to favour the lower paid.   J.P.

Bibl: D. Morris (ed), *The Economic System in the U.K.* (Oxford, 3rd ed., 1985).

incommensurability. EMPIRICIST and POSITIVIST views of scientific development have always presupposed that facts in some sense speak for themselves. Theories are derivative from them, and the best theory is that which explains the largest body of facts without ANOMALY. Many modern PHILOSOPHIES OF SCIENCE, by contrast, deny any such fundamental disjunction between fact and theory. Facts themselves are recognized only through already existing conceptual and linguistic schemes; they are 'theory-bound'. Appeal to the facts alone, therefore, can never decide which is the better of two rival scientific theories, because each theory makes sense of the facts within its own interpretative framework. This insight lies at the core of the notion of the incompatibility of PARADIGMS, or theories, as advanced in T.S. Kuhn's *The Structure of Scientific Revolutions*. SCIENTIFIC REVOLUTIONS occur by the sudden replacement of one theory by another. At that revolutionary moment, it is impossible to appeal to any so-called objective body of facts to adjudicate the claims of rival theories; the theories are INCOMMENSURABLE. Thus at some level, the theory switch is 'irrational'. Kuhn's holistic view obviously finds support from GESTALT psychology and from studies of visual PERCEPTION, as well as corresponding to the experience of many scientists.   R.P.

Bibl: T.S. Kuhn, *The Structure of Scientific Revolutions* (London, 2nd ed., 1970).

incommensurable. Two theories or sets of beliefs are held to be incommensurable if there is no means of interpreting or understanding one in terms of the other or of comparing them. For example, American Indian theories about how and why raindances cause rainfall, and meteorological theories about how and why chemical seeding of clouds causes rainfall, are said to be incommensurable. The notion is associated with RELATIVISM. It can take a strong form: for example, some relativists argue that changes in the meanings of theoretical terms in science entail that early 20th-century theories of atomic structure are incommensurable with theories about the ATOM in the late 20th century.   A.C.G.

Bibl: P. Feyerabend, *Against Method* (London, 1977).

incorporating (in LINGUISTICS), see POLYSYNTHETIC.

incorporation. The new industrial WORKING CLASS of the 19th century was widely held to be *in* society but not *of* it. Incorporation refers to the process over the past century whereby the workers themselves, together with many of their institutions and practices, have been brought into the existing institutional order and made a regular part of its working. Working class voters, LEFT-wing political parties, TRADE UNIONS, and strike activities, at first excluded and often forcibly suppressed, have become legitimate parts of the political and economic system of 20th-century societies. For some sociologists, such as T.H. Marshall and Reinhard Bendix, this represents the achievement of social and political 'citizenship' by the working class, enabling full and effective participation in the life of society. For MARXISTS such as Herbert Marcuse, incorporation rather refers to the loss by the working class of a distinctive radical and 'oppositional' culture, and its accommodation to the values and institutions of BOURGEOIS society. As such, it contributes to the 'deradicalization' of the working class. See also EMBOURGEOISEMENT; DOMINANT IDEOLOGY.   K.K.

Bibl: R. Bendix, *Nation-Building and Citizenship* (New York, 1964); H. Marcuse, *One-Dimensional Man* (London, 1964).

incorrigibility, see under DEFEASIBILITY AND INCORRIGIBILITY.

independence (in STATISTICS), see under CORRELATION.

independent assortment, see under MENDEL'S LAWS.

Independent Theatre, see under THÉÂTRE LIBRE.

indeterminacy.
(1) In music, the practice of not completely specifying the end results of a composition. Indeterminate music relies on

chance (see ALEATORY) or performer interpretation to complete a version of the piece which will thus exist in as many forms as it has performances. This abdication by the composer of some of his control over the final outcome of his music has been championed by John Cage (see also MOMENT FORM; MOBILE FORM; GRAPHIC SCORE; TEXT SCORE; EXPERIMENTAL MUSIC).　　　　　　　　　　B.CO.

Bibl: R. Kostelanetz, *John Cage* (New York, 1971).

(2) In PHYSICS, see UNCERTAINTY PRINCIPLE.

indeterminism. The opposite of DETERMINISM.　　　　　　　　　　　　　　　A.Q.

index number. A single measure of the change in a particular characteristic, e.g. price, of a group of entities such as goods. Index numbers measure the change in the characteristic from the base to the current period or from one region to another. The most commonly used indices are for prices and quantities. In measuring, for example, the change in the prices of a group of goods consumed by a group of consumers in two different years, an index has to allow for the different changes in the prices of the different goods. This could be done by multiplying each price by the quantity consumed of the good — these quantities are called *weights*. These products are summed and the index number is the ratio of the sum for the current period to the sum for the base period. The same quantities are used as weights in both periods, though an important choice has to be made whether to use base or current period quantities as weights. The index number is usually expressed by multiplying the ratio by 100. Indices of the increase in output, consumption, standard of living, etc. (i.e. quantity indices) can be constructed in a similar manner to price indices, but using prices as weights. An alternative means of constructing a price index is to multiply the relative increase in the price of each good by the good's share in total expenditure and summing. The index number problem is that, as a measure, it is only an approximation and the closeness of the approximation depends on how different the weights are in the base and current period. For example,

as the relative structures of consumption in the 19th and 20th centuries are very different, the two different sets of weights that could be used to construct an index of the change in prices between the 19th and 20th centuries could give very different estimates of the change. The index number problem has no theoretical solution.　　　　　　　　　　　　　　　　　　J.P.

Bibl: R.G. Lipsey, *An Introduction to Positive Economics* (London, 6th ed., 1983); R.G.D. Allen, *The Theory and Practice of Index Numbers* (London, 1975).

indicator, see under SCALE.

indifference curves. In ECONOMICS, the term used to denote a collection of different patterns of consumption between which an individual consumer is indifferent. Each indifference curve is associated with a particular level of UTILITY. In MICROECONOMICS it is usually assumed that the objective of a consumer is to maximize utility within the constraints of the prices of goods and services and the consumer's income. This can be represented by the consumer attempting to reach, given the budget constraint and prices, the indifference curve with the highest level of utility (see SUBSTITUTION).　　　　　　　　　　　　　　　　　　J.P.

Bibl: D. Begg *et al.*, *Economics* (London, 1984).

indigenous theology. Since the 1960s the determination has grown to study Christian THEOLOGY, and to give training to clergy and laity, in styles which are not imported from Europe or the U.S. The most flourishing example of what can be achieved is the LIBERATION THEOLOGY of Latin America, but BLACK THEOLOGY has exposed the traditions and aspirations of Christians with roots in Africa, and India has been the scene of a sustained attempt to restate Christianity in terms easily understood by inquirers more familiar with the rich spiritual heritage of HINDUISM. Theologians of the Caribbean islands, of the Chinese world, of Japan, of the South Pacific and of Australia have also taken pioneering steps to break free of their dependence on imports. Since 1976 the Ecumenical Association of THIRD

415

WORLD theologians has provided a platform in its periodic conferences and publications, but the largest initiatives have often come from intellectuals who remain more or less loyal to Roman CATHOLICISM.

D.L.E.

Bibl: V. Fabella and S.Torres (eds.), *Irruption of the Third World* (New York, 1983); D.L. Edwards, *The Future of Christianity* (London, 1987).

indirect euthanasia, see under EUTHANASIA.

individual psychology. A theory of personality originated by Alfred Adler whose essential principle is that human behaviour is an attempt to compensate for feelings of inferiority caused by physical, psychological, or social deficiencies. The basic human drive is the striving towards superiority which is expressed as a yearning towards perfection. Individual psychology emphasizes the subjective nature of the individual's goal striving, the innate creativity of psychological adaptation and the unity of personality. Healthy goals are largely social in orientation and centre on cooperation with others. This view is one of the earliest PSYCHOANALYTIC theories emphasizing the importance of environmental factors in personality. R.P.-S.

Bibl: H.L. Ansbacher and R.R. Ansbacher, *The Individual Psychology of Alfred Adler* (New York and London, 1967); H. Mosak, *Alfred Adler: His Influence on Psychology Today* (Park Ridge, N.J., 1973).

individualism.

(1) In political theory, a term both of praise and dispraise. LIBERALISM is founded on a belief in the sanctity of the individual and the individual conscience, which in time bred a more romantic and less Puritan enthusiasm for the diversity of individual character and a belief in the value of each person 'doing their own thing'. This has always been attacked by conservatives (see CONSERVATISM) who emphasize the need for social cohesion and for authority rather than individual liberty; more recently, it has been attacked by socialists (see SOCIALISM) as a doctrine which encourages selfishness and social conflict. Liberals retort that they are concerned to defend individual rights rather than selfishness.

(2) In social analysis, individualism is the doctrine that explanation must be rooted in the beliefs and desires of individuals and not in 'holistic' (see HOLISM) concepts such as 'national spirit' or 'the destiny of the proletariat'. It thus suggests that classical and NEOCLASSICAL ECONOMICS is the proper model for the other SOCIAL SCIENCES to follow, a claim as widely resisted as accepted. A.R.

Bibl: K.R. Popper, *The Open Society and Its Enemies* (London, 1945); *The Poverty of Historicism* (London, 1954); S.M. Lukes, *Individualism* (Oxford, 1966).

individualism, methodological, see METHODOLOGICAL INDIVIDUALISM.

individualized instruction; individualized learning. The organization of instructional materials in a form which allows each student to proceed at his or her own pace according to abilities and interests. Obvious examples are the Dalton Plan and the MONTESSORI METHOD. Another area in which the principle is applied is PROGRAMMED INSTRUCTION, whether through TEACHING MACHINES or prepared books. The object is to recognize individual differences and not let them be lost among the mass of learners in a classroom.

W.A.C.S.

individuation. In PHILOSOPHY a principle of individuation is a means of uniquely distinguishing or identifying particular items or individuals. To say of something *x* that it can be individuated is to say that it can be picked out or separated from other particulars *y* and *z*. It provides not only a criterion for discriminating among particulars but for counting them. A.C.G.

inductance, see under SUICIDE CONNECTION.

induction.

(1) In LOGIC, a form of reasoning that usually involves generalization, i.e. the INFERENCE from an instance or repeated instances of some conjunction of characteristics that the conjunction obtains universally. But the term is often used for any

inference whose premises do not ENTAIL its conclusions, i.e. they support it but do not, if true, logically exclude the possibility that it is false. The justification of induction has been a persistent problem. It seems to presuppose an inductive principle of the form: 'For any *A* and *B*, if all known *A*s are *B*, then all *A*s whatever are *B*.' So stated, however, the principle is obviously false, as is shown by the discovery of black swans in Australia at a time when all known swans were white. A currently favoured position is to contend that the PROPOSITION 'If all known *A*s are *B*, then *probably* all *A*s whatever are *B*' is ANA-LYTIC, and that it implicitly defines the CONCEPT of probability in the sense of CONFIRMATION.   A.Q.

Bibl: Bertrand Russell, *The Problems of Philosophy* (London, 1912), ch. 12; P.F. Strawson, *Introduction to Logical Theory* (London and New York, 1952), ch. 9.

(2) In MATHEMATICS, see MATHEMAT-ICAL INDUCTION.

(3) In classical EMBRYOLOGY, the process whereby a certain STIMULUS, such as a pin-prick or exposure to a particular chemical, initiates the formation of new TISSUES or organs from pre-existing CELLS.
                                        E.O.W.

(4) In BIOCHEMISTRY, the process whereby the addition of a particular substance (the inducer) causes CELLS to produce the ENZYMES required to accelerate the chemical transformation of the substance. For example, when the bacterium *E. coli* encounters lactose (the inducer), it rapidly manufactures the three enzymes required to absorb the lactose into the cell and to hydrolyse it to glucose and galactose.
                                        E.O.W.

induction motor. An electrical machine in which a circular arrangement of electro-magnets (usually embedded in slots in the inner walls of a hollow laminated-steel cylinder) is fed with alternating currents so phased as to produce a rotating mag-netic FIELD within the cylinder. A second (usually slotted) laminated-steel cylinder is mounted within the first cylinder and is free to spin on the output shaft. The slots of this second cylinder (*rotor*) usually con-tain solid copper or aluminium bars, all of which are connected together at each end of the rotor by thick conducting rings. The

rotating field drives the rotor by inducing electric currents in the rotor bars. Al-though these are often called EDDY CUR-RENTS and it is true that their origins are identical, induction-motor currents are generally distinguished by being forced to flow in orderly patterns. Induction motors supply over 95% of the world's power in electric motor drives. The reason for their popularity is the inherently robust nature of the rotor which requires neither electri-cal nor mechanical contact with the stationary part of the machine in order to operate. In a linear induction motor (see LINEAR ELECTRIC MOTOR) the electromag-nets are arranged in a straight line and produce unidirectional force on the sec-ondary, which often consists of a simple sheet of conducting material.   E.R.L.

Indus civilization. One of the major civili-zations of antiquity based on the Indus valley, with twin capitals at Harappa and Mohenjo-Daro and other smaller sites ex-tending over the Punjab, Sind, and Ka-thiawar, now mostly in Pakistan. The Indus civilization was brought to light in excavations by Sir John Marshall and Sir Mortimer Wheeler in the 1920s. It appears to have been fully developed *c.* 2300 B.C. (when it was in trading contact with Sumer) and to have been in decline by 1700 B.C. before its final destruction by hos-tile attack *c.* 1500. The buildings, which include large granaries and baths, are made of burnt brick, with an elaborate system of sewers and wells; sites show the earliest examples of gridiron town-planning. Standard weights and measures were used, and a hieroglyphic script which remains undeciphered. Apart from the ar-chaeological remains, nothing is known of its origins or history.   A.L.C.B.

Bibl: R.E.M. Wheeler, *The Indus Civil-ization* (London, 3rd ed., 1968).

industrial action. Industrial actions may be taken as a sanction against an employer in the course of COLLECTIVE BARGAINING. A STRIKE is the most dramatic and visible of these actions. Such actions are generally a sign that collective bargaining has broken down. There are however many other industrial actions which may have as profound an effect as a strike. Many of these have been developed over the past 20 years. Marches and demonstrations are most often used as a weapon against a government. When they are associated with the cessation of work, for however short a period, they become an industrial action. French and Italian unions use this weapon more often than most other union movements. Actions short of a strike include: the banning of overtime; strict adherence to working rule books; boycotts (the U.S. grape-pickers in 1967 onwards, by the public as well as TRADE UNION members); refusing to cover for absent colleagues (teachers in 1986), non-cooperation with management, the 'blacking' of goods (the ammunition on the *Jolly George* in 1919) or services and working without enthusiasm. Other actions are newer. The Upper Clyde Shipbuilders workers 'worked in' in 1971 and this has now become an established tactic in redundancy situations. Sit-ins and occupations, pioneered in the late 1960s by students in the U.S., France and Germany, were taken up by trade unions in the 1970/80s; for example the CGT sit-in at Peugeot/Talbot in 1982. Other actions such as the hijack of a train carrying Renault machinery from France to Spain by the CGT, or the amending of a computer program, come into a grey area of illegality. See also SYNDICALISM.   B.D.S.

industrial archaeology. Term coined in the 1950s, originally to refer to the study of the INDUSTRIAL REVOLUTION in England, Germany, Belgium, the U.S.A. and elsewhere from the evidence of material remains such as coal mines, textile mills, railways and so on. Industrial archaeology has been slow to establish itself as a serious academic subject, whether among archaeologists (most of them concerned with much more remote periods) or historians (accustomed to working with documentary evidence). It has, however, benefited from amateur enthusiasms for steam trains, LOCAL HISTORY, and so on, and has become associated with conservation movements. In Britain, a Register of Industrial Monuments has been compiled and there is an Association for Industrial Archaeology and also a *Review*. In the last few years the scope of this sub-discipline has widened, both chronologically and thematically.

Some industrial archaeologists now concern themselves with the artefacts and monuments of the second industrial revolution — aeroplanes, radios, cinemas, typewriters etc. — while widening their scope to include the entire MATERIAL CULTURE of INDUSTRIAL SOCIETIES. As they do so they are coming into closer contact with SOCIAL HISTORIANS.   P.B.

Bibl: K. Hudson, *World Industrial Archaeology* (Cambridge, 1979).

industrial democracy, see under DEMOCRACY; PARTICIPATION.

industrial dynamics, see under SYSTEMS.

industrial psychology. A branch of APPLIED PSYCHOLOGY covering applications of PSYCHOLOGY in the industrial field. Topics now classed under this title may be grouped thus: (1) fatigue, safety, accident-proneness, and mental health, all of which were originally matters of medical concern; (2) vocational guidance, selection, training, and appraisal where there are strong links to work in education; (3) personal relations, relations within groups, and relations within the structure of organizations, all of which have links with SOCIAL PSYCHOLOGY and SOCIOLOGY (industrial relations and conflict, which clearly involve psychological considerations, are, curiously enough, seldom treated in depth in works on industrial psychology); (4) interactions between human beings, machines, and the ENVIRONMENT constitute a special subject, usually called ERGONOMICS in the U.K. and *engineering psychology* in the U.S.A.; (5) in so far as matters in (3) and (4) lead to the study of control SYSTEMS they also come under the heading of CYBERNETICS.

The term 'industrial psychology' only appears after 1900, and the subject was at first concerned primarily with the efficiency and well-being of individual workers. Academically and in practice, its development in Britain came with the setting up of the Health of Munition Workers Committee in 1915. Important later studies were concerned with industrial fatigue. The development of psychological techniques for testing, selection, and appraisal contributed in the 1920s to the growth of *personnel work*. Over the same period industrial psychology was affected by ideas of SCIENTIFIC MANAGEMENT and time and motion studies of work processes aimed at increasing efficiency. These had successes, but also met opposition, and increasing interest in social psychology led during the 1930s to a heightened concern with human relations. Since 1945 the scope of the subject has widened again to take into account the contributions of managers and MANAGEMENT to the well-being and effectiveness of organizations. In these developments industrial psychology overlaps sociology. B.B.S.

Bibl: E.J. McCormick and J. Tiffin, *Industrial Psychology* (Englewood Cliffs, N.J., 6th ed., 1974).

industrial revolution. General term for the process of the rapid onset of continued economic change and advancement through the application of industrial processes to traditional forms of manufacture, the divorce of an economy from a restricted resource and agricultural base, and a sustained increase in general living standards and in urbanization. The term was first used by French observers in the 1820s (in an analogy with the French revolution), as a description of the process in which Britain in the late 18th and early 19th centuries became the first industrial nation. The first English use was by Engels and then, more widely, by Toynbee. The British experience was then to be followed by other western European nations and the U.S.A.; eastern Europe and Japan. The pathway of the industrial revolution was held to be one which economies would follow as they reached a certain stage of ECONOMIC DEVELOPMENT (a view particularly associated with the American economist W.W. Rostow), an assumption akin to that which underwrote the idea of the DEMOGRAPHIC TRANSITION. Recent work on the English (and first) industrial revolution has rejected many of the older certainties about the direction of causality and speed of change, placing emphasis on random factors and the slow and piecemeal character of change, and pointing to inconsistencies between indexes of change and the onset of full-scale INDUSTRIALIZATION making the general lessons less applicable to other circumstances. The classic industrial revolution

was accompanied by a shift from human and animal power to mechanical power (steam, and later gas and electricity). Commentators now talk of a second industrial revolution, with the advent of widespread computerization, and of a POST-INDUSTRIAL service-based (rather than manufacturing-based) economy.
D.S.

Bibl: P. Mathias, *The First Industrial Nation* (London, 2nd ed., 1982); S.S. Kuznets, *Economic Growth of Nations* (Cambridge, Mass., 1971).

industrial society. The type of society produced by INDUSTRIALIZATION. In social theory the term has rarely been neutral. FUNCTIONALISTS, taking their lead from Herbert Spencer and Emile Durkheim, have taken the optimistic view that industrial society tends towards social equilibrium and the orderly integration of its parts. After the initial disruption of the INDUSTRIAL REVOLUTION, and the creation of new CLASSES such as the industrial WORKING CLASS, industrial society gradually elaborated a new stable order based on an extensive DIVISION OF LABOUR. For some theorists, such as the American SOCIOLOGIST Talcott Parsons, industrial society also generates a new NORMATIVE consensus, based on such values as achievement, equality of opportunity, and LEGAL-RATIONAL procedures. MARXISTS on the other hand see industrial society as tending towards greater conflict and eventual breakdown. For them the chief feature of industrialism is its capitalistic character. Industrial society is a system of EXPLOITATION, giving rise to an inevitable conflict of classes which will ultimately lead to the overthrow of its CAPITALIST form and the substitution of a SOCIALIST order. The so-called COMMUNIST societies of eastern Europe, and of China and Cuba, are not, for most Marxists, proper examples of the new order. These were relatively backward and semi-developed societies when their 'socialist' revolutions occurred. Socialism can only come about when capitalist industrialism has been developed to its fullest extent, on a world scale. K.K.

Bibl: R. Aron, *The Industrial Society* (London, 1967); T. Burns (ed.), *Industrial Man* (Harmondsworth, 1969).

419

industrialization. A broad CONCEPT, generally thought of as a massive development of CAPITALISM, as the latter came to harness the new knowledge of science by means of MECHANIZATION in new processes of factory production. It entailed new relations between owners of CAPITAL, entrepreneurs, MANAGEMENT, and wage-labourers; and new physical concentrations both of industry and of population (see URBANIZATION). After early years of uncontrolled development, with many inhumanities, subsequent efforts of reform and political policy have been to *tame* industrialization and to control it for the increase of human welfare. It has thus been regarded as the central set of economic and attendant social features which first appeared with the INDUSTRIAL REVOLUTION in Britain in the late 18th and early 19th centuries, spread to other countries, and marks off 'the modern world' from all earlier periods of history.   R.F.

Bibl: S. Pollard, *Peaceful Conquest; the Industrialization of Europe, 1760-1970* (Oxford, 1981); C. Kerr *et al., Industrialism and Industrial Man* (Harmondsworth, 2nd ed., 1973); K. Kumar, *Prophecy and Progress* (Harmondsworth, 1978).

inertia. The ability of matter to resist ACCELERATION when acted on by forces (see NEWTONIAN MECHANICS). The measure of inertia is MASS. See also MACH'S PRINCIPLE.   M.V.B.

inertial guidance. A method — based on the tendency of a MASS to move uniformly in a straight line, i.e. on its INERTIA — for continuously correcting the course of a guided MISSILE. The ACCELERATION is monitored by measuring the forces exerted on devices inside the missile (see NEWTONIAN MECHANICS); the motion thus computed is compared with a preprogrammed flight plan.   M.V.B.

infallibility. The inability to err. This happy condition has been popularly ascribed to a number of politicians, scientists, etc., but is chiefly associated with the DOGMA of the Roman CATHOLIC Church (1870) that the Pope is infallible when teaching *ex cathedra* (in full official solemnity), and with the FUNDAMENTALISM of some PROTESTANTS. The number of occasions on which Popes have so taught, and the exact nature of the truth in the Bible, are matters debated even by those who accept such infallibility.   D.L.E.

Bibl: H. Küng, tr. E. Quinn, *Infallible?* (London and New York, 1971); F.A. Sullivan, *Magisterium: Teaching Authority in the Catholic Church* (New York and London, 1983).

inference. The process or product of reasoning or argument. In a piece of reasoning or an argument a *conclusion* is inferred or derived from a *premise* or premises; it is asserted as true, or probable, on the assumption of the truth of the premise or premises. Thus the connected sequence of assertions 'All men are mortal, Socrates is a man, so Socrates is mortal' is an inference in the sense of process of reasoning; 'Socrates is mortal' is an inference in the sense of product of reasoning. In a valid *deductive* inference the premises ENTAIL the conclusion, which thus cannot be false if they are true. In a sound *inductive* inference (see INDUCTION) the premises only *support* the conclusion, or render it probable. An inference of either kind can have both its premises and conclusions true and yet be invalid or unsound.   A.Q.

inferiority complex. A term developed by the Austrian-American psychiatrist, Alfred Adler, to describe feelings of resentment at being inferior. Adler was deeply influenced by Nietzsche's concept of a 'will to power'. Seeing people as aggressive and competitive, Adler saw suspicion, PARANOIA and an excessive focusing upon alleged slights as a functionally adaptive device to enable people to cope with 'underachievement'. The ambiguities of power thus played a role equivalent to sexuality in Freudian PSYCHOANALYSIS. Adler emphasized how such character traits as timidity, indecision, insecurity, shyness, cowardice and submissive obedience could be explained as responses to innate drives to power.   R.P.

infertility. Literally, the inability to conceive though it is interpreted as failure to have a child or children. It may be voluntary, due to coital abstinence or CONTRACEPTION. Involuntary infertility occurs in

10-15% of couples and may be due to problems in either partner or with coitus. Many individuals and couples are really subfertile rather than infertile. In the male infertility may be caused by GENETIC or endocrine disorders affecting the development of the testes, by testicular failure or removal, blockage of the vas and disorders of erection or ejaculation. In the female, causes include infrequent, irregular or absent ovulation (the release of an egg), blockage of the fallopian tubes, abnormalities of the uterus or cervix, and inability to have intercourse. General disease, obesity, poor NUTRITION, stress, smoking and alcohol can affect fertility adversely. Investigation of the couple is best conducted in a specialized infertility clinic where the history and examination are supported by investigations which include examination of the semen, mucus from the uterine cervix after intercourse (post-coital test), tests for ovulation and tubal patency. Ultrasound enables the ovaries and ripening eggs to be watched and the operations of laparoscopy and hysteroscopy allow the surgeon to inspect the interior of the pelvis and uterus respectively. Treatment to induce ovulation is often successful but tubal surgery to open or reconstruct blocked tubes is less so. Treatment of male infertility is generally less successful than of the female. ARTIFICIAL INSEMINATION by donor (AID) is acceptable to some couples when the male is infertile. A recent advance is 'in vitro fertilization' (IVF) pioneered in Cambridge and Oldham by R.G. Edwards and P.C. Steptoe where eggs are obtained from the ovary, fertilized outside the body by sperm and then replaced in the uterus. This technique was introduced for women who had badly damaged tubes and those who had suffered surgical removal of the tubes but is now also used for women with other problems and unexplained infertility. New methods are being developed including the placing of egg and sperm in the tube (GIFT). The chance of a pregnancy is about 1 in 10 overall and 1 in 3 to 4 where fertilized eggs are actually placed in the uterus. The possibility of egg donation for those who have lost their ovaries and surrogate pregnancy (another woman 'carrying' the pregnancy) where the woman has had a hysterectomy have raised the hopes of some as well as posing major ethical issues. (See also WARNOCK REPORT.) S.J.S.

infinite; infinity. Our imagination readily transcends the strictly finite. We can see that the sequence 0,1,2,3,... can be continued indefinitely, without limit. But the problem of harnessing this insight to MATHEMATICS is not easy and has not been finally resolved. Throughout the history of the subject two opposed tendencies are manifest. One, akin to NOMINALISM and IDEALISM, finds its expression today in *finitism* and INTUITIONISM. ABSTRACT objects such as numbers are considered as creations of the human mind. Hence although the law describing the above sequence can be grasped, and the members up to a given point can be constructed, the sequence itself must always remain uncompleted. One says that infinity is only *potential*. Because each real NUMBER is defined by an infinite sequence or SET, this view requires a radical reworking of ANALYSIS; standard theorems are replaced by more sophisticated, less intuitive, counterparts. It is not surprising, therefore, that most mathematicians follow the other tendency, which is akin to REALISM or PLATONISM. Here it is supposed that the *completed* sequence does, in some mysterious way, exist and so can be treated as an object; the infinite is actual. If care is taken to avoid PARADOXES and inconsistencies, one can treat infinite sets rather as if they were finite. The word *transfinite* is used to indicate this extension (e.g. transfinite arithmetic). This view is given a plausible, though partial, expression in the axioms of SET THEORY.

Cantor first showed that some sets are more infinite than others (see CARDINAL). In set theory there is an infinite hierarchy of orders of infinity. Recently many new *axioms of infinity* have been contrived which extend this hierarchy. They have interesting consequences, but stretch intuition to breaking point. R.G.

Bibl: Bertrand Russell, *Introduction to Mathematical Philosophy* (London and New York, 1919); R. Rucker, *Infinity and the Mind* (London and New York, 1982).

infinitesimals, see under ANALYSIS.

inflatables, see PNEUMATIC STRUCTURES.

inflation. In ECONOMICS, a term used to denote an increase in the level of prices or, more commonly, a significant and persistent increase in prices. Over history, there have been periods of falling prices, e.g. the Great DEPRESSION, as well as periods of inflation. Periods of inflation imply a decline in the purchasing power of the unit of MONEY. In theory, if the economy adjusts immediately and costlessly to inflation, no harm is caused. In reality, inflation does have a number of harmful effects. The informational content of prices is reduced as the change in the price of one product has to be seen in the context of changes in the prices of all other products. Information on the latter is likely to be limited and costly to acquire. Thus, decisions may be based on incomplete information and persons may make different decisions than if they were in possession of complete and certain information. The greater level of uncertainty about prices may lead to less INVESTMENT and ECONOMIC GROWTH. For such reasons, there are likely to be greater problems in firms maintaining sufficient LIQUIDITY. Money rates of interest may not adjust for increased inflation and the real interest rate, i.e. the money rate minus the inflation rate, may be reduced. Previous legal commitments or MONEY ILLUSION may lead to the lending of money at lower real interest rates than at the previous rate of inflation. This would redistribute income from lenders to borrowers. The effect of inflation on saving may be to reduce it, because of the lower real interest rate and uncertainty about the real interest rate, or increase it, because people wish to have more reserves to protect them against future uncertainty. The ability of different groups to adjust to inflation varies and this may lead to a redistribution of income, e.g. away from those on fixed money incomes. Changes in relative prices are often greater in periods of high inflation. Those consumers who consume relatively more of products whose prices have risen most quickly will suffer most from inflation, unless their incomes increase to compensate them. Thus, the different rates of price increases have consequences on the distribution of income.

Inflation implies a need for a greater quantity of money or higher velocity of circulation (see QUANTITY THEORY OF MONEY) to maintain FULL EMPLOYMENT. The velocity of money may increase as the economy adapts, e.g. the emergence of credit facilities outside the banking system and a shortening of the average period for which money is held. The ability of the velocity of circulation to change in the short run is likely to be limited. Thus, in times of inflation, it is necessary to increase the MONEY SUPPLY in order to maintain full employment. Inflation represents a tax on holdings of money that accrues to the government through the supply of money being increased.

MONETARISTS regard inflation as a consequence of inappropriate MONETARY POLICY. KEYNESIANS regard inflation as being caused by cost-push and demand-pull factors (see PHILLIPS CURVE). The latter occurs when AGGREGATE DEMAND is allowed to exceed the productive potential of the economy. The former is caused by a struggle over the distribution of NATIONAL INCOME, especially between different forms of labour, and rises in import prices. In this Keynesian view, accommodating monetary policy increases the supply of money to ensure full employment and is not itself the cause of inflation. An associated view is that the government should control the fixing of wages and prices through INCOMES POLICIES and, thus, secure price stability. Monetarists believe that, at best, incomes policies have only a short run effect and that inflation should be cured by the government not allowing the money supply to grow more quickly than is warranted by the growth in the productive potential of the economy. Eventually, the wage setting process will adjust to the government's monetary stance and inflation will be reduced and the economy will return to full employment. However, in the intervening period, which may be very long, serious and persistent UNEMPLOYMENT may occur. The eradication of inflation is made more difficult by people holding expectations (see RATIONAL EXPECTATIONS) of continuing and even increasing inflation.

The term *disinflation* means the reduction in the rate of inflation. This may be brought about through deflationary monetary and FISCAL POLICIES that reduce a high level of aggregate demand that is responsible for the wage and price increases. *Reflation* is the use of expansionary monetary and fiscal policies to increase the level of aggregate demand and is intended to bring the economy back to full employment. *Stagflation* occurs when there is high inflation, but a low level of economic activity and high unemployment. It is likely to occur when cost pressures and inflationary expectations force prices up, but the level of aggregate demand is low. Inflation is called *Hyperinflation* when prices increase extremely quickly, e.g. the inflation of over 50% per day that occurred in Germany in 1923. It is different in *scale* but not in *kind* to inflation. P.M.O.; J.P.

Bibl: D. Begg *et al., Economics* (London, 1984); J. Trevithick, *Inflation* (London, 1980).

inflationary universe theory/scenario. Phenomenon predicted by theoretical cosmologists to have occurred during the first moments of the universe's expansion from the Big Bang (see BIG-BANG HYPOTHESIS). The refinement of the Big-Bang cosmological theory including this idea is called the inflationary universe theory/scenario. If matter behaved in a particular fashion that is consistent with but not demanded by current theories of GRAND UNIFICATION and ELEMENTARY PARTICLES during the first 10-35 seconds after the beginning of the universe its expansion can undergo a period during which it is greatly accelerated. During this period the universe behaves as though there exists a positive COSMOLOGICAL CONSTANT. If inflation occurs it offers a natural explanation as to why the universe is so uniform and similar in its properties from one direction to another. This idea and the term 'inflation' were first introduced by Alan Guth in 1981. The theory was subsequently refined to exclude some undesirable features by several other cosmologists. It is not yet known whether this theory is true or false. It predicts that our universe must have a total density within one part in 10,000 of the critical level that must be exceeded if it is to recollapse in the future. It does not predict on which side of this critical dividing line the density does lie. It is not

known whether there does exist as much matter in the universe as is predicted by the inflationary theory but the issue is uncertain because of the possible existence of very large quantities of DARK MATTER. J.D.B.

Bibl: J. Trefil, *The Moment of Creation* (New York, 1983); J. D. Barrow and J. Silk, *The Left Hand of Creation: The Origin and Evolution of the Expanding Universe* (New York, 1983); G. Gibbons, S. W. Hawking and S. Siklos (eds.), *The Very Early Universe* (Cambridge, 1983); A. Guth and P. Steinhardt, 'The Inflationary Universe', *Scientific American*, May 1984.

inflecting (or *fusional*). In comparative LINGUISTICS, adjectives applied to a language (e.g. Latin) in which grammatical relations are expressed primarily by means of changes within the forms of words (the *inflections*). The term *fusional* implies a characteristic, generally absent from AGGLUTINATING languages, namely that different grammatical meanings are often combined within a single affix, e.g. in Latin *bonus* the *-us* simultaneously marks nominative, masculine, and singular. D.C.

information processing, see COMPUTING.

information storage and retrieval. A generic term for activities, usually using COMPUTERS, in which data of some sort are stored in an organized way so that they may be recovered in response to enquiries. The expression is used for two quite distinct activities. In one (sometimes known as *data retrieval*) the complexity arises from the detailed structure of the data and from their bulk, all enquiries being unambiguous as are the encodings of the data. In the other (sometimes known as *document retrieval* or *reference retrieval*) the complexity arises from the impossibility of describing the content of a document, or the intent of a request, precisely or unambiguously. In the first case the difficult question is 'What is the thing I am looking for?' and in the second 'Is this thing the one I am looking for?' R.M.N.

information technology. A term used, particularly in the context of the financing of research and teaching, to cover all areas concerned with the processing and transmission of information, including COMPUTERS, COMPUTING SCIENCE, INFORMATION THEORY and ELECTRONICS (particularly the technology of electronic communication). J.E.S.

information theory (or *communication theory*; for another sense of that term see COMMUNICATION, THEORIES OF). In CONTROL ENGINEERING, the treatment of the problem of transmitting messages: that is, of reproducing at one point either exactly or approximately a message selected at another point. The fact that a message may have a *meaning* is irrelevant to the engineering problem, which is concerned with the ability to encode, transmit, and decode an actual message selected from a set of possible messages with which the communication SYSTEM claims to deal. Success in this depends on the quantity of information that has to be processed in a unit of time, measured against *channel capacity*, i.e. the capacity of the available channels to handle it. Mathematical tools are developed to enable such measurements to be made and compared.

The essential problem arises because of the almost universal presence of NOISE in communication systems. Noise, which may be generated by faulty components, miscoding, or outside interference, cannot be eliminated; but its corrupting effects can be diminished to an *arbitrarily* small degree by the use of REDUNDANCY. The capability of this theory to compute precise relationships between signals and noise in redundant communication is its major contribution. S.BE.

Bibl: C.E. Shannon and W. Weaver, *The Mechanical Theory of Communication* (Urbana, Ill., 1949).

infra-red. Electromagnetic RADIATION whose wavelength can range from 8 ten-millionths of a metre to about 1 millimetre, i.e. just longer than visible light, but shorter than RADIO FREQUENCY waves. Bodies less than red-hot emit infrared radiation, so that photographic film sensitive to infra-red reveals 'hot spots' such as vehicle exhausts, even at night when there is no visible light. Infra-red radiation penetrates haze because it suffers less than visible light from DIFFRACTION by the small PARTICLES. M.V.B.

infrastructure. The roads, transport systems, communications, sewage facilities, etc., that are necessary to the functioning of the economy and that are not usually supplied in sufficient quantities by the PRIVATE SECTOR. These goods and services are really examples of PUBLIC GOODS and, thus, there is an implication that the state should supply them. J.P.

Bibl: J. Craven, *Introduction to Economics* (Oxford, 1984).

Ingsoc, see under ORWELLIAN.

inheritance of acquired characters. Most evolutionary theories before Charles Darwin's *Origin of Species* (1859) invoked the inheritance of acquired characters as the major mechanism for transformation of species. Lamarck's account, set out in his *Philosophie zoologique* (1809), is the most celebrated. Lamarck claimed that creatures had the capacity to adapt themselves during their lifetimes to environmental challenges (the lengthening neck of the giraffe forms the classic illustration), and that such modifications were passed on to their offspring. There could thus be cumulative improvement down the generations, eventually leading to the appearance of whole new SPECIES. Darwin did not reject the theory, but it played a relatively small part in his explanatory mechanism of species change (which depended fundamentally upon the NATURAL SELECTION of chance genetic variations). Debates between Lamarckians and Darwinians continued to rage long after Darwin's death, in the absence of any experimentally-grounded science of GENETICS which would explain the laws of inheritance. This situation was changed by the rediscovery at the beginning of this century of Mendel's HYBRIDIZATION experiments, which demonstrated that the genetic material contained in CHROMOSOMES was fixed and quite independent of any modifications brought about during the life history of the individual plant or animal. The eventual triumph of Mendelian genetics effectively spelt the demise of the theory of acquired characters. See also DARWINISM; LAMARCKISM; MENDEL'S LAWS. R.P.

Bibl: G. Allen, *Life Science in the Twentieth Century* (Cambridge, 1978).

inhibition, see under PAVLOVIAN.

initial teaching alphabet, see i.t.a.

initiation. The act of introducing someone to a new STATUS (e.g. adulthood), or to membership of an association or group (e.g. a Church, the House of Commons, the Freemasons, the graduate body of a university), or to a new experience (e.g. sexual). Initiation may be of any degree of formality; at its most formal, it is accompanied by RITUAL (*initiation rites*). See also RITES DE PASSAGE. R.F.

Bibl: A. van Gennep, tr. M.B. Vizedom and G.L. Caffee, *The Rites of Passage* (Paris, 1909; London and Chicago, 1960).

innateness hypothesis. In LINGUISTICS, the view, particularly found in GENERATIVE GRAMMAR, that the rapid and complex development of children's grammatical COMPETENCE can be explained only on the hypothesis that they are born with an innate knowledge of at least some of the universal structural principles of human language. The hypothesis has had a considerable impact in other fields, notably PSYCHOLOGY and BIOLOGY, though it is not accepted by everyone, even within linguistics. D.C.

inner direction, see under OTHER-DIRECTION.

innovation, see under TECHNICAL PROGRESS.

inorganic chemistry. The branch of CHEMISTRY concerned with the study of compounds based on ELEMENTS other than carbon. It embraces the preparation of new compounds, the elucidation of reaction mechanisms, and the measurement and rationalization of the physical and chemical properties of inorganic systems. Compounds containing carbon fall within the scope of the subject when interest is centred on another element or elements, and they are actively investigated, notably in *organometallic chemistry*. Certain areas of study interact with BIOCHEMISTRY, METALLURGY, and SOLID-STATE PHYSICS. B.F.

Bibl: F.A. Cotton and G. Wilkinson, *Advanced Inorganic Chemistry* (Chichester and New York, 4th ed., 1980); C.S.G. Phillips and R.J.P. Williams, *Inorganic Chemistry*, 2 vols. (Oxford, 1965-6).

input/output (I/O). The parts of a COMPUTER concerned with input (i.e. the instructions and data fed to it) and output (i.e. the results it supplies in response to these). Most of the I/O (which comprises the *peripherals*, or *peripheral devices*, and their controllers) is concerned with communicating with human beings and involves the production of some visible record. Input generally starts from keystrokes (as from a typewriter) which either provide a direct input to the computer (as in a TERMINAL) or produce a machine-readable intermediate form (punched cards or paper tape, MAGNETIC TAPE); at the same time a printed copy is usually produced, though in some cases (e.g. numerals printed in magnetic ink on cheques) the two are combined. Devices for reading printed or handwritten characters (OPTICAL CHARACTER-RECOGNITION) are still far from fully developed; they are expensive, and work well only with good quality printing or typescript. Their perfection would make a large difference to the use of computers.

Output for human consumption might be in evanescent form on a VISUAL DISPLAY. A permanent copy often comes from a *line-printer* — a device which prints a whole line at a time at rates up to about 1,000 lines per minute. Early line-printers had ugly and restricted character sets which gave the layman an unfavourable impression. More modern machines can print small and capital letters as well as a variety of other symbols. Better quality output (almost indistinguishable from letterpress) is possible using a LASER printer: this device uses a form of XEROGRAPHY in which the image is produced, not by photographing an original document, but by a scanning beam of modulated laser light. Graphical output is also possible on visual displays and laser printers or on graph-plotters, devices employing a computer-controlled pen.

Some computer applications, particularly *real-time* COMPUTING and PROCESS CONTROL, use I/O which is not for human beings. Their input includes direct sensing devices for position, temperature, etc., and their output may control some machine directly.   C.S.

input-output analysis. A technique that reveals the amount of goods, services and FACTORS OF PRODUCTION that are used in the production of other goods and services. For example, a motor car is produced using, among other things, labour, CAPITAL, steel, rubber and plastics. Economic data is used to estimate how much of each good, service and factor of production is used in the production of one unit of output of each good and service. This is represented in an input-output matrix. From this matrix of COEFFICIENTS, it is possible to compute the required structure of production that is necessary to give a particular pattern of final consumption of goods and services. The analysis can take account of INVESTMENT and inventories. As the coefficients of an input-output matrix are usually taken as fixed, it is implied that there is only one means of producing each good or service and that constant RETURNS TO SCALE exist. In reality, there are usually various ways of producing a particular good or service and, thus, SUBSTITUTION between different factors of production is possible. Over different ranges of output, diseconomies and ECONOMIES OF SCALE may exist. Additionally, TECHNICAL PROGRESS will result in changes in the input-output coefficients that define the production techniques. In practice, these coefficients are updated to reflect changes in the chosen production techniques and technical progress. Input-output analysis is often used in the FORECASTING and planning of the economy.
                                          J.P.

Bibl: W.J. Baumol, *Economic Theory and Operations Analysis* (London, 4th ed., 1977).

insider dealing/trading. Dealing on the stock market in the shares of a company on the basis of knowledge that is not known to the other shareholders — selling shares in advance of bad news being announced or buying on information about developments that cause the price to rise.

On all stock markets insider dealing is considered unethical and bad practice; in many countries, including the U.S. and Britain, it is a criminal act.   R.I.T.

instinct. A term used in too many different senses to be of further use in the present stage of the BEHAVIOURAL SCIENCES. Derived from Latin *instinguere* (to drive or incite), it has been applied (1) to the (presumed) internal system that controls complex behaviour even in the absence of proper external stimulation; (2) to the faculty governing behaviour that is 'not learned'. Modern analysis of both the short-term control of adult behaviour and of the development of the control systems during the growth of the individual have invalidated these uses of the word by showing (*a*) that most, if not all, behaviour patterns are at any moment steered jointly by internal and external determinants, and (*b*) that they develop partly under the influence of GENETIC instructions (which limit the range of possible behaviour) and partly by complex interactions with the ENVIRONMENT.

It is also used to denote (3) a major, functionally unitary behaviour system such as feeding, sexual behaviour, etc., and (4) the mere absence of premeditation ('I braked instinctively') — a condition which has so far defied scientific analysis.
                                          N.T.

Bibl: R.A. Hinde, *Ethology* (London, 1982).

institutions. In SOCIOLOGY, activities which are repeated or continuous within a regularized pattern that is NORMATIVELY sanctioned. Sociologists usually speak of four major complexes of institutions. *Political institutions* regulate the competition for POWER. *Economic institutions* are concerned with the production and distribution of goods and services. *Cultural institutions* deal with the religious, artistic, and expressive activities and traditions in the society. *Kinship institutions* focus on the questions of marriage and the family and the rearing of the young. Institutions are studied comparatively in order to see how different societies organize their political or religious life. Or a set of related institutions within a society may be studied as a social system in order to see how they affect each other. D.B.

instrumental conditioning, see OPERANT CONDITIONING.

insulin. The hormone (see ENDO-CRINOLOGY), secreted by the pancreas, the partial or complete lack of which results in diabetes; its discovery in 1921, by Frederick Banting and Charles Best in Toronto, has saved the lives of millions who would otherwise have died in diabetic coma. It is a *polypeptide* (see PEPTIDE) consisting of two chains, respectively of 21 and 30 AMINO ACIDS linked together by sulphur ATOMS. Its chemical formula was discovered in 1955 by F. Sanger of Cambridge, and its spatial configuration was worked out in 1970 by Dorothy Hodgkin of Oxford. It is formed in the body from a precursor, *proinsulin*, a fact discovered in 1968 by Donald Steiner of Chicago.

In medical practice insulin is given by injection; it cannot be given by mouth as it is destroyed in the stomach. If too much insulin is given, the blood sugar level falls too low, producing symptoms which if untreated can culminate in unconsciousness and convulsions; but when the dose is properly adjusted, and a satisfactory DIET given, the diabetic's blood sugar can be kept near normal values, and he can lead an almost normal life. D.A.P.

insurgency, see under WAR.

integer, see under NUMBERS.

integer programming. A technique of OP-TIMIZATION THEORY. Certain optimization problems lead to mathematical programming problems in which some or all of the variables can take only certain discrete values. Usually it is sufficient to consider only the case of integer values, and the resultant problems are called *integer programming problems*. Problems involving packaging objects or setting out patterns so as to waste as little space or material as possible often lead to integer programs, as do problems where processes have not only a running cost but a capital or starting cost associated with them. Integer programs are as a rule extremely laborious to solve. R.SI.

integrated circuit. A single electronic component containing a large number of GATES and other LOGIC circuits and their interconnections. The TRANSISTORS, resistors, capacitors, and their connections are generally deposited together on a single piece of silicon (the *silicon chip*). *Medium-*, *large-* and *very-large-scale integration* (MSI, LSI and VLSI) are distinguished by their packing density. In LSI this can amount to more than 10,000 gates on a square inch of semiconductor chip, and is approaching that of the human brain. C.S.;J.E.S.

integrated day. In education, the 'day' may sometimes stretch to a week or more as children work on projects that concentrate their minds on learning rather than being taught. Teachers become guides rather than instructors. Subjects tend to be avoided, though different knowledge is merged. For instance, children might work on something involving the use of mathematics, a modern language and science. J.I.

integration.

(1) Many quantities in GEOMETRY and PHYSICS are given multiplicatively: thus area = height $\times$ breadth, distance travelled = velocity $\times$ time. Integration is the process by which such a product may be evaluated when one of the factors (hereinafter 'y') is a FUNCTION f of the other: say $y = f(x)$. Intuitively the range of variation of x (say from a to b) is dissected into 'small' intervals of length, say x_1, x_2, ... x_n, in each of which the value of y (say y_1, y_2, ..., y_n) is approximately constant. The sum $y_1x_1 + y_2x_2 + ... + y_nx_n$ is then an approximation to the desired overall product; if the function f is reasonably smooth this approximation will tend to a definite LIMIT as the dissection is made finer and finer. This limit $_a\int^b ydx$, or $_a\int^b f(x)dx$, is the *definite integral* of f between the limits a and b. If a is given, but b is considered as a VARIABLE, then the integral is a function, say $F(b)$, of b. F is an *indefinite integral* of f; conversely f is the DERIVATIVE (rate of change) of F. This fact facilitates the calculations of F. The method may be extended to quantities (e.g. volumes) which are products of more than 2 factors, by introducing *multiple*

integrals. Nowadays the theory of integration is treated as part of MEASURE THEORY. R.G.

Bibl: W.W. Sawyer, *Mathematician's Delight* (New York, 1943; Harmondsworth, 1949).

(2) In social contexts, a term having three related, but distinguishable, meanings: (*a*) A situation of cohesion, deriving from consent rather than coercion, between the parts of a community sufficient to make it a workable whole. The conditions for this were the object of pioneering study by the French sociologist Émile Durkheim. (*b*) The process whereby any MINORITY group, especially a racial one (see RACE), adapts itself to a majority society and is accorded by the latter EQUALITY of rights and treatment. If such a process reaches the point of obliterating the minority's separate cultural identity, a preferable term is *assimilation*. (*c*) In American usage, the opposite of SEGREGATION; i.e. the process of combining into a single system any educational or other public facilities previously available only on a racially selective basis. M.D.B.

Bibl: E.J.B. Rose, *Colour and Citizenship* (London and New York, 1969).

intellectual history, see HISTORY OF IDEAS.

intellectuals. The word, as a noun (with which in its plural form *intelligentsia* is synonymous), emerged largely in the 19th century, first in Russia in the 1860s, to designate that section of the university-educated youth who were 'critically thinking personalities' (Pisarev's phrase) or 'nihilists' (Turgenev's term), those who questioned all traditional values in the name of reason and progress. In France it was used, pejoratively or proudly, of and by the Dreyfusards (see DREYFUS CASE). The resultant association of the category *intellectual* with the LEFT was reinforced by such views as those of Alexis de Tocqueville and of Marx who, in the *Communist Manifesto*, described the intellectuals as a section of the BOURGEOISIE who attached themselves to the WORKING CLASS with the function of shaping their ideas.

Yet, if one defines intellectuals as the culture-bearers of their society, then the majority, until World War II, were not of the left, while many were on the RIGHT, e.g. Maurras, Bernanos, Mauriac; Stefan George, Jünger, Gottfried Benn; D'Annunzio, Pirandello; Wyndham Lewis, Pound, Lawrence, Yeats. And if one sees the intellectuals as the defenders of humanist values, then the majority have been of the *clerisy* (Coleridge's term), the upholders of tradition and learning against the popular passions and politics of the day; Julien Benda's *La Trahison des clercs* (1927, translated as *The Betrayal of the Intellectuals*), with its attack on the intellectuals as seeking to 'govern the world', is a major statement of that position.

In general, one can say that the intellectuals are the custodians of the tradition of creative and critical thinking about the NORMATIVE problems of their society and the effort of men to relate themselves to symbols of meaning outside their immediate self-interest and experience. In social fact, however, an intellectual is often one who simply identifies himself as an intellectual, participates with other intellectuals in discussion of questions that are deemed intellectual, and is confirmed in that STATUS by those who are recognized, informally, as the leaders of the intellectual world. Indeed, with the expansion of higher education in almost all INDUSTRIAL SOCIETIES, and the growth of the cultural sectors (publishing, television, the arts), the intellectuals today constitute a distinct social CLASS. How this ROLE affects their 'historic function' (howsoever defined) is an unresolved problem. D.B.

Bibl: B. de Huszar (ed.), *The Intellectuals* (Glencoe, Ill., 1960); L.A. Coser, *Men of Ideas* (London and New York, 1965); A. Gouldner, *The Future of Intellectuals and the Rise of the New Class* (New York, 1982).

intelligence. A term that came into widespread use with the rise of the MENTAL TESTING movement in the early 20th century. Intelligence was considered to be an innate general COGNITIVE ability underlying all processes of complex reasoning. In practice, it was defined operationally in terms of performances on tests of ABSTRACT reasoning. This gave rise to the statistical abstraction (see STATISTICS) of the INTELLIGENCE QUOTIENT. There is little doubt that scores on intelligence tests correlate with educational achievement and occupational STATUS. The major controversy surrounding their use lies in the NATIVIST argument that 80% of the variability in I.Q. between individuals in Western societies is attributable to GENETIC factors. On this view, intelligence is a relatively fixed attribute which sets an upper limit on individual intellectual functioning.

An alternative to the static MODEL of fixed intelligence is offered by Piaget's theory (see PIAGETIAN). Adult intelligence is conceived not as an attribute but as a complex hierarchy of information-processing skills underlying an adaptive EQUILIBRIUM between the individual and the ENVIRONMENT. Furthermore, adult forms of intellectual organization are derived from qualitatively different forms characterizing thought in infancy and childhood. Piaget's theory describes a universal sequence of stages in intellectual development culminating in the FORMAL OPERATIONS of adulthood. Since intellectual development depends on environmental factors to provide the experiential basis for change, the theory precludes any attempt to ascribe intellectual functioning to genetic or environmental factors alone.

Piaget's approach had the advantage of directing attention to the process of cognitive growth but tended to ignore the role of the CULTURE in defining what is to be considered as intelligent behaviour. A third view is that intelligence consists of skill in a culturally defined context, and that, whereas pre-literate societies depend on action-based skills taught in the context within which they will be used, technological societies (see TECHNOLOGY) require abstract reasoning skills transmitted by means of formal schooling. Consequently, what is defined as intelligence in a technological society reflects factors that make for success in school. This theory of intelligence, unlike those that stress intellectual processes alone, takes into account the contribution to skilled performance made by motivational factors. Particular emphasis is placed on the role of poverty in making the child feel he belongs to a 'culture of failure', a feeling which will tend to limit his self-imposed educational

goals. Recent theories go even further in stressing the context-dependent aspects of intelligence. It has been argued that far from comprising one global faculty, intelligence consists of a series of relatively interdependent 'modules', each preadapted to serve particular forms of experience. The theory of multiple intelligence helps to explain prodigious abilities in art, mathematics, music or chess in persons who may be of average intelligence in other respects. This approach also helps to explain how some mentally retarded persons (*idiots savants*) may nevertheless show remarkable mathematical or musical ability. See also ARTIFICIAL INTELLIGENCE.   G.B.

Bibl: L.J. Kamin, *The Science and Politics of IQ* (London and New York, 1974); R.J. Sternberg, *Handbook of Human Intelligence* (Cambridge, 1982); H.J. Gardner, *Frames of Mind: The Theory of Multiple Intelligences* (London, 1983).

intelligence amplifier. A mechanical or electronic aid to human INTELLIGENCE or PROBLEM-SOLVING; e.g. a slide-rule, a calculating machine, or a COMPUTER. Language, and mathematical rules and notations, might also be regarded as intelligence amplifiers, and indeed they may be crucial for giving humans a problem-solving ability so much greater than that of other animals. Whether machines will ever be able not merely to amplify human intelligence, but to *replace* it, is an open question implicitly begged by the phrase ARTIFICIAL INTELLIGENCE.   R.L.G.

intelligence quotient. The expression of an individual's INTELLIGENCE either as a ratio of his MENTAL AGE to his chronological age, with 100 representing the MEAN (the so-called 'classical I.Q.') or as a standard score, also with a mean of 100 and with a standard deviation (see under VARIANCE) conventionally of 15 or 16 I.Q. points.
       W.E.C.G.

intelligent knowledge-based system (IKBS), see under EXPERT SYSTEM.

intelligentsia, see INTELLECTUALS.

intension, see under CONNOTATION.

intensionality, see under EXTENSIONAL-ITY.

intensive care. This involves the highest level of continuing patient care and treatment. It is provided in a specialized ward or unit where facilities for the critically ill are concentrated together with staff with special expertise in such matters. Its primary objective is the safe recovery of a patient from a life threatening complication back to normal ward care.   D.W.R.

intentional fallacy. Term proposed by W.K. Wimsatt and Monroe C. Beardsley (*The Verbal Icon*, 1954) to denote the converse of the AFFECTIVE FALLACY. Conceding that there is an 'intended' meaning to a literary work, Wimsatt and Beardsley none the less separate this from the 'actual' meaning — which is independent of the author (as from all the work's effects). The author's intention, on this view, may be taken as *evidence* in determining its 'actual', independent meaning; but it should not be confused with it; such evidence is 'external'. The theory is stimulating but not easy to accept: the work's meaning *is* in one important sense inseparable from the author's whole (no doubt largely subliminal) intention; it is impossible to pretend that we read, say, Keats's work without our own (perhaps unconscious) reference to what we know about his life or to what he thought he wanted to do; and any evidence of an author's intention is nearer to the 'actual' meaning than anything else available, certainly nearer to it than a critic's interpretation. The argument about this became increasingly oversophisticated and sterile; but Wimsatt and Beardsley eventually failed to convince even the academic world that their primary motive was not extra-critical: to separate writers finally from their works, and to have no further truck with biography.   M.S.S.

intentionality. The central concept in the PHENOMENOLOGY of Edmund Husserl, the specifically phenomenological act of the mind by which the ESSENCE of a mental phenomenon is constituted. The medieval Schoolmen had argued for the 'intentional inexistence of an object' as being characteristic of mental phenomena, and Bren-tano had developed this concept, assuming the existence of an individual subject thinking, but it was Husserl who gave a quite new importance to the idea, making it in fact the founding characteristic of phenomenological reflection. In Husserl's version, a series of up to six 'reductions' are carried out, and with each one, there is a reduction of the specificity of the phenomenon in question, and an increase in 'pure', that is to say, non-individual SUBJECTIVITY. The act of intentionality is presented, in *Ideas* I (1913) as co-extensive with the whole scope of phenomenology itself. Of this *intentional* act, one can say that it is active, not passive, thus replacing the passive *tabula rasa* MODEL of PERCEPTION dominant since Locke by a model which takes account of the intending, selecting, choosing and ordering capacities of the mind in the act of perception. One can also say of the intentional act, that it is an *entry into* the mental phenomenon, an act of decision, creating pattern, context and inter-relation for any perceived phenomenon, not merely noting its brute and isolated existence. Thirdly, it seems to involve deciding what value or meaning to attribute within an overarching structure or INTERSUBJECTIVE map of meaning. In Anglo-Saxon terms, the act of intentionality could be compared to what E.M. Forster is desiderating with his 'Only connect! Only connect the prose and the passion', that is to say, the intentional act is one which carries the full responsibility for the act of knowing along with it, and the responsibility in particular for deciding on a *context of meaning* which is to be attributed to the observed phenomenon. The intentional act is, fourthly, participatory, entering into the being and nature of what is attended to. Thus an entire phenomenology of emotional states is allowed for, admitted, and taken account of, in the intentional act: perceiving, judging, valuing and wishing (*Ideas*, para 84) enter into the judgment, and by extension, there could be a phenomenology of love and hate, desire and fear etc. — this possibility having been developed not by Husserl himself, but by some of his French and English successors. It is obvious that intentionality as an account of perception and analysis submits the concept of an 'objectively' available knowledge to a fundamental critique, though of course Husserl himself asserted that each of the 'reductions' brought the judgment nearer to objective truth, though, since this is achieved by a six-fold multiplication of essential subjectivity, his position is obviously paradoxical and needs close attention before it can be understood. Nevertheless, Heidegger, Sartre and Merleau-Ponty, and in England R.D. Laing, chose to understand the Husserlian position as one that could be developed existentially, and the suggestion that it is the subject himself who finally decides on what status to accord to what he experiences or analyses, and that this is, in some ultimate sense, a 'true' decision, has been one of the most fertile in 20th-century thought. See EIDETIC REDUCTION.   R.PO.

Bibl: E. Pivčević, *Husserl and Phenomenology* (London, 1970); Q. Lauer, *Phenomenology, Its Genesis and Prospect* (New York, 1965); P. Ricoeur, *Hermeneutics and the Human Sciences* (Cambridge, 1981).

interactionism, see under MIND-BODY PROBLEM.

intercontinental ballistic missiles (ICBM), see under MISSILES.

interdependence. Term widely used to describe the increased multiple channels of contacts between STATES and non-state actors in the international system. This has led to demands for a new approach to international political analysis from such writers as Burton and Keohane and Nye. The target for attack has been the predominant realist paradigm which is considered too state-centric and POWER-ORIENTED. Keohane and Nye posit that interdependence should be accepted as a necessary corrective to realism, Burton that it should supersede it with what he terms a 'WORLD SOCIETY/COBWEB MODEL'.   A.W.

interest group/pressure group. A POLITICAL SCIENCE term which may be taken as synonymous with *pressure group* as distinctions drawn between the two terms are unsatisfactory. It describes an association formed to promote a particular interest by influencing government. Interest groups may be distinguished from political parties by their relatively narrow range of concerns, and more clearly by their uninterest in electing their own candidates to public office and seeking direct control of government. They tend to flourish in states whose political organization allows multiple points of access, and where government activity touches on a wide range of social and economic interests. However, generalizations about their character, roles and tactics tend to founder on variety. They are a crucial unit of PLURALIST analysis of politics; more generally, they are often regarded as a useful supplement to the representative mechanisms of parties and elections. Some critics, however, are concerned either with inequalities of influence between groups of differing resources, with the fate of the unorganized in systems favouring interest-group politics, or with the fragmentation of political decision-making which their presence may encourage.   S.R.

Bibl: T. Moe, *The Organisation of Interests* (Chicago and London, 1980); J.Q. Wilson, *Political Organizations* (New York, 1973).

interests, theory of. The concept of an interest is much employed in political debate, especially when individuals or groups are asked to subordinate self-interest to the PUBLIC INTEREST; none the less, it is a term whose analysis has caused much difficulty. It cannot mean 'what an individual or group wants', since we often want what is not in our interests; but it must be connected to our wants, for the pursuit of ideals is not always in our interests, whether or not we ought to pursue ideals as well as interests. A plausible view is that what is in our interest is what will enlarge our chances of getting what we want; solicitors, for instance, look after our interests by securing the *means* to whatever we may want, not by doing what we want at the moment. Governments look after the public interest by securing the means which people at large can use for whatever individual purposes they have in mind, not by doing whatever the public wants. See INTEREST GROUP.   A.R.

Bibl: Brian Barry, *Political Argument* (London, 1965).

431

interface. In technical contexts, the connection between two pieces of equipment. The word is mainly used, in ELECTRONICS, of equipment handling information (e.g. TELECOMMUNICATION equipment or parts of a COMPUTER); the requirement that the behaviour of the various strands in the connection should satisfy fairly complicated overall conventions makes it useful to consider the whole connection as an entity. By analogy, the word is increasingly used in other contexts, e.g. that of intercommunication between various social groups.　　　　　　　　　　J.E.S.

interference (in EDUCATIONAL PSYCHOLOGY), see under TRANSFER.

interferons. A family of PROTEINS which were discovered by virtue of their ability to hinder the multiplication of viruses. It is known that in addition to being part of the body's defence against viruses, interferons can also suppress the multiplication of some CELLS. The original difficulties of producing interferon in sufficient quantities to test its clinical value have been overcome by GENETIC ENGINEERING and BIOTECHNOLOGY, and some limited uses of interferons in CANCER and viral therapy are emerging. See also VIROLOGY.　　P.N.

interior monologue, see under STREAM OF CONSCIOUSNESS.

intermediate nuclear forces. MISSILE systems with a range of up to 5,500 miles. In practice this consists of the Tomahawk (Cruise) and Pershing weapons deployed by NATO, and the SS20 missiles used by the Soviet Union. The intermediate missile systems were deployed by NATO in response to the Soviet deployment of the SS20, but, equally, in an attempt to lock the U.S. more tightly into the defence of Europe. The theory advanced for the deployment was that if the Soviet Union could be induced to renounce their intermediate missiles, then NATO could do the same (see ZERO OPTION). But now fears have been raised that this would also serve to 'decouple' the defence of the U.S. from that of Europe. Thus, the intermediate nuclear forces have become a token in the complex inter-alliance politics of NATO. See also CRUISE MISSILES.　　A.J.M.W.

internal clock, see under CHRONOBIOLOGY and BIOLOGICAL RHYTHM.

internal colonialism. A term that suggests that the relation between dominant and subordinate groups, or dominant and subordinate REGIONS, within a nation, can best be understood on analogy with the relationship between the metropolitan POWER and its colonies in an empire. First applied by MARXISTS such as Lenin and Gramsci in the analysis of regional inequalities within societies, it was later more generally applied to social inequalities of various kinds that had a distinctive regional basis. The general idea is that, as in a colonial empire, the dominant groups exist in relation to subordinate groups as 'core' to 'periphery'. Specifically, the analogy is meant to suggest (1) that the relationship between dominant and subordinate groups and regions is inherently exploitative, involving an unequal exchange between 'core' and 'peripheral' regions and groups; (2) that the exploited groups and regions, like colonial peoples, will generally be marked by easily identifiable differences, such as those of colour, language, or religion, from the dominant groups, and that these will be used to screen them out in the allocation of positions of prestige and power; and (3) that there will never be equality between regions, nor full civic integration of all groups, because regional inequality is a necessary feature of industrial development and a condition of the maintenance of the existing social order. In recent times, the concept of internal colonialism has been used with considerable effect to analyse the relations between England and the Celtic regions — Wales, Scotland, and Ireland — in the context of British national development. Its limitations however became apparent when applied to such cases as Quebec in Canada and the Basque and Catalan regions of Spain, all of which cry 'oppression' but none of which fits at all clearly the exploited 'colonial' role. See also SOCIOLOGY OF DEVELOPMENT.　　K.K.

Bibl: M. Hechter, *Internal Colonialism: the Celtic Fringe in British National Development* (London, 1975).

internal rate of return. That rate of interest that when used in the DISCOUNTING of an INVESTMENT gives a NET PRESENT VALUE of zero. It is a measure of the profitability of an investment. If it exceeds the actual interest rate, it is usually considered to be profitable to proceed with the investment. It has been noted that there may be more than one internal rate of return, in which case the usefulness of the concept as a criterion for investment is limited. However, this problem is usually regarded as a theoretical rather than a practical problem. A related but more substantial problem is that internal rates of return may well give a ranking of the desirability of investment projects different from that given by the net present values of the projects. J.P.

Bibl: J. Craven, *Introduction to Economics* (Oxford, 1984).

internal relations. Those RELATIONS of a thing to other things which are essential to it, which it logically cannot cease to have without ceasing to be the thing that it is. Being the square of 4 is essential to 16, or 'being the square of' internally relates 4 to 16, since any number that was not the square of 4 could not be 16. Hegelian IDEALISTS subscribe to a general doctrine about the internality of relations, according to which the type of ABSTRACT, ANALYTIC thinking used in science and everyday life ('understanding') apprehends the relations between things, inadequately, as external, while a higher, philosophical type of thinking ('reason') apprehends all relations as internal, a thesis foreshadowed in the philosophy of Spinoza. Idealists infer from this doctrine that what appear, and are commonly taken, to be complex pluralities, such as a nation or a work of art or the multitude of finite minds, are really unanalysable wholes or systematic unities (see HOLISM). A.Q.

internalization. The process whereby an individual learns and comes to regard as binding the values and NORMS of his or her social group, or of the wider society as a whole. It is the central psychological mechanism in SOCIALIZATION. SOCIOLOGISTS, unlike psychologists, have tended to see it as relatively unproblematic, and have often made it the basis of their shaky concepts of social order or social consensus. For this, they have sometimes been accused of holding to an 'over-socialized' conception of man. K.K.

International, the. Term applied historically to a succession of federations of working-class SOCIALIST parties and organizations. History distinguishes: the *First International,* the international Working Men's Association, founded in London in 1864 with the support of Karl Marx, which in 1872 split into followers of Marx and those who preferred Mikhail Bakunin's brand of ANARCHISM, and in 1876 was dissolved; the *Second International,* founded in Paris in 1889 as a loose federation, which failed to survive the conflict of socialist and NATIONALIST loyalties revealed by the outbreak of World War I in 1914; the *Third International,* or COMINTERN, founded in Moscow in 1919, which, it became quickly apparent, was only open to socialist parties which accepted the discipline and leadership of the Russian COMMUNIST Party, and was dissolved by Russian fiat in May 1943; the *Fourth International,* formed in 1938 by the followers of Trotsky (see TROTSKYISM); the *Labour and Socialist International,* which, recreated in 1923 from the surviving democratic socialist parties (see SOCIAL DEMOCRACY) of the Second International, ceased to function after the NAZI conquest of continental Europe; and the *Socialist International* founded in Frankfurt in 1951, with headquarters in London and a membership of 40 democratic socialist parties. D.C.W.

Bibl: G.D.H. Cole, *A History of Socialist Thought,* vols. 2-5 (London and New York, 1954-60).

International Bank for Reconstruction and Development, see under BRETTON WOODS.

International Court of Justice. This court, whose seat is at The Hague, was established by the charter of the United Nations in 1945. Its organization is governed by Articles 2-23 of the Statute of the Court and by Articles 1-18 and 32-37 of the Rules of the Court. The court subsumed all the functions of its predecessor, the Permanent Court of International Justice.

433

The present court consists of 15 judges who are elected by the General Assembly and the Security Council for terms of 9 years and are eligible for re-election. Furthermore, the parties to a dispute before the court are entitled to appoint *ad hoc* judges who sit only in the particular case for which they have been chosen.

The court has jurisdiction to hear contentious cases. Only STATES falling within any of the following three categories may be parties to litigation before the court: members of the U.N. who are *ipso facto* parties to the Statute of the Court; certain states which are not members of the U.N. but which have become parties to the Statute in accordance with Article 93(2) of the Charter; and certain states which are not parties to the Statute of the Court but comply with the conditions laid down by the Security Council Resolution of 15 October 1946. Although to all appearances the court is virtually accessible to all states, no state is necessarily obliged to take its disputes with other states to the court. This is because its jurisdiction in contentious cases depends upon the consent of the parties. Such consent may be expressed in a special agreement; or by accepting the court's jurisdiction in a treaty; or by undertaking in accordance with Article 36(2) of the Statute to accept as compulsory, in relation to any other state accepting the same obligation, the jurisdiction of the court in all legal disputes concerning (1) the interpretation of a treaty; (2) any question of INTERNATIONAL LAW; (3) the existence of any fact which, if established, would constitute a breach of an international obligation; (4) the nature or extent of the preparation to be made for the breach of an international obligation. When the court is seized of a dispute it applies, in accordance with Article 38 of the Statute, international treaties and conventions, international custom, the general principles of law recognized by civilized nations and judicial decisions and the teaching of the most highly qualified publicists as subsidiary means for the determination of the rules of law. Furthermore, the court may determine a case *ex aequo et bono* (i.e. according to the principles of equity) if the parties agree thereto. Apart from its jurisdiction to deal with contentious cases, the court has the competence to give advisory opinions on any legal question, at the request of the General Assembly of the U.N., the Security Council or other organs authorized to do so.   O.Y.E

Bibl: I. Brownlie, *Principles of Public International Law* (Oxford, 1979).

international education. A term increasingly employed to denote a variety of developments in both the form and content of education. International education appears to be a reflection of the emergence of international economic, political, and cultural linkages leading towards what some claim is an emergent global social system. Educators have responded to this perception in various ways: the administrative response is characterized by a move towards greater equivalence and standardization of certification (the development of widely accepted new qualifications such as the International Baccalaureate, etc.), and is also marked by an increase in the number of cooperative agreements reached between educational institutions in different countries, and attempts to coordinate aspects of educational policy on a regional basis (as with the EEC since 1976). At the curricular level many courses increasingly look beyond the confines of the sovereign state in order to address the growing complexity and interdependence of the issues arising from global interaction. The goal of international education is the development of cognitive awareness (some would claim affective and behavioural corollaries) of the international dimensions of economy, polity, society, culture, aesthetics, etc.
P.S.L.

international law, see under PUBLIC INTERNATIONAL LAW.

international liquidity. Those assets available to governments for settling debts between themselves and limited to the kinds of money held in the official reserves of nations, which are usually deposited with the CENTRAL BANK (see LIQUIDITY). Since World War II the main forms of international liquidity have been gold, reserves of acceptable foreign currencies (which have varied over this period) and *special drawing rights.* At the time of the BRET-

TON WOODS negotiations in 1944, Keynes suggested that a new international currency (*bancor*) be distributed by a new world central bank. Instead, in 1969, the IMF invented the Special Drawing Right, a new form of interest bearing deposit held at the IMF. The rules and regulations concerning Special Drawing Rights have varied. At the moment, IMF member and non-member countries can hold them and they can be exchanged for foreign currency; they are valued against a basket of five different currencies; the interest they bear is an average of five different interest rates; and there are various rules about minimum holdings and the transactions they can be used for. Special Drawing Rights were invented because of fears that international liquidity was increasing less quickly than world trade. Until their invention, international liquidity depended on the production of gold and holdings of acceptable foreign currencies. However, Special Drawing Rights account for less than 5% of world international liquidity.

Members of the European Monetary System deposit a proportion of their international foreign exchange reserves with the system. These deposits entitle members to draw funds from the system that are measured in European Currency Units. The European Currency Unit is a weighted sum of the different EEC currencies (see EXCHANGE RATE). Though the European Currency Unit is a theoretical unit, it is used as the unit of account in many of the transactions between European central banks and certain European financial and business transactions.   J.P.

Bibl: R.E. Caves and R.W. Jones, *World Trade and Payments* (Boston, 4th ed., 1985).

International Monetary Fund, see under BRETTON WOODS.

International Phonetic Alphabet, see IPA.

International School of Theatre Anthropology (ISTA), see under THIRD THEATRE.

international style. The title of a book by Henry-Russell Hitchcock and Philip Johnson published in New York in 1932, and now applied to the main stream of modern architecture. The label covers the functional architecture derived from *De* STIJL, influenced by the BAUHAUS, and characterized by a simple rectangular geometry of defined planes; it was to have been a style expressive of contemporary TECHNOLOGY and social programmes. Its chief exponents during its most vital period, the second quarter of the century, were Mies van der Rohe, Walter Gropius, Le Corbusier, and other more local figures, such as G.T. Rietveld in Holland or Skidmore, Owings & Merrill in the U.S.A., who ensured the wide diffusion of the style. It continues into the 1980s, though much criticized as an oversimplified solution and easily debased when used by lesser practitioners. See also CIAM; FUNCTIONALISM; MACHINE AESTHETIC; ORGANIC.   M.BR.

Bibl: J.M. Richards, *An Introduction to Modern Architecture* (Harmondsworth, 1940).

international trade unions. International TRADE UNIONS are less well established than the international companies which they theoretically confront. The International Labour Organization (ILO) is an agency of the UNO, and as such is impartial, with employers represented. There are three international trade union bodies. The International Confederation of Trade Unions (ICFTU) which houses most OECD unions; the World Federation of Labour (WFL), a Christian/Conservative body, and the World Federation of Trade Unions (WFTU), a COMMUNIST body. While all three have notional coordinating and communication roles between individually affiliated union centres and trade secretariats, their main practical function would seem to be fighting the COLD WAR in third world countries. International Trade Secretariats (ITCs) represent workers in an industry, for example the International Metalworkers Federation (IMF). The first secretariat was formed in 1871; there are now 16, but they have achieved little in terms of international COLLECTIVE BARGAINING; it is still undeveloped. A parallel European trade secretariat movement exists within the umbrella of the European Trade Union Confederation (ETUC). Large unions exist in many countries, but few cooperate with their colleagues overseas, indeed many compete fiercely domestically. The CGT in France (not an affiliate of the ICFTU) cooperates only under sufferance with its French colleagues. The largest U.S. union, the Teamsters, is not affiliated to the union centre, the AFL/CIO, and the CGIL in Italy competes politically and industrially with its rivals. However the German, Scandinavian and Benelux systems have non-competitive demarcation lines. The growth of the transnational corporation has been a feature of the 1970s and 1980s along with the growth of world manufacturing capabilities. In this period of growth the countervailing force of international trade unionism has stagnated.

B.D.S.

Internationals, see INTERNATIONAL, THE.

interpolation, see under EXTRAPOLATION.

intersex (or *sexual intergrade*). In sexually reproducing organisms, an organism of which the secondary sexual characters are intermediate between those of the two sexes. Thus an intersex is different from a *hermaphrodite*, in which the *primary* sexual organs of both sexes are represented on a single individual. In *bilateral gynandromorphism* each side of the body is of each sex. Intersexuality may be brought about by a derangement of the SEX CHROMOSOMES or by a dysfunction of the sex hormones (see ENDOCRINOLOGY). Hermaphroditism is common among plants and among sedentary or very slow-moving animals like snails. In hermaphrodites self-fertilization is always rare and sometimes impossible. Indeed, such a process would defeat the purpose of sexual reproduction, which is to bring about genetical commingling.

P.M.

intersubjectivity. A major concept in PHENOMENOLOGY, where the importance of SUBJECTIVITY is so pronounced. The creation of meaning is an active process, the result of INTENTIONALITY, and each individual proposes his own interpretation of the world, through his language and actions, to a world of countersubjects. Thus a world of intersubjectivity is continuously built up and held in being. An individual's

'intentional hypotheses' are 'fulfilled' if the world confirms or endorses them, and remain 'unfulfilled' if refused. Intersubjectivity is thus very much a local cultural creation, and thinkers following Weber, like Alfred Schutz, have tried to describe the modes of interpretation we need to grasp the conventions of intersubjective understanding. See also PHYSICALISM.

R.PO.

Bibl: A. Schutz, *The Phenomenology of the Social World* (London, 1972).

intertextuality. A term coined by Julia Kristeva in an essay of 1966 to describe the necessary interdependence that any literary text has with a mass of others which preceded it. A literary text is not an isolated phenomenon, it is 'constructed from a mosaic of quotations; any text is the absorption and transformation of another'. In this essay, Julia Kristeva was trying to describe to a French audience the nature and importance of the literary theory of Bakhtin, then virtually unknown in the west. Bakhtin's sense of the 'dialogical' nature of the novel led Kristeva to coin, however, a term which had an immense effect in founding a properly STRUCTURALIST literary vocabulary. She herself, and the contributors to *Tel Quel*, took intertextuality to represent a new freedom from univocity, ESSENTIALISM and all forms of non-political critique. Kristeva was quick to insist, also, that intertextuality simply replaces the phenomenological-BOURGEOIS notion of INTERSUBJECTIVITY, thus doing away at one stroke both with any theory of SUBJECTIVITY and any theory of an INDIVIDUALIST cast. Intertextuality is also, of course, both linguistic and SEMIOTIC, and hence recuperable by PSYCHOANALYSIS and by her own new theory of semanalysis.

R.PO.

Bibl: J. Kristeva, *Desire in Language* (Oxford, 1980); J. Culler, *Structuralist Poetics* (London, 1975).

interval estimation. In STATISTICS, a way of summarizing experimental evidence about the value of a PARAMETER by calculating from the data an interval with a given fairly high probability of containing the true parameter value. The interval is a *confidence interval*. It is important to remember that the true value of the parameter is a fixed quantity and the interval is a data-dependent (and hence randomly varying) object, and not vice versa. The probability that the (random) interval contains the (fixed) parameter value is the degree of confidence or confidence level. One speaks, for example, of a '95% confidence interval' as a contracted form of 'confidence interval at the 95% confidence level'. A common rule-of-thumb is to take sample $\pm 2 \times$ sample standard deviation (see VARIANCE) as a 95% confidence interval for the true MEAN. See also ESTIMATE.   R.SI.

interval scale, see under SCALE.

intimism. Term applied to the work of those late-19th-century painters who concentrated on domestic scenes, somewhat in the genre of Henri Fantin-Latour's early work, e.g. Georges Lemmen and such NABIS as Maurice Denis and Édouard Vuillard.   J.W.

intonation. In PHONOLOGY, systematic variations in the pitch of the voice serving to distinguish MEANINGS.   D.C.

intraocular pressure. The relative rigidity of the globe of the eye helps to promote its optical efficiency. Among the factors determining the rigidity of the globe is the fluid pressure within it and this is the so called intraocular pressure, or tension. The globe of the eye can be considered as a closed space enclosed by a non-distensible envelope, the sclera, the white of the eye, and within this closed space there is maintained a balanced exchange of fluid, the aqueous humour, which flows into and drains out of the eye so that in health the intraocular tension remains constant within quite narrow limits. In the event of reduced fluid draining out of the eye, or of excess fluid flowing into the eye, the fluid pressure within the eye will at once rise because of the non-distensible nature of the sclera. A rise in intraocular pressure reduces the perfusion of circulating blood and thus reduces the nutrition reaching the constituent parts of the eye, notably the retina and the optic nerve. Damage to these structures caused in this way is the central clinical feature of the eye disorder called glaucoma.   J.WI.

intraocular tension, see under INTRAOCULAR PRESSURE.

intron, see under SPLIT GENE.

introspection. Generally, the mind's awareness of itself; more specifically, its attentive scrutiny of its own workings as contrasted with the inattentive and unbidden consciousness which we have of our own mental states. Locke called it 'reflection' and Kant 'inner sense', thus emphasizing the ANALOGY between it and our awareness of what is external to our minds in sense-PERCEPTION. The notion raises various difficulties. One is that it seems to imply an unacceptable duality in the introspecting mind which it divides into an introspecting subject self and an introspecting object self. This consequence was embraced by Kant; Ryle, with his formula 'Introspection is retrospection', took the present self to be the introspector and the immediately past self to be the introspected. (But, it may be argued, one cannot retrospect or recollect any mental event of which one was not aware at the time it occurred.) Another difficulty is the infinite regress generated by the view of Locke and many other philosophers that mental states are self-intimating in the sense that they cannot occur unless the mind whose states they are is aware of them, for the introspecting is itself a mental state, or act, which must, on this view, itself be introspected.   A.Q.
Bibl: D.M. Armstrong, *A Materialist Theory of the Mind* (London and New York, 1968), ch. 15.

introspective psychology. The study of states and qualities of private experiences and feelings by means of self-reports, mostly verbal descriptions given by the introspector.   I.M.L.H.

introversion. In PSYCHOLOGY, a term introduced by Jung (see JUNGIAN) to denote a process whereby an individual frustrated in his attempts to develop relationships with others withdraws his concern and LIBIDO from them and turns it towards his own fantasies. In protecting his withdrawal, the individual develops behavioural means to defend himself from the enticements to establish relations with others. This process is somewhat similar to that underlying NARCISSISM. Later the process was reified (see REIFICATION) and generalized to refer to a PERSONALITY TYPE, the *introvert*, much of whose life seemed to be characterized by these processes and behaviours. Introversion is not a true opposite of EXTROVERSION, and frequently both co-exist as distinct phases of the same person.   T.Z.C.

intuition. In LINGUISTICS, the native-speaker's knowledge of or about his language, used as evidence in deciding questions of ACCEPTABILITY; also, the linguist's awareness of principles for evaluating analyses.   D.C.

intuitionism.

(1) In ETHICS, the theory that the fundamental moral TRUTHS are directly apprehended as true by a special faculty of moral knowledge. It takes two main forms, corresponding to two different conceptions of the nature of the fundamental moral truths. According to the first of these, which may be called particular or, less politely, unphilosophical intuitionism, my moral faculty apprehends PROPOSITIONS to the effect that something is my, or some particular person's, duty on a particular occasion, by ANALOGY with the way in which the faculty of sense-PERCEPTION apprehends particular empirical facts. This is roughly the view of Bishop Butler. According to the second, which may be called general or philosophical intuitionism, the moral faculty, here conceived as an aspect of the capacity to apprehend *a priori* truths, such as the propositions of LOGIC and MATHEMATICS, apprehends general principles of duty, for example that promises ought to be kept or that lies ought not to be told. Most ethical intuitionists are adherents of DEONTOLOGY, but some hold that moral intuition apprehends the goodness or badness of the consequences of action, either in particular cases (G.E. Moore) or in the form of general principles such as that pleasure is good (Rashdall).

(2) In EPISTEMOLOGY, any theory of knowledge which holds that there are (or must be if scepticism is to be repelled) some items of absolutely certain, self-evident, and incorrigible knowledge.

Peirce criticized the epistemology of Descartes for its intuitionism and defended FALLIBILISM against it.

(3) The philosophy of MATHEMATICS, developed by L.E.J. Brouwer, which is *finitist* (see INFINITE) in that it does not assume there is a totality of NUMBERS but arrives at conclusions about all numbers by MATHEMATICAL INDUCTION, and is 'constructivist' in that it rejects indirect proofs of mathematical existence by *reductio ad absurdum* (see DEMONSTRATION) and acknowledges only such mathematical entities as can be constructed from the natural numbers by intuitively acceptable procedures. In denying that the derivation of a contradiction from 'no number has the property P' entails that there is a number with the property P, which he holds to be true only if such a number can be positively constructed, the intuitionist has to reject the universal validity of the *law of the excluded middle* (that every proposition is either true or false) and admit a third TRUTH-VALUE, possessed by a class of propositions whose members are, in default of adequate proof, undecidable.

A.Q.

Bibl: A. Heyting, *Intuitionism* (Amsterdam, 2nd ed., 1966); W.D. Hudson, *Ethical Intuitionism* (London and New York, 1967); A. Quinton, *The Nature of Things* (London and New York, 1973).

invariant, see under CONSERVATION LAWS; TRANSFORMATION.

invention, see under TECHNICAL PROGRESS.

investment. (1) The creation of CAPITAL which is capable of producing other goods and services. As capital depreciates, there is a distinction between gross investment and net investment (the latter being the actual increase in the stock of capital). Investment can be carried out by either the private or public sector. Positive net investment increases the productive potential of an economy. In KEYNESIAN economic theory, gross investment is an important part of AGGREGATE DEMAND and thus plays an important role in determining NATIONAL INCOME. (2) The purchase of an asset (e.g. shares in a company) that represents existing or new capital. J.P.

Bibl: D. Begg *et al.*, *Economics* (London, 1984).

investment currency. The currency resulting from the sale of foreign securities or used for their purchase when such transactions are controlled and channelled through a market separate from the market in foreign exchange. A.C.

invincible ignorance. A term used in Roman Catholic THEOLOGY to describe the condition of those who because of their heredity, upbringing, or environment cannot see a religious or moral truth, e.g. the truth of CATHOLICISM, whatever efforts they may make, and who are therefore not to blame. The term, although apparently offensive, expresses the charitable attitude, now happily characteristic of Roman Catholics, towards both sinners and non-Catholics. D.L.E.

invisible astronomy. There have been two remarkable leaps forward in man's ability to discern the contents of the heavens. One came in the 17th century with the invention of the telescope. The other occurred in the 1930s when astronomers' traditional total reliance upon optical wavelengths for the observation of celestial bodies was supplemented by the use of cosmic radio waves. This was thanks to the discovery by the radio engineer, Karl Jansky, of extraterrestrial radio waves. RADIO ASTRONOMY, however, was quite slow to develop (it was given a big spur by studies of RADAR during World War II). From 1946 onwards, radio astronomers made increasing finds of radio stars (the first was found in Cygnus by T.S. Hey's team in Britain). Vast radio dishes came to be constructed at Arecibo (Puerto Rico), the Max Planck Institute in Bonn, Jodrell Bank, Cheshire, Goldstone, California and Parkes, New South Wales. Extragalactic finds have been central to the role of radio astronomy as an instrument of discovery, but finds within the GALAXY have been important too, including the discovery of QUASARS and PULSARS by the Cambridge team in the 1960s. R.P.

Bibl: F.G. Smith, *Radio Astronomy* (London, 1974).

invisibles. That component of a country's BALANCE OF PAYMENTS on current account which comprises receipts and payments for services (as distinct from 'visible' goods); cash gifts, legacies, and other transfers for which no service is rendered; and the two-way flow of interest, profits, and dividends between home and abroad. All these items, which may be on government or private account, make up the *invisible balance*. The phrase *invisible exports and imports*, however, is usually restricted to travel, financial, and other services such as sea transport, civil aviation, insurance, banking, merchanting, brokerage, etc. These items are also included, with visible trade, in the concept of 'exports and imports of goods and services'. Fuller definitions and figures for recent years are set out in the annual volume entitled *United Kingdom Balance of Payments*. P.J.

in vitro fertilization, see under INFERTILITY.

involuntary euthanasia, see under EUTHANASIA.

I/O, see INPUT/OUTPUT.

ion. An ATOM or MOLECULE which is electrically charged because of an excess or deficiency of ELECTRONS (see ATOMIC PHYSICS); excess of electrons results in a negatively charged *anion*, deficiency in a positively charged *cation*. Ions produced by fast charged particles form the basis of several detectors used in ELEMENTARY PARTICLE physics (e.g. the BUBBLE CHAMBER, CLOUD CHAMBER, and GEIGER COUNTER). Ions of chemical salts and ACIDS in solution provide the source of current in many electrical CELLS. Because of its conceptual simplicity the ionic MODEL is a very useful way of viewing many solids and solutions, but since electrons are at least partially shared between neighbouring atoms it is at best a good approximation. See also IONOSPHERE. M.V.B.; B.F.

ion engine. A propulsion device similar to the ROCKET, which is under development and intended for use on SPACE PROBES. The exhaust consists of rapidly moving IONS which are propelled backwards not

439

by the expansion due to the combustion but by ELECTROSTATIC repulsion.   M.V.B.

ion exchange. The exchange of *cations* or *anions* (see ION) between a solution and an insoluble solid. The ion exchange material consists of a chemically bonded (see BOND) framework carrying a surplus positive or negative charge which is neutralized by mobile counter-ions. The latter may leave the host framework only when replaced by ions with the same total electrical charge. Water-softeners act by exchanging calcium ions in hard water with sodium. The first synthetic ion exchangers were aluminosilicates, but today most are based on synthetic organic resins.   B.F.

ionization. The production of IONS.   M.V.B.

ionization potential. The ENERGY that must be supplied to an ATOM to remove an ELECTRON and thus create an ION. M.V.B.

ionosphere. The radio-reflecting layers in the atmosphere, on which over-the-horizon radio transmission depends. At heights above about 100 km, positive IONS are produced from ATOMS in the air by short-wave RADIATION from the sun; the resulting free ELECTRONS give rise to the radio reflections. See also PLASMA PHYSICS.   M.V.B.

IPA (International Phonetic Alphabet). The most widely used system for transcribing the sounds of a language, originally drawn up in 1889, but subsequently modified and expanded at various times by the International Phonetics Association. See also PHONETICS.   D.C.

IQ, see INTELLIGENCE QUOTIENT.

IRA, see IRISH REPUBLICAN ARMY.

IRBM (intermediate-range ballistic missiles), see under MISSILES.

IRCAM. The Institut de Recherche et de Coordination Acoustique/Musique is a prestigious centre for the study of music, ELECTRONIC MUSIC and acoustics set up in Paris under the coordination of the composer Pierre Boulez.   B.CO.

Irgun Zvai Leumi (Hebrew for 'National Military Organization'). An armed extremist Jewish underground organization founded in 1937 by ZIONISTS in secession from the main Palestinian Jewish self-defence organization, the Hagana. It engaged first in anti-Arab, then in anti-British activities, until the outbreak of war in Europe in September 1939. Remaining inactive until January 1944, it then resumed anti-British sabotage and TERRORIST activities. Irgun Zvai Leumi, acting independently of Hagana, was responsible for blowing up British offices in the King David Hotel, Jerusalem, in 1946 and for the massacre of Arab villagers at Deir Yasin in 1948. It was forcibly disbanded by the Israeli Government in September 1948.   D.C.W.

Irish National Liberation Army (INLA). A violently militant splinter group of the official IRA, the INLA has since 1973 carried out a campaign of assassination and violence in Ulster, Britain and, in concert with other TERRORIST groups, mainland Europe. It was responsible for the killing of Airey Neave MP by a car bomb on 30 March 1979.   M.W.
  Bibl: T.P. Coogan, *The IRA* (London, 3rd ed., 1987).

Irish Republican Army (IRA). The Irish Republican Army is a NATIONALIST paramilitary organization dedicated to the unification of Ireland into a single autonomous republic. It is a lineal descendant of the anti-British, revolutionary Fenian movement begun in 1858, reorganized as the Irish Republican Brotherhood (IRB) in 1873, and linked to the Fenian Brotherhood in the U.S. Defeated in the Easter Rising against British rule in 1916, the IRB and its paramilitary arm the Irish Volunteer Force evolved into the IRA in 1919. It fought against British occupation forces, rejected the Anglo-Irish agreement of 6 December 1921 which maintained British SOVEREIGNTY over the six counties of Ulster, and rebelled against the government of the newly formed Irish Free State which accepted that partition. It became an underground and marginal organization, involved in sporadic campaigns of bombing in Britain and raids into Ulster until the mid-1950s, and promoting the 'Border Campaign' of 1956-62.

In 1969 the violent ULSTER UNIONIST response to the CIVIL RIGHTS MOVEMENT revived the IRA's standing in the north. The Belfast-based northern leadership broke with the Dublin-based Army High Command in January 1970 to form the Provisional IRA (PIRA). After a short internecine struggle it dominated the Republican cause in Ulster, while the rump of the official IRA lapsed into insignificance.

Since 1970 the PIRA's fortunes and tactics have fluctuated. Until 1981 it relied largely on terrorist tactics in the attempt to force British withdrawal from Ulster. In that year, in concert with its political wing Provisional SINN FEIN, it adopted a strategy combining selective violence with conventional political activity — denoted by the phrase of PSF publicist Danny Morrison, 'a ballot paper in this hand and an Armalite in this hand'.   S.R.;M.W.

Bibl: T.P. Coogan, *The IRA* (London, 3rd ed., 1987); P. O'Malley, *The Uncivil Wars* (Belfast and Boston, 1983).

iron curtain. A phrase used to describe the enforced isolation of areas under the political domination of the Soviet Union from the rest of the non-Soviet world. Often used in German by the Nazi propaganda minister Goebbels, it was adopted in English by Churchill and popularized in his Fulton speech of March 1946. D.C.W.

irradiation, see under PAVLOVIAN.

irrationalism. The view either that the conduct of men *is* not or that it *should* not be guided by reason. On the whole the two views are sharply opposed, and the two parties could be called, respectively, *descriptive* and NORMATIVE irrationalists. (1) The descriptive irrationalists are, for the most part, rather disillusioned or sceptical social theorists. Mild examples are Bagehot and Graham Wallas, a more scornful one is Pareto. Marx and Freud, both themselves dedicated to rationality, can be regarded without distortion as descriptive irrationalists: Marx for his theory of the false consciousness of men in an alienating social system (see MARXISM; ALIENATION), Freud for his view that the

fundamental determinants of belief and conduct are UNCONSCIOUS and irrational (see FREUDIAN). Any theory (like the last two, or like Mannheim's sociology of KNOWLEDGE) which implies that all human thinking is irrational has a self-refuting tendency. (2) Among normative irrationalists may be included Rousseau for his emphasis on sentiment and natural impulse and his hostility to civilized sophistication; D.H. Lawrence for his glorification of primal instinct as against BOURGEOIS prudence and calculation; Kierkegaard for his insistence on the absurdity of the human situation; and, perhaps above all, Nietzsche. Normative irrationalism began and has continued as a protest against the consequences of INDUSTRIALIZATION.   A.Q.

isallobar. Meteorological te.m for a line on a map connecting places with equal change in barometric pressure over a given time period.   P.H.

Islam. Literally 'surrender' or 'submission' to God is the religion founded by the prophet Muhammad (c.570-632) in Mecca and Medina in eastern Arabia. The profession of faith which all Muslims must make is the *shahada*: 'there is no God but God, and Muhammad is the Prophet of God'. In addition pious Muslims should pray five times a day, give alms (*zakat*), fast from dawn to dusk during the holy month of Ramadan and if possible make the pilgrimage to Mecca (the *hajj*) at least once. These four rituals, with the shahada, are the five pillars of Islam. Muslims reject the epithet Muhammadan as implying a submission to the prophet which is rightfully owed only to God. The scripture of Islam is the Koran (or Quran), believed to be literally the word of God and the most perfect revelation of God to man. *Shari'a* is Islamic Holy Law, based on the Koran and the sayings and actions of Muhammad and his early companions (the *hadith*). The written word is thus central to Islam but many pious Muslims, generally known as Sufis, have also sought God through MYSTICISM and have formed religious orders to do so.

The most important sectarian division in Islam emerged within fifty years of the death of the prophet and concerned the

441

succession to the leadership, and its nature. For most Muslims — Sunnis — leadership passed to the first four 'orthodox' Caliphs and then to the Omayyad and Abbasid Caliphates. These successors to the prophet exercised only temporal power. Shi'is believe that the prophet's son-in-law, Ali (the fourth orthodox Caliph) was Muhammad's direct successor and established a line of succession, of which the twelfth leader (Imam) did not die but disappeared, retaining final authority until his eventual return; until then there can be no truly legitimate leader on earth. Shi'is generally have therefore an enduring suspicion of political authority, and this is no doubt strengthened by their MINORITY position. Of about 700 million Muslims in the world about 87 million are Shi'is. Only in Iran is Shi'ism the official religion although Shi'is are a majority in Iraq and a majority of the Muslims in LEBANON. Conflict between Sunnis and Shi'is stems more from NATIONALIST and communal feeling than theological difference. Like CHRISTIANITY Islam has many minority SECTS. The most important for late 20th-century politics are the Alawites, a Shi'i sect who, although only 10% of the population, captured power through the BA'ATH party and the army, and the more eccentric Druze (believing in reincarnation) in Lebanon, Syria and Israel. Wahhabis, named from their 18th-century founder, are puritanical and fundamentalist, form an essential part of the government and retain great influence in Saudi Arabia. The BAHA'I religion departed from Islam and is regarded as heretical by Muslims and therefore subject to persecution, especially in Iran where it originated in the mid-19th century.

Islam responded to the expansion of the west first by a movement of reform (the *tanzimat*) originating in the 19th-century Ottoman empire, and by a movement called pan-Islam — a largely western concept denoting Islamic resistance to the divisions imposed on Islam by imperial rule. The late 20th century has seen a resurgence of Islam, differing from the reform movement of the 19th century in its emphasis on Muslim fundamentalism. Its political content is not new since Islam has always been concerned with political organization; Muhammad was not only a prophet but a consummate politician who built a community in Medina. The most important fundamentalist organization, the Muslim Brotherhood, was founded in Egypt by Hasan al-Banna in 1928 and survived suppression by Nasser. The proliferation of Muslim groups can however be dated from the Egyptian defeat in the MIDDLE EAST WAR of 1967 which discredited 'Arab SOCIALISM' borrowed from the west. In a sense all ACTIVIST Muslim groups look for a return to the Shari'a, since Muslim law gives rules for personal STATUS and conduct as well as for political behaviour. The weakness of Shari'a is that it lacks rules to govern modern political and economic organization, so that neither Libya nor Iran have dispensed with legal systems adopted from the west and Saudi Arabia has added western codes to the Shari'a. The diversity of activist Muslim groups is immense and while some are EGALITARIAN others are CONSERVATIVE in economic doctrine. Of key importance is the lengths to which any one group will go in denying the legitimacy of a government. A purifying mission has always been part of the ethos of the Muslim Brotherhood, who tried to assassinate Nasser and from whom a splinter group assassinated Sadat. Other groups merely demonstrate for the adoption of Shari'a as STATE law or are content with strict personal behaviour and dress. Governments of Muslim countries, especially Arab governments alarmed by the added impact of the Iranian revolution, have tried to reinforce their legitimacy by stricter observance of Islam, especially in inessentials such as the banning of alcohol. Arab rulers have also made appeal to the idea of *jihad*, conventionally translated as 'holy war' but originally meaning 'effort'. It was in this sense that so secular a ruler as President Bourguiba called for a jihad of ECONOMIC DEVELOPMENT when Tunisia became independent. King Fahd called for a jihad against Israel when Begin claimed Jerusalem as its capital but this had no military sequel. Khomeini has invoked jihad against the government of Iraq whom he distinguishes from the Iraqi people since jihad cannot be waged against fellow Muslims.   W.K.

Bibl: E. Mortimer, *Faith and Power* (New York and London, 1982).

isobar. (1) In METEOROLOGY, a line of constant atmospheric pressure on a weather map. (2) In NUCLEAR PHYSICS, one of a pair of NUCLEI with the same number of NUCLEONS (cf. ISOTYPES).

M.V.B.

isogloss. In DIALECTOLOGY, a boundary line demarcating regions that differ in respect of a particular linguistic feature.

D.C.

isohyet. In METEOROLOGY, a line on a map connecting places with equal rainfall characteristics.

P.H.

isolating (in LINGUISTICS), see ANALYTIC (2).

isolationism. The doctrine that a nation's interests are best served by abstaining from intervention in the main issues of international politics. Variously practised in Imperial China, Czarist Russia, and late Victorian Britain ('splendid isolation'), it more specifically applies to American attitudes to the world of great-power politics before 1941. Historians distinguish between complete rejection of international entanglements, hemispheric isolationism (as embodied in the MONROE DOCTRINE), and isolationism which rejected involvement in Europe but not the Pacific sphere. Isolationism has normally been accompanied in America by a moralistic rhetoric which denounces colonialism, IMPERIALISM and European practices in world affairs. Between 1939 and 1941 it was most supported by Americans who regretted involvement in World War I or whose ethnic origins disposed them against pro-British, anti-German or anti-Italian policies.

S.R.

Bibl: C.S. Campbell, *The Transformation of American Foreign Relations 1865-1900* (New York, 1976); R.D. Schulzinger, *American Diplomacy in the Twentieth Century* (Oxford and New York, 1984).

isomer. A chemical SPECIES, usually molecular, which differs from other MOLECULES made up of the same ATOMS. Thus ethyl alcohol and dimethyl ether each have the same chemical constitution, C_2H_6O, but they have different chemical BONDS and properties. In *stereoisomers* the bonding is similar but the atoms are arranged spatially in a different way; *optical isomers* differ only by being mirror images of each other, in their effect on polarized light, and in their chemical reactivity with optical isomers of other compounds.

B.F.

isometric projection. In CARTOGRAPHY, a diagram in three dimensions, i.e. a block-diagram, usually drawn to illustrate features of GEOMORPHOLOGY, and giving the appearance of a relief model viewed obliquely. An isometric projection is not in perspective. It is true to scale in both its horizontal axes, but the scale of the vertical axis is usually exaggerated with respect to them. It can be made by using isometric graph paper or by constructing sections, using contours, along horizontal and vertical grid lines of a topographical map and projecting them onto a rhombus base.

M.L.

isomorphic. Adjective applied to two or more things that have the same STRUCTURE, i.e. whose corresponding parts have similar properties and RELATIONS. Thus two chains of identical shape are isomorphic even if one is made of wood and the other of metal. The 'things' may, however, be to a greater or lesser degree ABSTRACT, and the CONCEPT of *isomorphism* is important in MATHEMATICAL STRUCTURES. Consider for example the following four sequences of numbers:

   (*a*) 2, 4, 6, 8
   (*b*) 7, 14, 21, 28
   (*c*) 3, 5, 7, 9
   (*d*) 3, 6, 12, 24.

If we merely consider the number of elements in each sequence, and the fact that each element is smaller than its successor and larger than its predecessor, then they are all isomorphic. If, however, we describe them in more detail, we find that there are pairs which are isomorphic with each other but not with the rest. Thus (*a*) and (*b*) are isomorphic because in each the difference between successive elements is equal to the first element, while (*a*) and (*c*) are isomorphic because the difference between successive elements is always 2. At a still more abstract level, (*a*) and (*d*) are isomorphic because, if we let the operation of addition in (*a*) correspond to multiplication in (*d*), then in both sequences the successor of an element is got by applying the operation to the element and the number 2, i.e. in (*a*) the successor of *n* is *n* + 2, while in (*d*) the successor of *n* is *n* × 2. Thus, whether two things are isomorphic or not depends on how they are described. It is possible to prove that almost any two things are isomorphic, if descriptions at a high enough level of abstraction are used. So talk of isomorphism without a specification of the relevant types of description is liable to be vacuous, or at least slipshod and ambiguous.   A.S.

isomorphism. When two MATHEMATICAL STRUCTURES *A* and *B* are ISOMORPHIC, there must be at least one bijective FUNCTION *f* which maps each element *a* of *A* into a corresponding *b*(= *f*(*a*)) of *B*. Any such structure-preserving function is an *isomorphism*.   R.G.

isoquant. In ECONOMICS, the set of different combinations of inputs of production that can be used to give the same level of output of a product. There is an isoquant for each level of output of a product. The use of the inputs is assumed to be efficient in that the level of output associated with each combination is the maximum possible. In microeconomics it is assumed that the objective of the FIRM is to minimize the costs of producing a given level of output and this can be represented on a diagram of isoquants (see SUBSTITUTION).   J.P.

Bibl: D. Begg *et al.*, *Economics* (London, 1984).

isorhythm. The application of a single and reiterated rhythmic pattern to differing melodic shapes. The term was originally applied by F. Ludwig in 1902 to rhythmic patterns that recur in 14th-century motets. Recently isorhythmic patterns have been much exploited by contemporary composers, in particular Messiaen.   A.H.

isostasy. Term proposed in 1889 by C.E. Dutton for the principle that the surface features of the earth will tend towards an ideal condition of gravitational EQUILIBRIUM; the *isostatic theory* proposes that balance is achieved by sub-surface inequalities of mass and implies that there

is horizontal transfer of mantle material at depth. It is known that the earth's crust is less dense than the underlying mantle (see ASTHENOSPHERE), so that the situation can be likened to blocks of wood floating on water. The bigger the block of wood, the higher it sticks out of the water, and the deeper it sinks underneath. Similarly the increasingly higher blocks of the earth's crust above sea-level are balanced by greater thicknesses of crust below sea-level. The flow of the mantle is very slow, so that the attainment of isostatic equilibrium lags behind the more rapid changes of mass caused by certain geological processes operating on the earth's surface. This is why those parts of the earth's surface that were depressed under the load of the Pleistocene ice-sheets are still rising, even though the ice melted some 15,000 years ago.   J.L.M.L.

isotherm. In METEOROLOGY, a line on a map joining places with the same temperature at a particular instant or, more usually, the same average temperature over a certain period of time. Such temperatures are usually reduced to sea level, by an addition of 1° centigrade for every 165 m altitude of a station, in order to eliminate differences due to height. In GEOGRAPHY the most commonly used isotherms are those indicating mean monthly temperatures, especially for the mid-winter and mid-summer months of January and July.   M.L.

isotope geochemistry. The study of naturally-occurring ISOTOPES with a view to obtaining information on the origin and evolution of the earth's rocks and minerals, and hence ultimately of the earth itself. The most prominent use of isotopes in the EARTH SCIENCES — in this case of RADIO-ISOTOPES — is for the DATING of rocks. Because the decay characteristics of radioactive isotopes are known, it is easy to measure the relative proportions of the still-decaying isotopes and the decay products in a rock or rock mineral, and hence extrapolate (see EXTRAPOLATION) back to determine the time at which the decay process began. This is taken to be the time at which the rock formed and thus defines the rock's age. The first decay series to be so used, in the early 20th century, was uranium to lead, but the chief series in use today for rocks more than a few tens of thousands of years old are potassium to argon and rubidium to strontium. For younger rocks containing organic remains, and in ARCHAEOLOGY, RADIOCARBON DATING may be used.

Stable isotopes of the lighter elements are not always uniform in nature, their precise distribution being the result of numerous natural processes and of the temperatures at which these processes took place. The isotopic compositions of certain rocks and minerals may therefore be used to deduce the thermal histories of both rocks and natural waters. For example, the ratio of the isotopes oxygen-18 and oxygen-16 in the calcium carbonate shells of ancient organisms provides the temperature at which the carbonate formed and hence of the seawater in which it formed. Isotopes are important in studies of the earth's internal temperature. Radioisotopes emit heat when they decay. Much, though not all, of the earth's internal heat is thought to have been generated in this way throughout the planet's 4,600 million years of history — a figure derived from the analysis of radioisotopes in both the earth and meteorites.   P.J.S.

isotopes. ATOMS of the same chemical ELEMENT, having the same ATOMIC NUMBER, but differing from each other in respect of the number of NEUTRONS in the NUCLEUS; e.g. DEUTERIUM is an isotope of hydrogen.   M.V.B.

Israel, see under JUDAISM; ZIONISM.

issue networks. Term coined in 1978 by political scientist Hugh Heclo to represent his conceptualization of an increasingly characteristic form of policy-making in the U.S. federal government. Heclo regards an older concept of iron triangles — close, continuous relationships between INTEREST GROUPS, executive bureaux and congressional committees — as at best an incomplete guide to a changed political environment. Among the relevant changes are a proliferation of competing interest groups; the growth of more complex bureaucratic, intergovernmental and quasi-governmental sources of knowledge and influence and the devolution of congressional power to subcommittees and professional staffs. The result is a growth in large, amorphous policy communities or 'issue networks' composed of numerous institutional and individual actors competing for a voice in the development of policy. The term is acquiring widespread usage, although it has yet to be adequately tested. Its relevance to other political systems may be limited as it derives from the U.S.'s unusually fragmented and complex system.   S.R.

Bibl: A. King, *The New American Political System* (Washington, D.C., 1978).

i.t.a. (initial teaching alphabet). An alphabet invented by Sir James Pitman and first tried in schools in 1961; the number of characters has ranged, at various times, between 42 and 44. The intention is to help children to read without dealing with the oddities of English spelling (or capital letters). Starting on i.t.a. at the age of 5, children will normally be sufficiently fluent in reading to move on to traditional orthography (t.o.) by 7. Research shows that i.t.a. classes read more quickly and with better comprehension than t.o. classes, and do not show major difficulty in the transition to t.o. However, those taught by traditional methods normally catch up by the age of 9 or 10.   W.A.C.S.

Bibl: F.W. Warburton and V. Southgate, *i.t.a.: an Independent Evaluation* (London, 1969).

Italianization. Term used in connection with west European COMMUNIST parties. It refers to the ideological and strategic development of the Italian Communist Party during the 1960s and 1970s. In particular, the PCI's support for eurocommunism and its decision to seek an HISTORIC COMPROMISE with other major political parties.   S.M.

item analysis. An examination of the various items included in an EXAMINATION. Before new questions may be included, examiners must make sure that they do not overstretch the candidate's ability nor must they be too simple. In order to test them, the questions are first piloted among groups of candidates. Their answers are then analysed and the items are amended accordingly.   J.I.

IZL, see IRGUN ZVAI LEUMI.

Izvestia (*News*). A Soviet daily newspaper, since 1960 an evening paper, with a Sunday supplement *Nedelya* (*The Week*). Established in March 1917 as the organ of the Petrograd Soviet, in 1918 it was transferred to Moscow. Like PRAVDA, it is printed in many Soviet cities, and its local editions are similarly standardized by the inclusion of material transmitted from its Moscow central editorial office. It reflects the official government point of view and only on one or two occasions in Soviet post-war history has it diverged from *Pravda*, reflecting political dissension at the top. Its estimated circulation is 8 million. L.L.

Bibl: A. Buzek, *How the Communist Press Works* (London and New York, 1964).

J

Jack of Diamonds, see KNAVE OF DIA-
MONDS.

Jacobinism. The Jacobins were the most
radical of the French Revolutionaries, and
their intransigent commitment to the
cause of the REVOLUTION inspired many
subsequent radicals; Lenin explicitly compared his BOLSHEVIKS with the Jacobins
and the MENSHEVIKS with the more moderate Girondins. Although the Jacobins
were in principle committed to some kind
of popular DEMOCRACY, the impact of
Robespierre's personality and the exigencies of the time led them inexorably to
embrace DICTATORSHIP and terror. The
'English Jacobins' of the 1790s never followed them in this, and were, in fact,
notably non-violent in their RADICALISM.
After the French Revolution, 'Jacobinism'
became a non-specific label for any kind of
radicalism which put its trust in insurrection and leadership rather than in parliamentary methods and persuasion.   A.R.

James-Lange theory. The theory of EMO-
TION proposed principally by William
James (*Principles of Psychology*, 1890)
and resting upon the premise that emotion
is the perception of bodily changes that
occur when we respond to an emotion-
arousing situation. That is, we are afraid
'because' we flee rather than fleeing 'because' we are afraid. James elevated the
original idea of C.G. Lange's that emotion
was a change in the cardiovascular system
and gave it the elaboration here noted to
account for the distinctive quality of different emotions.   J.S.B.

jazz. A few key certainties can be distilled
out of the misty speculations surrounding
the origins of the music (the actual name
almost certainly had something to do with
sex). Without question it was a unique
product of the enforced wedding of African and European musical cultures in the
American south. Deprived of everything
else, the blacks enslaved on southern plan-
tations brought with them their musical
traditions. The work songs and spirituals
they evolved showed characteristics of
their African heritage: a rhythmic sophis-

tication and flexibility unknown in European music, a more supple sense of pitch
and ornamentation, and a free, emotional
style of delivery that reflected the need for
their music to express and relieve great
care. The work song especially informed
the compact, deeply felt declamation of
the BLUES. Influenced heavily by the
emerging blues form, jazz also made crucial use of the forms and materials of
European music particularly available in
the rich culture of NEW ORLEANS, where
the African elements mixed with marches,
dances like the quadrille and even popular
airs from operas. Such cross-fertilization
exposed black music to harmonic structures which African music largely lacked.
The process intensified in the later 19th
century as blacks gained access to orchestral instruments, particularly those of
brass bands, which they adapted to their
own expressive needs. Certainly by 1890 a
kind of proto-jazz had appeared in New
Orleans, a blend of all these elements,
identified especially by strong but flexible
rhythm and improvisation. New Orleans
remained the matrix of jazz into the 1920s,
by which time the music had established
itself not just in America but in Europe as
well. (See also CHICAGO, RAGTIME, SWING,
BEBOP, MAINSTREAM, FREE JAZZ, RHYTHM
AND BLUES, BOOGIE-WOOGIE.)   GE.S.

jazz age. A term used, mainly with reference to the U.S.A., for the decade between
the end of World War I and the Great
Crash (1929). The white DIXIELAND version of negro JAZZ which formed the base
of the period's characteristic dance style
reflected the general atmosphere of excitement and confidence of the era, created by
a popular faith in lasting peace and prosperity. Social, sexual, and cultural values
were permanently altered by the social
and material changes of this first period of
mass-consumption, which made available
silent movies, radios, cars, and other consumer goods. The flamboyance and economic confidence of the period is portrayed particularly well by Scott Fitzgerald, notably in *The Jazz Age, The
Diamond as Big as the Ritz,* and *The
Great Gatsby.* The jazz age was also, how-

ever, an age of hysteria over 'BOLSHEVISM' (e.g. the execution of Sacco and Vanzetti, 1927), gangster economics (e.g. the Teapot Dome scandal, 1923-4), a *prohibition* of alcohol which was everywhere defied (with pervasive attendant crime), and of intellectual anachronisms like the Scopes Monkey Trial, in which a schoolteacher was arraigned for the teaching of EVOLUTION.   P.S.L.

jazz poetry. Poetry designed to be read with JAZZ accompaniment. In the 1960s it had a considerable vogue in Britain and parts of the U.S.A., with Christopher Logue and Kenneth Rexroth, respectively, as leading exponents.   M.S.-S.

j-curve, see under DEVALUATION.

Jehovah's Witnesses. A basically American religious body, also called the 'Watch Tower Bible and Tract Society'. Founded by C.T. Russell and by J.F. ('Judge') Rutherford (1869-1941), it attacks the Christian Churches and calls on its adherents to reject military service and blood transfusion. It prophesies that 144,000 Jehovah's Witnesses will form the elect in heaven at the imminent end of the world, and will rule over the 'Jonadabs' or resurrected people of good will inhabiting a new earth. The Witnesses are more active than welcome in door-to-door EVANGELISM.
                                                D.L.E.
Bibl: H.H. Stroup, *The Jehovah's Witnesses* (New York, 1945).

jet engine. A device for propelling aircraft through the atmosphere. Air swept into the front of the engine provides the oxygen required to support the burning of fuel. The resulting heat makes the combustion gases expand through a nozzle at the rear. These gases leave the engine much faster than the air goes in at the front, so that forward motion is produced, on the ROCKET principle. See also RAM JET.
                                                M.V.B.

jihad ('holy war'), see under ISLAM.

job evaluation. A systematic description of a job and its comparison with other jobs in order to establish differential rates of pay.   R.I.T.

joint replacement. The term is generally understood to mean that a joint, such as a hip or knee, is replaced by an artificial joint, which has been very carefully manufactured to meet certain strict criteria with regard to design and materials. It is usual to replace joints totally, that is both articular surfaces. The joints in use are usually a combination of high density polyethylene and an inert material such as stainless steel. Replacement of the whole joint, or arthroplasty, is generally used in osteoarthritis or rheumatoid arthritis; occasionally a hemi-arthroplasty is used, for example after a fracture of the hip joint in an elderly person when only the femoral end of the joint is replaced.   N.H.H.

jouissance. A French, as well as an archaic English word, for enjoyment. In spite of its stronger sexual connotation in French, it has taken on a wider significance in psychoanalytical theory. It defines what lies beyond the FREUDIAN pleasure principle, and what escapes the EGO'S censorship (see SUPEREGO). When this censorship breaks down, as in nightmares or in psychotic states, jouissance manifests itself as unpleasure, in the form of the symptom. It is experienced as pleasurable only in a limited number of cases, as in the form of mystical ecstasy and in some forms of feminine sexual enjoyment (see FEMININE SEXUALITY).   B.BE.

Joycean. Characteristic or reminiscent of the writings of James Joyce (1882-1941), particularly of *Ulysses* (1922) and whatever portion of *Finnegans Wake* (1939) the person using the word may actually have read. The characteristics alluded to include a propensity for sordid and scatological subject-matter, an immense stylistic and technical range (including the use of SYMBOLISM and the STREAM OF CONSCIOUSNESS technique), and a verbal inventiveness (with an addiction to puns and portmanteau words) that takes the English language near, and in the later work beyond, the limits of readability.
                                                O.S.

Judaism. The RELIGION of the Jews. Founded on the experiences of Israel which are recorded in the literature known to Christians as the Old Testament, Judaism took its present shape after the destruction of the Kingdoms of Israel and Judah, the fall of the Temple, and the Jews' exile to Babylon in the 6th century B.C. During this exile and many later wanderings and sufferings, the Jews preserved their communal identity by their devotion to the study of the Law (*Torah*), a system of morality and religious teaching originating in the Hebrew Scriptures and added to by generations of Rabbis; by their close adherence to dietary regulations and insistence on male circumcision; by their observance of the weekly day of rest on Saturday (*Sabbath*); through their strong family life; and through the synagogues where they gathered for prayer and education.

Jewish experiences in the 20th century have included the NAZI extermination or 'HOLOCAUST' of most of European Jewry (following centuries of Christian ANTISEMITISM), and the culmination of ZIONISM in the establishment of the state of Israel in 1948. The chief challenge to traditional Judaism, both within Israel and in the *Diaspora* or dispersion among the 'Gentiles' (non-Jews), is SECULARIZATION. Should the old law still be observed as completely as possible, as the Orthodox Rabbis teach? Or is a far more LIBERAL interpretation, largely abandoning the use of Hebrew and the detailed laws about diet, etc., the best way of keeping the spirit of Judaism alive under modern conditions — as Reform Judaism (originating in 19th-century Germany) advocates? In the U.S.A., Conservative Judaism, a movement founded by Solomon Schechter (1847-1915), has had great influence as a compromise between the rigid and modernizing extremes. A similar attitude has been taught by Martin Buber (1878-1965). He derived a PERSONALIST and SOCIALIST philosophy and a renewed THEISM from his enthusiasm for the *Hasidic* mystical tradition originating in the 18th century. Buber summed up his message in his little book, *I and Thou* (1923).   D.L.E.

Bibl: L. Jacobs, *Principles of the Jewish Faith* (London and New York, 1964); J.L. Blau, *Modern Varieties of Judaism* (New York, 1966); H. Wouk, *This is My God, the Jewish Way of Life* (New York, 1970; London, rev. ed., 1973); D. Narmur,

Beyond Survival: Reflections on the Future of Judaism (London, 1982).

judicial review. The power of a court to pass on the validity of legislative or administrative actions. In the U.S., it is the basis for the power of the U.S. Supreme Court and its authority to declare state and federal laws void as unconstitutional. The principle was established in the then controversial decision Marbury v. Madison in 1803, but it gradually became the accepted view of judicial power in the U.S. The doctrine led to a great expansion of judicial power and activism in the late 19th century and throughout this century, and continues to be controversial among supporters of STATES' RIGHTS.   M.S.P.

Judson Dance Theater. Co-founded by Robert Dunn, Steve Paxton and Yvonne Rainer. It was established as a weekly meeting at the Judson Memorial Church, New York in 1962. It was a focus for experimental work founded in the POSTMODERN DANCE aesthetic and acted as a forum and catalyst for collaborative projects between artists. The focus of the work corresponded with the MODERNIST movement in that the arts sought to free themselves from convention. The informal and flexible nature of the Judson Dance Theater permitted 'non-dancers' to dance and choreograph furthering the demystification of dance. Until 1968 it acted as a platform, educating and challenging audience expectations by providing free concerts for the community.   L.A.

Bibl: S. Banes, *Democracy's Body: Judson Dance Theater 1962-1964* (New York, 1980).

Jugendstil, see ART NOUVEAU.

July 20th. The date in 1944 of an abortive *coup d'état* in Nazi Germany directed at the overthrow of Hitler. Involved in the conspiracy were anti-Nazis in the armed forces and the Prussian aristocracy, together with former diplomats, clergy, civil servants, and trade unionists. The *putsch* failed when Hitler escaped with his life, but it achieved considerable momentary success in Paris and Vienna. The German resistance suffered from the fact that, unlike the resistance movement in occupied countries, it ran in the face of national feeling in a time of war, and (particularly when the plot failed) was open to the charge of treason. The conspirators were hunted down and executed, often after being tortured. Their moral courage in risking their lives in protest against the Nazi regime has seemed more important subsequently than their failure to overthrow it.   A.L.C.B.

Bibl: P. Hoffmann, *History of the German Resistance 1933-1945* (London and Boston, 1977).

jumping gene, see under TRANSPOSABLE ELEMENT.

Jungian. Adjective applied to a theory of personality put forward by Carl Gustav Jung (1875-1961) as an alternative to the FREUDIAN view and rejecting the latter's emphasis on the centrality of sexual instincts. Jung left the psychoanalytical movement (see PSYCHOANALYSIS) in 1913 to practise *analytic psychology*, according to which man's behaviour is determined not only by the conflicts already present in his individual and racial history (the personal and COLLECTIVE UNCONSCIOUS) but also by his aims and aspirations. The character and indeed even the quality of dreams suggests the striving towards individuation; according to analytic psychology, man seeks creative development, wholeness, and completion. The individual personality contains memories, known as ARCHETYPES, of its ancestral history which can be studied through MYTHS. Jung postulated two basic PERSONALITY TYPES, characterized respectively by EXTROVERSION and INTROVERSION.   R.P.-S.

Bibl: A. Samuels, *Jung and the Post-Jungians* (London, 1985).

jurisprudence of concepts, see CONCEPTUALISM (2).

justice. Said by many writers to be the first of social virtues, justice has been the subject of intense argument in the last two decades. Recent discussion has centred on the work of John Rawls, Robert Nozick

and Friedrich von Hayek. John Rawls's *A Theory of Justice* (1971) argued that recent political theory had been too UTILITARIAN, too unconcerned with individual rights; by asking the question 'what rules would mankind contract to obey if they were to establish a social order in conditions where none of them could take advantage of their fellows?' he hoped to arrive at an account of justice which any dispassionate reader would accept. Rawls's view is that justice demands 'maximum equal liberty' and a distribution of economic benefits which makes the least favoured person as well off as possible — the so-called 'maximin' conception of justice, which concentrates on maximizing the minimum benefit. This view has been attacked both by Robert Nozick and F.A. von Hayek. In their view, justice is not a matter of how benefits are distributed, but a matter of protecting individual rights to resources. Hayek has argued that 'social justice' is a chimera, and that appeals to social justice imply that some authority or other, notably the STATE, has the right and the duty to distribute goods and opportunities as it sees fit. But this is incompatible with individual liberty, which requires that we should be able to use what is ours as we choose. Similarly Nozick denies that there is such a thing as 'DISTRIBUTIVE JUSTICE'. The concept implies an agency entitled to achieve it, but when we look closely, we can see that everything worth distributing already belongs to some owner or other. All the rights over goods and opportunities that there are, are in the hands of single individuals. The state cannot lay hands on any of these things without violating those individual rights. Goods and opportunities are justly distributed when they are in the hands of their rightful owners. Any EGALITARIAN claim for further redistribution is a reflection of the 'politics of envy' not of justice.   A.R.

Bibl: John Rawls, *A Theory of Justice* (Cambridge, Mass. and Oxford, 1971); Robert Nozick, *Anarchy, State and Utopia* (New York and Oxford, 1974); D. Miller, *Social Justice* (Oxford, 1976)).

K

Kadarism. The term used by western analysts to describe the policies of János Kádár, the present Hungarian leader. He has reformed the Soviet-type system previously in operation by liberalizing both the economy and, to a lesser extent, political life, while retaining fundamental features of SOCIALIST bloc countries, such as state ownership of the MODE OF PRODUCTION and loyalty to the Soviet Union. Coming to power after the suppression of the uprising of 1956 (see HUNGARY 1956) and having initially acted against the insurgents ruthlessly, from 1962 he pursued a policy of 'Alliance' between the Party and all sections of the population. This broke with the previous STALINIST practices of his predecessor, Mátyás Rákosi, which strengthened the power of the COMMUNIST Party. Kadarism involved an amnesty to former opponents of the regime, the reduction of censorship, the selection of specialists who were not Communist Party members to fill leadership positions in the state and the economy, and the introduction of greater DEMOCRACY within the Communist Party. In the economic sphere, Kádár granted more freedom to farmers and, by implementing the NEW ECONOMIC MECHANISM, to individual industrial enterprises. Kadarism has led to the most significant reform yet introduced into any system based on the Soviet model.
D.PR.

Bibl: H-G. Heinrich, *Hungary: Politics, Economy and Society* (London, 1986).

Kafkaesque. Adjective applied to situations and atmospheres, whether real or fictional, that recall the writing of Franz Kafka (1883-1924), particularly *The Trial* and its sequel *The Castle*. The essential ingredient is a nightmarish sense of having lost one's identity, and of bewildered helplessness against a vast, sinister, impersonal BUREAUCRACY which is intuitively felt to be evil, yet which appears to have a crazy kind of transcendent logic on its side. English novelists who have approached the Kafkaesque mode include Edward Upward, Rex Warner, and Nigel Dennis.
O.S.

Kampuchea-Vietnam, invasion of. In December 1978, 100,000 Vietnamese troops supported by 20,000 'Friendly Kampucheans' launched a full scale invasion of Kampuchea which resulted in the ousting of the KHMER ROUGE under Pol Pot and the fall of Phnom Penh on 7 January 1979. Relations between the two nations were tense from the onset of the Khmer Rouge regime in 1975, due to the purge by Pol Pot of the pro-Vietnamese faction in the party in 1973. The situation was worsened by the Kampucheans' treatment of ethnic Vietnamese during the programme of enforced ruralization, and spring 1977 saw the first armed border clashes. Supported by the Chinese leadership, who wanted to use their influence over Phnom Penh as a counterweight to Soviet influence in VIETNAM, Pol Pot increased his belligerence towards Hanoi, prompting the Vietnamese intervention in 1979. A pro-Hanoi government was installed, but a Chinese backed coalition of the old Khmer Rouge, and non-COMMUNIST forces led by Prince Sihanouk continue to wage GUERRILLA war against the Vietnamese from bases on the Thai border.
S.B.

Bibl: G. Evans, *Red Brotherhood at War* (London, 1984).

Kansas City. One of the proudest JAZZ cities and centre of the music in the American southwest. In the late 1920s and early 1930s, the region evolved the style with which Kansas City is synonymous, an amalgam of the BLUES, a new and deceptive level of technical accomplishment and a loose, driving beat. It was more sophisticated than NEW ORLEANS, freer than New York. Developed in BIG BANDS like those of Walter Page and Bennie Moten, the music reached its irresistible acme in the Count Basie band, which took America by storm in the SWING era. The light, propulsively swinging feel of his superb rhythm section was quintessentially Kansas City, as were the long, inventive lines of soloists like Lester Young. Both the subtlety of the beat and the freedom it encouraged became key ingredients in the rise of BEBOP (one of its

451

greatest pioneers, Charlie Parker, was from Kansas City). The style itself is one of the main currents in MAINSTREAM jazz. GE.S.

Karmarkar's method. An ALGORITHM for LINEAR PROGRAMMING problems invented by N. Karmarkar in 1985. It is a substantial improvement on the standard simplex method, taking only polynomial time rather than EXPONENTIAL TIME. Each iteration of the algorithm takes longer but the total number of steps is drastically reduced. J.M.

karyology, see under CYTOLOGY.

karyotype. The normal complement of CHROMOSOMES in a cell, as defined by their number, size and shape. P.N.

Katyn. The name of some woods near Smolensk where in April 1943 the Germans announced that they had discovered several thousand bodies of Polish officers and others who, they claimed, had been murdered by the Russians in 1940. The Soviet Government at once announced that these men (captured during the Soviet invasion of Poland in 1939) had fallen into German hands in 1941 and that the Germans had murdered them. Previously it had disclaimed all knowledge about some 15,000 Polish officers not among those released after the German invasion of Russia in 1941 and allowed to go to the Middle East to form a new Polish Army. Yet the 5,000 bodies found at Katyn were in the great majority men on the lists the Poles had submitted to the Russians. (The other 10,000 have never been accounted for.)

The Germans allowed a FORENSIC commission including prominent neutral experts to supervise part of the exhumation, which representatives of the Polish underground were permitted, and senior Allied officer prisoners compelled, to attend. All reported that the German story was clearly true; forensic, documentary, and other evidence showed that the massacre had taken place in April 1940. The facts, though accepted everywhere else, have still not been admitted by the Soviet leadership. Khrushchev is believed to have

urged frankness but to have been dissuaded by the Polish COMMUNISTS. R.C.

Bibl: J. Mackiewicz, *The Katyn Wood Murders* (London, 1951); General W. Anders (intr.), *The Crime of Katyn* (London, 1965).

Keller plan. A system of self-learning and self-testing where the pupil/student studies a unit at his/her own pace. On completion, the unit is discussed with a tutor who has to establish whether or not the student has passed and may go on to the next unit. J.I.

keratins, see under PROTEINS.

Keynesian. Description of the economic theories resulting from the ideas and writings of John Maynard Keynes. NEOCLASSICAL ECONOMIC THEORY proposes that the flexibility of wages and prices is sufficient to ensure FULL EMPLOYMENT. Keynes argued that money wages might not fall, because of the actions of TRADE UNIONS, and that, even if money wages fell, full employment would not be obtained. The latter proposition is based on the effects of a fall in money wages: producers may hire more labour and output increases; this increase in output generates an equal increase in NATIONAL INCOME; not all of the increase in national income is consumed, some is saved; this means that AGGREGATE DEMAND increases by less than the increase in output; the unsold output results in prices, output and employment being reduced and a downward spiral of falling wages, prices, output and employment is initiated. In the money market, Keynes noted that, if wages and then prices fall, the real value of the MONEY SUPPLY increases and the interest rate would have to fall to induce people into holding the existing supply of money. Keynes proposed that there is a lower limit below which the interest rate can not fall and, furthermore, that INVESTMENT was not responsive to reductions in the interest rate. Therefore, a fall in money wages and the consequent reduction in the interest rate can not be relied upon to increase aggregate demand and move the economy to full employment.

In the last 20 years, Keynes's work has been reinterpreted and been given more fundamental theoretical importance. This reinterpretation is examined through considering the response of the economy to the existence of involuntary UNEMPLOY-MENT. The involuntarily unemployed have a notional demand for goods and services, but this demand is not effective, as they have little or no income to pay for the notionally demanded goods and services. For a firm to hire more labour requires an increase in the demand for the firm's product. If all firms simultaneously hire more labour, the notional demand of the involuntarily unemployed is made effective — though some of the demand may be for consumption at a later date — and used to purchase the increase in output. However, an individual firm has no incentive to hire more labour, as such an action has a negligible effect on the demand for the firm's output. Consequently, if there is involuntary unemployment in the economy, it is not necessarily true that the economy will move towards full employment. For the labour market to move towards full employment, the notional demand of the involuntarily unemployed has to be backed up by actual income. In both interpretations of Keynes's work, involuntary unemployment persists because of deficient aggregate demand and it is the duty of the government to increase aggregate demand. Keynesian and MONETARIST theories are often considered as alternative views of the economy and they have been extensively contrasted and compared. See MULTIPLIER and ACCELERATOR.   J.P.

Bibl: R. Levacic and A. Rebman, *Macroeconomics* (London, 2nd ed., 1982); M.C. Sawyer, *Macro-economics in Question* (Brighton, 1982); B. Morgan, *Monetarists and Keynesians* (London, 1978).

KGB (Committee for State Security). The name, since 1953-4, of the Soviet secret police, one of the two organizations, the other being MVD, which share, with somewhat fluctuating lines of demarcation, responsibility for order and security. Roughly speaking, the KGB — like its predecessors Cheka, Vcheka, GPU, OGPU, NKVD, NKGB, MGB, several of which have been bywords for brutality (see, especially, YEZHOVSHCHINA) — is responsible for security troops, counter-espionage, counter-subversion, loyalty

supervision among the administrative, political, and military ÉLITES, and such features as trials of writers and others. Its other major role is organizing the greater part of the Soviet espionage and subversion effort abroad. Its current chief, Viktor Chebrikov, is a full member of the POLITBURO.   R.C.

Bibl: J. Barron, *The KGB* (London, 1974).

Khmer Rouge. COMMUNIST group led by Pol Pot who ruled Cambodia (Kampuchea) between 1975 and 1979. The Khmer Rouge came to power after the civil war in a coalition with Prince Norodom Sihanouk in 1975, but Sihanouk was soon replaced as head of state by Khieu Samphan and the country was renamed Democratic Kampuchea. Once in power, the Khmer Rouge set about implementing policies of extreme reform: abolishing money and private property, outlawing religion, forcibly removing the entire urban population to the countryside, and wiping out intellectuals and the old MIDDLE CLASSES through mass executions by DEATH SQUADS. A total of 2,700,000 Cambodians are estimated to have been killed before the Vietnamese ousted the Khmer Rouge government in 1979 (see KAMPUCHEA-VIETNAM). The remains of Pol Pot's supporters have since allied with non-Communist groups led by Sihanouk and Son Sann, and now profess to pursue non-Communist policies in the struggle to oust the Vietnamese.   S.B.

Bibl: F. Ponchaud, *Cambodia, Year Zero* (New York, 1978).

kibbutz (plural *kibbutzim*). A form of collective settlement which has played a key role in the creation of modern Israel. The first kibbutz was founded in 1909 by a group of pioneers from Russia. By 1965 there were 230, some of them up to a thousand strong. Allowing for individual variations, the kibbutz combines three functions: (1) *economic,* cultivation of the land, often with some industrial production as well; (2) *social,* providing communities in which SOCIALIST ideals can be put into practice, e.g. equality (see EGALITARIANISM), common property, communal living (including the rearing of children), and collective decision-making; (3)

453

military, acting as watch posts, and in times of trouble as strong points with their own garrison. In the 1960s over 80,000 Israelis were living permanently in kibbutzim. This was less than 5% of the population, but their contribution to the formation of Israel has been much greater than these figures suggest. A.L.C.B.

Bibl: S.N. Eisenstadt, *Israeli Society* (London and New York, 1967).

kilobyte (kb). 1024 (2^{10}) or, less commonly, 1,000 BYTES. J.E.S.

kiloton. A measure of the ENERGY released in a nuclear explosion equivalent to 1,000 tons of T.N.T. 1 kiloton equals about 100,000 kilowatt-hours. M.V.B.

kinaesthetic. Relating to those sensations produced by movements of the joints, tendons, or muscles, and those emanating from the balance organs of the inner ear. H.L.

kinematics. One of the two branches of MECHANICS. M.V.B.

kinesics, see under SEMIOTICS.

kinesthetic, see KINAESTHETIC.

kinetic art. The extension of the traditionally static arts of painting and sculpture to incorporate an element of motion (*a*) by making them mobile, (*b*) by a shifting sequence of static variations, or (*c*) by exploiting the spectator's movement around a static work so as to give it changing aspects. Though efforts in this direction have been made since the earliest times, the modern history of kineticism really starts with FUTURISM and its use of overlapping 'simultaneous' images and 'lines of force'. Other early attempts were Tatlin's tower (1919-20) and other CONSTRUCTIVIST works, Marcel Duchamp's rotating discs (1920), and László Moholy-Nagy's 'Licht-requisit' (1930). The real breakthrough, however, came with the American Alexander Calder's invention (*c.* 1931-2) of the *mobile*, a balanced contraption of brightly coloured weights swinging from wires.

By the 1950s many artists (and advertising agencies) were trying their hands at mobiles, and a widespread kinetic trend set in, with Nicolas Schöffer, proponent of 'spatiodynamism' (1948) and 'luminodynamism' (1957), as its most ambitious exemplar, and the Paris *Mouvement* exhibition at the Galérie Denise Reneé (1955) as its first collective manifestation. Subgroups have included the German *Gruppe Zero* (from 1958), the Paris *Groupe de Recherche d'Art Visuel* (1960-68), the Italian groups 'T' and 'N', the 'programmed art' of Bruno Munari, and the Soviet *Dvizhenie* collective led by Lev Nusberg.

Today virtually any practitioner of ABSTRACT ART is liable to include some element of motion or PERMUTATION in his work, the latter particularly if it is of a geometrical or OP ART kind. CONCRETE POETRY reflects a similar concern, and certain writers, mainly English and West German, have produced 'kinetic' poems where the movement consists in the calculated (or 'programmed') shifting of words and letters, line by line or page by page. There is also a quasi-cinematic or PSYCHEDELIC branch of the art in the LIGHT SHOW, which bears some relation to Moholy-Nagy's and Schöffer's researches as well as to earlier experiments in SYNAESTHESIA. J.W.

Bibl: G. Brett, *Kinetic Art* (London and New York, 1968).

kinetic energy. The ENERGY of matter in motion. Because of the CONSERVATION LAW satisfied by energy, kinetic energy can only be produced at the expense of some other form of energy, e.g. chemical energy in an explosive is converted into kinetic energy of rapidly expanding bomb fragments; a stone dropped over a cliff accelerates by converting the POTENTIAL ENERGY of GRAVITATION into kinetic energy. Naturally occurring kinetic energy can be converted into useful work, as when falling water enters a TURBINE, producing kinetic energy of rotary motion which in turn generates hydroelectric power. For a single particle in NEWTONIAN MECHANICS, kinetic energy = ½ × mass × (velocity)^2. M.V.B.

kinetography Laban, see under DANCE NOTATION.

Kinsey Report. A questionnaire-based study of sexual attitudes and behaviour, compiled by the American zoologist Alfred Kinsey (1894-1956) and others, and published in two volumes in 1948-53. By showing that many practices (e.g. *fellatio*) commonly regarded as PERVERSIONS were actually widespread it was influential in increasing sexual PERMISSIVENESS. It also indicated CORRELATIONS of social CLASS with sexual habits. It has been criticized for faults in interviewing and SAMPLING techniques, as well as for its title, *Sexual Behavior in the Human Male/Female*; only mid-20th-century North Americans are actually considered. H.L.

kinship. Term which covers named relationships between individuals — social relationships which may or may not have a biological basis. In its broadest sense kinship includes relations of consanguinity (based on blood or descent ties) and affinity (based on MARRIAGE). Kinship is based on a set of rules, and in establishing relationships between people it may prescribe behavioural NORMS. Kinship is both a part of IDEOLOGY (a means for thinking or classifying) and of PRAXIS (a means for organizing, e.g. economy). It mediates between the INFRASTRUCTURE and SUPERSTRUCTURE.

Early work in kinship was governed by an evolutionary (see EVOLUTION) perspective. Writers at the end of the 19th century, such as Maine and McLennan, were concerned with tracing the evolution of marriage and the FAMILY from an era they believed to have been characterized by promiscuity (or group marriage) to the MONOGAMY of modern societies. A major part of this debate concerned whether early societies were MATRIARCHAL (i.e., women held POWER and authority), but which were later replaced by societies characterized by PATRIARCHY. Morgan also worked within an evolutionary framework, but he focused attention upon kinship terminology and established it as an important area for analysis. He believed that kin terms held the key to the understanding of the history of kinship systems. In his classic book *Systems of Consanguinity and Affinity of the Human Family* (1871), Morgan distinguished between terminologies he described as *classificatory*

(groupings of kin into categories which include both lineal and collateral relatives, for example, father's brother and his sons are all referred to as 'brothers') and *descriptive* (terms with very limited and specific reference). The study of kinship terminology has continued to occupy a central place in kinship studies. It has represented an attempt in ANTHROPOLOGY to use native categories in understanding kinship practices.

Another important early innovation was the development by W.H.R. Rivers of the *genealogical method*. During the 1898 Torres Straits expedition, Rivers began to collect oral genealogies. He quickly discovered that this method gave access to the inner dynamics of a society and moreover, the complexity of these genealogies began to cast doubt on the widely-held view of the simplicity of the 'PRIMITIVE' mind.

The break with evolutionary theories came with Malinowski. He had been particularly influenced by Freud, and his work focused on relations within the family. He did not consider kinship as a system or as a part of SOCIAL STRUCTURE, but understood it in terms of individuals and their needs. It was Radcliffe Brown who developed the notion of kinship as a system. He studied the relationships established between individuals and the rights and duties associated with particular kin ROLES. Evans-Pritchard and Meyer Fortes both carried out extensive fieldwork in Africa where LINEAGES were a central feature of social organization. It was in this context that the concept of DESCENT, which became central to kinship studies, was elaborated. In 1949 Lévi-Strauss published *The Elementary Structures of Kinship* in which he argued that EXCHANGE was the critical feature of kinship systems and that marriage established alliances between different groups. Anthropologists quickly polarized into two camps (descent and alliance theorists) and for two decades debates raged over aspects of kinship. The division mirrored different ethnographic (see ETHNOGRAPHY) and theoretical perspectives: descent theorists worked in Africa and tended to be followers of the STRUCTURAL-FUNCTIONALISM of Radcliffe Brown; alliance theorists worked in south east Asia and were influenced by the

STRUCTURALISM of Lévi-Strauss. Since the early 1970s, under the influence of Marxist (see MARXISM) ideas, interest has developed in the relationship between kinship and aspects of the economy (land tenure, property, inheritance, production etc.). These approaches were anticipated in Leach's *Pul Eliya* (1961), but Goody has more recently explored the issues in *Production and Reproduction* (1976). A.G.

Bibl: A. Kuper, *Anthropology and Anthropologists* (London, 1983); A. Barnard and A. Good, *Research Practices in the Study of Kinship* (London, 1984); I. Langham, *The Building of British Social Anthropology: W.H.R. Rivers and His Cambridge Disciples in the Development of Kinship Studies 1898-1931* (Dordrecht, 1981).

Kirkpatrick theory. The theory of political development espoused by Georgetown University professor Jeane Kirkpatrick, adviser to the Reagan Administration and former U.S. Ambassador to the U.N. Drawing on the ideas of 17th-century British political philosopher Thomas Hobbes, Kirkpatrick argues that order is the fundamental value of any political system, absence of which precludes the enjoyment of any other values. Adhering to the theories of social modernization developed in the 1960s by Samuel Huntingdon in *Political Order in Changing Societies*, Kirkpatrick contends that stability can be found either in traditional societies or in modern social systems, but not in the transitional stage. In weak STATES, where governments lack true decision-making POWER and are confronted by fragmented and conflicting civilian interests, political stalemate arises, leading to prolonged instability and consequent vulnerability to externally backed 'TERRORIST' threats to order. Applying the analysis to Central America Kirkpatrick advocates that U.S. policy give priority to the reconstruction of a stable order in the area even if this has to be imposed by means of AUTHORITARIAN models. N.M.

Bibl: Jeane Kirkpatrick, 'The Hobbes Problem: Order, Authority and Legitimacy in Central America', in American Enterprise Institute, *1980 Public Policy Week Papers* (Washington D.C., 1981).

kitchen sink drama. Pejorative term for those English plays written from the late 1950s onwards (see ENGLISH STAGE COMPANY and THEATRE WORKSHOP) whose distinguishing feature was a portrayal of working- or lower-middle-class characters surrounded, in the view of their critics, by an undue degree of domestic squalor. 'The kitchen sink school' was a term applied first to the SOCIAL REALIST paintings of John Bratby and others showing at the Beaux Arts Gallery in London in the early 1950s, but has achieved lasting currency in relation to the theatre. M.A.

klangfarbenmelodie. A term used by Schoenberg in his 'Harmonielehre' (1911) to denote a melody where the sense of shape is given by different tone-colours (e.g. a clarinet and a violin playing the same note have a different musical colour) rather than different pitches as in a conventional melody. Schoenberg used the technique in the third of his 'Five Orchestral Pieces Op.16' (1909) and the technique was used by his pupils Alban Berg ('Wozzeck') and, to a much greater extent, Anton Webern. The technique is symptomatic of a general heightening of awareness of tone-colour in 20th-century music from Debussy through to ELECTRONIC MUSIC. B.CO.

Kleinian. This term refers to the theoretical and clinical set of psychoanalytic ideas introduced by Melanie Klein, who greatly influenced the approach of British PSYCHOANALYSIS. Klein's theoretical results derive from her pioneering work with children under three years of age, based on her newly introduced play technique. The infantile psychic apparatus is dominated at the oral stage by cannibalistic drives, sadistic in relation to the breast, which become the prototype of all one's future relationships to objects. These aggressive instincts have, as one of their consequences, the arousing of primitive anxieties, as the infant fears both that the breast will be destroyed by its sadistic attacks, and that the breast has powers of retaliation. The breast is then split into a 'bad' retaliating breast, and a 'good' one which the SUBJECT tends to introject to soothe its anxiety. This mechanism of splitting will invest all possible objects of the infantile world, and will remain a tendency throughout all adult life in the form of denial and idealization. Objects will be split into external and internal objects, into bad and good ones, so that the object is never whole, but rather partial (see PARTIAL OBJECT). Klein drew on Ferenczi's concepts of introjection and projection to establish the process by which the splitting and fragmentation of the infantile world occurs: this is introjective and PROJECTIVE IDENTIFICATION, where parts of the self or of the object (that is, of the internal and external world) are introjected or projected in a pathological exchange of roles. This is the paranoid-schizoid position, which is followed by the depressive position when the child develops a more correct relationship to its object (see OBJECT RELATIONS), where it can perceive it as a whole object, separated from itself. This gives rise to a sense of guilt about one's own AGGRESSION as well as to the major function of the reparative tendency, the expression of the life instinct struggling with the destructive impulses of the DEATH INSTINCT. The Kleinian approach is applied to adults, as insanity is viewed in this perspective as linked to the same phenomena that occur in infancy, where the adult world finds its roots.

B.BE.

Bibl: M. Klein, *Love, Guilt, and Reparation, and Other Works* (London, 1975).

Knave (or *Jack*) **of Diamonds** (Russian *Bubnovy Valet*). Originally the title of an art exhibition organized by the painter Michel Larionov in Moscow, December 1910, including David Burliuk, Goncharova, Exter, Falk, Kandinsky, Konchalovsky, Lentulov, Malevich, Mashkov, Survage, and the French painters Gleizes, Le Fauconnier, and L.-A. Moreau. An album of 18 reproductions was published with a cover by Goncharova. She and Larionov subsequently left the group in protest against its hardening into a formal society and its French orientation; the remaining artists held a second show, with more French participation, in 1912 and continued to exist as a group till 1916. A retrospective exhibition was held at the Tretiakov Gallery in 1927.

M.C.

Bibl: V. Markov, *Russian Futurism* (Berkeley, 1968; London, 1969); C. Gray,

The Russian Experiment in Art 1863-1922 (London and New York, 1970).

knocking. Pre-ignition and detonation in an internal combustion engine. Unbranched hydrocarbons, the major constituent of normal petrol, have a pronounced knocking tendency, measured as an octane rating, in high-compression car and aero engines. *Anti-knock* agents, chiefly tetraethyl lead, are frequently employed.

B.F.

knot theory. The study of knots, that is of closed loops in space, their classification and recognition (i.e. finding a list of all possible knots, and, given a knot, how do you know which one it corresponds to on the list). The recognition problem is partly solved by a collection of calculable INVARIANTS — principally numbers and polynomials (see EXPONENTIAL TIME) associated with any knot. Knot theory has applications in BIOLOGY, to the study of how DNA MOLECULES may knot and link.

J.M.

knowledge, sociology of. The study of how styles of expression and the character of IDEAS or systems of thought are related to different social contexts. Thus Marx, from whom the contemporary impetus to the sociology of knowledge largely derives, sought to relate art and ideas to particular historical circumstances and the kinds of CLASS systems prevailing at the time; and Max Weber, in *The Sociology of Religion*, analysed the way in which different kinds of religions were the creation largely of specific social groups (e.g. the relation of Confucianism to the Chinese literati and BUREAUCRACY). The effort to broaden the use of sociology of knowledge as a general scheme for the analysis of all ideas is, however, associated largely with three writers: Karl Mannheim, who relativized Marx's ideas to all thought, including MARXISM itself; Max Scheler, who divided the influences on thought into 'real factors' (different at different historical moments) and 'ideal factors' (a realm of timeless ESSENCES which constituted an absolute order of TRUTH); and Émile Durkheim, who argued that the basic rhythms of social life experienced by a society — its sense of space and time — were a function of its kind of social organization.

Objectors to the sociology of knowledge claim that it attaches insufficient importance to the *content* of knowledge, or to the truth or otherwise of a PROPOSITION; that a cultural SUPERSTRUCTURE, once created, retains a life of its own, and becomes part of the permanent cultural repertoire of mankind; that ideas and works of imagination are alike multivalent and it is crudely REDUCTIONIST to associate a set of ideas only with a particular political position (e.g. MATERIALISM with RADICALISM, and IDEALISM with CONSERVATISM), or to equate as 'BOURGEOIS' the contrasting work of Flaubert, Zola, Mann, Joyce, and Proust; and that art forms and ideas may unfold 'immanently', i.e. out of their inner logic and as a reflection on and extension of previous forms. See also IDEOLOGY.

D.B.

Bibl: K. Mannheim, *Ideology and Utopia* (London and New York, 1936); W. Stark, *The Sociology of Knowledge* (London and Glencoe, Ill., 1958); J.C. Curtis and J.W. Petras (eds.), *The Sociology of Knowledge* (London and New York, 1979).

Koch's postulates. The three CRITERIA, formulated by the German bacteriologist Robert Koch in 1876, which must be fulfilled if evidence of a causal connection between an illness and a bacterial infection (see BACTERIOLOGY) is to be accepted as valid. They are: (1) the bacterium is to be demonstrated in all cases of the disease; (2) its distribution in the body must correspond to the lesions, if any, associated with the disease — e.g. with ulcers, tubercles, or 'spots'; (3) the organism must be recoverable and cultivable in suitable media outside the body. Although this third criterion cannot always be applied, nevertheless, with reservations relating to the intrinsic difficulty of culturing certain organisms outside the body (e.g. the leprosy organism), Koch's postulates are still regarded as valid. P.M.

kolkhoz (*kollektivnoe khozyaystvo*), see under COLLECTIVIZATION.

Kolyma. The most notorious of Stalin's FORCED LABOUR camp areas, consisting of a large area round the valley of the River Kolyma down to the Arctic Ocean. Its main product was gold. During the period 1937-53, it is believed that up to four million prisoners died there, mainly of hunger and overwork. See also GULAG.

R.C.

Bibl: E.S. Ginzburg, tr. P. Stevenson *et al., Into the Whirlwind* (London and New York, 1967); R. Conquest, *Kolyma* (London and New York, 1978).

Komsomol (All-Union Leninist Communist Union of Youth). The youth organization of the COMMUNIST Party of the Soviet Union. It is responsible for those aged between 14 and 28. Compared with the more recreational activities of the Pioneer organization, which deals with the 7-14 age-group, it stresses political work and expects members to involve themselves in political life. A large proportion of those elected to membership of the Communist Party come from the Komsomol. Established in 1918, its members played a significant part in the COLLECTIVIZATION and INDUSTRIALIZATION campaigns in the early STALINIST period. According to its statutes it is required to inculcate in youth values which will enable it to build communism. In 1985 there were almost 42 million members, about three-quarters of the whole population in that age-group. Members are frequently encouraged to help out in industry and agriculture, but they also take part in the many social and sporting activities organized by the Komsomol. It publishes several newspapers, the most widely read being *Komsomolskaya Pravda*, and has its own tourist organization, Sputnik. D.PR.

Bibl: R.J. Hill and P. Frank, *The Soviet Communist Party* (London, 1981).

Korea. The name of one of the historic civilizations of East Asia, frequently used as a shorthand term for the Korean War of 1950-53. Having long lived under Chinese suzerainty, Korea was annexed by the Japanese in 1910 and after the Japanese defeat in 1945 was divided between a COMMUNIST state under Soviet patronage in the North and the American-supported regime of Syngman Rhee in the South. After the withdrawal of American forces in 1949, the Soviet-equipped armies of

North Korea crossed the partition line and launched a full-scale invasion of the South (25 June 1950). UNO forces, largely American and under American command, came to the support of the South. When they in turn carried the war north of the partition line (the 38th parallel) they were met by Chinese Communist forces. An armistice, concluded in July 1953, redivided the country along a line close to that of the original partition. The motivation for the original North Korean attack is unclear; but suspicions that it had been instigated by the Soviet authorities played a considerable part in inspiring the collective defence of Western Europe by NATO.

A.L.C.B.

Bibl: D. Rees, *Korea: the Limited War* (London and New York, 1964).

Krebs cycle (or *citric acid cycle* or *tricarboxylic acid cycle* or *TCA cycle*). The cycle, named after the biochemist Sir Hans Krebs (1900-1982), of oxidative processes within the CELL, the structural basis of which lies in the mitochondria (see CYTOLOGY).

P.M.

Kremlinology. Strictly, the study of Soviet politics at the higher levels, i.e. of the struggle for power and over policy between the leading members of the POLITBURO, who normally meet in the Kremlin in Moscow; loosely, any study of Soviet affairs. It implies deduction of what is or has been going on from such clues as emerge from behind the conventional facade of 'monolithic unity' among the leadership.

R.C.

Bibl: R. Conquest, *Power and Policy in the USSR* (London and New York, 1961); M. Tatu, *Power in the Kremlin* (London and New York, 1969).

kula. An elaborate system of gift EXCHANGE which links together different islands in New Guinea. The kula was studied by Malinowski, and his book *Argonauts of the Western Pacific* (1922) was used by Mauss in the development of a general theory of gift exchange. Different groups in the Trobriand islands are linked in a circuit of exchange. Two sets of objects, long red necklaces (*soulava*) and white shell bracelets (*mwali*) circulate in opposite directions. At the different points where these objects meet they are exchanged according to fixed rules and conventions. One partner makes his GIFT and the recipient is bound to make a return gift at the next meeting. The kula is a system of ceremonial exchange. The goods involved have no commercial value, but confer prestige. However, *soulava* and *mwali* are constantly in movement and no individual can hold on to an item for any length of time. Relationships established between partners in the kula ring are long term and bind together different groups through a complex system of exchange (see POTLATCH).

A.G.

Bibl: J.W. Leach and E.R. Leach (eds.), *The Kula: New Perspectives on Massim Exchange* (Cambridge, 1983).

kulak ('fist'). Originally a general Russian term for a grasping peasant, later defined as a peasant who employed labour. The COMMUNIST Party of the Soviet Union was concerned from early days to destroy this element of the peasantry, with the aid of the 'middle peasant', and the village poor. The COLLECTIVIZATION campaign of 1930-33 led to the elimination, by famine or in FORCED LABOUR camps, of about 10 million peasants defined officially as *kulaks*, though later Soviet figures show that many of them were in fact 'middle peasants'.

R.C.

Kunstgewerbeschule. Any 'School of Applied Art'; usually that at Vienna, an outstanding training-place for designers of all sorts in the opening years of this century, when the teachers included Koloman Moser and Josef Hoffmann, founder of the WIENER WERKSTÄTTE, and the students Oskar Kokoschka.

J.W.

Kuomintang (KMT). Chinese NATIONALIST revolutionary party formed in 1911 by Sun Yat-sen out of the remains of the *Tong Meng Hui* (Alliance Society). Despite winning a clear majority in the 1912 elections, it was outlawed a year later by Yuan Shi-kai. The KMT turned to the Soviet Union for support and advice, and swelled its ranks by admitting CCP members, and after Chiang Kai-shek became leader after the death of Sun Yat-sen in 1925, the Northern Expedition unified most of the country under nationalist control from Nanjing. In 1927, CCP members were expelled from the KMT, and despite the second united front with the COMMUNISTS in 1936 during the war with Japan, civil war followed, and the KMT was finally ousted from the Chinese mainland in 1949. It retreated to the island of Taiwan (Formosa), where it set up an administration which claimed to be the true and only government of all China; a claim that was acknowledged by the UNO until the People's Republic of China was admitted in 1971. The KMT has remained in power in Taiwan, with Chiang Kai-shek being succeeded on his death by his son, Chiang Ching-k'uo. Although the Taiwan regime has not been as incompetent and corrupt as the period of KMT tutelage on the mainland, constraints on opposition are tight, and political freedom remains severely limited. S.B.

Bibl: L. Eastman, *The Abortive Revolution* (Cambridge, Mass., 1974).

L

Labanotation, see under DANCE NOTATION.

labelling theory. An influential approach in the SOCIOLOGY of DEVIANCE. It argues that there is no behaviour that can be seen as *intrinsically* deviant: deviant behaviour is that which has been successfully defined or 'labelled' as such by those social groups with the POWER to make and enforce these definitions. Thus deviance does not inhere in the act itself, but in the response of others to the act. But once so-labelled by the reaction of others, the deviant is likely to be led on a career of further deviance. He or she develops a deviant SELF-IMAGE or self-conception based on the social reaction, and many come to be locked more or less permanently in a deviant ROLE. So for instance the individual whose behaviour comes to be labelled SCHIZOPHRENIC, and treated as such, is likely to adapt to the requirements of the role of a mental patient, and to intensify the 'schizophrenic' behaviour in such a way as continually to require treatment.

The humane impulse behind labelling theory is evident. Its radical rejection however of the possibility of physiological causes of deviance, and its antagonism — which does not follow logically from the theory — to any form of imprisonment or specialized medical therapy, has sometimes made its position seem naive if not outrightly callous. K.K.

Bibl: T. Szasz, *The Manufacture of Madness* (London, 1971); W.R. Gove, *The Labeling of Deviance: Evaluating a Perspective* (Beverly Hills, Ca., 1975).

labour, dilution of, see DILUTION OF LABOUR.

labour, forced, see FORCED LABOUR.

Labour and Socialist International, see under INTERNATIONAL.

labour hoarding. The practice adopted by some companies, during a decline in DEMAND, of retaining their labour force intact, thus reducing the productivity of labour and raising the average variable cost per unit of output. Though widely decried, this practice has a twofold rationale: in any subsequent recovery in demand it avoids (1) problems of attracting sufficient labour back into the industry, and (2) CAPITAL costs associated with the training of a new work force. D.E.

labour law. Since the inception of TRADE UNIONS in the 19th century there have been attempts to control them by legal means. These have varied widely in different countries. Unions, being organizations of workers, can be seen as a threat by some regimes which cannot countenance opposition. Labour legislation in such circumstances is highly restrictive, and often punitive; examples are common in Latin America and Africa. In the U.K. labour legislation has been changed many times. From the early Combination Acts (virtually outlawing unions), through the Taff Vale judgment giving unions rights, to the 1927 restrictive legislation and then on to the years since 1971 in which there have been rapidly changing laws, trade unions have been affected by specific legislation. The 1971 Industrial Relations Act attempted to manufacture specific legal instruments for unions but only the Industrial Tribunals have remained. The 1974 Employment Protection Act attempted to give collective rights to workers, but of these, only the conciliation body, ACAS remains. It ran into the problem that in traditional liberal British law the individual is paramount, but unions are collective organizations. The latest round of legislation, the Employment Acts, have concentrated on the removal of immunities from trade unions so that they may face actions for damages in the ordinary courts. Laws that fail in one country may work well in another. Labour courts are accepted in the U.S. and Australia but failed in the U.K.

In addition to specific laws, unions are bound by the general laws of their countries. These may affect PICKETING, demonstrations, STRIKES, ability to undertake political action or even prevent a union representing certain types of members. However different labour legislation may be, every country in the world has found it necessary to introduce it, and subsequently change it from time to time, and only rarely have these changes been to give trade union members greater rights.

B.D.S.

Bibl: K. Wedderburn *et al.*, *Labour Law and Industrial Relations* (Oxford, 1983).

labour theory of value. The theory, proposed by Adam Smith and Ricardo, and adapted by Marx, that any two products will exchange against one another in proportion to the amounts of labour necessary to make them. Thus, only labour can contribute to the value of a product. The part played by CAPITAL in production is allowed for, either by assuming that the same amount of capital is used per unit of labour in making every product, or by treating capital equipment as the product of past labour. By contrast, NEOCLASSICAL ECONOMIC THEORY allows the value of a good to be determined by its value in consumption (see UTILITY) and goods exchange at a rate determined by their relative use-values. The labour theory of value has difficulties in dealing with use-values, the interest rate, the value of natural resources and reducing different types of labour to a common unit. Even in COMMUNIST countries STATE ECONOMIC PLANNING does not adhere exclusively to a labour theory of value, though this theory remains central to communist and MARXIST ideology (see VALUE, THEORY OF).

E.H.P.B.;J.P.

Lacanian. Adjective referring to Jacques Lacan (1901-81), the French psychoanalyst. See SYMBOLIC, IMAGINARY, REAL, MATHEME, FORECLOSURE, IDENTIFICATION, PHANTASY, SUPPOSED SUBJECT OF KNOWLEDGE, DRIVE, OBJECT (A), SUBJECT, TRANSFERENCE, JOUISSANCE, NAME-OF-THE-FATHER, FEMININE SEXUALITY, DESIRE, MIRROR PHASE, BODY IMAGE, EGO, EGO-IDEAL, IDEAL EGO, SUPEREGO.

B.BU.;B.BE.

Bibl: B. Benvenuto and R. Kennedy, *The Works of Jacques Lacan: an Introduction* (London, 1986); J. Lacan, *Seminar One — Freud's Papers on Technique* (Cambridge, 1987).

Laffer Curve, see under SUPPLY-SIDE ECONOMICS.

laissez faire. A term used to describe an economy in which the activities of the government are kept down to an absolute minimum. See MARKET ECONOMY.

R.H.

Lake Baikal. The Siberian lake which became the centre of a protracted dispute over CONSERVATION, giving rise to the most successful environmental lobby in the Soviet Union to date. Between the late 1950s and the middle of the 1970s a number of scientists, journalists and authors protested to the government privately and publicly through articles in newspapers against the building of a cellulose cord factory on the shores of the lake. As Baikal is the largest freshwater lake in the world and many of the species which live there are unique to it, scientists considered any pollution of its waters by the factory to be very serious. Despite enormous difficulties in overcoming the vested interests of the cellulose industry, the campaign achieved some important successes. Although it failed to stop the building of the plant and some pollutants still find their way into the lake, elaborate waste-treatment facilities have been provided and in the long term the example of Baikal may prevent harm to the ENVIRONMENT in other cases. The achievements of the Baikal campaign show that a loose coalition, operating outside the accepted framework for articulating particular INTERESTS, can put pressure on the Soviet political ELITE to change government policies by drawing nation-wide attention to its cause.

D.PR.

Bibl: T. Gustafson, *Reform in Soviet Politics* (Cambridge, 1981).

Lamarckism. The conventional interpretation of the views on EVOLUTION held by the great French zoologist Jean Baptiste Pierre Antoine de Monet, le Chevalier de Lamarck (1744-1829) — the doctrine inadequately summarized as that of the 'inheritance of *acquired characteristics*'. In DARWINISM the heritable variations that are the subject of NATURAL SELECTION arise either spontaneously or not at all. Thus GENETIC information is self-engendered as part of the responding system. In Lamarckism the motive forces for evolutionary change are an animal's needs and the activities it undertakes in order to satisfy them. Thus, in the traditional example, a giraffe acquired the genetic specification for a long neck through generations of browsing upon the upper foliage of trees. A more sophisticated example is the ADAPTATION of micro-organisms which enables them to use new sources of nutriment or to combat a new ANTIBIOTIC. Lamarckism has a great inherent plausibility, because social evolution is so obviously Lamarckian in character — we learn generation by generation and can propagate our learning to the next generation. Nevertheless, whenever Lamarckism in a purely biological context has been exposed to a critical test it has been faulted. Indeed, according to our modern notions of PROTEIN synthesis (see NUCLEIC ACID) there is no known method by which any modification brought about in a living organism during its own lifetime can be IMPRINTED upon the genetic mechanism.

Lamarckism, like Darwinism, lends itself to political prejudices. If it were true that all human beings were born equal and that a man is what his environment and upbringing make him, then evolution could proceed only in the Lamarckian manner. It is therefore understandable that an extreme radical form of Lamarckism, bearing the same relationship to it as CALVINISM bears to Puritanism, was advocated in the Soviet Union by the agriculturalist Trofim Lysenko, after whom it has become known as LYSENKOISM. Lysenko's teaching became official doctrine in the COMMUNIST Party, and destroyed GENETICS in the Soviet Union as well as many of its practitioners. NEO-LAMARCKISM is the name given to an emphatic reiteration of Lamarckian beliefs by Nature-philosophers. Considered as an evolutionary procedure, Lamarckism is completely at odds with the central dogma of MOLECULAR BIOLOGY that genetic information flows only from NUCLEIC ACID towards protein or other products, and never the other way about.　　　　P.M.

Bibl: L.J. Jordanova, *Lamarck* (Oxford, 1984).

Lamb shift. Named after W. Lamb, American physicist (b. 1913). A small observed difference between energy levels in the hydrogen ATOM. This difference is predicted to exist by QUANTUM ELECTRODYNAMICS (QED) and arises because the single ELECTRON orbiting the PROTON which constitutes the hydrogen NUCLEUS interacts with the RADIATION field surrounding the atom to surround the nucleus by VIRTUAL PARTICLE pairs. This effect was first measured by Lamb.　　J.D.B.

Bibl: R. Feynman, *QED* (New York, 1986).

land art, see under CONCEPTUAL ART.

land reform. The reform of systems of land tenure to break up large estates and distribute ownership as widely as possible, with the consolidation of small holdings. Land reform has been a necessary development where large-scale ownership has been combined with small-scale tenant farming (often on a share-cropping basis) to produce a stationary system of agricultural management. It has been much employed by REFORMIST regimes, and also by revolutionary regimes as a necessary intermediary step towards COLLECTIVIZATION and breaking the power of the peasants.　　D.C.W.

Bibl: R. King, *Land Reform: a World Survey* (London, 1977).

land use planning. Provision for the use of land in accordance with a considered policy. The term is used mainly in connection with policies for the national and regional use of land, e.g. for agricultural and non-agricultural uses and, within the latter, for housing, industrial, recreational, or other use. Provision must necessarily be made also for multi-purpose uses, e.g. for recreation and forestry. The criteria for decisions and the administrative machinery for carrying decisions into practice differ between countries and over time.　　K.E.H.

Bibl: J.B. Cullingworth, *Town and Country Planning in Britain* (London, 9th ed., 1985).

landscape archaeology, see under ARCHAEOLOGY.

Langmuir-Blodgett films. Irving Langmuir exploited the fact that when a small quantity of oil or fatty acid is floated on a liquid (e.g. water) it spreads out to a very thin film that is only one MOLECULE thick. The molecules in the film are ordered so they are parallel to one another and by compressing the film to reduce its area and bring the molecules closer together (with a piston device) it can become solid. He found that such a film could be transferred on to a base material, such as a piece of glass, by slowly dipping the material into the liquid through the film and then withdrawing it. Katherine Blodgett then showed that by repeating this dipping process one could make multilayered films, either of the same or of different materials, in which each layer is ordered with respect to its neighbours — thus the technique is sometimes referred to as *molecular engineering*. The term L-B films is now applied to these multilayered structures in which there has recently been a great resurgence of interest since they can be made to have novel optical, magnetic or electrical properties. Possible applications are acoustic detectors, new TRANSISTORS and other ELECTRONIC devices, and very high definition INTEGRATED CIRCUITS (see SUPERLATTICE and LOW DIMENSIONAL MATERIALS).

H.M.R.

language, history of, see HISTORY OF LANGUAGE.

langue and *parole.* Terms introduced into LINGUISTICS by Ferdinand de Saussure (see SAUSSURIAN) to distinguish between language viewed as a complete system of forms and contrasts represented in the brains of the language-users, and language viewed as the act of speaking by an individual at a given time. It is similar to Chomsky's distinction between COMPETENCE AND PERFORMANCE. See also IDIOLECT.

D.C.

large numbers, laws of, see under PROBABILITY THEORY; STATISTICAL REGULARITY.

large-scale integration, see under INTEGRATED CIRCUIT.

laser (Light Amplification by Stimulated Emission of Radiation). A device invented in 1960 for producing an intense beam of light with a high degree of COHERENCE, by making all the ATOMS in a material emit light in PHASE. The system is prepared by illuminating it with a flash of light which raises all the atoms into the same *excited state* (see ENERGY LEVEL). When one of the atoms falls back into its *ground state* the light emitted stimulates a small fraction of the other atoms to radiate in sympathy, their light being in phase with that from the first atom. This weak coherent pulse is not allowed to escape but reflects back and forth between carefully spaced mirrors at each end of the specimen until all the atoms have been stimulated to radiate. One mirror is only partially reflecting, however, so that all the light eventually leaks out. The energy in the original illuminating flash (which is incoherent) has been converted into coherent light.

Laser light is used wherever coherence is necessary, e.g. in HOLOGRAPHY and METROLOGY, and wherever a highly localized source of ENERGY (obtained by focusing the beam) is required, e.g. in welding the cornea of the human eye.

M.V.B.

Bibl: O.S. Heavens, *Lasers* (London, 1971).

laser printer, see under INPUT/OUTPUT.

laser surgery. In the posterior regions of the eye the use of the LASER has helped most in the management of three distinct types of disorder. Firstly, in the treatment of that common ocular complication of long standing diabetes mellitus, diabetic retinopathy, the laser can improve the visual prognosis by destroying areas of diseased retina which, if left untreated, would provoke serious visual deterioration. So-called photocoagulative treatment of diabetic retinopathy has greatly improved its prognosis and this also applies to certain other retinal vascular disorders. In the treatment of retinal detachment, the laser provides one of the means by which a retinal break may be made to close by the induction of a focal inflammatory reaction in the structures underlying the retinal break in response to the focal laser burns. The laser beam may also have a role in the management of tumours in the posterior segment of the eye dependent on the nature, size and position of the tumour. Perhaps its greatest contribution so far has been in the treatment of glaucoma, a common eye disorder in which it is necessary to achieve a reduction in the level of the INTRAOCULAR PRESSURE. Application of the laser beam to the outflow channels for fluid at the front of the eye has in many instances been shown to lower the intraocular pressure and thus to benefit the management of chronic glaucoma. The laser may also be used to perforate structures within the eye. In the treatment of so-called closed angle glaucoma, the laser may be used to perforate the iris diaphragm thereby avoiding the need for an open eye operation to achieve the same end. Sometimes, following cataract surgery, a membrane may form in the eye which can further obscure the vision. The laser can punch a hole in this membrane thus avoiding the need for a surgical procedure in order to achieve an improvement in vision.   J.WI.

late modernism. Condescending term used by POST-MODERNISTS for architecture of the 1970s which is of interesting and high design quality but which does not conform with the post-modern canon. As the name suggests it particularly applies to design which ultimately derives from Modern Movement ideology, such as HIGH TECH. (See also MODERNISM.)   S.L.

latency period. In psychoanalytic theory (see PSYCHOANALYSIS), the stage of PSYCHOSEXUAL DEVELOPMENT that begins at the age of about five (in the resolution of the OEDIPUS COMPLEX or ELECTRA COMPLEX) and lasts until puberty. During this time sexual tensions are repressed or sublimated (see REPRESSION; SUBLIMATION) into other less conflictive activities. Cultural RELATIVISM in the expression of this phenomenon has been sufficiently emphasized by anthropologists to bring its universality into considerable doubt.   W.Z.

lateral thinking, see VERTICAL AND LATERAL THINKING.

lattice. A regular arrangement of lines or points. The ATOMS in a crystal lie approximately at points on a lattice, but the regularity is upset by (1) vibrations of the atoms about the lattice points (see SOLID-STATE PHYSICS), and (2) crystal DEFECTS such as DISLOCATIONS.   M.V.B.

Lautgedichte, see under CONCRETE POETRY.

law, administrative, see ADMINISTRATIVE LAW.

law, comparative, see COMPARATIVE LAW.

law, pure theory of. *Pure Theory of Law* is the title of a major contribution by Hans Kelsen to the philosophy of law and the theory of the State. First published in 1911, it presents a comprehensive account of the distinctive logical or formal structure of laws and legal systems, for the description of which it furnishes new concepts, of which the most novel and important is the concept of a *basic norm*. Kelsen called his theory 'pure' to mark its VALUE-FREE character and independence of moral or other evaluative judgement of the content of the law, and also to mark the distinction between this form of analytical study of the structure of the law and sociological studies of the law which are designed to furnish causal explanations or to establish other empirical relations between law and other phenomena.

The *basic norm* is introduced into the Pure Theory in order to explain both the systematic unity and the NORMATIVE character of law. It is not to be identified with the legal constitution of any state, or with any other form of positive law or social practice. It is, according to Kelsen, 'a juristic presumption or postulate implicit in legal thinking' prescribing that one ought to behave in the manner stipulated by the constitution and by the laws whose creation is authorized by the constitution. Kelsen believed that without such a presupposition or postulate only a sociological description and not a normative description could be given of the law and there could be nothing to unify separate laws into a single system. Hence, in Kelsen's view, the presupposition of the *basic norm* is implicit in the legal thought and the language commonly used by lawyers to describe the law.   H.L.A.H.

Bibl: H. Kelsen, tr. M. Knight, *Pure Theory of Law* (London and Berkeley, 1967); J. Raz, *The Concept of a Legal System* (Oxford, 1984); J. Raz, 'The

Purity of the Pure Theory', *138 Berne Internationale de Philosophie* (1981).

law, the rule of. Various meanings have been given to this phrase and it has sometimes been conceived as a factual summary of the basic principles of the British Constitution and sometimes as a statement of an ideal only partly embodied in actual constitutional practices. It was used by A.V. Dicey in his *Law of the Constitution*, first published in 1885, for three principles, which he thought desirable and which in his view underlay the British Constitution. These principles require (1) that a citizen's legal duties and his liability to punishment should be determined by the 'regular law', and not by the arbitrary fiat of officials or the exercise of wide discretionary powers; (2) that disputes between a private citizen and an official should be subject to the jurisdiction of the ordinary courts; and (3) that the fundamental rights of the citizen should not rest on a special guarantee by the Constitution but should arise from the ordinary law.

Contemporary versions of the rule of law stress the importance of two principles: (1) that the exercise of discretionary powers of rule-making and adjudication should be controlled by impartial tribunals in the light of stated general principles designed to secure that the power should be exercised fairly and within the limits prescribed by law; and (2) that as large an area of the law as possible and of the criminal law in particular should afford clear guidance to the citizen as to his rights and duties, and that he should be liable to punishment for breach of the law only if he had the capacity and a fair opportunity to conform his conduct to it.

H.L.A.H.

Bibl: A.V. Dicey, *Introduction to the Study of the Law of the Constitution* (1885; London and New York, 11th ed., 1985); R.F.V. Heuston, *Essays in Constitutional Law* (London, 3rd ed., 1969).

Law Commission. A commission set up by the Law Commission Act of 1965 to consider reforms of the law and make proposals to the British Government for the examination and reform of the laws. Various programmes have been laid by the Commission before the Lord Chancellor for the examination of different branches of the law, and some of these have been undertaken by the Commission itself or by other bodies. The Commission publishes informative annual reports of its activities and proposals and is also responsible for preparing legislation to provide for consolidation and revision of statute law.

H.L.A.H.

Law of the Sea. This branch of PUBLIC INTERNATIONAL LAW embraces the rules governing relations between STATES in maritime matters. Its main sources are: (1) *multilateral treaties*, e.g. the 1958 Geneva Conventions: on the territorial and contiguous zone; on the high seas; on the continental shelf; and on the fishing and conservation of living resources of the high seas. The 1982 Convention on the Law of the Sea, signed by 159 states but ratified by only 19, is unlikely to enter into force within the foreseeable future. Nonetheless, some of its articles re-state those provisions of the Geneva Conventions representing customary law. Its provisions on the exclusive economic zone reflect the customary law as it had existed before its completion in 1982. (2) *Customary international law*, e.g. the customary law rule that had evolved by the late 1950s recognizing coastal states; ownership over the resources of their continental shelf. (3) *General principles of international law*, e.g. the rule providing for exclusive jurisdiction of the flag state over ships on the high seas.

It is accepted that every coastal state enjoys SOVEREIGNTY over its *territorial sea* (3 to 12 miles), including the air space over it as well as its bed and subsoil. This sovereignty is subject to the obligation to allow a right of innocent passage to all foreign ships. By contrast, in the area known as the continental shelf, the coastal state can exercise only *sovereign rights* for the purpose of exploring the continental shelf and exploiting its natural resources without prejudice to freedom of navigation and overflight. A similar principle applies, *mutatis mutandis*, to claims by coastal states for *exclusive economic zones*. As regards the high seas, they are open to all nations; hence no state has a right to subject any part of them to its sovereignty. Coastal and non-coastal states alike are entitled to enjoy the freedom of the high seas, viz., navigation, fishing, laying submarine cables and pipelines and flying over such waters.   O.Y.E.

Bibl: R. Churchill and A. Lowe, *The Law of the Sea* (Manchester, 1983).

law and order. An expression used to refer to (1) social conditions in which there is general conformity to law, especially to the criminal law prohibiting such crimes as violence, theft, and disturbance of the peace, and to the firm administration of penalties imposed for breaches of the law; or (2) the conformity by law enforcement agencies themselves to the laws conferring and limiting their powers; or (3) respect for the rule of law (see LAW, RULE OF).
H.L.A.H.

Bibl: W.J. Chambliss and R.B. Seidman, *Law, Order and Power* (London and Reading, Mass., 1971).

Lawrentian. Adjective formed from the surname of D.H. Lawrence (1885-1930), whose novels and ideas had an enormous and liberating influence on his contemporaries and juniors. The adjective is now used in a generally non-pejorative sense (though it may occasionally refer to the crypto- or proto-FASCIST position allegedly occupied by Lawrence towards the end of his life) to refer to certain unique aspects of his writing and teaching, mostly to the latter. Qualities understood to be Lawrentian are: reliance, in human and sexual relationships, on 'blood', 'belly', 'loins', or 'bowels' (i.e. instinct) as against intellect (or, worse, 'sex in the head'); love of the particulars (birds, beasts, plants) of nature, and hatred of TECHNOLOGY; agrarianism as against URBANISM; tenderness as against sophistication; sexual candour (dubiously exemplified in *Lady Chatterley's Lover*) as against prudishness or PORNOGRAPHY (Lawrence's word for what he sexually disliked). 'Lawrentian' only approximates to Lawrence's own highly complex personality, especially in the matter of sex, since his portrait of himself in this respect did not coincide with what he was.   M.S.-S.

Bibl: F. Kermode, *Lawrence* (London, 1973).

laws of physics, see under MODEL.

L-B films, see under LANGMUIR-BLODGETT FILMS.

LDC (less developed country). A country which is in a state of UNDERDEVELOPMENT.   J.P.

LDP, see under LIBERAL DEMOCRATIC PARTY (Japan).

League of Nations. An international security organization created by covenant of the victors of World War I as part of the Treaty of Versailles, and established at Geneva in 1920. Its proposed method of maintaining peace was the application of economic and/or military SANCTIONS by member states against any nation committing aggression and ignoring the various procedures for the peaceful settlement of international disputes. The League's organs included a Council (with five permanent and four elected member powers) and an Assembly. The U.S.A. never joined it; Germany did not join until 1926 and withdrew in 1933; Japan withdrew in 1933; the Soviet Union joined in 1934 and was expelled in 1940.

During the 1920s the League enjoyed considerable authority and dealt successfully with a number of disputes. It also administered mandates and made some progress in developing various auxiliary international organizations such as the ILO and the Court of International Justice. During the 1930s, however, it failed to secure the support of the major powers in the face of Japanese, Italian, and German aggression that it was powerless to prevent, and did not survive World War II. At the end of that war it was replaced by the United Nations (see UNO).   D.C.W.

Bibl: F.P. Walters, *A History of the League of Nations* (2 vols., London and New York, 1952); G. Scott, *The Rise and Fall of the League of Nations* (London, 1973; New York, 1974).

learning by doing, see under TECHNICAL PROGRESS.

learning problems, see under DYNAMIC PROGRAMMING.

467

least-action principle. An alternative formulation of NEWTONIAN MECHANICS, which states that of all the conceivable paths along which a body may move between two points the path actually taken is such that a certain readily calculated property of the paths — the 'action' — is a minimum. A similar law in OPTICS (*Fermat's principle of least time*) governs the bending of light rays.

In the 18th century these principles were often regarded as indicating a 'desire for economy' on the part of Nature, which made objects 'choose' the minimal paths. However, this interpretation is untenable, because (1) a wide range of conceivable physical laws, including many known to be false, may be transformed mathematically into minimum principles, and (2) the action may occasionally be not a minimum but a *maximum* (when the paths or light rays have been through a focus). Least-action principles are useful in theoretical studies, such as the connection between Newtonian and QUANTUM MECHANICS.   M.V.B.

Leavisite. Adjective or noun formed from the name of the British literary critic F.R. Leavis (1895-1978) — and of his wife, Q.D. Leavis, whose *Fiction and the Reading Public* (1932) can perhaps be regarded as her most notable contribution to their working partnership. Since the 1930s Leavis has been, probably, the most powerful single influence on English studies: as a teacher at Cambridge University (and especially at Downing College), as founder and editor of *Scrutiny* (1932-53) and as the author of such books as *New Bearings in Poetry* (1932), *Culture and Environment* (with Denys Thompson, 1933), *Revaluation* (1936), and *The Great Tradition* (1949) — although his upward 'revaluations' (e.g. of T.S. Eliot, George Eliot, and above all D.H. Lawrence; see LAWRENTIAN) have been more generally accepted than his downward ones (e.g. of Milton, Shelley, and numerous English novelists). An outstanding exponent of the *practical criticism* (i.e. criticism based on close analysis of the text) pioneered by I.A. Richards, Leavis regarded the study of English as a unique opportunity for developing a general 'critical awareness'. His own critical awareness, however, too often led to critical and even personal acerbity, as in the TWO CULTURES controversy. The term 'Leavisite' is applied, pejoratively, not to Leavis himself nor to such former *Scrutiny* associates as L.C. Knights or D.J. Enright, but (as a noun) to his more dogmatic disciples, and (as an adjective) to the type of criticism or teaching which is concerned with the accurate 'placing' of literature (within Leavis's framework) at the expense of enjoyment.
                                                        O.S.

Bibl: E. Bentley (ed.), *The Importance of Scrutiny* (London and New York, 1948); G. Steiner, 'F.R. Leavis', in his *Language and Silence* (London and New York, 1967).

Lebanese Resistance Brigades, see under LEBANON.

Lebanon. An eastern Mediterranean state which has become synonymous with the collapse of civil order into chronic factional war. The state owes its character to French interest in the Christian inhabitants of the district of Mount Lebanon, which consequently became a privileged district of the Ottoman Empire after a civil war in 1861. This was followed by a French mandate over modern Lebanon as part of the post World War I settlement. The good days for Lebanon followed independence in 1943 when the leaders of the two most powerful communities, the Maronites and the Sunni Muslims, agreed an unwritten 'National Pact' (still operative in theory) distributing positions of authority according to religious affiliation, giving primacy to the Maronites (the presidency and command of the armed forces) with Sunnis second (the premiership) and Shi'i third (speakership). The most important change which undermined this delicate balance and led to civil war in 1975, was that Shi'i Muslims became more numerous, were impoverished by population growth and the severance of their homeland in the south from Palestine (now Israel), and so became a subversive force in the towns. Maronites, numbering about 900,000 (25%), claim their origins among Christian Arab tribes who in the 6th to 7th centuries defended themselves against Muslims and Byzantines. They now recognize the authority of the Pope. They retain the presidency but their effective control does not extend far beyond east Beirut. The Sunni Muslims (700,000 or 20%) have been eclipsed; linked to the Sunni world outside Lebanon they did not develop the same intensity of political cohesion and lacked an effective militia. The Shi'i, originating from the 7th-century split in ISLAM, number 1.1 million (30%) and have formed a political organization with a militia wing called Amal (acronym: Lebanese Resistance Brigades) now led by Nabih Berri. Amal seeks a reconstructed Lebanese system in which Shi'i have a fair part. Some Shi'i, calling themselves Hizbollahis (Party of God) under the leadership of Sheikh Muhammad Hussein Fadlallah, have close connections with Iran and seek the establishment of an Islamic Republic in Lebanon. The Druze number only 250,000 (8%) but have always had disproportionate influence because they are the most tightly knit, hierarchical and territorially compact community with disciplined voters in time of peace and a disciplined militia in fighting. Greek Orthodox, Catholics and Armenians are politically unimportant.

Palestinian refugees accommodated in camps in Lebanon were quiescent from 1948 to 1970 when Palestinian GUERRILLAS were expelled from Jordan by King Hussein. Their arrival destroyed the already precarious Lebanese balance, turned the refugee camps into guerrilla bases and established a PLO base in Lebanon which so far has not been destroyed.

Other Arab states have always pursued their rivalries within Lebanon but since 1975 the key protagonists have been Israel, whose invasion of Lebanon in 1982 failed in its objective of making Lebanon a Christian state under Israeli patronage, and Syria which has so far failed to reconstruct Lebanon under its paramountcy. At the beginning of the civil war alliances between rival groups, and between them and the outside powers, were made on the basis of political empathy or long term interest; as instability persists they are made as short term tactics dictate. The absence of civil order permits all kinds of terrorism: the suicidal efforts of zealots (the attack on the U.S. multinational force); TERRORISM as a political-military weapon (Syrian supported Amal actions); hostage-taking and the rent-a-bomb trade of mercenary terrorists.   W.K.

Bibl: H. Cobban, *The Making of Modern Lebanon* (London, 1985).

Lebensraum ('living room'). Term of biological origin meaning the area inhabited or habitable by a particular life-form (BIOSPHERE). It was introduced into political usage by German publicists after 1870 to justify Germany's territorial expansion. A central concept after 1919 in German ultra-NATIONALIST writing, including the propaganda literature of the NAZIS, it looked in particular to an expansion of Germany into eastern Europe, justifying this by the need for agricultural land to maintain the favourable balance between peasant and city-dweller on which the moral health of the German nation was supposed to rest. This was the ideological justification for Hitler's attack on Russia in 1941. See also GEOPOLITICS.   D.C.W.

Bibl: N. Rich, *Hitler's War Aims* (New York and London, 1974).

Lebenswelt (Lifeworld). An important concept in the later philosophy of Edmund Husserl. During the period 1934-8 he worked on a text we know as *The Crisis of European Sciences*, in which, dismayed by the current political débâcle and the complicity of science in it, Husserl sketched out a theory of a 'Life World' in which men and women historically exist, and which has its own *telos* and ethical reality. Individual epochs do more or less well in their responsibility towards the Lifeworld. In Husserl's view, the present epoch was, or was about to be, the most irresponsible ever. The telos of science and philosophy set up by the Greeks had been abandoned completely, and an ethical concern for the future of the Lifeworld had dropped to virtually zero. The Lifeworld is both part of, and yet distinct from, the physical world around us. It is partly constituted by intellectual, political and ethical INTENTIONALITY, a membrane of INTERSUBJECTIVITY and responsibility in which we encounter the OTHER, and with him, carry on, or fail to carry on, the ethical project which the Lifeworld is. So far as Husserl writing in the late 1930s could see, the very continuation of the

Lifeworld as a human project was in danger. R.PO.

Bibl: E. Husserl, *The Crisis of European Sciences* (Evanston, Ill., 1970).

Lebesgue measure, see under MEASURE THEORY.

Leboyer method of childbirth, see under CHILDBIRTH TECHNIQUES.

Le Chatelier's principle. Name given to the tendency of the environment to exert restoring forces on a system disturbed slightly away from stable, static or dynamic EQUILIBRIUM. M.V.B.

lect. In SOCIOLINGUISTICS, any collection of linguistic phenomena which has a functional identity within a speech community, such as a regional dialect, or a social variety. A continuum of varieties is recognized, for example distinguishing between a variety which has the greatest prestige within a community (the 'acrolect') and that which is furthest away from this norm (the 'basilect'). D.C.

Bibl: D. Bickerton, *Dynamics of a Creole System* (Cambridge, 1975).

le fantastique. A term used in French film criticism which has no direct equivalent in English, usefully encompassing not only horror films but fantasy (everything from SCIENCE FICTION to *Alice in Wonderland*), and even films basically realistic in theme which may have strange, dreamlike or seemingly supernatural elements. French film criticism is also inclined to categorize such films, the latter group in particular, as either *onirique* (meaning dreamlike, now frequently borrowed by English critics as *oneiric*) or *insolite* (unwonted, unusual, weird). T.C.C.M.

Left, the. Label applied to a range of radical political views (see RADICALISM) and to those holding them. It came into being as a metaphorical extension of the seating plan of the French Estates General in 1789, where the nobility sat on the King's right and the 'Third Estate' on his left. The division of opinion crystallized in the debates on the royal veto, with the more revolutionary deputies opposing it, the conservative ones favouring it, and those in the CENTRE proposing a compromise.

This perception of politics as a continuum in which the body politic is consistently divided by attitudes towards social change and social order resulted in the identification of the Left (or left wing) as the parties of change and of the RIGHT (or right wing) as the forces of the status quo. The left-right dichotomy was that of EGALITARIANISM *v.* inequalities, of reform (or REVOLUTION) *v.* tradition, of RADICALISM *v.* CONSERVATISM, of economic interventionism (see STATE ECONOMIC PLANNING) *v.* LAISSEZ FAIRE, of internationalism *v.* patriotism.

However, after World War I political attitudes no longer clustered so consistently along the old left-right division. Although the two terms continue to be used, they have undergone many shifts of meaning; and some of the old contradictory tendencies have appeared in new combinations. The Left could not be defined any more by its attitude to EQUALITY *and* change: the two were sometimes divergent. The Right was no longer necessarily an epitome of conservation and of the defence of the status quo; it could be radical, or even revolutionary like NAZISM. Nor was the Left necessarily internationalist; the emergence of national versions of COMMUNISM testified to this. Even inside the parties internal divisions were no longer always best described in terms of left and right. The Polish REVISIONISTS considered themselves to be to the left of Gomulka, whereas he denounced them as a rightist deviation (see DEVIATIONISM). The MAOIST Chinese similarly denounced Soviet 'revisionism' as a right-wing betrayal of communism, while Soviet Communists castigated the Maoists as 'leftist adventurers' *and* 'PETIT-BOURGEOIS nationalists'.

The emergence of the NEW LEFT contributed even more to the confusion and shifts in the meaning of the terms right and left. The perception of politics as a spectrum became more difficult, and a definition of 'the Left' in terms of traditional and consistent attitudes even more so. The label continues to be applied because it still helps to describe persistent divisions, but it often contributes more to the obfuscation of political realities than to the clarification of political issues.

L.L.

Bibl: D. Caute, *The Left in Europe* (London and New York, 1966); B. Crick (ed.), *The Socialist Heritage* (Oxford, 1987).

Left Book Club. A London publishing venture, founded early in 1936, which epitomized LEFT attitudes during the POPULAR FRONT period. Its publisher was Victor Gollancz and its co-founders were John Strachey and Professor Harold Laski; its editorial direction was a Communist INTELLECTUAL, John Lewis. Starting with some 10,000 members, within three years it increased five-fold. Although not all of its books were written by COMMUNISTS or FELLOW-TRAVELLERS, most of them were strongly pro-Soviet, and none was in any way critical of Stalin's Russia at the time of the Great Purge (see YEZHOVSHCHINA) and the MOSCOW TRIALS. The Club's success was interrupted by the 1939 Nazi-Soviet Pact, which was denounced by some of the Club's leaders, including Victor Gollancz. Its membership fell rapidly, and in 1948 it was dissolved.

L.L.

Bibl: V. Gollancz (ed.), *The Betrayal of the Left* (London, 1941); J. Symons, *The Thirties* (London, 1960; rev. ed., 1975).

legal positivism. A theory about the nature of law which defines it in a purely descriptive way in terms of the commands, or other *ex officio* pronouncements, of a sovereign or generally recognized authority, and without reference to moral considerations. It was first fully expounded by the 19th-century legal theorist, John Austin (see AUSTINIAN), who based his position on the ideas of Hobbes and Bentham. More recent developments of the doctrine have adjusted it to take account of the facts that not all laws are straightforwardly imperative in form and that not all constitutions contain so simply identifiable an ultimate source of law as that of Britain, whose legal system was Austin's prime example.

A.Q.

Bibl: H.L.A. Hart, *The Concept of Law* (Oxford, 1961).

legal professional ethics. Regulations concerning the conduct of lawyers in their professional capacity. In England, where there are two legal professions, these regulations are for the most part laid down by the Law Society for solicitors and the Senate of the Inns of Court and the General Council of the Bar for barristers, though certain overall provisions are made by Act of Parliament, e.g. concerning complaints about the Law Society's handling of complaints against solicitors. Ethics cover such matters as the conduct of counsel or solicitor advocates in court, fees, ADVERTISING (which is permitted in a limited way for solicitors, but not for barristers), training (including provision for articled clerkships for intending solicitors and pupillage for barristers), and arrangements for partnerships between solicitors. Firms of solicitors may not be incorporated, and barristers may not enter into partnerships of any kind, though they practise from sets of chambers which they share with other barristers, and in which they share a clerk or clerks. A lawyer offending against his profession's ethics will be disciplined by the Law Society or the Bar Council who, in serious cases, may strike a solicitor from the rolls or disbar a barrister.

D.C.M.Y.

Bibl: R.J. Walker, *The English Legal System* (London, 6th ed., 1985); H.G. Hanbury and D.C.M. Yardley, *English Courts of Law* (Oxford and New York, 5th ed., 1979).

legal-rational authority. A term associated particularly with the German SOCIOLOGIST Max Weber. It refers to an IDEAL TYPE of authority dependent not on tradition, as in the rule of elders or leaders in tribal and peasant societies, nor on personal CHARISMA, as with the authority of kings or religious prophets, but on the acceptance of certain formal rules and procedures as rationally valid and legally binding. For Weber, it is the form of authority increasingly characteristic of a modern INDUSTRIAL SOCIETY. Its principal agent and exponent is modern BUREAUCRACY, although Weber was well aware that in practice bureaucracy was quite capable of highly 'irrational' as well as flagrantly illegal behaviour.

K.K.

legal realism. A theory about the nature of law which, like LEGAL POSITIVISM, seeks to define it without reference to moral considerations, but goes even further in interpreting statements about legal rights and duties in a straightforward factual way. It defines a person's legal *rights* as whatever, as a matter of fact, the courts will decide that he should be allowed to do, his legal *duties* as whatever the courts will decide he is required to do. A common objection to this self-consciously hard-headed theory is that it can give no intelligible account of the reasoning of judges. A judge asking himself 'What are this man's legal rights?' is really, according to legal realism, asking 'What, in fact, am I going to say he should be allowed to do?'   A.Q.

legionnaires' disease. This form of pneumonia is caused by the bacterium *Legionella pneumophila* which was hitherto unrecognized as it was difficult to grow in the laboratory. The disease is now generally diagnosed by the finding of a rise in the concentration of ANTIBODIES in the patients' blood. The rise is sought in successive blood samples taken several days apart. About 150 to 200 cases are recognized every year in the U.K. and although the bacterium is sensitive to certain ANTIBIOTICS the disease still has a case fatality ratio of about 12.5%. About a third of British cases have become infected abroad, usually in southern Europe, although that distribution possibly reflects the distribution of susceptible travellers. About 70% of the patients are more than 50 years old and most are male. While sporadic cases arc found, outbreaks seem to occur in hotels, hospitals and other large institutions where the organism is found to be infecting water systems such as those in air conditioning or shower heads from both of which it is inhaled as an aerosol. Some water systems may be found to be infected on routine inspection and it is not yet clear why explosive outbreaks suddenly arise. The disease achieved notoriety from an outbreak among a group of American ex-servicemen (legionnaires) attending a convention at a hotel in Philadelphia in 1976. Twenty-nine out of about 180 cases died and it was only after some months of intensive work that the investigators succeeded in finding and growing the bacterium responsible. It is interesting to reflect that had the outbreak affected not the legionnaires but some other convention, this section might have been titled Candlemakers' disease or even Eucharistic Congress Syndrome.   W.R.L.

legitimacy. An interest in governmental legitimacy has two bases, either a SOCIOLOGICAL interest in a government's *de facto* ability to have its word pass for law, or a moral interest in the grounds on which governments ought to have their word pass for law. The first topic has come back into vogue because of a persistent anxiety as to whether modern STATES overstretch themselves in trying to provide 'cradle to grave' WELFARE for their subjects, the second has always exercised political philosophers since subjects first challenged their rulers' authority. Recently, a widespread concern for HUMAN RIGHTS has provoked the thought that if governments possess authority only in virtue of protecting their subjects' rights, few governments are wholly legitimate. (See POWER.)   A.R.

Bibl: J. Habermas, *Legitimation Crisis* (London, 1980); P. Sieghart, *Human Rights* (Oxford, 1983).

Lehrstück ('didactic play'). German term of the 1920s for a form of MUSIC THEATRE designed to instruct the performers rather than entertain an audience. The genre was introduced, apparently as a development of Hindemith's *Gemeinschaftsmusik*, or communual music intended for amateurs, at the 1929 Baden-Baden chamber music festival, when Brecht, Hindemith, and Kurt Weill produced the *Badener Lehrstück vom Einverständnis* and the 'radio Lehrstück' *Flug der Lindberghs* or *Lindberghflug* (later renamed *Der Ozeanflug*). The term was virtually annexed by Brecht, whose model appears to have been the Japanese No drama, which henceforward became an important constituent of his EPIC THEATRE. With Weill and Hanns Eisler he wrote, in 1930-34, further didactic works, some with an expressly COMMUNIST message, for performance by children or amateurs.   J.W.

Bibl: G. Skelton, *Paul Hindemith* (London, 1975).

Leicester school, see under AGRARIAN HISTORY.

leisure class. A term coined, with a characteristic degree of irony, by the American social critic Thorstein Veblen in 1899. The leisure CLASS is made up of all those — aristocrats, clergy, BOURGEOIS, *nouveaux riches* — who regard manual labour, and industrial occupations generally, as beneath them, and who devote themselves to government, warfare, religion, and sport. Though the values and life-styles of the leisure class are derived largely from the upper class of FEUDAL Europe, they have persisted in the outlook of the wealthier classes of INDUSTRIAL SOCIETY, and have even been strengthened by the vast private fortunes made possible by industrialism. The leisure class is not however interested in riches as such; it is concerned with its social standing in society, and hence indulges heavily in CONSPICUOUS CONSUMPTION. For Veblen this meant a misdirection of industrial effort, in the production of luxury goods for display purposes; though many economists argue that this is a necessary and beneficial stage of ECONOMIC GROWTH above the level of primary accumulation. Some critics today think that Britain is too heavily permeated by the values of the leisure class, leading to an aversion to industrial pursuits and a preference for the professions and public life.   K.K.

Bibl: T. Veblen, *The Theory of the Leisure Class* (London, 1925); M. Wiener, *English Culture and the Decline of the Industrial Spirit 1850-1980* (Cambridge, 1981).

lend-lease. An Act of the U.S. Congress, signed by President Roosevelt on 11 March 1941, while the U.S.A. was still neutral, to allow the supply of arms and general supplies to Britain and subsequently to other states at war with the AXIS powers. Its basic principle was the leasing of arms and armaments in return for undertakings to return their value after war was over. The Act did not allow for any extension once hostilities had ended, and its operations were abruptly terminated in 1945 by order of President Truman.   D.C.W.

Bibl: R. Dallek, *Franklin D. Roosevelt*

and American Foreign Policy, 1932-45 (Oxford and New York, 1979).

Leninism. The term refers to the version of MARXIST thought which accepts the validity of the major theoretical contributions made by Lenin to revolutionary Marxism. These contributions fall into two main groups. Central to the first was the conception of the revolutionary party as the vanguard of the PROLETARIAT. The workers, if left to their own devices, would concentrate on purely economic issues and not attain full political CLASS consciousness, and therefore the revolutionary seizure of power needed the leadership of committed Marxist ACTIVISTS to provide the appropriate theoretical and tactical guidelines. The role of the party was thus to be a 'vanguard' in the revolutionary struggle which would culminate in the overthrow of the CAPITALIST STATE and the establishment of a DICTATORSHIP OF THE PROLETARIAT under the HEGEMONY of the party.

The second major theoretical contribution made by Lenin was to draw the political consequences from an analysis of CAPITALISM as both international and imperialist. The phenomenon of IMPERIALISM divided the world between advanced industrial nations and the colonies they were exploiting. This situation was inherently unstable and led to war between capitalist nations thus creating favourable conditions for REVOLUTION. For Lenin, the 'weakest link' in the capitalist chain was to be found in UNDERDEVELOPED regions of the world economy such as Russia where the indigenous BOURGEOISIE was comparatively weak, but where there had been enough INDUSTRIALIZATION to create a class-conscious proletariat. The idea of world-wide SOCIALIST revolution beginning in relatively backward countries led to the inclusion of the peasantry as important revolutionary actors affording essential support to the proletariat in establishing a socialist order. Such socialist revolutions in underdeveloped countries would exacerbate the contradictions inherent in advanced capitalist economies and thus lead to the advent of socialism on a world scale.

As compared with the ideas of Marx and Engels, Leninism gives more emphasis to the leading role of the party, to backward or semi-colonial countries as the initial site of revolution, and to the peasantry as potential revolutionary agents. With the success of the BOLSHEVIK revolution in 1917, Leninism became the dominant version of Marxism and the official IDEOLOGY of the Soviet Union. Lenin's analysis of imperialism and his idea of the 'weakest link' also made his version of Marxism appealing to emerging ELITES in the THIRD WORLD. In the West, however, while Leninist principles are maintained by the small Trotskyist parties, many adherents of eurocommunism have begun to ask how far Leninist ideas reflected specifically Russian circumstances and should therefore be modified to fit the conditions of advanced capitalist societies.

D.T.M.

Bibl: N. Harding, *Lenin's Political Thought*, 2 vols. (London, 1977, 1981); D. Lane, *Leninism: A Sociological Interpretation* (Cambridge, 1981); A. Meyer, *Leninism* (New York, 1957).

lensing, see under GRAVITATIONAL LENS.

lepton. Any ELEMENTARY PARTICLE that does not react or decay with STRONG INTERACTIONS, but instead displays only the WEAK INTERACTION or interactions via the ELECTROMAGNETIC FIELD (e.g. the ELECTRON, the NEUTRINO). M.V.B.

lesbianism, see under HOMOSEXUALITY.

lettrism. Parisian literary movement founded in 1946, based on a poetic and pictorial concern with letters and signs, and identified particularly with Isidore Isou and Maurice Lemaître. Its works, generally regarded as inferior to comparable exercises in CONCRETE POETRY and by allied artists of a calligraphic bent, take the form of phonetic poetry, picture-writing (*hypergraphy*), and quasi-SEMIOTIC painting. J.W.

Bibl: I. Isou, *Introduction à une nouvelle poésie* (Paris, 1947).

leucotomy (or *lobotomy*). The operation of cutting the white matter of the brain. In its most drastic form, the *prefrontal leucotomy*, a cut is made in the front of the brain to divide connecting tracts between the frontal lobes and the thalamus.

Prefrontal leucotomy was introduced when it was noticed (and confirmed by experiments with animals) that injuries of the frontal lobes resulted in a blunting of the EMOTIONS — particularly AGGRESSION and ANXIETY. It was widely practised in the late 1940s and early 1950s, and brought undoubted relief to a number of patients with PSYCHOSIS or severe emotional disorders, but its exact value was never generally agreed, and it is now performed much less often, since better results can be achieved by treatment with drugs, which is reversible, controllable, and less drastic.

D.A.P.

Bibl: W.J. Freeman and J.W. Watts, *Psychosurgery* (Oxford and Springfield, Ill., 2nd ed., 1950).

level. In LINGUISTICS, a fundamental theoretical term which is used in a number of senses, in particular (1) to denote an aspect of the structure of language regarded as susceptible of independent study; three levels (PHONETICS, SYNTAX, SEMANTICS) are generally recognized (but see also DUALITY OF STRUCTURE; FORM); (2) in GENERATIVE GRAMMAR, to characterize the distinction between DEEP STRUCTURE AND SURFACE STRUCTURE ('varying levels of depth'); (3) especially by some American linguists, in the sense of RANK.

D.C.

levirate, see under BRIDEWEALTH.

lexeme. A term used by some LINGUISTS (e.g. John Lyons) to describe the basic abstract lexical unit which underlies the different inflectional forms of a word, e.g. *sleep, slept, sleeps, sleeping* are variants of a single lexeme, *sleep*. D.C.

lexical functional grammar. In LINGUISTICS, a grammatical theory that developed in the 1970s, in which grammatical relations are represented by means of a 'functional' analysis of sentence structure, and the LEXICON is assigned a more important role than it held in earlier models of TRANSFORMATIONAL GRAMMAR. D.C.

Bibl: P. Matthews, *Syntax* (Cambridge, 1983).

lexical word, see under WORD CLASS.

lexicography, see under LEXICON.

lexicology, see under LEXICON.

lexicometry, see under QUANTITATIVE HISTORY.

lexicon. The dictionary component of a linguistic analysis, in which all information about the meaning and use of individual lexical items in a language is listed. It is particularly used with reference to the SEMANTIC component of a GENERATIVE GRAMMAR. The study of the properties of the lexicon is sometimes called *lexis*, sometimes *lexicology*. The latter must be distinguished from *lexicography*, the principles and practice of dictionary-making. In neo-Firthian (see FIRTHIAN) LINGUISTICS, lexis has a more restricted sense, referring only to the formal, not the semantic, characteristics of the lexicon.

D.C.

lexicostatistics, see under GLOTTO-CHRONOLOGY.

lexis, see under LEXICON.

Liberal Democratic Party (*Jiyūminshutō*). The Liberal Democratic Party (LDP) is a broadly based CONSERVATIVE party which has ruled Japan independently since its formation in 1955, except that between the general elections of 1983 and 1986 it was in coalition with the minuscule New Liberal Club. Although its support is heaviest in the countryside (which receives disproportionate weight in Japan's lopsided electoral system) it has proved flexible enough to retrieve its electoral fortunes in the big cities, where up to the mid-1970s its support was declining. In this it has been helped by the fragmentation and unconvincing performance of the opposition parties.

As a party which has spent over 30 years in power, the LDP constitutes part of a complex network of POWER linkages with government ministries and significant INTEREST GROUPS. Politically it is not monolithic, being divided into a number of powerful factions (5 in 1986) which bargain for cabinet and party positions, and

channel electoral funding to their members (see LOCKHEED SCANDAL), but which are not clearly distinguishable in policy terms. In the Lower House general elections of July 1986 the LDP won 300 out of 512 seats — its best performance for many years.

J.A.A.S.

Bibl: Haruhiro Fukui, *Party in Power: The Japanese Liberal-Democrats and Policy-Making* (Canberra, 1970); T.J. Pempel, *Policy and Politics in Japan: Creative Conservatism* (Philadelphia, 1982).

liberalism/liberal.

(1) A political philosophy whose origins lie in the Renaissance and Reformation, which acquired firmer roots in the 18th century and its greatest coherence in the 19th. Since then it has remained a massive influence on the values of democratic societies, although truly liberal political movements and parties have lost ground. Although protean in nature and not easily reducible to a set of general propositions, liberalism springs from a vision of society as crucially composed of individuals (rather than, for instance, classes), and of their liberty as the primary social good. This liberty is to be defended in such rights as those to free political institutions, religious practice, intellectual and artistic expression. Particularly in the 19th century it was also held to include the right to property, a FREE MARKET and FREE TRADE and in all to require the careful limitation of government to those activities which preserve rather than inhibit individual freedom.

Liberalism has been less coherent in the 20th century. Doctrines such as FASCISM and variants of MARXISM challenged it by respectively stressing the principles of state POWER and EQUALITY. Changing patterns of economic organization and state activity also demanded a reappraisal of its relevance. American liberalism, as exemplified in the NEW DEAL and GREAT SOCIETY, adapted by accepting the state as an instrument to alleviate economic inequalities and protect the rights of minorities (see NEO-LIBERALISM). More generally, liberalism's difficulty in accommodating a more positive state and the inequalities of CAPITALIST societies has led to the term more often loosely connoting such values as tolerance, rationality, privacy,

MINORITY rights, PARTICIPATION. In recent years, however, major attempts have been made to apply older liberal economic ideas to the present. These are confusingly labelled both as neo-liberalism and as an essential element of new right thought.

A.L.C.B.; S.R.

Bibl: A. Arblaster, *The Rise and Decline of Western Liberalism* (Oxford, 1984); J. Gray, *Liberalism* (Milton Keynes, 1986).

(2) In RELIGION and THEOLOGY, the opinion that an individual, or a new generation, ought to have liberty to question and reject orthodox doctrines and DOGMAS if these seem contrary to reason or morality (see EMPIRICAL THEOLOGY), and to apply ordinary historical methods to the Bible and other sacred texts (see HIGHER CRITICISM). The greatest theologian with these attitudes was Friedrich Schleiermacher (1768-1834). Before 1914, particularly in the 'Liberal PROTESTANTISM' of Adolf von Harnack (1851-1930) and others, such an approach was often associated with an over-optimistic attitude to human progress and rationality. Hence BARTHIAN and other exponents of NEO-ORTHODOXY condemned much of it as a betrayal of the Christian Gospel.

D.L.E.

Bibl: B.M.G. Reardon (ed.), *Liberal Protestantism* (London and Stanford, 1968).

liberalism, economic, see ECONOMIC LIBERALISM.

liberation theology. A style of Christian THEOLOGY which emphasizes God's demand for social justice and defence and deliverance of the poor (as in the Exodus of Israel from Egypt). It derives its theoretical insights not only from the Bible but also from active participation in the lives and struggles of peasants, the landless and the urban WORKING CLASS. The economic and political situation is often analysed in MARXIST terms and the solution is often seen to lie in SOCIALISM. For this reason such theology has been criticized as being essentially political propaganda and warnings have come from Pope John Paul II and the Vatican. But the World Council of Churches has been an influential patron and the worldwide tendency of Christians to express the aspirations of Third World peoples, and of the marginalized groups in the industrial nations, has made this the most influential theological movement of the 1980s. Its earliest and most vigorous articulation has been in Latin America although it has been applied to African, Asian, European, etc., problems. It received decisive encouragement when in a conference at Medellin in Colombia in 1968 the Roman Catholic bishops of Latin America (or most of them) made a 'preferential option for the poor' after decades of acquiescence in regimes close to FASCISM. In Latin America theologians of this kind have not only been productive in the writing of books at a variety of levels; they have also been intimately associated with the popular BASIC COMMUNITIES.

D.L.E.

Bibl: Gustavo Gutierrez, tr. C. India and J. Eagleson, *A Theology of Liberation* (Mary Knoll, 1973, and London, 1974); J.M. Bonino, *Doing Theology in a Revolutionary Situation* (Philadelphia, 1975) and *Revolutionary Theology Comes of Age* (London, 1975); T. Witvliet, tr. J. Bowden, *A Place in the Sun: An Introduction to Liberation Theology in the Third World* (London, 1985).

libertarianism.

(1) The doctrine that no STATE can be legitimate which sets out to do more than enforce individuals' rights; extreme libertarians hold that no state whatever can be legitimate, and that we are not obliged to obey any authority to which we have not given our actual, and not merely our hypothetical, consent. Unlike orthodox CONSERVATIVES, libertarians believe it is no part of the state's duties to enforce private morality; prostitution, DRUG taking and sexual PERVERSION not involving harm to others are all within the individual's right to do what he chooses with his own resources. Conversely, libertarians are sceptical of the nation state's tendency to possess large military forces and to spend huge sums on so-called defence. Libertarians differ from 20th-century LIBERALS in disbelieving in social justice and in thinking the WELFARE STATE is simply robbery under the cover of law. The intellectual charms of libertarian doctrine are

greater than its impact on practical politics has thus far been.   A.R.

Bibl: Murray Rothbard, *For a New Liberty* (New York, 1974).

(2) A theory, opposed to DETERMINISM, about the nature of human action which holds that some human actions, those for which it is correct to hold the agent in question morally responsible, are not causally explicable, or not wholly so.
                                    A.Q.

libido.

(1) In early psychoanalytic theory (see PSYCHOANALYSIS), a FREUDIAN term for specifically sexual energies.

(2) Later, all psychic energies employed in the service of the LIFE INSTINCT.   W.Z.

life cycle. One or other of the regenerative processes in the BIOSPHERE; examples are the *nitrogen cycle*, the *carbon cycle*, and the *oxygen cycle*. The elementary constituents of the biosphere — carbon, hydrogen, oxygen, nitrogen, phosphorus, sulphur — enter into compounds which so far from being static undergo continuous cycles of use and re-use, synthesis and degradation. Nitrogen compounds are essential for living organisms and are probably the most important limiting factor in regulating their abundance. Yet in spite of its enormous abundance (about 80% of the atmosphere) very few organisms have the power to make use of nitrogen directly. For this reason the artificial fixation of gaseous nitrogen is the most important and biologically influential technological innovation since the INDUSTRIAL REVOLUTION. The amounts of nitrogen fixed in industrial processes for the manufacture of fertilizers are of the order of tens of millions of tons per annum and are probably on the same scale as the natural fixation of atmospheric nitrogen by marine MICRO-ORGANISMS and by the microorganisms that live in SYMBIOSIS with leguminous plants. The fixation of nitrogen has to compete with the denitrifying processes which in the latest stages of organic breakdown return nitrogen to the atmosphere, and with the wastage produced by the dissipation or misuse of sewage, which is normally rich in nitrogen compounds.

The *carbon cycle*, closely intertwined with the *oxygen cycle*, begins and ends with atmospheric carbon dioxide. Although living organisms are compounds of carbon, very much more carbon is locked up in the form of coal and other fossil fuels than in living organisms themselves. The crucial TRANSFORMATION in both the carbon cycle and the oxygen cycle is PHOTOSYNTHESIS. The chief agents fixing atmospheric carbon are terrestrial forests and marine phytoplankton. Carbon dioxide is returned to the air by respiration, by the combustion of fossil fuels, and as a terminal stage of the decomposition of organic matter. In both carbon and oxygen cycles an annual rhythm is superimposed upon a CIRCADIAN RHYTHM.   P.M.

life force, see under VITALISM.

life instinct (or *Eros*). In psychoanalytic theory (see PSYCHOANALYSIS), a FREUDIAN term for the supposed source of all the impulses and drives that serve the individual in self-preservation and reproduction. It is contrasted with the DEATH INSTINCT. See also LIBIDO.   W.Z.

life sciences, see BIOLOGY.

life space. In the TOPOLOGICAL PSYCHOLOGY of K. Lewin, the spatial representation of the entire psychological ENVIRONMENT as it exists for an individual person and within which he behaves according to interactions among various needs, values, obstacles, social pressures, aspirations, etc.   I.M.L.H.

life style.

(1) In psychoanalytic theory (see PSYCHOANALYSIS), an ADLERIAN term for a child's method, modified continuously throughout its life, of coping with feelings of inadequacy and of attaining superiority and STATUS.

(2) In popular usage, all the observable characteristics of a person, e.g. his manner of dress, way of speaking, personal appearance, domestic habits, and choice of friends, which serve to indicate his value system and attitudes towards himself and aspects of his ENVIRONMENT. These characteristics serve as a social signal to others, who react accordingly with feelings of trust, admiration, liking, etc., or the opposite. Latterly, most commonly in the

phrase 'life style politics', it has connoted an outlook less concerned with traditional public issues (rights and duties, liberty, EQUALITY, justice, etc.) and more with the quality of life, in respect of environmental concern, the nature of work and so on. Politically it is associated with the emergence of GREEN politics. H.L.;R.P.

life table (or *table of mortality*). A statistical MODEL used in DEMOGRAPHY to illustrate the effect of mortality on a population. A *current life table* shows how many persons would survive to any given birthday out of a given initial number of births (normally 10,000 or 100,000) if the current risks of dying at each age were applied to them. A *cohort life table* (or *generation life table*) traces the survivors of an actual COHORT of birth, when subjected to the mortality rates of different periods of their lives. The model was first used by John Graunt in 1660, though his method of constructing tables was faulty.
E.G.
Bibl: L.I. Dublin, A.J. Lotka, and M. Spiegelman, *Length of Life* (New York, rev. ed., 1949).

light amplifier, see under NON-LINEAR OPTICS.

light pen. A device used with a VISUAL DISPLAY to provide a graphical INPUT to a COMPUTER. It consists of a pen-like holder containing a PHOTO-ELECTRIC CELL and attached to the display by a flexible lead. When this is presented to the face of the display, the computer arranges that a spot of light should appear under it. This spot follows the movement of the light pen, leaving a trail behind it, so that the light pen appears to draw a line of light on the display. C.S.

light shows, see under MEDIA.

lightquantum. A concentration of radiant energy, basic to the quantum conception of the 'free radiation' of light, in contradistinction to the traditional wave theory of light propagation. QUANTUM THEORY proposes that light is emitted by a finite number of lightquanta. Such a view of the behaviour of light gained support from J.J. Thomson's investigation of X-ray IONIZA-

TION, but it took decisive shape in Einstein's perception that under certain conditions light acted in ways thermodynamically equivalent to the behaviour of a molecular gas. The idea of lightquantum initially met considerable resistance from most physicists, however, for whom it failed to explain DIFFRACTION and interference so well as the traditional wave theory. It received powerful support in the 1920s, however, through the experimental work of Arthur Compton and Peter Debye, and it was to prove highly influential in the development of later WAVE MECHANICS, at the hands of Heisenberg and Schrödinger. R.P.
Bibl: W. Wilson, *A Hundred Years of Physics* (London, 1950).

limen, see THRESHOLD.

liminality, see under RITES DE PASSAGE.

limit. A fundamental CONCEPT of MATHEMATICS. We give three examples of its use.
(1) Successive approximation to π may be made by calculating the perimeter p_n of a regular polygon with n sides inscribed in a circle of unit diameter. As n tends to infinity p_n tends to the limit π (see CONVERGENCE).
(2) The velocity of a body falling freely through the air tends to (but never actually reaches) a limit called the terminal velocity.
(3) A train travelling at a mile a minute tends to the first milestone as a limit as the second hand of a watch approaches the first minute, and reaches it at that time.
R.G.

limited war. WAR with limited aims. It can be contrasted with *total war*, which is aimed at the complete destruction of the enemy. The FALKLANDS WAR (1982) was an archetypal case: Argentina and Britain limited themselves to fighting for control of the islands, and refrained from attacks on each other's homeland; prisoners of war were humanely treated and speedily repatriated; and there were no deliberate attacks on the civilian population. Some limited wars have been characterized by particularly ruthless fanaticism, but even these have remained non-nuclear, have avoided a direct clash of arms between the superpowers, and have been limited in geographical extent. Some limited wars continue to defy international efforts at peaceful resolution, and carry ever-increasing risks of escalation.   P.W.

limits to growth. A concept popularized by the *Club of Rome*, an international group of philanthropic businessmen, scientists, and educationists who since 1968 have been intent on alerting the world to the looming crisis posed by rapid growth in many areas — population, industrial TECHNOLOGY, energy use, consumption of natural resources. Although stressing the interdependence of social and technical factors, the group has become particularly associated with the stress on the *physical* limits to growth. Sophisticated COMPUTER-based calculations carried out for the Club of Rome suggest that on current and projected rates of population and ECONOMIC GROWTH, the world's natural resources will be badly depleted by the early part of the next century. They also point to environmental destruction on a massive scale, together with intensifying international conflict as states struggle to increase their share of the world's diminishing resources.

A later contribution to the debate, associated especially with the economist Fred Hirsch, has stressed the *social* limits to growth. Beyond a certain level of economic growth, Hirsch argued, competition for scarce material goods is replaced or reinforced by competition for even scarcer 'positional' goods, such as clean air, open space, personal privacy, and satisfying work. Hirsch predicted an intensifying and, in the nature of things, self-defeating struggle between individuals and groups for such 'positional' goods. Only the development of a new social ethic, he thought, backed by public intervention and regulation, could prevent an AUTHORITARIAN, Hobbesian, resolution of the predicament.   K.K.

Bibl: D.H. Meadows *et al.*, *The Limits to Growth* (London, 1972); F. Hirsch, *Social Limits to Growth* (London, 1977).

limnology. The science which deals with the interrelationships between the BI-OLOGY, CHEMISTRY, and PHYSICS of inland water, including lakes, rivers, and marshes. The word derives from the Greek *limnē* (marshy lake), and some naturalists with a classical education prefer the term to be restricted to studies of muddy waters and bogs rather than clear lakes and rivers. Generally, however, it is synonymous with *hydrobiology* or *freshwater biology*.   K.M.

Bibl: T.T. Macan and E.B. Worthington, *Life in Lakes and Rivers* (London, 1951).

line and staff, see under MANAGEMENT STUDIES.

lineage. Line of DESCENT traced from a common ancestor. If the line is traced exclusively through the male, it is called PATRILINEAL; if traced exclusively through females, MATRILINEAL. A lineage may function as a group to which individuals are recruited on the basis of descent. Lineage and descent group are often used interchangeably as terms by anthropologists. Lineage may, however, be used to describe the total number of groups which may be traced from a single ancestor, but through the process of SEGMENTATION these groups may exist on the ground as separate units.

The term *segmentary lineage systems* was developed to describe the process of *fission* and *fusion*. For example in a patrilineal society, a brother may establish a new lineage segment by moving out from his elder brother's compound with his wives and children (fission). However, in the context of a FEUD, the two segments headed by sons of the same father would fuse to form a single unit (fusion).

The model of segmentary lineage systems was developed by anthropologists working in Africa (particularly by Evans-Pritchard and Meyer Fortes in *African Political Systems*, 1940) to understand political relations in ACEPHALOUS societies, that is those without centralized or state organization. The Nuer were a classic example. The notion of segmentary lineage systems has been criticized as a model developed by observers which does not correspond to ethnographic (see ETHNOGRAPHY) reality. It also does not represent a *folk model*, that is the model held by the actors of their own society. A.G.

Bibl: L. Holy and M. Stuchlik, *Actions, Norms and Representations* (Cambridge, 1983); A. Kuper, 'Lineage Theory: a critical retrospect', *Annual Review of Anthropology II*, 1982.

linear. Both in MATHEMATICS and in the real world the simplest non-trivial RELATION between two quantities x and y is that of proportionality. This is expressed by EQUATION (1): $y = cx$, where c is a constant. The GRAPH of y versus x is a straight line, and the relation is said to be *linear*. Even when the actual relation is less simple, equation (1) may give a serviceable approximation provided x and y are not too large. The best approximation is obtained by taking c to be the value of the DERIVATIVE of y at $x = 0$; if values of x and y are experimental data, c may be estimated statistically (see CORRELATION).

Generalizations of this notion permeate mathematics and theoretical PHYSICS. If y be considered as a FUNCTION of x, say $y = f(x)$, then a consequence of (1) is that f satisfies (2): $f(ax + bx') = af(x) + bf(x')$. This characterization of f can be applied when x and y are non-numerical. In particular if x and y are VECTORS and f satisfies (2) then f is called a *linear mapping*; it can be represented by a MATRIX. If x and y are themselves functions then f is called a *linear operator*. A *linear equation* in the unknowns $x_1, x_2,..., x_n$ has the form $a_1x_1 + a_2x_2 + a_nx_n = b$; the left-hand side is a *linear function* of (the vector whose components are) $x_1,..., x_n$. A linear TRANSFORMATION of coordinates is one in which the old coordinates are linear functions of the new coordinates and vice versa. R.G.

Linear A and B. Name given to two scripts used in Crete and Greece in the Bronze Age. Both are syllabic. They were first recognized on Crete by Sir Arthur Evans who proposed the name to distinguish them from the earlier hieroglyphic script. Linear B was deciphered in 1952 by Michael Ventris who showed the language used to be an early form of Greek. The subject-matter of the tablets so far translated is restricted to inventories. Linear A has not yet been deciphered. B.C.

Bibl: J. Chadwick, *The Decipherment of Linear B* (London, 1958; New York, 1963).

linear accelerator. A type of ACCELERATOR for IONS, which travel along a straight line down the common axis of hollow cylindrical ELECTRODES. The acceleration is produced in the gaps between adjacent electrodes by means of oscillating voltages. See also RADIOTHERAPY. M.V.B.

linear electric motor. An electric motor in which the systems of primary and secondary conductors are arranged in a straight line rather than around the surface of a cylinder, as in conventional rotary motors. All types of electric motor can be treated in this way but the most commonly used are the induction and synchronous types. In one form of linear INDUCTION MOTOR the secondary conductor is of liquid metal e.g. sodium and/or potassium where the liquid is used to carry heat from a NUCLEAR REACTOR. Applications of linear motors include vehicle propulsion, travelling crane, sliding door and actuator operation, baggage handling, metal sorting and conveyor belt drives. E.R.L.

Bibl: E.R. Laithwaite, *Propulsion without Wheels* (New York, 1968; 2nd ed., London, 1970).

linear planning. A system of structuring urban or large architectural forms about a line, usually a route of movement, with short subsidiary routes coming off this line at right angles. The principle stems from the work of the Spanish town-planner Arturo Soria y Mata, and has since been applied in a number of instances, though never on the scale of Soria's vision of a linear city from St Petersburg to Cadiz. M.BR.

Bibl: F. Choay, *The Modern City: Planning in the 19th Century* (London and New York, 1969).

linear programming. A technique of OPTIMIZATION THEORY developed during World War II. Many optimization problems can be put into a form in which the *objective function* and all the constraints are linear, and all the variables are nonnegative. Such problems are *linear programs*; G.B. Dantzig's *simplex method*, developed in the 1940s, provides an efficient method of solving them. R.SI.

linguistic philosophy. A form of ANALYTIC PHILOSOPHY, the historical successor to LOGICAL ATOMISM and LOGICAL POSITIVISM, first practised by G.E. Moore in a methodically unselfconscious way and developed as an explicit philosophical method by Wittgenstein from about 1930 and, later, by Gilbert Ryle and J.L. Austin. Like logical positivism, it is hostile to METAPHYSICS, but for a different reason: for the linguistic philosopher, the hallmark of a metaphysical PROPOSITION is its incompatibility with the COMMON SENSE view of the world, and he conceives his task to be that of unveiling the mistaken assumptions about the actual use of language on which the persuasiveness of metaphysical argumentation depends. Philosophical problems, on this view, require not solution but dissolution. Wittgenstein's style of linguistic philosophy has been reasonably described as 'therapeutic', for his concern with the rules of ordinary language extended only so far as was needed to dispel philosophical puzzlement. The Oxford philosophers of ordinary language approached it more systematically. Linguistic philosophers are generally suspicious of formal LOGIC, at least in the role of ANALYTIC instrument in which it was cast by their positivist predecessors. Sometimes the phrase 'linguistic philosophy' is applied to all varieties of analytic philosophy, but the narrower application described above is more usual among philosophers. A.Q.

Bibl: C.W.K. Mundle, *A Critique of Linguistic Philosophy* (Oxford, 1970).

linguistics. The scientific study of language. As an academic discipline, the development of this subject has been recent and rapid, having become particularly widely known and taught in the 1960s. This reflects partly an increased popular and specialist interest in the study of language and communication in relation to human beliefs and behaviour (e.g. in THEOLOGY, PHILOSOPHY, INFORMATION THEORY, literary criticism), and the realization of the need for a separate discipline to deal adequately with the range and complexity of linguistic phenomena; partly the impact of the subject's own internal development at this time, arising largely out of the work of Chomsky (see CHOMSKYAN) and his associates, whose more sophisticated analytic techniques and more powerful theoretical claims gave linguistics an unprecedented scope and applicability.

Different branches may be distinguished according to the linguist's focus and range of interest. A major distinction, introduced by Ferdinand de Saussure (see SAUSSURIAN), is between *diachronic* and *synchronic* linguistics, the former referring to the study of language change (also called *historical* linguistics), the latter to the study of the state of language at any given point in time. In so far as the subject attempts to establish general principles for the study of all languages, and to determine the characteristics of human language as a phenomenon, it may be called *general* linguistics. When it concentrates on establishing the facts of a particular language system, it is called *descriptive* linguistics. When its purpose is to focus on the differences between languages, especially in a language-teaching context, it is called *contrastive* linguistics. When its purpose is primarily to identify the common characteristics of different languages or language families, the subject goes under the heading of *comparative* (or *typological*) linguistics. (See also AGGLUTINATING; INFLECTING; ISOLATING; POLYSYNTHETIC LANGUAGE.)

When the emphasis in linguistics is wholly or largely historical, the subject is traditionally referred to as *comparative philology* (or simply *philology*), though in many parts of the world 'philologists' and 'historical linguists' are people with very different backgrounds and temperaments. The term *structural* linguistics is widely used, sometimes in an extremely specific sense, referring to the particular approaches to SYNTAX and PHONOLOGY current in the 1940s and 1950s, with their emphasis on providing DISCOVERY PROCEDURES for the analysis of a language's surface structure (see DEEP STRUCTURE); sometimes in a more general sense, referring to *any* system of linguistic analysis that attempts to establish explicit systems of relations between linguistic units in surface structure. When the emphasis in

481

language study is on the classification of structures and units, without reference to such notions as deep structure, some linguists, particularly within GENERATIVE GRAMMAR, talk pejoratively of *taxonomic* linguistics.

The overlapping interests of linguistics and other disciplines has led to the setting up of new branches of the subject, such as ANTHROPOLOGICAL LINGUISTICS, BIOLINGUISTICS, COMPUTATIONAL LINGUISTICS, ETHNOLINGUISTICS, MATHEMATICAL LINGUISTICS, NEUROLINGUISTICS, PSYCHOLINGUISTICS, SOCIOLINGUISTICS. When the subject's findings, methods, or theoretical principles are applied to the study of problems from other areas of experience, one talks of *applied* linguistics; but this term is often restricted to the study of the theory and methodology of foreign-language teaching.　　　　　　　　　　　　D.C.

Bibl: J. Lyons, *Introduction to Theoretical Linguistics* (London, 1968); G.C. Lepschy, *A Survey of Structural Linguistics* (Oxford, 1982); D. Crystal, *Linguistics* (Harmondsworth and Baltimore, 1985); R.H. Robins, *General Linguistics* (London, 1980).

linkage.
(1) In GENETICS, see GENETIC LINKAGE.
(2) In SYSTEMS ANALYSIS, any recurrent sequence of behaviour which originates in one system and produces a reaction in another.　　　　　　　　　　　A.L.C.B.

linkage politics. A method for the analysis of international relations, based on the notion of LINKAGE (2) — in this case the interaction between international and domestic policies. Three major types of linkage politics are distinguished: (1) the *penetrative*, e.g. 'the penetration' of Western Germany and Japan by the U.S.A. after World War II; (2) the *reactive*, e.g. an increase in the defence budget of one country in reaction to increased armament in another country which is felt to be unfriendly; (3) the *emulative*, e.g. the spread of SOCIAL WELFARE measures in Western countries, or of the demand for independence in colonial countries, as a result of seeing and emulating what their neighbours are doing. It is claimed that this method of analysis has the advantage of neither denying nor exaggerating the relevance of national boundaries. A.L.C.B.

Bibl: J.N. Rosenau (ed.), *Linkage Politics* (New York, 1969).

liquid crystals. The change of state between solid and liquid entails the releasing of the BONDS between MOLECULES which restrict their motion to small oscillations only, so that in the liquid state they are free to move randomly within the liquid. In a crystal the molecules are arranged in rows which in turn are arranged in layers. At the boundary between liquid and solid, for example at such a temperature that the crystal is just a solid, a very small temperature change causes the layers to slide over each other without altering the arrangement of the rows. A further slight temperature increase causes the rows to slide relative to each other, still maintaining the order within a row. Finally the rows themselves break up and the whole is now liquid.

During the intermediate stages the substance is neither liquid nor solid, exhibiting properties of both states, and is known as a liquid crystal. The same result can be obtained by applying an electrical voltage across the crystals, and where the changes of state are accompanied by changes in colour, the chemicals are used for such applications as digital displays on measuring instruments, pocket calculators, etc.　　　　　　　　　　　E.R.L.

liquidity. In ECONOMICS, the possession of or the ability to realize quickly adequate supplies of MONEY, relative to commitments. An asset is regarded as liquid when it can be used as money or can be changed into money at short notice and at a predictable price. An economy, or part of it, is liquid if it has sufficient level of liquid assets (see INTERNATIONAL LIQUIDITY).　　　　　　　　　　　J.P.

Bibl: D. Begg *et al., Economics* (London, 1984).

literariness. The central concept of the Russian FORMALISTS. Roman Jakobson, one of the founder members of the school, wrote in 1919: 'The real field of literary science is not literature but *literariness*; in other words, that which makes a specific work literary'. Literariness is closely connected with the distinguishing quality of DEFAMILIARIZATION.   R.PO.

Bibl: T. Bennett, *Formalism and Marxism* (London, 1979).

lithosphere. Prior to the theory of PLATE TECTONICS the terms lithosphere and *crust* were used synonymously for the outermost rock shell of the earth which is succeeded inwards by the mantle (see ASTHENOSPHERE). The term lithosphere is now used within the framework of plate tectonic theory for the relatively rigid outer zone of the earth, some 100 km thick, which includes the rock shell and part of the upper mantle. Thus only the term 'crust' is used for the rock shell. The boundary between the crust and the mantle is defined by an important seismological discontinuity, the *Mohorovicic discontinuity* (*Moho* for short).   J.L.M.L.

Little Review. An American literary magazine, founded in Chicago by Margaret Anderson in 1914 as a rival to Harriet Monroe's POETRY (CHICAGO). It began by printing many early American radical poets and writers and importing new European ideas; after Ezra Pound took over the foreign editorship, it acquired Joyce's *Ulysses* as well as verse and prose by Eliot, Wyndham Lewis, Hart Crane, and others. After a shift to New York it moved, in 1922, to Paris and took in DADA and SURREALISM, and various French and American expatriate writers. It ended in 1929.   M.S.BR.

Bibl: M. Anderson, *My Thirty Years' War* (London and New York, 1930).

Liturgical Movement. The movement to restore to the laity an active and intelligent part in the 'liturgy' (Greek *leitourgia*, people's work) or public worship of God by the Church, specially in Holy Communion. Originating in the French monastery of Solesmes under Abbot Guéranger (1805-75), this movement received the most authoritative expression and blessing in the 'Constitution of the Sacred Liturgy' of VATICAN COUNCIL II (1963), and has been the most conspicuously successful part of the AGGIORNAMENTO in the Roman CATHOLIC Church. It has also influenced other Churches, particularly ANGLICANISM.   D.L.E.

Bibl: G.E.A. Dix, *The Shape of the Liturgy* (London, 2nd ed., 1945); C. Jones et al., *The Study of Liturgy* (London, 1978).

Liverpool Poets. A group of writers from that city who coalesced in the early 1960s as a product of the Anglo-American JAZZ-POETRY movement and the local POP music wave which threw up the BEATLES. Strongly impregnated with local references, yet rooted in the wider modern movement, the work of Adrian Henri, Roger McGough, and Brian Patten was designed mainly for public performance, with or without music, and appealed to a largely pop audience. It was brought to the critics' somewhat disdainful attention by Edward Lucie-Smith's anthology *The Liverpool Scene* (London, 1967) and by Penguin Modern Poets no. 10, *The Mersey Sound* (Harmondsworth, 1967).   J.W.

Living Newspaper. A form of didactic political drama which uses journalistic techniques to present an account of a contemporary issue, usually in a satirical or agitational context. The Living Newspaper was developed as a form of AGIT-PROP drama by the Red Army during the Russian Revolution to reach a mass and largely illiterate audience (cf. the 'factory-wall newspaper'); in the U.S.A. the Federal Theater Project (see WPA) established a Living Newspaper unit in 1935; in England, the UNITY THEATRE presented the first of a number of Living Newspaper productions in 1938. See also DOCUMENTARY.   M.A.

Bibl: J. O'Connor and L. Brown (eds.), *The Federal Theater Project* (London, 1980).

Living Theater. A radical AVANT-GARDE troupe founded by Julian Beck and his wife, Judith Malina, in New York in 1947 and remaining in more or less nomadic but continuous existence until Beck's death in 1985. Beginning with poetic drama (Brecht, Eliot, Lorca) the group moved into improvisational REALISM with work like Kenneth Brown's *The Brig* (1965), set in a U.S. Marines detention cell. The Becks later moved the company to Europe where its members lived in communal poverty and became avowedly ANARCHIST.

483

The group's aim was 'to increase conscious awareness, to stress the sacredness of life, to break down the walls'. The calculated AGGRESSION and audience-harassment of shows like *Paradise Now* (1968) suggested that barriers were being erected rather than broken down, although later pieces like *Prometheus* (1978) aimed at participation rather than confrontation with audiences; but they never wavered in their rejection of AUTHORITARIANISM. Living Theater productions were invariably exciting experiences; but the break-up of the group surprised no one.   M.BI.

Bibl: T. Shank, *American Alternative Theatre* (London, 1982).

loader, see under ASSEMBLER.

lobotomy, see LEUCOTOMY.

local history. This includes the history of a village, a town, a country, or even a province and can involve the study of the landscape as well as the study of documentary evidence. Long the preserve of amateurs and antiquarians, local history has been invaded in the last generation by problem-oriented professional historians for whom the regional monograph is the obvious means of testing generalizations. This new local history flourishes most in France. In England there is a group of local historians associated with the University of Leicester and concerned in particular with AGRARIAN HISTORY.   P.B.

Bibl: W.G. Hoskins, *Local History in England* (Harlow, 3rd ed., 1984).

location. Geographical term used in two senses: (1) the absolute position of a place on the earth's surface, stated usually by reference to a coordinate reference system (e.g. latitude and longitude); (2) the relative location of a place in relation to other places. Studies of the changing impact of relative location on human activity have given rise to a theoretical branch of human GEOGRAPHY termed LOCATIONAL ANALYSIS.   P.H.

locational analysis. In GEOGRAPHY, term for the study of the location of economic activity dealing with the broad questions 'What is where, and why there?' The

where may be defined in broad *macrogeographic* terms as REGIONS or in narrower *microgeographic* terms as *sites*. It is usually concerned with the relative spatial qualities of proximity, CONCENTRATION, and dispersion, and with optimization of spatial arrangements. Major branches of analysis are concerned with the location of primary (agricultural) activities, secondary (industrial) activities, and tertiary (service) activities.   P.H.

Bibl: P. Haggett *et al., Locational Analysis in Human Geography* (London, 1977).

Lockheed scandal. The Lockheed scandal was Japan's biggest corruption scandal of recent times, involving Kakuei Tanaka (Prime Minister, 1972-4) and a number of other leading politicians and some business executives as well as an unsavoury ultra-rightist called Yoshio Kodama. The scandal broke in February 1976, during the prime ministership of Takeo Miki, as a result of congressional testimony in Washington by a leading executive of the Lockheed Corporation. Allegations were made that Tanaka had received large sums of money several years previously from Lockheed for the promotion of its Tristar airbuses in Japan. The affair convulsed the political world in Japan throughout 1976. Miki was unwilling to authorize a cover-up, top executives of the Marubeni Corporation and of All Nippon Airways were arrested, and in July Tanaka himself was briefly taken into custody and charged with violations of the Foreign Exchange and Trade Control Law. After a lengthy trial involving Tanaka and several other defendants, in October 1983 Tanaka was sentenced to 4 years imprisonment and a fine of Y500,000,000, though he was freed pending appeal. Although forced to resign from the LIBERAL DEMOCRATIC PARTY in 1976 Tanaka continued to exercise great influence within the party as leader of the Tanaka faction, and was in effect 'king-maker' to three successive prime ministers, Ōhira, Suzuki and Nakasone. His influence declined, however, after he suffered a stroke early in 1985. Despite many predictions in the late 1970s, the party survived the scandal and has gone from strength to strength.   J.A.A.S.

locus (plural *loci*). Position on a CHROMO-SOME occupied by one of a set of allelomorphic (see ALLELE) GENES. J.M.S.

logarithmic scale, see under SCALING.

logic.
(1) The study of INFERENCE. Logic does not simply describe the kinds or patterns of inference that are actually used; it is concerned with the rules of *valid* inference (see VALIDITY), by which those inferences whose premises really entail their conclusions (see ENTAILMENT) may be distinguished from those whose premises do not. Logicians, however, are not concerned with particular entailments except as examples, even though for each particular entailment ('This is red' entails 'This is coloured') there is a corresponding rule of valid inference (from 'This is red' infer 'This is coloured'), which can be applied on an indefinitely large number of occasions.

In the first place logic is *formal*. There are abstract patterns of inference of which an indefinite number of particular inferences, all of the same logical form, are instances (e.g., from 'No *A* is *B*' infer 'No *B* is *A*'). Logic may be said to have begun with the formulation of individual rules of this kind. Secondly, logic aims to be *systematic*. The first great logical systematizer was Aristotle, whose theory of the SYLLOGISM set out in a reasonably systematic (although not yet axiomatic — see AXIOMATICS) way all the rules for valid inference from two premises. The thoroughness of Aristotle's achievement obstructed the further development of the discipline, and its systematic elaboration caused it to be regarded as finally authoritative for more than 2,000 years and overshadowed logical discoveries in fields outside the range of his treatment. In the mid 19th century, however, Boole and De Morgan set out in mathematical form (see MATHEMATICAL LOGIC) an ALGEBRA of CLASSES closely related to Aristotle's logic of predicative terms. De Morgan also started the logical study of *relational predicates*, traditional logic having restricted itself to *attributive predicates*; an attributive predicate is a quality, a relational predicate is a relation, or, in some people's usage, the word for a quality (e.g.

an adjective) and the word for a RELATION (e.g. a transitive verb or a preposition) respectively. The major achievement of the modern period has been the mathematically rigorous system of Frege. The structurally similar, but less rigorous, system set out by Whitehead and Russell in *Principia Mathematica* (1910 onwards) had the advantage of a simple notation, and the really fertile period in modern logic may be dated from its publication. The main ingredients of logic, as currently conceived, are (1) the logic of compound PROPOSITION or PROPOSITIONAL CALCULUS or TRUTH-FUNCTION theory and (2) the logic of predicates or PREDICATE CALCULUS or QUANTIFICATION theory. The logic of classes of SET THEORY is now generally viewed as the fundamental discipline of mathematics rather than as a part of logic proper. See also MODAL LOGIC.
A.Q.

Bibl: W.C. and M. Kneale, *The Development of Logic* (Oxford, 1962); S.F. Barker, *The Elements of Logic* (London and New York, 1965); I.M. Copi, *Introduction to Logic* (London and New York, 6th ed., 1982).

(2) In COMPUTERS, the digital circuits, built up largely from GATES, which form the CPU and parts of other units. Their characteristic feature is that the electrical state of each part of the circuit is stable only at a limited number of values, i.e. the output of such a circuit is the 'logical' consequence of the various INPUTS according to the rules of, say, BOOLEAN ALGEBRA. This number is most commonly two, and the logic is then BINARY. There is a continuing tendency for logic circuits to become smaller and faster, and to use less power. See also INTEGRATED CIRCUIT.
C.S.

logical atomism. A theory about the nature of the facts that constitute reality, devised by Russell (in *Philosophy of Logical Atomism,* 1918) and Wittgenstein (in *Tractatus Logico-Philosophicus,* 1922) and associated with the technique of philosophical ANALYSIS. That technique shows that some PROPOSITIONS can be analysed into others and so may be seen as theoretically dispensable abbreviations for them. The propositions in which analysis terminates reveal the actual structure of the facts which, if they obtain, make the propositions true. Wittgenstein, when a logical atomist, held that 'all propositions are TRUTH-FUNCTIONS of elementary propositions', in other words that *atomic* propositions, which are singular, affirmative, and categorical and consist of logically proper names of simple entities together with an attributive or relational predicate, directly picture their verifying facts, while *non-atomic* propositions conceal them. Analysis, then, reveals the structure of the world by exhibiting every kind of true or significant proposition as being an atomic proposition, or some assemblage of atomic propositions, in which only unanalysable words for simple individuals and properties occur. Russell's logical atomism was less thoroughgoing than Wittgenstein's, since he doubted the reducibility (see REDUCTION) to strictly atomic form of negative and universal propositions and also of apparently INTENSIONAL propositions about beliefs. The LOGICAL POSITIVISTS accepted the idea of a terminal class of propositions, constituting the part of language that is in direct contact with the world (calling them *protocol* or *basic*, rather than atomic, propositions) but saw them as direct, non-inferential reports of experience, rather than as pictures of fact. A.Q.

Bibl: D.F. Pears, *Bertrand Russell and the British Tradition in Philosophy* (London and New York, 1967).

logical calculus. A systematic deductive presentation of a body of logical laws (see LOGIC) or truths of a broadly mathematical form. An ideally systematic form of presentation is that of an AXIOMATIC system. The chief logical calculi are the PROPOSITIONAL CALCULUS and the PREDICATE CALCULUS. Such calculi can be presented in non-axiomatic ways: with equal rigour and minimization of unproved assumptions by the technique of natural deduction (see DEMONSTRATION), or in a relatively informal way without the greatest possible economy of assumptions. A.Q.

logical construction, see under REDUCTION.

logical empiricism. The philosophical school which, mainly in the U.S.A., immediately succeeded LOGICAL POSITIVISM as a result of the migration to that country, after Hitler came to power, of several leading members of the VIENNA CIRCLE, in particular Carnap. The change of name had a more than merely geographical point; it also signified some change of doctrine, most notably a remission of the anti-METAPHYSICAL fervour of the original logical positivists and a lessness polemical concentration on the task of articulating or reconstructing in a logically explicit and rigorous form the CONCEPTS and theories of various forms of discourse, above all MATHEMATICS and NATURAL SCIENCE.
A.Q.

Bibl: J. Jøergensen, *The Development of Logical Empiricism* (Chicago, 1951).

logical form, see under PROPOSITION, TYPES OF.

logical positivism. A body of philosophical doctrine developed from the later 1920s by the VIENNA CIRCLE under the leadership of Schlick and Carnap. It asserted the meaninglessness of METAPHYSICS, which it held to consist of all PROPOSITIONS that are neither verifiable (see VERIFICATION) by empirical observation nor demonstrable as ANALYTIC, and conceived PHILOSOPHY as consisting purely of ANALYSIS, conducted with the assistance of formal LOGIC with a view to the logical reconstruction of mathematical and scientific discourse. Most logical positivists regarded religious and moral utterances as metaphysical and thus as meaningless. There was disagreement within the school (1) as to whether the basic propositions in which philosophical analysis terminates (see LOGICAL ATOMISM) refer to immediate experience (the majority view) or to material objects (see PHYSICALISM); (2) as to whether probability should be interpreted in terms of CONFIRMATION or frequency or both; and (3) as to whether TRUTH is a relation of correspondence between propositions and extra-linguistic reality or one of coherence between propositions. Logical positivism dissolved as a school at the end of the 1930s, but was continued in the U.S.A. in the slightly

different form of LOGICAL EMPIRICISM.
A.Q.

Bibl: V. Kraft, *The Vienna Circle* (New York, 1953).

logical realism, see under REALISM.

logical syntax (or *syntactics*). The discussion of the logical properties and significance of linguistic expressions in terms that refer only to the expressions themselves and not to their relations to extralinguistic reality. Exaggerated claims on its behalf by Carnap were abandoned after the successful development of logical SEMANTICS, primarily by Tarski, in the mid 1930s.
A.Q.

Bibl: R. Carnap, *The Logical Syntax of Language* (London and New York, 1937).

logical types, theory of. A theory, devised be Bertrand Russell, to avoid the logical PARADOXES or ANTINOMIES which arise from *self-reference*. (For example, the statement 'This statement is false', if taken to refer to itself, is false if true and true if false. Likewise the class of classes that are not members of themselves is a member of itself if it is not and is not if it is.) The theory of types lays down that a class must always be of a higher type than its members and thus that to say of a class that it either is or is not one of its own members is meaningless. The conclusion that grammatically well-formed sentences may be neither true nor false but meaningless, that there are logical as well as grammatical restrictions on the possibilities of significant combination of words, has been widely influential. It lent force to the attack of the LOGICAL POSITIVISTS, with the VERIFICATION principle, on METAPHYSICS, and it has inspired broader, informal investigations into the possibilities of significant combination of words, investigations that have issued in modern theories of CATEGORIES.
A.Q.

logicism. The school of MATHEMATICS which maintains that the fundamental CONCEPTS of mathematics can be defined in terms of the concepts, and its fundamental laws can be deducted from the laws, of LOGIC. It was the principal aim of both Frege and of Whitehead and Russell

in *Principia Mathematica* to establish this point. The crucial phase of the project is the definition of NUMBER in terms of the logical notion of class. A natural number, for logicism, is the class of all classes which are 'similar' in the sense of being equinumerous. The number 2 is the class of all pairs and the statement 'There are two chairs in this room' means the same as 'The class of chairs-in-this-room is a member of the class of pairs'. GÖDEL'S THEOREM that in any system containing arithmetic there must be truths that cannot be proved within the system undermined the project of deriving all of pure mathematics from logic.
A.Q.

logistics. All the activities and methods connected with supply of armed forces, including storage, transport, and distribution of ammunition, petrol, food, and so on. The term is of American origin and came into general use during and after World War II by reason of the dominant position of the U.S.A. in both the wartime and post-war alliances. The word is now acquiring a more general use to connote the supply organization of non-military field operations such as mountaineering expeditions or famine relief organizations.
A.F.B.

logograms, see under CONCRETE POETRY.

Lolita syndrome. A SYNDROME named after Vladimir Nabokov's *Lolita* (1955), whose theme is the unreasoning and self-destructive passion of a middle-aged man for a teen-age 'nymphet'. The condition is anticipated, in a psychologically more convincing manner, in the Chilean Vicente Huidobro's untranslated *Satyr, o El Poder de las palabras* (1939). M.S.-S.

Lomé Conventions. A series of trade agreements between the EEC and developing countries from Africa, the Caribbean and the Pacific. These agreements were implemented in 1975, 1980 and 1985. They were thought of as important movements towards a NEW INTERNATIONAL ECONOMIC ORDER. However, the actual achievements of these agreements have not been substantial. The conventions allow freer access to the EEC for many of the products of the developing countries,

487

mechanisms for stabilizing foreign exchange earnings from certain commodities and minerals and a channel for EEC aid.

J.P.

Bibl: C. Stevens, *The EEC and the Third World* (London, 1981).

London Group. An association of British artists, founded in November 1913, incorporating the CAMDEN TOWN GROUP and certain smaller groups. Its first president was Harold Gilman; Sickert was a prime influence; the original members included Wyndham Lewis and other leading VORTICISTS. They tended to admire the POST-IMPRESSIONISTS, notably Gauguin, van Gogh, and Cézanne, but in later years their sympathies became more diverse and in many cases more conservative. The group is still extant.

P.C.

Long March. The epic year-long 6,000 mile journey made by Chinese COMMUNIST forces after the KUOMINTANG'S fifth encirclement campaign dislodged them from their power base in Kiangxi province. During the course of the journey, Mao Zedong established himself as leader of the party by becoming chairman of the ruling Revolutionary Military Council at the Zunyi Conference, January 1935. Under constant attack from NATIONALIST forces, the depleted communist forces arrived in northern Shaanxi province in October 1935. However, the success of the Long March in merely surviving ensured the communists of a base from which to expand later. Swelled by the arrival of groups from other areas, a new Soviet base area was set up in Yan'an, which became the centre for anti-KMT GUERRILLA activities, and the model for post-1949 emulation.

S.B.

Bibl: H. Salisbury, *The Long March* (London, 1985).

long-range planning, see CORPORATE STRATEGY.

longitudinal. In PSYCHOMETRICS, adjective applied to a method or type of investigation in which selected variables are studied over time in the same sample of subjects, in contrast to *cross-sectional* methods, where similar variables are studied at different ages, but on different subjects at each age.

H.L.

Look, The, see THE LOOK.

lookalike (of COMPUTERS). A computer designed by one manufacturer so as to imitate the product of another, in particular by successfully running PROGRAMS written for the other. The imitated machine, whether a PERSONAL COMPUTER or a much larger machine, is usually an IBM product.

J.E.S.

loop gain. In CONTROL ENGINEERING, the degree of magnification of an input signal around a loop which is normally closed but which has been opened beyond the last element in order to measure such magnification.

E.R.L.

low dimensional material. A very thin film of material which is only a few atoms thick. The material has effectively only two dimensions and the motion and ENERGY of the ELECTRONS which try to travel across the film is severely restricted. This is particularly important in the case of SEMICONDUCTORS and very thin layers, or multiple layers of different materials, can be made which have electrical and optical properties which are different from those of the bulk materials. Such films are being used in the development of new types of LASERS, high-speed TRANSISTORS and optical detectors (see LANGMUIR-BLODGETT FILMS and SUPERLATTICE).

H.M.R.

LSD, see under DRUGS; HIPPIES.

LSI (large-scale integration), see under INTEGRATED CIRCUIT.

Lubyanka. The headquarters of the Soviet SECRET POLICE, on Dzerzhinsky Square, Moscow, containing the famous prison in which many of the leading 'State criminals' of the Soviet period have been held, and in whose basement they have been executed. It has become synonymous with the whole apparatus of interrogation, confession, and liquidation.

R.C.

luminodynamism, see under KINETIC ART.

Lumpenproletariat. Term coined by Karl Marx for the fluctuating antisocial elements within the poor of big cities from whom no CLASS identification or solidarity could be expected.   D.C.W.

Lutheranism. The Christian tradition begun when Martin Luther (1483-1546) inaugurated PROTESTANTISM. The Lutheran World Federation, mainly German, Scandinavian, and American, was formed in 1947. In these self-governing national or regional Churches some CATHOLIC practices, e.g. leadership by bishops, may be retained, but the dominating feature is the sermon, intended to proclaim God's grace. Luther's experience (much studied by modern scholars) convinced him that no one could become righteous before God through his own efforts; it was necessary to be 'justified' (accounted and then made righteous) by God's grace received through faith. This conviction has been at the heart of German Protestant THEOLOGY, which has thereby been liberated to embark on many intellectual adventures. Although European interest in God has diminished in the 20th century, the Lutheran form of CHRISTIANITY has flourished in the U.S. and Africa. In the 1980s it has about 65 million adherents.
D.L.E.

Bibl: J. Pelikan, *From Luther to Kierkegaard* (St Louis, 1950); E.H. Erikson, *Young Man Luther: a Study in Psychoanalysis and History* (New York, 1958; London, 1959).

Luxembourg Compromise. In 1965 the European Commission announced a 'package deal' linking farm price increases to two further measures designed to increase the powers of the European Commission and European Assembly vis à vis member states. The French government objected to the measures, removed its permanent representative from Brussels and for the next seven months boycotted the Community — the so-called 'empty chair' policy. The conflict centred upon the supranational aspirations of the Commission and the proposed extension of majority voting in the Council of Ministers. The crisis was resolved in 1966 by the Luxembourg Compromise which shifted the institutional balance of power away from the Commission in favour of the Council of Ministers (and by implication, national governments). While the Commission's right to initiate policy was confirmed it was agreed that it should consult more closely with member states' governments in drafting proposals. With regard to majority voting in the Council of Ministers it was agreed that if a member state has very important interests at stake, the Council will endeavour to reach a unanimous decision. In practice, the Luxembourg Compromise enables a single member state to veto a Community policy. This has seriously hampered Community policy-making (see EEC).   S.M.

Bibl: A. Daltrop, *Politics and the European Community* (London, 1984).

lymph. A term improperly used to describe any free fluid contained within or expressible from the TISSUES; more properly the plasma-like fluid contained within lymphatic vessels (or *lymphatics*) which drain all the tissues into the venous system. Lymph, like plasma (see SERUM) with which it is closely in EQUILIBRIUM, is a clotting fluid which is propelled along lymphatic vessels by ordinary bodily movements. The many valves in lymphatics ensure that circulation is one way only, i.e. towards points of entry into the venous system. The characteristic cellular constituent of lymph is the *lymphocyte* which plays an important role in immunology (see IMMUNITY). All lymphatics, and therefore all lymph, pass through regional lymph nodes (in common parlance 'glands') on the way from tissues to blood system. An accumulation of lymph due to blockage of lymphatics or to prolonged inactivity is known as *lymphoedema*, of which elephantiasis is an extreme and highly abnormal example.   P.M.

Lysenkoism. The Soviet version of LAMARCKISM; named after Trofim Lysenko, whose views became dominant in Soviet BIOLOGY, and especially agricultural science, in the mid 1930s. Many adherents of Mendelian (see MENDELISM) GENETICS were dismissed and liquidated at this time, in particular Nikolai Vavilov, Russia's leading biologist. However, Lysenkoism only gained a complete monopoly in 1948, when the Central Committee officially decreed its correctness. Some criticisms of it were permitted during Stalin's last months, but it was reimposed under Khrushchev and it was only in 1964, and particularly after Khrushchev's fall, that it became totally discredited — though a number of Lysenkoist 'scientists' continue to hold research posts.   R.C.

Bibl: Z.A. Medvedev, *The Rise and Fall of T.D. Lysenko* (London and New York, 1969).

lysosomes, see under AUTOLYSIS.

M

Mach number. The speed of a body flying through the atmosphere, divided by the local speed of sound. The Mach number (named after Ernst Mach) is less than 1 for *subsonic* speeds, greater than 1 for *supersonic* speeds, and greater than 5 for *hypersonic* speeds. Conventional aircraft fly subsonically (e.g. Mach 0.9 for the VC 10), but the Anglo-French Concorde flies at Mach 2.1. Considerable ENERGY is required to 'break the sound barrier' at Mach 1, because of the SHOCK WAVE which must be created. See also SONIC BOOM. M.V.B.

Mach's principle. The laws of NEWTONIAN MECHANICS are valid only if events are referred to certain special FRAMES OF REFERENCE. Observations show that these 'inertial frames' are those relative to which the distant matter of the universe is, on the average, not accelerating. In 1872 Mach suggested that the distant matter actually determines the inertial frames, by forces related to GRAVITATION; this principle was later given precise expression by Einstein in his general theory of RELATIVITY.
M.V.B.

machine aesthetic. A theory about the appearance of objects derived from a belief in how machine-made objects should look; the expression probably originated in Theo van Doesburg's statement: 'The new possibilities of the machine have created an aesthetic expressive of our time, that I once [in 1921] called "The Mechanical Aesthetic".' Objects were to look like machines (somewhat as in the paintings of Léger) and to look as if they were made by machines — which was taken to mean being made up from undecorated geometric solids such as the sphere, cube, cylinder, etc., even though this did not necessarily correspond with efficient machine production. See also BAUHAUS; FUNCTIONALISM. M.BR.
Bibl: R. Banham, 'Machine Aesthetic' (*Architectural Review*, April 1955).

machine code, see under ASSEMBLY LANGUAGE.

machine intelligence, see ARTIFICIAL INTELLIGENCE.

machine translation (also called *automatic* or *mechanical translation*). The use of a COMPUTER to facilitate the production of translations between natural languages. The PROGRAM contains a set of rules for analysing the orthography, identifying the vocabulary, and parsing the syntactic structure of both source and target languages, and another set of rules which places these in formal correspondence with each other so as to establish semantic equivalences. The urgent need for rapid translation in science and TECHNOLOGY has been the main motive for work in this area, and there has been limited success; but a great deal of human sub-editing still needs to take place before translations are acceptable, and in the more aesthetic areas of language use little progress has been made. The difficulties are not so much those of INFORMATION STORAGE AND RETRIEVAL as the inadequacy of available syntactic analyses of languages. Future progress is very much dependent on advances in the appropriate branches of theoretical LINGUISTICS. D.C.

machismo. Literally, maleness. The cult of virility in Latin America, especially Mexico, identified with a bull-like masculine aggressiveness, invulnerable and indifferent to the attacks of others, above all intransigent, withdrawn, inner-directed (see OTHER-DIRECTION), AUTHORITARIAN, absolutist; more loosely, a pejorative term applied by its adversaries to the advocacy of an active, military, interventionist U.S. foreign policy (e.g. in VIETNAM). D.C.W.
Bibl: P. Stevens, 'Mexican Machismo: Politics and Value Orientations', in F. Moreno and B. Mitrani (eds.), *Conflict and Violence in Latin American Politics (N.Y., 1971).*

Machtpolitik, see POWER POLITICS.

macrobiotics. The most doctrinaire of the ZEN-influenced food cults. The word itself has an illusory scientific flourish common to much neo-MYSTICISM (see also OCCULT-

ISM; SCIENTOLOGY). First preached by Georges Ohsawa, the message of this harmless fad is that all foods are either *yin* or *yang* or both. 'Yin', the shadow, is the passive, feminine principle of life; 'yang', the sun, is the active, masculine principle. The diet, which is generally abstemious and loosely vegetarian, prescribes an equal balance of 'yin' and 'yang' components, thus ensuring that the body of the consumer is in harmony with the mystical unity of the cosmos (nothing so small as the world). Most foods contain both 'yin' and 'yang', so complicated cutting is necessary to preserve the balance: an onion is 'yin' at the top and 'yang' at the bottom; it therefore has to be cut vertically rather than horizontally. Fish are supposed to be eaten whole (so as to include their 'yang' heads and tails), and the term *whole food*, which is common to many spiritually inclined vegetarian DIETS, is a macrobiotic keyword, indicating the correct, equipoised balance between 'yin' and 'yang'. More loosely, macrobiotics relates to dietary theories of the superior wholesomeness of vegetable food, and conforms to long-standing western traditions of vegetarianism. J.R.

macroeconomics, see under ECONOMICS.

macrolinguistics, see under MICROLINGUISTICS.

macromolecule. A MOLECULE consisting of a large number (hundreds or thousands) of ATOMS. The term is generally reserved for molecules whose atoms are arranged in long chains, e.g. DNA (see NUCLEIC ACID) and related biochemicals connected with life, or the POLYMERS used in the PLASTICS industry. M.V.B.

macroregion, see under REGION.

Maekawa report. Faced by mounting international criticism of Japan's balance of payments surpluses, the NAKASONE Government set up the Advisory Group on Economic Structural Adjustment for International Harmony in October 1985, under the chairmanship of Mr Haruo Maekawa, a former governor of the Bank of Japan. The Group, reporting in April 1986, recommended radical changes in economic management with a view to eliminating the current account surplus in the medium to long term. The Maekawa Group argued for shifting the thrust of ECONOMIC GROWTH away from exports into domestic demand by increasing wages, shortening the working week, reducing taxes and improving the social INFRASTRUCTURE. It also recommended encouragement for foreign INVESTMENT, both by Japan overseas and by foreigners into Japan, radical agricultural adjustment, further promotion of manufactured goods imports into Japan, promotion of EXCHANGE RATE stability at realistic rates, liberalization of financial and capital markets, and a variety of policy changes involving improved policies towards less developed countries (see UNDERDEVELOPMENT). J.A.A.S.

Mafia. The Sicilian word for a clandestine criminal organization so deeply rooted in Sicilian rural society as to amount to a counter-government administering its own law and justice. Established among the Italian immigrant community in the U.S.A., the Mafia became the basis of various organized crime syndicates operating according to the same alternative code as in Sicily, the code of *omerta*, the Italian word for 'connivance'. D.C.W.

Bibl: F.A.J. Ianni and E. Reuss-Ianni, *A Family Business* (London and New York, 1972).

magic. A form of activity in which different elements, physical and verbal, are manipulated in order to bring about certain results. The symbolic or RITUAL component of magic sets it apart from merely technical activity. James Frazer (*The Golden Bough*, 1911) described magic as founded upon a mistaken theory of CAUSATION. He and later writers (for example, Lévy-Bruhl) understood it as an expression of a form of PRIMITIVE mentality. Malinowski interpreted the importance of magic for the Trobriand Islanders as fulfilling an emotional need, the need for certainty and order in natural and social events. Later anthropologists pursued different levels of enquiry: what actually happens in magic (its internal structure), what beliefs underlie its practice (questions of rationality and irrationality), and its place in a particular society. A.G.

Bibl: J. Skorupski, *Symbol and Theory* (Cambridge, 1977); G. Lewis, *Day of Shining Red* (Cambridge, 1980).

magic number. The numbers of NEUTRONS or PROTONS in an atomic (see ATOM) NUCLEUS which is highly stable against RADIOACTIVE decay. The magic numbers are 2, 8, 20, 28, 50, 82, and 126, and the stability arises from the filling of complete shells (see ELECTRON SHELL) of nuclear ENERGY LEVELS, in a similar manner to the chemical stability of the inert gases. See also PERIODIC TABLE. M.V.B.

magic realism. Term coined by Franz Roh in 1924 to describe certain works of the NEUE SACHLICHKEIT artists, particularly their Munich wing. The still, smoothly painted pictures of figures and objects, with their mildly disquieting SURREALISM-and-water impact, are akin to the NEO-CLASSICAL art of certain Italians (e.g. Felice Casorati) in the METAPHYSICAL wake, as well as to that of the Royal Academy. Among its practitioners were the former member of the NEUE KÜNSTLER-VEREINIGUNG Alexander Kanoldt and the subsequent president of the NAZI Kunstkammer Adolf Ziegler. Though the names sound similar, the gay and decorative *Peinture de la Réalité poétique* associated with Maurice Brianchon and others is a very different affair. More recently, the term has been applied to a group of Latin American authors, the best known of whom is Gabriel Garcia Márquez. J.W.

magnetic monopole. A PARTICLE predicted to exist in nature by P. Dirac in 1931. It carries an isolated north (positive) or south (negative) magnetic charge. The existence of such a particle in nature would explain why electric charge comes in discrete fractions of the fundamental ELECTRON charge. It has yet to be detected experimentally although there were claims in 1972 and 1982 that a magnetic monopole had been observed. These observations have not been repeated with the same results and are controversial. GRAND UNIFICATION predicts that the process of grand unification at very high ENERGY must be accompanied by the production of stable magnetic monopoles with a MASS roughly equivalent to the energy at which grand unification occurs. (These are sometimes called Polyakov-t'Hooft monopoles.) This corresponds to a mass of about 10^8 gms and is 10^{16} times the mass of an atomic NUCLEUS. Until 1981 this property was regarded as a major argument against such theories of their existence because too many monopoles would be formed in the first moments of the universe's expansion from the Big Bang (see BIG-BANG HYPOTHESIS). The idea of inflation (see INFLATIONARY UNIVERSE THEORY) suggested by A. Guth in 1981 resolves this problem. The presence of magnetic monopoles in space would have adverse effects upon any cosmic magnetic fields. Such fields would be drained away, using their energies to accelerate monopoles. The existence of magnetic fields in planets, stars and interstellar space is therefore evidence against the existence of a significant population of monopoles in the universe. J.D.B.

Bibl: J. Trefil, *The Moment of Creation* (New York, 1983); R. A. Carrigan and W. P. Trower, 'Superheavy Magnetic Monopoles', *Scientific American*, April 1982.

magnetic reconnexion. In PLASMA PHYSICS and COSMOLOGY, it occurs when two plasmas interact with one another. An electric plasma always has a magnetic field associated with it. In principle such fields avoid one another and this prevents the two plasmas from interacting. It now appears that the magnetic fields of one plasma are able to link up with those of another and this is called reconnexion. This is important because when it occurs it is possible for one plasma to affect the behaviour of another plasma. For example the magnetic field due to the solar wind (from the sun's plasma) can influence the earth's magnetic field. The effect can also be observed in laboratory experiments such as in a TOKOMAK machine. H.M.R.

magnetic resonance. When a system is magnetized, the ENERGY LEVELS associated with the SPINS of its ATOMS and NUCLEI split into a finely-spaced sequence. If an ELECTROMAGNETIC wave of RADIO FREQUENCY is applied, its ENERGY will be strongly absorbed by the system whenever the frequency is such that the wave is in RESONANCE with two energy levels. The pattern of resonances as the frequency varies is a valuable tool giving detailed information about the structure of matter. See also NUCLEAR MAGNETIC RESONANCE.

M.V.B.

magnetic storm. A period of rapid variation of the earth's MAGNETISM, which can upset long-distance radio transmissions and cause compasses to give false readings. Magnetic storms are caused by ELECTRONS and PROTONS emitted by the sun. See also VAN ALLEN BELTS. M.V.B.

magnetic tape. A thin, non-metallic tape (usually of the order of 0.01 m wide), coated on one or on both sides with a very thin layer of ferromagnetic material (see FERROMAGNETISM). When such a tape is moved longitudinally at a fixed speed, very near to an ELECTROMAGNET (known as a *writing-head*), magnetization is induced from place to place along the tape, varying in intensity with the variations in the electric current that is being fed to the electromagnet. When the magnetized tape is subsequently moved again at constant speed, past a second electromagnetic device (known as a *reading-head*), the original sequence of electric currents is reproduced in the coil of the reading-head.

Magnetic tape is capable of very high accuracy of reproduction, and is used extensively for reproducing sounds (as an alternative to the gramophone record; see HI-FI) and for recording visual pictures seen by a television camera so that the tape can later be used to re-create the scenes on a television screen. Portable tape-recorders are now very popular for the enjoyment of music and other programmes that have been recorded on spools of tape specially housed in packages known as *cassettes* which can be inserted into the portable recorder and played back through a TRANSISTOR amplifier. Recent developments include the use of magnetic tape for digital recording.

Magnetic tape is also used extensively in COMPUTING, in both analogue and digital modes, as a form of backing STORE. The capacity is unlimited, but any attempt to use RANDOM ACCESS to this information tends to make the ACCESS TIME inordinately long. The consequent need to use SERIAL ACCESS makes the medium inconvenient for many applications. However, large business enterprises, postal systems, banks, etc. all depend a great deal on the tape storage system. E.R.L.; C.S.

magnetism. The branch of ELECTROMAGNETISM concerned with magnetic materials and their interaction with electric currents. Magnetic FIELDS are produced by moving electric charges, e.g. the current in the windings of an electromagnet. Thus the magnetism of solid matter arises from the orbital motion and SPIN of atomic (see ATOM) ELECTRONS, while the earth's magnetism (*geomagnetism*) is thought to be due to currents in its rotating liquid core. The smallest magnetic entities are spinning ELEMENTARY PARTICLES; these are DIPOLES, and no isolated north or south poles have been found. See also ARCHAEOMAGNETISM. M.V.B.

Bibl: E.W. Lee, *Magnetism* (New York, 1970).

magnetohydrodynamics (MHD). The ELECTRODYNAMICS of free ELECTRONS or IONS in a fluid (e.g. the IONOSPHERE). Motion of charges in the fluid can be produced by magnetic FIELDS, but it is not yet known whether a complete and stable *containment* can be achieved in this way (see PINCH EFFECT). The problem of containment is of tremendous technological importance, because, if the ENERGY of nuclear FUSION is ever to be tamed for peaceful purposes, the reacting substances must be kept together at temperatures so high that walls of any conventional material would vaporize. See also PLASMA PHYSICS.

M.V.B.

magneto-optics. In the 1840s, Michael Faraday discovered that, when placed in a magnetic field, the plane of polarized light rotates. In subsequent experiments, Faraday sought to disturb light magnetically, an endeavour later supported by Lord Kelvin's notion that the magnetic FIELD was a vortex within the aether. Experimentation and theorizing from H.A. Lorentz to J.J. Thomson began to reveal the particulate structure of light emissions, and the crucial role of ELECTRONS. Precise elucidation of magneto-optical phenomena, however, long defied physicists involved in the dilemmas of QUANTUM MECHANICS. The most important breakthrough was made in the 1920s by Wolfgang Pauli, who succeeded in explaining anomalies in the behaviour of electrons in terms of an 'EXCLUSION PRINCIPLE', which drew upon the concept of electron SPIN. Magneto-optics remains an area in which quantum explanations have proved superior to CLASSICAL PHYSICS.

R.P.

Bibl: M. Jammer, *The Conceptual Development of Quantum Mechanics* (New York, 1966).

magnetostriction. A change in the dimensions of a piece of ferromagnetic material (see FERROMAGNETISM) resulting from magnetization by an externally applied FIELD. The effect is greatest in nickel. Some materials expand in the direction of magnetization, others contract. This property is used to make mechanical oscillators that make high frequency acoustic waves capable of producing CAVITATION in objects. See ULTRASONICS. E.R.L.

magnetotaxis, see under TROPISM.

magnetotropism, see under TROPISM.

magnitizdat, see under SAMIZDAT.

Mahayana, see under BUDDHISM.

main store, see under STORE.

mainstream. A critical term coined in the late 1950s to designate a style of JAZZ neither self-consciously conservative, like TRAD, nor commitedly advanced and advancing, like the forms that followed BEBOP. Mainstream players are generally associated with the SWING era, in the middle of jazz's evolution — in fact the French term for the school is 'middle jazz'. By any name, the music exudes a timeless, mature appeal, a relaxed and confident energy. For once, a label performed a valuable service, by returning to public attention a large group of musicians — men like Roy Eldridge, Ben Webster or Jo Jones — who were still at the height of their powers, but who did not fit into the easy dichotomy of ancients v. moderns.

Indeed, today it is to such players that musicians are turning for insight into the real meaning of jazz tradition. GE.S.

maisons de la culture, see under ARTS CENTRE; CENTRES DRAMATIQUES.

maisons du peuple, see under ARTS CENTRE.

maladministration. Administrative fault, whether illegal or legal. The term has no significance for purposes of litigation in courts or other tribunals, but it is of prime importance in relation to extra-judicial remedies provided by ombudsmen, whose function is to investigate and report on complaints of injustice caused by the maladministration of administrative authorities in the process or procedure leading to an act or determination. It is only rarely defined in legislation governing the powers of ombudsmen throughout the world, and no United Kingdom legislation defines it for ombudsmen within the kingdom. This has been intentional because Parliament believes that ombudsmen should have a wide discretion to build up their own caselaw. Some maladministration involves conscious wrongdoing or turpitude, e.g. bias, perversity, intentional delay, but in practice most cases found are faults of inadvertence, e.g. inattention, unwitting delay, ineptitude, failure to follow procedures already laid down, or failure to establish proper procedures where their need has been established. D.C.M.Y.

Bibl: K.C. Wheare, *Maladministration and its Remedies* (London, 1973); D.C.M. Yardley, *Principles of Administrative Law* (London, 2nd ed., 1986).

male chauvinism, see under SEXISM.

malnutrition. Wrong NUTRITION caused either by a deficiency of a NUTRIENT or an excess of food. Deficiency diseases which have historically assumed epidemic proportions include scurvy (lack of vitamin C), beri-beri (lack of vitamin B1) and rickets (lack of vitamin D). Kwashiorkor and marasmus (lack of PROTEIN and energy) and iron-deficiency anaemia are common in developing countries. Obesity is included in the definition of malnutrition. See also FAMINE. A.E.B.

495

Bibl: A.E. Bender and D.A. Bender, *Nutrition for Medical Students* (Bristol, 1982).

Malthusianism. Theory of population, from the writing of Thomas Robert Malthus (1766-1834), seeing a check in the rate of population increase as desirable. The term is in most western languages, with many wayward meanings. Malthus wrote, in his 'Essay on the Principle of Population' (six editions, 1797-1826) that it was given that food was necessary, and that FERTILITY resulted from the continuing passion between the sexes; but that food production could only be increased in an arithmetical ratio whereas population increase was potentially greater, in a geometrical ratio. The laws of nature demanded that a balance be kept between population and resources, and there were therefore strong and operating checks upon the power of population. Those checks were of two sorts, 'positive' and 'preventive'. Positive checks were FAMINE, disease, and war; preventive checks took the form of prudential or moral restraint, namely late marriage, pre-marital chastity, and widespread celibacy. Malthus is forever associated with the positive check, and Malthusianism is generally taken to be its operation and the near-inevitability of disaster. In reality he saw the preventive check as important, especially in civilized nations; and his views became more optimistic. His ideas were as misunderstood in his own day as in ours. In later 19th-century Britain *neo-Malthusianism* emerged, which, quite contrary to what Malthus believed, advocated CONTRACEPTION (and induced ABORTION) to control population. Earlier writers had urged birth control, but the formation of the Malthusian (later Neo-Malthusian) League in 1861, and the celebrated Bradlaugh-Besant case of the late 1870s, paved the way for the advocacy of contraception (and of EUGENICS) in Britain and America. Since World War II FAMILY PLANNING has become a world-wide concern, not least with the population explosion in developing countries and changed attitudes to the VALUE OF CHILDREN in developed countries.   D.S.

Bibl: E.A. Wrigley and D. Souden (eds.), *The Works of Thomas Robert Malthus*, 8 vols (London, 1986), vols 1-3; R.A. Soloway, *Birth Control and the Population Question in England, 1877-1930* (London and Chapel Hill, N.C., 1982).

man-machine interface. An unwieldy term referring to the way that people use COMPUTERS. The hope is to design computers and PROGRAMS around the needs of the people who use computers rather than for the convenience of the machine itself. This can range from providing clear instructions to a novice using a computer to attempts in ARTIFICIAL INTELLIGENCE to allow INPUT/OUTPUT in spoken or written natural languages such as English. R.S.C.

management. The collection of persons responsible for the direction of the activities of an organization and the actual process of direction. Management covers all the activities of the organization, e.g. production, MANPOWER PLANNING, sales, finance and research. Management occurs in any organization providing a good or service, e.g. in national health services, the armed forces, charities and private companies. MANAGEMENT SCIENCE is the discipline of applying quantitative methods in management, e.g. see STATISTICS and OPERATIONS RESEARCH. In the plural form, it is the application of quantitative methods and SOCIAL SCIENCE in management. *Management by objectives* is the setting of objectives throughout an organization. This requires the identification of the functions of individuals and the different parts of the organization. By comparison, CORPORATE STRATEGIES emphasize the long term objectives of the company as a whole. SCIENTIFIC MANAGEMENT regards management's function as one of planning, leadership, organization, control and coordination. In particular, it involves the study of work practices and the taking of responsibility for organizing and supervising the work of individual members of the labour force. *Work measurement* is the establishment of the times needed for qualified workers to carry out specified tasks. *Method study* is the systematic study of work practices and of means of improving them. WORK STUDIES consider the efficient use of people and resources in carrying out tasks and makes use of the two latter techniques. Scientific management can use work studies to raise the productivity of the organization. This view of the function of management underlies the use of MANAGEMENT CONTROL SYSTEMS. A management control system is the procedures for planning expected performance, measuring actual performance and reporting differences between the two. Associated with this control are MANAGEMENT INFORMATION SYSTEMS, which are the systematic processes for providing information that management uses in making decisions. In the last few decades, developments in INFORMATION TECHNOLOGY and COMPUTER SCIENCE have made the collection and use of information easier and have been used to improve the quality of decision-making. The scientific management approach ignores the importance of social relationships in organizations. The *human relations* approach considers such relationships to be very important in determining the productivity of organizations and individuals. This latter approach has been criticized for its simplified view of harmony, job satisfaction, conflict, efficiency and social relationships in organizations. These criticisms have led to the SYSTEMS APPROACH being used to examine the social relations in organizations.   R.I.T.; J.P.

Bibl: G.A. Cole, *Management Theory and Practice* (Eastleigh, 1982).

management control system. Procedures and methods of planning the expected performance in managers' areas of responsibility, monitoring and measuring the actual performance, and reporting discrepancies between the two for managerial action. Examples include budgetary control based on INPUT costs; profit-responsible centres treating managers as autonomous units responsible for financial outputs as well as inputs; various multiple-criteria approaches, and PPBS methods suitable for non-profit organizations. A management control system will reflect the organizational approach and the CORPORATE STRATEGY of the enterprise.
R.I.T.

management information system. The rigorous study of the information needs of MANAGEMENT at operational, tactical, and strategic levels. Although decision-makers

have always needed information, such study is a recent development, concurrent with increasingly complex and interrelated decision situations, the use of a SYSTEMS APPROACH, and the potential use of COMPUTERS. Until now, most efforts to employ computers in information systems have concentrated on information flows within the organization, i.e. on monitoring the basic resources of men, machines, materials, or money. Recently, however, COMPUTER SIMULATION and other modelling methods (see MODEL) have been used with the aim of increasing and improving information about the external environment also.   R.I.T.

management science. The body of quantitative methods that can be applied to MANAGEMENT problems; predominantly, but not exclusively, the field of OPERATIONS RESEARCH. Contrast with SCIENTIFIC MANAGEMENT.   R.I.T.

Bibl: W.J. Baumol, *Economic Theory and Operations Analysis* (London and New York, 4th ed., 1977).

management studies. Studies related to MANAGEMENT. Management has, of course, been practised for as long as men have worked together to accomplish common tasks and needed to make decisions about scarce resources in uncertain situations. Only in the 20th century, however, has it been made a subject for serious study.

The measurement of work on the factory floor marked the beginning of so-called SCIENTIFIC MANAGEMENT. Then the foundations of the classical, or traditional, school of management thought were laid in the 1920s. This saw the process of managing as planning, control, coordination, organization, and leadership, quite distinguishable from the operating tasks that a manager might also undertake. Management was thought of in hierarchical terms with responsibility and authority delegated and subsequent accountability for performance expected. Classical thinking is reflected in the *organization chart* which pictures the hierarchical chain of command. Positions may be identified as *line* or *staff*, line responsibilities being in the chain of command for decision and actions, whereas staff positions are advisory. The *span of control* refers to the number of subordinates reporting directly to a manager.

Such ideas lie behind much of today's management practice and provide the conceptual underpinning of most MAN-AGEMENT CONTROL SYSTEMS. However, by the mid 20th century it had become apparent that management studied only as a set of functional activities was incomplete. Managers achieved their results through people. There followed a proliferation of ideas about the importance, for successful management, of understanding people, both as individuals and in groups. These viewpoints are referred to as the *behavioural approach* and classified as ORGANIZATION THEORY. Recently, an alternative set of insights into the process of management has been developed. This focuses on the use of information in decision-making, and is known as the SYSTEMS APPROACH. Relevant concepts are also found in DECISION THEORY. R.I.T.

managerial revolution. Phrase popularized by the ex-Trotskyite James Burnham in a book of that title (New York, 1941) predicting the rise of a new social CLASS, 'the managers', which would supplant the old capitalist class. Burnham saw Nazi Germany, the Soviet Union, and the NEW DEAL in the U.S.A. as variants of this new type and declared that 'the war of 1939 is the first great war of managerial society' as 'the war of 1914 was the last great war of capitalist society'. His class of managers was never precisely defined, but included production managers, administrative engineers (but not finance executives of corporations), government bureau heads, and the like. The prediction of the collapse of CAPITALISM was wrong. The 'theory' was highly simplified, and in the scope elaborated by Burnham it has been largely abandoned.

In a more restricted sense, however, the managerial revolution may be understood, in the usage of A.A. Berle and Gardiner Means (*The Modern Corporation and Private Property,* New York, 1933), as the shift *within* the modern corporation from the owner to the professional manager as the key figure in the enterprise. This is associated with a parallel change from 'ownership' to 'control' and with the decline of the importance of private property in contemporary capitalism. See also FIRM, THEORY OF. D.B.

Bibl: J. Scott, *Corporations, Classes and Capitalism* (London, 1979).

manic-depressive psychosis. A PSYCHOSIS in which an individual's behaviour alternates between extremes of mood. The manic phase is characterized by hyperactivity and occasionally by violent outbursts; in the depressive phase feelings of inadequacy, sadness, and lack of physical coordination are manifested. W.Z.

manifest function and **latent function.** Contrasted terms applied to the purpose served by a practice, custom, or INSTITUTION in a society. The two poles are not always quite the same, and in some cases only the context may determine whether the intended distinction is (1) between a manifest function of which the society's members are aware and a latent function of which they are not aware, or (2) between a proclaimed (manifest) and a real (latent) function. A.S.

manifold, see under GEOMETRY.

manoeuvrable re-entry vehicle (MARV). A MISSILE that has one or more warheads that may be controlled so as to avoid enemy defences. C.E.D.

manpower. A term, coined by the geographer Halford J. Mackinder, for the work force, with its quantitative and qualitative characteristics, available in a given place or area. J.G.

manpower planning, see under CORPORATE STRATEGY.

Manpower Services Commission (MSC). Body established by the British government under the Employment and Training Act of 1973 to run employment and training services to ease the growing burden of the nation's long-term unemployed. It works closely with other agencies, including the Trades Union Congress and the Confederation of British Industry, and has produced a number of schemes which have become internationally known, including the *Youth Training Scheme*

(YTS) which enables young school leavers aged 16-plus to be taken on by employers and trained in a given field. The employer is paid by the government for each trainee over a period of up to two years and the young person receives a small weekly wage also met by the government. The idea is that, if the youngster proves a good and acceptable employee, he or she may be taken onto the permanent payroll after the training period is over.   J.I.

mantle convection. Large-scale motion of the material comprising the earth's mantle, the region between the planet's outer shell (LITHOSPHERE) and the CORE. When the theory of CONTINENTAL DRIFT was proposed by Alfred Wegener early this century it attracted little support, largely because there seemed to be no mechanism by which moving continents could plough their way through the earth's solid surface. With the discovery of CREEP, however, it became clear that the solid mantle beneath the continents might be able to flow slowly under high pressure and over long periods of time, carrying the overlying continents along with it. When, during the 1960s, evidence from the MAGNETISM of rocks proved beyond doubt that the continents are indeed drifting (and that the oceanic lithosphere is spreading), mantle flow, or convection, became a necessity, although there is no direct proof that it actually exists. Some scientists no longer regard mantle convection as the engine driving the moving continents and ocean floors above; rather, they see sliding of the oceanic lithosphere under gravity as requiring compensating flows in the mantle below. Either way, the mantle must be able to move. When mantle convection was first proposed, it was envisaged as a system of large flow cells throughout the whole depth of the mantle. But with the discovery of the ASTHENOSPHERE, the layer of partially molten material immediately below the lithosphere, it became customary for a while to imagine convection limited to that narrow region. A more recent, and highly popular, model has convection occurring throughout the whole of the zone between the base of the lithosphere and a depth of 700 km, the limit of the deepest earthquake and the location of a boundary

(discontinuity) across which seismic waves are refracted (see SEISMOLOGY). A fourth possibility is that convection does take place throughout the whole mantle but as two separate, independent systems above and below 700 km.   P.J.S.

manufacture of madness. A term coined by the leading American 'antipsychiatrist' (see ANTI-PSYCHIATRY), Thomas Szasz, to describe the process whereby modern societies have allegedly chosen to designate sizable minorities of their populations insane as ways of isolating, labelling and scapegoating deviant individuals. Historically speaking, Szasz argues, the category of the insane has come to fulfil a role equivalent to that of lepers and witches in earlier centuries. This labelling depends upon a bogus concept of 'mental illness', illegitimately constructed by analogy with the somatic reality, physical illness. The notion of 'mental illness' masquerades as sympathetic, but in reality it functions as a stigma rather like the traditional category of sin. The rise of the psychiatric profession, the emergence of the asylum, and the passing of legislation depriving the mad of legal rights and personal freedoms are the socio-legal means whereby this 'manufacture' is accomplished. Szasz's case is not an argument against PSYCHIATRY as such, but against its abuse (as he sees it) by STATE and society.   R.P.

Bibl: Thomas S. Szasz, *The Manufacture of Madness* (London, 1973).

many worlds hypothesis. An interpretation of the theory of QUANTUM MECHANICS proposed by H. Everett III in 1957 under the title of 'The Relative State Formulation of Quantum Mechanics'. It is sometimes called the *Everett* or *Everett-Wheeler interpretation* of quantum mechanics. Unlike the COPENHAGEN INTERPRETATION it proposes that the WAVE FUNCTION never collapses and the quantum formalism describes the measurement process as well as the evolution of the wave function. This requires that the observer splits each time a measurement is made. The number of splittings is equal to the number of possible outcomes of the measurement. All the sequences of events that are logically possible do actually

499

occur in reality. These many worlds are believed to be causally disjoint and so we will only experience one of them. D. Deutsch has recently suggested that the development of quantum COMPUTERS could allow the existence of the parallel worlds to be tested by experiment. The many worlds interpretation of QUANTUM THEORY must be adopted by cosmologists attempting to create a quantum theoretical description of the entire universe because there is assumed to be no observer who could collapse the wave function of the entire universe as required in the Copenhagen interpretation. Most subscribers to the many worlds interpretation tend therefore to be cosmologists. (See also BELL'S THEOREM; COSMOLOGY; and ANTHROPIC PRINCIPLE.) J.D.B.

Bibl: B. de Witt and N. Graham, *The Many Worlds Interpretation of Quantum Mechanics* (Princeton, 1973); J. Wheeler and W. Zurek (eds.), *Quantum Theory and Measurement* (Princeton, 1983); P.C.W. Davies, *Other Worlds* (London, 1983).

Maoism. The political philosophy of Mao Zedong. The adaptation of MARXIST-LENINIST theory to suit the practical requirements of Chinese conditions, or as Mao himself put it in 1938, 'The Sinification of Marxism'. Maoism conflicts with orthodox MARXIST thought on fundamental levels, such as on the way to solve contradictions in society, definitions of the consistency of the BOURGEOISIE and the peasantry, and the ability to have a successful SOCIALIST revolution in a peasant based agrarian society. In fact while Maoism owes a lot to Lenin's *Theory of Imperialism* (1919), the importance of pure Marxist theory in the evolution of Mao's thought is not as important as the GUERRILLA heritage and the lessons learnt during the long struggle for POWER (see LONG MARCH). Because concrete conditions in China have changed over time, Maoism has also changed, to the extent that it has negated itself in many fields, such as the need or otherwise for decentralization. Despite this essentially pragmatic side of Maoism, certain ideas, such as the belief in the ability of political mobilization and storming tactics to solve economic problems, remained important for Mao, but on the whole, while the goal remained the same, the means by which that goal could be achieved depended heavily on Chinese PRAGMATISM. S.B.

Bibl: D. Wilson (ed.), *Mao Tse-tung in the Scales of History* (Cambridge, 1977).

mapping (in MATHEMATICS), see under FUNCTION; LINEAR.

maquette. French term for a scale MODEL, used in the English-speaking countries exclusively in its sense of a preliminary model for a work of sculpture. J.W.

marginal analysis. A marginal effect is the change in one VARIABLE caused by a small change in another. This concept is often encapsulated in the ratio of the two variables, e.g. marginal cost is the ratio of the additional cost of producing a small increase in the output of a product to the actual increase in output. The rigorous application of the concept of this ratio involves DIFFERENTIAL CALCULUS. Marginal analysis is used extensively in ECONOMICS, engineering and business. It provides a means of obtaining a maximum or minimum value of a variable (e.g. profit or costs) that depends on some factor that can be controlled. For example, a FIRM may wish to maximize profits and this is achieved by increasing output if the marginal revenue accruing from an increase in output exceeds its marginal cost. This process continues until the two marginal values are equal, i.e. when profit is at a maximum. This procedure can be followed for all variables (e.g. ADVERTISING) that affect profits. Marginal analysis lies behind many MICROECONOMIC theories (see NEOCLASSICAL ECONOMIC THEORY). This analysis can be used to estimate the effect of a change in one variable on another variable it determines. This is done by taking the product of the change in the determining variable and the appropriate marginal analysis ratio. For example, the marginal propensity to consume is the proportion consumed out of a small increase in NATIONAL INCOME. The effect on consumption of a change in national income can be estimated from the product of the change in income and the marginal propensity to consume. J.P.

Bibl: J. Craven, *Introduction to Economics* (Oxford, 1984).

marginal cost pricing. The setting of price equal to the marginal cost of production. Marginal cost is the additional cost of producing an extra unit of output (see MARGINAL ANALYSIS). If a consumer is rational (see RATIONALITY), a pattern of consumption is chosen such that the additional UTILITY — called the marginal utility — from an additional unit of consumption of a good is just equal to the loss in utility from the decrease in the consumption of other goods necessary to finance the additional consumption. If it is more/less, the rational consumer should increase/decrease consumption of this good and decrease/increase consumption of the other goods. Thus, for rational consumers prices affect the marginal utility of the consumption of different goods. If prices are equal to marginal costs consumers will implicitly make decisions about their pattern of consumption on the basis of their individual preferences and the marginal costs of supplying extra output. If all prices are equal to the marginal costs, this is often taken as implying ECONOMIC EFFICIENCY, though strictly this also requires efficiency in exchange, the minimization of costs, and the private costs and benefits of consumption and production being the same as social costs and benefits, i.e. there are no EXTERNALITIES. If certain prices are not equal to marginal costs, then, because of the interrelationships in the economy, it is not necessarily the case that efficiency is increased by setting more, but not all, prices equal to marginal costs. In spite of this, it is often suggested that economic efficiency would be increased by setting prices equal to marginal costs for as many groups of similar goods as is possible, e.g. the group of fuels sold in the energy market. Within each of these groups and between them, the chosen pattern of consumption would be determined by preferences and marginal costs and, thus, may be more efficient, though the pattern of the rest of consumption would not. A marginal cost may be less than average cost, in which case this pricing rule will result in firms making losses. The government may choose to finance these losses. This policy is likely to reduce the incentive to minimize costs. A further problem with this rule is the time span of the calculation of the marginal cost. If the adjustment of prices is costless, actual prices should be set equal to short-run marginal costs and long-run marginal costs should be used in considering investment plans. In the long run, this investment rule will give equality of long-run and short-run costs, and the price. It has been often suggested that the NATIONALIZED INDUSTRIES should set prices equal to long-run marginal costs.

J.P.

Bibl: R. Rees, *Public Enterprise Economics* (London, 2nd ed., 1984).

marginal costing. In MANAGEMENT, a comparison of costs based on the *marginal cost*, i.e. on the expenditure actually incurred by producing the next unit of a product or service; or, conversely, actually saved by not producing it. By contrast, *full recovery cost*, or *absorption cost*, includes both the direct expenditure incurred on the product (such as materials used and labour employed), which will vary directly with the volume produced, and an appropriate share of the overhead or fixed costs (such as staff salaries), which are constant for a period, irrespective of the level of activity or output.

R.I.T.

Bibl: C.L. Moore and R.K. Jaedicke, *Managerial Accounting* (Dallas, 4th ed., 1976).

marginal efficiency of capital. The INTERNAL RATE OF RETURN on the least productive piece of CAPITAL. Net INVESTMENT will occur up until the point that the interest rate is equal to the marginal efficiency of capital. In this way, with the interest rate and the price of capital goods, it determines the return on capital, the rate of investment and quantity of capital employed.

J.P.

Bibl: W.E. Kuhn, *The Evolution of Economic Thought* (Cincinnati, Ohio., 2nd ed., 1970).

marginal productivity theory of wages. The theory states that labour is paid a sum equal to the value of the output produced by employing an extra worker, keeping the use of all other FACTORS OF PRODUCTION constant (see MARGINAL ANALYSIS). The theory is often used with the assumption of PERFECT COMPETITION. Profit maximization implies that a firm employs labour up until the point that the additional revenue from employing an extra worker falls equal to the cost of an additional worker. As a perfectly competitive firm can employ as much labour as it wishes to at the market wage, this latter cost is the wage. The additional revenue generated by an extra worker is given by the additional output produced by the worker, i.e. the marginal product, multiplied by the price of output, as the perfectly competitive firm can sell as much output as it wishes to at the market price. This is equal to the value of the marginal product and, according to the law of DIMINISHING RETURNS, it must fall as more labour is employed. A similar theory can be developed for FIRMS that are not perfectly competitive. The theory has been criticized as it may be difficult for the firm to calculate the relevant variables, it may not be possible to increase the use of labour while keeping the use of other factors of production the same and social, legal, political and institutional effects may be important in determining wages.   J.P.

Bibl: J. Craven, *Introduction to Economics* (Oxford, 1984).

marginal rate of substitution, see under SUBSTITUTION.

marginal utility. The UTILITY or value yielded by the marginal, i.e. last, unit of consumption. The CONCEPT is important in DEMAND theory, since an individual consumption of a good will be determined by its marginal utility relative to other goods and its price relative to other goods. D.E.

Bibl: G.J. Stigler, *The Theory of Price* (London and New York, 3rd ed., 1978).

markedness. An analytical principle in LINGUISTICS whereby pairs of linguistic features, seen as oppositions, are given different values of positive ('marked') and neutral or negative ('unmarked'). For example, in English there is a formal feature (adding an ending, usually *s*) which marks the plural of nouns: the plural is therefore the marked form, and the singular is the unmarked form. In recent GENERATIVE GRAMMAR, a theory of markedness has

been proposed: here, an unmarked property is one which accords with the general tendencies found in all languages, whereas a marked property is one which goes against these tendencies.   D.C.

Bibl: A. Radford, *Transformational Syntax* (Cambridge, 1981).

marker, see under CONSTITUENT ANALYSIS.

market economy. A term synonymous with a free economy and free enterprise. Under certain conditions (see PERFECT COMPETITION), a market economy is economically efficient (see ECONOMIC EFFICIENCY).   J.P.

market failure (or *imperfection*). A market in which one or more of the assumptions of PERFECT COMPETITION is not valid. There is usually a presumption that a market failure is undesirable, e.g. external diseconomies (see EXTERNALITIES) and BARRIERS TO ENTRY. However, some market failure may be desirable, e.g. PATENTS and MONOPOLIES can lead to greater TECHNICAL PROGRESS.   J.P.

Bibl: D. Begg *et al.*, *Economics* (London, 1984).

market research. Developing or tailoring a product or service, its PACKAGING, presentation and MARKETING, requires a considerable insight into human habits and motivations in general, and those that directly affect a propensity to buy, in particular. Market research is undertaken, at all levels, the better to understand realized and unrealized customer wants and needs, in order to adjust all elements of the 'marketing mix' to achieve optimum effect. Clearly, the research process, in entering the realms of unrealized needs, will need to be deeply invasive at one level. In the past, market research, particularly qualitative research, was not a highly developed process in Japan, because it was considered impolite to wonder what went on in someone else's mind. There will still be those who view with deep concern, and perhaps with justification, the use to which all forms of research may be put.   T.S.

market socialism, see under TITOISM.

marketing. Now widely held to be the most important of industrial and commercial disciplines. In theory, before development, manufacturing or organization to provide service should be undertaken, the establishment of the nature and scale of consumer demand, and the price they are prepared to pay is regarded as a prerequisite. In practice, development is often undertaken in isolation, or manufacturing is embarked upon without regard to the market place. Or overseas suppliers and manufacturers seek the cost efficiencies of scale. Under such circumstances, marketing practitioners are called upon to develop levels of demand at profitable prices from the market place. It is widely believed that it is this retroactive practice of marketing that leads to pricing being the key distributive and competitive determinant. The result is, invariably, lack of profitability. Through the process of marketing come the functions of (1) marketing organization — the recruitment, training and structuring of the individuals or team also will, in concert, orchestrate a marketing programme; and (2) MARKET RESEARCH — the process of probing and evaluating and predicting the market's response to all stages of product work, from concept to death, and of the impact of the environment and the market place, especially competitive activity. Thus, marketing people, replete with information and an understanding of the market's predictable or observable response to quality, content, pricing, PACKAGING, presentation, distribution and service, manage the process of optimizing investment and return. So complex is the marketing process, and so essential to it a grasp of human nature and behaviour, that it can only be regarded as an art, rather than a science.   T.S.

Markov process, see under STOCHASTIC PROCESS.

Maronites, see under LEBANON.

marriage. A union established between the sexes which may be singular (MONOGAMY) or plural (POLYGYNY and POLYANDRY). It is governed by rules of ENDOGAMY and EXOGAMY, who one may or may not marry. Morgan described marriage as 'a bundle of rights' and as an institution it serves different functions: it establishes legal rights between spouses and the legitimacy of their children, it establishes a domestic group and it links different social groups through relations of affinity. The ceremony of marriage is a RITE DE PASSAGE, marking the change in social STATUS. The GIFTS and property exchanged at marriage symbolize the transfer of rights from one set of kin to another. Marriage presentations are usually in the form of BRIDEWEALTH or DOWRY. Marriage is not a universal institution. In *The Origins of English Individualism* (1978) Macfarlane's researches in HISTORICAL ANTHROPOLOGY established that in western Europe a certain proportion of men and women have always remained unmarried (spinsters, bachelors, maiden aunts etc.). The unmarried or celibate individual was socially recognized and accepted. Marriage has been the cornerstone of the alliance theorists — anthropologists who, in following Lévi-Strauss, have stressed the EXCHANGE of women as the critical element in KINSHIP systems. This approach understands primary recruitment to groups not on the basis of DESCENT, but as a result of marriage, or the establishment of links or alliances between social groups. In *The Elementary Structures of Kinship* (1949) Lévi-Strauss distinguished systems as elementary (characterized by a positive marriage rule, rules lay down who one should marry) and complex (without a positive marriage rule, rules on who one may not marry, but not on who one should marry).   A.G.

Bibl: Alan Barnard and Anthony Good, *Research Practices in The Study of Kinship* (London, 1984).

MARS (Modern Architectural Research Society), see under CIAM.

Marshall Plan or European Recovery Programme (ERP). An American plan for aid to European economic recovery after World War II; first publicly proposed in a speech at Harvard on 5 June 1947 by George Marshall, U.S. Secretary of State. The plan offered aid to all European nations, and demanded that they request assistance and act in concert. It reflected American fears that economically dislocated countries (e.g. France, Italy, West Germany) might fall to COMMUNIST movements, and placed the onus for East European non-involvement on the Soviet Union. Under Anglo-French leadership, plans were developed which led in 1948 to the launching of the ERP, and linked the U.S. Economic Cooperation Administration (ECA) with the Organization for European Economic Cooperation (see OEEC) in its implementation.　　　S.R.

Bibl: A. Bullock, *Ernest Bevin, Foreign Secretary* (London and New York, 1983); S. Hoffmann *et al.*, *The Marshall Plan: A Retrospective* (Westview, Conn., 1984).

MARV, see under MANOEUVRABLE RE-ENTRY VEHICLE.

Marxism. Marxism refers to the economic, social and political theory and practice of Karl Marx and its subsequent elaboration by his various followers. Although there is considerable dispute as to what Marxism is and what it is not, there is general agreement that most varieties of Marxism typically contain three main strands. Firstly, and most importantly, there is an explanation and critique of present and past societies. The explanation consists in according some privilege to the economic factor over other factors in accounting for social change and development. More specifically, prime importance is given to the forces of production (the tools and instruments that are at the disposal of human beings at any given time) and the relations of production (the way in which human beings organize themselves in order to use the same forces of production) as shaping the political and cultural arrangements in any given society. This view, known as HISTORICAL MATERIALISM, is often jejunely formulated in the proposition that the economic base determines the political and ideological SUPERSTRUCTURE. Although it is granted that the political and ideological elements can influence the economic structure, it is the development of the latter which produces social change: at a certain stage of their evolution the forces of production develop as far as they can under the existing economic and political organization of

society, which then becomes a barrier to their further development, and a period of social REVOLUTION starts in which new economic and political relationships, corresponding to the expanded forces of production, are established. In accordance with this latter, it is possible to pick out the Asiatic, ancient, FEUDAL and modern bourgeois MODES OF PRODUCTION as progressive epochs in the economic formation of society. The critical component in this first strand consists in the view that in these successive modes of production the crucial element in society — the forces of production — have been controlled by a minority who have used their economic power in order to exploit the mass of the population by appropriating the economic surplus for their own benefit. This inherently conflictual situation gives rise to a CLASS struggle which centres around the ownership and control of the means of production. All political INSTITUTIONS and cultural beliefs are shaped by the economic arrangements and those with economic power — the ruling class — so as effectively to bolster the unequal distribution of resources. This yields the Marxist concept of IDEOLOGY as a set of beliefs and practices which serve to maintain an asymmetrical allocation of economic and political power.

The second strand of Marxist thought is the notion of an alternative to a society based on exploitation and divided along class lines. In Marx's view this can only consist of a society based on the common ownership of the means of production in which the human potential stunted by the DIVISION OF LABOUR characteristic of class societies will be enabled freely to develop its manifold facets. Such a society will have no classes and therefore no need for a state apparatus defined as an instrument of class domination. In an initial stage, generally known as SOCIALISM, distribution of goods will be made in the first instance according to the contribution of each individual; later it will be possible to move to a COMMUNIST organization of society which will allow the famous principle of 'from each according to their ability and to each according to their needs', to be implemented. Any detailed description of such a society is bound, on Marxist assumptions, to be highly speculative.

The third strand is some account of how to move from the first to the second. Clearly the materialist conception of history outlined in the first strand comprises the view that the CAPITALIST mode of production is as transitory as all previous ones. Marxists have disagreed over the exact mechanism — whether, for example, it is the tendency of the rate of profit to fall or the growth of underconsumption — but there is general agreement that the capitalist system is inherently unstable, crisis-ridden and will inevitably collapse. However, socialism will also be the result of the revolutionary activity of those whom capitalist society is producing as its own gravediggers — the WORKING CLASS whose growing numbers and relative impoverishment will drive them to revolt. Following on a revolutionary upheaval, there will have to be a transitional period known as the DICTATORSHIP OF THE PROLETARIAT before a fully communist society can be inaugurated. The relationship of any Marxist-inspired party to the class it represents is subject to more varying accounts than any other aspect of Marxism. Since the era of the mass party only arrived after Marx's death, he himself did not have to cope with this problem and anyone — from a LENINIST proposing a highly centralized 'vanguard' party to lead workers (who would otherwise have the most inadequate views about politics) to a LIBERTARIAN socialist who believes that political POWER should be vested directly in workers' assemblies — can claim, without fear of refutation, that they are in the true Marxist tradition. See also NEO-MARXISM.

D.T.M.

Bibl: L. Kolakowski, *Main Currents of Marxism*, 3 vols. (Oxford, 1978); G. Lichtheim, *Marxism: An Historical and Critical Study* (London, 1961); D. McLellan, *Marxism After Marx* (London, 1980).

Marxism-Leninism. This term originated in the debates and struggle for power in the Soviet Union following Lenin's death and culminating in the ascendancy of Stalin. It thus came to mean the theory and practice of Marx and Lenin as narrowly defined by Stalin and was used as a yardstick of orthodoxy to refute all opposition and became part of the official self-description of the Soviet Union. Marxism-Leninism was taken up by the Chinese Communists under Mao as a description and justification of their policies. Currently the term Marxism-Leninism tends to be used by any Marxist party which has retained some sympathy for the policies of Stalin or Mao. See MARXISM; LENINISM; STALINISM; MAOISM.

D.T.M.

Bibl: J.P. Plamenatz, *German Marxism and Russian Communism* (London and New York, 1954); L. Schapiro, *The Communist Party of the Soviet Union* (London and New York, 2nd ed., 1970).

maser (Microwave Amplification by Stimulated Emission of Radiation). A device producing high levels of power at precisely defined frequencies in the MICROWAVE region. The basic principle is that of the LASER, but the lower frequency means that the ENERGY LEVELS of MOLECULES as well as ATOMS can be used. Masers are used as oscillators in RADAR, and as amplifiers.

M.V.B.

masochism. A PERVERSION in which sexual pleasure is derived from being subjected to pain, either self-inflicted or inflicted by another. It was named by Krafft-Ebing after Baron Sacher-Masoch, who described it in *Venus in Furs* (tr. G. Warner, 1925).

W.Z.

mass. A fundamental QUANTITY in PHYSICS. In NEWTONIAN MECHANICS, the mass of a body is a measure of its ability to resist ACCELERATION when acted on by forces. Mass is also a measure of a body's ability to attract other bodies by GRAVITATION. The scientific unit of mass is the kilogram, and masses are measured by comparison with the standard, which is kept near Paris. Einstein's MASS-ENERGY EQUATION shows that mass is not indestructible.

M.V.B.

mass culture. A culture — known also as POPULAR CULTURE, and usually contrasted with *high culture* — which is identified with those products produced primarily for entertainment rather than intrinsic worth, for artifacts to be sold in the market in response to mass taste, rather than by patronage, and with items created by mechanical reproduction such as the printing press, gramophone records, and art illustrations. The argument about mass culture, which goes back as far as Wordsworth, was revived in the 1950s with the spread of affluence (see AFFLUENT SOCIETY) and the fear that ADVERTISING (see ADMASS) was shaping cultural tastes; but it took a very different form. Though traditionalists such as F.R. Leavis still decried the break-up of the 'organic' community, and LEFT-wing writers such as Dwight Macdonald declared that mass culture had corrupted high culture, yet other writers such as Richard Hoggart (in *The Uses of Literacy*) argued that English WORKING-CLASS culture had a vitality of its own, while sociologists such as Edward Shils argued that the spread of serious music recordings and art works had upgraded mass taste and brought more people 'into' society. In the 1960s the debate took another turn with the rise of POP ART. A group of critics associated with the American magazine *Partisan Review* (Susan Sontag, Richard Poirier) became advocates of 'the new sensibility' which denied the validity of any distinction between 'highbrow' and 'lowbrow' art, proclaimed film as the important art of the 20th century, and argued that the music of the BEATLES and the Rolling Stones was as important as that of Schönberg for its evocation of popular responses. From that perspective, 'high art' is seen as élitist and artificial, and mass culture becomes a term of praise.   D.B.

Bibl: N. Jacobs (ed.), *Culture for the Millions?* (London and Princeton, 1961); S. Giner, *Mass Society* (London, 1976); A. Swingewood, *The Myth of Mass Culture* (London, 1977).

mass-energy equation. The famous EQUATION $E = mc^2$ deduced by Einstein from his theory of RELATIVITY. According to this theory matter is one of the many forms of ENERGY, and the equation predicts the amount of energy (E) that is released when a MASS (m) is annihilated (c is the speed of light in empty space). Conversion of mass takes place during NUCLEAR REACTIONS, such as FUSION and FISSION; it is responsible for the light of stars and the sun, and the power from NUCLEAR REACTORS and NUCLEAR WEAPONS. Only a small fraction of the mass involved disappears in these processes; if *all* the mass could be used up, the energy release would be far greater (e.g. the 'burning' of 1 kilogram every second would provide power at the rate of about 100,000 megawatts).   M.V.B.

mass extinction. An occasion in the history of life when an exceptionally large number of SPECIES became extinct. The best known mass extinction took place at the end of the Cretaceous Period about 65 million years ago, and included the dinosaurs. The mass extinction at the end of the Permian Period, about 225 million years ago, is the earliest well-documented mass extinction, and in it as many as 96% of species may have become extinct. The total number of mass extinctions in the history of life is uncertain, but there may have been as many as nine between the Permian and the present, at approximately 26 million year intervals. Four of these are reasonably well documented. It is unclear whether mass extinctions are the extreme of a continuum of extinction rates, or whether they differ in kind from a normal rate of extinction. The cause, or causes, of mass extinctions is controversial. The recent discovery, by L. Alvarez, that rocks at the CRETACEOUS-TERTIARY BOUNDARY have a high concentration of the RARE EARTH element iridium led him to suggest that extinction was caused by a catastrophic meteor impact, because iridium is found in particularly high concentrations in meteors. Other explanations of the iridium anomaly are possible, such as volcanism (see VOLCANOLOGY). Many other hypotheses have been put forward to explain mass extinctions. Humans are probably causing a mass extinction at present, by the destruction of the tropical rain forests.   M.R.

mass media, see under MEDIA.

mass picketing, see under PICKETING.

mass society. A society in which similar tastes, habits, opinions, and activities are shared by the large majority of the population who accordingly become less differentiated either as individuals or in terms of social CLASS, etc. In political terms, mass society is seen as a result of the processes of INDUSTRIALIZATION, the extension of suffrage and the erosion of SOCIAL STRATIFICATION. The emergent social order of mass society threatens a new volatility — of masses responsive to the direct manipulation of despots and tyrants or, vice versa, of governing ELITES unable to resist the whims of popular opinion. Among the claimed characteristics of mass society are an extensive BUREAUCRACY, a powerful MEDIA, a tendency to conformity, mediocrity and ALIENATION; on the positive side observers have also pointed to enlarged areas of public PARTICIPATION and increased CONSENSUS over societal ends and means.   P.S.L.

Bibl: S. Giner, *Mass Society* (London, 1976).

mass spectrometry. A technique for separating the different masses in a beam of IONS of the same charge. The ions are sent through a vacuum chamber containing electric and magnetic FIELDS, where they are deflected in accordance with the laws of ELECTRODYNAMICS by amounts depending on their masses, and focused onto a photographic plate. The proportions of the different ISOTOPES in a sample of an ELEMENT may be measured in this way, and ATOMIC WEIGHTS may be accurately determined (see also ANALYTICAL CHEMISTRY).   M.V.B.

mass terms. Terms referring to stuffs or substances which cannot be counted, which can only be measured by weight or volume. Thus 'air', 'water', 'butter' are mass terms, for whereas one can count tumblers of water or pats of butter, one cannot count water or butter. 'Count terms', by contrast, refer to countable items; one can count apples, therefore 'apple' is such a term. One way of distinguishing mass from count terms is to note that mass terms apply to substances about which one would ask 'is there more or less of it than before?', whereas count terms apply to items about which one would ask 'are there more or fewer of them than before?' Confusions over mass and count terms abound in colloquial usage: 'there were less people than last year' is incorrect for 'there were fewer people (etc)'. A.C.G.

massive retaliation. A STRATEGY envisaging a strategic riposte to all identifiable provocations or attacks. The term was adapted from a phrase in a speech by John Foster Dulles on 12 January 1954 in which he said that 'the way to deter aggression is for the free communities to be willing and able to respond vigorously at places and with means of our own choosing'. This phrase was subject to contemporary misinterpretation, for American strategy never envisaged any form of automatic nuclear riposte; the message Dulles was trying to signal to the Communist powers was (a) that they could not hope to hide behind aggression by proxy; (b) that they could not expect to limit any ensuing conflict to thresholds chosen by themselves; and (c) that any attack on the United States would involve reprisals against their homeland. The substance of this policy was NATO doctrine from 1954 until 1966 when it was modified in favour of FLEXIBLE RESPONSE. It remains, however, official French strategic doctrine.
                                                           A.F.B.

Bibl: see under DETERRENCE.

material culture, history of, see HISTORY OF MATERIAL CULTURE.

materialism. In ONTOLOGY, the theory that everything that really exists is material in nature, by which is meant, at least, that it occupies some volume of space at any time and, usually, that it continues in existence for some period of time and is either accessible to PERCEPTION by sight and touch or is analogous in its causal properties (see CAUSALITY) to what is so accessible. This denies substantial existence (1) to minds and mental states, unless these are identified with states of the brain and NERVOUS SYSTEM, and (2), ordinarily, in the style of NOMINALISM, to abstract entities of UNIVERSALS. The first of these denials is the more crucial and controversial. It is generally agreed that statements about mental events are not equivalent in MEANING to statements about physical events in the brain. Yet the obviously close correlation between brain and mind suggests that the event that is described in mental language as experiencing a pain may be the very same event, under a non-equivalent description, as some event in the brain. EPIPHENOMENALISM is a kind of diluted materialism inspired, like the stronger form, by the intimations of complete DETERMINISM in the material world which, if true, would deprive mental events (conceived, in the manner of DUALISM, as radically non-material) of any causal efficacy.

The DIALECTICAL MATERIALISM of Marx and Engels repudiates the mechanistic account of the relations between events given by standard materialism and allows, as do other, biologically inspired forms of emergent EVOLUTIONISM, that mind, while originating in matter, is distinct in nature from it. Materialism excludes the possibility of disembodied minds, whether of God or of the dead. Materialists, from the time of Democritus to the present, have usually been NATURALISTS in ETHICS, but that does not commit them to materialism in the colloquial sense of an overriding interest in the acquisition of material goods and bodily satisfactions.   A.Q.

Bibl: F.A. Lange, tr. E.C. Thomas, *The History of Materialism* (3rd ed., London, 1925; New York, 1950); K. Campbell, *Body and Mind* (New York, 1970; London, 1971).

materialism, heroic, see under ZEITGEIST.

materialist conception of history, see HISTORICAL MATERIALISM.

materials science. The systematic study of matter in bulk, unifying the disciplines of METALLURGY, POLYMER science, RHEOLOGY, and SOLID-STATE PHYSICS, and techniques such as CRYSTALLOGRAPHY, ELECTRON MICROSCOPY, and X-RAY DIFFRACTION, in an attempt to understand matter and develop useful new materials such as CARBON FIBRES.   M.V.B.

mathematical economics, see under ECONOMETRICS.

mathematical induction (or *Peano's fifth postulate*). The assertion that if the natural NUMBER 0 has some property *P*, and if further whenever *n* has *P* then so does *n* + 1, *then* all natural numbers have *P*. It expresses the fact that the natural num-

bers are precisely the things got from 0 by successive additions of 1, and is an important method of proof in NUMBER THEORY.
                                                            R.G.

mathematical linguistics. A branch of LINGUISTICS which studies the mathematical properties of language, usually employing CONCEPTS of a statistical or algebraic kind (see STATISTICS; ALGEBRA).   D.C.

mathematical logic (also known as *symbolic logic*). A term that covers a range of interconnected disciplines. Traditional LOGIC, because of its concern with logical form (see PROPOSITION), has from the earliest times used symbols to replace words. Leibniz proposed that logical arguments could be reduced to algebraic manipulations; for traditional logic (in particular for SYLLOGISMS) this was accomplished by De Morgan and Boole in the mid 19th century (see BOOLEAN ALGEBRA). However, as the work of Frege clearly showed, traditional logic does not suffice for mathematical argument. To support the thesis of LOGICISM he developed QUANTIFICATION theory and the theory of SETS (classes) and gave them an AXIOMATIC formulation. Russell's PARADOX showed that the logic of classes needed a more mathematically sophisticated formulation (see SET THEORY). Up to this point the development of the subject-matter and the development of the symbolism for it went hand in hand, but since then the distinction between the SYNTAX and the SEMANTICS of formal languages has become of crucial importance. Hilbert, in his version of FORMALISM, developed *proof theory*; through the study of formal proofs, considered simply as strings of symbols, he hoped to defend classical MATHEMATICS against the criticisms of INTUITIONISM by demonstrating that no proof would lead to a contradiction. GÖDEL'S THEOREM shows that such a demonstration must use new principles which are not formalizable in the system studied. Proof theory has thus become a recondite branch of mathematics; it is closely connected with RECURSIVE FUNCTION THEORY. The study of the semantics of formal languages, begun by A. Tarski in 1936, has blossomed into *model theory*. Here one pushes the AXIOMATIC METHOD to its limit by studying *all* possible interpretations (MODELS) of a given formal language or system of AXIOMS. The results are particularly valuable for abstract ALGEBRA.   R.G.; A.Q.

Bibl: G. Boole, *The Laws of Thought* (London, 1854; London and Chicago, 1952); A. Church, *Introduction to Mathematical Logic* (Princeton, 1956); J.N. Crossley *et al.*, *What is Mathematical Logic?* (London, 1972); D.R. Hofstadter, *Gödel, Escher, Bach* (Harmondsworth and New York, 1980).

mathematical psychology. A branch of PSYCHOLOGY concerned with devising statistical procedures (see STATISTICS) for extracting information from psychology data, and with constructing COMPUTER or mathematical MODELS that seek to simulate or represent human behaviour. See also COMPUTER SIMULATION.   J.S.B.

Bibl: G.A. Miller, *Mathematics and Psychology* (London and New York, 1964).

mathematical structure. Before the 19th century MATHEMATICS dealt with objects that belonged to a limited variety of well-defined species (e.g. geometric points, whole NUMBERS, real numbers) whose fundamental laws were given by intuition. Where intuition was lacking (e.g. COMPLEX NUMBERS) the 'objects' were treated with suspicion. In the 19th and 20th centuries there has been an enormous enrichment of mathematical imagination. New objects and new species were introduced, sometimes by formal postulates (e.g. non-Euclidean GEOMETRIES, QUATERNIONS), sometimes by construction (GROUPS were first introduced as sets of PERMUTATIONS), sometimes by new intuitions (e.g. the sets of Cantorian SET THEORY), often by a combination of these approaches. Gradually the AXIOMATIC METHOD emerged as the preferred way of handling the multitude of notions, each of which is seen as a particular case of the general CONCEPT (due to BOURBAKI) of mathematical structure. A *first-order structure* is defined by specifying a SET *A* of *elements* (e.g. the points of a line, the natural numbers) together with certain RELATIONS (e.g. betweenness) and/or certain FUNCTIONS (e.g. addition). For *higher-order structures* one specifies in addition certain relations of relations, functions of functions, and so on. What is significant to the pure mathematician is the pattern formed by the specified relations, functions, etc. All ISO-MORPHIC structures will exhibit the same pattern; so one defines the corresponding *abstract mathematical structure* (see EQUIVALENCE RELATION). Here the elements are colourless, structureless individuals, and the specified relations etc. are defined purely extensionally — by means of (possibly INFINITE) lists and tables. This means that totally arbitrary or chaotic patterns of relations etc. are counted as structures. Mathematically significant structures are singled out by imposing AXIOMS which the relations etc. are required to satisfy. The axioms may determine a unique abstract structure; more often they determine a whole family of similar structures (for examples see GROUPS and ORDERING RELATIONS). Such a family may itself be treated as a structure; see CATEGORY THEORY.   R.G.

Bibl: N.W. Gowar, *Basic Mathematical Structures* (London, 1973); R.O. Gandy, 'Structure in Mathematics', in E.D. Robey (ed.), *Structuralism* (Oxford, 1973).

mathematics. Until the mid 19th century the subject was correctly described as the science of NUMBER and QUANTITY (including the dimensional quantities of GEOMETRY). The thesis of LOGICISM and the introduction of the unifying CONCEPT of MATHEMATICAL STRUCTURE suggested a redefinition: the study of SETS and RELATIONS. The rise of the AXIOMATIC METHOD and of FORMALISM led some to describe it as the drawing of correct INFERENCES from AXIOMS. Both of these last views (which have been influential in the NEW MATHEMATICS) are disastrously misleading because they emphasize trivial facets and conceal what is important. Significant structures and difficult theorems are not discovered by playing around with relations and formal inferences. They are found by using imagination, intuition, and experience, and are often, initially, logically incoherent; logical packaging comes later. (A good mathematician once said: 'Test of good mathematician — how many bad proofs.') The standards of precision and rigour today are high, but this is not

509

what makes 20th-century mathematics a supreme achievement of the human intellect.

Mathematics arises from trying to solve problems. The problems come from three primary directions: (1) from the external world — the source of GEOMETRY, CALCULUS, and parts of TOPOLOGY; (2) from intellectual playfulness — from this comes NUMBER THEORY, PROBABILITY THEORY, much of ALGEBRA and COMBINATORIAL MATHEMATICS (see FOUR-COLOUR CONJECTURE), some of topology (see MÖBIUS BAND); (3) from reflecting on the power and the limitations of our intellect — see MATHEMATICAL LOGIC, INFINITY, GÖDEL'S THEOREM, RECURSIVE FUNCTION THEORY. The efforts to solve these primary problems produce not only manipulative techniques (such as ALGEBRA and the use of DIFFERENTIAL EQUATIONS, VECTORS, MATRICES, BOOLEAN ALGEBRA) but also new concepts and patterns of thought (for examples see COMPLEX FUNCTION THEORY, GEOMETRY, GROUP, SET THEORY, TOPOLOGY), which in turn produce new problems. It is these new patterns of thought, at one remove from the primary problems, which form the rich and intricate heart of mathematics. Because these patterns have been formed by *our* intellect, and so are conformable to our understanding, they modify or even revolutionize our view and knowledge of the external world. The theory of groups was invented to solve problems of pure algebra; it is now a part of the physicist's view of nature (see TRANSFORMATION; PARITY). R.G.

Bibl: L. Hogben, *Mathematics for the Million* (London, 4th ed., 1967; New York, 1968); J. Singh, *Mathematical Ideas* (London, 1972); M. Kline, *Mathematical Thought from Ancient to Modern Times* (New York, 1972); P.J. Davis and R. Hersh, *The Mathematical Experience* (London and New York, 1983).

matheme. A term in Lacan's version of PSYCHOANALYSIS. Lacan's clinical practice led him to formulate what he called the REAL, a limit both to the SYMBOLIC and to the IMAGINARY, and thus a stranger, strictly speaking, to the orders of representation, visualization, and signification. The matheme was Lacan's response to the problem of theorizing the real without falling into the traps characteristic of imaginary and intuitive representation, since the symbolic writing that constitutes a matheme is both devoid of a univocal signification and bars access to intuitive representation. Hence the mathemes are not to be understood, but to be used; the imaginary connotations carried by the idea of understanding are eliminated by a procedure that produces multiple effects of sense while allowing for a formalization of many aspects of psychoanalysis.

Bibl: J. Lacan, *Ecrits* (Paris, 1966; Eng. tr. London, 1977).

D.L.

matriarchy. In a limited sense the term means authority exercised by women over men (in contrast to PATRIARCHY, where men exercise power over women). Matriarchy, however, is frequently used more loosely to refer to female autonomy, mother-right, recognition of female principle, worship of goddess, matrilineage, women centred social organization etc. Matriarchy was of particular interest to writers at the end of the 19th century in their investigations of the evolution of society. An original state of matriarchy was postulated by Bachofen (*Das Mutterrecht*, 1861) and it became an important stage in the evolutionary schema of Morgan (*Ancient Society*, 1877) and Engels (*The Origin of the Family, Private Property and the State*, 1884). More recently the concept of matriarchy has been important in attempts to understand the origins of sexual oppression. A number of feminists (see FEMINISM) have drawn upon 19th-century and other historical accounts to discover early matriarchal (or gynocentric) organizations (e.g., E. Gould Davis, *The First Sex*, 1971). Those feminists working within an anthropological tradition have also considered the question of matriarchy. They have rejected evolutionary speculation, but investigated the nature of women's power (or lack of it) in contemporary societies (e.g., R. Reiter, *Towards an Anthropology of Women*, 1975). For the feminist movement the potential existence of matriarchy (in history or contemporary society) is important evidence to refute the notion that patriarchy is universal, fundamental and inevitable. It suggests the possibility of dissolving or bringing to an end the state of male domination. A.G.

Bibl: K. Millett, *Sexual Politics* (London, 1983); S. Rowbotham, *Dreams and Dilemmas* (London, 1983).

matri-clan, see under CLAN.

matrilineal. Tracing of DESCENT through a single female line from an ancestor. As with other forms of descent it may act as a principle governing relations between individuals over the inheritance of property or succession to office. It may also be the organizing principle of a social group, and the basis of membership of a specific matrilineal descent group. Audrey Richards' study of the Bemba of Central Africa (*Land, Labour and Diet in Northern Rhodesia*, 1939) was a classic example.

Typically, a matrilineal descent group is organized around resident women: mothers and sisters descended from a common ancestress. However, although the line of descent runs through women, the line of authority runs through men. Thus the relationship between a woman and her brother is central. But brothers cannot impregnate their sisters to perpetuate the lineage and thus men are brought from outside as husbands: *matrilocal marriage*. A husband acquires through MARRIAGE rights over the sexual and domestic services of his wife, but not over her reproductive powers. They remain part of her matrilineage under the control of her brother. Children of the marriage are similarly members of their mother's matrilineage and subject to the authority of her brother rather than her husband. Men as husbands are marginal, but as brothers they are central to a matrilineal descent group (see BRIDEWEALTH). A.G.

Bibl: L. Holy, *Strategies and Norms in a Changing Matrilineal Society* (Cambridge, 1985).

matrilocal marriage, see under MATRILINEAL.

matrix. In MATHEMATICS an $m \times n$ matrix A is a rectangular array of objects (usually NUMBERS) which has m rows and n columns, e.g. A might give the COEFFICIENTS in a set of linear EQUATIONS, or the components of a set of VECTORS. If this was all,

it would be nothing more than a handy piece of jargon. But in fact a matrix can always be considered as a linear mapping from an n-dimensional to an m-dimensional vector space. This gives rise to various operations on matrices; in particular, matrix 'multiplication' corresponds to the composition of FUNCTIONS. Problems about linear functions and equations can then be described in terms of these operations, and they in turn can be described in terms of algebraic manipulations on the entries. In this connection the *determinant* of a matrix A is of great value. It is a number computed from the entries and is zero unless the matrix is square (i.e. unless $m = n$); division by A is possible if and only if the determinant is non-zero. R.G.

matrix mechanics. An alternative formulation of QUANTUM MECHANICS which does not involve a WAVE FUNCTION, devised by Heisenberg in 1925. A dynamical quantity (e.g. MOMENTUM or SPIN) is represented mathematically by a MATRIX, instead of a number as in NEWTONIAN MECHANICS. These matrices form the basis of calculations aimed at predicting experimentally-measurable quantities, such as the intensities of lines in SPECTROSCOPY, the HALF-LIVES of RADIOACTIVE decay, and the ENERGY LEVELS of ATOMS. M.V.B.

matrix organization, see under ORGANIZATION THEORY.

mature/developed socialism. The term used in current Soviet IDEOLOGY to describe the stage which the Soviet Union has now reached in its progress from SOCIALISM to COMMUNISM. Leonid Brezhnev first defined it at the XXIV Congress of the Communist Party in 1971 although the idea had gained some currency earlier, and it featured as an important concept in the Constitution of 1977. It is intended to take into account the ECONOMIC GROWTH achieved since 1936, when Stalin announced that socialism had been created, while putting off the advent of communism to the distant future. The main feature of this stage of socialism is modernization and particularly the scientific and technical revolution, the encouragement of which will allow socialism to develop further and will create the conditions for the establishment of communism. Another characteristic of developed socialism is the achievement of a large measure of unity among the Soviet people which has allowed the Communist Party to become the vanguard of the people, not just of the PROLETARIAT as was the case under the DICTATORSHIP OF THE PROLETARIAT. This accords with the new doctrine of the ALL PEOPLE'S STATE. D.PR.

Bibl: N. Harding (ed.), *The State in Socialist Society* (London, 1984).

maximin, see under GAME THEORY.

maxims of conversation. Notions derived from the work of the philosopher H.P. Grice which are widely cited in current research in PRAGMATICS. The maxims are general principles which are thought to underlie the efficient use of language, and which together identify a general COOPERATIVE PRINCIPLE. Four basic maxims are identified. The *maxim of quality* states that speakers' contributions ought to be true. The *maxim of quantity* states that the contribution should contain more information than is necessary for the needs of the exchange. The *maxim of relevance* states that contributions should relate clearly to the purpose of the exchange. And the *maxim of manner* states that the contributions should be perspicuous — especially avoiding obscurity and ambiguity. D.C.

Bibl: S. Levinson, *Pragmatics* (Cambridge, 1983).

May 1968. The 'events' of May 1968 in France began with student protests in Paris about university conditions and proposed reforms. Violent clashes between students and police were accompanied by student occupations throughout the capital and in some provincial universities. By mid-May factory workers as well as some professional groups, supported by the major TRADE UNIONS, had joined the students; there was a general strike and factory occupations in support of AUTOGESTION. The crisis was resolved in early June 1968 by the government's promise to consult the students over university reforms and the *Grenelle* agreements, which provided workers with a high minimum wage, a shorter working week and an extra week's paid holiday. Although the events of May 1968 were at the time interpreted by many people as a revolutionary threat to the Fifth Republic, the GAULLIST government quickly re-established order and in the general election of June 1968 was re-elected with an overwhelming majority. Although student protests were the immediate cause of the events, the rapid escalation of the crisis suggests that there was widespread discontent in France at the time with the somewhat illiberal (albeit constitutional) nature of the Gaullist regime. S.M.

McCarthyism. The name, attributed to cartoonist Herbert Block (Herblock), for a brief but lurid phase in U.S. history from 1950 to 1954, in which Senator Joseph McCarthy led an hysterical and mendacious campaign against alleged COMMUNISTS in the U.S. government and other institutions. Although McCarthy's own main motive was self-promotion and his methods crude, his campaign enlarged an existing mood and attracted both substantial popular support and the tacit encouragement of Republican Party ELITES. By association, the term now denotes any attempt to persecute members of an organization by innuendo, implication of guilt by association, the suspension of usual rules of evidence and procedure, etc. S.R.

Bibl: D. Caute, *The Great Fear* (London, 1978).

mean. The mean of a SET of values is a further value calculated from them as a typical or representative value for the set; the word 'average' is sometimes used as a synonym. The most important type is the *arithmetic mean*, given by adding the values together and dividing the sum by the number n of summands. The *geometric mean* is the nth root of the product of the values, and the *harmonic mean* is the reciprocal of the arithmetic mean of the reciprocals; geometric and harmonic means are useful only when all the values involved are positive. In any technical context 'mean' (unqualified) denotes arithmetic mean: thus in STATISTICS the *sample mean* is the arithmetic mean of the observations making up the SAMPLE (see also MEASURE OF LOCATION). A *weighted arithmetic mean* is obtained by multiplying each value by some non-negative *weight* before summation and then dividing the sum of the products by the sum of the weights. R.SI.

mean deviation. In STATISTICS, the expected absolute value of the difference between the observed value of a RANDOM VARIABLE and a measure of its location (see MEASURE OF LOCATION). R.SI.

meaning. The sense, intension, or CONNOTATION of linguistic expressions, whether sentences as wholes or logically isolable parts of sentences; to be distinguished from the connected, but nevertheless different, reference, extension, or denotation of expressions. The meaning of a sentence is a function of the meaning of its constituents. The meaning of an expression is the rules which determine its use in discourse: semantic rules (see SEMANTICS) connecting it to things, properties, states of affairs, etc., and syntactical rules (see SYNTAX) governing its possibilities of combination with, and its logical RELATIONS to, other expressions. For a person to know the meaning of a word is for him to know the rules of its use; for a word to have a meaning is for there to be, among some group of speakers, a practice of using it in accordance with a set of rules. To identify the meaning of a word with the rules connecting it to objects in the world is not to say that these objects themselves are its meaning any more than the rules of a game are to be identified with the goalposts, wickets, and so forth with which the basic operations of the game are connected by the rules. Philosophical theorists of meaning, however, have an inveterate tendency to identify meanings either with the ordinary objects to which meaningful words refer or with more unusual entities specially recruited for the task. Those who take the ordinary object or objects referred to to be the meaning of a term overlook the fact that the bearer of a name is not its meaning: two names that do not mean the same can have the same bearer. Among the unordinary objects held to be the meanings of terms are such abstract entities as UNIVERSALS and CONCEPTS and such mental entities as images. A.Q.

Bibl: M. Platts, *Ways of Meaning* (London, 1979).

meaning-relation (also called *sense relation* or *semantic relation*). In LINGUISTICS, (1) a specific semantic association regularly interrelating sets of words in the LEXICON of a language, e.g. synonymy, antonymy (see SEMANTICS, SEMANTIC-FIELD THEORY); (2) the semantically relevant interrelationships between grammatical classes and structures, as well as between single words, e.g. the relations postulated by CASE GRAMMAR. D.C.

measure of location. In STATISTICS, an empirical DISTRIBUTION is often described by giving a typical value, e.g. 'Men are about 175 cm in height'. Such a value is called a *measure of location* or *norm* (for other meanings of the latter term see NORM). Measures of location in common use include the MEAN (or EXPECTATION), *median* (see PERCENTILE), MODE, and *midrange* (see DISTRIBUTION). R.SI.

measure theory. In MATHEMATICS, a branch of ANALYSIS (sense 1) which seeks to define notions of length, area, volume for 'figures' which are so intricate or unnatural that simple-minded definitions do not apply. The subject is closely bound up with INTEGRATION and with PROBABILITY THEORY. In particular, the introduction in 1902 of *Lebesgue measure* (and a corresponding *Lebesgue integral*) cleared up many anomalies of the traditional theory. R.G.

mechanical jurisprudence, see CONCEPTUALISM.

mechanics. The branch of PHYSICS dealing with the motion of matter. The subject is divided into two parts: *kinematics*, consisting of the precise geometrical description of position, velocity, ACCELERATION, ORBITS, etc.; and *dynamics*, where the causes of motion are analysed in terms of forces, interactions between objects, etc.

There are three main theories of mechanics in current use: NEWTONIAN MECHANICS is valid for systems which are large in comparison with ATOMS, moving slowly in comparison with light, and not subjected to very strong GRAVITATIONAL fields (such as those near BLACK HOLES). RELATIVITY mechanics includes Newtonian mechanics as a special case, and is also valid near the speed of light and for objects strongly attracted by gravity; it breaks down on the atomic scale. QUANTUM MECHANICS also includes Newtonian mechanics, but remains valid for atomic and nuclear systems. A completely satisfactory fusion of relativity and quantum mechanics has not yet been achieved.

Sometimes the term mechanics is used in a restricted sense, to refer to the purely Newtonian theory required for ASTRONOMY (planetary orbits etc.) and ENGINEERING (bridges, machines, vehicles, etc.).

M.V.B.

Bibl: R.H. March, *Physics for Poets* (New York, 1970).

mechanism. The theory that all CAUSATION is, in Aristotle's terminology, *efficient*, i.e. that for an event to be caused is for its occurrence to be deducible from the antecedent (in some cases contemporaneous) condition in which it occurs, together with the relevant universal laws of nature. The traditional opponent of mechanism is TELEOLOGY, the view that some, perhaps all, events must be explained in terms of the purposes which they serve, and thus that the present is determined by the future rather than by the past. Other views opposed to mechanism are ORGANICISM, the biological doctrines of EMERGENCE and VITALISM, and the position of the dominant school of quantum physicists (see QUANTUM MECHANICS).

A.Q.

mechanization. The central technological feature of INDUSTRIALIZATION. Men have always sought to enhance their power and lighten their labour by mechanical means (levers, wheels, pulleys, etc.) and by harnessing natural energies (windmills, watermills, etc.). In the 18th century, however, technological developments, notably in METALLURGY, made it possible to harness *hidden* energies (steam, gas, electricity, nuclear energy) and thus to power machines capable of performing certain routine skills automatically and much more rapidly than was possible by hand. Over the greatest part of industry, mechanization replaced the craftsman by the 'operative', thus transforming the nature of work, attitudes to work, and a wide range of human relationships. Blake, William Morris, and D.H. Lawrence are among those writers who in different ways have emphasized the DEHUMANIZING effects of mechanization; to their fears have been added that of massive UNEMPLOYMENT resulting from AUTOMATION. See also MODERNIZATION; TECHNOLOGY.   R.F.

media. A generic term used to indicate systems or vehicles for the transmission of information or entertainment such as radio, television, videotape, newspapers and magazines, hoardings, films, books, records, and tapes. Of these, the ubiquitous television, radio, and newspapers are generally classified as the *mass media*. Unlike the others, they form part of man's total ENVIRONMENT in MASS SOCIETY and cannot be ignored without conscious and sustained effort; far more commonly their use engenders a degree of passivity which makes them efficient for the moulding of tastes and preferences. Marshall McLuhan, however, has argued in recent years that the form of the media has a more significant effect on society and knowledge than the contents carried.

Mixed media is a recent term for the long-established CONCEPT (cf. GESAMTKUNSTWERK) of combining more than one form or area of communication, usually for dramatic effect. Thus opera combines drama, music, and singing, while *son et lumière* presentations combine light effects, narration, drama, and music. In contemporary terms, Andy Warhol's mid-1960s 'Exploding Plastic Inevitable' was the first in a succession of mixed-media presentations in which *light shows* (projected variations of pattern and colour either on a random basis or linked with the rhythm of music), films, video playback, and music were combined. Today many forms of artistic expression such as plays, concerts, and art exhibitions utilize mixed-media techniques. Another usage of the term media refers to the professionals employed in this sector who, on the grounds of their assumed cultural and political attitudes, are seen either to distort or dictate public taste. For many, the media has assumed a politically and culturally independent existence.   P.S.L.

Bibl: M. McLuhan, *Understanding Media* (London and New York, 1964); J. Curran *et al*. (eds.), *Mass Communication and Society* (London, 1977).

median, see under PERCENTILE.

medical ethics. May be considered under two headings, traditional, and critical or philosophical medical ETHICS. Traditional medical ethics concerns the moral obligations governing the practice of medicine and has been a central concern of the medical profession for at least 2,500 years. The Hippocratic oath required doctors to benefit their patients, and avoid harming them by, among other things, eschewing 'deadly medicines', ABORTION and the seduction of patients and their families, and by keeping secret whatever 'ought not to be spoken of abroad'. The profession has updated its codes of ethics, especially following medical atrocities in World War II. The World Medical Association has promulgated a series of ethical declarations on such topics as medical research, terminal illness, death and organ transplantation, abortion, and medical participation in torture (categorically forbidden). Regulation of professional standards varies in different countries. In Britain it is vested in the General Medical Council (GMC), established by the Medical Act of 1858 and modified in the Medical Act of 1983. The Council, mostly doctors but including non-medical members appointed by the Crown, is empowered to censure doctors and to remove or suspend them from medical practice. Advice on professional ethics is also provided by the British Medical Association (the main professional association or trade union) and to some extent by the medical protection societies, which in effect insure doctors against malpractice claims. There is a growing trend, which started in America in the 1970s, towards the teaching of critical or philosophical medical ethics in which medico-moral claims and their justifications are exposed to critical analysis in the light of counterarguments. R.GI.
Bibl: A.S. Duncan *et al*. (eds.), *Dictionary of Medical Ethics* (London, 1981); W.T. Reich (ed.), *Encyclopedia of Bioethics* (New York and London, 1978); British Medical Association, *Handbook of Medical Ethics* (London, 1984); General Medical Council, *Professional Conduct and Discipline: Fitness to Practise* (London, 1985); T.L. Beauchamp and J.F. Childress, *Principles of Biomedical Ethics* (New York and Oxford, 1983).

medical genetics. The application of GENETIC techniques to the problems of clinical medicine, and vice versa. Inherited disorders of bodily structure and function are classified according to their mode of inheritance, so that affected individuals and their relatives can be told the likelihood of the same disorder recurring in the family. The facts of the matter, and the consequences of the different options facing a family, are discussed in the process of genetic counselling. The estimation of recurrence risks may be precise, if the disorder is well characterized and its inheritance well understood, but in many cases this is not possible. There may be some doubt as to the precise diagnosis, or the stated recurrence risk may be derived from experience gained with similar familes rather than the application of genetic principles. Counselled families may opt to terminate a pregnancy where there is a high risk that the fetus is affected by an inherited disorder. Testing in the first half of pregnancy is possible for a fetus at risk of such a condition, to see whether or not the child would be affected. Such tests allow families to have normal children when they would find the risk of having an affected child to be otherwise too great. These tests are becoming possible for a rapidly lengthening list of inherited disorders, and make use of techniques to sample the fluid and membranes surrounding the fetus. They also utilize DNA (see NUCLEIC ACID) technology to identify those within a family who share specific lengths of their DNA, thus indicating that they may also share nearby genes. See also EUGENICS. A.CL.

medicalization. The tendency, increasingly marked in the U.S. but also shown elsewhere, as in the Soviet Union, to treat all socially undesirable or deviant behaviour as the fit object of medical science and medical treatment (for the opposite view, see LABELLING THEORY). Drugs are invented to treat children diagnosed as 'hyperactive'. Mental patients and prison inmates with particularly intractable problems of behaviour are diagnosed as suffering from constitutional conditions of insanity or AGGRESSION, and given the appropriate drug therapy. Political dissidents are seen as temperamentally disturbed and in need of medical 'correction'. The view is that most if not all social problems — violent crime, vandalism, ALCOHOLISM, HOMOSEXUALITY, political or moral dissidence — are the result of clinically identifiable 'diseases', which can be cured provided the medical profession is given the care of them. Critics, such as Ivan Illich, of the medicalization of social problems not unnaturally see in it an unwarranted extension of the POWER of the medical profession. More seriously, they see danger in the extension of the 'medical model' to problems with complex social causes, for which drugs appear a highly unsuitable form of treatment.   K.K.

Bibl: P. Conrad and J.W. Schneider, *Deviance and Medicalization: From Badness to Sickness* (St Louis, Missouri, 1980); I. Illich, *Limits to Medicine* (Harmondsworth, 1977).

medium-scale integration, see under INTEGRATED CIRCUIT.

megabyte (Mb). 1,480,576 (2^{20}) or, less commonly, 1,000,000 BYTES.   J.E.S.

Megale Idea, see under ENOSIS.

megalithic. Constructed of large stones: an adjective applied to a wide range of PREHISTORIC structures including stone circles (e.g. Stonehenge), standing stones and alignments, and many CHAMBER TOMBS. It used to be thought that megalithic structures were culturally connected, developing in the East and spreading by DIFFUSION to many parts of Europe; hence the terms 'megalithic religion' and 'megalithic saints'. More recently they have tended to be regarded rather as the outcome of a widespread constructional technique, though cultural connection between some areas adopting megalithic structures is still implied.   B.C.

megalomania. In ABNORMAL PSYCHOLOGY, a pathological state in which the individual over-evaluates his own importance.   W.Z.

megalopolis. Ancient Greek word for 'great city', revived since 1957 by Jean Gottmann to describe the American urban complex stretching from Boston to Washington. It has been accepted as meaning huge urban regions formed by chains of metropolitan areas. Gottmann saw in it a new pattern in the organization of inhabited space, a vast and dense concentration due to the evolution of society towards white-collar and transactional work and to the gregarious nature of people seeking opportunity. Other megalopolitan regions have been described in Japan, in northwest Europe, and along the Great Lakes.   J.G.

Bibl: J. Gottmann, *Megalopolis* (New York, 1961); H.W. Eldredge (ed.), *Taming Megalopolis* (2 vols., New York, 1967).

megastructure. In architecture, a large, multi-storey framework, normally in dense urban situations, which would embrace different kinds of activities and allow different spaces to take on a variety of forms, changing while the megastructure remained. Such notions were put forward in the 1960s by the Archigram Group in England, by Yona Friedman in France, and by the Metabolist Group in Japan. They are an enlargement and extension of Le Corbusier's original project of 1947-8 for the *Unité d'Habitation* at Marseilles where 'bottles' (dwellings) were to fit within a 'bin' (structural framework). Their enormous financial cost and likely high social cost have so far prevented any from being built.   M.BR.

Bibl: J. Dahinden, tr. G. Onn, *Urban Structures for the Future* (London and New York, 1972).

megaton. One thousand KILOTONS.   M.V.B.

meiosis. In GENETICS, two successive CELL divisions (forming a single *reduction division*) as a consequence of which the GAMETES (ova and spermatozoa) contain half the number of CHROMOSOMES present in the cells of the organism, female or male, that produces them; when fertilization occurs, this HAPLOID number is restored to the DIPLOID number. In meiosis one chromosome of each pair passes at random into one of two gametes; one of which will thus have a paternal and the other a maternal chromosome. For the genetic implications of this process see MENDEL'S LAWS. P.M.

Meissner effect, see under STRINGS.

melancholia, see DEPRESSION (2).

melanism. The occurrence of black pigmentation in organisms that are normally light-coloured — particularly in moths and in consequence of industrial processes. The black pigments in most coloured animals including human beings are *melanins* — oxidation products of the AMINO ACIDS dihydroxyphenylalanine (DOPA) or tyrosine. P.M.

membrane structures. Generally very thin skinned flexible STRUCTURES supported by masts or props and stabilized by cables. Guyed tents and boat sails are a crude form of this kind of structure which can now achieve remarkable spans and very dramatic configurations. In recent years, when membrane structures have become the subject of detailed COMPUTER analysis, they have almost exclusively been made from new-technology fabrics such as coated glass fibre. Flexible Teflon coatings have provided an answer to the problem of cleaning. The term also embraces PNEUMATIC STRUCTURES where the structural support is a combination of pressurized air and the shape of the enclosing structure. Because membrane structures are inherently flexible they are most commonly used only as roofing, detached from whatever enclosing structure is to be found underneath. S.L.

memory. Scholars in a number of disciplines are becoming increasingly interested in the process by which different cultures shape the memories of their members, or their views of the past, which can be seen as a kind of collective memory. A pioneer in this field was the French sociologist Maurice Halbwachs, author of *Les cadres sociaux de la mémoire* (1925). Since his day anthropologists and his-

torians have been concerning themselves with the reliability of ORAL TRADITION, while social psychologists and literary critics have analysed the manner in which experience is stereotyped and mythologized as it is recalled. Most recently, historians have become interested in the ways in which societies commemorate the past, studying festivals, museums, STATUS, war memorials and so on as so many forms of institutionalized collective memory with a crucial part to play in the formation of social identity (national, ethnic, religious, professional, etc.). Like the opposition between 'genuine' and 'invented' tradition, the contrast between spontaneous 'memory' and self-conscious REPRESENTATION now appears increasingly difficult to maintain. P.B.

Bibl: P. Nora (ed.), *Les lieux de la mémoire* (Paris, 1984).

Mendel's laws. In GENETICS, the laws of inheritance, specifically for inheritance in DIPLOID organisms in the absence of LINKAGE. Mendel did not himself formulate his discovery (1865) in one or a series of laws, but today his findings are often summed up in two laws: of SEGREGATION, by which a hybrid or *heterozygote* transmits unchanged to each GAMETE one or other of the two factors in respect of which its parental gametes differed; and of *independent assortment*, according to which factors concerned with different characteristics are recombined at random in the gametes. Mendel's laws are now known to follow from the way in which CHROMOSOMES and therefore genetic factors are apportioned to gametes and therefore the next generation. In bisexual organisms the chromosomes are present in pairs (in man, 23 pairs); within each pair one member has derived from each parent. In the formation of gametes these pairs are separated, and each gamete contains only one chromosome from each pair (e.g. a human gamete contains 23 instead of 46 chromosomes). Since segregation is entirely random, the chromosomes in any gamete may be anything from 100% paternally derived to 100% maternally derived. The number of gametes bearing a preponderance of paternally derived chromosomes must, however, be equal to the number bearing

517

a preponderance of maternally derived chromosomes.   J.M.S.; P.M.
Bibl: see under MENDELISM.

Mendelism. The branch of GENETICS dealing with the SEGREGATION of characters in sexual crosses of DIPLOID organisms; by extension, the theory of heredity deriving originally from the work of Gregor Mendel (1865). See also MENDEL'S LAWS.
                                                                J.M.S.
Bibl: C. Stern and E.R. Sherwood (eds.), *The Origin of Genetics* (London and San Francisco, 1966).

Mensheviks. Between 1903 and 1917, a political faction of the Russian Social Democratic Workers' Party; it constituted itself as a political party in August 1917. After the split between the Mensheviks and the Bolsheviks (for the origin of the names see BOLSHEVISM) a formal reunion occurred in 1906, but the struggle for the domination of the R.S.D.W.P. continued. The Mensheviks, of whom the most important were Plekhanov, Axelrod, and Martov, took the orthodox MARXIST view of Russia's development and rejected Lenin's view of the role of the Party (see LENINISM). The split was further complicated by issues such as underground versus legal forms of struggle, national defence versus revolutionary defeatism (see REVOLUTION), etc., which caused divisions among the Mensheviks themselves. Broadly speaking, however, the Mensheviks were 'softer' than the Bolsheviks and more ready to collaborate with other parties, including non-SOCIALIST ones, in the struggle for a democratic constitution (see DEMOCRACY) and against Czarist autocracy. Following the February 1917 revolution, the Mensheviks had a majority in most SOVIETS. After the Bolsheviks' seizure of power in October 1917, the Mensheviks tried to become a legal opposition, but the dissolution of the Constituent Assembly was followed by repressive measures against their Party, culminating in its suppression in 1922. In 1931 Stalin mounted a SHOW TRIAL against the Mensheviks in Moscow (only one of the accused was in fact a Menshevik). The Party maintained its existence abroad, and its leaders, such as F.I. Dan and R.A. Abramovich, continued until the late

1960s to publish commentaries on Soviet developments in the monthly *Sotsialisticheskiy Vestnik* (*Socialist Courier*).   L.L.
Bibl: A. Ascher (ed.), *The Mensheviks in the Russian Revolution* (London, 1976).

mental age. The level of mental development in a child, expressed in years and months, based on age norms for mental tests (see MENTAL TESTING) designed to measure INTELLIGENCE. See also INTELLIGENCE QUOTIENT.   H.L.

mental retardation. Variously defined, but most simply a condition attributed to those individuals placed, in respect of COGNITIVE attainments, in the bottom 2-3% of their age-group. Some 'mental retardates', however, particularly borderline cases, are so classified more on the basis of social than cognitive competence. Indeed, it has been suggested that in the British Mental Deficiency Act of 1913 (superseded in 1958) mental deficiency was defined almost exclusively in terms of social competence.
The study of 'idiots' goes back to antiquity. Over the last few centuries emergent PSYCHIATRY and PSYCHOLOGY came to distinguish clearly between the disturbed and the defective, and particular attention was vested in so-called 'idiot boys' or 'wild boys', feral children, whose educability could be put experimentally to the test. Mass education brought the problem of retardation to public attention in the late 19th century. For most of the 20th century the major contribution of psychologists to the scientific study of mental retardation has been in the area of techniques of cognitive assessment, and, to a lesser extent, the assessment of social and emotional maturity. In the first decade of this century, A. Binet and T. Simon in Paris developed a MENTAL AGE scale for the more systematic appraisal of judgement and reasoning in schoolchildren. Adapted and expanded forms of this scale, notably L.M. Terman's 1916 revision (known as the *Stanford-Binet test* — a later version being known as the *Terman-Merrill revision*), allied with the CONCEPT of INTELLIGENCE and 'innate mental ability' (C. Burt, 1921), served to condemn children and adults thus 'diagnosed' to society's

passive acceptance of their so-called condition. The establishment of special schools (see SPECIAL EDUCATION) and subnormality hospitals had the effect of maintaining and supporting professional and public assumptions, since the inmates not only conformed to expectations but exceeded them in that there was evidence of 'deterioration'.

In educational terms, retarded children were until comparatively recently distinguished in terms of whether they were 'educable' or merely 'trainable'. In Britain, until 1971 this was a crucial distinction, since those considered 'ineducable' were excluded from the educational system. For these children the distinction was based mainly on the results of an intelligence test (see MENTAL TESTING), the approximate borderline being an I.Q. of 50. Children in the I.Q. category of approximately 50-70 were considered EDUCATIONALLY SUBNORMAL, a term which now applies to all retarded children; in the U.S.A. a distinction is still made between 'educable' and 'trainable' mental retardates, although changes in thinking and educational practice have blurred the division.

Important changes in psychological thinking and practice with regard to mental retardation have become increasingly apparent from the early 1950s onwards — although the implications of new findings and, more importantly, new ways of thinking, have yet to be absorbed by the relevant professions, let alone society at large. In Britain, pioneer work was done by A.D.B. Clarke (1953) at the Manor Hospital in Surrey; he demonstrated the effectiveness of task analysis and training schedules in teaching adult retardates quite complex skills. Although intelligence testing remains an active process (the fourth revision of the Stanford-Binet Intelligence Scale was published as recently as 1985), an educational revolution has overtaken assumptions about what I.Q. implies. There is now a large body of empirical evidence which demonstrates that low I.Q. is not necessarily a barrier to learning of 'academic' skills such as literacy and numeracy if systematic instruction is given. Gillham (1986) suggests that mental handicap should be construed as a function of the degree of dependence on instruction. Helping the mentally handicapped to acquire skills typical of the population at large is part of the wider process of normalization. The recognition of special needs does not imply different goals for the handicapped. W.E.C.G.;R.P.

Bibl: A.D.B. Clarke and A.M. Clarke (eds.), *Mental Retardation and Behavioural Research* (Edinburgh, 1973); R. C. Scheerenberger, *A History of Mental Retardation* (London, 1983); M. Craft *et al.* (eds.), *Mental Handicap: A Multidisciplinary Approach* (London, 1985).

mental testing. The measurement, by means of reliable and validated tests, of mental differences between individuals or groups, or the different responses of the same individuals on separate occasions. The tests can be used clinically, as an aid to psychological diagnosis, and vocationally to help in appropriate work placement. Assessment by means of mental testing is used not only by psychologists, doctors, paramedical professionals, teachers and speech therapists, but also increasingly in the industrial and military fields in order to establish and select criteria of competency for particular tasks. All mental testing involves the interpretation of information about a person and his or her situation, and the prediction of his or her behaviour in new situations.

Mental testing may take many forms. *Analogy tests*, which involve the form of verbal reasoning 'A is to B as C is to D', are most commonly used in the assessment of INTELLIGENCE. *Aptitude tests* are designed to measure particular skills possessed by the subject, in order to predict what he might attain with specialized training. *Educational tests* are used to assess basic skills such as reading, arithmetic, spelling, and language comprehension. *Performance tests* measure skill in arranging or otherwise manipulating material (e.g. block designs, mazes) which is visually and spatially presented. *Personality tests* may be *unstructured* as in *story-* or *sentence-completion* (see also RORSCHACH TEST), or structured as in the *Eysenck Personality Inventory*, in which statements about feelings and ideas are presented to the subject for sorting or ticking; his responses can be interpreted to provide insight into his EMOTIONS, and his personal and social relationships.

Mental testing began with the work of A. Binet in 1905. It has been developed by Wechsler, Spearman, Cattell, Thurstone, and many others. Today it is attacked on social and political grounds: on the one hand by those (e.g. Szasz) who fear the misuse of the *results* by an arbitrary authority (such as the State or an institution) or a malignant individual, and on the other by those, mostly EGALITARIANS, who believe that the whole CONCEPT of mental testing is contaminated with unacceptable principles (see, for example, ÉLITISM; MERITOCRACY; RACE).   M.BE.

Bibl: P. Mittler (ed.), *The Psychological Assessment of Mental and Physical Handicaps* (London, 1978).

mentalism. The doctrine that mental states and processes exist independently of their manifestations in behaviour and can explain behaviour. It is thus opposed to BEHAVIOURISM and to the application of the latter known as SOCIAL BEHAVIOURISM. Its best-known proponent is A.N. Chomsky.   A.S.

Bibl: J.A. Fodor, *The Language of Thought* (Brighton, 1975); Z. W. Pylyshyn, *Computation and Cognition* (Boston, 1984); A. Sloman, *The Computer Revolution in Philosophy, Science and Models of Mind* (Brighton, 1978).

mentalities, history of (*mentalités collectives*), see HISTORY OF MENTALITIES.

mercantilism. A school of economic thought that arose in the 16th and 17th centuries and was interested in the relation between a nation's wealth, primarily measured by its reserves of gold and silver, and the balance of foreign trade. It was believed that the STATE was powerful and should intervene to discourage imports, through imposition of tariffs and other measures, and encourage exports through providing subsidies. A surplus on the balance of foreign trade would lead to a net inflow of precious metals, either directly or because of the relation between these metals and money. This inflow would, it was argued, increase the nation's wealth. In 1776, Adam Smith conducted a largely successful attack on mercantilism (see CLASSICAL ECONOMIC THEORY). Most modern economists disagree with mercan-

tilism, but such ideas have often reappeared, e.g. in the Great Depression, and underlie some of the calls for restrictions on imports and more incentives for exports (see PROTECTIONISM and NEO-MERCANTILISM).   R.L.; J.P.

Bibl: W.E. Kuhn, *The Evolution of Economic Thought* (Cincinnati, Ohio, 2nd ed., 1970).

merchandising. 'If you've got it, flaunt it' is an injunction that anyone with products or services to sell would invariably do well to take to heart. Not that explicit flamboyance is always appropriate. Environment is an important part of image building. But if the product is not visible, and not readily accessible, it may well pass even the most determined customer by. Shelf, counter, floor, window, even street display are part of the distributive cycle. But it's usually the way it's done that counts. Merchandising often requires specialized display and presentation skills which should not be underrated. Equally important is the skill of understanding the way the target audience will react to the form and environment of presentation.   T.S.

mereology. In PHILOSOPHY, the theory of part-whole relationships, prompted by such questions as 'is a whole something more than the sum of its parts, or not?' Answers depend upon what kinds of entity the whole and its parts are. The chief puzzle is that many wholes are indeed something more than the sum of their parts, in that they have properties the nature of which is not deducible from knowledge of the parts alone; and this requires explanation.   A.C.G.

merger. The coming together of two or more firms to form one new FIRM. The term is often used to encompass *takeovers*, where one firm acquires another firm. Mergers can have harmful effects in that they can increase MONOPOLY power, which is used to restrict output and raise prices. A beneficial effect of mergers is that they may give rise to ECONOMIES OF SCALE. However, such effects are likely to be economies in MANAGEMENT, planning, RESEARCH AND DEVELOPMENT and MARKETING, as the existing CAPITAL equipment of the merging firms may not be capable of being restructured to give economies in actual production. Larger firms may find it easier to carry the risk and costs of research and development. Thus, they may invest more in research and development. However, the decrease in COMPETITION resulting from a merger may reduce the incentive to produce inventions and INNOVATIONS. Most countries operate a mergers policy to deter and prevent those mergers that are regarded, on balance, as harmful. Mergers can be *horizontal*, between firms in the same industry; *vertical*, between firms at different stages of the production process; and *diversifying*, between firms in different industries (see CONGLOMERATE).   J.P.

Bibl: M.C. Sawyer, *The Economics of Firms and Industries* (London, 1981).

meritocracy. A word coined by Michael Young (*The Rise of the Meritocracy*, 1958) for government by those regarded as possessing merit; merit is equated with INTELLIGENCE-plus-effort, its possessors are identified at an early age and selected for an appropriate intensive EDUCATION, and there is an obsession with QUANTIFICATION, test-scoring, and qualifications. EGALITARIANS often apply the word to any ÉLITIST system of education or government, without necessarily attributing to it the particular grisly features or ultimately self-destroying character of Young's apocalyptic vision.   O.S.

Mertonian thesis, the. The MARXIST claim that CONSCIOUSNESS is determined by social being has defined the terms of debate for the SOCIOLOGY OF KNOWLEDGE during this century. Against Marx, Max Weber contended that ideas could be seen as shaping economic structures no less than the other way round. Specifically, PROTESTANTISM was a crucial factor in the growth of the 'spirit of CAPITALISM'. Weber's analysis was taken up, in the field of the history of science, by the American sociologist, R.K. Merton, who contended that the scientific movement of the 17th century was a response not primarily to socio-economic need but to the stimulus of Protestant THEOLOGY. CALVINISM and Puritanism in particular would lead believers to reject the dead-weight of authority and rely on personal experience and experiment. The

Calvinist VOLUNTARIST conception of God would encourage scientists to seek His ways in Nature, and would foster the notion of a scientific 'calling', encouraging UTILITARIAN ideas of the application of scientific knowledge for human improvement not just personal glory. Merton postulated a high statistical connection between Protestants and scientists in the 17th century. In their specific form, Merton's hypotheses have hardly stood the test of time, but his work has stimulated a lasting interest in the links between modern science and RELIGION.   R.P.

Bibl: R.K. Merton, *Science, Technology and Society in Seventeenth Century England* (New York, 1970; first published, 1938).

Merz. Name given by the painter, poet and typographer Kurt Schwitters (1887-1948) to his one-man DADA splinter movement in Hanover in the 1920s. Recalling the French term *merde* and the German *ausmerzen* (to extirpate), it supposedly derived from a fragment of the word *Kommerz* (commerce) on one of his COLLAGES of 1919. Thereafter he produced *Merz* 'pictures' (assemblages of rubbish), a magazine *Merz* (1923-32) to which Lissitzky, van Doesburg, and Hans Arp all contributed, *Merz* poems, *Merz* evenings with performances of his phonetic *Lautgedichte*, three *Merzbaus* (or environmental sculptures; see ENVIRONMENT), a *Merz* stage, a new alphabet or *Systemschrift*, rubber-stamp pictures (*Stempelbilder*), and some virtually CONCRETE 'picture poems' or *Bildgedichte*. All these shared in the revival of Dada in the 1950s.   J.W.

Bibl: W. Schmalenbach, *Kurt Schwitters* (London and New York, 1970).

mesomorph, see under PERSONALITY TYPES.

meson. A class of ELEMENTARY PARTICLE. Mesons are exchanged during the STRONG INTERACTION of NUCLEONS, and provide the 'glue' holding the atomic NUCLEUS together against the mutual repulsion of the PROTONS in it. This behaviour resembles that of ELECTRONS whose exchange forces hold molecules together, but mesons are unstable, and decay in less than a ten-millionth of a second into elec-

521

trons, NEUTRINOS, and GAMMA-RAYS. Mesons have masses ranging from 100 to 500 times that of the electron, and may occur with positive, negative, or zero electric charge. M.V.B.

messenger RNA, see under NUCLEIC ACID.

messianism. Belief in the salvation of mankind — or, more often, of the particular group which holds the belief — through the appearance of an individual saviour or redeemer. The word is derived from the Hebrew Messiah, a king of the line of David, who was to deliver the Jewish people from bondage and restore the golden age. The adjective *messianic* is frequently used to describe thinkers who (like Marx) foretell with prophetic power than human history is predestined to lead up to an apocalyptic dénouement in which the contradictions and injustices of the present order will be swept away and Utopia, the New Jerusalem, the classless society, established. See also MILLENARIANISM; UTOPIANISM. A.L.C.B.

Bibl: J.L. Talmon, *Political Messianism: the Romantic Phase* (London and New York, 1960); N. Cohn, *The Pursuit of the Millennium* (London and New York, rev. ed., 1970).

metabolism. Considered collectively, the processes of chemical transformation that occur in an organism, whether for the building up of bodily substances or secretions or for the liberation of energy. The predominantly synthetic or constructive elements of the processes of metabolism are known as *anabolism*; the characteristically degradative or destructive processes are known as *catabolism*. P.M.

metadyne. A name given to a cross-FIELD electric generator that originated at the Metropolitan-Vickers Electrical Company. Like the AMPLIDYNE it is used for monitoring large currents (such as those used by London Underground trains) by means of small currents, but is not fully compensated for voltage drops on load as is the amplidyne. E.R.L.

Bibl: C.V. Jones, *The Unified Theory of Electrical Machines* (London, 1967; New York, 1968).

metagrammar. In LINGUISTICS, some linguists use this term to refer to a GENERATIVE GRAMMAR which contains a set of *metarules*, i.e. rules which define the properties of other rules on the basis of information already present in the grammar. D.C.

Bibl: G. Gazdar *et al.*, *Generalized Phrase Structure Grammar* (Oxford, 1985).

metahistory. A synonym for the philosophy of history, in its double sense of reflection on the pattern of the past or the methods of historians. More recently, however, the term has been used by Northrop Frye and Hayden White to refer to the narrative structure of histories, which according to them are of four kinds, tragi-comic, tragic, romantic and satirical, whether the writers are aware that they have 'emplotted' their history in this way or not. P.B.

Bibl: H. White, *Metahistory* (Baltimore and London, 1973).

metal fatigue. The increased liability to fail of a metal that has been subjected to repeatedly variable stress for long periods. The degree of fatigue increases (i.e. the metal is liable to break as the result of smaller and smaller stresses) with the size of the average stress and with the magnitude and frequency of the stress changes. Metal fatigue was first brought to public attention as the result of early jet-plane crashes. See also CREEP. E.R.L.

metalanguage. In LINGUISTICS, any technical language devised to describe the properties of language. D.C.

metalinguistics. A term used by some linguists for the study of language in relation to other aspects of cultural behaviour. It is not, as etymology might suggest, the study of METALANGUAGE. D.C.

metallurgy. The branch of science and TECHNOLOGY which deals with metals and their alloys. Its existence as a distinct field of study (though it draws heavily on PHYSICS and CHEMISTRY) illustrates the importance of metals (particularly steel, aluminium, and copper) in everyday life. It is concerned with the extraction of metals from their ores; with the understanding of their properties in terms of ELECTRONIC and crystalline structure (see CRYSTALLOGRAPHY); with devising new alloys or new methods of treatment to meet particular needs. Metallurgy grew up as a practical, nearly empirical technology but is nowadays given academic respectability as a branch of MATERIALS SCIENCE.   B.F.

Bibl: A.C. Street and W.O. Alexander, *Metals in the Service of Man* (Harmondsworth, 6th ed., 1976); G.C.E. Olds, *Metals and Ceramics* (Edinburgh, 1968).

metamathematics. The logical investigation (see LOGIC) of the properties of axiomatically formulated mathematical systems (see AXIOMATICS), introduced by Hilbert and associated by him with a FORMALIST interpretation of the nature of MATHEMATICS. It is concerned to establish the CONSISTENCY, independence, and completeness of the AXIOMS of formalized deductive systems, that is the compatibility of the axioms with each other, the impossibility of deducing any one of them from the rest, and the deducibility from them of all the TRUTHS expressible in the vocabulary of the system. GÖDEL'S THEOREM proves the incompletability of any system that contains arithmetic.   A.Q.

metamorphosis. A more or less radical rearrangement of parts that occurs in the development of those animals of which the embryonic or larval forms differ greatly from the corresponding adult forms. Examples in early EMBRYOLOGY are *gastrulation* and *neurulation*; examples from a later stage of development are the metamorphosis of the familiar tadpole into the frog and of the lepidopteran caterpillar through a pupal stage into moth or butterfly.   P.M.

metaphor. It was Roman Jakobson who, in a major essay published in 1956, made a seminal distinction between metaphor and *metonymy*. Jakobson was concerned primarily with a study of aphasia (see NEUROPSYCHOLOGY), and distinguished two types of aphasia, one whose 'major deficiency lies in selection or substitution, with relative stability of combination and contexture'; and the other whose major deficiency lies in 'combination and contexture, with relative retention of normal selection and substitution'. It seemed to Jakobson that this led to a conclusion about language itself, and that metaphor and metonymy are actually *opposed*, because they are generated from antithetical principles. Metaphor belongs, it would seem, to the selection axis of language, allowing of the possibility of *substitution*. Metonymy, however, belongs to the combination axis of language, allowing for the perception of *contexture*. These oppositions correspond to the distinctions made by Saussure between the paradigmatic and the SYNTAGMATIC. Jakobson demonstrates the difference between the two types of thought-process by invoking literature, art and film. Lyrical song, ROMANTIC and SYMBOLIST poetry and the films of Charlie Chaplin, for instance, clearly operate according to the principle of metaphor, while the REALIST novel, such as Tolstoy's, demonstrates the metonymic principle of selection in full activity, along with the associated TROPE of synecdoche, as do the films of D.W. Griffith. The principle that the two forms of language are actually opposed both in principle and in origin had a galvanizing effect upon French STRUCTURALISM. Lévi-Strauss took Jakobson's distinction as one of the bases of his own binary METHODOLOGY, and Lacan, Barthes and the writers round *Tel Quel* all made great play with it.   R.PO.

Bibl: R. Jakobson and M. Halle, *Fundamentals of Language* (The Hague, 1956); R. Barthes, *Elements of Semiology* (London, 1967); D. Lodge, *The Modes of Modern Writing* (London, 1977).

metaphysical painting (*pittura metafisica*). An Italian movement so named by the artists Giorgio de Chirico and Carlo Carrà at Ferrara in World War I, and later joined by Giorgio Morandi. The mysterious, inhuman calmness of their pictures of empty city spaces, tailor's dummies, and banal 'ordinary things' — of which Chirico's dated largely from before the war — was influential in the development of pictorial SURREALISM, as well as having a muted echo in German MAGIC REALISM. Itself largely a reaction against FUTURISM and a re-evocation of Giotto and other Florentine masters, the movement largely petered out after about 1920, as both Chirico and Carrà became increasingly traditionalist. J.W.

metaphysics. The investigation of the world, or of what really exists, generally by means of rational argument rather than by direct or mystical intuition. It may be either *transcendent* (see TRANSCEND-ENCE), in that it holds that what really exists lies beyond the reach of ordinary experience (as in the picture of the world supplied by supernatural RELIGION), or *immanent*, in that it takes reality to consist exclusively of the objects of experience. Kant and the LOGICAL POSITIVISTS both denied the legitimacy of transcendent metaphysics, Kant on the ground that the *a priori* elements in thought (see APRIOR-ISM) yield knowledge only if applied to the data of experience, the logical positivists on the ground that sentences ostensibly about the world are not even significant unless susceptible of empirical VERIFICA-TION. The primary component of meta-physics is ONTOLOGY, in which metaphysi-cians ascribe existence to, or withhold it from, three major classes of things: (1) the concrete occupants of space and time, (2) minds and their states, conceived in the manner of DUALISM as in time but not space, and (3) abstract entities or UNIVER-SALS. A further ontological issue is the number of real existences there are of the preferred kind: is there just one real SUB-STANCE, as MONISTS like Spinoza and Hegel believe, or many? Metaphysicians also propound theories about the overall structure of the world. Is it a mechanical or deterministic system or does it contain chance events or the causally inexplicable emergence of novelty? A.Q.

Bibl: W.H. Walsh, *Metaphysics* (London and New York, 1963); K. Campbell, *Metaphysics* (Berkeley, 1976).

metapsychology. Considerations about PSYCHOLOGY with regard to its definition, purposes, PRESUPPOSITIONS, METH-ODOLOGY, and limitations, its status as a contribution to knowledge, and its rela-tions to other disciplines. I.M.L.H.

metastable, see under EQUILIBRIUM.

metastases, see under CANCER.

metasystem. A SYSTEM 'over and beyond' a system of lower logical order, and there-fore capable of deciding PROPOSITIONS, discussing CRITERIA, or exercising REGU-LATION (3) for systems that are themselves logically incapable of such decisions, such discussions, or of *self*-regulation. This is a CONCEPT used in CYBERNETICS and the SYSTEMS approach, and derives from theoretical MATHEMATICS. The emphasis is on *logical* order, not on 'seniority' in the sense of command. For example, one may observe a system in which playing-cards are dealt to a group of people who proceed to dispose of them according to a set of fixed rules which can be ascertained, and which completely determine winners and losers. Over and beyond this system is a metasystem which is expressed in entirely different terms: money. If the observer failed to understand the metasystem he would not appreciate what the game of poker is actually about. See also ALGE-DONIC. S.BE.

metatheory. The set of assumptions pre-supposed (see PRESUPPOSITION) by any more or less formalized body of assertions, in particular the CONCEPTS implied by the vocabulary in which it is expressed and the rules of INFERENCE by means of which one assertion in the system is derived from another. The idea is a generalization of that involved in the selection of features of deductive systems for investigation that is characteristic of AXIOMATICS or META-MATHEMATICS. A.Q.

meteorology. The study of short-term changes in the weather (temperature, rain-fall, humidity, sunshine, etc.), as con-trasted with CLIMATOLOGY, which deals with long-term changes. A picture of the state of the atmosphere is built up by observations from the ground and from SATELLITES; this forms the starting-point for COMPUTER calculations, based on AERO-DYNAMICS, aimed at forecasting future weather conditions. M.V.B.

Bibl: O.G. Sutton, *Understanding Weather* (Harmondsworth, 1960).

method study, see under MANAGEMENT; WORK STUDY.

method, the. A system of training and rehearsal for actors which bases a performance upon inner emotional experience, discovered largely through the medium of improvisation, rather than upon the teaching or transmission of technical expertise. Based on the theory and practice of Konstantin Stanislavsky (1863-1938) at the Moscow Arts Theatre, it was developed by the American director Lee Strasberg who in 1947, with Cheryl Crawford and Elia Kazan, founded the *Actors' Studio* in New York as a partial successor to the GROUP THEATRE. For some 15 years the Studio had a profound influence upon American film and theatre, in the work of actors including Marlon Brando, James Dean, and Paul Newman.

M.A.

Bibl: R.H. Hethmon (ed.), *Strasberg at the Actors' Studio* (London, 1966).

Methodism. A Christian denomination active throughout the English-speaking world, with about 26 million adherents. Founded by John Wesley (1707-91), it was originally so nicknamed because of its claim to be methodical in observing the devotional requirements of ANGLICANISM, but was organized as a virtually independent PROTESTANT Church in Wesley's lifetime. It has stressed its warm fellowship, its strict morality, its interest in social problems, and its keen EVANGELISM. It is well organized — in the U.S.A. under bishops. Theologically it is optimistic, believing that all men can be saved, can know that they are saved, and can reach moral perfection, but it has been criticized for a lack of sophistication and of intellectual liveliness. Recently it has been much influenced by the ECUMENICAL MOVEMENT for Christian reunion.

D.L.E.

Bibl: R.E. Davies, *Methodism* (Harmondsworth and Baltimore, 1963).

methodological individualism and **methodological holism.** Two contrasted approaches to the METHODOLOGY of the SOCIAL SCIENCES. They differ in their answers to such questions as the following: Is it necessary, or even relevant, to mention the beliefs, attitudes, decisions, or actions of individual people in attempting to describe and explain social, political, or economic phenomena? Is it necessary to postulate the existence of SOCIAL WHOLES which have purposes or functions or needs, or which cause events to occur; or are all mentions of such things really abbreviated references to the individual persons in the society concerned (e.g. can a nation or committee be said to have a mind of its own?)? Do SOCIAL STRUCTURES and social processes influence the attitudes, beliefs, decisions, etc. of individuals, or are all such influences to be explained simply in terms of person-to-person interaction? Is the study of society necessarily based on the study of its members, or is there some other means of observing or measuring social entities, like the will of the nation, perhaps through the study of large-scale historical processes?

In answering such questions, *methodological individualists* tend to discount the importance or scientific status of social wholes, while *methodological holists* tend to discount the influence of individuals on social phenomena. It can be argued that the whole dispute is as futile as a dispute between engineers as to whether what is important in a building or mechanism is its structure or the materials or components used. Clearly both are important, but in different ways. See also HOLISM.

A.S.

Bibl: A. Ryan, *The Philosophy of the Social Sciences* (London, 1979; New York, 1971).

methodology. In the narrowest sense, the study or description of the methods or procedures used in some activity. The word is normally used in a wider sense to include a general investigation of the aims, CONCEPTS, and principles of reasoning of some discipline, and the relationships between its sub-disciplines. Thus the methodology of science includes attempts to analyse and criticize its aims, its main concepts (e.g. EXPLANATION, CAUSALITY, *experiment, probable*), the methods used to achieve these aims, the subdivision of science into various branches, the relations between these branches (see REDUCTION), and so on. Some scientists use the word merely as a more impressive-sounding synonym for method.

A.S.

Bibl: E. Nagel, *The Structure of Science* (London and New York, 1961); C.G. Hempel, *Philosophy of Natural Science*

(London and Englewood Cliffs, N.J., 1966); K.R. Popper, *The Logic of Scientific Discovery* (London, 3rd ed., 1968; New York, 2nd ed., 1968).

metonymy, see under METAPHOR.

metrology. The precise establishment and comparison of the standard units of measurement. See also ATOMIC CLOCK; MKS UNITS; SI UNITS.   M.V.B.

metropolis. A Greek word for mother-city which has long meant the main city or largest centre of activity in a region or country. With modern URBANIZATION many cities grew very big, while suburbs and SATELLITE TOWNS sprawled around them. Metropolitan regions are thus formed around many large centres. The use of the term has spread with the phenomenon. 'Metropolitan' government, police, transport, encompassing the metropolis and the region in its orbit, are common concepts, while the term *metropolitanization* has been used to describe certain trends in the U.S.A. and other countries where the majority of the population lives in metropolitan areas. The term is also used in the sense of a city recognized as a major market for a certain category of goods or services.   J.G.
Bibl: S.R. Miles (ed.), *Metropolitan Problems* (London and Toronto, 1970).

mezzo-giorno. An economically UNDER-DEVELOPED area comprising the southern Italian mainland regions of Abruzzi, Molise, Campania, Puglia, Basilicata and Calabria together with islands Sicily and Sardinia. The Italian term *mezzo-giorno* means 'mid-day' and southern Italy is so-called because of the intensity of the mid-day sun. Per capita income in the *mezzo-giorno* lags behind that of northern Italy. Agriculture is the main form of employment; olive oil, fruit and vegetables are the main crops. ECONOMIC DEVELOPMENT programmes for the *mezzo-giorno* are assisted by the European Investment Bank and the Italian government. Economic planners have favoured bringing heavy industries (iron, steel, petro-chemicals, car manufacture) into the region.   S.M.

MGB, see under KGB.

MHD, see under MAGNETOHYDRODYNAMICS.

MI (Military Intelligence). The gathering of information, by clandestine as well as overt means, about the intentions of enemies or potential enemies and the means at their disposal to effect their intentions. In Britain MI has become in addition a cover name for a Security Service (MI5) and the Secret Intelligence Service (MI6), both civilian forces, the first operating purely on British territory and answerable on security problems through the Home Secretary to the Prime Minister, the other operating outside British territory and therefore answerable to the Foreign Secretary. Both intelligence services have found themselves at the centre of political rows in Britain, particularly when in 1986-7 the Thatcher government attempted to stop the publication of former MI5 officer Peter Wright's memoirs in a notorious court case in Australia.
D.C.W.; S.T.
Bibl: P. Knightley, *The Second Oldest Profession* (London, 1986); N. West, *MI5: British Security Operations 1909-1945* (London, 1981) and *A Matter of Trust: MI5 1945-1972* (London, 1982) and *MI6* (London, 1983).

Michelson-Morley experiment. It was believed in the late 19th century that the earth must be moving relative to the ETHER which was thought to support light waves; and that because the speed of light would be constant relative to the ether, its speed relative to the earth should vary with direction. In 1888 the American scientists Albert Michelson (1852-1931) and Edward Morley (1838-1923) tried to measure this difference in velocity for light travelling in different directions, but no effect could be detected. A large number of subsequent more accurate experiments all confirmed this result, except for that of Miller in 1924, who claimed to detect a tiny positive effect; but this was later shown to be due to an identifiable experimental error. It was concluded that the speed of light in a vacuum is independent of the relative motion of source and ob-

server, and this result became one of the postulates of RELATIVITY theory. M.V.B.
Bibl: see under OPTICS; RELATIVITY.

microbe. A lay term used to describe bacteria (see BACTERIOLOGY) and also, quite wrongly, infective particles like viruses (see VIROLOGY), which are not living organisms as bacteria are. P.M.

microbiology. The discipline concerned with bacteria and viruses in their wider aspects which grew up when it came to be realized, during the past 20 or 30 years, that BACTERIOLOGY and VIROLOGY were important not merely for their own sakes, but also because they might provide MODELS of such phenomena occurring in higher organisms as heredity (see GENETICS), development, and DIFFERENTIATION. P.M.

microchemistry. The branch of CHEMISTRY which deals with the manipulation and estimation of chemical substances in minute quantities. Microanalytical techniques typically allow one ten-thousandth of a gram of material to be determined with an accuracy of 1% or 2%. B.F.

microclimatology. The branch of CLIMATOLOGY concerned with small-scale atmospheric phenomena near the surface of the earth. P.H.
Bibl: R. Geiger, tr. from 4th German ed., *The Climate near the Ground* (Cambridge, Mass., 1965).

microcoding. The use of a computer PROGRAM intended to imitate the behaviour of another COMPUTER. They are often written in rebarbative PROGRAMMING LANGUAGES intended to be used only by the expert employees of a computer manufacturer but designed with an eye to their easy implementation in HARDWARE. The resulting SYSTEM is cheaper (though perhaps slower) than the direct hardware implementation of the imitated machine. J.E.S.

microcomputer. A COMPUTER using a MICROPROCESSOR and other components implemented in VLSI (see INTEGRATED CIRCUIT), and either packaged on its own or forming part of a larger SYSTEM. The low cost of this TECHNOLOGY has revolutionized the use of computers, so that microcomputers are now used in washing machines, video games, watches, and even embedded in credit cards. J.E.S.

microeconomics, see under ECONOMICS.

micro-electronics. The development of tiny TRANSISTORS, INTEGRATED CIRCUITS, and other ELECTRONIC components for use in COMPUTERS, INERTIAL GUIDANCE systems, spacecraft, etc. M.V.B.

microhistory. This term, first employed in Italian, is coming into use to describe a cluster of books on social and cultural history which attempt to see the world in a grain of sand and concentrate on a small community (like the village of Montaillou in Languedoc, studied by Emmanuel Le Roy Ladurie) or even an individual (like Menocchio Scandella, the miller-hero of Carlo Ginzburg's *Cheese and Worms*), in an attempt to reconstitute the experience of life in the past, which according to these scholars is lacking in quantitative 'macrohistorical' studies. The approach has become fashionable, is producing diminishing intellectual returns and sometimes degenerates into anecdote. However, at its best the microhistorical method can reveal the weaknesses and challenge the conclusions of traditional SOCIAL and CULTURAL HISTORY. How to link the two approaches is the current problem. P.B.
Bibl: E. Le Roy Ladurie, *Montaillou* (1975; English trans., London, 1978).

microlinguistics. A term used by some LINGUISTS for the study of the phonological and morphological LEVELS (sense 1) of language; but also used in a general sense for any analysis or point of view which concentrates on describing the details of linguistic behaviour as against general trends or patterns (to which the term *macrolinguistics* is sometimes applied). D.C.

micronutrients, see TRACE ELEMENT.

micro-organism. A term (with the same CONNOTATION as the layman's MICROBE) which stands generally for microscopically small organisms like bacteria, proto-

527

zoa, and the mycoplasmas, and also includes viruses (see VIROLOGY) — though this is an improper use because viruses are not in any strict sense living organisms.

P.M.

microprocessor. A COMPUTER processor (see PROCESSOR) implemented in VLSI on a single chip. See INTEGRATED CIRCUIT; MICROCOMPUTER.

J.E.S.

microregion, see under REGION.

microsome. A small cellular particle consisting mainly of ribonucleoprotein, identified in the 1930s by Albert Claude using the ultracentrifuge (see SEDIMENTATION). For a long time its real existence was in doubt, but now it is thought that microsomes represent a cellular element known as *ribosomes.* See also CYTOLOGY; NUCLEIC ACID.

P.M.

microstructure, see under EXCHANGE MODEL.

microsurgery, see under SURGERY.

microteaching. A technique in the training of teachers first used at Stanford University in 1960. A teacher takes a specially constructed lesson lasting from, say, 10 to 30 minutes with a class of about 5-10 pupils. The lesson is evaluated (under such headings as aims, content, and vocabulary) by an observer, the pupils, and the teacher; it is then reconstructed, re-presented, and re-evaluated. VIDEOTAPE is often used and the re-presentation is given to a different group of pupils. W.A.C.S.

Bibl: J.L. Olivero, *Microteaching* (Columbus, Ohio, 1970).

microtone. A fraction of a tone smaller than a semitone. Normally in Western music the octave is divided into 12 equal parts or semitones. It has been argued that a division into 24 quarter-tones would provide greater variety; in 1907, Busoni suggested 3 divisions to a semitone, making a scale of 36 chromatic notes, while the Czech composer Alois Haba has experimented with 6th- and even 12th-tones. From the point of view of sheer geographical distribution, microtonal music was, indeed, for centuries the predominant

idiom. Chinese, Japanese, Indian, Polynesian, Greek, Arabic, Bulgarian, Hungarian, and Andalusian music have this common factor. Yet attempts to introduce microtones into Western concert music have so far met with limited success. It is likely, however, that the infinite variability of pitch obtainable through ELECTRONICS and the simultaneous breakaway from traditional tone-colours may hasten their acceptance.

A.H.

microvascular surgery. The operating microscope has made it possible to join small arteries (greater than 1 mm in diameter) to restore blood flow to organs and TISSUES. While useful in PLASTIC AND RECONSTRUCTIVE SURGERY, results have been disappointing in the restoration of blood flow to the brian. Microvascular surgery on small aneurysms of the brain has proved more rewarding, and allows the accurate placement of small clips to these lesions and the removal of arteriovenous malformations of the brain and spinal cord. All these techniques make use of the operating microscope and specially designed micro instruments which allow the safe manipulation of these delicate structures under better illumination and with magnification.

A.D.M.

microwaves. The shortest radio waves, with wavelengths less than about 30 cm and frequencies greater than 1,000 megahertz (1 hertz = 1 complete vibration cycle per second; 1 megahertz = 1 million hertz). Microwaves are generated by oscillating electric circuits or MASERS, and used in RADAR and TELECOMMUNICATION systems.

M.V.B.

MIDAS (Missile Defence Alarm System), see under MISSILES.

middle class. Until recently, there would have been little to distinguish this term from its Continental synonym, BOURGEOIS, although the English term was always less value-loaded, carried less of the pejorative overtones that went with the borrowed foreign term. Increasingly in the 20th century, however, there has been a growth of distinctively middling ranks between the old middle class, the bourgeoisie proper, and the WORKING CLASS. As a result especially of the enormous expansion of private and public bureaucracies, there is now a white-collar salariat, a middle-level, middle-income 'service class' which differs markedly in outlook and prospects from the professional and proprietary middle class — better now thought of as decidedly *upper*-middle class. At the same time the new middle class is very different from the old PETITE BOURGEOISIE or lower-middle class of small farmers, small businessmen, and artisans. Since the new middle class currently amounts to over one-third of the employed population, and is likely to be about a half by the turn of the century, its attitudes and interests are bound to be increasingly represented in social and political life. What precisely these attitudes and interests are no one seems very sure of, and that includes the middle class itself; but it is already clear that neither the traditional RIGHT nor the traditional LEFT have much to offer it. The struggle for the soul, and the votes, of the middle class is likely to be central to the politics of the coming decades.   K.K.

Bibl: J. Raynor, *The Middle Class* (London, 1970); I. Bradley, *The English Middle Classes are Alive and Kicking* (London, 1982).

Middle East Wars. Generated from 1948 to 1973 from hostility between Israel and the Arab states, complicated by the interests of the great powers. The wars of 1948-9 arose from Arab refusal to accept the creation of the state of Israel in May 1948. The Arab defeat left Israel with more territory than the UNO partition plan for Palestine had recommended and Jerusalem was divided between Israel and Jordan. The armistice lines which thus became Israeli borders invited Arab infiltration and made Israel strategically vulnerable. At the same time it was cut off from navigation to the south.

The SUEZ war, October-November 1956, originated from President Nasser's NATIONALIZATION of the Suez Canal which the British government saw as a threat to their world power and the French to their imperial interests in Algeria. Israeli interest in securing the south by an occupation of Sinai produced a loosely jointed alliance and an invasion of Egypt first by Israel, then by Britain and France under the pretext of a 'police action'. The war was a turning point for all participants. In Britain it was a *cause célèbre* because the government deceived parliament as to the alliance with Israel; it confirmed the loss of British world power as the Suez action was opposed by the U.S. In France the Israeli alliance was uncontroversial but the eventual independence of Algeria was taken a step further. Israel, under unique pressure from the U.S., withdrew from all occupied territory and abandoned war as a means of changing the BALANCE OF POWER until 1982. President Nasser won prestige in the Arab world as well as Egypt and was confirmed in his anti-IMPERIALIST Arab policies.

The complex origins of the Six Day War (June 1967) can best be summarized as an attempt by Nasser to recoup the losses of the Yemen war and a faltering economy by challenging Israel and winning a limited political-military victory. Instead Israel responded to Egyptian moves, including the withdrawal of consent to the UN force in Sinai and a blockade of the straits of Aqaba, by a brilliant air strike which effectively decided the battle with Egypt. This was followed by the occupation of Sinai, and counter attacks on Jordan and Syria, leaving Israel in occupation of the Sinai, the Gaza strip and the West Bank and the Golan heights. Possible Russian support for Egypt was held off by the U.S.

The October War (1973) known, from its timing, as the Yom Kippur War in Israel and the war of Ramadan in Egypt, was initiated by President Sadat in alliance with Syria and with the support of the Arab oil producers as part of a strategy to recover the Sinai. A successful penetration of the Israeli line on the Suez Canal was followed by an Israeli recovery. The Soviet Union and the U.S. resupplied their clients, Egypt and Israel respectively, and U.S. forces were put on full alert against possible direct Russian intervention. Arab use of the OIL WEAPON had no direct effect on the war but heightened U.S. interest in the region. Kissinger's shuttle DIPLOMACY then led to disengagement agreements between Israel and Egypt and Israel and Syria. The October war was a prelude to the Egypt-Israel peace treaty of 1979.

W.K.

Bibl: P. Mansfield, *The Arabs* (London, 1985); N. Safran, *Israel, The Embattled Ally* (Cambridge, Mass., 1981).

middle range, theories of the. Term introduced by Robert K. Merton (1949) for theories, especially in SOCIOLOGY, which aim to integrate observed empirical regularities and specific hypotheses within a relatively limited problem-area — as opposed to either entirely *ad hoc* explanation or attempts at a quite general theory of SOCIAL ACTION or SOCIAL STRUCTURE as in, say, STRUCTURAL-FUNCTIONAL THEORY or CONFLICT THEORY.   J.H.G.
Bibl: see under REFERENCE GROUP.

MIDI. Musical Instrument Digital Interface, which is a standardization set up in the 1980s to govern the intercommunication between ELECTRONIC MUSICAL devices: e.g. SYNTHESIZERS, SEQUENCERS, etc. Machines with this system can be very simply linked up to control one another.
                                          B.CO.

mid-oceanic ridge, see under OCEANIC RIDGE.

mid-range, see under DISTRIBUTION.

militancy, see under ACTIVISM (sense 2).

Militant. A British political organization which claims not to be, and which is often wrongly referred to as, the *Militant Tendency*. It is an essentially TROTSKYITE group, which attempted to disguise its existence and structure behind that of its newspaper *Militant*. Its long term goal is to lead the transformation of the United Kingdom to a SOCIALIST and, ultimately, COMMUNIST society. Its tactics include attempts to penetrate the Labour Party, particularly at the level of parliamentary constituency parties and in municipal politics. Since 1983 the party's leadership has tried to check Militant's influence. Its publicly-stated programmes are non-revolutionary and rather anachronistic; they are designed to broaden Militant's appeal and raise WORKING-CLASS political consciousness rather than to offer a serious contribution to debate within the Labour Party.   S.R.
Bibl: M. Crick, *The March of Militant* (London, 1986); P. Taaffe, *What We Stand For* (London, 1981).

Militant Tendency, see under MILITANT.

military-industrial complex. A phrase coined by speechwriters for President Eisenhower's farewell address to the American electorate in 1960, in which he warned of the growing influence on economic and foreign policy of the armaments industries and the military establishment, who shared a common interest in constantly growing defence budgets and a militaristic approach to international relations. The theme was surprisingly close to the thoughts of the American LEFT, who adopted the phrase with relish. It survives, denoting more elaborate arguments, in MARXIST and elitist critiques of American government.   S.R.
Bibl: S. Melman, *The War Economy of the US* (New York, 1971).

Military Intelligence, see MI.

millenarianism (or *millennialism*). The belief and practices of those who seek, by way of a religious and/or political movement, to secure a comprehensive, salvationary solution for social, personal, and political predicaments. The term has been used by historians and social scientists as a comparative focus for the study of many movements in many parts of the world which have developed sectarian or messianic or salvationary programmes of social transformation (see, e.g., CARGO CULTS). There has been much controversy about the psychological or economic roots of such programmes, their links in specific cases with magical practices, and their utility for the diverse societies in which (or in relation to which) they have been promoted. The term originated — like the related term *chiliastic* — in the myth of Christ's return after 'a thousand years', but the idea has pre-Christian roots and is reflected in Jewish and Islamic thought.
                                          S.J.G.
Bibl: N. Cohn, *The Pursuit of the Millennium* (London and New York, rev. ed., 1970); B. Wilson, *Magic and the Millennium* (London and New York, 1973).

mimicry. In BIOLOGY, similarity of form or behaviour of one SPECIES to another. For example, the viceroy butterfly, which is not poisonous to birds, is almost identical in appearance to the gold and black coloured monarch butterfly, which is poisonous. The two species inhabit similar regions of the southern U.S. The viceroy gains protection from birds by mimicking the monarch. Cases of mimicry in which one species (the model) is poisonous and the other (the mimic) is not are called *Batesian mimicry.* In other cases, both species may be poisonous; these are called Müllerian mimicry. Other types of mimicry are also known. M.R.

mind, philosophy of. The philosophical investigation of minds and their states and our knowledge of them. Starting traditionally from the DUALIST assumption that the mental is radically distinct in nature from the physical, it was principally concerned with the apparent causal relations between mind and body: PERCEPTION in one direction and the operations of the will in the other. More recently the main problem has been that of our knowledge of the minds of others, to whose states we have no direct, introspective access but which we must infer from their perceptible manifestations in speech and behaviour (see INTROSPECTION; BEHAVIOURISM). A persistent problem is whether the mind is a substantial entity, distinct from the thoughts and experiences that make up its history, or whether it is simply the related totality of its experiences. Increasingly, biochemical research is demonstrating organic substrates for 'mental acts'. It remains unclear precisely how brain activity and CONSCIOUSNESS should be conceptually related. A connected issue is that of personal identity. Are two experiences those of the same person by reason of association with a persisting mental substance, or with the same human body, or because of some special relation between the two, e.g. that the later contains a memory, or the possibility of a memory, of the earlier one? A further problem concerns the question of whether the mind is pre-programmed. Chomsky's LINGUISTICS claimed that the use of language was not learned but innate, suggesting a revival of the basic Cartesian notion of an innate human rationality distinct from the conditioned responses postulated by behaviourists. See also MIND-BODY PROBLEM; CHOMSKYAN. A.Q.;R.P.

Bibl: J. Shaffer, *Philosophy of Mind* (Englewood Cliffs, N.J., 1968).

mind-body problem. The set of issues that have emerged from the human tendency to postulate a fundamental difference between the realm of mind on the one hand and physical nature on the other. It is generally accepted that any attitude towards the dichotomy creates major, perhaps insoluble, problems of philosophical ANALYSIS. Traditionally, there have been four main attitudes: (1) *Physical monism* (see also MONISM) is probably the most widely accepted among natural scientists, assuming as it does that all phenomena of mind and of nature can be reduced to the laws of PHYSICS and BIOLOGY. (2) *Neutral monism* (or *mental monism*) holds that all is mind, and that the CONCEPT of nature is itself a CONSTRUCT of mind that can only be known through hypotheses tested by reference to experience. This view, which received its contemporary expression in the late 19th century from Ernst Mach, is today expressed as a METHODOLOGICAL principle, based on the premise that, since nature cannot be known directly but only by the mediation of a human observer, one defines nature and mind alike by the kinds of observations one makes and the nature of the INFERENCES one draws — whether these refer to a postulated 'external' system of physical nature, or to the 'internal' system called mind. (3) *Interactionism* (see also PSYCHOSOMATIC) holds that there are two interacting spheres, mind and body: a view that received its first definitive elaboration in the writings of Descartes. The issue of how the two spheres interact without each destroying the self-sufficiency of the other's body of principles remains moot. (4) The classical doctrine of *psychophysical parallelism,* usually attributed to Leibniz, is the view that physical and psychical events run a parallel course without affecting each other. For a fifth, less widespread, view see EPIPHENOMENALISM.

The modern development of the notion has been deeply affected by Darwinian evolutionism (see EVOLUTION), which

531

stressed the ultimate unity and continuity between animal existence and emergent CONSCIOUSNESS. In particular, William James and other American FUNCTIONAL-ISTS around the turn of this century postulated an adaptive functionalism which treated mind rather like other organic faculties. C. Lloyd Morgan argued that the evolution of organized complexity produced a qualitatively distinct level of being, while the school of Pavlov (see PAVLOVIAN) in the U.S.S.R. stressed the evolutionary interaction between conscious action and ENVIRONMENTAL DETER-MINATION. Scientifically speaking, classic mind/body dualism cannot survive the implications of evolutionism.   J.S.B.;R.P.

Bibl: G. Ryle, *The Concept of Mind* (London, 1949); A. Flew (ed.), *Body, Mind, Death: Readings* (New York, 1964); D.A. Oakley, *Brain and Mind* (London, 1985).

mineralogy. The study of minerals, the naturally occurring solid substances which make up the earth's crust, meteorites, and lunar rocks. The use of word 'mineral' for sand and gravel and also for plant nutrient elements derived from the soil suggests that the elasticity of the English language has been over-stretched.   J.L.M.L.

miners' strike. The term usually refers to the bitter industrial dispute between the National Union of Mineworkers (NUM) and the British government and National Coal Board (NCB), from March 1984-March 1985. The strike is widely regarded as the most significant in post-war Britain, raising questions about DEMOCRACY in TRADE UNIONS, the government's capacity to impose its vision of economic modernization, and acceptable techniques of policing industrial disputes. Views of its origins vary widely. Some critics assert that the government not only prepared for, but keenly sought a strike to break the power of a union whose strength and activity in the 1970s was abhorrent to THATCHERISM. Others claim that the NUM was drawn without adequate consultation into untenable positions by a leadership committed to a longer and deeper revolutionary struggle. Neither view is complete or ad-equate; the strike's beginnings and evolution require detailed assessment.   S.R.

Bibl: G. Goodman, *The Miners' Strike* (London, 1985).

minimal art (or *ABC art, art of the real*). A term which came into use in the 1960s to describe art in which all elements of expressiveness and illusion are minimized, and which thus encroaches on the territory of what is (or was thereto) regarded as ANTI-ART. In painting, this movement has been identified with *post-painterly abstraction*, exemplified by the flat colour-fields and uncomplicated geometry of Barnett Newman and Ellsworth Kelly; forerunners include Rodchenko and Malevich. But minimalists have turned increasingly to sculpture in their quest for the inexpressive. Donald Judd, Robert Morris, and others in the later 1960s produced arrangements of large, fairly regular coloured forms, or *primary structures*, often designed to be seen in relation to a particular ENVIRONMENT. A well-publicized example is Carl André's *120 Fire-Bricks* at the Tate Gallery. Still more 'minimal' exhibits have consisted of piles of earth and photographs of simple natural features.   P.C.

Bibl: G. Battcock (ed.), *Minimal Art* (New York, 1968; London, 1969); Tate Gallery Catalogue, *The Art of the Real* (London, 1969).

minimal music. Type of music arising in America in the 1960s, probably in reaction to the extreme complexities of AVANT-GARDE MUSIC. Minimal music uses in contrast very simple harmonic and melodic progressions which are usually tonal or modal (see ATONALITY) and frequently involves large amounts of repetition of small phrases (e.g. Terry Riley's 'In C'). See also PHASE SHIFTING; PROCESS MUSIC.   B.CO.

Bibl: M. Nyman, *Experimental Music: Cage and Beyond* (London, 1974).

minimal surfaces. If a (twisted) wire loop is dipped into a soapy solution and withdrawn, a soap film will be formed. The surface tension forces the film to assume the shape which minimizes its area; such a shape is a minimal surface. The mathematical study of these is a very rich subject involving a mixture of GEOMETRY and partial DIFFERENTIAL EQUATIONS.

J.M.

minimax, see under GAME THEORY.

minimum lending rate, see BANK RATE.

minorities. Groups distinguished by common ties of DESCENT, physical appearance, language, CULTURE or RELIGION, in virtue of which they feel or are regarded as different from the majority of the population in a society. In modern usage the term tends to connote real, threatened or perceived discrimination against minorities, although in exceptional cases (e.g. South Africa) a minority may hold power over a majority. Before the 19th century, the only minorities to play any role in national or international politics were religious. With the growth of national consciousness (see NATIONALISM), national minorities acquired significance. Thus in domestic politics national minorities protested their grievances (e.g. Czechs in the Habsburg Empire), while in international affairs the existence of minorities provided grounds for one nation to claim to interfere in the affairs of another (e.g. Hitler's use of German-speaking minorities to put pressure on the Czechoslovak and Polish states). In the 20th century minorities distinguished by other characteristics such as RACE, ethnic identity as immigrants, or sexual preference have joined the range of groups pressing political claims for equality of treatment with that accorded the majority (see AFFIRMATIVE ACTION).

A.L.C.B.;P.B.M.;S.R.

Bibl: G. Kinloch, *The Sociology of Minority Group Relations* (Englewood Cliffs, N.J., 1979).

miracle. Traditionally in Christian THEOLOGY, as in many non-Christian religious traditions, a miracle was an event so clearly different from normal events that it revealed divine power. The supreme miracle of this sort was the human life of Jesus, God the Son (the 'second person' of the Holy Trinity), beginning in conception by the power of the Holy Spirit without a father's intervention, continuing in many miraculous acts and climaxing in the resurrection, when the tomb was empty because the body had been 'raised' gloriously. But in modern times many Christians have become doubtful or sceptical about miracles including these, either because it is thought that science has revealed unbreakable 'laws' or at least regularities in the 'order' of nature, with convincing explanations of phenomena previously regarded as supernatural, or because particular accounts of miracles seem to be MYTHS or at least to be of dubious historical value (see BIBLICAL CRITICISM). Some Christians have therefore opted for a consistently non-miraculous religion (see DEISM). Others have thought that belief in THEISM necessarily involves the acceptance of God's ability to perform some miracles but that stories about them should be assessed for their probability on the basis of the evidence. Others, however, have continued to trust the Bible or the Church's tradition entirely (see FUNDAMENTALISM). Often it has been agreed that an event can be explained either in scientific language (e.g. 'healing miracles' may be a result of the faithful mind's influence over the body) or in religious terms as something wonderful and therefore specially able to disclose God. The Latin for 'object of wonder' is *miraculum*. Similar modern debates have taken place in JUDAISM and, to a much lesser extent, in other religions.

D.L.E.

Bibl: C.S. Lewis, *Miracles* (London and New York, 1947); Richard Swinburne, *The Concept of Miracle* (Oxford, 1970).

mirror phase. In PSYCHOANALYSIS, the mirror phase is Lacan's original formulation of the structure of imaginary IDENTIFICATION. In this moment the child assumes an imaginary unity to its BODY IMAGE, in the way that some animals alienate their true nature, in mimetically hiding in their surroundings. One consequence of the EGO's determination by such NARCISSISTIC forms is the generation of the ego-functions of jealousy and aggressivity, and it is the glossing structure of this narcissistic ego that is repeatedly assaulted and wounded by the themes of the OEDIPAL triangle. The relation of the Oedipal drama to the mirroring ego was later described by Lacan in terms of the relationship of the SYMBOLIC to the imaginary. According to Lacan, the Oedipal intrusions into the mirror phase operate a Symbolic CASTRATION, which introduces into the ego functioning the humanizing structure of DESIRE.   B.BU

MIRV, see under MULTIPLE INDEPENDENTLY TARGETED RE-ENTRY VEHICLE; MISSILES.

mise-en-scène. Term originally employed in theatre to designate the contents of the stage and their arrangement, and adopted by cinema critics to refer to the content of the film frame. This includes the arrangement of the profilmic event (elements of the 'real world' which are set up for the camera, or which the camera captures — persons, settings, costumes, props). *Mise-en-scène* also refers more broadly to what the spectator actually sees on the screen — lighting, composition and iconographic features of the cinematic image; and to the relationship between onscreen space and offscreen space created by the framing of the image, in particular through the 'mobile framing' of the image produced by the depolyment of telescopic (zoom) lenses or camera movements such as tracking and panning.   A.KU.
   Bibl: David Bordwell and Kristin Thompson, *Film Art: An Introduction* (Reading, Mass., 1979).

missiles. Self-propelled projectiles employed in WAR and carrying explosive warheads. In *short-range missiles,* employed against tanks or low-flying aircraft, the warhead consists of ordinary explosive. In *medium-range* (MRBM), *intermediate-range* (IRBM), *intercontinental* (ICBM) and *anti-ballistic missiles* (see ABM) the warhead is nuclear. The term 'ballistic' in this latter range of missiles describes the trajectory of the missile. Missiles may be ground-to-ground, ground-to-air, sea-to-air, or air-to-ground, and may be fired from ground platforms, from under the sea (see TRIDENT), or from an airborne platform, although in this latter category development costs and technical problems have combined to prevent the development of all but short-range 'stand-off' missiles (i.e. missiles whose range enables them to be launched from aircraft flying out of range of conventional anti-aircraft defences). Certain ballistic missiles, including *submarine-launched ballistic missiles* (SLBM), may be equipped with *multiple, independently targetable, re-entry vehicles* (MIRV). In this case, there are a number of warheads to the missile, each of which may be targeted independently in succession, and delivered from the outer atmosphere. Mention should also be made of the CRUISE MISSILE, a flat-trajectory missile, comparable in speed and performance to pilotless aircraft, launchable from any kind of platform from torpedo tube to aeroplane, and adaptable to all tactical and strategical purposes. See also NUCLEAR WEAPONS.   D.C.W.

missing link. In the popular mind, the 'missing link' is a SPECIES intermediate between *homo sapiens* and the apes, the discovery of which would finally demonstrate the truth of EVOLUTIONARY theory. (The continuing 'missingness' of the link is sometimes, by contrast, argued by anti-evolutionary CREATIONISTS as evidence against DARWINIAN theory.) Evolutionary scientists do not expect to find, within the fossil record, links of that kind (apparent finds are characteristically elaborate hoaxes). For Darwinians, true missing links found in fossilized condition are species intermediate between present beings and their own distant forebears. Thus finds of 'prehistoric' man would be expected to have more affinities with the precursors of other modern primates than with the current primates themselves — as in fact has been demonstrated by major anthropoid finds over the last half-century, in particular in East Africa. In previous centuries, belief in the GREAT CHAIN OF BEING, a continuous graded series of creation leading from God, through mankind and down to the merely inanimate stone encouraged the notion that each species was 'linked' to the next species above and below in the 'chain'. No species could be truly missing, or that would constitute a 'gap' in creation. R.P.
   Bibl: A.O. Lovejoy, *The Great Chain of Being* (Cambridge, Mass., 1936).

missing mass problem, see under DARK MATTER.

missing matter, see under DARK MATTER.

MIT school. In LINGUISTICS, those scholars who, following A.N. Chomsky, Professor of Linguistics at the Massachusetts Institute of Technology, adopt a generative conception of language; see CHOMSKYAN; GENERATIVE GRAMMAR.
D.C.

mitochondria, see under CYTOLOGY and SYMBIOSIS.

mitosis. In CELL BIOLOGY, the usual process by which the NUCLEUS divides during CELL division. Each CHROMOSOME splits into two, one of the resulting duplicates passing to each of the daughter cells. The process is important in ensuring that the daughter nuclei have identical sets of chromosomes, and hence of GENES.
J.M.S.

mixed ability grouping. U.K. term for classes containing pupils of varying abilities. This idea was born earlier than the comprehensive schools system but blossomed with the opening of the first comprehensives. It was felt that all children should be equal — a philosophy of EGALITARIANISM which has since been proved false. Truly mixed ability classes required teachers of well above average standards, otherwise, there was a danger of brighter children being neglected as teaching concentrated on the lowest ability pupils. Paradoxically, primary school classes have almost invariably been mixed ability classes.
J.I.

mixed economy. An economy in which a substantial number, though by no means all, of the activities of production, distribution, and exchange are undertaken by the Government, and there is more interference by the State than there would be in a MARKET ECONOMY. A mixed economy thus combines some of the characteristics of both CAPITALISM and SOCIALISM in a compromise which corresponds in varying degree to the actual state of affairs in many industrialized countries outside the COMMUNIST group of states, e.g. the U.K. See PUBLIC SECTOR; PUBLIC GOOD.
R.H.

mixed media, see under MEDIA.

mixed strategy, see under GAME THEORY; NASH EQUILIBRIUM.

MKS units. A set of fundamental units used in science, based on the metre, kilogram, and second for length, MASS, and time, and forming the basis of the currently employed SI UNITS.
M.V.B.

mobile form. In music, the structure of a piece which is composed of sections whose order or relationship to each other is not completely specified by the composer but left to the performer or to chance. The music may therefore be different each time it is performed and this variety has something of the qualities of the MOBILE sculptures of A. Calder. An important pioneer of this form is the composer Earle Brown, and both Boulez and Stockhausen have used a similar technique (see MOMENT FORM; EXPERIMENTAL MUSIC).
B.CO.

mobiles, see under KINETIC ART.

mobility, social, see SOCIAL MOBILITY.

mobilization, social, see SOCIAL MOBILIZATION.

Möbius band. The one-sided surface with a single edge that is obtained by giving a strip of paper one twist and gluing the ends together. It is of interest in TOPOLOGY as being the simplest way of constructing topological spaces that have unfamiliar or unexpected properties (e.g. a cut round the band does *not* separate it into two pieces).
R.G.

modal logic. The part, or kind, of LOGIC concerned with INFERENCES whose constituent PROPOSITIONS embody the CONCEPTS of necessity and possibility and their opposites, CONTINGENCY and impossibility. These four concepts are interdefinable, with the aid of the concepts of negation and disjunction: thus, 'p is possible' means the same as 'It is not necessary that not-p'; 'p is impossible' as 'It is necessary that not-p'; and 'p is contingent' as 'It is not necessary either that p or that not-p'. Modern modal logic was initiated by C.I. Lewis because of his dissatisfaction with the concept of IMPLICATION found in the standard propositional logic of Russell.

535

But it has developed into an addition to, rather than an improvement upon, extensional logic (see EXTENSIONALITY) using material implication. See also MODALITY.

A.Q.

Bibl: G.E. Hughes and M.J. Cresswell, *Introductions to Modal Logic* (London and New York, 1968).

modal propositions, see under MODALITY.

modality. In MODAL LOGIC, a logical property of certain PROPOSITIONS known as *modal propositions*; a modal proposition is any proposition which states of a certain fact either that it is necessary or that it is possible. The use, now common, of 'modality' as a pretentious synonym for the 'mode' or 'way' in which something happens is confusing and unnecessary. D.P.

mode. In STATISTICS and PROBABILITY THEORY, (1) the most probable value in a DISTRIBUTION; in this sense it is sometimes used as a MEASURE OF LOCATION. (2) More generally, a value which is more probable than any *nearby* value. A distribution having more than one mode is called *bimodal* or *multimodal*, as appropriate, and often arises as the result of mixing simpler *unimodal* distributions. R.SI.

mode of production. A CONCEPT of central importance in MARXISM, though now widely employed by non-Marxist SOCIOLOGISTS as well. The mode of production encapsulates the relationship between the forces or means of production — TECHNOLOGY, natural resources, human labour, economic instruments such as banking and insurance — and the social relations of production — essentially CLASS or property relations — which determine the pattern and direction of the development of the productive forces. The forces of production, for Marx, are never found in a 'natural', neutral, or random state. They are always organized and developed by particular groups — classes — in their own interest. These groups use their possession and control of the means of production to dominate other groups, on whose labour however they depend for their superior wealth and POWER.

This is the general form of the relationship between the forces and the relations of production. The precise form varies over time. Thus, according to Marx, in the modern CAPITALIST mode of production the BOURGEOISIE, the owners of land, factories, machinery and so on, directly dominate and exploit the PROLETARIAT, who own nothing but their labour power which they must sell to the capitalist in return for wages. The proletariat are however formally and legally free, unlike the slaves in the slave mode of production of the ancient world, where the slave owners had legal rights over the bodies of the slaves. In the FEUDAL mode of production, typical of the European middle ages, the landowning ruling class did not have direct control of the substantial forces of production — land, cattle, tools — left in the hands of the peasantry; it did however have ultimate control of the land through its control of the type of tenure, and it controlled the distribution of the peasants' produce. Finally Marx distinguished the 'Asiatic' mode of production, the form characteristic for many millennia in the ancient empires of Asia as well as certain parts of eastern Europe and the Near East. Here the STATE — monarch, emperor, or BUREAUCRACY — controls the means of production, generally land but also certain crucial economic instruments such as irrigation systems. This admission of the possibility of the existence of a political ruling class has, not unnaturally, led some critics to see current COMMUNIST systems in eastern Europe as based on the Asiatic mode of production. So far as the West is concerned, Marx discerned a historical succession of modes of production, through 'primitive communism', slavery, feudalism and capitalism. The next and final mode of production would be SOCIALISM where the 'associated producers' — the proletariat acting as a collectivity on behalf of the whole society — would own and control the means of production, dispensing forever with the need for a subordinate exploited class. So far this has happened nowhere in the West; and in contemplating those places, such as Russia and China, where socialist REVOLUTIONS are alleged to have occurred, the suspicion must remain that modern socialism runs the real danger of reviving, at a vastly higher and more effective level, the ancient mode of ORIENTAL DESPOTISM — the 18th-century term for what Marx called the Asiatic mode of production. See also ALTHUSSERIANISM. K.K.

Bibl: B. Hindness and P.Q. Hirst, *Precapitalist Modes of Production* (London, 1975).

model. A representation of something else, designed for a special purpose. This representation may take many forms, depending upon the purpose in hand. A familiar purpose is to remind ourselves of something we already know about. Thus a model aeroplane, a model of Shakespeare's birthplace, or a photograph, all represent an original; they recall to our minds what that original looks like. But the purpose may be discovery. Thus a model aeroplane placed in the controlled environment of a wind-tunnel may be used for experiments that will predict how a real aeroplane built to this design would behave in the sky. A third purpose for a model is explanation, e.g. when the solar system is proposed as a model of the ATOM. Again, the model need not necessarily 'look like' whatever it represents. A system of gravitational equations can model the behaviour of the planets as they move around the sun. Such a model is usually called a *theoretical* model.

All models have one characteristic in common, whatever their purpose. This characteristic is the *mapping* of elements in the system modelled onto the model. It is possible for every relevant element to be mapped, in which case the model is an absolute replica (e.g. a paste copy of a piece of precious jewellery). Such a model is the result of an ISOMORPHIC mapping, and the ordinary person cannot distinguish the fake from the real thing. But an expert knows the difference, because he investigates the stones at a level of abstraction (see ABSTRACT) where the mapping is no longer isomorphic. More usually, models openly lose in complexity compared with the original. But if this loss of detail is irrelevant to the purpose in hand the model is still effective. We may not need every rivet in the model aeroplane to be mapped in order either to recognize the plane, or even to experiment with it in a wind-tunnel. When complexity is deliberately sacrificed in the modelling process,

according to definite scientific rules set up to govern the TRANSFORMATION, the mapping is called *homomorphic*.

The steps in building a *theoretical model* can be outlined as follows: (1) The variables to be used in characterizing and understanding the process must be specified. (2) The forms of the relationships connecting these variables must be specified. (3) Ignorance and the need for simplicity will ensure that all relationships other than identities are subject to error and so, for purposes of efficient statistical estimation, these *error terms* must be specified. (4) The PARAMETERS of the model must be estimated and the extent of its IDENTIFICATION ascertained; if this is inadequate, the model must be reformulated. (5) Finally, the model must be kept up to date and used, so that an impression can be formed of its robustness and reliability.

Theoretical models are of many kinds: static or dynamic; partial or complete; aggregated or disaggregated (see AGGREGATION); DETERMINISTIC or STOCHASTIC; descriptive or optimizing (see OPTIMIZATION). In PHYSICS, when models are well established they are formalized as *laws of physics* and their use for prediction and design becomes a part of ENGINEERING. In ECONOMICS, although the position is rapidly changing, models have usually been static, partial, aggregated, deterministic, and descriptive. Despite the limitations of such models, this experience has enabled model-builders to walk; and it is fortunate for economics that they have consistently ignored the arguments of those who claim that if one cannot run it is pointless to be able to walk.

Nevertheless, partly because they tackle much more complicated situations, as compared with physical models, economic and social models tend to be mathematically more naive and to lack experimental verification. In the less exact SOCIAL SCIENCES, moreover, the term 'model' is often used of the results of step (1), or at most steps (1) and (2), as numbered above, and these results may not be expressed in mathematical form. In SOCIOLOGY, especially, 'model' may be almost interchangeable with IDEAL TYPE.

In interdisciplinary studies (such as OPERATIONAL RESEARCH or CYBERNETICS) processes that are well understood in one scientific context may be used to investigate the properties of some other system altogether. This often looks as though analogies are being drawn; but a formal model involving homomorphic mapping is something more potent than an analogy. Since mappings are, strictly speaking, mathematical transformations, models are frequently expressed in mathematical notation. This accounts for the popular misconception that the models used in science are necessarily mathematical models.

The use of COMPUTERS has increased the complexity of models which can be handled, but complexity provides no guarantee of validity. Experience shows that simple and apparently reasonable rules often have remote consequences which are extravagant and that 'mid-course correction' (or FEEDBACK) is necessary to produce an acceptable result. Unfortunately feedback of this sort is very difficult to incorporate in a model.

S.BE.; C.S.; R.ST.; J.R.T.

model theory, see under MATHEMATICAL LOGIC.

modem (MOdulator/DEModulator). A device connected between a SERIAL COMMUNICATIONS socket of a COMPUTER and a TELECOMMUNICATION system (such as the public telephone network). Its purpose is to transform the information output by the computer into a form which can be accurately transmitted over the system without interfering with any other communication taking place over the system or endangering the safety of anyone working on it. It also provides the reverse function for information to be received by the computer. J.E.S.

moderator. Any material which slows down NEUTRONS without absorbing them. Moderators such as HEAVY WATER are used in NUCLEAR REACTORS, because CHAIN REACTIONS based on FISSION proceed more efficiently with slow THERMAL NEUTRONS. M.V.B.

Modern Churchmen. The name taken by a group of LIBERAL theologians within ANGLICANISM, perhaps most influential in the 1920s. Leaders included H.D.A. Major and W.R. Inge. See also MODERNISM.

D.L.E.

Bibl: H.D.A. Major, *English Modernism* (Cambridge, Mass., 1927); A.M.G. Stevenson, *The Rise and Decline of English Modernism* (London, 1984).

Modern Dance. A broad term used to describe a variety of CONTEMPORARY DANCE styles whose vocabulary is not rooted in CLASSICAL BALLET, entertainment revue or musical theatre. Modern Dance originated in the U.S.A. and Germany in the early 20th century. The work of pioneering modern dancers Loie Fuller, Isadora Duncan and Ruth St Denis arose from a desire for female emancipation and individual expression and demanded a new dance aesthetic which informed, provoked and enlightened its audience. Leaning heavily on subjective content, in direct contrast to the narrative characteristic of ballet, each first-generation modern dancer devised a system of movement relevant to their thematic concerns and movement theories. Fuller exaggerated costume and light to make performance not performer the central focus, Duncan danced barefoot, demonstrating her rejection of the academic restraints imposed on dance in classical ballet, and Ruth St Denis made exotic and extravagant dances and provided a disciplined intensive performance training, with her husband Ted Shawn later establishing the DENISHAWN school. In the 1920s Martha Graham (see GRAHAM TECHNIQUE), Doris Humphrey and Charles Weidman rejected Denishawn, concerning themselves with creating serious works of social significance and developing personal techniques. This second generation brought more percussive, forceful expression into their work, e.g. Graham's *Contraction and Release*, and Humphrey/Weidman's *Fall and Recovery*. European Modern Dance emerged from the German Expressionist Dance (*Austrucktanz*) led by Mary Wigman, and reflected the cultural and political upheaval in Europe, employing expressive gesture as an emotional response and a particular use of space and improvisation. Wigman, former student of Rudolph von Laban (see MODERN EDUCATIONAL DANCE) and Dalcroze (see EU-

RYTHMICS), established a school in New York (directed by Hanya Holm). Third-generation modern dancers in the U.S.A. generally accepted principles laid down by second generation except the more AVANT-GARDE DANCE artist Cunningham who spawned rebellion, culminating in the POST-MODERN DANCE movement. In Britain the influence of Graham gave rise to the Place School and this in turn provoked change giving rise to NEW DANCE.   L.A.

Bibl: J. Morrison Brown (ed.), *The Vision of Modern Dance* (London, 1980); D. McDonagh, *Complete Guide to Modern Dance* (New York, 1976); R. Copeland and M. Cohen (eds.), *What is Dance?* (New York, 1983).

modern educational dance. Based on Rudolph von Laban's analysis of movement, and introduced by Lisa Ullman into the physical education curriculum of primary and secondary schools in the 1950s. It is used as a means of developing the child's self-expression through the creative use of a self-discovered movement vocabulary, thus encouraging the child to be both creative and interpretive.   L.A.

Bibl: R. Laban, *Modern Educational Dance* (London, 1948).

modernism.

(1) Although the adjective 'modern' has (cf. AVANT-GARDE and CONTEMPORARY) been applied to many different phenomena at different times, 'modernism' (or 'the modern movement') has by now acquired stability as the comprehensive term for an international tendency, arising in the poetry, fiction, drama, music, painting, architecture, and other arts of the West in the last years of the 19th century and subsequently affecting the character of most 20th-century art. The tendency is usually held to have reached its peak just before or soon after World War I, and there has for some time been uncertainty about whether it has ended. Orwell and Cyril Connolly were pronouncing its demise during World War II, but the *avant-garde* events of the post-war period require explanation. Frank Kermode has argued for continuity, suggesting 'a useful rough distinction between two phases of modernism': *palaeo-modernism* and *neo-modernism*, the former being the earlier

developments, the latter being SURREALIST and post-surrealist developments. Others, especially in America (Ihab Hassan, Leslie Fiedler, etc.) have proposed a sharp distinction, a new *post-modernist* style amounting to a reaction against modernist FORMALISM, a choric, global village art, the product of a 'post-cultural' age, emphasizing developments dealt with here under ALEATORY, ANTI-ART, ANTI-LITERATURE, AUTO-DESTRUCTIVE ART, POST-MODERNISM and NEW NOVEL.

As a stylistic term, modernism contains and conceals a wide variety of different, smaller movements, usually reckoned to be those post-dating NATURALISM and characterized by the anti-positivistic (see POSITIVISM) and anti-representational leanings of many late-19th-century artists and thinkers. It would thus include the tendencies of SYMBOLISM, IMPRESSIONISM, and DECADENCE around the turn of the century; FAUVISM, CUBISM, POST-IMPRESSIONIST, FUTURISM, CONSTRUCTIV-ISM, IMAGISM, and VORTICISM in the period up to and over World War I; and EXPRESSIONISM, DADA, and SURREALISM during and after that war. A number of these movements contain large theoretical differences among themselves, but certain stylistic similarities. Thus ATONALISM in music, anti-representationalism in painting (see ABSTRACT ART), VERS LIBRE in poetry, fragmentation and STREAM OF CONSCIOUSNESS presentation in the novel, FUNCTIONALISM in architecture, and in general the use of spatial (see SPACE) or COLLAGE as opposed to linear or representational forms, are recurrent features. Another common characteristic noted by critics is the presence of an element of, in Frank Kermode's word, 'decreation' — of technical introversion, or an often ironic self-awareness — in modernist forms. A rough cycle from the late ROMANTICISM of Symbolism and Impressionism through the 'hard', 'classical', or 'impersonal' image and then to the modern psychological romanticism of Surrealism also seems visible in literature and visual forms.

Modernism stretched across the European capitals, reaching the peak of activity and achievement in different countries at different times: in Russia in the immediately pre-Revolutionary years, in Germany in the 1890s and again just before

World War I, in England in the pre-war years from about 1908, in America after 1912; in France it is a plateau rather than a peak — though sloping off after about 1939. There was great cross-fertilization between countries and also among the different arts: a complicated interaction between the merging of forms — poetry becoming like music, etc. — and intense specialized exploration within the forms ensued. Modernism had a high aesthetic and formal constituent, and can often be seen as a movement attempting to preserve the aesthetic realm against intellectual, social, and historical forces threatening it. But it has been seen as a change larger than simply formal. Its relation to modern thought and modern PLURALISM, to the military, political, and ideological (see IDEOLOGY) dislocations of the century, is considerable. Indeed its forms, with their element of fragmentation, introversion, and crisis, have sometimes been held to register the collapse of the entire tradition of the arts in human history. They can be seen either as a last-ditch stand on behalf of the aesthetic in the face of barbarism (as in much Symbolism), or as a probe towards something new. What is clear is that, presentationally and in attitude and belief, modernism does represent a radical shift in the social STATUS and function of the artist, of his art, and of form; that it is the style of a changed SPACE-TIME CONTINUUM; and that hence the modernist arts require, for their comprehension, criteria different from those appropriate to earlier art.   M.S.BR.

Bibl: S. Spender, *The Struggle of the Modern* (London and Berkeley, 1963); R. Ellmann and C. Feidelson (eds.), *The Modern Tradition* (New York, 1965); I. Howe (ed.), *The Idea of the Modern in Literature and the Arts* (New York, 1968); F. Kermode, 'Modernism', in *Modern Essays* (London, 1971); M. Bradbury and J. McFarlane (eds.), *Modernism: 1890-1930* (Harmondsworth, 1976).

(2) In THEOLOGY, the movement to modernize doctrine by taking into account the results of HIGHER CRITICISM and scientific discovery, and the conditions of modern CULTURE. In England and the U.S.A. the term has been used for the MODERN CHURCHMEN and other advocates of religious LIBERALISM, but its chief use has been as a label for the outlook of a group of Roman Catholic thinkers. This group was given both its public identity and its death sentence by the ENCYCLICAL *Pascendi* issued by Pope Pius X in 1907. Its leaders were Alfred Loisy (1857-1940) and George Tyrrell (1861-1909), priests who felt challenged by critical studies of Christianity's origins. They rejected the call of Liberal PROTESTANTISM to return to the 'pure' origins, and welcomed the development of Christianity in history. They regarded Roman Catholic DOGMAS and devotions as valuable, because helpful, symbols of faith and spiritual life, but believed that a fuller CATHOLICISM was being born. The Pope condemned them as heretics, and the later Roman Catholic AGGIORNAMENTO had to take care not to be identified with them.   D.L.E.

Bibl: A.R. Vidler, *A Variety of Catholic Modernists* (London, 1970).

modernization. The term now used by, e.g., Eisenstadt and Rostow, for all those developments in modern societies which follow in the wake of INDUSTRIALIZATION and MECHANIZATION. They include the loosening of boundaries between social CLASSES and an increase in SOCIAL MOBILITY; the growth of EDUCATION; new procedures of industrial negotiation; the extension of franchise; the development of social services, etc.   R.F.

Bibl: S.N. Eisenstadt, *Modernization: Protest and Change* (London and Englewood Cliffs, N.J., 1966); W.W. Rostow, *Politics and the Stages of Growth* (London and New York, 1971).

modular, see under MODULE.

modulation. In PHYSICS, any variation in the properties of a high-frequency wave (e.g. a radio wave or a LASER beam), produced by a signal of a much lower frequency. Broadcasting relies on the AMPLITUDE MODULATION or FREQUENCY MODULATION of a carrier wave.   M.V.B.

module. In architecture, a standard unit of measurement used in order to create proportional relationships between parts and the whole (as in the Classical Orders and Le Corbusier's Modulor), and to control building design, and thus the manufacture and assembly of building elements. An imaginary grid to which length and thicknesses relate is used to define the position of these elements. Buildings planned on the basis of the module are described as *modular*. The need, common to virtually all building, for some form of dimensional coordination becomes acute in PREFABRICATION, for which the use of the modular principle is particularly appropriate.

M.BR.

moho (Mohorovicic discontinuity), see under LITHOSPHERE.

moieties. 'Halves', paired social groups. Moieties are similar to CLANS in that recruitment is based loosely on DESCENT and they are higher-order social groupings. Moieties are usually named after places of origin or natural phenomena. Identity is expressed through a TOTEM or common SYMBOL. Societies with moieties are usually described as having features of *dual organization*.

Among certain groups in East Africa (for example, the Turkana) moieties are an important feature of social organization. According to Gulliver (*Social Control in an African Kingdom*, 1963) all Turkana men are divided into two moieties, stones and leopards, and the division extends between and within generations. A man is always in the opposite moiety of his father. The moiety division is expressed at feasts when stones and leopards sit separately to eat, but each serves meat to the other group.

Moieties have long interested anthropologists as exogamous (see EXOGAMY) and RITUAL groups. Early studies of Australian KINSHIP systems identified the importance of dual organization: in particular moieties functioned as marriage or exogamous groups. Radcliffe Brown built on this early work, but the principle of dual organization was most fully investigated by Lévi-Strauss (*Structural Anthropology*, 1963).

A.G.

Bibl: I. Langham, *The Building of British Social Anthropology: W.H.R. Rivers and His Cambridge Disciples in the Development of Kinship Studies 1898-1931* (Dordrecht, 1981).

moiré effect. An illusory effect of shimmering movement, produced by superimposing one configuration of multiple lines or dots upon another very similar to it, so that the two do not quite coincide. An effect of this kind may be seen in everyday objects, such as sets of railings, or finely threaded materials (*soie moirée*, watered silk); in the 1960s moiré patterns were cultivated by OP and KINETIC artists, and employed in COMPUTER GRAPHICS. P.C.

Bibl: J. Tovey, *The Technique of Kinetic Art* (London and New York, 1971).

molecular biology. A branch of BIOPHYSICS of which the purpose is to interpret biological structures and functions in explicit molecular terms. Thus much of IMMUNOLOGY and BIOCHEMISTRY is now interpretable on a molecular basis. Molecular biology is the basis of GENETIC ENGINEERING and PROTEIN ENGINEERING. The techniques of molecular biology have added a new dimension to such diverse studies as BIOSYSTEMATICS, ENDOCRINOLOGY and MOLECULAR MEDICINE. Günther Stent distinguishes two main streams of thought in molecular biology which correspond fairly exactly to the British and the American traditions of research. The British tradition of molecular biology is predominantly structural; it may be said to have begun with W.T. Astbury's demonstration in the 1940s of an essentially crystalline and therefore molecular orderliness in the structures of, for example, hairs, feathers, and PROTEIN fibres, and to have culminated in the elucidation by Crick and Watson (1953) of the crystalline structure of NUCLEIC ACID and the interpretation by Perutz and Kendrew (1957) of the structure of myoglobin. These achievements rest upon the use of X-RAY DIFFRACTION analysis, pioneered from 1912 onwards by Laue and W. and L. Bragg. The two traditions of research overlap considerably and converge in the elucidation of the GENETIC CODE, the 'dictionary' relating to the sequence of nucleotides in nucleic acids (DNA and RNA) with the AMINO ACIDS whose nature and order of assembly into polypeptides (see PEPTIDES) or proteins they specify. The central dogma of molecular biology is that coded information can pass only from

541

DNA to protein and never the other way about; and this irreversibility of information flow is the reason for the falsity of Lamarck's idea (see LAMARCKISM) of the INHERITANCE OF ACQUIRED CHARACTERS.

P.M.;P.N.

Bibl: Bruce Alberts *et al.*, *Molecular Biology of the Cell* (New York, 1983).

molecular clock. The theory that EVOLUTION, at the molecular level, proceeds at a relatively constant rate. With the development of techniques of the high speed sequencing of PROTEINS in the 1960s, it became possible to compare the protein sequences of different SPECIES. Cytochrome-c Was one of the earliest proteins to be thoroughly studied in this way. The degree of difference between the cytochrome-c structure of different species was found to be almost exactly proportional to the time since the two species had split from a common ancestor. For species whose evolutionary relationships are not known, the degree of molecular difference can therefore be used to measure their evolutionary relations (see BIOSYSTEMATICS). How accurately the molecular clock ticks is a matter of controversy. In 1968 the Japanese geneticist Motoo Kimura argued that the constancy of molecular evolution is incompatible with NATURAL SELECTION, and that evolution at the molecular level must take place by chance changes: this is called the neutral theory of molecular evolution. M.R.

molecular engineering, see under LANGMUIR-BLODGETT FILMS.

molecular genetics, see under GENETICS.

molecular medicine. A term that is loosely applied to the application of MOLECULAR BIOLOGY to the understanding and correction of medical problems. P.N.

molecule. The smallest structural unit of a material which can participate in a CHEMICAL REACTION. Molecules consist of ATOMS held together by chemical BONDS arising from exchange forces. See also CHEMICAL EQUATION; MACROMOLECULE; EXCHANGE ENERGY. M.V.B.

moment form. Musical term used by Stockhausen with reference to certain of his works where he feels that the listener's attention may concentrate on the actual musical event happening at that instant ('moment') rather than on the progression and relationships of events over the duration of the whole piece of music. With this relaxed view of structure Stockhausen allows the performer to re-arrange the 'moments' or short sections of the piece in a manner similar to that in MOBILE FORM. The concept of moment form is full of inherent contradictions that Stockhausen has never fully resolved. B.CO.

Bibl: R. Maconie, *The Works of Karlheinz Stockhausen* (London, 1976).

momentum. A measure of the ability of a moving body to resist forces acting on it. For a single PARTICLE obeying NEWTONIAN MECHANICS, momentum = MASS × velocity. This is, mathematically, a vector quantity (see VECTOR; QUANTITY) because the velocity of a body is directed along its line of motion. For a system that is isolated (i.e. not acted on by forces from outside), momentum obeys a CONSERVATION LAW which is very useful in analysing the motion of interacting parts of the system. In a NUCLEAR REACTION, for example, the total momentum before a collision (of incident particle + target) is the same as the total momentum afterwards (of all the reaction products), whatever the interactions during impact. Conservation of momentum is the basis of the motion of ROCKETS. M.V.B.

monads. According to the PHILOSOPHY of Leibniz, the ultimate substantial constituents of the world. Leibniz argued that everything complex must be made of simple and indivisible parts and that, since everything extended is divisible, the ultimate simples must be unextended and so mental or spiritual in nature. But while monads are all consciousnesses, they need not be self-conscious or endowed with APPERCEPTION, although some are. God and human souls, according to Leibniz, are monads; and everything that exists that is not a monad, such as a material object, is a collection of monads. A.Q.

Bibl: Bertrand Russell, *A Critical Expo-*

sition of the Philosophy of Leibniz (Cambridge, 1900).

monetarism. An economic theory that is based on the view that economic markets operate most effectively without government intervention. For example, labour markets will always operate so as to move the economy towards FULL EMPLOYMENT. In the monetarist view production and prices in markets respond quickly to changes in the economy and, consequently, the economy moves quickly towards EQUILIBRIUM. From this assumption, various monetarist propositions have been derived. This has resulted in confusion over what the term monetarist means, especially as what constitutes a monetarist view of the working of the economy has varied considerably between different economists, over time and across countries. The different monetarist views can be explained as follows. (1) It is considered that the most important reason for holding MONEY is for its use in economic transactions. Starting from equilibrium in the whole economy, an increase in the MONEY SUPPLY will increase holdings of money and this will cause people to spend more. At full employment the effect of this extra expenditure is not to bring forth extra output, but to increase prices. This increase in prices reduces the real value of the money supply; this process continues until the increase in prices is equal to the initial increase in the money supply. At this point, the real value of the money supply has returned to its original level. The increase in the supply of money has had no effect on the equilibrium values of employment, output and the interest rate. The QUANTITY THEORY OF MONEY states that the price level increases at the same rate as the money supply and in particular, the level of employment remains the same. (2) As monetarism assumes that the economy is at or moving towards full employment, FISCAL POLICY can have little or no effect on the level of employment and real output. An increase in government expenditure financed by an increase in the money supply will, according to the first monetarist view, have little or no effect on the level of employment and real output. Government expenditure financed by greater borrowing will increase the interest rate and *crowd out*, i.e. replace, INVESTMENT in the rest of the economy. The level of AGGREGATE DEMAND and, thus, output remains unchanged, though as investment has fallen (assuming the increase in government expenditure is not investment) the productive potential of the economy has been reduced. Monetarist theories have been developed to incorporate expectations about prices (see RATIONAL EXPECTATIONS). If the economy is in equilibrium, an upward shift in aggregate demand — say, because of an increase in government expenditure — will increase only prices as output is, by monetarist assumption, at the full employment level. FIRMS react to higher prices by increasing output through hiring more labour at higher money wages. Labour may not realize that this increase in money wages should be adjusted for the increase in prices, i.e. they may suffer from MONEY ILLUSION. If this adjustment does not occur, the increased money wages attract a larger supply of labour and employment increases. However, as labour adjusts for the increase in prices, the supply of labour is reduced and employment falls. If these expectations of inflation continue to be held, but aggregate demand shifts back, unemployment will rise as labour perceives real wages to be lower than they actually are. This unemployment will persist until expectations adjust to the true value of INFLATION. (3) The use of fiscal and monetary policies to stabilize the economy is unlikely to be successful, as too little is known about the working of the economy, especially with regard to the lags in the effects of economic policies. The government should attempt to balance the budget and increases in the money supply should be consistent with stable prices. (4) There are a number of monetarist views about the operation of the economy which have crucial implications for economic policy. The monetarist view is that these relationships are such that markets will always return to equilibrium. Monetarism is often discussed as the major alternative economic theory to KEYNESIAN economics.

J.P.

Bibl: J. Craven, *Introduction to Economics* (Oxford, 1984); M.C. Sawyer, *Macro-economics in Question* (Brighton,

1982); B. Morgan, *Monetarists and Keynesians* (London, 1978).

monetary policy. The policy of a government or CENTRAL BANK in varying the quantity of money in circulation, the cost and availability of credit and the composition of NATIONAL DEBT. The classical instruments used for this purpose are discount policy (changes in the central bank's lending rate) and open-market operations (purchases or sales of government debt by the central bank designed to put more or less money in circulation). Other instruments of monetary policy include government control over bank lending, directly or indirectly, and regulation of the rates of interest to be charged by banks and other financial institutions. Economists differ as to the importance of monetary policy (in comparison, for example, with FISCAL POLICY) in regulating the level of economic activity. As government's budget deficits have to be financed by borrowing or the creation of MONEY, monetary policy is closely linked to the level of the budget deficit, i.e. fiscal policy.   A.C.; J.P.
Bibl: D. Begg *et al., Economics* (London, 1984).

money. Any thing which is generally acceptable as a medium of exchange. Money must be a store of wealth and thus be durable; otherwise people would not want to hold it. In times of very rapid INFLATION (hyperinflation) money loses its value and people avoid holding it. Money is also a unit of account, as it is convenient to express all prices and financial instruments in terms of the same money unit. Money is useful in that it simplifies economic transactions, as the double-coincidence of wants that is necessary for barter is avoided (see MONEY SUPPLY; MONEY CREATION).   J.P.
Bibl: J. Craven, *Introduction to Economics* (Oxford, 1984).

money creation. A bank can create MONEY by lending out money that is deposited with the bank. The ability of banks to create money is limited by their need to maintain sufficient liquid reserves and for them to comply with official regulations concerning the holding of reserve assets. Changes in these regulations can be used to control the MONEY SUPPLY. In this and other ways (see MONETARY POLICY) the government can create money.   J.P.
Bibl: D. Begg *et al., Economics* (London, 1984).

money illusion. The failure to distinguish between real and MONEY income. For example, an individual who experiences a 10% rise in both prices and money income and feels better, or worse, off is said to suffer from money illusion.   J.P.

money supply. The amount of MONEY in the economy. As it is possible to finance payments in a variety of notes and coins, bank cheques and building society cheques, similarly it is possible to define money in a variety of ways. The wider the definition of money, the less readily accepted forms of money that are included in the definition. A fairly wide definition of the money is sterling M3, but not the widest; it includes notes and coins in circulation and PRIVATE and PUBLIC SECTOR sterling current and deposit bank accounts (see MONEY CREATION).   J.P.
Bibl: D. Begg *et al., Economics* (London, 1984).

mongolism (*mongolian idiocy*), see DOWN'S SYNDROME.

monism. In PHILOSOPHY, (1) the theory that there is only one truly substantial thing in the universe, as in Spinoza's doctrine of SUBSTANCE, also described as God-or-Nature (*deus sive natura*), and Hegel's doctrine of the *absolute idea* (see ABSOLUTE; IDEA); this kind of monism is a limiting case of HOLISM; its opposite is *pluralism*. (2) The theory that there is really only one fundamental *kind* of thing in the universe, whether it be material, as in MATERIALISM, mental as in IDEALISM, or abstract as in Platonic REALISM. The two forms of monism are variously combinable; Spinoza held that his Substance had thought and extension as attributes, as well as other unknown ones, whereas Hegel, as an idealist, was a monist in both senses. Materialists ordinarily acknowledge a plurality of individual things or substances, but Parmenides, in the 6th century B.C., did not. See also MIND-BODY PROBLEM; NEUTRAL MONISM.   A.Q.

monoclonal antibody. CLONING of a single ANTIBODY-producing CELL results in a large number of cells each making the same monoclonal antibody. Before the technique for producing monoclonal antibodies was available, antibodies had to be extracted from the serum of experimental animals; since an animal produces a multiplicity of antibodies against any one substance, each antibody coming from a different clone of cells, the SERUM antibody is known as polyclonal. Monoclonal antibodies are of great value both in experimental biology and in IMMUNOASSAYS.
P.N.

monoculture. An agricultural system, such as is used for sugar cane and continuous wheat production, in which the same crop is planted successively on the same land, in contrast to systems in which a sequence of crops is planted in rotation. Some users of the term are particularly concerned to emphasize the extension of such simplified cropping over large areas of countryside, and occasionally it has been applied to all systems except those in which several crops are grown mixed together on the same fields on farms where livestock are an integral part of the system. The simplicity of monocultural systems makes for economy in certain production costs, but they tend to break down because of the build-up of pests and diseases or the deterioration of the soil, with consequent reduction in yields. K.E.H.

monogamy. A form of MARRIAGE in which each partner has only one spouse. Monogamy is found most commonly in Europe and Asia. In India the idea of an exclusive bond between husband and wife was taken to its extreme with the institution of *suttee*, when a woman followed her deceased husband onto the funeral pyre. The practice of monogamy has been associated with certain economic conditions and forms of property inheritance. It is particularly found in societies where property is transmitted bilaterally and DOWRY is the common form of marriage payment. Monogamy has been linked to societies based upon intensive or plough agriculture. Land is scarce and intensively worked. Landholding is a crucial element in social differentiation and wealth is carefully preserved between generations. Each partner brings property to marriage and with the establishment of a single conjugal fund, monogamy acts for its concentration and against the dispersal of wealth. A.G.

Bibl: Jack Goody, *Production and Reproduction* (Cambridge, 1976).

monopoly. The only FIRM producing a certain good or service. A monopolist can restrict output and, thus, charge a higher price than would be obtained in PERFECT COMPETITION. The restriction of output below an efficient level results in a loss of SOCIAL WELFARE, compared with that which can be obtained in perfect competition. The power to restrict output and raise the price, and the definition of a monopoly, depend on the number and closeness of substitutes for the product of the monopoly and BARRIERS TO ENTRY. A legal monopoly is one derived from a privilege conferred by government. A natural monopoly exists when ECONOMIES OF SCALE make it inefficient for there to be more than one firm and, if they exist, the smaller and more inefficient firms will go out of business. It has been argued that monopolies have beneficial effects, as they are more likely to invest in RESEARCH AND DEVELOPMENT and generate TECHNICAL PROGRESS. A monopoly may have a greater incentive to invest in research and development, as the results of such effort are less likely to be imitated because of its monopoly position. Monopolies may have easier access to finance, find it easier to carry the burden of risk and cost of investments and obtain economies of scale in carrying out research and development. Alternatively the lack of rivals may mean monopolies have no spur to invent and innovate and develop and that the most favourable industrial structure for technical progress is one of a few large, rival firms (see OLIGOPOLY). The lack of rivals may also result in monopolies not minimizing costs of production (see COMPETITION). G.B.R.; J.P.

Bibl: M.C. Sawyer, *The Economics of Industries and Firms* (London, 1982).

monopoly policy, see under ANTI-TRUST OR MONOPOLY POLICIES.

545

monorail. A transport system for goods or passengers in which the vehicles are suspended by wheels or other means that operate along the surface of a *single* rail or beam, as opposed to the dual rail of a conventional railway. Monorails have lost favour since the early part of the 20th century as they can be shown to be more costly than an equivalent bi-rail system.

E.R.L.

monosystemic, see under FIRTHIAN.

monotheism, see under THEISM.

Monroe Doctrine. A political doctrine of hemispheric influence, first enunciated in a message to the U.S. Congress by President James Monroe on 2 December 1823. It had four elements: two aimed at restricting the activities of European powers, two those of the U.S. The former were: (1) The American continents were not to be considered as subjects for annexation by European states; (2) any interference by such states in the affairs of the Americans would be taken as threatening to U.S. interests and security. The latter were: (1) the U.S. would not interfere with existing European colonies in the American continents; (2) nor would she intervene in 'the wars of the European powers in matters relating to themselves'. Although the latter have been largely redundant since U.S. entry into World War I in 1917, the former give the Doctrine continuing relevance in that it is still invoked in attempts to justify a U.S. monopoly of external influence in Central and South America. As such it is widely regarded in those regions as a symbol of U.S. domination.

D.C.W.;S.R.

Bibl: A. DeConde, *A History of American Foreign Policy* Vol. 1 (New York and London, 1978).

montage. French term for the assembling and erection of mechanical apparatus. Used internationally in the arts:

(1) For the technique of *photomontage* devised by the Berlin DADA group *c*. 1918 and practised mainly by Raoul Hausmann, Hannah Höch, and John Heartfield. This was an application of COLLAGE to photographic and other illustrative material, which Heartfield later adapted to political caricature. Countless designers have come to use it for large-scale display and decorative schemes.

(2) In the cinema, as the ordinary term for editing (the placing of one shot or scene next to another to make a narrative or thematic point). The early Soviet filmmakers, influenced by D.W. Griffith's development of *parallel montage* (the simultaneous conduct of two or more narrative themes) in *Intolerance*, gradually developed complex intellectual theories of montage through the experiments first of Kuleshov from 1917, then of Dziga Vertov in his *Kino-Pravda* documentaries from 1922 on, until Eisenstein, elaborating his theory of the *montage of attractions* (the juxtaposition by cutting of seemingly disparate shots to produce a shock or 'attraction'), not only gave montage pride of place in the art of film-making, but raised it into what was to prove a cumbersome mystique.

(3) More loosely, for almost any type of compilation made up of disparate elements, particularly where there is a mechanical quality about the work.

J.W.; T.C.C.M.

Montague grammar. A movement in LINGUISTICS in the mid-1970s which owes its impetus to the thinking of the American logician Richard Montague (1930-70). The approach uses a conceptual apparatus derived from the study of the SEMANTICS of formal (logical) languages, and applies it to the study of natural languages. D.C.

Bibl: D.T. Dowty *et al., Introduction to Montague Semantics* (Dordrecht, 1981).

Monte Carlo methods. In STATISTICS and PROBABILITY THEORY, the estimation of quantities (which are perhaps too difficult to calculate analytically) by construction of a probabilistic process which is then simulated (see SIMULATION) using RANDOM NUMBERS; the Laws of Large Numbers (see STATISTICAL REGULARITY) will guarantee that after a large number of runs of the simulation the estimated PARAMETERS of the MODEL are unlikely to be far from the true values. Thus one method of finding the area inside a closed curve is to enclose it within a polygon of known area and consider the frequency with which points from a uniform DISTRI-

BUTION on the polygon fall inside the curve. The successful application of Monte Carlo methods depends critically on designing the simulation experiment to take maximum account of known information; design techniques of this kind are called *variance-reduction methods*. R.SI.

Montessori method. Educational method associated with Maria Montessori (1870-1952). After qualifying, in 1894, as Italy's first woman doctor, she worked in Rome, first with feeble-minded children, later with normal children aged 3-7. Her specially designed auto-didactic apparatus and furniture provided a challenging environment which exercised the child's physical mechanisms and his discrimination of length, size, weight, texture, shape, and colour. The Montessori method and classroom were commended by progressives as both 'scientific' and sensitive, but the dominating Dottoressa was not always an acceptable champion of her own doctrines. In the Anglo-Saxon world the FROEBEL METHOD has been preferred.

W.A.C.S.

MOOP, see MVD.

moral panic. A term generally used in relation to the creation of a certain kind of social hysteria by the mass MEDIA in modern society. The mass media, it is claimed, in the indulgence of the sensationalism which is one of their principal values, exaggerate relatively trivial acts of violence or misbehaviour to the proportions of a major social or moral crisis. This perception is then taken over by various individuals and institutions of authority — the police, the law courts, community workers, churches, schools, parents — who are often themselves prisoners of the media in their understanding of society. Acting on these media images, these individuals and institutions seek to stamp out the particular activities which have been highlighted, thus confirming their reputation as grave social evils while at the same time paradoxically enhancing their appeal to other so far unaffected individuals who are attracted by their notoriety. Thus in the 1960s in Britain, the media built up a moral panic over the relatively harmless activities of certain youth groups, such as

the 'Mods' and 'Rockers', leading to a glamorization of their cultural styles, and occasioning pitched battles — staged sometimes for, or by, the media — between rival groups on public holidays at seaside resorts on the south coast. These violent incidents then became the fuel for alarmist speeches by politicians and churchmen, and the imposition of tough penalties by magistrates. This in turn stimulated defiant responses from the young, amplifying the behaviour first complained of.

Similar moral panics have been created over 'mugging' — the media suggesting a problem of American proportions — and teenage promiscuity. While the mass media continue to be regarded as the primary producers of moral panics, the term is now used of any kind of collective social or moral hysteria that is artificially, sometimes deliberately, generated. See also LABELLING THEORY. K.K.

Bibl: S. Cohen, *Folk Devils and Moral Panics* (London, 1972); S. Hall, *Policing the Crisis: 'Mugging', the State, and Law and Order* (London, 1978).

moral theology. A term, more familiar in CATHOLICISM than in PROTESTANTISM, covering the discussion of the relevance of religious, especially Christian, belief to ethical problems (see ETHICS). Most of the discussion has been about a minimum standard of conduct for Christians who do not aspire to the heights of sanctity, and has sometimes resulted in a semi-legal, even hair-splitting, code listing possible concessions to human appetites. This is pejoratively called 'casuistry', a word which can, however, have the nobler meaning of applying moral philosophy to particular cases. See also ANTINOMIANISM; SITUATION ETHICS. D.L.E.

Bibl: J. Macquarrie and J. Childress (eds.), *A New Dictionary of Christian Ethics* (London and Philadelphia, 1986).

Mormons. A basically American religious body properly called 'The Church of Jesus Christ of the Latter-Day Saints'. Founded by Joseph Smith and Brigham Young, it attracted attention by its establishment, around Salt Lake City, of the State of Utah (1847, admitted into the U.S.A. in 1895), by the bizarre nature of its holy book (the

Book of Mormon), and by its practice of polygamy (now abandoned). In the 20th century it has become well-known for its world-wide EVANGELISM and for its practice (based on 1 Corinthians 15) of baptizing the names of the dead. It is now respected for its moral purity, if not for its THEOLOGY.   D.L.E.

Bibl: L.J. Arrington and D. Bitton, *The Mormon Experience* (New York and London, 1979).

morpheme. In LINGUISTICS, the minimal unit of grammatical analysis, i.e. the smallest functioning unit out of which words are composed. Morphemes are commonly classified into *free forms* (morphemes which can occur as separate words) and *bound forms* (morphemes which cannot so occur — traditionally called *affixes*); thus *unselfish* consists of the three morphemes *un*, *self*, and *ish*, of which *self* is a free form, *un-* and *-ish* bound forms. Morphemes are generally regarded as abstract units; when realized in speech, they are called *morphs*. Some morphemes are represented by more than one morph according to their position in a word or sentence, such alternative morphs being called *allomorphs*. Thus the morpheme of plurality represented orthographically by the *-s* in, e.g., *cots*, *digs*, and *forces* has the allomorphs represented phonetically by [s], [z], and [iz] respectively; in this instance the allomorphs result from the phonetic influence of the sounds with which the singular forms of the words terminate.   D.C.

morphogenesis. The sum of the processes by which an animal or plant develops its distinctive form. These processes are (1) *determination*, in which the fate of certain CELLS or TISSUES is determined; (2) DIFFERENTIATION, in which various cells or tissues undergo diverging courses of development; and (3) growth, in which cells enlarge, multiply, or both. See also EMBRYOLOGY.   E.O.W.

morphology.
(1) In BIOLOGY, a term introduced by Goethe to denote a science dealing with the very essences of forms — and so distinguished from workaday descriptive sciences like ANATOMY. In Goethe's mind

the word probably had a slightly mystical neo-Platonic significance.   P.M.

(2) In GEOGRAPHY and GEOLOGY, a term used to denote the form of landscapes or elements of the natural landscape. Thus E. Raisz has defined and standardized symbols for forty 'morphologic types' such as cone volcanoes, scarplands, plains, and has added a further ten based on natural vegetation to diversify the category of plains. More recently the term *urban morphology* has been used, with reference to urban landscapes, to differentiate different parts of a town according to form and structure.   M.L.

Bibl: E. Raisz, 'The Physiographic Method of Representing Scenery on Maps' (*Geographical Review*, 21, New York, 1931).

(3) A branch of LINGUISTICS, traditionally defined as the study of word structure, but now more usually as the study of the properties of MORPHEMES and their combinations.   D.C.

Bibl: P.H. Matthews, *Morphology* (Cambridge, 1974).

morphophonology (sometimes called *morphonology* and, especially in American linguistic work, *morphophonemics*). In LINGUISTICS, the analysis and classification of the different phonological shapes available in a language for the representation of MORPHEMES.   D.C.

mortality. The process in which deaths occur in a population. Crude death rates measure the number of deaths as a proportion of the population; more is revealed by other, age-specific measures, notably expectation of life, the average number of additional years a person would expect to live (most commonly measured from birth, but also measurable from any other age). The greatest single determinant of death rates is age, with highest levels of mortality in the first years of life and in old age. A distinction is usually made between exogenous mortality, the operation of infectious diseases such as smallpox or influenza (often with high mortality) and such factors as FAMINE, which will tend to predominate in less developed or past societies; and endogenous mortality, death from such causes as cardio-vascular disease and CANCERS, which tend to be more prevalent in developed societies.   D.S.

Bibl: H.S. Shryock *et al.*, *The Methods and Materials of Demography* (condensed edition) (New York and London, 1976).

Moscow trials. The three great Soviet SHOW TRIALS whose leading victims were Zinoviev, Kamenev, and others (August 1936); Pyatakov, Radek, and others (January 1937); and Bukharin, Yagoda, and others (March 1938). The term is sometimes used to include earlier public trials such as the Shakhty Trial of 1928, the 'Industrial Party' Trial of 1930, the Menshevik Trial of 1931, and the 'Metro-Vickers' Trial of 1933 (when the main accused were British engineers). The principle of these rigged trials was that of public confession by the accused, though some of the earlier ones named were not wholly successful in this respect. See also YEZHOVSHCHINA.   R.C.

Bibl: Robert Conquest, *The Great Terror* (London and New York, rev. ed., 1971).

Moslem, see under ISLAM.

Moslem Brotherhood, see under ISLAM.

Mössbauer effect (discovered by Rudolf Ludwig Mössbauer in 1958). The emission of GAMMA RAYS with very precisely defined frequencies by an atomic NUCLEUS in a solid. The nuclear velocities, whose DOPPLER EFFECTS broaden the range of frequencies in a gas, may be reduced virtually to zero in a solid, because the MOMENTUM due to recoil and random heat motion is absorbed by the whole crystal LATTICE.

Very small frequency shifts can be measured with these Mössbauer gamma rays; this has led to many applications of the effect in SOLID-STATE PHYSICS, and to a successful test of the prediction from the theory of RELATIVITY that GRAVITATION will cause a RED SHIFT in the frequency of PHOTONS.   M.V.B.

most favoured nation clause, see under BILATERALISM.

motif writing, see under DANCE NOTATION.

motivation. (1) Originally and properly, the process of motivating, i.e. of providing with a motive ('Iago represents a failure in motivation on Shakespeare's part'). (2) Increasingly, a slightly pretentious synonym for motive or motives ('Iago's motivation is obscure'). (3) Most recently and loosely, any or all of the following: ambition, determination, energy, initiative, intellectual curiosity, physical stamina, moral fibre. Somebody lacking in these qualities is said to be *unmotivated* (as Lady Macbeth didn't say, 'Unmotivated! Give me the daggers').   O.S.

moveable property, see under DESCENT.

Movement, the. Name originally given in the mid 1950s to a conservative and anti-romantic tendency then manifesting itself in British poetry. The term is misleading in that there was never any 'movement'; Robert Conquest's *New Lines* (1956), which included poetry by Donald Davie, Kingsley Amis, Philip Larkin, John Wain, Elizabeth Jennings, Thom Gunn, and others, was programmatically retrospective, and very soon after this some British poets, including Gunn himself, Edwin Morgan, and Iain Crichton Smith, came under such very different influences as Robert Lowell's 'confessionalism' (a writing of one's own life story by way of the strictly clinical facts), EXISTENTIALISM, and the 'post-SURREALISM' of John Ashberry. The Movement's tendency — traditionalism in form, irony, 'robustness', distrust of CULTURE, an empirical approach — is most characteristically seen in Philip Larkin, arguably Britain's best post-war poet. The Movement was a reaction against the NEW APOCALYPSE and similarly loose British poetry of the 1940s, a response to the ingenuity of William Empson, and a belated, partial recognition of the achievement of Robert Graves and of (this has been less well acknowledged) Norman Cameron, who in the 1930s and 1940s had been overshadowed by Auden and Eliot. Beyond this it amounted to nothing, and it should be noted only as a tendency.   M.S.-S.

Bibl: M.L. Rosenthal, *The New Poets* (New York, 1967).

MRBM (medium-range ballistic missiles), see under MISSILES.

MS. Abbreviation for (1) manuscript; (2) motor-ship; (3) MULTIPLE SCLEROSIS; (4) either Mrs or Miss: an ambiguous style of address favoured by those women, especially members of the Women's Liberation movement (see FEMINISM), who resent the implication that their marital status, unlike that of men, is an integral part of their persona.   O.S.

MSI (*Movimento Sociale Italiano*; also an abbreviation for *medium-scale integration*, for which see INTEGRATED CIRCUIT). Italian NEO-FASCIST party founded in 1946, anti-DEMOCRATIC and anti-COMMUNIST in character. Forced to work through the Italian parliamentary system, it has directed its main efforts towards attempting to draw the dominant CHRISTIAN DEMOCRAT party into a RIGHT-wing anti-Communist and anti-SOCIALIST coalition.
                                                D.C.W.

MT, see MACHINE TRANSLATION.

multicultural; multiethnic; multiracial. Concepts which grew out of the policy of INTEGRATION (rather than assimilation) developed with respect to minority groups. They imply the recognition and acceptance of social diversity, PLURALISM. The concepts differ in the selection of the significant features of this diversity. Sociologists working in the field of RACE relations have been concerned with racial diversity (difference based upon physical features) while those working within an anthropological tradition have focused upon CULTURE or ETHNICITY (R. Miles, *Racism and Migrant Labour*, 1982). The idea of multiculturalism is now widely accepted in education, but is the subject of much debate.   A.G.
   Bibl: A. James and R. Jeffcoate (eds.), *The School in the Multicultural Society* (New York, 1982); H.V. Carby, 'Schooling in Babylon' in *The Empire Strikes Back* (London, 1982).

multidimensional scale, see under SCALE.

multidimensional scaling, see under SCALING.

multi-factor analysis, see under FACTOR ANALYSIS; MULTIVARIATE ANALYSIS.

multilateralism.
   (1) The doctrine advanced against *unilateralism*, that DISARMAMENT should be undertaken by all nuclear powers at the same time, and in concert. The two conflicting approaches to disarmament are not particular to NUCLEAR WEAPONS, but emerged in the debates over disarmament in the 1930s. Multilateralism is the traditional diplomatic approach, based on mutual concession and advantage, subject to control and verification. It is the professional's choice. By contrast, unilateralism appeals to a popular constituency: no STATE possessing nuclear weapons has taken up a unilateralist stance. Some nations refuse to allow nuclear weapons on their territory, most recently New Zealand. Unilateralism has proved most popular in the United Kingdom, through the Campaign for Nuclear Disarmament (see PEACE MOVEMENT). This recently joined with various unilateralist groups in Europe to form END, to cover the whole of Europe, on both sides (in theory) of the Iron Curtain. Where the multilateral approach depends on agreement between states, the unilateral approach suggests that a single power renouncing nuclear weapons would upset the balance in a positive fashion. At one time, it was believed that the force of moral example alone would be sufficient for other nations to follow such a lead. More recently, the argument for unilateralism has rested more solidly on the grounds of self-interest. It suggests that many states are the unwilling hosts to nuclear arsenals, and would be happy to see them go; if one state in Europe renounced nuclear weapons, others would be relieved to let them go as well. This argument is seen to be more potent and thus more dangerous by the advocates of multilateralism. A.J.M.W.
   Bibl: Daniel Frei, *Assumptions and Perceptions in Disarmament* (New York, 1984).
   (2) In international trade, see under BILATERALISM.

multinational company. A company that operates in several countries. Since World War II they have grown rapidly in size and number, and have contributed significantly to world ECONOMIC GROWTH and trade. Their growth is a reflection of their access to funds for INVESTMENT and their technical and ENTREPRENEURIAL abilities. As they are not restricted in where they produce and sell their output, they can locate in areas of the world which are most profitable for their operations. This may be thought to be ECONOMICALLY EFFICIENT. Many governments provide incentives to attract multinational firms. Whether multinational firms provide a net benefit to the host country is a contentious issue. They may employ and train local labour, invest, generate income and profits which can be taxed, transfer technology, produce exports and provide COMPETITION for local firms. Alternatively, they may use CAPITAL intensive techniques of production that employ relatively small amounts of labour, and the technology may not be adapted to the circumstances of the host country, e.g. if labour is relatively cheap the technology used should be labour intensive (see APPROPRIATE TECHNOLOGY). The skilled and managerial labour used may not be recruited from the host country; investment funds may be raised in the host country — thus, depriving funds for alternative domestic investment; TAXATION on profits may be evaded; profits may be moved out of the host country; the incentives used to attract the firms may be costly and different countries may compete to provide the most attractive incentives. These issues are complicated and it is difficult to generalize about the net benefits or costs of the operation of multinational firms.   J.P.

Bibl: R.E. Caves, *Multinational Enterprises and Economic Analysis* (Cambridge, 1982).

multiphonics. In music the use of unusual fingering and breathing techniques to produce two or more notes simultaneously (chords) from a single wind instrument. An important pioneer in the development of these techniques is the composer Bruno Bartolozzi who has developed series of finger positions to produce not only chords but MICROTONE scales and unusual tone colourings from woodwind instruments.   B.CO.

Bibl: B. Bartolozzi, *New Sounds for Woodwind* (London, 1967).

multiple-choice method. In MENTAL TESTING and other forms of examination, a method of questioning in which the answer must be selected from alternatives provided by the questioner. Such fixed-alternative questions are capable of ingenious refinements and, for some purposes, are preferable to conventional free-answer or open questions. See also CONVERGERS AND DIVERGERS.   I.M.L.H.

multiple independently targeted re-entry vehicle (MIRV). A MISSILE that has several warheads, each one being directed to different enemy targets. MIRV can also refer to any one of the warheads. C.E.D.

multiple sclerosis. A disease, usually progressive, of the central NERVOUS SYSTEM, characterized by remissions and paroxysmal increases in severity, and caused by demyelization of the white matter of the brain or spinal cord or both.   H.L.

multiples. Two- or three-dimensional art objects (other than lithographs, screenprints, etchings, and relief prints) that are made in bulk, usually in signed and numbered limited editions.   A.K.W.

multiplicative axiom, see AXIOM OF CHOICE.

multiplier effect. The effect on final NATIONAL INCOME of a change in a component of AGGREGATE DEMAND. The multiplier itself is the ratio of the change in final national income to a change in aggregate demand — changes in the different components of aggregate demand give rise to different multipliers. For example, starting from the whole economy being in EQUILIBRIUM, an increase in INVESTMENT will result in an increase in payments to the owners of those domestic FACTORS OF PRODUCTION, e.g. labour and CAPITAL, used in the additional investment. A portion of this latter increase in national income will be spent on domestically produced goods and services. This additional expenditure will find its way to those domestic factors of production used in producing the extra output that is consumed. A portion of *this* increase in national income will be spent on domestically produced goods and services and so on. At each stage of this process, not all of the increase in national income is spent on domestically produced goods and services. The remaining portion is saved, used to pay taxes or to purchase foreign goods and services. At each step, the size of the increase in national income gets smaller and is eventually negligible. At this point a new final and higher level of equilibrium national income has been established (see ACCELERATOR and KEYNESIAN).   J.P.

Bibl: J. Craven, *Introduction to Economics* (Oxford, 1984).

multipolarity. An intellectual MODEL of the international political system which claims that political power is likely to become effectively concentrated and exercised by several major world powers, a process known as multipolarization. Like BIPOLARITY in the 1950s and 1960s, multipolarity in the 1970s played a role in determining U.S. foreign policy, having arisen to accommodate the resurgence of China, Japan, and Western Europe as world powers. Whereas the two 'superpowers' were set apart from the rest by the possession of nuclear capability, the determining factor in the recent evolution of several world powers has been an aggregation of economic strength.   D.E.

multi-programming, see under COMPUTING.

multi-racial education. Lessons, generally integrated in most subjects, that show children that there are other RACES, other colours, languages and religions and that tolerance of all must be practised, while prejudice can be hurtful and damaging. Morning assemblies at schools, traditionally in Britain of a Christian denominational variety, have gradually been replaced by multi-racial assemblies, particularly in schools whose rolls comprise large proportions of pupils from immigrant backgrounds and homes where other religions than CHRISTIANITY are devoutly followed.   J.I.

multitrack recording. From the initial monophonic tape recorders have developed machines that can record up to twenty-four tracks (and beyond) of music either simultaneously or one after another. The advantages of recording music in this way are immense. Firstly, a single instrumentalist or singer can be overdubbing (recording additional tracks over the first) to create a multivoiced piece of music by him/herself. Secondly, individual mistakes in the recording can be corrected by 'dropping in' without having to re-record the entire piece or the other parts. Thirdly, the individual tracks of music can be treated separately to enhance them without affecting the rest of the music. Developments in recording techniques have led to the reduction in size of multitrack recorders (these are now available in a cassette format), the syncing or linking up of several recorders and other musical devices (see SEQUENCERS) and to the multitrack recording of DIGITAL MUSIC. Classical musicians have tended to be wary of this 'artificial' way of recording music but it has become an indispensable tool in POPULAR, ELECTRONIC and film music where the producers and engineers who manipulate the sound often have as much control over the music as the musicians.
                B.CO.

Bibl: A. Mackay, *Electronic Music: The Instruments, Music and Musicians* (London, 1975).

multivariate analysis. The statistical analysis of data involving more than one type of measurement or observation. Various subdivisions may be distinguished. Thus the CORRELATION or REGRESSION relation of a single variable (e.g. a person's weight) with several other variables (e.g. age, sex, social class) is known as a *multiple correlation* or *regression analysis*. The term multivariate analysis is often restricted to problems where more than one such dependent variable (e.g. both height and weight) are being analysed simultaneously. In some problems no external variables (such as age or sex) with which to correlate are available; and the correlation structure may be expressed in terms of an internal set of hypothetical components or *factors* (see FACTOR ANALYSIS; CLUSTER ANALYSIS).   M.S.BA.

multiversity. A word coined by Clark Kerr, former President of the University of California at Berkeley, to indicate the enormous variety of purposes in a university like California set down on about 100 campuses, many of which are universities in themselves. In a university in Newman's sense (*The Idea of a University*, 1852) the parts are those of an organism. In a multiversity, on the other hand, many parts can be added or subtracted with little effect on the whole. W.A.C.S.
Bibl: C. Kerr, *The Uses of the University* (Cambridge, Mass., 1963).

Munich. The capital city of Bavaria, which became the symbol of APPEASEMENT after the 'summit' conference of 29-30 September 1938 attended by Hitler (Germany), Mussolini (Italy), Chamberlain (Britain), and Daladier (France). Acting under the German threat of war the conference (without Czech participation) awarded to Germany the fortified frontier areas of Czechoslovakia inhabited by the Sudeten-German minority. 'Munich' has since become synonymous with any illjudged, pusillanimous, and self-defeating attempt to buy off would-be aggressors at the expense of third parties under the cloak of 'satisfying their legitimate claims'. D.C.W.
Bibl: J.W. Wheeler-Bennett, *Munich; Prologue to Tragedy* (London, 1966); T. Taylor, *Munich: the Price of Peace* (London, 1979).

muon. An ELEMENTARY PARTICLE in the MESON family. M.V.B.

museé imaginaire (*museum without walls*), see IMAGINARY MUSEUM.

music notation. Various developments in notation have taken place to deal with new ideas in 20th-century music. Paradoxically some of these are related to giving the performer greater freedom (see GRAPHIC SCORE, TIME NOTATION, SPRECHSTIMME) while others relate to music which is much more detailed and exact (see PARAMETERS, MULTIPHONICS, MICROTONE). A whole new area of music notation deals with ELECTRONIC MUSIC and COMPUTER MUSIC. For electronic music which appears as finished tape recordings the idea of a score may seem redundant but composers of electronic music have continued to produce them for various reasons including copyright, analysis, visual aids and most importantly as guides in electronic works which combine tape and live performance. The special qualities of electronic music (unpitched notes, complex colourings, supercomplex or random rhythms etc.) are often outside the scope of conventional music notation and composers have used a wide variety of new graphic symbols on the one hand and complex mathematical and acoustical details on the other to try and represent the music. Only rarely however are these electronic scores produced for the purpose of the re-creation of the music. B.CO.
Bibl: K. Stone, *Music Notation in the Twentieth Century* (New York, 1980).

music theatre. Originally, as used by the composers György Ligeti and Mauricio Kagel, a form of musical performance that takes place on a stage, with some theatrical aids such as props and costumes. In London in 1956 Alexander Goehr and John Cox formed their 'Music Theatre Ensemble' which extended this concept to cover the performance of works by Schönberg, Kurt Weill, Goehr, Maxwell Davies, and others, some of them involving a dramatically significant text. It is to be distinguished from opera, but like opera is on the whole of musical rather than theatrical interest. J.W.

musicology. The academic study of music, with particular reference to its history and to questions of authenticity and AESTHETICS. Although musicologists often disagree about the interpretation of points of historical detail, their combined researches have opened up vast areas of music which were previously unexplored or neglected. For many years such research was treated with indifference or derision by the average concert-performer; but since about 1950 the validity of the musicological contribution to the actual performance of early music has been widely accepted. While complete authenticity is a chimera (since we cannot hear, e.g., 17th-century music with 17th-century ears and minds), the search for it is always stimulating and revealing to the performer. Notable musicologists include Arnold Dolmetsch, Albert Schweitzer, Otto Deutsch, Alfred Einstein, Oliver Strunk, Egon Wellesz, the composer Peter Warlock (Philip Heseltine), Thurston Dart, Robbins Landon and many others.   A.H.

musique concrète, see CONCRETE MUSIC.

musique d'ameublement, see under FURNITURE MUSIC.

Muslim, see under ISLAM.

Muslim Brotherhood, see under ISLAM.

mutant. (1) A GENE which has undergone MUTATION within the particular stock of organisms under observation; (2) an organism bearing such a gene.   J.M.S.

mutation. A change in GENE, or in the structure or number of CHROMOSOMES. Mutation is important in the study of EVOLUTION, because it is the ultimate origin of all new inheritable variation.
J.M.S.

mutually assured destruction. The principle of symmetry in nuclear relationships, so that nuclear aggression by one STATE will bring massive and inevitable retaliation. It depends on both sides having a balance of defensive and offensive forces. Often known as the BALANCE OF TERROR, or by its rather unfortunate acronym MAD, mutually assured destruction has successfully underpinned Soviet-U.S. strategic relationships since the 1960s. But it offers no alternative to an escalating ARMS RACE, in an area where both sides have a massive oversupply of offensive weapons. Any sudden rush to change the shape of the nuclear equation is seen as destabilizing and therefore dangerous, so all efforts at limitation and control have been limited and cautious. Many attempts have been made to make the doctrine of mutually assured destruction more adaptable to new requirements and new technology (see FLEXIBLE RESPONSE), but with no striking success. Indeed, the concept is inherent in the politics which surround NUCLEAR WEAPONS, since they are designed to deter rather than to be used. The logic of mutually assured destruction has

been reinforced by recent theories concerning the NUCLEAR WINTER which suggest that the use of nuclear weapons would interrupt the FOOD CHAIN and cause a global catastrophe.   A.J.M.W.

Bibl: David Carlton (ed.), *The Dynamics of the Arms Race* (London, 1985); Lawrence Freedman, *The Evolution of Nuclear Strategy* (London, 1983).

Muzak. Muzak is actually a proprietary name but without a capital m it has gradually become synonymous with *piped* or *canned music.* This is music, generally bland arrangements of light classical and popular tunes, which is played in lifts, supermarkets and factories. Scientific studies have been done that would seem to show that the correct timing of different speeds and types of music can subconciously increase the listener's work output. Objections to this type of music have been made on the grounds that the listeners have no choice as to whether they wish to hear the music or not, but presumably many people welcome this form of aural background and feel that it adds warmth and colour to certain environments. For an early anticipation of muzak see FURNITURE MUSIC and for a contemporary interpretation see AMBIENT MUSIC.   B.CO.

MVD (Ministry of Internal Affairs). One of two Soviet organizations, the other being the KGB, which share, with somewhat fluctuating lines of demarcation, responsibility for order and security. Roughly speaking, MVD (as opposed to KGB) is devoted to the non-secret elements of police organization: the maintenance of overt order, and the regulation and, where necessary, repression (including corrective labour camps) of the ordinary population. For a time (1962-8) it was rechristened MOOP — Ministry for the Defence of Public Order.   R.C.

My Lai. Complex of villages in South VIETNAM where in 1968 U.S. troops massacred the entire population under the impression that they were supporters of the VIETCONG and that the village was a Vietcong stronghold. In 1971 Lieutenant William Calley and his immediate superior, Captain Ernest Medina, were court-martialled in the U.S.A., the former being sentenced to 20 years, the latter acquitted. The incident did much to polarize American opinion on the issue of patriotism versus justice, as it did to publicize the decline in morale and discipline of the U.S. Army in Vietnam.   D.C.W.

mycology. The study of the fungi, which include the yeasts, penicillins, and familiar fungi like mushrooms and toadstools, and are clearly enough demarcated from plants and animals to deserve the status of a kingdom of their own.   P.M.

myopathy. Any disease, disorder or dysfunction of muscle. Three types of muscle exist in the animal kingdom. These are smooth or unstriated muscle (found, for example, in the walls of blood vessels or of the various parts of the gastrointestinal tract); striated muscle (because of the cross-striations within the individual muscle fibres examined microscopically), skeletal muscle (as all such muscles have attachments to bone) or voluntary muscle (as contraction of this type is under the control of the will); and the highly specialized cardiac muscle of which the heart is almost wholly constituted. Whereas various forms of cardiomyopathy involving cardiac muscle have been described, the term myopathy is generally used in medicine and veterinary practice to identify disorders of voluntary muscle in man and animals, of which several hundred different types have been described. In man, these include many types of inherited muscle disease of which the muscular dystrophies are the most common, all of them progressive in varying degree and all producing muscular weakness and wasting. Some are due to autosomal dominant, others to autosomal recessive and yet others to X-linked recessive GENES (especially severe Duchenne type muscular dystrophy, which is usually fatal by the age of 20). Many other forms of myopathy are metabolic, some resulting from dysfunction of endocrine organs or toxic or nutritional factors, others from specific enzymatic deficiencies or other biochemical abnormalities involving individual components of the muscle CELL or its covering membranes. Others are inflammatory, some (like polymyositis and dermatomyositis) being due to disordered immunity, while others are due to infection with bacterial, viral or parasitic agents. Many rare congenital myopathies also exist, identifiable through specific morphological abnormalities of the muscle cell. Diagnosis usually depends upon the clinical history and physical examination, a variety of biochemical tests such as estimation of various ENZYMES in the blood SERUM, *electromyography* (examination of the electrical activity of muscles at rest and during contraction, usually with needle electrodes) and upon the examination of samples of muscle removed by biopsy through the light and/or ELECTRON MICROSCOPE, using various preparative and staining techniques including HISTOCHEMISTRY.   J.N.W.

Bibl: J.N. Walton (ed.), *Disorders of Voluntary Muscle* (Edinburgh and London, 4th ed., 1981).

mysticism. The direct experience of the divine as real and near, blotting out all sense of time and producing intense joy. The divine may be conceived as in PANTHEISM, so that the experience is interpreted as a glad union with all nature (as celebrated in much poetry), or it may be thought of as the bliss of ending all separate existence, as in the BUDDHIST idea of *Nirvana*. The experience may be limited to specially mysterious, sacred, or 'numinous' objects, as described in Rudolf Otto's *The Idea of the Holy* (1917), or it may simply be valued as a more intense or ecstatic awareness of the surrounding reality, an awareness which is close to the state of mind produced by psychedelic DRUGS. The possibility of such mysticism is one of the factors accounting for the popularity of COMPARATIVE RELIGION amid the modern West's materialism. But in Christianity, as in JUDAISM and ISLAM and as often in Buddhism and HINDUISM, the aim of mysticism has been a closer knowledge and adoration of God, leading to the 'beatific vision' of God and to eternal joy in his presence, or even in union with him (see THEISM).

Among Christians in the 20th century there has been much interest in the literature of mysticism, and also some sustained practice of the art of contemplating God in secret. In THEOLOGY, however, mysticism has often been accused of belittling the historical self-revelation of God (safeguarded by orthodoxy) and of being remote from the problems of daily life. (G.K. Chesterton wrote that mysticism begins in mist, centres in 'I', and ends in schism.) 'Mystical theology' is given a place in CATHOLICISM, but only alongside MORAL THEOLOGY and 'ascetical' theology, which deals with self-discipline and the humbler levels of prayer.   D.L.E.

Bibl: W.T. Stace, *Mysticism and Philosophy* (London and Philadelphia, 1961); R.C. Zaehner, *Mysticism, Sacred and Profane* (Oxford, 1957; New York, 1961); V. King, *Towards a New Mysticism* (London, 1980).

myth. A 'sacred' narrative, from which legends and fairy tales are not always clearly distinguishable. In a common tradition of analysis, myth is above all explanatory (how something came to be as it is). In the anthropological tradition best represented by B. Malinowski (1884-1942), myths are seen as justifications ('charters') of INSTITUTIONS, rights, etc. But the most recent anthropological discussions have been conducted with reference to Lévi-Strauss's thesis that the meaning of a myth lies below the narrative surface, being detectable by a close analysis of the individual incidents and items in the narrative, by their regrouping, and by their study in the context of the transformations they undergo in all versions of the myth. They then reveal an endless struggle to overcome 'contradictions'. The anthropological study of myth links with psychological, literary, and classical studies, and with POLITICAL SCIENCE and SOCIOLOGY. In the latter, myth is often no longer a 'sacred' narrative but, so to say, a whole value-bestowing area of belief. See also STRUCTURALISM.   M.F.

Bibl: S. Hugh-Jones, *The Palm and the Pleiades* (Cambridge, 1979); E. R. Leach and A. Laycock, *Structuralist Interpretations of Biblical Myth* (Cambridge, 1983).

mythopoeia. Deliberate and conscious MYTH-making; a writer's return to the PRIMITIVE habit of non-logical anthropomorphization and ritualization. Some artists, reacting against the sophistications of DEISM, RATIONALISM, and ATHEISM, have set out to remythologize the material of their experience, to rediscover 'belief', but in personal and diverse ways. Thus, Blake's mythopoeic system is a response to the thinking of the Enlightenment, Yeats's to the loss of Christian faith; all contemporary mythopoeic activities may be described as responses to the sense of existential disappointment (see EXISTENTIALISM) generated by godless TECHNOCRACIES.   M.S.-S.

N

Nabis, les. French artists' group, formed in 1888 under the impact of Gauguin's PONT-AVEN pictures, with Pierre Bonnard, Édouard Vuillard, Maurice Denis, Paul Sérusier, and the sculptors Georges Lacombe and Aristide Maillol as leading members. Their term 'Nabi', deriving from a Hebrew word for prophet, suggests the MYSTICISM tinged with THEOSOPHY that later turned Denis and (at BEURON) Jan Verkade into religious painters. But the main feature of their work in the 15 years of the group's activity was the application of Gauguin's flat surfaces (SYNTHETISM) and bright colours to calmer, more domestic or intimate subjects. Unlike their IMPRESSIONIST precursors they also ventured into theatre design, book and magazine illustration, posters, screens, and other aspects of applied art. In painting, however, they became overshadowed by the FAUVES, who made more spectacular use of much the same pictorial language.　　J.W.

Bibl: C. Chassé, tr. M. Bullock, *The Nabis and their Period* (London and New York, 1969).

Nachträglichkeit. Freud's 'theory of deferred action', in which the memory of past events is reconstituted in conformity with the present intentions, fears and DESIRES of the SUBJECT. The past is not recalled 'as it was', but in a form and context which is useful to the subject *now*. It is thus an act of INTENTIONALITY and is part of the life-project of the subject, since the way the past is recalled is operative in forming the way that the future is intended. The concept has been of importance in the theorizing of Lacan.　　R.PO.

Bibl: A. Wilden, *System and Structure* (London, 1972).

naive art, see under PRIMITIVE (2).

naive realism, see REALISM, NAIVE.

Nakasone's reforms. After a decade of short-term prime ministerships the coming to power in 1982 of Mr Yasuhiro Nakasone ushered in a period of more determined and radical leadership in Japan. Nakasone was a leader with serious reservations about the post-war settlement imposed on Japan by the American Occupation, and frequently spoke of a 'settling of accounts with the post-war period'. The reforming efforts of his government focused principally on the PUBLIC SECTOR, finance, trade, TAXATION, education and defence. Inheriting from his predecessor a commission on administrative reform, he strove to cut back the public sector and in particular promoted PRIVATIZATION of the Japan National Railways, which were seriously in deficit. In the interests of 'internationalizing' the economy, he encouraged liberalization of the financial system and promoted a more open trading regime (see MAEKAWA REPORT). He sought taxation reform to eliminate a serious budget deficit and to reduce tax loopholes and abuses.

His government set up a commission on education with a wide brief to recommend educational reform. His major concerns in this field were alleged lack of discipline in schools, the influence of the MARXIST-influenced Japanese Teachers Union, and the need to promote creativity in a system characterized by mass uniformity and an EGALITARIAN ethic. Concerning defence, Nakasone sought to reduce inhibitions against military spending inherited from the post-war period, and to strengthen and expand the security relationship with the U.S. In all these areas of reform a limited degree of success was obtained.　　J.A.A.S.

Name-of-the-Father. Term adopted by the French psychoanalyst Jacques Lacan for its echoes of the religious invocation 'in the Name of the Father'. It emphasizes the SYMBOLIC function of the father as representative of law and authority. The attribution of procreation to a real father is not self-evident; the father gives his name in order to function as a paternal authority. Freud had already come to realize the importance of the paternal function in the Oedipal triangle of mother-father-child in his work with neurotics. The father who intervenes, as the prohibitor of INCEST, to separate mother and child from their symbiotic and devouring relation, becomes for the UNCONSCIOUS the father-to-be-killed, and after that, the dead father. This unconscious father is the symbolic father who ties the SUBJECT to the law. But if in the neurotic there is always a flaw in relation to the Name-of-the-Father, in the psychotic the paternal function has not worked as a principle of separation from the mother — it is FORECLOSED. The father represents in the Oedipal stage the third term which prohibits the arbitariness of the mother-child relation, thus changing the structure of infantile reality. The Name-of-the-Father, by introducing the prohibition of incest as a primordial law, replaces the order of nature by the order of CULTURE.   B.BE.

nand-gate, see under GATE.

nanosecond. 10^{-9} sec (one thousand-millionth of a second). A typical time interval in the HARDWARE of a COMPUTER, e.g. for the operation of a GATE. In PHYSICS it is the time taken for light to travel about one foot.   C.S.

narcissism. In psychoanalytical theory (see PSYCHOANALYSIS), extreme love of self. *Primary narcissism,* in which sexual energy is directed toward the self, is characteristic of the pre-genital stages of PSYCHOSEXUAL DEVELOPMENT, whereas *secondary narcissism* refers to feelings of pride experienced when the EGO identifies with the ideas of the SUPEREGO.   W.Z.

narcoanalysis, see under TRUTH DRUG.

Nash equilibrium. A CONCEPT in GAME THEORY, which has been used in ECONOMICS. A number of individuals or firms, with possibly conflicting interests, are in a Nash equilibrium if each of them is following the best STRATEGY he can, given the strategies being followed by others. J.F. Nash showed in 1950 that such an EQUILIBRIUM exists rather generally if *mixed strategies* (i.e. strategies involving a random choice of action) are allowed. However, the concept allows no role for the formation of coalitions, or agreements to make side-payments.   J.A.M.
Bibl: M. Waterson, *Economic Theory of the Industry* (Cambridge, 1984).

Nation of Islam. A BLACK religious and political movement in the U.S., whose members are often referred to as Black Muslims. It was founded in Detroit during the Depression by W.D. Fard, who preached an eclectic mixture of black supremacism and doctrines derived from *Sunni* ISLAM. After Fard's disappearance in 1943 the movement's leadership passed to Elijah Mohammad, who combined its doctrines with an appeal particularly aimed at dispossessed and delinquent young blacks. The Nation grew during the 1950s, partly stimulated by the charismatic Malcolm X, to a membership of between 70,000 and 100,000 in 1960. Its politics were incoherent; in essence they rested on aims for an independent state for American blacks. The movement was at odds with more moderate black organizations of the CIVIL RIGHTS MOVEMENT, and lost much of its political impetus when Malcolm X left in March 1964. During the 1970s it was characterized by internal strife, and by attempts to establish links with radical Islamic movements abroad. After its leadership was assumed by Elijah Mohammad's son Wallace in 1975, the Nation adopted more orthodox Islamic doctrines and in 1978 was renamed the World Community of al-Islam in the West. In 1981 Louis Farrakhan, a former dissident Black Muslim, founded a revived 'Nation of Islam', which has a fluctuating political voice which veers between black NATIONALISM and more moderate rhetoric. In 1984 his apparent ANTISEMITISM was a handicap to the RAINBOW COALITION.   S.R.
Bibl: M. Marable, *Race, Reform and Rebellion* (London, 1984); A.L. Reed Jr, *The Jesse Jackson Phenomenon* (Yale, 1986).

national accounting. The statistics of the NATIONAL INCOME, e.g. private and public consumption and INVESTMENT, saving, exports and imports. These variables are related to each other by various identities (see GDP and GNP). They provide a statistical description of the economy. However, the definitions and conventions used in national accounting raise many problems, e.g. the statistics for the national income of a country take no account of the (dis) advantages conferred by a lack/abundance of natural resources. J.P.

Bibl: D. Begg *et al., Economics* (London, 1984).

National Bolshevism. A polemical term in use in Germany between the wars to describe a policy of NATIONALIST resistance to the Treaty of Versailles and the West based on alliance with the other 'pariah power', Bolshevik Russia, against their common enemies. The idea was first started by Karl Radek in 1919; its paradoxical appeal attracted groups on both extremes of the political spectrum, nationalists on the RIGHT (like Reventlow and Moeller van den Bruck) and dissident COMMUNISTS and SOCIALISTS on the LEFT. It did not survive the NAZI capture of power. A.L.C.B.

Bibl: K. von Klemperer, 'Towards a 4th Reich? The History of National Bolshevism in Germany' (*Review of Politics*, 13, 1951), pp. 191-211.

national debt (or *public debt*). The interest-bearing debt of a central government, sometimes extended to include the debt of state or local governments and public enterprises. The debt instruments may be marketable (bonds and Treasury bills) or non-marketable (deposits at savings banks and the like) and of varying maturity, from deposits withdrawable at sight to irredeemable bonds. The composition is influenced by MONETARY POLICY. The debt is accumulated through government borrowing (see FISCAL POLICY), and may be held by either home or foreign residents. The interest on the debt is paid by tax or other government receipts. Where the debt is partly held by foreign residents, the payment of interest and the principal has to be in foreign exchange and represents a debit on the BALANCE OF PAYMENTS. Except in this sense, the national debt does not constitute a burden on the economy. P.M.O.

Bibl: J. Craven, *Introduction to Economics* (Oxford, 1984).

National Front (France). The political party, *Le Front National* (FN), was founded in 1972 by its present leader, Jean-Marie Le Pen. Like the British National Front, it is an extreme RIGHT-wing party which is anti-IMMIGRANT and racist in outlook. The twin themes of immigration and 'insecurity' occupy a central position in the rhetoric of the FN while the Party's policies include restoration of the death penalty, a ban on ABORTION and the repatriation of immigrants from France. Public support for the FN has grown rapidly since 1980: in the French general election of March 1986 the FN won 9.65% of the vote and 35 of the 577 National Assembly seats. The FN is also now influential in many local councils. Support for the FN is highest in industrial areas which have large migrant communities and high levels of unemployment. The Party's leader, Jean-Marie Le Pen, was a Poujadist deputy during the Fourth Republic, a fanatical supporter of the Algérie-Française movement and a supporter of the Far Right candidate, Maître Tixier-Vignacour, in the 1965 presidential elections. S.M.

national income. The income generated, in a given period of time, by the economic activity of the residents of a country. The term is used so as to correspond to either GNP or NET NATIONAL PRODUCT, i.e. the value of economic activity after deduction of the depreciation of CAPITAL. The latter usage is the more meaningful, as it refers to the income available for spending on goods and services after allowance is made for keeping capital intact. Incomes are included in national income only insofar as they arise from production, i.e. it does not include transfer payments such as welfare benefits. J.P.

Bibl: D. Begg *et al., Economics* (London, 1984).

National Socialism, see NAZISM.

nationalism. (1) The feeling of belonging to a group united by common racial, linguistic and historical ties, and usually identified with a particular territory. (2) A corresponding IDEOLOGY which exalts the nation STATE as the ideal form of political organization with an overriding claim on the loyalty of its citizens.

Developing first in Western Europe with the consolidation of nation states, nationalism brought about the reorganization of Europe in the 19th and 20th centuries and has been the prime force in the political awakening of Asia and Africa. In the first half of the 19th century it was associated with DEMOCRACY and LIBERALISM; its greatest prophet, Mazzini (1805-72), gave a generous interpretation of the 'principle of nationality', seeing the individual nations as subdivisions of a larger world society which ought to live together in peace. In the later 19th century, however, nationalism assumed aggressive, intolerant forms (*integrative nationalism*) identified with military and trade rivalries, national expansion at the expense of other peoples, and IMPERIALISM. In the 20th century it has been an essential element in FASCISM and other TOTALITARIAN movements, but also a moving force in the rebellion and liberation of colonial peoples and in the resistance of nations and national MINORITIES threatened with subjugation by more powerful states.

In its African and Asian manifestations, nationalism has assumed three analytically distinct forms which sometimes conflict and at others are interwoven. (a) Territorial nationalism sustains the states created by decolonization which often contain different ethnic groups, such as Zambia, Kenya, Uganda, Malaysia, India. (b) Ethnic nationalism expresses the wishes of such groups to revise national boundaries to form ethnically homogeneous states, as for example the Tamil, Kurdish, Ibo or Kikuyu peoples. (c) There is also the 'pan' or 'superstate' variant, which seeks to unify a number of culturally similar or geographically contiguous states into a larger state or confederation of states (see PAN-AFRICANISM; PAN-ISLAM). In many Western countries, the ethnic nationalisms of regionally-concentrated cultural or linguistic groups have challenged their nation state and sought a weaker or independent relationship, as in Canada, France, Spain and Britain.

Nationalism has been a powerful source of inspiration in the arts; it formed one of the dynamic elements of ROMANTICISM in 19th-century Europe and has more recently shaped artistic expression in the 'new nations' of Africa and Asia. Despite the rival claims of CLASS war on the one hand and internationalism on the other, nationalism as a mass emotion has been the most powerful political force in the history of the world. A.L.C.B./S.R.

Bibl: E. Kamenka (ed.), *Nationalism* (London, 1976); E. Gellner, *Nations and Nationalism* (Oxford, 1983).

nationalization. The acquisition by the government of property held by private persons or companies to form nationalized industries. Nationalization may be accompanied by compensation, paid in money or government bonds to the previous owners, or it may be by expropriation. Nationalization may be for the direct political purpose of SOCIALISM or it may be for the more limited objective of increasing the government's control of the economy. There are economic arguments for the STATE providing PUBLIC GOODS, correcting for EXTERNALITIES and controlling NATURAL MONOPOLIES. The degree of control governments exert over nationalized industries varies between industries and countries. In Western Europe, since World War II, most countries have had nationalized railways and electricity supply systems, and coal mines and steel firms have sometimes been nationalized. In France and Italy, certain motor car firms are in the PUBLIC SECTOR. For many years, nationalization has been an important political issue, e.g. ownership of the gas industry in Britain has passed from private into public ownership and back again (see PRIVATIZATION). M.V.P.; J.P.

Bibl: R. Rees, *Public Enterprise Economics* (London, 2nd ed., 1984).

nationalized industries, see under NATIONALIZATION.

nativism. In DEVELOPMENTAL PSYCHOLOGY, the theory that perceptual (see PERCEPTION) or other faculties are innate and not dependent on experiential stimuli or REINFORCEMENT for their development. See also NATURE/NURTURE. H.L.

NATO (North Atlantic Treaty Organization). An organization established on 4 April 1949 in a treaty signed by Belgium, Canada, Denmark, France, Iceland, Italy, Luxembourg, the Netherlands, Norway, Portugal, Britain, and the U.S.A.; Greece and Turkey acceded on 18 February 1952, West Germany on 9 May 1955. NATO is a permanent military alliance set up to defend Western Europe against the threat of Soviet aggression. In addition to integrated multinational commands, its organs consist of a Council, an International Secretariat, and various committees established to formulate common policies on political, social, and economic issues as well as military ones. Its founders' belief in a common Atlantic political and cultural heritage gradually dwindled with the growing European resentment of American leadership. The French withdrawal in 1966, and the Greek withdrawal of 1974 from the integrated command structure were signs of a growing estrangement, as was the general European rejection of the American NEUTRON BOMB suggestions of 1978. The seeming dropping by the Americans of the idea of 'MUTUALLY ASSURED DESTRUCTION' in favour of a limited nuclear WAR and the placing of 'Euromissiles' to counter the Russian SS 20s on American bases in Europe led to the resurgence of the European PEACE MOVEMENT and to increased anti-American feeling in Europe. Soviet premier Gorbachev has skilfully exploited these splits in the Alliance to put pressure on the U.S. in various ARMS CONTROL discussions.

D.C.W.;A.WI.

Bibl: E.H. van der Beugel, *From Marshall Aid to Atlantic Partnership* (Amsterdam and New York, 1966); P.H. Trezise, *The Atlantic Connection* (Washington, 1975).

natural childbirth, see under CHILDBIRTH TECHNIQUES.

natural justice. The practical application by the English courts of NATURAL LAW theories in the form of two basic presumptions to be enforced unless in any instance there is express statutory provision to the contrary. They are (1) that no man may be a judge in his own cause; and (2) that no man is to be condemned unheard. Actions or decisions which, in the absence of express statutory authority, breach either presumption are void. Accordingly a court will quash the decision of an administrative authority if any member of the authority had a personal interest in the issue, unless this is expressly permitted by an Act of Parliament. Similarly an office-holder may not be validly dismissed from office unless he has first been adequately informed of the charge against him, and then been heard in his own defence and permitted to bring witnesses or produce evidence. These presumptions have in recent years become the basic judicial test of fair dealing by the administration.

D.C.M.Y.

Bibl: D.C.M. Yardley, *Principles of Administrative Law* (London, 2nd ed., 1986); H.W.R. Wade, *Administrative Law* (Oxford and New York, 5th ed., 1982); P. Jackson, *Natural Justice* (London, 2nd ed., 1979).

natural law. Rules of law laid down by nature. Though many theorists through the ages have recognized the importance of natural law, and have often argued that human law is subordinate to it, they have interpreted what it is and how it has been derived in many different ways. Aristotle believed that natural laws were universally recognized, e.g. the law of murder, and never changed. The Stoic philosophers considered natural law to be based on rational thought. St Thomas Aquinas argued that it was the reflection of divine wisdom in human beings, and many Christian philosophers have asserted that human laws and even national sovereigns are subordinate to the law of God. INTERNATIONAL LAW, regulating relations between independent states, has been much influenced by natural law theories. Locke based his ideas of life, liberty and estate upon NATURAL RIGHTS, which also influenced the French Declaration of Rights, 1789, and the United States Declaration of Independence, 1776, and Bill of Rights, 1791. The effect of natural law theories upon practical English law is seen in the development of equity by the Court of Chancery, the doctrine of unreasonableness as the test of negligence (see COMMON LAW and TORTS), parental rights in FAMILY LAW, the rules of natural justice, and civil liberties (see HUMAN RIGHTS). Natural law ideas are often about an ideal, e.g. the Universal Declaration of Human Rights. H.L.A. Hart believes there is a minimum content of natural law, but few today think that natural law is immutable.

D.C.M.Y.

Bibl: R.W.M. Dias, *Jurisprudence*

(London, 5th ed., 1985); J. Finnis, *Natural Law and Natural Rights* (Oxford, 1980).

natural monopoly, see under MONOPOLY.

natural rights. Declared by Bentham to be 'nonsense on stilts', the doctrine of natural rights has enjoyed something of a revival in recent years, though under the label of 'human' rather than 'natural' rights. The most extravagant versions of the doctrine that 'nature' endows us with natural and inalienable rights to life, liberty and the pursuit of happiness have fallen into disrepute along with a faith in reason and reason's dictates. On the other hand the view that no government is lawful which fails to secure the rights of its citizens is widely held, and is supported by the United Nations Universal Declaration of Human Rights. These rights are, evidently, more fundamental than rights which merely happen to be enshrined in the local law, and are, in that sense, natural rights. In spite of Bentham's scepticism about rights which were nowhere spelled out by their creator, the 20th century has felt a great need for a doctrine which will justify the view that governments exist in order to enforce rights which the government did not create and is not entitled to abrogate.   A.R.

Bibl: M. Cranston, *What are Human Rights?* (London, 1953); R.M. Dworkin, *Taking Rights Seriously* (London, 1979).

natural sciences. Roughly speaking, those branches of organized knowledge concerned with the material aspects of existence. But the CONCEPT of 'Nature' is so all-embracing, historically variable, and dependent upon METAPHYSICAL assumptions that it cannot be given an *a priori* definition. Traditionally, the natural world was contrasted with the 'supernatural' realm of THEOLOGY, but the modern convention is to draw a distinction between the natural sciences and the SOCIAL SCIENCES and/or BEHAVIOURAL SCIENCES, related perhaps to the elements of CONSCIOUSNESS and choice in the sphere of human relations. The core disciplines of PHYSICS and CHEMISTRY (once called *natural philosophy*), GEOLOGY, and BIOLOGY (*natural history*) encroach on PHILOSOPHY through MATHEMATICS and spread vaguely into PSYCHOLOGY. This categorization has no practical significance, but is a convenient classification scheme for academic purposes (e.g. the Natural Sciences Tripos: an examination curriculum at Cambridge University).   J.Z.

natural selection. The mechanism of evolutionary change, suggested simultaneously by Darwin and Wallace in 1858. The theory asserts that EVOLUTION occurs because those individuals of a SPECIES whose characteristics best fit them for survival are the ones which contribute most offspring to the next generation. These offspring will tend to have the characteristics by virtue of which their parents survived, and in this way the adaptation of the species to its ENVIRONMENT will gradually be improved. It is now generally accepted that natural selection, acting on MUTATIONS which are in their origin nonadaptive, is the primary cause of evolution. (See also DARWINISM.)   J.M.S.

Bibl: C. Darwin, *On the Origin of Species* (1859; London, 6th ed., 1872; New York, 1873).

natural unit of time, see under PLANCK TIME/ERA.

naturalism.

(1) In ETHICS, the doctrine that the CRITERION of right action is some empirical feature of the natural world such as the happiness of sentient beings or the self-preservation of an individual, group, or SPECIES. Agreeing that moral utterances are genuine PROPOSITIONS, which can be known to be true or false, it maintains that the facts that verify them (see VERIFICATION) are of an ordinary empirical kind and not of a supernatural character (as in MORAL THEOLOGY) or constituents of an autonomous realm of moral values, accessible only to a special moral faculty (as in INTUITIONISM). It is this doctrine, in the first instance, that G.E. Moore taxed with committing the NATURALISTIC FALLACY.

(2) More generally, any PHILOSOPHY which sees mind as dependent upon, included within, or emergent from, material nature, and not as being prior to or in some way more real than it. Its direct opposite is not *supernaturalism*, which holds that the realm of the divine is the

only or primary reality, but ANTINATU-RALISM. IDEALISM is antinaturalistic but is not always supernaturalistic. A.Q.

(3) An approach to PSYCHOLOGY and SOCIAL SCIENCE which assumes that human beings are essentially physico-chemical SYSTEMS, and can be studied in exactly the same way as the rest of the physical world. For the opposite view, and for an intermediate position, see ANTI-NATURALISM. A.S.

(4) In literature and drama, a tendency — consequent on but distinguishable from REALISM — influential in Western Europe from the 1870s to the 1890s (for its Italian version see VERISM) and in the U.S.A. and Russia from the 1890s. A form of literary POSITIVISM, naturalism is basically post-Darwinian and inclined towards an environmentalist and often evolutionary explanation of life (see ENVIRONMENT; EVOLUTION); it often takes the form of close reportage and documentation and involves systematized views of connection and CAUSALITY; and it is disposed to regard the literary act as an 'experiment' on the scientific model. This last analogy is established by Zola in the most explicit book on the subject, *Le Roman expérimental* (1880); his own Rougon-Macquart series of novels exemplifies classic naturalism, based on intensive research into social conditions and forces and on physiological and evolutionary principles. In the theatre the leading naturalist was Ibsen, whose influence spread massively over Europe in the last two decades of the 19th century. In America the delayed reaction to naturalism was perhaps the result of neglecting the vast forces for social change, and the moral and social problems, that arose in American society at its high point of IN-DUSTRIALIZATION; but with Frank Norris, Stephen Crane, and Hamlin Garland in the 1890s a tradition developed which has been remarkably persistent. By this date naturalism in Europe was giving way to a new AESTHETICISM and SYMBOLISM: Strindberg was overtaking Ibsen, and the IM-PRESSIONISTIC element in naturalism was pushing through to create the uncertain surface of much MODERNIST writing and painting. Naturalism was the transition point at the end of an era in Europe; in some countries and in some writers it has persisted significantly into the new century. M.S.BR.

Bibl: H.M. Block, *Naturalistic Triptych* (New York, 1970); R.N. Stromberg (ed.), *Realism, Naturalism and Symbolism* (London and New York, 1968); L.R. Furst and P.N. Skrine, *Naturalism* (London, 1969; New York, 1971).

(5) In French painting, an analogous movement which derived from mid-19th-century REALISM, and to conservative eyes soon seemed a safer alternative to the IMPRESSIONISM which was springing from the same roots at the same time. Its prophet was the critic Castagnary; its product the stock art of the Third Republic, as exemplified by the former Musée du Luxembourg.

In senses (4) and (5), the term is used pejoratively by COMMUNIST critics, who tend to see naturalism as the dispassionate, more or less detailed photographic rendering of a non-tendentious scene, and compare it unfavourably with realism, and even more with SOCIALIST REALISM. The latter, however, in Western eyes, is often extremely naturalistic. J.W.

naturalistic fallacy. In ETHICS, a term coined by G.E. Moore for the alleged mistake of defining 'good' in terms of ordinary empirical expressions such as 'pleasant' or 'desired' or, indeed, of giving any ANALYSIS of 'good', that is to say any definition intended to elucidate its MEANING. Moore branded ethical NATURALISM, which involves such analyses or definitions, as fallacious, and defended ethical INTUITIONISM, taking goodness to be a characteristic of states of affairs that cannot be discerned by ordinary empirical observation but only by an autonomous moral faculty. The phrase has come to be applied to any account of ethical terms or utterances which identifies them in meaning with any terms or utterances of a factual or descriptive kind and, in particular, with any INFERENCE that purports to derive a NORMATIVE conclusion from purely factual premises, any passage in reasoning from 'is' to 'ought'. In this form it is the negative starting-point of EMOTIVISM and all other ethical theories which classify VALUE-JUDGEMENTS as some form of discourse that is not propositional (see PROPOSITION). A.Q.

Bibl: G.E. Moore, *Principia Ethica* (Cambridge, 1903), ch.1.

nature versus nurture. In DEVELOPMENTAL PSYCHOLOGY, the controversy over ascribing due weight to GENETIC facts on the one hand and ENVIRONMENTAL ones on the other as factors responsible for the characteristics of an organism. See also NATIVISM. H.L.

Nazism. Term formed from the abbreviation for National Socialist German Workers' Party, a political movement founded in 1919 and taken over by Adolf Hitler (1889-1945) in the early 1920s to become the basis on which he established his twelve-year DICTATORSHIP (1933-45) in Germany. Nazism originated as a movement of protest against the surrender of 1918 and the Treaty of Versailles (and the WEIMAR REPUBLIC, which Hitler held to blame for both), but it was only in 1930, with the economic DEPRESSION and the mass UNEMPLOYMENT, that the Nazis succeeded in attracting mass support. Taken into partnership by a RIGHT-wing coalition in January 1933, Hitler rapidly disposed of his partners, liquidated the opposition parties, and established a TOTALITARIAN regime based on monopoly of power by the Nazi Party.

Nazism shared many of the features of FASCISM in other countries. Its special characteristics were (1) the Nazi Party, which proved capable of matching the success of the WORKING CLASS movement (COMMUNISTS and SOCIAL DEMOCRATS) in mobilizing a mass following in a highly industrialized state, and the methods used to achieve this; (2) a racist IDEOLOGY which proclaimed the racial superiority of the 'Aryan' RACE and specifically of its best exemplar, the German people, a 'master race' (*Herrenvolk*) with an inalienable claim to LEBENSRAUM at the expense of other inferior races such as the Slavs in Central and Eastern Europe; (3) a virulent ANTISEMITISM that denounced the Jews as the mortal enemies of the German people and found expression before World War II in the NUREMBERG LAWS and during the war in the FINAL SOLUTION, a plan, largely carried into effect, for the extermination of the Jewish population of Europe; (4) the creation of the SS as an instrument of arbitrary power responsible solely to Hitler to put the ideological commitments of (2) and (3) into effect without regard to the traditional institutions of the state and the legal system; (5) the realization of German ambitions, backed by German military power, to establish their HEGEMONY over Europe, which were a principal cause of World War II; and (6) the personality of Adolf Hitler, who as Führer (Leader) of the German people showed a ruthlessness, only equalled by Stalin, in carrying out the programme contained in (2), (3) and (5) above, and a determination to see Germany destroyed rather than admit defeat. A.L.C.B.

Bibl: K.D. Bracher, *The German Dictatorship* (London and New York, 1970); Joachim Fest, *Hitler* (London and New York, 1974); Walter Laqueur (ed.), *Fascism* (New York, 1976; London, 1979).

NDP (net domestic product), see under GDP.

NEAC, see NEW ENGLISH ART CLUB.

Néant, le. Sartre's French equivalent of Heidegger's *Das Nichts*, both meaning the same as NOTHINGNESS. The notion is important to EXISTENTIALISM, where it refers variously to the object of objectless ANXIETY (i.e. to that anxiety that isn't about anything), to death, and to the indeterminacy of human nature until it is realized by acts of free choice. ANALYTIC PHILOSOPHERS criticize the metaphysical affirmations in which it occurs as misinterpreting a formal concept of LOGIC, that of negation, as a genuine name or *referring* expression (see CONNOTATION), as in the Lewis Carroll exchange: 'I see nobody on the road.' 'I only wish *I* had such eyes. To be able to see Nobody!' A.Q.

nebula. A GALAXY, or a cloud of incandescent gas within our own galaxy, which appears as a misty object in the heavens. M.V.B.

necessary and sufficient conditions. PROPOSITION A is a *necessary condition* of proposition B if B's truth and A's falsity are incompatible; proposition A is a *sufficient condition* of proposition B if B's falsity and A's truth are incompatible.

I.M.D.L.

Needham thesis. Joseph Needham (1900-), a biochemist by training, became deeply involved in the study of Chinese science while on duty in China during World War II. For Needham, Chinese science posed a fundamental dilemma to the historian. Until the 15th century it had easily outstripped Western science and TECHNOLOGY in both its theoretical and applied dimensions. Thereafter, Chinese science had fallen relatively stagnant at precisely the time when European science underwent its most fundamental revolution. Why? A Marxist, Needham attributed it to China's failure to undergo a parallel bourgeois REVOLUTION to the West, ushering in a CAPITALIST economy which would act as a spur to scientific and technological change. The centralized authority of the Emperor valued intellectual orthodoxy above INNOVATION, and the mandarinate bureaucratized knowledge. Scholars remain divided as to whether Needham's stress upon what China failed to achieve is a fruitful approach to understanding the true nature of Chinese science. R.P.

Bibl: J. Needham, *Science and Civilization in China* (Cambridge, 1954-).

negative income tax. A tax system that guarantees a minimum income and applies a high rate of tax on all other incomes up until a break even point, at which the tax paid is equal to the minimum guaranteed income. The tax rate above this point is lower. This high initial tax rate is necessary to recoup the costs of guaranteeing a minimum income and to target the benefits, as much as possible, at the poorest households. This high rate of tax gives rise to a POVERTY TRAP. With a reasonable guaranteed minimum income and even a high initial tax rate, the break even point is quite high. This implies that the scheme is costly and that not all the benefits go to the poorest households. See SOCIAL DIVIDEND. J.P.

Bibl: M.J. Artis, *The UK Economy* (London, 11th ed., 1986).

negative population growth (NPG). A population in which the number of births plus immigrants is less than the number of deaths plus emigrants. Singapore is an example of a country in which disincentives to FERTILITY have resulted in negative population growth. S.T.

negentropy, see under ENTROPY (2).

négritude. A term coined in the 1930s, and much used since World War II, to express the sense of a common Negro inheritance and destiny among French-educated Negro INTELLECTUALS in Africa and the Caribbean. It embraces the revolt against colonialist values (see IMPERIALISM), glorification of the African past, and nostalgia for the beauty and harmony of traditional African society, which is seen as being founded on BLACK emotion and intuition as opposed to Hellenic reason and LOGIC. *Négritude* is, however, a universalist concept, which owes a great deal to its French, or even Parisian, intellectual origins, and it is very different from traditional African tribalism. Although it has helped the black cause, it has also been criticized by blacks themselves as resting on a doubtful belief in intrinsic cultural blackness and as neglecting contemporary political realities. The main exponents have been L.-S. Senghor (President of Senegal) and Aimé Césaire, and the chief political critic Frantz Fanon. A useful discussion of the various issues involved is to be found in 'Orphée noir', Sartre's Introduction to Senghor's *Anthologie de la poésie nègre et malgache* (1948). J.G.W.

neighbourhood. Term embodying the idea of a recognizable physical unit which is also a social unit. The idea has been highly influential in urban planning, and especially in the post-war NEW TOWNS. It stems from a view of the medieval small town as an ideal entity which requires re-creation if the anonymity of the METROPOLIS is to be avoided. Such neighbourhoods have as a rule been taken as equivalent to the catchment area of a primary school. It has, however, been argued that the real social contacts of a mobile PLURALIST society are not so geographically circumscribed. M.BR.

neoclassical economic theory . A school of economic thought based on the view that

565

markets function efficiently and, in particular, adjust to EQUILIBRIUM. The theoretical justification for this view is that markets satisfy the assumptions of PERFECT COMPETITION and adjust to a COMPETITIVE EQUILIBRIUM. This theory is associated with MARGINAL ANALYSIS and has dominated much of economic thought and analysis for the last century. In content, it has similarities to the schools of economic thought associated with ECONOMIC LIBERALISM, FREE MARKETS, MONETARISM, LAISSEZ-FAIRE and SUPPLY-SIDE ECONOMICS. Many forms of economic analysis are based on its assumptions, e.g. TRADE THEORY, or on situations when the assumptions do not hold, e.g. EXTERNALITIES and PUBLIC GOODS.   J.P.

Bibl: M. Blaug, *Economic Theory in Retrospect* (London, 5th ed., 1985).

neo-classicism.

(1) In architecture, a movement between 1750 and 1850 which became the first international style, ranging from St Petersburg to Virginia, and strongly influencing the modern movement, both intellectually and visually. It was inspired by the recent archaeological discoveries in Greece and Rome, by the rational ideas of the Enlightenment and the resulting notions of 'apparent utility' developed by Laugier, and by the rejection of baroque and rococo forms in favour of simple geometric, largely rectilinear, shapes derived from antique sources. Neo-classicism was strongest in France and Germany and its influence on such 20th-century architects as Mies van der Rohe can be traced directly back through Behrens to Schinkel (1781-1841). A perverted form was associated with TOTALITARIAN Germany, Italy, and the U.S.S.R. during the 1930s.

M.BR.

Bibl: H. Honour, *Neo-Classicism* (Harmondsworth, 1968).

(2) In painting and sculpture, the evocation of the 'noble simplicity and calm grandeur' declared by Winckelmann to characterize the art of the Ancients. The style spread rapidly from the mid 18th century: Canova, David, and Flaxman, then Ingres and Thorwaldsen, were leading exponents.

More recently Picasso displayed a thoroughly neo-classical style, especially in his line-drawings of the 1920s, sometimes even taking classical subjects. The term has also been applied (though more obscurely) to various works of the same period: the Ingres-inspired paintings of Matisse, the METAPHYSICAL PAINTING of de Chirico and Carrà, and the serene still-lifes of Morandi. Just as 18th-century neo-classicism had supplanted the exuberance of baroque, so did these productions of the 1920s represent a return to passivity and restraint after the turbulent experiments of the preceding decade.   P.C.

(3) In music, a 20th-century reaction against the emotional extremes of Wagner and his immediate followers, a conscious rejection of ROMANTICISM, and a harking back to 18th-century models. This postulated a certain detachment from the musical material and a suppression of personal involvement on the part of the composer. Paradoxically it was Stravinsky, whose *Rite of Spring* had revolutionized musical thought, who in turn became an anti-revolutionary, reverting to 18th-century patterns and textures in the bulk of the compositions he wrote between about 1920 and 1950. Of these, *Pulcinella* (1919, based on music by Pergolesi, with actual quotations), the Octet for Wind Instruments, the Piano Concerto, the Symphony in C, the ballet *Apollo*, and *The Rake's Progress* are notable examples of the neo-classical style. Hindemith, Casella, Malipiero, and to a lesser extent Bartók are other composers who tried to find a satisfactory contemporary equivalent to classical ideals.   A.H.

neo-colonialism, see under IMPERIALISM.

neo-conservatism. (1) A recent American variant of CONSERVATISM propagated by members of the nation's intellectual ELITE, often through journals such as *The Public Interest* and *Commentary*. Neo-conservatives differ over many issues, but are to an extent unified by a common temperament and vision. Many are former radicals and from Jewish and Catholic backgrounds. Disillusionment with Soviet COMMUNISM encouraged some to re-evaluate the virtues of capitalist DEMOCRACY; others were threatened by what they saw as the turbulence and philistinism of the 1960s and driven to a concern with social stability and cultural values. Neo-conservatives tend to see themselves as sophisticated realists with an informed pessimism about the limitations of human nature and a sceptical view of the potential of the state either as an economic manager or an agent of social progress. They tend to defend CAPITALISM as a system which promotes democratic political forms and individual freedoms as well as affluence. Neo-conservatism also asserts the need for society to share a firm set of values, perhaps to be drawn from non-FUNDAMENTALIST religion. In foreign policy contradictions abound, but the emphasis lies on 'realism', a constant distrust of the Soviet Union, and a rejection of the HUMAN RIGHTS policy of the Carter administration.   S.R.

Bibl: G. Peele, *Revival and Reaction* (Oxford and New York, 1984); P. Steinfels, *The Neo-Conservatives* (New York, 1979).

(2) A term which some commentators apply to a body of CONSERVATIVE thought which has developed in Britain since the mid-1970s. It is distinct from the New RIGHT in that it attempts to reinstate supposedly conservative values rather than to smuggle elements of 19th-century LIBERALISM into conservative IDEOLOGY. As such it probably does not deserve the prefix 'neo'; its emphasis lies on familiar themes of social cohesion and stability, national integrity and purpose. Its voice on concrete policy issues is heard most in such areas as immigration and RACE relations, education and the family.   S.R.

Bibl: R. Scruton, *The Meaning of Conservatism* (London, 1984).

neo-Darwinism, see under DARWINISM.

Neo-fascism. A term characterizing the values, aims and methods of political groups or movements reminiscent of and sometimes explicitly based upon those of pre-1945 FASCISM. It is applied to such cases as the Movimento Sociale Italiano (MSI) in Italy and the NATIONAL FRONT in France, and more loosely in political rhetoric directed at extreme RIGHT-wing factions everywhere.   S.R.

neo-Firthian, see under FIRTHIAN.

neo-Freudian. Adjective used to describe several schools of PSYCHOANALYSIS which modified the view of Freud and his followers that the individual is motivated by instinctual drives which control the psychic energy, called LIBIDO, behind all human action. The neo-Freudians expanded the motivating forces to include both maturation and environmental factors, thereby rejecting the concept of libido with its link to the EROS instinct. The neo-Freudians are so called because they broke away from classical pyschoanalysis during Freud's lifetime; those who altered his views after his death in 1939 are generally known as EGO-PSYCHOLOGISTS. The most influential of the neo-Freudians is Erik Erikson who achieved recognition well beyond psychoanalytic circles for his specification of the epigenetic stages through which the personality develops throughout life. For Erikson, the fundamental personality problem is the adjustment of the individual to the external, social world. At each period of the life cycle, from infancy through old age, the individual faces particular EGO crises concerned with the sense of identity. Resolution of the crisis leads to the acquisition of ego strengths which in turn enable the ego to master the demands from both inner and external world associated with subsequent stages of the life cycle. In this way Erikson depicts the ego from a psychosocial perspective. Other prominent neo-Freudians include Karen Horney, Heinz Hartmann, and Erich Fromm.   R.P-S.

Bibl: C. Monte, *Beneath the Mask: An Introduction to Theories of Personality* (New York, 1980).

neo-Hegelianism. A revival of the philosophical IDEALISM of Hegel. Prominent neo-Hegelians have been, in Britain, the school of T.H. Green (1836-82) and F.H. Bradley (1846-1924), whose most loyal (if idiosyncratic) member was J.E. McTaggart (1866-1925) and most recent R.G. Collingwood (1889-1943); in France, Léon Brunschvicg (1869-1944); in Italy, Benedetto Croce (1891-1970).   A.Q.

neo-imperialism, see under IMPERIALISM.

neo-Impressionism. French school of painting deriving from IMPRESSIONISM but based on the more scientific approach of Georges Seurat, whose readings in SPECTROSCOPY led him to elaborate two techniques of rendering effects of light, both laborious by comparison with the Impressionist sketch: (1) *divisionism*, or the splitting of the spectrum into dabs of pure primary colour, and (2) *pointillisme*, or the reduction of those dabs to small dots. The term neo-Impressionism was coined by the critic Félix Fénéon in the Brussels magazine *L'Art moderne* on 19 September 1886, the year when Seurat's masterpiece *Un Dimanche d'été à la Grande Jatte* (now in the Art Institute of Chicago) was shown at the last Impressionist Exhibition. Among its adherents were Camille Pissarro and his son Lucien, Paul Signac, H.E. Cross, and Maximilien Luce; van Gogh too was influenced during his last few years in France. The school was ANARCHIST or SOCIALIST in its sympathies; this was sometimes reflected in the choice of subjects, especially Luce's. Outside France it embraced the Belgians Théo van Rysselberghe and Henri van de Velde (the subsequent ART NOUVEAU designer and architect), the Dutchman Jan Tooroop, the Italians Giovanni Segantini and Gaetano Previati, and through them the FUTURIST painters, who included a form of divisionism in their 'Technical Manifesto' of 1910.   J.W.

Bibl: R.L. Herbert, *Neo-Impressionism* (New York, 1968).

neo-Kantianism. A school of German philosophers in the late 19th century, inaugurated by Liebmann's invocation of 1865: 'back to Kant'. In effect it was a revival of aprioristic (see APRIORISM) EPISTEMOLOGY encouraged by the failure of METAPHYSICS, as expounded by Hegel and subsequent speculative thinkers, to do justice to developments in MATHEMATICS and the NATURAL SCIENCES. Leading neo-Kantians were Lange, Cohen, Natorp, and Cassirer in Germany, Renouvier in France, Adamson in Britain.   A.Q.

Bibl: T.E. Willey, *Back to Kant* (Detroit, 1978).

neo-Lamarckism. Neo-Lamarckism built upon the fundamental evolutionary concept advanced by Lamarck in his *Philosophie Zoologique* (1809), that species change was largely the product of the INHERITANCE OF ACQUIRED CHARACTERS. It flourished in the late 19th century and early 20th century, most prominently in France, in an attempt to formulate a theory free from the apparent defects of Darwin's theory of EVOLUTION by the NATURAL SELECTION of chance variations. To many natural historians, Darwin's random and tiny variations could not provide a credible basis for the appearance of wholly new SPECIES. Adaptive, purposive, uni-directional change must surely be required for the establishment of new species, for which the inheritance of modifications undergone during a creature's life span (e.g., for Lamarck the stretching of a giraffe's neck to gain access to high leaves) seemed the best explanation. Darwin's accent upon accident also seemed morally unacceptable. Neo-Lamarckism's stress upon acquired characters restored a place within evolution to purpose. In France, neo-Lamarckism was closely linked to philosophical movements, such as Bergson's VITALISM. In the U.S.A., by contrast, it was the favoured theory of palaeontologists such as Alpheus Packard and E.D. Cope, seeking to make sense of the complex historical interaction of organism and ENVIRONMENT as revealed by the fossil record. Nowadays few scientists look to neo-Lamarckism to resolve the residual problems of DARWINISM. See also LAMARCKISM.   R.P.

Bibl: P.J. Bowler, *The Eclipse of Darwinism* (London, 1983).

neo-liberalism. An American hybrid of uncertain character, which may be more a label attached to a package of politically expedient positions than any important revision of LIBERAL thought. The term was coined by Charles Peters, editor of the *Washington Monthly*, to encompass the ideas developed since the mid-1970s by a diverse group of INTELLECTUALS and politicians. Neo-liberalism rejects some of the orthodoxies which characterized American liberalism in its NEW DEAL and GREAT SOCIETY phases. It rejects a KEYNESIAN role for the state in the economy, accepts elements of conservative critiques of the WELFARE STATE, and seeks to detach the

Democratic Party from uncritical endorsement of TRADE UNIONISM. It purports to favour selective state intervention in the economy, mainly to assist restructuring of production towards new industries and services, and to find forms of WELFARE provision which are neither excessively bureaucratic nor conducive to welfare dependence. Neo-liberalism demonstrates a concern for social PLURALISM and tolerance which represents less of a break with the liberalism of the 1960s. Its ambiguous foreign policy perspective tends to be masked by an emphasis on defence issues, in which the movement stresses the need for military reform and urges a greater reliance on conventional armaments and EMERGENT TECHNOLOGY to complement reductions in nuclear arms.   S.R.

neolithic, see under THREE-AGE SYSTEM.

neolithic revolution. Term introduced by V.G. Childe to describe the development of food-producing economies in the Middle East during the so-called New Stone Age, i.e. between 9000 and 6000 B.C. Childe regarded this as the first major step forward in man's development: it was followed by the URBAN REVOLUTION and the INDUSTRIAL REVOLUTION. Recent work has tended to emphasize the complexity of the processes involved and a time span greater than Childe envisaged. As a broad generalization, however, the term still has some value.   B.C.
    Bibl: S. Cole, *The Neolithic Revolution* (London, 3rd ed., 1963).

neo-Malthusianism, see under MALTHUSIANISM.

neo-Marxism. A term used to refer to mainly post-war developments in MARXIST thought, particularly in the West, which considerably revises the classical Marxist tradition. Two strong early influences on neo-Marxism were the young Lukács and Gramsci. Lukács laid emphasis on the HEGELIAN aspects of Marx's thought and developed a striking critique of the BOUR-GEOIS world-view as reified — that is, unacceptably static, fragmented and objective. Gramsci re-evaluated the role of the SUPERSTRUCTURE in Marxist theory by

stressing the role of INTELLECTUALS in politics and discussing the importance of HEGEMONY in the sense of the process by which the PROLETARIAT gained leadership over all the forces opposed to CAPITALISM and welded them into a new political bloc capable of resisting and eventually overthrowing the hegemony of the bourgeoisie.
    Whereas both Lukács and Gramsci were political activists, neo-Marxism as it emerged from World War II was much more academic. It has been characterized by two opposite tendencies both of which sought to rejuvenate Marxism with the aid of some more contemporary philosophy. The first, largely embodied in the FRANK-FURT SCHOOL and the later Sartre, stressed the subjective side of Marxism. Whereas Sartre attempted to combine a form of Marxism with his own version of EXISTEN-TIALISM, the Frankfurt School was most influenced by PSYCHOANALYSIS and their work tended to move from the traditional Marxist version of politics and economics to a more general critique of bourgeois culture. The second trend was influenced by STRUCTURALIST ideas and conceived of Marxism as a science. The work of the most prominent of these Marxists, Louis Althusser (see ALTHUSSERIAN), in particular his concept of the problematic and his insistence on the relative autonomy of the sciences, was a good antidote both to all types of REDUCTIONISM and to extreme forms of Hegelian Marxism. Nevertheless, neo-structuralist Marxism, too, was cut off from the influence of the conditions of social production and ultimately appeared as the preserve of an intellectual ELITE disconnected from the revolutionary activity of the WORKING CLASS. As the influence of structuralism declined there have been recently, and particularly in the Anglo-Saxon world, some interesting attempts to re-examine Marxist concepts with the aid of linguistic analysis and GAME THEORY.   D.T.M.
    Bibl: P. Anderson, *Considerations on Western Marxism* (London, 1976); N. McInnes, *The Western Marxists* (London, 1972); D. McLellan, *Marxism after Marx* (London, 1980).

neo-mercantilism. A term coined by the economist Harry Johnson, for modern rationalizations of policies designed to

569

protect home producers from overseas competition, or to subsidize exporters, especially by indirect and selective methods. Old-fashioned MERCANTILISM was based on the belief that a country's wealth consists of its stocks of precious metals, which should be increased by securing a favourable balance of trade. Mercantilism gained a second wind within the Great Depression of the 1930s, when countries tried to export their UNEMPLOYMENT by trade restrictions and competitive DEVALUATIONS. This beggar-my-neighbour approach to employment policies has not disappeared from popular political debate. But an attempt has been made to give PROTECTIONIST policies a new respectability by the cult of 'technologically advanced industries' (which very often do not pay commercially) as the key to growth, and by the argument that CUSTOMS UNIONS such as the EEC must be held together by highly protectionist farm policies. S.BR.

Bibl: H.G. Johnson (ed.), *The New Mercantilism* (Oxford, 1974).

neo-modernism, see under MODERNISM.

neonatology. The paediatric care of newborn babies is now part of everyday PAEDIATRICS. It entails the routine supervision of mature healthy babies and those who are born prematurely or of low birth weight. They may require treatment in Special Baby Care Units. Such babies require specialized skilled nursing in conjunction with specialized paediatric management. During the lying-in period the paediatrician can detect early changes which, if recognized and treated promptly can avoid serious harm to the baby's growth and development: jaundice and a fall in the blood sugar are two of the commonest such happenings. D.M.

neo-orthodoxy. A term used to describe the insistence of BARTHIAN and other PROTESTANT theologians (especially Reinhold Niebuhr in the U.S.A.), *c.* 1920-60, on the TRANSCENDENCE of God and thus on some of the central themes in 'orthodox' LUTHERANISM and CALVINISM, but with a new conviction that God's self-revelation must be interpreted afresh. See also CRISIS THEOLOGY. D.L.E.

neo-plasticism, see under STIJL, DE.

neo-Prague school, see under PRAGUE SCHOOL.

neo-rationalism. In architecture of the 1970s and later more commonly known as rationalism. An entirely European movement, its protagonists were nicknamed Rats in the English speaking world. The Rationalists, arguing from a somewhat MARXIST standpoint, were in line with POST-MODERNISM in rejecting the visual formulae of the Modern Movement — but detested the elements in post-modernism which celebrated the visual vernacular of CAPITALISM. Their argument was that the true architectural model was a stripped-back version of classical buildings. In practice their built designs often have the appearance of the stripped classicism of the interwar years — leading their opponents to link it with the architecture of the TOTALITARIAN regimes of those times. S.L.

neo-realism. Term originally used by Umberto Barbaro in 1943 to define the poetic REALISM characteristic of the pre-war French cinema, in particular the Carné-Prévert films, which he held up as an object lesson to Italian film-makers at a time when Visconti's *Ossessione* (1942, a raw, uncompromisingly honest adaptation of James Cain's *The Postman Always Rings Twice*) had finally broken the stranglehold of MIDDLE-CLASS gentility in the FASCIST cinema's 'white telephone era'. The great days of Italian neo-realism began in 1945 with Rossellini's *Rome, Open City*, continued with films by Rossellini, De Sica, Visconti, Lattuada, and De Santis, and ended some five years later under opposition (financially expressed) from church and state. A product of political and social circumstances (the legacy of fascism and World War II), the movement was essentially a bitter outcry against widespread poverty and injustice. Though the Italian neo-realist films were disparate in approach and method, the term is now usually applied to films (of any nationality) following the guidelines laid down by Cesare Zavattini, scriptwriter and theorist of the movement: 'real' people, not professional actors, human situation rather than plot, humble setting (peasant, slum, outcast society), social indignation. Neo-realism is not to be confused with NOUVEAU RÉALISME.   T.C.C.M.

Bibl: R. Armes, *Patterns of Realism* (London and South Brunswick, 1971); P. Leprohon, tr. R. Greaves and O. Stallybrass, *The Italian Cinema* (London and New York, 1972).

neoteny. An evolutionary process (see EVOLUTION) in consequence of which organisms become sexually mature and therefore in effect adult at a stage corresponding to embryonic or foetal stage of their ancestors. Neoteny has, unquestionably, been a most important evolutionary stratagem — one which makes possible what Hardy has called an 'escape from specialization'. The chordates themselves (see ZOOLOGY) probably arose neotenously from animals akin to sea-urchins. Again, the ostrich has some characteristics reminiscent of a foetal bird, and human beings have some characteristics of foetal apes — e.g. the relatively enormous size of the brain. In the latter context neoteny has been referred to as *foetalization*.   P.M.

neo-thermal period, see under POLLEN ANALYSIS.

neo-Thomism. The renewed appreciation in Roman CATHOLICISM of the teaching of St Thomas Aquinas (1226-74). The study of St Thomas (who was greatly indebted to Aristotle) was enjoined on all students of THEOLOGY by Pope Leo XII in 1875, but has been made more fruitful in the 20th century (e.g. in the varied writings of Jacques Maritain, 1882-1973) by greater consideration of the issues raised in CRISIS THEOLOGY and CHRISTIAN EXISTENTIALISM. The more rigid type of Thomism is known as *scholasticism*.   D.L.E.

Bibl: E.H. Gilson, tr. L.K. Shook, *The Christian Philosophy of St Thomas Aquinas* (London and New York, 1957).

neo-vernacular. Originally in the mid-1970s a British critics' term of abuse for housing design which imitated vernacular building. The word neo-vernacular has now begun to lose its pejorative sense as more and more architects, housing speculators and local authorities in the U.K. erect this kind of housing. The essential ingredients are pitched roofs, brick walls, porches and, latterly, tile hanging, harling, dormers, strapwork, and leaded window glass. Neo-vernacular estate developments normally have picturesque, winding layouts and an attempt is normally made in more expensive developments to enhance the appearance of village rusticity by varying the mixture of decoration applied to the facades.   S.L.

NEP (New Economic Policy). A policy introduced by the Soviet Government in March 1921 after the 10th Congress of the BOLSHEVIK Party. Ending the policy of 'war communism' (see COMMUNISM), it aimed at restoring the economy by concessions to private trade and industry and by abandoning the pressure on peasant smallholders. Before NEP these were forced to provide the State with compulsory deliveries of agricultural products and were considered to be the natural enemies of SOCIALISM. But although under NEP the State retained control over the 'commanding heights' of the economy — heavy industry and foreign trade — the new policy encountered opposition inside the Party from RADICAL elements, who considered it a betrayal of the workers in the interest of the peasant and of socialism for the sake of State CAPITALISM.

The economic consequences of NEP were beneficial, and the country recovered economically, reaching in 1927 the production level of 1913. Politically, NEP produced a relaxation in internal Soviet policies, but at the same time Party discipline was strengthened by the elimination of the right to factional disagreement, and the Party increased its hold over the State. By the time NEP was abandoned by Stalin in 1929 the Party was well on the way to monolithic STALINISM, with oppositionists defeated and the resistance from the Party RIGHT (led by Bukharin) to compulsory COLLECTIVIZATION and forcible INDUSTRIALIZATION neither organized nor effective. The new policies which replaced NEP after 1929 amounted in effect to a 'second revolution', this time implemented 'from above'. NEP thus proved to be an interval, a tactical retreat, perhaps shorter than Lenin envisaged when he introduced it.   L.L.

Bibl: E.H. Carr, *The Bolshevik Revolution, 1917-23,* vols. 2, 3 (London and New York, 1952-53).

nephanalysis. Meteorological term for the analysis of cloud patterns, e.g. in the interpretation of synoptic conditions. Its use is now generally reserved for the study of global weather by SATELLITE monitoring where nephanalysis may provide early-warning indication of hurricane centres. See also REMOTE SENSING.   P.H.

Bibl: E.C. Barrett, *Viewing Weather from Space* (London and New York, 1967).

nephrology. The science of renal PHYSI-OLOGY and the speciality devoted to the care of patients with renal diseases. Nephrology is a comparatively recent discipline which has evolved rapidly during the last 30 years. Prior to World War II early scientific foundations were laid with conceptual formulations such as renal 'clearance' of endogenous and exogenous materials. Refinement of chemical analysis of body fluids and urine opened up study of the regulatory functions of the kidney. Micropuncture and microperfusion of isolated tubules have permitted the assessment of single nephron function. HORMONE assays have led to an increasing appreciation of the roles of the kidney as an ENDOCRINE organ. Diseases of the kidney have become better understood as a result of cumulative clinical data to establish their natural history. Imaging techniques, RADIOLOGICAL (including tomography and computed axial tomography), ULTRASONIC and those using RADIO ISO-TOPES are now widely available for patient investigation. Percutaneous renal BIOPSY carries few risks in experienced hands and is usually performed under some imaging control. Biopsy samples are studied by light, immunofluorescence and ELECTRON MICROSCOPY and the modern classification of glomerular diseases has replaced earlier descriptions. Treatment of patients with renal diseases has advanced most dramatically because of methods for replacement of the failing organ: excretory function can be replaced by either haemo- or peritoneal dialysis (see HAEMODIALYSIS) and both excretory and endocrine functions by successful renal transplantation. Because of the specialized skills in investigating and treating patients with renal diseases, it seems likely that physicians specializing in nephrology will need to be represented on the staff of all large hospitals.   A.J.W.

nervous system. The part of the body responsible for sensation, the excitation of muscular action, and the correlations between sensory input and motor performance that make complex behaviour possible. The nervous system is conventionally subdivided into the *central nervous system,* which is the seat of the major correlating functions of the nervous system, and the *peripheral nervous system,* which establishes the connections between on the one hand the sense organs and the central nervous system, and on the other hand the central nervous system and the muscular system. Whereas in lower vertebrates the brain is dominated by the olfactory functions, and the correlation centres are relatively little developed, the higher vertebrates are distinguished by the enormous development of the *new brain* or *neopallium,* which represents as it were the hypertrophy of the correlative elements of the brain. Contrasted with the neopallium is the *ancient brain* or *archipallium,* consisting of the *brain stem,* the *thalamus.* In addition to the central and peripheral nervous system, it is conventional to distinguish an *autonomic nervous system,* specially concerned with unconscious or 'automatic' functions, such as the movements of the gut, the state of dilatation of the blood vessels, etc.   P.M.

net barter terms of trade, see under TERMS OF TRADE.

net domestic product (NDP), see under GDP.

net national product (NNP), see under GNP.

net present value, see under DISCOUNTED CASH FLOW; DISCOUNTING.

net reproduction rate. A statistical PARAMETER expressing a population's prevailing FERTILITY when duly weighted by its MORTALITY. When computed for the female part of the population only and for female births, it represents the ratio of live female births in successive generations, so that a rate higher than unity (i.e. 1 to 1) signifies a true biological increase in population numbers even allowing for mortality, while a rate less than unity indicates that the population is not biologically holding its own. At one time the net reproduction rate was regarded as a thermometer for measuring a nation's reproductive health. This use of the rate, and all other such single measures (e.g. the rate of natural increase measured by the so-called 'MALTHUSIAN parameter') are discredited, for it is realized that the net reproduction rate is very much influenced by small short-term variations in the pattern of family-building which do not necessarily have much significance for the long-term reproductive welfare of a population.

P.M.

network.

(1) In COMPUTING and TELECOMMUNICATION, a SYSTEM providing for the transfer of information between any of a number of sites. They normally consist of a large number of *nodes* (normally computers, sometimes known as exchanges) connected by communication channels. The nodes might be responsible for such things as the choice of the optimum route for a message and retransmission in the event of failure. The most well known example is the public telephone system. Networks for the interconnection of computers divide into two main classes: *local-area networks* (LANs), which are entirely confined to one building or closely neighbouring buildings and do not use the public system, and *wide-area networks* (WANs) in which the site may be spread worldwide, perhaps even having nodes on communication SATELLITES. The former, because of the greater reliability of the communications, can achieve much higher transfer rates; the latter are much slower but much more tolerant of communications failures.

J.E.S.

(2) In ANTHROPOLOGY, a concept elaborated by J.A. Barnes (*Class and Community in a Norwegian Island Parish*, 1954) as a means for studying the internal dynamics of society. As an analytical tool, a network cuts across the divisions drawn between rural/urban and simple/complex societies. A network comprises a field of social relations. It may be analysed as a personal or ego-focused network (ties which radiate from an individual) using interactional criteria, or as a general network (an abstract MODEL in which society as a whole is understood as being made up of different elements linked through multiplex relationships) using structural critera.

In the case of a personal network a number of critical features have been identified for study. They concern the nature of links: the diversity of ties between an individual and others, the content of transactions between individuals, the direction in which goods and services move, the frequency, duration and intensity of interaction. It may be difficult, however, to specify the limit of a personal network and the total number of networks focusing on an individual may not have been activated at the time of analysis. The structural aspects of a general network refer to the patterning of the total number of links within a society: the size, density and connectedness of networks. Anthropologists have particularly utilized network analysis in the study of the system of PATRONAGE widespread in Mediterranean societies (see POLITICAL ANTHROPOLOGY; EXCHANGE; BROKER; CLIENT).

A.G.

Bibl: J. Boissevain, *Friends of Friends* (Oxford, 1974).

network analysis. In OPERATIONAL RESEARCH, the use of a MODEL designed to represent a SYSTEM as a concatenation of points connected together to depict a special sort of relationship between them. For a particular type of network analysis see CRITICAL PATH ANALYSIS.

S.BE.

network grammar. A class of grammars which have developed out of the concerns of COMPUTATIONAL LINGUISTICS and ARTIFICIAL INTELLIGENCE to show how language understanding can be simulated. A 'network' is a certain way of representing the structure of a sentence — a series of *states* (points at which alternative grammatical possibilities exist, in analysing a construction) and *paths* (the points of transition between states). The grammatical analysis of a text is known as a *parse*.

D.C.

Bibl: M. Halle *et al.* (eds.), *Linguistic Theory and Psychological Reality* (Boston, 1978).

network theory, see under IDIOTYPE.

Neue Künstlervereinigung (New Association of Artists). Munich group from which the BLAUE REITER derived. It was formed in 1909 under Kandinsky's chairmanship as a breakaway from the local SEZESSION and included the Russian Alexei Jawlensky as well as such Germans as Adolf Erbslöh and Alexander Kanoldt. Its main achievement was to introduce Germany to the work (in its 1910 exhibition) of Picasso, Braque, Rouault, and other French contemporaries. J.W.

Neue Sachlichkeit. New Objectivity, or New Matter-of-Factness. A German term for architectural FUNCTIONALISM, used also in the other arts, where it came to stand for much of the reaction against EXPRESSIONISM during the 1920s. Thus (1) in painting it was popularized by G.F. Hartlaub, who defined it as 'the new realism bearing a socialistic flavour' and in 1925 used it as the title of an exhibition at the Mannheim Kunsthalle which featured coolly and impersonally representational pictures by Max Beckmann, Otto Dix, and the ex-DADAISTS Grosz and Schlichter, besides a group of MAGIC REALIST works. These latter apart, its main characteristics were hardness of outline, smoothness of finish, a bald but often distorted or caricatured literalism, and a choice of subjects that concentrated on modern technical apparatus and the less cheerful aspects of the big cities and their inhabitants. Differing from Soviet SOCIALIST REALISM in its debt to other movements, this easily merged into the 'proletarian' art (see PROLETARIAT) favoured by the German COMMUNISTS from 1928 to 1933. (2) By extension the same label was applied in literature, where it described the socially critical fiction and documentary reportage of Ludwig Renn, Hans Fallada, and Egon Erwin Kisch, and the satirical verse of Erich Kästner and Kurt Tucholsky; again, a 'proletarian' school of writing developed from this. (3) Where the remaining arts adopted a similarly cool approach — as with the music of Hindemith and Kurt

Weill, the theatre of Brecht and Erich Engel, or the typography of Jan Tschichold — the term was again often used, as was the related idea of 'utility' or GEBRAUCHS (-*musik, -lyrik, -grafik*). J.W.
Bibl: J. Willett, *The New Sobriety: Art and Politics in the Weimar Period, 1917-33* (London, 1978).

Neue Sezession, see under SEZESSION.

neurasthenia. One of the most commonly diagnosed psychiatric conditions between the 1880s and the 1930s, although it is rarely deployed nowadays. The diagnosis was developed by the American psychologist, G.M. Beard, who characterized it as a state of abnormal tiredness or nervous prostration, associating it with a particular PERSONALITY TYPE and appearance (thin, infantile looks, flaccid). Most commonly diagnosed as a female complaint, psychiatrists often saw it as symptomatic of the 'new woman', and frequently blamed intellectual overstimulation. R.P.
Bibl: S.P. Fullinwider, *Technicians of the Finite* (Westport, Ct., 1982).

neuroanatomy, see under NEUROPSYCHOLOGY.

neurocybernetics, see under CYBERNETICS.

neuroendocrinology. The branch of ENDOCRINOLOGY that is concerned with the action of NEURONS and their secretions, including the NEUROPEPTIDES. P.N.

neuroglia, see under NEURON.

neurolinguistics. A new and developing branch of LINGUISTICS, sometimes called *neurological linguistics*, which studies the NEUROLOGICAL preconditions for language development and use in man. D.C.

neurology. The branch of medicine that deals with disorders of the NERVOUS SYSTEM. Because it has to do with physical abnormalities of the brain and peripheral nervous system neurology is to be distinguished from PSYCHOLOGY and PSYCHIATRY. For the application to psychology of knowledge derived from neurology see NEUROPSYCHOLOGY. P.M.

neuron (or *neurone*). The cellular element of the NERVOUS SYSTEM. In terms of CYTOLOGY, the conducting element of the nervous system consists of neurons and a number of supporting CELLS which are known collectively as the *glia* or *neuroglia*. Although neurons do not undergo cell division they are typical cells in that they consist of a cell body (perikaryon) out of which grow long cytoplasmic extensions — axons or dendrites, known collectively as 'nerve fibres', along the surfaces of which the nerve impulse is propagated.
P.M.

neuron theory. The theory that the NEURON is the fundamental structural element of the NERVOUS SYSTEM. See also CYTOLOGY.
P.M.

neuropathology. Disorders of the NERVOUS SYSTEM; also the study of such disorders. Neuropathology (in the first sense) can take one of two forms — inactivation of a neural control mechanism or its inappropriate action. It may result from flawed genetic instruction (see GENETIC CODE), mechanical damage, inflammation, deprivation of blood supply, or replacement or compression of NEURONS by tumour TISSUE. It can be investigated by clinical neurological examination (see NEUROLOGY), by electrical recording from neural tissue, by RADIOLOGICAL techniques, by MAGNETIC RESONANCE imaging and by microscopic and chemical analysis of neural tissue and surrounding fluids. Samples may be obtained during life (biopsy) or after death (autopsy).
M.K.

Bibl: *Greenfield's Neuropathology* (London, 4th ed., 1985).

neuropeptide. A PEPTIDE produced by and released from a NEURON, acting as a chemical messenger between the neuron and nearby CELLS, including other neurons (see NEUROENDOCRINOLOGY).
P.N.

neurophysiology, see under NEUROPSYCHOLOGY.

neuropsychology. The study of changes in behaviour that result from alteration in the physical state of the brain. These behavioural changes are not only of scientific interest by virtue of their implications for knowledge of the way the brain is organized. They also have clinical diagnostic interest as indicators of the location of brain disease, and clinical rehabilitative interest in that they reveal the mechanism of the difficulty the patient is experiencing.

The nature of brain organization is inferred from brain-behaviour relationships. Damage to particular areas of the brain induces characteristic and recognizable changes in behaviour. It is then inferred that the affected area of brain was necessary to the integrity of the processes that normally underlie the behaviour in question. Thus damage to the most complex and evolutionarily recent area of brain, the paired cerebral HEMISPHERES, is apt to disturb higher mental functioning, which includes PERCEPTION, memory, language, reasoning, and motor skill. Different localized cerebral areas are implicated by damage underlying disordered perception (*agnosia*), memory (*amnesia*), language (*aphasia*), and motor skill (*apraxia*); widespread diffuse cerebral damage degrades the ability to reason (*dementia*). This localization of function within the cerebral hemispheres goes further, and each of the disorders mentioned can take a variety of specific forms according to the precise location of the damage.

The mental functions so far discussed involve the analysis of external events and the programming of specific responses. These functions tend to be represented in the left cerebral hemisphere of right-handed subjects, and are said to manifest left *cerebral dominance*. The right hemisphere also has its characteristic responsibility, namely for the ability to orient the body in space and to articulate input into an immediate and a remembered spatial framework. Thus it lends context to the precise and focused activities of the left hemisphere. In a few left-handers, cerebral dominance may be less marked or even reversed. In children, delays in the development of lateralized COGNITIVE processes may be correlated with delayed language development, or in older children with delayed availability of reading skills (DYSLEXIA). Certain mental processes are represented in both hemispheres, and only suffer when damage is bilateral. Bilateral injuries may cause pathological forgetting (*amnesia*); its victim can neither remember events from the recent past nor learn new information. Still other forms of brain damage change the patient's emotional makeup, e.g. they may produce apathy and lessened motivation to act.

In animals, brain-behaviour relationships can be studied by inflicting operative damage on preselected areas of the brain and observing the behavioural results. In man, opportunities for such observations arise through naturally occurring disease and operative remedial efforts. The neuropsychologist requires expertise in relation both to behaviour and to brain structure (*neuroanatomy*) and function (*neurophysiology*) if he is to make full use of the opportunity his science offers to elucidate the organization of those processes that outstandingly characterize the human species. See also NEUROLOGY; TWO HEMISPHERES.   M.K.

neurosis (or *psychoneurosis*). In PSYCHIATRY and ABNORMAL PSYCHOLOGY in the West, a term used for one of the main classes of mental illness. Though there is no generally accepted way of defining the class (for the relationship between the neuroses and the PSYCHOSES see the latter), it is helpful to say that they are states of mental conflict, which, in different ways, represent exaggerations of our normal difficulties, and our normal impulses, feelings, etc. They include a wide range of states that have traditionally been subdivided (in part) as follows:

(1) *Anxiety states*, including PHOBIAS. The ANXIETY is beyond normal limits in intensity, and is unwarranted by the objective situation.

(2) *Obsessional states* (see OBSESSION), including compulsive states (see COMPULSION). In these the person develops ideas or impulses which he wishes to resist as distasteful, but from which he cannot free himself, and which often drive him into ritualistic conduct (e.g. compulsive body-washing) that can be time-consuming and exhausting.

(3) *Hysteria*. The person's functioning, in some respect or other (e.g. eyesight, digestive system, sexual functioning, motor abilities), is upset and unable to work satisfactorily. The disorder cannot be accounted for organically, and may run quite counter to what is known about the way the body works. But the symptoms enable the person to play the role of someone who is ill, and this in turn brings him certain immediate advantages in his particular situation (e.g. the battle-weary soldier who develops leg trouble).

The establishment in psychiatry of the neuroses was the outcome, in particular, of the work of the psychotherapists, e.g. Janet and Freud (see FREUDIAN). The generally recommended method of treatment is PSYCHOTHERAPY, though other methods (e.g. OPERANT CONDITIONING) have been developed. Prognosis depends on the severity of the condition, but there seem to be factors at work in these states that contribute slowly to spontaneous improvement and recovery. This fact makes it particularly difficult to establish the effectiveness of the therapy employed.
                                                    B.A.F.

Bibl: M. Gelder *et al., Oxford Textbook of Psychiatry* (Oxford, 1983).

neurosurgery. The clinical practice of SURGERY of the central NERVOUS SYSTEM includes operative procedures on the brain, the spinal cord, their coverings the meninges and their adjacent bone and ligamentous structures. Benign tumours (meningioma, acoustic neuroma) can be totally removed using modern operative techniques which include the operating microscope, the ULTRASONIC scalpel and LASER beams. Haemorrhage from Berry aneurysms and arteriovenous malformations is prevented by operative removal of these lesions, with the prospect of total cure. *Stereotaxic surgery* permits BIOPSY of other tumours, and the selective production of lesions to relieve pain and disorders of movement. The insertion of drainage tubes will relieve raised intracranial pressure from hydrocephalus (accumulation of abnormal quantities of cerebrospinal fluid in the ventricular system of the brain). Management of head injured patients (approximately 1 million attend hospitals in Britain per year) is directed towards the early detection and removal of blood clots which compress the brain. Correction of spinal cord and nerve compression by disc protrusions, bone abnormalities and tumours may alleviate pain and relieve disabling paralysis. The development of computer tomography (see RADIOLOGY) and NUCLEAR MAGNETIC RESONANCE imaging has improved the accuracy of diagnosis in neurosurgery. Research into the mechanisms of brain damage by compression, raised intracranial pressure, reduced cerebral blood flow and brain swelling promises hope to patients suffering from severe head injury, stroke and intracranial haemorrhage. Controversy exists regarding operative procedures for relief of narrowing and occlusion of arteries. Similar controversy surrounds the removal of HORMONE secreting tumours of the PITUITARY gland and the timing of surgery for ruptured aneurysms. There is very little to offer to patients with metastatic CANCER of the central nervous system and to patients with intrinsic tumours of the glial cells of the brain (gliomas).   A.D.M.

Bibl: B. Jennett and S. Galbraith, *An Introduction to Neurosurgery* (London, 4th ed., 1983).

neutral monism. The theory that the ultimate constituents of the world are individual momentary experiences, in themselves neither mental nor physical but of which, differently arranged, both minds and material things are composed. The ground for the theory is that such experiences are the sole direct object of empirical knowledge. It is, above all, the philosophy of Mach and his British allies, Clifford and Pearson, but was first called 'neutral monism' by William James, who took it to be the ontological consequences (see ONTOLOGY) of his 'radical EMPIRICISM'. It was adopted by Russell, largely under James's influence, around 1914. In broad terms it extends PHENOMENALISM from material objects to minds, conceiving them too, in the manner of Hume, as no more than ordered collections of experiences.   A.Q.

Bibl: Bertrand Russell, *Our Knowledge of the External World* (London and New York, rev. ed., 1926).

neutrality. Foreign policy option open to a STATE, enforced by acceptance in treaty form (e.g. Switzerland and the guarantee of its neutrality by the Treaty of Vienna in 1815). A difficult option in that it relies on the respect of great powers, and is often abused as with Belgium in 1914 and Poland in 1939. Some states, such as Switzerland, have opted for an 'armed neutrality' based on a militia army of some strength. Such states have been used by powers as useful 'neutral' territory for contact with their opponents, as with Switzerland and Sweden in World War II. Often referred to in the 20th century as neutralism.   A.W.

neutrality, affective, see under PATTERN VARIABLES.

neutrino. A type of stable ELEMENTARY PARTICLE emitted during the decay of NEUTRONS and MESONS. Neutrinos are difficult to detect because they have zero MASS and are electrically neutral, and hardly interact at all with measuring apparatus. The original prediction of their existence was a triumph of pure reason: it was necessary to postulate 'carriers' of MOMENTUM, ENERGY, and SPIN in order to satisfy the CONSERVATION LAWS for these quantities during neutron decay. Neutrinos differ from PHOTONS in that their QUANTUM for spin is ½ instead of 1. See also SUPERSYMMETRY.   M.V.B.

neutron. An electrically neutral ELEMENTARY PARTICLE (discovered by Chadwick in 1932) which is one of the two components of an atomic NUCLEUS, the other being the PROTON. In isolation, a neutron is unstable, and undergoes RADIOACTIVE decay with a HALF-LIFE of about 12 minutes into a proton, an ELECTRON, and a NEUTRINO. A neutron is slightly heavier than a proton.   M.V.B.

neutron bomb. Nuclear explosions are a cocktail of different mixes of RADIATION: NEUTRONS, GAMMA RAYS, ALPHA and BETA PARTICLES. These plus blast and heat create the various lethal effects of atomic weapons. The ideal battlefield nuclear device is one which kills the enemy forces, but does not produce long-lasting radiation or great physical damage from blast or heat. The aim of enhanced radiation weapons, usually known as the neutron bomb, is to achieve just that effect.

These weapons are engineered to produce the maximum short-term radiation emission over a limited distance. This radiation can penetrate armour plate and kill tank crews, leaving the vehicle unharmed. Often these devices are intended for delivery by BATTLEFIELD NUCLEAR WEAPONS, and at present they can be designed to have a limited killing radius of about 2 km. In theory, therefore, they make the nuclear battlefield a more plausible option for strategists, all part of the concept of a 'winnable' nuclear encounter. As such, they have been attacked as destabilizing the current nuclear balance, and the U.S. has postponed development and deployment. But they involve no technical breakthrough, nor even much alteration to current production systems, so the neutron bomb can confidently be expected in the arsenal, although perhaps secretly rather than openly, given the political cost of opting for 'dirtier' NUCLEAR WEAPONS.   A.J.M.W.

neutron star, see under PULSAR.

new age music. A MARKETING concept rather than a musical one, this catalogue of music, originating in America in the 1980s, embraces a diverse range of style including classical, non-western and ELECTRONIC MUSIC. Some of its common features however are immaculate glossy presentation (records often using DIGITAL MUSIC recordings), instrumental music rather than vocal music and a tendency to avoid extremes. This music is therefore very suitable as a sophisticated form of background music (see AMBIENT MUSIC; MUZAK).   B.CO.

New Age, The. A London-based weekly review taken over in 1907 by A.R. Orage, and brilliantly edited by him until 1922, *The New Age* was a central literary, cultural, and political clearing-house of GUILD SOCIALIST political bias, carrying the work of G.B. Shaw, Arnold Bennett, H.G. Wells, F.S. Flint, Ezra Pound, T.E. Hulme, Wyndham Lewis, Katherine Mansfield, Marinetti, and other important radical (see RADICALISM) or new writers. It is a superb atmospheric record of a tempestuous period, displaying, for example, the changing response from REALIST to post-realist and POST-IMPRESSIONIST developments in literature and the general impact of European MODERNISM, strongly supporting the idea of a literary 'Risor-

gimento', and carrying many novel works and manifestos.   M.S.BR.

New Apocalypse. A short-lived, youthfully grandiloquent, and undisciplined movement in British poetry during World War II. The name comes from the first of three anthologies of this 'new Romantic tendency, whose most obvious elements are love, death, an adherence to myth and an awareness of war': *The New Apocalypse* (1940). This was edited by J.F. Hendry; the other two, *The White Horseman* (1941) and *The Crown and the Sickle* (1945), were edited by him and Henry Treece. Of the many poets (e.g. Hendry himself, Vernon Watkins, G.S. Fraser, Norman MacCaig) who contributed to the anthologies, few deserve to be described as 'new apocalyptics'. They held that one of their members, the forgotten poet the late Nicholas Moore, was 'greater than Blake'. The group introduced into British poetry an awareness of contemporary American verse.   M.S.-S.

New Christian Right. The name given to the movement of FUNDAMENTALIST and EVANGELICAL Christians in the U.S. which is based on the belief that political involvement has become a moral obligation. Although its breadth and organizational variety contains differences of emphasis and tactics, its elements are united in an attempt to redirect the political agenda towards social values derived from its members' religious beliefs. It is particularly concerned to prohibit ABORTION, to reintroduce prayer and 'Christian values' to public schools, and to oppose any diversity of sexual mores.

Its precise origins lie in a reaction against Supreme Court decisions sustaining the legality of abortion in 1972 and 1973, and in governmental moves in 1978 to remove the tax-exempt status of private religious schools which appeared to be racially segregated. More generally, it is a reaction against what its members regard as threats posed by 'secular HUMANISM' — its term for the socially liberal, culturally experimental values of recent decades. Its key institutions include the Moral Majority, founded in 1979 and led by Rev. Jerry Falwell; Christian Voice, founded in 1978 by Rev. Robert Grant, and Roundtable, formed in 1979 as an ELITE networking organization of leaders of New Christian Right and other CONSERVATIVE groups.

The movement's impact in national elections has been less than its leaders hoped, and its values have not been wholeheartedly adopted within the legislative agenda of REAGANISM. But the movement, which is strongest in the south and parts of the midwest, has had some success at state level. It has also sustained arguments over issues which liberals (see LIBERALISM) thought had been resolved, and thus helped move the locus of political debate to the RIGHT. It also provides an important source of money, ACTIVISTS and votes for right-wing candidates in elections, and as such is carefully nurtured by leaders of the more conventional and business-oriented right. Critics of diverse ideological persuasions have accused the New Christian Right of a dangerous intolerance and zealotry which threatens to undermine the need for tolerance and disestablished religion in a society of great ethnic, racial, religious and cultural diversity.   S.R.

Bibl: G. Peele, *Revival and Reaction* (Oxford and New York, 1984); R.C. Liebman and R. Wuthnow (eds.), *The New Christian Right* (New York, 1983).

New Criticism. An ill-defined term generally taken as referring to 20th-century literary criticism's self-purification: to the reaction against the view of criticism as the mere expression of personal preferences, and to the belief that precision, method, and some theory are required. When J.E. Spingarn first coined the term (1910) he used it to describe a new trend in scholarship and the application of extraliterary, statistical, STYLOMETRIC devices. On this basis, Caroline Spurgeon's work on Shakespeare's imagery was 'old criticism' so far as her inferences were concerned; but her statistical METHODOLOGY was entirely 'new'. The names — predominantly American — of those most frequently designated 'new critics' are I.A. Richards, Allen Tate, Cleanth Brooks, John Crowe Ransom, Kenneth Burke, William Empson, R.P. Blackmur, and Yvor Winters. Ransom's *The New Criticism* (1941) found fault with Richards, T.S. Eliot, Empson, and Winters,

and suggested that it was time for a new 'ontological' critic to appear. This demonstrates how little — scholarship and philosophical over-scrupulosity apart — the new critics have in common; and this variegated movement later diversified itself still further into: proponents of pure aesthetic theory (Wimsatt, Beardsley, Krieger); would-be scientific BIBLIOGRAPHERS (Fredson Bowers); and more eclectic critics who write from a particular point of view, though with due care and attention to the text. Several important critics (e.g. Lionel Trilling, Northrop Frye) were never considered as 'new' in this specific sense. The New Criticism has long given way to, first, STRUCTURALISM and then to DECONSTRUCTION. However, since it is difficult to produce truly readable criticism of individual authors along the lines laid down by these theories, the New Criticism is still largely practised, if sometimes with perfunctory bows to them.   M.S.-S.

Bibl: R. Wellek and A. Warren, *Theory of Literature* (London and New York, 1949; Harmondsworth, 3rd ed., 1963).

new dance. A term referring to a new style of British MODERN DANCE which emerged in the early 1970s both in performance and studio work. The new dance aesthetic is somewhat akin to POST-MODERN DANCE in that it was initiated from a desire to remove oppressive characteristics of dance training and return to the basics of movement and stillness. Influences include CONTACT IMPROVISATION, tai chi, RELEASE DANCE and alignment work.   L.A.

New Deal. A phrase of contested genesis which occurred in Franklin D. Roosevelt's acceptance speech at the 1932 Democratic Party nominating convention, and became the label for the main features of domestic policy in Roosevelt's presidency from 1933 to World War II. The New Deal was characterized by policies designed to rescue the economy from the Great Depression, to exert greater REGULATORY control over economic activity, and to extend the state's responsibilities for the WELFARE of its citizens — especially the elderly and unemployed. Its methods were experimental and results patchy; World War II rather than the

New Deal restored employment levels, while its WELFARE STATE framework was limited by a longstanding American intolerance of state remedies for poverty. Nevertheless, it averted greater social unrest and more violent class conflict, and laid the foundations for post-war LIBERALISM. Among its effects (not all intended) were the incorporation of labour unions into a more legitimate role in industrial relations and politics; a shift in the balance of governmental authority from state to federal level; an elevation of the presidency to a more central position as the major source of policy initiatives. It may also be said to have created a fragmented style of politics in which organized interests (see INTEREST GROUPS) developed comfortable relations with the relevant parts of the governmental apparatus, rendering difficult the imposition of electoral choice or the representation of unorganized interests.   S.R.

Bibl: J. Braeman *et al.* (eds.), *The New Deal*, 2 vols. (Columbus, Ohio, 1975); M.A. Jones, *The Limits of Liberty* (Oxford, 1983).

new economic history, see under ECONOMIC HISTORY.

new economic mechanism. The economic system in operation in Hungary since 1968 which amounts to the most radical departure from the Soviet model yet introduced in a country of the SOCIALIST bloc. The STATE still largely owns the means of production (although the PRIVATE SECTOR has been expanded), but the old planning organs have been decentralized and the market has a greater role. Individual enterprises have been given more independence in dealing with the labour force and determining production levels and are encouraged to sell products rather than to fulfil the plan, which now limits itself to defining long-term goals. However, in practice the state still has the power to control enterprises indirectly by using financial incentives such as subsidies and by guiding INVESTMENT policies. In addition, trading links were established with Western Europe to an extent unusual within the socialist bloc. After initial successes, since the middle of the 1970s the economy has run into serious difficulties. The economic reforms have also produced sharp inequalities in wealth and a growth in UNEMPLOYMENT resulting from management's attempts to increase productivity. Discontent among the WORKING CLASS has increased and there has been significant opposition to the reforms within the COMMUNIST Party and the TRADE UNIONS.
D.PR.

Bibl: H-G. Heinrich, *Hungary: Politics, Economy and Society* (London, 1986).

New Economic Policy, see NEP.

New English Art Club (NEAC). A society of artists founded in 1885 whose members were critical of the Royal Academy and the traditions which it fostered. Augustus John, Wilson Steer, and Walter Sickert were all members at some time. Many of these artists looked to France for artistic inspiration: they tempered their own work with a little mild IMPRESSIONISM. By 1910, however, the NEAC itself seemed old-fashioned to those artists who formed the CAMDEN TOWN GROUP.   P.C.

Bibl: D.S. MacColl, 'The New English Art Club' (*The Studio*, March 1945).

New General Catalogue of Nebulae and Clusters of Stars (NGC). A catalogue in which over 8,000 nebulae, GALAXIES and clusters are listed numerically.   C.E.D.

New International Economic Order (NIEO). In 1974, the UNO General Assembly committed itself to working for a new economic order that would dramatically change the existing international economic structures in favour of developing countries. This commitment and various other similar declarations, e.g. the NORTH-SOUTH DIALOGUE, are based on the view that critical economic decisions are made by the developed countries among themselves, insufficient funds are lent to developing countries by international agencies, developing countries are disadvantaged in international trade, particularly by the low prices paid for their exports of primary products and the tariffs imposed by developed countries, and MULTINATIONAL CORPORATIONS treat host countries unfairly. The major aims of this movement are for the renegotiation of the debts of developing countries, more favourable

TERMS OF TRADE, a larger share in world trade for developing countries, a greater share of world manufacturing output, the transfer of TECHNOLOGY, more development aid, a change in the attitudes and decisions of developed countries and that developing countries should have a greater say in the making of decisions affecting themselves and the world economy. J.P.

Bibl: M.P. Todaro, *Economic Development in the Third World* (London, 3rd ed., 1985).

New Left. A political tendency which emerged in several countries in the late 1950s and 1960s through disenchantment with the conventional LEFT. Its idealism was generally more intense; it was partly based on a new emphasis on Marx's concept of ALIENATION and on other aspects of NEO-MARXIST thought. It also came to embrace elements of ANARCHISM, SYNDICALISM, TROTSKYISM, MAOISM and CASTROISM. In Britain the New Left's emergence was stimulated by the disillusionment of many British COMMUNISTS with the Soviet Union (see STALINISM), by changes in MARXIST analysis and by non-communist radicals. These strands came together in the founding of the *New Left Review* in 1960. In the U.S. the origins of the New Left are usually traced to the Port Huron Statement, a manifesto issued in 1962 by Students for a Democratic Society (SDS), an organization which became a key component of the New Left. More generally the movement's impetus came from radicalizing effects of the CIVIL RIGHTS MOVEMENT, campus revolts against the university system, and the war in VIETNAM. In France, West Germany and Japan the New Left of the 1960s was also a predominantly student and MIDDLE-CLASS phenomenon. It stimulated the events of MAY 1968 in Paris, widespread unrest in universities, and such TERRORIST splinter groups as the Baader-Meinhof group in Germany and the Japanese RED ARMY Faction. By the end of the decade the movement had fragmented; in varying proportions in each country, ACTIVISTS entered more conventional left politics, fringe terrorist organizations, or tendencies such as the GREEN MOVEMENT or radical FEMINISM, while others withdrew from politics. The more sophisticated elements of New Left thought have retained some currency in intellectual debate. L.L./S.R.

Bibl: A. Matusow, *The Unraveling of America* (New York, 1984); R. Gombin, *The Origins of Modern Leftism* (Harmondsworth, 1975).

new novel (*nouveau roman*). The name given to a new kind of ANTI-NOVEL, i.e. to the kind of work produced by a group of French novelists (notably Alain Robbe-Grillet, Nathalie Sarraute, and Michel Butor) who have tried deliberately to adapt the technique of novel-writing to what they consider to be the requirement of mid-20th-century sensibilities. Although they are not, and do not claim to be, a school, they all reject such features of the traditional novel as character-drawing, linear narrative, and obtrusive social or political content. Instead, they offer elaborate, and often apparently gratuitous, structures, as well as minute notation of psychological and physical detail. All are strongly avant-gardist (see AVANT-GARDE), i.e. they believe that each new generation of artists must reveal fresh aspects of reality, and they are convinced of the inseparability of form and content. They can be seen both as following on from EXISTENTIAL PSYCHOLOGY and PHENOMENOLOGY, and as reacting against Sartre's theory of COMMITMENT, which was the prevailing literary doctrine when Robbe-Grillet, the most prominent member of the group, first emerged in the mid-1950s. Typical novels are Robbe-Grillet's *La Jalousie* (1957), Sarraute's *Les Fruits d'or* (1963) and Butor's *L'Emploi du temps* (1957), and the two major theoretical statements *Pour un nouveau roman* (1963) by Robbe-Grillet and *L'Ère du soupçon* (1956) by Sarraute. This wave of experimentalism has been important mainly in France, though there have been echoes elsewhere, e.g. Uwe Johnson in Germany, Susan Sontag in America, Christine Brooke-Rose and Rayner Heppenstall in England. J.G.W.

Bibl: J. Sturrock, *The French New Novel* (London and New York, 1969).

New Orleans. The traditional birthplace of JAZZ, and home to a jazz style which still possesses much of its original character. Compounded of BLUES, marches, RAG-

TIME and dances like the quadrille, it emerged in the 1890s in black dance halls and social clubs, performed customarily by a three-man front line, which roughly but exuberantly filled the basic musical functions: trumpet or cornet played a strong lead supported by the trombone, while a clarinet spun upper-register embroidery. Below them, piano, string bass or tuba and banjo provided the firm rhythmic pulse. Indeed, all the instruments contributed to the warm, throbbing pulse which is still the music's stamp. In its classic form, individual virtuosity mattered less than the ensemble effect, and, except for short breaks, solos were relatively rare. All that would be changed, however, by New Orleans's most famous son and jazz's first genius, Louis Armstrong.   GE.S.

new theology. A phrase used on two occasions to describe the ferment of ideas contained in a short book by an English writer: *The New Theology* by R.J. Campbell (1907) and *Honest to God* by John A.T. Robinson (1963). Each book emphasized the nearness, rather than the TRANSCENDENCE, of God, and preached a radically simplified and LIBERAL Christianity.   D.L.E.

Bibl: D.L. Edwards (ed.), *The Honest to God Debate* (London and Philadelphia, 1963).

new towns. In recent years, and particularly since World War II, the growth of cities has become so rapid as to endanger the quality of life within them. Even the establishment of a *green belt* of open land around them (e.g. London) or a series of such (e.g. Copenhagen) failed to solve the problems created by large numbers of people COMMUTING to and from their work in the cities. In Britain it became Government policy to minimize commuting by the creation, beyond the green belts, of new towns in which industry and commerce were encouraged to provide employment. Under the New Towns Act of 1946, 8 new towns, starting with Stevenage, were created within a 30-mile radius of London, while 14 others relieved pressure on other crowded cities. In the case of the London ring the attraction and domination of London itself has proved too

great, and these new towns have remained SATELLITE TOWNS.   M.L.

new wave (*nouvelle vague*). Loose journalistic term coined by Françoise Giroud, on the analogy of 'new look' (clothing styles introduced by Christian Dior in the late 1940s) and the NEW NOVEL (*nouveau roman*), to define the sudden influx of new talent into the French cinema in 1959-60, when 67 new directors embarked on their first feature films. Spearheading the movement were the *Cahiers du Cinéma* group of critics (François Truffaut, Jean-Luc Godard, Claude Chabrol, Eric Rohmer, Jacques Rivette). The commercial and artistic success of their first films, made very quickly, cheaply, and without established stars, revolutionized production in the French film industry. But the methods characteristic of the early *nouvelle vague* films — improvisation, hand-held cameras, location shooting, minimum technical crews — were exigencies of economy rather than a matter of principle. The only real unifying principle behind the movement, which included documentarists (Alain Resnais, Chris Marker) and young film-makers from within the industry (Louis Malle, Roger Vadim), was the belief, constantly reiterated by the *Cahiers du Cinéma* critics, that a film should be the conception of one man, the AUTEUR, rather than a commercial package arbitrarily put together by a studio or a producer. In its English form, the term has subsequently been applied to any sudden creative surge in the cinema, e.g. in Britain immediately after the French *nouvelle vague*, or in Australia in the 1970s and 1980s.   T.C.C.M.

Bibl: P. Graham (ed.), *The New Wave* (London and New York, 1968).

new wave (in popular music), see under PUNK.

new working class, see under WORKING CLASS.

New Writing. A bi-annual founded in London by John Lehmann in 1936 to give voice to younger writers 'conscious of the great social, political and moral changes going on round them', rally anti-FASCIST voices, and emphasize the international dimension of this entire tendency. The venture — retitled *Folios of New Writing* (1940-41) and *New Writing and Daylight* (1942) — carried many major writers of its period: Spender, Auden, Isherwood, Edward Upward, William Sansom, Rex Warner, Orwell, Pasternak, Silone, and André Chamson, as well as a good number of working-class authors. An important extension was *Penguin New Writing* (1940-50), which through the war years carried much important writing, including valuable reportage and DOCUMENTARY, and a broad interest in all the arts, to a wide audience.   M.S.BR.

New York school. A general term applied to artists working in New York City in the 1940s and 1950s, primarily in the AB-STRACT EXPRESSIONIST style. School in this case connotes no more than a sense of community, energy and ambition among artists as diverse as Jackson Pollock, Arshile Gorky, Franz Kline, Adolph Gottlieb, Willem de Kooning, Hans Hofmann, and Barnett Newman. It is now used, analogously to ÉCOLE DE PARIS, to encompass subsequent artistic styles with an American flavour. See also ACTION PAINTING.   A.K.W.
Bibl: D. Ashton, *The New York School. A Cultural Reckoning* (New York, 1973).

newly industrializing countries. (NICs). Since the 1950s these countries have experienced rapid ECONOMIC GROWTH and the shares of manufacturing in their national output and exports have also increased rapidly. These increases have usually been matched by declines in the shares of agriculture and primary exports. These transformations in the structure of their economies are usually regarded as the cause of their rapid economic growth (see ECONOMIC DEVELOPMENT). This process of INDUSTRIALIZATION is usually attributed to the countries' policies of promoting manufactured exports. The relative importance of government intervention and FREE MARKET policies in the economic success of these countries is a contentious and unresolved issue. Examples of NICs are South Korea, Taiwan, Hong Kong, Singapore and, perhaps, Brazil.
                    J.P.

Bibl: B. Balassa, *The Newly Industrializing Countries in the World Economy* (Oxford, 1981).

Newspeak, see under ORWELLIAN.

Newtonian mechanics. One of the three great theories of MECHANICS. The basic principle is that the forces exerted on a material system by its interaction with other matter produce an ACCELERATION of the system — i.e. a *change* in its velocity or MOMENTUM. The precise law is: *acceleration = force ÷ mass* (see MASS). This means that if there is no force acting on a system its acceleration is zero, and the system persists unaltered in its state of rest or motion. (By contrast, in an earlier mechanics deriving mainly from Aristotle, it was believed that force was necessary to maintain motion itself, so that a body far from all others would come to rest.)

Newtonian mechanics is prevented from being a tautology by a series of 'laws of force' which state the various ways in which systems can interact. Fortunately there appears to be only a small number of basically different forces in nature; GRAVITATION, ELECTROMAGNETISM, STRONG INTERACTIONS, and WEAK INTERACTIONS. Other forces such as friction can be explained in terms of these.

When dealing with the interactions between the parts of a composite system, it is necessary to add a further postulate: the force on body A exerted by body B is equal in magnitude but opposite in direction to that on body B exerted by body A (i.e. 'action and reaction are equal').

Abundant verifications of Newtonian mechanics are provided by experiments and observations ranging from the motion of the heavenly bodies (see CELESTIAL MECHANICS) to the CONTINUUM systems studied in RHEOLOGY. For systems of atomic dimensions Newtonian mechanics no longer holds, and must be replaced by QUANTUM MECHANICS, while for systems moving near the speed of light or in enormous gravitational fields it must be replaced by RELATIVITY. See also MACH'S PRINCIPLE; PHYSICS.   M.V.B.
Bibl: P. Harman, *Metaphysics and Natural Philosophy* (Brighton, 1982).

NGC, see under NEW GENERAL CATA-
LOGUE OF NEBULAE AND CLUSTERS OF
STARS.

NGU, see NON-GONOCOCCAL URETHRITIS.

NIC, see under NEWLY INDUSTRIALIZING
COUNTRIES.

Nicaragua. Central American Republic
with an economy based on primary export
crops, mainly coffee, cotton and sugar.
Subject to repeated invasions by the U.S.
in the first quarter of the 20th century,
Nicaragua was occupied by U.S. marines
from 1927-1934. Washington withdrew its
troops under Franklin D. Roosevelt's
Good Neighbor Policy, but left behind a
surrogate force in the Nicaraguan National Guard, which supported 45 years of
dictatorship by the Somoza family (1934-
1979). *Somocismo* was characterized by
extreme centralization of power, corruption and wide-scale HUMAN RIGHTS
abuses. Anastasio Somoza Debayle was
overthrown in July 1979 by a popular
uprising led by the Sandinista National
Liberation Front (FSLN), after a prolonged civil war which claimed over
50,000 lives. (See SANDINISTA; CONTRAS;
REAGAN DOCTRINE.)   N.M.
   Bibl: G. Black, *Triumph of the People*
(London, 1981).

NIEO, see under NEW INTERNATIONAL
ECONOMIC ORDER.

Night of the Long Knives. The dramatic
events of the weekend of 29 June-2 July
1934 in Germany when, on the orders of
Hitler, Ernst Roehm and the leadership of
the brown-shirted SA were liquidated.
The SA Stormtroopers had been an indispensable element in the NAZIS' rise to
power but had become a major embarrassment in Hitler's relations with the German Army, which were the key to his
succeeding the dying Hindenburg as Head
of State and Commander-in-Chief as well
as Chancellor. Goering and Himmler
(whose black-shirted SS carried out the
executions) were the moving spirits in organizing the killings. Hitler was apparently convinced by the argument that the
SA leaders were plotting a second and
more radical REVOLUTION; but the

smoothness with which the operation was
carried out and the absence of any resistance suggested that this was a pretext with
little substance. Amongst the 150-200 estimated to have been killed were a number
(such as Gregor Strasser and General von
Schleicher) who had no connection with
the SA but were victims of earlier feuds.
The events were the turning-point of the
Nazi regime: they opened the way to
Hitler's succession to Hindenburg with
the approval of the Army. At the same
time Hitler's assumption of personal responsibility for the executions, carried out
without any pretence of a trial, made clear
the ruthless character of the regime, and
the role played by the SS laid the foundation for their supremacy among its instruments of power.   A.L.C.B.
   Bibl: M. Gallo, *The Night of the Long
Knives* (New York, 1972; London,
1973).

nihilism. An attitude or viewpoint denying
all traditional values and even moral
truths. The word was invented by Turgenev in his novel *Fathers and Sons* (1861)
to describe that part of the radical Russian
intelligentsia (see RADICALISM; INTELLEC-
TUALS) which, disillusioned with the slow
pace of reform (see REFORMISM), abandoned the LIBERAL faith of their predecessors and embraced the belief that the
destruction of existing conditions in
Russia justified the use of any means. The
chief ideologist of revolutionary UTILI-
TARIANISM in politics, ETHICS, and AES-
THETICS was D.I. Pisarev (1840-68), who
was portrayed as Bazarov in Turgenev's
novel and who proudly accepted the new
label. Many members of subsequent generations of the Russian intelligentsia
adopted nihilistic postures, from P.G.
Zaichnevsky, who summoned his contemporaries 'to the axe', to Sergei Nechaev,
author of a *Revolutionary Catechism*,
who was portrayed as the unscrupulous
Peter Verkhovensky in the novel by Dostoyevsky variously translated as *The
Devils* or *The Possessed*. The term has
subsequently been applied to various radical movements outside Russia: the NAZI
victory in Germany in the 1930s was described as a 'REVOLUTION of nihilism'.
                                          L.L.

Bibl: *J. Gouldsblom, Nihilism and Culture* (Oxford, 1980).

nitrogen cycle, see under LIFE CYCLE.

Nixon doctrine. Also known as the *Guam Doctrine* after its enunciation at Guam in 1970 to the press and then to American client President Marcos in the Philippines. The doctrine was contained in a speech made by President Nixon on 3 November 1969. It reflected the belief, prompted by the increasingly unpopular entanglement of the U.S. in VIETNAM, that the nation should not readily involve itself in another land war on behalf of an allied or client state. The doctrine's propositions were that the U.S. would keep its treaty commitments; would 'provide a shield' to protect allies or states whose survival mattered to U.S. interests against threat from a nuclear power; and would deal with other types of aggression towards such states by providing economic aid, military advice and material but not troops. Thus the U.S. signalled its preference for using smaller states as surrogates to execute anticommunist policy, such as the military regimes of Central and South America, of the Shah in Iran and Marcos in the Philippines. The doctrine eschewed any judgment of regimes' characteristics except for their resistance to COMMUNISM, stability, and disposition towards the U.S.　　S.R.
Bibl: S. Hoffmann, *Primacy or World Order* (New York, 1978); T. Szulc, *The Illusion of Peace* (New York, 1978).

NKGB, see under KGB.

NKVD, see under KGB.

NNP (net national product), see under GNP.

no first use. A declaration that a STATE would never be the first to use NUCLEAR WEAPONS: in effect, the renunciation of the use of nuclear weapons for offensive purposes. This is a political as much as a strategic doctrine, since it relates to the current military relationship of NATO to the Warsaw Pact. It is relatively easy for the Warsaw Pact to renounce first use, since they have a considerable superiority in conventional weapons. However, some Western experts argue that NATO defence should not be so dependent on a nuclear strike, and that Western strategy should move to NON-NUCLEAR DEFENCE.
　　　　　　　　　　　　A.J.M.W.

noble gases (or *rare gases* or *inert gases*). The ELEMENTS helium, neon, argon, krypton, xenon, and radon, which are gaseous at room temperature. Chemically, the gases are only weakly reactive.　　M.V.B.

noise. Any random disturbance superimposed on a signal. Electrical noise arises from random heat motion in circuit components, and constitutes a nuisance in TELECOMMUNICATIONS and HI-FI, where much effort is devoted to producing a high 'signal-to-noise ratio'. An incoherent combination of frequencies over a wide band is termed *white noise*.　　M.V.B.

nomadism. Anthropological term for the LIFE STYLE in which human groups follow a wandering life. It is usually restricted to livestock-keeping groups whose movements are directly related to the search for pasture. Examples of such pastoral nomadism are increasingly rare; the Lapps of northern Scandinavia and the Kirghiz of Turkestan come nearest to the model. See also TRANSHUMANCE.　　P.H.

nominalism. In PHILOSOPHY, the denial of real existence to abstract entities or UNIVERSALS. In its extreme, original form it answers the question 'What is there in common in the SET of things to which some general term is truly applicable?' by 'Nothing but the general term'. This seems to make the CLASSIFICATION of things into kinds wholly arbitrary. What is often called nominalism is the view — that of Hobbes and, in a way, of Locke and Hume — that what is common to the individuals denoted by a general term is their similarity to one another. Critics object that the similarity between the members of a set of things is as much an abstract entity as the common property which, according to REALISTS, they all exemplify.　　A.Q.
Bibl: D.M. Armstrong, *Nominalism and Realism* (Cambridge, 1978).

nomothetic, see under IDIOGRAPHIC.

non-alignment. The refusal of states to take sides with one or other of two principal opposed groups of powers such as existed at the time of the COLD WAR. Non-alignment was less ISOLATIONIST than the neutralism which it superseded, and was associated with the concept of *positive* NEUTRALITY, i.e. of collective intervention to prevent BIPOLARITY from degenerating into open military conflict; as in the conference of non-aligned powers held at Belgrade in 1961 in which some 35 Mediterranean and Afro-Asian powers took part. Subsequent conferences have demonstrated a common belief in the need for a NEW INTERNATIONAL ECONOMIC ORDER and the Non-Aligned Movement was a principal influence on the setting up of UNCTAD. They have also demonstrated (especially at Havana, 1979) ideological splits about the role of 'brother states' such as the U.S.S.R. with Cuba a leading proponent of a more active anti-U.S. stance. Current concerns are APARTHEID and U.S. policy towards Latin America, and the REAGAN DOCTRINE.   D.C.W.;A.WI.

Bibl: L. Mates, *Non-Alignment: Theory and Current Policy* (Belgrade and New York, 1972).

non-deterministic program. In COMPUTING, a PROGRAM which does not necessarily behave in exactly the same way whenever it is run with the same input data. This might be because it incorporates instructions which allow the HARDWARE or OPERATING SYSTEM to make a random choice when alternative actions are equally suitable. Most commonly non-determinism arises because of the varying speeds of different parts of the system. For example, a time-sharing operating system is non-deterministic, because the order in which things happen depends on the speed at which the various users work; the system must normally nevertheless ensure that a sufficiently deterministic environment is presented to each independent user. Sometimes, particularly in DISTRIBUTED COMPUTING, the overall effect is required to be non-deterministic. Non-deterministic programs are the hardest to think about, to write and particularly (because it might be impossible to produce a repetition of the circumstances which led to failure) to DEBUG.   J.E.S.

non-Euclidean geometry, see under GEOMETRY.

non-figurative art, see under ABSTRACT ART.

non-gonococcal urethritis. Non-gonococcal urethritis (NGU), or *non-specific urethritis* (NSU), refers to inflammation of the male urethra not caused by GONORRHOEA. The majority of cases are caused by sexually transmitted microbes: *Chlamydia trachomatis* causes 50%, genital mycoplasmas (*Ureaplasma urealyticum*) 20% and other bacteria and PROTOZOA 5%; the cause of the remainder is unknown. Men with NGU usually notice painful urination and a urethral discharge, but symptomless infections are quite common. The disease is normally treated with a course of one of the tetracylines. It is very important to locate and treat sex partners who are at risk, because if they are infected with CHLAMYDIA they are liable to develop SALPINGITIS. NGU is the commonest SEXUALLY TRANSMITTED DISEASE affecting men in Europe and the U.S.A., and its incidence continues to rise, probably because of inadequate contact-tracing efforts.   J.D.O.

Bibl: Y.M. Felman (ed.), *Sexually Transmitted Diseases* (London, 1986).

non-intervention. The opposite view to the right of intervention maintained by the great powers of the 19th century as an accepted part of INTERNATIONAL LAW. According to the then accepted view, one STATE was within its rights in intervening (if necessary by force) in the affairs of another state, where the second state's government was unable or incompetent to exercise SOVEREIGN powers, particularly in the protection of the rights, property, and persons of nationals of the first state. This view was challenged by the Argentinian jurist, Carlos Calvo, who in 1868 maintained that all sovereign states enjoyed absolute equality. The MONROE DOCTRINE denied *European* rights to intervene in the Americas; the Calvo doctrine and that put forward by the Argentinian, Dr Louis Drago, in 1903 and embodied in part of Article I of the second Hague Convention of 1907, were directed to prevent *U.S.* intervention. After the BOLSHEVIK revolution the doctrine became an integral part of the treaties negotiated by the Soviet Union with its non-Soviet neighbours. In times of civil war, as in the Spanish Civil War, the major powers have adopted non-intervention as a kind of self-denying ordinance intended to avoid ESCALATION into international conflict, but usually (as in the case of Spain) with very unequal results.   D.C.W.

non-linear mathematics/physics. There are many mathematical functions which depend on, say, x and y but which are not directly proportional to x and y. Instead they depend on x^2, y^2 and other powers of x, y. Similarly in PHYSICS there are SYSTEMS in which the response of the system, e.g. the amount by which a spring is stretched, is not exactly proportional to the force which is applied, but again it might depend on other powers of the force. In ACOUSTICS, ELECTRONICS and OPTICS there are non-linear devices, i.e. those for which the signal that emerges is not an exact replica of the one which entered. Non-linearity is not necessarily an undesirable property. It leads to new types of mathematical functions (CHAOS) and useful technological devices, such as those for the extraction of speech, music, or pictures from radio signals (see NON-LINEAR OPTICS and SOLITONS).   H.M.R.

non-linear optics. When an intense beam of light — an ELECTROMAGNETIC wave — passes through certain materials (e.g. lithium niobate) their ATOMS or MOLECULES do not respond to the light linearly, i.e. in a manner directly proportional to the strength of the electromagnetic wave. Instead their response is greater than this and is termed non-linear (see NON-LINEAR MATHEMATICS/PHYSICS). The effect is to modify the character of the transmitted light in ways similar to that in which electronic circuits can affect radio waves. For example, frequency doubling can occur so that a red beam can emerge with part of it changed to blue. The difference frequency between two incident beams can be generated and in this way certain INFRA-RED frequencies can be produced which are not within the range of conventional LASERS. Non-linear devices can be designed to provide *light amplifiers, beam splitters* and guides and the MODULATION of light beams by speech and other signals. All these are essential in the technology of FIBRE-OPTIC communications.   H.M.R.

non-nuclear defence. The use of conventional forces, enhanced by technologically advanced weapons systems, to resist attack by a superior enemy. Where NUCLEAR WEAPONS conventionally provide the margin of superiority, advanced but non-nuclear weapons will perform the same function. Another approach is to use BATTLEFIELD NUCLEAR WEAPONS, but these carry the potential risk of wider nuclear war which a non-nuclear defence does not. A third approach, involving renunciation of nuclear weapons (see MULTILATERALISM) without making the investment in advanced TECHNOLOGY and other resources, is not held to be militarily credible. See also DEEP STRIKE; EMERGENT TECHNOLOGY.   A.J.M.W.

non-objectivism. Russian ABSTRACT ART movement led by Alexander Rodchenko during World War I.   J.W.

non-proliferation, see under PROLIFERATION.

non-representational art, see under ABSTRACT ART.

non-specific urethritis, see NON-GONOCOCCAL URETHRITIS.

non-theistic religion. RELIGION not involving belief in God or gods. Although in the Western world religion is usually thought to imply such belief (see THEISM), this is not true historically (see BUDDHISM; CONFUCIANISM; PANTHEISM). Many modern AGNOSTICS value teachings traditionally associated with religion, notably reverence for nature and for other people, self-discipline, and the spirit of service to society. See also DEATH OF GOD THEOLOGY; HUMANISM.   D.L.E.

non-verbal communication. The larger inter-personal context within which all verbal communications take place. All human actions are suffused with meaning. Hence all actions communicate meanings. How I reach for, hold, and drink from, my teacup is a communicative act as well as an instrumental act. As one speaks, one's tone, speed, pause structure, gestures, facial expression, and degree of proximity to one's auditor modulate the meaning of the communication. These latter activities are the non-verbal context in which speech is embedded. Without such a context, all speech would be ambiguous. An important stimulus to the concept lies in Karl Polanyi's idea of TACIT KNOWLEDGE, the acquisition and communication of wisdom through the fingers and other body organs. See also EXPRESSIVE MOVEMENT.

T.Z.C.

Bibl: R.L. Birdwhistell, *Kinesics and Context* (Philadelphia, 1970; London, 1971); R.A. Hinde, *Non-Verbal Communication* (London, 1972); Roger Poole, *Towards Deep Subjectivity* (New York and London, 1972).

non-violent resistance. A STRATEGY or policy of resisting an adversary's attack or an occupation of one's country by non-violent means; the appeal to world opinion, political resistance, or CIVIL DISOBEDIENCE. Recent examples are Gandhi's organization of resistance to the British Raj during its final decades, the prevailing policy of the Norwegian resistance movement in World War II, and the decision of the Czechs to offer no military resistance to the Soviet invasion of their country in August 1968, but to rely on civil disobedience and global publicity. A recent example of domestic civil disobedience is, in the U.S.A., the National Association for the Advancement of Colored People's campaign for CIVIL RIGHTS. A.F.B.

Bibl: A. Roberts (ed.), *The Strategy of Civilian Defence* (London, 1967; Harrisburg, Pa., as *Civilian Resistance as a National Defense*, 1968).

non-zero-sum, see under GAME THEORY.

noosphere. A neologism introduced in an essay written in 1949 by the nature-philosopher Teilhard de Chardin on the model of BIOSPHERE and atmosphere and signifying the realm or domain in which mind is exercised. Teilhard's contention (see EVOLUTIONISM) was that in the ordinary course of the EVOLUTION of living

things the biosphere is being supplanted by the noosphere. P.M.

noradrenalin, see under ADRENAL GLAND.

norm.

(1) Established and expected form of social behaviour. Norms are sets of implicit social rules, MODELS of what should happen. Durkheim developed the notion of norms in his analysis of SOCIAL FACT, that is the conventions of behaviour and standards of value which exist independently of individuals and which exercise a coercive influence. Breaches of norms can result in the imposition of SANCTIONS (sense 2). It is important to draw a distinction between social norms (what individuals think ought to happen) and statistical norms (what actually happens). A.G.

Bibl: L. Holy and M Stuchlik, *Actions, Norms and Representations: Foundations of Anthropological Inquiry* (Cambridge, 1983).

(2) In Soviet usage, the basis of the piece-work system which long predominated in industry there, and in which the worker's pay depended on his reaching or exceeding a 'norm' of output. The 'progressive norm' method involved continual raising of the norm required for the basic wage; thus levels achieved by STAKHANOVITES tended to become obligatory for all. The norm system also prevailed among prisoners in labour camps (see FORCED LABOUR), whose bread ration was tied to their output. The past decade has seen a decline of the system, which now applies to well under half of Soviet industrial workers. R.C.

norm-referenced, see under PSYCHOMETRICS.

norm-referenced test, see under CRITERION-REFERENCED TEST.

normal distribution (or *Gaussian distribution*). In PROBABILITY THEORY and STATISTICS, a probability DISTRIBUTION on the line; the density function is a bell-shaped curve given by the formula

$f(x) = (2\pi)^{-1/2} \exp(-\frac{1}{2}x^2)$.

The normal distribution has MEAN 0 and VARIANCE 1; it is symmetrical about the mean. Scale change and translation along the line yield the more general normal distribution of mean u and variance σ^2. The importance of this distribution is twofold. First, the Central Limit Theorem of probability theory states that under suitable conditions, if random variables are added together and the sum is standardized to have mean 0 and variance 1, then as the number of summands tends to infinity the distribution of the standardized sum converges to the normal distribution. For example, if a fair coin is tossed repeatedly and $+ 1$, $- 1$ are scored for heads and tails respectively, then the score divided by the square root of the number of tosses converges to the normal distribution as the number of tosses increases. Second, it is found, for reasons related to the Central Limit Theorem, that empirical distributions in a wide variety of situations often conform closely to the normal distribution; it is thus common in statistics to assume that distributions encountered in such contexts are normal until the contrary is established. Many other important statistical distributions, including the chi-squared distribution and Student's t-distribution, are derived from the normal distribution.   R.SI.

normal temperature and pressure (NTP), see under STANDARD TEMPERATURE AND PRESSURE.

normalization. Already current in the sense of (industrial) standardization, the word was used in post-1945 European contexts to signify a return to friendly relations between STATES, ruling parties, etc. (as after the Moscow-Belgrade breach); then specifically of Gustáv Husák's counter-REFORMIST policy in Czechoslovakia from 1969, with restoration of complete control by pro-Soviet leaders and reintegration into the Soviet bloc in all aspects.   D.V.

normative. In general, concerned with rules, recommendations, or proposals, as contrasted with mere description or the statement of matters of fact. The words *evaluative* and *prescriptive* are used in much the same way, though 'normative', unlike the other two, tends to imply — cf. NORM — that the standards or values

involved are those of some social group rather than of an individual. Specific applications include the following.   A.S.

(1) In PHILOSOPHY, the label is applied to VALUE-JUDGEMENTS by EMOTIVISTS and other adherents of the doctrine of the NATURALISTIC FALLACY, who conclude that the TRUTH or falsity of value-judgements cannot be assessed. LOGIC, likewise, is sometimes called a normative science because it does not simply classify forms of INFERENCE that are actually followed but critically selects, and by implication recommends, those it regards as VALID. A valid inference, after all, is one whose conclusion *ought* to be accepted if its premises are.   A.Q.

(2) In LINGUISTICS, the adjectives *normative* and *prescriptive* are applied interchangeably to the largely outmoded view that there are absolute standards of correctness in language, and that the aim of linguistic analysis is to formulate rules of usage in conformity with them. This attitude is opposed to the aims of *descriptive* linguistics, which emphasizes the need to describe the *facts* of linguistic usage — how people actually speak (or write), not how they (or the grammarians) feel they ought to speak.   D.C.

north-south dialogue. A dialogue concerning the need for a NEW INTERNATIONAL ECONOMIC ORDER and emphasizing the mutual benefits to be gained from the transformation of the political and economic relationships between developed and developing countries. The COMMUNIST and CAPITALIST countries have competed with each other to exert military, political and economic POWER over developing countries and the cessation of such aggressive acts would have many benefits for individual countries and the world. Those supporting a north-south dialogue stress the moral imperative for action to promote ECONOMIC GROWTH and development in the THIRD WORLD and the effects of such action on economic growth in developed countries, through increased demand for their goods and services. J.P.

Bibl: A.P. Thirlwall, *Growth and Development* (London, 3rd ed., 1983).

nothingness (*le Néant*). In Sartre's *Being and Nothingness* (1943) nothingness is the polar opposite of BEING. Being is primordial, but *being-for-itself*, that is to say, the consciousness possessed by an individual being, is capable of conferring nothingness, negation or absence upon the world, which is a uniquely human property, and only possible because of the activities of the imagination. In Sartre's famous example, he enters the café looking for his friend Pierre, but Pierre is *not there*. The searching glance decides on the absence of Pierre, and imposes 'nihilation' upon an apparently real and full world. When nothingness is used as an activity in BAD FAITH, the subject decides to accord reality to what is not the case, thus reneging on his own freedom.   R.PO.

Bibl: J.-P. Sartre, *Being and Nothingness* (London and New York, 1957); M. Warnock, *The Philosophy of Sartre* (London, 1965).

notional and formal. Adjectives applied respectively to grammatical analysis which does, and does not, assume a set of undefined extralinguistic notions as its basis. 'Notional' often has a pejorative force for linguists reacting against the widespread notionalism of traditional GRAMMAR.   D.C.

noumena (or *things-in-themselves*; German *Dinge-an-sich*). Terms used by Kant to refer to the things that underlie our experience both of the physical world and of our own mental states (called by him the *phenomena* of outer and inner sense) and that are not themselves objects of possible experience.   A.Q.

nouveau réalisme. A phrase (literally, 'new realism', but bearing no relationship to either REALISM or NEO-REALISM) coined by the French critic Pierre Restany to describe artists' work in Paris in the late 1950s and early 1960s that incorporated junk and common objects into *assemblage* and COLLAGE forms. The French artist Arman is the figure most associated with this style, which is akin to POP and *assemblage* art. Yves Klein, Jean Tinguely, Daniel Spoerri, and Martial Raysse can also be counted within this movement.   A.K.W.

Bibl: H. Martin, *Arman* (New York, 1973).

nouveau roman, see NEW NOVEL.

nouvelle vague, see NEW WAVE.

nova. A star whose brightness suddenly increases by up to 10,000 times through the ejection from it of incandescent gases.
                         M.V.B.

NPV (net present value), see under DISCOUNTED CASH FLOW; DISCOUNTING.

NRT, see under CRITERION-REFERENCED TEST.

NSU, see NON-GONOCOCCAL URETHRITIS.

NTP (normal temperature and pressure), see under STANDARD TEMPERATURE AND PRESSURE.

nuclear disarmament, see under PEACE MOVEMENT; NUCLEAR WEAPONS, LIMITATION AND CONTROL; MULTILATERALISM.

nuclear family. A co-resident domestic group of husband, wife, and children. This simple family structure contrasts with the *extended family*, to which kin are added extending the group laterally (kin of the same generation) or vertically (another generation). Most developed INDUSTRIAL SOCIETIES have the nuclear family as the dominant IDEAL TYPE, while many other parts of the world are characterized by various extended family forms. SOCIAL MOBILITY and geographical mobility are a stronger feature of the nuclear family than other family systems, while the instrumental importance of KINSHIP relations is likely to be weaker. The belief that the nuclear family is a product of modern industrial society is a tenacious one, but is belied by much historical evidence. Before the INDUSTRIAL REVOLUTION in much of western Europe, and in England in particular, the nuclear family was frequently the norm. This undermines theories which place emphasis on the structure and interaction of the nuclear family in itself as producing tension and stress, divorce, delinquency, and the weakening of cultural transmission. Particularly through the growth of divorce and consensual unions, by the mid 1980s only about a third of all households in Britain conformed to the nuclear family ideal type, but its powerful symbolism is evident in its ubiquitous use in ADVERTISING and consumer images.

P.S.L.;D.S.

Bibl: R. Wall *et al.* (eds.), *Family Forms in Historic Europe* (Cambridge, 1982); F. Mount, *The Subversive Family* (Oxford, 1980).

nuclear fission, see under FISSION.

nuclear freeze, see under COMPREHENSIVE TEST BAN TREATY.

nuclear freeze movement. In the early 1980s American public concern at the proliferation of NUCLEAR WEAPONS increased, partly because the election of President Reagan seemed both to decrease the likelihood of major ARMS CONTROL efforts and to cool relations between the U.S. and U.S.S.R. The Nuclear Freeze Movement was a highly variegated, loosely co-ordinated response. It consisted of numerous local or factional groupings, including many church-based elements and associations of scientists, united by the wish for a mutual, verifiable halt in the production or deployment of nuclear weapons by the U.S.A. and U.S.S.R. as a prelude to arms reduction. At its peak in June 1982 the movement co-ordinated a rally of 750,000 in New York, and numerous state legislatures, city councils and New England town meetings passed pro-freeze resolutions. The movement succeeded in forcing the issue into the institutional arena, as with the Senate resolution introduced by Senators Kennedy and Hatfield. It was influential in Reagan's decision to reopen START in Geneva in June 1982, and arguably in his shift towards a more positive arms control position in the months preceding the 1984 elections. The movement is not defunct, but suffers from problems of distinguishing its commitment from that claimed by the government. See NUCLEAR WEAPONS, LIMITATION AND CONTROL.　　　　S.R.

Bibl: L. Robins (ed.), *The American Way* (Harlow, Essex and New York, 1986).

nuclear fusion, see under FUSION.

nuclear magnetic resonance. The application of MAGNETIC RESONANCE to the SPIN of the NUCLEUS. See RADIOLOGY.　　M.V.B.

nuclear physics. The study of the atomic NUCLEUS and its constituent NUCLEONS, and the NUCLEAR REACTIONS between nuclei. See also QUANTUM MECHANICS.

M.V.B.

nuclear reaction. In NUCLEAR PHYSICS, any process resulting in structural changes in an atomic NUCLEUS. Generally the ATOMIC NUMBER alters so that it is possible to transmute small amounts of one ELEMENT into another, thus fulfilling the dream of the medieval alchemists; this could not be achieved in any purely CHEMICAL REACTION since only the outer ELECTRONS are involved (see ATOMIC PHYSICS). FUSION reactions are responsible for starlight and the operation of the hydrogen bomb, and FISSION reactions are involved in RADIOACTIVITY, NUCLEAR REACTORS, and the atomic bomb. See also QUANTUM MECHANICS.　　M.V.B.

nuclear reactor (originally called *atomic pile*). A device (of which the prototype was completed in 1942 under the direction of Enrico Fermi) in which a controlled CHAIN REACTION is set up, based on nuclear FISSION. It contains a core of fissile materials, which when bombarded by NEUTRONS yields up a portion of its ATOMIC ENERGY as heat. This heat is then transported out of the fissile core by a variety of methods. The material undergoing fission (usually an ISOTOPE of uranium) is normally mixed with a MODERATOR to increase the efficiency of the NEUTRONS. The speed of the reaction is controlled by adjusting rods of neutron-absorbing material such as cadmium. Nuclear reactors generate (1) ENERGY, which is used to drive TURBINES, which in turn drive electric generators; and (2) RADIOACTIVITY which is used in the production of isotopes (e.g. TRACE ELEMENTS) for industry and medicine.

Nuclear reactors are classified in a variety of ways, and the types mentioned in the following sentences are selected from several classifications. A *breeder reactor* is one in which fissile material is produced in greater quantities than it is consumed, so that even if part of the final product is used in the same reactor there will still be a surplus for use elsewhere. A *fast reactor* is one in which no moderator is used, but this absence is compensated by a high concentration of core material. A *thermal reactor* is one in which the bombarding agents are THERMAL NEUTRONS. A *pressurized-water reactor* is one in which water under pressure (of the order of 2,000 lbs per square inch) is used both as moderator and coolant. In a *boiling-water reactor* water acts as a coolant only. In a *gas-cooled reactor* (in which graphite is used to slow the neutrons) the heat is carried away by a gas (originally carbon dioxide, later helium) which can be used at very high temperatures (up to 1,000°C) and then operate directly on the blades of a gas turbine. M.V.B.; E.R.L.

Bibl: see under QUANTUM MECHANICS.

nuclear submarine. A submarine powered by a compact NUCLEAR REACTOR. This gives it virtually unlimited range underwater, constrained only by the crew's ability to live submerged for long periods. However, refuelling, although an infrequent occurrence, requires an elaborate (and often vulnerable) base facility. In use, nuclear submarines are designed either as hunter killers, which are used to attack other submarines or surface vessels, or MISSILE launchers. These offensive weapons can either be submarine launched ballistic missiles (SLBM) or more recently, CRUISE MISSILES. Current developments have extended the range of submarine launched weapons very considerably, and advances in low frequency radio communications have resolved many of the command and control problems (see C³I) which once restricted their strategic role. However, simultaneous improvements in underwater detection have made the nuclear submarine more vulnerable.

A.J.M.W.

nuclear war, see under WAR.

nuclear weapons. Arms which depend on the principles of nuclear FISSION to produce an awesome explosive force and RADIOACTIVE fallout. The explosion comprises a blast effect, with winds of several hundred mph, and a fire storm, with temperatures rising to 1,000°C. The longer lasting, more widespread effects come from the scattering of fallout, which causes RADIATION sickness and long-term diseases. The power of these weapons is calculated in kilotons, equivalent to one thousand tons of TNT; now the power is more often described in megatons (MT), one million tons of TNT. The largest current warheads are of up to 25 MT, but current thinking is to carry a number of smaller warheads on each delivery vehicle, which has a much greater destructive potential. The lethal effect of fallout depends on many factors related to the size and type of the weapon, and whether it explodes in the air or on the ground. Radioactive contamination can be carried on the wind for great distances: the fallout from the nuclear accident at the CHERNOBYL power station in the Soviet Union in 1986 spread over much of Europe. One consequence widely predicted from a nuclear war is a NUCLEAR WINTER, in which the debris thrown up by the explosions, and the smoke from the firestorms will keep the light of the sun from the earth.

Nuclear weapons systems are traditionally designated as being strategic or tactical; the BATTLEFIELD NUCLEAR WEAPON is a recent development. The distinctions are now becoming blurred. The theory is that strategic weapons are those which can be launched from a nation's own territory against an enemy; by extension it also includes bombers carrying nuclear bombs and submarines carrying submarine launched ballistic MISSILES. The categories were created in terms of the confrontation between the U.S. and the Soviet Union. So tactical or theatre nuclear weapons are defined as those with a range of less than 5,500 km, which means that they cannot be fired from the Continental U.S. against Russia, and vice versa. Generally speaking the (larger) strategic weapons now tend to carry multiple nuclear warheads (MULTIPLE INDEPENDENTLY TARGETED RE-ENTRY VEHICLES — MIRVs). This has given new life to the older strategic systems. The elaborate system of strategic and tactical nuclear weapons has created its own language and philosophy (see DETERRENCE; MUTUALLY ASSURED DESTRUCTION). All depend on the unique destructive power of nuclear weapons, and the uniform horror with which they are regarded. But there is a new tendency among theorists to 'normalize' nuclear weapons, regarding them as just another war-fighting technique. This has given a great impetus to the scheme for NON-NUCLEAR DEFENCE. A.J.M.W.

Bibl: C. Bertram (ed.), *Strategic Deterrence in a Changing Environment* (London, 1981).

nuclear weapons, limitation and control. The attempt to restrict the possession of NUCLEAR WEAPONS to a small group of nations; to reduce nuclear stockpiles (see ARMS CONTROL). The means of exercising control were through long-running negotiations. Two *Strategic Arms Limitation Talks* (SALT 1 and 2) produced agreements between 1969-79. SALT 2 was never ratified by the U.S. Congress, although its provisions were observed. In 1982, a round of *Strategic Arms Reduction Talks* (START) were opened. The new designation was political, reflecting U.S. President Reagan's determination to reduce overall numbers rather than limit growth in nuclear arsenals. The position was complicated by the development of INTERMEDIATE NUCLEAR FORCES after 1979, providing a fresh area for dispute. The logical termination of START was the *zero option*, which grew from a determination to reduce intermediate nuclear forces in Europe to zero on each side, into a plan for the complete elimination of nuclear weapons as a consequence of President Reagan's STRATEGIC DEFENCE INITIATIVE. All the various nuclear weapons control and limitation talks have been bilateral, between the U.S. and the Soviet Union. Other nuclear powers, Britain and France, have not been included; their possession of nuclear weapons has bedevilled recent (post-1985) discussions. The Non-Proliferation Treaty designed to stop the spread of nuclear weapons was first signed in 1968 by the then nuclear powers; by 1986 more than 100 other countries had joined the agreement. But those countries with both the desire and the capacity to develop nuclear weapons —Israel, India, Pakistan, South Africa — refused to sign, as did existing nuclear powers, China and France. A.J.M.W.

Bibl: P. Bracken, *The Command and Control of Nuclear Forces* (New Haven, Conn. and London, 1983).

nuclear winter. The term 'nuclear winter' was coined to describe the potential climatic effects of nuclear war but it is also a useful metaphor for the acute disruption of global civilization that will result from nuclear war and the cumulative threat to life on earth that is posed by the existence of NUCLEAR WEAPONS. In the early 1980s, the atmospheric chemists Paul Crutzen and John Birks realized that the smoke and debris thrown up into the atmosphere by nuclear blasts and fires may be sufficient to generate a substantial climatic change. Later work, by the pioneering TTAPS group (Turco, Toon, Ackerman, Pollack and Sagan) and other climate modellers, confirmed that temperatures could fall by tens of degrees Celsius turning summer into nuclear winter. A major investigation undertaken by SCOPE (the Scientific Committee on Problems of the Environment, a standing committee of the International Council of Scientific Unions) concluded that the sensitivity of the BIOSPHERE is such that even minor environmental stress, coupled with the loss of industrial production in the nuclear nations, international trade, aid and other aspects of modern civilization, would result in starvation on a global scale. Nuclear winter has highlighted the need to consider the long-term consequences of the use of nuclear weapons and, some have claimed, has added a new dimension to the nuclear debate. There has been much discussion of the implications of the new findings for DISARMAMENT, ARMS CONTROL, weapons development, nuclear strategy and civil defence. The global nature of the threat of nuclear winter has strengthened the involvement of the non-nuclear nations in the arms debate. P.M.K.

Bibl: O. Greene et al., *Nuclear Winter: the Evidence and the Risk* (Oxford, 1985).

nucleic acid. Nucleic acids are of crucial importance in all living organisms and in viruses (see VIROLOGY) as the sole vectors of genetic information. They are giant polymeric (see POLYMER) MOLECULES of which the structural unit is a *nucleotide*, a compound built up of (1) a sugar, either ribose (in ribonucleic acid, RNA) or deoxyribose (in deoxyribonucleic acid, DNA), (2) a nitrogen-containing base, and (3) a phosphoric acid. These nucleotides are joined together linearly to form a *polynucleotide* through the combination of the phosphoric acid of one nucleotide with the sugar constituent in its neighbour and so on. In DNA the nitrogenous bases are adenine, thymine, guanine, and cytosine; in RNA uracil substitutes for thymine. Each such base defines a distinct nucleotide, and these are the symbols of the GENETIC CODE by means of which genetic information is embodied and transmitted. It was shown by Watson and Crick (1953) that DNA has a binary structure: each molecule consists of two strands aligned to each other in such a way that adenine is linked non-covalently (see COVALENCY) with thymine, and guanine with cytosine. The two strands have a helical twist — which gives them the form of the famous DOUBLE HELIX. The first crucial piece of information that nucleic acids are the vectors of genetic information came from the work of Avery and his colleagues (1944) showing that the agent responsible for bacterial TRANSFORMATIONS of the kind that had been observed by Griffith was indeed DNA itself. PROTEINS are synthesized according to information coded in DNA. The flow of information from DNA into protein begins with the 'transcription' of the DNA into a single stranded RNA. *Splicing* of the RNA removes any *introns*. The result is *messenger RNA*, the information in which is 'translated' according to the genetic code through the mediation of *transfer RNA* which assembles individual AMINO ACIDS into *polypeptides* (see PEPTIDES) and proteins. Although under special circumstances reverse transcription can occur, translation is irreversible and there is no known mechanism by which information can flow from protein into nucleic acid. This is the central dogma of MOLECULAR BIOLOGY. P.M.;P.N.

Bibl: Bruce Alberts *et al.*, *Molecular Biology of the Cell* (New York, 1983); Benjamin Lewin, *Genes II* (Bristol, 1985).

nucleon. A generic term for either of the two types of ELEMENTARY PARTICLE, i.e. PROTONS and NUCLEONS, which form the NUCLEUS of an ATOM, and which may be regarded as different states of the same PARTICLE. M.V.B.

nucleonics. Engineering based on NUCLEAR PHYSICS. M.V.B.

nucleoprotein, see under NUCLEUS.

nucleosynthesis. The production of atomic NUCLEI by a sequence of NUCLEAR REACTIONS. The end products may be the result of breaking up heavy nuclei by nuclear FISSION or amalgamating light nuclei by nuclear FUSION. *Primordial nucleosynthesis* is the sequence of nuclear fusion reactions which occurred during the first three minutes of the universe's history. The BIG-BANG HYPOTHESIS of the universe's early history and primordial nucleosynthesis correctly predicts the abundances of hydrogen, helium-3, helium-4, deuterium and lithium in the universe. This is one of the principal pieces of evidence for the Big-Bang COSMOLOGY.

Nuclei heavier than helium-4 are not produced in significant abundance by primordial nucleosynthesis. They are produced by *stellar/explosive nucleosynthesis* — nuclear reactions within the interiors of stars, and in SUPERNOVAE. The detailed results of this process were first calculated by W. Fowler, F. Hoyle and G. and M. Burbidge in 1957 and explain the relative abundances in the universe of those atomic nuclei not produced by primordial nucleosynthesis. J.D.B.

Bibl: S. Weinberg, *The First Three Minutes* (London, 2nd ed., 1983); R. Wagoner and D. Goldsmith, *Cosmic Horizons* (San Francisco, 1984); R. Kippenharm, *One Hundred Billion Suns* (New York, 1984).

nucleotide, see under NUCLEIC ACID.

nucleus.

(1) In ATOMIC PHYSICS, the tiny central core (discovered by Rutherford in 1912) containing most of the mass of an ATOM. The nucleus is composed of PROTONS and NEUTRONS, held together by STRONG INTERACTIONS resulting from the exchange

of MESONS. (The sole exception is hydrogen, which consists of a single proton.) Most ISOTOPES found in nature are stable, but some are unstable, and their nuclei undergo RADIOACTIVE decay. Nuclei of the TRANSURANIC ELEMENTS are all unstable because the number of protons is sufficient for their long-range ELECTROSTATIC repulsion to overcome the strong interactions. See also QUANTUM MECHANICS.   M.V.B.

(2) In CYTOLOGY, the administrative centre of the CELL. The nucleus, which with rare exceptions (e.g. the red blood corpuscles of mammals) is possessed by all plant and animal cells, is separated from the main bulk of the CYTOPLASM by a membrane of its own, distinct from the outer cell membrane. It is the repository of all the cell's genetic information and of all the information, therefore, that specifies in exact detail the synthesis of the PROTEINS of the cell. Whenever the division of the nucleus is not accompanied by a division of the cytoplasm a binucleate cell results. By special experimental methods, particularly the use of ultraviolet-inactivated Sendai virus (see VIROLOGY), two different cells can be fused in such a way that two nuclei of different origins may be housed within one cell body. Such a cell is called a *heterokaryote*, and its study can throw light upon, e.g., the properties of a CANCER cell which are responsible for its malignancy. Nuclei are composed mainly of *nucleoprotein*, which is a salt-like compound of deoxyribonucleic acid (see NUCLEIC ACID) and a basic protein such as a histone or protamine; and virtually all the DNA of the cell is housed within the nucleus. If a cell such as a ZYGOTE is deprived of its own nucleus and its place is taken by a nucleus from a cell of some other type from a later embryo, the zygote may nevertheless develop with a fair approximation to normality — an experiment with demonstrates that the GENOME of all cells in the body derived by MITOSIS from the zygote is the same. Thus DIFFERENTIATION must consist in some process by which genetic potentialities of the cell are realized in different ways in different cells.   P.M.

Nuffield approach. An approach, sponsored by the Nuffield Foundation, to curriculum development in British schools. The characteristic approach has been for Project staff, often seconded from universities and schools for three or four years, to try out proposals and many kinds of apparatus in the classroom and laboratory before proceeding to publication. There have been Nuffield projects in chemistry, physics, biology, general science for junior and younger children, mathematics, English and European languages, classics, and social science. The term is also used to describe the development and practice of a particular style of science-teaching involving the use of experiments rather than lectures or demonstrations.   W.A.C.S.

null hypothesis. This is the theory, mainly used in statistical analyses, that all things are equal — or, at least, that there is no vital difference between them. Thus an analysis may start from a level base. If one is testing two or more separate groups for their standards in a subject, be it reading, mathematics or whatever, one would test each group, making sure that they comprise large samples, are evenly distributed and do not show any notable differences. Differences, if any, will show up once the test answers have been analysed.   J.I.

number. In MATHEMATICS, a term with several distinct meanings:

(1) The *natural numbers* $\{0, 1, 2, 3, ...\}$ (with or without 0) come first; according to Kroenecker they come from God, all else being the work of man. They may be thought of as the finite CARDINAL NUMBERS or ORDINALS, or as a MATHEMATICAL STRUCTURE satisfying axioms which were first clearly stated by Peano in 1889. The simplest, if impractical, system of *notation* is to represent the number n by n successive strokes. The Greeks and Romans used various combinations of letters, inadequate for representing arbitrary large numbers. The decimal system, derived from Babylonia, India, and the Arabs, can be generalized to an arbitrary *base b*. The choice of b is pragmatic. The decimal system ($b = 10$) seems well suited to the human brain; $b = 8$ and $b = 12$ have also been used. The BINARY SCALE is suitable for COMPUTERS or other devices whose components may be in either of two states ('on' or 'off').

(2) The *integers* $(0, \pm 1, \pm 2, ...)$.

(3) The *rational numbers*: all (improper) fractions of the form p/q where p and q are integers and $q \neq 0$, with the identification $p/q = p/rq$ for any integer $r \neq 0$.

(4) The *real numbers*. As early as the 6th century B.C. it was known to the Pythagoreans that *incommensurable ratios*, or *irrational* numbers, exist: e.g. $\sqrt{2}$. Intuitively, once an origin and a unit of measurement have been fixed there is a one-to-one correspondence between the real numbers and the points of a straight line; for this reason the set of real numbers is called the CONTINUUM. Despite a brilliant attempt in Euclid, book 5, it was not until about 1870 that Cantor and Dedekind gave satisfactory definitions. The easiest definition to convey (though not to theorize with) is to say that every real number can be expressed as an infinite decimal: $\pm n.a_0 a_1 a_2 \dots$ where n is a natural number and $a_0, a_1, a_2 \dots$, is an *arbitrary* sequence of decimal digits. Observe that there is still an appeal to intuition for the understanding of 'arbitrary'; for further discussion see SET. Not all real numbers are the roots of algebraic equations (see ALGEBRA). Those which are not (e.g. e and π) are *transcendental*.

(5) The COMPLEX NUMBERS; the algebraic numbers form a subset of these.

(6) 'Number' used also to be applied to the elements of other mathematical structures occurring in algebra; but it is nowadays confined to (1)-(5) above.   R.G.

Bibl: R. Dedekind, *Essays on the Theory of Numbers* (New York, 1963); R.L. Wilder, *Evolution of Mathematical Concepts* (Milton Keynes, 1978).

number theory (or the *higher arithmetic*). The study of the natural NUMBERS. Topics considered range from trivial conundrums to deep and difficult theorems. Areas of perennial interest include the following: (1) *Prime numbers*. The chief theorem (first proved in 1896) states that $x/\log_e x$ is an ASYMPTOTIC approximation to the number of primes less than x (more accurate estimates are now known). Famous unproved conjectures are that there are infinitely many primes p such that $p + 2$ is also prime, and *Goldbach's conjecture* — that every even number greater than 4 can be expressed as the sum of two primes.

COMPLEX FUNCTION THEORY plays a large part in the investigations. (2) *Diophantine equations*. These are algebraic (see ALGEBRA) EQUATIONS with the stipulation that the solutions must be integers. There is a general problem of deciding whether a solution exists (see RECURSIVE FUNCTION THEORY), and there is the study of the solutions of equations having some particular form; e.g. Pell's equation $x^2 - Ay^2 = 1$ has been extensively studied. The subject merges with algebraic number theory and with algebraic GEOMETRY. The most famous unsolved problem is FERMAT'S LAST THEOREM. (3) *Additive* number theory: a typical problem is to give an asymptotic expression for the number of ways in which a number x can be expressed as the sum of cubes.

Number theory is fascinating because it combines the particular (each number has, so to speak, a personality of its own) with the general, and because simply stated problems may require sophisticated ideas for their solution. Number theorists sometimes congratulate themselves on the lack of application of their work. The current tendency is to concentrate attention on those problems and methods which will cast light on other MATHEMATICAL STRUCTURES; practical application remains infrequent.   R.G.

Bibl: H. Davenport, *The Higher Arithmetic* (London, 5th ed., 1982).

numeracy. A word coined, on the analogy of literacy, in the Crowther Report (1959). It represents understanding of the scientific approach to study in terms of observation, measurement, assessment, experiment, and verification, and more specifically some mastery of interpretation of mathematical and statistical evidence. The Report argued that sixth forms (16-18), whatever their specialization, should continue with education in numeracy, so that an 18-year-old leaving school, whether to go to university or not, will have a facility with quantitative statements as well as verbal ones.   W.A.C.S.

Bibl: Crowther Report, *15 to 18* (London, 1959); Dainton Report, *Enquiry into the Flow of Candidates in Science and Technology into Higher Education* (London, 1968).

numerical analysis. In general, the science and art of computing approximate solutions to problems formulated in mathematical terms. In particular it must cope with the operations of the CALCULUS. For example, a DERIVATIVE will be replaced by the ratio of corresponding *finite* increments in ARGUMENT and value; the *calculus of finite differences* is the study of this process and its applications. The numerical analyst must not only use ingenuity and skill in choosing methods which will yield approximations that converge rapidly towards the true solution (see CONVERGENCE), but must also investigate with complete rigour the degree of error involved. The advent of high-speed digital COMPUTERS has greatly enhanced the importance (and the difficulty) of the subject. R.G.

Bibl: A. Graham, *Numerical Analysis* (London, 1973).

numerical scale, see under SCALE.

numerological criticism. An ambitious attempt to apply number symbology to literary works. It owes much to Vincent Hopper's *Medieval Number Symbolism* (1938), Edgar Wind's *Pagan Mysteries in the Renaissance* (1958), and G. Duckworth's *Structural Patterns and Proportions in Vergil's Aeneid* (1962), and takes as its exemplar K. Hieatt's *Short Time's Endless Monument* (1960), a convincing examination of Spenser's *Epithalamion* in terms of the 24 hours of Midsummer's Day. Numerological criticism as now understood begins with Alastair Fowler's *Spenser and the Numbers of Time* (1964); this was followed by studies of the (alleged) numerological significance of the works of Fielding and others, and of the numerological element in medieval poetry. Numerological criticism of the grand sort is by no means universally recognized as valid, important or interesting. That being said, the earlier the work the more likely it is to contain some numerological significance. M.S.-S.

Bibl: C. Butler, *Number Symbolism* (London, 1970).

nuptiality. The frequency of marriage (or more generally, consensual unions) in a population. Attention in research is usually focused on the formation of unions, especially first marriages which have considerable implications for FERTILITY. The most useful measures the mean ages at marriage and proportions never-married. With many developed societies having rising rates of divorce or the dissolution of unions, there is now considerable demographic and sociological interest in the process whereby unions end and re-form. E.G.;D.S.

Bibl: H.S. Shryock *et al., The Methods and Materials of Demography* (condensed edition) (New York and London, 1976); J.A. Sweet, 'Marriage and divorce', *International Encyclopedia of Population* (New York, 1982), pp. 429-36.

Nuremberg Laws. A series of antisemitic decrees (see ANTISEMITISM) promulgated by Hitler at the Nazi Party conference in Nuremberg on 15 September 1935. These defined Jews as those with three Jewish grandparents, those practising JUDAISM, and those married to Jews. The Nuremberg Laws denied them any rights of state or local citizenship; forbade marriage, and any sexual relations, between 'Jews' and 'non-Jews'. Other decrees excluded Jews or half-Jews from public office; from owning businesses, economic enterprises, or land; and from practising as doctors, lawyers, writers, journalists, teachers in schools and universities, etc. The Nuremberg Laws, reducing the Jews to the status of second-class citizens, were the beginning of a process which led to the FINAL SOLUTION. D.C.W.

Nuremberg Trials. The trial at the end of World War II of 24 former NAZI leaders, and the 12 subsequent trials of major war criminals from the Army, the ministries, the legal community, doctors, business, etc., on charges of crimes committed before and during the war. These included the planning and waging of aggressive war, GENOCIDE, the ill-treatment of prisoners of war and deportees, crimes against humanity, the use of FORCED LABOUR, and general breaches of the laws of war. The legal justification for such trials of the vanquished by the victors has been a matter of subsequent dispute among jurists. Of the 177 men indicted, 25 were sentenced to death, 20 to life imprisonment, and 25 acquitted. D.C.W.

Bibl: B.F. Smith, *Reaching Judgment at Nuremberg* (New York, 1971).

nutrients. The basic elements of food as required by the body, namely PROTEINS, fats, CARBOHYDRATES, 13 VITAMINS and 20 mineral salts. A.E.B.

nutrition. The branch of PHYSIOLOGY that deals with the nature and utilization of foodstuffs. From the human standpoint the essential foodstuffs are PROTEINS, CARBOHYDRATES, and fats, together with mineral salts and VITAMINS. The energy values of foods are measured in terms of calories or kilocalories, i.e. the thermal energy released upon complete combustion in a calorimeter. In addition to mineral salts certain essential ELEMENTS must be present, notably iodine in combination because of the dependence of the THYROID upon it. P.M.

Bibl: R. Passmore and M.A. Eastwood, *Human Nutrition and Dietetics* (London, 1986).

nylon. The first 'tailor-made' POLYMER (developed in the 1930s). It is useful because it can easily be formed into fibres by extrusion through small holes. M.V.B.

O

O and M, see ORGANIZATION AND METH-
ODS.

OAU, see under ORGANIZATION FOR AFRI-
CAN UNITY; PAN-AFRICANISM.

object (a). A term used by the French
psychoanalyst Lacan who regarded the
object (a) as his most important contribution to analytical theory: the object, says
Lacan, falls, and each particular object (a)
(breast, faeces, look, voice) has its own
time of falling. By falling, we can understand the idea of remainder, or waste
product, such that when the SUBJECT takes
on signifiers in the OTHER, there is a remainder which cannot be taken up into
the signifying chain (see SYMBOLIC). This
remainder signifies all that is left of the
living nature of the subject, since the signifying chain, with its autonomous structure
of repetition, is in a sense 'beyond' life —
it carries on regardless of the contingencies of human activity, and thus Lacan
could equate it with the death drive. On
the other hand, where life is to be found is
on the side of what is cut off by the
signifying chain, that is, the object. This
object (a) is what is offered as a response
to the DESIRE of the Other, and thus comes
to function as the cause of desire.   D.L.
   Bibl: J. Lacan, *The Four Fundamental
Concepts of Psychoanalysis* (London,
1977).

object relations. A post-FREUDIAN emphasis on the interrelation between subject
and object, rather than on the study of the
subject only. This theory derives from
Freud's description of the development of
the libidinal stages, but whereas he viewed
the object as secondary in relation to the
subject's problems of libidinal attachment,
many post-Freudians saw the object as an
integral part of the subject's psychic development, which starts from PARTIAL OB-
JECTS such as the breast, and then leads on
to the whole person perceived as another
subject. Michael Balint stressed the necessity of looking at the subject as interacting with others, and as being determined
by this process, so that clinical work as a
consequence should concentrate on a per-

son-to-person relationship, on the modes
of the original mother-child dual relation.
The KLEINIAN theory of object relations is
based on the infant's relation to his primary perceptions of the external object as
part of himself and the ensuing frustra-
tions at having to perceive it as separated
and independent of his instinctual demands. The object is then split into 'bad'
unaffording parts, and 'good' parts collud-
ing with the baby's satisfaction. In this
way the object is endowed with moral and
pragmatic qualities: it is not only good or
bad, but it acts upon the subject by persecuting or reassuring him. The object
relation process functions, for Klein, as an
assessment of the subjective stage of psychic development and integration. The
Freudian oral, anal, and genital stages of
libidinal development are applicable to the
object relations theory; starting from
sadistic and persecuting oral and anal
stages, where the objects and the self are
split into pieces (paranoid-schizoid position), the infant has to develop a relation
to a whole, independent but not persecuting object. This passage from a partial to
a whole relation to the object is called the
depressive position, whose overcoming in
turn introduces the child to the genital
stage. These various modes of relation to
the object can overlap, alternate, or combine with each other. The difficulty of this
approach is in sorting out the ambiguity of
the status of the object: whether it is as a
real object that it determines the infantile
phantasized relation, or whether it is as a
phantasy object that it operates.   B.BE.

objective correlative. Term coined by T.S.
Eliot in his essay, 'Hamlet' (1919): 'The
only way of expressing emotion in the
form of art is by finding an "objective
correlative": in other words, a set of objects, a situation, a chain of events which
shall be the formula of that *particular*
emotion; such that when the external
facts, which must terminate in sensory
experience, are given, the emotion is immediately evoked.' Eliot maintains that
Hamlet is dominated by an emotion which
is 'in *excess* of the facts as they appear'. As
with DISSOCIATION OF SENSIBILITY, Eliot's

dictum cannot be erected into a universal law (and has been disputed in its application to Hamlet), but it provides an excellent description of the sort of immature writing where intense emotions remain inexplicable and unengaging because they lack a context which will evoke and define them. D.J.E.

objective function, see under OPTIMIZATION THEORY.

objective idealism, see under IDEALISM.

objective tests. Educational tests in which questions are so presented that there can only be one right answer and the examiner's own interpretation is eliminated from the marking process. The instructions and the length of time allowed are standardized, and usually such tests are made up of a number (or 'battery') of short sub-tests. They can be constructed in words, diagrams, symbols, or mathematical terms. See also MULTIPLE-CHOICE METHOD. W.A.C.S.

objectivism. An American poetic movement of the early 1930s, short-lived but influential. According to William Carlos Williams, whose *Collected Poems 1921-1931* was published by the Objectivist Press in 1934: 'Objectivism looks at the poem with a special eye to its structural aspect, how it has been constructed ... It arose as an aftermath of IMAGISM, which the Objectivists felt was not specific enough, and applied to any image that might be conceived.' Other poets associated with the movement were George Oppen, who founded the Objectivist Press (originally TO: The Objectivists); Carl Rakosi; Louis Zukofsky, who edited *An Objectivist's Anthology*; and Charles Reznikoff. Ezra Pound gave postal encouragement. M.S.-S.

objet trouvé (found object). Any strange, romantic, or comic bit of stone, wood, or manufactured bric-à-brac which is presented by the finder as an art object. The term was much used by the SURREALISTS to whom such objects, whether found or fabricated, became from the late 1920s onwards as significant as their pictures or sculptures. J.W.

obsession. In ABNORMAL PSYCHOLOGY and PSYCHIATRY, a form of NEUROSIS marked primarily by an emotionally charged idea that may persistently impose itself on the subject's conscious awareness; in this sense, the phrase *obsessional disorder* is widely used. In popular usage, any excessive preoccupation. W.Z.

obsidian dating, see under DATING.

obstetrics. The medical management of pregnancy, labour and the period of recovery after delivery (the puerperium). Care may start before conception with education and the encouragement of social and dietary habits to favour the eventual delivery of a healthy baby. Ante-natal care involves regular consultation with, and examination of, the pregnant woman by a doctor or midwife, as well as preparation for labour and the care of the child. It is intended to exclude abnormality, prevent complications and where problems occur to identify and treat them early so that serious consequences are avoided. Investigations include blood tests to determine the blood group, the presence or otherwise of anaemia, ANTIBODIES and infections such as SYPHILIS and rubella. Ultrasound (see RADIOLOGY) is used to confirm early pregnancy, measure the size of the embryo or fetus and to confirm the duration of pregnancy; it also reveals multiple pregnancy, major abnormalities, the site of the placenta and growth retardation. Prenatal diagnosis of fetal health, abnormality and disease is becoming increasingly important as new techniques facilitate this, though ethical considerations must balance the technological advances and the arguments for and against abortion when the fetus is abnormal; chorion villus BIOPSY obtains tissue from the fertilized ovum at 8-10 weeks which can be used for CHROMOSOME and other examinations. Fetal cells for this purpose may also be obtained by aspiration of a sample of the amniotic fluid in which the fetus lies, usually at 16 to 18 weeks. Measurement of α feto PROTEIN in the mother's blood or amniotic fluid and ultrasound scanning are used to detect spina bifida. The fetal monitoring is regular or continuous measurement or recording of fetal activity or function to confirm fetal well-being and to detect early signs of danger, for example due to oxygen lack, before there is permanent damage or death. Biochemical methods are now less used and records of fetal movement, fetal heart and uterine contractions (cardiotocography) and ultrasound are most widely used. Delivery may be normal with maternal effort or assisted by an obstetrician using forceps, a vacuum cap (ventouse) or caesarean section. After delivery the baby is examined and treated if necessary; later the mother will be given help in the care and feeding of her child with appropriate emotional support and physical care. Pregnancy and labour are now very safe thanks to improved health, education, social conditions and obstetric care but death of the mother (c. 1 in 10,000 in the U.K.), fetus or child (perinatal mortality c. 10 per 1,000 births) can still occur.   S.J.S.

Bibl: N.A. Beischer and E.V. Mackay, *Obstetrics and the Newborn* (London, 1986).

occlusion. In METEOROLOGY, the complex frontal structure formed when a cold FRONT overtakes a warm front. Occlusions are associated with widespread precipitation along and in advance of the surface position of the occluded front.   P.H.

occultism. The occult is the mysterious that lies below the surface of things; occultism is the exercise of magical procedures to influence this, by a knowledge of it. Elements of MAGIC, WITCHCRAFT, etc. have persisted in all civilizations; anthropologists insist that these features may be present in the RITUALS of all types of society (modern as well as PRIMITIVE), and they have not been dissipated by modern science. With the supposed 'flight from reason' during recent decades, occultism has enjoyed a popular revival. The Society for Psychical Research was founded in Britain in 1882, and in recent years a growing literature has examined telepathy, hypnotism, clairvoyance, the evidence for survival beyond death, and, in general, those supranormal faculties of man which still seem to lie beyond the range of testable knowledge.   R.F.

Bibl: Reader's Digest, *Folklore, Myths and Legends of Britain* (London, 1973).

occupation. The ways in which men obtain their livelihood are commonly divided into: (1) *primary occupations*: the production or extraction of raw materials, e.g. agriculture, fishing, hunting, lumbering, and mining; (2) *secondary occupations*: the production of man-made goods or the processing of raw materials. The growth of secondary at the expense of primary occupations is a feature of the early stages of INDUSTRIALIZATION; (3) *tertiary occupations*: the provision of services (see SERVICE INDUSTRY) rather than the production of goods. Some expansion of tertiary as well as secondary occupations takes place in the early stages of industrialization, but the marked growth of tertiary at the expense of both primary and secondary occupations is one of the distinguishing characteristics of advanced INDUSTRIAL SOCIETIES.   A.L.C.B.

occupational health. Although its origins may be traced to the early years of the INDUSTRIAL REVOLUTION, occupational health has greatly developed in the last 50 years, emerging as a specialist field in most developed countries. It comprises two main elements, occupational medicine and occupational hygiene. The latter is the province of scientists and engineers engaged in the assessment and physical control of environmental hazards at the place of work. This may involve such diverse procedures as measurement of noise levels with their component frequencies, measurement of respirable dust or of the concentrations of chemicals, such as vapours or aerosols, in the workplace. 'Comfort factors' such as lighting, glare, temperature and humidity are increasingly receiving attention. Occupational medicine changed its name from industrial medicine as the speciality widened its application to occupations outside manufacturing industry and mining. The speciality is concerned both with the effects of work on health and with the effects of health on work. The effects of work on health encompass hazards from physical agents (e.g. noise, RADIATION, work at increased barometric pressure), work with chemical agents (which may produce acute or long term effects including CANCER), the handling of microbiological agents (e.g. hepatitis B, AIDS, and work with genetically

601

manipulated organisms) and the psychological stresses associated with the work organization and environment. In this respect occupational medicine may be regarded as a special branch of environmental medicine, where the environment is amenable to control and monitoring and where the selected population (the workforce) may, when necessary, be put under close medical surveillance. Study of the effects of health on work includes such diverse subjects as the medical criteria for fitness to fly planes or to drive trains and cranes, both at entry to the job and after illness. It embraces occupational REHABILITATION after accident or illness and the study of patterns of sickness absence and of the factors which influence it.

W.R.L.

Bibl: A. Raffle *et al., Hunter's Diseases of Occupations* (London, 1987).

occupational therapy. In medical practice, the treatment of physical or mental disability by purposive occupation. Originally activities like farming helped to combat apathy of long-stay patients in mental hospitals. Later, handicrafts provided soothing diversions for the physically or mentally sick. Modern occupational therapy is much more actively therapeutic, aiming to foster interest and self-confidence, to overcome disability, and to develop fresh skills enabling patients to perform a useful function in the community. Activities are tailored to the needs of individual patients, and range from games to typing, domestic science, and light industrial work supervised by technical instructors. Group activities are emphasized as a means of encouraging social interaction. Occupational therapy now forms an integral part of the treatment of many illnesses, particularly chronic physical or mental handicap, whether in hospital or not.

D.H.G.

Bibl: E.M. MacDonald (ed.), *Occupational Therapy in Rehabilitation* (London, 4th ed., 1975).

oceanic ridge (mid-oceanic ridge). Any section of the more or less linked system of rugged mountain ranges that rise from the floors of all the world's major oceans. The system has no single name; in the Central and South Atlantic it is called the mid-Atlantic ridge, in the North Atlantic

to the southwest of Iceland it is the Reykjanes ridge, in the Pacific it is the East Pacific rise and so on. It is about 80,000 km long overall, has an average width of about 1,000 km, rises to 2-3 km above the ocean floors on average (but with individual peaks rising to 5 km and some even breaking surface to form islands, e.g. Bouvet Island, Jan Mayen Island) and has a rift valley along the axis for much of its length. It is the earth's largest and longest mountain chain. The oceanic ridge system is a crucial element in PLATE TECTONICS. The central rift valleys are the sites at which molten material rises continuously from the ASTHENOSPHERE below, cools, solidifies and becomes new oceanic LITHOSPHERE which then spreads away from the ridges in both directions. Oceanic ridges are thus the chief manifestations of the earth's volcanism, in comparison with which the conventional, land-based conical volcanoes are as almost nothing. Detailed examination of rift valleys from submersibles has revealed the presence of current tectonic activity in the form of fresh lavas, active fissures, high heat flow and HYDROTHERMAL VENTS (see SUBDUCTION ZONE).

P.J.S.

oceanography. Scientific study of the phenomena associated with the ocean waters that cover 70% of the earth's surface. The main branches are *physical oceanography* (concerned with waves, ocean currents, tides, and circulation systems); *chemical oceanography* (e.g. analyses of the constituents of ocean water); *biological oceanography* (e.g. study of marine fauna), and *geological oceanography* (e.g. study of ocean basins, MORPHOLOGY of the sea bottom, oceanic sediments). Scientific oceanography dates from the mid 19th century with growing interest in deep-sea biology, marked by the establishment of research centres such as the Stazione Zoologica in Naples, founded in 1872. The *Challenger* voyages in the 1870s are an early landmark in the development of special research exploration voyages. Current interest in oceanography is widening its scope to include broader issues of a legal, economic, and ECOLOGICAL nature. Leading centres for oceanography include the Scripps Institution of Oceanography at La Jolla, California, the Woods Hole Oceano-

graphic Institute in Massachusetts, and the National Institute for Oceanography at Wormley, England.   P.H.
W.A. Anikouchine and R.W. Sternberg, *The World Ocean: An Introduction to Oceanography* (New York, 1981).

OCR, see under OPTICAL CHARACTER READER/RECOGNITION.

October War, see under MIDDLE EAST WARS.

OECD (Organization for Economic Cooperation and Development). An intergovernmental organization which was established in a convention of 1961 comprising the 20 original members of the OEEC, and subsequently including Yugoslavia (1961), Japan (1964), Finland (1969), Australia (1971) and New Zealand (1973). The objectives of the convention are to promote policies that encourage ECONOMIC GROWTH and employment in member countries and the rest of the world, and that contribute to world ECONOMIC DEVELOPMENT and the expansion of world trade. The OECD is also interested in science, education, social affairs and the relations between developed and developing countries. It is based in Paris and the reports and forecasts of its economic secretariat are widely reported and influential in the formation of opinions.   W.B.; J.P.

Oedipus complex. In psychoanalytic theory (see PSYCHOANALYSIS), the normal emotional crisis brought about, at an early stage of PSYCHOSEXUAL DEVELOPMENT, by the sexual impulses of a boy towards his mother and jealousy of his father. Resultant guilt feelings precipitate the development of the SUPEREGO (conscience). Its female counterpart is the ELECTRA COMPLEX.   W.Z.

OEEC (Organization for European Economic Cooperation). A Paris-based intergovernmental organization established under a convention of 16 April 1948 and comprising, finally, 18 European countries (Austria, Belgium, Denmark, France, Germany, Greece, Iceland, Ireland, Italy, Luxembourg, the Netherlands, Norway, Portugal, Spain, Sweden, Switzerland, Turkey, and the U.K.), plus Canada and the U.S.A. as associate members. Its primary aim was to assist in the post-war reconstruction of its members' economies on a cooperative basis, notably through the administration (1948-52) of the MARSHALL PLAN. After this American aid ended, OEEC continued to play an important role in liberalizing trade between member countries and establishing a multilateral international-payments machinery. In September 1961, after it had become clear that little further progress in eliminating restrictions on international trade, payments, and movements in labour and CAPITAL was possible within the existing framework, and that more attention should be given to the problem of UNDERDEVELOPMENT, OEEC was replaced by the more broadly based OECD.   W.B.

Off-Broadway. A collection of some 30 theatres surrounding New York's Broadway on all sides but the west, best known for the development of new dramatists such as Edward Albee and Jack Gelber, and the revival of old masters like Eugene O'Neill. The movement and the term date back to 1915 when the PROVINCETOWN PLAYERS and the *Washington Square Players* established themselves in Greenwich Village. Dedicated to good production of good plays in intimate surroundings, the movement acquired a new lease of life in 1952 with a notable revival of Tennessee Williams's Broadway failure, *Summer and Smoke*. But, despite much excellent work in the 1950s and 1960s, soaring costs and the desire for commercial success gradually turned Off-Broadway into a replica of Broadway itself, and the really experimental work began to take place off Off-Broadway in coffee houses, cabarets, churches, and warehouses. See also ALTERNATIVE THEATRE and, for a British equivalent, FRINGE, THE.   M.BI.
Bibl: M. Gottfried, *A Theater Divided: the Postwar American Stage* (Boston, 1969).

off-line computing, see under COMPUTING.

OGPU, see under KGB.

603

oil crisis. The crises precipitated by OPEC's substantial increases in the price of oil in 1974 and 1979. The use of oil is crucial to most economies, as the substitution of other forms of energy for oil is difficult or can only take place over a long time span. These price increases raised awareness about the use and exhaustion of finite reserves of fossil fuels (see ENERGY CRISIS). They also contributed to the world economic recession and the steep rise in inflation during the 1970s. The funding of increased oil import bills has been an important cause of the DEBT CRISIS.   J.P.

Bibl: P.R. Odell, *Oil and World Power* (London, 8th ed., 1986).

oil weapon. Used by the Arab states during the OCTOBER WAR in 1973, it consisted of a monthly percentage reduction (5%) and an embargo on oil exports to the U.S. and the Netherlands. Led by Saudi Arabia and based on a decision of the Organization of Arab Petroleum Exporting Countries (OPEC), it was too short-lived (from October 1973 to March 1974) to have a direct effect on events. But the unusual unanimity of the Arab states and the subsequent fourfold increase in the price of oil agreed by OPEC gave a sense of euphoria to the Arab producers and a corresponding sense of alarm among consumers. Neither the political cohesion nor the market conditions necessary for a renewed use of the oil weapon have so far recurred.   W.K.

oligarchy. A new application, for our times, of the old theory that rule can only be by the few, never by the many. It has been developed especially in relation to the institutions of modern mass DEMOCRACIES, such as political parties and TRADE UNIONS. As Robert Michels was among the first to point out in 1911, formally democratic organizations with large memberships face a constant tension between efficiency and democratic control. In seeking to survive and to prosper, they tend to produce oligarchies of full-time officials. These have the expertise and experience to control the life of the organization, and can generally smother, head-off, or ignore the views of dissident and usually disunited members. They can also usually modify the IDEOLOGY and formal goals of the organization, according to their perception of its long-term interests. 'Who says organization', said Michels, 'says oligarchy.' The 'iron law of oligarchy' has been shown at work in a host of modern organizations, with striking effect in the case of those formally committed to radical or democratic goals and procedures, such as SOCIALIST parties and trade unions. It is one explanation of the 'de-radicalization' of working class political parties. Michels has been accused of a Machiavellian cynicism (or detachment), as have proponents of similar elitist views such as Mosca and Pareto. But so far it has proved difficult to show how large-scale organizations can function adequately if subject to constant intervention by the mass membership. COOPERATIVE, decentralized enterprises, such as that of Mondragon in the Spanish Basque provinces, seem to be successful only where there is a strong local tradition of communal self-help.   K.K.

Bibl: R. Michels, *Political Parties: A Sociological Study of the Oligarchical Tendencies of Modern Democracy* (1911; Eng. trans., New York, 1962); T.B. Bottomore, *Elites and Society* (Harmondsworth, 1966).

oligopeptide, see under PEPTIDE.

oligopoly. An industry in which a good or service is provided by only a few FIRMS, which implies that the actions of any one of them affect the circumstances of the other firms. Oligopoly is often thought to be close to the reality of much of manufacturing business. A firm's choice of STRATEGIES will be influenced by its view of how rivals will react to its actions. Firms may collude and attempt to act as a MONOPOLY. Collusion will be more difficult, the larger the number of sellers and the more different the interests of the sellers. Collusion may be difficult to arrange and, in practice, may take the form of price leadership and tacit rules of behaviour, e.g. not encroaching on other firms' territories. Explicit or tacit collusion will be limited by the possibility of entry of new firms into the industry (see BARRIERS TO ENTRY and GAME THEORY).   G.B.R.; J.P.

Bibl: J. Craven, *Introduction to Economics* (Oxford, 1984).

ombudsman. A state official entrusted by the legislature with very wide powers enabling him to intervene in the bureaucratic and administrative process in the interests of individual citizens whose complaints he investigates. The institution originated in Swedish practice as early as 1809 and has since been copied in civilian matters by Finland (1919), Israel (1950), Denmark (1953), Norway (1962), New Zealand (1962), and Britain (1967). In military matters Norway and West Germany have similar officials. The successful operation of the institution depends on the width of the official's powers and on his powers of initiative, two elements notably restricted in the British case. D.C.W.

Bibl: R. Gregory and P. Hutchesson, *The Parliamentary Ombudsman* (London, 1975).

Omega Workshops. Established by Roger Fry in 1913 to provide a livelihood for young artists who undertook decorative work anonymously for a small weekly wage. Adversely affected by the war, the Omega was dissolved in 1919. Q.B.

oncogene. A GENE that contributes to tumour formation. The most convincing examples of oncogenes are those in TUMOUR viruses; if the oncogene of such a virus is experimentally removed, the virus no longer causes tumours. From the notion that the oncogenes of such viruses had their origins in the animals that are the target for the viruses, came the discovery of what are presumed to be the progenitors of oncogenes. Since, in healthy animals, these progenitor genes direct the production of PROTEINS that are important for normal CELL growth — particularly HOR-MONE-like substances or their RECEPTORS — it is misleading to call them oncogenes. Instead the term *proto-oncogene*, which indicates their potential subversion, is often used. It is possible to detect oncogenes in some human tumours, where it is reasonable to suppose that, for example, a CARCINOGEN has directly or indirectly converted a proto-oncogene into an oncogene. But the relative importance of oncogenes in the development of human tumours is by no means clear. P.N.

oncology. The branch of medical science concerned with CANCER. The prefix onco- (from a Greek word meaning 'mass' or 'bulk') denotes something to do with a tumour; thus *oncoviruses* are tumour-causing viruses (see VIROLOGY), an *oncogen* (or CARCINOGEN) is an agent giving rise to tumours, and an ONCOGENE is a gene that has a role in cancer. P.M.;P.N.

ondes martenot (*ondes musicales*). An electrophonic instrument invented by Maurice Martenot in 1928 and similar to the THEREMIN, having a keyboard and capacity for glissandi. It now generally replaces the theremin and has solo roles in major works of Messiaen, notably *Turangalîla*. J.G.R.

on-line computing, see under COMPUTING.

onomastics. The study of the origins and forms of proper names, especially of people and places. D.C.

ontogeny. The course of growth within the lifetime of a single member of a SPECIES. It is contrasted with PHYLOGENY. J.S.B.

ontology. The theory of existence or, more narrowly, of what really exists, as opposed to that which appears to exist but does not, or to that which can properly be said to exist but only if conceived as some complex whose constituents are the things that really exist. It is the primary element in METAPHYSICS. Some ontologists have argued that many things exist that are not commonly acknowledged to do so, such as (1) abstract *entities* and (2) NOUMENA (Kant's 'things-in-themselves') inaccessible to empirical observation; others have argued that many things commonly thought to exist do not, e.g. material things, the theoretical entities of NATURAL SCIENCE, mental states conceived as something other than DISPOSITIONS to behaviour, and objective value-properties. The ontology of a theory or body of assertions is the SET of things to which that theory ascribes existence by referring to them in a way that cannot be eliminated or analysed out (see ANALYSIS) by REDUCTION. A.Q.

Bibl: A. Quinton, *The Nature of Things* (London, 1973).

op art. A scientifically-oriented ABSTRACT ART movement in the 1960s concerned with perceptual dynamics and retinal stimulation. Geometric forms, colour dissonance, and KINETIC elements were used to achieve optical effects, illusions, afterimages, and MOIRÉ patterning, and to stress the act of perception as the central meaning. Artists involved in this somewhat *passé* movement were: Julio Le Parc, founder of the Groupe de Recherche d'Art Visuel in Paris in 1960; Victor Vasarely in Paris; Bridget Riley in England; and Richard Anuszkiewicz in New York. Its more romantic counterpart was PSYCHEDELIC ART.   A.K.W.

Bibl: W.C. Seitz, *The Responsive Eye* (New York, 1965); F. Popper, *Origins and Development of Kinetic Art* (London, 1968; New York, 1969).

opacity, referential. In philosophical discussions of reference a term is said to be 'referentially opaque' when it is not being used in a straightforward way to refer to some object. For example, in 'Tom is happy' the name 'Tom' is being used simply to refer to a given individual. This is shown by the fact that if Tom has a second name, say 'Philip', then one can substitute 'Philip' for 'Tom' in the sentence 'Tom is happy' and its TRUTH-VALUE will remain unaffected. Here therefore 'Tom' is being used in a 'referentially transparent' way. But this is not the case in 'I believe that Tom is happy'. Suppose that I do not know that Tom's other name is 'Philip'. Then although I believe that Tom is happy I do not believe Philip is happy; substituting 'Philip' for 'Tom' will therefore change the truth-value of the sentence. Thus 'Tom' is here occurring in a referentially opaque context. Opaque contexts are generated in other ways too; for example, referring terms falling within the scope of the modal adverbs 'necessarily' and 'possibly' (see MODAL LOGIC) also suffer from referential opacity.   A.C.G.

Bibl: L. Linsky, *Reference and Modality* (Oxford, 1971).

OPEC. The Organization of Petroleum Exporting Countries was formed, in 1960, by Venezuela, Saudi Arabia, Iran, Iraq and Kuwait as a response to the major oil companies reducing payments to host countries for crude oil. In the first decade, new members joined the organization; OPEC's production of oil increased and OPEC was generally cautious; it bargained for only small increases in the payments made by the oil companies to host countries. In the early 1970s, a toughening in the attitude of the organization and, in particular, Libya and Algeria, revealed its potential power as a CARTEL. In OCTOBER 1973 the Arab-Israeli war led to OPEC raising the price of oil. The war brought forward rather than caused the increase in the price of oil because the demand for oil had increased rapidly; it is difficult to substitute other energy sources for oil; production in certain countries was being restricted; and OPEC had developed into a reasonably strong cartel, with a strong desire to increase the price of oil to match increases in the prices of goods imported by member countries. In January 1974, the actual and threatened Arab oil embargoes led to panic in oil markets and allowed the price of oil to be raised again. Over the period 1975-78, world INFLATION reduced the real value of oil prices. The Iranian crisis of 1978 reduced the supply of oil and made possible further large increases in the price of oil. Though oil prices fell slightly through the early 1980s, the Iran-Iraq war and the political instability it generated helped to maintain prices at a fairly high level. In 1986, Saudi Arabia attempted to impose some discipline on the cartel, by carrying out its threat to refuse to continue with its traditional role of altering its own production in order to stabilize the price of oil. This act, combined with other strains in the cartel, production from new non-OPEC oil fields, OPEC's smaller share of the world's supply of oil and substitution away from the use of oil, led to a large fall in the price of oil in early 1986. See OIL CRISIS, OIL WEAPON, ENERGY CRISIS and DEBT CRISIS.   J.P.

Bibl: I. Seymour, *OPEC: Instrument of Change* (London, 1980); P.R. Odell, *Oil and World Power* (London, 8th ed., 1986).

Open Cities and Special Economic Zones. Areas of low TAXATION and high INVESTMENT in China designed to act as a window into China, and attract vital foreign currency and TECHNOLOGY into the country in an attempt to stimulate ECONOMIC GROWTH. There are 18 open cities and 4 special economic zones, the most famous being Shenzhen on the China-Hong Kong border, and Xiamen (Amoy). Bearing a more than passing resemblance to the much hated treaty ports of the pre-liberation era, their job was to stimulate international interest in trading with China, and also to facilitate the return of Hong Kong by showing that China was prepared to tolerate areas of CAPITALISM within her jurisdiction. Recently, their importance has declined with the extension of the right to make trade arrangements with foreign companies being extended to all units of production without first having to seek government approval.   S.B.

Bibl: H. Harding (ed.), *China's Foreign Relations in the 1980s* (New Haven, Conn., 1984).

open class, see under WORLD CLASS.

open court reading plan. A reading method used in many American schools where children are taught the sounds of letters by breath and touch. For instance, the sound for 'h' in reality cannot be 'aitch' or even 'huh'. Children 'breathe' the soundless 'h' onto their hands or arms, thus 'feeling' it properly. The method proved highly successful and children were found to read at well beyond their norm.   J.I.

open door policies. A term relating to the conditions of confinement within mental hospitals. The legal framework within which lunatic asylums developed in the 19th century was that of compulsory confinement. Only those certified by due legal process were to be admitted as patients. This strict legalism was enacted in order to prevent the occurrence of detention as a form of psychiatric abuse. Increasingly, this situation was found psychiatrically counter-productive. The precise requirements of certification too often meant that patients were not admitted until their PSYCHOSES had become severe; moreover, discharge was an equally cumbersome process. The English Mental Treatment Act of 1930 effectively changed this situation, encouraging voluntary admissions (and hence a greater right of self-discharge) and thus greater 'permeability' between asylum and community. This open door policy was greatly extended by an Act of 1959, as a consequence of which the great majority of patients attending mental hospitals are voluntary.   R.P.

Bibl: Tom Butler, *Mental Health, Social Policy and the Law* (London, 1985).

open entry. University or college which admits students regardless of their qualifications as long as they are willing to study. The City University of New York tried this scheme for a while but found that it became quickly overcrowded and that the drop-out rate was extremely high.   J.I.

open plan. An arrangement of spaces, usually in domestic or office architecture, where the division between areas is implied by screens, columns, changes of level, or different ceiling heights, rather than defined by walls. It was largely developed by Frank Lloyd Wright in his house plans from the mid-1890s onwards and owes something to his familiarity with the traditional Japanese house. A variant, *le plan libre*, was practised by Le Corbusier, taking advantage of skeletal construction. Its acceptance is largely due to the emergence of efficient heating systems and the great reduction in the number of household servants; in the case of offices it allows the regrouping of work areas with the least disturbance.   M.BR.

open-plan schools. Schools where the architecture provides for minimal or no visual and acoustic separation between teaching-stations. Commonly between two and eight teachers and their pupils share a large teaching-space to which one or more quiet rooms or learning-bays may be connected. Teachers necessarily work in view and hearing of one another; effective teaching therefore requires them to cooperate in decisions about deployment of groups of children, scheduling, curriculum, teaching and learning problems. The focus of decision-making is typically shifted from the individual teacher to the team (see TEAM-TEACHING), and vertical grouping is facilitated. Some pupils and teachers thrive in the atmosphere of an open-plan school, but others feel lost and insecure and would be happier and better cared for in self-contained classrooms. A prime target for criticism in open-plan schools is the noise level, and adequate soundproofing is of great importance.

E.L.-S.

open prison (or *prison without bars*). An establishment with minimal or token security, and in general a less restrictive regime than that of an ordinary prison; a feature of prison systems in Britain, the U.S.A., and Scandinavia since the 1930s. Inmates are selected, for short sentences or the latter part of long ones, on the basis of their constituting negligible escape risks. There is little evidence to suggest that open prisons have more than humanitarian value.

T.M.

open society. Sir Karl Popper's (see POP-PERIAN) term for the free society, where all are able to criticize effectively those who hold authority in it. Popper quotes and approves of Pericles: 'Although only a few may originate a policy, we are all able to judge it.' This entails a forthright attack on TOTALITARIAN doctrines; on 'closed' hierarchies of social and political organization which do not allow individuals to rise according to merit; on indoctrination in education; on HISTORICIST social theories which predict the destiny of human society on the basis of 'unalterable laws' of historical development; and on totalitarian programmes for the reform of 'society as a whole' — which can easily replace one AUTHORITARIANISM by another. See also SOCIAL ENGINEERING.

R.F.

Bibl: K.R. Popper, *The Open Society and its Enemies*, 2 vols. (London and Princeton, rev. ed., 1967).

open stage. A term first used by Richard Southern (1953) to denote any form of staging in which the actor is not separated from the audience by a proscenium arch. The move towards open staging in this century is part of the reaction against NATURALISM which, in the theatre, is associated with realistic stage setting seen through the 'picture frame' or 'fourth wall' of the proscenium opening. The tech-

niques of the open stage were developed in the first half of this century in productions by William Poel, Max Reinhardt, Jacques Copeau, Vsevolod Meyerhold, and Nikolai Okhlopkov, and in the design of Walter Gropius's unrealized TOTAL THEATRE project for Piscator (1927). The principles of open staging have been increasingly incorporated in theatre architecture since the 1940s.

The principal forms of open stage are *thrust stage*, in which an acting area with a scenic or architectural background is surrounded on three sides by an audience; *end stage*, in which an audience faces the stage in a rectangular auditorium; *transverse stage*, in which an audience is seated on two opposite sides of a performing area; and THEATRE IN THE ROUND. An *adaptable theatre* is one designed to allow a variety of forms.

M.A.

Bibl: S. Joseph, *New Theatre Forms* (London and New York, 1968); R. and H. Leacroft, *Theatre and Playhouse* (London and New York, 1984).

Open University. Originally called the *University of the Air*, the Open University (headquarters at Milton Keynes in Buckinghamshire) offers degree courses (and a variety of non-degree courses) to people who have not the qualifications required for ordinary university entrance. Students who in 1985 numbered about 80,500 register from their own homes and most work for degrees on a cumulative COURSE CREDIT system, normally over at least four years. The teaching is provided through specially prepared books and book lists, weekly television and radio programmes (broadcast by the British Broadcasting Corporation), regionally organized study centres, written work on a correspondence basis, local counsellors and tutors recruited regionally, and full-time summer courses in university centres.

W.A.C.S.

operant conditioning (also known as *instrumental conditioning*). A form of CONDITIONING in which behaviour is controlled through systematic manipulation of the consequences of previous behaviour; a sophisticated branch of American BEHAVIOURIST psychology developed by B.F. Skinner (see SKINNERIAN). A central idea is that of REINFORCEMENT. Knowledge of (or control over) the delivery of reinforcements in a given situation is both a NECESSARY AND A SUFFICIENT CONDITION for the prediction (or control) of behaviour.

Although Skinner's ideas originated in studies of rats and pigeons in restricted experimental ENVIRONMENTS (see SKINNER BOX), he has extended his conceptual analysis to human behaviour, including language. Techniques derived from operant conditioning have proved useful in PSYCHIATRY, EDUCATIONAL PSYCHOLOGY, and INDUSTRIAL PSYCHOLOGY. D.H.

Bibl: B.F. Skinner, *The Behaviour of Organisms* (London and New York, 1938); *Verbal Behavior* (New York, 1957; London, 1959).

operating system. A PROGRAM, generally large, complicated, and expensive, which regulates the flow of work through a COMPUTER or provides helpful facilities for its user. The user is often more affected by the properties of the operating system than by those of the machine. C.S.

operational research (U.K. term; in the U.S.A., *operations research*). The adoption of a numerate approach to empirical processes involving decision-taking, particularly in government and commerce. Among the many mathematical techniques used in operational research are OPTIMIZATION THEORY; DYNAMIC PROGRAMMING and control theory (see CONTROL ENGINEERING); DATA ANALYSIS, including most classical STATISTICS together with many recent nonprobabilistic techniques; and SIMULATION, usually involving both the production of a mathematical MODEL of a system and of a PROGRAM to run the model on a COMPUTER. The term was coined (and gained wide currency) during World War II to describe the increasingly scientific approach then adopted in the planning of military operations; and this is an area in which the techniques continue to be very widely used. The problems now tackled by operational research methods also include: minimal-cost adequate diet; minimal-cost distribution from supply points (depots) to demand points; optimal location of manufacture and distribution centres relative to raw-material sources and markets; effects

and relative priorities of different forms of transport modernization; choice of container size for packaging mixed consignments; stock control; maintenance and inspection schedules; analysis of marketing information; design of 'product profiles'; forward planning and needs prediction in public utilities and social services. See also CRITICAL PATH ANALYSIS. R.SI.

Bibl: S. Beer, *Decision and Control* (London and New York, 1966); S. Vajda, *Planning by Mathematics* (London, 1969; New York, 1971); P. Whittle, *Optimization under Constraints* (London and New York, 1971); C.H. Waddington, *OR in World War II* (London, 1973).

operationalism. A theory that defines scientific CONCEPTS in terms of the actual experimental procedures used to establish their applicability. Expounded by Bridgman in 1927, it identifies length, for example, with the set of operations by which length is measured. It is a radically EMPIRICIST doctrine and very close to that version of the VERIFICATION principle which defines the meaning of a PROPOSITION as 'the method of its verification'. Einstein's famous rejection of the concept of absolute simultaneity, on the ground that the simultaneity of events is always relative to the FRAME OF REFERENCE of the observer who is assessing it, is operationalist in spirit. A.Q.

Bibl: P.W. Bridgman, *The Logic of Modern Physics* (New York, 1927).

operations research, see OPERATIONAL RESEARCH.

operator. In MATHEMATICS, a synonym for FUNCTION, often used when the arguments are non-numerical or themselves functions. R.G.

operon. A group of GENES brought into action simultaneously. The concept is based on studies of gene action in bacteria (see BACTERIOLOGY) by Jacob and Monod (Nobel Prize, 1965). J.M.S.

ophthalmic surgery, see under OPHTHALMOLOGY; LASER SURGERY.

ophthalmology. A discipline which devotes itself to the study and treatment of disorders of the visual system. While the discipline forms a part of the overall curriculum of medicine, its practice is mainly the province of the specialist. Disorders of the visual system are widely varied in nature. Some may be amenable in treatment to the skills of the physician while others may require the skills of the surgeon. J.WI.

opportunity cost. In ECONOMICS, that which is forgone by taking a particular action, e.g. a decision to invest in a particular project prevents the associated resources being used elsewhere in the economy. It is measured by considering the consequences of the best alternative use of the resources, e.g. the best alternative INVESTMENT project. The alternative forgone is not necessarily financial, but it is usual to measure opportunity cost in terms of money. The concept is fundamental to the definition of ECONOMIC EFFICIENCY. In PERFECT COMPETITION, price represents the opportunity cost to the consumer of the purchase of a good and the opportunity cost of producing the good (see MARGINAL COST PRICING). In COST-BENEFIT ANALYSIS and applied economics, it is often necessary to value goods and inputs for which there are no directly observable markets. This can be done by considering the opportunity cost involved in the consumption of the good or use of the input (see SHADOW PRICE). J.S.F.; J.P.

Bibl: J. Craven, *Introduction to Economics* (Oxford, 1984).

optical character reader (OCR). A computer peripheral device enabling letters, numbers or other characters usually printed on paper to be optically scanned and input to a storage device, such as MAGNETIC TAPE. The device uses the process of optical character recognition, which is also abbreviated to OCR. C.E.D.

optics. The branch of PHYSICS devoted to the study of light. There are four conceptual levels, appropriate to different phenomena: (1) *Geometrical optics*, where light is considered as *rays* travelling according to the laws of refraction and reflection. This is sufficient for the understanding of lenses and mirrors in cameras, telescopes, etc. (2) *Physical optics*, where

the interference and DIFFRACTION effects due to the *wave* nature of light are taken into account — in order to explain, for example, the limit to the fine detail that can be discerned even with a perfect lens, or the operation of HOLOGRAPHY. (3) ELECTROMAGNETISM, where the *physical nature* of light waves as undulating ELECTROMAGNETIC FIELDS is studied. Thus light is seen in a new perspective, as just one frequency band in the spectrum of electromagnetic RADIATION. (4) *Quantum electrodynamics*, where the application of QUANTUM MECHANICS to the electromagnetic field explains the parcelling of light ENERGY into discrete PHOTONS which are most easily discernible at very low levels of illumination. M.V.B.

Bibl: A.C.S. van Heel and C.H.F. Velzel, tr. J.L.J. Rosenfeld, *What is Light?* (London and New York, 1968).

optimal foraging. The theory that animals adjust their behaviour in searching for and exploiting food in such a way as to maximize their rate of intake of energy. When feeding, animals have to decide (presumably unconsciously) by what method to search for food, how long to spend searching and (once a patch of food has been found) how long to spend exploiting a patch before moving on to search for another. When exploiting a food resource, the animal also should decide which food items to eat and which to leave. The mathematics of *optimality theory* has been used to predict how these decisions should be taken in a specified set of circumstances of food distribution and abundance. The predictions have been extensively tested by experiment, especially on birds. John Krebs has been a leader in this research. The theory assumes that the behaviour of animals has evolved under NATURAL SELECTION. M.R.

optimal policy, see under DYNAMIC PROGRAMMING.

optimization; optimization theory. The problem of optimization is that of making the best possible choice out of a set of alternatives; the context to which the term usually refers is the mathematically expressed version of the problem, which is the maximization or minimization of some function (the *objective function* or *criterion function*); the set of alternatives is frequently restricted by *constraints* on the values of the variables. Many of the practical applications of optimization lie in OP-ERATIONAL RESEARCH. Simple examples of an optimization problem include designing an electronic network to carry out specified logical operations (e.g. in a COMPUTER) using as few components as possible, and finding the most efficient transportation pattern to carry supplies of a commodity from supply points to demand points, given the amount of commodity available at each supply point and the amount needed at each demand point, and the unit cost of transporting the commodity from any of the former to any of the latter. See also DYNAMIC PROGRAMMING; GRADIENT METHODS; INTEGER PROGRAMMING; and perhaps most importantly, LINEAR PROGRAMMING. R.SI.

optometry. A term coined in the U.S.A. but coming into wider use in the U.K. to denote the clinical practice of measuring the refractive state of the eye; in other words the measurement of any optical error present in the eye together with an estimation of the ophthalmic lenses required to correct that error, usually so as to give the best VISUAL ACUITY. J.WI.

OR, see OPERATIONAL RESEARCH.

oracy. A word formed by analogy with 'literacy' (the ability to read and write) and meaning mastery of the skills of speaking and listening. It was coined by Andrew Wilkinson in the 1960s to draw attention to the neglect of the oral skills in education despite the fact, confirmed by research, that the ability to communicate in speech is a necessary precondition of learning to read and write and an essential stage in human development. Like NUMERACY, oracy has proved a convenient coinage that has now come into general use. A.L.C.B.
Bibl: J. Britton, *Language and Learning* (London and Coral Gables, Fla., 1970).

oral character, see under PSYCHOSEXUAL DEVELOPMENT.

oral history, see under ORAL TRADITION.

oral tradition. Defined by Vansina as 'oral testimony transmitted verbally from one generation to the next one or more'. Oral tradition is one of the basic sources for the study of ETHNOHISTORY. Its reliability is still controversial. The conventional wisdom of historians has been that oral tradition is valueless or that it is impossible to determine its value. This view has been challenged by historians working on African societies which paid great attention to the correct transmission of their traditions.
It is convenient to reserve the term *oral history* for the study of CONTEMPORARY HISTORY through interviews, often tape-recorded, with eye-witnesses. There has been a rise of interest in oral history in Britain in the 1970s, and a journal, *Oral History*, has been founded. P.B.
Bibl: J. Vansina, *Oral Tradition as History* (London, 1985).

orbit. The path or trajectory along which an object travels in space according to NEWTONIAN MECHANICS. For example, the nearly circular orbit of the moon around the earth arises because the attracting force of GRAVITATION produces an inward ACCELERATION — i.e. the tangential velocity of the moon constantly changes in *direction* by bending inwards, while remaining constant in magnitude. See also BALLISTICS; CELESTIAL MECHANICS. M.V.B.

orbital. In the QUANTUM description of the ATOM, Bohr (in 1911) introduced the concept of an orbit in which the ELECTRONS followed planet-like motions around the NUCLEUS. Modern wave-mechanical treatments (see QUANTUM MECHANICS) do not allow the path of the electron to be pinpointed (see UNCERTAINTY PRINCIPLE), but there is a relation between the WAVE FUNCTION used to describe an electron in an atom or MOLECULE and its spatial distribution. The region within which there is a reasonable (say 95%) probability of finding an electron is termed an orbital. B.F.

ordering relations. In MATHEMATICS, a number of variants of the familiar RELATION 'less than'. They are characterized by AXIOMS; let '<' denote any such relation.

If $<$ is only required to be transitive and irreflexive it is called a *partial* ordering; an example is the relation of (strict) inclusion between SETS. If, in addition, it is required that for any x and y either $x < y$ or $y < x$ or $x = y$, then $<$ is called a *linear* or *simple* ordering; this corresponds to the ordinary use of 'less than'. If, further, it is required that any (non-empty) set of elements has a least element, then $<$ is a *well-ordering*. A familiar example is provided by the natural NUMBERS. But other *transfinite* well-orderings exist; e.g. the numbers may be arranged in a new order as follows: 0, 2, 4, ..., 1, 3, 5, ... Well-orderings are a useful tool in the study of INFINITE sets. R.G.

Bibl: N.W. Gowar, *Basic Mathematical Structures* (2 vols., London, 1973-4).

ordinal (number). The abstract CONCEPT defined by the EQUIVALENCE RELATION of ISOMORPHISM between well-orderings (see ORDERING RELATION). R.G.

ordinal scale, see under SCALE.

organic. In architecture (for its meaning in art see BIOMORPHIC), adjective used (1) principally by Frank Lloyd Wright (1869-1959) as a term of approval for certain buildings, including his own, which were usually asymmetrical and integrated closely with the particular features of the site; in this sense the term is opposed both to 'classical' and to the INTERNATIONAL SYTLE; (2) often in its more literal sense of being abstracted from the forms of nature, especially in the case of ornaments such as the arabesque; (3) occasionally to describe buildings, or parts of buildings, organized on a direct biological analogy such as that of the human body. See also FUNCTIONAL-ISM. M.BR.

Bibl: F.L. Wright, *The Future of Architecture* (New York, 1963).

organic chemistry. One of the main branches of CHEMISTRY. Originally defined as the chemistry of substances formed by living matter, but since 1828, when it was shown that organic chemicals could be produced from inanimate material, better described as the chemistry of compounds containing carbon (except for some compounds containing metal

IONS). Over half a million organic compounds have been described, including petroleum products, rubber, PLASTICS, synthetic fibres, dyes, explosives, perfumes, insecticides, fertilizers, ANTIBIOTICS, VITAMINS, ALKALOIDS, hormones (see ENDOCRINOLOGY), sugars, and PROTEINS. The organic chemist is concerned with the extraction and identification of naturally occurring materials, the synthesis and study of a wide range of compounds, and the relationship between molecular structure and physiological action. B.F.

Bibl: J.D. Roberts and M.C. Caserio, *Modern Organic Chemistry* (New York, 2nd ed., 1977).

organic conductors. In ORGANIC CHEMISTRY, most materials are electrical insulators because the ATOMS are so tightly bound that neither the IONS nor the ELECTRONS can break away and move through the material very easily. Thus an electric current cannot flow. However, in some long-chain or layered structures, certain electrons can break free so that these materials can become either conductors or SEMICONDUCTORS. The conductivity is usually very different along the layers than across the layers. Since, in general, organic materials are light in weight and are relatively cheap to produce, considerable development in the field is stimulated not only by the possibility of producing materials with novel and potentially useful properties, but also with the idea of replacing present-day devices, such as rechargeable batteries, by cheaper and lighter ones (see POLYMER FILMS). H.M.R.

organic foods/organic farming. Food production without the use of inorganic fertilizers but relying on manure or compost. It is claimed to be a more natural way of producing food that does not depend on outside resources. Since it yields less food per farm and is more labour intensive than current western farming methods it is suggested as a useful aid in reducing European food surpluses. Claims that organic foods are richer in NUTRIENTS are not true and claims that the taste is preferred are not borne out in trials. A.E.B.

Bibl: A.E. Bender, *Health or Hoax* (Goring-on-Thames, 1985).

organic labour state. The model formulated by the British commentator Neil Harding to characterize the nature of Soviet-type STATES. It suggests that in these systems the maximization of production is considered to be the main objective of both the state and society, which are organically linked and neither of which has a separate identity. Society is regarded as 'an organically developing system of production relations' which only the state can coordinate. As a result the state controls the main forces of production and grants rewards and rights to its citizens dependent on their contribution to production. A single political party puts forward policies which will lead to the realization of economic goals. As these goals are in the interests of all members of society, any opposition to the party is considered unacceptable. This model has been criticized by some analysts for failing to take account of the diverse *interests* which have some influence on state authorities, and for overemphasizing the state's economic objectives at the expense of political concerns such as ensuring the conformity of the population. D.PR.

Bibl: N. Harding (ed.), *The State in Socialist Society* (London, 1984).

organicism. In PHILOSOPHY, the theory that some, or all, complex wholes have the kind of systematic unity characteristic of what are literally organisms. An organism is held to differ from a mere mechanism or aggregate by reason of the dependence of the nature and existence of its parts on their position in the whole. A hand is, or remains, a hand only if united to a living body. The notion has been applied to social INSTITUTIONS and to the universe at large (for example, in the philosophy of Whitehead). The organic analogy implies not only that the parts of the whole are unified by INTERNAL RELATIONS but that the whole has a characteristic LIFE CYCLE or course of development as organisms typically do. A.Q.

organismic psychology. Any approach to PSYCHOLOGY which emphasizes that an organism, in developing from the single-CELL egg onwards, functions as a complex and many-sided but essentially unitary psychobiological whole which must be studied by proceeding from this whole to its parts rather than vice versa. For the opposite approach see ELEMENTARISM.

I.M.L.H.

Bibl: K. Goldstein, *The Organism* (New York, 1939).

organization and methods (O and M). The study of clerical methods and office work systems with the object of improving them. R.I.T.

Bibl: G.E. Milward, *Organization and Methods* (London and New York, 1967).

organization man. Term used by William H. Whyte in *The Organization Man* (1956) to denote a character-type encountered in modern bureaucratized social systems — that of individuals who work for large-scale organizations, primarily in managerial roles within American corporate business enterprises, but also within scientific establishments; and who in various senses 'belong' to such organizations. They are dominated by a SOCIAL ETHIC rather than the PROTESTANT ETHIC. This fact or self-perception of 'belonging' or 'togetherness' affects the LIFE STYLE and wider social aspirations of such individuals — influencing, via education and IDEOLOGICAL pressures, the way in which they see themselves and their societies, and including a level of standardized mediocrity and conformity. S.J.G.

Organization of African Unity (OAU). An association of African states, established in 1963 to fight colonialism and promote unity among African nations.

C.E.D.

Organization of American States (OAS). Consultative body of the Latin American nations and the U.S., established at the Ninth Pan-American Conference held at Bogota in 1948. The OAS set up an institutional and legal framework for the hemisphere based on the guidelines of the UN Charter, in the belief that there existed a community of interests between North and South America. The OAS endorsed the CIA-instigated overthrow of the leftist Arbenz government in Guatemala in 1954 and then in the same year passed a resolution (which became known as the Caracas Declaration) to exclude COMMUNIST influence from the hemisphere — in effect an updating of the 1823 U.S. MONROE DOCTRINE. The organization expelled Castro's CUBA in 1962 following alleged Cuban interference in the internal affairs of Venezuela, and supported the U.S. 1962 trade embargo on Cuba until 1975. It also gave backing to the U.S. 1965 invasion of the Dominican Republic. In 1979, however, the OAS rejected a U.S. motion to introduce an OAS peacekeeping force to prevent a revolutionary victory in NICARAGUA.   N.M.

organization theory. The study of the functions, structure, relationships and behaviour of organizations and their relationships with the external environment. There are many different aspects to this broad subject: (1) the effect of MANAGEMENT's interest in workers' problems (see HAWTHORNE EFFECT); (2) the effect of a BUREAUCRATIC form, in the sociological, Weberian sense, on the structure, relationships, behaviour and efficiency of an organization; (3) the implications of managers who see work as being performed in response to their commands and managers who see work as being a potential source of satisfaction and self-fulfilment; (4) different techniques of management that can be used in organizations; (5) the effects of an organization's TECHNOLOGY, size, range of products and geographical spread; (6) the *matrix* of relationships crossing the traditional organizational structure, e.g. the setting up of a project team with members drawn from different parts of the organization; (7) the motivations and systems of learning and perception of individuals and groups that may be established in the organization; (8) the reaction of organizations to external and/or unpredictable events.   R.I.T.; J.P.

Bibl: D.S. Pugh (ed.), *Organization Theory* (London, 2nd ed., 1984).

organizational development. Intervention in an organization with the intention of increasing the capacity to resolve conflict between external factors, internal values and leadership styles.   R.I.T.; J.P.

Bibl: C. Argyris, *Management and Organizational Development* (New York, 1971).

organizer. All animals belonging to the chordate line of descent (see ZOOLOGY) undergo, early in development, a fundamental METAMORPHOSIS known as *gastrulation* (see EMBRYOLOGY). The effect of gastrulation or of an equivalent process is to form an embryo which in addition to an outermost layer or ectoderm contains inside it an *archenteron* or rudimentary gut. The central NERVOUS SYSTEM begins as a median dorsal tubular formation in the ectoderm overlying the roof of this primitive gut. In a number of classical experiments the German embryologist Hans Spemann showed by operations on amphibian embryos that the primitive central nervous system or nerve tube arises in response to some influence emanating from the roof of the archenteron. To this important region of the embryo he accordingly gave the name *organizer*. The nature of the influence emanating from this organization centre is not yet known. A region equivalent to the organizer of amphibian embryos is found in other vertebrate embryos. Thanks to the work of Needham and Waddington it is generally agreed that one element in the action of the organizer is a purely evocative chemical STIMULUS which realizes the potential of the overlying ectoderm to roll up into a nerve tube. The other element in its action is more strictly an organizational one, i.e. one which imposes a pattern. The ectoderm responds to the action of the organizer only when it is in a state of so-called *competence* — a condition of reactivity which is soon lost in the course of development.   P.M.

organometallic chemistry, see under INORGANIC CHEMISTRY.

or-gate, see under GATE.

oriental despotism. A term common in the political vocabulary of the 18th century, and employed with particular effect in Montesquieu's *Spirit of the Laws* (1748), to compare and contrast the arbitrary and despotic political regimes of the eastern hemisphere with the constitutional republics and limited monarchies of the west. In current usage the term has largely been superseded by or subsumed under the MARXIST concept of the 'Asiatic' MODE OF

PRODUCTION. It has however been partly revived to suggest a fundamental continuity between the political system of the old oriental empires and that of COMMUNIST states such as the Soviet Union and China. K.K.

Bibl: K.A. Wittfogel, *Oriental Despotism* (New Haven, 1957).

origin of species, see under EVOLUTION.

ornament. Until recently western architects have taken the view that buildings should be undecorated — that any deviation from plainness should derive directly from the shape or colour of materials or the building's structural system — as opposed to being merely applied to a building. Various attempts have been made to establish a terminological distinction between the two, between ornament and decoration. But with the abandonment of the basic Modern Movement aesthetic rules the difference has become redundant. S.L.

orogeny (orogenesis). The processes by which the world's major mountain ranges, or orogenic belts, are formed (e.g. the Alps, Himalayas and Andes). Strictly speaking, an orogeny is a period of mountain building (which may last for tens of millions of years) and orogenesis refers to the processes involved; but the distinction has largely been lost by lax usage, and only pedants now insist upon it. Orogenic belts are exceptionally thick accumulations of sedimentary (see SEDIMENTATION) and volcanic rocks. They are also structurally extremely complex, comprising a highly compressed, deformed and metamorphosed (altered by high pressures and temperatures) mixture of continental crust and marine sediments together with oceanic crust and even bits of the earth's mantle. The complexity, composition and huge mass of mountain belts long presented geologists with their greatest dilemma, the most popular, but not entirely convincing, explanation being that the ranges were the 'crinkles' on the surface of an earth that was cooling and contracting. When independent evidence for contraction failed to appear, the true solution had to await the discovery of PLATE TECTONICS during the 1960s.

The details are poorly understood even now, but the key to mountain building is undoubtedly the motion of the plates of the earth's LITHOSPHERE. Oceanic lithosphere, created continuously at OCEANIC RIDGES and gradually forced sideways, ultimately plunges back into the earth's interior at SUBDUCTION ZONES along the edges of certain continents (e.g. South America). Where subduction and continent meet there is intense deformation, volcanic activity and uplift, resulting in an orogenic belt of the Andean type. When a moving ocean floor brings a continent into the subduction area, however, there is an even greater confrontation, for continental material is too light to subduct. As the continents collide and are inexorably forced into coalescence (e.g. India with the main body of Asia) there is even greater deformation and uplift, converting the orogenic belt into one of the Alpine-Himalayan type.

Ranges such as the Himalayas, Alps and Andes are still being formed; but older, extinct orogenic belts (e.g. the Urals and Appalachians) also exist in various states of erosion, suggesting that plate tectonic processes of some sort must have operated on the earth for at least 2,000 million years. P.J.S.

orography. The branch of physical GEOGRAPHY which is concerned with mountains and mountain systems. See also TECTONICS; OROGENY. M.L.

Orphism (or *Orphic Cubism*). In 1913 the paintings of Delaunay, Duchamp, Léger, and Picabia were described by Apollinaire as 'orphic', in the sense that they were more abstract (see ABSTRACT ART) and offered a more purely abstract aesthetic pleasure than did other CUBISTS; but the artist to whom this epithet has clung most firmly is Robert Delaunay, with lyrical, non-representational colour formations of 1910-14. He was joined by Sonia Terk (whom he married) and František Kupka; and his geometrical patterns influenced the work of Kandinsky, Marc, and Klee (see BLAUE REITER). The inheritors of his theories of the primacy of colour were the Americans Stanton Macdonald-Wright and Morgan Russell, who were followers of Delaunay in Paris in 1912, and who have been regarded as the initiators of the first distinctively American art movement, *synchromism*. P.C.

Bibl: R. Delaunay, ed. P. Francastel, *Du Cubisme à l'art abstrait: documents inédits* (Paris, 1957); W.C. Agee, 'Synchromism, the First American Movement' (*Art News*, October 1965).

Orthodoxy, Eastern. The faith of the ancient Christian Churches of Russia, Greece, and the Middle East, with their modern offshoots in the U.S.A. and elsewhere, all of which are in communion with the Ecumenical Patriarch of Constantinople. These Churches are self-governing and reject the Pope's claims. In general they are conservative although not uniform, and the secret of their survival despite some persecution (e.g. in the Soviet Union) is their EUCHARISTIC worship, which feeds a spiritual life that can be profound. Some smaller Eastern Churches, e.g. the Nestorians, are not 'orthodox' because they do not accept the decisions of the Ecumenical Councils about CHRISTOLOGY; but the most important causes of these continuing divisions are sociological. In the 1980s Orthodox Christians in the world appear to number about 170 million, although exact numbers, especially in the Soviet Union, are difficult to ascertain. See also CATHOLICISM; ECUMENICAL MOVEMENT. D.L.E.

Bibl: T.R. Ware, *The Orthodox Church* (Harmondsworth and Baltimore, 1963).

orthogenesis. When a long succession of evolutionary changes (see EVOLUTION) seems to proceed in a single direction it is sometimes said to display orthogenesis. The term is falling out of use and serves no useful purpose in evolution theory. P.M.

orthopaedics. The literal translation from the Greek is 'straight child'. Nicholas Andry (1658-1742), a French physician, wrote a book on *The Art of Correcting and Preventing Deformities in Children*, and this gave the speciality its name. Orthopaedics has for many years included the management of a whole range of bone and joint diseases (congenital and acquired) in children and adults. It includes such conditions as bone and joint infections, tuberculosis, tumours of bone, rheu-

matoid and osteo-arthritis and various spinal conditions, such as a prolapsed lumbar disc. In the last 20 years JOINT REPLACEMENT has revolutionized orthopaedic procedures, to the considerable benefit of patients. A further example of the rapidly changing scene in orthopaedics is the development of arthroscopic surgery of the knee and microsurgery (see SURGERY). With regard to children, some of the common problems that are dealt with by orthopaedic surgery are hip diseases, including congenital dislocation, congenital foot deformities, scoliosis and leg equalization procedures. N.H.H.

Orwellian. Characteristic or reminiscent of the writings of George Orwell — though the word is mainly used with reference to a not particularly characteristic work; his nightmarish vision, published in 1949, of the year *Nineteen Eighty-Four*. In this novel the world is divided into three TOTALITARIAN super-states, each permanently at war with one or both of the others. Life in the state known as Oceania includes such features as *Big Brother*, whose black-moustached face gazes down from a million posters; the *Thought Police*, who make good the boast that 'Big Brother is watching you'; and the *Newspeak* language, 'designed to meet the ideological needs of *Ingsoc*, or English Socialism'. The vocabulary of Newspeak shrinks every year, the ultimate object being to make heretical thoughts (*crimethink*) 'literally unthinkable'; meanwhile *Oldspeak* (i.e. English) has borrowed from it such deliberately unlovely words as *prolefeed* ('rubbishy entertainment and fictitious news' for the submerged masses or *proles*), *doublethink* ('the power of holding two contradictory beliefs in one's mind simultaneously, and accepting both of them'), and unperson. The best-known Orwellian *mot*, however, comes from his fable of Soviet COMMUNISM, *Animal Farm*: 'All animals are equal but some animals are more equal than others'. O.S.

osmosis. The process whereby, when a volume of, say, cane sugar solution is separated from a volume of pure water by a membrane which is permeable by water but not by sugar, water enters the sugar-containing compartment to dilute the solution and increase its volume. Very high *osmotic pressures* may be developed in this way. Osmosis plays a most important part in all biological transactions involving water transport or water imbibition in plants and animals. With reference to some chosen standard, solutions having an equal, higher, or lower osmotic pressure are referred to as *isotonic, hypertonic*, and *hypotonic* respectively. Osmotic pressure may sometimes be a disruptive force. Thus the red blood corpuscles soon swell up and burst in hypotonic solutions, and shrivel up and crinkle ('crenate') in hypertonic ones. P.M.

ostensive. A term applied to definitions which correlate words, not to other linguistic expressions (as in the verbal definitions of a dictionary), but to actual things that are representative instances of the correct application of the word. Every verbal definition of the form '*A* means the same as *B*' has to presume that *B* is already understood if it is to explain the meaning of *A*. It is usually argued that there must therefore be some verbally undefinable, or at least undefined, terms (the colour-words are a favourite example) where meaning is explained in some NON-VERBAL or *ostensive* way so that the process of verbal definition has a stock of already understood terms to start from. See also PARADIGM CASE. A.Q.

osteology. The term means a study of the anatomy of the bones and joints of the skeleton. It includes not only the detailed anatomical features of a bone and its muscle and ligamentous attachments, but also the clinical structure of the bone and the blood circulation within it. It includes also a study of the normal growth and development of bones and joints. Osteology is part of the course of study for pre-clinical medical students. N.H.H.

Ostpolitik ('Eastern Policy'). The policy of working for an end to the hostile relations between the Federal German Republic (West Germany) and its eastern COMMUNIST neighbours: Soviet Russia, Poland, Romania, Czechoslovakia, Hungary, and the German Democratic Republic (East Germany). Inaugurated by Willy Brandt, Foreign Minister and then Chancellor of the Federal Republic (1969-1974), it led to treaties with Poland and the U.S.S.R. (ratified May 1972), and to *de facto* recognition of the Oder-Neisse frontier with Poland and of the German Democratic Republic. Brandt's *Ostpolitik* was seen by its advocates as opening the way to improved relations between the Western powers (not just the Federal Republic) and the Communist bloc, and was a forerunner of the policy of DÉTENTE.

A.L.C.B.

Bibl: R. Tilford (ed.), *The Ostpolitik and Political Change in Germany* (Farnborough, Hants, and Lexington, Mass., 1975).

Other, the (*autrui*). In PHENOMENOLOGY the Other is a constituting factor in the self-image that a subject builds up. In Husserl's fifth *Cartesian Meditation*, in the work of Sartre and of Merleau-Ponty, and notably in later EXISTENTIAL PSYCHIATRIC usage such as R. D. Laing's, the Other is the perceiving, conscious, meaning-conferring other person who helps, or forces, the conscious subject to define his own world picture and his own view of his place in it. Knowledge, as defined in phenomenological description, is thus precisely not SOLIPSISM, as is often averred, but precisely the opposite. Knowledge is a world picture built up, partly through the instrumentality of other people in the world in INTERSUBJECTIVITY, and is thus a social, socializing and socialized process through and through. The Other socializes and intersubjectivizes PERCEPTION because of the fact of EMBODIMENT. R.PO.

other-direction. A quality ascribed by David Riesman in *The Lonely Crowd* (New Haven, 1950) to persons (or their characters) predominantly influenced by a 'need for approval and direction from others'. Riesman emphasizes (1) orientation towards the individual's contemporaries ('either those known to him or those with whom he is indirectly acquainted through friends or the mass media') and (2) a capacity for 'a superficial intimacy with and response to everyone'. Other-direction is contrasted with *tradition-direction* and *inner direction*. S.J.G.

otherness. Term often used in radical philosophical DISCOURSE to describe the condition of non-conformity to social NORMS or of disenfranchisement through the activities of the STATE or other institutions in which POWER is vested (e.g., the professions). The other in this usage becomes marginalized, beyond the pale.
S.T.

outer planets. The planets Jupiter, Neptune, Pluto, Saturn and Uranus. Jupiter, Neptune, Saturn and Uranus are also called *giant planets*. Saturn and Uranus have been observed at close quarters by the American Voyager SPACE PROBES. Compare TERRESTRIAL PLANETS.
J.D.B.

output. For the precise meaning of this word in COMPUTING and ECONOMICS, see respectively INPUT/OUTPUT and INPUT-OUTPUT ANALYSIS. In more general discourse, it should be applied only to quantifiable (see QUANTIFICATION) phenomena such as a writer's output in words; to speak of, say, the 'output' of a political system is to imply (1) that this too can be quantified (which it cannot); and perhaps (2), by analogy with the output of a farm or factory, that all such 'output' is beneficial (which may not be the case).
O.S.

outsider. Word given currency for a few years by Colin Wilson's ill-considered mish-mash of pseudo-Nietzschean and other ideas in *The Outsider* (1956). His 'outsiders' included Kierkegaard, Nietzsche, T.E. Lawrence, Kafka, and Hemingway — an oddly disparate group. In this sense the word admits of no precise definition; all that can be said is that the term as used by E.M. Forster ('the artist will tend to be an outsider') is here given a 'superman' flavour: the artist should not merely stand apart from society to concentrate upon his own function within it, but should raise himself above it and become a superior being. Essentially this was a reprehensible and mischievous misunderstanding of Nietzsche's conception of the 'overman'.
M.S.-S.

overdetermination, see under ALTHUSSERIANISM.

overheating. The inflationary consequences (see INFLATION) of excessive pressure on resources during a period of expansion in demand. So long as there are idle resources such an expansion usually leads first to increased employment and OUTPUT, and it is only at a later stage, as shortages and bottlenecks develop, that the pressure expends itself increasingly in higher prices.
A.C.

overidentification, see under IDENTIFICATION.

overkill. A polemic term used primarily by advocates of minimum DETERRENCE who argue that both the U.S.A. and the U.S.S.R. already possess a nuclear capability far exceeding that which is necessary for mutual destruction. It is also used in non-military contexts, e.g. of the excessive use of chemical poisons in dealing with agricultural pests.
A.F.B.

Bibl: R. Lapp, *Kill and Overkill* (New York, 1962; London, 1963).

overpopulation. A word whose different senses have been distinguished by W.A. Lewis as follows: (1) A country is said to be overpopulated if it could achieve a larger total output with a smaller population and a larger output per head. This assumes that the population structure in terms of age, skilled labour, and sex remains the same, whereas population change does not assume this. (2) In a more extreme sense a country is said to be overpopulated when its population is so large relative to its resources that any change would have no effect on total output; Mauritius, with very limited resources and space and a very large population, is a case in point. (3) The term sometimes means that the population is larger than can be fed without importing food; this usage can only really be justified when referring to the world population as a whole, since, however desirable self-sufficiency may be in a country, its absence can easily be rectified by trade — nor are countries which produce a surplus necessarily underpopulated. (4) The term is sometimes used to indicate that a country is using up irreplaceable resources at an excessive rate — a vague use which leads to no positive conclusions concerning the right size of population in relation to resources.

Germaine Greer criticizes the use of the word in any context, particularly the sociological. She maintains that its use reflects a preconceived idea on the part of the user, usually from the developed world, as to how people, usually in the THIRD WORLD, should live.   M.L.

Bibl: W.A. Lewis, *The Theory of Economic Growth* (London and Homewood, Ill., 1955); G. Greer, *Sex and Destiny* (London, 1984).

OVRA (Organizzazione di Vigilanza e Repressione dell' Antifascismo: Organization for the Observation and Repression of Anti-Fascism). The Italian FASCIST political secret police set up in 1927; an unpleasant organization, if somewhat less efficient than its German or Soviet equivalents (see GESTAPO; KGB).   D.C.W.

ownership and possession. It is difficult to give a precise and consistent meaning in English law to the concept of property, which is a patchwork of different 'estates' and 'interests' denoting shades of proprietary right. Nevertheless ownership denotes the right of a person in the fullest degree to the use and enjoyment of land or goods, including their disposition or destruction, though it remains subject to rules of law protecting the rights of others, and in the case of land to rules imposed by statute concerning e.g. planning control and powers of compulsory acquisition. The ownership of land may also be subject to rights of the public or of a neighbour to cross it by e.g. a footpath. Whereas ownership is essentially a right, albeit not absolute, possession is primarily a matter of fact, of physical occupation of land or retention of custody of goods. The owner of land need not necessarily be in current possession of it, and his ultimate right may be subject to current occupation by someone else: even a squatter may enjoy some limited legal protection. A thief of goods will have current possession of them, though unlawfully, and the owner's right to recover them is not thereby diminished.   D.C.M.Y.

Bibl: G.C. Cheshire and E.H. Burn, *Modern Law of Real Property* (London, 13th ed., 1982).

oxidation. Originally regarded as the increase of oxygen associated with a given ELEMENT, oxidation is now defined more generally as any CHEMICAL REACTION which removes ELECTRONS from an ATOM. Since the total number of electrons is unchanged in a reaction, oxidation is always matched by a corresponding *reduction*. There is often scanty knowledge of the real distribution of electrons, so that atoms are assigned oxidation states by a set of simple rules. An element has zero oxidation state; for an ION, the oxidation number is equal to the electronic charge. In COVALENT compounds the electrons are assigned to the more ELECTRONEGATIVE atoms participating in a BOND, e.g. in the reaction of hydrogen and oxygen to give water each hydrogen atom is oxidized to the $+1$ state. The assignment of oxidation states in such compounds can become increasingly arbitrary, and the concept then has little or no significance.   B.F.

oxygen cycle, see under LIFE CYCLE.

ozone/ozone layer. Oxygen whose MOLECULES consist of three ATOMS instead of the usual two (see ALLOTROPE). Ozone is a powerful oxidizing agent with deleterious effects on many organic substances (see OXIDATION). Ozone in the lower atmosphere, near ground-level, is largely the product of human activity. It results from the action of sunlight on a range of pollutants, most notably carbon monoxide, nitrogen oxides and hydrocarbons from car exhausts. Hydrocarbons released by the oil and gas industry may also be a factor. It is a prime component of PHOTOCHEMICAL smog. High ozone levels can be responsible for asthma attacks in humans, cause decay in many materials ranging from rubber to textiles, and may be implicated in the marked forest decline in parts of central Europe. It is important to distinguish between ozone near the Earth's surface and the 'ozone layer' in the high atmosphere, the STRATOSPHERE. The ozone layer is also vulnerable to human activity but because of the different chemistry at height in the atmosphere the threat is that the ozone layer may become depleted. The ozone layer in the high atmosphere shrouds the surface from biologically-damaging ULTRAVIOLET radiation

(UV-B). A rise in surface UV-B levels may be associated with an increased incidence of skin CANCER and reduced efficiency of the immune response. The main pollutants that may affect the ozone layer are the chlorofluorocarbons (CFCs). Concern about this problem has led to some restrictions on the use of CFCs, most notably in their use as aerosol can propellants. A 'hole' appeared in the ozone layer over Antarctica during the 1980s but it is not clear whether this is a natural fluctuation or the first sign of depletion induced by POLLUTION. M.V.B.; P.M.K.

Bibl: Environmental Resources Ltd, *Acid Rain* (London, 1983).

P

Pacem in Terris. An ENCYCLICAL issued by Pope John XXIII in 1963, stating the urgent problems of the peaceful development of the world and urging Catholics (see CATHOLICISM) to work for peace and justice in collaboration with others. It was a landmark in the AGGIORNAMENTO.

D.L.E.

pacemakers. The use of electrical stimuli delivered to the heart to support the rhythm artificially. A specially made solid catheter, filled with conduction material and coated with an insulating layer, is inserted through a large vein (most commonly the subclavian) and passed into the tip of the right ventricle. It is connected either to an external source (temporary) or an implanted lithium battery placed beneath the subcutaneous tissues of the anterior chest wall (permanent). It increases the heart rate to a fixed rate of 72 beats per minute and is inhibited by the heart's own rhythm. Originally used exclusively for complete heart block, there are now much wider indications for its use. New developments include an additional wire in the atrium (dual chamber pacing), multiprogrammability and rate increases with exercise. L.J.F.

pacifism. The belief and, consequently, conduct of those who believe that WAR and the employment of organized armed force are unjustifiable. Until the 20th century this was a view held only by such minority Christian groups as the QUAKERS and the PLYMOUTH BRETHREN. The word 'pacifism' first came into use at the beginning of the 20th century to describe movements advocating the settlement of disputes by arbitration and the reduction of armaments. Efforts to influence national policy in favour of the UNILATERAL renunciation of war have continued (e.g. the CND, Campaign for Nuclear Disarmament), in face of the objection that a nation which adopted such a policy would be more likely to encourage than discourage aggressive action. From the time of World War I, the word has also been used to describe the refusal of individuals, on grounds of conscience, to undertake military service, whatever the consequences to themselves. States have varied a great deal in their treatment of such a refusal. In only a small number of countries has the right to conscientious objection been recognized; in the majority it is treated as a breach of the law and often harshly punished. See also NON-VIOLENT RESISTANCE.

A.L.C.B.

package. In educational technology, a unit of material which is worked out and presented by someone other than the teacher and which can be repeated and reproduced. Examples are the processed programmes used in TEACHING MACHINES, the tapes and books found in a language laboratory, and television programmes. These teaching resources offer advantages when there is a class of varied ability and speed of understanding, and may allow a unique experience such as an outstanding foreign film or broadcast play to be brought into the classroom. See also INDIVIDUALIZED INSTRUCTION. W.A.C.S.

Bibl: L.C. Taylor, *Resources for Learning* (Harmondsworth, 2nd ed., 1972).

packaging. Time was when packaging was to contain and protect a product. It may well still have to perform that function, but now the packaging must allure the customer as well. In a world full of commercial images, each vying for the attention of would-be customers, impact and impression are, if anything, more important than protection. The specialist skill of packaging combines engineering and design skills at a high commercial level. Packaging has, thus, become one of the most important disciplines in MARKETING communication. T.S.

paediatrics. The medical care of ill children has become a speciality in the U.K. in the last 50 years in contrast to the previous care of ill children by family doctors and adult physicians. Whereas the main work is still diagnosis and treatment it now also involves the promotion and maintenance of health, the earliest possible detection of deviations from health and their correction and REHABILITATION

621

after treatment. The fall in the number of infectious diseases and the overall improvement in children's health has seen a dramatic drop in those with rickets, tuberculosis and gastro-enteritis. The involvement in the care of the newborn infant is now widespread and entails care of premature and low birth weight babies in special care units. There has also been a growth of interest in the psychological and emotional wellbeing of children, exemplified in the more humane care of children in hospital with unrestricted visiting for parents. Children with special needs have attracted more interest as have those taken into care, those suffering non-accidental injury and sexual abuse. Preventive and developmental paediatrics involving the school health services provide for regular supervision of children's dental health and auditory and visual monitoring. Speciality within paediatrics has grown apace in the last 10 years and kidney and heart TRANSPLANTS have become a part of hospital paediatrics with considerable team involvement. D.M.

pair bonding. The habit of forming a sexual pair for purposes of breeding. Pair bonding is rare among animals considered as a whole, but is found in a few shrimps, insects, and fish, several species of mammals, and the majority (over 95%) of species of birds. Pair bonding is usually associated with the co-operative rearing of young, and is probably found in species in which the young can only survive if looked after by two parents. Pair bonds are formed after a prolonged period of courtship. Once formed, they are maintained by a variety of behaviour patterns. In some birds, pairs sing duets. Mammalian pairs may mark their partners; male tupaid tree shrews, for example, spray urine on their mates. The duration of a pair bond may be for a single breeding cycle or longer; or, as in kittiwakes for example, it may depend on the pair's breeding success — successful pairs tend to stay together, unsuccessful pairs to split up. M.R.

palaeobotany. The study of the floral remains of the past, encompassing POLLEN ANALYSIS, DENDROCHRONOLOGY, and the identification of wood, charcoal, cultivated grain, weed seeds, and fibres. One rapidly expanding branch, *palaeoethnobotany*, is concerned with the evolution of cultivated plants. B.C.

Bibl: J.M. Renfrew, *Palaeoethnobotany* (London, 1973); G. Dimbleby, *Plants and Archaeology* (London, 1978).

palaeoclimatology. The study of the climates of the past — a study which depends on many branches of science, mainly GEOLOGY but also CLIMATOLOGY and METEOROLOGY. The basic data have been principally geological, derived in particular from PALAEOBOTANY, whereas explanations are presented in an astronomical or meteorological framework. Evidence of climates of the past is drawn from three main sources, BIOLOGY (e.g. the restricted HABITAT of corals), lithology (e.g. evaporites), and GEOMORPHOLOGY (e.g. glacial landforms). J.L.M.L.

palaeodemography. The study of the population dynamics of communities living in the distant past. Attempted by archaeologists with untestable degrees of success. .B.C.

Bibl: F.A. Hassan, *Demographic Archaeology* (London, 1981).

palaeoethnobotany, see under PALAEOBOTANY.

palaeogeography. The reconstruction of the GEOGRAPHY of a given REGION, essentially the distribution of land and sea, at a particular time in the past. Palaeogeography is an exercise in STRATIGRAPHY, using the biological and lithological characters which are determined by the depositional ENVIRONMENT preserved in the sedimentary rocks of a particular period. It is assumed that depositional environments of the past, certainly from Cambrian times (see under GEOLOGICAL TIME CHART), were similar to those of today. J.L.M.L.

palaeolithic, see under THREE-AGE SYSTEM.

palaeo-modernism, see under MODERNISM.

palaeontology. The science which deals with the fossil remains (*palaios* is the Greek word for 'ancient') of animals and plants found buried in rocks. The term, in practice, is restricted to the study of animal remains; fossil plants are dealt with by PALAEOBOTANY. Fossils are of importance to GEOLOGISTS as time-markers which help to establish the succession of strata in the earth's crust. They also throw light on the geographical conditions under which rocks were laid down and on the PALAEO-GEOGRAPHY and PALAEOCLIMATOLOGY of the world as a whole. Any succession of fossil-bearing rocks shows a fossil succession which corresponds to the biological process of EVOLUTION and adds greatly to the understanding of this. Finally palaeontology is of value to ARCHAEOLOGY for the evidence fossil remains afford of the early domestication of animals and of other local environmental conditions of archaeological sites.　　　A.L.C.B.

palaeopathology. The use of ancient human remains for the study of disease, injury, and NUTRITION. Normally only skeletal material is available, but occasionally (as in the case of the Danish bog burials, the bodies preserved in permafrost conditions in the Altai Mountains, and mummified remains) hair, skin, flesh, and entrails survive for scrutiny.　　　B.C.

Bibl: C. Wells, *Bones, Bodies and Disease* (London and New York, 1964); D.R. Brothwell, *Digging Up Bones* (London and Oxford, 1981).

palaeoserology. The study of ancient BLOOD GROUPS by testing samples of human TISSUE preserved under ideal conditions, or, more often, spongy bone tissue. The technique is not far advanced, and its limits of reliability have still to be defined.　　　B.C.

palaeozoology. The branch of PALAEON-TOLOGY which deals with fossil animals and the historical record they embody. For most practical purposes the record begins in Cambrian times (see GEOLOGI-CAL TIME CHART). Until the acceptance of the theory of EVOLUTION fossil remains made very little sense — Cuvier (1769-1832), the leading zoologist of his day, could describe a fossil ichthyosaur as *homo diluvii testis* (man witness of the Flood). The fossil record is biased in as much as soft-bodied animals normally leave no fossil traces.　　　P.M.

Palestine Liberation Organization (PLO). A conglomerate organization led by Yasser Arafat whose own movement, Fatah, is the strongest, but not dominant component. Its aim is the creation of a Palestinian state. The essence of Palestinian national resistance starts from the proposition that Palestinians were driven out of the land which, in an era of decolonization, should have become a Palestinian state and that other Arab states will only, at best, help the Palestinians to regain what is rightfully theirs. Fatah (meaning victory, and a reverse acronym from Harakt Tahrir Filastin — Palestine Liberation Movement) was founded by Arafat, in the aftermath of SUEZ. In May 1964 pressure from Palestinians and other radical Arabs for action against Israel led President Nasser to sponsor the creation of the Palestine Liberation Organization under the leadership of Ahmad Shuqayri and under Egyptian control, but after the 1967 war (see MIDDLE EAST WARS) Fatah became the most powerful faction within the PLO with Arafat as chairman of the executive. But the PLO retained an institutional structure based on consensus politics which in practice gives negative power to small groups. The Palestine National Council can alone change the charter, which embodies the maximalist aims for the recovery of the whole of Palestine. Neither it nor the executive committee coordinates the political and military activities of the constituent factions, namely: the Popular Front for the Liberation of Palestine (NEO-MARXIST descendant of George Habbash's Arab National Movement), the more formally MARXIST-LENINIST Democratic Front for the Liberation of Palestine (Nayif Hawatmeh), the military-terrorist Popular Front for the Liberation of Palestine-General Command (Ahmad Jabril), the Syrian-controlled Saiqa and the Iraqi-controlled Arab Liberation Front. The PLO has the support of Palestinians in the occupied territories and the Palestinian diaspora, is recognized by Arab states as the sole representative of the Palestinians and has achieved limited diplomatic recognition elsewhere. It lacks military force to chal-

623

lenge Israel and uses TERRORISM as a weapon, but seldom within Israel or the occupied territories. In Israel there is no constituency for negotiation with the PLO. In consequence survival has been the organization's main achievement.

W.K.

Bibl: A.D. Miller, *The PLO and the Politics of Survival* (New York, 1983).

palynology. The study of pollen, especially of fossil pollen grains, for which see POLLEN ANALYSIS.

K.M.

pan-Africanism. Less a movement for a united Africa than a quasi-NATIONALIST set of beliefs in the uniqueness and spiritual unity of black Africans, beginning among American and West Indian negroes returning to Africa from the 1850s on, and linked with the cultivation of cultural NÉGRITUDE among black Africans from French African colonies. Pan-African conferences met in London, Paris, and New York in 1900, 1919, 1921, 1923, and 1927 and in Manchester in 1945. The first to be held in Africa met in Accra in 1958. Since the attainment of independence by most African states, pan-Africanism has expressed itself through the ORGANIZATION OF AFRICAN UNITY, its support for liberation movements in remaining colonized states and in pressure for international action against the APARTHEID regime in South Africa. D.C.W.; S.R.

Bibl: C. Legum, *Pan-Africanism* (London and New York, 1962); J. Mayall, *Africa; the Cold War and After* (London, 1971).

Panama Canal treaty. A treaty governing the operation and defence of the Panama Canal, signed by the U.S. Carter Administration and Panama in September 1979 and entering into force in October 1979. It replaces the 1903 treaty which established the U.S.-owned Panama Canal Company and the U.S.-administered Panama Canal Zone. By the provisions of the new treaty Panama gains full SOVEREIGNTY rights over the former Canal Zone and is to accept control of the Canal itself by the year 2000. A second part commits the U.S. and Panama jointly to maintaining the permanent neutrality of the Canal. U.S. congressional amendments have given the U.S. leeway to intervene militarily to reopen the Canal (if its operations were to be interrupted) even after the end of 1999. N.M.

Bibl: David N. Farnsworth and James W. McKenney, *US-Panamanian Relations 1903-1978: A Study in Linkage Politics* (Boulder, Co., 1983).

pan-Arabism, see under ISLAM.

Panch Shila. 'Five Principles' publicly adhered to by Jawaharlal Nehru, Prime Minister of India, and Chou En-lai, Premier of the People's Republic of China, in 1954; NON-INTERVENTION in the internal affairs of other states, mutual respect for territorial integrity and SOVEREIGNTY, mutual non-aggression, mutual aid, and peaceful COEXISTENCE. The same principles were adopted by the states attending the BANDUNG CONFERENCE the following year. D.C.W.

panentheism, see under PANTHEISM.

pangenesis. Now obsolete theory of HEREDITY according to which particles travelled from all parts of the body to the GONADS, where they were incorporated into the GAMETES. It was suggested by Darwin (1868) to account for the supposed INHERITANCE OF ACQUIRED CHARACTERISTICS. J.M.S.

pan-Germanism. A movement aiming at the union of all German-speaking peoples into a single state, strengthened by racial theory on the one hand, HISTORICIST and GEOPOLITICAL arguments on the other. It was embodied as a political movement, the *Alldeutscher Verband*, in 1894, and was at first mainly confined to academics, INTELLECTUALS, and publicists. It captured the imagination of the German High Command during World War I and was embodied into the doctrines of the RIGHT, both parliamentary and anti-parliamentary, under the WEIMAR REPUBLIC, emerging as an essential element in NAZISM. D.C.W.

Bibl: G.A. Craig, *Germany, 1866-1945* (Oxford, 2nd ed., 1981).

panic, theatre of, see THEATRE OF PANIC.

pan-Islam, see under ISLAM.

panpsychism. The theory that everything that really exists in the world is a mind or CONSCIOUSNESS. Leibniz's theory of MONADS is, in effect, a form of panpsychism, as in Berkeley's view that the only true SUBSTANCES are minds, finite or infinite. The 'personal idealists' (see under PERSONALISM) of the late 19th century who reacted against the absorption of finite personalities into the all-engulfing ABSOLUTE of Hegel tended towards pan $>$ DX $<$ psychism. It was explicit in the METAPHYSICS of McTaggart, for whom reality consisted exclusively of finite selves. A.Q.

panspermia. The theory that life on earth originated on another planet. Whether life exists on other planets is unknown (see EXOBIOLOGY) but if it does, it could conceivably have been transported here, and have seeded life on earth. The transport could have been deliberate and active, by means of a rocket, or passive, if for instance small organisms hitched here on comets. The difficulties for the theory are: (1) the small chance of successful transport, and (2) the small chance that life evolved on another planet would be appropriately built for life on earth (see ADAPTATION). The appeal of the theory is that it makes less improbable the origin of life from inorganic systems, by multiplying the number of places where it could have happened. M.R.
Bibl: F. Crick, *Life Itself* (London, 1981).

pantheism. The worship of nature (Greek *pan*, all) as divine (Greek *theos*, god). Pantheism is usually connected with MONISM, the philosophy which avoids a radical distinction between the Creator and his creation and which seeks to explain all that exists in terms of a single reality, which can be conceived of in highly spiritual terms. Its roots are close to polytheism, the worship of many gods often connected with natural phenomena such as mountains, rivers, or storms; but pantheism is different because it rejects both the TRANSCENDENCE and the personality of gods or God, and because it refines the PRIMITIVE response to nature in a sophisticated and RATIONALIST way, attempting to have RELIGION without the intellectual difficulties of THEISM. Some forms of HINDUISM are pantheistic; most notably, the 8th-century teacher Samkara denied any duality between the world and the Supreme. In the West, the word 'pantheism' was coined, by the DEIST John Toland in 1705, for an intellectual system stated by the Dutch Jewish philosopher Baruch Spinoza in his *Tractatus Theologico-politicus* (1670). In the 19th century both the poetry of William Wordsworth and Hegelian (see HEGELIANISM) PHILOSOPHY tended in this direction. For a 20th-century movement among Christians with the same tendency, see PROCESS THEOLOGY; but Christian thinkers usually prefer the term *panentheism* coined by K.C.F. Krause (1781-1832), meaning that everything exists in (Greek *en*) God. This is thought to preserve the idea of God as Creator. D.L.E.
Bibl: K. Ward, *The Concept of God* (Oxford, 1974).

pantonal music. Music whose component parts are at times identifiable in terms of various conventional 'keys', without any one key being established as predominant. It is thus intermediate between polytonal (see POLYTONALITY) and ATONAL MUSIC, with borderlines so uncertain and subjective that Schoenberg sometimes applied the adjective 'pantonal' to music that is normally called atonal. A.H.

paper chromatography. A CHROMATO-GRAPHIC technique in which chemical separation is effected on an absorbent filter paper. The stationary PHASE is water supported by the cellulose MOLECULES of the paper, and the mobile phase, usually based on an organic solvent, flows by capillary action. Uses include the separation of AMINO ACIDS and PEPTIDES in the investigation of PROTEIN structures, the analysis of body fluids (e.g. for sugars) and the separation of inorganic IONS. Quantities down to 10^{-7} grams (one ten-millionth of a gram) may be detected. B.F.

par values, see under PARITY.

paradigm. A term given a technical meaning within the PHILOSOPHY OF SCIENCE by

T.S. Kuhn's *The Structure of Scientific Revolutions*. Countering standard EMPIRICIST versions of the growth of scientific knowledge, Kuhn denied that hypotheses or theories were simple products of INDUCTION from sense experience. A more 'HOLISTIC' notion of visual and intellectual perception applied: theories were comprehensive orderings of reality, in which the whole was in some sense prior to its parts and made sense of its individual components. Theories gave meaning to facts rather than, in any simple sense, arising out of them. All scientific thinking and practices operated within theoretical frameworks, or, as Kuhn termed them, paradigms. Kuhn's conception of paradigm-bound science was widely criticized on two grounds. First, the notion of paradigm was itself too vague (the term seemed to be used to describe both whole sciences and individual concepts within them). Second, by viewing the development of science as a succession of self-contained paradigms (e.g., Ptolemaic ASTRONOMY, Copernican astronomy), Kuhn was committing the RELATIVIST fallacy, and denying that science approximated ever nearer to a true account of reality.

R.P.

Bibl: T.S. Kuhn, *The Structure of Scientific Revolutions* (London, 2nd ed., 1970).

paradigm case. A representative instance of a CONCEPT, used to provide an OSTENSIVE definition of it. In so far as some concepts must be ostensively defined for the process of verbal definition to have a starting-point, it follows that if any word is to have MEANING at all some must truly apply to actual things. This argument from paradigm cases was introduced by G.E. Moore to rebut comprehensive sceptical theories, such as that no proposition is certain or that no material object is known to exist. How, he asked, could the word 'certain' or words for material objects have meaning at all unless there are actual instances for them to be ostensively learned from? The argument assumes, questionably, that some particular words must be ostensive (a stronger claim than that there must be some ostensive words), that it is possible to establish which they

are, and that 'certain' and words for material objects are among them.   A.Q.

paradigmatic, see under SYNTAGMATIC.

paradox. A statement which appears acceptable but which has unacceptable or contradictory consequences. Three kinds of paradox have proved important in the development of LOGIC and MATHEMATICS. (1) Paradoxes of the INFINITE. Zeno of Elea argued thus: space is infinitely divisible; so an arrow must pass through infinitely many points in its flight; therefore it can never reach the target. This (like many variants) is resolved by the theory of CONVERGENCE to a LIMIT: an *infinite* sequence can have a *finite* limit. (2) SEMANTIC paradoxes. Epimenides the Cretan said (and was believed by Saint Paul): 'The Cretans are always liars.' If true, the statement would have made the speaker an invariable liar, and would therefore have been false. Therefore it must be false. (For another example see HETEROLOGICAL.) (3) Paradoxes of SET THEORY. Bertrand Russell considered the class (or SET) *R* which consists of just those classes that do not belong to themselves. Then *R* belongs to itself if and only if it does not.

Paradoxes of types (2) and (3) are said to involve *self-reference*. Following a suggestion of Poincaré, Russell proposed the resolution of paradoxes on the *vicious-circle principle*: an object (such as a PROPOSITION, predicate, or class) is illegitimate if its definition involves a totality to which itself belongs. Thus Epimenides' saying refers to *all* statements by Cretans, itself included, and so is not a proposition, does not express anything. The proposal was worked out in great detail as the *ramified theory of types* of Russell and Whitehead in *Principia Mathematica*; but the theory has proved unsatisfactory from almost every point of view. It is now customary to distinguish sharply between (2) and (3). The semantic paradoxes are resolved by distinguishing levels of language: Epimenides' saying is at a higher level, it is *metalinguistic* (see METALANGUAGE); the lies it refers to are those of ordinary discourse, and so it does not apply to itself and may therefore be true. The set-theoretic paradoxes are avoided in axiomatic set theory; another solution is provided by the *simple theory of types*. In this theory, individuals are of type 0, sets (or predicates) of individuals are of type 1, sets of sets of individuals are of type 2, and so on. Sentences like 'an individual is equal to a set' or 'a set of type 2 belongs to a set of type 1' are regarded not as false but as ungrammatical, meaningless. A paradox should be distinguished from an ANTINOMY. See also CLOCK PARADOX.

R.G.

Bibl: E. P. Northrop, *Riddles in Mathematics* (London, 1945).

paradoxical sleep, see REM SLEEP.

paralanguage. In suprasegmental PHONOLOGY, a range of vocal effects (e.g. giggle, whisper; see also INTONATION) that contribute to the tones of voice a speaker may use in communicating meaning. They are at present less susceptible of systematic description than the other areas of phonology, and are considered by many linguists to be marginal to the sound-system of the language. For some scholars, the term also subsumes kinesic phenomena (see SEMIOTICS). D.C.

parallelism.

(1) In COMPUTING, the ability of parts of a machine or SYSTEM to work simultaneously on different problems or sub-tasks. J.E.S.

(2) In PSYCHOLOGY, see under MIND-BODY PROBLEM.

parameter.

(1) In MATHEMATICS, originally a particular auxiliary COORDINATE used in describing *conic sections*; the term is still used for an auxiliary VARIABLE in terms of which others are expressed by *parametric* equations. R.G.

(2) In its modern usage in mathematics and its applications, particularly in ECONOMICS, it denotes a quantity that is constant in the MODEL or circumstances under consideration. This quantity may take a different value in other models or circumstances. For example, the marginal propensity to consume (see MARGINAL ANALYSIS) is thought to increase with income, though over small enough ranges it may be assumed to be a constant, i.e. it is a parameter. D.E.; J.P.

(3) In STATISTICS, a summary measure such as the MEAN of a characteristic of members of a population. R.G.

(4) In music, a term often used since 1950 to denote the different aspects of a musical sound (e.g. duration, loudness, pitch, tone colour, attack, spatial location etc.). B.CO.

paranoia. In ABNORMAL PSYCHOLOGY and PSYCHIATRY, a type of PSYCHOSIS in which the individual experiences delusions, typically of persecution and/or grandeur. It is often accompanied by hallucinations.

W.Z.

parapsychology (or *psychical research*). The scientific study of actual or alleged paranormal phenomena (such as ESP and PSYCHOKINESIS). I.M.L.H.

Bibl: H.L. Edge *et al., Foundations of Parapsychology* (London, 1986).

parasitology. The scientific study of parasites. Parasites are organisms that live and feed on organisms of other species. Some such parasites live on humans and cause fearful disease. Perhaps 200 to 300 million people are suffering at present from schistosomiasis, for example; and parasites are so ubiquitous and dangerous that the biologist J.B.S. Haldane once suggested they were the main influence in human evolution.

Parasites may be simple one-celled organisms or complex multi-celled structures. PROTOZOA are the simplest organisms in the animal kingdom, consisting of a single nucleated CELL. Malaria, amoebic dysentery, sleeping sickness, giardiasis and trichomoniasis are all caused by protozoa. Although insects and bugs (arthropods) such as mosquitoes, lice and fleas are primarily vectors of pathogens, some can be directly injurious to man (see VECTORS OF DISEASE). They can cause pain, ALLERGY and psychological problems such as entomophobia and delusionary parasitosis. The third group of parasites are complex multi-cellular worms such as threadworms, hookworms, tapeworms, filaria, schistosomes and guinea worms. Many of these, such as tapeworms and hookworms, live and breed in the intestines, but others such as filaria live in blood vessels, muscles and the brain. Parasitic diseases require specialist attention. Some like malaria, sleeping sickness and schistosomiasis can be fatal. Unlike many bacterial and viral infections, parasitic infections do not lead to immunity from further infection with the same parasite and repeated infections are common.

The most important part of parasitology is its medical application, which seeks to control human parasites. Parasitologists study the often complex and multi-staged LIFE CYCLES of parasites, how they are transferred between hosts, and the factors affecting their abundance. This knowledge can be put to use in controlling the parasite. Schistosomes, for example, parasitize aquatic snails as intermediate hosts before entering humans, and it would in principle be possible to control the disease by killing the infected snails (or bolstering their resistance to schistosomes) or by preventing people from coming into contact with them. Parasites may be controlled at the next stage, as they seek to enter the host, by improving the host's resistance. Humans resist parasites by means of their immune system (see IMMUNITY), which acts to recognize and kill foreign matter that enters the body. Injecting a small dose of the parasite, in harmless form, can prime the immune system and immunize the body against the parasite. Finally, if the parasite has successfully entered its host it can be attacked directly, for instance by chemical poisons. The techniques developed to control parasites vary with the life cycles and survival strategies of different parasite species, and have been more successful in some cases than others. M.R.;A.P.H.

Pareto optimum. The formal conditions, named after the Italian sociologist and economist, under which general ECONOMIC EFFICIENCY is obtained. The condition is said to exist when there is no reorganization of the economy which makes one or more persons better off without making one or more others worse off. This concept of efficiency is fundamental to much of microeconomic theory and normative economics. Though a Pareto optimum is efficient, the resulting distribution of income may be undesirable. In particular, there may be other Pareto optima that have a greater SOCIAL WELFARE.
R.L.; J.P.

parity.
(1) In PHYSICS, a precise mathematical description of left-right SYMMETRY or 'handedness'. For systems of atomic size or larger, nature makes no fundamental distinction between left and right, so that an object and its mirror image are equally compatible with the laws of physics. (Left- and right-handed systems need not actually occur *equally often* in nature: by an accident of EVOLUTION, almost everybody's heart is on his left side, but the reverse occasionally occurs with no ill effects.)

A perfectly symmetrical isolated system has a value of the parity which can be calculated from the WAVE FUNCTION; as the system evolves it remains symmetrical, and the parity does not alter — it is an *invariant* (see CONSERVATION LAWS). For the WEAK INTERACTIONS between ELEMENTARY PARTICLES, however, parity is not conserved, e.g. an apparently symmetrical NEUTRON decays into components with a definite 'handedness'; on this level it appears that nature does know left from right. M.V.B.

Bibl: M. Gardner, *The Ambidextrous Universe* (New York, 1964; London, 1967).

(2) In ECONOMICS, the word has at least two distinct meanings:

(*a*) *Par values* of the BRETTON WOODS currency system are the fixed EXCHANGE RATES between currencies and the international accepted standard of value, the dollar. This system of fixed exchange rates collapsed in the early 1970s.

(*b*) The *purchasing power parity theory* states that exchange rates are mainly determined by the relative price levels in different countries. As not all goods and services are traded, it is the price levels of tradables that are relevant to determining exchange rates. The prices at which trade actually takes place depend on subsidies, taxes and transport costs. Exchange rates are also affected by relative interest rates and inflows and outflows on the CAPITAL, as well as the current account of the BALANCE OF PAYMENTS. J.P.

Bibl: D. Begg *et al., Economics* (London, 1986).

Parkinson's Law. A principle formulated by the British political scientist, C. Northcote Parkinson (*Parkinson's Law*, London, 1958) to the effect that 'work expands so as to fill the time available for its completion'. As a corollary Parkinson states that 'a perfection of planned layout is achieved only by institutions on the verge of collapse'. *Parkinson's Law* and similar popular studies such as *The Peter Principle* (which states that employees tend to be promoted above the level at which they are efficient) serve to counteract the tendency for MANAGEMENT to take itself too seriously. P.S.L.

parliamentarianism. The view that the best form of government is a parliamentary form, conforming more or less to the 'Westminster model'. By association, the idea that reform and social change should take place only by means of legislative measures agreed on by an elected parliamentary government, as opposed to being pushed through by the rulers of a one-party system or on a dictator's unsupported say-so. A.R.

parole. In PENOLOGY (for its meaning in LINGUISTICS see under LANGUE), a shorthand term applied to the premature release of a convicted prisoner on expiry of part of his sentence, with provision for recall if he violates the parole terms; thus to be distinguished from *remission* which cannot be revoked once the prisoner is released. Originating in the 19th century 'tickets of leave' system for transported convicts, parole is widely used in the U.S.A., in combination with indeterminate sentences, but was introduced into Britain only by the Criminal Justice Act, 1967. The granting of parole is discretionary, following consideration by local Review Committees and the Central Parole Board, with special arrangements for life sentences; supervision is the responsibility of the Probation and After-Care Service. T.M.

Bibl: D.A. Thomas (ed.,), *Parole* (Cambridge, 1974).

parsec (PARallax-SECond). A unit of distance in ASTRONOMY. 1 parsec = 3.26 light-years = 19 million million miles. M.V.B.

Parsonian. Derived from or resembling the sociological theories of Talcott Parsons. Parsons (*b.* 1902), professor of SOCIOLOGY at Harvard for most of his life, became the leading American sociological theorist of his generation. His approach, a type of STRUCTURAL-FUNCTIONAL THEORY, was most influential in the 1950s. Though his ideas have changed continuously, four main themes emerge. (1) Individual personalities, societies, and CULTURES can all be analysed as self-equilibrating SYSTEMS and described in terms of a common conceptual framework, that of *action systems*. (2) Action systems contain four *subsystems*, performing functions of pattern maintenance, integration, goal-attainment, and adaptation. (3) As SOCIAL ACTION systems, societies evolve towards greater functional specialization of STRUCTURE: e.g. modern political and economic INSTITUTIONS largely correspond with the analytical subsystems 'polity' and 'economy' which perform the goal-attainment and adaptation functions. (4) SOCIAL STRUCTURE is analysable into four components (values, NORMS, collectivities, ROLES), and the institutionalization of certain *core values*, through the NORMATIVE regulation of collective activities and individual role performances, primarily determines the stability and functioning of societies. Critics of Parsonian theory have asserted that it contains only verbal categorizations from which no testable PROPOSITIONS follow; or that it can (perhaps) explain stability but not change; or even that it merely expresses a conservative preference for a society devoid of significant disagreements over values. Although it has inspired much empirical research, its claim to be scientific is not yet established. J.R.T.

Bibl: W. C. Mitchell, *Sociological Analysis and Politics: the Theories of Talcott Parsons* (London and Englewood Cliffs, N.J., 1967).

partial object. A psychoanalytic concept which refers to the predominance in the infantile psychic world of parts of whole objects, such as the breast and faeces. Melanie Klein introduced, as her way of taking up Karl Abraham's theory of partial love, her theory of the development of OBJECT RELATIONS, which develop in connection with the different psychosexual stages (see DEVELOPMENTAL THEORY), and the evolution of the relation to the object as a whole. She introduced the concept of 'part-object' as central in her theory of object relations. Even though partial, the infantile objects have the uppermost power in the infant's psychic world; they are endowed with threatening or reassuring qualities, and they are split according to their moral qualities into 'good' or 'bad' objects in the same sense as one would ascribe these properties to individuals. A massive splitting mechanism characterizes the primitive oral and anal stages, which will persist throughout all adult life, in spite of the development of the third, genital stage, which introduces the establishment of a relation to whole objects. B.BE.

participation. A slogan which came into widespread use in the 1960s to express what the EEC calls 'the democratic imperative', defined as the principle that 'those who will be substantially affected by decisions made by social and political institutions must be involved in the making of those decisions'. It is argued that the size and complexity of modern MASS SOCIETIES, the centralization of political POWER, the growth of BUREAUCRACY, and the concentration of economic power all mean that the traditional guarantees of DEMOCRACY need to be strengthened and extended in order to check the tendency for more and more decisions affecting people's lives to be made in secret by small groups which are often remote and not easily identified or called to account, since they act in the name of the State, of a local authority, or of some large, impersonal business corporation.

So far as politics is concerned, the principle is as old as democracy itself. The problem is how to implement it — a problem likewise as old as democracy itself, but made vastly more difficult by the scale and comprehensiveness of modern government and by the need for clear-cut and rapid decisions, failure to produce which is no less a matter for protest on the part of those who demand greater participation. The new feature in the period since World War II is the proposal to extend participation to fields other than politics, e.g. to higher education, where it was the major demand of all student protests in the late 1960s and early 1970s, and, of much greater importance, to industry and business. The practice (*Mitbestimmung* or *codetermination*) by which employees take a part in MANAGEMENT decisions was introduced by the Federal Government of Germany in 1952, has spread in various forms to other countries in Western Europe, and has been adopted as an objective by the EEC. In the U.K. the 1977 BULLOCK REPORT, *Industrial Democracy*, proposing a variant of the German system, was rejected by the employers. Since then the TRADE UNIONS have resolutely failed to agree on a common policy. Other forms of participation, notably the growth of interest in cooperatives and profit sharing and share ownership schemes, have superseded the EEC initiative (which, after 15 years, is still in draft). In the U.S., progress was started when Frazer of the Auto Workers Union went onto the Chrysler Corporation board, but the example has not been repeated. Within the EEC structures the concept of 'social partners' has attempted to provide a platform for participation from the top down.

A.L.C.B.; B.D.S.

particle. A relative term, in common use throughout PHYSICS, denoting any object which may be considered as a moving point, characterized by a few simple properties such as MASS and SPIN. The concept is an idealization, valid whenever the internal structure, size, and shape of the object are irrelevant to the phenomenon being considered. Thus, for instance, such a complicated system as the earth may be treated as a particle for many purposes of ASTRONOMY, and it is sufficient to treat ATOMS as particles in order to explain much of the behaviour of matter in bulk. Particles interact with one another via FIELDS. See also ATOMIC PHYSICS; ELEMENTARY PARTICLE; WAVE-PARTICLE DUALITY.

M.V.B.

particle collider. Device for accelerating ELEMENTARY PARTICLES to very high energies and colliding them together in a region surrounded by sensitive detection instruments. New elementary particles are sought in the debris of the collisions. (See also ACCELERATOR.) J.D.B.

particular, see under UNIVERSAL.

particularism, see under PATTERN VARIABLES.

Pascal. A HIGH-LEVEL PROGRAMMING LANGUAGE designed for use in teaching how to write well-structured PROGRAMS. It has found considerable popularity in other contexts, particularly with users of PERSONAL COMPUTERS.   J.E.S.

pass laws. The term denoting the body of South African law requiring blacks to carry at all times passes permitting their movement within the nation. The pass laws evolved in the 1950s from earlier restrictions on black mobility. They became an essential part of the apparatus of APARTHEID, being designed to control the geographical distribution of blacks while managing their role in the labour market. Always an object of black opposition, the laws became increasingly difficult to administer as resistance grew. Their abolition was successfully demanded in 1985 by the newly formed Confederation of South African Trade Unions, although the replacement measure of identity cards to be carried by members of all races did not satisfy many opponents of the regime.   S.R.

passive euthanasia, see under EUTHANASIA.

Past and Present. A journal founded in 1952 by a group of young MARXIST historians (including its first editor John Morris, Christopher Hill, Eric Hobsbawm) to challenge the dominance of political history and Western European history in more orthodox periodicals. Under the editorship of the late Trevor Aston it became one of the best-known historical journals in the English-speaking world, associated with a greater variety of approaches to history than before but continuing to emphasize SOCIAL HISTORY and the history of the world outside Europe.   P.B.

pastiche, see under POST-MODERNISM.

patent. An exclusive legal right to the use of an invention or innovation (see TECHNI-

CAL PROGRESS). The information embodied in an invention or innovation may be regarded as a PUBLIC GOOD whose use should not be artificially restricted. If the use of this information can not be restricted, imitation occurs. Imitation reduces the economic rewards to invention and innovation and, thus, the incentive to invent and innovate. A restriction on imitation is justified, if the costs of a legal MONOPOLY are more than offset by the technical progress following from the greater incentives for successful invention and innovation.   J.P.
  Bibl: P. Stoneman, *The Economics of Technological Change* (Oxford, 1983).

pathology. The study in all its aspects of departures from normality in respect of health and bodily function. Since all illnesses represent departures from normality it could be said, and by pathologists has been said, that pathology comprehends all medicine. Pathology is subdivided into a number of branches, notably *pathological* (gross) *anatomy* such as is laid bare on the post-mortem slab; HISTOPATHOLOGY, dealing with structural abnormalities at the TISSUE level, and nowadays *cellular pathology*, comprehending any attempt to interpret abnormalities of form or function at a cellular structural level; and *chemical pathology*, which has to do with diagnosis and interpretation of disease at a biochemical level (see BIOCHEMISTRY) — thus it is the chemical pathology laboratory which undertakes the analysis of blood samples for evidence of impaired liver function, or tests urine samples for evidence of impaired kidney function or metabolic (see METABOLISM) abnormalities, including the 'inborn errors of metabolism' (e.g. phenylketonuria, alkaptonuria, and galactosaemia) first recognized and defined by Sir Archibald Garrod (1857-1936). In these disorders a defective genetical programming has the consequence that some ENZYME necessary for metabolism is missing so that intermediate metabolites, some of which may be toxic, accumulate in the body, or some biochemical function is missing altogether. The consequences of these single enzyme defects are often widespread throughout the body: thus both phenylketonuria and galactosaemia may have secondary effects on the central NERVOUS SYSTEM leading to an impairment of mental function, while galactosaemia may be associated with cataract. In many modern departments of pathology the experimental approach is supplanting the merely descriptive.　　　　　　　　　　P.M.

Bibl: H.W. Florey (ed.), *General Pathology* (London and Philadelphia, 4th ed., 1970).

patriarchalism. In the writings of historians of political thought, it refers to the 17th-century doctrine that the authority of kings over their subjects is of the same kind as that of fathers over their children, and in both cases is absolute and arbitrary. The political theory of John Locke was a wholesale refutation of this doctrine and therefore a justification of the 'Glorious Revolution' of 1688.　　　　　　A.R.

Bibl: G. Schochet, *Patriarchalism in Political Thought* (Oxford, 1975); E. Figes, *Patriarchal Attitudes* (Greenwich, Conn., 1971).

patriarchy. Derived from the Greek 'rule of the father'. The term describes authority and control exercised by men over women. Patriarchy is used as a concept by feminists (see FEMINISM) to refer to what is perceived to be a fundamental and universal state of male dominance. Patriarchy is both a state of affairs (i.e. men control social institutions) and an IDEOLOGY (embedded in languages). Kate Millett's *Sexual Politics* (1969) was a landmark in the study of patriarchy. Questions of GENDER, the nature of the family and the process of socialization were highlighted in understanding the nature of male supremacy. For Millett, the political relationship between the sexes was central to patriarchy, and male power was expressed and contained in the sexual act itself. Other feminists have pursued the question of male power in studies of PORNOGRAPHY and rape (e.g. A. Dworkin, *Pornography*, 1981 and S. Brownmiller, *Against Our Will*, 1975). The examination of the material bases of patriarchy (rather than the ideological or pyschological) has focused upon the place of women in public (in the workplace) and in private (in the home). One strand of this debate has drawn on the work of Engels (*The Origin of the Family,*

Private Property and the State, 1884) to locate the origins of patriarchy within a particular MODE OF PRODUCTION. Firestone has taken Engels's MATERIALIST interpretation in a new direction. Patriarchy is understood to have its foundations in biological materialism, establishing the primacy of sex class over economic CLASS (S. Firestone, *The Dialectic of Sex*, 1970). Other writers have avoided evolutionary speculations and biological materialism. Patriarchy is understood as historically variable and as stemming from a complex of factors, particularly from the articulation of public and private domains.　A.G.

Bibl: H. Eisenstein, *Contemporary Feminist Thought* (London, 1984).

patri-clan, see under CLAN.

patrilineal. Refers to the tracing of DESCENT through a single line from an ancestor, the male line. Patrilineality may act as a principle governing relations between people in terms of the inheritance of property or succession to office. It may also be the basis for the recruitment to a social group, a patrilineal descent group. A society may be described as patrilineal, but need not necessarily have patrilineal descent groups. A patrilineal descent group consists of the male descendants of a particular ancestor, his brothers and sons. The degree of corporateness may vary, but usually the women — sisters and daughters — marry out of the LINEAGE. The men bring in women as wives. Husbands pay BRIDEWEALTH and thereby acquire rights over the domestic, sexual and reproductive powers of their wives. This MARRIAGE arrangement is called *patrilocal* (men stay put, women move). POLYGYNY is common in patrilineal societies and the wives perpetuate the lineage of their husbands by bearing children. ANCESTOR WORSHIP may be found in association with a patrilineal descent group.　　　　　　　　　A.G.

Bibl: D. Parkin, *The Cultural Definition of Political Response: Lineal Destiny Among the Luo* (London, 1978); Rubie S. Watson, *Inequality Among Brothers: Class and Kinship in South China* (Cambridge, 1985).

patrilocal marriage, see under PATRILINEAL.

patronage. NETWORK of strategic links through which individuals gain access to resources. It is a system founded upon an unequal distribution of POWER. The patron has standing, wealth, contacts and in entering into a relationship with him a CLIENT is offered access to the sources of power. The relationship between patron and client is complex and involves a diversity of transactions. It is usually long term and cast in terms of quasi or spiritual KINSHIP. There is a strong element of personal loyalty and essentially the relationship is voluntary rather than contractual. It is closely linked with the concept of HONOUR. Systems or networks of patronage most commonly involve relationships between individuals (not corporate groups).

It has been suggested that patronage is a feature of societies where at the local level there is little corporate sense or group solidarity, for example the bilateral (see BILATERAL/COGNATIC DESCENT) societies of the Mediterranean. There is very limited autonomous access to sources of power except through structures of mediation. A number of writers have also understood certain forms of religious practice as an integral part of this particular social configuration. For example CATHOLICISM has been linked to systems of patronage. In Catholicism access to spiritual power is through the mediation of a priesthood or hierarchy of saints.   A.G.

Bibl: S.N. Eisenstadt and L. Roniger, *Patrons, Clients and Friends* (Cambridge, 1984); Caroline White, *Patrons and Partisans* (Cambridge, 1980).

pattern variables. In PARSONIAN theory, a set of paired terms specifying the ranges of variability within which persons engaging in social interaction orient themselves to one another. They were originally formulated as (1) *affectivity v. affective neutrality* (does the relationship involve EMOTION, or not?); (2) *self-orientation v. collectivity-orientation* (is the other person to be appraised in relation to my personal goals, or to those of some larger group?); (3) *universalism v. particularism* (does the other person represent a category, or something unique?); (4) *achievement v. ascription* (does the other's STATUS depend on his achievements, or on attributes

beyond his control?); (5) *specificity v. diffuseness* (is the other's participation based on some specialized interest or qualification, or not?). For the most part, people assume and adjust orientations without reflection or conscious effort, because standardized expectations about behaviour in social ROLES are learned, as more or less habitual responses, in the form of NORMATIVE 'patterns'. There is only a limited number of such patterns culturally available to a society. Any pattern is in principle capable of description in terms of the five variables. This is the simplest version; in later work Parsons has modified this scheme in order to integrate it with other parts of his theory.   J.R.T.

Bibl: T. Parsons, 'Pattern Variables Revisited' (*American Sociological Review*, 25, 1960), pp. 467-85; T. Parsons and E.A. Shils (eds.), *Toward a General Theory of Action* (Cambridge, Mass., 1959).

Pavlovian. Relating to the work or views of the Russian physiologist I.P. Pavlov (1849-1936). Studying in Petersburg University, Pavlov developed a lasting passion for nervous PHYSIOLOGY. His major contribution to science came in the fields of the circulation of the blood, the physiology of digestion (for which he was awarded a Nobel Prize) and the physiology of the brain (his most famous work).

Pavlov maintained that the NERVOUS SYSTEM controls all physiological activity, and saw its function as being, in addition to the conduction of nervous impulses, one of setting up patterns of excitation for the control of functions and also of inhibiting impulse patterns once they had been started in the nervous system. Above all, however, he conceived of the nervous system as being involved in making connections between neural patterns so that there could be set up associations in the nervous system that mirrored associations between stimuli in the external world, as well as between incoming stimuli and responses that had been made to them in the past. The principal result of this form of connecting activity in the nervous system, known as CLASSICAL CONDITIONING, shows that the nervous system is adaptive, permitting the organism to anticipate crucial events by virtue of their being signalled by those events which precede them, thus also permitting the organism to respond in advance with an appropriate reaction. Pavlov considered the importance of the CONDITIONED REFLEX to be its role in the general organization of higher nervous systems. This organization he saw as the basis for the formation of human temperament. In his later writings, Pavlov distinguished between classical conditioning and the SECOND-SIGNAL SYSTEM.

Pavlov also emphasized the adaptive value of *inhibition*, the process by which it was possible for the organism to withhold response in the nervous system initially to protect the nervous system from firing too intensely, and which later provided a means of delay in response appropriate to the nature of the situation. He extended this notion of the adaptive function of inhibition by suggesting that sleep was itself an extension of inhibition which allowed the nervous system to recover. Pavlov was also much interested in the problem of generalization of response to an array of stimuli. This problem he attempted to solve by the doctrine of *irradiation*, a process whereby responses would be made not only to the stimuli to which they had initially been conditioned, but also to a range of similar stimuli. He extended the concept of irradiation well beyond its original meaning, and talked about the irradiation of inhibition and excitation to account for certain general response tendencies important to the development of temperament and character. Towards the end of his life Pavlov's interest moved increasingly towards PSYCHIATRY. Pavlov's lasting importance lay partly in directing neurophysiological research increasingly in the direction of the study of animal behaviour, and partly came through showing the crucial significance of conditioned reflex activity within a largely vitalist (see VITALISM) framework.　　　　　　G.M.; J.S.B.; R. P.

Bibl: B. Simon (ed.), *Psychology in the Soviet Union* (London and Stanford, 1957); I.P. Pavlov, *Experimental Psychology and Other Essays* (New York, 1957; London, 1958); J.A. Gray, *Pavlov* (London, 1979).

pax Americana. The concept of a peace imposed by North American rule or, more broadly, the settlement of conflict on U.S. terms and in accordance with U.S. interests. A variation on the term *pax romana*, it has been used in recent years primarily with reference to the current crises in Central America.　　　　　　N.M.

Peace Movement. The umbrella term given to diverse groups, organizations and political efforts in several countries since the mid-1970s and to their antecedents such as those of the late 1950s and early 1960s. The term is arguably a misnomer, as the movement is less concerned with international frameworks for peace, more with its explicit objective of the abolition of NUCLEAR WEAPONS. Its modern form evolved in Britain and in the Netherlands through opposition to the NEUTRON BOMB; it expanded in both countries and more widely in western Europe in response to the planned introduction of more and new nuclear weapons including CRUISE and Pershing II, and to the foreign and defence policies of President Reagan in the U.S. after 1980.

The movement assumes different forms and is of different strength in the Scandinavian nations, West Germany, Belgium, the Netherlands, Italy and Britain. In Britain its main voice is the *Campaign for Nuclear Disarmament* (CND) which was founded in 1958, reached its first peak of activity in 1961-2 and diminished until the mid-1970s. It now has a national and local membership of respectively some 100,000 and 250,000; it pursues tactics including peaceful DIRECT ACTION, mass demonstrations and support for the smaller, less organized but highly publicized 'peace camp' of women at the U.S. Air Force base at Greenham Common in Berkshire.

There are analogous movements elsewhere which oppose either current or any levels of production or deployment of nuclear weapons, as in New Zealand, Japan and the U.S. (see NUCLEAR FREEZE MOVEMENT), and movements in east European countries which form part of broader critiques of their regimes.　　　　　　S.R.

Bibl: *Journal of Peace Research*, Vol. 23, No.2 (Oslo, June 1986); J. Minnion and P. Bolsover, *The CND Story* (London, 1983).

peaceful coexistence, see COEXISTENCE, PEACEFUL.

peacekeeping. The interposition of UNO forces, armed only for self-defence, between antagonists on the assumption that they will keep the peace if they are denied any easy way of attack and are protected from the escalation of accidental firing or skirmishes. UN forces, usually drawn from small powers, played this role so successfully that they have been largely forgotten, for example between Greeks and Turks in Cyprus and between Israelis and Syrians on the Golan heights. The withdrawal of the post-SUEZ UN Expeditionary force from Egypt at Nasser's request was the prelude to the MIDDLE EAST WAR (1967). The UN Interim Force in LEBANON, established after a limited Israeli invasion of Lebanon in March 1978, enjoyed a hazardous life before and after Israeli forces swept through its lines in their second invasion (June 1982). A Multinational Force (American, British and French contingents) established outside the UN in August 1982, supporting the Lebanese Army and supervising the withdrawal of the PLO, found itself trying to make rather than keep the peace; its mission ended disastrously especially for the Americans who suffered a suicidal TERRORIST attack. W.K.

pecking order, see under DOMINANCE.

pedestrian segregation. The separation of vehicles and pedestrians on plan or section or both so as to avoid conflict between the two; Venice is the classic prototype. Serious proposals started in the 19th century when London's horse-drawn traffic created great problems; Olmsted and Vaux's plan of about 1868 for Central Park is an early American example and the principle was further elaborated by Le Corbusier in 1935 in *La Ville radieuse*. Most examples today consist of the closure of existing streets to vehicles, frequently to provide pedestrian shopping precincts, and the building of pedestrian decks raised above cars; in housing areas separation is often based on the RADBURN LAYOUT. M.BR.

pedology. A component part of SOIL SCIENCE concerned with the study of soils as naturally occurring phenomena, particularly their MORPHOLOGY (see also HORIZON), CLASSIFICATION, and distribution on the land surface. The aims of pedology are to describe the properties of soils and to identify the processes which have produced particular soils. The subject has suffered from the lack of a universal system of soil classification. J.L.M.L.

peer group. A group of people who regard themselves, or who are regarded, as of approximately equal standing in the larger society to which they belong; standing can be defined in terms of a very wide range of CRITIERIA. M.BE.

Peinture de la Realité poétique, see under MAGIC REALISM.

PEMEX (Petroleos Mexicanos, Mexican Petroleum). The STATE oil company of Mexico, created in 1938 after NATIONALIST President Lazaro Cardenas had expropriated the entire petroleum industry. Since 1950 it has had a monopoly of drilling, transporting, refining and marketing of Mexico's immense oil and gas resources (by 1979 Mexico had proven hydrocarbon reserves of over 40 billion barrels). It leases concessions for the operation of retail service stations. Particularly since 1972, when the first large discoveries were made in the Tabasco and Chiapas regions, PEMEX has played an extremely important role in the Mexican economy, and the Director of PEMEX is a member of the Cabinet. N.M.
  Bibl: George Philip, 'Oil and Politics in Latin America', *Cambridge Latin American Studies* (1982), chapter 17.

penetrance. In GENETICS, the frequency with which a dominant GENE (or a recessive gene in a homozygote) manifests itself in the phenotype (see GENOTYPE). The fact that penetrance is not always 100% implies that some genes require a particular environment before they are expressed. J.M.S.

penis envy. In FREUDIAN theory, the female desire to possess male genitals; a desire arising initially out of the small girl's assumption that because she lacks a penis she must at some stage have been castrated (see CASTRATION ANXIETY). Postulated as universal by Freud, the phenomenon has been challenged on theoretical grounds by some psychologists, and on experiential grounds by some women.

W.Z.

penology. The study of the punishment and treatment of criminals. Penology originated in, and has remained closely linked with, the movement of penal reform which developed at the end of the 18th century, notably in the writings of the Marquis de Beccaria (1738-94) in Italy, and of John Howard (1726-90). Jeremy Bentham (1748-1832) was concerned to develop the principles of UTILITARIANISM as a basis for the treatment of offenders. Numerous theorists in the 19th century in Britain and the U.S.A. were influential in the introduction of new methods of treating offenders, notably within what were termed *penitentiaries*. The subject has expanded to cover all aspects of the treatment of offenders, including prisons, institutions for young offenders, and mental treatment, as well as all forms of noncustodial disposal such as probation and fines.

T.M.

Bibl: R.J. Gerber and P.D. McAnany (eds.), *Contemporary Punishment* (London, 1972); W. Carson and P. Miles (eds.), *Crime and Delinquency in Britain* (London, 1976).

pentecostalism. The gift of the Holy Spirit is described in the Bible (Acts 2) as having descended on the 50th day (Greek *pentekoste*) after the Jewish Passover festival, with extraordinary resultant phenomena. In the 20th century many Christians have claimed to experience the same gift (in Greek, CHARISMA) and phenomena, and are referred to as the *Charismatic Movement*. Some have remained in the historic Churches but may have organized themselves in Pentecostal Churches, specially in the U.S.A. and Latin America, with a strong emphasis on informality, confidence, and joy, and a THEOLOGY mostly FUNDAMENTALIST. The largest such Church is the 'Assemblies of God, U.S.A.' The rapidly spreading 'independent' Churches in Africa, which are free from Western control and influence, have many similar characteristics. See also QUAKERS.

D.L.E.

Bibl: W.W.J. Hollenweger, tr. R.A. Wilson, *The Pentecostals* (London and Minneapolis, 1972).

people's democracy. A COMMUNIST euphemism for regimes which display the machinery of public participation in government while denying the electorate any real choice between political parties. Such regimes are usually distinguished by the absence of those legal and constitutional restraints on the use of the power of the State which are essential to DEMOCRACY or to any genuine PARTICIPATION by 'the people' in the processes of government.

D.C.W.

Bibl: F. Fejtö, tr. D. Weissbort, *A History of the People's Democracies* (London and New York, 1971); F.J. Kase, *People's Democracy* (Leyden, 1968).

peptide. A relatively simple polymeric molecule formed by the conjunction of AMINO ACIDS (see POLYMER; MOLECULE). The simple or short-chain peptides are called *oligopeptides* and include many biological effectors such as hormones (see ENDOCRINOLOGY) — e.g. oxytocin and vasopressin — whereas the larger, long-chain *polypeptides* grade directly into PROTEINS which are essentially polypeptides, e.g. the trophic hormones of the anterior PITUITARY, INSULIN, etc. P.M.

percentile. In STATISTICS there is often a need to describe an empirical DISTRIBUTION roughly. One way to do this is to state a few scale values dividing the distribution in predetermined proportions. A scale value such that there is an $x\%$ chance of an observation falling to the left of it is an $x\%$ *percentile*. The 25% and 75% percentiles (with half the distribution between them and a quarter on either side) are the *quartiles* and the 50% percentile (with half the distribution on either side of it) is the *median*, which is sometimes used as a MEASURE OF LOCATION. R.SI.

percept, see SENSE DATUM.

perception. In general, awareness or appreciation of objects or situations, usually by the senses. Historically, perception was a branch of OPTICS. Till the 17th century it was commonly assumed that vision depended upon rays issuing forth from the eye, rather than emitted from the object and striking the eye. From the 18th century, perception became embodied within emergent SENSATIONALIST psychology. Specific technical meanings are related to the many theories of perception still extant in PHILOSOPHY, PSYCHOLOGY, and PHYSIOLOGY. It is a theory-laden word, and so changes its meanings and implications across rival theories. There are, in particular, two essentially different theories of perception:

(1) That perceptions are *selections of reality*: i.e. they are essentially like, and made of the same stuff as, objects of the external world. This notion has a strong appeal to philosophers wishing to accept perceptions as the unquestionable basis of empirical TRUTH. Errors of perception — illusions and hallucinations — are clearly embarrassing for such a theory; and indeed the *argument from illusion* (see ILLUSION) claims to disprove it. How can we know that a perception is true, if we have reason to believe that other perceptions appearing just as sound are illusory?

(2) That perceptions are not any kind of selection of reality; but are rather *accounts, descriptions*, or, most interesting, *hypotheses* of the object world. On this view perception is only indirectly related to reality, and there is no difficulty over illusions. But, correspondingly, it offers no guarantee that any particular perception can be relied upon as true. Thus all knowledge based on perceptions is essentially uncertain; perceptions must be checked before they can be relied upon, and even then perhaps no set of perceptions can be *completely* trusted as true. It is generally accepted that this holds also for all scientific observations, instrument-readings, or signals.

The status of perception may be very like that of scientific hypotheses. What we see is affected by what is likely; and we can be driven into error by following assumptions which are not appropriate for the available sensory data. This is a development of Hermann von Helmholtz's notion that perceptions are unconscious inferences from sensory and memory data.

Some illusions may be fallacies of perceptual inference. Furthermore there has been considerable dispute as to the status of perception. One school (essentially EMPIRICIST) stresses that perceptions are built up through slow, gradual, complex, acquired learning processes. Another (the GESTALT) sees perceptual organization as more innate and holistic.   R.L.G.;R.P.

Bibl: Maurice Merleau-Ponty, *The Phenomenology of Perception* (London, 1962); R. L. Gregory, *Eye and Brain* (3rd ed., London, 1977; New York, 1978) and *The Intelligent Eye* (London and New York, 1970); D. Vernon, *The Psychology of Perception* (London, 1962).

perceptual defence. A process of unconscious 'censorship' that prevents PERCEPTION of unacceptable events, objects, words, etc., as when TABOO words presented briefly in a *tachistoscope* are 'normalized' into an acceptable form. It is usually contrasted with *perceptual vigilance*, a state of increased sensitivity to threatening or unacceptable events.   J.S.B.

Bibl: F.H. Allport, *Theories of Perception and the Concept of Structure* (London and New York, 1955).

perceptual realism, see under REALISM.

perfect competition. A hypothetical state referring to a market or the economy as a whole. The conditions of such a state are: (1) within each industry, each firm produces an identical product; (2) each firm and individual consumers pursue their own material objectives; (3) there is no restriction on what persons or firms can buy or sell; (4) each firm and person is small and has no effect on the prices at which goods, services and inputs are traded; (5) there is perfect information (this assumption can be relaxed); (6) there are no EXTERNALITIES. A COMPETITIVE EQUILIBRIUM is an equilibrium of a perfectly competitive economy. A competitive equilibrium is ECONOMICALLY EFFICIENT and, thus, is usually considered as desirable. The desirability of the PRICE MECHANISM, COMPETITION and FREE MARKETS is based on this view. However, the distribution of income in a perfectly competitive economy is not necessarily desirable. In economic markets that most closely resemble perfect competition, e.g. certain markets for agricultural produce, there have been examples of chronic and wasteful instability. Though the above assumptions are unrealistic, perfect competition is often used as a MODEL of markets and the economy.   J.P.

Bibl: J. Craven, *Introduction to Economics* (Oxford, 1984).

perfect equilibrium. A concept in ECONOMICS and GAME THEORY, introduced by R. Selten. It disallows threats or plans that are not credible. As in a NASH EQUILIBRIUM, each player (competing firm, negotiator, or combatant) does what best serves his own interests, given the strategies of others. The special feature is that these strategies should never require actions that are not best for the player at the time when they are to be taken. For example, it is inadmissible to attempt deterrence by threatening actions that would not, in the event, be rational, once the past must be taken as given. The concept provides a powerful theory of bargaining. If accepted, it also means that reputation and nuclear DETERRENCE can be explained only by supposing that each participant thinks there is some chance that others would irrationally adhere to unenforceable commitments.   J.A.M.

Bibl: K.G. Binmore and P.S. Dasgupta, *Bargaining* (Oxford, 1986).

performance art. A kind of art which in its purest form would claim to be a branch of the visual arts differing from painting or sculpture only in its use of live performers as material and, as a consequence, having only a temporary existence within finite limits of time. Many of the HAPPENINGS AND EVENTS of the 1960s and 1970s were of this kind. However, the introduction of language, music and the technical skills of actors and dancers tends to enlarge the aesthetic response evoked by performance art and place it in a theatrical context. Some performance groups, notably the People Show (founded 1966) in its early years, owed their disruptive effects to the aesthetics of DADA and Artaud's THEATRE OF CRUELTY.   M.A.

Bibl: J. Nuttall, *Performance Art* (London and Dallas, 1979); R. Goldberg,

Performance: Live Art 1909 to the Present (London, 1979).

performance tests, see under MENTAL TESTING.

performative. In LINGUISTICS, deriving from the work of the philosopher J.L. Austin (1911-60), a type of sentence where an action is 'performed' by virtue of a sentence having been uttered, e.g. *I apologize..., I promise..., I baptize you....* Performative verbs have a particular significance in SPEECH ACT theory, as they mark the ILLOCUTIONARY force of an utterance in an explicit way. Performative utterances are usually contrasted with *constative* utterances: the latter are descriptive statements which, unlike performatives, can be analysed in terms of TRUTH-VALUES.   D.C.

Bibl: S. Levinson, *Pragmatics* (Cambridge, 1983).

period analysis, see under COHORT ANALYSIS.

period-luminosity relation. A fundamental problem of ASTRONOMY has been the nature of *variable stars*, i.e., ones whose brightness changes. They were first discovered in the 16th century. By the end of the 18th century, thanks largely to the observations of Delta Cephei by John Goodricke, the regularities of their variations had been ascertained. The introduction of photography into astronomy in the 1840s vastly increased the number of variable stars (or CEPHEIDS) known: some 19,000 variable stars are known to exist today. The major problem with such stars has been establishing the relation between observed brightness and real luminosity; for this, the work of Ejnar Hertzsprung (1873-1967) and Henry Norris Russell (1877-1957) towards the understanding of their periodicity has been crucial. On this basis, Edwin Hubble (1889-1953) was able to demonstrate that spiral nebulae were external GALAXIES, and Walter Baade further built upon Hubble's findings to show that the galaxies were about twice as distant as previously thought.   R.P.

Bibl: R. Smith, *The Expanding Universe* (Cambridge, 1982).

periodic functions. The FUNCTION $f(t)$ is *periodic with period T* and *frequency* $1/T$ if $f(t + T) = f(t)$ for all values of t. Mathematically and physically the simplest periodic functions are those describing *simple harmonic motion*; they have the form $f(t) = A \sin(2\pi t/T + \theta)$ or equivalently $f(t) = a \cos(2\pi t/T) + b \sin(2\pi t/T)$. Such a function has as its graph a *sine wave*; it is recognized by the ear as a pure tone, in SPECTROSCOPY as a spectral line, and is the ideal form of alternating current. Other periodic functions can be broken down into simple harmonic constituents by FOURIER ANALYSIS. R.G.

periodic table. An arrangement of the chemical ELEMENTS into rows and columns; it was discovered by the Russian chemist Mendeleev in 1869. The ATOMIC NUMBER increases across each row and from one row to the next, while the chemical properties (e.g. VALENCY) of the elements in each column are similar (e.g. the 'inert gases' helium, neon, argon, etc. lie in the same column). The physical basis of the periodic table is explained by ATOMIC PHYSICS: elements in a given column contain the same number of ELECTRONS in the unfilled outer ELECTRON SHELL, while elements in a given row have the same number of filled shells. M.V.B.

peripheral devices (*peripherals*), see under INPUT/OUTPUT.

peripheral nervous system, see under NERVOUS SYSTEM.

permanent education. A CONCEPT based on the belief that education ought not to be concentrated into childhood and adolescence but should be seen as a lifelong process. The term comes from France, where advocates of *éducation permanente* lay stress on the value of a return to education in adult years for vocational or other utilitarian purposes. Alternative terms for this are *in-service training* (for teachers) and *post-experience education* (for managers). But there is no reason why permanent education should be limited to vocational purposes, and in this larger sense it has much the same meaning as adult or continuing education. W.A.C.S.

Bibl: *Adult Education* (Russell Report, London, 1973).

permanent revolution. An expression first used by Marx in his *Address to the Communist League* (1850), but mostly associated with Trotsky who between 1904 and 1906 developed it into a theory which put Russia potentially at the forefront of world REVOLUTION. The argument rested on the idea that it was possible to have a SOCIALIST revolution in an economically backward country. Trotsky held that in Russia the BOURGEOISIE was too weak to oppose the Tsarist autocracy in its own interests and envisaged a direct revolutionary confrontation between the autocracy and the PROLETARIAT. While the proletariat might begin by demanding merely LIBERAL reforms, it could only retain power by making the revolution 'permanent' and immediately proceeding to implement socialist policies — a viewpoint to which Lenin himself was converted during the course of 1917. A second element in the notion of permanent revolution was that the establishment of socialism in the Soviet Union could only be successful if the revolution were to spread to the more advanced CAPITALIST countries — a viewpoint originally shared by all the BOLSHEVIKS, but later contested by Stalin with his slogan of 'socialism in one country'. Permanent revolution is thus the central concept of what came to be known as TROTSKYISM. D.T.M.

Bibl: B. Knei-paz, *The Social and Political Thought of Leon Trotsky* (Oxford, 1978); L. Trotsky, *Permanent Revolution* (New York, 1962).

permissiveness. The view that the individual's pursuit of pleasure should, provided no harm is done to others, be unrestricted by external factors such as laws or by internal guilt arising from social conventions. The 'permissive society', a cliché of the late 1960s, was exemplified by the decline of stage and film censorship, by public acquiescence in the relaxation of certain moral and social conventions, and by a series of legislative derestrictions on HOMOSEXUALITY between consenting adults, ABORTION, divorce, etc. Although legislation of this type indicates toleration rather than endorsement, there has subsequently been a public reaction which seeks a return to more rigid moral and social conventions and prescriptions. There have recently been attempts to trace the sources of endemic social problems back to 1960s permissiveness, but this narrowly political reaction appears not to be widespread.   P.S.L.

permutation. In MATHEMATICS, traditionally, any rearrangement of a finite SET A of objects. More abstractly it is a FUNCTION f which assigns to each a in A an object b in A (the new occupant of a's place) such that to distinct ARGUMENTS there correspond distinct values and such that every b in A is a value of f for some argument. The latter definition applies equally well to INFINITE sets; it includes the identity function ($f(a) = a$). The set of all permutations of A form a GROUP.
                                                                R.G.

permutational. Adjective applied to works of art where a prescribed set of elements, rules, or dimensions is subjected to variation, whether controlled by the artist or of an ALEATORY kind. Essential to music (especially SERIAL MUSIC), such treatment may also occur in the visual arts (notably in OP ART), in writing (as in anagrams and word-games and some kinds of CONCRETE POETRY), and in photography and film. It can also lead to the production of subtly varied MULTIPLES, particularly when guided by a COMPUTER as in COMPUTER GRAPHICS; the art then lies in the structure and sequence of the data fed to the machine.   J.W.

Peronism. An IDEOLOGY associated with the name of Juan Perón (1895-1974), elected ruler of Argentina (1946-1955) and his wife Eva (Evita). It involved: in domestic affairs, the mass demagogic organization of the Argentinian WORKING CLASS in labour unions and a workers' militia against the upper-middle-class ELITES; an organization backed by mass social-security and other redistributive methods on the one hand, and repression on the other; in foreign affairs, the espousal of the so-called 'Third Position', whereby Argentina was to steer a middle course between CAPITALISM (the U.S.) and COMMUNISM (the U.S.S.R.); the inflamma-

tion of Argentinian national feelings against the U.S. and the claim that Argentina should lead Latin America. Perón proved unable to solve the economic problems facing his country and lost much support after Evita's death in 1952; but his prestige was such that it brought him back to the presidency by popular acclaim in 1972. On his death in 1974, the Peronist cause was briefly led by his second wife and successor as president, but foundered with the revelations of incompetence and corruption that followed her 1976 overthrow by the military. The Peronist movement is still influential in Argentinian politics, however, and is particularly strong among the labour unions.
                                                        D.C.W.;N.M.

Bibl: Frederick C. Turner and José Enrique Miguens (eds.), *Juan Perón and the Reshaping of Argentina* (Pittsburgh, Pa., 1983).

personal computer. A MICROCOMPUTER designed to satisfy the needs of a single user without requiring an expert operator. The absence of the need to share the computer among several independent users greatly simplifies the task of the OPERATING SYSTEM; the art is to provide a repertoire of useful facilities which can be easily used by beginners. The advent of these machines has had an enormous impact on computer sales and applications. At present the U.K. leads the world in sales of computers per head of population, but it uses them very largely for video games: the proportion of machines with DISC STORES, almost essential for their use as an aid to thought, is lower than elsewhere.
                                                              J.E.S.

personal idealism, see under PERSONALISM.

personalism. A form of IDEALISM which holds that everything real is a person or an element in the experience of some person. Inspired more by Berkeley than by Leibniz (whose MONADS, although described as souls, are too simple to count as persons), it is generally opposed to the absolute idealism of Hegel in which all finite persons are absorbed into an ABSOLUTE which transcends personality (see TRANSCENDENCE). The *personal idealism* of such dissenters from absolute idealism as McTaggart and Rashdall around the turn of the century is perhaps the most philosophically significant form of personalism, but it has been more recently exemplified in modern French NEO-THOMISM, and there has been a continuing tradition of personalism in the U.S.A. with a strong theistic tendency (see THEISM).　　　　　　　A.Q.

personalistic psychology. An approach to PSYCHOLOGY that takes as its FRAME OF REFERENCE the individual person as a unique, unitary being, and relates fractional studies of PERCEPTION, learning, and the like to this personal frame of reference.　　　　　　　　　　I.M.L.H.

Bibl: W. Stern, tr. A Barwell, *Psychology of Early Childhood* (London and New York, 2nd ed., 1930).

personality cult. The formula employed by Soviet advocates of COLLECTIVE LEADERSHIP against any of their number who seems to be accumulating too much personal power and consequent public adulation. It was first employed after Stalin's death in 1953 to discredit those who attempted to capitalize on his memory, and was one of the central themes of Khrushchev's denunciation of the STALINIST era in his 'secret speech' to the 20th congress of the Soviet Communist Party (25 February 1956). The accusation was subsequently employed to discredit Khrushchev himself after his resignation in 1964. It was also used in China by the successors of Mao Tse-tung to criticize his methods of leadership.　　　　　　　　　D.C.W.;D.PR.

Bibl: R. Conquest, *Power and Policy in the U.S.S.R.* (London and New York, 1961).

personality tests, see under MENTAL TESTING.

personality types. Idealized descriptions of personality derived either by statistical procedures (e.g. FACTOR ANALYSIS) or by theoretical postulation or by some more or less skilful combination of the two. Historically and in contemporary practice, types are based upon differences in physiological hormonal functioning (see ENDOCRINOLOGY) that reflects itself in temperament, as in the CLASSIFICATION by Galen of the *phlegmatic*, the *choleric*, the *melancholic*, and the *sanguine* that were outward manifestations of the so-called bodily humours. One of the most successful efforts to describe personality types in relation to body type is W.H. Sheldon's. By careful anthropomorphic measurement, he has been able to distinguish three basic physical types (most individual subjects appearing as a mix): the round, soft *endomorph*, the square, muscular *mesomorph*, and the long, thin *ectomorph*. By the use of personality tests (see MENTAL TESTING), Sheldon established temperamental qualities associated with these. With endomorphy goes *viscerotonia*, a certain passivity and pleasure in sensation; with mesomorphy, *somatotonia*, a pleasure in physical activity; with ectomorphy, *cerebrotonia*, a pleasure in the exercise of COGNITIVE activities. Another attempt was made by Jung, in his postulation not only of the well-known types characterized by INTROVERSION and EXTROVERSION, but also of types contrasted in terms of orientation towards the world: sensation-oriented v. thought-oriented, feeling-oriented v. instinct-oriented. The isolating of *function types* that may be mixed in any given individual is most closely associated with H.J. Eysenck. Work on *value types*, represented principally by the Allport-Vernon-Lindzey *Study of Values* (1951), is aimed at establishing dominant value orientations (i.e. political, aesthetic, social, religious, theoretical) and has achieved considerable predictive success. See also CONVERGERS AND DIVERGERS.　　　　　　　J.S.B.

perspectivism. In PHILOSOPHY, the theory that there are alternative systems of CONCEPTS and assumptions, not equivalent to each other, in whose terms the world may be interpreted and as between which there is no authoritative external way of making a choice. It is to be found in the philosophy of Nietzsche, for whom belief systems are instruments serving the impulse to survive and succeed and, in a less passionate and more domesticated form, in Ortega y Gasset. Broadly analogous conclusions have been reached by Ajdukiewicz and Quine (the latter under WHORFIAN inspiration). They maintain that there are, or can be, different languages which are not translatable into each other and which supply their speakers with quite different pictures of the world. Like other sceptical hypotheses of comparable generality, perspectivism invites the question: is it not itself just one perspective on thought and language among others, with no greater claim to validity than they have?   A.Q.

PERT (programme, evaluation, and review technique). A form of CRITICAL PATH ANALYSIS, in which expected timings of stages in a project are used to calculate a range of probable completion times, of varying degrees of pessimism or optimism. Many COMPUTER-assisted routines used by MANAGEMENT for project scheduling and control are derived from the PERT method, which was devised in 1958 by the U.S. Navy for the POLARIS submarine project.   R.I.T.

Bibl: A. Battersby, *Network Analysis for Planning and Scheduling* (London and New York, 3rd ed., 1978).

perversion. Deviation from the NORMS of sexual practice; for examples see HOMO-SEXUALITY; MASOCHISM; SADISM; SADO-MASOCHISM. Attitudes to such perversions or (the more neutral word) deviations have shifted, increasingly since the KINSEY REPORT (1948-53) and the Wolfenden Report (1957), from censorious condemnation to greater PERMISSIVENESS.   O.S.

Pestalozzi methods. Educational principles associated with Johann Heinrich Pestalozzi (1746-1827), a Swiss from Zurich. Pestalozzi (who at the age of 5 was left fatherless) stressed the importance of the mother and the home in the early education of a child, and the need to call on the personal sensory experience of children in helping them to develop ideas, and to use their surroundings in teaching them to synthesize experience. Pestalozzi's ideas and methods were widely influential in Prussia through the influence of Fichte and were brought to England by the Mayos and Kay-Shuttleworth.   W.A.C.S.

Bibl: K. Silber, *Pestalozzi* (London, 1960).

PET scanning. Positron emission tomography (PET) has been developed to study brain function and damage from outside the brain. It makes use of certain RADIO-ISOTOPES that, on decay, produce SUB-ATOMIC PARTICLES known as POSITRONS. As the positrons react with surrounding brain matter a particular form of energy is generated. This can be recorded by detectors outside the brain and computed into an image that represents the distribution of the radioisotope in slices across the brain. PET scanning is being used to investigate regional and temporal activities in the healthy and diseased brain and, in particular, to explore the basis and diagnosis of psychiatric disease. It has an unparalleled potential for the study of the chemicals that transmit information between brain NEURONS via their RECEPTORS. Like other techniques that require expensive and sophisticated equipment, as well as considerable interpretative skills (such as NMR scanning — see RADIOLOGY — which it complements), PET scanning is a valuable clinical and research tool which can only be afforded by the most affluent countries.   P.N.

Peter Principle, see under PARKINSON'S LAW.

petit bourgeois. A member of the French *petite bourgeoisie*, as opposed to the *haute bourgeoisie* (see BOURGEOIS). The *petite bourgeoisie* were men of small-scale wealth and property, owners of individual shops, single houses, small plots of urban land, small workshops and factories, etc. The limited scale of their wealth was widely regarded as being paralleled by their limited horizons, narrow minds, and obscurantist attitude to art and culture. Hence the hyphenated adjective *petit-bourgeois* is most often used pejoratively — a connotation emphasized by the common anglicization of *petit* (or *petite*) as petty. See also POUJADISM.   D.C.W.

petrography. A division of PETROLOGY concerned with the description and CLASSIFICATION of rocks. Most rocks are aggregates of mineral grains, and an important part of the subject is the investigation of the texture of rocks, i.e. the shape and relationship of their constituent grains.   J.L.M.L.

petrology. The study of rocks, their composition (see under PETROGRAPHY), occurrence, and genesis. Three main classes of rocks are recognized, igneous, sedimentary, and metamorphic. *Igneous* rocks are those which have solidified from hot molten material called magma which is generated below the earth's crust (see LITHOSPHERE) and rises to cool on or just below the surface; *sedimentary* rocks are formed on the earth's surface, mainly on the sea floor, by the deposition of mineral matter weathered and transported from rocks on the land surface; *metamorphic* rocks are produced by the deep-seated alteration of pre-existing rocks due to the action of the few branches of GEOLOGY in which observation and analysis are supported by experimental work. J.L.M.L.

PGR (psychogalvanic response), see under GALVANIC SKIN RESPONSE.

pH. A convenient measure of the acidity or alkalinity of a solution (see ACID; ALKALI). Defined as the logarithm of the reciprocal of the hydrogen ION concentration, pH values in aqueous solutions range from 0 to 14. Pure water has a pH of 7. B.F.

phagocytes. CELLS which can nourish themselves by the direct entrapment and engulfment of solid particles, which are taken into the CYTOPLASM and digested by hydrolytic ENZYMES. *Phagocytosis*, the name given to this process of ingestion by cells, was discovered by the Russian zoologist Mechnikov, who may have attached undue importance to its role in bodily defences. Phagocytosis occurs in the amoeboid PROTOZOA and also among white blood corpuscles, particularly the monocytes, polymorphs, and the cells lining lymphatic sinuses. In the living organism phagocytosis of bacteria (see BACTERIOLOGY) is greatly promoted by the action of antibodies (see IMMUNITY). Thus bacteria which would not be phagocytized in their native state may come to be so if they are coated by an antibody. P.M.

phallic character, see under PSYCHOSEXUAL DEVELOPMENT.

phantasy. In Lacan's view, the phantasy is produced by the subject when confronted with the enigma of the DESIRE of the OTHER; the subject responds by offering to the Other his own loss, his own disappearance. The static, frozen aspect of phantasy is accounted for in terms of the object (see OBJECT(A)), the lost object that the subject brings into play to block the sliding of the signifying chain (see SYMBOLIC). On a structural level, phantasy is the neurotic's relation to JOUISSANCE. D.L.

pharmacology. The branch of BIOLOGY that deals with the properties and mode of action of DRUGS and other biological effectors, particularly those of external origin and thus conventionally excluding hormones, the subject-matter of ENDROCRINOLOGY. Pharmacology consists partly of a taxonomy or functional CLASSIFICATION of drugs (particularly in relation to chemical structure), partly study of their fate in the body and their metabolic transformations (see METABOLISM), and partly of an investigation of their mode of action, particularly at a cellular level; this investigation involves the identification of special drug receptors on the CELL surface and a detailed analysis of how the drug alters the cell's behaviour. It includes the study of anaesthetics, antidotes to drugs, and drug addiction. (The measuring, dispensing, and formulation of drugs is the subject-matter of *pharmacy*.) Among the biological agents that are not drugs in the conventional sense but come under the study of pharmacology are the ANTIBIOTICS. A most important branch of pharmacology is that which has to do with the standardization and testing of drugs — procedures specially necessary for those drugs which, being of biological origin, are often not chemically characterized and therefore not open to ordinary chemical methods of measurement and potency testing. Safety control is another important — sometimes vitally important — procedure associated with the preparation, marketing, and medical use of agents of biological origin such as hormones, antibodies (see IMMUNITY), and antibiotics. P.M.

phase. (1) In PHYSICS, an angle specifying position along a wave, or the extent to which two waves are 'in register'. One

643

complete cycle (crest + trough) corresponds to 360°. Thus waves which are a quarter wavelength out of step have a phase difference of 90°, while waves whose phase difference is 180° are half a wave out of step, and still interfere destructively if superimposed, because the crests cancel the troughs. (2) One of the chemically identical but physically different states of the same system; e.g. ice, water, and steam, or graphite and diamond (see also ALLOTROPE). M.V.B.

phase conjugate mirror. In PHYSICS, an optical device which reverses the PHASE of any light which it reflects. The most striking result of this is that, irrespective of the angle of the beam of light to the mirror, it is always reflected back along its original path, whereas with an ordinary mirror this would only occur if the light struck the mirror at right angles. The effect of phase conjugation goes much further than this, however, since any distortion which is produced in the wave before it enters the mirror will be reversed on reflection and the net effect is that distortion-free effects can be produced. Some examples are (1) an image of a picture or a diagram can be projected with complete faithfulness — this is being developed to produce microcircuits (see MICROELECTRONICS) containing very fine detail. (2) A point source of light, say from a LASER, can be focused back to a point (rather than to a tiny blob) — a property which is being exploited in the development of laser FUSION for power generation. (3) In fundamental physics the mirror is used in SPECTROSCOPY to produce and study lines of atomic spectra without the usual broadening which is introduced by atomic motion and collisions. The mirror effect is actually produced by the interference of beams of light in a NON-LINEAR OPTICAL medium. A hologram (see HOLOGRAPHY) is produced in the medium which when illuminated by another beam of light 'undoes' any distortion which was present in the beam which originally produced the hologram. H.M.R.

phase modulation. The variation of the PHASE of a high-frequency wave in proportion to the strength of another wave of much lower frequency. Phase modulation is very similar to FREQUENCY MODULATION. M.V.B.

phase shifting. The technique frequently used by Steve Reich of moving the emphasis or the starting point of a repeating musical phrase often against a solid rhythmic background or against itself. This change in the aspect of a musical phrase often makes the listener misinterpret what is basically a very simple technique and frequently hear countermelodies in the music that were not specifically intended by the composer. The technique often produces a hypnotic effect and forms an important part of PROCESS MUSIC. Phase shifting is also sometimes used to denote the electronic technique of slightly moving the phase or orientation of a soundwave against itself thus producing a richer sound. B.CO.

Bibl: S. Reich, *Writing about Music* (New York, 1974).

phatic language. In LINGUISTICS, a term deriving from the anthropologist Malinowski's phrase *phatic communion*, and applied to language used (as in comments on the weather or enquiries about health) for establishing an atmosphere rather than for exchanging information or ideas. D.C.

phenology. Study of the times of recurring natural phenomena. Used primarily within BIOLOGY for study of seasonal variations, e.g. in plant flowering times or bird migration. P.H.

phenomena (in PHILOSOPHY), see under NOUMENA.

phenomenalism. The theory, propounded by J.S. Mill, that material things are 'permanent possibilities of sensation'. It has been elaborately developed by ANALYTIC PHILOSOPHERS in this century, expressed in a more linguistic idiom as the (REDUCTIONIST) theory that statements about material things are equivalent in meaning to statements about actual and possible SENSE-DATA, the sense-data that an observer would have if certain conditions were satisfied. It seems an irresistible consequence of a radically EMPIRICIST theory of meaning together with the widespread philosophical assumption, created by the *argument from illusion* (see IL-LUSION), that material objects are not directly perceived (the *sense-datum theory*). But both of those premises are open to question. A.Q.

Bibl: A.J. Ayer, *The Foundations of Empirical Knowledge* (London and New York, 1940).

phenomenology.

(1) In PHILOSOPHY, a method of enquiry elaborated by Edmund Husserl as a development of his teacher's, Brentano's, conception of 'descriptive', as opposed to 'genetic', PSYCHOLOGY. It takes philosophy to begin from an exact, attentive inspection of one's mental, particularly intellectual, processes in which all assumptions about the causation, consequences, and wider significance of the mental process under inspection are eliminated ('bracketed'). Husserl was insistent that phenomenology is not an empirical technique. It is an *a priori* (see APRIORISM) investigation or scrutiny of ESSENCES or MEANINGS, the objective logical elements in thought that are common to different minds. The phenomenological method has been applied by others, notably Max Scheler, to less austerely intellectual subject-matter, and Husserl's pupil Heidegger used it for the investigation of the extreme states of mind in which, according to EXISTENTIALISM, the situation of man in the world is revealed. A.Q.

Bibl: H. Spiegelberg, *The Phenomenological Movement* (2 vols., The Hague, 2nd ed., 1965).

(2) In the PSYCHOLOGY of PERCEPTION, a doctrine or school which postulates that the significant role of SENSE-DATA lies in the form of the object as perceived, however erroneously or distorted, by the individual, and not in the object itself nor in material descriptions, locations, or identifications of the object that follow the rules of physical science. H.L.

Bibl: M. Merleau-Ponty, tr. C. Smith, *Phenomenology of Perception* (London and New York, 1962).

(3) In SOCIOLOGY, Husserl's method (see 1, above) was adapted by Alfred Schütz to investigate the assumptions involved in everyday social life. In the sociology of KNOWLEDGE, phenomenologists have concentrated on the way in which COMMON-SENSE knowledge about society feeds back, through SOCIAL ACTION, into the moulding of society itself. Other developments range from highly generalized descriptions of how people in different types of society think and feel about the world and their place in it, to analyses, in ETHNOMETHODOLOGY, of the unconscious routines by which people manage their inter-personal contacts. Critics of phenomenological sociology mistrust its aprioristic tendencies (see APRIORISM), and are impatient with its preference for description and uncontrolled hypothesis over EXPLANATION. When explanations are offered, it is claimed, they are disappointingly trite. J.R.T.

Bibl: Alfred Schütz, tr. G. Walsh and F. Lehnert, *The Phenomenology of the Social World* (Evanston, Ill., 1967).

phenotype, see under GENOTYPE.

pheromone. A chemical scent that is released by one organism and produces a specific response in another organism. Female moths, for example, attract their mates by releasing pheromones; when the male senses its species' pheromone it flies upwind, which brings it to the female. The full importance of pheromones in the lives of animals is unknown, because they are difficult for humans to detect. They are, however, used by all the main kinds of animals, to mediate all the main kinds of behaviour. The use of pheromones is probably most strongly developed in ants, which use different pheromones to coordinate all the behaviour patterns of their complex social lives — ants use, for example, a variety of 'recruitment' pheromones in exploiting food, 'propaganda substances' in battles between colonies, and 'alarm' pheromones to warn of danger. M.R.

Phillips curve. A negative relationship between UNEMPLOYMENT and INFLATION that was proposed and given sound empirical justification by A. W. Phillips in 1958. The downward slope of the convex Phillips curve implies that as unemployment declines the rate of change in wages and prices rises; the convexity implies that to obtain equal decrements in unemployment requires successively larger increases in inflation. Until the late 1960s the Phillips curve was seen as an important economic policy MODEL that showed a widely accepted and used trade-off between unemployment and inflation. In the U.K. the empirical justification for the curve broke down in the mid-1960s. The curve was explained by the proposition that an excess demand for labour forced up money wages (and thus, prices) and excess demand for labour is associated with low levels of unemployment. The shape of the curve was explained by the downward inflexibility of wages at low or negative levels of excess demand for labour and the flexibility of wages at higher levels of excess demand.   R.L.; J.P.

Bibl: J. Craven, *Introduction to Economics* (Oxford, 1984).

philology, see under LINGUISTICS.

philosophical linguistics. A branch of LINGUISTICS which studies (a) the role of language in relation to the understanding and elucidation of philosophical concepts, and (b) the philosophical status of linguistic theories, methods, and observations. D.C.

Bibl: J. Lyons, *Semantics* (Cambridge, 1977).

philosophical theology. A term sometimes equivalent to PHILOSOPHY OF RELIGION, but more usually applied to the discussion of the rationality of Christian faith within the tradition of Christian THEOLOGY, e.g. by EMPIRICAL or CRISIS theologians or in CHRISTIAN EXISTENTIALISM or NEO-THOMISM.   D.L.E.

Bibl: J. Richmond, *Faith and Philosophy* (London and Philadelphia, 1966).

philosophy. A term that cannot be uncontroversially defined in a single formula, used to cover a wide variety of intellectual undertakings all of which combine a high degree of generality with more or less exclusive reliance on reasoning rather than observation and experience to justify their claims. The chief agreed constituents of philosophy are EPISTEMOLOGY, or the theory of knowledge, METAPHYSICS, and ETHICS. There is a philosophy of every major form of intellectual activity of less than wholly general scope: science (see SCIENCE, PHILOSOPHY OF), HISTORY (see METAHISTORY), RELIGION (see RELIGION, PHILOSOPHY OF), art (see AESTHETICS), and others. These departmental philosophies are either epistemologies of the type of knowledge involved or metaphysical accounts of the domain of objects which that knowledge concerns. (The distinction is often marked as that between the critical and the speculative philosophy of whatever it may be.) Until fairly recent times LOGIC was so closely associated with philosophy as, in effect, to form part of it; but today logic is as often taken to be a part, a very fundamental part, of MATHEMATICS. The philosophical theory of logic, however, that is to say SEMANTICS, in a wide sense, or the theory of MEANING, is very much part of philosophy and, to a large extent, has replaced epistemology as the fundamental philosophical discipline. In the colloquial sense of the word, philosophy is a set or system of ultimate values. This is rather the subject-matter of identical with ethics. The rational pursuit of such a value-system must rest on a general conception of the nature of the world in which values are sought, the goal of metaphysics. Metaphysics, in its turn, presupposes a critical investigation of the various sorts of knowledge-claim and method of thinking from and by which a general picture of the world (or WELTANSCHAUUNG) might be constituted, in other words epistemology. The main preoccupations of technical or academic philosophy are all to be found in the writings of Plato and Aristotle and, less comprehensively, in the work of their ancient Greek predecessors, and a continuous tradition of philosophical discussion derives from them. If a single short formula is insisted on, the least objectionable is that philosophy is *thought about thought*; this distinguishes philosophy from those various kinds of first-order thinking about particular parts or aspects of what there is (i.e. science, history, and so on) whose ideas, methods, and findings constitute the subject-matter of philosophy.   A.Q.

Bibl: J.A. Passmore, *Philosophical Reasoning* (New York, 1962; London, 2nd ed., 1970); A. J. Ayer, *The Central Questions of Philosophy* (London, 1973).

philosophy of history, see METAHISTORY.

philosophy of mind, see MIND, PHILOSOPHY OF.

philosophy of religion, see RELIGION, PHILOSOPHY OF.

philosophy of science, see SCIENCE, PHILOSOPHY OF.

phi-phenomenon. A type of illusory perceptual impression of movement produced when, e.g., two stationary, spatially separated lights are flashed in brief succession. 'Phi' refers specifically to an impression of pure movement dissociated from PERCEPTION of an object. See also GESTALT.
I.M.L.H.

phlebology. A field of medicine dealing with the diseases of veins. Veins transport the blood to the heart and contain 70% of the blood volume, taking part in the regulation of cardiac output, hydrostatic pressure in the microcirculation, and body heat exchange. Composed of muscle fibres, collagen and some elastic tissue, veins have valves which are folds of the intimal layer, functionally important for the 'venous muscle pump'. Numerous collateral veins are preformed in the extremities. Common venous diseases are varicosis (a malfunction of valves), thrombosis (the obstruction by a blood clot) and the post thrombotic syndrome. Thrombosis occurring in deep veins can result in fatal pulmonary embolism. Its risk factors are heart disease, SURGERY, malignancy, trauma, clotting abnormalities, pregnancy, obesity and oral contraceptives. Varicosis supposes a genetical predisposition. Treatment of venous diseases depends on the individual case and is applied by specialists from various fields. It can consist of drugs, physical therapy or surgery. Therefore the definition of phlebology differs slightly depending on the school of thought. E.E.

phobia. An ANXIETY state (see also NEUROSIS) marked primarily by an intense fear out of proportion to the actual danger present in the feared situation or object. Phobias are diagnosed also by their intractability to the effects of direct experience with the relevant situations or objects.
W.Z.

phonaesthetics; phonesthetics. In LINGUISTICS, the study of the aesthetic properties of sound, especially the sound symbolism attributable to individual sounds (such as the *ee* of teeny, *wee*, etc. suggestive of smallness).
D.C.
Bibl: S. Ullman, *Language and Style* (Oxford, 1964).

phoneme. In LINGUISTICS, the minimal unit of PHONOLOGICAL analysis, i.e. the smallest unit in the sound-system capable of indicating contrasts in meaning; thus in the word *pit* there are three phonemes, /p/, /i/, /t/, each of which differs from phonemes in other words, such as *bit, pet,* and *pin.* Phonemes are abstractions (see ABSTRACT), the particular phonetic shape they take depending on many factors, especially their position in relation to other sounds in the sentence. These variants are called allophones, e.g. the /t/ phoneme has (amongst others) both an alveolar allophone (the sound made with the tongue contacting the alveolar ridge above and behind the teeth, as in *eight*) and a dental allophone (the sound made with the tongue further forward, against the teeth, as in *eighth* because of the influence of the *th* sound which follows).

In GENERATIVE GRAMMAR, the phoneme concept is not used: the sound features themselves (e.g. alveolar, nasal), referred to as *distinctive features*, are considered to be the most important minimal units of phonological analysis.
D.C.
Bibl: P. Hawkins, *Introducing Phonology* (London, 1984).

phonemics, see PHONOLOGY.

phonetic poetry, see under CONCRETE POETRY.

phonetics. A branch of LINGUISTICS which studies the characteristics of human sound-making; normally divided into *articulatory* phonetics (the processes of sound articulation by the vocal organs), *acoustic* phonetics (the transmission of vocal sound through the air, often referred to as ACOUSTICS), and *auditory* phonetics (the perceptual response to human sound).

The term *instrumental* phonetics is used for the study and development of mechanical aids for the analysis of any of these aspects. The name *general* phonetics is often used to indicate the aim of making phonetic principles and categories as universal as possible. See also IPA; PHONOLOGY. D.C.

Bibl: D. Abercrombie, *Elements of General Phonetics* (Edinburgh and Chicago, 1967); J.D. O'Connor, *Phonetics* (Harmondsworth and Baltimore, 1973); P. Ladefoged, *A Course in Phonetics* (New York, 1982).

phonology. A branch of LINGUISTICS, sometimes called *phonemics*, which studies the sound-systems of languages. It is normally divided into *segmental* and *suprasegmental* (or *non-segmental*) phonology: the former analyses the properties of vowels, consonants and syllables, the latter analyses those features of pronunciation which vary independently of the segmental structure of a sentence, e.g. INTONATION, rhythm, PARALANGUAGE. See also PROSODIC FEATURES. D.C.

Bibl: P. Hawkins, *Introducing Phonology* (London, 1984); R. Lass, *Phonology* (Cambridge, 1984).

phonon. An elementary vibration in a crystal. Heat is conducted by an incoherent superposition of short-wave phonons (see COHERENCE), while sound in solids is a coherent superposition of phonons whose wavelength is much longer than the distance between neighbouring ATOMS in the crystal LATTICE. M.V.B.

phosphorescence. The delayed emission of light from substances that have previously been exposed to it. M.V.B.

photino, see under SUPERSYMMETRY.

photobiology. The branch of BIOLOGY that deals with the influence of light on various biological performances. It includes PHOTOSYNTHESIS, the deposition of melanin (see MELANISM) in the skin through the action of sunlight, the emission of light by such organisms as glow-worms, and the behavioural responses towards sources of light of organisms such as moths and beetles. P.M.

photochemistry. The study of CHEMICAL REACTIONS induced by light. It was recognized early in the 19th century that only the light absorbed by a MOLECULE produces a photochemical change (the first law of photochemistry). Stark and Einstein (1912) were responsible for the second law, which states that, when a molecule is activated and caused to react, one quantum of light has been absorbed. Photochemical reactions are of great importance; they include PHOTOSYNTHESIS, production of the OZONE LAYER in the upper atmosphere, photochemical oxidation (e.g. the fading of dyes in light), photographic processes, and the chemistry of vision. B.F.

photoelectric cell. A device for detecting the presence of light and measuring its intensity, as in a photographer's light meter. PHOTONS arriving at the surface of a suitable material (e.g. selenium) interact with ELECTRONS in it, thus producing measurable electrical effects. M.V.B.

photogram. ABSTRACT or near-abstract photograph produced without a camera by the action of light and shade on sensitized paper. A DADAIST technique first employed by Christian Schad in Geneva in the winter of 1919-20 and subsequently by Man Ray in Paris; hence the alternative names *schadograph* or *rayograph*. J.W.

photolysis. The decomposition of a MOLECULE by light (see PHOTOCHEMISTRY). B.F.

photomicrograph. A photograph taken by attaching a camera to a microscope. M.V.B.

photomontage, see under MONTAGE.

photon. The ELEMENTARY PARTICLE or 'quantum' of ENERGY in which light or other electromagnetic RADIATION is emitted or absorbed when an ELECTRON, in an ATOM (see ATOMIC PHYSICS) or MOLECULE, changes its ENERGY LEVEL. The energy of a photon is equal to its frequency multiplied by PLANCK'S CONSTANT. Between emission and absorption, when the light is travelling through space, the intensity is usually so high that many photons are present, and classical OPTICS based on ELECTROMAGNETISM provides a sufficiently accurate description; this is an example of the WAVE-PARTICLE DUALITY. A burst of light containing no more than a few photons is detectable by the naked eye.   M.V.B.

photosynthesis. A highly complex oxidative-reduction reaction between carbon dioxide and water which takes place the presence of CHLOROPHYLL and involves the absorption of solar energy. In plants photosynthesis takes place in *chloroplasts*, small organelles within plant cells. The reaction results in the production of glucose and of higher CARBOHYDRATES which provide the food (and thus the energy) required by animals. In addition, the oxygen in the atmosphere is renewed by photosynthesis, so the whole LIFE CYCLE of the earth ultimately depends upon this reaction.   K.M.

phototaxis; phototropism, see under TROPISM.

phrase-structure grammar, see under GENERATIVE GRAMMAR.

phrenology. A would-be science with some popularity in the 19th century but now completely discredited by the findings of NEUROPSYCHOLOGY. It supposed that mental faculties were located in distinct parts of the brain and could be investigated by feeling bumps on the outside of the head.   I.M.L.H.

phylogeny. An animal's pedigree in terms of evolutionary descent (see EVOLUTION). It is contrasted with ONTOGENY, which is essentially its development (see EMBRYOLOGY). The so-called law of RECAPITULATION is sometimes, following Ernst Haeckel (1834-1919), put in the form 'Ontogeny repeats phylogeny'. See also BIOSYSTEMATICS.   P.M.

phylum. A group of organisms united by basic similarity (or *homeomorphy*) of ground plan. Thus the chordates (see ZOOLOGY) form a phylum because all pass through a *neurula* stage (see EMBRYOLOGY) in which the basic layout is essentially similar throughout.   P.M.

physical chemistry. A major branch of chemistry concerned with the measurement and understanding of chemical processes. It deals with chemical THERMODYNAMICS, in particular the position of chemical EQUILIBRIUM and the forces between chemical SPECIES (ATOMS, IONS, or MOLECULES) in the gaseous, liquid and solid states. The rates of CHEMICAL REACTION and their mechanisms are a central study. Other major areas are the determination of molecular structure and the investigation of the allowed ENERGY LEVELS for chemical species in different environments. Since many of these topics might equally well be studied by physicists, there is practically no distinction, except academic convention, between physical chemistry and *chemical physics*.   B.F.

Bibl: W.J. Moore, *Physical Chemistry* (London and Englewood Cliffs, N.J., 5th ed., 1972).

physicalism. The theory that all significant empirical statements can be formulated as statements referring to *publicly* observable physical objects. LOGICAL POSITIVISM, in its early stages, combined the desire to legitimize scientific statements as the paradigm of what is significant and knowable with a commitment to the view that the empirical basis of MEANING and knowledge is *private* sense-experience (see PRIVACY; SENSE-DATUM). Neurath held that the scientific requirement of *intersubjectivity* (i.e. of being publicly observable) must extend to its foundations and converted Carnap from his previous 'methodological SOLIPSISM'. Neurath saw physicalism as establishing the unity of science, contending that there is no difference of method or, fundamentally, of subject-matter between the NATURAL SCIENCES and the SOCIAL SCIENCES. In its original form physicalism interpreted statements about mental events in a BEHAVIOURISTIC way as statements about the DISPOSITIONS of living human bodies to behaviour of various kinds. The doctrine has been revived by exponents of the IDENTITY THEORY of mind and body (see also MIND-BODY PROBLEM), notably Smart, for whom mental events are in fact events occurring in the brain and NERVOUS SYSTEM.   A.Q.

Bibl: J.J.C. Smart, *Philosophy and*

Scientific Realism (London and New York, 1963).

physics. The study of the motion and interactions of matter, and the TRANSFORMATIONS between different kinds of ENERGY. On an abstract level, the subject is based on the 'six great theories' of NEWTONIAN MECHANICS, QUANTUM MECHANICS, RELATIVITY, ELECTROMAGNETISM, THERMODYNAMICS, and STATISTICAL MECHANICS. These theories make contact with the brute facts of nature via bodies of experimental data and interpretation devoted to particular kinds of system, e.g. ATOMIC PHYSICS, NUCLEAR PHYSICS, CRYOGENICS (low-temperature physics), SOLID-STATE PHYSICS, PLASMA PHYSICS, ASTRONOMY, etc. (For *chemical physics* see PHYSICAL CHEMISTRY.) However, none of the 'great theories' seems capable of explaining the interactions between ELEMENTARY PARTICLES or their origin in COSMOLOGY, and these subjects constitute the frontiers of physics today. M.V.B.
Bibl: R.P. Feynman, *The Character of Physical Law* (Cambridge, Mass., 1965); Tony Hey and P. Walters, *The Quantum Universe* (Cambridge, 1987).

physiography. A term, now falling into disuse, for the purely descriptive aspect of GEOMORPHOLOGY. J.L.M.L.

physiology. The branch of BIOLOGY that deals with function rather than structure and constitution. There are as many branches of physiology as there are distinct organ and TISSUE systems, e.g. NEUROLOGY, ENDOCRINOLOGY, etc. P.M.

physiotherapy. A systematic method of assessing musculoskeletal and neurological disorders of function, including pain and those of PSYCHOSOMATIC origin, and dealing with or preventing these problems by natural methods based essentially on movement, manual therapy and physical agencies. Physiotherapy is involved with all problems of function and the ability and mobility of the population from birth to death; from antenatal preparation, through childhood disability, physical and mental handicap, accidents and illness to dealing with the problems of elderly people. C.J.; D.L.W

phytogeography. The branch of BIOGEOGRAPHY which studies the geographical distribution of plants. Over a limited area plant distribution depends mainly on the soil type, determined by the GEOLOGY of the underlying rock. The other main factors are climatic (see CLIMATOLOGY). Agriculture has now changed the plant cover of the whole landscape in developed countries, and man, by burning the bush for instance, has affected other, less developed areas. This means that stable natural vegetation is becoming increasingly rare, and many of the original CONCEPTS of phytogeography cannot now be easily demonstrated. K.M.
Bibl: M.I. Newbigin, *Plant and Animal Geography* (London and New York, rev. ed., 1957).

phytopathology. The study of the diseases of plants; alternatively, the study of diseases caused by vegetable organisms, such as fungi. See also MYCOLOGY. K.M.

Piagetian. An adjective referring to Jean Piaget (*b.* 1896) and his theory of intellectual development. The theory is distinguished by an account of intellectual development as a universal sequence of mental stages (see STAGE OF DEVELOPMENT). The order of the stages is invariant, the later incorporating and resynthesizing the earlier. Development is divided into three broad stages: the SENSORY-MOTOR period (from birth to 18 months), in which the infant constructs a picture of a stable world divided into objects which retain their identity through space and time; the CONCRETE OPERATIONS period (from 2 to 11), in which the young child acquires classificatory principles of number, class, and quantity for organizing such objects; and the FORMAL OPERATIONS period (from 12 onwards), in which the adolescent acquires the ability systematically to coordinate his own classificatory principles.

Piaget has taken a characteristic position over various central psychological controversies. INTELLIGENCE is seen neither as a resonance to the external world (EMPIRICISM) nor as the unfolding of a predetermined system (NATIVISM), but as the progressive coordination between an organized intellectual system and the external world, beginning with the initial coordination between reflex and stimuli. Nor is intellectual development guided by cultural and social tools such as language. Instead, Piaget argues that intellectual development guides the usage of those tools.

The theory has contributed to the recent growth of COGNITIVE PSYCHOLOGY and contemporary interest in mental operations as opposed to observable behaviour (see BEHAVIOURISM). Nonetheless, even within cognitive psychology, Piaget remains distinctive. First, he adopts a developmental approach to COGNITION, and second, he concerns himself with epistemological categories (see EPISTEMOLOGY) and issues such as the nature of space (see SPACE PERCEPTION), quantity, and causality, rather than with psychological categories such as short-term memory, attention, and retrieval, etc. See also ACCOMMODATION; ASSIMILATION; CONSERVATION; DEVELOPMENTAL PSYCHOLOGY. P.L.H.

Bibl: J. Piaget, tr. M. Cook, *The Origin of Intelligence in the Child* (London, 1953; New York, 1963); J. Piaget, tr. C. Maschler, *Structuralism* (London and New York, 1971); J. Piaget, tr. B. Walsh, *Biology and Knowledge* (Edinburgh and Chicago, 1971); J. Piaget, tr. W. Mays, *The Principles of Genetic Epistemology* (London, 1972).

picketing. Picketing is the practice of the posting of strikers or their agents to intercept non-strikers and/or third-parties to the dispute and to persuade them not to cross the 'picket-line', thereby adding to the effectiveness of the strike. The persuasion and the interception should be peaceful. In the U.K. picketing is constrained by two sets of laws, one specific to picketing (viz. pickets must only be placed at the place of work of the strikers; only strikers may picket etc.) and common law (viz. laws of obstruction, trespass and riot, see LABOUR LAWS). Since individual police discretion is required these laws are applied inconsistently.

Historically, picketing has also been used as a human barrier to prevent the movement of people or supplies into or out of a plant or office. In the U.S. in the 1920s and 1930s in the car and steel industries these tactics led to violence and deaths. In the U.K. *mass picketing* came to promi-nence in the 1973/4 miners strike at the Saltley coke works and at the photographic printers Grunwick in 1976. In more recent times the 1984/5 miners strike and the 1986/7 mass picket outside News International in Wapping have both seen violence, notwithstanding massive police presences.

Flying pickets are a variation on the mass pickets. They consist of workers who are prepared to travel speedily, and in considerable strength, to picket at a workplace where they themselves do not work. This tactic was pioneered in 1972 in the construction industry dispute and 1974 in the miners dispute. It is now illegal in the U.K. *Secondary picketing*, that is a picket at a place of work not directly involved in the dispute, is also illegal. B.D.S.

picture-writing, see under LETTRISM.

pidgin. In SOCIOLINGUISTICS, a language with a markedly reduced GRAMMAR, LEXICON, and stylistic range, which is the native language of no one. Pidgin languages are formed when people from two different speech communities try to communicate (e.g. for trading purposes) without the aid of an interpreter. These languages flourish in areas of economic development, as in the pidgins based on English, French, Spanish, and Portuguese in the East and West Indies, Africa, and the Americas. Pidgins develop into CREOLES when they become the mother-tongue of a community. D.C.

Bibl: P. Trudgill, *Sociolinguistics* (Harmondsworth, 1984).

pinch effect. When a large electric current flows, the resulting MAGNETISM exerts a force on the moving ELECTRONS, tending to push them towards the axis of current. If the conductor is a fluid (e.g. a PLASMA or liquid metal), then a constricting effect — the pinch effect — is produced. The resulting instability is similar to the break-up of thin water jets into droplets caused by surface tension. See also MAGNETOHYDRODYNAMICS. M.V.B.

piped music, see under MUZAK.

pituitary. In ENDOCRINOLOGY, the most important endocrine gland in the body. It contains two elements of different origins and functions, on the one hand the epithelial element which began as a sort of median nose — an inpushing of the outermost layer of the skin towards the floor of the thalamic region of the brain — and on the other hand a neural element on the floor of the thalamus. The anterior pituitary derived from the epithelial element secretes *hormones* whose chief function is to control the activities of other endocrine organs, e.g. the GONADS, the THYROID, and the ADRENAL cortex. This anterior part of the pituitary is brought under the control of the brain by the action of intermediaries or 'releasing substances'. The neural element of the pituitary gland produces secretions such as oxytocin and vasopressin, the effects of which are similar to those of the autonomic NERVOUS SYSTEM. The hormones of this part of the gland are in fact manufactured in the hypothalamus and transported down the highly modified nerve CELLS to the posterior part of the pituitary, whence they are liberated into the bloodstream, as with other endocrine glands.   P.M.

PK, see PSYCHOKINESIS.

PL/1. A HIGH-LEVEL PROGRAMMING LANGUAGE sponsored by IBM to supersede FORTRAN and COBOL. It has not yet done so.   C.S.

place. Although the term 'place' is routinely used to identify a specific location or portion of worldly space, whether this be a room in a house or the TERRITORY of a whole country, it has also acquired a particular pertinence for a perspective within human GEOGRAPHY known as HUMANISTIC GEOGRAPHY. In this context place — or, to be more precise, 'sense of place' — connotes the myriad values, beliefs, feelings, hopes and fears that human beings attach both individually and collectively to certain settlements, regions, environments and landscapes. Distance from a place is hence to be measured, not simply in terms of physical distance, but in terms of the extent to which people feel that they belong to or are 'at home in' this place. And, similarly, attention needs to be paid to whether people perceive places as 'authentic' — as rooted in a set of time-honoured

local traditions and customs — or as 'inauthentic' — as littered with buildings, institutions and suchlike that are somehow alien, perhaps through being manifestations of a curiously 'placeless' modern western CULTURE. (For a rather different treatment of place by geographers, see CENTRAL PLACE.)   C.P.

Bibl: E. Relph, *Place and Placelessness* (London, 1976).

Planck era, see under PLANCK TIME.

Planck's constant. A universal constant (generally written *h*) first introduced by Max Planck in 1900, which relates the mechanical properties of matter to its wave properties (see WAVE-PARTICLE DUALITY). The ENERGY of a PARTICLE determines its frequency according to the EQUATION *frequency = energy ÷ h*, while the MOMENTUM of a particle determines its DE BROGLIE WAVELENGTH. The extreme smallness of Planck's constant makes NEWTONIAN MECHANICS an excellent approximation to QUANTUM MECHANICS in normal circumstances.   M.V.B.

Planck time/era. A unit of time obtained from combining three FUNDAMENTAL CONSTANTS of nature: the velocity of light, Newton's constant of GRAVITATION, and Planck's quantum of action. It has a value of 10^{-43} seconds. It was first derived by Max Planck in 1900 (although a similar quantity had been computed by George Johnstone Stoney in 1874). The Planck time is the earliest time in the history of the universe to which our current scientific theories are believed to apply. The interval of cosmic history beginning at the Big Bang (see BIG-BANG HYPOTHESIS) (assumed to be the start of time) and lasting for the Planck time is called the Planck era by cosmologists. During this period no known theory of nature remains consistent. The structure of the material universe during this epoch is sometimes called *space-time foam*.

The Planck time is an example of a *natural unit of time*; that is, it is not defined in terms of man-made artefacts but by reference to the fundamental constants of nature. There also exist related standards of mass and length called the

Planck mass (10^5 grammes) and Planck length (10^{33} centimetres). J.D.B.

Bibl: E. R. Harrison, *Cosmology* (Cambridge, 1981).

plane of the ecliptic, see under ECLIPTIC.

planetary rings. Systems of small rocks and PARTICLES observed orbiting around the planets Saturn, Jupiter and Uranus. Saturn's rings were first discovered by Galileo in 1610. The rings are probably no more than 5 km thick and appear to consist of constituent particles between one mm and tens of metres in size. They may have arisen when material failed to condense into moons (see GALILEAN MOONS) during the formation process of the central planet. Six principal rings of Saturn (A, B, C, D, E and F) are known. The most recently discovered is the F (or 'braided') ring. There may exist other fainter rings. All these rings exhibit complicated internal structure and constituent ringlets. J.D.B.

planetesimal theory. One of a number of hypotheses proposed for the origin of the SOLAR SYSTEM which have as a common starting-point the disruption of the primitive sun by an external force. T.C. Chamberlin and F.R. Moulton proposed that planetesimals, fragments which aggregated to form the planets, were derived from the break-up of the primitive sun and another star, on their close approach to each other. There are, however, serious physical and chemical objections to all theories involving disruption of the sun. Chemical evidence alone suggests that it is very unlikely that the planets were formed from the interior of the sun. J.L.M.L.

Bibl: see under EARTH SCIENCES.

planetoid, see ASTEROID.

planetology, see under EARTH SCIENCES.

planning. In POLITICAL ECONOMY, the mode of thinking which stresses the advantages of a central planning authority to coordinate the development of the national economy, or, more loosely, of government intervention in some form (as opposed to a LAISSEZ FAIRE approach). In the wake of the CAPITALIST chaos of the 1930s, the Soviet example of planning, and especially its emphasis on heavy industry, exercised considerable intellectual appeal. By the post-war period, not only had the Soviet Union, Eastern Europe, and China all adopted rigorous central planning, but the majority of the THIRD WORLD countries also favoured a planned approach. Meanwhile most Western industrial countries have adopted MIXED ECONOMIES of varying shades. See also STATE ECONOMIC PLANNING. D.E.

plan-séquence. A term in French film vocabulary signifying an entire sequence or segment of a film shot in one unbroken take, where otherwise a cut might be used to indicate a displacement from one viewpoint to another. Sometimes rendered in English as *sequence shot,* but the looser term 'long take' (briefly made fashionable as 'the ten-minute take' by Alfred Hitchcock's experiment with the technique in *Rope*) remains in more current usage. Film theorists, notably the French critic André Bazin, have attempted somewhat simplistically to divide film-makers into two broad groups: those who followed the principles of MONTAGE to heighten reality, and those who attempted to let the camera record reality by refusing to cut away from it. T.C.C.M.

plasma, see under SERUM.

plasma physics. The study of fluids containing a large number of free negative and positive electric charges, e.g. the IONOSPHERE or the gases in which a FUSION reaction is occurring. Such systems are strongly affected by electric and magnetic forces, so that their complicated motions (e.g. the PINCH EFFECT) must be interpreted within MAGNETOHYDRODYNAMICS. M.V.B.

plasmagene. A GENE or group of genes not incorporated into a CHROMOSOME. It once seemed that the presence in CELLS of structures such as MITOCHONDRIA and chloroplasts (see PHOTOSYNTHESIS) which arise only from pre-existing structures of the same kind indicated the existence of a hereditary mechanism profoundly different from the Mendelian one (see MENDELISM). These structures are now known to contain DNA (see NUCLEIC ACID), and it seems that the difference concerns the way in which DNA is transmitted from cell to cell rather than the process of self-replication upon which HEREDITY depends. See also EPISOME.　　　　J.M.S.

plasmid, see CLONING.

plastic. Any normally solid material which can flow slowly as a result of pressure or heat (see RHEOLOGY); generally the term is restricted to POLYMERS with this property.　　　　M.V.B.

plastic (reconstructive) surgery. The SURGERY to restore or reconstruct damaged, diseased or congenitally malformed TISSUE to normal form. This is achieved by the transfer of similar living tissue from adjacent or more distant parts of the body or by the reshaping of the malformed tissue itself. The major part of plastic surgery involves the treatment of head and neck and skin cancers, injuries of the soft tissues of the face, hands and legs, burns, and of birth deformity such as cleft lip and palate, birthmarks and deformed hands. Tissue transfer and repair has been developed from skin grafting to transfer of composite tissue such as muscle and bone and, more recently, whole limbs using suture of individual arteries, veins and nerves under the operating microscope. The origins of the art are recorded in Egyptian writings of 2000 B.C. (case histories of treatment of a fractured, deformed nose), and in Indian scripts of 600 B.C. (describing how cheek skin could be cut to repair deformities of ears and face). During the 17th and 18th centuries successful surgical experiments were made with transferring tissue from undamaged to mutilated parts, but the advent of ANAESTHESIA in the 1840s allowed the surgeon the time to carry out the more intricate procedures previously denied. Early skin grafting for burns was introduced by Sueve in the U.S.A. in 1905. The First World War trench injuries provided the impetus for Harold Gillies (1882-1960) and Pomfret Kilner (1890-1964) to set up plastic surgery units within hospitals where specialist care could be provided. Specialist provision for victims of burns injuries became available during and after the Second World War at the instigation of Archibald McIndoe (1900-1960), though the first Burns Unit in Britain had been set up a hundred years before in Edinburgh.　　　　J.V.H.K.

Bibl: I.A. McGregor, *Fundamental Techniques of Plastic Surgery and their Surgical Applications* (Edinburgh, 1980).

plate tectonics. A hypothesis of global TECTONICS which postulates large-scale horizontal movements of the rigid outer shell of the earth, termed the LITHOSPHERE, over a plastic layer of the upper mantle, the ASTHENOSPHERE. The theory has developed as a result of recent discoveries of patterns of remanent magnetism of the ocean floor which make it virtually certain that oceanic crust is being continually created by upwelling of mantle material along a worldwide mid-ocean fracture system (see OCEANIC RIDGE). The oceanic lithosphere so created spreads laterally at a rate of a few centimetres a year, moving in opposite directions on either side of the mid-oceanic fracture system, and eventually sinks down to be reabsorbed in the mantle under certain continental margins. The major zone of sinking is the circum-Pacific region from the Philippines to Chile. Six major plates of the lithosphere, five of them carrying continental crust, are moving relative to each other across the earth's surface away from the mid-ocean fracture, and in doing so they seem to determine the major tectonic features of the earth. See also CONTINENTAL DRIFT.　　　　J.L.M.L.

Platonic realism, see under REALISM.

Platonism. The theory that ABSTRACT entities or UNIVERSALS really exist, outside space and time, in an autonomous world of timeless ESSENCES. (Plato, indeed, held that such Ideas or Forms are the *only* things that really or wholly exist, on the ground that it is only of them that we have absolutely certain knowledge, namely, in MATHEMATICS.) One argument for the existence of universals is that there are statements, known to be true, which refer to them. Critics object that such references can be eliminated by ANALYSIS: 'Honesty is the best policy', with its apparent implication of the existence of honesty-in-general, is just an idiomatic abbreviation for 'Anyone who acts honestly acts prudently'. But it has been argued by Quine that any language mathematically rich enough for the needs of science must contain irreducible references to classes (see SET THEORY), and that classes are abstract entities. If *a priori* knowledge (see APRIORISM) is conceived by ANALOGY with PERCEPTION, abstract entities provide suitable objects for acts of rational insight or intellectual intuition. A.Q.

Bibl: Bertrand Russell, *The Problems of Philosophy* (London, 1912), chs. 9, 10; W.D. Ross, *Plato's Theory of Ideas* (Oxford, 1951).

pleasure principle. In psychoanalytic theory (see PSYCHOANALYSIS), a FREUDIAN term for the principle of mental functioning that characterizes UNCONSCIOUS, primitive instincts (the ID), which are driven to gratification without regard to their consequences either socially or for the individual's adaptation. It is usually contrasted with the REALITY PRINCIPLE. W.Z.

pleiotropy. The development of apparently unrelated characteristics under the influence of a single GENE. It is thought that each gene has only one primary function, and that pleiotropic effects arise because a single primary effect can have many consequences. J.M.S.

PLO, see under PALESTINE LIBERATION ORGANIZATION.

Plowden Report (1967). The two-volume report *Children and their Primary Schools* (London, H.M.S.O.) by a committee set up under the chairmanship of Lady Plowden 'to consider primary education in all its aspects and the transition to secondary education'. The report considered organization and content, staffing and resources, child development, school health and welfare services, the school management system, and the independent schools for this age range, and has had many tangible results from its 197 recommendations. W.A.C.S.

PLR (Public Lending Right). The principle that authors should receive some kind of payment when their works are borrowed from public libraries. Public Lending Right may be operated in various ways; and there are different means of raising the money — e.g. by direct government grant, by a levy on the rates, etc. It exists in Denmark, Sweden, and several other countries, but not in the U.S.A. In Great Britain, where the idea was pioneered by the novelist and writer John Brophy and then by his daughter Brigid Brophy and an association she formed called Writers Action Group (now dissolved, its aims fulfilled). Legislation to implement it was announced in the Queen's Speeches of 1974 and 1975, and in 1983 it was put into effect. It is based on a loan-sample and has been widely accepted, but is unfair — as is also accepted — to the poverty-stricken authors and editors of reference books. The anomalies — mainly that those least in need get most — cannot be ironed out. M.S.-S.

plural society. A society containing within it two or more communities which are distinct in many (predominantly cultural) respects — colour, belief, RITUAL, practices both institutionalized (e.g. form of marriage and family) and habitual (e.g. preferred food, dress, leisure) — and which in many areas of social behaviour remain substantially unmixed; a society whose elements acknowledge, or are constrained by, an overall political authority, but are strongly disposed to the maintenance of their own traditions and are therefore motivated towards SEPARATISM. In plural societies the problem of preserving order and freedom is especially great; a slender unity easily breaks into warring national, racial, or religious groups. All societies other than the very simplest are pluralist in possessing local, regional, and CLASS communities, but the concept has come strongly to the fore since World War II when many hitherto subjected and newly immigrant (or refugee) groups feel the right to equal STATUS, and when, with movements of population, many societies (e.g. Britain) now contain distinctive cultural groups. The plural society has created moral, legal, and political problems of a new degree of difficulty — from APARTHEID at one extreme to the all-embracing statement of EQUALITY in the constitution of the U.S.A. at the other — and has rendered any analysis of social cooperation and conflict in terms of the orthodox concepts of SOCIAL STRATIFICATION (slavery, serfdom, CASTE, estate, class) much too simple. The more detailed analysis required has been provided in discussions of the composition of a population by F.H. Giddings (in *The Elements of Sociology*, London, 1898) and of cultural communities and INTEREST GROUPS by Gustav Ratzenhofer (e.g. as expounded by Albion W. Small in *General Sociology*, Chicago, 1905). See also CULTURE.   R.F.

Bibl: H.M. Kallen, *Cultural Pluralism and the American Idea* (Philadelphia, 1956); M. Ginsberg, 'Cultural Pluralism in the Modern World', in R. Fletcher (ed.), *The Science of Society and the Unity of Mankind* (London and New York, 1974).

pluralism. In political thought (for its meaning in PHILOSOPHY see MONISM), a term with three meanings, not always clearly distinguished: (*a*) institutional arrangements for the distribution of political POWER; (*b*) the doctrine that such arrangements ought to exist; and (*c*, a somewhat slipshod usage) pluralist *analysis*, i.e. the analysis of power distributed in this way. It is frequently used to denote any situation in which no particular political, ideological, cultural, or ethnic group is dominant. Such a situation normally involves competition between *rival* ÉLITES or INTEREST GROUPS, and the PLURAL SOCIETY in which it arises is often contrasted with a society dominated by a *single* élite where such competition is not free to develop.   M.BA.

Bibl: R.A. Dahl, *Who Governs? Democracy and Power in an American City* (New Haven and London, 1967); S. Lukes, *Power* (London, 1974).

plurisignation. Term introduced by Philip Wheelwright, in *The Burning Fountain* (1954), as a substitute for William Empson's AMBIGUITY, which, in his view, had an irrelevantly pejorative CONNOTATION, and was over-restrictive. 'Real plurisignation differs from simply punning or witwriting ... Empson's use of the term "ambiguity" generally refers to the plurisignative character of poetic language; his

word is inappropriate, however, since ambiguity implies an "either-or" relation, plurisignation a "both-and".' 'The plurisign, the poetic symbol, is not merely employed but enjoyed'; 'it is a part of what it means'. The term extends the Empsonian CONCEPT by relating it to the mystico-religious connotation of words.

M.S.-S.

plutocracy. Word of Greek origin for the rule of the wealthy, a state in which citizenship or POWER is defined by great wealth. A strict example of such a state is difficult to find; the Venetian republic probably comes closest, while the high property franchise obtaining in France under Louis Philippe (1830-48) and the roles open to the wealthy in American politics in the last decades of the 19th century gave these societies distinctly plutocratic elements.   D.C.W.

plutonium. The most important TRANSURANIC ELEMENT. Plutonium (atomic number 94) is produced artificially in a NUCLEAR REACTOR from naturally occurring uranium by a succession of NUCLEAR REACTIONS which follow NEUTRON absorption. Unlike the uranium 238 ISOTOPE, which constitutes 99.3% of natural uranium, the chief isotope of plutonium (atomic weight 239) is a fissionable material and can be used in atomic bombs and to fuel nuclear reactors. Large-scale production of plutonium and separation from uranium began towards the end of World War II, and the first plutonium-containing bomb was exploded in New Mexico in 1945. Fast breeder reactors produce excess plutonium in addition to generating power.   B.F.

Plymouth Brethren. A Christian SECT, originating in 1830 in Plymouth, England, but now widely distributed and vocal, although still not large. Its doctrines are generally FUNDAMENTALIST, and one section, the 'Exclusive' Brethren, interpret biblical passages about the 'holy' people as forbidding marriage or friendship with non-members. The 'Open' Brethren are somewhat more liberal.   D.L.E.

pneumatic structures. Enclosures in which a membrane is air-supported by means of the difference in pressure between the inside and outside. As a rule air is pumped into such an enclosure through fans, and this air also acts as the mechanical ventilation. To prevent its escape, the membrane is tightly sealed and entrance is through an air lock. The membrane has to be in sufficient tension to withstand wind and snow loads. Much of the technology derives from lighter-than-air balloons and dirigibles.

Pneumatic structures can be erected and dismantled quickly and have thus so far been mostly used for temporary buildings, and in HAPPENINGS, play areas, etc., where they are often called *inflatables*. Some of the most complex examples were seen at Expo '70 in Osaka. Small, totally enclosed forms have been used as furniture.   M.BR.

Bibl: R.N. Dent, *Principles of Pneumatic Architecture* (London, 1971).

poetics. The theory and/or practice of poetry; alternatively, an exposition of such theory or practice.   O.S.

Poetry Bookshop. A bookshop set up in December 1912 at 35 Devonshire Street, London, by Harold Monro (1879-1932), as an adjunct to his middle-of-the-road *Poetry Review* (succeeded by *Poetry and Drama*). His hope of bringing poetry out of the study and 'back into the street' was hardly realized; but the Poetry Bookshop, housed in a splendid 18th-century mansion, played an important part in bringing poetry to those who really wanted it. There were readings; indigent poets were offered lodgings. Most of the readings and poems were bad; but the poets included Robert Frost, Rupert Brooke, T.E. Hulme, Wilfred Owen, and Conrad Aiken.   M.S.-S.

Bibl: J. Grant, *Harold Monro and the Poetry Bookshop* (London, 1967).

Poetry (Chicago). One of the first and chief of American 'little magazines'. It began in Chicago in October 1912, edited by Harriet Monroe, with Ezra Pound as foreign correspondent, and had much to do with the modern revolution in poetry; it included work by T.S. Eliot, William Carlos Williams, Wallace Stevens, and Marianne Moore (all largely via Pound) as well as more 'native', middle-western voices like Vachel Lindsay and Carl Sandburg. Harriet Monroe, basically sympathetic to the latter tradition, finally lost Pound to Margaret Anderson's rival LITTLE REVIEW. Though the early years are the best, the journal's tradition continues, subsequent editors including Morton D. Zabel and Peter de Vries. M.S.BR.

Bibl: H. Monroe, *A Poet's Life* (New York, 1938).

Poetry Workshop, see GROUP, THE.

point block (often called *tower block*). A tall narrow block placed in a city or landscape so that its simple geometry is clearly discernible, as in Le Corbusier's plan (1922) for the centre of a city for three million people. The geometry is usually that of a rectangular block or a cylinder, and not the pyramidal form of so many SKYSCRAPERS.   M.BR.

point estimate, see ESTIMATE.

pointillism.

(1) In music, the use of melodic lines so disjointed that the individual notes seem to stand alone and not to refer to each other, sounding rather like points of sound. The music of Anton Webern (see SECOND VIENNESE SCHOOL) is often referred to as pointillist due to his fragmentation of the musical fabric by the use of silences in between the notes and by his frequent changes of tone colour in a single melody (see KLANGFARBENMELODIE). This fragmentation was taken to even greater extremes in the 1950s by composers of the POST-WEBERN SCHOOL.   B.CO.

(2) In fine arts, see under NEO-IMPRESSIONISM.

Poisson distribution. In STATISTICS and PROBABILITY THEORY, a DISTRIBUTION on the non-negative integers which attaches probability $\lambda^n e^{-\lambda}/n!$ to the integer n. Both the MEAN and the VARIANCE of the distribution are equal to the value of the PARAMETER λ. The distribution arises naturally in a number of ways, and is often used in applied probability as a model for the occurrence of a rare event in a large number of trials — for example, the number of misprints per page in a newspaper has approximately a Poisson distribution.

R.SI.

Polaris missile, see under TRIDENT.

polarization. (1) In OPTICS, the state of affairs in which light or other radiation has different properties in different directions at right angles to the direction of propagation. (2) The process whereby, when an electric FIELD acts on matter, positive and negative charges separate. (3) The process whereby a social or political group is divided on, for example, a political or religious issue into two diametrically opposed sub-groups, with fewer and fewer members of the group remaining indifferent or holding an intermediate position.

A.S.

polarography. A method of chemical analysis, invented by Heyrovsky around 1920, involving the measurement of current-voltage curves as mercury, which forms one ELECTRODE, drops steadily from a fine capillary through a solution. It can be used to determine dilute concentrations of any metal ION or organic SPECIES which can be reduced at the dropping electrode, as well as to investigate OXIDATION-reduction chemistry in solution.

B.F.

polaroid camera. A camera (invented by Land in 1947) producing positive contact prints a few seconds after exposure, without requiring a darkroom. A roll of positive paper covered with pods filled with developer is stored in the camera. This paper and the exposed film are brought into contact and withdrawn from the camera through pressure rollers which burst the pods. Development is complete in a few seconds, and the print can be peeled off.

M.V.B.

police powers. In the U.S., the federal government is, in theory, the government of generally delimited powers, while the states retain inherent powers over the public health, safety, welfare, and morals. These state powers are referred to as the 'police powers'. Federal review of state activities is permitted only to determine whether state actions under their police powers violate a specific constitutional limitation. This distinction between the powers of state and national government is the basis of the American federal system, and also explains why the U.S. is not a complete legal union.

M.S.P.

Politburo. The most powerful institution in the Soviet COMMUNIST Party and the main policy-making body of the U.S.S.R. As the Political Bureau of the Central Committee, it is officially responsible for directing the activities of the Communist Party in between plenary sessions of the Central Committee, which nominally elects it. However, in practice Politburo members are recruited by co-option and they have much more say over policy than does the Central Committee. It meets once or twice a week and is particularly concerned with foreign and national security affairs, although it also deals with internal economic questions. Its membership is small: in 1986 it had 12 full members and 7 candidate (non-voting) members. Its most influential member is the General Secretary to the Central Committee, at present Mikhail Gorbachev. Representatives of important government departments such as the Ministry of Foreign Affairs and more recently the KGB are usually included in its membership, together with the chiefs of key party regional organizations, such as Moscow, Leningrad and the Ukraine. Having risen to prominence after its establishment in 1919, it lost much of its power under Stalin in the period after the YEZHOVSH-CHINA, but since 1953 it has been restored to its central position.

D.PR.

Bibl: R.J. Hill and P. Frank, *The Soviet Communist Party* (London, 1981).

political anthropology. Study of the political organization and patterns of leadership found in non-industrial societies. It was effectively established as a field of study by the publication in 1940 of *African Political Systems* edited by Evans-Pritchard and Fortes. The TYPOLOGY the editors drew up was based upon a distinction between centralized (state) and uncentralized (stateless) societies. It had an enormous impact in ANTHROPOLOGY, but for many years constrained analysis. This classification of political systems increasingly came in for criticism because of its failure to correspond to ethnographic (see ETHNOGRAPHY) reality. It was a static MODEL which could not incorporate the dynamics of political life.

Leach's *Political Systems of Highland Burma* (1954) broke with the African oriented model. It focused upon political process and the transformations effected at the level of structure. The latter was a model or an ideal which the Kachin people themselves held, but it was constantly changing as a result of political activity. The Manchester school under Max Gluckman developed political anthropology in a different direction. Gluckman was interested in the role of conflict and the balance of oppositions in the creation of social equilibrium (*Custom and Conflict in Africa*, 1956). The study of political process, the competition for POWER, became central to analysis as fieldworkers increasingly broadened their range of enquiry beyond traditional small scale societies. Focus was increasingly on individuals and the strategies employed to attain power. In particular the development of GAME THEORY (F.G. Bailey, *Stratagems and Spoils*, 1969) and NETWORK theory (J. Boissevain, *Friends of Friends*, 1974) have reflected the new orientation in political anthropology.

A.G.

Bibl: T.C. Lewellen, *Political Anthropology: An Introduction* (Boston, Mass., 1983); D. Riches (ed.), *The Anthropology of Violence* (Oxford, 1986).

political culture. A term meant to encompass political values and attitudes wider than intimated by the more formal political system, and to some extent upholding it. A political culture is formed by the practice of politics. It is the sum of the dispositions created by the regular operation of the political system of a particular society. A political culture can encourage participation and involvement by the majority of citizens, as tends to be the case in democratic politics, especially the smaller ones (ancient Athens, 18th-century Geneva). Or it can promote attitudes of passivity and acquiescence, as in AUTHORITARIAN or TOTALITARIAN political systems (Tsarist Russia, NAZI Germany).

A political culture is largely formed by the political system, but it depends for its persistence and vitality on the support of other social INSTITUTIONS. In modern societies, there is a complex and sometimes contradictory relation between the attitudes and values developed in formal political practice, and those formed by other institutions such as the family, school, church, and the mass MEDIA. Somewhat idealistically, the 'civic culture' of western DEMOCRACIES is said to exhibit a basic congruence of democratic values and practices across all the major social institutions. What is learned and practised in the family and school matches and confirms the practices of the political system. Elsewhere, the lack of fit between the political system and other institutions can undermine the system. Thus in Germany in the 1920s, the authoritarian tradition still persistent in the German family and educational system is seen as an important cause of the weakness and eventual demise of the democratic WEIMAR REPUBLIC.

K.K.

Bibl: G.A. Almond and S. Verba, *The Civic Culture* (Boston, 1983); R.E. Dowse and J.A. Hughes, *Political Sociology* (Beverly Hills, Ca., 1986).

political economy. The management of the economy of the STATE. By the end of the 18th century the scope of political economy was limited by a number of writers (Du Pont in France, Verri in Italy, Sir James Steuart and Adam Smith in Great Britain) to problems connected with the *wealth* of a state. Although at this time considerations of the moral, political, and social desirability of economic policies and also the administrative problems involved were still included in treatises on political economy, during the early 19th century they were gradually excluded. Throughout that century there were discussions of the definition of political economy and of other METHODOLOGICAL issues. Attempts were made to define the relation between political economy and other SOCIAL SCIENCES, particularly SOCIOLOGY and politics. Distinctions were made between a pure scientific study of economics and the VALUE-JUDGEMENTS that are implied in the political choice of actual economic policies. Towards the end of the century the term political economy was being grad-

POLITICAL SCIENCE

ually superseded, in English-speaking countries, by the single word ECONOMICS. This change was partly for convenience, but it also reflected the hope that it would be possible to separate out the positive from the normative aspects of economics. How successful economics has been in making this distinction is a matter of dispute. The change of name may have altered the popular image of economists slightly but it has not abolished the problems or the discussion of scope and method.   M.E.A.B.; J.P.

Bibl: L. Robbins, *Political Economy Past and Present* (London, 1976).

political science. The study of the organization and conduct of government. This has existed since the time of Aristotle at least. But so long as reflection upon politics remained substantially inseparable from the speculations of 'moral philosophy' about society in general, it could assert no sustained claim to be a discipline in its own right. Only during the later 19th century was its independence adequately established, under British, French, and American leadership. Even then, its subject-matter remained uncomfortably ill-defined. The new discipline was distinguishable from *political philosophy*, however, in having empirical rather than NORMATIVE interests — i.e. in describing things as they are rather than as they ought to be. The comparative study of governments bulked large, and was indicative of a dominant concern with INSTITUTIONS. In the second half of this century, however, there has been a considerable shift of emphasis towards behavioural issues (see BEHAVIOURAL SCIENCES). Political scientists now devote much time to probing into the patterns of SOCIAL ACTION and behaviour which underlie the operation of political institutions and which condition such phenomena as the competition for POWER or the making and implementation of public decisions. The consequent involvement in matters of attitude and motivation, VALUE and COGNITION, suggests the extent of common ground — and the difficulties of demarcation — with, especially, POLITICAL SOCIOLOGY and SOCIAL PSYCHOLOGY.   M.D.B.

Bibl: J. Blonde, *The Discipline of Politics* (London, 1981); A. Finifter (ed.), *Pol-*

itical Science: the State of the Discipline (Washington, 1983).

political sociology. A field of study which came into existence to emphasize the sociological dimensions of politics. Major political issues include ÉLITES (see also POWER ÉLITE); LEGITIMACY and effectiveness (e.g. Max Weber's analysis of three types of authority: traditional, CHARISMATIC, and LEGAL-RATIONAL); the relation of economic to political development (e.g. Samuel P. Huntington's study of turbulence in the new states created after World War II, *Political Order in Changing Societies,* 1968); DISTRIBUTIVE JUSTICE (see also RELATIVE DEPRIVATION); conditions of DEMOCRACY (attempts to relate effective democracy to the degrees of literacy, PARTICIPATION, the character of voluntary associations, the nature of national character, and the strength of tradition in different societies); TOTALITARIANISM; conditions of REVOLUTIONS; and the political ROLE of social groups, such as the WORKING CLASS or the INTELLECTUALS. Behavioural studies have concentrated in three areas: types of party systems (one-party, two-party, multi-party) and the social bases of parties and political division (e.g. CLASS, RELIGION, RACE); the comparative structure of governments (e.g. centralized and decentralized, presidential and parliamentary); and public opinion.   D.B.

Bibl: B. Moore, *The Social Origins of Dictatorship and Democracy* (London, 1967); R.E. Dowse and J.A. Hughes, *Political Sociology* (Beverly Hills, Ca., 1986).

pollen analysis. The recognition and counting of pollen grains preserved in a sample of soil or peat. The technique relies on the fact that the exine (outer coat) of pollen is both distinctive as between SPECIES and resistant to decay. The pollen is extracted from a suitable sample and examined under the microscope, the different species being identified and their relative commonness assessed by counting the different grains within a representative area of the microscope slide. There are two principal applications: the establishment of a general pattern of climatic change within the *neothermal period* (following the end of the Ice Age), and the study of local ENVIRONMENTS to assess the effect of man's activities on the flora. The first application has allowed the definition of a number of vegetational zones which have been calibrated by RADIOCARBON DATING methods, thus providing a sequence by means of which associated archaeological material can be dated. The second application has been extensively used to examine the initial effects of forest clearance and the introduction of a food-producing economy on a virgin area.   B.C.

Bibl: K. Faegri and J. Iversen, *Textbook of Pollen Analysis* (Oxford and New York, 2nd ed., 1964).

pollution.
(1) Pollution is usually related to the place or medium affected, e.g. air pollution, water pollution, pollution of the ocean. However, the word is often used very loosely to cover the presence of substances considered objectionable even when these are present in such small amounts that no recognizable harm is done to the ENVIRONMENT. Also the term pollution is used to imply the presence of chemical substances produced by man's activities, and not to the natural existence of even higher levels of the same substances. Thus, if a factory discharges lead into a river, this is thought of as polluted even if the lead is diluted down to harmless (though chemically measurable) levels, whereas lead naturally leached from rocks, yielding levels which can seriously damage fish, may not produce such an emotional reaction.

These loose uses of the word should be discouraged, and it should only be used when damage occurs. Thus polluted air is air which is unpleasant or dangerous to breathe, polluted water has a nasty taste or is harmful to the animals and plants living in it. Air containing the unpleasant or harmful substances at levels which are only detectable by very accurate chemical analysis, and where no discomfort or damage is suffered by man or animals breathing it, should not be considered as polluted, though it may be difficult to be completely certain that absolutely no damage is done. Thus, though gross pollution is easily recognizable, as levels fall the gradation to harmless contamination may be difficult to define.   K.M.

Bibl: K. Mellanby, *Pesticides and Pollution* (London, 1969) and *The Biology of Pollution* (London, 1972); Royal Commission on Environmental Pollution (Chairmen: Lord Ashby, Sir Bryan Flowers), *Reports*, 1-5 (London, 1971-76).

(2) (purity/impurity). Notions particularly developed by Mary Douglas and Edmund Leach. Early work by Steiner (*Taboo*, 1956) suggested the existence of objects or states surrounded by restrictions. They were regarded as unclean, polluting and dangerous. Ideas of purity and impurity were more fully elaborated in the wake of Lévi-Strauss and STRUCTURALISM. States of purity/impurity arise from the process of classification. Douglas described pollution or impurity: 'dirt is matter out of place' (*Purity and Danger*, 1966). Pollution arises from the disruption of cultural categories or from the area between categories. It is closely associated with power. Pollution can be the state of an object or a person, and in this condition they are regarded as contagious and surrounded by restrictions. Objects commonly designated as impure include semen, nail clippings and menstrual blood. Persons who are impure are frequently those in the process of movement between social states in a RITE DE PASSAGE.   A.G.

Bibl: E.R. Leach, *Social Anthropology* (London, 1982).

polyandry. Term used to describe a form of plural MARRIAGE in which a woman has several husbands. Most commonly, a set of brothers share a single wife: *fraternal* or *adelphic polyandry*. In these cases often only the eldest of the set of brothers undergoes the formal marriage ceremony, the younger brothers becoming husbands *de facto* as they come of age. Sexual access to the wife is on the basis of seniority, but frequently the conditions in which polyandry occurs influence this arrangement. For example, in Ladakh, each household is required to pay labour tribute to the monastery. Brothers take it in turn to perform these services and while one is absent the one left behind has access to the wife.

Early writers associated polyandry with 'group marriage' and with the existence of MATRIARCHY. It was understood as rep-

661

resenting an early stage in the evolution of marriage forms. Later anthropologists have tried to relate its appearance to specific economic conditions. This has been difficult since although polyandry may have superficial cross-cultural similarities, the economic reasons for its appearance in any one society may be quite different. A.G.

Bibl: M.C. Goldstein, 'Pahari and Tibetan Polyandry Revisited', *Ethnology* 17, 1978.

polyarchy. A term coined by Robert Dahl (1953) to characterize the working of contemporary American government in which rule by the majority is unfeasible, and DEMOCRACY has come to mean rule by various minorities. Literally, it means 'rule by many' as distinct from what Aristotle feared, namely 'rule by the many'. Dahl's point was that although 'the people' did not and could not govern, nevertheless a lot of people did govern, in contradistinction to dictatorial and TOTALITARIAN regimes where almost everyone was shut out of the corridors of power. A.R.

Bibl: Robert Dahl, *A Preface to Democratic Theory* (Chicago, 1953); *Polyarchy* (New York, 1974).

polycentrism. The process of splintering a unitary organization or movement into independent centres of power; also the resulting diversification. The term was first used by Togliatti to describe the developments in world COMMUNISM after the 20th Congress of the Soviet Communist Party (1956), but it refers now not just to the breakdown of what was once regarded as a political monolith under Stalin, but to the emergence of independent Communist parties in general. The process started with the Soviet-Yugoslav dispute, which produced in Yugoslavia the first Communist state no longer dominated by the ideological authority (see IDEOLOGY) of Moscow. Yugoslavia had acquired its own MARXIST ideological legitimacy in TITO-ISM. After Stalin's death, the number of splits between Communist parties and Communist states increased and the tendency towards national communism was reinforced, eventually leading to the establishment of independent Communist

centres of power, which attempted to take greater account of local conditions in their political line. The divisions within international communism resulted not only in some Communist states (like Albania or Romania) pursuing an independent line and some parties (like the Italian or the Dutch) insisting on their autonomy, but also in some providing a point of ideological attraction (like MAOISM or CASTROISM). The Sino-Soviet split to some extent polarized the world Communist movement, providing at the same time the opportunity for NEUTRALISM vis-à-vis the dispute. But although in some respects this extended the possibilities for the political autonomy of the national parties, in other respects it limited such possibilities by the need for support from one or other of the powerful antagonists. This need for support, however, and the demand for solidarity amongst Communist parties, has not prevented the diversification of Communist ideology and the evolution of national Communist parties, as was shown in the statements made by the French, Italian, and other Communist parties at the Conference of European Communist Parties held in Berlin in 1976. These national parties stressed their independence from the Soviet Union, while, however, giving no hint of any weakening of Leninist (see LENINISM) DEMOCRATIC CENTRALISM, which constitutes a fundamental constraint on the evolution of national Communist parties. L.L.

Bibl: W. Laqueur and L. Labedz (eds.), *Polycentrism* (New York, 1962); L. Labedz, *International Communism after Khrushchev* (Cambridge, Mass., 1965); A. Westoby, *The Evolution of Communism* (Oxford, 1987).

polydentate ligand, see under CHELATE.

polyembryony. A state of affairs in which an animal regularly gives birth to a number of genetically identical offspring. Although the production of identical twins is the simplest example of polyembryony, the term is usually reserved for the regular production of multiplets such as those of the nine-banded armadillo. Polyembryony arises by fission of the ZYGOTE, which may occur more than once, each daughter CELL giving rise to a whole organism, or to fission of the embryo at a somewhat later stage. It must thus be distinguished from the conventional multiple births in which litter mates resemble each other no more closely than ordinary brothers and sisters (except, of course, in age). Each member of such a litter is the product of a distinct egg cell fertilized by a distinct spermatozoon. P.M.

polyethylene, see POLYTHENE.

polygene. When a single characteristic is influenced by GENES at many LOCI, its inheritance is said to be polygenic or multifactorial. The genes concerned have sometimes been called polygenes, but they probably differ from other genes only in having a small effect on the characteristic under study. J.M.S.

Bibl: D.S. Falconer, *Introduction to Quantitative Genetics* (Edinburgh and New York, 1960).

polygyny. A form of legitimate plural MARRIAGE (as opposed to illegitimate, i.e. bigamy) in which a man has several wives. Polygyny is occasionally found in Eurasia and it is usually a strategy to provide an heir when an existing wife has failed to produce offspring. It is most commonly found in Africa where approximately 35% of marriages are estimated to be polygynous. A young man would make his first marriage with a woman of a similar age. Later he would acquire other wives through the payment of BRIDEWEALTH and the age differential between the spouses would continue to increase.

Co-wives and their children usually occupy separate huts within the man's compound, but the degree of solidarity between them is very variable. Tensions between co-wives may lead to accusations of WITCHCRAFT. One strategy which reduces hostilities in a polygynous situation is for a man to marry sisters: *sororal polygyny*.

The incidence of polygyny has been linked to certain economic conditions in Africa. It has been suggested that polygyny is associated with extensive or hoe agriculture where labour is the critical factor in production and women play an important role in cultivation. Thus the more wives a man has the greater will be the productivity. Other anthropologists

(Goody, *Polygyny, Economy and the Role of Women*, 1973) have linked polygyny not with women as producers, but as reproducers: that is, their ability to produce children which alleviates labour scarcity and allows expansion in the areas of economic activity. A.G.

Bibl: D. Parkin, *The Cultural Definition of Political Response: Lineal Destiny Among the Luo* (London, 1978).

polymer. Any material consisting of MACROMOLECULES formed by the linking of many similar chemical units into long chains. NYLON, POLYTHENE, and many other synthetic PLASTIC substances, as well as PROTEINS and other materials vital to life, are all polymers. Prediction *a priori* (see APRIORISM) of the properties of polymers from the fundamental laws of PHYSICS is very difficult, because of the great structural complexity of these systems. Therefore polymer science is interdisciplinary, and techniques from BIOLOGY, CHEMISTRY, and ENGINEERING are being employed to understand, e.g., the physical basis of inheritance (see DNA under NUCLEIC ACID) and the RHEOLOGY of bulk polymers such as wood. M.V.B.

polymer films. Of interest because of their potential use for producing materials with special optical and electronic properties. Depending on the material, they can be made by condensation from a vapour or by ELECTROLYSIS. Some of these films are electrically conducting. Very thin layers formed by electrolysis (a very cheap and simple process) have been used to make certain INTEGRATED CIRCUITS (see ORGANIC CONDUCTORS). H.M.R.

polymorphism. The presence in a single population of more than one genetically distinct type, each at a frequency too high to be explained by repeated MUTATION alone. The study of polymorphism is important for an understanding of EVOLUTION, which depends on populations being variable. J.M.S.

polynomial time, see under EXPONENTIAL TIME.

polynucleotide, see under NUCLEIC ACID.

polypeptide, see under PEPTIDE.

polyploid (noun or adjective). (A CELL) containing more than two sets of CHROMOSOMES. In an *autopolyploid* the chromosomes all come from a single SPECIES; in an *allopolyploid* from two or more species. Allopolyploids arise by HYBRIDIZATION between species followed by a doubling of the chromosome number. They are often sexually fertile, even if the DIPLOID hybrid is not. The process has been important in the origin of wild and domestic plant varieties, including wheat and cotton, but is rare or absent in animals.   J.M.S.

polyrhythm. The mixture of markedly differing rhythms, done in such a way as to be a striking feature of the music rather than a mere incidental; in particular, the combination of rhythms based upon different pulses or metres. Dating from the Middle Ages and brought to a point of perfection by the Elizabethan madrigalists, polyrhythm became relatively unimportant in the music of the 18th and 19th centuries, though examples occur in the finale of Mozart's Oboe Quartet and the ballroom scene in *Don Giovanni*. In the 20th century composers as diverse as Charles Ives, Michael Tippett, and Olivier Messiaen have been fascinated by the exploration of polyrhythm.   A.H.

polysynthetic (or *incorporating*). In comparative LINGUISTICS, adjectives sometimes applied to a type of AGGLUTINATING language (e.g. Eskimo) which displays a very high degree of synthesis in its word forms, single words typically containing as much structural information as entire sentences in ISOLATING languages.   D.C.

polysystemicism, see under FIRTHIAN.

polytheism, see under PANTHEISM; THEISM.

polythene (or *polyethylene* or *alkathene*). A synthetic POLYMER whose chemical inertness and flexibility, and the ease with which it can be shaped, result in a variety of industrial and domestic applications (plastic bags, buckets, etc.).   M.V.B.

polytonality. The simultaneous combination of several tonalities, each instrumental line adhering to one key regardless of possible conflict with other lines. Used occasionally in the past for humorous purposes (e.g. Mozart's Musical Joke), it was much exploited in scores by Milhaud (e.g. the Serenade in the 3rd Symphony), Bartók, Stravinsky, Holst (e.g. the Terzetto for Flute, Oboe, and Viola), and others. Like BITONALITY, it serves to preserve some of the stability conveyed by traditional tonality, while adding harmonic bite.

A.H.

polyunsaturated fats. Fats that contain many UNSATURATED chemical bonds. Polyunsaturated fats are thought to be the most healthy dietary form of fat because saturated fats tend to increase the amount of cholesterol in the body and an excess of cholesterol contributes to hardening of the arteries.   P.N.

polywater. A recently-discovered dense semi-PLASTIC material formed near the surface of fine glass tubes on which water has been condensed. Polywater is probably an effect of impurities leached from the glass, rather than an ALLOTROPE of water as originally believed.   M.V.B.

Pont-Aven. School of French painting, centred on the small Breton town of that name, which was much frequented by artists in the late 19th century, notably Gauguin around 1886-89. With a few younger painters, including Émile Bernard and Paul Sérusier, he there established his characteristic way of painting Breton subjects, using simplified outlines, flat two-dimensional surfaces, and clear colours. This SYNTHETISM became, through Sérusier, the launching platform for the NABIS.   J.W.
  Bibl: C. Chassé, *Gauguin et le groupe de Pont-Aven* (Paris, 1921).

pop. An abbreviation of 'popular' used in the arts since the 1950s to signify work employing aesthetic or symbolic elements calculated to appeal to a modern mass audience. The basis of the calculation is normally commercial, though the use made of the elements is often not. Originating in some measure as an updated and industrialized version of the FOLK concept, it differs in its overtones both from the German *volkstümlich* and from the French *populaire*, and is a purely Anglo-Saxon term which other cultures have had to import. The three main usages are:

(1) *Pop music*. Term used for a broad range of commercial music arising in the 1950s and 1960s in the U.S. and Europe and aimed to a large extent at the growing youth market. Pop music has its roots in the popular song styles of the first half of the century but has been influenced by rock and roll, country music, ROCK MUSIC, SOUL MUSIC, REGGAE, etc. This has led to a diverse range of formats and styles but dominant among these are the three minute song, recorded on a single and performed by a vocalist accompanied by electric guitars, electric bass, drums and various other instruments including more recently ELECTRONIC MUSICAL instruments. Pop music is often criticized for its disposable nature (in contrast to serious music and rock music) and for the massive influence of fashion and commercial interests on its production. These concerns can undoubtedly lead to stagnation and a smothering of other musical styles but among the vast amount of pop music produced there is an astonishing amount of highly original music.   B.CO.

(2) *Pop poetry*. A type of easily intelligible poem, akin to the pop lyric and often appealing to the same age-group, which is written primarily for public reading (often in combination with JAZZ; see JAZZ POETRY) and is associated particularly with the LIVERPOOL POETS whose rise followed that of the Beatles.

(3) *Pop art*. A term first used in the mid-1950s by the critic Lawrence Alloway to describe such elements as flags, jukeboxes, PACKAGING, comic strips, badges, and chromium-plated radiator grilles, then transferred to the often sophisticated, startling, ironic, or nostalgic constructions which highbrow artists began to make out of them. Based largely on the visual trappings of American industry (including the entertainment industry) and contemporary FOLKLORE (from Batman to Marilyn Monroe) much the same symbols served both British (Richard Hamilton, David Hockney, Peter Blake), and American

painters (Jim Dine, Andy Warhol, Roy Lichtenstein) who throughout the 1960s used a DADA-like COLLAGE technique and the silk-screen printing process to convey their many-levelled visions. Sometimes isolating the most mundane objects — e.g. the soup-tin or the mass-produced hamburger — they were echoed by sculptors like Claes Oldenburg, who made inflated versions of these in all kinds of materials. Lettering and sign-language were further elements which sometimes became dominant. Though the term remained Anglo-American a similar imagery and approach could be found among continental artists associated with NOUVEAU RÉALISME, and it has also affected the cinema, notably certain films of Jean-Luc Godard and the Beatles' cartoon film *The Yellow Submarine*. Fashion, packaging, and GRAPHIC DESIGN quickly conformed, the whole complex sometimes being known as the *pop scene*.   J.W.

Bibl: G. Melly, *Revolt into Style* (London, 1970; New York, 1971).

Popperian. Adjective referring to Karl Popper (*b*. Vienna, 1902), Professor of Logic and Scientific Method at London University 1949-69, and especially to his views on (1) the nature of scientific procedure and (2) the philosophical foundations for social reform.

(1) Popper's arguments for *deductivism*, or the *hypothetico-deductive method*, are expressed in *The Logic of Scientific Discovery* (1934; English translation 1959). He contends that a scientific theory can never be accorded more than provisional acceptance, and that even this cannot properly depend upon VERIFICATION of the kind made orthodox by Bacon and Mill. Their *inductivism* (see INDUCTION) suggests that the scientist must accumulate and classify particular observations and thereafter generalize the regularities which these exhibit. Popper retorts that no number of cases of *A* being *B* can establish that all *A*s are *B*. Yet he also notes that such universal statements, though unprovable, remain in principle *disprovable*. According to this principle of *falsifiability*, a theory holds until it is disproved; and falsification, not verification, is the appropriate object of the observational and experimental procedures of

665

science. Enlargement of our provisional knowledge begins with the conversion of hunches or other imaginative insights into hypotheses. Then, once the conditions for their falsification have been established by the application of deductive LOGIC, such hypotheses must be tested through sustained search for negative instances.

(2) The same distrust of dogmatism pervades Popper's more political writings such as *The Open Society* (1945) and *The Poverty of Historicism* (1957). He argues that social theories based on mistaken notions of certainty (e.g. 'scientific' MARXISM) breed AUTHORITARIANISM and unrealistic blueprints for total change; they embody a 'holistic' (see HOLISM) insistence that the individual possesses value only in so far as he subserves the needs of the whole. To this Popper opposes his own brand of METHODOLOGICAL INDIVIDUALISM, which seeks to understand 'all collective phenomena as due to the actions, interactions, aims, hopes, and thoughts of individual men, and as due to traditions created and preserved by individual men'. Popper's preference is for programmes of 'piecemeal SOCIAL ENGINEERING', that accord not only with individuals' competing aspirations but also with the spirit of critical self-scrutiny involved in the principle of 'falsification' outlined above.   M.D.B.

Bibl: B. Magee, *Popper* (London and New York, 2nd ed., 1982).

popular culture. Historically, popular culture refers to the oral, folk or 'little' tradition of the pre-literate mass; this vernacular cultural tradition is usually distinguished from the more esoteric high or 'great' literate culture characterized by its association with objects, texts and scores that are accessible through an extended and developed sense of AESTHETICS. While all have access to popular culture, high culture implies limited ingress. The sensitivity of popular culture to social change contributes to its ephemeral and transient character, and has prompted various conceptualizations and methodological approaches to the phenomenon. In the 1950s Hoggart, Williams and others extended the serious analysis of CULTURE and the question of aesthetics to include EVERYDAY visual, stylistic, and material reflections of the experience of ordinary people

and their response to real or imagined structural subordination. Popular culture has since become understood in terms of active processes and practices as well as objects and artefacts, and encompasses a variety of phenomena including mail order catalogues, the design of cars and other consumer durables, clothes, food fashions, football matches, videotapes, Christmas, etc. It has been suggested that popular culture has the capacity to subvert, even invert (Burke cites the historical function of the carnival (see CARNIVALIZATION) to 'turn the world upside down') the established HEGEMONIC order. Cultural elitists have traditionally criticized and attempted to neutralize or improve the culture and LIFE STYLE of the masses.

However, since 'the people' do not constitute an undifferentiated collectivity, their culture will vary according to their structural location and the perceptions that this entails, which has led to SUBCULTURAL analysis. Current POST-MODERNIST fascination with popular culture reflects the rediscovery of 'the people' by 18th- and 19th-century European INTELLECTUALS; then as now, the cultural system of the masses was undergoing changes (industrial capitalism, growing literacy, impact of the print MEDIA, SECULARIZATION and participatory politics). Contemporary concerns with MASS SOCIETY, the commodification of leisure, identity, etc., under consumer CAPITALISM have led to an erosion of the distinction between ELITE and popular culture, and now cultural SEMIOTICS deconstructs (see DECONSTRUCTION) all REPRESENTATIONS and signs to expose their uniform ideological significance. See also MASS CULTURE; HISTORY FROM BELOW.   P.S.L.

Bibl: P. Burke, *Popular Culture in Early Modern Europe* (London, 1978); I. Chambers, *Popular Culture: The Metropolitan Experience* (London, 1986).

popular dance. Sometimes termed social dance, has its roots in the SOCIAL STRUCTURE of society, in particular interclass relationships, changing attitudes towards women and patterns of social conventions, and the level of TECHNOLOGY. Popular dance therefore reflects the spirit of the age in any particular society and this term covers all forms of dancing related to recreation and leisure. Historically court dancing and folk dance come into this category, unlike CLASSICAL BALLET or MODERN DANCE. Popular dance plays a significant role in the general pattern of any society, for example in Britain ballroom dancing in the 19th and early 20th century, rock and roll of the 1950s, the dance crazes of the 1960s like the twist, and free form dance of the 1970s. Most recent innovations in popular dance have emerged in the street dance of the South Bronx, New York, where *body popping* and *break dancing* have developed into *hip hop* culture finding expression across all the arts. This form of popular dance clearly exemplifies its social roots inspired by repetitive drum machine sequences, robotics, and the body conscious competitive athleticism of the 1980s.   L.A.

Bibl: F. Rust, *Dance in Society* (London, 1969); B. Nadell and J. Small, *Break Dance* (London, 1984).

Popular Front. A COMMUNIST-inspired policy in the 1930s, aimed at bringing about the collaboration of the LEFT and CENTRE parties against RIGHT-wing movements and regimes. It was launched in July 1935 at the 7th Congress of the CO-MINTERN, after the abandonment of the policy of attacking social democrats (see SOCIAL DEMOCRACY) as 'social FASCISTS', which had contributed to the victory and consolidation of power by the NAZIS in Germany. The new policy of broad Left alliances brought Popular Front governments to power in France and Spain in 1936, and in Chile in 1938. In France the Popular Front government of Léon Blum (which did not include Communists, although it was to some extent supported by them) was replaced by that of Daladier after the coalition broke down in April 1938. In Spain the electoral victory of the Popular Front under President Azaña resulted in a CONFRONTATION with the Spanish Right and the civil war which ended in 1939 with the victory of Franco.

Generally, the Popular Front policy came to an end after the conclusion of the Nazi-Soviet pact (August 1939). The new Comintern line, radically changed, lasted until the attack of Hitler on the Soviet Union in June 1941. This attack once again led the Communists to seek cooper-ation with other parties in an 'anti-fascist front'.

Since World War II the policy of collaboration with SOCIALIST and 'BOURGEOIS' parties has undergone a variety of modifications, particularly since the emergence of POLYCENTRISM. It was abandoned in 1947 with the establishment of the COMINFORM and a new tough ('Zhdanov') line, but resumed by various Communist parties after Stalin's death, and particularly since the Soviet REHABILITATION of Tito (see TITOISM) in 1955. This tendency has continued. Coalition tactics have played an important part in the practice of Communist parties, particularly in France, Italy and Spain.   L.L.

Bibl: D.R. Brower, *The New Jacobins: The French Communist Party and the Popular Front* (Ithaca, 1968); *Journal of Contemporary History,* special issue on *Popular Front* (no. 3, 1970).

population biology. The study of all aspects of the structure and function of populations, in so far as they can be distinguished as comprising the unit of organization between the organism and the ECOSYSTEM. The subject includes the discipline of POPULATION GENETICS; population ECOLOGY, including DEMOGRAPHY; and many aspects of SOCIOBIOLOGY.

E.O.W.

population genetics. The study of genetic variation and change in populations; fundamental for an understanding of EVOLUTION, and also of animal and plant breeding.   J.M.S.

Bibl: J.F. Crow and M. Kimura, *An Introduction to Population Genetics Theory* (New York, 1970).

population pressure. The tension between the size of a population and the economic resources (above all food) at its disposal. The outcome of population pressure is usually seen in declining living standards, and ultimately in the operation of a MALTHUSIAN check, positive or preventive. Such pressure has characterized many developing nations in recent decades, with considerable distress, producing many fears of the outcome from continued rapid population growth. Defining pressure in other ways, demographers often make a distinction between 'low pressure' and 'high pressure' demographic regimes. The former have relatively low FERTILITY and high marriage ages (as was historically the case in much of western Europe), the latter high fertility and low marriage ages (as many Asian countries have exhibited); fertility controls and change are considerably easier to accomplish in low pressure regimes.   D.S.

Bibl: A. Sauvy, *General Theory of Population* (London and New York, 1969).

populism. A form of politics which emphasizes the virtues of the uncorrupt and unsophisticated common people against the double-dealing and selfishness to be expected of professional politicians and their intellectual helpers. It can therefore manifest itself in LEFT, RIGHT or centrist forms. On the left, it flowered in Russia, where the Narodniks believed that Russia might be spared the horrors of CAPITALISM and move directly to a form of SOCIALISM based on the peasant COMMUNE or Mir. Russian populism had distinguished liberal adherents such as Alexander Herzen, and wilder revolutionary adherents such as Bakunin and Tkachev. In the U.S., too, populisms have been seen as equally likely to be driven by right-wing fears of social and political change or by left-wing hopes for such change. Senator La Follette's Progressive Party represented the latter, the forces behind Senator Joseph McCarthy (see MCCARTHYISM) the former. American LIBERALS such as Edward Shils, Seymour Lipset and Daniel Bell have described all varieties of populism as pathological. Populism flourishes only when orthodox democratic politics does not.
                                        A.R.

Bibl: F. Venturi, *The Roots of Revolution* (London and New York, 1960); G. Ionescu and E. Gellner (eds.), *Populism* (London and New York, 1969).

pornography. Literally defined as the depiction of whores, but conventionally meaning representations (in literature, film, video, drama, the visual arts etc.) intended to produce sexual excitement. A distinction is usually made between 'hardcore' pornography — explicit and violent — and 'soft-core' pornography which is regarded by some as less harmful. But these definitions can only be provisional as the term 'pornography' is the subject of a debate in which different ideological (see IDEOLOGY) groupings produce their own definitions of pornography, and attempt to gain a consensus for those definitions through public campaigning.

Of three broad groupings, one might be categorized as the 'Moral Right', exemplified in Britain by Mary Whitehouse and her National Viewers and Listeners Association. They regard themselves as guardians of public morality and the sanctity of the family, taking an interpretation of Christian values as their authority. Sex itself is seen as wrong unless legitimized by marriage, and almost any representation is perceived as able to 'deprave or corrupt'. Through parliamentary lobbying and MEDIA publicity they seek to impose legal restraints on the portrayal of all sexually stimulating material.

Many feminists (see FEMINISM) find themselves in uneasy alliance with the 'Moral Right' when they seek to ban certain representations of sexuality. But their critique of pornography is very different. Feminists see pornography as an expression of male violence against women, as in the slogan 'Pornography is the theory, rape is the practice'. They challenge the Moral Right's defence of the family, which, no less than pornography, reinforces the institution of PATRIARCHY. Feminists describe a wider range of material as pornographic, objecting to the use of images of women (or parts of women) in ADVERTISING. Indeed some have described Western civilization as a 'pornographic culture'. The problem with this argument is that if society is wholly pornographic it is difficult to maintain a traditional distinction between pornographic and erotic representations, between 'wholesome' and 'unwholesome' representations. Consequently, some feminists, such as Griffin, posit a sexuality existing prior to, or outside, pornographic culture. But this contradicts a central argument of feminism (and of the Moral Right), namely that you cannot separate the individual from culture, the private from the public, pornography from sexual crimes.

Since the 1960s feminism has challenged and largely abandoned the liberal position on pornography, a position recently assumed by the Williams Committee (U.K., 1979). It asserts a clear distinction between the public and private realms: it is quite all right to enjoy pornography in private since this does not impinge on the public sphere, an area where private freedoms may conflict. Provided pornography does not harm those involved in its production, and is not imposed on those who do not wish to consume it, the law need not intervene (see PERMISSIVENESS). Consequently the Williams Committee disputed claims that pornography precipitates sexual crimes, merely recommending the restriction of hard-core material to special shops, without window-displays so as not to offend the casual passer-by. The debate will continue.   R.C.C.

Bibl: S. Griffin, *Pornography and Silence* (London, 1981); J. Ellis, 'Photography/Pornography/Art/Pornography' in *Screen* Vol. 21, No. 1, 1980.

portfolio selection. The INVESTMENT in a range of financial and real assets which diversifies the risk and gives a balance between income, CAPITAL appreciation and risk. In selecting the best balance, the investor may purchase a wide range of assets. In selecting a portfolio, as the range of assets held is broadened, the investor should also take account of the increased costs of purchasing, monitoring and selling of assets.   J.P.

Bibl: D. Begg *et al.*, *Economics* (London, 1984).

port-of-trade. Widely used in ARCHAEOLOGY. A defined location on the interface between discrete territories, specializing in the exchange of goods and raw materials between two or more socioeconomic systems.   B.C.

positive economics, see under ECONOMICS.

positive neutrality, see under NON-ALIGNMENT.

positivism. The view that all true knowledge is scientific, in the sense of describing the coexistence and succession of observable phenomena. So named by Comte, it was the leading principle of his comprehensive philosophical system, which took the unsophisticated form, for the most part, of an encyclopedic CLASSIFICATION of the findings of scientific enquiry. Positivism is a scientifically oriented form of EMPIRICISM. The word is now most commonly used as an abbreviation for LOGICAL POSITIVISM. In view of its close association with PHENOMENALISM and REDUCTIONISM generally, it is sometimes opposed to REALISM, particularly in the interpretation of the nature of the unobservable theoretical entities that occur in scientific discourse.   A.Q.

positron. The positively charged antiparticle (see ANTI-MATTER) corresponding to the ELECTRON.   M.V.B.

positron emission tomography, see under PET SCANNING.

possession, see under OWNERSHIP.

possible worlds. In PHILOSOPHY, situations or states of affairs which are free of internal inconsistency and which therefore do or can exist. The term is standardly employed to denote a situation or 'world' which, whether or not it in fact exists, nevertheless *could* do so. Leibniz originated the notion in arguing as follows: God could have created any contradiction-free world he chose. However, his goodness would prompt him to create only the very best such world. Therefore this world — the one we inhabit — must be the best of all possible worlds. In contemporary philosophy the notion is used in attempts to explain the modal concepts 'necessity' and 'contingency'. By means of it *necessary truth* is described as truth in every possible world, and *contingent truth* as truth in at least one possible world. It is claimed to be an important concept for investigating other issues in philosophy and LOGIC besides, but its use is controversial. In its strictest contemporary sense, the concept belongs to the SEMANTIC interpretation of quantified MODAL LOGIC.
                                        A.C.G.

Bibl: A. Plantinga, *The Nature of Necessity* (Oxford, 1974).

post-capitalist; post-economic, see POST-INDUSTRIAL SOCIETY.

posterior distribution, see under STATISTICS.

Post-Impressionism. An English term for modern French art from IMPRESSIONISM to World War I. It derived from the Post-Impressionist Exhibitions organized by Roger Fry at the Grafton Gallery, London, in 1910 and 1912, and was used to embrace all the artists revealed there, i.e. the NEO-IMPRESSIONISTS, Gauguin and the PONT-AVEN school, Cézanne, the FAUVES, and the early CUBISTS, and also (by adoption) the work of van Gogh. Hence there is no equivalent in German or French. J.W.

Bibl: A.C.H. Bell, *Since Cézanne* (London and New York, 1922); C.J. Holmes, *Notes on the Post-Impressionist Painters* (London, 1910); *Post-Impressionism: Cross-currents in European Painting* (London, 2nd ed., 1981).

post-industrial society. A term coined by the American sociologist Daniel Bell to describe the new SOCIAL STRUCTURES evolving in INDUSTRIAL SOCIETIES in the latter part of the 20th century which (he believes) point the way to the emergence of a new form of society in the U.S.A., Japan, the U.S.S.R., and Western Europe in the next century. What Bell calls the 'axial principle' of post-industrial society is 'the centrality of theoretical knowledge as the source of innovation and of policy formation for the society'. Economically, it will be marked by the change from a goods-producing to a service economy; occupationally, by the pre-eminence of the professional and technical CLASS; and in decision-making by the creation of new 'intellectual technology'.

The same term has been used by other writers with a different emphasis on the features which they believe will mark post-industrial society, e.g. the search by young people for a world beyond materialism (Kenneth Kenniton, Paul Goodman); or the displacement, as a result of technological change, of the WORKING CLASS from the ROLE assigned to it by MARXISTS as the historic agent of change in society (various NEO-MARXISTS). Other terms which have been used to convey the same idea of the emergence of a new form of society are 'post-economic'; 'post-capitalist' (Ralf Dahrendorf); 'post-maturity' (W.W. Rostow); and 'technetronic' (Z. Brzezinski). A.L.C.B.

Bibl: D. Bell, *The Coming of Post-Industrial Society* (New York, 1973; London, 1974).

post-modern classicism. As POST-MODERNISM took over as the reigning AVANT-GARDE architectural stance in the western world certain models became more preferred than others. Classical architecture was the main preference — more accurately the details of classical buildings: keystones, rustication, arches, friezes, fountains, columns, pilasters, domes, vaults and the like. This was partly because the well defined language of classical architecture was reasonably easily grasped by architects, who all had a cursory training in the history of architecture, partly because clients recognized classicalism from the 19th-century buildings remaining in their cities and believed that they were getting buildings which related to that tradition. Thus designing post-modern classical buildings was a pragmatic response to the market and the fact that other architects would understand the architectural 'jokes'. Increasingly the joke element (never admitted to people outside the closed architectural circle) faded as post-modernists began to take themselves with great seriousness — including an attempt by some of them to restyle themselves under the heading *symbolic architecture* in which the various details of a building could be explained one by one — providing buildings with a deeper 'meaning' than that given by inventive re-use of formal historical elements. S.L.

post-modern dance. A form of AVANT-GARDE DANCE in the U.S.A that emerged from Cunningham's inspiration in the 1960s and broke from the more traditional MODERN DANCE. Post-modern dancers influenced by Anna Halprin, James Waring and Robert Dunn reacted against the expressiveness of modern dance, narrative choreographic content, musical formulae and demands for technical excellence. The post-modern aesthetic proposed changes in structure and performance attitude, and that conceptual development of theories or systems of movement might be a reasonable framework to look at movement for its own sake. This aesthetic proposed that dance be akin to real life, using the body in a relaxed, casual and ordinary way, i.e. pedestrian movement, that REAL TIME be used, that attention be deliberately drawn away from skill or virtuosic technique, and that flaws and limitations were not to be hidden from the audience. Since the body was the subject for the dance it raised direct questions about sexual politics. Analytic post-modern dance used recognizable processes of construction, e.g. accumulation, tasks, systems, ALEATORIC structure, rules etc. to shape this anti-illusionist approach.   L.A.

Bibl: S. Banes, *Terpsichore in Sneakers* (Boston, 1980); D. Jowitt, *Dance Beat: Selected Views and Reviews 1967-76* (New York, 1977).

post-modernism. An increasingly familiar if still controversial term for defining or suggesting the overall character or direction of experimental tendencies in Western arts, architecture, etc., since the 1940s or 1950s, and particularly more recent developments associated with POST-INDUSTRIAL SOCIETY. The term contains its own paradox, suggesting that MODERN-ISM is decisively over, and a new artistic era has succeeded; at the same time it implies that successor movements are dependent on it, as well as in some degree in revolt against it. In fact most attempts at definition suggest that what has been called, by J.-F. Lyotard, 'the post-modern condition' arises from the broad if belated acceptance of modernism and its AVANT-GARDE aspirations as the dominant 20th-century tradition — hence centralizing the avant-garde but requiring advance beyond its conventions. This has given the contemporary, post-1945 artist an inordinate, pluri-cultural range of styles, techniques and technologies, but has also created an uncertainty and indeterminacy about their use and their authority. Hence post-modernism is often associated with a revolt against authority and signification, and a tendency towards pastiche, parody, quotation, self-referentiality, and eclecticism.

So in architecture post-modernism now refers largely to building design subsequent to the Modern Movement of Mies van der Rohe, etc., and a move away from functionalism towards colourful play and eclectic quotation (e.g. the architecture of Robert Venturi). In painting the tendencies on from the 1950s acceptance of AB-STRACT EXPRESSIONISM have been seen as 'post-modern'. In music, the work of Messiaen, Stockhausen and John Cage, again marked by eclecticism and ALEA-TORY qualities, has been similarly identified. In literature the term has been used to relate a wide variety of tendencies in fiction, drama and poetry subsequent to James Joyce and inclining to what John Barth has called 'the literature of exhaustion', a writing conscious of the 'used-upedness' of forms. In the novel this ranges among phenomena as different as the French NOUVEAU ROMAN, the CUT-UP novel (William S. Burroughs), the self-reflexive novel (Nabokov, middle Beckett, Borges), the non-fiction novel (Mailer, Capote), the cybernetic novel (Pynchon, Gaddis), the MAGIC REALIST novel (Marquez, Cortazar), to name but a few. Again there is the implication of eclecticism, as likewise in poetry and drama. Similarly, merged forms — HAPPENINGS, multi-media arts, crossovers of high and POP arts, from the late 1950s on — are generally seen as 'post-modern'.

The strongest philosophical context is that of STRUCTURALISM and DECONSTRUC-TION, and the sense of collapsed signification and challenged HUMANISM it expresses as a late 20th-century demystificatory philosophy. Recent debate — particularly that between the German philosopher Jurgen Habermas and the French post-structuralist Lyotard — has implied that post-modernism is the art of an age of counter-revolutionary politics, avant-garde exhaustion and defeated PROGRESS-IVE impulses, by contrast with modernism. But just as modernism contained both the radical and the conservative, so has post-modernism, which owed much to the radical movements of the 1960s. Modernism was a movement of many segments, directions, and inner disputes; so is post-modernism, though it is harder, being contemporary, to identify. It is a still amorphous body of developments and directions marked by eclecticism, pluriculturalism, and often a post-industrial, hi-tech frame of reference coupled with a sceptical view of TECHNICAL PROGRESS. Like structuralism and deconstruction, it seems both to revolt against and seek to recover humanism. To date it remains best seen as a complex map of late 20th-century directions rather than a clearcut aesthetic and philosophical IDEOLOGY.

M.S.BR.

Bibl: Christopher Butler, *After the Wake* (Oxford, 1980); J.-F. Lyotard, *The Postmodern Condition* (Paris, 1979; Manchester, 1984); Charles Newman, *The Post-Modern Aura* (Evanston, 1985).

post-painterly abstraction, see under MINIMAL ART.

postulational method, see under AXIOMATICS.

post-Webern school. Collective name given to those composers in the 1950s who were influenced by the work of Anton Webern. The most important of these composers are Boulez and Stockhausen and some of the areas they developed were total serialism (see SERIAL MUSIC), POINTILLISM and MOBILE FORM.

B.CO.

Bibl: R. Smith Brindle, *The New Music* (London, 1975).

potassium-argon dating, see under DATING.

potential. A mathematical representation of a FIELD in PHYSICS. In a field of force due to GRAVITATION, for example, the POTENTIAL ENERGY of a body at any point is obtained by multiplying its mass by the value of the potential there. Other potentials describe ELECTROMAGNETIC forces, and the velocity field in a flowing fluid.

M.V.B.

potential energy. The ENERGY that a system has as a result of its position in a FIELD of force. For example, a spring which has been compressed or extended against its elastic forces, and a pair of positive electric charges pushed together against their mutual repulsion, are both systems whose potential energy has increased, because they are capable of doing work while returning to their original states. On the other hand, an apple that has fallen to the ground has lost GRAVITATIONAL potential energy, because work must be done on it to return it to its original height.

M.V.B.

potlatch. 'To give'; potlatch is a form of institutionalized *gift exchange* (see GIFT; EXCHANGE). It was found among the Kwakiutl and other Indian communities of the American north-west. A detailed study of potlatching was made by Boas (*Kwakiutl Ethnography*, 1897) and his work was used by Mauss in his development of a theory of gift exchange. A potlatch is a public distribution of goods and the holder of a potlatch makes a claim to STATUS on the basis of his POWER to give. Goods for redistribution may have been accumulated through a cycle of smaller potlatches and from the NETWORK of gifts and loans which bind kin or members of a DESCENT group. In giving the potlatch the holder binds the recipients in a relationship of debt. The system is fiercely competitive with each holder trying to outdo rivals in generosity.

It has been suggested that the potlatch has a sound economic rationale. It redistributes food from those with surplus to those experiencing temporary shortage. At the same time it allows the holder to convert perishable goods into durable status. On occasions a potlatch may involve a dramatic public destruction of property and the holder lays down a challenge to his rivals to outbid him in the amount they can destroy. There are a number of similarities between the potlatch system of the Kwakiutl and the kinds of ceremonial exchange, for example the KULA and moka, found in New Guinea.

A.G.

Bibl: C.A. Gregory, 'Gifts to Men and Gifts to God: Gift Exchange and Capital Accumulation in Contemporary Papua', *Man* vol. 15, no. 4, 1980.

Potsdam. The site of the last great conference between the U.S.S.R, U.S. and Britain of World War II (see also YALTA), held after the German capitulation from 17 July to 2 August 1945. The main actors were Stalin, Truman and Churchill, the latter being replaced by the new Prime Minister Attlee during the conference. The three powers attempted to resolve a series of questions including war reparations, the boundaries of Poland, treatment of Germany's European allies and the post-war political character of Germany. The contemporaneous successful testing in the U.S. of the atomic bomb encouraged President Truman to lead the issue of the Potsdam Declaration, which demanded the unconditional surrender of Japan, whose resistance was met with the decision to drop an atomic bomb on HIROSHIMA.   S.R.

Bibl: A.W. de Porte, *Europe Between the Superpowers* (New Haven, Conn., 2nd ed., 1986).

Poujadism. A set of attitudes derived from a political movement founded by Pierre Poujade, a French small-town shopkeeper, in 1953. These embodied lower-middle-class, PETIT BOURGEOIS resentment at the increasing interference of the State by taxation, investigation of tax evasion, and other regulatory power over their economic freedom of action. Poujadism was essentially hostile to the State as anything more than the provider of LAW AND ORDER, and therefore to MODERNIZATION or any encouragement of large-scale labour or business organization. The Poujadist Association for Defence of Shopkeepers and Artisans won 50 seats and three million votes in the 1956 parliamentary elections, but disintegrated in the political crisis of 1958 with the advent of GAULLISM.   D.C.W.

poverty trap. A situation in which a poor household on increasing its income from employment loses (low) income-related benefits and pays a high rate of tax on the increase in income. Thus, the actual benefit of finding employment or better paid employment is reduced. It has been suggested that this may discourage persons in these households from searching for and taking employment. In certain circumstances, the loss of benefits and the increase in tax payments can exceed the increase in income. In devising tax and benefit systems, it is desirable, but difficult, to avoid the construction of poverty traps.   J.P.

Bibl: J. Craven, *Introduction to Economics* (Oxford, 1984).

powder metallurgy. The production from a powder, without melting, of compact pieces of metal in a usable form. The process, first demonstrated by William Wollaston at the end of the 18th century, involves pressing and heating the powder in the required shape so that SINTERING causes the PARTICLES to adhere strongly. It is of value particularly for metals such as tungsten, which cannot be melted under commercial conditions. The incorporation of a second substance, e.g. graphite in bearings, may also be readily effected.

B.F.

power. One of the central CONCEPTS of political theory, which sociologists have sought to define by distinguishing it from *authority* on the one hand, and from *force* on the other. *Power* is the ability of its holders to exact compliance or obedience of other individuals to his *will*, on whatsoever basis. Yet, as Rousseau observed in *The Social Contract* (Book I, chapter 3), 'The strongest man is never strong enough to be always master unless he transforms his power into right and obedience into duty'.

Authority is an attribute of social organization — a family, a corporation, a university, a government — in which command inheres in the recognition of some greater competence lodged either in the person or in the office itself. Relations between states — in the absence of any common framework of law or consensus — are usually power relations. Relations between individuals and groups, if regularized and subject to rules, traditional or legal, tend to be authority relations.

Force is a compulsion, sometimes physical (when it then becomes violence), invoked by wielders of power and authority. Force may be utilized in support of authority, as the spanking of a child or the imprisonment of a felon. And the threat of force often lies behind the use of power to enforce a power-holder's will. Yet there are examples of the use of power (i.e. will) in history without force, such as Gandhi's *satyagraha* (NON-VIOLENT RESISTANCE) to British authority.

In political theory, the State alone,

among modern associations, can make legitimate use of police and military force in the exercise of its authority. In contemporary social theory, the important component in the exercise of authority is LEGITIMACY, the rightful rule or exercise of power, based on some principle (e.g. consent) jointly accepted by the ruler and the ruled.　　　　　　　　　　　D.B.

Bibl: B. de Jouvenel, tr. J.F. Huntington, *Power* (London, rev. ed., 1952); S. Lukes, *Power* (London, 1974).

power élite. A phrase coined by the American sociologist C. Wright Mills for those who stand at the heads of the major institutional hierarchies of modern society — the corporations, the military, and the State — and who, through their pooled interests, become 'an intricate set of overlapping cliques [sharing] decisions having at least national consequences'. The theory has been criticized by MARXISTS for its focus on ÉLITES, rather than on CLASSES, and by LIBERALS for preaching a conspiracy theory of POWER; for confusing *arenas* of action (e.g. the political system) with INSTITUTIONS; for loosely asserting a shared degree of interests between institutional sectors, rather than organized groups; and for failing to focus on decision-making and decisions, rather than on institutional hierarchies.　　　D.B.

Bibl: C.W. Mills, *The Power Elite* (London and New York, 1956); G.W. Domhoff, *Who Rules America Now?* (New York, 1983).

power politics. An emotive phrase applied to the employment of calculations of comparative POWER and influence made by those responsible for the major powers' conduct of foreign policy, as in the phrase 'playing power politics'. Critics of power politics wish to substitute for it the rule of ETHICS, law, and justice in international relations; others hold that, so long as the world is divided into independent sovereign states, there is no alternative to international relations being based upon considerations of power, and that it is self-deception to pretend otherwise.　A.L.C.B.

Bibl: I. Claude, *Power and International Relations* (New York, 1962); M. Wight, *Power Politics* (London, 1946, rev. ed., 1977).

PPBS (programme, planning, and budgeting system; also known as *programme budgeting*). A method of determining the allocation of resources in the PUBLIC SECTOR organizations, such as EDUCATION, local authorities, and the social services, in which profit criteria are inappropriate. In contrast to the traditional budgeting of expenditure by cost item and spending department, PPBS identifies expenditures with the basic programmes of activity. Originating in the U.S. Treasury, the methods have been employed (under various names) in many organizations, including the former Greater London Council. See also COST-BENEFIT ANALYSIS.　R.I.T.

Bibl: D. Novick, *Program Budgeting* (London and Cambridge, Mass., 1965).

PR. Abbreviation for either PROPORTIONAL REPRESENTATION or PUBLIC RELATIONS.

practical criticism, see under LEAVISITE.

pragmatics. In LINGUISTICS, the study of language from the viewpoint of the users, especially of the choices they make, the constraints they encounter in using language in social interaction, and the effects their use of language has on the other participants in the act of communication. This field, which deals with such diverse topics as politeness, conversational interaction, DEIXIS, PRESUPPOSITION and SPEECH ACTS, is attracting a great deal of interest in the 1980s, but it is not as yet capable of clear definition or delimitation from such areas as SEMANTICS and SOCIO-LINGUISTICS.　　　　　　　　D.C.

Bibl: S. Levinson, *Pragmatics* (Cambridge, 1983); G.N. Leech, *Pragmatics* (London, 1983).

pragmatism. In PHILOSOPHY, a version of EMPIRICISM, developed in the U.S.A. by C.S. Peirce, William James, and John Dewey, which interprets the meaning and justification of our beliefs in terms of their 'practical' effects or content. Peirce's pragmatic maxim was a theory of MEANING which identified the content of a PROPOSITION with the experienceable difference between its being true and its being false. James put forward a pragmatic theory of TRUTH as that which it is ultimately satisfying to believe, either because the expectations a true belief excites are actually fulfilled or, in the less empirical case of the propositions of THEOLOGY and METAPHYSICS, because they contribute to the satisfactoriness of, and effectiveness in, the conduct of life. Dewey stressed that aspect of pragmatism which holds knowledge to be an instrument for action, rather than an object of disinterested contemplation. In general, pragmatists emphasize the conventional character of the CONCEPTS and beliefs with which we seek to understand the world as opposed to the 'intellectualism' which sees them as a passive reflection of the fixed, objective structure of things. An incentive to this view has been the idea that mutually inconsistent scientific theories can each be compatible with all the known empirical data so that only non-logical features of simplicity, convenience, and utility can provide a reason for selection between them. A.Q.

Bibl: A. Rorty (ed.), *Pragmatic Philosophy* (New York, 1966); A.J. Ayer, *The Origins of Pragmatism* (London and San Francisco, 1968).

Prague. The capital of Czechoslovakia and the scene of three major crises of 20th-century European history, each of which is frequently named after it.

(1) Prague, 1939. In March 1939 Hitler ordered the occupation by force of the capital and the rest of Czechoslovakia, which had already been truncated by the MUNICH agreement of 1938. Apart from the consequences for the Czech people, who spent the next six years under German 'protection', this new and undisguised act of aggression ended any illusions that Hitler would be satisfied with the incorporation into the Third Reich of territories with a German-speaking population, and confronted the other powers with the choice between acquiescing in Hitler's domination of Europe or steeling themselves to fight in order to prevent it. A.L.C.B.

(2) Prague, 1948. In February 1948 the Czechoslovak COMMUNIST Party, with its adjunct the Slovak Communist Party, seized power and replaced the coalition government, in which they were already the largest single element, with a virtual single-party dictatorship. The coup was achieved by a combination of mass demonstrations and threats, while technically remaining within the forms of the constitution; the term *coup de Prague* has come to be used generally for any quasi-constitutional change backed by street pressures. As in the case of (1), apart from the consequences for the people of Czechoslovakia themselves, Prague 1948 ended illusions in the West that the Soviet Union would be satisfied with anything less than complete control through local Communist regimes of the countries within her sphere of influence in Eastern and Central Europe, and led to an intensification of the COLD WAR. R.C.; A.L.C.B.

(3) Prague, 1968, refers to two developments which attracted worldwide attention. The first, known as the *Prague Spring* (from an annual music festival in the capital), was the attempt by reforming elements in the Czechoslovak Communist Party, with growing public support, to liberalize domestic affairs ('SOCIALISM with a human face') and achieve some international freedom of action without abandoning overall Party control or Warsaw Pact membership. Replacement of Antonin Novotný by the more open-minded Slovak, Alexander Dubček, as Party leader in January earned the backing of Slovak autonomists for a cautious reform programme. The second development was the open intervention of the Soviet Union to suppress the CZECH REFORM MOVEMENT, which led to the invasion of Czechoslovakia by Soviet armed forces in August 1968 and the replacement of Dubček by the conservative Gustáv Husák eight months later. The Party Congress held secretly during the invasion in Prague-Vysočany was then annulled, censorship reimposed, the ideas of the reformists abjured in favour of so-called NORMALIZATION, and their spokesmen decried as REVISIONIST or counter-revolutionary. D.V.

Bibl: H.G. Skilling, *Czechoslovakia's Interrupted Revolution* (Princeton, 1976).

Prague School. In linguistics, a group of LINGUISTS (notably R. Jakobson and N. Trubetskoy) working in and around Prague in the late 1920s and early 1930s.

Their primary contribution was the formulation of an influential theory of PHONOLOGY in which sounds were analysed into sets of distinctive oppositions. More recently, a *neo-Prague* school has concentrated on developing syntactic theory in terms of the SAUSSURIAN notion of functionally contrastive constituents of sentences (see SYNTAGMATIC AND PARADIGMATIC): this is known as FUNCTIONAL SENTENCE PERSPECTIVE (FSP). D.C.

Bibl: J. Vachek (ed.), *A Prague School Reader in Linguistics* (London and Bloomington, 1966).

Prague Spring, see under PRAGUE (3).

Pravda (*Truth*). A Soviet daily newspaper, the official organ of the Soviet COMMUNIST Party. It was founded in 1912 and published legally in Czarist Russia until 1914, when it was banned because of its 'revolutionary defeatism'. It reappeared after the 1917 February revolution and since October 1917 has been the leading Soviet journal. Published in Moscow since 1918, it appears seven days a week, and its editorials provide the best indication of the current Party line. Its editors have included Stalin and Bukharin; its estimated circulation is 8,300,000 — slightly higher than that of IZVESTIA. Under Gorbachov, *Pravda* has surprised some western observers by taking a more critical view of certain aspects of Soviet society than it had done previously. L.L.; S.T.

praxis. This Greek term for 'action' or 'practice' was given a special meaning in the early philosophy of Karl Marx (see MARXISM). It refers to the idea of 'the unity of theory and practice'. Thought or theory, Marx claimed, cannot be seen as separate from practice, as some abstract standard or contemplative ideal. It arises out of practice, and is developed and modified by it. Marx considered that the split between 'ideal' and 'reality', between an irrational world and a RATIONALIST critique of it, could only be overcome by the development of a theoretical consciousness among social groups engaged in the practice of changing the real world. The praxis of the PROLETARIAT, therefore, would consist in the growth of a SOCIALIST consciousness arising out of the conditions of life of the proletariat and its attempts to transform them. K.K.

Bibl: L. Kolakowski, *Main Currents of Marxism*, vol.I (Oxford, 1981).

prebiotic chemistry. The study of the chemical events that led to the origin of life on Earth. Although it has been shown that complex biological MOLECULES can be formed from simple chemicals under the conditions that are thought to have prevailed in prebiotic times, these experiments are far removed from the experimental creation of life and there is no prospect of that being achieved in the foreseeable future. As a result a few people have been driven to take seriously the concept of PANSPERMIA, even if that simply passes the problem on to another time and place. P.N.

precasting, see under CONCRETE.

precession, see under GYROSCOPE.

precisionism. A name given to American REALIST painting in the 1920s and 1930s that combined ideas and techniques of photography and CUBISM in its representation of the contemporary industrial landscape. So-called Precisionists Charles Sheeler, Charles Demuth, and Preston Dickinson painted machine forms and domestic architecture with dryness, clean detail, and sharp focus that occasionally bordered on abstraction (see ABSTRACT ART). A.K.W.

Bibl: B. Rose, *American Art Since 1900* (London and New York, 1967); S. Hunter, *American Art of the 20th Century* (New York, 1972).

precognition. The direct awareness of future events, or true prophecy, as contrasted with the rational prediction which derives beliefs about the future, which there is good reason to think true, from the present state of things together with more or less well-confirmed laws of nature. Memory, as distinct from apparent memory, implies that the event remembered really has happened. Likewise precognition implies that the event precognized really will happen. It can be argued that precognition is impossible in so far as the notion of knowledge that is logically included in it entails (see ENTAILMENT) that the state of knowing is caused by the fact known. For if there were precognition a future event would have to cause a present one and a cause can never be temporally subsequent to its effect. This, however, is a semantic point. It does not mean that people cannot have true, uninferred beliefs about the future but only that, since this cannot be causally explained, it cannot be called knowledge. A.Q.

preconscious. In psychoanalytic theory (see PSYCHOANALYSIS), a word used in two ways. (1) To refer to thoughts, which, although not actually present in CONSCIOUSNESS, are nevertheless capable of being brought into consciousness by ordinary recall and effort. By contrast, UNCONSCIOUS thoughts can be recovered only — if at all — by the aid of technical methods, such as PSYCHOTHERAPY and psychoanalysis (see also REPRESSION). (2) To refer to the part of the mental system, or apparatus, that contains these preconscious thoughts. B.A.F.

predicate calculus. One of the two chief LOGICAL CALCULI, consisting of a formal system of notation, AXIOMS, and rules for handling QUANTIFICATION. See also AXIOMATICS. R.G.

prediction theory, see under EXTRAPOLATION.

pre-emptive strike, see under STRATEGIC CAPABILITY.

prefabrication (or *industrialized building*). The manufacture of building elements for subsequent assembly at the site in an attempt to shift the major effort to the controlled conditions of the factory. The factory may be either a distant plant making complete bathroom units, for instance, or an enclosure on or near the site making CLADDING panels of precast CONCRETE.

Prefabrication in any serious sense began in the 19th century with the manufacture of cast- and wrought-iron structural members, particularly where these, together with glass, were marketed to provide complete greenhouses. After 1945 systems of industrialized building were developed in which a coordinated range of components could be assembled to provide whole schools or flats. In the U.S.S.R. and Eastern Europe the method was widely used for housing. Industrialized systems, however, have not yet shown the economic benefits claimed for them, while the visual effect has frequently been undistinguished. M.BR.

Bibl: B. Kelly, *The Prefabrication of Houses* (London and New York, 1951).

preference. An international trading arrangement between two countries or more whereby one or both give favourable treatment to the other(s) by removing or lowering its existing tariffs. Preferences run counter to an alternative principle in trading arrangements, which argues that trading arrangements should be entirely nondiscriminatory, a principle enshrined in GATT. Preferences have become highly controversial as the expanding EEC makes preferential arrangements with an increasing number of countries in the Mediterranean area as well as in Africa. D.E.

Bibl: B. Sodersten, *International Economics* (London, 1980).

preformation and **epigenesis.** Alternative interpretations, thought in Victorian times to be mutually exclusive, of the development of animals and plants. Preformationists believed that the adult simply enlarges or unfolds from a miniature precursor, e.g. homunculus; epigenesists that development results from the evocative influences of the ENVIRONMENT shaping the germ into its adult form. The truth is now known to lie somewhere between the two: the genetic instructions which are followed in development are certainly preformed — or at all events inherited — but their working out and realization is epigenetic in pattern, i.e. depends upon an interplay between environmental STIMULI and the effects of neighbouring CELLS upon the genetic programme built into them. See also EMBRYOLOGY. P.M.

prefrontal leucotomy, see under LEUCOTOMY.

prehistory. The study of the past of a given region before the appearance of written

677

records relevant to that region. See also ARCHAEOLOGY.   B.C.

preon, see under ELEMENTARY PARTICLES.

prepared piano. A piano whose timbre is altered by the attachment of a variety of objects (metal, rubber, wood, glass, etc.) to the strings and hammers so as to produce intriguing and unexpected sounds. It resulted from the compositional investigations of the American John Cage (*b.* 1912). Part of the effect lies in the denial of expectation: seeing a piano, the audience has a preconceived notion of the sound it will make.   A.H.

Preppie. An early POPULAR CULTURE manifestation among young people of a return after the 1960s (see PERMISSIVE; HIPPIE) to a more conventional and conformist LIFE STYLE, attitudes and external appearance. Loosely based on folk memories of 1950s elitist East Coast American prep school styles (specific brands of button-down shirts, shoes and trousers and short neat haircuts) its display of 'higher' cultural SYMBOLS reflects a distancing from COUNTER-CULTURAL forms.   P.S.L.

prequark, see under ELEMENTARY PARTICLES.

Presbyterianism. A system of church government. In the New Testament, an 'elder' (Greek *presbuteros*) is a leader of a Christian congregation. Returning to that system as part of their Calvinist (see CALVINISM) THEOLOGY, Presbyterian churches have been established around the world, including the Church of Scotland. 'Elders' lead a local church; one of them is 'the Minister' who preaches, and representatives gather in a 'Presbytery' which supervises church life in an area. Both EPISCOPALISM and the independence of the congregation are rejected. In the 1980s about 43 million Christians belong to such churches and more than five times as many adhere to 'united' churches influenced by this tradition but often having bishops with limited powers.   D.L.E.

prescriptive, see under NORMATIVE.

prescriptivism, see under EMOTIVISM.

present-value method, see under DISCOUNTED CASH FLOW.

presidentialism (France). The 1958 Constitution of the Fifth Republic was written by General de Gaulle (President of the Republic 1958-1969) and close associates such as Michel Debré (Prime Minister from 1958-1962). De Gaulle (see GAULLISM) believed that the parliamentary system of government which had existed during the Fourth Republic (1945-1958) had been a major cause of the political instability and eventual collapse of this regime. The primary objective of the authors of the 1958 Constitution, therefore, was to establish a powerful political executive which would no longer be at the mercy of parliament. This was achieved in two ways: the legislative powers of parliament were substantially reduced; and executive power shared between a prime minister, who is 'in general charge of the work of the government' and a powerful president who 'ensures by his arbitration the regular functioning of the organs of government and the continuity of the STATE'. Presidents of the Third and Fourth Republic had — with few exceptions — been little more than ceremonial figureheads; the 1958 Constitution thus marked a decisive departure.

Since 1962 the president has been directly elected by universal suffrage every seven years. In addition to the traditional power enjoyed by a head of state, the French president has the constitutional right to appoint (though not to dismiss) the prime minister, to send a bill to the Constitutional Court for judgment on its constitutionality and to appoint three of the nine members of that Court, to request a referendum and to dissolve the National Assembly. Most controversial of all, the president may under Article 16 (the so-called emergency powers provision) take whatever measures he/she sees fit 'when there exists a serious and immediate threat to the institutions of the republic, the integrity of its territory or the fulfilment of international obligations'.

The Constitution is, however, extremely vague when it comes to defining the powers of the president and all incumbents (most notably General de Gaulle himself) have, by their interpretation of the document and their actions, further increased the powers of the president. Successive presidents have chosen and dismissed government ministers as well as prime ministers. Equally, all presidents have followed de Gaulle in declaring that foreign policy falls within the presidential domain. And while all presidents have declared themselves to be above the fray of politics, they have increasingly intervened to marshal party and parliamentary support for government policy. Thus, whatever the intentions of the framers of the Constitution, presidential supremacy was quickly established. Two factors (the imprint of General de Gaulle upon the office; and the introduction in 1962 of a directly-elected president) were decisive in the consolidation of the presidential regime.

This trend towards full-blown presidentialism was nevertheless challenged following the legislative elections (which take place every five years) of March 1986. In those elections, the SOCIALIST government which had been elected in 1981, was defeated by the RIGHT-wing opposition parties. The socialist president, François Mitterrand, who had been elected in 1981, thus became (with two years of his presidency remaining) the first president of the Fifth Republic to face a hostile majority in the National Assembly. Since March 1986 the assertive Gaullist prime minister, Jacques Chirac, has been forced to 'cohabit' with the socialist president. COHABITATION (which has attracted considerable public support) has prompted much debate on the subject of the respective constitutional powers of the president and prime minister. Chirac has declared his right to govern while Mitterrand has refused to sign government decrees on PRIVATIZATION and social reform, thus forcing the prime minister to obtain parliamentary approval for his policies.

Presidents of the Fifth Republic: 1958-1969 General Charles de Gaulle (Gaullist); 1969-1974 Georges Pompidou (Gaullist); 1974-1981 Valéry Giscard d'Estaing (Republican); since 1981 François Mitterrand (Socialist).   S.M.
Bibl: V. Wright, *The Government and Politics of France* (London, 1983); M. Anderson, *Government in France — an Introduction to the Executive Power* (London, 1970).

pressure group, see under INTEREST GROUP.

pressurized-water reactor (PWR). A NUCLEAR REACTOR using water as a coolant and moderator at a pressure that is too high to allow boiling to take place inside the reactor. The fuel is enriched uranium oxide cased in zirconium.   C.E.D.

prestige goods economy. Useful concept borrowed by archaeologists from ANTHROPOLOGY. An economy in which social STATUS is maintained by the acquisition and selective distribution of goods acquired from outside the system.   B.C.
Bibl: J. Friedman and M.J. Rowlands, *The Evolution of Social Systems* (London, 1977).

prestressing, see under CONCRETE.

presupposition.
(1) In PHILOSOPHY, the logically NECESSARY CONDITION of some state of affairs which must be satisfied if the state of affairs is to obtain. Thus the uniformity of nature has been held to be a presupposition of the rationality of inductive reasoning (see INDUCTION); the real existence of UNIVERSALS to be a presupposition of our ability to classify things into kinds as we do with predicative general terms; memory, less controversially, to be a presupposition of our having a CONCEPT of the past. Philosophy has sometimes been held, not unreasonably, to be a matter of the pursuit and critical examination of the presuppositions of the varieties of human thinking. Kant's theory of the synthetic *a priori* principles of the understanding (see APRIORISM) is, in effect, an account of the presuppositions of Newtonian PHYSICS; his ethical theory of the CATEGORICAL IMPERATIVE an account of the presuppositions of a particularly rigorous form of Protestant morality. R.G. Collingwood held that in different ages men conduct their thinking within the framework of different sets of absolute presuppositions, ultimate assumptions about the nature of things which form, for their time, the limits of critical thinking. Presupposition as de-

fined above (P.F. Strawson uses the term somewhat differently) is a species of ENTAILMENT.   A.Q.

(2) In LINGUISTICS, and especially in SEMANTICS and PRAGMATICS, what a speaker assumes in saying a particular sentence, as opposed to what is actually asserted.   D.C.

Bibl: S. Levinson, *Pragmatics* (Cambridge, 1983).

price mechanism. The response of SUPPLY AND DEMAND to prices, which can be used to bring order and coordination to a wide range of economic activities. The term can refer either to the spontaneous adjustments of the market-place or to the deliberate governmental adjustment of prices. On either interpretation, the price mechanism is at least a partial alternative to more direct intervention. In the short run it can be used to prevent shortages and surpluses; in the long run its main use is to adapt the structures of production to consumer requirements. Its successful working depends on the movement of prices *relative to each other*, whereas the containment of INFLATION is concerned with the average movement of *all* prices. Failure to appreciate this distinction has been the source of much confusion. The efficient operation of the price mechanism in the market-place lies behind the view that markets should be left to operate freely (see FREE MARKET; LAISSEZ FAIRE; ECONOMIC LIBERALISM; PERFECT COMPETITION).   S.BR.; J.P.

Bibl: D. Begg *et al., Economics* (London, 1984).

primary occupation, see under OCCUPATION.

primary structures, see under MINIMAL ART.

prime ministerial government. A term popularized in 1963 by R.H.S. Crossman's contention that a series of political changes had undermined cabinet government in Great Britain, combining to elevate the office of prime minister to greater power and authority than that granted by the constitution. As the argument was put by Crossman and others, it emphasized the prime minister's extensive resources of patronage; power to dissolve Parliament; control over cabinet agenda, procedure, and committees; opportunities for MEDIA exposure, and such like. The case was at best overstated, neglecting, for example, a host of constraints on a prime minister's actions, the vagaries of individual temperament, and the different environment of Conservative and Labour governments. The argument was, however, revived in the late 1970s by Tony Benn and other Labour Party reformers, whose wish to place tighter restraints on the prime minister may have derived less from reverence for the constitution than from their aim to strengthen the non-parliamentary party at the expense of its parliamentary leadership.   S.R.

Bibl: R.H.S. Crossman, 'Introduction' in W. Bagehot, *The English Constitution* (London, 1963); A. Benn, *Arguments for Democracy* (London, 1981); P. Norton, *The Constitution in Flux* (Oxford, 1982).

prime mover. In attempting to explain directional change in past societies archaeologists may seek a single motive force such as population growth, plague, climatic change, while conscious of the dangers of monocausal explanation. B.C.

primitive. Adjective used:

(1) Traditionally, to define the subject-matter of ANTHROPOLOGY. Its use derives from the discipline's evolutionary heritage (see EVOLUTION), and it is often nowadays redefined to try to avoid evolutionary assumptions: thus primitive societies are said to be small in scale, nonliterate, and based upon simple technologies; indeed, 'small-scale' (likewise 'tribal'; see TRIBE) is often used as a euphemism corresponding to 'UNDER-DEVELOPED' and 'developing' in ECONOMICS and POLITICAL SCIENCE. But it is arguable that anthropology, though it has properly eliminated 'savage', will always need 'primitive', from which it should strive to remove the last vestige of cultural and political condescension. All men are 'cultured' by definition; some CULTURES/societies are more complex (less primitive) than others.

By taking primitive forms and manifestations as the centre of its interest, anthropology deals in a special way with many of the problems studied by the various social and human sciences. For example, alongside the work done in economics, political science, and jurisprudence, there lie anthropological treatments of primitive economic organization, primitive systems of politics and government, and primitive forms of law. Again, RELIGION, MYTH, music, and visual art are all studied in their primitive manifestations by anthropologists, their special treatment sometimes being signalled by the prefix ethno- (as in ETHNOMUSICOLOGY). M.F.

Bibl: E. R. Leach, *Social Anthropology* (London, 1982); C. Larner, *Witchcraft and Religion* (Oxford, 1984).

(2) In late-19th-century art criticism, to categorize European pre-Renaissance painting, especially of the 14th and 15th centuries; thereafter it acquired a different, alternative sense with the growing appreciation of non-Western and non-academic art. After 1900 this sophisticated interest in exotic or naive work — e.g. negro sculpture and Bavarian glass paintings, with their influence respectively on CUBISM and the BLAUE REITER — combined with a new approach to child art to create a vogue for untutored contemporary 'primitives' like Henri Rousseau (1844-1910), the retired toll-collector (*douanier*) who became a spare-time or 'Sunday' painter and exhibited with the FAUVES in 1905. Leaders of this trend in France, where it affected the whole ÉCOLE DE PARIS, included Picasso, Apollinaire, and the critic Wilhelm Uhde. More recently, with the wave of international exhibitions of naive art in the 1960s, the concept has become greatly extended, covering e.g. the art of Yugoslav peasants (in the Zagreb Museum of Primitive Art), Eskimos, Haitians, 18th- and 19th-century dilettantes, do-it-yourself architects, and extremely old ladies. Chimpanzee art, which also attracted some attention in that decade, relates more to ACTION PAINTING. J.W.

Bibl: O. Bihalji-Merin, *Modern Primitives* (London and New York, 1961).

primitivism. In RELIGION (for primitivism in art see PRIMITIVE), either the desire to imitate the 'primitive' (i.e. first) Christians or, more commonly, an interest in, usually with an admiration for, the vitality of African, West Indian, etc. tribal religion, in which the supernatural and the natural, the dead and the living, the individual, the family, and the TRIBE are all bound together by a corporately accepted system of imagery, RITUAL, and behaviour. See also SHAMANISM. D.L.E.

Bibl: J.V. Taylor, *The Primal Vision* (London, 1963); C. Lévi-Strauss, *The Savage Mind* (London and Chicago, 1966).

primordial nucleosynthesis, see under NUCLEOSYNTHESIS.

prior distribution, see under STATISTICS.

prisoner's dilemma, see under GAME THEORY.

privacy. In EPISTEMOLOGY, being known to, or knowable by, only one person. It is in this sense that the thoughts and feelings of which a person is introspectively aware (see INTROSPECTION) within his STREAM OF CONSCIOUSNESS are held to be private. More precisely, a thing is private in this epistemologically important sense if it is knowable *directly* and without INFERENCE by only one person. My smile is, of course, as much mine and no one else's as my feelings are, but this makes it proprietary rather than private and is of little epistemological interest (though my smile, unlike my bicycle, cannot be mine at one time and somebody else's at another). The mental states of another are indeed private in the sense defined but that does not exclude me from having indirect, inferential knowledge of them. A.Q.

Bibl: A.J. Ayer, *The Concept of a Person* (London and New York, 1963).

private good. The consumption of a private good by one person means that it cannot be consumed by another person. Examples of private goods are food and energy. A distinction is usually made between private and PUBLIC GOODS, though it is difficult to classify certain goods and services in just one of these categories.

J.P.

private language. In the PHILOSOPHY of Wittgenstein, a language which is intelligible only to its user; for example, a language whose expressions refer to its user's private sensations and inner psychological states and which is therefore intelligible only to himself. Wittgenstein invented the idea of private language in order to deny that there can be any such thing: he argued that language is essentially public because it is a rule-governed activity, in which learning the rules and subsequently checking that they are being followed correctly requires a shared public context of language use.   A.C.G.

Bibl: L. Wittgenstein, *Philosophical Investigations* (London, 1953).

private sector. That part of the economy that is not owned and controlled by the government. In terms of output, it includes the economic activity of private firms, charities and non-profit-making organizations. On the expenditure side, it refers to the expenditure of these bodies and also the expenditure of individuals. The economy can be categorized into the private and PUBLIC SECTORS. (See also PRIVATIZATION.)   J.P.

privatization. The substitution of private for public ownership and supply of a good or service. Privatization of a good or service that can be supplied by a COMPETITIVE market may allow prices and costs to be reduced and output increased. If the industry is a natural MONOPOLY, e.g. the telephone network, privatization will not result in a competitive market and ECONOMIC REGULATION of the private industry is necessary. It may be possible to separate off a part of a publicly owned monopoly and privatize it to form a competitive market. For example, the retailing of telephones to the public could, perhaps, be made into a competitive market, but truly competitive markets in the supply of telephone lines and exchanges are unlikely. Private ownership and interest in the running of a privatized company may result in greater ECONOMIC EFFICIENCY. However, privatization of the supply of PUBLIC GOODS is unlikely to be efficient. In the form of privatization where the state pays a private firm to provide a good or service, there may be difficulties in defining the good or service adequately and monitoring the quality of the output supplied. Privatization of firms in the PUB-

LIC SECTOR is a source of revenue to the STATE, though the state loses any future profits such firms would have made. Empirical studies have varied in their conclusions about the economic efficiency of privatization, but they tend to suggest that for cost and price reductions to be obtained requires the presence of competition. The desirability of privatization is a very contentious economic and political issue (see NATIONALIZATION).   J.P.

Bibl: E. Roll, *The Mixed Economy* (London, 1982).

probabilistic explanation, see under EXPLANATION.

probability density, see under DISTRIBUTION.

probability theory. The mathematical theory of processes involving uncertainty; the traditional illustrative cases are those of tossing a coin, rolling a die, and drawing a card from a pack; and it was in the context of gaming odds that early probabilistic calculations were carried out from the 17th century onwards. Proper theorems (as distinct from mere calculations) including versions of the Central Limit Theorem (see below) were proved by Laplace and others, but the subject only began to be taken seriously by pure mathematicians with Kolmogorov's definitive characterization of the theory, around 1930, as a branch of the pure mathematical discipline of measure theory. Although probability theory draws heavily on analysis for its techniques, it has a strong flavour of its own in consequence of its role as a mathematical MODEL for empirical phenomena, and probabilistic methods can on occasion feed ideas and proofs back into analysis. The major results of the theory include a class of theorems known as *Laws of Large Numbers*, which identify the probability of an event with its long-run frequency in the limit as the experiment is repeated. These theorems are enshrined in folklore as the 'law of averages', usually in a highly incorrect form (see STATISTICAL REGULARITY). Another major theorem is the *Central Limit Theorem*, which may be thought of as stating that suitably standardized distributions arising from the summation of large numbers of independent errors converge in the limit to the NORMAL DISTRIBUTION. The work of Markov in the early 20th century led to interest in probabilistic systems evolving through time; these are now known as STOCHASTIC PROCESSES. Probability theory forms the foundation on which STATISTICS is built, but in recent years the phrase 'applied probability' has come to mean the study of particular stochastic processes thought to be reasonable mathematical models for such empirical processes as the spread of epidemics, the inheritance of GENES, the interaction of components of a biological environment, and the growth of crystals and POLYMERS.   R.SI.

Bibl: W. Feller, *An Introduction to Probability Theory and its Applications* (London and New York, 3rd ed., 1968); I. Hacking. *The Emergence of Probability* (Cambridge, 1975).

problem-oriented language. In COMPUTING, a PROGRAMMING LANGUAGE designed with a particular class of problem in mind rather than a particular type of COMPUTER. See also ASSEMBLY LANGUAGE; HIGH-LEVEL PROGRAMMING LANGUAGE.
C.S.

problem-solving. That form of activity in which the organism is faced with a goal to be reached, a gap in the 'route' to the goal, and a set of alternative means, none of which are immediately and obviously suitable. It is studied by psychologists in a variety of forms: circumventing detours, solving puzzles and mathematical problems, finding a common basis of classification for a diverse array, solving chess problems, etc. The most widely held view of the problem-solving process in contemporary PSYCHOLOGY is some variant of what is called *means-end* analysis, illustrated best, perhaps, by the *General Problem Solver* (G.P.S.) PROGRAM of A. Newell and H.A. Simon (1957), a COMPUTER program designed to simulate a human problem-solver's procedure.

G.P.S. begins by comparing the present state of solution of the problem with the desired outcome and first determines a set of differences in terms of selected outcome attributes; thus, in the well-known cannibals and missionaries example, it notes

that there are too many missionaries on one side of the river. The program has available a number of *transformation-rules* (see AXIOMATICS) for altering current states in the direction of desired outcomes. The transformation highest on the list is applied; if it does not succeed, G.P.S. then tries out other means of solution, or seeks to change the situation so that other means can be applied. A rule for recognizing dead ends is included so that a stop order can be imposed, after which the next transformation on the list is tried. The notice order for spotting differences between desired outcome and present state, and the order of application of transformations, are HEURISTICS or 'rules of thumb' based on knowledge of how real problem-solvers proceed. It is apparent from this account that such phenomena as *functional fixedness* (being stuck too long with an incorrect hypothesis) and other, human-like errors are committed by the program as a function of its presuppositions, and it is this feature that makes G.P.S. not a 'super-problem-solver' but a recognizably 'human' one.

Current research is concentrated on determining some of the biases inherent in programs designed in this way in order to locate more clearly the nature of the difficulties in human problem-solving.   J.S.B.

Bibl: A. Newell and H.A. Simon, *Human Problem-Solving* (Englewood Cliffs, N.J., and Hemel Hempstead, 1972).

process control. The use of an on-line COMPUTER to control a continuous process such as a chemical plant. See also COMPUTING.   C.S.

process music. A type of music where certain processes are set in action or followed by the performers. It quite frequently has a certain mechanical inevitability and the logical resolution produced by the completion of the process (sometimes cyclical) is often an important quality. An important innovator is Steve Reich (e.g., 'Pendulum Music').   B.CO.

Bibl: S. Reich, *Writing and Music* (New York, 1974).

process theology. A modern form of Christian THEISM which takes account of modern science, especially the knowledge of EVOLUTION, and which teaches that God's way of working in the world is a slow process, patiently overcoming the elements of chance and evil present in the universe and including in itself all the good that is brought about. The emphasis is on God's involvement rather than his self-sufficiency, his love rather than his omnipotence. The chief philosopher in this movement was A.N. Whitehead (1861-1947); the chief popularizer of a Christ-centred vision of the meaning of evolution was Pierre Teilhard de Chardin (1881-1955). In NEO-ORTHODOXY, however, the position has been attacked as encouraging PANTHEISM.   D.L.E.

Bibl: P. Teilhard de Chardin, tr. B. Wall et al., The Phenomenon of Man (London and New York, 1959); N. Pittenger, Picturing God (London, 1982).

processor. The part of a COMPUTER where the data-processing is carried out. This includes the arithmetic and logical operations as well as the control of the sequence of instructions and of INPUT/OUTPUT. Though logically the most complicated part of a computer it represents only a small fraction of its cost. C.S.;J.E.S.

producers' goods, see under CONSUMERS' GOODS.

productivists, see under CONSTRUCTIVISM.

productivity. In LINGUISTICS, a major defining characteristic of human language, the creative capacity of language-users to produce and understand an infinite number of sentences using a finite set of grammatical rules. In this respect, human language is often contrasted with the extremely limited range of signals which constitute the communication systems of animals.   D.C.

productivity bargaining. A form of COLLECTIVE BARGAINING, developed in the U.K. in the early 1960s, in which higher rates of pay are traded against employees' acceptance of changes in inefficient methods of production. The use of machinery that embodies old technology, wasteful working practices, lines of demarcation of

tasks between different grades of labour, and contrived overtime are all examples of inefficient production practices. The objective of productivity bargaining is to raise real wages, but reduce average costs by increasing overall productivity. In the U.K. there have been many notable successful examples of productivity bargaining.   J.P.

Bibl: H.A. Clegg, The Changing System of Industrial Relations in Great Britain (Oxford, 1979).

professionalization. One of the key features of the emergence of 'modern society', it has been claimed, is the transformation of many occupations into professions. This process involves the development of formal entry qualifications based upon education and examinations, the emergence of regulatory bodies with powers to admit and discipline members, and some degree of state-guaranteed monopoly rights. Advocates of professionalization argue that it is a movement which helps protect the public from the hazards of a 'caveat emptor' market place situation, in which their ignorance would put them in jeopardy. Critics by contrast see it as essentially an oligarchic tendency, in which corporate power serves to increase an occupation's leverage against the public through reducing competition or public accountability (see OLIGARCHY).   R.P.

Bibl: W.J. Reader, Professional Men (London, 1966).

profile. Metaphorically, a summary description giving the main features of some person, state of affairs, process, social group, organization, etc. In particular, if the relevant qualities can be measured, the profile may consist of a set of numbers, one for each quality. These can be expressed also as a diagram or graph, by labelling one axis with the names of the qualities and the other with the possible numerical values, making a mark at the appropriate distance above the label for each quality, and joining up the marks by means of straight lines.   A.S.

Profintern. Red International of Labour Unions founded in Moscow in July 1921 to implement point 10 of the programme adopted by the Second Congress of the

COMINTERN in 1920, and to establish a rival to the International Federation of Trades Unions (see INTERNATIONAL TRADE UNIONS). Initially (1921-8) its main tactic was the capture of national TRADES UNION movements by 'boring from within'. In 1928-35 this was replaced by the formation of competing unions, a policy abandoned in turn in 1935 for that of the POPULAR FRONT. After 1937 the Profintern was moribund.   D.C.W.

profit-sharing. Term applied to a number of arrangements under which most of the employees of a firm receive a part of its profits in accordance with an agreed scheme. A common arrangement is for the balance of net profits after payment of a fixed rate of return on share capital to be divided in fixed proportions between shareholders and employees; each eligible employee participates in proportion to his earnings. The transfer to employees may be made in the form of shares. Under *co-partnership* employees hold shares and, as shareholders or through consultative bodies, have a voice in the conduct of the business. See also PARTICIPATION.
                                        E.H.P.B.

program (so spelled in Britain as well as the U.S.A.). A list of statements or commands in some PROGRAMMING LANGUAGE whose purpose is to cause a COMPUTER to carry out some desired operation. The versatility of modern computers springs from the fact that a single machine can be made to do a large number of different and often complex tasks by presenting it with suitable programs. See also PROGRAMME; SYSTEMS.   C.S.

programme. This spelling is used in England (but not the U.S.A.) for all meanings except the technical one in COMPUTING. A firm's computer programme is its policy for buying and using computers, its computer PROGRAMS are the detailed sets of instructions given to its COMPUTER to make it carry out particular tasks.   C.S.

Programme, Evaluation, and Review Technique, see PERT.

programme music. Music normally without words but directly associated with extra-musical subject-matter such as literature (e.g. Berlioz, *Roméo et Juliette*) or natural phenomena (e.g. Debussy, *La Mer*). The concept is particularly associated with 19th-century ROMANTICISM and the symphonic poem (e.g Liszt, *Les Préludes*), but is much older; its survival in the 20th century, despite being an obvious target for anti-Romantic reaction, suggests that it is a natural form of musical expression. To its forms must now be added 'mechanical romanticism' (Honegger, *Pacific 231*). Extra-musical connotations for instrumental music are implicit even in Stravinsky's preference for *Le Sacre du Printemps* in the concert hall rather than as a ballet. Programme music may be related to the GESAMTKUNSTWERK, although the non-musical elements are usually left to the imagination. On these grounds Ernest Newman even argued that the symphonic poem should supersede the music drama.   J.G.R.

Programme, Planning, and Budgeting System, see PPBS.

programmed art, see under KINETIC ART.

programmed instruction. The technique of presenting material to be learned (*programmed learning*) in an order and form which is designed to make the learning process easy and to bring out the interconnectedness of the material, but which is altered in response to, and correction of, the learner's error patterns as shown in corrective FEEDBACK. In this last respect, it is often useful to use a COMPUTER as an aid, a technique sometimes called *computer-assisted instruction*. See also TEACHING MACHINE.   J.S.B.

programming. The process of constructing the detailed set of instructions required to make a COMPUTER perform some specific task. This involves the choice (or invention) of a suitable ALGORITHM, decisions about the representation and organization of data, and consideration of the action to be taken if a machine malfunction is detected or the PROGRAM is presented with inconsistent or incorrect data. The programmer must also take account of the structure of the computer on which the program is to be run, and in particular of the nature of its STORE and OPERATING SYSTEM. He may use FLOW CHARTS (which need a further stage of CODING) or may work directly in a PROGRAMMING LANGUAGE. See also SYSTEMS.   C.S.

programming language. The notation in which computer PROGRAMS are expressed. There are by now several hundred different programming languages which can be divided roughly into ASSEMBLY LANGUAGES, each closely based on a particular type of COMPUTER, and HIGH-LEVEL PROGRAMMING LANGUAGES, which are more often PROBLEM-ORIENTED. All programming languages are *artificial*, i.e. deliberately invented; they differ from *natural* languages, which have developed gradually, by having a perfectly rigid syntax, a much smaller vocabulary, and no emotive power.   C.S.

progressive. Adjective used to characterize:

(1) Generally, believers in the possibility and desirability of progress, i.e. of a moral and social improvement in the human condition, a view which implies a certain optimism about human nature.
          A.L.C.B.

(2) Political parties or movements seeking to achieve such progress by removing institutions which obstruct it and advocating measures which they believe will promote it (e.g. universal free EDUCATION). In this sense all LEFT-wing parties, LIBERALS, radicals (see RADICALISM), SOCIAL DEMOCRATS, SOCIALISTS and COMMUNISTS (before they come to power), can be counted as progressive. The term is also attached to a broad and highly diverse movement in the U.S. from about 1900 to the beginning of World War I which pressed for various changes in the role of government as an agent of ECONOMIC REGULATION and social reform, and which then later prompted local or short-lived Progressive Parties. Elements of U.S. progressive thought resurfaced in the NEW DEAL.   S.R.

(3) Generally used in education to describe a school whose ethos or teaching methods are different from the more formal or 'fundamental' schools. It is not easy to define since some schools would label themselves progressive when they are almost REACTIONARY. Sometimes, it might perhaps be progressive to be reactionary, but generally the term implies 'modern' methods. For example, there are some schools (King Alfred's, London, or Bedales) where children call teachers by their first names, wear no uniform and take part in the school's government. Other schools considered progressive in Britain include the Round Square schools, a group of independent schools based on the Kurt Hahn ethos of educating 'the whole man' by mixing straight lessons with outdoor activities. Although 'progressive' is often interpreted to describe a school which pays little attention to the academic and EXAMINATIONS, this would be a gross oversimplification, although, generally, such schools tend to concentrate more on the happiness of the child than his/her love for learning.   J.I.

Bibl: (1) J.B. Bury, *The Idea of Progress* (London and New York, 1920); (3) W.A.C. Stewart, *Progressives and Radicals in English Education 1750-1970* (London, 1972).

prohibition, see under JAZZ AGE.

project work. A teaching method (in Dewey's phrase, the 'problem method') in which a topic, preferably one within the pupils' everyday experience, is approached from a number of angles. Much used in primary schools, project work cuts across traditional divisions between subjects and involves the pupils actively in the solving of problems: thus, a project on baking might incorporate elements traditionally taught as mathematics, science, history, English, and creative arts, and involve a group visit to a bakery as well as individual quests for information in the school and local public libraries. A single project may be studied by just one child, a whole class, or even an entire school. In turn, its study might be periodic (e.g. once a week for a term), or take up most of the students' time over some set period (e.g. one or two weeks, but this can also extend to a whole term).   W.A.C.S.; E.L.-S.

Bibl: G. Cowan, *Project Work in the Secondary School* (London and New York, 1967); G. Kent, *Projects in the Primary School* (London, 1968).

projection. In PSYCHOLOGY, the tendency to attribute to others unacceptable impulses and traits that are present in oneself. In extreme cases it may be pathological in nature, though generally it is one of the normal DEFENCE MECHANISMS.   J.S.B.

projective geometry, see under GEOMETRY.

projective/introjective identification. A term derived from the psychoanalytic concept of PROJECTION: the ejection into the outside world of something which the subject refuses in himself. M. Klein (see KLEINIAN) expanded the modalities of this psychic mechanism in her explorations in the field of the analysis of young children. The infant projects outside those parts of the self (see PARTIAL OBJECT) which are defined as 'bad internal objects' in its defence against depressive anxiety due to the psychic process of separation from the mother. Klein coined the term 'projective identification' in connection with the paranoid-schizoid position of the infant in relation to his first object, the maternal breast (see OBJECT RELATIONS). The baby projects split-off parts of the self, or later the whole of one's self, into the external object in order to harm and control it. This mechanism corresponds to primitive oral infantile phantasies of sadistic attacks and invasions into the inside of the mother's body. In this way the object, breast or mother's body, is perceived as having acquired the characteristics of the projected 'bad' parts of the self which thereby becomes identified with the object of its own projection. The introjective identification works at the level of a retaliation of the object which was attacked by the projective identification in the first place. Pathological projective identification functions as a result of minute disintegration of the self, whose parts are then projected into the object and disintegrated. This pathological process explains the adult psychotic sense of disintegration (see PSYCHOSIS).   B.BE.
    Bibl: M. Klein, *The Psychoanalysis of Children* (London, 1932).

prokaryote. A fundamental division of living things, made up of CELLS that lack a separate NUCLEUS. All living things are either prokaryotes or EUKARYOTES, according to their cellular structure. Prokaryotic cells have little internal differentiation, and their DNA floats around in the cell rather than (as in eukaryotes) being enclosed in a separate nucleus. The bacteria and ARCHAEBACTERIA are the main kinds of living prokaryotes; they are practically all single-celled. Prokaryotes are probably ancestral to the eukaryotes.
    M.R.

prolefeed; proles, see under ORWELLIAN.

proletariat. The word first appeared (Latin *proletarius*, from *proles*, offspring) in the Servian constitution of the sixth century B.C. in which military service and taxes were required of the landowners and other classes. Those who could not serve the State with their property did so with their offspring; hence the idea of service by labour. The term disappeared by the end of the second century of the Christian era but reappears after the enclosure movements of the 15th and 16th centuries, to designate men made landless and able to live only by selling their labour power. It was central in the *Étude sur l'économie politique* (1837) by the Swiss economist Sismondi, the founder of the underconsumption theory of economic crises. It was used by Proudhon, Cabet, Louis Blanc, and other French radicals and was popularized by the German social critic Lorenz von Stein in *Der Sozialismus und Communismus des heutigen Frankreichs* (1842).
    The term is, however, associated predominantly with Marx. In the *Critique of Hegel's Philosophy of Right* (1843) he talks of the proletariat as a 'CLASS in radical chains' and ends with the peroration: 'Philosophy cannot be realized without the abolition of the proletariat, the proletariat cannot abolish itself without realizing philosophy.' And the *Communist Manifesto* (1848) begins with the ringing declaration: 'The history of all human society, past and present, has been the history of class struggle. Freeman and slave, patrician and plebeian, lord and serf ... the bourgeois age ... has simplified class antagonisms ... society is splitting into two great hostile classes ... BOURGEOISIE and proletariat.' Yet it also seems likely that he

used the term largely for dramatic effect. In *Das Kapital* (1867-94) it appears only infrequently; Marx uses instead the more specific (and in English more familiar) terms 'wage-labourers', 'factory hands', 'the WORKING CLASS'. Nonetheless it became an important concept in the COMMUNIST movement of the 1920s, not least among artists and INTELLECTUALS; and following the PROLETKULT a number of 'proletarian' cultural groupings sprang up, particularly in Germany and the U.S.S.R. They were liquidated, for differing reasons, by Hitler and Stalin respectively in the early 1930s.   D.B.; J.W.

Bibl: L. Benson, *Proletarians and Parties* (London, 1978).

Proletkult. Workers' cultural organization conceived in 1909 by the Russian SOCIALIST exiles Alexander Bogdanov, A.V. Lunacharsky, and Maxim Gorky, who saw it as a third arm of the revolutionary movement, catering for the PROLETARIAT'S spiritual life while the unions and the party looked after its economic and political interests. After holding its first conference in Petrograd in 1917 the Proletkult briefly flourished under the wing of Lunacharsky's Education Commissariat, but was distrusted by Lenin, who reduced its powers; in 1922 it lost its subsidy and thereafter petered out. Its influence, however, persisted, whether in the vocabulary of the much more aggressively 'proletarian' cultural groupings of the later 1920s or in the actual achievements of its often non-proletarian members, such as Eisenstein, whose first theatrical and film ventures (e.g. *Strike*, 1925) it sponsored.   J.W.

Bibl: M.E. and C. Paul, *Proletcult* (London, 1921); B. Thomson, *The Premature Revolution* (London, 1972).

proliferation. In political contexts, an increase in the number of states possessing the technological capacity needed for independent production of and control over NUCLEAR WEAPONS. Thus the Treaty of 1968, by which three nuclear powers (U.S.A., U.S.S.R., and Britain) undertook not to transfer such TECHNOLOGY, and some 100 other signatory states not to develop it, is entitled the Treaty on the Non-Proliferation of Nuclear Weapons.
                    A.F.B.

Bibl: L.A. Dunn, *Controlling the Bomb: Nuclear Proliferation in the 1980s* (London and New York, 1982).

promotions. The tactical precipitation of an enhanced level of take-up of a product or service. The promotion may take the form of enhanced MERCHANDISING, or more obvious presentation; or an incentive to buy through discount or added value. However it is shaped, there are probably no more effective forms of promotion than increased value for money. A great deal of time and ingenuity has been expended on finding new or different ways of expressing value for money packages, but, in the end, there is nothing that is new.   T.S.

pro-natalism. Policies or theories to encourage the growth rate of a population by raising FERTILITY. Pro-natalist ideas have long had religious motivations (following the exhortation to 'go forth and multiply'), and Roman Catholic (see CATHOLICISM) official teachings continue to have a strong pro-natalist character. Pro-natalist government policies have often stemmed from a belief that large numbers would produce a strengthened nation, e.g. in late 19th- and 20th-century France, and in recent decades in the U.S.S.R., often giving financial or moral incentives to high fertility; or that population growth would reduce structural problems associated with an ageing population, or enhance the quality of family relations. The counter to pro-natalist ideas is associated with MALTHUSIANISM and EUGENICS, where the containment or selectiveness of population growth is perceived as a general benefit.
                    D.S.

proof theory, see under MATHEMATICAL LOGIC.

prophylaxis. A preventive measure or protected state, particularly with respect to infectious diseases and achieved through a mechanism of IMMUNITY. Prophylaxis may be achieved by the prior injection of (1) a relatively innocuous organism closely related to the one against which protection is desired (e.g. against smallpox virus by cowpox virus); (2) a virulent but attenuated organism, i.e. a *vaccine* (e.g. against poliomyelitis by virus particles inactivated by treatment with, e.g., formaldehyde, Salk vaccine); or (3) heat-killed or otherwise inactivated bacteria or bacterial extracts known as *toxoids*, which retain their immunizing power but cannot cause disease (e.g. prophylaxis against diphtheria and tetanus — a procedure far superior to treatment by means of antiserum, which is fraught with dangers). See also VIROLOGY.   P.M.

proportional representation. A political principle, often referred to simply as PR, aspired to by most of the world's democratic states although not by Britain or the U.S. It refers to the system used to elect legislatures, and requires that a representative body be elected by a method which seeks to reflect as far as possible the exact distribution of voting preferences within the electorate. There are several different kinds of electoral system which are based on PR, of which the commonest are the single transferable vote and additional member (or 'party list') systems. PR has long been opposed by the major parties in Britain, who disguise their main concern that its adoption would disadvantage them behind the claim that it would not produce stable and authoritative governments, but would tend to produce coalitions, which they allege are not liked by the British.

S.R.

Bibl: V. Bogdanor, *What is Proportional Representation?* (Oxford, 1984).

proposition, types of. In LOGIC and EPISTEMOLOGY, propositions may be distinguished in respect (1) of their *logical form*, as for example (*a*) singular, particular, or universal, (*b*) affirmative or negative, (*c*) categorical (see CATEGORY), hypothetical, or otherwise complex, (*d*) existential, attributive, or relational; (2) of their kind of TRUTH or VERIFICATION, as *a priori* (see APRIORISM) or empirical (see EMPIRICISM), necessary or contingent (see CONTINGENCY), ANALYTIC or synthetic (three distinctions that do not obviously, but may fundamentally, coincide); (3) of their subject-matter, as physical, psychological, experiential, scientific, historical, moral, philosophical, and so forth; (4) of their epistemological status as basic or intuitive

on the other hand or as inferred or derivative on the other. The first of these classifications is of primary interest to logic; the other three are the concern of epistemology.   A.Q.

propositional attitudes. Mental acts of believing, intending, hoping, wishing, fearing and others like them are directed upon a particular mental content which can be represented by a proposition; thus (where 'p' stands for any proposition) we attribute beliefs etc. to someone by saying 'he believes that p', 'hopes that p', 'fears that p', and so on; for example, 'Tom believes that the earth moves'. Believing and the rest are thus characterizable as *attitudes towards propositions*. Propositional attitudes are important in PHILOSOPHY because among other things they figure in accounts of the nature of mind and in explanations of behaviour, action, and mastery of language. The TRUTH-VALUE of a statement ascribing a propositional attitude to someone is independent of the truth-value of the proposition, embedded in the 'that' clause, towards which the given attitude is being taken. For example, it can be true that 'Tom believes that Santa exists' despite the falsity of the proposition 'Santa exists'. For this reason some philosophers say that, unlike 'believing', 'knowing' does not name a propositional attitude because 'Tom knows that p' can only be true if 'p' is true. Attitudes with this property might be called 'cognitive' attitudes to distinguish them from propositional attitudes.   A.C.G.

propositional calculus. One of the two chief LOGICAL CALCULI, consisting of a formal system of notation for representing combinations of PROPOSITIONS together with AXIOMS and rules (see AXIOMATICS) which determine the RELATIONS between them. The most frequently used *connectives* by means of which the combinations are formed are negation, conjunction, disjunction (*A* and/or *B*), and implication (if *A*, then *B*). In the *classical* propositional calculus every proposition is taken to be true or false, and the connectives correspond to TRUTH-FUNCTIONS. In INTUITIONISM (3) the connectives have different meanings and obey different rules.   R.G.

prosodic feature. In PHONOLOGY, any systematic variation in pitch, loudness, speed, or rhythm that carries a difference in meaning. See also INTONATION. In FIRTHIAN linguistics, prosodic features (or *prosodies*) are any features which can be found throughout a sequence of sounds; thus if all the sounds in a word were nasal, the nasality would be considered a prosodic feature.   D.C.

prosopography. The study of collective biography, usually but not necessarily the biography of ÉLITES such as peers or Members of Parliament. Prosopography is one of the most important types of QUANTITATIVE HISTORY. The prosopographical method has been employed regularly by historians since about 1930, in particular by political historians such as Sir Lewis Namier, and is increasing in popularity because it lends itself to computerization (see COMPUTERS). The great advantage of the method is that it gives a firm basis to some kind of general statement about groups. It has been criticized for taking the ideas out of history, because it is easier to card-index a man's economic interests or family relationship than his fundamental values.   P.B.
    Bibl: L. Stone, 'Prosopography' (*Daedalus*, 100, 1971, pp. 46-74).

prostaglandins. A family of fatty acid derivatives, members of which are produced by most TISSUES of the body. A wide variety of biological activities seem to be mediated by prostaglandins. Because they are involved in the contraction of the uterus during childbirth, certain prostaglandins can be used to induce therapeutic ABORTIONS.   P.N.

prosthesis. Any artificial device which does duty for a bodily organ or member. Thus false teeth and artificial kidneys are equally prostheses.   P.M.

proteases, see under ENZYMES; PROTEINS.

protectionism. Government interference in international trade. Free trade is the absence of government interference. Free trade is beneficial since it allows countries to specialize in the production of goods and services that they have a comparative advantage in and, consequently, world production and real income increases (see TRADE THEORY). There are many forms of interference: banning of or quotas on certain imports; regulations on the quality of imports; international agreements limiting the level of a country's exports; tariffs on imports; and subsidies on exports. For the century prior to the 1930s, many countries, but not all, followed free trade policies. The Great Depression led to many countries adopting protectionist policies and world trade declined. Since World War II, many, but not all, of the restrictions on free trade have been removed; this increased freedom has mainly been the result of the efforts and negotiations of GATT. However, there have been a number of cases of protection of particular industries. Protectionist policies may be beneficial to a country, as they can increase employment and output. Tariffs can change the TERMS OF TRADE in favour of a country and, thus, increase its real income. Tariffs raise revenue for the government. An infant industry can be protected in its growing stages and, at a later stage, it may give rise to ECONOMIES OF SCALE and beneficial EXTERNALITIES. Protecting an industry increases the rewards to the owners of those FACTORS OF PRODUCTION employed in the industry and imposes costs on the rest of the economy through higher prices. The protection of industries has often been a political measure, to favour those with interests in the industry. Protected industries may become inefficient because they lack the spur of international competition to force them to minimize costs. It is often argued that any net economic benefits from a protectionist policy occur at the expense of other nations.   J.P.
    Bibl: B. Sodersten, *International Economics* (London, 2nd ed., 1980).

protein. Giant polymeric (see POLYMER) MOLECULES, found in all living organisms, and built up of AMINO ACIDS united to each other by the so-called *peptide bond*, CO-NH. The elementary composition of a protein thus depends directly upon its constitution in terms of amino acids. Proteins contain carbon, hydrogen, oxygen, and nitrogen, and most proteins contain also sulphur and phosphorus. In skeletal structure the protein is a giant polypeptide (see PEPTIDE); the first protein of which it could be said that its structure was fully elucidated was myoglobin (by Perutz and Kendrew, 1957). The functions fulfilled by proteins are protean. ENZYMES are proteins, and so are connective TISSUE fibres including tendons and ligaments, while hairs and nails are formed by insoluble proteins of the class known as *keratins*. When proteins are altered in such a way that they lose their distinctive structures or become insoluble, they are said to be *denatured*. Heating a protein normally causes irreversible coagulation, such as occurs in cooking an egg. The main classes of soluble protein are: albumins, globulins, and fibrous proteins such as fibrinogen out of which blood clot fibres are formed. In digestion, proteins are broken down by hydrolytic enzymes into raw peptides or individual amino acids. The enzymes that break down proteins are known as *proteases*. Protein synthesis (see NUCLEIC ACID) is directed by information encoded in GENES. Experimental modification of the information results in the synthesis of modified proteins, a procedure known as PROTEIN ENGINEERING.   P.M.;P.N.

Bibl: R. Passmore and M.A. Eastwood, *Human Nutrition and Dietetics* (London, 1986).

protein engineering. The modification of the structure of a PROTEIN. Usually the modified protein is made by protein synthesis from its GENE, after the gene has been deliberately altered according to the rules of the GENETIC CODE. Protein engineering is used both in the pursuit of BIOTECHNOLOGY and as a way of testing hypotheses concerning the contribution of parts of a protein to its overall function.
P.N.

Protestant ethic. A phrase deriving from Max Weber's proposition, put forward in 1905-6, that, while CAPITALISM has existed throughout most of history, a particular *spirit* of capitalism, that of methodical accumulation and a rationalistic ethic, is found only in Western Europe and after the 16th century, in Protestant countries or among Protestant sects within Catholic countries. Though disputed by a number of writers who have argued that the spread

of capitalism in Holland was due primarily to economic causes, or that the rise of capitalism was a general phenomenon whose inhibition in Catholic countries was due largely to the Counter-Reformation, Weber's thesis has been one of the most influential ideas in contemporary SOCIAL SCIENCE. Many writers still assume that the Protestant ethic undergirds contemporary capitalism; but Weber specifically argued that 'victorious capitalism', resting largely on materialist and hedonistic incentives, 'needs [the support of the Protestant ethic] no longer'. The pursuit of wealth, he maintained, had become stripped of its religious and ethical meaning.   D.B.

Bibl: M. Weber, tr. T. Parsons, *The Protestant Ethic and the Spirit of Capitalism* (London, 1930); G. Marshall, *In Search of the Spirit of Capitalism* (London, 1982).

Protestantism. The RELIGION of those who make an EVANGELICAL protest against what are believed to be corruptions in CATHOLICISM, urging a return to a more purely biblical faith; so called from a *Protestatio* issued in 1529 as part of the LUTHERAN Reformation. In the 19th and 20th centuries the U.S.A. has come to share the leadership of Protestantism with Europe, but Protestantism has experienced a need to redefine its position more positively, both in its attitude to Catholicism and in its adjustment to modern thought (see MODERNISM). Where the Bible is not treated in a FUNDAMENTALIST way, the central problem for Protestantism is authority. If the only real authority is the individual's conscience, it is not clear why a Church is needed at all.
D.L.E.

Bibl: M.E. Marty, *Protestantism* (London and New York, 1972).

protocol. In COMPUTING, a set of conventions enabling two COMPUTERS to send messages to each other; it involves such things as acknowledgement of accurate receipt, retransmission in the event of error and the format of the message itself. The more unreliable the communications medium, the more elaborate must the protocol be. Computers connected over a NET-

WORK must observe a standard protocol.
J.E.S.

protohistory. The study of the past of a given region at a time when it is referred to, but only sporadically, in written records. Protohistory follows PREHISTORY but precedes the period served by regular written sources sufficient to create a cohesive history.
B.C.

proton. A positively charged ELEMENTARY PARTICLE about 2,000 times heavier than the ELECTRON. Protons are stable, and constitute one of the two structural units of the atomic NUCLEUS, the other being NEUTRONS.
M.V.B.

proto-oncogene, see under ONCOGENE.

protoplasm. An obsolescent term intended to designate the ingredient of living systems that was truly living — a sort of biological ether that permeated or lay between otherwise inert structures. With the realization that the distinctive characteristics of living things are above all else organizational, the entire conceptual background or 'protoplasm' has collapsed; nevertheless nature-philosophers, unlike practising scientists, do still confront themselves with questions like 'Are connective tissue fibres really alive?'
P.M.

protozoa. A sub-kingdom of single-CELL animals comprising some 30,000 SPECIES of both free-living (e.g. amoeba) and parasitic (e.g. the malaria parasite, plasmodium; trypanosoma) forms. The protozoa also comprehend chlorophyll-bearing AUTOTROPHIC organisms intermediate between animal and plant cells — the phytomonadines. Marine planktonic protozoa with hard 'skeletons' or shells are an important element in the formation of marine geological deposits. Some protozoa produce what are in effect ANTIBIOTICS. Thus a paramecium belonging to one of the so-called 'killer' races produces an infective particle — in effect a virus which kills members of 'non-killer' races. Susceptibility to this infection (kappa) is under strict genetic control. Because of its sexual process the GENETICS of paramecium is now very thoroughly understood. The protozoa generally are ubiquitous in distribution.
P.M.

Bibl: D.L. Mackinnon and R.S.J. Hawes, *An Introduction to the Study of Protozoa* (Oxford, 1961).

protozoology. The branch of ZOOLOGY that deals with PROTOZOA.
P.M.

Proustian. Adjective formed from the name of Marcel Proust, the author of the outstanding French fictional work of the 20th century. *A la recherche du temps perdu* (1913-27). It may refer to Proust's method of reliving the past in the present by means of memory, and thus purporting to triumph over time; to the long, evocative sentences which constitute his normal style; to his remarkable feeling for nature, works of arts, and historic buildings; or to the characteristic *belle époque* high society of aristocrats, men of fashion, and *demi-mondaines* that he describes.
J.G.W.

provenance. The place at which something has been found, or from which it has originated. Provenance is often important in such fields as the attribution of works of art, TEXTUAL CRITICISM, and BIBLIOGRAPHY, and invariably so in ARCHAEOLOGY. In the case of archaeology it normally implies only location; it lacks the stratigraphical precision (see STRATIGRAPHY) of CONTEXT.
B.C.

Provincetown Players. An American experimental theatre group founded in Provincetown, Mass., in 1915 and active in New York from 1916 to 1929. It was intimately connected with the early work of Eugene O'Neill, whose first play *Bound East for Cardiff* it presented in 1916.
M.A.

Provos. (1) *Provokants.* An urban movement of Dutch radical youth of an anti-industrialist, individualist, anti-ESTABLISHMENT kind, distinguished by its members' uniform of white socks, their preference for the bicycle (as 'non-pollutant'; see POLLUTION), and the unconventional humour of their campaigns. In the late 1960s individual provos stood for election to municipalities. (2) Abbreviation for the 'provisional' faction of the IRISH REPUBLICAN ARMY.
D.C.W.

proxemics, see under SEMIOTICS.

psephology. The study of elections, voting patterns, and electoral behaviour. The word is a recent coinage, being derived as an academic jest from the *psephos* (pebble) deposited in urns by voters in classical Athens.   D.C.W.

Bibl: I. Maclean, *Elections* (London, 1980).

pseudo-alleles. A term originally used to describe genetic units which appeared to be single entities or GENES when judged by the test of having a single primary function, but which could be split by CROSSING OVER. The term is obsolete, since it is now known that all functional units or genes can be so split.   J.M.S.

pseudo-statement. Term introduced, though not formally defined, by I.A. Richards in the context of the age-old controversy, fiercely revived in this century, about whether poetry (and, by extension, literature) is COGNITIVE or emotive, or both. In *Science and Poetry* (1926) Richards presented an emotive theory of poetry; in *Poetries and Sciences* (1970), however, he puts poetry forward as a medium containing special knowledge, exclusive to itself. Philip Wheelwright's proposition of 'poetic statement' as a substitute for Richards's term has the virtues of simplicity, and of avoiding the pejorative CONNOTATIONS of 'pseudo-'. What Richards really meant, however, and what is really important, is that poetic statements are different from empirical statements: they are non-verifiable, and they are not supposed to be verifiable; but they do order our impulses, and are therefore useful. 'A pseudo-statement is a form of words which is justified entirely by its effect in releasing or organizing our impulses and attitudes ... a statement, on the other hand, is justified by its truth.' Richards has stuck to this: 'In fluid [poetic] statements a great many precise meanings may be free to dispose themselves in a multiplicity of diverse ways' (1955).   M.S.-S.

pseudo-symmetry, see under QUASI-CRYSTAL.

psichiatria democratica. A movement to reform the care of the mentally ill in Italy, developed from the 1970s above all by Franco Basaglia. It has concentrated on replacing traditional mental hospitals with neighbourhood residences. Fired by a political POPULISM associated with the COMMUNIST Party, Basaglia campaigned in particular against compulsory confinement and custodial restraint, and met success in 1978 when the Italian Parliament abolished all new admissions to mental hospitals, concentrating treatment for acute cases upon special wards of general hospitals. In certain North Italian centres such as Bologna, effective community care units have been established. In other areas, the demise of the public mental hospital has led either to the neglect of disturbed people, or the emergence of a new 'private sector' of specialized mental units.   R.P.

Bibl: Peter Sedgwick, *Psycho Politics* (London, 1982).

psychedelic art. Art primarily concerned with sensory PERCEPTION, distortion, and hallucinations similar to those mental states produced by DRUGS such as LSD and mescaline. Such art often combines visual, aural, and KINETIC elements borrowed from TECHNOLOGY to heighten the spectator's sensory experience. Light and sound ENVIRONMENTS could be considered within this category, but psychedelic art can take so many diverse forms that its association with any one technique or medium is precluded. It has a more sober and more organized equivalent in OP ART.
A.K.W.

Bibl: D. Davis, *Art and the Future* (New York, 1973); and see under PRECISIONISM.

psychiatric society. A term, developed above all by the French psychiatrists Robert and Françoise Castel, to characterize the alleged domination of 20th-century western polities by the rationales of the 'psy complex' (PSYCHIATRY, PSYCHOANALYSIS, PSYCHOTHERAPY, PSYCHOLOGY etc). Earlier societies, it is argued, responded punitively to malefactors and deviants (see DEVIANCE). Modern society, following the principle of an economy of coercion, chooses to regulate disturbing elements not punitively but therapeutically, by treatment and mental readjustment. Moreover, whereas the 19th-century psychiatric goal was the asylum, utterly segregated from society, in the present century psychiatry has entered the community, through voluntary therapy, the introduction of psychology into schools and the workplace and psychiatry into the judicial domain. In this vision, the 'psy complex' can be seen as a hegemonic value system, playing the equivalent role to a new religion.   R.P.

Bibl: Robert Castel, Françoise Castel and Anne Lovell, *The Psychiatric Society* (New York, 1981).

psychiatry. The branch of medicine concerned with the study and treatment of mental illnesses and of other disorders, both behavioural and physical, in which psychological factors are important as causes or clinical features. As an independent medical specialism, psychiatry hardly existed before the 19th century, and its emergence was heavily associated with the concomitant rise of the lunatic asylum and mental hospital throughout Europe. As typically practised, pyschiatry has leaned heavily upon its medical bases, and has made presuppositions about the organic source of mental disturbances. Herein it may be distinguished from PSYCHOANALYSIS and the various PSYCHOTHERAPIES.

A psychiatrist is a physician with advanced training in the treatment of the severe mental illnesses (PSYCHOSES) such as SCHIZOPHRENIA and MANIC-DEPRESSIVE PSYCHOSIS, the less severe NEUROSES and emotional disorders, PSYCHOSOMATIC disorders, MENTAL RETARDATION, and behavioural anomalies such as the addictions and sexual deviations.

As a branch of medicine, psychiatry has its foundations in the basic biological sciences (see BIOLOGY); it also derives fundamental CONCEPTS and methods from the BEHAVIOURAL and SOCIAL SCIENCES, particularly PSYCHOLOGY and SOCIOLOGY, and to a lesser extent ANTHROPOLOGY and ETHOLOGY. In its medical aspects, psychiatry uses modes of investigation derived from ANATOMY, PHYSIOLOGY, BIOCHEMISTRY, NEUROLOGY and other related sciences; these methods are applicable to a range of psychiatric disorders, especially

those associated with demonstrable disease of the brain or with conditions such as EPILEPSY or ALCOHOLISM. In medical practice, psychiatric principles are playing a growing role in the treatment of physical illnesses, as it is increasingly recognized that psychological factors may determine the manifestations, course, and outcome of such disorders.

The practice of modern psychiatry extends over a wide range of subspecialities, in some of which the 'medical model' of treatment is less applicable. For example, *child psychiatry* is largely but not exclusively concerned with emotional and conduct disorders in children; *forensic psychiatry* is concerned with the behavioural deviations and delinquents and criminals (see DEVIANCE; DELINQUENCY; CRIMONOLOGY). PSYCHOANALYSIS, the FREUDIAN theoretical system and method of treatment, has been influential in the U.S.A.; most British psychiatrists, though acknowledging that Freud's contribution has been radical and stimulating, are not psychoanalysts. Sharply contrasted with the individualist approach of psychoanalysis is the recent development of *community psychiatry*, which is concerned with the provision and delivery of a coordinated programme of mental health to a specified population. This applies particularly in the light of current policies of reducing institutional confinement in mental institutions.

In recent years much attention has been paid to social factors as determinants of psychiatric disorders. *Psychiatric social workers* have been trained to deal with occupational, domestic, economic, and family problems. Psychiatric research has been concerned with socio-economic variables such as social isolation and SOCIAL MOBILITY, emigration, economic deprivation, etc. and the extent to which they are correlated with differences in the prevalence and outcome of mental illnesses and abnormal behaviour such as suicide.

The contribution of the science of psychology should be emphasized. In psychiatry extensive use is made, for example, of PSYCHOMETRIC techniques and statistical devices applied to the measurement of COGNITIVE functions and personality. Behavioural methods derived from learning-theory principles are being increasingly used in the treatment of neuroses. Above all, perhaps, today's psychiatry looks to chemical and pharmaceutical containment and cure of mental disorders. For a rejection of conventional psychiatry see ANTI-PSYCHIATRY.   D.H.G.;R.P.

Bibl: A.M. Freedman and H.I. Kaplan (eds.), *Comprehensive Textbook of Psychiatry* (Baltimore, 1967); W. Mayer-Gross, E. Slater, and M. Roth, *Clinical Psychiatry* (London and Baltimore, 3rd ed., 1969); P. Hays, *New Horizons in Psychiatry* (Baltimore, 1964: Harmondsworth, 2nd ed., 1971); M. Shepherd (ed.), *Handbook of Psychiatry* (Cambridge, 1982).

psychic determinism, see under PSYCHO-ANALYSIS.

psychical research, see PARAPSY-CHOLOGY.

psychoanalysis. (1) The PSYCHOLOGY and the PSYCHOTHERAPY associated with the work of Freud and the FREUDIAN traditions. (2) More broadly, the whole family of SCHOOLS OF PSYCHOLOGY, stemming from the original work of Breuer and Freud in the 1880s and 1890s. (In both senses, the word is popularly used to refer *only* to the therapy, and not to the theory on which this is based.) Themes or doctrines common to these traditions include the following:

(a) The doctrine of *psychic determinism*. This amounts to a directive to refuse to accept an item of behaviour (e.g. a slip of the tongue, a casual remark) as a matter of chance, but to look instead for its psychological significance to the individual (see FREUDIAN SLIP).

(b) The doctrine of the UNCONSCIOUS. This amounts to the thesis that there are mental processes which operate outside the realm of an individual's awareness, and which play a key role in his life and in the explanation of his behaviour (whether it be a slip of the tongue or a neurotic collapse).

(c) The doctrine of *goal-directedness*. Human functioning is much more goal-directed than we ordinarily suppose. Hence this doctrine lays stress on the MOTIVATION of human thought, behaviour, etc., and prescribes that we look for

the unconscious motives that, on (b) above, go to determine and explain our conduct.

(d) The doctrine of *development*. This emphasizes the importance of experience, and especially early experience, in the development of the individual towards adulthood.

(e) The doctrine of *treatment*. The proper form of treatment for the NEUROSES is psychotherapy. For all other non-organic disorders, psychoanalysts would confess (probably) to having a professional preference for psychotherapy, but (in general) they would not urge that it should always or even generally be adopted in these cases. For they recognize the great practical limitations of psychotherapy and the advantages to be had from using other recognized methods of PSYCHIATRY.

The main psychoanalytic schools stem from the work of Freud, Jung, and Adler, and the differences between them centre round their different psychologies (see FREUDIAN; JUNGIAN; ADLERIAN). Thus, Jung rejected Freud's view of the sexual LIBIDO and extended the notion of the individual unconscious to cover that from which the individual CONSCIOUSNESS emerges, i.e. the COLLECTIVE UNCONSCIOUS; and he developed his own view of personality and PERSONALITY TYPES. Adler also rejected Freud's theory of libido, and emphasized the inter-personal relations in the family as a chief source of the LIFE STYLE of the person, which could be unrealistic, and so lead to neurosis. Some psychologists and psychiatrists have argued that what helped to produce these different schools in the first instance, and what helps to maintain them now, are defects in psychoanalytic method. If an analyst develops any ideas of his own about human nature, and if he feeds them into the therapeutic situation (which it is very difficult *not* to do), then he is liable to get material out of his work that goes to confirm his ideas about human nature.

All traditions of psychoanalysis report roughly the same proportion of improvement in their patients. This raises the interesting speculation that, in so far as improvement is *due* to psychoanalytic therapy, this results from the inherent nature of the psychotherapeutic situation in psychoanalysis, and not from the particular doctrines that the analyst uses in his treatment. See also LACANIAN, KLEIN-IAN, EGO-PSYCHOLOGY, OBJECT RELATIONS, EXISTENTIAL PSYCHIATRY, DEVELOPMENTAL THEORY, EGO, SUBJECT, TRANSFERENCE, IDENTIFICATION, PHANTASY, DRIVE, REAL, IMAGINARY, SYMBOLIC, FEMININE SEXUALITY, MIRROR PHASE.   B.A.F.

Bibl: R.L. Munro, *Schools of Psychoanalytic Thought* (London, 1957); J. Laplanche and J.-B. Pontalis, *The Language of Psychoanalysis* (London, 1973).

psychoanalytic criticism. Literary criticism influenced by the work of Sigmund Freud or, more recently, Jacques Lacan. Early PSYCHOANALYTIC critics like Marie Bonaparte on E.A.Poe or Ernest Jones on *Hamlet*, analysed the texts by uncomplicatedly assuming that literary works merely mirror the UNCONSCIOUS obsessions or NEUROSES of the writer, or of the characters themselves in a novel or play; and that in order to establish the nature of these obsessions, they could interpret basic 'FREUDIAN' symbols as if these had an exact and unchanging denotative value. A good deal of freeing conceptual work was achieved by Jakobson's essay on METAPHOR and metonymy of 1956. In the hands of Lévi-Strauss, Lacan and Barthes, this opposition was exploited to achieve a conceptually less naive view of the relation of representation to reality. The importance of language as a self-subsistent entity in the literary work, the way in which metaphor and metonymy can be seen as homologous with CONDENSATION and *displacement*, the two major techniques at work in Freud's account of dream-work, led eventually to Lacan's extreme outer position, in which language achieves complete independence of the writer and indeed enjoys its own unconscious. Critics writing under the influence of Lacan present the literary text as a set of free-floating 'signifiers' for which no 'signifieds' can be established, and in which there is in no significant sense an originating consciousness, a SUBJECTIVITY, a 'presence'.

Major conceptual innovations in Freudian psychoanalytic criticism have been made in America by Harold Bloom (*The Anxiety of Influence*, 1973) and the YALE SCHOOL; and by Norman Holland (*Five Readers Reading*, 1975), David Bleich (*Subjective Criticism*, 1978) and the 'Buffalo School'. Psychoanalytic criticism has also influenced the READER-RESPONSE theoreticians. In all these forms of influence, the emphasis has been on the writer, the reader, or the relation between the two. Properly LACANIAN criticism, however, seems to have abandoned concern for these relationships, and to have developed a METAPHYSIC of its own. In this metaphysic, the text is unknowable and independent, and indifferent both to its writer and its readers. The complex 'philosophy' of Lacan himself is deployed as if it were of use in analysing literature, and his antihumanistic bias is deployed to justify reading the text as a diagram for everything which we can't have and everything which isn't possible. The Phallus (the principle of REALITY and exclusion) constantly blocks DESIRE and commits human beings to senseless repetition and frustrated 'slippage' from one 'signifier' to another. When applied to literary texts, the formal application of Lacanian theory seems to do nothing but darken counsel. But the attractiveness of Lacan's theories to FEMINIST critics has something of the paradoxical about it, as it is obvious from Lacan's own texts that he is more 'phallocentric' than the patriarch Freud himself. Nevertheless, FEMINIST CRITICISM emanating from France, and including in particular Julia Kristeva, Luce Irigaray and Helene Cixous, has established the Lacanian form of psychoanalytic criticism as the most powerful form of IDEOLOGICAL theorizing now on offer. In its endless negativity, French Lacanianism has resulted in a kind of SOLIPSISM in which women are locked into a consideration of the physical construction of their own bodies, or the irreparable loss of their mothers, in a way which excludes an analysis of the male psyche altogether. An insistence upon 'sexual difference', partly derived from Lacan and partly from Derrida, has become an entrenched position from which all forms of male presence and activity can be harassed, and in particular all forms of self-deluded belief in male adequacy. It is not clear from this how the political situation will be changed in any way, though their emphasis on 'difference' is often equated, in their writings, with the taking of a 'political', 'radical' or even 'revolutionary' position. R.PO.

Bibl: E. Wright, *Psychoanalytic Criticism* (London, 1984); T. Moi, *Sexual/Textual Politics* (London, 1985).

psychodiagnostics. The assessment of personality characteristics and possible psychiatric disorder through interpretation of either (1) objective behavioural indices such as gait, facial expression, and GRAPHOLOGY; or (2) the way in which a person, in terms of his motivational CONSTRUCTS, responds to a series of inkblots (see RORSCHACH TEST). See also MENTAL TESTING.
G.M.

psychodrama. In PSYCHOTHERAPY, a technique in which the patient plays out a ROLE in the dramatic enactment of a particular situation, in order to help him understand his subjective and interpersonal feelings. W.Z.

psychodynamic. An adjective, used in PSYCHIATRY and PSYCHOLOGY, for which there is no accepted definition. In one usage it is applied to theories which represent symptomatic behaviour as determined by an interplay of forces within the mind of an individual subject without involving awareness. This is exemplified by FREUDIAN psychoanalytic theory (see PSYCHOANALYSIS), which postulates intrapsychic conflicts between UNCONSCIOUS mental activities, such as primitive sexual and aggressive impulses, and those parts of the mind (EGO and SUPEREGO) concerned with morality. The adjective is also applied, in a wider sense, to behavioural symptoms and indicates that these are regarded as being determined by both intra-psychic and extra-psychic factors, the latter including, for example, parental influences, family conflicts, occupational and other stresses. D.H.G.

psychogalvanic response (PGR), see under GALVANIC SKIN RESPONSE.

psychogenic, see under PSYCHOSOMATIC.

psychohistory. A term coined in the 1960s to describe an approach to historical subjects which attempts to take into account SUBCONSCIOUS and private elements of human experience studied by psychologists, particularly of the FREUDIAN school. Although attempts have been made to apply this approach to collective experiences (e.g. WITCHCRAFT; Puritanism; MILLENARIANISM), or, by Norbert Elias, to the 'process of civilization', the examples which have attracted most attention have been biographical studies, beginning with E.H. Erikson's *Young Man Luther* (1958). Other examples are biographies of Gandhi (by Erikson) and Newton (by Frank Manuel), and Lyndon Johnson (by Doris Kearns).

The method has been sceptically received by most historians on the grounds that the evidence available is insufficient to produce more than conjectural conclusions. On the other hand, to write history, and especially to write biography, without assumptions about PSYCHOLOGY is impossible, and Erikson, for example, in his study of Luther faced certain crucial problems more seriously than earlier historians had been willing to do. The controversy continues. A.L.C.B.; P.B.

Bibl: F.E. Manuel, 'The Use and Abuse of Psychology in History', in *Freedom from History* (New York, 1971; London, 1972); D. Stannard, *Shrinking History* (Oxford, 1980).

psychokinesis (PK). In PARAPSYCHOLOGY, movement of physical objects caused by somebody not using physical forces; e.g. making a dice fall in a certain position merely by willing it to do so. PK is probably not involved in movements of divining rods and ouija boards since such movements can, like automatic writing, result from unconscious muscle movements. It is sometimes alleged to be responsible for poltergeist hauntings and for the performances of people, like Uri Geller, who produce movements of and in objects without using any apparent physical force. PK is the kinetic counterpart of ESP and poses the same challenges to scientific investigation. I.M.L.H.

psycholinguistics. A branch of LINGUISTICS which studies variation in linguistic behaviour in relation to psychological notions such as memory, PERCEPTION, attention, and acquisition. D.C.

psychological medicine, see under PSY-
CHOLOGY.

psychological parallelism, see under
MIND-BODY PROBLEM.

psychological warfare, see under WAR.

psychologism. The interpretation of philosophical problems as questions of a factual
kind to be answered by PSYCHOLOGY.
Locke and Hume both explicitly endorsed
this conception of philosophical enquiry,
although they were not wholly bound by
it in practice. Their theory of MEANINGS as
images causally dependent on previous
sense-experiences and Hume's account of
the associative mechanisms underlying the
CONCEPTS of cause and identity are influential examples of psychologism. Critics
have argued that psychologism treats
questions of ANALYSIS and justification,
which concern the correct use of words
and the *right* formation of beliefs, as questions about the actual mental associates of
the use of words and the psychological
causation of belief, thus misinterpreting
what is logically NORMATIVE as if it were
psychologically descriptive. Husserl's PHE-
NOMENOLOGICAL theory of philosophy as
the intuitive scrutiny of ESSENCES was
negatively inspired by a rejection of the
psychologism of Mill, particularly about
MATHEMATICS. Again, the contemporary
philosophy of MIND is not a very abstract
and general *part* of psychology, but an
examination of its PRESUPPOSITIONS. A.Q.

psychology. A word variously defined as
the study of mind, the study of behaviour,
or the study of man interacting with his
social and physical ENVIRONMENT. Historically, pyschology was a late emergence
as an independent science and discipline,
traditionally being variously subsumed
within THEOLOGY, LOGIC, PHILOSOPHY and
learning theory. In England and France,
the lineage from Locke through Condillac
to the ideologues put the psychological
study of mental operations (such as memory, imagination and judgement) and the
validation of knowledge on the map as a
science in its own right. The word psychology as such was rarely used until the
19th century.
The definition one prefers has theoreti-

cal and methodological consequences (see
METHODOLOGY), since it conceptualizes
what is central in one's concern about man
and predisposes one to study different aspects of human experience and behaviour
and their determinants. But, while its
'schools' and their theoretical debates
have at times been divisive, the field has
taken a fairly definite shape with respect
to subject-matter studied, methods used,
and professions created. At the same time,
psychology has not achieved the degree of
organization of its knowledge characterizing such NATURAL SCIENCES as PHYSICS or
CHEMISTRY, principally because it still
lacks fundamental central CONCEPTS comparable to the CONSERVATION LAWS of the
physical sciences.
If one takes the ultimate aim of psychology to be the systematic description
and explanation of man at the fullness of
his powers, as a thinking, striving, talking,
enculturated animal (see ENCULTURA-
TION), it has often proved most advantageous to pursue that aim by comparative
study. Psychology typically divides into
fields of study based on the comparisons
used. When, for example, one compares
man with other organisms at different
levels of EVOLUTION, there emerges the set
of disciplines known as COMPARATIVE PSY-
CHOLOGY. Since its tools of analysis must
be as manageable when working with animals as with man, much of the work in
comparative psychology looks for its explanations in terms of the relation of brain
and behaviour, of blood chemistry and the
endocrine (see ENDOCRINOLOGY) system
of GENETICS, and of the functional ADAPTA-
TION of organisms to their natural environment in response to SELECTION
PRESSURES. But although in theory one is
looking for direct comparisons, in practice
no phenomenon need be excluded, since
every phenomenon has its analogue (if not
its homologue) elsewhere in the animal
kingdom; e.g. communication in bees or
dolphins is analogous to human speech,
the capacity of a chimpanzee to recognize
and differentiate his own image in a mirror
from that of another animal is analogous
to human self-awareness.
A second comparison, that between
adult and child, is the basis of DEVELOP-
MENTAL PSYCHOLOGY; a field including
studies of growth in other species as well

as in man. Developmental studies, strongly influenced by the work of Piaget, have centred increasingly in recent years on the growth of adult powers of PERCEPTION, reasoning, memory, language, and moral judgement; but analysis of the factors that may affect these (e.g. the growth and transformation of motives, the role of mother-child interaction and of the family, personality formation) has also continued. The developmental approach has also been used to explore in increasing detail the effects of different CULTURES on the growth of mental processes and motives. Since much of development is strongly affected by formal or informal schooling, the principal application of work in this field is through EDUCATIONAL PSYCHOLOGY and CHILD PSYCHOLOGY.

A third comparison is between man operating effectively and man afflicted either by PSYCHOPATHOLOGY or NEUROPATHOLOGY, the two often being difficult to distinguish. This comparison is the basis of ABNORMAL PSYCHOLOGY, and it serves in its applied form as a field ancillary to PSYCHIATRY. A fourth comparison, of human and animal behaviour in different social settings, forms the basis of SOCIAL PSYCHOLOGY, which has recently been freed, by a marked growth in research, from an ETHNOCENTRISM often criticized by ANTHROPOLOGY. Fifth and last, there is a new and fruitful comparative study of the difference between 'natural' man functioning in his 'natural' surroundings and COMPUTER-built MODELS of man functioning in hypothesized environments, with PROGRAMS embodying assumptions about human behaviour and human environments. The assumptions are tested by direct comparison of outcomes. The study of ARTIFICIAL INTELLIGENCE is a good example. There is nowadays massive debate as to how far artificial minds should be understood psychologically, in the same terms as human ones.

But psychology can also be characterized in two other ways: by its choice of processes to be studied, and by its method of analysis. With respect to the processes studied, the distinctions can most easily be made in terms of an INPUT-OUTPUT metaphor. One part of psychology tends to specialize more on input processes; *sensory processing*, PERCEPTION, *short-term memory*, and HABITUATION. Generally, the object of such study is to discern the manner in which organisms transduce or transform ENERGY changes in the physical environment, converting them into sensations or percepts. It was in this enterprise that psychology was founded as an experimental science, in research that still continues rigorously in PSYCHOPHYSICS. At the other extreme, psychologists are concerned with the nature of response processes, e.g. with skill, EXPRESSSIVE MOVEMENT, motives and drive states, language, and various forms of social behaviour. Between the two are studies of the processes that mediate between input and output, e.g. attention, the organization of memory and learning, the formation of attitudes, and concepts and rules whereby the organism can regulate response systematically with respect to stimulus changes, in a fashion that is systematic but not a direct reflection of the nature of the stimulation.

It is from work of these three types that psychology derives the processes used to explain the differences and similarities that emerge from its comparative studies. Another important subfield of psychology over the last century has been *psychological medicine*, aiming to understand the cognitive basis of mental disfunction and the misconstrual of reality. The stress on failures in cognition (memory, etc.) and the attempt to relate these to neurological defects (see NEUROLOGY) retains the distinction between psychological medicine and most departments of psychiatry proper.

With respect to methods of analysis, psychology inevitably uses a variety of approaches (EXPERIMENTAL, observational, clinical, even literary) and tools (field studies, mathematical and computer modelling). Even more striking than its growth as a university subject has been its proliferation as an applied field (see APPLIED PSYCHOLOGY) in industry (see INDUSTRIAL PSYCHOLOGY), EDUCATION, medicine, ENGINEERING, politics, and the armed forces. See also BEHAVIOURISM; COGNITIVE PSYCHOLOGY; DEPTH PSYCHOLOGY; DIFFERENTIAL PSYCHOLOGY; DYNAMIC PSYCHOLOGY, EXISTENTIAL PSYCHOLOGY; FACULTY PSYCHOLOGY; GENETIC

PSYCHOLOGY; GESTALT; GROUP PSYCHOLOGY; HERBARTIAN PSYCHOLOGY; HORMIC PSYCHOLOGY; HUMANISTIC PSYCHOLOGY; INDIVIDUAL PSYCHOLOGY; INTROSPECTIVE PSYCHOLOGY; MATHEMATICAL PSYCHOLOGY; ORGANISMIC PSYCHOLOGY; PERSONALISTIC PSYCHOLOGY; PSYCHOLINGUISTICS; SCHOOLS OF PSYCHOLOGY; STRUCTURAL PSYCHOLOGY; TOPOLOGICAL PSYCHOLOGY. J.S.B.;R.P.

Bibl: P. Lloyd et al., Introduction to Psychology: an Integrated Approach (London, 1984).

psychology of religion, see RELIGION, PSYCHOLOGY OF.

psychometrics. The techniques of quantifying human mental traits, particularly the statistical treatment of MENTAL TESTING. Until recently, these techniques were almost exclusively concerned with sorting people into different categories, especially for educational and vocational placement. QUANTIFICATION is usually accomplished by devising test items that show maximum discrimination between individuals, and by the use of standard test STATISTICS that emphasize the internal consistency of the items to one another. Such tests are *norm-referenced*, i.e. individual scores are determined by reference to the scores achieved by a relevant group, most often a group of the same age.

Psychometrics, and consequently the mental testing movement, were initiated in 1883 by the English biologist Sir Francis Galton during his investigations into HEREDITY (see EUGENICS). His statistical methods for the analysis of data on individual differences were developed by his students and their associates, particularly Karl Pearson (1892) and Charles Spearman, into a test theory which held up very well under subsequent formal mathematical analysis. Pearson's extensive work on CORRELATION, together with the introduction by Spearman (1904) of the CONCEPT of FACTOR ANALYSIS, was the breakthrough that launched the mental testing movement, pioneered by J. McK. Catell (1890) and E.L. Thorndike (1904) in America, and in Europe by A. Binet and T. Simon (1905), who produced the first influential measures of scholastic aptitude. In Britain Cyril Burt, an associate of

Spearman and devotee of Galton, began in 1909 a lifetime's work on the testing of INTELLIGENCE and achievement.

The development of group testing during World War I (for classifying recruits according to intellectual level) gave additional impetus to a movement which has steadily expanded and proliferated. Today, in most industrialized countries, there are large establishments devoted to the construction, application, and interpretation of standardized tests which are widely used for educational and vocational selection, and which play an important part in the determination of life-chances.

In recent years, opposition to mental testing has grown. On the one hand, it is attacked by those who claim that its meritocratic rhetoric masks the perpetuation of existing inequalities in the distribution of power and opportunities (see ÉLITISM; RACISM; MERITOCRACY); American psychometricians, for example, have revealed the loading of most vocabulary tests in favour of whites by devising other such tests which are loaded in favour of blacks, and in which the normal higher white rating is reversed. On the other hand, it is criticized for having failed to evolve new forms to meet changing applications, particularly in the field of education. Here a major effort has been made during the last decade to improve the quality of the curriculum; but appropriate procedures for measuring the efficacy of educational treatments rather than the performance of students have yet to be devised.

Recently there has been a tendency to replace norm-referenced tests by CRITERION-REFERENCED ones, whose primary function is to compare individual performance, not with other individual performances, but with a specific criterion, such as how well the subject might need to perform a specified task, or how well he might reasonably be expected to perform if given adequate instruction. Since tests are traditionally validated against how particular groups perform, and since test statistics are based on concepts of individual differences, the classical ways of judging tests through 'validity' and 'reliability' are not suited to criterion-referenced tests.

How to judge their quality remains a formidable problem.   B.M.
Bibl: R.L. Thorndike, *Applied Psychometrics* (New York, 1981).

psychoneurosis, see NEUROSIS.

psychopathology. The study of abnormal mental states, which developed out of the sustained observation of asylum patients in the 19th century, in the context of an overriding theory of mental and racial DEGENERATION. Psychopathology has commonly linked mental and emotional abnormality to physical and organic defect, suggesting some hereditary and biological component; but behavioural inputs (such as childhood experiences) are acknowledged to play major parts in individual psychopathology. Central to 20th-century developments has been the formulation of the disease concept, SCHIZO-PHRENIA, focusing attention on the 'psychopathic type', i.e., abnormals not necessarily suffering from delusions but who seem to lack human engagement with others or any normal conscience concerning their own actions.   R.P.
Bibl: F. Kraupl Taylor, *Psychopathology* (London, 1966).

psychopharmacology. The study of the behavioural effects of DRUGS (sense 1). It is Janus-like: it may aim principally at the CLASSIFICATION of drugs according to the similarity of their effects on behaviour, or at the classification of types of behaviour according to the similarity of their susceptibility to the effects of drugs. The former aim has usually been more prominent, but the latter may eventually prove more important. With regard to the former, the existing pharmacological classifications have proved very unhelpful in predicting effects of drugs on behaviour, while it is often difficult to see any pharmacological similarity between drugs that are indistinguishable in their behavioural effects. Furthermore, drugs that have a relatively precise pharmacological action frequently turn out to have remarkably unspecific behavioural effects, while drugs that have highly specific effects on behaviour have very wide-ranging and unspecific effects on the chemistry of the brain. Thus psychopharmacology is very much a disci-pline in its own right and not merely an INTERFACE between its two parents, PSY-CHOLOGY and PHARMACOLOGY. See also NEUROPSYCHOLOGY.   J.A.G.

psychophysics. The study of relations, especially quantitative, between psychological characteristics of perceived properties and physical characteristics of STIMULI, e.g. between the heard loudness and pitch of a tone and the intensity and frequency of the ACOUSTIC stimulus. Pioneered in Germany around 1850 by G.T. Fechner, psychophysics is a field in which work has continued vigorously.   I.M.L.H.
Bibl: see under PERCEPTION.

psychoprophylaxis, see under CHILDBIRTH TECHNIQUES.

psychosexual development. The processes whereby human beings reach a mature expression of their sexual impulses, including attitudes and values concerning their sexuality. In Freud's view, psychosexual development included the earliest feelings of affection of the boy for his mother or the girl for her father (see OEDIPUS COMPLEX; ELECTRA COMPLEX) and the development of *erogenous zones* connected with which there was some pleasure or tension created by relations with the mother or foster-mother. The first phase was the *oral phase* related to the child's preoccupation with the intake of food: the child's mouth was conceived of as a centre not only for nutriment but for exploration, and, provided there were no difficulties with feeding, the child was thought to develop expectations concerning gratification. The second phase was the *anal phase*: the crises connected with the bowel movements, and the approval these were given by the mother, were thought to be a focus for the organization of early sexual tendencies. The development of stronger and more direct sexual feelings towards the mother (in boys; the father in girls) were thought, next, to produce CASTRATION ANXIETY, leading to the suppression of sexual feelings during the pre-adolescent LATENCY PERIOD. Adolescence then produced a resurgence of sexuality in the *phallic phase* (a somewhat curious expression for a phenomenon postulated of girls as well as boys), with the emphasis more on expression of sexual feelings as such (e.g. through masturbation) than on sexual relations with a partner, including the sharing of gentler, more tender feelings. Full or 'genital' maturity took the form, finally, of sexuality expressing itself in the context of a mature relationship with a loved partner whose satisfaction and well-being also provided an important aspect of sexual gratification.

It was proposed in psychoanalytic theory (see PSYCHOANALYSIS) that either indulgence or frustration at any stage of psychosexual development would lead to FIXATION at that stage with character traits emerging in the adult reflecting unrequited requirements. In consequence one speaks of an *oral character* or an *anal character* or a *phallic character* as reflecting these early fixations.

Studies of sexual development have shown that it follows no fixed course but is highly influenced by the NORMS of the CULTURE or SUBCULTURE in which the child grows up. The FREUDIAN theory of it has also been criticized for assuming the invariable presence of castration anxiety and the latency period, as have most theories, including the Freudian, for their inadequacy in describing the course of psychosexual development in women. See also DEVELOPMENTAL THEORY.   J.S.B.

psychosis. In PSYCHIATRY and ABNORMAL PSYCHOLOGY in the West, a term used for one of the main classes of mental illness. In the present state of psychiatric knowledge it is not possible to classify the majority of mental illnesses on the basis of causal factors, and modern systems of CLASSIFICATION go back to the work of Emil Kraepelin (1856-1926), a German psychiatrist who endeavoured to establish definite psychiatric diseases and to bring order into psychiatric taxonomy. Psychoses are usually distinguished from NEUROSES, personality disorders, PSYCHOSOMATIC disorders, and MENTAL RETARDATION, and are themselves divided into the *organic* and the so-called *functional* psychoses. Within the original terminological framework, psychoses were seen essentially as disturbances of consciousness, without any necessary organic correlate. As such they included functional disorders, and could comprehend the less

serious mental complaints. Over the last century, terminological confusion between psychoses and neuroses was common, as is exemplified by Freud's alternative usages of neuropsychosis and psychoneurosis. In organic psychoses, such as general paralysis of the insane and delirium, there is a demonstrable physical abnormality in the brain. In functional psychoses, such as SCHIZOPHRENIA and the affective psychoses, no underlying physical disease has been discovered; but the mental and physical symptoms, together with the results of GENETIC research, are thought by many psychiatrists to indicate underlying morbid endocrine or biochemical changes (see ENDOCRINOLOGY; BIOCHEMISTRY).

Traditionally, much attention has been paid to the time-honoured distinction between psychoses and neuroses. Probably the origins of this distinction were mainly social and historical: psychotic (mad, insane, or lunatic) patients were those whose behaviour was so deranged that they were placed in madhouses or asylums, while neurotics were treated in physicians' consulting-rooms. There is no single characteristic by which psychoses can be defined. Psychoses have been said to be distinctively characterized by greater severity of illness; total dissolution of the personality; lack of insight into the illness; inability to distinguish between subjective experience and reality; the presence of delusions and hallucinations; the occurrence of a marked personality change which cannot be interpreted as an understandable development of the personality or reaction to psychological TRAUMA. Exceptions are readily found to all these criteria. Nevertheless, psychiatrists of similar training can achieve a high level of agreement in classifying patients as neurotic or psychotic.

While most psychiatrists agree that a system of diagnostic classification is necessary, the term psychosis is not of great value in clinical practice. Other, less inclusive diagnostic categories are more useful, and decisions as to treatment and prognosis are based on other considerations.   D.H.G.

Bibl: M. Lader, *Priorities in Psychiatric Research* (Chichester, 1980).

psychosomatic. Adjective derived from the Greek words for 'soul' and 'body' and used in medical and PSYCHIATRIC contexts — it can be applied to a patient or to his disorder — to imply a relationship between mental and physical states of health; *psychosomatics* is the study of this relationship. Historically, the traditional humoral theory of disease made no clear distinction between mind and body and so saw all disease as to some degree psychosomatic. The rise of scientific medicine in the 19th century tended to stress the organic substrate, but the visible presence of such conditions as HYSTERIA ensured a hearing for psychosomatic interpretations of apparently organic dysfunctions. The adjective is most commonly used in the context of physical conditions, e.g. gastric or duodenal ulcers or severe headaches, that derive from stress states. Most theories of psychosomatic illness offer inadequate explanations both of why some individuals 'somatize' their symptoms of stress while others do not (manifesting ANXIETY or DEPRESSION instead), and of 'organ choice', i.e. why one person develops ulcers, another chronic fatigue. Contemporary research indicates that in stress there is massive involvement of the adreno-cortical system, and that this can express itself in a variety of physical symptoms by maintaining in the bloodstream high levels of circulating catecholamine which may disrupt different organ systems. Psychosomatic disorders are to be distinguished from *psychogenic* (i.e. those originating exclusively in the mind). See also ABNORMAL PSYCHOLOGY; MIND-BODY PROBLEM.   J.S.B.;R.P.

psychosurgery. The use of surgical means against mental disease (e.g., trepanning the skull to release pressure and tension) has a long history, but became a movement only in the present century with the work of Egas Moniz (1874-1955) at Lisbon. A distinguished neurologist, Moniz believed that functional PSYCHOSES largely stemmed from diseases of the frontal area of the brain. By removing parts of the frontal lobes he expected to provide relief or cure. He performed his first lobotomy (see LEUCOTOMY) in 1935, and the operation spread in the 1940s, finding loud advocates in the U.S.A. in particular. It was found that lobotomized patients were less violent, but that many were turned into 'zombies', lacking ambition and energy. Psychosurgery was widely criticized because it was imprecise and irreversible, and since the 1970s its use has been drastically curtailed.   R.P.

psychotherapy. A sub-class of the methods used — either within PSYCHIATRY or outside it — for treating sufferers from mental abnormalities. The sub-class is easier to delimit by giving examples of what it *includes* (e.g. PSYCHOANALYSIS, counselling, ordinary psychiatric interviews, transactional analysis, the nonverbal movement and body therapies) and what it *excludes* (e.g. ELECTROCONVULSIVE THERAPY, PSYCHOPHARMACOLOGY, surgical interference with the brain, OPERANT CONDITIONING, the desensitization technique of BEHAVIOUR THERAPY) than by a formal definition. But perhaps the most fruitful way of trying to distinguish between psychotherapy and other methods is in terms of the sort of situation and interaction set up in the former between patient and therapist and deliberately used for therapeutic purposes. This revolves essentially around a special relationship between patient and therapist that is produced and maintained by the rules of operation the particular therapist employs. Thus, a psychoanalyst will operate in accordance with certain rules which will generate a characteristic type of situation and relationship between patient and analyst, in which, e.g., the development of TRANSFERENCE is a key feature. In contrast, a counsellor in the tradition of Carl Rogers will operate in a different way, and this will produce a different type of situation and relationship, in which transference is minimal and the development of spontaneity in the verbal expression of feeling becomes important.

Historically, psychotherapy became an accepted part of contemporary psychiatry partly or largely as the result of the growth and influence of psychoanalysis. Likewise, the different methods of contemporary psychotherapy are, in large measure, developments out of psychoanalytic practice. In the last three decades, however, many therapists have become increasingly dissatisfied with psychoanalytic practice because of its length and slowness, the few patients who can be reached by it, its great expense, and its rigidities, which (allegedly) restrict its effectiveness. Accordingly, many psychotherapists have struck out in novel directions in attempts to overcome the limitations of traditional psychoanalysis, e.g. by shortening the duration of therapy, and by a variety of group techniques such as GROUP THERAPY and PSYCHODRAMA. About the results of psychotherapy it is very difficult to establish any claims, whether positive or negative, because of the massive complexity of the issue, and the comparative crudities of our current techniques of investigation. At best, perhaps, it can be said that we have some grounds for thinking that psychotherapy can be of use when it is appropriately used and skilfully operated.

Despite the doubts and difficulties that surround it, psychotherapy has had an immense impact on Western culture. Thus, it has greatly affected our ways of thinking about and organizing human relations in various departments of life, e.g. educational practice, prison organization, and the selection and training of business managers. Material produced by psychotherapy has formed the evidential base for a number of theories (FREUDIAN, JUNGIAN, etc.) about human nature which are of great interest, and, if true, of enormous importance. These theories have stimulated psychologists in their efforts to uncover the hard facts about human nature, and have permeated our thought and attitudes in ways not yet adequately charted.

B.A.F.

Bibl: S.Bloch (ed.), *Introduction to the Psychotherapies* (Oxford, 1979).

psychotic, see under PSYCHOSIS.

public debt, see NATIONAL DEBT.

public good. The consumption of a public good by some people allows others to consume the same good. The consumption of a pure public good means that all other persons necessarily consume the same quantity of the good. Examples of public goods are clean air, knowledge and defence. Often it is technically difficult or prohibitively expensive to exclude persons from consuming public goods. If private

firms cannot force individuals to pay for the consumption of a public good, they will be unwilling to supply them. A function of the state is to supply public goods, the costs of which are covered by taxes. The incidence of this TAXATION and the distribution of the benefits resulting from consumption of public goods can have important redistributive impacts. If the incidence of taxation is according to the estimated benefits derived from consumption, a FREE-RIDER problem exists. This problem exists as the level of supply of the public good is altered only by a negligible amount by an individual's payment of the taxes associated with the stated benefit. Thus, individuals have an incentive to underestimate the strength of their preferences for publicly supplied public goods. If everyone adopted this strategy, there would be no supply of public goods. As taxes are rarely levied in this way, the free-rider problem is unlikely to be of practical importance. However, it remains difficult to find out the true demand for public goods. Many public goods, e.g. mass transport systems, have low costs of exclusion and there is considerable economic and political debate on whether they should be supplied by the PRIVATE or PUBLIC SECTOR (see EXTERNALITIES and PRIVATE GOOD). J.P.

Bibl: D. Begg *et al., Economics* (London, 1984).

public housing. Dwellings financed directly by governmental agencies and/or local authorities, and rented to tenants. It assumes the provision of housing as a basic social service for those groups unable to compete in the housing market, or as a service to a much wider group, depending on the political outlook of the country. In Britain the ratio between private and public housing built since 1945 has fluctuated around 40:60, with the larger share going to one or other sector according to political control. In the U.S.A. the proportion of public housing is very much smaller, in the U.S.S.R. very much greater. M.BR.

Bibl: D.V. Donnison, *The Government of Housing* (Harmondsworth, 1967).

public interest. A term used to distinguish the public interest from the selfish interests of some individual or group (see IN-

TEREST GROUP). Of interest to political theorists because of the plausibility of the thought that while individuals and small, well organized groups can be trusted to promote *their* interests, the unorganized mass of the population cannot be expected to look after the public's interest in the same way — from which the familiar view that it is the task of the state to defend the public interest follows quite naturally. See also INTERESTS, THEORY OF.   A.R.

Bibl: Brian Barry, *Political Argument* (London and Boston, 1965).

public interest immunity. The protection of documents from production in court as evidence by reason of the public interest. In England until 1968 the courts automatically granted this immunity or privilege in respect of all documents or classes of documents for which the Crown, in proper form, claimed that production would be injurious to the public interest. But in that year the House of Lords established the modern rule whereby any such claim must be tested by the court to determine whether or not the public interest in keeping the document confidential should properly outweigh the other public interest that justice be done. Thus 'class claims' to immunity no longer succeed, and all individual claims are examined by the courts on their merits.
                                                        D.C.M.Y.

Bibl: D.C.M. Yardley, *Principles of Administrative Law* (London, 2nd ed., 1986); H.W.R. Wade, *Administrative Law* (Oxford and New York, 5th ed., 1982).

public interest theory, see under ECONOMIC REGULATION.

public international law. A term used to define a body of rules which are regarded as binding by states in their relationship with each other, e.g. STATE responsibility for breach of international obligations, or observance of diplomatic privileges and immunities. Although it is only states that are subjects of international law, individuals and institutions figure increasingly in the international domain. The sources of international law outlined in Article 38 of the Statute of the INTERNATIONAL COURT OF JUSTICE are: (1) international conventions, whether general or particular, establishing rules expressly recognized by the contesting states; (2) international custom, as evidence of a general practice accepted as law; (3) the general principles of law recognized by civilized nations; and (4) judicial decisions and the teachings of the most highly qualified publicists of the various nations, as subsidiary means for the determination of the rules of law. Where a conflict arises between the rules of international and municipal law, an international tribunal will opt for the former. By contrast, where the conflict arises before a municipal court, it will be resolved on the basis of the constitutional rules of the state in which that court is situated. An apparent defect of the international system is its lack of an effective central organ for the enforcement of legal rights. Nonetheless, due to the role of reciprocity in international relations and the deterrent effect of counter-measures, in practice international law operates efficaciously.   O.Y.E.

Bibl: I. Brownlie, *Principles of Public International Law* (Oxford, 1979).

public-key crypto system. A type of code which is believed to be unbreakable. There are two parts to using a code: the coding procedure and the decoding procedure. For traditional codes, if one knew the first, then it was an easy matter to deduce the second. However, in the mid 1970s it was realized that it was possible to have a code where the coding procedure is public knowledge but the decoding procedure is essentially unobtainable. This is made possible by some elementary NUMBER THEORY related to prime numbers (viz. Fermat's little theorem). The coding procedure involves knowing a very large number which is the product of two (or more) prime numbers. In order to crack the code one needs to know those prime numbers, but the ALGORITHMS available for finding the prime factors of a given number are very slow (so for a huge composite number, it may take a COMPUTER thousands of years to find its prime factors).   J.M.

Bibl: Ian Stewart, *The Problems of Mathematics* (Oxford, 1987); Martin Helleman, 'The Mathematics of Public-key Cryptography', *Scientific American*, August 1979.

Public Lending Right, see PLR.

public relations. Anything enjoys the benefits, or disadvantages, of external perceptions, whether they want to or not. The management of public relations, for a business (or for the product of a business) is, in many ways, more difficult than the management of paid for communication. Press, television and radio are the main MEDIA of public relations. Relationships with the media are often a case of 'damned if you do, damned if you don't'. Historically, many businesses have managed their public relations on the basis of saying nothing, and being prepared to pay to avoid mention — this on the basis that, if all other communication is being carefully managed and controlled, then nothing is left to chance. In the era of investigative and exposé reporting even silence cannot guarantee non-mention, and public relations practitioners have learnt to ride tigers.

Just like the ADVERTISING process, effective management of public relations starts with a clear definition of key target audience(s), and an explanation of consumer benefits. The most effective medium is selected for the communication of benefits to the target, with a due recognition that, to adapt McLuhan, the medium can affect the message. Then no effort is spared in ensuring that key journalists are the recipients of detailed product information on a regular basis.

T.S.

public school. (1) In the U.S.A., any primary school or secondary school supported by public funds. (2) In Britain, a term paradoxically applied to certain private or independent schools for pupils of, mostly, 13 to 18, the most famous of which, founded in the Middle Ages (e.g. Eton, Winchester), have long been the nurseries of the British governing CLASS. Variously defined, public schools show, typically, these features: (*a*) foundation or considerable enlargement during the 19th century, in the heyday of British imperial expansion (see IMPERIALISM); (*b*) an inherited ethos which stems from Thomas Arnold's declared aim (1828) of turning out 'Christian men' and emphasizes such virtues as 'gentlemanly conduct' (Arnold's phrase), discipline, self-discipline, public service, and the 'team spirit'; (*c*) a wide range of extra-curricular activities; (*d*) above-average academic standards and results, helped by (*e*) an above-average staffing ratio; (*f*) pupils who are predominantly or exclusively boarders, and (*g*) of one sex only (though coeducation is increasing); (*h*) very high fees. Their supporters stress (*b*), (*c*), and (*d*); opponents emphasize the unfairness of (*e*) and (*h*), the psychological effects of (*f*) ('an undeveloped heart', according to E.M. Forster), the sexual dangers inherent in (*g*) and the ÉLITISM and social divisiveness of the whole system.

In America the nearest equivalents to the British public schools, found mainly on the east coast, and today mainly coeducational, are known as *college preparatory schools*; in Britain a *preparatory school* is one that prepares pupils (from, in general, the age of about 9) for the entrance examination of the public schools, many of whose features it shares.

O.S.

public sector. That part of economic activity that is owned and controlled by the government, central or local. It includes nationalized industries, public corporations, those firms that are owned by the government but are not directly controlled by them, and those bodies providing services and goods such as education, health, etc. Until recently, the relative size of the public sector has been increasing in most CAPITALIST economies (see AFFLUENT SOCIETY). It has been suggested that such an increase is undesirable (see PRIVATIZATION and NATIONALIZATION). In SOCIALIST countries most of the economic activity takes place in the public sector.

J.P.

pulmonary disease, see under RESPIRATORY DISEASE.

pulsar. A very regularly pulsating astronomical source of RADIATION. Such sources were observed in 1967 by A. Hewish and J. Bell-Burnell and were for a time suspected of being signals from intelligent extraterrestrials (see SEARCH FOR EXTRATERRESTRIAL INTELLIGENCE). Subsequently they were explained as very rapidly rotating *neutron stars*. They have a mass roughly equal to that of the sun but a diameter similar to that of a planet like the Earth. As a result their density is 10^{14} times greater than that of water and roughly equal to that inside the atomic NUCLEUS. Radiation is beamed away from a region on the surface of the rotating neutron star which we see every time the neutron star rotates to point the beam in our direction. The effect is similar to that seen when a lighthouse beam rotates. Almost every known pulsar is an isolated star but there exists a *binary pulsar* which is a very important site for examining the predictions of the general theory of RELATIVITY. In this system the pulsing of the pulsar is regular to a higher precision than can be measured by any terrestrial clock. The binary pulsar has been observed to be losing energy very slowly, revealed by a tiny change in the pulsing frequency. This change is equal to that predicted to occur due to loss of energy by GRAVITATIONAL radiation, according to Einstein's theory of general relativity. The most famous pulsar is that residing at the centre of the Crab nebula, an expanding remnant of an exploding star (SUPERNOVA) first observed in the 11th century. A very large number of pulsars are known with a wide range of pulse periods. They possess large (typically 100 million tesla) magnetic fields and are surrounded by a complex magnetosphere of electrically charged PARTICLES. A detailed theoretical explanation of the source of the pulses has not yet been found and is an active area of study.   J.D.B.

Bibl: I. Shkovskii, *Stars* (San Francisco, 1981).

pulsating universe. A hypothetical system in COSMOLOGY. The EXPANSION OF THE UNIVERSE resulting from the explosion postulated in the BIG-BANG HYPOTHESIS is supposed to slow down and eventually become a contraction under the mutual GRAVITATION of the GALAXIES. When all the matter is compressed into a small region of space, nuclear forces (e.g. STRONG INTERACTIONS) would result in another explosion, and the cycle would repeat itself indefinitely, with a period of about 100,000 million years. Whether the universe is in fact pulsating, or whether it will expand indefinitely, depends on the total amount of matter in it; at present the

experimental evidence suggests contained expansion rather than recontraction.
                                                                    M.V.B.

punctuated equilibrium. The theory that EVOLUTION proceeds mainly in fits and starts, rather than at a constant rate (GRADUALISM). Evolutionary changes, as seen in the fossil record, often appear to take place in sudden jumps. This had generally been attributed to the gaps in the record, but in 1972 two American palaeontologists, Niles Eldredge and Stephen Gould, argued that the jumps reflect the way evolution normally proceeds. The 'jumps' in the fossil record are on the human time scale rather slow; in one well documented case among the snails of Lake Turkana, the sudden evolutionary event took 5,000-50,000 years. How generally evolution proceeds in the punctuated or the gradual mode is a matter of factual controversy. Punctuated equilibrium has sometimes been suggested by publicity-hungry biologists and gullible journalists to be anti-Darwinian; however, it is not.
                                                                    M.R.

punk. A British youth SUB-CULTURAL movement that rose to prominence in 1976, in many ways created and effectively destroyed by MEDIA exposure. (It impinged upon public consciousness by way of the Sex Pistols' — a renowned early punk band — use of bad language on a popular TV programme.) Punk started life as both a style — anti-fashion — and a musical form — fast, aggressive, raw and deliberately unprofessional. Like most youth sub-cultures, it refers simultaneously to a COLLECTIVE CONSCIOUSNESS, an aesthetic, musical innovations and unmistakable stylistic signals, and the punk movement — later transformed into '*new wave*' — stressed cultural rebelliousness, self-parody, NIHILISM, surrealism and iconoclasm. In many respects, punk was a reaction to the classless liberal PERMISSIVENESS of the 1960s. Sixties YOUTH CULTURE reached further up the age and CLASS scale than any previous manifestations, and punk started off by reclaiming lost territory for the young — increasingly workless — WORKING CLASS. Punk music was intended to be open access — anyone can play; no heroes, no leaders — and was a response to the expense and absurdity of megastar and supergroup idolatry that had beset 'progressive' ROCK; it was also a reaction to the campness of glitter rock. Punk was symbolically rather than actually violent; despite fears that swastikas and NAZI regalia would be taken at face value, punk veered slightly LEFT in terms of political orientation, and the musical commentary on RACISM, UNEMPLOYMENT and urban disorder ranged from radical to anarchic.

The strain of simultaneously carrying cultural criticism, political consciousness, stylistic élan, and musical innovation soon began to dilute punk which, as a distinctive mass-based phenomenon, died in the transition from youth sub-culture to diffuse cultural and intellectual movements. Overexposure began to destroy the authenticity of punk to the point where it became an all-encompassing description for a whole range of eclectic youth styles, from the infamous spiky hair, bondage trousers and ripped clothing, through the purple streak and studded belt of the suburbanite to the studied coolness of the new wave. Though commentators were quick to label it 'dole queue rock', the phenomenon was as Bohemian as it was PROLETARIAN and, save for a few latter-day adherents, most young people have reverted to more predictable consumer habits beloved of the commercial interests that dominate the youth market. Art theory and sub-culture had, however, intersected, and POST-MODERN theory was given a tremendous boost.   P.S.L.

purchasing power parity theory, see under PARITY.

pure line. A pure line of organisms is a lineage which has become virtually homozygous (see GENE), so that genetic VARIATION has been extinguished. Pure lines can be achieved in self-pollinating plants and in laboratory animals such as guinea-pigs and mice which have been bred together, parent to offspring or brother to sister, for upwards of 50 successive generations. Sex differences apart, the members of such pure lines resemble each other as closely as if they were identical twins.   P.M.

pure theory of law, see LAW, PURE THEORY OF.

purism. An aesthetic movement proposed in 1918 by Amédée Ozenfant and the architect Le Corbusier (Charles-Édouard Jeanneret) in their book *Après le Cubisme* which advocated the restructuring of CUBISM. Reacting to the prettification of Cubism after 1916 by painters such as Braque, and to the NEO-CLASSICISM of Picasso, purism sought to maintain the representation of clearly identifiable objects and forms and a logical composition. No significant school developed, despite the interest of other artists such as Fernand Léger, and some analogies in the work of Giorgio Morandi and certain NEUE SACHLICHKEIT artists.   A.K.W.

Bibl: A. Ozenfant, tr. E.E. Asburn, *Foundations of Modern Art* (London, 1931; New York, 1952); Tate Gallery Catalogue, *Léger and Purist Paris* (London, 1970); R.E. Krauss, 'Léger, Le Corbusier, and Purism' (*Artforum*, April 1972).

purity, see under POLLUTION (2).

purposive explanation, see under EXPLANATION.

purposivism. A label for any approach to PSYCHOLOGY which asserts that man is a purposeful, striving creature who is, in large part, responsible for his own conduct and destiny, e.g. McDougall's HORMIC PSYCHOLOGY, COGNITIVE PSYCHOLOGY, EXISTENTIAL PSYCHOLOGY, HUMANISTIC PSYCHOLOGY. The opposite assertion is that man's conduct is nothing but the fully determined outcome of his heredity (see GENETICS), his past experience, and his present ENVIRONMENT.   I.M.L.H.

Bibl: M. Wertheimer, *Fundamental Issues in Psychology* (London and New York, 1972).

PWR, see under PRESSURIZED-WATER REACTOR.

Q

QCD, see under QUANTUM CHROMODY-NAMICS.

QED (quantum electrodynamics), see under FIELD THEORY.

QSO, see under QUASAR.

Quadragesimo Anno. An ENCYCLICAL issued by Pope Pius XI in 1931, 40 years after RERUM NOVARUM, restating Roman CATHOLIC teaching on social problems. Both COMMUNISM and LAISSEZ FAIRE were condemned, and a preference for GUILD SOCIALISM was implied.   D.L.E.

Quakers. Members of a religious body, so nicknamed soon after its foundation by George Fox (1924-91); its official title is the Society of Friends. Dispensing with many of the outward forms of religion such as creeds, professional clergy, and traditional words in worship, the Quakers have commended themselves by their philanthropy, their PACIFISM, and their basis in Christian (see CHRISTIANITY) MYSTICISM. Their nickname was suggested by their trembling or excitement when gripped by religious ecstasy (see PENTECOSTALISM), but nowadays in their worship calm, although spontaneous, words arise from a corporate silence.   D.L.E.

Bibl: H. Loukes, *The Quaker Contribution* (London and New York, 1965).

quality circle. A MANAGEMENT process in which a small group of employees involved in a particular area of an organization are formed into a team with the purpose of finding ways of improving the efficiency of the organization (e.g. the RECYCLING of waste materials from the production process). Quality circles originated in the field of quality control and they have been applied to many other areas of organizations. They are widely used in Japan.   R.I.T.; J.P.

Bibl: G.A. Cole, *Management: Theory and Practice* (Eastleigh, 1982).

quantification.
(1) In general, the expression of a property or quality in numerical terms. Proper-ties that can usefully be expressed in these terms are said to be *quantifiable*; descriptions, theories, and techniques couched in such terms are said to be *quantitative.* Despite the widespread myth that only quantitative measurements and descriptions are of use to science, many *non-quantifiable* things, i.e. things that cannot be usefully measured on numerical SCALES, can be given precise objective descriptions that can play a valid role in scientific theories and EXPLANATIONS. Thus LINGUISTS describe the structures of sentences, CHEMISTS describe the structures of chemical MOLECULES, COMPUTER scientists describe computational processes, and PSYCHOLOGISTS may one day be able to describe the structure of mental processes, using precise mathematical language including *non-numerical* symbols. MENTALIST psychology and ARTIFICIAL INTELLIGENCE have taken the first steps in this direction. It is arguable that much research effort has been wasted — particularly in the SOCIAL SCIENCES, but perhaps also in the NATURAL SCIENCES, e.g. BIOLOGY — in attempting to force non-quantifiable processes into quantitative moulds, instead of searching for more relevant kinds of mathematical representation.   A.S.
(2) In LOGIC, the referring aspect of PROPOSITIONS which do not refer to a particular, designated individual but to all members or some members of a class (universally and existentially quantified propositions, respectively). In the PREDICATE CALCULUS, or logic of quantified statements, the basic, universally quantified formula 'For all x, if x is A then x is B' is not quite equivalent in meaning to its counterpart in ordinary language, 'All A are B'. It is entailed by it (see ENTAILMENT), but does not entail it, since the latter is not true unless there are some A things (i.e. unless it has 'existential import') whereas the former is, vacuously, true if there are none. The quantificational interpretation of universally and existentially general statements justifies its deviation from ordinary language by its systematic formal manipulability and by its perspicuousness. On the second part, it

709

makes explicit the ambiguity of 'Everybody loves somebody' which it represents either as 'For any x there is some y that x loves' or as 'There is a y that every x loves'. Besides 'all' and 'some' and their synonyms, language contains other quantificational expressions: 'most', 'many', 'several', 'a few'. A.Q.

quantitative history. Any serious attempt to present statistical evidence in a work of historical research. Economic historians took the lead in the 1920s with studies of price history. Political historians followed, using the methods of PROSOPOGRAPHY. More recently, quantitative methods have transformed SOCIAL HISTORY and have even made some impact on the HISTORY OF IDEAS, e.g. in the studies of *lexicometry* (the study of the frequency of theme words in a corpus of texts) carried out for 18th-century France. Quantitative historical studies received a great boost in the 1960s, when academics began to get access to COMPUTERS for their research projects. The profession is still divided about the reliability and the significance of the results. See also ECONOMIC HISTORY; SERIAL HISTORY. P.B.
Bibl: R. Floud, *An Introduction to Quantitative Methods for Historians* (London, 1973).

quantitative linguistics. A branch of LINGUISTICS which studies the frequency and distribution of linguistic units, using statistical techniques. The subject has both a pure and an applied side: the former aims to establish general principles concerning the statistical regularities governing the way words, sounds, etc. are used in the world's languages; the latter investigates the way statistical techniques can be used to elucidate linguistic problems, such as authorship identity. D.C.
Bibl: J. Lyons, *Introduction to Theoretical Linguistics* (Cambridge, 1968).

quantity theory of money. A theory relating the price level in an economy to the MONEY SUPPLY and the volume of goods produced. Its simplest form is $MV = PT$, where M is the supply of money, V the velocity of circulation (i.e. the average number of times a unit of money changes hands within the given period), P the price level, and T the quantity of goods produced. This relationship is true by definition, i.e. it is an identity (see IDENTIFICATION, sense 1). Only if the velocity of circulation is assumed to be constant does the theory became of causal importance. Thus, writing the theory in the form $P = (MV)/T$. with V constant and a fixed level of output the formula shows that the price level is proportional to the money supply. This theory is one of the basic tenets of MONETARISM. D.E.; J. P.
Bibl: J. Craven, *Introduction to Economics* (Oxford, 1984).

quantum chemistry, see under THEORETICAL CHEMISTRY.

quantum chromodynamics. Quantum FIELD THEORY of QUARKS and GLUONS, so called because these particles possess an attribute called 'colour' which is an analogue of electric charge. QCD describes how quarks and gluons interact together. It possesses the property, called ASYMPTOTIC freedom, that interactions between quarks and gluons become weaker at high energies and these PARTICLES behave as though they were free of any forces at very high energies. The intuitively reasonable converse of this property, called confinement, would result in all coloured particles being confined to exist in combinations of zero total colour charge at low energies. This remains unproven but is supported by all the unsuccessful experimental attempts to observe free quarks. PROTONS and NEUTRONS are combinations of three quarks with zero net colour. MESONS are combinations of a quark and an anti-quark with zero net colour. J.D.B.
Bibl: F. Close, *The Cosmic Onion* (London, 1984); H. Fritzsch, *Quarks* (New York, 1983).

quantum electrodynamics, see under FIELD THEORY.

quantum electronics. A branch of engineering devoted to the design and construction of MICROWAVE power generators (e.g. the MASER) whose operation is based on QUANTUM MECHANICS. M.V.B.

quantum fluid. In PHYSICS the behaviour of individual ATOMS is dictated by QUANTUM MECHANICS, but quantum effects are usually so small that they are not easily detected. As the temperature is reduced, however, the atoms move more slowly and in two liquids, helium 4 and helium 3, their motions, instead of being quite random, appear to become correlated with one another. The complete assembly of atoms then appears to act as a single unit whose behaviour as a single entity is determined by quantum mechanics. This transition to what is called a quantum fluid occurs at very low temperatures (2.17 K for helium 4 and 0.002 K for helium 3) and is accompanied by a range of properties which are not observed in any other liquid. The most outstanding of these is the phenomenon of *superfluidity* — these liquids appear to have no viscosity and so they are able to flow through extremely fine channels or tubes without any apparent resistance. The term quantum fluid is also applied to the assembly of ELECTRONS in certain materials when they become SUPERCONDUCTING. In this case it is the electrons which, instead of moving independently as they do at high temperature, interact and behave as a single system. This manifests itself in the complete disappearance of the electrical resistance of the material.   H.M.R.

quantum Hall effect. Discovered by Klaus von Klitzing (Nobel Prize for physics, 1985). It is an extension of the HALL EFFECT technique when applied to a very thin layer of SEMICONDUCTOR (the active region of a special type of TRANSISTOR, the mosfet, was actually used). In a very high magnetic field at low temperatures the Hall voltage across the sample does not change gradually as the current through the material is increased. Instead it exhibits a series of regularly spaced quantum jumps or steps whose height is accurately related to the quantity h/e^2, which involves the FUNDAMENTAL CONSTANTS h (PLANCK'S CONSTANT) and e (the charge on the ELECTRON). These steps can be measured with high precision and so the effect can be used to check the value of h/e^2 and it can also be used to establish a standard of electrical resistance.   H.M.R.

quantum mechanics (or *wave mechanics*; developed in the 1920s by Born, Dirac, Heisenberg, Jordan, and Schrödinger). The system of MECHANICS, based on the WAVE-PARTICLE DUALITY of matter and RADIATION, which must be used to describe systems so small that NEWTONIAN MECHANICS breaks down.

Whereas in CLASSICAL PHYSICS the state of a system is specified by a precise simultaneous determination of all relevant 'dynamical variables' (position, MOMENTUM, ENERGY, etc.), the UNCERTAINTY PRINCIPLE asserts that this specification cannot be made for small-scale systems. Thus complete DETERMINISM is lost, and in quantum mechanics systems are specified by stating the *probability* of given values for position, momentum, etc. This indeterminacy can be seen very clearly whenever a single atomic event can be observed (e.g. in RADIOACTIVITY); usually, however, experiments measure an average value resulting from the cumulative effect of many atomic events (e.g. a 'line' in SPECTROSCOPY comes from the radiation of many ATOMS).

Probability enters the framework of quantum theory as the intensity of a *wave* whose frequency and wavelength are related to its energy and momentum by PLANCK'S CONSTANT; from a knowledge of the WAVE FUNCTION, all observable properties of the system may be calculated. ENERGY LEVELS, which appear *ad hoc* in BOHR THEORY, arise naturally in quantum mechanics from the interference of waves travelling round ORBITS. For example, waves describing ELECTRONS in an atom will only be in PHASE after successive circuits if a whole number of DE BROGLIE WAVELENGTHS fits into an orbit, and this only occurs at certain discrete energies; between these energies, the waves making successive circuits interfere destructively and the wave function is zero. For large systems or large QUANTUM NUMBERS, the energy levels lie too close together to be differentiated, and Newtonian mechanics affords a very accurate approximate description; this is the 'correspondence principle' between the two theories.

The INDETERMINISM in quantum mechanics (which is embodied in the COMPLEMENTARITY PRINCIPLE) has caused much controversy: Einstein wrote 'God does not play dice', while others have tried to construct theories in which 'hidden variables' operate on a very fine scale to determine, for example, the precise moment when a given atom will radiate, or a NUCLEUS decay. Despite these doubts about its conceptual foundations, quantum mechanics is supported by a great mass of experimental evidence (e.g. in ATOMIC PHYSICS and SOLID-STATE PHYSICS), and must be regarded as one of the greatest intellectual triumphs in all PHYSICS.   M.V.B.

Bibl: B. Hoffmann, *The Strange Story of the Quantum* (Harmondsworth and Gloucester, Mass., 2nd ed., 1963); J. Andrade e Silva and G. Lochak, tr. P. Moore, *Quanta* (London, 1969); G. Gamow, *Thirty Years that Shook Physics* (New York, 1966; London, 1972).

quantum number. A number used to label the state of a system in QUANTUM MECHANICS. For example, the ENERGY LEVELS of an ELECTRON in an ATOM have the quantum numbers 1, 2, 3, etc. (starting from the *ground state* — see ENERGY LEVEL), two further numbers label the rotational state, and a fourth (half-integral) quantum number describes the SPIN. Whenever the quantum number is an integer, it is equal to the number of oscillations of the WAVE FUNCTION.   M.V.B.

quantum statistics. The QUANTUM MECHANICS of systems of identical PARTICLES (e.g. ELEMENTARY PARTICLES). The STATISTICAL MECHANICS of such systems depends on whether or not the particles are *fermions* (e.g. ELECTRONS and NUCLEONS), which obey the EXCLUSION PRINCIPLE, or *bosons* (e.g. MESONS and PHOTONS), which do not. See also BOSE-EINSTEIN STATISTICS; FERMI-DIRAC STATISTICS; SPIN.   M.V.B.

quantum theory. A major branch of modern physical theory, developed above all by Max Planck from 1900 onwards, arguing for the emission of light or radiant energy from light-sources in discrete amounts, or 'quanta'. In 1905, Einstein lent his support to the theory by using it to explain photoelectricity (i.e. the ejection of ELECTRONS from metal surfaces). Following on from Planck and Einstein's work, it became necessary to view light as possessing both the qualities of waves and those of PARTICLES. Niels Bohr then extended quantum theory to the field of SUB-ATOMIC PARTICLES, arguing that electrons could 'jump' from one ORBIT of ENERGY to another, thereby causing the radiation PHOTONS (or light quanta).

This new perception that light sometimes acts like waves and sometimes like particles was subsequently extended to other fields of physics by Schrödinger, Heisenberg and De Broglie, in particular in the development of WAVE MECHANICS. Though challenging traditional NEWTONIAN MECHANICS, quantum theory is now established as a corner-stone of modern PHYSICS, even though its philosophical problems (concerning reality and causality) remain contentious.   R.P.

Bibl: L.I. Schiff, *Quantum Mechanics* (London, 1968).

quantum wave function, see WAVE FUNCTION.

quark. In PHYSICS, one of three different hypothetical PARTICLES which might be the structural units from which many of the ELEMENTARY PARTICLES are constructed. Quarks have the unusual property that their electric charges are multiples of *one-third* of the charge on the ELECTRON. Despite extensive searches, no quarks have yet been observed.   M.V.B.

quarter-tone, see under MICROTONE.

quartile, see under PERCENTILE.

quasar. Astronomical object which appears to be the most distant yet found in the universe. They emit enormous quantities of ENERGY, equal to the output of hundreds of GALAXIES, despite being compact and starlike in appearance. Their name arose as a contraction of Quasi-stellar object (or Quasi-stellar radio source) and is abbreviated as QSO. They were discovered in 1963 by J. Bolton and C. Hazard but many hundreds have since been discovered. They possess very high RED SHIFTS of their emitted light and this is now unanimously interpreted as being indicative of their high recession speeds and hence great distance from us. The greatest measured red shift is currently

4.1. The fact that their unusual observed light spectra could be simply explained as the red shifted spectra was first pointed out by M. Schmidt in 1964. The large amounts of energy emanating from very small regions in the quasar have led to a theoretical picture of the quasar phenomenon in which a central BLACK HOLE accretes material which radiates large quantities of RADIATION en route to being captured by the black hole (see ACCRETION). The light emission from quasars resembles that from other unusual types of galaxy (Seyfert galaxies, BL Lacertae objects and radio galaxies — these are known collectively as *active galaxies*) which emit large quantities of radiation. Some quasars are surrounded by faint material which suggests that quasars might be the bright central regions of very distant active galaxies whose outer regions are too faint to be generally visible. It is believed that quasars are associated with the formation of the very first galaxies in the universe. A number of quasars have been found to possess identical companions nearby on photographic images. This is believed to be the result of a very massive intervening object acting as a GRAVITATIONAL LENS and producing two images of a single object. Some unconventional explanations have been offered for the high red shifts of quasars which do not associate them with high recession velocities and hence argue that quasars are not at very great astronomical distances from us. These explanations do not seem to be consistent with all known facts about quasars. J.D.B.

Bibl: J. Silk, *The Big Bang* (San Francisco, 1980); N. Henbest and M. Martin, *The New Astronomy* (Cambridge, 1983).

quasicrystal. Material in which the ATOMS seem to be arranged on a regular pattern but nevertheless do not lie on one of the LATTICES or have one of the SYMMETRIES which are absolutely necessary if they are to fill all the space available without leaving any awkward gaps. There are only 14

of these space-filling lattices. The most obvious is a set of cubes packed tightly together. Similarly in two dimensions we are familiar with the problem of completely covering a floor with regularly-shaped tiles. We could use squares or hexagons but we could not use pentagons without leaving some areas uncovered. It therefore came as a complete surprise when DIFFRACTION studies on certain evaporated metal films (e.g. an aluminium-manganese alloy) indicated that they apparently had a five-fold symmetry. These were called quasicrystals. TOPOLOGICAL studies have now shown that it is possible to have local regions of five-fold symmetry provided that at larger distances the five-fold patterns are rotated with respect to one another. The search for new *pseudo-symmetries* and the implications they have for the theory of solids is continuing. H.M.R.

quaternion. A generalization of the notion of COMPLEX NUMBER discovered by Sir W.R. Hamilton in 1843; the first example of objects whose multiplication is not COMMUTATIVE. For many purposes they have been superseded by VECTORS. R.G.

queuing theory. Methods for determining the best ways of serving queues. For example, if a business firm's vehicles are repaired when they break down, the number arriving for repair on any day is uncertain, and it is not immediately obvious how large a repair shop the firm should run. It is not usually possible to describe the behaviour of the queue by explicit mathematical expressions, and indirect methods of computation have to be used. As a group of problems in applied PROBABILITY THEORY, the field hardly deserves the title of a 'theory'. J.A.M.

Bibl: D.R. Cox and W.L. Smith, *Queues* (London and New York, 1961).

Qumran, see under DEAD SEA SCROLLS.

R

race/racism. A classificatory term, broadly equivalent to subspecies. Applied most frequently to human beings, it indicates a group characterized by closeness of common descent and usually also by some shared physical distinctiveness such as colour of skin.

Biologically, the CONCEPT has only limited value. Most scientists today recognize that all humans derive from a common stock and that groups within the SPECIES have migrated and intermarried constantly. Human populations therefore constitute a GENETIC continuum where racial distinctions are relative, not absolute. Any remaining categorization of races then relates only to gradients of frequency delineating the varying geographical incidence of particular genetical elements common to the whole species. It is also acknowledged that visible characteristics, popularly regarded as major racial pointers, are not inherited in any simple package and that they reflect only a small proportion of an individual's genetical make-up.

The educationally delicate question of correlation between race and INTELLIGENCE has remained more disputable. Since the later 1960s controversy has surrounded attempts by Arthur Jensen and others to demonstrate here a dominance of nature over nurture, but no adequate evidence has emerged to prove that some races are, for distinctively biological reasons, superior to others in intelligence or cultural potential.

Socially, race has a significance dependent not upon science but upon belief. Men depict themselves and see one another in terms of groups which, however frail their objective basis, thereby assume social importance. *Race relations* arise between groups whose interaction is conditioned by belief in the fact and relevance of their racial difference. The resulting behaviour is best studied within the wider sociological context of inter-group relations generally. South Africa is the outstanding contemporary example of a state where domestic social and political relations are structured principally around racial criteria (see APARTHEID). *Racial prejudice*, in its usual hostile connotation, covers attitudes hastily or unreasonably formed to the detriment of those deemed racially alien. *Racialism* is preferably reserved to describe actions that discriminate, in most instances adversely, in regard to other races. But the term is now less commonly used than either racial prejudice or racism.

Hitherto, however, this last label has maintained a valuably distinctive application to IDEOLOGY. There it covers particularly those systematic doctrines about the central significance of racial inequality that constituted a major, though still underestimated, theme in Western thought from at least 1850 until 1945. At first widely supported by scientists, these ideas were soon linked with SOCIAL DARWINISM. They contributed to the ethos of IMPERIALISM, and in Europe to ANTISEMITISM. Landmarks in this literature of racist DETERMINISM are A. de Gobineau's *Essay on the Inequality of the Human Races* (1853-5) and H.S. Chamberlain's *Foundations of the Nineteenth Century* (1899). The theory and practice of NAZISM marked a culmination. But even now the tradition's basic idiom of virtuous purity and vicious blending, though biologically discredited, remains embedded in much popular thinking about race. See also ETHNICITY.   M.D.B.

Bibl: M. Banton, *The Idea of Race* (London, 1977); J. Barzun, *Race: a Study in Superstition* (London and New York, rev. ed., 1965); E. Cashmore and B. Troyna, *Introduction to Race Relations* (London, 1983); N. Stephan, *The Idea of Race and Science in Great Britain 1800-1968* (London, 1982).

radar (RAdio Detection And Ranging). A system whereby short pulses of MICROWAVES are sent out from an aerial, which may be on land, or on a ship or aircraft. Any objects in the path of the beam cause echoes which are received back at the source. The time delay and nature of these echoes (viewed as a display on a CATHODE RAY TUBE) give information about the distance and nature of the reflecting object. See also SONAR.   M.V.B.

Radburn layout. A form of layout separating pedestrians and traffic, developed by Clarence Stein and first applied by him at Radburn, New Jersey, in 1928. It consists of one or more *superblocks*, a superblock being an area containing a complex of houses (and/or shops, schools, offices, etc.) built around a central green or pedestrian space. Each superblock is ringed by a peripheral road off which short cul-de-sacs provide access for vehicles. For pedestrians, access is via the green areas which are linked to each other by underpasses or overpasses. The basic principle was first seen in Jefferson's plan for the University of Virginia; later examples include housing estates, Lancaster University, and NEW TOWN shopping centres.

M.BR.

Bibl: C.S. Stein, *Toward New Towns for America* (Cambridge, Mass., 1957; Liverpool, 2nd ed., 1959).

radiation. Waves or PARTICLES travelling outwards from a source; also the emission of such waves or particles. The term usually refers to electromagnetic waves (see ELECTROMAGNETIC FIELD). These cover an enormous frequency range (the 'electromagnetic spectrum') of which visible light (see OPTICS) constitutes only a very small part.

The principal kinds of electromagnetic waves, in order of increasing wavelength, are: GAMMA RAYS, X-RAYS, ULTRA-VIOLET radiation, visible light, INFRA-RED radiation, MICROWAVES, and RADIO FREQUENCY waves. Frequency and wavelength are related by the EQUATION *wavelength × frequency = speed of light in empty space*, and the speed of light is 300 million kilometres per second. See also BLACK-BODY RADIATION; QUANTUM MECHANICS; SPECTROSCOPY.

M.V.B.

radiation biology (or *radiobiology*). The branch of BIOLOGY that deals with the immediate and long-term effects of RADIATIONS, particularly ionizing radiations (see IONIZATION) and the useful purposes which such radiations may be made to serve. Penetrating ionizing radiations such as X-RAYS and GAMMA RAYS have a disruptive effect on DNA (see NUCLEIC ACID) and can therefore lead to MUTATION (see RADIATION GENETICS). They also suppress CELL division — a property that is put to good use in the RADIOTHERAPY of tumours, for it is characteristic of radiation and of radiomimetic drugs (i.e. drugs whose pharmacological actions mimic those of irradiation) that they both cause CANCERS and also, under different conditions of administration, discourage their growth. A characteristic biological effect of radiation and radiomimetic drugs on warm-blooded animals is that of interfering with the manufacture of red blood corpuscles because of the destruction of stem cells. For a cognate reason, such radiations also diminish IMMUNITY (sense 2). In experimental animals the transplantation of bone marrow is a feasible method of repairing radiation injury in so far as it affects the manufacture of red blood corpuscles, but the GENETIC effects of radiation are cumulative, irreversible and, in general, harmful.

Radiobiology also includes the preparation and use of radioactively labelled ELEMENTS and compounds to serve as TRACERS in studies of METABOLISM. The use of radioactive substances (see RADIOACTIVITY) for this purpose needs to be controlled by strict regulations, and the same applies to the use of radioactive substances in painting watch dials etc. In all civilized countries legislation has been introduced to reduce to a minimum the population's exposure to radioactive substances whether produced by atomic or NUCLEAR WEAPONS or by atomic power plants (see ATOMIC ENERGY; NUCLEAR REACTOR).

P.M.

radiation genetics. A branch both of GENETICS and of RADIATION BIOLOGY that grew up under (1) the influence of H.J. Muller's discovery that ionizing (see IONIZATION) RADIATIONS can induce MUTATION, and (2) the realization that certain industrial processes and offensive weapons may increase the dosages of radiation to which human beings are exposed. P.M.

Bibl: P.C. Koller, *Chromosomes and Genes* (Edinburgh, 1968; New York, 1971).

radical. In CHEMISTRY, a term used since the time of Lavoisier — though now rarely — to denote a building block in the construction of a chemical compound. A radical is often merely one ATOM, but is frequently a group of atoms which behaves as a single atom or ION. Thus ethane (C_2H_6) can be considered as the combination of two methyl (CH_3) radicals, while the ammonium ion and the sulphate ion are examples of inorganic radicals.　　B.F.

radical chic. A phrase coined in 1970 by Tom Wolfe, American journalist, to describe specifically a benefit concert given by Leonard Bernstein for the Black Panthers (see BLACK POWER) and, more generally, the current fashion of adopting radical political causes (see RADICALISM) in New York society. He likened this trendy romanticizing of primitive souls, e.g. American Indians and Chicano grapeworkers, to the French 19th-century phenomenon denoted by the phrase *nostalgie de la boue* (literally, 'hankering after mud').　　A.K.W.

radical geography. A perspective which insists that the world's human GEOGRAPHY can only be properly understood by considering the way in which geographical distributions of all sorts are shaped by the inequitable and socially divisive workings of economy and society. Proponents of this perspective are extremely critical of geography as SPATIAL SCIENCE, which isolates geographical distributions from their socio-economic context when seeking to 'explain' them by reference to the known laws of GEOMETRY and the hypothesized laws of spatial organization. In reaction to this type of geographical inquiry a number of more recent studies have adopted either a WELFARE stance, and have thereby endeavoured to relate spatial disparities in wealth, welfare and resource-ownership to inequalities inherent in regional, national and even international SOCIAL STRUCTURES, or a MARXIST stance, which aims to sharpen these welfare accounts by tracing the links between spatial disparities, social inequalities and the economic logic of an underlying MODE OF PRODUCTION (which in most cases is found to be CAPITALISM). There are many difficulties with these radical geographies, particularly given the danger of slipping into a DETERMINISM — and notably an economic determinism — insensitive to the often ambiguous contribution of human thought and action (see

HUMANISTIC GEOGRAPHY), but there can be little doubt that they comprise a significant and provocative break from previous traditions of geographical inquiry.　　C.P.

Bibl: D. Harvey, *Social Justice and the City* (London, 1973); D.M. Smith, *Where the Grass is Greener: Living in an Unequal World* (Harmondsworth, 1979).

radicalesbianism, see under FEMINISM.

radicalism. A tendency to press political views and actions towards an extreme. Historically, radicalism has always been associated with dissatisfaction with the status quo and an appeal for basic political and social changes. But the meaning of the word has varied in different periods and countries, ranging from the moderate CENTRE, like the *Parti Républicain Radical et Radical Socialiste* which was influential in France before 1939, but was neither radical nor SOCIALIST, to the extreme ultra-REVOLUTIONARY radicals of the post-war NEW LEFT. Although in some countries, e.g. the U.S.A., 'radicalism' is mostly used with reference to the LEFT (where radicals are clearly distinguished from LIBERALS), it can also be characteristic of the RIGHT; notable examples are FASCISM and NAZISM. The term is also used in the wider sense of a disposition to challenge established views in any field of human endeavour, e.g. in the arts or scholarship.　　L.L.

Bibl: Melvin J. Lasky, *Utopia and Revolution* (Chicago and London, 1976).

radioactivity. The spontaneous decay of certain types of atomic NUCLEUS. Decay usually takes place by emission of an ALPHA PARTICLE or by the decay of one of the nuclear NEUTRONS and emission of the resulting BETA PARTICLE; thus radioactivity generally results in a change in ATOMIC NUMBER. It is not possible to predict the precise moment at which a given unstable nucleus will decay. However, the HALF-LIFE can be calculated by means of QUANTUM MECHANICS.

Most naturally-occurring ISOTOPES are stable; the exceptions either have long half-lives (e.g. several thousand million years for uranium) or else are produced continuously by various processes (e.g. radium is a decay product of uranium, and radiocarbon is produced in a NUCLEAR REACTION by COSMIC RAYS — see RADIOCARBON DATING). A great number of short-lived radioisotopes can be produced artifically in NUCLEAR REACTORS (see also TRACE ELEMENT). The health hazards of radioactivity arise from the ENERGY liberated when PARTICLES collide with atomic nuclei in living matter. This causes mechanical damage to TISSUES, and affects the GENETIC structure of CELLS, often resulting in MUTATION.   M.V.B.

radio astronomy. A branch of ASTRONOMY, in which RADIO TELESCOPES are used to study electromagnetic RADIATION at RADIO FREQUENCIES emitted by sources outside the earth. Most of the radio sources are GALAXIES, but the sun and the planet Jupiter, as well as PULSARS, QUASARS, and SUPERNOVAE, all emit radio waves. Apart from visible light, radio waves (in the 1 cm to 10 metre wavelength band) constitute the only ELECTROMAGNETIC radiation capable of reaching the ground without being absorbed in the atmosphere or reflected by the IONOSPHERE. The revolution in COSMOLOGY in the last two decades has been stimulated largely by the discoveries of radio astronomy, especially the COSMIC BACKGROUND RADIATION.   M.V.B.
Bibl: J.S. Hey, *The Radio Universe* (Oxford and New York, 1971).

radiobiology, see RADIATION BIOLOGY.

radiocarbon dating. In ARCHAEOLOGY, a method of DATING pioneered by W.F. Libby, who first proposed it in 1946. It is based on the rate of decay of the radioactive (see RADIOACTIVITY) ISOTOPE C^{14} incorporated in organic matter. C^{14} is produced from nitrogen^{14} by cosmic RADIATION in the upper atmosphere and is absorbed by living matter in the form of carbon di.xide. The proportion of C^{12} to C^{14} remains constant in the atmosphere and in living plants and animals, but as soon as the organism dies, and further absorption of carbon dioxide ceases, the proportion of C^{14} to C^{12} is steadily decreased by the decay of the unstable radioactive isotope. If we know the HALF-LIFE of C^{14} and the ratio of C^{14} to C^{12} in a sample it is, in theory, possible to work out

the absolute age at time of death for a substance which was once alive. The validity of the method as an absolute dating technique rests on two basic assumptions: that the half-life of C^{14} can be accurately determined, and that C^{14} has been produced at a constant rate. Early calculations used a half-life of 5,568 $\pm$ 30 years (the 'old half-life'), but recent recalculation suggests that 5,730 is a better approximation (the 'preferred half-life'). Comparison between radiocarbon dates and historical dates (e.g. obtained from dating Egyptian woodwork) has for some time shown a certain lack of CORRELATION. Recent studies involving the radiocarbon dating of tree rings of known age (see under DENDROCHRONOLOGY) have confirmed the discrepancy. It is now suggested that the production of C^{14} was not constant throughout time and that it is necessary to recalibrate 'radiocarbon years' against tree-ring dates to arrive at 'real years'.

Dates are always quoted $\pm$ x years, representing the standard statistical error, 4300 $\pm$ 50 B.C. means that there is a 2:1 chance of the date lying between 4250 and 4350. Dates are often published B.P. (before the present), the present being 1950. In the wake of the confusion following the apparent need to recalibrate, some writers have adopted the procedure of quoting the date 'b.c.' meaning 'radiocarbon years' and offering a recalibrated date 'B.C.' to represent an approximation to 'real years'. Each data assessment is uniquely numbered according to international agreement. It is accepted that this laboratory number should always be quoted.   B.C.
Bibl: T. Watkins, *Radiocarbon: Calibration and Prehistory* (Edinburgh, 1975).

radio frequency. A vibration frequency in the range 10,000 Hertz to 100,000 million Hertz (1 Hertz = 1 complete vibration cycle per second). Radio frequency electromagnetic RADIATION includes the relatively long waves used for broadcasting, as well as the MICROWAVES used for RADAR.   M.V.B.

radio isotope. Any ISOTOPE of an ELEMENT which is RADIOACTIVE. Some radio-

RADIOLOGY

isotopes occur naturally but others may be produced artificially by NEUTRON irradiation or by bombardment with helium and other light NUCLEI. They are widely used in diverse fields including medicine (e.g. in RADIOTHERAPY), GEOLOGY, and ARCHAEOLOGY (see RADIOCARBON DATING) as well as PHYSICS, CHEMISTRY, BIOLOGY, and ENGINEERING. Radioactive TRACES provide information on the mechanism of CHEMICAL REACTIONS, diffusion processes, chemical analysis, rates of wear, etc. B.F.

radiology. The study of the human body by the utilization of X-RAYS which were discovered by Wilhelm Conrad Röntgen in 1895. As a beam of X-rays passes through the body it is attenuated to different degrees by different TISSUES. The pattern of the X-ray beam emitted from the patient is then recorded on photographic film. *Computed tomography* (CT) uses X-rays to produce an image of a thin slice of a patient in cross-section. The machine is designed so that the X-ray source circles the body through 360° and the information obtained is recorded by special detectors. This information is then analysed in a COMPUTER and the image produced is displayed on a television monitor. The advantage of CT over conventional radiology is that very fine differences in the attenuation of X-rays can be delineated and it is possible to identify tissues and abnormalities not visible on a conventional X-ray film. *Ultrasound* has been widely used in medicine since the early 1970s. An ultrasound pulse is produced by a TRANSDUCER. The pulse penetrates the tissues of the body and produces an echo at tissue interfaces. These echoes are recorded and displayed on a television monitor. Ultrasound is mainly used for examination of abdominal and pelvic organs and is particularly useful for the assessment of pregnancy. Advances in ultrasound have led to the development of transducers which can measure blood flow through major vessels and can record cardiac abnormalities. NUCLEAR MAGNETIC RESONANCE (NMR) is a new development in clinical medicine. The patient is placed in a magnet and hydrogen atoms within the body are excited by a RADIO-FREQUENCY pulse. The hydrogen atoms line up in the direction of the magnetic field. The pulse is then switched off and the hydrogen atoms relax, giving up energy as they do so. Different tissues relax at different rates and this information provides the basis of magnetic resonance imaging. The images produced demonstrate ANATOMY and PATHOLOGY in a similar way to CT but since they are obtained in a different way, different and sometimes more detailed information is obtained. See also PET SCANNING. J.H.

radio stars, see under INVISIBLE ASTRONOMY.

radio telescopes. The 'eyes' of RADIO ASTRONOMY, which receive and locate the direction of RADIO FREQUENCY electromagnetic RADIATION reaching the earth. Because the wavelength is thousands of times greater than that of visible light, radio telescopes are gigantic structures. The steerable parabolic dishes which focus the radio waves (in the same way as the mirrors of ordinary telescopes) may be hundreds of feet across, while *radio interferometers*, which locate direction by measuring the PHASE difference between the waves reaching different aerials in an array, may extend over several miles.

M.V.B.

radiotherapy. The use of ionizing RADIATION in the treatment of CANCER based on the ability of many normal TISSUES to recover from the CELL killing effects of radiation more efficiently than malignant tissues. Radiotherapy has a major curative role in cancers which have not spread far from their sites of origin at the time of diagnosis. Ionizing radiations in the form of X-RAYS or GAMMA RAYS are generated by LINEAR ACCELERATORS or produced as decay products of radioactive ISOTOPES such as cobalt 60 or iridium 192. Linear accelerators enable sharply defined beams of X-rays to be directed accurately at deep seated tumours from different directions, thereby ensuring maximum dose to diseased tissues with minimal exposure of surrounding healthy tissues. Radioactive isotopes in the form of small tubes, needles or wires can be inserted temporarily inside or around diseased organs to treat cancers of the uterine cervix, mouth, tongue and breast, for example, resulting in the cure of selected patients without recourse to radical SURGERY. J.R.Y.

ragtime. An ancestor of JAZZ with a firm identity of its own. It began to emerge in the late 19th century in the southern and southwestern U.S., the hotbed of BLACK musical CULTURE, and came to be particularly associated with the towns of St Louis and Sedalia, in Missouri. It blossomed into maturity in the gay nineties as an ideal accompaniment to the ebullient dance of the era, the cakewalk. Ragtime's chief characteristic is snappily syncopated melodies over a regular march-like, oompah bass. Though performed by instrumental combinations, it was and is primarily a piano genre, and its most famous compositions were written for the instrument, like 'Maple Leaf Rag' and the many other works by Scott Joplin, the medium's greatest composer. Though the syncopation is an obvious link, ragtime is a more limited and more formal genre than jazz, lacking the expressive depth supplied by the BLUES, and demanding strict fidelity to the written score. It could be said to have anticipated SYMPHONIC JAZZ, influencing classical composers like Debussy and Stravinsky. GE.S.

rainbow coalition. The term was first applied to the unsuccessful mayoral campaign of BLACK candidate Mel King in Boston, Massachusetts in 1983, in which King attempted to construct an electoral coalition which united racial and sexual MINORITIES, FEMINISTS, progressive clergy, the PEACE MOVEMENT and LEFT-labour ACTIVISTS. The strategy became, in modified form, that of Jesse Jackson's attempt to win the Democratic Party's presidential nomination in 1984. The movement led by Jackson sought to tilt the balance of power within the party towards its less advantaged and more radical supporters, and to raise issues which the party's 'mainstream' wished to avoid. These included continuing problems of racial inequality; REAGANISM's lack of sympathy for feminist causes and GAY rights; the moral premises of America's foreign and defence policies. The coalition in 1984 failed to develop convincingly from its largely black base, partly because of Jackson's inability to distance himself from Black Muslim (see

NATION OF ISLAM) supporters such as Louis Farrakhan. Since 1984 the movement has tried to convert itself into a stable organization, but is still characterized by internal tensions and predominantly black support. S.R.

Bibl: A.L. Reed Jr, *The Jesse Jackson Phenomenon* (Yale, 1986); M. Marable, *Black American Politics* (London, 1985).

RAM (Random Access Memory), see under SEMICONDUCTOR STORE.

ram jet. An internal combustion engine of the simplest form, consisting of nothing more than a steel tube, a fuel inlet, and a sparking-plug. By suitable shaping of the tube the air passing through it can be subjected to the same four-stroke cycle as that in a motor-car engine. It is used in very high-speed flight. At Mach 1 (see MACH NUMBERS), the SHOCK WAVE improves the compression by decelerating the air to subsonic speeds. At higher Mach numbers, two shock waves are needed for the dual purpose of slowing down the air and raising its pressure. At Mach 3, pressure ratios as high as 36:1 are obtainable. The 'VI' 'flying bombs' of World War II were propelled in this way. E.R.L.

ramified theory of types, see under PARADOX.

random access. A method of using a computer STORE in which no account is taken of the physical location of the information. It is much easier to use than SERIAL ACCESS but with some forms of store, e.g. MAGNETIC TAPE, it may be several thousand times slower. See also ACCESS TIME. C.S.

random number. To generate statistical SIMULATIONS or to ESTIMATE by MONTE CARLO METHODS, it is often convenient to program a COMPUTER to produce a sequence of random numbers — i.e. numbers which take any value in a fixed interval with equal probability. The numbers generated are actually *pseudo-random* — in fact deterministic, but with the appearance of randomness — and recently many hitherto unsuspected defects have been discovered in the conventional ways of generating such numbers. R.SI.

random variable. Any way of obtaining a number which describes the outcome of an experiment in PROBABILITY THEORY. Thus with the experiment 'toss a coin 10 times' we might associate the random variables 'number of heads', 'length of longest sequence of heads', etc.; with the experiment 'draw a card', the random variable 'number of pips'. See also DISTRIBUTION. R.SI.

random walk, see under STOCHASTIC PROCESS.

range (in STATISTICS), see under DISTRIBUTION.

rank. A CONCEPT in some theories of LINGUISTICS which suggests that the relationship between linguistic units and structures is best viewed taxonomically in terms of composition, a particular structure being described in terms of units which operate at a 'lower' level or rank. It is an important concept in neo-Firthian (see FIRTHIAN) linguistics, where sentence, clause, group, word, and MORPHEME are placed on a *rank scale*. See also LEVEL.
D.C.

rank-size relations. The distributions which result when objects in some collection are arranged by rank-size order (i.e the largest first, the next largest second, and so on). Rank-size studies have been particularly used by biologists in the study of SPECIES abundance and by urban geographers in the analysis of city sizes by population. P.H.
Bibl: G.K. Zipf, *Human Behaviour and the Principle of Least Effort* (London and New York, 1965).

rapid-eye-movement sleep, see REM SLEEP.

rapping, see under REGGAE.

rare earth. Any ELEMENT with ATOMIC NUMBER between 57 and 71. Rare earths are all metals, closely similar in their ELECTRON SHELL structures and chemical properties. M.V.B.

Rastafarianism. A BLACK religious and socio-political movement first articulated by Marcus Garvey (d. 1940) in Jamaica during the 1930s, though having roots in the Caribbean's earlier experiences of colonialism. It came to prominence as a specific vehicle for the expression of black identity in white societies such as Britain in the 1970s, while continuing to manifest itself in the West Indies. The conceptual order of the Rastafarian is centred on Ras Tafari (Haile Selassie, Emperor of Ethiopia 1930-1974, d.1975, regarded as divine), the shared identity and interests of all black people, the decadence of white social, political structures and values (known as Babylon), the eventual return to Zion (Africa), and the use of ganja (cannabis) as a sacrament to achieve spiritual enlightenment. The millennial (see MILLENARIANISM) PAN-AFRICANISM of the movement must be seen primarily as a symbolic response to the predicament of deracinated and marginalized blacks in white industrial cultures. It combats low self-esteem, dissolves inferiority and subordination, and fosters a new separatist sense of identity rooted in the past and ordering the future. Two particularly recognizable attributes of (male) Rastafarians are their physical appearance — dreadlock hairstyles (multiple coiled locks of hair), the red, green, black and gold colours — and their predilection for REGGAE music. Female Rastafarians are encouraged to adopt modest dress and a generally supportive stance. Its many youthful adherents bestowed SUBCULTURAL connotations on the phenomenon, and the struggle to have religious legitimacy conferred upon it continues.
P.S.L.
Bibl: P.B. Clarke, *Black Paradise: The Rastafarian Movement* (London, 1986).

Rate Support Grant (RSG). The biggest proportion of education in Britain is financed through locally collected taxes — the rates. The local education authorities (LEAs) spend much of this money on school books, equipment, special supply teachers, and transport, as well as the upkeep of local colleges and polytechnics. The Department of the Environment contributes a block allocation of money to LEAs to use on all kinds of services, including education. The LEA spends about 85% of its total resources on education. Of the amount, the government contributes between 60 and 65% (depending on what economy measures have been ordered). It is this amount which is known as the rate support grant. Until recently, local authorities were free to spend the RSG on their own chosen service. In the 1980s, the government has tended increasingly to dictate the sector, even the items within the sector, on which the money should go. This is known as a 'specific grant' and has incurred the wrath of most local authorities who claim that their autonomy is being eroded.   J.I.

ratio scale, see under SCALE.

rational expectations. In ECONOMICS, an expectation of a VARIABLE that makes use of all the available information and that is the same as the true expected value, i.e. the conditional mathematical expectation. For an expectation to be rational, it has to be held by all other persons, as different expectations may result in the variable taking different actual values. The formation of expectations can have very important effects on the economic system (see MONETARISM). Rational expectations have been a popular way of modelling expectations. For a rational expectation of a variable to be held implies that there is an explicit or intuitive understanding of the causes of changes in the variable. However, it has been argued that, as an expectation is formed about a variable which is uncertain (see UNCERTAINTY), it is unlikely that a rational expectation can be formed as the forces determining the variable are not completely understood. The ECONOMETRIC testing and modelling of rational expectations in economic behaviour has only been a subject of serious study since the 1970s.   J.P.

Bibl: C.L.F. Attfield *et al., Rational Expectations in Economics* (Oxford, 1985).

rational number, see under NUMBER.

rationalism. Either (1) APRIORISM; or (2) the opposite of IRRATIONALISM, in which sense it denies the acceptability of beliefs founded on anything but experience and reasoning, deductive (see DEMON-STRATION) or inductive (see INDUCTION); or (3), a little datedly, disbelief in the supernatural. In PHILOSOPHY the first meaning is commonest. The 'Rationalists' are the great 17th-century metaphysicians (see METAPHYSICS) Descartes, Spinoza, and Leibniz, who believed that the general nature of the world could be established by wholly non-empirical demonstrative reasoning.   A.Q.

rationality. Behaviour that satisfies two conditions: consistency and fulfilment of certain aims. Consistency can be interpreted in a number of ways. A weak form of consistency is that in the same circumstances the same course of action is always taken. A stronger form of consistency is that if action A is taken rather than action B and action B rather than action C, then action A would be taken rather than C — this property is called transitivity. The second condition of rationality requires that decisions are made purely on the basis of achieving certain aims. The aims may be those of the person or group selecting the course of action or those that society regards as appropriate. The action of an individual taking his own life may be regarded as rational, if he prefers death to any other possible future. However, society may regard his death as an undesirable aim, in which case society would not regard the act of suicide as rational. If it assumed that the preferences, i.e. aims, of an individual are only revealed and defined by choices of courses of action, then, according to the individual's revealed aims, the individual's behaviour must be rational by definition.

In ECONOMICS, the assumption of rational behaviour is important. At the level of the consumer, it is assumed that, within the constraints of actual income and prices, the most preferred pattern of consumption is chosen (see UTILITY). By assumption, this choice is rational from the perspective of the consumer's preferences. It is rational from society's perspective, if society considers an individual to be the best judge of what is in his own best interests, i.e. if the notion of INDIVIDUAL-ISM is accepted. However, society rarely agrees with this proposition (e.g. society's view about the consumption of tobacco and its subsidization of the consumption of health services). If society accepts the notion of individualism, SOCIAL WELFARE can be considered to be a function of the utilities or preferences of the different consumers. The IMPOSSIBILITY THEOREM suggests that it is not possible for society to be rational as it is impossible to construct a SOCIAL CHOICE rule that satisfies the two conditions of rationality and other acceptable assumptions.   J.P.

Bibl: B. Barry and R. Hardin (eds.), *Rational Man and Irrational Society* (London, 1982).

rationalization. A DEFENCE MECHANISM whereby the individual justifies his behaviour by imposing on it a plausible rational explanation.   W.Z.

Raumbühne, see under SPACE (2).

rayograph, see PHOTOGRAM.

rayonism. Method of painting evolved by Michel Larionov in Moscow in 1912 and expounded in his pamphlet *Luchism,* 1913 (Italian translation *Radiantismo,* 1917). Since the eye sees objects by means of rays of light, the colour relationship and intersection of these can be used in non-objective compositions. Rayonist works by Larionov and Goncharova figured in the Target (*Mishen*) exhibition in Moscow, 1913, and in Paris (1914; also a retrospective exhibition in 1948). The movement, which bears some relationship to FUTURISM and its 'lines of force', was short-lived, and few of the manifesto's other signatories made a name. In the mid 1950s Goncharova again produced some rayonist works.   M.C.

Bibl: W. George, *Larionov* (Paris, 1966); M. Chamot, *Nathalie Gontcharova* (Paris, 1972); and see under KNAVE OF DIAMONDS.

r&b, see under RHYTHM AND BLUES.

R&D, see under RESEARCH AND DEVELOPMENT.

reactionary. Adjective or noun applied to those who not merely resist change but seek to put the clock back and return to some earlier order of society which is seen as having possessed characteristics (discipline, respect for authority and privilege, a hierarchical structure, sense of duty) which the present is felt to lack. The word *reaction* was much used by 19th-century radicals (see RADICALISM) who spoke of the 'forces of reaction' (the Catholic Church, absolutist monarchies and hereditary aristocracies) blocking progress towards a more just, equal, and enlightened society. Contemporary radicals would characterize the forces of reaction differently but would have as little doubt as their predecessors that such forces exist and are still bent upon blocking change and annulling reforms already achieved.

The words 'reaction' and 'reactionary' are commonly regarded as the opposite of 'progress' and PROGRESSIVE. Few people, however, would describe themselves as reactionary, and the term is thus most frequently pejorative. It is employed mainly by the LEFT although both the NAZIS and the FASCISTS also used it, in their case to describe the resistance of traditional INSTITUTIONS to their RIGHT-wing radicalism.   A.L.C.B.

reactor, see NUCLEAR REACTOR.

reader-response theory. An influential school of thought in literary theory, mostly based in America, but influenced by RECEPTION THEORY critics such as Wolfgang Iser. Leading exponents are Norman Holland, Stanley Fish, David Bleich, Walter Benn Michaels, Michael Riffaterre and Jonathan Culler. These critics emphasize the important role of the reader in establishing the 'meaning' of any literary text, thus subverting the emphasis which is traditionally laid upon the text as an 'objective' entity whose nature and meaning are to be established by the self-effacing reconstructions of the reader or critic. Reader-response theory emphasizes, on the contrary, that the 'meaning' any literary work is accorded will depend to a very large degree on the 'subjective' contributions of the reader as he or she reads, hence the title of one of Norman Holland's most important books, *5 Readers Reading*, where it is the 'identity theme' of the reader which in fact constitutes the meaning of the work which is being read. This is argued by comparing 5 different sets of perfectly acceptable responses to a single literary text, Faulkner's story 'A Rose For Emily'. Holland sees himself as writing *transactive criticism*, i.e. a criticism which is a free interchange between subjectively offered text and subjectively constituted reading. Holland's influence on other members of the 'Buffalo School' (for instance, David Bleich's *Subjective Criticism*, 1978) has been pervasive. Drawing on insights in Iser's *The Implied Reader* (1974), reader-response criticism has insisted upon a diminished objectivity of the given text, an insistence which has fitted in harmoniously with the doctrine of DECONSTRUCTION. Instead of an unknowable Kantian DINGE-AN-SICH, the literary text now becomes a matter of subjective agreement between 'writer' and 'reader'. Stanley Fish has emphasized the degree to which even the very act of reading, the travelling eye across the line, can set up and constitute properties of the text which the original author had deliberately left in a 'virtual state' — a state which has to be 'fulfilled' by any given reader. This is connected to the PHENOMENOLOGICAL doctrine of INTENTIONALITY and indeed reader-response criticism, in its insistence upon the MEANING-CONFERRING nature of the act of reading is phenomenological through and through. This is clearly visible in Iser's second famous book, *The Act of Reading* (1978) which creatively disagrees with the work of Roman Ingarden, Husserl's disciple, without for all that abandoning the basic theoretical assumption that all reading is a phenomenological act, deeply complicit with various kinds of intentionality. R.PO.

Bibl: J. Tomkins, *Reader-Response Criticism* (Baltimore, 1980).

readymades. Term adopted in the U.S.A. by the painter Marcel Duchamp to describe his DADA-like use, for exhibition and similar purposes, of incongruous manufactured objects such as the porcelain urinal which he submitted to a New York jury in 1917. These continued to feature in his *oeuvre* after his return to Paris in 1919, being put forward, in an ironic-nihilistic spirit, as works of art rendered so by the arbitrary decision of the artist. J.W.

Reagan doctrine. Term used by Karl Krauthammer in the April 1985 edition of *Time* to describe President Reagan's foreign policy. Can be seen as a reaction to the 'VIETNAM syndrome' and President Carter's emphasis on U.S. promotion of HUMAN RIGHTS. The U.S. ambassador to the UNO expressed its essence by writing that 'the central goal of our foreign policy should be... the preservation of civilized conceptions of our own national interest'. This has been translated into a constant evocation of the Soviet threat, described by Reagan as the 'evil Empire', and a return to the support of AUTHORITARIAN régimes in their suppression of revolutionary movements. The doctrine justifies limited intervention to suppress such movements, but avoiding if possible the use of U.S. combat personnel by engaging local forces to do the job (as with the CONTRAS in NICARAGUA and UNITA in Angola) in what has been termed 'low intensity combat' (by Robert Pfaltzgraff). Some doubt has been shed on the compatibility of such actions with international law (see PUBLIC INTERNATIONAL LAW) and has led to increased criticism of U.S. foreign policy towards the THIRD WORLD, both within and outside the U.S. A.W.

Bibl: F. Halliday, *The Making of the Second Cold War* (London, 1986).

Reaganism. The term given, mainly by the European MEDIA and the LEFT, to the ideological character of the rhetoric and policies of Ronald Reagan's two terms as President of the U.S. The term has an imprecise meaning; Reagan is not noted for depth or clarity of conceptual thought, and the fragmented structure of U.S. government inhibits consistency and coherence in policy-making. It may, however, be seen as a variant of American CONSERVATISM which bears some New RIGHT influences and which rejects many of the premises of NEW DEAL liberalism which dominated American politics from 1932 to the 1970s. Reaganism aims to reinvigorate the U.S. economy by reducing government regulation of business, which is taken to stifle innovation and reduce flexibility; and by tax cuts whose rationale is derived from SUPPLY-SIDE ECONOMICS. The economic recovery since 1983 was arguably more the result of massive in-

creases in defence expenditure, and hence was accompanied by an unprecedentedly large budget deficit. It also claims a commitment to reducing the size and cost of the federal government, partly by devolving programmes to state level, partly by cuts in WELFARE expenditure. These aims have been largely frustrated by the resistance of state governments and congressional opposition. Reaganism's proclaimed commitment to conservative social values such as the defence of the FAMILY, the protection of religion, and a resistance to FEMINISM, have been pursued less through legislation than by more modest tactics such as the appointment of conservatives to the federal judiciary. In foreign policy, some distinctive strands are discernible behind the inconsistencies created by executive-branch disunity and electoral imperatives. Policy is largely shaped by emphasis on East-West relations, to the extent that some observers identify a second COLD WAR. The Soviet Union is regarded with suspicion and, sporadically, open hostility, and it is stressed that any attempt at ARMS CONTROL must be undertaken with caution and from a strong bargaining position (see REAGAN DOCTRINE). S.R.

Bibl: J.L. Palmer and I.V. Sawhill (eds.), *The Reagan Record* (Cambridge, Mass., 1984); M. Davis, *Prisoners of the American Dream* (London, 1986).

real. A critical notion which emerged in Lacan's work in the early 1950s as a limit concept in relation to the SYMBOLIC. The real, in one sense, is simply what is excluded from the symbolic, excluded from the network of signifiers which build up the reality of the world, and which is hence impossible to know. Given that a major part of the analytic experience is concerned with this real, Lacan attempted to theorize it using an algebra consisting of what he baptized as MATHEMES: in this way, he thought, it was possible to transmit, through symbolic letters, what otherwise escaped knowledge and, specifically, linguistic representation. D.L.

real number, see under NUMBER.

real time. (1) In music, the ability of an ELECTRONIC MUSIC or COMPUTER MUSIC device to react quickly enough to produce music at the speed at which it is performed. Early electronic and computer music often required much greater amounts of setting up and computing time than the actual duration of the music itself, but recent advances in technology have made real time instruments common thus facilitating live (as opposed to prerecorded) electronic music.

Real time composition is also used to refer to a method of programming sequencers and drum machines in contrast to STEP TIME COMPOSITION.

(2) In dance, the performing of an action (e.g. walking) in the amount of time that it would take in real life rather than in some artificial, perhaps music dominated time scale. Real time is an important facet of POST-MODERN DANCE. B.CO.

real-time computing, see under COMPUTING.

realignment. A term of American origin denoting a major shift in the partisan allegiance of substantial blocks of voters, which then becomes the stable base of a new balance of political forces for a long period. In its more formal version, a realignment may develop over several elections or occur at one 'critical' election; it reverses the majority and minority status of parties in a two-party system; is accompanied by a rise in PARTICIPATION, a heightened intensity of debate, and the emergence of new issues in the political arena. Some authorities find the concept more appropriate to the past than the present, believing that the modern U.S. electorate is in a phase of *dealignment*, in which many voters have replaced their former allegiance with great fluidity of choice. Both terms are now applied to other electorates, with variations in precise meaning. S.R.

Bibl: J.E. Chubb and P.E. Peterson (eds.), *The New Direction in American Politics* (Washington D.C., 1985); H. Drucker *et al.*, *Development in British Politics 2* (Basingstoke, 1986).

realism.

(1) In PHILOSOPHY, a term applied to two distinct theories: (*a*, as opposed to IDEALISM) the theory that there is a world

of material things in space which do not depend for their existence on the fact that some mind is aware of them; and (*b*, as opposed to NOMINALISM) the theory that abstract entities or UNIVERSALS really exist in a world of their own, not in space and time, whether they have instances or not. The first view is sometimes called *perceptual realism*, or, less happily, *epistemological realism*; the second is usually called *Platonic realism* (see also PLATONISM), sometimes *logical realism*. *Perceptual realism* defends one of the most elementary convictions of COMMON SENSE against the consequence of the *argument from illusion* (see ILLUSION) that only private SENSE-DATA or appearances are directly perceived, doing so usually on the ground that since sense-experiences occur independently of the perceiver's will they must be attributed to a cause external to him. That conclusion is compatible with any concept of the intrinsic nature of the external cause of sense-data, including Berkeley's God, so perceptual realists go on to argue that there is some likeness, if only partial, between sense-data and their external causes, e.g. that the former at least correspond in shape, size, and relative position to the latter (see REPRESENTATIONALISM). *Platonic realism* infers (see INFERENCE) the real existence of abstract entities from the fact that there are true statements (see TRUTH) whose subject-terms are abstract nouns and (as its PRESUPPOSITION) from our ability to classify individual things together as being of various kinds and sharing various properties. The two forms of philosophic realism are, in LOGIC, entirely independent; neither implies, nor excludes, the other. They share the name because each asserts the existence of a type of problematic entity. A.Q.

(2) In the arts, a key term used to define both a general, recurrent characteristic of nearly all art and a specific historical movement. Realism in the general sense — what Harry Levin calls the 'willed tendency of art to approximate to reality': to attempt precise imitation of external and historical experience, to make empirical observations, to follow laws of probability, to seem true — has magnetized artists as diverse as Homer, Breughel, and Defoe. During the 19th century, however, realism grew from a technique into a powerful theoretical aim: first and foremost in painting, but also in fiction and drama. Reacting against ROMANTICISM and philosophical IDEALISM, suspicious alike of MYTH, RELIGION, and abstraction (see ABSTRACT), it concentrated heavily on the here-and-now, and developed new techniques for the detailed, accurate representation of life in all its social and domestic aspects.

In France between 1848 and 1870 it was a key aesthetic movement; it had a political component, was to some extent a child of the 1848 Revolution, and carried radical implications (see RADICALISM). Its primary theoreticians were Champfleury and Duranty; as exemplary artists they took Courbet and Degas, whose 'plebeian' realism contrasted and interacted with Flaubert's 'higher' version. A key line runs from Balzac to Flaubert to the Goncourts, and into NATURALISM. In England, Mrs Gaskell, George Eliot, and George Moore are representative; in Russia, Gogol, Turgenev, and Tolstoy; in Germany, Raabe, Fontane, and early Mann; in the U.S.A., James and Howells. The realist sensibility embraces arguments as various as George Eliot's view of Dutch genre painting as a model for the novelist; the Goncourts' demand that the novel provide the social history of the lower classes; and Flaubert's claim of 'no lyricism, no beauty, the author's personality absent'.

Both in painting, via Courbet, Manet, and Degas, and in literature, realism evolved (*a*) towards IMPRESSIONISM, stressing the aesthetic and perceptual technique, the new way of setting down what was seen; and (*b*) towards naturalism, emphasizing the scientific and evolutionary elements that help interpret the subject. Erich Auerbach in *Mimesis* has emphasized, however, the long historical dimension of realism, and its role in attaching art to familiar experience through numerous, sceptical techniques. Realism cannot logically be formless, nor beyond form; it is itself an aesthetic and contains certain logical structures. However, one of its triumphs is to limit complex techniques and mannerisms so that (as Ortega y Gasset puts it) art becomes 'humanized'. Thus it emphasizes character, controls fantasy and idealism, and insists on experience, fact, and the sceptical view in the spirit of

W.D.Howells's 'Is it true — true to the motives, the impulses, the principles that shape the life of actual men and women?' Today it is usually identified as a BOURGEOIS phase of style, associated with EMPIRICISM and INDIVIDUALISM, but deep-seated concepts of realism persist in forms as varied as SOCIALIST REALISM and CHOSISM.　　　　　　　　　M.S.BR.

Bibl: E. Auerbach, tr. W.R. Trask, *Mimesis* (Princeton, 1953); G.J. Becker (ed.), *Documents of Modern Literary Realism* (Princeton, 1963); R. Barthes, tr. A. Lavers and C. Smith, *Writing Degree Zero* (London, 1967); F.J. Hemmings (ed.), *The Age of Realism* (Harmondsworth, 1974); J.P. Stern, *On Realism* (London, 1973).

realism, critical. A theory of PERCEPTION which denies that the perceiver is ever directly aware of material objects which exist independently of him but holds that he can derive knowledge of independent material things from the appearances or SENSE-DATA which are directly present to perceptual consciousness. Dawes Hicks in Britain, Lovejoy and Santayana in the U.S.A., were the chief critical realists so to describe themselves. The word 'realism' marks a contrast with IDEALISM or PHENOMENALISM, which takes objects to be wholly constructed out of appearances or ideas; 'critical' indicates a rejection of the naive realism (see next entry) which takes our perception of material objects to be commonly immediate or direct.　　A.Q.

realism, naive (or *direct realism*). The theory that in PERCEPTION we are as a rule directly and non-inferentially (see INFERENCE) aware of material objects which exist independently of us. Its does not imply that we always perceive things as they really are, nor does it imply that we ever perceive more than a small selection of what is true about a material object. It rejects the consequence derived from the *argument from illusion* (see ILLUSION) that what are directly perceived are never material objects, but always private SENSE-DATA or impressions. Its adherents, disliking the derogatory epithet 'naive', often describe themselves as direct realists.
　　　　　　　　　　　　　　A.Q.

Bibl: D.M. Armstrong, *Perception and the Physical World* (London and New York, 1961).

realistic grammar. In LINGUISTICS, an approach to grammatical analysis which aims to be psychologically real, in that it contributes to the explanation of such areas of linguistic behaviour as comprehension and memory. A contrast is intended between this approach and earlier, formal characterizations of GRAMMAR on the basis of intuition alone. The aim is to 'realize' a TRANSFORMATIONAL GRAMMAR within a psychological model of language use, so that the model genuinely represents users' knowledge of their language.
　　　　　　　　　　　　　　D.C.

Bibl: M. Halle *et al., Linguistic Theory and Psychological Reality* (Boston, 1978).

réalités nouvelles, see under ABSTRACT ART.

reality principle. In psychoanalytic theory (see PSYCHOANALYSIS), a FREUDIAN term for the principle governing the functioning of the EGO. The reality principle imposes constraints on the PLEASURE PRINCIPLE by delaying gratification until the desired object or state can realistically be achieved and by causing an impulse towards such a goal to be modified into a socially acceptable form.　　　　　　　　W.Z.

Realpolitik. Term originated by the German publicist Ludwig von Rochau in his *Grundsätze der Realpolitik* (1853), a critique of the lack of realism in the policies followed by the German Liberals during the years 1848-9. The term was particularly applied to Bismarck's policy during and after the years of German unification, and is to be distinguished from a policy of selfish self-interest or from a ruthless reliance on naked power. The phrase has been used, by American theorists of international politics opposed to the IDEOLOGICAL elements in traditional American foreign policy, to cover the integration of POWER, morality, and self-interest into a 'policy of the possible'.　　　　D.C.W.

Bibl: H.J. Morgenthau, *Politics among Nations* (New York, 4th ed., 1967).

Rebel Art Centre, see under VORTICISM.

recapitulation. The notion embodied in the familiar phrase that in development an animal 'climbs up its own family tree' — i.e., that the development of an individual animal recapitulates its ancestry. In this naive form *recapitulation theory* is associated with the name of Ernst Haeckel (1834-1919; see also PHYLOGENY) and is entirely discredited. The element of truth in it is the unquestioned fact, sometimes referred to as von Baer's principle (see EMBRYOLOGY), that the embryos of related animals resemble each other more closely than do the corresponding adults. As an animal develops from a ZYGOTE we can determine its affinities with increasing confidence: first the embryo will be recognizable as a CHORDATE, then as a vertebrate, then as a mammal, then as a primate and finally, maybe, as a man.

P.M.

reception theory *(Rezeptionsästhetik).* A school of literary theory associated with the University of Konstanz and grouped around the journal *Poetik und Hermeneutik* from 1964 onwards. Unlike READER-RESPONSE THEORY which is made up of a set of independent reflections on the importance of the reader in the act of reading, the Konstanz theory has a certain corporate identity. In America the best known member of the school has been until recently Wolfgang Iser, although the most famous statement of its aims is Hans Robert Jauss's essay 'Literary History as a Challenge to Literary Theory' (1970). Attempting to avoid the impasses of MARXISM and FORMALISM, neither of which take much account of the reader, Jauss proposes that a literary work should in future be studied in terms of the impact it has upon its contemporaries. In order to establish this impact it is necessary to discover the 'horizon of expectations' that environs the new work. The indebtedness of this concept to Jauss's old teacher Gadamer, and his own use of the Husserlian concept of *horizon* is evident. Jauss instances and analyses the differing receptions accorded to Flaubert's *Madame Bovary* and Feydeau's *Fann,* both of which appeared in 1857.

R.PO.

Bibl: R. Holub, *Reception Theory* (London, 1984).

receptor. Structural or molecular grouping in, or on the surface of, a CELL which has an affinity for a pharmacological or immunological agent (see IMMUNITY; PHARMACOLOGY). Thus in IMMUNOLOGY an *antigen* on a cell surface may be thought of as a receptor for the *antibody* whose formation it may excite if administered in a suitable way. Likewise cells which are specifically affected by them are presumed to have receptors for various drugs. The same applies to hormones (see ENDOCRINOLOGY) and the cells they act upon, resulting in SIGNAL TRANSDUCTION and RECEPTOR-MEDIATED ENDOCYTOSIS.

P.M.;P.N.

receptor-mediated endocytosis. After a hormone (see ENDOCRINOLOGY) or an equivalent signalling MOLECULE binds to its RECEPTOR one result is SIGNAL TRANSDUCTION. Another is that the complex of hormone and its receptor is removed from the surface of the CELL to the interior within small vesicles. Receptor-mediated endocytosis, as the process is known, ensures that the signal delivered by the hormone is short-lived. The notion survives that the hormone and its receptor can trigger responses within the interior of the cell but it is more likely that the hormone is simply destroyed there, while the receptor is recycled to the surface of the cell.

P.N.

Bibl: B. Alberts *et al., Molecular Biology of the Cell* (New York, 1983).

recession, see under DEPRESSION (3).

recessive, see under GENE.

recidivism. Literally, a 'falling back' into crime. A recidivist is strictly any offender who is convicted on more than one occasion, but for practical purposes most criminologists (see CRIMINOLOGY) are concerned to study the problem within defined time limits, e.g. percentages of offenders reconvicted in one, five, ten years. Penologists (see PENOLOGY) normally consider that recidivists merit special treatment, and many countries provide for special sentencing related to the offender's total criminal record as well as the offence of which he may be convicted. Such provisions are known variously as 'preventive detention', 'extended sentence', 'double-track systems', or arrangements made in the interests of 'social defence'. Factors explored in connection with recidivism have included age at first conviction, type of offence, the isolation of the offender in the community without family or friends, and the extent to which his criminal record increases the chances of his being further detected and convicted.   T.M.

Bibl: S. Box, *Deviance, Reality and Society* (London, 2nd ed., 1981).

recombinant DNA, see under GENETIC ENGINEERING.

recombination (in GENETICS), see CROSSING OVER.

reconstructive surgery, see under PLASTIC SURGERY.

rectification. A general term used in Chinese politics to refer to campaigns directed against those whose ideas don't conform with the official line. The idea is to criticize others and, more importantly, to accept criticisms in order to rectify mistakes and realize the errors of one's past. First used in Yan'an in 1942 (see LONG MARCH), rectification campaigns have been used throughout the post 1949 period, such as in the Oppose Bureaucracy Oppose Corruption movement of 1952. Because of the responsiveness of the masses to the centre's, particularly Mao's, directives, rectification can be used as an opportunity to purge those cadres or leaders whose positions are becoming too powerful. See, for example, the way Liu Shaoqi and Deng Xiaoping were identified as 'capitalist roaders' during the GREAT PROLETARIAN CULTURAL REVOLUTION, and the expulsion of 10% of the party membership after the 'Three Anti' campaign of summer 1952.   S.B.

Bibl: F.C. Teiwes, *Politics and Purges in China* (New York, 1979).

rectifier. A device which allows an electric current to flow in one direction but not the other (e.g. a diode THERMIONIC value, or a

TRANSISTOR). If an *alternating* voltage is applied to a rectifier, a *direct* current flows.   M.V.B.

recursion (or *recursiveness*). In LINGUISTICS, the attribute of rules which may be applied an indefinite number of times in the generation of sentences, e.g. a rule which would introduce an adjective before a noun.   D.C.

recursive function theory. The study of what can and what cannot be done by an ideal COMPUTER (limitations of space and time being entirely ignored). Its importance for MATHEMATICS comes through the general acceptance of *Church's thesis*: any effective, or routine, or ALGORITHMIC process in mathematics can be performed by an (ideal) computer. The first such 'computer' considered — in 1936, before modern computers existed — was a TURING MACHINE. Let P be a property of natural NUMBERS or of finite sequences of symbols ('words'); P is *decidable* (or *computable*, or *solvable*) if there is a PROGRAM for an ideal computer such that when any number n or word W is given as INPUT the computer will (eventually) print 1 if n or W has the property P and 0 otherwise, e.g. 'being prime' is decidable. The most significant from a great range of results are: (1) 'W is a theorem of the PREDICATE CALCULUS' is undecidable; (2) 'W is a diophantine equation (see NUMBER THEORY) which has a solution' is undecidable. But, in contrast to (1): (3) 'W is a correct proof in the predicate calculus' is decidable; (4) 'W is a theorem of "elementary" Euclidean GEOMETRY' is decidable ('elementary' is a technical term; Euclid's theorems all satisfy it). The theory is closely linked with GÖDEL'S THEOREM, and with INTUITIONISM (sense 3).   R.G.

Bibl: B.A. Trakhtenbrot, tr. J. Kristian *et al., Algorithms and Automatic Computing Machines* (Boston, 1963); D.R. Hofstadter, *Gödel, Escher, Bach* (Harmondsworth and New York, 1980).

recursiveness, see RECURSION.

recycling.

(1) The recovery of scrap material after use, followed by re-processing in order to permit of further use, sometimes of a dif-

ferent kind, as when waste paper is used in the manufacture of cardboard. The word has become a battle-cry among those concerned with the POLLUTION of the ENVIRONMENT and with the need for CONSERVATION of the earth's resources. In this context it usually refers to the decomposition of biodegradable materials after use so as to form nutrients for fresh organic growth, this in turn renewing the source of the original materials.

(2) In ECONOMICS, accumulated surpluses on a country's current and/or capital accounts of the BALANCE OF PAYMENTS may be put back into international financial circulation. This recycling can be conducted through the country's CENTRAL BANK, or, as is more common since the early 1970s and the era of freer foreign exchange (see EXCHANGE CONTROL), through the decisions of private individuals, firms and financial institutions. This recycling is important to the growth of world trade and the stability of the world financial system. See DEBT CRISIS; EURODOLLARS; OIL CRISIS.   J.P.

Bibl: R. B. Johnston, *Economics of the Euro-market* (London, 1982).

Red Army. (1) Originally, a catch-phrase for the Soviet Army. (2) Recently, a terrorist organization (*Sekigun*) of extremist if vague revolutionary views which emerged from the Japanese radical (see RADICALISM) student movement in 1969. It is characterized by (*a*) its rejection of Japanese CHAUVINISM on the one hand and of NONVIOLENT RESISTANCE on the other; (*b*) the elimination of internal disagreement by kangaroo courts ready to inflict death on convicted dissidents; (*c*) the large part played by women in its ranks; and (*d*) the transference of its activities, following drastic pressure from the Japanese police, to bases and activities in Europe and the Middle East. These include the action at Lod airport in Israel in May 1974 in which 26 were killed and 71 injured by indiscriminate machine-gunning of airport users; the hijacking of airliners to Korea in 1970 and in Amsterdam in 1973; an attack on an oil refinery in Singapore in February 1974; the seizure of the French Embassy at The Hague in September 1974; and the hijacking of an airliner at Dacca in September 1977. Following this last incident

the Red Army was heard from less frequently. Japanese police estimated that in 1980 it included about 30 members. During the 1980s reports spoke of it working with the Popular Front for the Liberation of Palestine in the Bekaa Valley of LEBANON.   D.C.W.;J.A.A.S.

red giant. A very large relatively cool star near the end of its life (see HERTZSPRUNG-RUSSELL DIAGRAM). Red giants may be hundreds of times larger than the sun in diameter, but their densities are extremely low — some are more tenuous than air.
               M.V.B.

Red Guards. A civilian revolutionary (see REVOLUTION) militia formed mainly among students and idealistic youth in China during the period of the GREAT PROLETARIAN CULTURAL REVOLUTION, as a response to Mao Zedong's appeal to maintain revolutionary fervour and attack bureaucratic and administrative inertia. After clashing with the work teams sent into educational establishments by Deng Xiaoping and Liu Shaoqi in order to restore their authority, the Red Guards became noted for their excesses of enthusiasm and vindictiveness against their opponents, and even against rival Red Guard factions. With the country at a standstill and in a state of virtual civil war, the People's Liberation Army stepped in to restore effective control of society, and the students were ordered to return to their studies in November 1967. The name has come to be connected with the indiscriminate destructive excesses of the cultural revolution, and the blind loyalty of hot-headed idealistic youth in their support of a party or IDEOLOGY.   D.C.W.;S.B.

Bibl: G.A. Bennet and R.N. Montaperto, *Red Guard* (London and New York, 1971).

red shift. A displacement towards the red of the spectral lines of distant GALAXIES and some stars. It is usually interpreted as a DOPPLER EFFECT; this implies that the galaxies are receding, and the red shift constitutes the main evidence for the EXPANSION OF THE UNIVERSE.   M.V.B.

redaction criticism, see under HIGHER CRITICISM.

Redemptor Hominis. The first ENCYCLI-CAL issued by Pope John Paul II, in 1979. It combined an orthodox insistence on the uniqueness of Christ with a generous attitude to all assertions of human rights against oppressive systems, and was in part inspired by the new Pope's experience of the struggles of the Polish church under Communism. He claimed that 'every man without any exception whatever has been redeemed by Christ', who provides him 'with the light and strength to measure up to his supreme calling'. D.L.E.

Bibl: J. Whale (ed.), *The Pope from Poland: An Assessment* (London and New York, 1980).

reductio ad absurdum, see under DEMONSTRATION.

reduction; reductionism.

(1) In PHILOSOPHY and related subjects, the process whereby CONCEPTS or statements that apply to one type of entity are redefined in terms of concepts, or analysed in terms of statements, of another kind, normally one regarded as more elementary or epistemologically (see EPISTEMOLOGY) more basic. *Reducible* is the adjective describing a type of entity that is considered susceptible of reduction; *reducibility* is the property of such a type of entity; *reductionism* is the systematic practice of reduction (also the view that reduction constitutes the business of philosophy). If entities of one kind, nations for example, are regarded as reducible to entities of another, in this case individual people, they are said to be CONSTRUCTS or *logical constructions* out of the latter.

Reduction is seldom an uncontentious activity, and to list some of the many varieties of reductionism (which may be contrasted with HOLISM) is to list a series of controversies: whether (as in PHENOMENALISM) material objects are reducible to SENSE-DATA; whether mental events and processes are reducible to physiological, physical, or chemical events and processes in human brains (see PHYSICALISM; MATERIALISM; BEHAVIOURISM; *physical monism* under MIND-BODY PROBLEM); whether SOCIAL STRUCTURES and social processes are reducible to relationships between and actions of individuals (see METHODOLOGICAL INDIVIDUALISM);

whether (as denied by VITALISM) biological organisms are reducible to physical systems; whether (as in LOGICAL POSITIVISM) philosophy is reducible to ANALYSIS; whether (as in LOGICISM) MATHEMATICS is reducible to LOGIC. The reductionist sometimes justifies his activity as a principle of economy in EXPLANATION, a principle that has obviously paid off in science; the anti-reductionist argues the existence of irreducible or EMERGENT PROPERTIES.

Some of the points at issue, however, are more apparent than real, and stem largely from terminological confusion (exacerbated in some cases by plain prejudice). Thus, a *logical construction* (see above) also needs to be distinguished from an aggregate or whole whose constituents are literally parts of it; e.g., the phenomenalist claims, not that a material thing is literally *composed* of sense-data, but merely that everything that can be said about material things can in principle be stated in assertions that refer only to sense-data. Some versions of reductionism, moreover, are purely METHODOLOGICAL, involving only the claim that the study of phenomena of type *A* has to be restricted to the study of evidence provided by class *B*; thus a methodological behaviourist might argue that, although mental events and processes exist, they can only be studied in terms of the behaviour they produce (see BEHAVIOURISM; MENTALISM). A.Q.; A.S.; J.S.B.

Bibl: A.J. Ayer, *Language, Truth and Logic* (London, rev. ed., 1946), ch. 2; E. Nagel, *The Structure of Science* (London, 1961), chs. 11, 14; A. Koestler and J.R. Smythies (eds.), *Beyond Reductionism* (London, 1969; New York, 1970).

(2) In CHEMISTRY, the addition, to an ATOM or MOLECULE, of ELECTRONS or electropositive groups such as hydrogen IONS, or the removal of electrons or electronegative groups such as oxygen ions. The opposite of OXIDATION. M.V.B.

reduction division, see under MEIOSIS.

redundancy.

(1) In INFORMATION THEORY, the representation of data by longer strings of symbols than are necessary to distinguish between all the possible different data items in a context. Redundancy is a bad thing if it leads to unnecessary expense in

storage or transmission of representations of data, but a good thing if it permits reconstitution of data whose representation has been accidentally corrupted. Compare 19F3 with nineteen sebenty three; each has one character wrong.

R.M.N.

(2) In CYBERNETICS, usage (1) is familiar, but the term is also applied to extra channels in a network that are intended to guard a whole system against the failure of an entire channel. It is possible to calculate mathematically how much redundancy is required to reduce the risk of a mistake (getting the message wrong in (1), or failure of the system in (2)) to an *arbitrarily* small degree.   S.BE.

Bibl: C.E. Shannon and J. McCarthy (eds.), *Automata Studies* (Princeton, 1956).

re-entry. In ASTRONAUTICS, the return of a space vehicle through the earth's atmosphere. It is during re-entry that the vehicle is subjected to the highest temperature, great heat being generated by the friction and pressure between air and vehicle. Radio contact with the vehicle is lost for most of the re-entry period.   E.R.L.

reference. In LINGUISTICS, the relationship between linguistic forms and the objects, events, etc. (*referents*) in nonlinguistic experience to which these forms refer. Most linguists are careful to distinguish reference from *sense*, which is a purely intralinguistic property arising from the MEANING RELATIONS between words.   D.C.

reference class, see under FREQUENCY THEORY.

reference group. Term introduced by Herbert H. Hyman (in *Archives of Psychology*, 1942) for a social collectivity, real or imagined, in relation to which an individual regularly evaluates his own situation or conduct. A *comparative* reference group is one which serves as a standard against which the individual appraises his achievements, social circumstances, life-chances, rewards, etc., and which thus influences the level of his expectations and, in turn, his degree of relative satisfaction or deprivation; thus the structure of comparative reference groups among members of different occupations has been shown to be important in determining the extent to which wage differentials are regarded as legitimate and the level at which wage claims are made. A NORMATIVE reference group is one which the individual perceives as a source of values and GROUP NORMS of which he approves, and with whose members he would wish to identify himself; thus a socially aspiring individual may take the ÉLITE of his local community as a normative reference group, and seek to emulate their LIFE STYLE, manners, tastes, opinions, etc. in the hope of being himself accepted into the élite.   J.H.G.

Bibl: R.K. Merton, *Social Theory and Social Structure* (New York, 2nd ed., 1957), chs. 8, 9.

reference retrieval, see under INFORMATION STORAGE.

referential language, see EMOTIVE AND REFERENTIAL LANGUAGE.

reflation, see under INFLATION.

reflex, conditioned, see CONDITIONED REFLEX.

reformism. A policy of social and economic reform by gradual stages rather than by REVOLUTIONARY change. The term has been applied in particular to a tendency in the SOCIALIST movement to abandon the idea of revolutionary violence and to rely instead on the slow transformation of social INSTITUTIONS through democratic means. It found its expression in British FABIANISM, French *réformisme*, German REVISIONISM, Russian 'economism', etc., but it was only in countries with a parliamentary suffrage that the constitutional framework favoured such a gradualist approach. It eventually became the hallmark of the Socialist INTERNATIONAL. The establishment of the COMMUNIST International reflected the split in the labour movement between the evolutionary and the revolutionary attitudes, a split resting upon fundamental differences of attitude towards DEMOCRACY and MARXISM.

Some socialist parties, like the British Labour Party, never embraced Marxism; some, like the German Social Democrats (see SOCIAL DEMOCRACY) abandoned it later. The further evolution of the socialist movement has produced a growing differentiation between moderate and radical elements (see RADICALISM). The latter have tended to prefer the socialist, the former a social-democratic label. In some countries, like Italy and Japan, this division has led to the establishment of separate socialist and social-democratic parties. In others it tends to create a growing gap between the moderate and LEFT-wing groups in labour and socialist movements.

L.L.

Bibl: J. Joll, *The Second International* (London, 1955; New York, 1966); W.E. Paterson and I. Campbell, *Social Democracy in Post-War Europe* (London and New York, 1974); L. Johnston, *Marxism, Class Analysis and Socialist Pluralism* (London, 1986).

refugee, see under IMMIGRANT.

refurbishment. Term used in architecture to describe the rehabilitation and fitting out anew of older buildings. Refurbishment has become a major activity of many British architects in the 1980s as land shortages, ultra-conservative planning laws and a widespread public rejection of the work of post-war architects have made designing, developing and erecting new buildings a difficult task. With the decline of older industries in the Western world and their buildings, together with an admiration for older industrial buildings, refurbishment of those buildings which can be used in new and profitable ways has also been a major factor in retaining snippets of the architectural heritage of many countries. S.L.

reggae. A BLACK musical form with African and American RHYTHM AND BLUES roots which emerged in Jamaica during the 1960s. The immediate antecedents of reggae were *ska/blue beat* and *rock steady*, all music and dance styles that share the firm percussive beat counterposed by a bass off-beat. The wider significance of reggae is due to three factors: it constitutes yet another significant black contribution to popular music; it transcended its ethnic dimensions and became a SUB-CULTURAL phenomenon (white

YOUTH CULTURE adopted reggae in various ways, from the skinheads' approval of street machismo to the *two-tone* phenomenon of deliberately multi-racial bands purveying an anti-racist message); it was closely associated with the RASTAFARIAN movement and the growth of black consciousness during the 1970s.

During the early and mid-1970s reggae became the dominant channel through which Rastafarian ideals were effectively communicated to young blacks in the urban industrial centres of the west. Reggae musicians drew extensively on the Rastafarian conceptual universe for their lyrics, developing a musical style from this source, and imparting a vicarious sense of unity to groups in industrial society who saw themselves as under pressure (this included elements of white youth). The dissemination of this message to a more differentiated and international audience was partially achieved through the emerging superstar status of the most renowned reggae musician, Bob Marley, who died prematurely of cancer in 1981. Though the connotations of black redemption have faded from reggae, it is still a characteristically black genre, and it has spawned more contemporary black cultural and musical forms such as *toasting* and *scratching, rapping* and *hip hop*. P.S.L.

régime theory. An increasingly fashionable way of explaining the relationships in international society as demonstrated by INTERDEPENDENCE. Concentrates on the regional and international attempts to show how régimes will form as 'principles, norms, rules and decision-making procedures around which actor expectations converge in a given issue area' (Krasner, 1982). It retains the state as principal actor in the international system, especially at the stage of régime formation, with the notion of the state 'hegemon' (see HEGEMONY). Can be applied to any area of international politics, from trade to HUMAN RIGHTS. Has been criticized as being an intellectual fad, and as a disguising of objective power relationships.

A.W.

Bibl: S. Krasner (ed.), *International Organization*, Spring 1982.

region. Geographical term for a homogeneous area of the earth's surface with characteristics which make it distinct from the areas that surround it. The distinction may be based on natural or man-made characteristics or a combination of both. Scale distinctions are made between large-scale regions of continental proportions (*macroregions*) down to very small structures (*microregions*); similarly, regions with common region-wide characteristics (*uniform regions*) are distinguished from those in which the characteristic is most strongly discernible at or near the centre of the region and least strongly at the boundaries (*focal regions*). P.H.

Bibl: D.Gregory, *Regional Transformation and Industrial Revolution* (London, 1982).

regional planning. A term applied usually to planned intervention by central government so as to adjust regional inequalities within a state. It is also used to describe intervention by two or more governments to meet the conjoint problems of a shared natural REGION (e.g. a river basin). P.H.

Bibl: J. Friedmann and W. Alonso (eds.), *Regional Development and Planning* (Cambridge, Mass., 1964).

regional science. An interdisciplinary field within the SOCIAL SCIENCES that focuses on the integrated study of economic and social phenomena in a regional setting. The term is particularly associated with W. Isard's research group at the University of Pennsylvania which draws heavily on mathematical MODELS to frame regional-science theories. See also REGION. P.H.

Bibl: W. Isard, *Introduction to Regional Science* (London, 1975).

regionalism. Geographical term for sociopolitical movements which seek (1) to foster or protect an indigenous CULTURE in particular regions, or (2) to decentralize central government to an intermediate level between that of the State and the traditional units of local government. The movement has been traditionally strong in France and Spain, and has become of increasing importance in Great Britain

with the establishment in the 1960s of Regional Economic Planning Councils. P.H.

register. (1) In neo-Firthian (see FIRTHIAN) *linguistics*, a regular, situationally-conditioned, and distinctive range in language use, e.g. 'scientific', 'upper-class', 'formal' registers. (2) In COMPUTING, the fastest type of computer STORE. D.C.; C.S.

regression. (1) In STATISTICS, it is common to attempt to explain the variation in some observed quantity as a combination of some simple kind of dependence on values set by the experimenter, together with an error term (see ERROR ANALYSIS). Such a representation is called a *regression*. It is found, for example, that the rate at which a cicada chirps is linearly related to the difference between the ambient temperatures, but any particular observation may as a result of random error fail to lie exactly on this regression line: this example is of *linear regression*. The design of experiments to obtain good ESTIMATES of regression coefficients is an important statistical problem. R.SI.

(2) In PSYCHOLOGY, a DEFENCE MECHANISM whereby an individual responds to stresses such as fear, frustration, isolation, etc. by reverting to behaviour characteristic of a less adult, more primitive and impulsive stage of development. In psychoanalytic theory (see PSYCHOANALYSIS) the regression is either to an earlier state of libidinal interest and sexual organization (see LIBIDO; PSYCHOSEXUAL DEVELOPMENT) or to an earlier stage of EGO development. In the former, the person regresses from adult genitality to earlier (pre-genital) oral or anal sexual interests. In the latter, the person deals with the danger threatening him by behaving in a more childlike and generally dependent way. W.Z.; B.A.F.

regression analysis, see under MULTIVARIATE ANALYSIS.

regulation.

(1) In EMBRYOLOGY, the process of CELL reorganization or readjustment that occurs in the restoration of an organic defect or incompleteness; more especially, the phenomenon whereby, if a sea urchin's or

733

starfish's embryo at the two-cell stage is divided into the two separate cells, each one will grow up into a whole organism. This phenomenon was made the basis of very far-reaching philosophical speculations by Hans Driesch (1867-1941). P.M.

(2) In ENGINEERING, a quantity that expresses — unexpectedly, in view of the normal meaning of the word — the degree of imperfection of a device or SYSTEM. Familiar examples are electrical transformers and electrical transmission systems, where the regulation is the amount by which the voltage falls when the appliance or load is connected, and driving motors, where it is the amount by which the speed of the motor falls when its load is coupled to the motor. Both voltage and speed regulation are usually expressed as a percentage of their respective values when no load is connected. See also VARIABLE SPEED.   E.R.L.

(3) In CYBERNETICS, any systematic behaviour within a system that tends to restrict fluctuations of any variable. This systematic behaviour will be embodied in a set of physical connections, which will need some form of ENERGY to operate them. However, the critical commodity used by any regulator is *information*. All regulators detect discrepancies from some expectation (which may be not a fixed value, but the varying output of some other part of the system) and FEEDBACK information to make adjustments that reduce the discrepancy.   S.BE.

(4) In ECONOMICS, see under ECONOMIC REGULATION.

rehabilitation.

(1) Rehabilitation is the combined and co-ordinated use of medical, social, educational and vocational measures for training and retraining the individual to the highest possible level of functional ability. The main aim is maximum restoration of physical, mental and social capabilities. Good rehabilitation requires a team approach involving the patient, family doctor, consultant, appropriate paramedical therapists, social worker, the family and employer. Rehabilitation of the physically disabled will involve the services of many paramedical and other support groups, for example, PHYSIOTHERAPISTS, OCCUPATIONAL THERAPISTS, speech therapists, so-

cial workers, also the voluntary agencies.
D.L.W.; D.D.

(2) In POLITICS, a term used particularly of the posthumous acquittal and restoration to Party favour of COMMUNISTS executed during the purges in Russia and in Eastern Europe in the Stalin epoch. In Russia, it is applied largely to political leaders executed in secret, to Army leaders, and to certain writers. Of those accused in the public MOSCOW TRIALS only half a dozen have been publicly rehabilitated, though statements have been made which are incompatible with the guilt of any of the others. Rehabilitation on criminal charges does not always imply complete political rehabilitation as well. A further process, sometimes known as *derehabilitation*, has also been noted, by which certain Party officials (e.g. F. Raskolnikov) restored to Party favour in the early 1960s have been denounced as traitors once again.   R.C.

Reichian. Relating to the beliefs or the followers of Wilhelm Reich (born in Austria in 1897, died in the U.S.A. in 1958). Reich's career began in orthodox PSYCHOANALYSIS, but he quickly developed original theories, relating NEUROSIS to sexual frustration and failure to achieve complete orgasm. This led to a complex therapeutic approach called *character analysis* or *bio-energetics*. Reich's interest in sexual energy led to his 'discovery' of the *orgone*, a 'life force' (for Bergson's earlier version of this, see VITALISM) which he found to be blue in colour, and to be present in living and inorganic matter throughout nature and interstellar space. His commitment to the 'Orgone Energy Accumulator' (a metal box which, he claimed, concentrated orgone energy and cured illness) led to his imprisonment in 1955 for selling medical equipment prohibited by the U.S. Food and Drug Laws. The technique of 'bio-energetics' as a therapy for neurosis is again popular (along with other GROUP THERAPY techniques), and the film *Mysteries of the Organism* has helped to keep Reich's views in the public gaze. It is still not clear whether he was a charlatan or a genius; the truth doubtless lies somewhere between the two.   M.J.C.

Bibl: M. Sharaf, *Fury on Earth: a Bi-*

ography of Wilhelm Reich (London, 1983).

reification. The act of regarding an abstraction (see ABSTRACT) as a material thing.

An analysis of any relationship in a complex world involves a process of simplification through a set of abstractions in which certain aspects of a given phenomenon are selected and stressed for HEURISTIC purposes. These abstracted elements of reality may be reduced to an IDEAL TYPE or a conceptual MODEL. If they are taken as a complete description of the real phenomenon and the resulting abstractions endowed with a material existence of their own, the process exemplifies what A.N. Whitehead called in his *Science and the Modern World* (1962) 'the fallacy of misplaced concreteness', which is in effect a special case of the fallacy of reification. (See also *reductionism*, under REDUCTION.)

Reification as a CONCEPT with a special meaning was used with particular emphasis by Karl Marx (see MARXISM). For him, reification (*Versachlichung, Verdinglichung*) meant that the 'social relation between men ... assumes for them the fantastic form of a relation between things'. In CAPITALIST society, he saw it as the result of ALIENATION (*Entäusserung*) or the estrangement (*Entfremdung*) of labour, a separation of the worker from the product of his work. Marx wrote that 'the general social form of labour appears as the property of a thing' and is 'reified' through the 'FETISHISM of commodities'. This is a social situation which is determined by 'the action of objects which rule the producers instead of being ruled by them'.

Marx's concepts of reification and alienation have been used as key terms by the NEW LEFT. In their popular form alienation was taken to mean the estrangement of man from an oppressive society, reification the treatment of men as objects of manipulation, as things rather than as human beings. In the theoretical writings of the Marxist forerunners of the New Left, such as Lukács and the philosophers of the FRANKFURT SCHOOL, the concept of reification has been applied to all pre-REVOLUTIONARY activities and INSTITUTIONS, including science (which for Hork-heimer is a 'reified IDEOLOGY'), TECHNOLOGY (which for Marcuse is a 'vehicle for reification'), and general intellectual concepts (which for Lukács are instances of reification).   L.L.

reinforcement. In the context of OPERANT CONDITIONING, the supplying of a consequence for certain behaviour which will *strengthen* that behaviour, i.e. make it more likely to recur in the same situation. In *positive reinforcement*, the behaviour is strengthened by the contingent presentation of a reward (e.g. food); in *negative reinforcement*, the behaviour is strengthened by the contingent removal of an aversive stimulus (e.g. electric shock, loud noise). Sometimes, *negative reinforcement* is extended to include the case where behaviour is made *less* likely to recur as the result of contingent presentation of an aversive stimulus, an operation properly termed *punishment*. The behaviour may be abolished (*extinguished*) if reinforcement no longer follows it; the abolition procedure is known as *extinction*. The rules that specify when and under what circumstances an operant response should be reinforced are known as *schedules of reinforcement*; such schedules may require e.g., a minimum time interval between responses, or the occurrence of a set number of unreinforced responses between successive reinforced ones.   D.H.

Bibl: C.B. Ferster and B.F. Skinner, *Schedules of Reinforcement* (New York, 1957).

relational grammar. A development of GENERATIVE GRAMMAR of the mid-1970s which takes as central the notion of grammatical *relations* (such as subject and object) rather than the categorial terms of earlier models (such as noun phrase and verb phrase).   D.C.

Bibl: P. Matthews, *Syntax* (Cambridge, 1981).

relations. What is ascribed to groups of two or more individual things by the predicates of sentences in which there is separate mention of two or more things. Logicians distinguish various formal properties of relations. (1) A relation is *symmetrical* if A's standing in it to B entails (see ENTAILMENT) that B stands in it to *A* (e.g. '*A* is married to *B*'), *asymmetrical* if *A*'s standing in it to *B* entails that *B* does *not* stand in it to *A* (e.g. '*A* is older than *B*'), *non-symmetrical* if it possesses neither of these properties (e.g. '*A* loves *B*'); (2) a relation is *transitive* if *A*'s standing in it to *B* and *B*'s standing in it to *C* entails that *A* stands in it to *C* (e.g. 'is the same age as'), *intransitive* if the two conditions just mentioned entail that *A* does *not* stand in it to *C* (e.g. 'is one year older than'); (3) a relation is *reflexive* if everything must have it to itself (e.g. 'is as tall as'), *irreflexive* if nothing can have it to itself (e.g. 'is older than'), otherwise *non-reflexive* (e.g. 'loves'). Relations that involve the CONCEPT of sameness or identity (EQUIVALENCE RELATIONS) are ordinarily transitive and symmetrical (and therefore reflexive); relations that involve that of more or less are ordinarily transitive and asymmetrical. See also INTERNAL RELATIONS; ORDERING RELATIONS.   A.Q.

relative deprivation. A CONCEPT introduced by the American sociologist S.A. Stouffer in 1949 and based upon the proposition that people's attitudes, aspirations, and grievances depend largely upon the FRAME OF REFERENCE in which they are conceived. Thus, when one COMMUNITY observes another comparable community or REFERENCE GROUP to be relatively prosperous, a feeling of deprivation arises which, prior to comparison, did not exist. The concept is a useful reminder of human envy, but fails to establish criteria for determining the point at which deprivation becomes absolute as well as relative.   P.S.L.

Bibl: W.G. Runciman, *Relative Deprivation and Social Justice* (London and Berkeley, 1966).

relativism. The view that beliefs and principles, particularly evaluative ones, have no universal or timeless validity but are valid only for the age in which, or the social group or individual person by which, they are held. It is most inviting as a reaction to the differences of moral belief as between different societies, but many of these differences can be reconciled if it is recognized that both the actual and the expected consequences of an action can differ from one society to another as a result of their differences in knowledge and circumstances. It is a common but not inevitable associate of HISTORICISM in the original sense of that word. It is implicitly present in the ethical speculations of the ancient Greek Sophists and, encouraged by the findings of ANTHROPOLOGY (see RELATIVISM, CULTURAL), was revived in the 19th century.   A.Q.

Bibl: S. Lukes and W. Runciman, 'Relativism: Cognitive and Moral' in *Proceedings of the Aristotelian Society* (London, 1974), pp. 165-208.

relativism, cultural. CULTURES (see ANTHROPOLOGY) are relative in the trivial sense that what is right and good in one society may not be in another. 'Cultural relativism' is usually restricted, however, to an anthropological doctrine most forcefully expounded by Melville J. Herskovits (1895-1963) according to which the values and institutions of any culture must be taken to be self-validating. In so far as this doctrine entails a stance of moral relativism, it is subject to the criticism (among others) that we are often obliged to judge the actions of members of other societies by standards which are not theirs. The question of relativism has been at the heart of much anthropological debate. It concerns fundamentally the unity of man. It has emerged in the form of discussions concerning rationality, 'PRIMITIVE mentality', modes of thought, etc. In ECONOMIC ANTHROPOLOGY it took the form of a debate between formalists and substantivists. Relativism has been most persistent in the attempts to interpret and understand certain practices and beliefs, particularly WITCHCRAFT, SORCERY and MAGIC.

M.F.;A.G.

Bibl: E. Gellner, *Relativism and the Social Sciences* (Cambridge, 1985); J. Overing (ed.), *Reason and Morality* (London, 1985); I.C. Jarvie, *Rationality and Relativism* London, 1984).

relativity. A system of MECHANICS developed by Einstein early in this century, based on the principle that it must be possible to express the physical laws governing the motion of a body in a manner which is independent of the motion of any observer who may be studying the body. In other words, no absolute FRAME OF

REFERENCE exists. Relativity is divided into two parts:

(1) In the *special* (or *restricted*) *theory* (1905), only frames of reference moving relatively to one another with constant velocity are considered. In addition, the status of a basic postulate is given to the result of the MICHELSON-MORLEY EXPERIMENT, i.e. that the speed of light in a vacuum is the same for all observers (a result inconsistent with NEWTONIAN MECHANICS). The principal deductions are: (*a*) The TRANSFORMATIONS between the position and time of an event as viewed by differently moving observers imply that the separate CONCEPTS of absolute space and absolute time must be replaced by the four-dimensional CONTINUUM of SPACE-TIME. In particular this leads to many surprising predictions such as the CLOCK PARADOX. (*b*) The MASS of a body increases with its speed, becoming infinite at the speed of light (see REST MASS); thus an INFINITE force would be necessary to 'cross the light barrier', and the speed of light is a natural upper limit in mechanics (but see TACHYON). (*c*) Matter is a form of ENERGY (see MASS-ENERGY EQUATION). These deductions have all been abundantly verified for ELEMENTARY PARTICLES moving near the speed of light in experiments with ACCELERATORS and in NUCLEAR REACTORS.

(2) The *general theory* (1916) goes on to consider transformation between *any* frame of reference which may have a mutual ACCELERATION. In addition, the fact that GRAVITATION attracts bodies so that they all fall with the same acceleration (which appears as a coincidence in Newtonian mechanics) is built into the basic structure of the theory. The space-time continuum is not 'flat' (i.e. *Euclidean*) as in the special theory, but 'curved' (i.e. *Riemannian*; for these terms see GEOMETRY). The curvature is produced by matter (see MACH'S PRINCIPLE), and PARTICLES move along 'straight lines', or GEODESICS, in this curved space — analogous to the 'great circles' connecting points on the two-dimensional continuum of points on the earth's surface; thus gravitation is explained as geometry.

On the comparatively small scale of the solar system, general relativity predicts that the motion of planets and light rays will differ slightly from that expected in Newtonian mechanics, and these effects have been confirmed — although not as precisely as the predictions of special relativity. The difference between Newtonian mechanics and general relativity is, however, much greater near BLACK HOLES and on the vast scales contemplated in COSMOLOGY.   M.V.B.

Bibl: H. Bondi, *Relativity and Common Sense* (New York, 1964; London, 1965); F. Close and C. Sutton, *The Particle Explosion* (London, 1987).

relaxation. A general term used in PHYSICS to denote the process whereby a system attains EQUILIBRIUM by neutralizing a disturbing force. For example, when a solid is suddenly stretched, large elastic forces are set up, which gradually relax to zero as CREEP occurs. Electric conduction in metals is a relaxation effect: the ELECTRONS neutralize an applied voltage by adjusting the rate at which they collide with IONS.
                                  M.V.B.

relaxation time. The time taken for RELAXATION to occur. In RHEOLOGY, solids are characterized by long relaxation times (e.g. about a year for glass), fluids by short relaxation times (e.g. one thousandth of a second for water), while viscoelastic materials occupy an intermediate position (e.g. 'potty putty', whose relaxation time is several seconds, bounces elastically under the sudden force of impact, but flows slowly under the more persistent force of GRAVITATION).   M.V.B.

release dance. A movement form which works towards releasing habitual movement conditioning, thereby encouraging an efficient and economic use of the body. In the mid 1930s in the U.S.A., Mabel Ellsworth Todd instigated release work in her study of posture and alignment, movement energy, breathing and relaxation. Dancers, most notably Mary Fulkerson working at Dartington College, Devon, and Joan Skinner and Marsha Paludon, developed release work from this therapeutic approach into a creative form of dance. Fulkerson uses simple early learning patterns, imagery, focus on breathing and qualities of stillness to arrive at an intuitive, KINAESTHETICALLY aware and expressive form of dance which de-emphasizes technique and virtuosity, and provides an experience for everyone who wishes to dance. Release dance is not a definitive school but is dependent on individual teachers and shares with ALEXANDER TECHNIQUE general principles of movement re-education. L.A.

Bibl: M. O'Donnell Fulkerson, *Language of the Axis* (Dartington, 1977).

releaser. (1) In ETHOLOGY, a translation of German *Auslöser*, a term coined by Lorenz in 1935 to denote those structures, movements, sounds, scents, etc. which act as social signals. Releasers in this narrow sense are intricately adapted, as far as is compatible with other requirements, to their dual function of conspicuousness and unambiguity. The majority are intraspecific, i.e. they serve to ensure cooperation between members of one SPECIES; examples are the breeding colours of many animals, the songs of songbirds, and other mating-calls. Other releasers are used in inter-species relationships, such as SYMBIOSIS on the one hand, and repulsion of predators on the other. Releasers are often structures or behaviour patterns that have originally had another function and have evolved their special signalling properties as a secondary ADAPTATION (*ritualization*) to the need for effective communication.

(2) By extension, the word is often misleadingly applied to *any* external STIMULUS complex that 'releases' or elicits behaviour. Thus the silvery colour of many pelagic fish may 'release' hunting behaviour in predatory fish such as the pike, even though the function to which it is adapted is the opposite one of concealment. N.T.

religion. An attitude of awe towards God, or gods, or the supernatural, or the mystery of life, accompanied by beliefs and affecting basic patterns of individual and group behaviour. In Latin *religare* means 'to bind', and religion is traditionally what most deeply binds a society, but the 20th century has been, more than any previous age, an age of SECULARIZATION. Paradoxically, the many challenges to inherited patterns of belief and behaviour in religion have made this a fertile age in THEOLOGY, and an unprecedented dialogue between

the world's great religious traditions has opened both on the scholarly and the popular levels (see COMPARATIVE RELIGION). The opinion is growing that none of these faiths will be able to make an adequate response to the secular challenge without learning from each other as well as from modern thought. One of the reasons for the success of COMMUNISM has been its ability to bind a society with new ideals and hopes when the traditional religion of that society no longer seems sufficiently plausible or vital. Not for nothing was Karl Marx descended from a long line of Jewish rabbis and deeply influenced by the semi-Christian philosopher, Hegel. NATIONALISM has also been a religion in a loose sense. It has also been associated with the revival of traditional religion as the assertion of cherished national values against the influence either of communism (as in eastern Europe) or of the west (as in the Middle East). Certainly religious belief has failed to disappear at the speed expected by many when the modern age began. D.L.E.

religion, philosophy of. The logical study of religious language and ideas. The main stimulus in 20th-century study has come from LINGUISTIC analysis of traditional THEOLOGY and devotion, and from EXISTENTIALIST challenges to religious statements not rooted in experience. See also EMPIRICAL THEOLOGY; PHILOSOPHICAL THEOLOGY. D.L.E.

Bibl: H.D. Lewis, *Teach Yourself Philosophy of Religion* (London, 1968); N. Smart, *The Philosophy of Religion* (London, 1979).

religion, psychology of. The analysis of religious experience (both MYSTICISM and more everyday phenomena), not necessarily admitting or denying its validity but relating it to the rest of PSYCHOLOGY. The main challenge has come from Sigmund Freud's (see FREUDIAN) treatment of all religious belief as an unhealthy illusion. In contrast, the JUNGIAN approach has been to stress the universality and life-interpreting functions of the basic SYMBOLS used in religion, although this need not mean that the symbols correspond with eternal realities. In addition to these great attempts to make sense (or nonsense) of the whole of religion, there have been many less judgemental case-studies, largely with an American background, of the functions of religious beliefs and customs in personal existence.   D.L.È.

Bibl: W. James, *The Varieties of Religious Experience* (London and Cambridge, Mass., 1902); G.W. Allport, *The Individual and his Religion* (London and New York, 1951); R.H. Thouless, *An Introduction to the Psychology of Religion* (London, 3rd ed., 1982).

religion, sociology of. The dispassionate study of the behaviour of groups influenced by religious beliefs. This can involve surveys of the adherents of a religious body in a given area, or may extend to the discussion, inevitably more speculative, of the interaction of social and emotional pressures in the beliefs of a whole society, e.g. the PROTESTANT ETHIC in its relations to the values of CAPITALISM. It may even embrace a general theory of the origins and functions of RELIGION in the life of mankind. The pioneers in these FUNCTIONALIST enquiries were Max Weber (1864-1920), who stressed religion's role as giving 'meaning' to social life; Émile Durkheim (1858-1917), who believed that through religious RITUAL the social group periodically reaffirms its identity and values; and Bronislaw Malinowski (1884-1942), who analysed religion as escape from the stress of powerlessness, e.g. in the face of death. There has been special interest in the role of religious SECTS in protesting against the social order of the day, and in the role of the more 'respectable' churches in maintaining it, as in Ernst Troeltsch, *The Social Teaching of the Christian Churches* (1912). There is disagreement among sociologists about whether, in view of the central role of religion in the past, society can ever be thoroughly secular (see SECULARIZATION).   D.L.E.

Bibl: B. Wilson, *Religion in Secular Society* (London, 1966); P.L. Berger, *The Social Reality of Religion* (London, 1969) and *Religion in Sociological Perspective* (Oxford, 1982).

REM sleep (rapid-eye-movement sleep; also known as *paradoxical sleep*). A normal sleep pattern in which most dreaming takes place. It is characterized by the sudden occurrence of ELECTRO-ENCEPHALOGRAPH arousal, the slowing of physiological functions such as the heart rate, and rapid eye movements. It is a 'deeper' sleep, and harder to arouse the sleeper from, than *slow-wave sleep*, with which it alternates.   H.L.

Bibl: G. Luce and J. Segal, *Sleep* (New York, 1966; London, 1967).

remedial education. Special forms of teaching given to pupils who have failed to reach a level expected of them. Such teaching (to be distinguished from the more fundamental SPECIAL EDUCATION) is short-term and looks for measurable improvement in specific fields such as reading. Much depends on the teacher's ability to restore the pupil's confidence and by encouragement to instil a sense of purpose and, by degrees, achievement.   W.A.C.S.

remission, see under PAROLE.

remittance. Money sent by a migrant working abroad to his or her family back home. It is usually sent at regular intervals and in the early days of migration it represented a substantial part of the wage packet. Expenditure in the new country is minimized to allow a greater amount of money to be remitted. Remittances are the expression of the obligations a migrant worker owes to his or her family. They also symbolize the continuing link between the migrant and the homeland. A migrant who falls behind in payments will not return to the home village and will have brought shame upon the family.

Remittances are spent in different ways by the family: to pay off debts, to buy land and agricultural equipment, to educate children, to pay marriage costs (DOWRY) or to purchase luxury goods. The economic and social STATUS of the family is enhanced by monies received. Whole communities may become dependent upon remittances and governments in the underdeveloped world rely heavily on this cash inflow from abroad. Remittances usually decline over time and ties weaken as a migrant community develops in the new country.   A.G.

Bibl: J.L. Watson (ed.), *Between Two Cultures* (Oxford, 1977).

remote sensing. Surveying the earth's surface from aircraft or SATELLITES using instruments to record different parts of the electromagnetic spectrum. Conventional photographic techniques using the visible light-band have been greatly extended over the last two decades to include the INFRA-RED and RADAR bands of the spectrum. Monitoring of the earth's surface by remote sensing from orbiting satellites has permitted major advances in the understanding of its surface, geological structure, mineral-resource potential, ocean circulation, and atmospheric phenomena. See also NEPHANALYSIS.   P.H.

repertory. (1) The collection of plays in active production at a theatre in one season, each play taking its turn in a constantly changing programme. Long established on the Continent, the system of playing 'in repertory' is still not widespread in Britain: only the National Theatre, the Royal Shakespeare Company, and a handful of regional theatres have adopted the practice. (2) A British theatrical movement in which plays are mounted by a permanent company for limited runs of anything from one to four weeks (the very opposite of Continental repertory). Initiated by Miss A.E.F. Horniman at the Gaiety Theatre, Manchester, in 1907, the movement has provided an excellent training-ground for actors and directors. With help from the Arts Council, the British repertory movement achieved a flourishing condition, comprising some 60 subventioned theatres scattered throughout the land, but lost some of its vigour in the years of declining public subsidies after 1979.

In the U.S.A. the nearest equivalent is *summer stock* (short seasons of interesting plays taking place outside the big cities and often graced by visiting stars), but in New York successive attempts to set up a permanent company have come to grief. Only OFF-BROADWAY's Negro Theater Ensemble is currently permanent and flourishing.   M.BI.

Bibl: G. Rowell and A. Jackson, *The Repertory Movement* (Cambridge, 1984).

replacement theory. In MANAGEMENT and ECONOMICS, a theory that provides a method for deciding upon the most economic strategy for replacing equipment. The productivity of equipment may decline over time; there may be more productive alternative types of equipment; and the present equipment may fail or require maintenance. The theory compares the discounted (see DISCOUNTED CASH FLOW; DISCOUNTING) costs incurred under different strategies — it is possible to allow for RISK by discounting expected costs. In making this decision, the relevant variables to consider are the lifetimes of the equipment, initial and operating costs, depreciation, the productivity of different types of equipment and the likelihood of equipment failures.   J.P.

representationism. In PHILOSOPHY, the theory that our knowledge of material objects is gained through our direct PERCEPTION of the private impressions or SENSE-DATA which they cause us to experience and which, in some way or other, they resemble. In Descartes and Locke the resemblance is held to extend only to the 'primary qualities', i.e. the mathematically measurable, spatial qualities with which PHYSICS is principally concerned. On this view the secondary qualities of colour, texture, sound, smell, and taste are subjective, at least to the extent that there is no similar property in the material objects that cause us to perceive them. The crucial difficulty for the theory is the justification of the thesis that there is a resemblance between objects and our impressions of them, when the first term of the relation is not accessible for purposes of comparison with its perceived effects. The aim of representationism is to show that the sense-datum theory does not imply SOLIPSISM.   A.Q.

representations. It is no new idea that art, literature and even the human mind do not mirror reality but represent it according to unconscious or semi-conscious conventions, but it is relatively recently that such representations have become a focus for interdisciplinary research, involving literary critics, social anthropologists, art historians and intellectual historians, leading in 1983 to the foundation of a special journal. The phrase 'collective representations' was a favourite of the French sociologist Emile Durkheim and corresponded to what some historians now call mentalities (see HISTORY OF MENTALITIES). In early 20th-century Germany, a concern with views or representations of the world was central to the SOCIOLOGY OF KNOWLEDGE. More recently, the study of representations has been encouraged and influenced by STRUCTURALISM, with its presentation of cultures as systems of signs. The cultural codes which underlie representations were an abiding concern of the late Michel Foucault, who suggested that these deep structures were a proper subject for 'intellectual archaeology' rather than history.　　　　P.B.

Bibl: *Representations* (Berkeley, 1983-).

repression. In psychoanalytic theory (see PSYCHOANALYSIS), a FREUDIAN term which is used largely to refer to two distinct processes. (1) *Primal repression.* An infant or child defends itself against the threat of excessive tension by attaching energy to some object or activity — which energy functions antithetically, or counter, to the threatening tension. (2) *Actual repression,* or *repression proper.* When an adult is threatened by the excessive tension that might arise if some UNCONSCIOUS wish, or impulse, moved into CONSCIOUSNESS, this danger is signalled by ANXIETY, and is met in various ways, e.g. by withdrawing energy from the idea of the threatening impulse, so that it cannot move into consciousness but remains unconscious. Repression proper is a function of the EGO, and is unconscious in its operation. See also DEFENCE MECHANISM.

　　　　B.A.F.

repressor. In GENETICS, a substance, produced by a *repressor gene*, which inactivates another GENE or group of genes (OPERON).　　　　J.M.S.

reproduction rate. Measures which indicate the extent to which a population is reproducing itself. The gross reproduction rate is the number of daughters a woman would have if throughout her lifetime she were subjected to current age-specific fertility rates; the more revealing net reproduction rate is the number of daughters she would have if subjected to CURRENT FERTILITY and MORTALITY (with a value of 1.0 indicating exact replacement).

　　　　E.G.;D.S.

Bibl: H.S. Shryock *el al., The Methods and Materials of Demography* (condensed edition) (New York and London, 1976).

Rerum Novarum. An ENCYCLICAL issued by Pope Leo XIII in 1891, applying some of the key ideas of Roman Catholic (see CATHOLICISM) MORAL THEOLOGY to the conditions created by the INDUSTRIAL REVOLUTION. The Pope taught that workers should be paid a 'just wage', i.e. enough to support a family in frugal comfort, and should be allowed to combine, e.g. in TRADE UNIONS, to achieve this.　　　　D.L.E.

research and development (R&D). Basic research is the pursuit of scientific knowledge that may or may not have commercial uses. Applied research is the application of scientific knowledge to the discovery of or modification of INVENTIONS with the direct intention of later commercial gain. Development is the process in which inventions are transformed into new production techniques and products for commercial gain. The economic benefits of research and development are more ECONOMICALLY EFFICIENT production and new goods and services that satisfy a wider range of wants. It is often suggested that these economic benefits are large, relative to the costs, and there is insufficient INVESTMENT in research and development. Research and development can be costly and subject to UNCERTAINTY, and successful projects may be imitated. These effects may deter private firms from investing in research and development (see TECHNICAL PROGRESS). Basic research may suffer most from these effects as the commercial opportunities and gains are more uncertain and most of the benefits accrue to other firms through an increase in the stock of scientific knowledge. As the knowledge from successful research and development has the attributes of a PUBLIC GOOD, it is often suggested that the state should undertake and finance such activities on behalf of society. A problem with this suggestion is that it requires the state to be capable of making decisions about which projects should be funded.   J.P.

Bibl: P. Stoneman, *The Economics of Technological Change* (Oxford, 1983).

resistentialism. A fictitious philosophical school invented by Paul Jennings in 1948. Foreshadowed by the 19th-century thinkers Freidegg and Heidansiecker, the school has as its leading luminary Pierre-Marie Ventre. Ventre 'reversed the traditional mechanism of philosophy, which until then had been the consensus of what men think about Things: Resistentialism is concerned with what Things think about men. Briefly, they are Against us (*Les choses sont contre nous*).' Resistentialism crystallizes definitively ideas which have long been in circulation: one's shoelaces are always impossibly tangled into knots when one is in a particular hurry, the better the carpet the more often the toast falls butter-side-down, and so on. Harassment of the animate by the inanimate is seen not as the just punishment for hubris, but as an inevitable consequence of the animate/inanimate dichotomy. The absence of any physical basis for resistentialism is more than counterbalanced by its appeal as a psychological theory.   R.SI.

resistivity surveying. In ARCHAEOLOGY, a technique for discovering buried features by measuring differences in the resistance of the subsoil. It is based on the principle that man-made disturbances such as a buried ditch or wall retain water in differing degrees as compared with the undisturbed soil. Since resistance depends on water content, where an area containing buried features is surveyed with a resistivity meter disturbances will appear as anomalous readings. Recent improvements include continuous recording on punched tape and COMPUTER plotting.
                                                B.C.

resonance. The sympathetic vibrations of a system subjected to an oscillating force whose frequency is close to one of the 'natural frequencies' of the system. Examples: (1) a child on a swing raises it by 'pumping' ENERGY into it at its natural frequency; (2) the tuning of radio receivers is based on 'resonant circuits' which oscillate only when stimulated by electromagnetic RADIATION of the correct RADIO FREQUENCY; (3) a PHOTON can be absorbed by an ATOM only if its frequency corresponds to an energy equal to the difference between two ENERGY LEVELS of the atom. See also MAGNETIC RESONANCE.   M.V.B.

resource centres. Storage centres, in schools, for educational materials such as books, press cuttings, film strips, charts, maps, models, periodicals, and children's work. In PROJECT WORK these materials are available to pupils as well as teachers. Resource centres are an attempt to facilitate efficient and economic use of costly apparatus and materials. They are frequently found in conjunction with TEAM TEACHING and similar methods. While including books, they represent a more comprehensive and flexible provision of educational materials than the books in a library.   W.A.C.S.

Bibl: N.W. Beswick, *School Resource Centres* (London, 1972).

resources, natural. That part of the material components of the ENVIRONMENT, including both MASS and ENERGY, physical and biological, that can be used by man. As such, resources are bounded by concepts of UTILITY, and resource estimates change with changing technological and socio-economic conditions. A distinction is conventionally drawn between *non-renewable resources* (sometimes termed *stock resources*), like coal and oil deposits, and *renewable resource* (sometimes termed *flow resources*), like tidal power. See also CONSERVATION.   P.H.

respiratory (pulmonary) disease. Respiratory disease constitutes the commonest cause of morbidity in Great Britain. *Causes.* (1) Infection by bacteria, viruses, etc. produces inflammation of the respiratory tract: tracheitis, bronchitis, pneumonia, pleurisy, with or without effusion (fluid). Chronic bronchitis/emphysema is a serious cause of chronic respiratory disability. Tuberculosis (consumption, phthisis), once a fatal plague, but now curable, still ravages the less developed areas of the world. (2) ALLERGY, e.g. asthma. (3) Circulatory, e.g. thrombo-embolism (blood clot). (4) Tumours, especially malignant, such as carcinoma of the bronchus (lung

CANCER) which is responsible for more than 30,000 deaths per annum in England and Wales. (5) Traumatic and mechanical effects, which may result in collapse of the lung from pneumothorax (air in the pleural space). (6) Environmental and occupational factors: atmospheric POLLUTION and exposure to noxious dusts, e.g. coal-miner's pneumoconiosis (dust disease of the lungs) and asbestosis. At the personal level, cigarette smoking is the greatest single cause of chronic bronchitis and lung cancer. (See ENVIRONMENTAL CAUSES OF DISEASE; OCCUPATIONAL HEALTH).

Diagnosis. (1) The commonest symptoms are cough, sputum, blood spitting (haemoptysis), breathlessness (dyspnoea) and chest pain. Clinical examination includes listening (auscultation) to the chest by means of a stethoscope. (2) Imaging by means of RADIOLOGY (chest X-RAY), including screening the lung movements (fluoroscopy) and X-rays taken in one plane (tomography); also by newer scanning techniques such as computer assisted tomography (CAT) and NUCLEAR MAGNETIC RESONANCE (NMR). (3) Laboratory investigations include BACTERIOLOGICAL and VIROLOGICAL examination of sputum and other secretions; also HAEMATOLOGICAL and immunulogical blood tests. (4) Respiratory function tests, which measure various parameters of respiration such as vital capacity, lung volume, force of expiration, alveolar gas diffusion, etc. (5) Bronchoscopy consists of the per-oral passage of an illuminated tubular instrument into the bronchi. The more flexible fibre-bronchoscope facilitates this examination. (6) BIOPSY of TISSUE obtained via the bronchoscope or by trans-thoracic needling of the lung may provide microscopic confirmation of the diagnosis.

Treatment. (1) ANTIBIOTICS, appropriate to the infection. (2) Broncho-dilator drugs, to relive broncho-constriction, as in asthma. (3) Oxygen administration. (4) PHYSIOTHERAPY, to assist expectoration of sputum. (5) SURGERY when indicated, e.g. to drain a lung abscess or an empyema (pus in the pleura). The thorax may be opened (thoracotomy) to remove a diseased lobe of a lung (lobectomy) or an entire lung (pneumonectomy). (6) CHEMOTHERAPY and RADIOTHERAPY, in the case of malignant disease not amenable to sur-

gery. (7) Artificial ventilation, when the patient's breathing cannot maintain adequate respiration. A.SA.

Bibl: J. Crofton and A. Douglas, *Respiratory Diseases* (Oxford, 3rd ed., 1981).

respondent conditioning, see CLASSICAL CONDITIONING.

rest mass. The MASS of a system as measured by an observer at rest relative to it. According to the special theory of RELATIVITY, the mass of a body moving relative to the observer is greater; the difference is appreciable only near the speed of light. M.V.B.

restriction enzyme. An essential tool of GENETIC ENGINEERING, the natural function of restriction ENZYMES is to protect the bacteria that make them from any invading foreign DNA (see NUCLEIC ACID). Each restriction enzyme recognizes and cuts particular permutations of NUCLEOTIDES in DNA. P.N.

restrictive practices. Industrial and commercial agreements or arrangements which operate in restraint of free COMPETITION even though they may be valid under the ordinary law of tort or contract. In the U.K. since the enactment in 1948 of the MONOPOLIES and Restrictive Practices Act, they have been subjected to various forms of legal control, notably the Restrictive Practices Act of 1956, which created a new judicial tribunal, the Restrictive Practices Court, to investigate agreements or arrangements designed to restrict in various ways the supply of goods and to declare them void if they are found to operate contrary to the PUBLIC INTEREST. Examples of such restrictive practices are agreements regulating the prices to be charged for goods supplied to customers, or the quantities to be supplied, or the conditions of supply. H.L.A.H.

Bibl: R.B. Stevens and B.S. Yamey, *The Restrictive Practices Court* (London, 1965).

Resurgence of Islam, see under ISLAM.

retaliation, massive, see MASSIVE RETALIATION.

retardation, mental, see MENTAL RETAR-
DATION.

retro-rocket. A small ROCKET whose
thrust is directed forwards to slow down a
SPACE PROBE, e.g. when making a soft
landing on the moon or planets.   M.V.B.

returns to scale. The relation between a
proportionate increase in the use of all the
inputs in production of a product and the
proportionate increase in output. Returns
to scale are increasing/constant/
decreasing if the proportionate increase in
output is greater than/equal to/less than
the proportionate increase in output. It is
usually assumed that increasing returns to
scale exist over a certain range of output
(see ECONOMIES OF SCALE). At higher levels of output the difficulty of managing
large organizations may give rise to decreasing returns to scale. At an abstract
level, the exact doubling of inputs must
give rise to twice as much output. Thus,
the returns to scale considered in practice
implicitly refer to situations where it is not
possible to increase all inputs exactly.
                                                    J.P.
    Bibl: J. Craven, *Introduction to Eco-
nomics* (Oxford, 1984).

reverse transcription. The transcription of
RNA into DNA (see NUCLEIC ACID).

revisionism.
    (1) A CONCEPT denoting a critical re-
interpretation of MARXIST theories and/or
a doctrinal deviation (see DEVIATIONISM)
from the official ideological position (see
IDEOLOGY) among COMMUNIST factions,
parties, and states. In Communist polemics, the relationship of revisionism to
orthodoxy appears to be a secular counterpart to that of HERESY to religious DOGMA.
The term dates from the 1890s, when the
German Social Democrat (see SOCIAL
DEMOCRACY) Eduard Bernstein attempted
to modify Marxist ideas in the light of
historical experience. In the Communist
movement it became a term of opprobrium for any attempt to revise official
interpretations of the Marxist canon. It
has been invoked particularly since the
emergence of Communist POLYCENTRISM.
After the 20th Congress of the Soviet
Communist Party (1956), which under-

mined Party infallibility by admitting
Stalin's errors, revisionism became a label
frequently used to denounce the ideas,
policies, and general ideological positions
of the opposing Communist parties, Soviet
and Chinese, Yugoslav and Albanian, all
of which claimed to be orthodox. Their
own doctrinal innovations they described
not as revisions but as 'a creative development of MARXISM-LENINISM' or its application to local conditions.
    Bibl: L. Labedz (ed.), *Revisionism*
(London, 1962).
    (2) A term applied before World War II
to the claims of such countries as Germany, Hungary, and Bulgaria to the territories which they had lost in World War
I.   L.L.
    (3) A tendency in American HISTORI-
OGRAPHY in the 1960s and early 1970s to
rewrite the history of the COLD WAR and
shift the blame for it onto the U.S.A. This
trend was strongly reinforced by the faults
and failure of U.S. policy in VIETNAM,
which revisionist historians argued were
not a divergence from but a consequence
and illustration of an IMPERIALIST foreign
and economic policy followed by the
U.S.A. from the end of World War II. The
revisionists' attack on the orthodox version of U.S. post-war policy represented
the second stage in the historiography of
the Cold War. This in turn has been succeeded by a third stage which offers a
more balanced appreciation of the complexities of the situation in the 1940s and
represents a synthesis of the first two.
                                                  A.L.C.B.
    Bibl: R.J. Maddox (ed.), *The New Left
and the Origins of the Cold War* (London
and Princeton, 1973); R. Aron, tr. F. Jellinek, *The Imperial Republic: the United
States and the World, 1945-1973* (Englewood Cliffs, N.J., 1974; London, 1975).

revolution. A term (meaning rotation or
turn) which was applied by Copernicus to
the movement of celestial bodies in his
treatise *De Revolutionibus Orbium Coe-
lestium* and which in the 17th century,
after the astronomical revolution, began to
be applied metaphorically to political and
social upheavals. From this it has developed to mean any fundamental or complete change in the mode of production
(the INDUSTRIAL REVOLUTION, technologi-

cal revolution, etc.), in the political and social system (the French Revolution, and Russian Revolution, etc.), or in some aspect of social, intellectual, or cultural life (SCIENTIFIC REVOLUTION, GREAT PROLETARIAN CULTURAL REVOLUTION, etc.). But it is sudden radical changes in the political, social, and economic structure of society that form the subject of revolutionary theories and of the theories of revolution. These are concerned not with mere changes of rulers ('palace revolutions'), but with changes of ruling CLASSES, of the methods of rule, and of social INSTITUTIONS, with the revolutionary passions and actions which lead to these changes, and with their consequences.

Revolutionary theories, like MARXISM or LENINISM, not only advocate revolution; they also try to explain how it comes about. The classical Marxist approach looked for the 'causes' of revolution in the development of 'the forces of production' which, by clashing with 'the conditions of production', engender industrial class-struggle to the point of explosion. Leninism shifted the emphasis from 'objective' to 'subjective' conditions for revolution, stressing the role of the revolutionary organization, the Party.

Most contemporary sociological theories (see SOCIOLOGY) focus on the need for MODERNIZATION as a 'root' cause of modern revolutions; they point to the confluence of the aspirations of the 'advanced intelligentsia' (see INTELLECTUALS) and the miseries of the 'backward peasantry'. However, the theories of revolution concentrating on UNDERDEVELOPMENT fail to explain the absence of revolutionary developments in some backward countries and their presence in some industrial ones. On the other hand, the experience of the 20th century points to the abandonment of Marxian *Gesetzmässigheit,* i.e. of the belief that the stages of social development leading to revolution conform to a system or regular (and predictable) 'laws'. Such a belief cannot survive 'revolutions of underdevelopment' and the decoupling by the NEW LEFT theoreticians of the 'subjective' from the 'objective' conditions for revolution, a separation that goes beyond Leninist VOLUNTARISM (as in the early theories of Régis Debray) and renders the old Marxist debate about the relation between BOURGEOIS and SOCIALIST revolutions obsolete.

Some contemporary analysts of the revolutionary phenomenon go beyond the relation between revolution and ECONOMIC DEVELOPMENT (Marx), underdevelopment (Lenin), and 'over-development' (the New Left), or even the question of 'modernization'. Their view of revolution transcends purely economic causation or even sociological DETERMINISM. They emphasize the recurrence of UTOPIAN and MILLENARIAN motives in history, and look for chiliastic elements in contemporary secular movements (Norman Cohn, Eric Voegelin). In this perspective, the history of the revolutionary idea may throw more light on the phenomenon of revolution than do either the existing revolutionary theories or the existing theories of revolution. See also PERMANENT REVOLUTION. L.L.

Bibl: E. Voegelin, *From Enlightenment to Revolution* (Durham, N.C., 1975); M.J. Lasky, *Utopia and Revolution* (London and Chicago, 1977); T.Skocpol, *States and Social Revolutions* (Cambridge, 1979).

revolutionary science. Classic PHILOSOPHIES OF SCIENCE, such as EMPIRICISM and POSITIVISM, argued that science evolved. Facts steadily accumulated, and broader, more comprehensive theories emerged automatically out of them. In some way, science approximated nearer towards the truth. T.S. Kuhn's *The Structure of Scientific Revolutions* (1970) aimed to scotch this view. For Kuhn, science operates for long stretches without any fundamental change. This is normal science, within a PARADIGM — a period in which the implications of existing theories are worked out in detail. Kuhn speaks of 'puzzle solving'. Very occasionally, however, science is revolutionized. Within the existing paradigm, ANOMALIES increasingly build up, and eventually a new theory is required, which can incorporate those anomalies. With the catastrophic speed of a REVOLUTION, the new paradigm ousts the old. Kuhn regards this as a revolutionary act, because it is, in his view, an irrational moment in science. The new theory establishes itself not because of any objective, rational superiority but through a leap of faith by the scientific community. The new science does not augment the old;

it destroys and buries it. For this reason, Kuhn's critics have accused him of undermining belief in the progressiveness of science, and of retreating into a kind of RELATIVISM. These are charges which Kuhn has, not completely convincingly, denied. In historic reality the notion of scientific revolutions is quite ambiguous. The period between Copernicus and Newton is often termed 'The Scientific Revolution', but the time-span involved there, over 150 years, makes the process sound more like EVOLUTION than revolution.

R.P.

Bibl: T.S. Kuhn, *The Structure of Scientific Revolutions* (London, 2nd ed., 1970).

revolving stage. A turntable stage whose earliest recorded use was in Roman theatres in the 1st century B.C. The first such device installed as permanent equipment was used in Japanese Kabuki theatre around 1760; its first recorded use in modern Europe was at Munich in 1896. Difficulties in fitting three or more sets into one circle led to the invention of sliding stages, rising and falling stages. The most elaborate of these were installed in cabaret theatres such as the Pigalle in Paris in the 1920s. But the basic turntable stage is now a standard feature of most large theatres, greatly facilitating changes of scene.

M.BI.

Bibl: R. and H. Leacroft, *Theatre and Playhouse* (London, 1984).

rewrite rules, see GENERATIVE GRAMMAR.

Reynolds wedge action. A HYDRODYNAMIC effect which is the operating principle of lubricating devices such as ball and roller bearings. The frictional resistance to relative motion of two adjacent metal surfaces is greatly diminished if the surfaces can be inclined at a slight angle to one another, because the force necessary to squeeze the lubricant (oil or — for very rapidly moving surfaces — air) through the wedge-shaped space between them prevents the surfaces from coming into contact and thus possibly 'seizing up'.

M.V.B.

Rezeptionsästhetik, see under RECEPTION THEORY.

RF, see RADIO FREQUENCY.

rheology. The branch of NEWTONIAN MECHANICS dealing with the deformation and flow of materials which are neither solid nor completely liquid, such as non drip paint, bread dough, modelling clay, glacier ice, and lead on roofs. See also RELAXATION; RELAXATION TIME.

M.V.B.

rhesus factor, see under IMMUNITY.

rheumatology. The sub-specialty of internal medicine devoted to the study and management of disorders of the musculoskeletal system. Rheumatic disorders, such as soft tissue rheumatism, osteoarthritis, rheumatoid arthritis and ankylosing spondylitis, are the most common clinical problems within the specialty but the field is much wider, comprising other inflammatory and immunological disorders which affect muscles and joints, e.g. the so-called 'connective tissue' disorders such as systemic lupus erythematosus, scleroderma, polymyositis, dermatomyositis, overlap connective TISSUE disease and vasculitic syndromes such as polyarteritis nodosa, polymyalgia rheumatica and giant cell arteritis. Many systemic diseases produce locomotor symptoms and signs and so involve the rheumatologist. Gout, a disorder of uric acid METABOLISM, is perhaps the best known of these but other metabolic disorders, infections (both bacterial and viral) and inflammatory disorders, such as sarcoidosis, can cause arthritic disease. The causes of the major rheumatological disorders are not known but the pathology of rheumatoid arthritis and the connective tissue disorders is characterized by inflammatory reaction and disordered immune response, and in ankylosing spondylitis GENETIC factors play an important role. Treatment of rheumatological disorders centres round relieving the symptoms of inflammation with anti-inflammatory and ANALGESIC drugs, suppressing the disordered immune response and minimizing physical disability with the aid of paramedical specialists such as PHYSIOTHERAPISTS and OCCUPATIONAL THERAPISTS.

D.D.; D.L.W.

rhythm and blues. Another of the labels applied to black music which the form's determined vitality and variety has dislodged. As a genre, rhythm and blues in the late 1920s and 1930s came to stand for BLUES-based music that was not JAZZ — simpler harmonically and rhythmically, more ruggedly emotional, performed by soloists or duos instead of bands. Recordings of the style were known as 'race records', turned out specifically for black audiences. In fact rhythm and blues was merely a catch-all for the current evolutionary stage of the blues, whether 'city' or 'country', played or sung. By the 1940s 'r&b', as it came to be known, had developed a more concerted version, reflecting the influence of the BIG BANDS of the SWING era; it crossed brass and saxes with its own traditional accessibility to produce a heady mixture of driving, good-time music that defied bodies not to dance. The most widely-known of these infectious 'jump bands' was probably Louis Jordan's Tympany Five, though other groups, like that of Junior Parker, had strong local followings. As this strain became identified with r&b, the old guitar and vocal form of the music followed its own course. Less commercial than the jump bands, it claimed a different audience, and, partly as a result of the rise of rock and roll, achieved a vogue of its own. ROCK performers of the 1950s, like Bill Haley, showed the influence of the jump bands, but gutty, passionate performers like Muddy Waters and B.B. King inspired 1960s groups like The Rolling Stones. Despite some surface similarities, partisans of blues (as the form came simply to be called to distinguish it from commercialized r&b), insisted on the superior authenticity and integrity of their music over rock. But in the late 1960s and 1970s it began to be supplanted by a new metamorphosis of black music, SOUL.   GE.S.

ribbon development. In GEOGRAPHY, the extension of a town or village in the cheapest possible way, i.e. next to its main services and thus alongside its main roads. Many industrial towns of Britain, e.g. those of south-west Lancashire, were linked in this way. Post-war development has tended to infill such areas so that building has taken place between the rib-

bons. In contrast, the Rhondda valley mining villages in Wales, confined from the start by topography, the position of coal seams, and the practices of the coal-mining industry, are linear in shape but not, strictly speaking, examples of ribbon development since their shape was unavoidable.   M.L.

ribosome, see under NUCLEIC ACID.

rich clusters, see under GALAXY CLUSTERS.

Right, the. Label applied to a range of political views at the other end of the political spectrum from the LEFT (q.v. for the origin of both terms), and to those holding such views. Originally, the Right comprised those who defended the monarchical INSTITUTIONS attacked by the French Revolution. During the 19th century the term was associated with authority, patriotism, tradition, strong government, property, the Church, and the Army. In France it remained monarchist even after the establishment of the Third Republic, but it was everywhere evolving from its aristocratic affinities towards the protection of CAPITALIST interests against the threat of SOCIALISM. It was now opposed not only to EGALITARIANISM, but also to State intervention in the economy, which the ultra-right French Legitimists and Bismarck had strongly favoured.

But the new Right was concerned not just with economic policies. It became increasingly influenced by the attitudes and ideas of romantic NATIONALISM. After World War I a new radical (see RADICALISM) Right emerged which was sharply different from the traditional conservative Right (see CONSERVATISM). It was no longer preoccupied simply with the defence of the established order, but often hostile to the interests of the upper classes; its most extreme form was Hitler's National Socialism (see NAZISM). In line with its mystique of the nation and the State, it was hostile to economic LAISSEZ FAIRE and in favour of strong economic controls for its TOTALITARIAN and military aims.   L.L.

(2) After World War II the Right remained diverse in values and configuration; in many democratic states its domi-

nant factions accepted the KEYNESIAN approach to economics and the principles of the WELFARE STATE. By the 1970s the perceived inadequacy of such approaches in the face of mounting economic difficulties and social problems prompted a resurgence encapsulated by the term NEW RIGHT. It is a phrase denoting a number of complex and loosely connected intellectual currents and political tendencies, ranging from elements of LIBERTARIANISM to the AUTHORITARIANISM of its French variant. Components of New Right thought have shaped the character of REAGANISM and THATCHERISM. Those include economic theories associated particularly with Friedman and Hayek, often described as NEO-LIBERAL, which exalt capitalism not only for its productive capacity, but claim it to be uniquely conducive to the maintenance of political and social liberty. The New Right thus opposes a strongly interventionist or ownership role for the State in the economy. Its social philosophy is ambiguous; its stress on individual freedom contradicts conventional conservatism's preference for hierarchy and obligation, but shares its concern for the maintenance of law and order.   S.R.

Bibl: N. Bosanquet, *After the New Right* (London, 1983).

ring modulator. An ELECTRONIC MUSIC device which takes in two sounds and adds and subtracts the frequencies of their harmonics. This results in complex sounds that bear strange relationships to the originals: e.g. if one of the sounds is rising in pitch the resultant sound rises (sum) and also falls (subtraction). Frequently a live sound (e.g. piano) and a simple electronic sound are combined in this way, thus producing instantaneous complex sounds usually of a bell-like nature (as in Stockhausen's 'Mantra').   B.CO.

Rio Treaty. The Inter-American Treaty of Reciprocal Assistance signed by representatives of 18 Latin American countries and of the U.S.A. at Rio de Janeiro in August 1947, as a mutual defence alliance against armed aggression and other situations threatening the peace of the American continents. Regular meetings of foreign ministers of the signatories provide a consultative organ. The Treaty became a model for other regional security pacts such as NATO and SEATO.   D.C.W.

Bibl: G.C. Smith, *The Inter-American System* (London and New York, 1966).

RISC (Reduced-Instruction-Set Computer). A class of COMPUTER processor designs in which the size of the instruction repertoire is reduced to a minimum. This means that actions which on some PROCESSORS could be done in one instruction require a whole sequence; on the other hand, the greater simplicity means that the processor can be made to run much faster.   J.E.S.

rishon, see under ELEMENTARY PARTICLES.

risk. The circumstances where all the different possible outcomes of a course of action are known and the probabilities of the outcomes occurring are known (see PROBABILITY THEORY). These probabilities are either objective, in that there would be widespread agreement about their values, or subjective, in that they reflect the perceptions of an individual and may not be held by other observers. See UNCERTAINTY, EXPECTED UTILITY, SCENARIO ANALYSIS and FORECASTING.   J.P.

Bibl: J. Hey, *Uncertainty in Economics* (Oxford, 1979).

risk analysis. An application of DECISION THEORY whereby SIMULATION, introspection and various techniques are used to form *probability density functions* (see DISTRIBUTION; FUNCTION) of the different possible outcomes corresponding to the alternate courses of action. It has been extended to cover decisions which have to be made sequentially. This version of the procedure uses a *decision tree* and is known as *stochastic decision tree analysis*. Risk analysis is used in ECONOMICS, MANAGEMENT and ENGINEERING. See also EXPECTED UTILITY; RISK; UNCERTAINTY.

H.TH.; J.P.

Bibl: H. Raiffa, *Decision Analysis* (London, 1968).

rite de passage. Rites of transition, a term developed by Van Gennep (*The Rites of Passage*, 1909; Eng. trans., 1960) to describe the movement of an individual from one state to another. The transition is marked by RITUAL and involves IN-ITIATION. In this way society recognizes and legitimates change. Examples of *rite de passage* include MARRIAGE, circumcision, coronation and mortuary rituals. Van Gennep identified three elements in *rite de passage*. (1) Rite of separation, temporary removal of an individual from society while preparing for the change. (2) Rite of marginality/*liminality*, moment of transition, initiation. (3) Rite of aggregation, new STATUS affirmed and the individual is reincorporated into society. The middle element or liminal phase is potentially dangerous as the individual is between social ROLES. In this phase the initiate is subject to restrictions and TABOO.

A.G.

Bibl: M. Bloch and J.P. Parry (eds.), *Death and the Regeneration of Life* (Cambridge, 1982); J.S. La Fontaine, *Initiation: Ritual Drama and Secret Knowledge Across the World* (Harmondsworth, 1985).

ritual. Formalized behaviour or activity in accordance with rules and procedures specified by society. The 'peculiarity' or 'alerting' quality of ritual sets it apart from other social activity. Ritual may be individual and private (i.e. a sorcerer casting his spells) or social and public (i.e. SACRIFICE). The clarity of the boundary between ritual and non-ritual varies. Certain rituals are very clearly marked off from the rest of social activity. Ritual may have an elaborate internal structure (beginning, middle and an end) and this may be seen in RITES DE PASSAGE: circumcision, mortuary rites and so on.

Ritual has both instrumental and expressive aspects: it is an activity (it does something) and it is a statement (it says something). Anthropologists working in the FUNCTIONALIST tradition (Malinowski, Radcliffe Brown, Gluckman) have attempted to understand the *function* of ritual by situating it within a specific social context. Others have focused upon the content of ritual and pursued its meaning rather than its function. These anthropologists are usually subdivided into 'intellectualists' and 'symbolists'. An intellectualist approach (ritual concerned with providing an explanation of the world) may be seen in the work of Stephen Hugh-Jones (*The Palm and the Pleiades*, 1979). The symbolists have highlighted the expressive or emotional content of ritual. V.W. Turner's work (*The Forest of Symbols*, 1967) has been important in establishing this approach.

A.G.

Bibl: G. Lewis, *Day of Shining Red* (Cambridge, 1980); M. Bloch, *From Blessing to Violence* (Cambridge, 1986).

ritualization, see under RELEASER.

RNA (ribonucleic acid), see under NUCLEIC ACID.

robot. A term originally introduced to describe a machine built to resemble a human in appearance and functioning. Later the use of the word was extended to any device which performed a function previously only thought to be possible by a human, e.g. traffic lights which do the job of a policeman on point duty, but which do not resemble a policeman in appearance or action. As more and more mechanical devices were used in conjunction with automatic control systems to replace human operators in factories concerned with mass production or in situations hazardous to humans, the study of these machines became a subject in its own right, known as robotics. This embraces the subjects of automatic control, COMPUTERS and MICROPROCESSORS, as well as many facets of electrical, ELECTRONIC, mechanical and chemical ENGINEERING.

E.R.L.

rock music. The collective name for a diverse range of popular musics coming to prominence in the 1960s with its roots in rock and roll and heavily influenced by SOUL music. Rock music normally uses amplification, electronic instruments (in particular the electric guitar) and drums, and its forms range widely from simple song structures (often BLUES) to long and complex improvisatory forms. The term rock music is often used interchangeably with POP music but the former is generally held to be less commercially oriented, more diverse and eclectic and aimed at a more knowledgeable audience. Many subcategories exist within rock music including *progressive rock* (more experimental, and less song-dominated), *heavy metal* (using extreme volumes, insistent rhythms and giving prominence to electric guitars and drums), *glam rock* (with emphasis on the appearance, make-up and clothes of the performers) etc. Rock music is also frequently linked to other musical types as in jazz rock (see FUSION) and *folk rock*. Rock music has been crucial to the development of ELECTRONIC MUSIC and recording techniques and its links with YOUTH CULTURE, style and politics are also extremely important (see PUNK).   B.CO.

Bibl: S. Frith, The Sociology of Rock (London, 1978).

rock steady, see under REGGAE.

rocket. A propulsion device for SPACE PROBES, MISSILES, etc., in which fuel is burned and the combustion gases emitted backwards at high speed. The *total* MOMENTUM of rocket + fuel does not change (see CONSERVATION LAWS), so that the increasing backward momentum of all the hot gases can only be produced by a compensating forward ACCELERATION of the rocket. Unlike the JET ENGINE, therefore, the rocket does not require an atmosphere; indeed, air friction slows it down.
                                        M.V.B.

Rogers plan, see under DEEP STRIKE.

role; role theory. In SOCIAL PSYCHOLOGY, 'role' connotes the bundle of formal and predictable attributes associated with a particular social position, as distinct from the personal characteristics of the individual who occupies that position. The waiter or the doctor, for instance, is called upon to perform a professional role expected of him by his public audience which may be quite at variance with his own inclinations of the moment. Roles as official and publicly recognized as these are frequently supported by uniforms and strict linguistic codes. But most social 'roles' are so inexactly defined that they are barely more than intuitively felt guidelines to the correct behaviour for a particular social situation.

The earliest systematic uses of the term were in G.H. Mead's social psychology (see SYMBOLIC INTERACTION), which emphasized the importance of 'taking the role of the other', and the role-playing therapy invented by J.L. Moreno (see SOCIOMETRY; PSYCHODRAMA). Later it became current in social ANTHROPOLOGY, where it lent itself especially to describing the rights and duties associated with positions in KINSHIP systems. Sociological theorists often adopted it, together with STATUS, as a suitable term for the basic elements from which SOCIAL STRUCTURES are built up, and various attempts have been made to use it as an interdisciplinary CONCEPT, bridging the gap between, on the one hand, the treatment of social systems and INSTITUTIONS by sociologists and political scientists and, on the other hand, the experimental study of personality, motivation, and group processes by social psychologists. The STRUCTURAL-FUNCTIONAL and NORMATIVE emphasis given to 'role' in PARSONIAN theory was not accepted by all students of standardized behaviour, and prompted a rediscovery of the original dramaturgical metaphor, which had suggested a degree of conscious theatre in EVERYDAY social life, and which had been largely forgotten when the term became part of a technical vocabulary.

It was in this sense that Erving Goffman expanded the term in *The Presentation of Self in Everyday Life* (1956), where he elaborated two key concepts: *role distance* (the extent to which the individual may free himself from the demands of mere adequacy in a given role, and exploit the possibilities of play and improvisation above and beyond the necessities of 'correct' behaviour); and *role conflict* (what happens when the individual finds himself in the position of playing two or more roles at once — when, for example, the doctor has to minister to a member of his own family, thereby confusing his professional and fatherly roles). Armed with these more subtle and modified terms, Goffman presented a most influential analysis of social behaviour as an elaborately mounted drama, in which virtually no area of human activity, public or private, was excluded from the essentially histrionic demands and conditions of the 'presented' self. From 1960 a great variety of ETHNOMETHODOLOGIES proliferated, all stressing the ritual nature of stylized public performance and the need for an adequate HERMENEUTICS to interpret it.

During the 1960s, the term became part of the commonplace idiom of social workers and political journalists. *Role*, along with other dramaturgical vogue words (notably, *scenario*) was used to describe any kind of staged or impersonated performance, especially those in public life. The main problem with the concept of 'role' is its lack of constraint; it is a tearaway word which tends to carry all of human behaviour indiscriminately away with it.   J.R.; J.R.T.

Bibl: J.A. Jackson (ed.), *Role* (London, 1972).

ROM (Read-Only Memory), see under SEMICONDUCTOR STORE.

Roman Catholicism, see under CATHOLICISM.

roman-fleuve ('river-novel'). French term, used originally perhaps with ironical intent, for the multi-volume novel which attempts to cover a large area of society or to follow the fortunes of a family through more than one generation. (The term *fleuve* has no specific connection with the concept of the STREAM OF CONSCIOUSNESS.) Balzac's *La Comédie humaine* and Zola's *Les Rougon-Macquart* can be classed retrospectively as *romans-fleuves*, but the term appears to have been first used with reference to Romain Rolland's *Jean Christophe* (1906-12). More recent French examples are *Les Thibault* by Roger Martin du Gard, *La Chronique des Pasquier* by Georges Duhamel, and *Les Hommes de bonne volonté* by Jules Romains. English and American examples include Galsworthy's *Forsyte Saga,* Anthony Powell's *The Music of Time*, and Upton Sinclair's Lanny Budd series.
                                                            J.G.W.

Romanticism.
(1) In the ARTS generally and in PHILOSOPHY, an overwhelming international tendency which swept across Western Europe and Russia at the end of the 18th and beginning of the 19th century, in reaction against earlier NEO-CLASSICISM, MECHANISM, and RATIONALISM. Arising in an age of social and internal REVOLUTIONS, involving a new model of being, Romanticism had much the same relationship to

the 19th century the MODERNISM has to the 20th. More than simply a return to nature, to the UNCONSCIOUS, the realm of imagination or feeling, it was a synthesizing temper that transformed the entire character of thought, sensibility, and art; many of its preoccupations and notions remain central to the modern mind, including interest in the psychological and the expressive, in the childlike, the revolutionary, the nihilistic, the PLEASURE PRINCIPLE. It was a specific revolt against formality and containment in art, ideas, and notions of man, an assertion of the primacy of the perceiver in the world he perceives; hence theories of the imagination as such are central to it. In central Romantic thought, the organic relation of man and nature, of the interior and the transcendent imagination, is proposed; but much Romanticism is about loss of contact and 'dejection', and can lead to the hallucinatory or fantastic as a mode of perceptual redemption. Hence its relation to the tradition of 'romance', and its disposition towards fantasy, MYTH, the picturesque, the Gothic, the Faustian and Promethean. Romanticism takes different forms in different national strands (despite its internationality and its primary interest in the foreign and strange, it contains deep NATIONALISTIC and POPULIST assumptions), ranges from strongly INDIVIDUALISTIC to revolutionary-collective concerns, and extends from IDEALISM and neo-PLATONISM to an agonized NIHILISM. Hence definitions of it vary widely. In fact, it is as much an international sensibility as a style or a philosophy; and its writing, painting, music, architecture, and thought, some of it intensely subjective and solipsistic (see SOLIPSISM), some of it strongly marked by distancing and fantasy, amount to an eclectic new worldview or WELTANSCHAUUNG which shifts the prevailing idea and function of the artist and of man himself and his ROLE in the world.

Romanticism is usually held to have originated in French (especially Rousseau) and German (notably Herder, Kant, Fichte, Schelling) thought; to have strong roots in German *Sturm und Drang* writing of the 1770s; to have spread to England and then America, returned to France somewhat later, and to have

751

shaped or affected all Europe in varying degrees at different times. Clearly related to dislocations in thought and SOCIAL STRUCTURE consequent on three revolutions — the American, the French, and the INDUSTRIAL — and to the new, self-conscious isolation of the artist or INTEL-LECTUAL in a post-patronage era, it dominates perhaps three literary generations, from the 1790s to the 1840s. It then splinters, on the one hand towards REALISM, which philosophically amends it, on the other towards latter-day versions like SYMBOLISM and AESTHETICISM. There is now much argument whether we still live in a Romantic age of style and sensibility; one strand in modernism assaults Romanticism's 'split religion' (T.E. Hulme's phrase) but another (e.g. Symbolism, EXPRESSIONISM) seeks to restore it. Certainly its revolutionary and pre-FREUDIAN overtones affect much modern art and thought. M.S.BR.

Bibl: H. Honour, *Romanticism* (London, 1979); M.H. Abrams, *The Mirror and the Lamp: Romantic Theory and the Critical Tradition* (London and New York, 1953); N. Frye (ed.), *Romanticism Reconsidered* (New York, 1963); J.B. Halsted (ed.), *Romanticism* (Boston, 1965).

(2) In architecture, a tendency that largely derives from the Picturesque movement of the 18th century, especially as embodied in English landscape practice. In modern architecture it manifests itself not so much as a return to an earlier period as in an emphasis on natural materials and forms. In America it is exemplified by the ORGANIC architecture of Frank Lloyd Wright, which evolved from the work of H.H. Richardson and Louis Sullivan. In Europe, where it was influenced by ART NOUVEAU, it is an alternative tradition to that of the INTERNATIONAL STYLE. The most notable examples come from Alvar Aalto, who dominated Finnish architecture from the 1930s until his death in 1976. His freely and flowingly arranged forms, whether in buildings, furniture, or light fittings, have that appearance of being naturally composed which the tenets of the Romantic movement require. M.BR.

Bibl: V.J. Scully, *Modern Architecture* (London and New York, 1961).

(3) In music, a movement belonging largely to the first half of the 19th century, and exhibited notably in the works of Beethoven, Weber, Schubert, Schumann, Chopin, Berlioz, Liszt, Verdi, and Wagner. It received its stimulus partly from German literature of the late 18th century (A.W. Schlegel, Tieck, Novalis), and partly from the ideals associated with the French Revolution. It is characterized by a tendency among composers to view music as an expression as much of their psyche as of their craft; through the power of association they sought to embody their own ideals and passions in their music; in so doing they cultivated an extremely personalized and sometimes exaggerated style. Reflected in their music is a series of opposing forces: between the individual and society; between intimacy and bombast; between the fusion of poetry and music and the pronounced self-sufficiency of instrumental music. Constant is the belief in music's power to translate human experience and to express human ideals. The term is often extended to include late-19th-century NATIONALIST composers (Dvořák, Tchaikovsky, Grieg), and the 'late Romantics' Bruckner, Mahler, and Richard Strauss. For reactions against Romanticism see IMPRESSIONISM; NEOCLASSICISM. E.H.

Bibl: A. Einstein, *Music in the Romantic Era* (London and New York, 1947).

Rorschach test. A projective test designed by the Swiss psychiatrist Hermann Rorschach consisting of ten bilaterally symmetrical inkblots to which the subject is asked to associate. Interpretation of the subject's responses is believed by its adherents to yield a description of general personality characteristics as well as UNCONSCIOUS conflicts. Responses are interpreted according to their content, their uniqueness or commonness, and the proportion and particular features (colour, shading, etc.) which have been used in forming the percept. Due to a lack of agreement over what this test measures, its popularity has declined sharply since the 1960s and it is now infrequently used in the diagnosis of mental illness. R.P.-S.

Bibl: M. Rickers-Ovsiankina, *Ror-*

schach Psychology (Huntington, N.Y., 1977).

Rosenthal effect. In EDUCATIONAL PSYCHOLOGY, a form of self-fulfilling prophecy, named after the American psychologist Robert Rosenthal, who demonstrated that high expectations of pupils' aptitude, on the part of teachers, even when these expectations were based on fictitious test scores, produced an improvement in the pupils' subsequent performance. W.Z.

Bibl: R. Rosenthal and J. Jacobson, *Pygmalion in the Classroom* (London and New York, 1968).

round characters, see under FLAT CHARACTERS.

Royal Court Theatre. A London theatre twice associated, since its opening in 1871, with important movements in the English theatre. From 1904 to 1907, under the management of J.E. Vedrenne and Harley Granville-Barker, it presented new plays by Shaw, Galsworthy, and Granville-Barker himself. In 1956 it became the home of the *English Stage Company* under the management of George Devine (1910-66): John Osborne, John Arden, Arnold Wesker, Edward Bond and Caryl Churchill are among the dramatists whose work was first presented by the Company. M.A.

Bibl: D. Kennedy, *Granville Barker and the Dream of Theatre* (Cambridge, 1985); R. Findlater (ed.), *At The Royal Court* (Ambergate, 1981).

Royal Institution. A body formed in 1799 to perform and publicize scientific research; its most famous directors were Humphry Davy and Michael Faraday. Although evening meetings are held throughout the year, the Institution is best known for its Christmas lectures delivered in London by eminent scientists before an audience of schoolchildren. M.V.B.

Royal Society of London. One of the oldest scientific societies, founded in 1662. As well as organizing discussion meetings and administering various funds for the support of scientific research, the Society publishes its *Proceedings* and *Philosophical Transactions*, which rank among the world's leading scientific journals. To be elected one of the few hundred Fellows of the Royal Society is one of the highest honours that can be bestowed on a British scientist by his peers. M.V.B.

RSG, see under RATE SUPPORT GRANT.

rule of law, see LAW, RULE OF.

rule, work to, see WORK TO RULE.

S

sacralization, see under SACRIFICE.

sacrifice. Seeks to establish a relationship, through an intermediary, between society and the supernatural order. Important elements in sacrifice include donor, RITUAL officiant, sacrificial object and recipient. The kind of intermediary is not randomly chosen, but culturally specified, and it is linked symbolically with the donor. Sacrifice has both instrumental aspects (that is an intention to bring something about) and expressive aspects (says something about the social and supernatural order). In establishing contact with the 'other world' sacrifice can involve elements of purification, symbolic exchange and communion. The classic work *Sacrifice: its Nature and Function* (1899) by Hubert and Mauss has exercised an important influence in ANTHROPOLOGY. It represented the movement away from the evolutionary theories of sacrifice developed by Robertson Smith and James Frazer.

Evans-Pritchard in *Nuer Religion* (1956) took over from Hubert and Mauss the concepts of *sacralization* (spirit from gods come to man) and *desacralization* (man gets rid of spirit) and linked them respectively to his distinction between collective and personal sacrifice. Collective sacrifice was connected with changes in social STATUS, confirming a RITE DE PASSAGE. Personal sacrifice was concerned with the warding off of potential dangers. Although Evans-Pritchard concentrated on the reasons for the performance of sacrifice, he did not neglect what actually happened in sacrifice. Other anthropologists (e.g., Leach, *Culture and Communication*, 1976) have particularly taken up this aspect and in utilizing a structural (see STRUCTURALISM) method, they have examined its internal logic.   A.G.

Bibl: L. De Heusch, *Sacrifice in Africa: A Structuralist Approach* (Manchester, 1985).

sadism. A PERVERSION in which sexual pleasure is derived from inflicting pain on others. It was named by Krafft-Ebing after the Marquis de Sade, who described its practice in *Justine* (1791) and other works. The word is often used loosely to denote cruelty of any kind.   W.Z.

sado-masochism. The coexistence in the same person of both SADISM and MASOCHISM, or their alliance as the complementary halves of a two-person relationship. However, the adjective *sadomasochistic* is usually reserved for fantasies of destruction or being destroyed, causing pain or receiving pain, which are thought by psychoanalysts to relate back to the anal stage of development — specifically, the anal-sadistic phase (age 2½ to 4 years; see PSYCHOSEXUAL DEVELOPMENT). Such fantasies are much more common in conditions such as PARANOIA and SCHIZOPHRENIA than in DEPRESSION, but can occur in obsessional (see OBSESSION) NEUROSIS and certain PHOBIAS. They occur in the majority of children as a developmental phenomenon.   M.J.C.

salami tactics. The technique whereby one element in a governmental coalition achieves a monopoly of POWER by destroying its allied parties section by section; in particular as employed in Eastern Europe after 1945. The phrase derives from a frank account by the Hungarian COMMUNIST leader Mátyás Rákosi of how the majority Smallholders Party and the SOCIAL DEMOCRATIC Party had each in turn been bullied into 'slicing off' first their RIGHT wing, then their CENTRIST members, until only close collaborators of the Communists remained.   R.C.

salpingitis. Inflammation of the fallopian tubes (which lead from the ovaries to the uterus). Most infections are caused by sexually transmitted microbes, e.g. *Neisseria gonorrhoea* and CHLAMYDIA *trachomatis* which ascend from the lower genital tract. A woman with salpingitis complains of abdominal and pelvic pain, often with fever and a vaginal discharge. The diagnosis is made by either pelvic examination or by use of a laparoscope inserted through the abdominal wall, which enables the pelvic organs to be closely inspected. The results of salpingitis, particularly if ANTIBIOTIC treatment is delayed, include pelvic abscesses, chronic pelvic pain and INFERTILITY due to fibrosis and blocking of the fallopian tubes. Most attacks would be prevented by the accurate diagnosis and treatment of SEXUALLY TRANSMITTED infections while confined to the lower genital tract. J.D.O.

Bibl: World Health Organization, *Nongonococcal urethritis and other selected sexually transmitted diseases of public health importance* (Geneva, 1981).

SALT (Strategic Arms Limitation Talks), see under NUCLEAR WEAPONS, LIMITATION AND CONTROL.

samizdat ('self-publication'). A Russian coinage, in general use since about 1966, for the circulation in typescript (including carbons) of literary and political books and articles refused by, or not submitted to, regular publishers. The format is designed to evade legal restrictions on printing and duplicating — though (as many cases have shown) people may afterwards be charged with the possession or circulation of 'anti-Soviet material'. The large and striking literature in *samizdat* ranges from such novels as Solzhenitsyn's *The First Circle* to political analyses such as Academician Andrei Sakharov's *Progress, Coexistence and Intellectual Freedom* and Ivan Dzyuba's *Internationalism or Russification*, together with much poetry and various periodical publications, notably the *Chronicle of Current Events*. The analogous *tamizdat* ('published there') consists of work in Russian published in the West and reaching the U.S.S.R. more or less clandestinely, as have copies of Pasternak's *Dr Zhivago. Magnitizdat* refers to such material as dissident songs and poetry (or foreign broadcasts) recorded on tapes which circulate unofficially in the U.S.S.R. R.C.

Bibl: P. Reddaway (ed.), *Uncensored Russia* (London and New York, 1972).

sample; sampling. In STATISTICS, the data themselves, or the random selection from which they are obtained, are often called the sample; sampling is the process of collecting such data. Thus an experiment to determine the height distribution of adult males in Britain might involve the selection of a random sample of say, 5,000, from a total population of around 20 million. The problem of sampling is to ensure that the sample is in some sense a fair representation of the underlying population; a sample which is not is sometimes said to be *biased*. Ideally selection procedures should be such that every individual has an equal chance of being chosen, but in a population which is known to be divided into sub-populations it may be advantageous to sample from each subpopulation in the correct proportions. A *Gallup Poll* is a SURVEY of voting intentions carried out in this manner. R.SI.

sanctions.

(1) In politics, coercive measures taken to secure fulfilment of international obligations. Such measures may be deterrent or — e.g. the French occupation of the Ruhr in 1923 when Germany failed to pay reparations —punitive in nature. Article 16 of the LEAGUE OF NATIONS Covenant envisaged the application of economic and military sanctions against states in breach of the Covenant; economic sanctions involve the severance of economic and financial relations with the offending state, military sanctions involve acts of war. Experience, especially during the Italo-Abyssinian conflict of 1935-6, and in the British attempts to bring pressure on the Southern Rhodesian regime which declared its independence in 1965, has shown economic sanctions to be a somewhat ineffective weapon. Their utility has again become a matter of debate in the case of sanctions against South Africa. D.C.W.

(2) The response, positive or negative, to modes of behaviour. Anthropologists distinguish between positive sanctions or rewards for socially approved behaviour (prizes, titles, decorations) and negative sanctions, responses to breaches of NORMS. Sanctions support the norms and customs of society. The term sanctions, however, most commonly refers to negative sanctions (i.e. the response to transgressions). They have particularly interested anthropologists who have studied societies without formal legal systems.

In his study of the Trobriand Islanders (*Crime and Custom in Savage Society*, 1926), Malinowski focused upon the importance of social reciprocity and he understood the threat of its withdrawal as the ultimate sanction against a breach of norms. Radcliffe Brown's approach was more theoretical and had CROSS-CULTURAL application. In *Structure and Function in Primitive Society* (1952) he constructed a TYPOLOGY of sanctions. He drew a distinction between *organized* (e.g., law) and *diffuse* (e.g., WITCHCRAFT, ostracism) sanctions and he distinguished between *primary* (actions by the whole community) and *secondary* (private) sanctions (see CUSTOM; FEUD; TABOO). A.G.

Bibl: E.R. Leach, *Custom, Law and Terrorist Violence* (Edinburgh, 1977).

Sandinista. A member or, more loosely, a supporter of the Sandinista National Liberation Front (FSLN), a GUERRILLA organization formed in 1962 with the aim of presenting a coherent political and economic response to *Somocismo*, and now the vanguard party of the Nicaraguan REVOLUTION. Taking its name from General Augusto Sandino who led an anti-IMPERIALIST struggle against the 1927-1934 occupation, FSLN IDEOLOGY draws on three distinct sources: (1) third world NATIONALISM, (2) post-Medellin Conference Latin American CATHOLICISM and (3) MARXISM. Since coming to power the FSLN have pursued redistributive policies to attack the extreme concentration of economic resources which characterized Somoza's NICARAGUA, but have not sought to eliminate the PRIVATE SECTOR. Education, health care and literacy programmes have been implemented and a NON-ALIGNED foreign policy pursued. Elections in November 1984 gave the FSLN 63.5% of the vote. See also CONTRAS. N.M.

Bibl: G. Black, *Triumph of the People* (London, 1981); David Nolan, *The Ideology of the Sandinistas and the Nicaraguan Revolution* (Miami, 1984).

sandwich course. A course in a college, polytechnic, or technological university organized to allow a period of college-based study to alternate with a period in industry planned as an integral part of the work. A 'thick' sandwich consists of two years in university, one year in industry, and a final year in university, and is the norm in high-level programmes. A 'thin'

sandwich, usually consisting of six-month layers, is found in lower-level diploma and certificate programmes. W.A.C.S.

Bibl: L. Cantor and I.F. Roberts, *Further Education in England and Wales* (London, 1969; New York, 1970).

sarcomas, see under CANCER.

satellite. Any body constrained by GRAVITATION to revolve in a circular ORBIT around a much more massive body. For example, the planets are satellites of the sun, while the moon and all the artificial communications satellites are satellites of the earth. M.V.B.

satellite town. In expanding, a town causes the formation of industrial or residential centres which depend upon it, which are separate from it, and without which its activities cannot be considered. Such a centre is often called a satellite town. V.G. Davidovich has defined a satellite by three characteristics, all of which require that communications between a central town (which may rank as a METROPOLIS) and its satellites are easy and frequent: (1) people living in a satellite town come to work in the central town; (2) the central town guarantees a certain number of services, notably cultural services, for its satellites; (3) the satellites accommodate the town's population for relaxation, e.g. in parks, sports centres, and public houses.

J. Beaujeu-Garnier has distinguished between a *consumer satellite* (i.e. a dormitory town) and a *production satellite*, for which the term satellite town should be reserved. Under this classification, the satellite town is one in which some provision is made for the industrial and commercial employment of its inhabitants independently from employment provided by the metropolis, e.g. the NEW TOWNS developed in Britain after World War II as a means of decongesting London. M.L.

Bibl: V.G. Davidovich and B.S. Khorev (eds.), *Satellite Towns* (Washington, 1962); J. Beaujeu-Garnier and G. Chabot, tr. G.M. Yglesias and S.H. Beaver, *Urban Geography* (London and New York, 1967).

satori, see under ZEN.

saturated. In ORGANIC CHEMISTRY, term used to describe a compound which will not react by adding other chemical SPECIES. In such compounds each carbon ATOM is singly bonded (see BOND) to four neighbouring atoms as in methane, and ethyl alcohol. See also UNSATURATED.

B.F.

Saussurian. Characteristic of, or a follower of, the principles of Ferdinand de Saussure (1857-1913), especially as outlined in his posthumous *Cours de linguistique générale* (Paris, 1916), translated by W. Baskin as *Course in General Linguistics* (New York, 1959). His conception of language as a system of mutually defining entities underlies much of contemporary structural LINGUISTICS. See also the distinctions between synchronic and DIACHRONIC, LANGUE AND PAROLE, SYNTAGMATIC AND PARADIGMATIC; see also COMPARATIST; SEMIOLOGY.

D.C.

Say's Law. An ECONOMIC LAW which is often taken as stating that 'SUPPLY creates its own DEMAND'. In an accounting sense, the law must be true as NATIONAL INCOME, output and expenditure are, by definition, equal (see GDP). The law must also be true in a barter economy, as the supply of a good constitutes a demand. If production occurs and is just added to stocks, no extra demand has materialized. Additionally, supply may even fall in the next period. An alternative statement of the law is that the value of the planned supply of all goods equals the value of the planned demand for goods. This interpretation, first given by Keynes, is that of an EQUILIBRIUM condition rather than a truism, as is the case in the first definition. The different definitions and interpretations of Say's Law have caused much dispute and confusion.

J.P.

scalar, see under VECTOR.

scale. In the sense of an objective basis for measuring, comparing, or classifying things, a scale may belong to one or more of several identifiable types. A scale that makes it possible to describe things in terms of some numerical quantity, e.g.

length in miles, weight in tons, or voltage, is called a *numerical scale.* The simplest type of scale assumes merely that objects can be arranged in a definite order, and then assigns numbers or labels to positions in that order, as when social CLASSES are ranked as 'upper', 'upper middle', 'lower middle', or 'working', or when objects are assigned one of the numbers from 1 to 7 according to their hardness as measured in a standard test; this is called an *ordinal scale.* In such scales, only the order is usually significant, and differences between positions carry no usable information; e.g., if the INTELLIGENCE QUOTIENTS of four persons are 96, 101, 146, and 156, then although the difference between the first two numbers is half the difference between the second two it is not possible to deduce that half as much teaching is required to bring the first person to the level of the second as is required to bring the third to the level of the fourth. When the differences or intervals *are* significant, as with measurement of temperature (the difference between 96°C and 101°C being physically related to the difference between 146°C and 156°C), the scale is called an *interval scale.* However, *ratios* between numbers on this scale are meaningless: something with a temperature of 80°C is not twice as hot as something with a temperature of 40°C, but merely twice as far from an arbitrary zero point, i.e. one that does not correspond to zero amount of anything. When the zero point of a scale is *not* arbitrary, as with measurement of lengths or weights, the scale is called a *ratio scale.*

Some phenomena cannot be measured along any single scale, but can be decomposed into constituent parts that are measurable on several different scales. Thus it can be argued that there is no single measure of the wealth of a nation. If, however, it is possible to agree on a way of assigning numbers to the separate *aspects* of wealth — e.g. the amount of food consumed per head, the average quality of housing, the standard of EDUCATION and medical care provided, the variety of entertainments available — then the wealth of the nation can be measured by giving a *set of numbers*, one for each type. This is called a *multidimensional scale*, each component being an *indicator* of the nation's wealth. See also QUANTIFICATION (1); SCALING. A.S.

scale, economies of, see ECONOMIES OF SCALE.

scale, returns to, see RETURNS TO SCALE.

scale-and-category grammar. A theory of GRAMMAR developed by Halliday and other neo-FIRTHIAN scholars in the early 1960s, and so named because it analyses grammatical patterns into a small number of theoretical *categories*, interrelating these through the use of *scales* (see, e.g., RANK). The grammatical analysis presupposes a general MODEL of language which distinguishes three basic LEVELS of *substance, form* and *context*. D.C.

Bibl: M.A.K. Halliday, 'Categories of the Theory of Grammar' (*Word*, 17, 1961, pp. 241-92).

scaling. The activity carried out by a statistician when he selects one out of several possible SCALES of measurement, e.g. when he decides whether to measure seeds by length or volume or weight. For biometric data (see also BIOMETRY) there are often good reasons for working with the logarithm of the observed quantity; this is called a *logarithmic scale*. Sometimes scaling problems can involve variation in more than one dimension; the resolution of such *multidimensional scaling* problems involves lengthy and complicated computation (see COMPUTING), but the techniques involved are very powerful weapons of DATA ANALYSIS for a wide variety of problems. R.SI.

scanning. The systematic traversal of a region by a narrow beam, e.g. the 'flying spot' of ELECTRONS which builds up a television picture by varying in brightness while scanning the screen of a CATHODE RAY TUBE in a total of 625 lines traversed too quickly for the eye to follow. M.V.B.

scenario, see under ROLE; SCENARIO ANALYSIS; TECHNOLOGICAL FORECASTING.

scenario analysis. A scenario is a description of what might happen in the future. Scenario analysis is used to evaluate the outcomes of policies and plans in a range of different futures (i.e. scenarios). It is a way of testing the robustness of policies and plans to different possible futures. In this way, scenario analysis is superior to FORECASTING techniques that only predict one single future. The evaluation of a plan or policy implies the need for PROBABILITIES to be attached to the occurrence of the different possible futures. This is rarely carried out because of the inherent difficulty of predicting futures that are characterized by UNCERTAINTY. In this sense, scenario analysis suffers from the same problem as the forecasting of a single future. Scenario analysis often uses relatively unstructured, non-quantitative MODELS of the future that allow investigation of aspects of the future that may be very different from the past and present. This can be an advantage, especially when considering the long term, and compares favourably with more rigid, structured models of the future, e.g. ECONOMETRIC models. However, the informal nature of the models that are often used in scenario analysis means that it is difficult to evaluate the validity of the models and resulting scenarios and, in particular, the probabilities of the different scenarios occurring. Scenario analysis has been used extensively in economic, business, strategic and engineering studies (see EXPECTED UTILITY). J.P.

Bibl: S. Makridakis and S.C. Wheelwright, *Forecasting Methods and Applications* (Chichester, 1978).

Schadenfreude. German term for pleasure derived from the misfortunes of others. In English it tends to be used, more or less jokingly, to describe satisfaction at what is felt to be a just retribution. Its occasional occurrence is thus a perfectly normal feeling; excessive proneness to it indicates an unkind or malicious nature, but is quite distinct from SADISM. O.S.

schadograph, see PHOTOGRAM.

scheduled territories, see under STERLING AREA.

schedules of reinforcement, see under REINFORCEMENT.

Schenker analysis. The analysis of primarily tonal music using the methods of Heinrich Schenker. Schenker's analytical techniques are based on the extraction of basic harmonic and linear progressions (*urlinie*) from masterpieces of classical tonal music, in particular the music of Beethoven. Schenker breaks the musical work down into layers: the foreground, the actual musical surface; the middleground, the music stripped of complexities; the background, the essential essence of the music (see also THEMATIC ANALYSIS). B.CO.

schizoid. In PSYCHIATRY, a term associated with the name of Kretschmer, who believed that the whole population fell along a normal curve of distribution (see NORMAL DISTRIBUTION) from MANIC-DEPRESSIVES at one end to schizophrenics (see SCHIZOPHRENIA) at the other. The group which was closest to the schizophrenic end of the curve, but not psychotic (see PSYCHOSIS) and therefore not abnormal, was the group he called schizoid.

Today the word is characteristically applied, independently of Kretschmer's theory, to a PERSONALITY TYPE whose main features are aloofness, detachment and a tendency to suppress the outward show of emotion. This usage is imprecise and apt to vary from one clinical worker to another, while the CONCEPT which it reflects is based on the impressionistic judgements of clinicians, and has not yet been satisfactorily validated by objective methods. Some workers, nevertheless, find it useful, especially some pscyhoanalysts. B.A.F.

schizophrenia. In PSYCHIATRY and ABNORMAL PSYCHOLOGY, a term introduced by Eugen Bleuler in 1910, replacing the older term, 'dementia praecox', to denote forms of mental illness characterized by a lack of connection (splitting of the mind) between mental functions, which seem to the observer incongruous with one another and not understandable. Schizophrenia is traditionally classed as a PSYCHOSIS, and the wide range of symptoms subsumed under it includes disorders of thought, such as delusions; sense deceptions, such as hallucinations; abnormalities of mood, such as unresponsiveness or incongruous reactions to situations; and behavioural disturbances such as loss of drive and social withdrawal.

The causal factors are probably multiple: GENETIC factors undoubtedly play a part, though how much is disputed; BIOCHEMICAL disorders in the brain may be influential but are as yet unproven; disturbances of early parent-child relationships have been suggested but without convincing evidence. Although causation remains obscure, in the past 20 years the course of schizophrenia has been improved by two developments. First, symptoms are frequently alleviated by drugs (phenothiazines), particularly in the acute stage. Second, active social and psychological treatment measures may greatly reduce long-term handicaps resulting from social withdrawal and from lack of suitable occupation and stimulation.

D.H.G.

Bibl: M. Lader, *Priorities in Psychiatric Research* (Chichester, 1980).

scholasticism, see under NEO-THOMISM.

schools of psychology. Psychological issues, being many-sided and complexly interrelated, can be regarded from many viewpoints which, although different, are not necessarily contradictory, and which vary according to the psychological aspect being studied, the method of study, and the theoretical FRAME OF REFERENCE within which the study is set. These diverse approaches can themselves be classified in different ways and are sometimes grouped into so-called schools so as to highlight theoretical similarities and divergences. There is no agreed repertoire of schools but the phrase 'schools of psychology' most often refers to certain groupings that dominated theoretical PSYCHOLOGY, particularly in America, during roughly the first half of this century, when psychology was asserting its independence from other disciplines.

According to R.S. Woodworth (*Contemporary Schools of Psychology*, 1931, revised 1948 and 1964), whose historical interpretation is widely accepted in America, there were six main schools. STRUCTURALISM sought by systematic introspection to discover the elementary contents of CONSCIOUSNESS, while FUNC-

TIONALISM was concerned with the activities by which the mind worked (see also COGNITIVE PSYCHOLOGY). ASSOCIATIONISM wanted to study isolated psychological elements in their interconnection, while GESTALT psychology asserted the priority of whole-characteristics and resisted segmentation into elements. BEHAVIOURISM insisted that only objective behaviour, and not subjective experience, be studied. PSYCHOANALYSIS attempted in a distinctive way to understand the motivational forces governing conscious and unconscious phenomena. Of these six, only behaviourism and psychoanalysis survived the mid-century as distinctive schools separated from the eclectic, middle-of-the-road orientation of most psychologists who bow to the breadth and diversity of their subject-matter by accepting that no one theory or method or field of specialization has proper monopoly and that complex problems are profitably approached, even simultaneously, from different viewpoints.   I.M.L.H.

Schwinger process, see under VIRTUAL PARTICLES.

science, philosophy of. This has included a number of distinct traditions of thought. Within NEO-KANTIAN German culture in particular it has set about answering the question: what makes the universe intelligible? and has focused upon the status of such concepts as time and space. Anglo-Saxon philosophy of science over the last century, by contrast, has been preoccupied with investigating and confirming the validity of scientific knowledge, above all with showing that NATURAL SCIENCE forms the normal, even the only, mode of true knowledge (as distinct from received authority or mere subjective assertion). As a discipline, the philosophy of science has wavered between description (being an account of what scientists actually do) and prescription (what scientists ought to do to advance truth).

An older view, much touted by Victorian scientists, championed the use of INDUCTION as recommended by Francis Bacon. The business of science was to maximize facts; in due course scientific laws would emerge, almost spontaneously, from the sheer weight of data. The attrac-

tion of this idea lay in minimizing the risk of being misled by false theories. Eventually, simple induction was accepted as being unrealistic. Popular in the middle of this century was *hypothetico-deductivism*, the notion that facts should lead to hypotheses which would guide further investigation leading to the testing of hypotheses, and so forth, in a progressive manner. Sir Karl Popper's 'falsificationism' formed a radical variant on this (see POPPERIAN). Science could only be truly critical if investigators systematically strove to *disprove* every theory advanced: or, in other words, science could never prove any theory correct, merely falsify all the untrue theories. Popper's sceptical perception that science could never be sure it had obtained truth was underlined by T.S. Kuhn's idea that science proceeds through a series of 'revolutions' which successively destroy old theories (PARADIGMS) replacing them with new ones (see REVOLUTIONARY SCIENCE). New theories form radical discontinuities, involving new perceptions (GESTALTS). Old and new theories are incommensurable. Scientific progress is thus unprovable, and science possibly thus appears as relativistic (see RELATIVISM) as other modes of knowledge. The implication that science is unavoidably subjective has been carried further by sociological philosophies, which have stressed that scientific language is itself contaminated by everyday associations, and that scientific reasoning contains elements of rationalization tainted with personal interests and IDEOLOGY. Defenders of a more sophisticated version of scientific objectivity such as Lakatos and Laudan have countered with appeals to the long-term capacity of science to sift truth from error through experimental testing. Ironically, these rival philosophies have revealed that the metaphysical bases of science are far more dubious than ever imagined.   R.P.

Bibl: R. Harre, *Philosophies of Science* (Oxford, 1972); R. Bhaskar, *The Possibility of Naturalism* (Hassocks, Sussex, 1979); G. Buchdahl, *Metaphysics and the Philosophy of Science* (Oxford, 1969).

science, sociology of. The study of the social relations and INSTITUTIONS of the scientific community. Typical problems are: (1) How efficiently is scientific knowledge communicated by journals, conferences, etc.? (2) How can the SCIENTIFIC METHOD persist virtually unchanged, when scientists come from countries differing radically in their political IDEOLOGIES? M.V.B.

Bibl: B. Barnes (ed.), *Sociology of Science* (Harmondsworth, 1972); S. Richards, *Philosophy and Sociology of Science* (Oxford, 1983).

science fiction. Unsatisfactory but firmly established term for an Anglo-American literary genre that shows average human beings confronted by some novelty, usually daunting: an invasion from another planet, a plague, space-travel, time-travel, a non-human civilization, a society ruled by machines, etc. There are anticipations in tales of wonder from the 17th century onwards and notably in the works of Jules Verne, but the first and still the greatest true exponent was H.G. Wells in *The Time Machine* (1895), *The War of the Worlds* (1898), etc. Until about 1940 most stories involved gadgetry, simple menace, or fantastic adventure. The next 25 years widened the range to include political, economic, technological, and psychological speculation. In the later 1960s the so-called New Wave imitated the stylistic and presentational trickery of the ANTI-NOVEL, but this has passed and the genre has returned to its traditional themes, though with an added emphasis on the potentialities of the mind and on philosophical questions. Often ostensibly concerned with the future, science fiction at its best throws a fresh light on today. Leading writers include Brian W. Aldiss, Isaac Asimov, J.G. Ballard, Arthur C. Clarke, Philip K. Dick, Harry Harrison, Damon Knight, Ursula Le Guin, Frederik Pohl, and Robert Silverberg. The abbreviations SF and sf are approved by practitioners and connoisseurs; sci-fic and sci-fi are not. K.A.

Bibl: B.W. Aldiss, *Billion-Year Spree* (London and New York, 1973).

science indicators. One goal of science has been to create a 'science of science', enabling the study of its own development and history to be put upon a quantitative basis. At the same time, society has increasingly needed reliable ways to judge the performance of science itself, particularly as science has demanded ever greater state funding. To meet these needs, science indicators have been devised. These focus upon statistical measures of the resources allocated to science, scientific output and productivity, measured in terms of publications, conferences, citations of papers, patent registrations, employment expansion, capacity to win support from industry, and so forth. Their deeper value remains in doubt however, because science may choose to orient itself precisely in directions which score well amongst the indicators. In any case the measure of qualitative worth remains unfathomable. R.P.

Bibl: Y. Elkana *et al., Toward a Metric of Science* (New York, 1978).

scientific law. A general statement of fact, methodically established by INDUCTION, on the basis of observation and experiment, and usually, though not necessarily, expressed in mathematical form. In so far as it is empirical, a scientific law is not a necessary, demonstrable (see DEMONSTRATION) truth; in so far as it is methodically derived from intentionally acquired evidence, however, it differs from everyday commonsensical generalization. Ideally, scientific laws are strictly universal or deterministic (see DETERMINISM) in form, asserting something about all members of a certain class of things, but they may also be 'probabilistic' or statistical and assert something about a methodically estimated proportion of the class of things in question. There is a problem about the distinction of laws from 'accidental' generalization, statements that just happen to be true about all the things there are of the kind to which they relate. The distinction is marked, but not explained, by the fact that laws do, but accidental generalizations do not, imply COUNTERFACTUAL conditionals. Only if 'All *A* are *B*' is a law does it imply that if this thing, which is actually not *A*, had been *A*, it would have been *B*. This logical peculiarity lends some support to the view that scientific laws do not just describe universally pervasive regularities but assert some necessary connection between the kinds of properties mentioned in them. A.Q.

scientific management. Term coined by Frederick Winslow Taylor in 1911 to describe the techniques he adopted to increase the output of workers. Controversial at the time (it was the subject of a Congressional Hearing in 1912), the approach is today seen as mechanistic and anachronistic. Contrast with MANAGEMENT SCIENCE.   R.I.T.

Bibl: F.W. Taylor, *The Principles of Scientific Management* (London and New York, 1911).

scientific method. The procedure by which, as a matter of definition, SCIENTIFIC LAWS, as contrasted with other kinds of general statement, are established. The orthodox view is that this procedure is inductive (see INDUCTION), but several philosophers of science have criticized *inductivism* (see POPPERIAN) as misrepresenting the actual procedure of scientists. Two phases of scientific activity need to be distinguished: the initial formulation of hypotheses, which seems mainly, as the anti-inductivists maintain, to be a business of inspired guessing that cannot be mechanized, and the CONFIRMATION of hypotheses thus formulated, which does appear to be a comparatively pedestrian and rule-governed undertaking.   A.Q.

Bibl: K.R. Popper, *The Logic of Scientific Discovery* (London and New York, 1959).

scientific revolutions, see under ANOMALY; REVOLUTIONARY SCIENCE.

scientism. The view that the characteristic inductive methods (see INDUCTION) of the NATURAL SCIENCES are the only source of genuine factual knowledge and, in particular, that they alone can yield true knowledge about man and society. This stands in contrast with the explanatory version of DUALISM which insists that the human and social subject-matter of history and the SOCIAL SCIENCES (the GEISTESWISSENSCHAFTEN) can be fruitfully investigated only by a method, involving sympathetic intuition of human states of mind, that is proprietary to these disciplines.   A.Q.

scientology. An organization of a quasi-religious character founded in the U.S.A. in 1952 by the late L. Ron Hubbard and purporting to bring its members complete mental health. It has been widely accused of authoritarian attitudes and of indoctrinating, hypnotizing, and BRAINWASHING its members so as to destroy their social links with non-members, including even close relatives. Several Australian states, New Zealand, Canada, and Great Britain have held official enquiries into its practices, and measures aimed at adversely publicizing its activities or drastically reducing their scope have been adopted in a number of them.   D.C.W.

Bibl: J.G. Foster, *Enquiry into the Practice and Effects of Scientology* (London, 1971).

scratching, see under REGGAE.

scratchpad. A form of computer store (see COMPUTER; STORE).   C.S.

Scrutiny, see under LEAVISITE.

SDI, see STRATEGIC DEFENCE INITIATIVE.

SDRs (Special Drawing Rights), see under INTERNATIONAL LIQUIDITY.

SDS (Students for a Democratic Society). A radical (see RADICALISM) American student organization which was a key element in the NEW LEFT of the 1960s. It was formed in 1960 from the residues of the nearly moribund student branch of the League for Industrial Democracy, and grew through its attempts to unify disparate protests against such matters as the ARMS RACE, nuclear testing, restraints on freedom of speech and the denial of CIVIL RIGHTS to BLACK Americans. In 1962 its Port Huron Statement provided a manifesto for a burgeoning movement, although its emphasis on HUMANIST themes and participatory DEMOCRACY was soon transcended. The SDS became committed to supporting the more radical elements in black politics, to opposing the VIETNAM War as a manifestation of American IMPERIALISM, and to protesting against universities as agents of a repressive system of quasi-LIBERAL, pro-CAPITALIST values. Its attempts to construct a coherent IDEOLOGY out of numerous fragments are variously seen as innovative or incoherent, and accentuated schismatic tendencies which fatally divided the organization by 1969. Of its remaining functions, the WEATHERMEN were most significant. S.R.

Bibl: K. Sale, *SDS* (New York, 1973); A. Matusow, *The Unraveling of America* (New York, 1984).

search for extraterrestrial intelligence. Usually referred to by the acronym SETI. Searches for signals from intelligent extraterrestrial life were first made by Frank Drake's Osma Project (1960) which listened for radio signals from Epsilon Eridani and Tau Ceti, the two nearest stars resembling our sun. No signals were detected. Other search strategies have since been suggested. A continuing listening channel is employed using the 'Haystack' radio telescope in the U.S.A. Freeman Dyson pointed out that the waste heat from advanced technological civilizations might be visible as INFRA-RED radiation. A search has also been made at special frequencies (for example 21 cm radio waves) which are associated with universal properties of nature likely to be known to any scientifically advanced civilization. A programme to transmit signals from Earth has also been initiated using similar principles. NASA SPACE PROBES to the outer planets, which will eventually be pointed out into deep space, carried information and pictures aimed at informing inhabitants of other planets of our own existence, location, physical characteristics and cultural development. Any form of communication with extraterrestrials is constrained by the enormous distances involved. Each signal to a nearby star would take many years to travel between there and the Earth at the speed of light.

Theoretical estimates of the likelihood of making contact with extraterrestrial intelligence are extremely uncertain. The most famous attempt is the Drake equation. This gives the probability that intelligent life which eventually attempts interstellar communication will evolve in a star system as the product of the probability that a star will possess planets, the number of habitable planets in a SOLAR SYSTEM possessing planets, the probability that life evolves on a habitable planet and the probability that an intelligent species will attempt interstellar communication in a reasonable time. The evaluation of esti-mates for these probabilities requires knowledge of EXOBIOLOGY, the range of living systems that are possible in non-terrestrial environments.

A common argument against the likely success of SETI is the *Fermi paradox* which argues that advanced lifeforms could so easily have made contact with us that we must conclude that they do not exist. A counter-argument called the *zoo hypothesis* by J. A. Ball in 1973 suggests that a very advanced lifeform might choose to leave us undisturbed as an object for study. At present there exists no positive evidence for the existence of any intelligent extraterrestrial lifeform.   J.D.B.

Bibl: I. S. Shklovskii and C. Sagan, *Intelligent Life in Space* (New York, 1966); C. Ponnamperuma and A. G. Cameron (eds.), *Interstellar Communication: Scientific Perspectives* (Boston, 1974); J. D. Barrow and F. J. Tipler, *The Anthropic Cosmological Principle* (Oxford, 1986).

searching-instinct. According to the work of Imre Hermann (1889-1984) the instinct for grasping plays a particularly privileged role in the development of the human mind. The associated searching-instinct comes into operation whenever the grasping-instinct finds itself without an object; the frustration of the instinct for grasping thus repeatedly produces the joint operation of this pair of antagonistic instincts acting as a couple. Hermann's analysis of the process of thinking takes place within the field of these two variables, since thinking includes within it this function of seeking. Hermann claims that there is a *parallelism* — an identity of structure — between forms of thinking, and the possible forms of instinctual conflict. He does not hope to reduce thinking to a PSYCHO-PATHOLOGY, but by establishing structures common to bodies of theory and the formation of the UNCONSCIOUS, to show how each domain in turn is able to explain problems in the field of the other.

In particular, Hermann claimed that the developments introduced into the psyche by the generation of language structure (PRE-CONSCIOUS word-representations), by idealization, and by love based on the admission of separation, are best described by the type of spatial structure known as a hyperbolic non-Euclidean GEOMETRY; that the structure of the SUPEREGO is best described by the restricted space of an elliptical non-Euclidean geometry (that in Jacques Lacan's work in this field is represented as a 'cross-cap'; see LACANIAN); and that the transition from the first geometry to the second is represented clinically by the depressive moment — and the reverse transition by the hypermanic moment — of certain psychotic states. His psychobiographies of creative mathematicians attempted to present their work as struggling with the mental conflicts whose structure was congruent with the themes of their work; he was in this way able to extend this class of results to the problem of the creation of the mathematical theory of sets (see SET THEORY), and to MATHEMATICAL LOGIC.   B.BU

SEATO (South-East Asia Treaty Organization). An organization established at Manila on 8 September 1954 in a treaty signed by Australia, Britain, France, New Zealand, Pakistan, the Philippines, Thailand, and the United States. Its purpose was to provide a defensive alliance on the model of NATO for the protection of the South-East Asia and South-West Pacific areas including, by an agreed protocol, Laos, Cambodia, and South VIETNAM. SEATO, however, lacked the long-term commitment of members' forces that was a feature of Nato; French and British commitments were always marginal, and Pakistan withdrew after the Indo-Pakistani war of 1971. In September 1975 it decided to phase itself out of existence.
                                                    D.C.W.

second-order theorizing. Making theories about theories. The term has no unique field of application, but two typical kinds of second-order theorizing can be broadly distinguished: (1) epistemological, logical, mathematical, etc. theories about the formal properties of other theories, e.g. demonstrating their structural similarity, justifying their claims to validity, or explicating their assumptions (see METATHEORY); (2) sociological, psychological, historical, etc. theories about how theories come into being, persist, or change. The first-order theories which compose the subject-matter of second-order theorizing are perhaps most commonly those of the NATURAL SCIENCES and SOCIAL SCIENCES. J.R.T.

Bibl: T.S. Kuhn, *The Structure of Scientific Revolutions* (Chicago, 2nd ed., 1970); K.R. Popper, *Objective Knowledge* (Oxford, 1972).

second-signal system. In PSYCHOLOGY, a PAVLOVIAN term used to differentiate a physical stimulus that was directly conditioned and linked to a response (see CONDITIONED REFLEX) from one that has been categorized in language and can thus be associated by meaning with a range of other similarly coded STIMULI. Pavlov aimed to distinguish CONDITIONING in animals from learning in man, in which the ordinary laws of conditioning were superseded by linguistic association.   J.S.B.

second-strike capability, see under STRATEGIC CAPABILITY.

second Viennese school. The collective name sometimes given to the composer Arnold Schoenberg and his two most famous pupils Anton Webern and Alban Berg due to their connections with Vienna (the first Viennese school being Mozart, Haydn and Beethoven). Among the important developments in the work of these three composers are ATONALITY and SERIAL MUSIC.   B.CO.

Bibl: O. Neighbour *et al., Second Viennese School* (London, 1980).

secondary occupation, see under OCCUPATION.

secondary picketing, see under PICKETING.

secretion. The synthetic product of an organ or gland, whether liberated externally (e.g. sweat, tears) into a body space (e.g. digestive juices) or directly into the blood stream, as with a ductless gland (see ENDOCRINOLOGY).   P.M.

sect. Term used to describe an exclusive social group which has mobilized around a charismatic religious or political leader. Boundaries are usually clear and separate those who are members of the sect from those who are not. Membership is voluntary, but usually involves total commitment to the sect. The term sect was developed by Ernst Troeltsch (1865-1923) in his studies of CHRISTIANITY. Following from his work, sects were often employed as a concept in opposition to church. Sect represents HERESY, unorthodoxy and opposition in contrast to an official legitimate authority. A.G.

Bibl: Bryan Wilson, *Religion in Sociological Perspective* (Oxford, 1982); S.J. Tambiah, *The Buddhist Saints of the Forest and the Cult of Amulets* (Cambridge, 1984).

secular Christianity. The attempt to restate CHRISTIANITY in sympathetic response to SECULARIZATION. The movement has been stimulated by the thought of Dietrich Bonhoeffer (1906-45), particularly by his *Letters and Papers from Prison*, sent to friends before he was hanged by the NAZIS. The emphasis is on this world rather than the supernatural, behaviour rather than belief, freedom rather than obedience, and a bold maturity rather than conservatism; but the ATHEISM which runs through the DEATH OF GOD THEOLOGY is usually avoided, notably by the devout Bonhoeffer. D.L.E.

Bibl: P. van Buren, *The Secular Meaning of the Gospel* (London and New York, 1963); E. Bethge, tr. E. Mosbacher *et al.*, *Dietrich Bonhoeffer* (London and New York, 1970).

secularism. The rejection of RELIGION after SECULARIZATION. See also ATHEISM; HUMANISM. D.L.E.

Bibl: C.D. Campbell, *Toward a Sociology of Irreligion* (London and Valley Forge, Pa., 1971).

secularization. The decline of RELIGION. This has been more marked in the 20th century than in any previous period of recorded history, and the concentration on this age (Latin *saeculum*) instead of on the divine has become the real orthodoxy of the modern ESTABLISHMENT. At its minimum, secularization means the decline of the prestige and POWER of religious teachers. It involves the ending of State support for religious bodies; of religious teaching in the national schools; of relig-

ious tests for public office or civil rights; of legislative protection for religious doctrines (e.g. the prohibition of CONTRACEPTION); and of the censorship or control of literature, science, and other intellectual activities in order to safeguard religion. Individuals are then free to deviate openly from religious DOGMAS and ETHICS. In all or most of these senses, secularization now seems desirable to many religious believers as well as to all AGNOSTICS (see SECULAR CHRISTIANITY). In the U.S.A., for example, Church and State are strictly separate, although most Americans are personally attached to one or other of the Christian churches; and the Republic of India is officially 'secular', although most Indians are devout Hindus (see HINDUISM).

The term can, however, also mean the decline of widespread interest in religious traditions, so that the religious bodies no longer attract many practising supporters or enjoy popular respect. Most industrial workers suspect religion of being 'opium for the people' to keep them quiet under injustice, while the influence of religion has also been blamed for the stagnation of rural life. INTELLECTUALS tend to resent religion's record of interference with freedom of opinion and behaviour, preferring HUMANISM. In COMMUNIST countries such as the Soviet Union and China there have been systematic, official attempts to suppress religion as antisocial. At its maximum, secularization would mean the end of all interest in religious questions and attitudes, including MYSTICISM. There is, however, little evidence that the 20th century has reached this last stage. On the contrary, both communism and the worldwide YOUTH CULTURE seem to owe some of their popularity to the inclusion (in secular form) of religious features such as idealism, uniformity of dogma, and hero-worship. See also RELIGION, SOCIOLOGY OF. D.L.E.

Bibl: D.L. Edwards, *Religion and Change* (London, 1969) and *The Future of Christianity* (London, 1987); V. Pratt, *Religion and Secularization* (London and New York, 1970); B. Wilson, *Religion in Sociological Perspective* (Oxford, 1982).

sedimentation. The slow natural settling of substances under the influence of

765

gravity (see GRAVITATION) — especially the formation of sedimentary rocks, such as chalk, slate, and shales, by the compacted calciferous or siliceous skeletons of myriads of minute sea animals, especially PROTOZOA. The term normally refers to the settling out of particulate matter (see PARTICLE). It can also, however, be extended to the sedimentation of MOLECULES — a process normally impeded by BROWNIAN MOTION.

Sedimentation is enormously speeded up by increasing gravitational forces — achieved in laboratories by the use of the CENTRIFUGE, an apparatus which enables most precipitates formed in CHEMICAL REACTIONS to be thrown down as a sediment in a matter of minutes where otherwise they might take hours to undergo natural sedimentation. By this means, blood is separated into red blood CELLS (the lowest stratum), white blood cells (the next above), and plasma. Svedberg's *ultracentrifuge* is widely used to separate particulate suspensions in suspending media differing from them only very slightly in density. In this apparatus centrifugal forces up to 100,000 times that of gravity can be achieved as a matter of routine. Large molecules, particularly of the larger PROTEINS, can also be thrown down by such strong centrifugal forces.   P.M.

segmentary lineage system, see under LINEAGE.

segmentation, see under EMBRYOLOGY.

segregation.
(1) In GENETICS, the apportioning out of CHROMOSOMES to GAMETES, and thereby of genetic factors to the next generation; see MENDEL'S LAWS.   P.M.
(2) The establishment by law or custom of separate (and inferior) facilities for social or (the most usual sense) racial (see RACE) and ethnic groups as in the 'Jim Crow' legislation of the Southern states of the U.S.A. providing separate educational, recreational, and other facilities for whites and blacks. Segregation inevitably results in discrimination in favour of one group over the other or others. The word has been extended to cover a whole range of discriminatory practices including the denial of employment and voting rights

and prohibition against intermarriage. In South Africa the term APARTHEID is used; see also DESEGREGATION.
(3) In SOCIOLOGY, the process by which individuals and groups settle in those areas of a community already occupied by people of similar social characteristics or activities.   D.C.W.

segregation, pedestrian, see PEDESTRIAN SEGREGATION.

seismology. A subject which began as the study of earthquakes but has widened its field to cover all the movements of the solid earth. The types of earth movement range from fast vibrations due to earthquake bodywaves, with a period of one second, to diurnal earth tides caused by the attraction of the sun and moon. The bulk of our knowledge about the interior of the earth has depended on seismic studies.   J.L.M.L.
Bibl: R.H. Tucker *et al.*, *Global Geophysics* (London and New York, 1970).

Sekigun, see RED ARMY (2).

selection pressure. A figurative expression of the magnitude of the force of NATURAL SELECTION. One of the conundrums of pre-Mendelian DARWINISM was to devise some means of measuring this force. The problem was solved independently and in slightly different ways by J.B.S. Haldane (1892-1964) and R.A Fisher (1890-1962). Common to both is the principle that selection pressure is measured by the rate at which one ALLELE replaces another in the course of EVOLUTION. Fisher's system is modelled closely on demographic practice (see DEMOGRAPHY) and amounts to allocating a NET REPRODUCTION RATE to the possessors of a particular GENE or GENOTYPE.   P.M.

self-actualization. In EXISTENTIAL PSYCHOLOGY, a term used by Abraham Maslow for the processes whereby an individual comes to understand himself and thereby develops his talents and capacities with acceptance of his limitations.   W.Z.

self-determination. Originally the right of the subjects of a state to choose their own government or form of government (a concept embodied both in the American Declaration of Independence of 1776 and in the French revolutionary Declaration of the Rights of Man of 1789). From this, by way of the nationalist assumption that the state must reflect the national group, self-determination came to encompass additionally the idea of national groups seceding from multinational states and empires in order to set up their own national state. (See NATIONALISM; SEPARATISM.) As such it played an important part in Allied propaganda during World Wars I and II (e.g. in the FOURTEEN POINTS), was embodied at various points in the Charter of UNO, and became the main basis for anti-IMPERIALISM.   D.C.W.

self-image. The impression an individual has of himself, which may differ greatly from the impression he gives others.
                                    W.Z.

self-orientation, see under PATTERN VARIABLES.

self-reliance. Calls for self-reliance followed the growing dissatisfaction of THIRD WORLD governments and INTELLECTUALS from north and south with prevailing patterns of development (see UNDERDEVELOPMENT). The idea was conceived as a response to ties of 'DEPENDENCE' and articulated at the international level mainly in the UNCTAD. The idea was first formulated by Mao Tse-tung as 'regeneration by our own efforts' in 1945 according to Johan Galtung, but can be dated back to Soviet ideas of AUTARKY in the 1920s. Draws its inspiration from Marxist (see MARXIST) STRUCTURALIST ideas in its present form, particularly centre-periphery analysis. Key dates in its recent development are the Arusha Declaration of 1967 and the NEW INTERNATIONAL ECONOMIC ORDER of 1974. Has led to calls for 'south-south' trade which have not to date led to any noticeable shifts in world trade patterns.
                                    A.W.
  Bibl: Galtung, O'Brien and Preiswerk (eds.), *Self-Reliance: A Strategy for Development* (Geneva and London, 1980).

self-similarity, see under FRACTAL.

selfish DNA. Sequences of DNA (see NUCLEIC ACID) that can proliferate by copying themselves through the GENOME of an organism. 'Normal' DNA consists of the GENES that encode all the bodily structures and functions, and is copied only once per CELL division. Selfish DNA encodes nothing, and therefore does not influence the PHENOTYPES of a body, and is capable of having extra copies of itself made. No examples of selfish DNA have been identified with certainty, but the idea was proposed to account for several kinds of much repeated sequences of DNA that can be found in all organisms and that have no known function in the body.
                                    M.R.

selfish gene. The selfish gene is DARWINISM in sharper form. It is a restatement of EVOLUTION by NATURAL SELECTION at the level of the GENE, rather than the more traditional level of the individual. Natural selection will always favour genes that are 'selfish', that is genes which have effects that promote their own survival at the expense of alternative competing genes. Most gene survival is achieved by building a body that is good at surviving and reproducing, and of acting in its own self-interest — that is, a selfish individual. However, gene survival may also be enhanced by the individual acting altruistically. This will be the case if the individual directs its altruism at others who share copies of the gene for altruism that are identical by descent (kin selection) or if there is a high chance that altruism will be reciprocated at a later date (reciprocal altruism). Using these arguments, Richard Dawkins's book, *The Selfish Gene* (1976), showed that group selection explanations of altruism — that altruism had evolved for the good of the group or SPECIES — were highly implausible. Genes are replicators, entities that produce copies of themselves with the occasional error; individuals and groups are only vehicles, entities through which replicators influence their own survival. Dawkins further developed these ideas in *The Extended Phenotype* (1982).   A.P.

selling. A pursuit as old as humanity. It is persuasive communication, requiring a complete and detailed knowledge of the characteristics of product and service and, particularly, benefits for any particular audience; and benefiting from as complete an understanding or sensitivity to the needs, wants and motivations of the buyer, as possible.

Long regarded as the gift of speaking, it is now understood to be, first and foremost, especially suited to those who are good at listening, understanding the needs and desires of the audience, and matching what they are selling to those needs and desires. But real selling skills are rare. And a world that depends on buying and selling has had to learn both to exploit, to the greatest possible degree, the rare personal talents, and to organize and synthesize the skills, using both human beings and even, more recently, machines, to substitute as best they may. IBM, for example, have a high reputation for the sales skills of their employees. In fact, they harness a carefully managed blend of excellent product training and knowledge with a high degree of motivation and incentivization, directed in the most focused way possible to the potential customers with the greatest prospects.   T.S.

semantic-field theory. In LINGUISTICS, the view that the vocabulary of a language is not simply a listing of independent items (as the headwords in a dictionary would suggest), but is organized into areas, or *fields*, within which words interrelate and define each other in various ways. The words denoting colour are often cited as an example of a semantic field: the precise meaning of a colour word can only be understood by placing it in relation to the other terms which occur with it in demarcating the colour spectrum.   D.C.

semantic relation, see MEANING-RELATION.

semantics.
(1) The branch of LINGUISTICS that studies MEANING in language (and sometimes in other symbolic systems of communication). Much neglected by early linguists, it is now the central focus of theoretical interest, though no adequate semantic theory has yet been developed. One influential approach is that of *structural* semantics, the application of the

principles of structural linguistics to the study of meaning through the notion of MEANING RELATIONS. See also COMPONENTIAL ANALYSIS.   D.C.
Bibl: F.R. Palmer, *Semantics* (London, 1981).

(2) In PHILOSOPHY and LOGIC, (*a*) the study of the RELATIONS between linguistic expressions and the objects in the world to which they refer or which it is their function to describe. This discipline was inaugurated by the Polish logician Alfred Tarski in the 1930s as the field in which lay his own influential investigations into the CONCEPT of TRUTH, in opposition to the view that all logical and philosophical problems about the MEANING of linguistic expressions could and should be treated within (logical) SYNTAX, namely the study of the relations of linguistic expressions to each other; (*b*) more generally, the philosophical theory of meaning as a whole, in which to semantics narrowly conceived as in sense (*a*) are added both syntax and *pragmatics*, the study of the dependence of the meaning of linguistic expressions on their users, and on the circumstances in which and the purposes for which they are used. Carnap employed the word SEMIOTICS in this sense to bring these three disciplines together, but in this sense it has not caught on.   A.Q.
Bibl: C. Morris, *Foundations of the Theory of Signs* (Chicago, 1938).

semeiology, see SEMIOLOGY.

semiconductor. A material which is normally an electrical insulator but becomes a conductor either when the temperature is raised ('intrinsic semiconductor') or when 'doped' (see DOPING) with a small number of 'impurity' ATOMS of another ELEMENT ('extrinsic semiconductor'; see also SOLID-STATE PHYSICS).

The ease with which their electrical characteristics can be adjusted accounts for the importance of semiconductors in TECHNOLOGY, the principal application being the TRANSISTOR. The elements germanium and silicon are commonly-used intrinsic semiconductors; almost any atoms may be used as impurities, provided their VALENCE differs from that of the bulk.
                                        M.V.B.

semiconductor store. A form of COMPUTER store (or 'memory') implemented by SEMI-CONDUCTORS, almost always in the form of INTEGRATED CIRCUITS. Sometimes the STORE is read-only (ROM): the information is written into the store at the time of manufacture and cannot be subsequently altered. Sometimes the read-only STORE is 'programmable' (PROM): the store is purchased blank, but the required information may be 'burnt into' the store by the user himself, usually by a process involving abnormally high currents. Sometimes the PROM is erasable (EPROM): the chip may be restored to its black condition (usually by exposing it to ULTRA-VIOLET light) and subsequently 'reprogrammed'. The other main type is read-write store (known as *random access memory*, or RAM): the information stored is 0 or 1 depending on whether current is flowing in a particular TRANSISTOR (static RAM), or whether a particular capacitor is charged (dynamic RAM). The former is faster, and normally used for REGISTERS; the latter is cheaper (though special circuitry is required for regular refreshing of the charged capacitors to prevent information being lost through leakage), and is often used for *main store*. Rapid improvements in semiconductor technology have led to enormous increases in the capacity of store available: a pocket calculator may now contain more store than an early computer filling an entire room.   J.E.S.

semiology (or *semeiology*). The general (if tentative) science of signs: systems of signification, means by which human beings — individually or in groups — communicate or attempt to communicate by signal: gestures, advertisements, language itself, food, objects, clothes, music, and the many other things that qualify. The subject was proposed by the linguist Ferdinand de Saussure (see SAUSSURIAN), but influentially developed by the French writer Roland Barthes. Barthes's complex Gallic METHODOLOGY has seemed overrecondite or obscure to some Anglo-Saxons; but the value of many of his insights, if not of his system, is undisputed.   M.S.-S.

Bibl: R. Barthes, tr. A. Lavers and C. Smith, *Elements of Semiology* (London and New York, 1968).

semiotic poetry, see under CONCRETE PO-ETRY.

semiotics. The study of patterned human behaviour in communication in all its modes. The most important mode is the auditory/vocal, which constitutes the primary subject of LINGUISTICS. The study of the visual mode — of systematic facial expressions and body gestures — is generally referred to as *kinesics*. The study of the tactile mode — e.g. inter-personal movement and touch activity — is sometimes called *proxemics*. Semiotics can also mean the study of sign and symbol systems in general; for which an alternative term is SEMIOLOGY. A similar approach to animal communication is called *zoosemiotics*.   D.C.

Bibl: T.A. Sebeok, A.S. Hayes, and M.C. Bateson (eds.), *Approaches to Semiotics* (The Hague, 1964).

sensationalism. In PHILOSOPHY, the theory that the only things which ultimately and irreducibly exist, and to which everything else that exists is reducible, are sensations. It has close affinities with NEUTRAL MONISM and differs from it only in describing the elements of reality as mental rather than as neither mental nor physical. Mach was a sensationalist, as, with some qualification, were Hume and J.S. Mill. If all factual knowledge comes from PERCEPTION and, as the SENSE-DATUM theory maintains, only sensations or sense-impressions are perceived, it seems to follow that we can know nothing to exist apart from sensations (and what can be constructed from them).   A.Q.

sense-datum. The private impression or appearance which, if the *argument from illusion* (see ILLUSION) is correct, is the direct and immediate object of PERCEPTION. The *sense-datum theory* is the belief that this is so. Sense-data have also been called sensations, sensa, presentations, representations, percepts, and (by Locke and Berkeley) IDEAS. A visual sense-datum is commonly taken to be a colour-patch or array of colour-patches in, or constituting, the visual field; a tactual sense-datum is a felt, textured, resistant surface. The sense-datum theory is presupposed by REPRESENTATIONISM and

PHENOMENALISM which seek to avoid SOLIPSISM by explaining how belief in an external world can be rationally grounded in direct knowledge confined to sense-data. A.Q.

Bibl: A.J. Ayer, *The Foundations of Empirical Knowledge* (London, 1940), chs. 1, 2.

sense-relation, see MEANING-RELATION.

sensorium. Biological term for the sensory system of the body considered in its entirety. It includes the entire NERVOUS SYSTEM as well as the grey matter of the brain and spinal cord. M.BE.

sensory deprivation. The condition produced by cutting off all patterned stimulation from the visual, auditory, tactual, and other sensory systems (including those activated from within the organism) by such devices as diffusing goggles, *white noise* (see NOISE), padded gloves and clothing, and flotation in a liquid medium. Its effect is to produce feelings of unreality and loss of identity, together with a marked decline in such intellectual operations as reasoning, comparison, and learning. Beyond a certain duration, subjects may report quasi-psychotic symptoms (see PSYCHOSIS). The work on this phenomenon has underlined the necessity of continuous sensory activity for the maintenance of effective functioning. Sensory deprivation is not to be confused with BRAINWASHING, with which it is sometimes associated in science fiction. See also KINAESTHETIC; NEUROPSYCHOLOGY. J.S.B.

Bibl: P. Solomon *et al.* (eds.), *Sensory Deprivation* (Cambridge, Mass., 1961).

sensory-motor. In DEVELOPMENTAL PSYCHOLOGY, adjective applied to the period of early infancy (from birth to 18 months) when many coordinations of PERCEPTION and action emerge. See also PIAGETIAN. P.L.H.

sensum, see SENSE-DATUM.

separation of powers. The doctrine that the agencies through which the three basic and essential functions of the government of an independent country (legislative, executive and judicial) are exercised should be quite separate from each other. It is put into practice as far as possible in the U.S.A., under the constitution of which the federal legislative power is conferred on Congress, the executive power on the president and the judicial power on the courts, but there are some overlaps both in the constitution itself (e.g. the president's power to veto bills passed by Congress; presidential nomination of judges for the Supreme Court, subject to confirmation by the Senate) and in its practical application (e.g. executive's participation in creation of subordinate legislation; the courts' power to judge the constitutionality or otherwise of actions of the president and acts of Congress). In the United Kingdom there is no attempt to keep the three agencies separate. Thus ministers are or will become members of one or other House of Parliament; most judges are appointed by the Queen on the advice of the Lord Chancellor, who is himself a cabinet minister, speaker of the House of Lords and president of the Judicial Committee of the House of Lords, which is the ultimate court of appeal, and whose members are all members of the upper House of Parliament; and the supreme legislative authority of Parliament (see SOVEREIGNTY) may always override or alter the powers or functions of other agencies. The virtue of the doctrine lies nevertheless in bringing attention to the undesirability of too much power being vested in any one person or INSTITUTION, and to this end it is a valuable constitutional guide. D.C.M.Y.

Bibl: D.C.M. Yardley, *Introduction to British Constitutional Law* (London, 6th ed., 1984).

separatism. The demand of a particular group or area to separate from the territorial and political SOVEREIGNTY of the state of which it forms a part, e.g. the desire of Basques in Spain for an independent Basque state, or the demand of French-speaking nationalists in Quebec for their own state. See also NATIONALISM; SELF-DETERMINATION. D.C.W.

separatists. Section of women within the feminist movement (see FEMINISM) which does not engage at all with men. It grew out of radicalesbianism, women who sought freedom from heterosexual commitments through women-focused relationships. Lesbianism is not merely a personal orientation, but it is also a political statement. Lesbian separatists in establishing relationships exclusively with women have attempted to escape from PATRIARCHY, male definitions and male power. For lesbian separatists heterosexuality is one of the pillars of male authority. Their position is founded on the idea that women are only able to fully develop on their own terms in relationships with other women: authentic relationships are between women.

Universalism (i.e. claiming to speak for all women) has been inherent in many statements by lesbian separatists and their neglect of the differences of RACE and CLASS has drawn criticism (e.g. 'Many Voices One Chant', *Feminist Review*, Autumn 1984). Other sections of the women's movement have been critical of the UTOPIAN implications of lesbian separatism and its spurning of political activity.

A.G.

Bibl: C. Bunch, *Building Feminist Theory* (London, 1981); E. Eisenstein, *Contemporary Feminist Thought* (London, 1984).

sequencer. An electronic device for controlling and playing SYNTHESIZERS automatically. These devices can normally store pitch and rhythmical information and more recently other PARAMETERS of a sound including dynamics, tone colour, vibrato etc. These devices were originally simple analogue machines (which gave out a series of control voltages) but nowadays MICROPROCESSORS are almost always used for their ability to process and store large amounts of information and they communicate this information digitally sometimes using MIDI.

B.CO

Serapion Brothers. A Russian literary group named after E.T.A. Hoffmann's hero. It was formed in Petrograd in 1921 by the young writers Fedin, Kaverin, Lunts, Ivanov, Zoshchenko, Nikitin, Slonimsky, Gruzdev, Tikhonov, Elizaveta Polonskaya, and Pozner, most of whom were to become leading Soviet writers and literary critics. Their literary work was initially guided by Zamyatin and the nov-

elist, literary critic, and leading FORMALIST theoretician Victor Shklovsky.

The Serapions stood for creative freedom, and in their writings shunned any form of political partisanship or UTILITARIANISM. They had no formal organization and no common aesthetic platform or literary tradition, being united mainly by their concern for literary craftsmanship. Along with other writers of moderate political outlook who wrote about the Revolution and Civil War, the Serapions were dubbed by Trotsky FELLOW-TRAVELLERS of the Revolution.

M.E.

Bibl: M. Slonim, *Soviet Russian Literature* (New York, 1964).

serial access. A method of using a COMPUTER store in which the information is used in sequence determined by its physical location in the STORE. This is much more difficult to use than RANDOM ACCESS and for some problems proves impossible. The need to use serial access exerts an overwhelming and often disastrous influence on the choice of ALGORITHM. See also ACCESS TIME.

C.S.

serial communications. A term indicating that a message is transmitting one BIT at a time. It may be *asynchronous*, in which the transmission itself indicates when each BYTE is beginning, or *synchronous*, in which the transmission is synchronized with timing signals sent separately. The former is employed for communication between a COMPUTER and a TERMINAL; the latter is more complicated but can offer a higher channel capacity (see INFORMATION THEORY). Either may be used for communication between computers, perhaps using MODEMS or a NETWORK. J.E.S.

serial history (*l'histoire sérielle*). Term current in France from about 1960 among the ANNALES SCHOOL for attempts to study long-term trends rigorously as continuities and discontinuities within a series. What is needed for this approach to be fruitful is a long sequence of relatively homogeneous data. Wheat prices, births, and Easter communicants have all been studied in this way. As these examples suggest, 'serial history' is a new term for an older practice: it is one kind of QUANTITATIVE HISTORY.

P.B.

771

Bibl: P. Chaunu, 'L'histoire sérielle (*Revue Historique*, 243, 1970, pp. 297-320).

serial music. Music organized according to a system devised by Schoenberg and later extended by Webern, Boulez, Stockhausen, and others. Around 1910 disillusionment with the lines of development established in the last two decades of the 19th century seems to have set in, and Stravinsky with *Le Sacre du Printemps* and Schoenberg with *Pierrot Lunaire* broke completely new ground. Stravinsky, however, was not to turn to serialism until after 1950; it was Schoenberg who consciously grasped the problems raised by the break-up of tonality (see ATONAL MUSIC). The latter between 1910 and 1920, devised the *serial* method of composing. Serial music is not, however, necessarily atonal; certain composers, e.g. Alban Berg (notably in his Violin Concerto), Frank Martin, Humphrey Searle, and Karl Blomdahl, have employed serial techniques within a recognizably tonal framework.

Serialism is a PERMUTATIONAL method rather than a style. Every serial composition is based on the concept of a *tone-row*, a sequence that uses, normally but not invariably, all twelve notes of the chromatic (semitone) scale in an order which is chosen for the purpose, and which varies from work to work. (The term *twelve-note* (or *dodecaphonic*) applies only to works which follow this norm, not to works — e.g. Stravinsky's *In Memoriam Dylan Thomas*, based entirely on a 5-note row — where the series is of more or fewer than 12 notes.) Normally no note may reappear in the row after its initial appearance, lest it should assume the characteristics of a tonal centre, and establish a sense of traditional key. Initially, the row is conceived in 4 guises: (*a*) the row itself; (*b*) its *inversion* (i.e. with falling intervals replacing rising ones and *vice versa*); (*c*) its back-to-front or *retrograde* form; and (*d*) the inversion thereof. To add to his resources, the composer may also transpose the whole series so that it begins on any one of the 12 semitones. There are thus 48 possible PERMUTATIONS of the original row.

Serial method is a discipline that concerns the composer alone, and not his audience. In no sense is it a complex extension of a traditional form such as fugue. It is simply a new grammar and syntax for handling a new concept of musical language. A later development, around 1950 and associated with Messiaen, Boulez, and Stockhausen, was *total serialization*, i.e. the strict organization of rhythm, silences, and even dynamics (gradations of volume and timbre). It was doubtless in reaction against this that the drift towards ALEATORY music began.

A.H.

serial order effect. The well-established tendency for the beginnings and the ends of lists to be memorized more easily than the middle, and for the middle to be forgotten more quickly.

J.S.B.

seriality. In Sartre's *Critique de la dialectique* (1960) this is the condition under which selfishly motivated individuals live in an ALIENATED society. A bus queue, for example, consists of a collectivity of individuals, united in their desire to catch a bus, but each wanting to catch the bus for his or her own selfish reasons. The collectivity of seriality is thus illusory. The condition can be transcended by establishing a *group* which has common goals and where the aim of each is the aim of all. Naturally, in this group the individual will have been subject to an 'oath' of allegiance, which is enforced by 'terror' and ultimately, 'lynching'.

R.PO.

Bibl: R.D. Laing and D. Cooper, *Reason and Violence* (London, 1964); M. Warnock, *The Philosophy of Sartre* (London, 1965).

seriation. The arrangement of different types of artifact in a series, either simple or complex, taking into account TYPOLOGY, ASSOCIATION, and DATING.

B.C.

Bibl: G.L. Cowgill, 'Models, Methods, and Techniques for Seriation', in D.L. Clark (ed.), *Models in Archaeology* (London and New York, 1972), pp.381-424.

series. In MATHEMATICS, the sum of a sequence of terms. For infinite series see CONVERGENCE.

R.G.

serology. The branch of IMMUNOLOGY that deals with antibodies and other effector agents, e.g. *complement*, which are found in and carried by SERUM.   P.M.

serum. The fluid part of the blood after blood has clotted, as distinguished from *plasma,* which is the fluid part of the blood in its native state. Serum, like plasma, is a yellow PROTEIN-containing fluid, but serum is normally free from CELLS because red and white blood corpuscles and blood platelets are caught in the fibres of the clot when blood clots. After a meal, particularly a fatty meal, very large numbers of fat droplets in an emulsified state may be present.   P.M.

service industry. An industry which provides customers with services rather than tangible objects. Service industries range from coach tours and retailing to the banking facilities of the CITY of London and teaching or broadcasting. The view that they are unproductive is sheer superstition, although the productivity of some service industries is inherently much more difficult to measure than that of, say, CONSUMER DURABLES. (What is the productivity of a teacher, and is it reduced if the numbers in his class go down?) See also OCCUPATION; QUANTIFICATION.   S.BR.

servomechanism. In CONTROL ENGINEERING, an automatically operating control device actuated by the difference between the actual and desired value of some variable determining the behaviour of a SYSTEM, and using some external source of power to drive the actual value towards the desired. See also FEEDBACK.   S.BE.

set. In MATHEMATICS and LOGIC, a collection of objects, itself considered as a single abstract object. Except in *axiomatic set theory* (see AXIOMATIC METHOD; SET THEORY), 'set' and 'class' are synonymous. Two sets are identical if they have the same members. (It is convenient also to admit a unique *empty set*: unique, because the set of unicorns and the set of centaurs each have, in their negative way, the same members.) Sets are to be distinguished (1) from the predicates signifying the properties that define them (the predicates 'featherless biped' and 'man' differ in

meaning but define the same class); (2) from mere assemblages. Thus, the United Nations is a set whose 180-odd members are nations; each nation can in turn be considered as a set of people, but these individuals are not members of the U.N. Similarly, to each object A (e.g. a person) there corresponds its *unit class* whose only member is A and which is distinct from A (it is a set, not a person). As with FUNCTIONS, mathematicians no longer think that a set must be defined by an expressly stated property; it is determined by its members and these can be chosen at random. (In fact functions can be defined in terms of sets, and sets in terms of functions, so that it is a matter of convenience which notion is taken as primary.)

Some useful notions concerning sets are now familiar to every schoolchild who learns the new mathematics, so it is appropriate to give them here. A *subset A* of a set B is a set which is included in B; every member of A is a member of B. Conventionally the empty set and B itself are counted as subsets of B. If A and B are sets, then the *union* of A and B consists of the members of either, the *intersection* of A and B consists of members of both (it is empty if A and B are *disjoint*) and the complement of A in B consists of those members of B which are not members of A. Under these operations the subsets of a given set form a BOOLEAN ALGEBRA.
                                        R.G.; A.Q.
Bibl: R.L. Wilder, *Evolution of Mathematical Concepts* (Milton Keynes, 1978).

set of numbers, see under SCALE.

set theory. SETS (or classes) occur naturally in MATHEMATICS, but their importance was only appreciated after G. Cantor (1845-1918) had developed the theory of INFINITE sets. His ideas formed the basis for the LOGICISM of Frege and Russell. The discovery of various PARADOXES showed that the naive theory of classes is contradictory. Cantor himself made a distinction between collections (such as the totality of *all* abstract objects) which are too all-embracing to be treated as wholes and smaller totalities (such as the set of all real NUMBERS) which can be regarded as single objects; nowadays the former are called *proper classes*, the latter are called *sets*. On this basis modern *axiomatic set theories* (see AXIOMATIC METHOD) have been erected. They provide a foundation for contemporary mathematics and are apparently free from contradiction. The various theories differ in strength; e.g., the AXIOM OF CHOICE may be included or rejected. All of them are incomplete; that is, there are important questions concerning infinite sets which cannot be decided on the basis of the AXIOMS (e.g. the CONTINUUM hypothesis). This reflects an inadequacy of contemporary intuition. Opinions differ as to how far this inadequacy may eventually be overcome.   R.G.

Bibl: A. Fraenkel and Y. Bar-Hillel, *Foundations of Set Theory* (Amsterdam, 1958); W.S. Hatcher, *Foundations of Mathematics* (London and Philadelphia, 1968).

SETI, see under SEARCH FOR EXTRA-TERRESTRIAL INTELLIGENCE.

setting. A form of internal school organization by which children are grouped in 'sets' which can vary in membership from subject to subject, instead of in forms or classes which remain together for all subjects (streaming). Since all the children in any set are of comparable ability in that subject, group teaching is facilitated and the pupil can go at his own pace.
                W.A.C.S.

settlement. The forms and processes of population distribution over the land. Settlement may be classified as urban, rural, suburban, or pioneer. Settlement policies, redistributing people within a territory, are needed in case of migration or rapid population change. Such problems as overpopulation, resettlement, decentralization, and planning of new towns, have usually been controversial. See also DENSITY; EKISTICS; URBANIZATION.   J.G.

sex chromosomes. CHROMOSOMES which differ in number or structure between the sexes. The commonest pattern is that found in man and other mammals, in which females have two large chromosomes, the X chromosomes, and males have one X chromosome and a smaller Y chromosome. Spermatozoa bearing X and Y chromosomes are produced in approximately equal numbers, and the sex of the new individual is determined at the time of fertilization by the type of sperm fertilizing the X-bearing egg.

Characteristics determined by GENES on the X chromosome are inherited differently from those determined by other genes. Such characteristics are said to show SEX LINKAGE. Examples in man are haemophilia and red-green colour blindness. There are few or no genes on the human Y chromosome other than those determining maleness.   J.M.S.

sex linkage. A form of LINKAGE that arises when more than one genetic determinant is present on a SEX CHROMOSOME, particularly the X chromosome. With a sex-linked recessive (see GENE) disease such as haemophilia (at least in one of its forms) the condition can be inherited only through females. On the average, half the sons of a maternal carrier of the haemophilia gene will be afflicted and half her daughters will be carriers like herself.
                P.M.

sex ratio. The ratio of males to females at birth or at any other age. We may take it that the norm for bisexual organisms is unity (1 to 1) over the reproductive period, but in large industrial populations and wherever there is adequate provision for antenatal, maternal, and infant welfare the ratio exceeds unity and in England is about 1.06 (106 male births to 100 female births). Later in life the ratio falls below unity because females have a better life expectancy at all ages and women therefore preponderate in the most senior age groups. It has been repeatedly observed that the sex ratio rises at or towards the end of major wars. The exact causes of this are not known but it is not helpful to describe it as 'nature's way of making good' the disproportionate loss of male lives.   P.M.

sexism. A word coined, on the analogy of racism (see RACE), for a deep-rooted, often unconscious system of beliefs, attitudes, behaviour and INSTITUTIONS in which distinctions between people's intrinsic worth are made on the grounds of their biological sex and GENDER roles. Whether consciously or not, the sexist sees woman (or man) as suffering from innately inferior capacity in areas of performance deemed significant, and behaves accordingly. As with racism, the term though not the phenomenon tends in practice to be restricted to one-way attitudes only, i.e. to male sexism. In the aggressive form of sexism known as 'male chauvinism' the paradigm is one of an assumed innate male supremacy in all the most important areas of activity (with the possible exception of child-rearing), accompanied by a predisposition to treat women as anonymous objects for male sexual pleasure and material wellbeing. For a female response to male sexism, see FEMINISM.   P.S.L.

sexual intergrade, see INTERSEX.

sexually transmitted disease. An infectious disease which is contracted only through sexual intercourse. In the U.K. a Royal Commission, reporting in 1916, designated SYPHILIS, GONORRHOEA and CHANCROID as the *venereal diseases*; the first two of these can be transmitted to babies during pregnancy or delivery. Since then it has become clear that there are many other sexually transmissible diseases. In some (e.g., genital HERPES, CHLAMYDIAL infection) this is the route of infection in the great majority of cases, but in others (e.g., AIDS, hepatitis B, genital yeast infection) sexual contact is one of several ways in which infection can be acquired. Because of the difficulty of categorizing many conditions in this 'all or nothing' way, the term venereal disease (which in any case has an inescapable stigma) is less used today. In England, the following are reportable as sexually transmitted diseases from hospital clinics: syphilis, gonorrhoea, chancroid, donovanosis (granuloma inguinale), lymphogranuloma venereum, NON-SPECIFIC URETHRITIS, trichomoniasis, genital candidosis (yeast infection), scabies, pubic lice, genital herpes and genital warts. To this day, only syphilis, gonorrhoea and chancroid are statutory sexually transmitted diseases.   J.D.O.

Sezession. Name given in the German-speaking countries to a number of art organizations seceding from the official academies around 1900, to start their own exhibitions. The first was that in Munich (1892), the most important that in Vienna (1897), which gave the name 'Sezession' to the Austrian ART NOUVEAU style and is associated particularly with the paintings of Gustav Klimt, its president from 1898 to 1903. In 1900 a Berlin Sezession was formed, with the IMPRESSIONIST Max Liebermann as its first president and Ernst Barlach and Max Beckmann among the early exhibitors. A *Neue Sezession* which split off in 1910, with the BRÜCKE painters and others, lasted only two years.   J.W.

SF, see SCIENCE FICTION.

SGHWR, see under STEAM-GENERATING HEAVY-WATER REACTOR.

shadow economy, see BLACK ECONOMY.

shadow matter, see under SUPERSTRINGS.

shadow prices. In ECONOMICS, estimates of the marginal social costs or benefits of goods, services and inputs. In general, prices emerge from the interaction of SUPPLY AND DEMAND in markets. In the case of PERFECT COMPETITION, prices can be taken as measures of the marginal social value of the associated good, service or input. However, markets do not exist for many goods, services and inputs. In many markets, prices do not indicate the marginal social value of the good, service or input, i.e. there are MARKET FAILURES. In these two cases, economic analysis may require the estimation of shadow prices. In the case of an unknown social marginal benefit or cost, the concept of OPPORTUNITY COST implies a fairly direct means of calculating the shadow price. If a directly observable market for a good or service does not exist, shadow prices can be calculated from other markets where a similar product is consumed. For example, the value of time can be estimated by investigating the trade-off between the time spent in making the same journey by different modes of travel and the cost of the different modes. In the case of market imperfections, the existing price can be corrected for the imperfections. The concept of shadow prices originated in LINEAR PROGRAMMING. Shadow prices are used extensively in applied economic analysis and COST-BENEFIT ANALYSIS.　　J.S.F.; J.P.

Bibl: R. Sugden and A. Williams, *The Principles of Practical Cost-Benefit Analysis* (London, 1978).

shadow world, see under SUPERSTRINGS.

shamanism. A variety of RELIGION which reveres the ability of the tribal priest-doctor (Russian *shaman*) to influence the good and evil spirits controlling life. It is found among various peoples of northern Asia, and also among the American Indians, specially in the north-west. See also PRIMITIVISM.　　D.L.E.

Bibl: M. Eliade, tr. W.R. Trask, *Shamanism* (London and New York, 1964).

shame culture and **guilt culture.** Terms apparently introduced into ANTHROPOLOGY by Ruth Benedict in *The Chrysanthemum and the Sword* (1946) to distinguish between CULTURES which rely, respectively, 'on external sanctions for good behaviour' and 'on an internalized conviction of sin'. Societies differ, no doubt, in the extent to which individuals are expected to consult their own consciences and monitor their own behaviour; but no society could dispense either with the internalization of NORMS (how otherwise could men influence one another?) or with the systematic surveillance of an individual's conduct by his fellows. The terms spring from a phase in the development of psychological anthropology and now have little currency.　　M.F.

Bibl: M.E. Spiro, 'Social Systems, Personality, and Functional Analysis', in B. Kaplan (ed.), *Studying Personality Cross-Culturally* (New York and Evanston, Ill., 1961).

Shanghai Communiqué. The document signed by Chinese Premier Zhou Enlai, and U.S. President Richard Nixon on 27 February 1972, at the end of the president's historic visit to China. The communiqué consisted of seven major parts: (1) a formal statement of the visit; (2) a joint appreciation of the contacts made; (3) a U.S. declaration on foreign policy; (4) a Chinese declaration on its alliances with North Korea and North VIETNAM;

(5) a joint statement about the principles of foreign policy held by both sides; (6) a summary of differing points of view on the Taiwan issue; (7) a joint declaration on expanding cultural and political relations between the two nations. Although the communiqué expressed more differences than common ground between the two, and full diplomatic relations were another six years in coming, the communiqué marked a new thrust in Chinese foreign policy, and signalled a much wider international acceptance of China as an important power in world affairs.　　S.B.

Bibl: G. Segal, *The Great Power Triangle* (New York, 1982).

Shari'a, see under ISLAM.

Sharpeville. A town in South Africa where on 21 March 1960 the South African police fired on African demonstrators against the PASS LAWS, killing 67 and wounding 186, including 48 women and children. The catch-phrase 'Remember Sharpeville' has been much used by advocates of international action to force the South African government to grant full rights to its coloured and black African populations (see APARTHEID).　　D.C.W.

Shavian. Characteristic or reminiscent of the writings of George Bernard Shaw (1856-1950). Nouns to which the adjective is frequently applied are wit, irreverence, paradox, ebullience, insouciance.　　O.S.

shell structure of atoms and nuclei, see under ELECTRON SHELL; MAGIC NUMBER.

shellshock. A psychiatric disorder which first became apparent during World War I when soldiers in large numbers developed paralysis in the face of battle. Whereas some traditional military authorities regarded it as malingering and cowardice and urged court martials, medical opinion tended to view shellshock as akin to the grand HYSTERIA with which they were familiar in their practices with female patients. Electric shock treatment (faradization) was commonly used, though more enlightened doctors attempted psychotherapeutic means to restore courage. It was considered essential for the victim's own morale and manliness, as well as for the nation's war effort, to restore him to the front. R.P.

shiggs, see under SUPERSYMMETRY.

Shi'i Muslims, see under ISLAM; LEBANON.

Shinto. The official RELIGION of the Japanese. This 'way of the gods' (Chinese *shin tao*) was defined in the 6th century, in a patriotic response to the introduction of Mayahana BUDDHISM, and its chief scriptures date from the 8th century. Essentially a way of purification and of respectful communion with the divinities and spirits of the Japanese tradition, Shintoism also became identified with the honours accorded to the Emperor (Japanese *Mikado*) as a descendant of the sungoddess. When the Americans occupied Japan in 1945, Shintoism was therefore subjected to one of the many reforms it has received. D.L.E.
Bibl: J.M. Kitagawa, *Religion in Japanese History* (London and New York, 1966).

shock wave. A sound wave in which the air pressure, temperature, and density vary suddenly instead of in the usual oscillatory manner. Shock waves arise whenever ENERGY travels at supersonic speeds, as in explosions and SONIC BOOMS. M.V.B.

show trials. Trials run on the principles of the MOSCOW TRIALS, e.g. in Eastern Europe in the 1940s and 1950s: the trials of László Rajk and others in Hungary (1949), of Traicho Kostov and others in Bulgaria (1949), and of Rudolf Slánsky and others in Czechoslovakia (1952). R.C.

shuttering, see under CONCRETE.

shuttle diplomacy, see under DIPLOMACY.

SI units (Système Internationale d'Unités). The system of units used at present for scientific work. SI units are built on the MKS system, extended to include electric current, temperature, luminosity, and molecular weight. M.V.B.

sick jokes, see under BLACK COMEDY.

signal transduction. The CELLS of a TISSUE or organ respond to many external signals, frequently hormones in a fluid that bathes them. Since cells are surrounded by a membrane that is not permeable to large MOLECULES, hormones instead bind to a RECEPTOR on the cell membrane. The consequence is signal transduction, in which an internal response is generated to the external signal. The internal response involves one or more second messengers — small molecules that mediate the first stages of the internal response. It remains uncertain whether the process of RECEPTOR-MEDIATED ENDOCYTOSIS contributes to the ultimate internal response of the cell. (See also ENDOCRINOLOGY.) P.N.
Bibl: B. Alberts *et al., Molecular Biology of the Cell* (New York, 1983).

significance (in STATISTICS), see under STATISTICAL TEST.

significant form. A term coined by Clive Bell in 1913 to describe the essential quality of a work of art, that which (he believed) evoked a special 'aesthetic emotion'. It was supposed to consist of certain forms and relations of forms, including colour. The theory of significant form was briefly influential in English AESTHETICS, especially as it coincided with the rise of the POST-IMPRESSIONISTS. P.C.
Bibl: A.C.H. Bell, *Art* (London and New York, 1914).

silicon chip, see under INTEGRATED CIRCUIT.

silicones. A group of synthetic silicon-containing compounds in which the silicon ATOMS are held together by BONDS to oxygen atoms acting as 'bridges'. Each silicon atom is attached to at least one organic RADICAL. Apart from simple compounds (strictly called *siloxanes*), silicon and oxygen can be linked in branched or unbranched chains to generate oils and POLYMERS which find use as water-repellents, lubricants, and rubbers. They are more resistant to heat than carbon-linked polymers, and the viscosity of the oils changes little over a wide temperature range. B.F.

simplex method, see under LINEAR PRO-GRAMMING.

simulation. A technique of applied PROB-ABILITY THEORY (and hence of OPER-ATIONS RESEARCH) used to compare a STO-CHASTIC model with reality by actually generating particular random results from the MODEL. RANDOM NUMBERS are usually used to produce the simulation, commonly on a COMPUTER.   R.SI.

singularity. In many branches of MATH-EMATICS one makes use of FUNCTIONS which are for the most part well-behaved, but behave badly at certain ARGUMENTS, e.g. they are undefined, or become INFI-NITE (e.g. $1x$ at $x = 0$) or are discontinuous or fail to have a DERIVATIVE. These arguments are the *singularities* of the function in question.   R.G.

Sinn Fein. A Gaelic phrase meaning 'ourselves alone'; the name for an Irish political party which was founded in 1907 to promote the cause of independence from British rule and became the political voice of the Irish Republican Brotherhood and its successor the IRA. In the British general election of December 1918 it won 73 seats and seceded to form a separate assembly which proclaimed Irish independence in January 1919. It refused to accept the partition of Ireland in 1921, and remained the political wing of the IRA, pursuing an abstentionist policy towards the Dail (Irish parliament). In 1970 it split along the same lines as the IRA into 'provisional' and 'official' wings. The latter abandoned abstentionism, moved to the left and in 1982 completed its disassociation from the IRA, changing its name to the Workers' Party. Provisional Sinn Fein has since 1970 produced a fluctuating strategy which has increasingly stressed more active involvement in electoral politics in Northern Ireland.   S.R.

Bibl: P. O'Malley, *The Uncivil Wars* (Belfast and Boston, 1983).

Sino-Vietnamese conflict. On 7 February 1979 the Chinese government ordered 75,000 to 85,000 troops to cross the border with VIETNAM to 'teach Hanoi a lesson' after the Vietnamese had deposed Pol Pot and the KHMER ROUGE in KAMPUCHEA.

After suffering high casualty levels and drawing no Vietnamese troops from Kampuchea, the Chinese withdrew. Although armed hostility still officially exists, the hostilities were over by March 1979. The Chinese claim that one of the main reasons for their action was to support the ethnic Chinese who had been heavily persecuted in Vietnam, and indeed, two-thirds of all Vietnamese boat people were ethnically Chinese. At the real crux of the matter, however, was China's disputes with the Soviet Union who backed Hanoi, and Beijing's subsequent attempt to support its anti-Soviet beachhead in east Asia, namely Pol Pot, who had been deposed by the Vietnamese in January 1979.   S.B.

Bibl: M. Yahuda, *China's Foreign Policy after Mao* (London, 1983).

sintering. The process by which an agglomerate of fine PARTICLES binds together on heating. DIFFUSION of ATOMS in a solid leads in stages to a smoothing of particles, shrinkage of the agglomerate as necks between adjacent particles form and widen, and a final densification in which individual particles grow and pores are eliminated. Sintering is important in POWDER METALLURGY and the manufacture of CERAMICS.   B.F.

SITE. AVANT-GARDE U.S. architectural group which has from the 1960s ignored the architectural conventions about buildings as serious three-dimensional creations. In a number of designs, notably for a supermarket chain, they devised Magrittesque facades with apparently peeling and crumbling and broken brickwork, or with sections of the interior store display fixed permanently into the facade. A maverick group, even for the POST-MODERNISTS, their basis has been that architecture is capable of being treated as a form of street art.   S.L.

site catchment analysis. The study of the interrelationship between a COMMUNITY and the territory which it exploits. The occupants of each SETTLEMENT utilize a tract of land and in doing so create changes within the natural ENVIRONMENT. In site catchment analysis the territory upon which the settlement or community is dependent is defined in terms of the total material needs of the community, and explanations are sought for the processes by which the environment is utilized. The CONCEPT has recently been introduced into ARCHAEOLOGY from GEOGRAPHY. It is of particular value in the early prehistoric period (see PREHISTORY), but its usefulness in periods of complex social organization needs to be demonstrated. B.C.

Bibl: M. Chisholm, *Rural Settlement and Land Use: an Essay in Location* (London, 2nd ed., 1966; New York, 1970).

situation ethics. The insistence, against the legalism characteristic of much conventional morality and MORAL THEOLOGY, that the right solution of any moral problem depends much more on the situation itself than on any general, external code; and that the key to the solution is always love. This position is criticized as leading to ANTINOMIANISM. D.L.E.

Bibl: J. Fletcher, *Situation Ethics* (London and Philadelphia, 1966).

situational analysis; situational logic (terms introduced by Karl Popper, 1945). An approach to the explanation of SOCIAL ACTION in which a detailed reconstruction of the circumstances of action (including both objective conditions and the participants' aims, knowledge, beliefs, values, and subjective 'definitions' of the situation) is taken as a basis for hypothesizing rational courses of action for the individuals involved, through which their observed behaviour may be rendered intelligible; i.e. through which its subjective logic in relating means to ends under given constraints may be appreciated. The approach has a close affinity with that of VERSTEHEN as advocated by Max Weber, but rejects any reliance on intuition as in the HERMENEUTICS of Dilthey or Collingwood. J.H.G.

Bibl: I.C. Jarvie, *Concepts and Society* (London and New York, 1972); K.R. Popper, *Objective Knowledge* (Oxford, 1972).

Situationism. The radical philosophy of a group of mainly French social and cultural critics whose views first appeared in an avant-garde magazine *Internationale Situationniste*, from 1958 onwards. Heavily influenced by SURREALISM and DADAISM, their thinking took on a greater political significance when it emerged as the main influence on the student radicals active in the MAY 1968 events in Paris. The Situationists denounced all conventional LEFT-wing RADICALISM — including MARXISM — as hidebound and anachronistic. Instead of the take-over of the state and economy that was the aim of most revolutionaries, they demanded a 'REVOLUTION of everyday life' that would transform personal relationships and cultural outlooks. Through changes in attitudes to sex, family life, work, and the urban environment, there would take place a thoroughgoing cultural politicization that would eventually substitute itself for the conventional institutions of politics. The Situationists were the inspiration of many of the best known graffiti that covered the walls of Paris in May '68: 'demand the impossible'; 'do not adjust your mind, there is a fault with reality'; 'Je suis Marxiste, style Groucho'. K.K.

Bibl: R. Vaneigem, *The Revolution of Everyday Life* (1967; Eng. trans., London, 1972); C. Gray (ed.), *Leaving the 20th Century: The Incomplete Work of the Situationist International* (London, 1974).

Six, les. A group of six composers, five of them French, brought together by Jean Cocteau in 1917. Although said to be influenced by and disciples of the French composer Erik Satie, no common aesthetic identity can really be observed except for an occasional and fashionable cynicism. Auric, Milhaud, Poulenc, and Germaine Tailleferre were each to develop their own musical styles; Durey's talent soon faded, while the Swiss Honegger felt no particular admiration for Satie. As a significant artistic force their influence proved negligible, their collective name being little more than a convenient label attached by critics to a certain aspect of French 20th-century music that moved in a different direction from the IMPRESSIONISM of Debussy. A.H.

Six-Day War, see under MIDDLE EAST WARS.

ska, see under REGGAE.

skeuomorph. An archaeological term for an object made in a form similar to that which it would have had if it had been made in another material. *Skeuomorphism* — the close copying of form and function in a substitute material — is often well demonstrated by pottery types; e.g. in southern Britain in the 6th century B.C. a small bowl was produced with a sharply angled shoulder, furrowed decoration, an idented (or omphalos) base, and a surface covering of hematite to give a glossy red-brown appearance. Many of these characteristics are alien to a ceramic technique but are evidently adopted to give the pot the appearance of contemporary bronze vessels. A modern plastic bucket still retains skeuomorphic features, reflecting its galvanized iron ancestry. B.C.

skewness, see under DISTRIBUTION.

Skinner box. A device developed by B.F. Skinner (see SKINNERIAN) for training animals to learn appropriate responses. The animal is placed in an isolating box provided with little more than one or more buttons or levers to press. Correct responses produce escape, food, water, etc. Using techniques of AUTOMATION, the investigator can register a cumulative record of response to different conditions of *reinforcement* (see OPERANT CONDITIONING), etc. W.Z.

Skinnerian. In PSYCHOLOGY, adjective applied to a type of experiment (see also SKINNER BOX) and a type of EXPLANATION associated with the American BEHAVIOURIST B.F. Skinner. The typical experiment involves an *operant response* (see OPERANT CONDITIONING), like pressing a button or lever, followed immediately by a REINFORCEMENT that increases the probability of the operant response being repeated. At a theoretical level, the term applies to explanations that eschew any reference to internal mediating or mental processes. J.S.B.
   Bibl: B.F. Skinner, *The Behaviour of Organisms* (London and New York, 1938).

skyscraper. Term applied since the 1880s, particularly in America, to tall multi-storey buildings; their actual height has progressively increased from W. Le B. Jenney's 10-storey Home Insurance Company, Chicago (1883-5) to the 102-storey Empire State Building, New York (1931) and even higher recent buildings in both cities. Their evolution stemmed from high land values and was made possible by the development of the skeleton frame, the lift, the water closet, and central heating. See also CHICAGO SCHOOL; POINT BLOCK; STRUCTURES. M.BR.
   Bibl: H.R. Hitchcock, *Architecture: Nineteenth and Twentieth Centuries* (Harmondsworth and Baltimore, 1958).

SLBM (submarine-launched ballistic missiles), see under MISSILES.

slepton, see under SUPERSYMMETRY.

slice of life. A term originally applied (*tranche de vie*) to fiction of the French NATURALISTS, particularly Zola, one of whose conscious aims was to present a cross-section of society (usually lower-class) in its actual, unselected, totality.
M.S.-S.

Sloane ranger. A LIFE STYLE encapsulation of shifts in the situation of the London upper-middle class, influenced by economic, political, and social changes of the 1970s, and finding visible expression in clothing, leisure activities and characteristic modes of speech. First publicly labelled by Peter York in an article in *Harpers & Queen* in October 1975, the female Sloane ranger sports a semi-uniform dress style based on the classic Look — headscarf, jacket, pearls and Italian shoes. Sloane ranger males — referred to as Hooray Henries — tend to work in the CITY in such 'gentlemanly' occupations as banking, stockbroking or law, or become estate agents and wine merchants. Female Sloanes are typically employed as personal assistants by prestige-conscious enterprises engaged in ADVERTISING, antiques, cuisine and other growth industries of the AFFLUENT SOCIETY. The limited vocabulary of the Sloane patois, their ENDOGAMOUS rituals, and their country and sporting orientations have all contributed to the caricaturing of the group, whose emergence and subsequent prominence in the public consciousness seem to reflect the rediscovery of social CLASS distinctions in Britain after the euphoric, expansionist 1960s (for another reflection see PUNK).

P.S.L.

Bibl: P. York, *Style Wars* (London, 1983).

slump, see DEPRESSION.

SNCC (Student Non-Violent Coordinating Committee), see under NEW LEFT.

sneutrino, see under SUPERSYMMETRY.

soap opera. A type of serial fiction originated in the late 1920s by American, mainly female, radio programme makers, characterized by an emphasis on human relations, domesticity and daily life. So called because they were originally sponsored by soap manufacturers, with the advent of television they took on a new lease of life, and the genre continues to flourish in American daytime serials such as *All My Children*, and in British early evening serials like *Coronation Street, Crossroads* and *EastEnders*. It has also moved into prime-time television with more lavish productions such as *Dallas* and *Dynasty*. Soap opera now attracts serious critical attention, notably from feminist film and TV theorists interested in understanding the special appeal of the genre to female audiences. These writers have pointed to the cultural significance of the unending quality — the 'indefinitely expandable middle' — of soap opera narrative, to the kinds of 'cultural competences' required in order to 'read' soap opera, and to the ways in which viewing soaps slots into women's work and social relations in home and family.   A.KU.

Bibl: I. Ang, *Watching Dallas: Soap Opera and the Melodramatic Imagination* (London, 1985).

social, see under SOCIETAL.

social action. In politics, activity by an interested group aimed at securing some particular reform, or support for a cause. In SOCIOLOGY, the most general term used for the subject-matter of the science:

human activity regarded from the point of view of its social context. Theorists have disagreed as to where and how the boundary should be drawn. Some (e.g. Weber) have distinguished sharply between, on the one hand, natural events and the scientific procedures appropriate to studying them, and, on the other hand, human actions, which can only be identified through the ideas and purposes of conscious agents and which therefore call for different methods of study. Others (e.g. Durkheim) have minimized this difference and aimed to study human actions naturalistically, as SOCIAL FACTS. A further difference is between theorists who regard social action as synonymous with human action (e.g. because it involves conceptual thinking and hence language, a social product) and others who define social action as a sub-class of human actions, involving direct interaction between persons, or a conscious reference to the expectations of others. Talcott Parsons's (see PARSONIAN) synthesis of Weber's and Durkheim's approaches located social action within social systems, treating CULTURE and personality as other types of action system. This synthesis stressed purposive interaction, but proposed a naturalistic and functional analysis in terms of the SYSTEMIC properties of its results. The vogue of Parsonian FUNCTIONALISM provoked a reaction in favour of a more subjective, neo-Weberian 'action approach'. Where functionalists preferred EXPLANATIONS in terms of adaptive responses to social expectations by 'actors' who are presumed to have learned and accepted the NORMS pertaining to their ROLES, action theorists emphasize the agent's own 'definition of the situation', his power of rational choice, and his ability to negotiate interaction or manipulate expected role performances. This approach shares common ground with the theory of SYMBOLIC INTERACTION and with PHENOMENOLOGY.   J.R.T.

Bibl: T. Parsons, *The Structure of Social Action* (London and New York, 1937); P. Winch, *The Idea of a Social Science* (London and New York, 1958); M. Weber, tr. A.M. Henderson and T. Parsons, *The Theory of Social and Economic Organization* (London and New York, 1964), ch. 1; A. Dawe, 'Theories of

Social Action' in T.B. Bottomore and R. Nisbet (eds.), *A History of Sociological Analysis* (New York, 1978).

social anthropology, see under ANTHRO-POLOGY.

social behaviourism. An approach, linked with the name of B.F. Skinner, to the analysis and modification of social systems within the framework of BEHAVIOUR-ISM (1). It turns directly to the relationship between behaviour and the ENVIRONMENT, and neglects supposed mediating states of mind. It is based upon the idea that behaviour is shaped and maintained by the consequence of previous behaviour, and also that the environment can be manipulated so that preferred responses are rewarded and so reinforced (see OPERANT CONDITIONING). The claim that if properly used it would solve the problems of mankind has been criticized because the direction of the changes in behaviour cannot be derived from the theory. It raises the question of which basic values are to be chosen and inculcated, and by whom. M.BE.

Bibl: B.F. Skinner, *Beyond Freedom and Dignity* (New York, 1971; London, 1972).

social benefits, see under EXTERNALI-TIES.

social biology. The study of the application of BIOLOGY to social problems, from food production, POLLUTION, overpopulation, etc., to the long-range goals of social and ecological (see ECOLOGY) planning. To be distinguished from SOCIOBIOLOGY. E.O.W.

social choice. Choices made by, or on behalf of, a group (such as a committee, or an assembly or a nation). Much of the theory of social choice is concerned with rules for basing group decisions on the preferences of the members of the group, e.g. the simple majority rule (see SOCIAL WELFARE and IMPOSSIBILITY THEOREM). The subject includes institutional decision procedures and the theoretical analysis of the VALUE JUDGEMENTS underlying different means of making social choices. Any criticism of social choice is based on some underlying theory (often implicit) on what should have been chosen or done in view of the preferences or interests (see INTER-ESTS, THEORY OF) of the members of the society (seen as individuals, CLASSES or groups) and the scope of the subject is, therefore, very wide. A.K.S.; J.P.

Bibl: J. Bonner, *Politics, Economics and Welfare* (Oxford, 1984).

social compact, see under SOCIAL CON-TRACT (2).

social construct. A CONSTRUCT devised to aid in the analysis and understanding of social phenomena. It is a deliberate abstraction (see ABSTRACT) from reality which focuses on particular aspects and ignores others in order to open up new lines of thought and new areas of investigation. Its function is HEURISTIC, not descriptive. Examples are the CONCEPTS of STATUS and ROLE. A.L.C.B.

social construction of mental illness. A radical wing of the ANTI-PSYCHIATRY movement since the 1960s has denied the objective reality of insanity as an authentic disease. Instead, it has contended that mental illness is best seen as a subjective category, designed to register and replicate social difference (above all, DEVI-ANCY). Various types of evidence are adduced to support the case. First, comparative studies of concepts of madness in different CULTURES (east/west, advanced/PRIMITIVE, etc.) indicate no uniform, stable medical categories. Second, historical studies demonstrate massive transformations in what has been designated insane (one age's saint is the next age's madman). Third, CLASS, GENDER and STATUS distinctions often govern diagnosis. 'Social construction' theorists commonly ascribe the supposed rise of mental illness over the last two centuries to an optical illusion, created by the emergence of the psychiatric profession and of institutions (mental hospitals) for housing the insane. Opponents have argued for a real organic substratum of mental disease. They have also contended that the 'social constructionist' analysis, while seeking to sympathize with the insane, actually demeans them. R.P.

Bibl: Peter Sedgwick, *Psycho Politics* (London, 1982).

social contract.

(1) The unwritten agreement between the members of a society to behave with reciprocal responsibility in their relationships under the governance of the 'State' which, in *social contract theory* (or CONTRACT THEORY) is presupposed by the existence of that society. The idea is of ancient origin (cf. Plato, Lucretius, etc.) but it was chiefly used as a tool for criticizing established, traditional authority when the modern nation states were breaking away from Christendom, and seeking both autonomy and just internal constitutions. Its chief exponents were Hobbes, who argued that the social contract *created* mutual obligations which did not exist prior to the constituted State; Locke, who argued that moral principles and obligations existed before the creation of the State, so that men could change the State if it failed to uphold these principles; and Rousseau, who devoted a famous work to the subject.   R.F.

Bibl: M. Lesnoff, *Social Contract* (London, 1983).

(2) The name given to the attempt by the 1974-79 Labour government in Britain to secure voluntary TRADE UNION agreement to restrain demands for pay increases, in exchange for an increase in the social wage (via increase in WELFARE provision and social security and restraint on price increases). First described before the government achieved office as the *social compact*, the change of name was intended to evoke an inappropriate comparison with much older, weightier and broader notions of the 'contract' between citizen and state (see above). The policy was only of limited success in 1975-77, after which high levels of INFLATION, the fragmented behaviour of trade unions and constraints on spending policies imposed by the International Monetary Fund (see BRETTON WOODS) undermined its fragile foundations (see also WINTER OF DISCONTENT).   S.R.

Bibl: J. Palmer, *British Industrial Relations* (London, 1983).

social costs, see under EXTERNALITIES.

social credit. A theory of economic and social development, largely discredited, which rests on the proposition that modern economies suffer from a deficiency of purchasing power. The remedy for this situation, according to Major C.H. Douglas, who first propounded the theory in the inter-war years, was to increase purchasing power by controlling prices and creating 'social credit' which would be distributed to consumers by discounts paid to retailers, and also by 'dividends' paid to citizens for the heritage of earlier generations. Social Credit came to power in Alberta, Canada, in 1935 on a programme of issuing social credits based on the real worth of the land, but never implemented its theory while in office.   D.E.

Bibl: C.H. Douglas, *Social Credit* (London and New York, 3rd ed., 1933).

social dance, see under POPULAR DANCE.

social Darwinism. The application of the concept of EVOLUTION to the historical development of human societies which lays particular emphasis on 'the struggle for existence' and 'the survival of the fittest'. Though not rooted in DARWINISM (the idea preceded publication of the *Origin of Species*) such theories had a great popular vogue in the late 19th and early 20th centuries, when they were applied to the rivalries of the Great Powers and provided a pseudo-biological justification for POWER POLITICS, IMPERIALISM, and war. Hitler picked up these ideas in Vienna before 1914 and made them a feature of NAZISM.   R.F.; A.L.C.B.

Bibl: G. Jones, *Social Darwinism and English Thought* (Atlantic Highlands, N.J., 1980); R. Hofstadter, *Social Darwinism in American Thought* (New York, 1959).

social democracy. A term whose history is at odds with its present meaning. In the 19th and early 20th centuries, the followers of Marx were 'social democrats', and Lenin's BOLSHEVIKS were members of the Russian social democratic party. After the split between REFORMIST and revolutionary socialists which began soon after Lenin's seizure of power in the Russian Revolution of October 1917, 'social democrats' were those who insisted that only the parliamentary road to SOCIALISM could achieve socialism without an excessive cost in violence, DICTATORSHIP and political suppression. Among the things that social democrats have insisted on is the value of independent TRADE UNIONS and the indispensability of civil rights. Today, social democrats are committed to the maintenance of the WELFARE STATE and a belief in the STATE's role in maintaining prosperity and achieving a more just society than the market alone would do, but have few or no theoretical or IDEOLOGICAL commitments beyond that. Indeed, the British SOCIAL DEMOCRATIC PARTY has espoused the belief in the SOCIAL MARKET which was formerly the distinguishing ideal of the anti-socialist CHRISTIAN DEMOCRATIC PARTY in West Germany.   A.R.

Bibl: J. Vaizey, *Social Democracy* (London, 1971; New York, 1972); D. Owen, *Face the Future* (London, 1980).

Social Democratic Party (SDP). Launched on 26 March 1981, realizing an idea for a new British political party first publicly aired by Roy Jenkins in a television lecture on 22 November 1979, shared by many moderate or modernizing members of the Labour Party, and loosely by many voters dissatisfied with the policies of and increasing distance between the dominant Labour and Conservative parties. The SDP attempts to unite faith in market mechanisms for most economic functions with selective STATE intervention and a commitment to a greater equality; offers with varying enthusiasm proposals for the decentralization of political authority and other constitutional changes including electoral reform (see PROPORTIONAL REPRESENTATION), and proposes innovative schemes for the regeneration of the economy and restructuring of the WELFARE STATE. The SDP formed ties with the Liberal Party: this Alliance's support was inadequately reflected in the 1983 and 1987 general elections. The Liberal leadership then sought a more complete merger, thus threatening to absorb much of the SDP while isolating its leader and some adherents.   S.R.

Bibl: I. Bradley, *Breaking the Mould* (Oxford, 1981).

social dividend. A tax system that guarantees a minimum income which is free of tax. The minimum income is paid in cash or as a tax credit. All other income is taxed. Thus, there is an income, the break-even income, at which the tax paid is equal to the minimum guaranteed income. Compared to a Negative Income Tax System (NITS), the tax rate below the break-even point is lower. This implies a higher break-even point and a wider distribution of the benefits of the system. This means that a social dividend system is more costly and requires higher tax rates above the break-even point.   J.P.

Bibl: M.J. Artis, *The UK Economy* (London, 11th ed., 1986).

social drama. Phrase coined by the British social anthropologist Victor Turner, who (beginning with his fieldwork experiences in East African villages, and later widening out and generalizing) analysed social situations, especially situations of conflict, as if they were plays, distinguishing four main phases which he described as the 'breach' of normal social relations; the 'crisis', or widening of the breach; 're-dressive action', and finally, the phase of 'reintegration'. This idea was taken up by other anthropologists, by social historians, and finally (bringing the wheel full circle) by students of literature. The metaphor of the world as a stage goes back of course to the ancient Greeks, and it was given a somewhat different twist (comic rather than tragic) by the American sociologist Erving Goffman in his *Presentation of Self in Everyday Life* (1956), at much the same time that Turner was working out his ideas.   P.B.

Bibl: V. Turner, *Dramas, Fields and Metaphors* (Ithaca, N.Y., 1974).

social dynamics, see under SOCIAL STATICS.

social engineering. The planning of social change according to a blueprint, and the associated TECHNOLOGY of social design and manufacture. The basic idea is as old as Plato's Republic and broad enough to encompass party political manifestos, but the force of the metaphor in modern times derives from a belief in the power of science-based technological thinking to solve social problems. In this respect related terms are SOCIAL TECHNOLOGY, SOCIAL INTERVENTION, UTOPIANISM and

TECHNOCRACY. In its strongest sense the term connotes a belief in the human capacity to invent a future which is discontinuous with the past. In this sense related terms are GENETIC ENGINEERING and behavioural engineering, which is associated with the psychologist B.F. Skinner and explores the possibility of altering individual behaviour through manipulation of the environment, and EUGENICS, which raises in acute form the ethical problems inherent in any approach to social reform that sees it as a technological problem of product specification and design.

The term has also been embedded in a significant political debate related to the nature of historical change, but its usage in this context has been confusing. Sir Karl Popper, for instance, in attacking both Plato's elitism and Marx's social physics as enemies of the OPEN SOCIETY, argues for piecemeal social engineering, a label he attaches to an evolutionary process of social experimentation that is essentially indeterminate, akin to his view of SCIENTIFIC METHOD. But this usage conflicts with more common, and arguably more accurate, application to PROBLEM-SOLVING approaches, like normative TECHNOLOGICAL FORECASTING for example, whose feasibility rests upon closed or authoritarian values determination. Given this confusion, the term may be regarded as a floating resource in ideological discourse.
B.M.

Bibl: K.R. Popper, *The Poverty of Historicism* (London, 1957); B.F. Skinner, *Walden Two* (New York, 1948).

social ethic. Term used by W.H. Whyte in *The Organization Man* (1956) to denote 'that contemporary body of thought which makes morally legitimate the pressures of society against the individual. Its major propositions are three: a belief in the group as the source of creativity; a belief in "belongingness" as the ultimate need of the individual; and a belief in the application of science to achieve the belongingness'. Whyte stresses the paradox that though 'practical' in its use within modern corporate INSTITUTIONS it is, in essence, a 'utopian faith'. See also OTHER-DIRECTION.
S.J.G.

social fact. The term used, especially by Émile Durkheim, to make clear the distinctive subject-matter of SOCIOLOGY and to emphasize the psychological creativity of human society. It is not the case, Durkheim argues, that human association is 'sterile' — a mere AGGREGATION of a number of individuals whose mental characteristics already exist, in given, permanent form, before association takes place. On the contrary, association is a *creative* process, producing new experiences, and new levels of experience; without it, indeed, the human 'person' could not come to exist. Social facts are therefore a qualitatively distinct *level* of facts in nature, requiring careful analysis and investigation at this level, and therefore a new and appropriate science — sociology. This, of course, was the essential, initial statement of Comte, which Durkheim reiterated and emphasized. See also COLLECTIVE CONSCIOUSNESS; CULTURE; FOLKWAYS; SOCIAL STRUCTURE; STRUCTURE; SUBCULTURE.
R.F.

Bibl: E. Durkheim, tr. S.A. Solovay and J.H. Mueller, ed. G.E.G. Catlin, *The Rules of Sociological Method* (Chicago, 1938), ch. 1; A. Giddens, *Durkheim* (London, 1978).

social gospel movement. The attempt of many influential liberal Protestants (see LIBERALISM; PROTESTANTISM), specially in the U.S.A. from *c.* 1880 to 1930, to bring 'the Kingdom of God' closer by working for the improvement of society, usually along SOCIALIST and PACIFIST lines. The most influential theologian was Walter Rauschenbusch (1861-1918). The evolutionary optimism involved was later attacked by NEO-ORTHODOX thinkers such as Reinhold Niebuhr. But this was not the end of the passionate concern of American Christians to improve and perfect society.
D.L.E.

Bibl: R.T. Handy (ed.), *The Social Gospel in America* (New York, 1966).

social history. A subject at one time left to amateur historians, defined as the history of everyday life, and studied mainly from literary sources. Since about 1950, however, the subject has undergone a revolution. It has become the history of social groups or CLASSES, and of changes in the SOCIAL STRUCTURE, carried out by professional historians or sociologists, using the methods of QUANTITATIVE HISTORY. This revolution has made the traditional term an embarrassment to some, but the alternatives suggested, 'sociological history', 'the history of society', 'societal history', and 'social structural history', have not become generally accepted. See also GENTRY CONTROVERSY; PAST AND PRESENT.

P.B.

Bibl: E.J. Hobsbawm, 'From Social History to the History of Society' (*Daedalus*, 100, 1971, pp. 20-43).

social intervention, see under SOCIAL ENGINEERING.

social learning. Term used by the American psychologist A. Bandura as the basis of a psychological theory that emphasizes the role of COGNITIVE, vicarious, and self-regulatory factors in human behaviour. While recognizing that people learn by direct experience, social learning theory stresses that they also learn, with fewer attendant hazards and burdens, by observing the example of others. Theories that portray behaviour as the product of external rewards and punishments alone are criticized as ignoring the part played by self-evaluation. Social learning theory acknowledges three ways in which REINFORCEMENT operates: people regulate their actions on the basis of consequences they experience directly, of those they see happening to others, and of those they create for themselves. Transitory experiences are coded into imaginal, verbal, and other symbols for memory representation, and thus have lasting effects, since these internal representations of behaviour patterns and their probable consequences serve as guides for action on later occasions. Social learning theory stresses the reciprocal influence between people and the environment: behaviour is influenced by environmental contingencies, but the contingencies are partly of people's own making.

A.B.

Bibl: A. Bandura, *Social Learning Theory* (Englewood Cliffs, N.J., 1977).

social market. A social market society is one in which a fundamentally CAPITALIST economy is supported by government provision of WELFARE and educational services which are intended to make it possible for every member of the society to participate fully in the advantages of the MARKET ECONOMY. The concept seems to have been first employed by the German politician Chancellor Erhard, and has had some impact on the thinking of the British Social Democrats.

A.R.

social medicine. In one sense, the interface between SOCIOLOGY and medicine; in a more practical sense, the practice of medicine considered as a social service. It thus comprehends (1) analysis of MORTALITY or sickness by geographical regions or by OCCUPATION — analyses of the kind that led to the recognition of a CORRELATION between smoking and the incidence of lung CANCER, and one between the degree of hardness of water and the incidence of cardiovascular disease; (2) investigation of FERTILITY and the means that must be taken to promote it or, where necessary, to reduce it; (3) investigation of the actual or possible contributions of the disabled to society and the means which may be taken to restore them to ordinary life; (4) a large part of hygiene and sanitary engineering, especially that part which deals with the elimination or containment of infectious organisms; (5) devising and promoting the legislation and other activities that safeguard the nation's health, e.g. the institution of vaccination or quarantine programmes; (6, of especial importance in an epoch of increasing longevity) medical care of the aged and the steps that must be taken to secure their position in society (see GERIATRICS). Social medicine is thus very closely bound up with the legislative and administrative provisions that are necessary if its findings are to be translated into practical use. In the U.K. the Department of Health has for some time been also the Department of Social Service.

P.M.

social mobility. The movement of individuals, families, or groups from one social position to another which is usually designated higher or lower on some socially evaluative scale (see SOCIAL STRATIFICATION; STATUS). The idea that each person in a society should have an equal chance to rise, or gain a place commensurate with his talents, is a fruit, largely, of the modern

EGALITARIAN idea. In modern INDUSTRIAL SOCIETY, social mobility is largely occupational mobility, and education is the chief means of access to a higher (i.e. more skilled) position — though family background and cultural advantages give the children of the upper and MIDDLE CLASSES a better start than children of the WORKING CLASS. The major change in modern society, however, is the status change upward in the entire slope of the occupational structure as the number of unskilled jobs decline under AUTOMATION and the number and proportion of white-collar and office employments expand in the POST-INDUSTRIAL phase of society.   D.B.

Bibl: A. Heath, *Social Mobility* (London, 1981).

social mobilization. The movement of individuals, families, or social groups to political consciousness within society, leading them either to greater influence and PARTICIPATION or to apathy and ALIENATION. Social mobilization is fostered by a movement of populations from rural to urban settings, from illiteracy to literacy, from barter to MARKET ECONOMIES, from traditional to modern social organizations (see MODERNIZATION). New political demands result. Depending upon governmental response, social mobilization reinforces either NATIONALISM and social solidarity (as occurred after the French Revolution) or distrust of political INSTITUTIONS. After 1945 the social mobilization of Asian, African, and Latin American societies undermined traditional polities and also the IMPERIAL ties on which they rested. The process also offers challenges to developed states; an example is the remobilization of ethnic populations in Western Europe and the British Isles.   R.R.

Bibl: K. Deutsch, *Nationalism and Social Communication* (Cambridge, Mass. and New York, 1953); J.P. Nettl, *Political Mobilization* (London, 1967).

social overheads. The costs imposed on the public purse by private agents, costs for which they do not necessarily have to pay unless the tax burden is suitably adjusted. The stock examples are the schools, roads, sewage facilities, etc. associated with urban and industrial development.   S.BR.

social precedence, see under AGGRESSION.

social psychology. A branch of PSYCHOLOGY, usually defined as the scientific study of human social behaviour. The study as we know it is very much the product of the last 100 years. Drawing to some degree on older studies of mass HYSTERIA, crowd behaviour, panic phenomena and the supposed distinctive dispositions of the different social CLASSES, social psychology developed to a large degree out of McDougall's theory of instincts, Mead's pioneering work on role-playing (see ROLE THEORY) and the sympathetic studies of the Freudians Erich Fromm and Karen Horney on the shaping importance of social institutions (see NEO-FREUDIAN).

In order to test its theories and hypotheses, social psychology endeavours to use methods of laboratory experimentation and of controlled research in 'natural' surroundings. Its theories often attempt to explain and systematize the complexities of human social behaviour in terms of wide-ranging generalizations about the individual psychological roots of various aspects of social interaction such as competition, cooperation, conformity, the functioning of small groups, the exercise of social influence, the development of social motives in the individual, relations between human groups, etc. Most of this work has been done in the context of Western societies, but efforts at cross-cultural validation (see CROSS-CULTURAL STUDY) have also been made.

The need to formulate and empirically test its theories has often led social psychology to look for its data to the study of individual reactions rather than to characterizing the properties or reactions of larger social aggregates. Typical is its emphasis on the study of individual attitudes, their formation and change. Much has been gained in precision by this approach, but there is increasing dissatisfaction with some of its constraints. Social psychology is today in process of change, characterized by a continuous search for new CONCEPTS and methods capable of bringing present individualistic concepts of man in society nearer to the social complexities of human life and to a more adequate analysis of man as both a creature and a creator of his society. In research methods, this is reflected in the growing influence of ETHOLOGY, and of other attempts to study behaviour in 'natural' settings. In the development of theory, there is much preoccupation with the study of human social communication and with the manner in which social behaviour is determined or affected by the conceptions about his society that each individual assimilates from the CULTURE. There is also increasing suspicion of the value of premature and often disappointing attempts to reduce the complexities of human social behaviour and experience to 'simpler' or 'elementary' laws of functioning.

Nowadays a social psychologist is someone who functions simultaneously as a 'man from Mars' and as a social anthropologist (see ANTHROPOLOGY), the former because he needs to achieve detachment from his material, and be aware of the social origins of his theoretical assumptions, the latter because he cannot hope to study human social conduct unless he relates it to the context of values, NORMS, and social expectations by which social action is powerfully affected.

Social psychology's subject-matter lies in the area between the biological (see BIOLOGY) and the SOCIAL SCIENCES. Evolutionary, genetic, and physiological perspectives (see EVOLUTION; GENETICS; PHYSIOLOGY) contribute to the understanding of how and why man became the kind of social animal he is; they also define his limitations, particularly in relation to the laws governing his development, both as a SPECIES and as an individual. But, in order to adapt, man has also created much of his ENVIRONMENT, not only social but also physical. He survived as a species because of his flexible ability to construct new modes of existence for himself. The understanding of these modes of adaptation requires a level of analysis that transcends the biological. Obviously, the range of SOCIAL CHOICES and ACTIONS open to individuals is dependent also upon individual psychological processes. In order to study the actual content of human social behaviour, therefore, social psychologists must look at the manner in which individuals perceive and conceptualize social and physical events, and at their motives,

values, and norms developed in reaction to these idiosyncratic views of the world.

While social psychology is one of the oldest of human preoccupations, its importance for our understanding of the human condition remains to be proved. It is at present widely used in application to studies of consumer habits, voting behaviour (see PSEPHOLOGY), worker morale, and RACE prejudice, and is an established part of many industrial, political, and military organizations.   H.TA.;R.P.

Bibl: P. Kelvin, *The Bases of Social Behaviour* (London and New York, 1970); K.J. Gergen and M.M. Gergen, *Social Psychology* (New York and London, 1981).

social realism. Socially concerned yet objectively presented works of REALIST art or literature of several different formal schools. To be distinguished from SOCIALIST REALISM.   J.W.

social sciences. Those disciplines that attempt, in a more or less systematic and objective manner, to study social systems, SOCIAL STRUCTURES, political and economic processes, and interactions between different groups or different individuals, with a view to establishing knowledge capable of being tested. Examples are ANTHROPOLOGY, ECONOMICS, POLITICAL SCIENCE, SOCIAL PSYCHOLOGY, SOCIOLOGY and some aspects of LINGUISTICS and cognitive science.

Social sciences are sometimes contrasted with NATURAL SCIENCES (e.g. PHYSICS, CHEMISTRY, GEOLOGY) on the grounds that there are essential differences between 'natural' physical systems and situations involving human beings (see ANTI-NATURALISM). One way of classifying social scientists (not social sciences) is by their attitudes to this issue. At one extreme are those who write like would-be physicists, using much mathematical and technical jargon, and scorning evidence not collected by elaborate formalized procedures; at the other extreme are those who sound more like novelists, literary critics, preachers, or philosophers. Though fashions change, economists tend to fall in the former category, anthropologists in the latter. The first group of social scientists sees the natural and social sciences as having common aims (i.e. EX-PLANATION, prediction, and increased control over happenings in the world) and requiring common methods, e.g. the use of numerical SCALES of measurement, the use of experiments and statistical techniques (see STATISTICS) to search for CORRELATIONS between variables, and the construction of mathematical MODELS to represent STRUCTURES and processes under investigation. The second group sees the social sciences, like the HUMANITIES, as aiming to enhance self-understanding, rather as art criticism helps one to understand a painting, or PSYCHOANALYSIS helps a patient to understand himself. This is sometimes called a HERMENEUTIC approach.

Parallel to the above contrast is a division of social scientists into those who adopt the BEHAVIOURAL approach and those who are MENTALISTS. A third contrast concerns the scale of the system studied; see METHODOLOGICAL INDIVIDUALISM AND METHODOLOGICAL HOLISM. For an attempt to cut across some of the distinctions and controversies and form a new synthesis see STRUCTURALISM; for a new discipline in which rapid progress is being made in developing and testing suitable conceptual tools see ARTIFICIAL INTELLIGENCE.   A.S.

Bibl: T. Raison (ed.), *The Founding Fathers of Social Science* (Harmondsworth, 1969); S. Andreski, *Social Sciences as Sorcery* (London, 1972); P. Manicas, *History and Philosophy of the Social Sciences* (Oxford, 1987).

social statics and **social dynamics.** The application to SOCIOLOGY of a distinction, valid for all sciences, which Auguste Comte made between two types of method: *statics*, which analyses the distinctive nature of the subject-matter (in the case of sociology, the distinctive nature of social systems or societies), and *dynamics*, which applies this analysis to establishing testable knowledge about the varieties of the subject actually existing in the continuing processes of nature and history. A common fallacy is the belief that social statics (and certain schools of theory, such as FUNCTIONALISM) regard society in a static way, studying it at one particular point of time, whereas social dynamics studies societies 'on the move'.

Neither Comte nor anyone else held that a human society could ever be *static*; indeed, Comte insisted that one of the distinctive features of societies was their essentially changing, cumulative, historical nature.   R.F.

Bibl: A. Comte, tr. J.H. Bridges *et al., System of Positive Polity,* vols. 2 and 3 (London, 1875-7).

social stratification. The process that occurs when individual inequalities — of physique, strength, wealth, power, etc. — become systematic, are given positive and negative evaluation, and organized into patterns that are recognized, if not accepted, by most members of a society. There are two general theories of stratification: the FUNCTIONALIST theory, derived from the work of Émile Durkheim and Talcott Parsons, in which every society necessarily grades its activities because some functions are valued more than others; and a contrary theory, derived from Rousseau, Proudhon, and Marx, which argues that POWER, not functional necessity, is the basis of stratification. Max Weber accepted, in part, the MARXIST notion that stratification is a manifestation of unequal power in society, but argued that stratification exists along three different dimensions, economic, social, and political. Some writers, deriving from the Saint-Simonian tradition, have argued that stratification may exist as a functional necessity, and create levels of command in a society based on technical competence, but these need not be converted into material advantage and into exploitative or power relations; this is the foundation for a theory of a MERITOCRACY. See also CLASS; SOCIAL MOBILITY.   D.B.

Bibl: F. Parkin, 'Social Stratification', in T.B. Bottomore and R. Nisbet (eds.), *A History of Sociological Analysis* (New York, 1978).

social structure. The discernible framework, form, shape, pattern, of the interrelationships of men in a society. It is always an outcome both of deliberate purpose in specific activities and of the manifold unforeseen consequences of all activities, and it can be analysed into its major elements, e.g. its political, legal, military, religious, educational, and family organization. All these, however, are interconnected both by INSTITUTIONS (e.g. marriage, which links the family, religion, law, property relations, political authority, etc.) and by groups, within many of which the same individuals have varying functions, ROLES, and STATUS. In any society, therefore, the total social structure can be broken down into the specific roles, and sets of roles, which individual persons have to fulfil. See also STRUCTURE; SUPERSTRUCTURE.

R.F.

Bibl: S.F. Nadel, *The Theory of Social Structure* (London, 1965); M. Haralambos, *Sociology: Themes and Perspectives* (London, 1983).

social studies. The wide variety of studies which concern themselves with urgent social problems (e.g. RACE, DRUGS, poverty), or with areas of social life (e.g. the development of transport, home-making, leisure activities, the mass MEDIA). Though supposedly resting on the foundations of the SOCIAL SCIENCES, social studies frequently fail to exercise scientific stringency. Indeed, they may even not attempt to do so, being concerned merely to make people aware of problems, of ways of investigating and discussing them, and of political policies which might be designed to solve them. In schools and colleges they may simply be elementary studies introducing children and young people to methods of analysing their own experience and the world in which they live.

Social studies also enter into courses for the training of social workers. This has led to a conflict of standards between them and the social sciences; but social workers are increasingly turning to social sciences for a more systematic study of the problems with which they are concerned.

R.F.

Bibl: R. Richardson and J. Chapman, *Frontiers of Enquiry* (London, 1971).

social technology, see under SOCIAL ENGINEERING.

social theory. Used loosely, this term connotes all those areas of thought that concern men and women as social beings. Its more precise, modern use denotes what would more accurately be termed 'sociological theory'. In this usage social theory is to be distinguished (1) from SOCIAL SCIENCE, i.e. speculative and analytic ideas are distinguished from those statements that claim scientific, falsifiable status (see POPPERIAN); (2) from the social INSTITUTIONS or practices it seeks to explain; (3) from economic, political, or psychological theory (see ECONOMICS; POLITICAL SCIENCE; PSYCHOLOGY).

M.BA.

Bibl: R. Bernstein, *The Restructuring of Social and Political Theory* (London, 1985).

social welfare. In ECONOMICS, the WELFARE of society as a whole (see WELFARE ECONOMICS). Its measurement requires VALUE-JUDGEMENTS and this raises problems. The welfare of an individual is often taken as the person's UTILITY. Social welfare is usually regarded as being a function of these utilities. Individuals may not make decisions in their own best interests, in which case utility and individual welfare are not the same. As measuring social welfare requires comparing welfare of different individuals, it is difficult to see how an acceptable consensus can be reached about the relation between social and individual welfare (see IMPOSSIBILITY THEOREM). This negative view has led economists to attempt to distinguish between changes in ECONOMIC EFFICIENCY and changes in the distribution of welfare across individuals. By considering the former, economists have tried to avoid making value-judgements and have restricted their attention to criteria and statements which are VALUE-FREE. However, the use of value-judgements appears to be unavoidable and should be made explicitly. For example, the evaluation of NATIONAL INCOME, ECONOMIC GROWTH and different policies using COST-BENEFIT ANALYSIS all imply or require value-judgements. Ultimately, the evaluation of social welfare not only relates to choice between alternative economic policies, but requires value-judgements about alternative social systems.

J.P.

Bibl: J. Bonner, *Politics, Economics and Welfare* (Brighton, 1986).

social whole. Generally, the larger social context within which a particular SOCIAL FACT requires to be seen before it can be sufficiently explained or understood. In sociological analysis, the CONCEPT operates at different levels. Thus, the full significance of a particular form of MARRIAGE can only be understood within its wider context of the family and KINSHIP system; but this in turn can only be understood within the wider context of the property relations, the religious doctrines and RITUAL, the political authority and WELFARE provisions, of the society as a whole. This 'whole society', again, may only be fully understood as part of a wider CULTURE AREA, or as having been fragmented from, or having separated itself from, a wider civilization (e.g. the European nations from medieval Christendom). See also SOCIAL STRUCTURE.   R.F.

socialism. A word with a wide variety of meanings but generally understood as a social system based on the common ownership of the means of production and distribution. Although the modern origins of socialism go back at least as far as Winstanley and the Diggers in the period of the English Civil War the term socialism first began to be widely used in the 1830s. It was the combined product of the Enlightenment, of the LIBERAL and EGALITARIAN principles of the French Revolution, and the impact of industrialism. Although most early socialist thought was UTOPIAN and of French inspiration, as in such thinkers as Fourier and Saint-Simon, it was the English Chartists who, in the 1830s and 1840s, created the first mass WORKING-CLASS movement to give expression to socialist ideas for DEMOCRACY, EQUALITY, and COLLECTIVISM.

The ideas of Marx and Engels resulted in a more precise version of socialism which attempted to give a historical, MATERIALIST, and scientific basis to the socialist project. Although Marx was quite willing to refer to his ideas as socialist, the success of Lenin and the BOLSHEVIKS in 1917 led to a contrast between COMMUNISM and socialism. In orthodox communist theory, socialism referred to a transitional stage between the PROLETARIAN revolution and a communist society which still lay in the future. Outside the communist bloc, socialism became associated with the more REFORMIST tendencies of the SOCIAL DEMOCRATIC parties.

As an historical phenomenon, therefore, the socialist movement has been essentially confined to the European left. In European countries it has successfully pressed for the extension of universal suffrage, social reforms, improved working conditions, and a greater economic role for the state in controlling the market mechanism and the ravages of an unrestrained CAPITALISM. In the countries of Asia and Africa socialist movements have been occupied with immediate problems of eradicating illiteracy, improving health standards, and promoting economic, mainly agrarian, development. The extent to which the Soviet Union and eastern Europe are properly described as socialist is a matter of continuing controversy. More generally it can be said that socialism is currently going through a period of re-appraisal. Originating in the optimistic, PROGRESSIVE climate of the 19th century, socialists now have to come to terms with the realization of the global scarcity of natural resources, the recalcitrance of many societies to fundamental reform, and the very limited sources of actual socialist projects. Nevertheless, the inability of capitalism to live up even to its own principles of liberty and equality, should ensure the survival of socialist ideas at least for the foreseeable future.   D.T.M.

Bibl: R. Berki, *Socialism* (London, 1979); S. Hampshire and L. Kolakowski (eds.), *The Socialist Idea: a Reappraisal* (London, 1977); G. Lichtheim, *A Short History of Socialism* (London, 2nd ed., 1985).

Socialist Courier, see under MENSHEVIKS.

Socialist International, see INTERNATIONAL.

socialist realism. The Soviet official formula for the COMMUNIST Party's demands of the creative artist, whatever his medium. First proclaimed by Maxim Gorky and the politicians N. Bukharin and A.A. Zhdanov at the Soviet Writers' Congress of 1934, this recipe has never been precisely defined, though its essence has proved to consist in the harnessing of the late-19th-century REALIST techniques of art (Repin), fiction (Turgenev), and theatre (Stanislavsky) to the portrayal of

791

exemplary Soviet characters (the 'positive hero') and a rosy future (the 'positive conclusion'). Socialist realism has, however, been regarded as incompatible not only with any kind of pessimism but also with FORMALISM, COSMOPOLITANISM, and other forms of DEGENERACY. While its practical application has been modified since the heyday of STALINISM, so that formerly unacceptable innovators like Mayakovsky and Brecht could be posthumously covered by it, this doctrine remains a serious obstacle to the development of the Soviet arts, not least because of the vagueness of its relevance to music and architecture, where for many years it seemed to signify the use (respectively) of FOLK tunes and mock-classical ornamentation, as favoured by the party leaders. Outside the U.S.S.R. it has been a great embarrassment to many Communist parties, particularly the French, so that its interpretation and practical implementation now vary widely from country to country. Socialist realism is to be distinguished from SOCIAL REALISM.   J.W.

Bibl: L. Aragon, *Pour un réalisme socialiste* (Paris, 1935); A. Zhdanov *et al.*, *Problems of Soviet Literature* (London, 1935).

socialization. In DEVELOPMENTAL PSYCHOLOGY, the early stages of induction of an infant or child into a CULTURE's values, rules, and ways of operating. It is one of the major topics of CROSS-CULTURAL STUDIES. In the early work on socialization, major emphasis was placed on the control of motivation by systems of reward and punishment (see OPERANT CONDITIONING), with special reference to critical stress points in development: early bowel-training, control of AGGRESSION, the transition into adolescent sexuality (an emphasis attributable to FREUDIAN theory). More recent studies have been more concerned with the process whereby children learn underlying rules and properties of the culture, an approach partly influenced by the emergence in ANTHROPOLOGY of STRUCTURALISM, with its insistence upon the connected role patterns characterizing cultures. See also PSYCHOSEXUAL DEVELOPMENT.   J.S.B.

Bibl: P.H. Mussen (ed.), *Carmichael's*

Handbook of Child Psychology (New York, 4th ed., 1983).

societal. A term which in current usage functions mostly as a pseudo-scientific and pompous variant of 'social'. Nevertheless, a case for retaining it can be made in view of the exceedingly wide range of meaning of 'social' as in 'social work', 'social event', 'social inadequacy', and 'social revolution'. 'Societal' could be defined as a term which refers to the attributes of society as a whole: its STRUCTURE or the changes therein. 'Social' would remain a wider term which not only includes 'societal' but can also be applied to interpersonal relations as well as to attributes or acts of an individual which affect other human beings.   S.A.

societal history, see under SOCIAL HISTORY.

sociobiology. The study of all aspects of social behaviour up to and including the evolution of social behaviour in man (see EVOLUTION, SOCIAL). It consists of five major topics: group size, age composition, mode of organization including the forms of communication, DIVISION OF LABOUR, and time budgets of both the group and its members. A theory of sociobiology which will unify all this information is one of the great but manageable tasks of BIOLOGY in the next two to three decades; it is likely to be formulated on the basis of the first principles of population ECOLOGY and POPULATION GENETICS. Sociobiology is to be distinguished from SOCIAL BIOLOGY.
          E.O.W.

Bibl: J.F. Eisenberg and W.S. Dillon (eds.), *Man and Beast: Comparative Social Behavior* (Washington, 1971); E.O. Wilson, *The Insect Societies* (Cambridge, Mass., 1971) and *Sociobiology: the New Synthesis* (Cambridge, Mass., 1975); R. Dawkins, *The Selfish Gene* (Oxford, 1976); J. Krebs and N.B. Davies, *An Introduction to Behavioural Ecology* (Oxford, 1986).

sociogram. A presentation in diagrammatic form of the relations among members of a social group. Although originating in the eclectic body of doctrine known as SOCIOMETRY, it is frequently employed without reference to the tenets of that creed. The credibility and informativeness of a sociogram greatly depend on the skill of its author. K.H.

Bibl: M.L. Northway, *A Primer of Sociometry* (Toronto, 2nd ed., 1969).

sociolinguistics. A branch of LINGUISTICS which studies the relationship between language and society, e.g. the linguistic identity of social groups, the patterns of national language use. There is some overlap in subject-matter between this branch and ANTHROPOLOGICAL LINGUISTICS. See also DIALECTOLOGY. D.C.

Bibl: P. Trudgill, *Sociolinguistics* (Harmondsworth and Baltimore, 1984).

sociological jurisprudence. An approach to the study of the law which starts from the conviction that no statutes or codes, however detailed, can relieve the courts of the task of choosing between conflicting social interests and considering the weight of different values recognized by the community. Jurists impressed by these facts, e.g. the American jurist Roscoe Pound, have urged the need for a sociological jurisprudence drawing upon all the SOCIAL SCIENCES to provide the courts with an analysis and classification of the various interests which they are called upon to adjust and of the different values which influence the law's development, and a realistic account of the legal system, including the judicial process itself.

H.L.A.H.

sociology. The study of societies: both the observation and description of social phenomena, and the articulation and application to these phenomena of a coherent conceptual scheme. In so far as there are several competing schemes, sociology is less fully a discipline than, say, ECONOMICS (with its general EQUILIBRIUM theory), and needs to be considered historically, by reference to the three different streams which one can identify in the rise of modern sociology:

(1) Curiosity about how a society hangs together. The major impulse here is NEWTONIAN MECHANICS, which inspired many efforts (e.g. Malebranche, Berkeley) to create an analogous 'social physics' that would account for, say, the distribution of human populations on the basis of some single principle, or (Montesquieu) explain the variations between societies and peoples by reference to climate, soil, numbers, or some combination of these physical attributes. Rousseau contrasted the 'state of nature' with society, and postulated a SOCIAL CONTRACT in which the wills of all are fused into a single personality, the community. Finally, the French Revolution suggested to de Maistre and Bonald the role of common faiths or MYTHS in holding a society together.

(2) A theory of social EVOLUTION which derives either from the Enlightenment belief in progress as developed by Auguste Comte, from the immanent development of consciousness or man's material powers (Hegel and Marx), or from SOCIAL DARWINISM (Herbert Spencer). These three independent skeins of thought together gave a powerful impetus to the idea of SOCIETAL change and a progressive direction of history.

(3) A curiosity about the actual facts of social life that became translated into systematic empirical enquiry. Notable examples are Frédéric Le Play's *Les Ouvriers européens* (2nd ed., 6 vols., 1877-99), the famous 'blue books' which Marx and Engels used to document their statements about the English WORKING CLASS, and Booth's *Labour and Life of the People in London* (9 vols., 1892-7) with its quantitative data and case studies.

Most of the concerns and problems of contemporary sociology, if not the conceptual structures as well, derive in large measure from four men:

(1) For Karl Marx (1818-83), all SOCIAL STRUCTURE was CLASS structure, and the history of all societies was the history of class struggles. In his fundamental METHODOLOGY, Marx argued that social existence determines CONSCIOUSNESS, and that IDEOLOGY is merely a SUPERSTRUCTURE, economic relations being the substructure. (See MARXISM; BOURGEOIS; PROLETARIAT.)

(2) Herbert Spencer (1820-1903) saw society in organismic terms and aimed to construct a social MORPHOLOGY of societies in terms of their structure and function. Sociology's fields were the family, political organization, ecclesiastical structures, the system of restraints (i.e. social control), and industry or work; its task

was 'to give an account of [how] successive generations of units are produced, reared, and fitted for cooperation'.

(3) For Émile Durkheim (1858-1917), the major focus of sociology was social solidarity, or social cohesion: society consisted of a 'collective conscience', a moral force, at the centre of which is a core of values or beliefs that is considered sacred. (Society is thus the source of RELIGION.) Durkheim saw social change in terms of the breakdown of 'segmentation', i.e. the replacement of isolated social structures by complex and interdependent modern society, with its competition, specialization, and structural differentiation.

(4) For Max Weber (1864-1920) the focus of sociology was on types of action, of which economics and law were the MODELS of rational action, and religion of non-rational action. His encyclopedic work, based on the COMPARATIVE METHOD, covered the great religious systems of the world, the studies of large bureaucratic systems, and the interrelations of economics, law, and society. Much of it is definitional, and Weber was concerned to identify the different kinds of authority (traditional, CHARISMATIC, and rational), the different kinds of POWER (*Macht* or force and *Herrschaft* or coordinated domination), the evolution of BUREAUCRACY (PATRIARCHAL, patrimonial, and legal-rational), and the different kinds of rational conduct. He also aimed to unfold the complex process by which rationality, in its various forms, developed in the West rather than other CULTURES. Modern CAPITALISM was defined on the basis of a rationalizing spirit and the creation of large rationalized organizations, and capitalism and SOCIALISM were two variants of a larger, more inclusive entity, bureaucratic society.

Spencer, Durkheim, Weber, and also Ferdinand Tönnies (1855-1936) all conceptualized social change in terms of contrasting modal types of societies (roughly speaking, traditional and modern), with sufficient overlap to allow for an assimilation of the terms to one another. In the one kind of society, relations were personal, communal, primary, with strong similarity of attitudes, and in orientation to the past. In the other, relations are impersonal, bureaucratic, differentiated, open,

and mobile, and men look to the future. Whereas Marx placed his sequence of societies — FEUDAL, capitalist, and socialist — completely within a historical frame, the implicit intention of the other four was to use these historical types as building blocks for the ahistorical analysis of different kinds of social relations in any society.

The most comprehensive effort to use sociological concepts purely as analytical elements, outside historical frameworks, has been made by the American sociologist Talcott Parsons (see PARSONIAN; PATTERN VARIABLES). In the period after World War II Parsons was the dominant figure in American and indeed Western sociology; more recently there has been a reaction against his schemes as being too abstract and a return to historical categories and problems of social change and social conflict.

Among the key *unit-ideas* of sociology Robert Nisbet listed COMMUNITY, authority, STATUS, the sacred, and ALIENATION. To the extent, however, that sociology becomes a discipline, it has to achieve this status through the articulation of a coherent set of interrelated CONCEPTS which can be applied to phenomena and codified as theories, or through the construction of simplifying MODELS which facilitate EXPLANATION. Unlike economics, sociology has no systematic theories which are formalized in mathematical terms. There are, instead, a number of different kinds of models: the *structure-function* model (see STRUCTURAL-FUNCTIONAL THEORY), associated with the work of Talcott Parsons and Robert Merton; EXCHANGE MODELS, associated with George Homans and Peter Blau; *conflict models* (see CONFLICT THEORY); *evolutionary models* (see EVOLUTION; TECHNOLOGY); *ecological models* (see ECOLOGY); and a growing number of *mathematical models*, which seek to formalize the RELATIONS or VARIABLES which are stated in the other models. Finally, one can look at sociology not as a scientific discipline, defined by its concepts and methods, but, in a view derived from the humanities, as a mode of consciousness, as a way of observing the subtle and complex ways in which men interact with one another, and of reporting these interactions in their complexity rather than simplifying them as a science necessarily does.

A survey, necessarily brief, cannot take into account the thousands of detailed empirical studies which seek to relate social phenomena (e.g. social class to occupation, crime to migration, family roles to value changes) in systematic enquiry.

D.B.

Bibl: R. Nisbet, *The Sociological Tradition* (London, 1967); R. Aron, tr. R. Howard and H. Weaver, *Main Currents in Sociological Thought* (London and New York, 1965); K. Kumar, *Prophecy and Progress* (Harmondsworth, 1978); L.A. Coser, *Masters of Sociological Thought* (New York, 1971); N. Abercrombie, S. Hill and B.S. Turner (eds.), *Dictionary of Sociology* (Harmondsworth, 1984).

sociology of development. A branch of the general study of the development of non-industrial or industrializing societies. It shares with MODERNIZATION theory a concern with values and INSTITUTIONS going beyond the purely economic, although it accepts that economic changes are at the core of the development process. The early SOCIOLOGY of development tended to assume too readily that development in the THIRD WORLD would follow the pattern of earlier western development. The process of INDUSTRIALIZATION was taken to be largely a neutral, technical matter, and on the whole beneficial. The more recent view, mainly under MARXIST influence, has been that non-western development takes place largely in the shadow of western societies, and under their direction and control. It has emphasized that third world societies have to some extent been 'de-developed' or UNDERDEVELOPED in the interest of western economies, so that for instance from being exporters of food, as many traditionally were, they have been converted into net importers. A related perception is that many of the development and aid programmes offered by western governments, or by such agencies as the World Bank (see BRETTON WOODS) under western control, have western assumptions built into them that are not necessarily appropriate to the societies in question, and which work ultimately to the advantage of the west. Overall the sociology of development has been concerned to stress the continuing dependence of non-western societies on those of the west, despite the attainment in most cases of formal political independence. (See also DEVELOPMENT ECONOMICS.)

K.K.

Bibl: A.G. Frank, *Capitalism and Underdevelopment in Latin America* (New York, 1969); H. Bernstein (ed.), *Underdevelopment and Development* (Harmondsworth, 1976).

sociology of knowledge, see KNOWLEDGE, SOCIOLOGY OF.

sociology of religion, see RELIGION, SOCIOLOGY OF.

sociology of science, see SCIENCE, SOCIOLOGY OF.

sociometry. The attempt to analyse interpersonal relations in such a way that the results can be plotted in diagrammatic form, on a SOCIOGRAM. Replies to a questionnaire about individual friendship and leadership choices are plotted by means of connecting lines to indicate which members of a particular social group are the effective leaders, the isolates, or the popular 'stars'. This approach to small-group social relations formed part of the idiosyncratic approach to social life adopted by its founder, J.L. Moreno. Although Moreno hoped that his technique would have very wide applicability, it is now seen as merely one of the available methods of obtaining popularity or leadership ratings from members of a social group.   M.BA.

Bibl: J.L. Moreno, *Who Shall Survive?* (New York, 1953).

soft X-rays, see under X-RAY ASTRONOMY.

software. In COMPUTING, the PROGRAMS as opposed to the HARDWARE. Although properly applied to all programs, the term is often reserved for the large and complex programs which are needed to assist all users whatever their particular application. These programs, which include the OPERATING SYSTEM, COMPILERS, ASSEMBLERS, and INPUT/OUTPUT controls, are generally written by the COMPUTER manufacturer and supplied with the machine. Their cost, and particularly the cost of enhancing them after their initial delivery, is often greater than that of the system's hardware; and the precise effect in this area of copyright and similar legislation is still far from clear. C.S.; J.E.S.

software engineering. The attempt to treat the production of COMPUTER software as a branch of ENGINEERING. As in other branches of engineering, increasingly rigorous MATHEMATICAL techniques are used to produce an artefact which satisfies its specification with predictable reliability, efficiency and cost. (See SOFTWARE.)
J.E.S.

soie moirée, see under MOIRÉ EFFECT.

soil erosion. The partial or complete removal of the soil of farmland by the action of running water or wind. Rain collecting as surface water can flow down sloping land as a sheet removing the fertile top soil, or it can concentrate in channels to cut deep gullies. In regions of low rainfall soils are liable to dry to an incohesive state. Strong winds which sweep the coarse soil particles along the surface are capable of carrying the finest dust up into the atmosphere to be deposited hundreds of miles away (see DUST BOWL).

The basic cause of soil erosion is the unavoidable removal, during harvesting, of much of the vegetative cover, and the consequent exposure of bare soil; overgrazing of grassland by stock can also reduce the plant cover to a point where soil erosion is inevitable. Vegetation protects the soil from the impact of raindrops which break down soil aggregates into smaller and therefore more easily removable individual particles. It also combats wind erosion by reducing wind velocity and by trapping moving soil. J.L.M.L.

soil science (or *agrology*). The study of the soil, embracing PEDOLOGY and also *edaphology*, i.e. the study of the soil as the natural medium in which plants grow. The object of soil science is the UTILITARIAN one of improving plant production through a better understanding of plant/soil relationships. The science is concerned therefore with investigating the reasons for the varying fertility of soils so as to conserve and improve the productivity of land. J.L.M.L.

solar cell, see under CELL (2).

solar system. Collection of astronomical objects bound to the sun by the GRAVITATIONAL attractive force of the sun. It includes the nine known planets (Mercury, Venus, Earth, Mars, Jupiter, Saturn, Uranus, Neptune and Pluto) and a large number of moons (or SATELLITES) of those planets, a large belt of ASTEROIDS (sometimes called minor planets or planetoids) lying between the orbits of Mars and Jupiter, numerous comets, meteoroids and rocks. There are only about 200 asteroids larger than 100 km in diameter but probably tens of thousands smaller than one km. These bodies orbit around the sun and all except the comets orbit in the same direction in orbits lying in the same plane. Mercury, Venus, Mars and Earth are called inner planets, the others OUTER PLANETS. The solar system moves as a whole around the centre of the Milky Way GALAXY in a circular orbit at a speed of about 250 km per second.

The *astronomical unit* (abbreviated AU) is the average distance from the Earth to the sun, 149,597,870 km. The planets within the solar system extend to about 50 AU from the sun but the smaller bodies can move more than 100,000 AU from the sun. The age of the solar system can be estimated from the age of its oldest constituents. Stony meteorites (carbonaceous chondrites) are known to be as old as 4.6 billion years. There have been various theories for the origin of the solar system. The vortex theory of Descartes (1644), the tidal theory of Buffon (1785), the nebular theory of Kant (1755) and Laplace (1796). The favoured modern theory is the ACCUMULATION THEORY in which small planetesimals collide with each other and coalesce, eventually growing to the size of planets. It is not known whether other stars have planetary systems around them but it is very likely that many do. J.D.B.

Bibl: W. Hartman, *Astronomy: The Cosmic Journey* (Belmont, 1978).

Solidarity. The name of the federation of independent TRADE UNIONS set up in Poland in August 1980 which developed into a mass movement for the reform of the political system. It was formed after strikes in the Baltic shipyards forced the authorities, in the GDANSK AGREEMENTS, to allow the existence of trade unions free of Party control, to grant economic concessions and to accept demands for some political freedoms. Led by Lech Walesa, an unemployed electrician, and enjoying the support of the Roman CATHOLIC Church, its membership grew to 10 million, in addition to the 2½ million who joined Rural Solidarity. Its criticism of existing political and economic arrangements became more radical, and at its conference in 1981 it called for the establishment of a 'self-managed republic', an idea with SYNDICALIST connotations which directly challenged the leading role of the Party. During the period of Solidarity's existence the COMMUNIST Party was forced to introduce more internal democracy, but its leadership was put under pressure to reject reform by the Soviet Union which threatened intervention. In December 1981 martial law was imposed by General Wojciech Jaruzelski and Solidarity was driven underground.

D.PR.

Bibl: N. Ascherson, *The Polish August* (Harmondsworth, 1981).

solid-state device. In ELECTRONIC circuits, a unit consisting principally of a piece of semiconducting material connected to ELECTRODES so that the element may be used to control the flow of current. Such devices include TRANSISTORS and THYRISTORS. Among their advantages over electronic and THERMIONIC valves is that they require no heating element. See also SEMICONDUCTOR; SOLID-STATE PHYSICS. E.R.L.

solid-state physics. A branch of PHYSICS, whose intense development in recent decades has been stimulated by the demands of TECHNOLOGY and by the understanding of solids made possible by QUANTUM MECHANICS. There are two main parts to the subject:

(1) The study of the crystal LATTICE on which the ATOMS are arranged: DEFECTS in the regularity of this lattice (especially DISLOCATIONS) are responsible for the brittleness, ductility, hardness, etc. of sol-

ids, while the random vibrations of atoms about the lattice positions (see PHONON) determine how well solids conduct heat or electricity.

(2) The study of the ELECTRONS in solids: instead of the ENERGY LEVELS characteristic of ATOMIC PHYSICS, the electron states are grouped into 'energy bands', separated by 'energy gaps'. Solids whose most energetic electrons lie at the top of a band are *insulators*, except when the next energy gap is very narrow, in which case the solid is a SEMICONDUCTOR. If the electrons only half fill a band, the solid is a *metal* which conducts electricity to a degree determined by lattice vibrations (see also SUPERCONDUCTIVITY).

In the HI-FI industry, the phrase 'solid state' is used honorifically to denote any apparatus containing TRANSISTORS.

M.V.B.

Bibl: A. Holden, *The Nature of Solids* (New York, 1965).

solipsism. The theory that nothing really exists but me and my mental states. Not surprisingly, philosophers are more frequently accused of being solipsists than ready to admit to being of that opinion. If the ultimate source of all factual knowledge is taken to be INTROSPECTION or self-awareness, and if immediate experience is held to be the only thing that is directly known, solipsism is a consequence hard to avoid. The usual recourse for doing so, among philosophers committed to some version of the SENSE-DATUM theory, is the causal argument from the involuntary character of sense-experience proper, as contrasted with images. A taint of solipsism, even if it is dismissed as 'METHODOLOGICAL', attaches to the alternative, PHENOMENALIST, way of reconciling the existence of an external world with the sense-datum theory. A.Q.

soliton. A type of wave which can propagate in a non-linear system or medium without ENERGY loss. An everyday example of a soliton is the sharp bow wave from a boat. This is able to maintain its shape and travel a considerable distance before it dies away. Solitons have the property that they are able to pass through one another and then reform without distortion and hence they can be used to represent various types of PARTICLE. H.M.R.

soma. Name used (1) by August Weismann (1834-1914) for the 'ordinary' parts of the body in contrast to the GERM PLASM; (2) by Aldous Huxley for a harmless but generally elevating DRUG much used by the inhabitants of his BRAVE NEW WORLD (1932). P.M.

somatotonia, see under PERSONALITY TYPES.

Somocismo, see under NICARAGUA; SANDINISTA.

son et lumière, see under MEDIA.

sonar (SOund NAvigation Ranging; also called *echo sounding*). A technique whereby short pulses of *ultrasound* are emitted under water, and the time delay and nature of any echoes are interpreted to yield information about the presence and location of shoals of fish, submarines, the sea bed, etc. Sonar was developed because radio waves cannot be transmitted through water, so that RADAR cannot be used. See also ANIMAL SONAR. M.V.B.

sonic boom. The sound caused by passage of a SHOCK WAVE from a supersonic aircraft. The shock takes the form of a cone whose tip is pulled along by the aircraft as it continually overtakes the sound waves it produces, in an extreme form of the DOPPLER EFFECT. The boom, which sounds more like a crack, is heard by an observer on the ground as the cone passes through him; this may occur many seconds after the aircraft has passed overhead. Sometimes two booms are heard, one from the nose and one from the tail. M.V.B.

sonography, see under UROLOGY.

sorcery. Refers to a technique employed to attain certain aims, based on the principles of MAGIC. Unlike WITCHCRAFT, which is thought to be involuntary or unconscious (a person may be a witch without knowing it), sorcery is conscious and intentional. A sorcerer deliberately employs spells and physical materials to bring about results. The status of sorcery,

however, is morally ambiguous: it may be socially beneficial or harmful.

All individuals may use sorcery. They have access to the means, but their STATUS and the purpose to which it is directed define whether sorcery is being used to legitimate or subvert the social order. Sorcery may be used by persons in recognized positions of authority to bring benefits to society (to drive out evil and threatening forces). These same individuals, if they use sorcery for their own ends, will be acting illegitimately as evil sorcerers. Sorcery as a technique may be employed by those without power to challenge or lay claim to established and legitimate positions of authority (see RITUAL). A.G.

Bibl: S.J. Tambiah, 'On Flying Witches and Flying Canoes: The Coding of Male and Female Values', in J.W. Leach and Edmund Leach (eds.), *The Kula* (Cambridge, 1983); L. Holy and M. Stuchlik, *The Structure of Folk Models* (London, 1981).

sororal polygyny, see under POLYGYNY.

sortal. In philosophy, a UNIVERSAL which provides a means of grouping particular things into kinds or species. For example, 'dog' and 'cat' are sortals; the criteria for applying these terms are exactly the criteria for separating dogs from cats or for grouping all dogs together. 'Water', 'butter' (see MASS TERMS) are not sortals.
A.C.G.

soul. Part musical style, part social attitude, soul became the dominant force in BLACK music in the 1960s. More positive in outlook and more public than the BLUES, its close antecedent is gospel music, the traditional voice of the black community, with its spirit of passionate freedom transferred from the church to the disco. Soul emerged as a force at the same time as that community was declaring its rightful identity in American life: in one of his biggest hits, soul's biggest star, James Brown, exhorted his brothers and sisters to 'say it loud, I'm black and I'm proud'. As a musical genre it was and is urban, aggressive, ecstatic, making equal use of high energy and high tech. The skills of recording engineers and producers (like Motown's Barry Gordy) are as formidable and necessary as those of the performers, and the result is as smooth, polished, potent as a racing car. If the simple individuality of the blues has been lost, many blacks regard the older form as 'slave time' music anyway, with associations better forgotten. For them, soul represents the authentic voice of contemporary black aspiration and deserves all its commercial success.   GE.S.

Bibl: P. Garland, *The Sound of Soul* (Chicago, 1969).

sound-law. In PHILOLOGY, a term referring to a hypothetical phonetic principle governing regular changes in sounds at different periods in a language's history. Such a hypothetical principle is derived from the analysis of uniform sets of correspondences operating between the sounds at these different periods.   D.C.

sound sampling. The technique of converting a sound into numbers (with an ANALOGUE TO DIGITAL CONVERTER), storing this information, processing it and finally reproducing the original sounds or variations on them, frequently controlled by a musical keyboard. A sound sampler enables a musician to sample for example a violin note (or notes — multi-sampling) and then play a piece of violin music from the keyboard. Unlike SYNTHESIZERS which can only approximate real instrumental sounds, sampled sounds are frequently indistinguishable from their originals. In many areas of music (notably ADVERTISING and television music) sound samplers are gradually replacing conventional instruments (with opposition from musicians' unions) because of their flexibility and cheapness (a single musician using MULTITRACK RECORDING and sound sampling can reproduce a complete orchestral piece). On the more experimental side sound samplers can sample 'non-musical' sounds (e.g. cars, weather, speech) and transform them into musical material in the manner of MUSIQUE CONCRÈTE but with the advantage of live, REAL TIME performance. As sound samplers become cheaper and more realistic they are set to have a more profound effect on every aspect of musical life than any other musical innovation this century.   B.CO.

Bibl: R. Hammond, *The Musician and the Micro* (Blandford, 1983).

source criticism, see under HIGHER CRITICISM.

sovereignty. Literally, the possession of ultimate legal authority; a STATE is sovereign when its rulers owe allegiance to no superior power and are themselves supreme within the local legal order; an individual may be said to be 'sovereign over himself' when he need ask permission of no one else to do as he chooses in a given area. The interest of the CONCEPT lies in the theoretical problems it produces; the U.S., for instance, is plainly a sovereign state, but commentators have never agreed where sovereignty is located within the U.S. — the Supreme Court can veto congressional legislation if it is unconstitutional, but Congress and the states can alter the constitution. No one body possesses supreme authority in all areas — does the U.S. possess a sovereign, then?
                                              A.R.

Bibl: B. de Jouvenel, *Sovereignty* (Cambridge, 1957); H.L.A. Hart, *The Concept of Law* (Oxford, 1962).

Soviet dissent. The term used for any opposition to the position or policies of the COMMUNIST Party which is not articulated through legitimate institutions. As MARXIST-LENINIST ideology considers that the Communist Party expresses the will of the Soviet people, challenges to its authority or policies which ignore the leading role of the Party are regarded as attacks on the people and the state and should thus be suppressed. The dissent movement is small and ideologically heterogeneous. While all groups argue in favour of greater freedom of speech and expression and urge a consistent respect for HUMAN RIGHTS, other demands are more diverse. They range from the rejection of modern secular society by writers such as Alexander Solzhenitsyn, to proposals by Andrei Sakharov for a movement towards a more liberal, democratic state, to the democratic LENINISM of Roy Medvedev. Other groups campaign more specifically for national or religious autonomy. Dissident groups were strongest between the late 1960s and early 1970s when the authorities drove them underground and forced many members to emigrate. However, the agreement by the Soviet Union to observe human rights in the HELSINKI Final Act of 1975 gave rise to the establishment by dissidents of several organizations to monitor its implementation.

Mikhail Gorbachev, the recently elected General Secretary of the Communist Party, towards the end of 1986 inaugurated a new policy which has led to the release of several well-known dissidents. In December Andrei Sakharov was released from internal exile and the cases of many others are to be reviewed. The government has also promised that a larger number of Jews will be allowed to emigrate from the Soviet Union than previously, and the prominent Jewish dissident, Anatoly Shcharansky, has been allowed to leave for the West.   D.PR.

Bibl: R. Tökés (ed.), *Dissent in the USSR* (London, 1975).

Soviets. Originally workers' councils which first emerged in Russia during the 1905 revolution. In 1917 they appeared again as Soviets of Workers' and Soldiers' Deputies. After General Kornilov's attempt to halt the Revolution (September 1917), many important Soviets switched allegiance and transformed a MENSHEVIK into a BOLSHEVIK majority. The Petrograd Soviet, led by Trotsky, established a Military Revolutionary Committee which became an instrument for the Bolshevik seizure of power under the slogan 'All Power to the Soviets'. Since then they have lost their autonomy, becoming the COMMUNIST Party's 'transmission belts to the masses' and eventually the principal INSTITUTIONS in the formal structure of power.

The Supreme Soviet, constitutionally the highest organ of state in the U.S.S.R., consists of two chambers: the Soviet of the Union and the Soviet of Nationalities. Its deputies are elected for five years (virtually unanimously, in one-candidate constituencies). All their decisions are also passed unanimously (by a show of hands).
                                                    L.L.

Bibl: J. Hough and M. Fainsod, *How the Soviet Union is Governed* (Cambridge, Mass., rev. ed., 1979).

sovkhoz, see under COLLECTIVIZATION.

Soweto, see under BLACK CONSCIOUSNESS.

space.
(1) In METEOROLOGY and ASTRONOMY, space is considered to be the region lying beyond the limit of the earth's atmosphere.   M.L.
(2) In the arts, space has become an increasingly important concept with the development of ABSTRACT ART, notably as rationalized by the CONSTRUCTIVISTS. Among the term's uses and abuses are (*a*) the space-stage, or *Raumbühne*, of Friedrich Kiesler and Karl Heinz Martin in the 1920s; (*b*) the 'spatio-dynamism' of Nicolas Schöffer's KINETIC works; (*c*) the 'spazialismo' manifesto of the Movimento Spaziale (Milan, 1954); (*d*) the French 'Espace' movement of 1951; and (*e*) the poetic 'spatialism' of Pierre Garnier, a freer form of CONCRETE POETRY.   J.W.
(3) GEOGRAPHY can be described as the study of how events and phenomena are distributed and linked together across space. Geography before the 1960s was principally concerned with the uniqueness of peoples in specific PLACES, REGIONS and ENVIRONMENTS and sought to produce regional geographies. With the rise of geography as a SPATIAL SCIENCE, space came to the fore as the prime organizing CONCEPT. It began to be thought that all geographical distributions, irrespective of their time and place, were governed by — and therefore could be 'explained' in terms of — universal laws of spatial organization and human spatial behaviour, and this introduced an 'absolute' view of space as a distinctive entity possessing its own causal powers (see CAUSALITY). This view has recently been attacked for its 'spatial fetishism', but that revision is itself under attack for downplaying the role of space.
                                                    C.P.
Bibl: R. D. Sack, *Conceptions of Space in Social Thought* (London, 1980).

space frames, see under STRUCTURE (2).

space perception. The process in vision whereby we locate the positions, sizes, and distances of objects in external space. Problems arise because any size of image in an eye — a retinal image — may be given by a small near object or by a correspondingly larger and more distant object. So the size of retinal images is not sufficient to determine how large or how distant an object is, or appears. The two eyes work together to give *stereoscopic* depth; but this does not function for distant objects, because the 'base line' given by the eye separation is too short, only 2½ inches. The visual world seems to be scaled for size and distance by acceptance of typical features, such as perspective convergence and texture gradients, present in the retinal image as 'clues' to size and distance. This implies that the brain must carry out quite complicated computations to estimate scale. When the available 'clues' are not typical they may mislead PERCEPTION, to produce distortions of visual space, such as some of the well-known visual illusions in perspective drawings. See also GESTALT; VISUAL CLIFF.

R.L.G.

space probe. A ROCKET equipped with instruments, which is sent into space to study RADIATION, COSMIC RAYS, etc.

M.V.B.

space-stage, see under SPACE (2).

space-time. A mathematical CONSTRUCT, representing the arena of events. In NEWTONIAN MECHANICS, the three dimensions of space and the FOURTH DIMENSION of time can be clearly separated; this means that the distance separating two events, and the time interval between them, are independent of the motion of the FRAME OF REFERENCE from which they are studied.

But according to RELATIVITY this absolute separation between space and time cannot be made; *both* the time and the distance between events will vary with the motion of the observer. The only 'absolute' quantity, which can truly be said to belong to the events themselves independently of any observer, is the so-called 'interval', a mathematical analogue of distance in four-dimensional space-time.

M.V.B.

space-time foam, see under PLANCK TIME/ERA.

span of control, see under MANAGEMENT STUDIES.

Spartacists. Anglicization of the *Spartakusbund*, a LEFT-wing REVOLUTIONARY splinter group (named after the leader of the Roman slaves' revolt of 73-71 B.C.), which broke away from the German SOCIAL DEMOCRATIC movement in 1917 under the leadership of Rosa Luxemburg and Karl Liebknecht. The Spartacists attacked the continuation of the war, supported the BOLSHEVIK revolution in Russia, and called for the overthrow of the government by direct action and a SOCIALIST revolution in Germany to be carried out by setting up workers' and soldiers' SOVIETS. In the period of revolutionary disorder that followed the abdication of the Kaiser (9 November 1918) the Spartacists (who reconstituted themselves as the Communist Party of Germany on 30 December) led a series of mass demonstrations against the compromise policy of Ebert's republican government and in January 1919 occupied a number of public buildings and newspaper offices in Berlin. They were driven out by force and their two leaders shot by army officers. The murder of Liebknecht and Rosa Luxemburg ensured them a place in COMMUNIST hagiography which criticism of Lenin's tactics and their dislike of large-scale organization and party discipline would certainly have denied them had they lived.

D.C.W.

Bibl: J.P. Nettl, *Rosa Luxemburg* (2 vols., London and New York, 1966); N. Geras, *The Legacy of Rosa Luxemburg* (London, 1976).

sparticle, see under SUPERSYMMETRY.

spatial diffusion, see under DIFFUSION (3).

spatial music. There are quite a few instances in the history of music of composers taking an interest in the spatial placing of the performers in their music (e.g. Wagner, Ives) but it is only in the last 40 years that an intense interest in this aspect of music has arisen. The main catalyst for this enthusiasm is undoubtedly the use in ELECTRONIC MUSIC of multiple speaker systems which give the composer the ability to place sounds in specific locations around and among the audience and even to move sounds around in various ways during a performance. Specific architectural environments have even been built to house such works. The use of space has spread to instrumental music such as Stockhausen's 'Gruppen' which uses three orchestras situated around the audience.

B.CO.

spatial science. A perspective which surfaced in human GEOGRAPHY during the 1960s, and which attempted to replace the discipline's older focus on the uniqueness of particular peoples and PLACES — the hallmark of *regional geography* — with a desire to discover the universal laws of spatial organization supposedly governing how human beings everywhere and at every time distribute their settlements, farms, factories, shops, roads and other productions across the physical landscape. In addition, this perspective embraced a concern to discover the universal laws of *spatial behaviour* supposedly governing how human beings everywhere and at every time organize their use of these myriad spatial distributions. In searching for universal laws — and in employing statistical, mathematical and modelling techniques as tools vital to this search — geography as spatial science succumbed to both a NATURALISM (sense 3) and a little-examined commitment to the philosophy of POSITIVISM. While many interesting findings have emerged from this 'new' geographical departure, it is now being heavily criticized by advocates of HUMANISTIC GEOGRAPHY and RADICAL GEOGRAPHY for neglecting, respectively, the creative role of human beings and the complex socio-economic contexts in which geographical distributions are always embedded. See also LOCATIONAL ANALYSIS and SPACE.

C.P.

Bibl: R. Abler *et al.*, *Spatial Organization: The Geographer's View of the World* (Englewood Cliffs, N.J., 1971).

spatialism, see under SPACE (2).

spatiodynamism, see under KINETIC ART.

Spear of the Nation, see under AFRICAN NATIONAL CONGRESS.

Special Drawing Rights (SDRs), see under INTERNATIONAL LIQUIDITY.

Special Economic Zones, see under OPEN CITIES.

special education. As defined in Great Britain, education provided to meet the special needs of pupils with marked disabilities of body or mind. Such provision is made under the 1944 Education Act and subsequent regulations, the children (from the age of two and upwards) being classified as blind, partially sighted, deaf, partially hearing, delicate (including diabetics, asthmatics, heart cases), educationally sub-normal (ESN), EPILEPTIC, maladjusted, physically handicapped, or speech-defective. Special education is provided in many forms: particular arrangements in ordinary schools, special classes, boarding-houses or hostels, hospitals, guidance clinics of many kinds, special schools, and home-visiting. Training in the teaching of handicapped children is widely offered in colleges and Institutes of Education, usually in the form of one-year courses for teachers already possessing normal qualifications and school experience.

In the U.S.A. the classifications of special educational need are similar to those in Great Britain, although under the heading of the education of exceptional children the intellectually gifted are also included. Special education is administered at Federal, State, and local levels, funds for training and research coming from Federal sources, direct services to children from State and local ones.

W.A.C.S.

species.
(1) The terminal element in the taxonomic hierarchy of BIOSYSTEMATICS. This, however, is a description rather than a definition. Definitions range from the ruthlessly pragmatic view that a species is anything regarded as such by a competent systematist, to the assertion that a species is essentially a 'point-cluster in n-dimensional character space'; both definitions are equally unhelpful. In any event the CONCEPT of species has been profoundly modified by POPULATION GENETICS. It is now universally agreed, however,

that no species consists of identical individuals, so that no one individual and no one genetic formula is representative of a species as a whole. A species is an actually or potentially inter-fertile assemblage of unlike individuals of which the genetically defining characteristics can only be represented by a 'GENE pool', the elements of which are variously recombined and reassorted in the process of sexual reproduction. In EVOLUTION a new species may arise by genetic transformation of an existing species leading to the establishment of a new and distinctive gene pool; or, under unequal selective pressures, a single species may divide into two. The practical problem in systematics at a species level is that of actually attaching a particular name to a particular plant, animal, or museum specimen. Yet if the genetical view is correct the exact typological characterization of species in this way cannot be possible, though an attribution may be made of such a high degree of likelihood that it is virtually a certain one. The element of personal judgement in such decisions is only to be deplored when experts disagree. It follows from the genetic conception of species that some measure of reproductive isolation, whether by geographical or other means, is a necessary precondition for speciation, for otherwise the gene pool would not maintain its integrity.   P.M.

(2) In CHEMISTRY, a general term which may be used to describe an ELEMENT, MOLECULE, RADICAL, or ION.   B.F.

specificity, see under PATTERN VARIABLES.

spectrographic analysis. A method of quantitative analysis involving a study of the light emitted when a substance vaporizes. It is based upon the fact that the light produced by each element, when split by a prism, yields a characteristic pattern of black lines crossing its spectrum. In practice a small sample of the substance to be analysed is caused to vaporize between graphite ELECTRODES, the light emitted being recorded, usually on a photographic plate. Since the method requires relatively small quantities of material it is particularly useful in ARCHAEOLOGY for analys-

ing artifacts such as bronze implements and weapons.   B.C.

spectrometry, mass, see MASS SPECTROMETRY.

spectroscopy. The analysis of electromagnetic RADIATION emitted by matter. By means of a spectroscope (simply a glass prism in the case of visible light) the different frequencies or colours in the radiation are spread out into a spectrum. Each frequency has been emitted as the result of transitions of ELECTRONS in the source from one ENERGY LEVEL to another. The distribution of energy levels is different for all substances and all states of temperature, pressure, etc., so that the intensities with which the various frequencies occur in the spectrum provide a precise and powerful method for determining the nature of the source. The spectra of the sun and stars consist of continuous coloured bands emitted by the dense hot core, crossed by thousands of sharp dark lines caused by absorption by ATOMS in the tenuous relatively cool atmosphere (see also ASTROPHYSICS).   M.V.B.

speech act. In LINGUISTICS, a notion derived from the philosopher J.L. Austin (1911-60), to refer to a theory which analyses the role of utterances in relation to the behaviour of speaker and hearer in interpersonal communication. It is not an 'act of speech', in a purely physical sense, but a communicative activity (a 'locutionary' act), defined with reference to the intentions of the speaker while speaking (the ILLOCUTIONARY force of his utterances) and the effects he achieves on his listener (the 'perlocutionary' effect of the utterances). Several categories of speech acts have been proposed, such as *directives* (e.g. begging, commanding), *commissives* (e.g. guaranteeing, promising), and *expressives* (e.g. welcoming, apologizing).   D.C.

Bibl: S. Levinson, *Pragmatics* (Cambridge, 1983).

speech recognition. A term that often refers to the recognition of speech by a machine (see MAN-MACHINE INTERFACE). The speech signal is converted to a digital ENCODING (see DIGITAL-TO-ANALOGUE

SPEECH SYNTHESIS

CONVERTER) which is then analysed by a COMPUTER and compared with other previously analysed samples of known speech. Very reliable recognition of known single word commands from known speakers can be achieved, with less reliability for unknown speakers. Utterances involving more than one word usually requires the speaker to pause between each word. Recognition of continuous, natural speech is not yet practically realizable.

The major difficulty in speech recognition is that the PHONETIC and LINGUISTIC properties of speech are not always reflected in the physical properties of its signal in a direct way. For instance, different utterances of the same words by just one person can produce great variations in the speech signal. Nor is it easy to extend the information gained by analysing utterances of known words by known speakers to allow comparison against utterances of unknown words by unknown speakers.

R.S.C.

speech synthesis. The simulation of human speech by artificial means. Early attempts used mechanical MODELS of the human vocal tract, air being pumped through while the model was manipulated in accordance with the hypothesized processes of articulation. More recently, electronically generated noise has been modified so as to simulate the resonances of the different parts of the vocal tract. It is now possible, using COMPUTERS, to produce synthesized speech which sounds extremely natural; but the process is laborious and expensive, and the possibilities of producing general-purpose artificial talking devices are still very distant. The main importance of speech synthesis is as a technique in experimental PHONETICS for evaluating hypotheses about the perceptual analysis of speech: if a particular acoustic feature is believed to be a significant determinant of a sound's recognizability, this can be tested by synthesizing the sound with the feature present in varying degrees, and rating the products for intelligibility and naturalness. D.C.

speleology. The exploration and study of caves, especially the interconnected caverns formed by the dissolving action of ground water percolating through limestone strata. Understandably, perhaps, a rather neglected field of GEOLOGY.

J.L.M.L.

sphere of influence. Geographical term denoting a TERRITORY over which a state is acknowledged to have preferential rights of a political or economic kind but over which it exercises little or no effective government. Spheres of influence may be declared unilaterally as in the MONROE DOCTRINE (1823), in which the U.S.A. stated its special interest in the Western hemisphere, or multilaterally as in the agreement over African territory between France, Germany, and Britain in the last quarter of the 19th century. One of the classic cases of bilateral agreement was the Anglo-Russian 1907 agreement dividing Persia into a northern Russian sphere, a southern British sphere, and a neutral sphere between. P.H.

Bibl: N.J.G. Pounds, *Political Geography* (New York, 1963).

spin. Rotation of a body about an axis. Within PHYSICS the term usually refers to SUBATOMIC PARTICLES, in which case the magnitude and direction of spin are restricted by QUANTUM MECHANICS. The spin QUANTUM NUMBER may be either half-integral (in which case the particles are *fermions*, e.g. the ELECTRON with spin ½) or integral (in which case they are *bosons*, e.g. the PHOTON with spin 1). See also QUANTUM STATISTICS. M.V.B.

Spinelli initiative. The Italian COMMUNIST, Altiero Spinelli, veteran FEDERALIST and national politician, has campaigned since the war for a federal European Community (see EEC). Elected to the European Parliament in 1979, Spinelli in 1981 put forward a comprehensive plan for institutional reform of the European Community. His proposals were federalist in nature and involved granting more powers to the supranational institutions (the Commission and the European Parliament) and reducing the policy-making influence of national governments within the Council of Ministers. The Spinelli initiative formed the basis of the Draft Treaty on European Union which was formally endorsed by the European Parliament in February 1984. This Draft Treaty on European Union then formed the basis of subsequent discussions on EC institutional reform in the Council of Ministers which culminated in the Single European Act of January 1986. This provided for only minor adjustments in the institutional balance of power within the European Community and was for that reason criticized by Spinelli.　　　S.M.

spin-off. A useful, usually unplanned, by-product or side-effect of some activity. For instance, spin-off from the space exploration programme includes the improvement of domestic electronic equipment such as radios and television sets. The term is normally restricted to desirable side-effects. Radioactive contamination of the environment by nuclear power stations, for example, would not normally be described as a spin-off, though perhaps it might if the RADIATION was found to kill off only undesirable people.　　　A.S.

Spiralen Group, see under COBRA.

spirit possession. State of dissociation or trance brought about in a person by a spirit entering the body. It involves a dramatic public performance. It may be involuntary and spontaneous possession which can be violent and uncontrolled. Spirit possession may express illness or mental instability, but it can also represent a claim to social recognition. Lewis suggested (*Ecstatic Religion,* 1971) that it was used by the peripheral or powerless (for example, women) to attain a social ROLE and STATUS. Those who undergo voluntary and controlled possession are known as spirit mediums or shamans (see SHAMANISM). They may be specially trained and initiated into the role or may have established a relationship with a spirit after spontaneous possession. Spirit mediums can seek the causes of misfortune through contact with the spirits. In entering into a relationship with the spirits a medium can placate and control their influence in society.　　　A.G.
Bibl: M. Lambek, *Human Spirits: A Cultural Account of Trance in Mayotte* (Cambridge, 1981).

splicing. The removal of INTRONS (see SPLIT GENE) from RNA (see NUCLEIC ACID). See also GENE SPLICING.　　　P.N.

spline functions. Mathematical FUNCTIONS obtained by fitting together polynomials at junction-points called knots. They are used in ENGINEERING, and also in DATA ANALYSIS.　　　R.SI.

split-brain. In NEUROPSYCHOLOGY, a separation of the right and left lobes of the cerebral cortex effected by sectioning the great commissure (*corpus callosum*). In man, when such an operation is performed, the result is that the left cortex appears to be dominant and superior in processing information received in linguistic form, the right for dealing with SENSORY-MOTOR messages.　　　J.S.B.
Bibl: M.S. Gazzaniga, *The Bisected Brain* (New York, 1970).

split gene. While the DNA (see NUCLEIC ACID) of a GENE encodes the instructions for the production of a PROTEIN, most genes of higher organisms, but very few genes of micro-organisms, do not carry the instructions in a continuous stretch of DNA. Instead the genes are split, with *exons,* the stretches of DNA that contain a part of the information, interrupted by *introns* or intervening sequences, stretches that do not encode instructions. After TRANSCRIPTION of a split gene into RNA, the introns are removed by GENE SPLICING. The unexpected discovery of split genes in 1977 has profoundly influenced ideas on gene and protein evolution. Exactly why many genes should be split is still a puzzle, but the most likely answer is that it allows and reflects the construction of genes, and hence proteins, in modular fashion. The most advantageous combinations of modules will be selected in the course of EVOLUTION. In addition, variations in gene splicing enable more than one protein to be made from a single gene, overthrowing the long-standing dictum of 'one gene — one protein'.　　　P.N.
Bibl: B. Alberts *et al., Molecular Biology of the Cell* (New York, 1983).

sprawl. In GEOGRAPHY, a term usually applied to an irregularly spread or scattered group of buildings, whether similar or different in kind. *Urban sprawl* is a spread of residential areas, shopping centres, and small industries without any apparent plan. M.L.

sprechstimme/sprechgesang. A vocal technique developed by Arnold Schoenberg which is half-way between talking and singing (literally speech voice/speech song). The singer follows the written rhythm of the melodic line and begins each note on the written pitch and then allows the pitch of the voice to fall as in speech. The most impressive use of *sprechstimme* is in Schoenberg's 'Pierrot Lunaire' and the technique has occasionally been used by other 20th-century composers. B.CO.
Bibl: C. Rosen, *Schoenberg* (Glasgow, 1976).

sprung rhythm. A term coined by Gerard Manley Hopkins (1844-89): 'One stress makes one foot, no matter how many or how few the syllables', and 'the feet are assumed to be equally long or strong and their seeming inequality is made up by pause or stressing'. Hopkins added, 'it is natural in Sprung Rhythm for the lines to be *rove over*, that is for the scanning of each line immediately to take up that of the one before', so that the stanza is to be scanned as a whole, from beginning to end, and for its full effect the verse should be read aloud. Thus, from 'The Wreck of the Deutschland' (1876):

Thou hast bóund bónes and véins in me, fástened me flésh,
And áfter it álmost únmade, whát with dréad,
Thy dóing: and dóst thou tóuch me afrésh?

Hopkins noted that Sprung Rhythm can be found at times in old English alliterative verse, the Psalms, Elizabethan plays, and nursery rhymes, and 'it is the rhythm of common speech and of written prose, when rhythm is perceived in them'. It does much to account for the dramatic expressiveness of his own poetry. D.J.E.

squark, see under SUPERSYMMETRY.

S-R connection, see STIMULUS-RESPONSE CONNECTION.

St Ives School. Since Whistler and Sickert spent a few weeks painting in the west Cornish fishing village of St Ives early in 1884, artists, mostly of an 'academic' persuasion, have worked there in their hundreds until the present day. The term is unprecise. It is usually applied to the MODERNIST artists of the place (Alfred Wallis, Ben Nicholson, Barbara Hepworth, Naum Gabo, Patrick Heron, Bernard Leach, Roger Hilton and others) though 'St Ives School' is also applied to more traditional artists living there. D.BR.
Bibl: Tate Gallery, *St Ives 1939-64: Twenty-five Years of Painting, Sculpture and Pottery* (London, 1985).

stabile. Term coined by the American sculptor Alexander Calder for his static, non-'mobile' works (see KINETIC ART). But a *teatro stabile* is the Italian version of a REPERTORY theatre (sense 2). J.W.

stabilizers, see AUTOMATIC STABILIZERS.

stable population. A population which has an unchanging sex and age structure, which is closed to migration, and which therefore increases or decreases in size at a constant rate. A stationary population is a special case of a stable population, where births equal deaths and there is ZERO POPULATION GROWTH. The concept of the stable population is in itself an unreal abstraction, but has been an important tool in formal demographic analysis (see DEMOGRAPHY) and in understanding complex demographic inter-relationships. E.G.;D.S.
Bibl: A.J. Coale, *The Growth and Structure of Human Populations* (Princeton, 1972); H.S. Shryock *et al., The Methods and Materials of Demography* (condensed edition) (New York and London, 1976).

stage of development. In DEVELOPMENTAL PSYCHOLOGY, each of successive developmental periods, especially of INTELLIGENCE. Each stage is assumed to be characterized by a relatively stable structure. In PIAGETIAN theory, the sequence of stages is invariant, later stages incorporating and resynthesizing the structures of earlier stages. P.L.H.

stagflation, see under INFLATION.

Stakhanovism. A movement associated with the name of Alexei Stakhanov, a miner in the Ukraine who in 1935 devised a system of increasing his OUTPUT by the skilled organization of a group of subordinate workers. Others followed him in other industries, and the Stakhanovites became the official heroes of Soviet labour. They were, moreover, paid according to an incentive scheme which put them into the richest section of the community. For this and other reasons they tended to be unpopular with rank-and-file workers. The word has been applied, by extension, to anyone putting in particularly effective and energetic work in any field. R.C.

Stalinism. The policies and methods associated with the rule of Joseph Stalin (1879-1953) and his followers in the Soviet Union. They included bureaucratic (see BUREAUCRACY) terrorism and the propagation for obligatory acceptance, both in Russia and in Eastern Europe, of fictions which were accepted as DOGMAS in the COMMUNIST movement while Stalin was alive.

Stalinism emerged when Stalin began to consolidate power during and after his struggle to succeed Lenin (d. January 1924). His policy of 'SOCIALISM in one country' meant in effect the enforced COLLECTIVIZATION of agriculture and forcible INDUSTRIALIZATION in the Soviet Union. In implementing these aims, Stalin expanded police controls over the population, using harsher and more ruthless means to achieve his ends. Purges (see YEZHOVSHCHINA), FORCED LABOUR camps, the use of secret police (see KGB; MVD), and other TOTALITARIAN methods were combined with the PERSONALITY CULT of Stalin to enforce conformity and present a picture of a benevolent ruler protecting with infinite wisdom his happy and prosperous people from the hostile 'CAPITALIST encirclement'. All the resources of state propaganda, the monopoly of information, SOCIALIST REALISM in literature, the rewriting of history, etc., were used to inculcate this vision of reality

internally and to propagate it externally. The victory of the Soviet Union in World War II and its post-war expansion were used to indicate the historical inevitability of its world-wide triumph.

The process of 'de-Stalinization' which began with Khrushchev's 'secret speech' to the 20th Party Congress in 1956 and the repudiation of 'the errors of the personality cult' weakened the Soviet Union's authority in the international Communist movement, strengthened the POLYCENTRIC tendencies in it, and raised the question of Stalinism's role in Soviet history. The attempts to dissociate Stalinism from MARXISM-LENINISM as the basis of ideological (see IDEOLOGY) legitimacy, both internally and externally, during the de-Stalinization period were minimized after the fall of Khrushchev. Later developments in the U.S.S.R. have underlined the durability of the Stalinist legacy and the continuous impact of his rule on Soviet INSTITUTIONS and on Communist orthodoxy. L.L.

Bibl: B. Franklin (ed.), *The Essential Stalin* (Garden City, N.Y., 1972; London, 1973); A. Solzhenitsyn, tr. T.P. Whitney, *The Gulag Archipelago* (London and New York, 1974-6); S.F. Cohen, *Rethinking the Soviet Experience* (New York, 1985; London, 1986); A. de Jonge, *Stalin* (London, 1986).

standard deviation, see under VARIANCE.

standard of living. A wide and rather vague concept that refers to the welfare of an individual or society (see WELFARE ECONOMICS). All those factors affecting the welfare of an individual should be taken into account, e.g. consumption of goods and services, leisure, the ENVIRONMENT, health and the political system. The standard of living is often naively and incorrectly associated with just the income of an individual or society. It is difficult or impossible to obtain agreement about what should be included in a measure of the standard of living and how the different components should be weighted (see INDEX NUMBER). Additionally, in the case of a society, there is the problem of assigning weights to the standards of living of the different members of society (see SOCIAL WELFARE). J.P.

Bibl: J. Craven, *Introduction to Economics* (Oxford, 1984).

standard temperature and pressure (STP). Standard conditions of 0°C and 101.325 kPa (or 760 mmHg) pressure. Also called normal temperature and pressure (NTP).

C.E.D.

Stanford-Binet test, see under MENTAL RETARDATION.

star wars, see under STRATEGIC DEFENCE INITIATIVE.

starred forms. In LINGUISTICS, a linguistic FORM (sense 1) preceded by an asterisk to indicate that it is either a historical reconstruction or a deviant utterance (see ACCEPTABILITY) in a language or IDIOLECT.

D.C.

START (Strategic Arms Reduction Talks), see under NUCLEAR WEAPONS, LIMITATION AND CONTROL.

state. It is surprisingly difficult to define the state; it is reducible neither to government and administration nor to the nation, yet impossible to detach from both. Insight into the CONCEPT may be gained by asking what leads us to call some societies 'stateless'; it is primarily that they lack a way of changing the rules or NORMS which govern their behaviour and they lack a way of choosing those who are to exercise that POWER. Innumerable theorists have speculated about just what leads to the creation of a state where none existed before — the needs of WAR, economic and technical change, population pressure have all been offered. MARXISTS and their critics have long debated whether states are the passive victims of economic forces or free agents playing an active role in stimulating and directing economic change. Recently, theorists have been impressed by the paradox that states are increasingly able to wield overwhelming force against the subjects of their and other states, but less able to secure the loyalty of their subjects by managing the domestic economy or supplying the WELFARE services which modern states are expected to supply.

A.R.

Bibl: A. Giddens, *The Nation State and Violence* (Oxford, 1986); W. Jordan, *The State: Authority and Autonomy* (Oxford, 1985).

state economic planning. The STATE's control or intervention in the economy in an organized manner. This planning replaces, either completely or partly, the PRICE MECHANISM as a means of coordinating the economy and, thus, contrasts with the LAISSEZ-FAIRE approach. This planning requires a large volume of information and a large administration, when compared with the simplicity of the price mechanism in PERFECT COMPETITION. In varying degrees and types, the Soviet Union, Eastern European countries and China use planning to control and direct the economy. Given the rudimentary position of the economies and markets of developing countries, many of them make great use of economic planning, though such a policy has its critics. Most economists accept the need for some state economic planning, even if it only concerns the provision of PUBLIC GOODS, TAXATION, and MONOPOLY and MONETARY policies. See INPUT-OUTPUT ANALYSIS.

J.P.

Bibl: J. Craven, *Introduction to Economics* (Oxford, 1984).

state terror/death squads/the disappeared. The implementation by the security forces of a nation of a series of extra-legal operations as part of a clearly defined programme of government, intended to stifle any resistance to the established order by creating a psychosis of terror amongst the population. Carried out in the name of eliminating 'COMMUNIST subversion', such measures include routine assassinations, political imprisonment (usually involving the use of torture) and summary executions. Particularly in Guatemala and EL SALVADOR death squads are a primary means of applying a policy of state terror. These organizations, which governments claim are beyond official control, in fact have the approval and often the patronage of the government and the army. They hold lists of people suspected of being 'communists' (in practice they tend to target anyone who is involved in local, church or political organizations which lie outside official control) and systematically kill them. Their characteristic method is to seize victims at night, torture and kill them (often by strangulation), disfigure the bodies by amputation and/or mutilation of face, hands and genitals and dump them in public places, such as along roadsides, as a 'warning'. Such killings often follow denunciations by neighbours, employers or local security officers, which are a product of the climate of fear created by state terror. A further method used in state terror is the disappearance, a kidnapping of a targeted figure by the security forces, who then deny all knowledge of the victim's whereabouts and refuse to acknowledge that he has been detained by them. The tactic enables the government to avoid abiding by legal provisions for the defence of personal freedom and safety. Typically, victims are seized openly — on the street or at work or home — by small groups of armed but plain-clothes men who drive away in unnumbered vehicles. The disappeared are normally tortured and murdered, although a few people have 'reappeared'. The term is most often associated with Argentina, where thousands of people disappeared under the military regime which came to power in 1976, pledged to wage a 'Dirty War' against communism. Disappearances have also taken place in Brazil, Chile, Haiti, Mexico, Uruguay, El Salvador and Guatemala.

N.M.

Bibl: George Black, *Garrison Guatemala* (London, 1985).

states' rights. In the U.S.A., the political doctrine that the several states of the Union should enjoy the exclusive exercise of powers not specifically granted to the Federal Government. The advocates of states' rights oppose the steady extension of federal jurisdiction as undesirable and unconstitutional. In 1815 this was the cry of the New England states; but since the 1850s and the Civil War (which ended the claim that states could secede), the argument of states' rights has been characteristic of the southern states, especially since the CIVIL RIGHTS MOVEMENT secured the support of the law and of federal law enforcement agencies for DESEGREGATION by appeal to the Supreme Court in 1954. See also FEDERALISM.

D.C.W.

Bibl: J. Peltason, *Understanding the Constitution* (New York, 10th ed., 1985).

stationary population, see STABLE POPULATION.

statistical explanation, see under EXPLANATION.

statistical linguistics, see under QUANTITATIVE LINGUISTICS.

statistical mechanics. A basic theory of PHYSICS developed in the 19th century by Boltzmann, Maxwell, and Willard Gibbs, in which the behaviour of matter in bulk is explained in terms of forces and collisions between vast numbers of constituent ATOMS and MOLECULES interacting according to the laws of MECHANICS. It would be impossibly complicated to compute the trajectories of all the atoms, and in any case their initial positions and velocities cannot be measured with sufficient precision. Therefore, the laws of mechanics are supplemented by the methods of PROBABILITY THEORY, in order to calculate AVERAGE values of dynamical quantities. For example, air pressure is calculated from the average MOMENTUM of air molecules continually striking solid surfaces, while temperature is calculated from the average KINETIC ENERGY of random molecular heat motion.

The behaviour of bulk matter is *irreversible* — it is easier to demolish a house than to build one — so that the future can always be distinguished from the past; this 'arrow of time' is expressed by the second law of THERMODYNAMICS, according to which ENTROPY always increases. But the laws of mechanics are *reversible* (see SYMMETRY), and any closed system must eventually return approximately to its original state, no matter how highly ordered this was. This apparent contradiction is resolved by statistical mechanics, within which the laws of thermodynamics can be shown to hold with overwhelming probability rather than certainty. The chances of observing a spontaneous return to order are remote, because the average time between such returns far exceeds the age of the universe as at present estimated from COSMOLOGY. The implication that the direction of time is defined only for large-

809

scale systems has caused considerable controversy, still not completely resolved.

Despite a century of intensive development, only relatively simple phenomena can be accurately described by statistical mechanics. A proper statistical theory of melting and boiling is still lacking, as is a detailed atomic explanation of the RHEOLOGY of bulk matter.   M.V.B.

statistical regularity, or the 'law of averages' in PROBABILITY THEORY and STATISTICS, is correctly viewed as the *laws of large numbers* and other limit theorems in practical operation; if an event of probability *p* is observed repeatedly and the repetitions are independent, then the observed *frequency* — the number of times the event actually occurs divided by the number of times the experiment is repeated — becomes close to *p* as the number of repetitions becomes large. There is a common misconception that some form of mysterious compensatory mechanism involving memory is required to bring this convergence about; this sort of mistake is enshrined in the advice to air travellers always to carry a bomb — because the chance that there are *two* bombs on a plane is so small as to be negligible. (Such reasoning is perhaps an illegitimate extension of the doctrines of RESISTENTIALISM.) The gambler's run of good or bad luck is of a similar nature; there is no reason to believe that such runs occur with other than the frequency which probability theory predicts.   R.SI.

statistical test. A rule for deciding from the data whether to retain the initial (*null*) *hypothesis* or whether to reject it in favour of a specified *alternative hypothesis*. For example, if a coin were tossed 100 times and landed heads 93 times, most experimenters would regard this as good evidence for rejecting the null hypothesis that the coin was fair in favour of the alternative hypothesis that it was biased towards heads. The test in this case might take the form 'reject the null hypothesis if the number of heads is N or more, otherwise retain it', where N is fixed in advance by the experimenter. A large value of N would lead to a small probability of wrongly rejecting the null hypothesis but a large probability of wrongly retaining it; these

are called *errors* of the *first* and *second kinds* respectively. Similarly a small value of N would give a small probability of an error of the second kind at the cost of a large probability of an error of the first kind. The probability of an error of the first kind is the *size* or *significance level* of the test, and 1 minus the probability of an error of the second kind is the *power* of the test. Usually the significance level is chosen in advance, typically as 5%, and a test is designed to give the largest possible power at that significance level — there is an extensive theory of the design of such tests, based on the work of Neyman and E.S. Pearson.   R.SI.

statistics. A word with different meanings for different people, and with different meanings in the singular and plural. To the layman a statistic is a piece of numerical information, often of a singularly useless variety; statistics are a multiplicity of these, often assembled with the intention of baffling or confusing him, or concealing something underhand — witness the familiar slander 'lies, damned lies, and statistics'. To the statistician such information is 'data', which he tends to view in the same jaundiced light as does the layman: statistics is the analysis of such data, usually with a probabilistic MODEL as a background (*classical statistics*; but see DATA ANALYSIS); 'statistic' is a technical term for a function of the data; and a statistician is a man who is prepared to estimate the probability that the sun will rise tomorrow in the light of its past performance. Early attempts at statistical reasoning can be traced back to classical antiquity, but it was the work of Karl Pearson and R.A. Fisher around the early years of the 20th century which first gave the subject coherence. Statistical theory has always been noted for deep and acrimonious divisions between various schools of thought, particularly for that between orthodox and BAYESIAN statisticians. In recent years DECISION THEORY has tended to unify the subject again by revealing that some of the differences are more apparent than real.

The basic idea of statistics is to regard some repeatable empirical phenomenon (the experiment: say, tossing a coin) as being governed by a probabilistic model not all of whose PARAMETERS are known (the probability of landing 'heads' is the unknown parameter in the coin-tossing experiment). The object of statistical analysis is to use the data obtained from repeated experimentation to provide information about the parameter values. This may take the form of hypothesis testing (STATISTICAL TEST) — failing to reject a null hypothesis (coin fair) or rejecting it in favour of an alternative hypothesis (coin biased); or of *point estimation* — giving a good guess (ESTIMATE) for the values of the parameters (say, probability of heads is 0.65); or of INTERVAL ESTIMATION — giving an interval for each parameter (confidence interval) (or a region for the set of parameters) in which the value of the parameter is likely to lie (say, $0.55 \leqslant$ probability of heads $\leqslant 0.75$); or — the Bayesian approach — of altering the weights (*prior distribution*) attached to the parameter values as degrees of belief so as to obtain a new system of weights (*posterior distribution*). Sometimes a statistic is used simply to summarize information about the data — for example the *sample mean* (see MEAN) of a set of observations may be used as a MEASURE OF LOCATION of the distribution, or a HISTOGRAM may be plotted to show it in more detail.   R.SI.

status. In SOCIOLOGY, a term used (1) neutrally, to designate a *position* in the SOCIAL STRUCTURE, such as the status of a father, or of a legislator (cf. ROLE, which defines the expectations of conduct assigned to a status); (2) to describe different social *evaluations* — in the form of rank, prestige, etc. — of a person or group. In pre-CAPITALIST society, status was often fixed and recognized by distinctive dress; in modern society, status distinctions are marked by different LIFE STYLES. In premodern societies status was often accorded on the basis of birth; in contemporary industrial society prestige is usually associated with the rankings of OCCUPATIONS.

Status as a dimension of SOCIAL STRATIFICATION, rather than a motive, is a feature of the analytical sociology of Max Weber. Weber contrasted status with CLASS on the one hand and POWER on the other, and used the term *status groups* to designate certain segregated groups, e.g.

CASTES or ethnic groups, who are marked off by distinct CRITERIA from other social groups in the society. Lenski has used the term *status inconsistency* to deal with the common phenomenon of individuals (e.g. blacks with high occupations) being ranked differently on different scales; and the theory of status inconsistency has been applied to discrepancies in political behaviour and RACE and class contact. The opposite of status inconsistency, *status consistency*, is sometimes called *status crystallization*.   D.B.

Bibl: G. Lenski, *Power and Privilege* (London and New York, 1966); F. Parkin (ed.), *The Social Analysis of Class Structure* (London, 1974).

status symbol. Any visible sign of a person's social STATUS (sense 2). It may indicate either affluence, as with a Rolls Royce car or lavish entertaining (see also CONSPICUOUS CONSUMPTION), or nonfinancial standing, as with the aristocrat's coat of arms, the don's gown, or the barrister's wig. Evidence from ANTHROPOLOGY refutes the widely held misconception that the status symbol is a product of modern CONSUMER SOCIETY. See KULA; POTLATCH; SYMBOL.   M.BA.

Bibl: E.R. Leach and J. Leach (eds.), *The Kula* (Cambridge, 1983); M. Douglas and B. Isherwood, *The World of Goods* (Harmondsworth, 1980).

statutory instruments. In modern English ADMINISTRATIVE LAW, all those regulations and orders of a legislative character which are made by government departments and which, under the Statutory Instruments Act of 1946, must be published and laid before both Houses of Parliament before they come into operation. In some cases statutory instruments require for validity an affirmative resolution of one or both Houses; in other cases, they are valid unless annulled by an adverse resolution of either House.

H.L.A.H.

Bibl: J.E. Kersell, *Parliamentary Supervision of Delegated Legislation* (London, 1960); C.K. Allen, *Law and Orders* (London, 3rd ed., 1965).

STD, see under SEXUALLY TRANSMITTED DISEASE.

steady-state hypothesis. A theory proposed by Hoyle, Bondi, and Gold in 1948, in which the observed EXPANSION OF THE UNIVERSE is compensated by a continuous creation of matter throughout space, at a rate which need not exceed 10^{-43} kilograms per cubic metre per second — too low to be directly observable. The theory had the attractive feature of requiring neither an initial moment of creation nor a limit to extension of space; nevertheless, it has now been superseded by the rival BIG-BANG HYPOTHESIS, both as a result of the latest evidence from RADIO ASTRONOMY, which suggests that the distribution of GALAXIES is evolving rather than being in a steady state, and also because of the discovery of the COSMIC BACKGROUND RADIATION. See also COSMOLOGY.   M.V.B.

steam-generating heavy-water reactor (SGHWR). A NUCLEAR REACTOR using heavy-water as the MODERATOR, light-water (H_2O) as the coolant and uranium oxide cased in zirconium alloy as the fuel.
C.E.D.

Steiner schools. Schools based on the principles of Rudolf Steiner, the founder of ANTHROPOSOPHY. The first such school was founded by Steiner himself in 1919, in a cigarette factory in Stuttgart; it was closed by the NAZIS and reopened in 1946. There are now over 70 Steiner schools throughout the world and about 120 special schools for handicapped children, who are understood and treated against a background of belief in *karma* or reincarnation. Children in Steiner schools do not learn reading or number work until after 7 years of age, and much emphasis is given to art, drama, EURYTHMY, and music. There is no streaming, and entry to a class is determined by chronological age.
W.A.C.S.

Bibl: L.F. Edmunds, *Rudolf Steiner Education* (London, rev. ed., 1962).

stellar nucleosynthesis, see under NUCLEO-SYNTHESIS.

stellar populations. Once observational ASTRONOMY began the systematic task of mapping out the GALAXY in the 18th century, the nature of the distribution of stars within that wider whole became intensely problematic. Did stars have any relations with their neighbours? Was the galaxy merely a random heap of stellar masses? Most astronomers traditionally assumed that all parts of the galaxy were made up of the same sorts of stars. This view was challenged in the 1940s through the work of Walter Baade (1893-1960), using the 100 inch telescope at Mount Wilson Observatory in America. Baade resolved into stars the Andromeda galaxy and the nucleus of the Andromeda galaxy, and in doing so noticed that the brightest stars of the nucleus were to a remarkable degree fainter than the stars of the outer regions. This was a surprising finding; and on the basis of it, Baade invoked the concept of stellar populations, involving the assumption that different luminosities were possessed by seemingly similar stars in different populations. Baade proposed two different populations (Types I and II) but since his work, additional types have had to be introduced.   R.P.

R.W. Smith, *The Expanding Universe* (Cambridge, 1982).

stenothermous, see under ZOOGEOGRAPHY.

step time composition. The programming of music into a COMPUTER, SEQUENCER, or drum machine using equal units of time as the rhythmical basis thus producing music with a precise mechanical accuracy. Conversely, in REAL TIME composition the machine is programmed by the composer performing the music into it, and it subsequently attempts to reproduce the nuances of a human performer.   B.CO.

stereo. In sound reproduction, a system whereby a programme is recorded simultaneously, on what are effectively two separate channels, by means of two microphones (A and B) forming with the sound source S an angle ASB, equal to the angle XLY formed, when the recording is played back, by the listener (L) and the two loudspeakers (X and Y) that are transmitting the recordings of microphones A and B respectively. In the gramophone-record type of storage it is usual to record both channels within the same groove in the surface by using two different 'walls' of the groove for the different recordings. *Four-way stereo* or *quadriphonic sound* makes use of four microphone-recorders and plays back through four loudspeakers placed, for example, in the four corners of a room with the listener in the centre. The 'three-dimensional' effect of these types of reproduction adds greatly to the 'realism' experienced by the listener.   E.R.L.

stereochemistry. The study of shapes of MOLECULES or complex ionic SPECIES. Stereochemistry is particularly concerned with the immediate atomic environment of an ATOM or ION and is thus intimately connected with descriptions of chemical bonding (see BOND).   B.F.

stereoisomer, see under ISOMER.

stereoscopy. Term, deriving from the invention of the stereoscope by Sir Charles Wheatstone in 1838, for the artificially induced illusion of relief in visual PERCEPTION.

(1) In photography, two separate photographs, taken from slightly different points of view corresponding to the position of two human eyes, are mounted side by side on a card. When viewed through the angled prisms of the stereoscope, the two views blend into one, giving the appearance of depth or solidity. The process is very important in aerial photography (both for military and for survey purposes), and in medical photography.

(2) In the cinema, experimental stereoscopic processes have been demonstrated since the early 1930s, most successfully during the Festival of Britain in 1951, but were not developed commercially until 1952 when (for the same reason as the introduction of CINEMASCOPE) the first '3-D' feature film, *Bwana Devil*, was launched in a process called Natural Vision. Combining the use of polaroid glasses and twin projection of superimposed images, the process had a certain success as a novelty, but proved too cumbersome for general commercial dissemination, though it is still occasionally used. In Russia, a process involving a grille of copper wires (later, optical lenses) to split the images thrown by two projectors —

thus dispensing with the need for special glasses — has been developed.   T.C.C.M.

Bibl: N.A. Valyus, tr. H. Asher, *Stereoscopy* (London and New York, 1966).

stereotaxic surgery, see under NEUROSURGERY.

stereotype. An over-simplified mental image of (usually) some category of person, INSTITUTION, or event which is shared, in essential features, by large numbers of people. The categories may be broad (Jews, gentiles, white men, black men) or narrow (women's libbers, Daughters of the American Revolution), and a category may be the subject of two or more quite different stereotypes. Stereotypes are commonly, but not necessarily, accompanied by prejudice, i.e. by a favourable or unfavourable predisposition towards any member of the category in question.   O.S.

sterilization. The destruction, by surgical or other medical means, of the reproductive capacity of an organism. Since the 1960s, voluntary sterilization of persons has become a much sought after form of permanent CONTRACEPTION. However, compulsory or coercive sterilization, particularly of the mentally retarded, social deviants and non-white, multiparous women, has been a major violation of HUMAN RIGHTS in the 20th century. (See also EUGENICS.)

Sterilization is generally effected in women by a surgical operation known as tubal ligation, in which the fallopian tubes are cut and tied. This operation is not reversible. In men, sterilization is normally carried out by means of vasectomy, in which the vas deferens, under a local anaesthetic, is cut. It is occasionally possible to reverse vasectomy.   S.T.

Bibl: S. Trombley, *The Right to Reproduce: A History of Coercive Sterilization* (London and New York, 1988); Germaine Greer, *Sex and Destiny* (London and New York, 1984).

Sterling Area. A term long applied to a group of countries which have used sterling as a reserve currency, and as a trading currency for a substantial part of their transactions. From World War II onwards the grouping became a more formal one for EXCHANGE CONTROL purposes and was known as the *Scheduled Territories*. Since the early 1970s sterling and other EXCHANGE RATES have been allowed to float and only the U.K., Channel Islands, the Isle of Man and Gibraltar remain within this area. The special COMMONWEALTH trading relationships, which originally provided part of the purpose of the Sterling Area (although Sterling Area and Commonwealth were never conterminous), have been overtaken by the progressive liberalization and internationalization of world trade. Other privileges enjoyed by Sterling Area members, such as access to borrowing in the London CAPITAL market, have become less important as international capital transactions have moved increasingly into the EURODOLLAR market. P.J.

steroids. A class of organic compounds which contain a characteristic group of four carbon rings (a hydrogenated cyclopentanophenanthrene carbon skeleton). A number of steroids are physiologically important, including cholesterol, cortisone, testosterone (male sex HORMONE), estrone (human estrogenic hormone), and progesterone (human pregnancy hormone). Oral CONTRACEPTIVES are steroids. B.F.

stigma. A concept associated especially with the work of the American SOCIOLOGIST Erving Goffman. A stigma is a personal or social attribute which is discrediting for the individual or group in the eyes of society as a whole. There are stigmas of the body — blemishes or deformities, such as pygmyism; stigmas of character, such as HOMOSEXUALITY or mental illness; and stigmas of social collectivities, such as membership of races or tribes regarded as inferior by the majority social groups. Stigmas are different from other forms of DEVIANCE, such as political deviance, in that usually an attempt is made to conceal them. One technique for doing so is 'passing': that is to say, adopting a pose or disguise which hides the stigma in question and allows the individual to 'pass' as a member of normal society or the majority group. Many American BLACKS with light-coloured skins have in this way successfully passed as whites in American society. (See also TOTAL INSTITUTION.) K.K.

Bibl: E. Goffman, *Stigma: Notes on the Management of Spoiled Identity* (Englewood Cliffs, N.J., 1964).

Stijl, De. The name (1) of a Dutch magazine first published in June 1917; (2) of the group which founded it; (3) eventually, of a whole movement. The aim of the magazine was 'to make modern man aware of new ideas that have sprung up in the plastic arts', i.e. of a pure form of abstraction (see ABSTRACT ART) which was to be 'the direct expression of the universal' and which they simply labelled 'the style'. It found its clearest expression in the paintings of Piet Mondrian, who called his attempts to paint without reference to any objective reality *neo-plasticism*, and whose rectangular primary-coloured paintings had direct counterparts in the architecture and furniture of Gerrit Rietveld. The group's intellectual leader was Theo van Doesburg, architect, painter, poet, and critic, who visited the Weimar BAUHAUS and ensured the introduction there of *De Stijl* ideas. Shortly after his death, the influence of the movement began to decline. This Dutch contribution to modern art left, however, an international legacy of a purity and vividness in abstraction which has been paralleled but hardly equalled. See also INTERNATIONAL STYLE. M.BR.

Bibl: H.L.C. Jaffe, *De Stijl, 1917-1931* (London and Amsterdam, 1956).

stimulus. An event which excites a nerve impulse, either by direct action upon the sensory nerve fibre or, more usually, through a TRANSDUCER such as a sense organ. A uniform stimulus of unvarying intensity soon ceases to excite an impulse (see ADAPTATION). See also ALL-OR-NONE LAW; SUMMATION. P.M.

stimulus-response connection (S-R connection). In PSYCHOLOGY, the basic unit of learning according to BEHAVIOURIST learning theory. C.E.D.

stochastic decision tree analysis, see under RISK ANALYSIS.

stochastic music. Term invented by the composer Iannis Xenakis, in 1956 for his musical compositions which use mathematical structures, and in particular PROBABILITY THEORY, to organize the sounds. A feature of this music is often the formation of clouds of sound built up from distributions of small individual elements. Xenakis frequently uses computers (see COMPUTER MUSIC) to help him with the calculations involved in the composition of his music.   B.CO.

Bibl: I. Xenakis, *Formalized Music* (Bloomington, Ind., 1971).

stochastic problems, see under DYNAMIC PROGRAMMING.

stochastic process. In PROBABILITY THEORY, a system involving time-dependence. For example, suppose that a 'drunkard's walk' is defined by repeated tosses of a coin: when the coin lands heads, the drunkard takes a step forwards; when tails, backwards. This is a stochastic process of a particularly simple kind, in that its future behaviour depends only on its present state and not on the route by which that state was reached — the process has no memory; such a process is called a *Markov process*. The progress of an epidemic, the behaviour of the economy or an ECOSYSTEM, BROWNIAN MOTION, the flow of traffic, and the serving of a queue all represent complicated empirical phenomena for which stochastic processes provide MODELS.   R.SI.

stock response. The reader's ready expectation that, for example, in verse 'June' will be followed by 'moon', 'dove' by 'love', and his predictable reaction to well-worn themes or situations. The term is used in connection with undemanding art which presents conventional subject-matter or appeals to fixed attitudes. 'Against these stock responses the artist's internal and external conflicts are fought, and with them the popular writer's triumphs are made' (I.A. Richards, *Principles of Literary Criticism*, 1924). Though seemingly a permanent phenomenon, stock responses are affected by fashion: the unhappy ending is now as conventional and looked-for as the happy ending, the ANTI-HERO as the hero. D.J.E.

stop-go. An alternation of government measures involving the periodic restriction and subsequent expansion of AGGREGATE DEMAND and a consequent suspension and resumption of the growth of output. The term came into current use in Britain about 1960 after a succession of BALANCE OF PAYMENTS crises and accompanying 'packages' of restrictive measures. 'Stop-go' policies were criticized for not achieving the goals of a stable level of employment and growth in output; causing more fluctuations in economic activity than would have occurred anyway; being one of the causes of the rapid increase in INFLATION during the 1970s; and not being a technically feasible policy because of the lack of understanding about the working of the economy and its unpredictable effects. See KEYNESIANISM; MONETARISM.   A.C.; J.P.

store. The most expensive part of a COMPUTER, where the information (both PROGRAM and data) is kept. The neutral term *store* is to be preferred to *memory* to avoid the danger of anthropomorphizing computers. There are many forms of store which differ widely in their cost and ACCESS TIME, and in the attempt to reconcile the requirements of speed, a large store, and tolerable cost, computers are generally made with several forms of store. These may include, in decreasing order of speed, (1) a few *registers* (store built from LOGIC units); (2) a few hundred WORDS of fast *working store* (sometimes called a *scratchpad store*) which may include some ASSOCIATIVE STORE; (3) a *main store*, generally on cores; and (4) a *backing store* generally on DRUM, DISC, or MAGNETIC TAPE. Using these different levels of store to best advantage is one of the most difficult parts of PROGRAMMING.   C.S.

STP, see under STANDARD TEMPERATURE AND PRESSURE.

strangeness. A property of some of the more exotic ELEMENTARY PARTICLES whose lifetime before decay is millions of times greater than expected. This must arise from some characteristic of their internal structure, corresponding to a 'strangeness QUANTUM NUMBER' which is zero for ordinary particles.   M.V.B.

815

Strategic Arms Limitation Talks (SALT), see under NUCLEAR WEAPONS, LIMITATION AND CONTROL.

Strategic Arms Reduction Talks (START), see under NUCLEAR WEAPONS, LIMITATION AND CONTROL.

strategic capability. The war-making or reprisal capability of those states that possess long-range aircraft or MISSILES has become differentiated according to its technical characteristics. Thus *first-strike capability* characterizes a force which is sufficiently vulnerable (e.g. bombers on airfields) to be destroyed by an enemy strike and which therefore must be employed first in a *pre-emptive strike* if the possessor state is not to be disarmed; an example is the attack on Egyptian airfields by the Israeli Air Force on 5 June 1967. *Second-strike capability* characterizes a force capable, through a combination of RADAR early warning systems and missiles in underground silos or in submarines, of surviving a first strike in sufficient strength to inflict unacceptable damage on the adversary. *Counter-force capability* characterizes a strategic force capable of crippling the adversary's strategic military installations and troop concentrations while leaving a reserve for the destruction of his cities and industries; the U.S.A. is thought to have possessed such a capability in relation to the U.S.S.R. in the early 1960s, and both probably still possess it in relation to China. Its antithesis, *counter-value capability*, characterizes a force sufficient only to destroy or damage an adversary's cities and industries; the British and French nuclear forces are of this kind. See minimum DETERRENCE.   A.F.B.

Bibl: H. Kahn, *Thinking about the Unthinkable* (London and New York, 1962).

Strategic Defence Initiative (SDI, or Star Wars). A programme of space-based defensive weapons designed to intercept attacking strategic MISSILES. This plan was announced by U.S. President Ronald Reagan in March 1983. His aim was to replace MUTUALLY ASSURED DESTRUCTION with Mutually Assured Security, by offering to share the TECHNOLOGY of the Strategic Defence Initiative. A budget of $30 billion was allocated to the project, which then attracted wide support from military and industrial interests. Critics have suggested that the SDI, or Star Wars project (from another speech made by President Reagan) is a destabilizing influence in the complex world of nuclear STRATEGY. It pushes aside the tacit understanding of the U.S. and the Soviet Union over ABM (anti-ballistic missiles), as well as engendering, in practice, a massive increase in arms spending. Other critics have suggested that it will never work, since it requires a degree of functional certainty which no possible COMPUTER system can provide. The system comprises ground- and space-based surveillance equipment, and destructive weapons mounted in space. These are either X-RAY lasers, which generate their own LASER beams to attack incoming missiles; or some versions are reflectors which concentrate rays projected from terrestrial bases. Other systems use guided missiles to create a lethal screen which will destroy incoming warheads. The essential quality of all the systems is their complexity, since they have to distinguish between true and false warheads, as well as avoiding an attacker's countermeasures. Soviet efforts have concentrated on using X-ray lasers as devices to attack space-based weapons from the ground. Broadly speaking, both the major powers are now involved in this area of research, with the U.S. leading in systems building, and the Soviet Union breaking new ground with particle beam and laser weapons.   A.J.M.W.

Strategic Nuclear Force, see under FORCE DE FRAPPE.

strategic studies. A widely used term first proposed in 1958 to the founders of the Institute of that name in London by its first Director, Alastair Buchan, to connote the scholarly analysis of the role of military and para-military force in international relations. The field of strategic studies is considerably wider and more political in character than military or war studies and embraces not merely problems like defence and DETERRENCE but also ARMS CONTROL and the economic and social consequences of armaments, ARMS RACES, and DISARMAMENT. Though the central focus of the field is the reinforcement of international security or peace, 'security' has so many meanings (social security, internal security, national security, personal security, commercial securities, etc.) as to make it valueless as a descriptive term, while 'peace' or 'conflict' studies and research, as evolved in Scandinavia and elsewhere, are either based on behavioural rather than political assumptions or else largely concerned with one aspect of the field, namely disarmament.   A.F.B.

strategy. The general conduct of WAR in its broadest aspects, to serve the ends of policy. It should not be confused with the training, deployment and operational use of military forces, which are properly described as tactics. The term 'strategy' is also widely used in other fields, such as mathematical and BUSINESS GAMING, but these usages are essentially derivative or metaphorical and will not be considered here.

The development of nuclear and thermonuclear weapons has revolutionized modern strategic thought. Prior to their invention, the political leaders of the major powers considered the use of military forces as a perfectly legitimate instrument of foreign policy to be used when diplomatic negotiation failed to achieve their objectives. But once both the U.S. and the U.S.S.R. had acquired weapons of much greater destructive power than the atomic bomb dropped at Hiroshima and Nagasaki, it became clear that a major war between the superpowers and their respective allies could cause their MUTUALLY ASSURED DESTRUCTION, and the launching of an aggressive war ceased to be a rational policy for these powers. The BALANCE OF TERROR or mutual nuclear DETERRENCE between the superpowers thus depends on each side communicating a credible threat of devastating nuclear RETALIATION in the event of a major attack on the territory or other vital interests of the other. As there has never been a nuclear war the theory of deterrence is HYPOTHETICO-DEDUCTIVE rather than empirical, leaving much room for uncertainty and serious problems of interpretation and application. How does each side know where the line between vital and expendable interests lies at any given time? How can one be sure that the other side believes that the NUCLEAR WEAPON sanction would be used against them? How far is *extended deterrence*, or the extension of nuclear protection over allied countries' territory, a credible policy in the eyes of the guarantor and protected populations and the potential enemy? Supporters of the theory of nuclear deterrence argue that for nearly 40 years it has prevented a major war between the superpowers. Both supporters and critics agree, however, that mutual nuclear deterrence could break down. A LIMITED WAR could escalate, drawing in superpowers and/or other nuclear armed states, and develop into limited nuclear war. Most theorists accept that, in practice, it would be hard to impose any limits or restraints once the nuclear threshold has been crossed. There is also the danger of nuclear war developing as a result of proliferation of nuclear weapons to unstable and fanatical regimes. A quite different form of destabilization of nuclear deterrence could result from the development of an effective strategic defence system against ballistic missiles. Both superpowers have major research programmes on what is loosely called 'Star Wars' technology (see STRATEGIC DEFENCE INITIATIVE). Scientific experts are deeply divided as to the feasibility of such a project. What can be safely assumed is that if one side does make a really major breakthrough in developing an effective strategic defence system, and in the meantime such systems have not been brought firmly under the constraints of ARMS CONTROL agreements, the side with the strategic defence capability would have achieved overwhelming strategic superiority. The debate on the implications of strategic defence at least had the effect of rewakening interest in the now rather dated but pioneering work of the major nuclear strategists such as A. Beaufre, B. Brodie, A. Buchan and H. Kahn. However, while the balance of terror continues to hold, the COLD WAR between east and west continues to take different forms. Economic, diplomatic and propaganda methods are the major instruments of competition between the superpowers and their respective alliance systems. In addition limited and unconventional war, incurring less risks and far lower costs, remain major strategic weapons. REVOLUTIONARY war aimed at seizing control in specific THIRD WORLD civil STATES, helped and encouraged by the Soviet Union and other COMMUNIST regimes, has become a favoured weapon of communist expansion in contemporary international relations. Modern strategy's understandable fascination with speculation about nuclear weapons and their utilization should not lead to a neglect of these other very widespread and influential modes of warfare. P.W.

Bibl: The publications of the International Institute for Strategic Studies, particularly the *Annual Military Balance* and *Strategic Survey*.

stratification. The most obvious characteristic of sedimentary rocks is that they invariably occur as layers known as beds or strata. Each bed, which may be anything from less than a centimetre to over a metre thick, is of broadly uniform composition and represents a period of uniform conditions in the depositional ENVIRONMENT. The upper and lower surfaces of beds are known as *bedding* or *stratification planes*. The study of stratified rocks is termed STRATIGRAPHY. Bedding is a pervasive structure of sedimentary rocks which persists after deformation of the rock body. It is therefore a fundamental reference plane in TECTONICS. J.L.M.L.

stratification, social, see SOCIAL STRATIFICATION.

stratificational grammar. A theory of GRAMMAR developed by S.M. Lamb in the 1960s, the name reflecting his choice of the term stratum to refer to the various interrelated LEVELS of linguistic structure recognized by the theory. D.C.

Bibl: S.M. Lamb, *Outline of Stratificational Grammar* (Washington, 1966).

stratigraphy. The principle used in GEOLOGY and ARCHAEOLOGY which states that a layer must be earlier than the one which *seals* it (i.e. which can be physically demonstrated to lie above it). Stratigraphy is the basis of all modern archaeological excavations. Most sites occupied for any period of time show a superimposition of layers, the careful observation of which

provides the raw material for constructing a sequence. Particular attention is paid to the recognition of the surface from which any feature, e.g. a wall footing, post-hole, or pit, is cut, since depth alone is not a criterion by which the stratigraphic position of an artifact can be assessed. The position of an artifact or structure in a stratified sequence is referred to as its CONTEXT. A well-stratified site provides a relative chronology which can be calibrated by means of dated artifacts or absolute dating methods (e.g. RADIOCARBON). *Horizontal stratigraphy* is the linear development of a site whose focus gradually shifts. It is particularly appropriate to the study of cemeteries. B.C.

Bibl: P. Baker, *The Techniques of Archaeological Excavation* (London, 1977).

stratosphere. Meteorological term for the upper layer of the earth's atmosphere lying immediately above the TROPOSPHERE. Its lower boundary varies from 7 or 8km high above the poles to about 16km at the equator, and it extends upward to a height of around 60km above the ground. Despite its great thickness the stratosphere contains only one quarter of the mass of the atmosphere, and about 10% of its water vapour. Very few clouds occur in the stratosphere but a major feature is the *mid-latitude jet streams*, very strong and highly localized westerly winds. P.H.

stream of consciousness. Phrase coined by William James in his *Principles of Psychology* (1890) to describe the ceaseless, chaotic, multi-levelled flow that characterizes human mental activity: 'let us call it the stream of thought, of CONSCIOUSNESS, or of subjective life.' Bergson's account of the mind (1889) is also much concerned with this, and was highly influential in the development of stream-of-consciousness fiction, which attempts, often by means of *interior monologue*, to capture the exact nature of this flow. Pre-Jamesian examples include Sterne's *Tristram Shandy* (1767) and Édouard Dujardin's *Les Lauriers sont coupés* (1887); modern exponents include James Joyce (Molly Bloom's interior monologue in *Ulysses*), Virginia Woolf, and the less intrinsically important and distinctly more prosaic Dorothy Richardson (*Pilgrimage*, 1916-57). Originally, as in Dujardin, and then Richardson, the stream-of-consciousness technique was an extension of REALISM; it has since taken two forms. In one the author — e.g. Dorothy Richardson — merely attempts to mime or imitate mental activity (the extreme example is the German Arno Holz's '*Sekundenstil*', which tries to represent the passing of seconds). In its other, more fruitful form the author is aware that he can only *simulate* mental activity: he deliberately abandons realistic, descriptive techniques (though of course aiming at a deeper realism) in order to achieve his artful — and artistic — purpose. This form is fundamentally EXPRESSIONIST, although, as in Joyce, it may give the appearance of realism. Virginia Woolf hovers uncertainly between the two forms. Four main techniques of stream-of-consciousness fiction have been noted: soliloquy, omniscient narration of mental processes, and both indirect and direct interior monologue. The most sophisticated and revealing forms of stream-of-consciousness fiction were until recently to be found in the works of Latin Americans: João Guimarães Rosa, Miguel Asturias, Juan Rulfo, and others. But the Latin American novel now tends to parody itself (and the authors their own artistic successes), and the truly vigorous exercise of stream of consciousness is seen only in individual and occasional works. M.S.-S.

Bibl: R. Humphrey, *Stream of Consciousness in the Modern Novel* (Berkeley, 1954); W.H. Sokel, *The Writer in Extremis* (Stanford, 1959).

street dance, see under POPULAR DANCE.

street furniture, see under TOWNSCAPE.

strict (or *absolute*) **liability.** In English law, as in that of most civilized countries, a person accused of a crime is generally not liable to conviction if he did not intend to do what the law forbids or know that he was doing it, and took reasonable care to avoid doing it. In the case of some offences, however, e.g. breaches of law regarding adulteration of food or drugs and driving offences, most but not all of which carry minor penalties, a man may be liable to conviction without proof of such knowledge, intention, or lack of reasonable care. Such offences are known as offences of strict liability. H.L.A.H.

Bibl: G.L. Williams, *Criminal Law* (London, 2nd ed., 1961); P.A. Jones and R. Card, *Introduction to Criminal Law* (London, 9th ed., 1980).

strikes. A strike is defined as a refusal by employees to continue working; a temporary withdrawal of labour or stoppage of work, generally at the behest of a TRADE UNION. A strike is the ultimate weapon which can be used by groups of workers in order to exert pressure on an employer, or a third party, in the course of COLLECTIVE BARGAINING. While thought to be exclusively associated with trade union action, strikes pre-date trade-unions. The Sabine women, Spartacus and his followers and the 17th-century London apprentices who downed tools to force the reduction of oysters from their diets, were all strikers. The term was first used in its present context in the Annual Register of 1768. Indeed employers can strike: viz. the strike of bus *owners* in Chile prior to Allende's deposition. Not all strikes are successful. The Greyhound workers strike in 1982 and the air traffic controllers in 1980 in the U.S.A. were both unmitigated disasters for the unions. The British MINERS STRIKE of 1984/5 was similar.

The right of workers to withdraw their labour is considered to be a basic HUMAN RIGHT. It is enshrined in the legislation, or the constitution, of many industrialized states. It is rarely an untrammelled right. Many groups of workers (viz. the military, police, government workers) are forbidden to strike by national legislation in many countries. In addition there are often legal requirements as to balloting of strikers and a minimum notice period before a strike can be called. These requirements change as government policies change. Strikes may be of a limited or an indefinite duration. They may affect workers nationally or locally. It is rare to find a strike which does not have adverse effects on third parties (viz. the unburied dead in Liverpool in 1979). For this reason strikes are held to be unpopular by the public at large. However a strike of telecommunication workers in Australia which gave the public free telephone calls was immensely popular. Strikes may have a political connotation; directly and indirectly. The 'General Strike' in Britain in 1926 was seen as a direct challenge to the government, as was the miners strike of 1984/5. In 1973 Edward Heath called, and lost, an election over the miners dispute, and in 1979 it is widely thought that James Callaghan lost the election through the strikes in the 'WINTER OF DISCONTENT'. While the U.K. and U.S. have no history of political strikes, France, Italy, Germany all have. Most of these strikes were (are) of a limited duration only.

B.D.S.

strings. Linear distributions of MASS-energy arising in some theories of ELEMENTARY PARTICLES. Vacuum strings could arise during a particular type of change in the material state of the universe during the first moments of the universe's expansion from the Big Bang (see BIG-BANG HYPOTHESIS). They would exist as a network of tubes of ENERGY which gradually become stretched and straightened by the EXPANSION OF THE UNIVERSE. An analogous phenomenon is observed to occur when matter is cooled to low temperature and is termed the Meissner effect. The existence of vacuum strings may explain the clustering patterns of GALAXIES in the universe but there is as yet no direct evidence for their existence. Sheet-like forms of energy (called domain walls) are also possible in principle but would produce observational effects in the universe which are not seen.

Strings and domain walls arise because underlying SYMMETRIES of nature break in disconnected ways in different parts of space and these linear or sheet-like structures form at the boundaries between regions of different symmetry. They are sometimes called topological defects (see also MAGNETIC MONOPOLE). M. Green and J. Schwarz have suggested a new theory of the ultimate nature of matter in which the most fundamental entities are not points, as is usually assumed, but linear structures called SUPERSTRINGS. The theory of superstrings requires the universe to possess more than three spatial dimensions and offers the first self-consistent approach to combining QUANTUM THEORY and general RELATIVITY into a single unified theory of all physical phenomena (see GRAND UNIFICATION and ELEMENTARY PARTICLES). It is hoped that the masses of all elementary particles and the values of all FUNDAMENTAL CONSTANTS of nature will ultimately be predicted and explained by superstring theories. Vacuum strings are not superstrings but superstring theories may give rise to vacuum strings.

J.D.B.

Bibl: P. C. W. Davies, *Superforce* (London, 1984); H. Pagels, *Perfect Symmetry* (New York, 1985); M. Green, 'Superstrings', *Scientific American*, September 1986.

strong anthropic principle, see under ANTHROPIC PRINCIPLE.

strong interaction. The strongest force known, which is an attraction acting over extremely short distances between NUCLEONS, and thus enabling the atomic NUCLEUS to resist the ELECTROSTATIC mutual repulsion of its PROTONS. Strong interactions are caused by the exchange of MESONS, and are about a million million times stronger than WEAK INTERACTIONS.

M.V.B.

structural-functional theory (also known as *structural-functionalism*; to be distinguished from STRUCTURALISM). A mode of theorizing in SOCIOLOGY (developed from FUNCTIONALISM in social ANTHROPOLOGY) in which societies, or smaller units such as communities or organizations, are conceptualized as SYSTEMS, and the attempt is then made to explain particular features of their SOCIAL STRUCTURE in terms of their contribution — i.e. the function they fulfil — in maintaining the system as a viable entity. Thus RITUAL and ceremonial practices may be explained as serving to reinforce shared beliefs and values and to maintain solidarity among different groups within a society — even though this function may be quite unrecognized in the purposes of those engaging in ritual and ceremony. Structural-functional theory is thus able to treat SOCIAL ACTION from the standpoint of unintended as well as intended consequences. A major problem which it faces is that of specifying precise criteria for the viability of social systems, whether in the sense of their 'survival' or of their 'efficiency'. Structural-functional theory has also been criticized by exponents of CONFLICT THEORY for its neglect of the part played by *coercion* in organizing social activities and preserving social stability. See also PARSONIAN.   J.H.G.

Bibl: A.R. Radcliffe-Brown, *Structure and Function in Primitive Society* (London, 1952); N.J. Demerath and R.A. Peterson (eds.), *System, Change, and Conflict* (London and New York, 1967); J. Elster, *Ulysses and the Sirens* (Cambridge, 1979).

structural linguistics, see under LINGUISTICS.

structural psychology. A SCHOOL OF PSYCHOLOGY concerned with the systematic, experimental, elementaristic (see ELEMENTARISM) study of conscious experience. By analogy with CHEMISTRY'S periodic table, the aim is to isolate and classify the elementary constituents of CONSCIOUSNESS without regard to their function. I.M.L.H.

structural reform. The process of assisting parts of an agricultural industry which are uneconomic (because farms are small or badly laid out or suffer from other deficiencies) to become capable of providing acceptable living conditions. Among the reasons why farm incomes may be low compared with those in other sectors of the economy, or even in other parts of a country's agricultural industry, are the small size of farms, the farmers' lack of business and technical skills, and poor access roads and other elements of the INFRASTRUCTURE. Since they had too little to sell, measures to improve prices of farm products (see DEFICIENCY PAYMENTS) could not solve the problems of these farmers. Consequently various countries, including those in the EEC, have introduced measures designed to encourage the early retirement of farmers and the amalgamation and consolidation of farms. K.E.H.

Bibl: M. Tracy, *Agriculture in Western Europe* (London, 1982).

structural semantics, see under SEMANTICS.

structural unemployment, see under UNEMPLOYMENT.

structuralism.

(1) In LINGUISTICS, any approach to the analysis of language that pays explicit attention to the way in which linguistic features can be described in terms of STRUCTURES and SYSTEMS. In the general, SAUSSURIAN sense, structuralist ideas enter into every school of linguistics. Structuralism does, however, have a more restricted definition, referring to the BLOOMFIELDIAN emphasis on the processes of segmenting and classifying the physical features of utterances (i.e. on what Chomsky later called SURFACE STRUCTURES), with little reference to the abstract, underlying structures (Chomsky's DEEP STRUCTURES) of languages or their meaning. It is this emphasis which the CHOMSKYAN approach to language strongly attacked; for GENERATIVE linguists, accordingly, the term is often pejorative. D.C.

Bibl: G.C. Lepschy, *A Survey of Structural Linguistics* (Oxford, 1982).

(2) In the (other) SOCIAL SCIENCES (but see also SCHOOLS OF PSYCHOLOGY), a movement characterized by a preoccupation not simply with structures but with such structures as can be held to underlie and generate the phenomena that come under observation, or, to use the Chomskyan distinction mentioned in (1), with deep structures rather than with surface structures. The outstanding contributor in the social sciences is Claude Lévi-Strauss. For him a social structure is not a web of social relationships that may quickly be abstracted from concrete behaviour, but a MODEL. Further, any set of relationships making up a structure must be transformable by systematic change in the relationships. In his first major structuralist work, *Les Structures élémentaires de la parenté* (1949), Lévi-Strauss strove to demonstrate that the wide variety of KINSHIP behaviour and INSTITUTIONS rests ultimately upon a principle of communication that is the driving force behind INCEST prohibitions and the EXCHANGE of women in MARRIAGE. In that study modes of action and modes of thought were treated together, but his later work on TOTEMISM and MYTH has concentrated upon modes of thought. Structures have,

821

of course, to be devised for each body of material selected for study, but in the last analysis they are all referable to basic characteristics of the mind (apparently considered to operate on a binary principle); and it is perhaps this feature of structuralism that distinguishes it most sharply from other movements in contemporary ANTHROPOLOGY. Like them, it starts from cultural variety, but unlike them it busies itself with the ultimate basis from which the variety is generated. See also EVOLUTION, SOCIAL AND CULTURAL; EXOGAMY; FUNCTIONALISM. M.F.

Bibl: C. Lévi-Strauss, tr. C. Jacobson and B.G. Schoepf, *Structural Anthropology* (London and New York, 1963); E. Gellner, *Relativism and the Social Sciences* (Cambridge, 1985); J. Sturrock, *Structuralism* (London, 1986).

(3) In architecture: despite the grave doubts of the father of structural anthropology, Claude Lévi-Strauss, a number of architects in the early 1970s believed it possible to transfer its basic METHODOLOGY to architectural thinking and analysis. Sceptical contemporaries highlighted the probability that architects were attracted by the name structuralism and the fact that it sought to give order. The belief by some architectural protagonists that they would eventually grasp the essential and underlying pattern of architecture is not known to have been realized. S.L.

structure.

(1) A word with a wide range of familiar meanings which has perhaps been overworked and even misused (as has *structured*, meaning often no more than 'organized') since the advent of STRUCTURALISM. Literally it is the basic framework, form, or outline of a material artifact: a building (see below), a vehicle, ship, aeroplane, chair, dress, etc.; objects with the same structure are said to be ISOMORPHIC. But it is also applied, by extension, to works of art and literature (a play, novel, symphony) and to elements of social organization (a political constitution or INSTITUTION, a system of EDUCATION). In nature all the distinctive forms of life, and in societies all the distinctive forms of association, have discernible structures which permit analysis in terms of their elements

and the ways in which these operate together in the living whole. Whether in human artifacts, or in emergent natural and social forms, elements of structure are clearly and closely associated with their *functions*; hence the significance of STRUCTURAL-FUNCTIONAL THEORY in the NATURAL SCIENCES and SOCIAL SCIENCES. See also DIACHRONIC; MATHEMATICAL STRUCTURE; SOCIAL STRUCTURE; SUPERSTRUCTURE. R.F.

Bibl: A.R. Radcliffe-Brown, *Structure and Function in Primitive Societies* (London, 1952).

(2) Specifically, in architecture, that part of a building which carries loads and resists stresses such as those caused by wind or ground movement. The exploitation of structure, and especially of its ability to span large spaces, to CANTILEVER, and to create expressive roof shapes, has been a major feature of 19th- and 20th-century architecture. Innovations have taken a number of specific forms.

The *frame*, characteristic of the CHICAGO SCHOOL, had a great liberating effect by separating the properties of enclosure and load-bearing previously assumed by a masonry wall. Steel or CONCRETE columns were able to support floors containing much lighter walls that served merely to separate spaces and act as weather barriers. Planning was also freed from the necessity to superimpose walls on each other.

Extremely thin, light roof construction became possible through the use of *curved concrete* forms, often curved in two dimensions, as in an eggshell. The best-known examples are by Maillart, Nervi, and Felix Candela in Mexico.

Folded plates are in a sense planar *shells* in which strength is achieved by the folding of surfaces. A familiar example is a corrugated roofing sheet. A complex form can be seen in the conference hall of the Unesco (see UNO) building in Paris (1953-7), designed by Nervi.

Space frames are created by joining a large number of struts to produce a lattice work in three dimensions. These lightweight roof or floor structures can span in two directions, and can be supported by irregularly spaced columns at wide intervals.

Tensile structures that do not have to

resist buckling can be made smaller in cross-sectional area and thus lighter. Attempts have therefore been made to create roof membranes carried by cables in tension. Several such structures were built in Munich for the 1972 Olympic Games.

The tensile strength of steel has also been used in bridge construction to achieve wide spans in suspension structures as well as the strength that can be attained by a tube with intervening membranes, as in a bamboo stem, and which when rectangular in cross-section becomes a *box-girder*. See also DYMAXION; PNEUMATIC STRUCTURES. M.BR.

Bibl: E. Torroja, tr. J.J. and M. Polivka, *Philosophy of Structure* (Berkeley, 1958); F. Otto (ed.), tr. D. Ben-Yaakov and D. Pelz, *Tensile Structures* (3 vols., Cambridge, Mass., 1967-71).

structure-conduct-performance theory. The view that the structure of an industry is the major determinant of the conduct and, thus, the performance of the industry and firms. *Structure* is defined by such factors as size and number of firms in the industry, BARRIERS TO ENTRY, type of product, existence of substitutes and complements to the industry's products, price and income ELASTICITIES for the product and related products, the supply of inputs, retailing of the product and TECHNOLOGY used in production. *Conduct* encompasses the behaviour and objectives of firms and their reactions and attitudes to the behaviour of rivals. *Performance* is defined in terms of such VARIABLES as growth, ECONOMIC EFFICIENCY, TECHNICAL PROGRESS, profitability, employment, exports and ADVERTISING. This theory has been central to the study of the economics of industries. For example, it has been suggested that the industrial structure of MONOPOLY and profit-maximizing behaviour (conduct) leads to the restriction of output and higher prices. This implies higher than average profits (performance). The theory has been criticized in that conduct and performance affect industrial structure (e.g. technical progress and advertising may raise new barriers to entry). Also, it is not clear that different industries are sufficiently similar to permit generalizations about structure, conduct and performance. J.P.

Bibl: M.C. Sawyer, *The Economics of Industries and Firms* (London, 1981).

Sturm, Der. A complex of Berlin cultural enterprises founded by Herwarth Walden around his magazine of that name (1910-32), which was the chief organ of German EXPRESSIONISM before 1914 and did much to introduce the ideas of the FUTURISTS, CUBISTS, and other innovators into Germany. There was a *Sturm* gallery (from 1912), *Sturm* readings featuring the near-phonetic poetry (see CONCRETE POETRY) of August Stramm, a *Sturm* theatre under Lothar Schreyer (later of the BAUHAUS), and even a *Sturm* march composed by the founder. After World War I the *Sturm* lost ground, its one important new recruit being Kurt Schwitters, whose energies went rather into MERZ. J.W.

stylistics. A branch of LINGUISTICS which studies the characteristics of situationally-distinctive uses of language (see REGISTER), with particular reference to literary language, and tries to establish principles capable of accounting for the particular choices made by individuals and social groups in their use of language. D.C.

Bibl: D. Crystal and D. Davy, *Investigating English Style* (London, 1969; Bloomington, 1970).

stylometry. A specialized branch of STYLISTICS: the methodical study of an author's chronology or development by analysing the proportions of parts of speech to one another in a particular work, his shifting preoccupations of thought or imagery, and other such factors. Such analyses are best made with the aid of COMPUTERS, which, when modestly and properly programmed, can solve many problems of attribution. M.S.-S.

subatomic particle. Any PARTICLE smaller than an ATOM, i.e. the atomic NUCLEUS and the ELEMENTARY PARTICLES. M.V.B.

subconscious. A term of popular PSYCHOLOGY used to refer to those mental items and processes that are outside the range of an individual's awareness. Though frequently used as a synonym for unconscious, it is not equivalent to UNCONSCIOUS in FREUDIAN theory, primarily because it blurs the distinction between unconscious and PRECONSCIOUS. Moreover, though apt to be associated rather with the psychology of Jung (see JUNGIAN), it is not equivalent, either, to Jung's CONCEPT of the personal unconscious, since, in his theory, it is used to refer to the part, or aspect, of the personal unconscious which is closer to the COLLECTIVE UNCONSCIOUS, and not to those parts which are closer to CONSCIOUSNESS.   B.A.F.

sub-culture. Despite centripetal tendencies, no society has a uniform system of meanings, perceptions or artefacts common to all elements of its population. The location of a social group in relation to POWER, authority, STATUS, its own sense of identity — ethnic, occupational or otherwise — leads to the development of a sub-culture whose function it is to maintain the security and identity of the group in question, and to generate a set of meanings that enable it to tolerate the exigencies of its situation. In a weak sense all recognizable subgroupings in society, from coal miners to executive directors, croupiers to Royalty, have their own patois, hierarchy of values and characteristic modes of appearance and behaviour, but this over-extension of sub-culture can lead to its virtual redundancy as an analytical tool. Sub-culture is primarily useful in summarizing visible and symbolic resistance to real or perceived subordination, high levels of ROLE or status ambiguity, etc., and this usage illuminates the IDEOLOGICAL and material responses of such diverse groups as ethnic MINORITIES, the poor, academic underachievers, youth, women, 'deviants', etc. By far the most extensive usage of the concept has been in relation to YOUTH CULTURE with its series of visibly sub-cultural responses — PUNKS, skinheads, mods, HIPPIES, etc. A problematic element of sub-cultural analysis is the nature of the accommodative relationship between dominant and sub-cultural forms (see POPULAR CULTURE; UNDERGROUND).   P.S.L.

subduction zone. A linear or arcuate region of the earth at which the spreading oceanic LITHOSPHERE bends downwards and re-enters the planet's interior, where it melts and becomes assimilated at depth. The angle of descent, which is usually about 45° (but can be somewhat shallower or steeper in particular cases) is marked by intense earthquake activity, the result of the large stresses induced in the descending lithospheric slab. The surface expression of a subduction zone is often a long trench up to 10 km deep, which compares with the 3-5 km depth of the typical ocean basin. Subduction zones, the most important of which lie around the edge of the Pacific, play a crucial part in PLATE TECTONICS. New lithosphere created at OCEANIC RIDGES spreads away from the ridges and is ultimately 'destroyed' at subduction zones at the same rate at which it was formed (see OROGENY).   P.J.S.

subject. In LACANIAN psychoanalytic theory, the notion of the subject developed out of Lacan's polemic with EGO PSYCHOLOGY, and he formulates it as in opposition to the EGO which is regarded, following Freud, as the pole of resistances in speech (Lacan would later, theorize resistance not in terms of the ego but in terms of the object). The IMAGINARY register of the ego is what blocks the relation to the OTHER, and it is thus a primary task of analysis to bring the subject into prominence. It is important to note that the subject for Lacan is a barred subject ('$'), that is, a subject barred by the signifier: born into a world of language, the child must assume signifiers in the Other and literally subject himself to the autonomy of the SYMBOLIC structures at play. Similarly the subject is barred in that it does not know what it wants: there are no signifiers in the Other to pin down exactly what the subject wants. Thus the bar in $ indicates not a signifier, but the lack of a signifier, a signifier that is missing from the Other. In clinical terms, this barred subject, or lack of a signifier, emerges in the moments of discontinuity in DISCOURSE, in slips of the tongue, in mistakes, and so on. It can thus be taken, in one sense, as a temporal moment, emerging in an instant only to disappear: a rigorous theorization of this pulsation is given by Lacan in his elaborations of the reciprocal operations of alienation and separation.   D.L.

Bibl: J. Lacan, *The Four Fundamental*

Concepts of Psychoanalysis (London, 1977).

subjective idealism, see under IDEALISM.

subjectivism. In ETHICS, the theory which holds that impersonally formulated VALUE-JUDGEMENTS, such as 'This is good' and 'That ought to be done', are in reality only statements about the likes and dislikes, desires and aversions of the speaker. More generally, any ethical theory which denies the ultimate resolubility in principle of disagreements about questions of value. More generally again, but on a somewhat different tack, any theory which takes private experience to be the sole foundation of factual knowledge is subjectivist, even if it admits that objective knowledge can be derived from this subjective basis. A.Q.

subjectivity. The role that subjectivity plays in philosophical reflection has worried and intrigued philosophers since Plato disagreed with Protagoras. Subjectivity takes on a major role in romantic (see ROMANTICISM) EPISTEMOLOGY, but becomes central to the philosophical enterprise itself in the work of Søren Kierkegaard in the mid-19th century. Kierkegaard insisted that philosophical judgements must be subjective and EXISTENTIAL and implied that the amount of objectivity available to us is vanishingly small and anyway not co-extensive with the claims of philosophers or scientists. It is in the PHENOMENOLOGY of Edmund Husserl that subjectivity is accorded a constitutive role, though Husserl's own understanding of how consciousness achieves ever greater subjective purity as a result of the EIDETIC REDUCTION is a paradoxical one, and he uses the concept of subjectivity in a way which does not refer to the subjectivity of any one experiencing or reflecting individual. Nevertheless, Husserl's inscription of subjectivity into the philosophical programme bore a plentiful harvest in the phenomenological work of Sartre (1943) and Merleau-Ponty (1945) where subjectivity and EMBODIMENT were made matters of fundamental importance for the first time since Descartes had banished them from the proper purlieus of philosophical awareness. The work of the French phenomenologists had a particular impact upon EXISTENTIAL PSYCHIATRY, which has its founding document in R.D. Laing's *The Divided Self* (1960), and upon existential psychotherapy, in the work of Peter Lomas and David Smail.

The effect of this phenomenological tradition has been to point up the degree to which a world constructed by an individual subjectivity is as 'real' and as 'true' to that individual as any reality or truth imposed from outside, and therefore that it is to the subjectively constituted world of meaning that we must attend if we wish to be of any help in the PSYCHIATRIC situation. Psychiatrists of the Laingian school have thrown into doubt the assumed 'objectivity' of the world from which the patient is claimed to have departed, for it is now obvious that social constructs are themselves INTERSUBJECTIVELY created and sustained and are not in any sense necessary or necessarily 'true'. This is the essential contribution of existential phenomenology to psychiatric theory. It makes possible the retrieval of INTENTIONAL meaning and dispenses the analyst from imposing 'objective', 'scientific' or 'medical' HEGEMONIC meanings over signs and embodiment which plead to be understood in their own terms. R.PO.

subjectivity in cinema. A concept used in cine-PSYCHOANALYSIS in considering how spectatorship in cinema works as a set of psychic relations. The model of the human subject most commonly deployed in this context is that advanced by Jacques Lacan (see PSYCHOANALYTIC CRITICISM; LACANIAN). A.KU.

Bibl: Rosalind Coward and John Ellis, *Language and Materialism* (London, 1977).

sublimation. In psychoanalytic theory (see PSYCHOANALYSIS), a FREUDIAN term for the gratification of instinctual impulses, usually sexual or aggressive in nature, through the substitution of socially acceptable behaviour for prohibited drives. See also DEFENCE MECHANISM; REPRESSION; SUPEREGO. W.Z.

subliminal. Adjective applied to stimulation operating below the THRESHOLD (*limen*) of PERCEPTION. There is much concern that subliminally presented messages can alter attitudes, but this has not been borne out by research.   H.L.

submarine-launched ballistic missiles, see under MISSILES.

sub-optimization, see under SYSTEMS.

subsistence agriculture. Farming intended primarily to supply the food and clothing needs of the farmer and his dependants. Subsistence agriculture accounts for a substantial part of the agricultural industries of many low-income countries. The term is occasionally used in high-income countries to refer to the activities of those who run small farms, which would be uneconomic as business enterprises, largely for the satisfaction of having home-grown foodstuffs and the amenities of country life, while earning their living in other ways.   K.E.H.
   Bibl: C. Clark and M.R. Haswell, *The Economics of Subsistence Agriculture* (New York, 3rd ed., 1968; London, 4th ed., 1970).

subsonic, see under MACH NUMBER.

substance. In PHILOSOPHY, either (1) a concrete individual thing, to which existence can be attributed in an unqualified way (everything else that exists being reducible to it; see REDUCTION), or (2, sometimes called *substratum*), that which, as distinct from the properties which a concrete thing may share with other things, confers its individuality on it. Substance in the first, Aristotelian, sense is a complex, composed of properties together with an individuating substratum or substance in the second sense. Many philosophers have held that there are no individuating substrata, and thus that a thing is no more than the collection of its properties. Mental substances, the soul or self, is often conceived as the substratum of the series of mental states that make up the biography of a person. See also INTUITIONISM.
                A.Q.

substitution. In ECONOMICS, substitution is an important element in economic decisions. RATIONAL consumers will substitute between different goods in order to obtain that pattern of consumption which is most preferred and is feasible, given prices and income. For any two goods, this can be represented by considering the rate at which the goods can be substituted for each other while leaving the consumer at the same level of UTILITY (see INDIFFERENCE CURVE). This rate is called the marginal rate of substitution and, in achieving the most preferred feasible consumption pattern, the rational consumer should, for each possible pairing of goods, equate the marginal rate of substitution to the ratio of the prices of the two goods. Similarly, firms minimize costs of production by substituting between FACTORS OF PRODUCTION until the marginal rate of substitution between any two factors is equal to the ratio of the prices of the factors (see ISOQUANT). Substitution underlies much of the production and consumer demand theory of microeconomics.   J.P.
   Bibl: D. Begg *et al., Economics* (London, 1984).

substrate, see under ENZYMES.

substratum, see SUBSTANCE.

sub-system, see under SYSTEMS.

subtopia. A term first used by Ian Nairn in the *Architectural Review* to denote certain areas beyond or within suburbs, areas which were 'the world of universal low-density mess' and included such things as 'abandoned aerodromes, fake rusticity, wire fences, traffic roundabouts, gratuitous notice boards, car parks and Things in Fields'. Nairn's campaign aimed to emphasize the distinction between town and country and to preserve the characteristics of each. In its more extreme forms, however, it became an attack on any low-density building in SUBURBIA.   M.BR.
   Bibl: I. Nairn, *Outrage* (London, 1955).

subtractive synthesis, see under ADDITIVE SYNTHESIS.

suburbanization. The development of the suburbs, outskirts, or urban fringe of a TOWN rather than the concentrated growth of the centre. J. Beaujeu-Garnier and G. Chabot have defined the French *banlieue* or urban fringe as the space under the jurisdiction of a town proclaimed by the 'ban' in the Middle Ages. For a long time these suburbs were limited to the immediate neighbourhood of the town, but the growth of towns and the development of COMMUNICATIONS in modern times has given a greater complexity to such a suburb, so that it is better described as an aureole round the town. Suburban life tends to become concentrated at points where communications are easiest. Such growth centres often use neighbouring villages and small towns as support. Jean Gottman has defined such a suburbanized zone as that area round a town centre where less than 25% of the active population works on agriculture.　　　　M.L.

Bibl: R.A. Walker, 'A Theory of Suburbanization' in M.J. Dear and A.G. Scott (eds.), *Urbanization and Urban Planning in Capitalist Society* (London and New York, 1981), pp. 383-430.

suburbia. At first a realization by the 19th-century MIDDLE CLASS of the arcadian idyll through which the industrial city need only be used for work and shopping (see also GARDEN CITIES). Successive waves of SUBURBANIZATION dealt with progressively lower socio-economic groups and resulted in lower space standards, and thus the end of the idyll. Suburbs tended to be one-CLASS communities, remote from places of work, and dedicated largely to the supposed interests of children. Their spread in continuous rings around all great cities was made possible by a new mobility but resulted in prolonged journeys to work (see COMMUTING), until recent relocation of offices and factories in suburban localities has tried to reverse the trend.　　　　M.BR.

Bibl: L. Mumford, *The City in History* (Harmondsworth and Baltimore, 1966).

Suez. Term used to denote the international crisis of October-November 1956 and the decline of British power which it is taken to symbolize. The crisis followed the NATIONALIZATION by Egypt of the Suez Canal and the other assets of the Suez Canal Company, the main part of whose shares were owned by the British government and by French private shareholders. The British and French governments used the pretext of an Israeli attack on Egypt, in the planning of which they had colluded, to attempt a forcible occupation of the Canal Zone, ostensibly to ensure its security. Their action attracted widespread international condemnation, including crucially that of the U.S., and was abandoned in the face of a collapse of international confidence in sterling and a widening breach in Anglo-American relations. The episode is regarded as the last and unsuccessful attempt by Britain and France to assert great-power status.　　S.R.

Bibl: F.S. Northedge, *Descent From Power: British Foreign Policy 1945-73* (London, 1974).

sufficient condition, see NECESSARY AND SUFFICIENT CONDITIONS.

suffragette. Term applied to women who were members of the suffragist movement, but specifically advocating votes for women. By 1860 the discourse of republicanism and citizenship prevalent in Britain, France and the United States had stimulated the interest of MIDDLE-CLASS women. They began to claim political and civil rights denied to them.

The importance of an historical perspective in contemporary FEMINISM has led to a re-examination of early suffragette activity. There has been a shift, however, in attention from the leaders, e.g. the Pankhursts, to the rank and file or local activists (e.g. Selina Cooper).　　A.G.

Bibl: J. Liddington, *The Life and Times of a Respectable Rebel* (London, 1984); O. Banks, *Faces of Feminism* (Oxford, 1986); J. Mitchell and A. Oakley (eds.), *What is Feminism?* (Oxford, 1986).

suicide connection. Name given to a technique employed for the rapid reversal of the motion of very large electric motors; e.g., a 15,000-horsepower motor may be reversed from full speed forward to full speed reverse in three seconds. The problem is to neutralize very rapidly the ENERGY stored in the magnetic FIELD within the motor, and to overcome the field's *inductance*, i.e. reluctance to have its value changed. It is solved by reconnecting the motor's field and armature circuits so that the motor becomes a *generator* and the whole of the vast KINETIC ENERGY of the rotating armature becomes converted to electrical energy which is fed to the field coils to cancel their stored magnetic field. The technique is used chiefly in rolling mills, where repeated passage of the *billet* (bar of metal) through the rolls calls for very rapid reversal of the drive. E.R.L.

summation. A STIMULUS below a certain THRESHOLD of intensity does not excite a nerve impulse. The repetition of sub-threshold stimuli may, however, eventually end in the discharge of an impulse. The property to which repeated sub-threshold stimuli owe their efficacy is known as *summation*. See also ALL-OR-NONE LAW. P.M.

summer stock, see under REPERTORY.

summit diplomacy. Personal negotiations held face to face between heads of state or government of the major powers in the hope of resolving their mutual conflicts. The term originated with Winston Churchill's call for a 'parley at the summit' in his election speech of 15 February 1950. Originally it carried connotations of hostility to traditional diplomatic methods of negotiation as tending to enhance rather than reduce those failures in communication held by liberal idealists to be the point of origin of most international conflicts. After the failure of the Paris summit conference in May 1960, the device fell into disrepute in the West, although since the early 1960s the practice has met with success on occasion, as with Nixon's visit to China in 1972 and the CAMP DAVID accords of 1979. The abortive Rejkjavik summit between Gorbachev and Reagan in 1986 and the less than conclusive meeting at Geneva in 1985 seem to have led to renewed criticism of an idea that raises unrealistically high expectations of instant success. D.C.W.;A.W.

Bibl: K. Eubank, *The Summit Conferences, 1919-1960* (Norman, Oklahoma, 1966); A. Eban, *The New Diplomacy* (New York, 1983).

Sunni Muslims, see under ISLAM; LEBANON.

superblock, see under RADBURN LAYOUT.

supercluster, see under GALAXY CLUSTERS.

superconductivity. The complete disappearance of electrical resistance observed (first by Onnes in 1911) when certain materials are cooled below a certain *transition temperature* (generally a few degrees above ABSOLUTE ZERO). An electric current set up in a superconducting circuit will persist undiminished for years without requiring a CELL to drive it around. These 'persistent currents' may be employed as memory elements in COMPUTERS, while on a much larger scale their magnetic FIELDS may power rapid-transit vehicles between cities, levitated above superconducting track. The transition to and from the normally-conducting state is sudden, and easily induced by changes of temperature or magnetic FIELD; this has led to 'superconducting switches', applicable to large complex systems like computers where economy of space is important. In these technological applications, promise has so far outstripped performance. M.V.B.

Bibl: see under CRYOGENICS.

superego. (1) In FREUDIAN psychoanalytic theory (see PSYCHOANALYSIS), a term for that part of the structure of the mind which is concerned with controlling excitation from the ID and the activity of the EGO. This control is largely UNCONSCIOUS, but manifests itself in CONSCIOUSNESS in the pronouncements of conscience and feelings such as guilt and shame. The superego is developed in the child through subtle and complex identifications with the parents, and by introjecting them as controlling or guiding models, with their corresponding moral attitudes. B.A.F.

(2) In LACANIAN psychoanalytic theory, the incorporation of certain verbal residues, leading to an interiorization of the law. The broken nature of this internalization leads to the establishment of a law unable to represent conflict and DIALECTIC. Despite the claims of the SUPEREGO to be able to judge, it in fact establishes a tyrannical and merciless system of imperatives; the function of censorship that it introduces has as one of its aims to keep beyond any access the structural relationship of the SYMBOLIC to DESIRE. B.BU.

superfluidity, see under QUANTUM FLUID.

supergravity, see under SUPERSYMMETRY.

superlattice. In PHYSICS new SEMICONDUCTING materials are being made by depositing very thin layers of different materials, only a few tens of ATOMS thick, on top of one another. It is now possible to form each layer in a very perfect crystalline state and the final assembly of many layers is called a superlattice or *heterostructure*. The different layers couple with each other so that the heterostructure has new properties which are unlike those of its constituent layers. Among the materials which are used are gallium arsenide and alternating silicon/germanium layers. By DOPING with, say, aluminium or indium in the various layers, it is possible to alter the electrical and optical properties in a controlled way so that their characteristics can be tailor made for the production of devices such as LASERS and light sensors. The term is also used to describe crystals of certain ALLOYS. In general the constituent atoms in such materials are arranged in a random manner on the permitted LATTICE, but sometimes after suitable heat treatment an ordering process can occur so that all the atoms of one type are in one particular position — say, at the corners of cubes, whilst the other type of atom are all at another set of regular sites — say, at the centres of the cubes. When this occurs the alloy is said to have formed a superlattice.

H.M.R.

supernova. An exploding star, which may be millions of times brighter than the sun. It is thought that the contraction of a RED GIANT due to the GRAVITATION of its MASS may cause nuclear FUSION reactions which accelerate the contraction, thus producing a catastrophic collapse and the emission of vast amounts of ENERGY. With the naked eye only two supernovae have been observed in the past thousand years, but with the aid of telescopes many have been seen in other GALAXIES. See also DWARF STAR.

M.V.B.

super-particle, see under SUPERSYMMETRY.

supersonic, see under MACH NUMBER.

superstrings. A new theory of the most elementary structure of the universe proposed by M. Green and J. Schwarz in 1984. Whereas previous theories of ELEMENTARY PARTICLE behaviour are quantum FIELD THEORIES in which the basic entities are 'points' of zero extent, superstring theories possess lines (STRINGS) as the basic elements. These strings possess a tension which collapses them down to points in a low energy environment. Superstring theories will therefore give rise to the conventional quantum field theories in the low energy limit. These theories were shown by Green and Schwarz to possess remarkable mathematical properties. Unlike the conventional quantum field theories they do not possess infinities when physical quantities are calculated. They develop an old idea that elementary particles are microscopic strings by the addition of SUPERSYMMETRY. They appear to offer a possible route to combining the general theory of RELATIVITY and QUANTUM THEORY. There are only two possible underlying SYMMETRIES which can dictate the form of the theory. One of these appears unrealistic and so the superstring theory is uniquely determined. It is believed that this theory allows the FUNDAMENTAL CONSTANTS of nature and the properties of all elementary particles to be calculated mathematically. For this reason the theory is sometimes referred to as a possible *theory of everything* (and denoted by the acronym TOE). As yet there is no observational evidence for or against superstring theories and a means of calculating their observational predictions has yet to be found. It is the principal current area of research into elementary particle PHYSICS. Superstring theory appears to predict the existence of an entire population of elementary particles which possess only very WEAK INTERACTIONS comparable in strength to GRAVITATIONAL interactions with other bodies. The population is called *shadow matter* or the *shadow world*. J.D.B.

Bibl: M. Green, 'Superstrings', *Scientific American*, September 1986.

superstructure. According to Marx and Engels's theory of HISTORICAL MATERIALISM, the primary reality in the world is matter and its quantitative combinations; the qualitative characteristics of differing natural forms are secondary, emerging from the nature and changes of such combinations. In history, the material STRUCTURE (basis) of any society (its economic system; its productive forces — including its socio-economic CLASSES) is the primary reality, and on this rests a qualitative *superstructure* of INSTITUTIONS. This superstructure has two sides, or perhaps layers. First, there are the legal and institutional forms of the social system, the State, the machinery of law, government, and official power; second, there is the IDEOLOGY of the system, the body of ideas and beliefs — moral, political, religious, and philosophical — which serve to ratify the society's institutional arrangements, particularly its property system or mode of distributing the fruits of the productive process. Marx's view is that the predominant direction of causal influence is from base to superstructure: major historical change begins in the economic base and leads to a more or less revolutionary transformation of the superstructure. R.F.; A.Q.

Bibl: K. Marx, Preface to *A Contribution to the Critique of Political Economy*, in *Karl Marx: Selected Works* (London and New York, 1968).

supersymmetry. Theoretical idea in ELEMENTARY PARTICLE physics which aims to effect a unification between BOSONS (which possess integral units of QUANTUM MECHANICAL spin) and FERMIONS (which possess half-integral units of quantum mechanical SPIN) in nature. Supersymmetry transforms bosons into fermions and vice versa. This symmetry requires that there exist a new population of elementary particles: every boson possesses a new super-partner possessing half-integral spin, while every fermion possesses a super-partner with integral spin. For example, the super-particle of the PHOTON is called the photino and that of the NEUTRINO, the sneutrino. The other particle to super-particle partnerships are as follows: LEPTONS (sleptons), GLUONS (gluinos), W bosons (winos), Z bosons (zinos), gravitons (gravitinos), Higgs boson (Higgsino or shiggs), QUARKS (squarks). The super-particles are termed sparticles. None have yet been observed but they are expected to be too heavy to have shown up in past ACCELERATOR searches. They are being searched for in the current accelerator experiments at CERN in Geneva. SUPERSTRING theories and some GRAND UNIFIED THEORIES possess supersymmetry. Supersymmetry is a global gauge field theory. If the gauge symmetry is made local then the theory encompasses GRAVITY and is called supergravity. J.D.B.

Bibl: H. Pagels, *Perfect Symmetry* (New York, 1985).

supply and demand. The usual term for the market forces governing prices, in the absence of administrative control, OUTPUT and the distribution of income. These forces make themselves felt through the PRICE MECHANISM, as responses in the quantities offered for sale (supply) or the quantities that consumers are prepared to buy (DEMAND) when the market price changes. Normally the responses are equilibrating since a rise in price tends to enlarge the supply and reduce the demand, and *vice versa* (the ECONOMIC LAW of supply and demand); but they may at times be disequilibrating (for example, if a change in price excites expectations of a further change in price in the same direction). Emphasis on supply and demand implies, not that there should be no interference with the price mechanism, but that control dampens market reactions and risks perpetuating a shortage or surplus. The more any form of economic organization relies on market forces, the more freedom it must allow to supply and demand to respond to changes in price. The operation of market forces will, in the case of PERFECT COMPETITION, result in ECONOMIC EFFICIENCY, but there is no reason to suppose that the resulting distribution of income is or is not desirable. Additionally, the operation of the law of supply and demand will not deal efficiently with MARKET FAILURES such as PUBLIC GOODS, EXTERNALITIES, MONOPOLIES, etc. A.C.; J.P.

Bibl: J. Craven, *Introduction to Economics* (Oxford, 1984).

supply-side economics. The view that TAX-ATION has severely reduced the incentives for work and INVESTMENT and that ECO-NOMIC GROWTH can be increased by large reductions in the taxation of the supply-side of the economy. This view contrasts with the KEYNESIAN approach which proposes that the level of AGGREGATE DE-MAND is important in determining the level of OUTPUT and employment. Supply-side economics proposes that a reduction in the taxation of incomes and profits will result in people working harder and investing more. An example of this view is the Laffer Curve, which considers the relation between tax revenue and the rate of tax. A zero tax on, say, income would give no tax revenue; increases in the tax rate would take larger proportions of income. According to the Laffer Curve view, as the rate of tax increases the incentive to work is reduced, and people choose to work less hard and earn less income. Thus, as the rate of tax increases, the tax base decreases in size. It is suggested that there is a tax rate at which tax revenue reaches a maximum and many countries have tax rates beyond this point. If this is true, a reduction in the tax rate would increase income and tax revenue. Most economists believe that actual tax rates are below this point, though taxation may have an effect on the incentive to work.   J.P.
Bibl: E.J. Neil (ed.), *Free Market Conservatism* (London, 1984).

supposed subject of knowledge. This notion is set at the heart of the theory of TRANSFERENCE elaborated by Lacan, and presents an immediate difficulty in translation. Although it would seem to indicate a knowledge supposed to a subject, Lacan is careful to point out that what is supposed is not a knowledge (which is already there in the UNCONSCIOUS), but a SUBJECT. Hence, transference love is connected to knowledge, the supposed subject being the analyst, and if the analyst is loved because of this knowledge, we can say that the patient loves the analyst because of what he lacks. The LACANIAN practice of PSYCHOANALYSIS attempts to interpret from a position which would undermine this fiction, however necessary it may be in the transference, of a supposed subject of knowledge, to demonstrate to the subject that there is always an irremediable split between a subject and knowledge, never a union.   D.L.

suprematism. A form of more or less geometric ABSTRACT ART propounded by the Russian ex-CUBIST Kasimir Malevich (1878-1935) in a manifesto of 1915 and exemplified in his classic painting of a white square on a white background (now in the Museum of Modern Art, New York). Though it influenced Lissitzky, Rodchenko, and other CONSTRUCTIVISTS, his movement was virtually stifled by their campaign against pure art and easel painting, only to be revived at the BAUHAUS (which published his book *The Non-Objective World*) and again in the 1960s, when there were exhibitions of his work in Stockholm and Amsterdam. In his own country it is still held to be FORMALISM, and accordingly unacceptable.   J.W.
Bibl: K.S. Malevich, tr. X. Glowacki-Prus and A. McMillin, ed. T. Andersen, *Essays on Art* (London and Chester Springs, Pa., 1969).

surface structure, see under DEEP STRUCTURE.

surfactant (or *surface-active agent*). A substance (e.g. a detergent) which accumulates at a surface and makes it easier for the surface to spread. This lowering of the surface tension is used to encourage the 'wetting' of a material, and surfactants are also used to assist FLOTATION PROCESSES.   B.F.

surgery. A method of treatment, the means whereby wounds can be repaired after injury, organs removed or parts of the body reconstructed on account of injury, disease or deformity. The basic procedures include incision (cutting into) to release infection and tension, or to gain access to parts and organs; excision (cutting out) and suturing (sewing together). The surgeon's knowledge begins in the sciences related to structure and function in health and disease (ANATOMY, PHYSIOLOGY and PATHOLOGY) and continues by involvement in research programmes. As John Hunter (1728-1793) demonstrated, advance in surgical knowledge and of the surgeon as an informed professional can only develop against a background of research. This concept reappeared in the 19th century when Lister applied Pasteur's discovery of MICRO-BIOLOGY to prevent and overcome the infection of wounds which had until then made impossible any technical advance beyond a crude craft. At the same time ANAESTHETIC agents were discovered. Further advances came with World Wars I and II with regard to the treatment of wounds, haemorrhage and shock (blood transfusion). With the arrival of penicillin in World War II surgeons began to operate on chest wounds with increasing confidence. This led to modern thoracic surgery, and with the development of machines to pump oxygenated blood, bypassing heart and lungs, it became possible to stop the heart, open it and repair or replace torn or worn-out valves, to rectify heart deformities in children and also to bypass, with veins taken from the leg, those obstructions of the coronary arteries which cause angina (see CORONARY AR-TERY BYPASS GRAFTING; CORONARY AR-TERIOGRAPHY). Rigorous control of infection enables the surgeon to implant artificial parts, e.g., plates and screws for broken bones, artificial hip joints for arthritis, artificial arteries to replace or bypass those which are obstructed or distended and bursting (aneurysms). The science of IMMUNOLOGY has enabled surgeons to *transplant* cooled but living organs from one person to another. Just as blood for transfusion must be matched between donor and recipient, so must organs (tissue typing), and rejection of the graft due to any other differences is suppressed by immunosuppressive drugs. Thus the kidney, heart, liver, lung and pancreas can be transplanted at all ages, with varying results. Transplant of the cornea for a type of blindness does not require such immunological control. Developments in PHYSICS contribute significantly to advances in surgery. The operating microscope enables the surgeon to sew together minute vessels and nerves. Severed limbs can be rejoined and special skin and muscle and nerve grafting is possible. *Microsurgery* facilitates eye surgery, e.g. lens removal and artificial lens implantation for cataract. It has advanced surgery on the brain and spinal cord, and oper-

ations can extend to the innermost part of the ear for deafness, including the implantation of micro-electrical circuits. Other developments in physics include the use of the LASER to replace the scalpel (see LASER SURGERY) and of ULTRASONIC devices to locate obstructions in arteries, stones in the gallbladder and the kidney, and even to allow destruction of kidney stones without the use of the surgeon's scalpel. Now the space programme is producing new knowledge which can be applied to the healing of wounds and to the production of acceptable CELLS for transplantation and as compounds which may reduce the need of the surgeon's knife. Strange as it may seem, the surgeon of today works with the scientist toward the means of dispensing with surgical operations, though it has to be remembered that the wounded in particular will always be in need of a well trained surgeon. See also PLASTIC (RECONSTRUCTIVE) SURGERY.

A.J.H.R.

Bibl: H. Bailey and R. Love, rev. A Rains and H. Ritchie, *Short Practice of Surgery* (London, 19th ed., 1984).

surplus value. A concept in MARXIST theory, specifically related to the LABOUR THEORY OF VALUE. Engels called it Marx's principal 'discovery' in ECONOMICS. It refers to the value remaining when the cost of maintaining the worker — his subsistence costs — has been subtracted from the total value of the product he produces. If a worker has a ten-hour working day, only a part of that day — say eight hours — is needed for him to produce goods equal in value to his subsistence costs. In the remaining two hours, the worker creates surplus value, which is appropriated by the CAPITALIST as profit. The concept of surplus value is hence central to the Marxist theory of EXPLOITATION in capitalist society. Some Marxists, especially those of a TROTSKYIST persuasion, have argued that surplus value may be appropriated, and hence exploitation continue, even in those economic systems where private ownership of capital has been abolished. In eastern Europe, they say, the state as 'collective capitalist' appropriates the surplus value created by the workers, and distributes it among the political and bureaucratic ELITES who control the state. K.K.

Bibl: A. Gamble and P. Walton, *From Alienation to Surplus Value* (London, 1972).

Surrealism. French literary movement evolving from the Paris wing of DADA during 1920-23, thereafter establishing itself also in the visual arts, theatre, and cinema, to become the last (to date) of this century's great international modern currents. Though the name had been coined in 1917 by Guillaume Apollinaire, the true spiritual ancestors of the movement were Rimbaud, the newly rediscovered poet Lautréamont, the German and other late-18th-century ROMANTICS (including de Sade), and the SYMBOLISTS. Its animator was the poet André Breton, who in 1919 founded the review *Littérature* with his friends Louis Aragon and Philippe Soupault, joined later that year by Paul Éluard, and there published his first experiments in *automatic writing*: a random stream of words coming from that SUBCONSCIOUS which the movement now deliberately set out to explore. Already aware of the manifestoes and activities of Zurich Dada, as well as Tzara's poems, in the winter of 1919-20 Breton joined forces with Picabia and Tzara himself to create a comparable succession of Parisian shocks and scandals, whose aggressive, continually newsworthy tactics thenceforward became an integral part of his movement. In 1924, with Dada outside France effectively dead and his new allies discarded, Breton and his friends formally constituted the Surrealist group. Its manifesto, proclaiming the inferiority of REALISM to 'psychic automatism' and 'previously neglected forms of association' of a magical, irrational, hallucinatory sort, appeared that October; its new, politically-tinged review *La Révolution Surréaliste* two months later.

Though visual art was neglected in the manifesto and its place at first far from clear, a distinctive Surrealist art gradually developed. Its main model was the METAPHYSICAL PAINTING of de Chirico, with its disquieting perspectives and poeticizing of the banal, but the more Dadaist work of Arp, Ernst, Duchamp, and Picabia also contributed and some attempt was made to annex Picasso and Paul Klee. In 1923 André Masson began to make 'automatic drawings' (or largely random doodles), influencing the light-hearted BIOMORPHIC art of Joan Miró who, with Arp, represented the more ABSTRACT wing of the movement. But the surreal poetry of de Chirico's pictures — a blend of strikingly dead subject-matter, at once familiar and improbable, with a smoothly academic technique — was not developed further until the emergence, during the second half of the 1920s, of such artists as Yves Tanguy, the Belgians René Magritte and Paul Delvaux, and finally the Spaniard Salvador Dali, who settled in Paris at the end of 1929. Basing himself on a 'paranoiac-critical method' (delirium tempered by a Meissonier-like meticulousness), Dali depicted soft watches, decomposing human limbs, and other glutinously biomorphic props lost in endless arid landscapes. By a mixture of technical skill and brilliant self-projection he became, for the public of the next two decades, the quintessential surrealist.

As a literary movement, Surrealism spread mainly to those areas where French cultural influence was strong, e.g. Latin America, the Middle East, Spain, and Eastern Europe, though it had its followers (such as David Gascoyne) in England, while there was an important group in pre-1939 Czechoslovakia. As a political force, dedicated to a concept of REVOLUTION that became increasingly TROTSKYIST, it was always negligible, its pretensions, which were largely those of Breton himself, leading only to disagreements (hence the secession of Aragon and Eluard in 1932 and 1938 respectively) and mystification. In the visual field, however, as also in Antonin Artaud's THEATRE OF CRUELTY and Luis Buñuel's films, it had a world-wide impact, particularly as a result of the London Surrealist Exhibition of June 1936, of Dali's window-dressing and HAPPENINGS in New York of 1939, of the posters of A.M. Cassandre and other epigones, and finally of the arrival in the U.S.A. of Breton, Ernst, Masson, Tanguy, and other refugees from German-occupied France. Gimmicks apart — and certainly it had these — Surrealism acted throughout the second quarter of this century as a universally intelligible plea for a revival of the imagination, based on the UNCONSCIOUS as revealed by PSYCHOANALYSIS, together with a new emphasis on magic, accident, irrationality, symbols, and dreams. Not the least of its achievements was that it led to a major revaluation of comparable romantic movements in the past.   J.W.

Bibl: *Minotaure* (Paris, 1933-9); A. Breton, tr. D. Gascoyne, *What Is Surrealism?* (London, 1936); M. Nadeau, tr. R. Howard, *The History of Surrealism* (New York, 1965; London, 1968); W.S. Rubin, *Dada, Surrealism and their Heritage* (New York., 1968); D. Ades, *Dada and Surrealism Reviewed* (London, 1978).

survey. A method for estimating characteristics of a population by analysis of a SAMPLE, whose members are so selected that the techniques of STATISTICS may be employed to assess the accuracy with which inferences may be made from sample to population. Its aim is not perfect precision but the control and estimation of random error (see ERROR ANALYSIS). Its preferred techniques of investigation are interviewing, the postal questionnaire, and observation. It contrasts with other methods of empirical social enquiry such as participant observation and the case study in that it typically uses more rigorously standardized procedures for eliciting information, and seeks to minimize the exercise of judgement in the recording of responses. A survey is distinguished from an enumeration or registration by the fact that a respondent or interviewee participates in a representative capacity. The method is at its best in eliciting information by methods which the informant regards as significant but not intrusive, but it can be misleading when it involves assessment of matters remote from his or her present concerns.

Survey analysis is regarded with suspicion by some because its complex techniques are often not sustained by adequate data, because analysis may be undertaken to give scientific legitimation to a preformed policy or IDEOLOGY, and because the mass MEDIA have low standards of reporting both the technical details and the institutional affiliations of survey enquiries. Nevertheless it remains an indispensable means for investigating the degree of VARIANCE of a characteristic, and the extent to which characteristics co-

vary. A non-trivial general proposition about a population can, in strict logic, be established or refuted only by analysis of data which represent that population to a known degree of approximation. Surveys are especially valuable for effecting comparisons and detecting trends.   K.H.

Bibl: C.A. Moser and G. Kalton, *Survey Methods in Social Investigation* (London and New York, 3rd ed., 1985).

survival of the fittest, see under DARWINISM.

survival value. The degree to which any qualification contributes to an organism's survival and the perpetuation of its kind.
                                                     P.M.

SUSY GUTS, see under GRAND UNIFICATION/GRAND UNIFIED THEORIES.

suture. A concept used in variants of film theory based upon LACANIAN psychoanalysis to refer to certain qualities of the spectator's engagement with cinema as a process of signification (see SUBJECTIVITY IN CINEMA). In this context, Stephen Heath defines suture as 'the relation of an individual-as-subject to the chain of its discourse where it figures missing in the guise of a stand-in'. This refers to the argument that the source of enunciation in cinema is characteristically invisible in the film text (see CINEMATIC ADDRESS). Suture is the process whereby the gap produced by that absence is filled by the spectator, who thus becomes its 'stand-in', the subject-in-the-text.   A.KU.

Bibl: S. Heath, *Questions of Cinema* (London, 1981).

swami. In HINDUISM, a formal title given to a specially honoured spiritual teacher. GURU is a more informal term.   D.L.E.

sweet. A term used especially in the SWING era to distinguish between those BIG BANDS that played JAZZ and those that played softly for the customers. Jazz fans sneered at the sweet bands, but for the musicians the relationship was more complex. Given the commercial context of popular music, even HOT bands had to play sweet from time to time — Count Basie recorded a fulsome version of

'Danny Boy' complete with 'Irish' tenor — and jazz stars often admired the technical accomplishment of the better sweet bands as well as envying their audience appeal. In a classic case, the great Louis Armstrong recalled with unfeigned relish the time he sat in with Guy Lombardo and his Royal Canadians, a band that epitomized everything sweet and, to Armstrong lovers, sickening.   GE.S.

swing. Variously, a JAZZ style and a jazz essence. As a genre, swing followed NEW ORLEANS and CHICAGO in the course of the music's development. It dominated and named the Swing era, which lasted roughly from the middle 1930s into the middle 1940s, and whose typical medium was the BIG BAND, touring the country playing arranged music, interspersed with improvised solos, for dancing. In character, jazz in the swing style was subtler than the earlier forms, though generally still closer to them harmonically and rhythmically than to the music of the BEBOP revolution that followed. At its best, as in the playing of Benny Goodman (known as the King of Swing for the popularity of his band) and men like Lester Young, Coleman Hawkins and Johnny Hodges (to name a very few) it conveys an effortless, timeless maturity, fully justifying its later designation as MAINSTREAM. As a vital quality of jazz, swing refers to its rhythmic aspect, that feeling of lift and drive that makes it unique. To swing is not simply to play rhythmically. RAGTIME does not swing, nor (depending on the particular listener) do the earliest forms of jazz, being too strictly tied to the underlying pulse. Swing in its mature sense depends on a subtle pulling away from the beat, blending tension and relaxation in perfect equilibrium. Describing it in abstract terms is impossible, but it is perceptible immediately, distinguishing the jazz player from any other musician, and jazz from any other music.   GE.S.

syllabics (or *syllabic verse*). Name given to a type of prose arranged to look like verse, written in the late 1950s and early 1960s, which was based simply on syllable-count (the number of syllables in the line, irrespective of their duration or accentual value). The verses in question (by, for example, George Macbeth) were invariably crude or flat or both; but serious experimentation had earlier proved fruitful in the work of genuine poets such as Robert Graves, Herbert Read and Marianne Moore, who did not care to draw attention to the new techniques they were trying out. A fairly cogent if incomplete discussion, by a practising poet, occurs in Roy Fuller's *Owls and Artificers*. The discussion of this subject — though never using the term syllabics — has a long history. There are experiments in English quantitative verse by Edmund Spenser, Tennyson and others; Robert Bridges also gave much thought to the problem, which is essentially one of making quantity (length of syllable) felt in an accentual context. The 'experimenters' of the 1960s thought that they had invented a new kind of verse, but it was chopped up prose because no distinction between syllables of different lengths was made (or, doubtlessly) noted. This episode was therefore irrelevant.   M.S.-S.

syllogism. In LOGIC, a deductive argument in which a *conclusion* is derived from two *premises* and in which each of the three PROPOSITIONS asserts or denies that all or some things of a certain kind are also of another kind. Each of the terms, or kinds, mentioned in the conclusion occurs in only one premise, together with a term (the *middle term*) which occurs in both premises but not in the conclusion. Thus in the syllogism 'All men are mortal, all Greeks are men, so all Greeks are mortal', 'men' is the middle term; 'mortal', the second term in the conclusion, is the *major term*, and the premise in which it occurs the *major premise*; and 'Greeks', the first term of the conclusion, is the *minor term*, and its premise the *minor premise*. The order of terms in the premises can be reversed, jointly or severally. This yields four patterns of term-arrangement or 'figures'. Each of the three propositions may be of any of the four recognized logical forms: all A are B, no A are B, some A are B, some A are not B. There are thus 256 possible syllogistic forms: 64 possible form-combinations multiplied by the four figures. Of these only 19 are valid. The theory of the syllogism was developed to a high degree of systematic completeness by Aristotle. A.Q.

symbiosis.
(1) The original meaning: in BIOLOGY, the state of affairs in which two often very dissimilar organisms live together in mutual dependence and for mutual benefit, each making up for the other's shortcomings. Thus a lichen is a symbiotic union of fungus and single-celled green alga. The compound organism, unlike a fungus, is AUTOTROPHIC. Symbiosis may have played an important part in EVOLUTION. Thus mitochondria (see CYTOLOGY) may have originated as symbiotic bacteria (see BACTERIOLOGY), and CHLOROPLASTS may have originated in the same way by union of non-CHLOROPHYLL-containing CELLS with single-celled green algae. A phenomenon which may be regarded as a step on the road towards full symbiosis is *commensalism*, in which two organisms 'dine at the same table': thus a sea anemone may grow on the shell which houses a hermit crab, and various little crustacea live within the giant respiratory chambers of, for example, sea squirt. The field of study dealing with symbiosis is sometimes known as *symbiotics*. P.M.
(2) In SOCIOLOGY, relations of mutual dependence between different groups within a community are described as *symbiotic* when the groups are unlike and the relations complementary; as *commensal* when they are like and the relations are supplementary. A.L.C.B.

symbol. Based upon a relationship of metaphor (X stands for Y) but the relationship is arbitrary. For example, a red rose is a symbol for love. Symbols have the ability to link previously separate areas of conceptual experience and allow the human mind to go beyond what is known or observed. This bridging process opens up an area of connotation which gives symbols their multifaceted, ambiguous qualities.

Anthropologists have pursued the study of symbols along two lines: meaning and function. Those influenced by Lévi-Strauss and the structuralist method (see STRUCTURALISM) have studied symbols and the nature of symbolization as a COGNITIVE process. This approach has considered 'the logic by which symbols are connected' (Leach, *Culture and Communication*, 1976). Meaning is generated from the combinations, relationships and transformations of different elements within a symbolic context. The second approach has focused upon the function of symbols for individual expressiveness and social requirements. This has located symbols within a specific social context and highlighted their emotional content. Recent work has tried to link these two lines of enquiry by understanding the power and effectiveness of symbols as arising from the dissonance between intellectual and emotional properties. A.G.

Bibl: M. Augé, *The Anthropological Circle* (Cambridge, 1982); G. Lewis, *Day of Shining Red* (Cambridge, 1980).

symbolic. The symbolic is a term introduced into PSYCHOANALYSIS by Lacan, and designates the set of pre-existing structures into which the child is born, for example, KINSHIP relations, language, and other combinatorial structures. We cannot, however, simply identify the symbolic with language, since the latter involves REAL and IMAGINARY dimensions: if there is a specifically symbolic side to language, it is on the side of the signifier whereby each element takes on its value due to its difference from other elements in the chain-like structure. D.L.

symbolic interaction. The aspect of human behaviour on which G.H. Mead based his ROLE THEORY. Mead argued that what distinguishes man from the other animals is the enormous number of symbolic or conventional meanings which his highly complex NERVOUS SYSTEM and the faculty of language enable him to store in his memory and to express by particular words and actions. These agreed meanings are learned through the process of symbolic interaction, i.e. of seeing yourself as you are seen by others, which is a necessary condition of playing roles; thus as a child you learn the role of bus-passenger-at-a-request-stop by taking the role of the driver, i.e. by imagining him seeing your raised hand, realizing you are trying to attract his attention, and stopping. This account of the learning process is extremely vulnerable to criticism from a

SKINNERIAN or BEHAVIOURIST standpoint; while Mead's insistence that the self is merely the sum of the social roles an individual plays can be taxed with failing to take into account GENETIC or PERSONALITY factors. See also CHICAGO SCHOOL (1).   M.BA.

Bibl: A. Strauss (ed.), *The Social Psychology of G.H. Mead* (London and Chicago, rev. ed., 1964); P. Rock, *The Making of Symbolic Interactionism* (London, 1979).

symbolic logic, see MATHEMATICAL LOGIC.

Symbolism. A general literary term and technique; but, specifically, the name of a central late-19th-century movement in the arts which marks the turn from ROMANTICISM to MODERNISM. Historically there are many Symbolist movements and tendencies, but Romanticism opened new possibilities by attaching special value to the imagination, the seer-poet, and the poetic path toward a transcendent world (Blake, Shelley, Poe). France, the 1850s, and Baudelaire form the starting-point for fresh developments: the matching of the Swedenborg-type theory of 'correspondences' (connections within the visible, or between the visible and invisible, worlds), with a prime role for the hyper-aesthetic imagination of the poet, who digests the 'storehouse of images and signs' in the visible world and relates them to create 'a new world, the sensation of newness'. Language itself had a transcendent content: thus Baudelaire's sonnet on the vowels. In 1886, Jean Moréas held that Symbolism had replaced all prior movements, and asserted the TRANSCENDENCE of art. In Rimbaud, Verlaine, Gautier, Nerval, Mallarmé, and Valéry, these ideas evolve into complex interplays of a subjective, magical poetic vision and the idea of a timeless, epiphanic image (see EPIPHANY) which art pursues and releases by its rhythmic, metaphoric, or linguistic action. As in Romanticism, the poet risks his own senses and experience for occult discovery through the imagination: Valéry emphasizes his special 'psychophysiology', Yeats his 'visions'. However, Symbolism emphasized much more than Romanticism the need to *create* form; a high premium is set on the fictionalizing act itself; linguistic mechanisms are stressed; technique becomes an end in itself; the idea of the 'supreme fiction' emerges. The world is seen less as an imaginative power than as a bundle of fragments; when the notion of cultural, historical, and linguistic crisis is added, this leads the way to much 20th-century modernist thought.

Hence the 'Symbolist movement' was particularly concentrated in the transitional 1890s: in Paris, with the Mallarmé circle, Huysmans, and Valéry; in Britain, with Yeats, Wilde, Symons; not much later in Germany (Stefan George);, Austria (Rilke), and Russia (Bely, Blok, etc.). Though strongly focused on the SYNAESTHESIA of poetry, it stressed the relation of all art-forms. It is evident in fiction (late James, Joyce, Proust), drama (Strindberg, Maeterlinck), music (Debussy, Scriabin), painting (Redon, Gauguin), and dance. Edmund Wilson rightly sees Symbolism coming through into familiar modernism; much early EXPRESSIONISM is really Symbolism (Trakl, Schönberg, Kandinsky). Gradually the transcendent element in Symbolism, its devotion to penetrating the veil beyond time, fades. IMAGISM and SURREALISM are distinguishable from it because the neo-Platonic bias goes. However, much modernist writing is Symbolist in spirit, because of the high value it places on form, holistically conceived (see HOLISM), as against materialistic, realistic, historical, or DOCUMENTARY presentation. See also AESTHETICISM; DECADENCE.   M.S.BR.

Bibl: Arthur Symons, *The Symbolist Movement in Literature* (London, 1899); Edmund Wilson, *Axel's Castle* (London and New York, 1931); A.G. Lehmann, *The Symbolist Aesthetic in France, 1885-1895* (Oxford, 2nd ed., 1968); P.G. West (ed.), *Symbolism: an Anthology* (London, 1980).

symmetry. The property possessed by any system which remains essentially unaltered after various operations have been performed on it. Examples: (1) the image of a stocking in a mirror is indistinguishable from the original; thus stockings, unlike shoes, possess *left-right symmetry* (see also PARITY). (2) Patterned wallpaper and crystal LATTICES are unaltered after being moved through a distance equal to the spacing between two of their elementary units; these systems have *translational symmetry*. (3) If the velocities of all the PARTICLES of a system are reversed, the system will pass successively through its former states; thus the laws of MECHANICS have *time-reversal symmetry* (see also GROUP; STATISTICAL MECHANICS; TRANSFORMATION). M.V.B.

symmetry, group, see under GROUP.

symphonic jazz. To some people the name is a contradiction, since the essence of JAZZ is spontaneity and individuality, the opposite of the symphony's massed forces and regimentation. But in fact composers and jazzmen have long been tantalized by the possibility of harnessing the distinctive flavour of jazz to the formal expressiveness of classical music. Among the first attempts were Darius Milhaud's *La Création du Monde* (1923) and George Gershwin's *Rhapsody in Blue* (1924). Action from the other side came in the 1930s with the extended compositions Duke Ellington wrote for his BIG BAND, *Creole Rhapsody* and *Reminiscing in Tempo*, just the first of numerous attempts throughout his career to wed his own improvisatory style to a more substantial structure. A notable product of the 1940s was Igor Stravinsky's *Ebony Concerto*, written for Woody Herman's band, but much more Stravinsky than Herman. By the 1950s, jazz musicians absorbed in serious musical study produced a spate of works employing classical forms that were given the collective label 'third stream'. But in the 1960s, with jazz beginning to suffer an identity crisis under pressure from FREE JAZZ and ROCK, such ambitions waned. It may be that mutual awareness and respect for what the two genres have to offer will enrich them both, without some form of self-conscious union. GE.S

synaesthesia. The experience, whether real or hallucinatory, in which a stimulus applied to one sense elicits a response from one or more others; also, the literary device that corresponds to this experience, as in 'silvery trumpet-note', 'scarlet stench', 'loud, stinking colour'. First used in this latter sense by Jules Millet in 1892, synaes-thesia (*synesthésie*) occurs in all poetry, but was especially popular among the RO-MANTIC and SYMBOLIST poets (as in Baudelaire's sonnet 'Correspondances') of the 19th century — mainly because mentally disturbed or drugged people claim to have experienced it. The CONCEPT enjoyed some facile revival in the DRUG-dominated 1960s, as 'sense-overload' and other such journalistic notions. The PSYCHEDELIC light-show (see MEDIA) was a practical manifestation. M.S.-S.

synaesthesis. Term coined by James Wood, I.A. Richards, and C.K. Ogden in *The Foundations of Aesthetics* (1922) to describe the harmony allegedly achieved by a work of art, which is said to raise the receptor to an awareness of beauty by its equilibrium: its capacity to balance strong emotions. M.S.-S.

synapse. The special interface between neighbouring NEURONS which according to the CELL theory are the cellular basis of the NERVOUS SYSTEM. Nerve impulses can travel in either direction along a nerve fibre from a point of stimulation in the middle. The impulses are polarized at the synapse, across which they travel in one direction only. Transmission across the synapse is chemically mediated rather than simply electronic in character. P.M.

synchrocyclotron, see under ACCELERATOR.

synchromism, see under ORPHISM.

synchronic, see under DIACHRONIC; LINGUISTICS.

synchronicity. JUNGIAN term for an acausal connecting principle that would give meaning to series of coincidences (e.g. the frequent recurrence of a particular numeral over a short period of time) not explicable through notions of simple causality, as well as to the experiences labelled DÉJÀ VU and PRECOGNITION. In this CONCEPT, Jung argued against the classical elementaristic view of experience, in favour of a view of events as participants within a structured whole (see STRUCTURALISM). Hence, on this view, the meaning of events is to be found in terms of their structural relationships, as well as their causal antecedents. Jung's structuralism entails a form of experiential harmony — harmony among events, and a harmony between the structure of our understanding and the event structure.   T.Z.C.

synchronism. In ARCHAEOLOGY, to establish a synchronism means to demonstrate, usually by means of TYPOLOGY, the contemporaneity of CULTURES, artifacts, or structures. Thus the synchronism of two disparate settlements might be argued on the basis of both containing like ASSEMBLAGES of distinctive tool types. Synchronisms over larger areas may be constructed with reference to the occurrence of characteristic types extensively traded. Until the advent of RADIOCARBON DATING this was one of the few methods available for correlating PREHISTORIC cultures.

B.C.

synchronous orbit. The path in space of an artificial SATELLITE which always remains directly above a fixed point on the equator. It is necessary for the ORBIT to be a circle about 22,500 miles above the earth; this figure is calculated from NEWTONIAN MECHANICS, using the MASS and radius of the earth and the fact that the orbit must be traversed in exactly one day. Synchronous satellites are used for intercontinental TELECOMMUNICATIONS.   M.V.B.

synchrotron, see under ACCELERATOR.

syncopation. The transference of musical accents onto the subsidiary pulses of a musical measure. Normally, the music has a regular pulse or time, of which 3-beat (waltz) and 4-beat (march) are the commonest. The natural accentuation falls on the first beat of 3, and on the first and (to a lesser degree) third beats of 4. In a syncopated rhythm the accent is shifted, although the main pulse continues in the background, even if only by implication. Examples of syncopation can be found as early as the 14th century; it has been a marked feature of much 20th-century music, and in JAZZ is all-pervasive.   A.H.

syncretism. Fusion, in PERCEPTION or thought (including dreams), of incompatible elements; e.g. an inchoate dream image of someone who is at once mother and brother, or man and horse.   I.M.L.H.

syndicalism. A militant TRADE UNION movement which started in France (*syndicat* is the French word for trade union) in the 1890s, and aimed at transferring the control and ownership of the means of production, not to the State, but to the unions themselves. The movement derived partly from the anti-parliamentary ideas of Proudhon and partly from the reaction of the workers against both the 'parliamentarism' of the SOCIALIST Party and the exclusive emphasis placed on politics by such MARXIST leaders as Jules Guesde. The syndicalists rejected politics, regarding CLASS struggle in the form of INDUSTRIAL ACTION as more effective; the fight on the shop floor was eventually to lead to a 'general STRIKE' (which Georges Sorel later made into the cornerstone of his theory of DIRECT ACTION). Socialist INTELLECTUALS were regarded with suspicion, and the need for workers' solidarity as a precondition of the success of any industrial and trade-union action was stressed in the *Charter of Amiens* (1906) and other texts of the Confédération Générale du Travail, in the pronouncements of the famous British leader of 'industrial unionism', Tom Mann, and in those of the organizers of the American Industrial Workers of the World (the '*Wobblies*').

Another factor permeating the syndicalist movement was the Bakuninist ANARCHIST tradition, particularly in France, Switzerland, Italy, and Spain, countries where in its early phase syndicalism appeared in its REVOLUTIONARY form of ANARCHO-SYNDICALISM. In other countries, syndicalism as a reaction to a still decentralized economy was seen, in Bertrand Russell's words, as 'the anarchism of the market place'. As an IDEOLOGY legitimizing direct industrial action by the workers, syndicalism has left a strong legacy in their trade-union organizations, but as a political current it disappeared from the scene as an effective force before World War I.   L.L.

Bibl: G. Sorel, tr. T.E. Hulme, *Reflections on Violence* (New York, 1914; London, 1916); F.F. Ridley, *Revolutionary Syndicalism in France* (London, 1970).

syndrome. (1) In medicine, the specific combination of symptoms distinguishing a particular disease, e.g. DOWN'S SYNDROME stemming from John Down (1828-96) who studied it. (2) By extension, distinguishable conditions of mind (and even social-psychological conditions) regarded as pathological, e.g. SCHIZOPHRENIA. (3) In popular current usage, a specific characteristic, set of characteristics, or behaviour pattern that has come to be symbolized by or associated with one person (real or fictitious) or group; e.g. the LOLITA SYNDROME.   R.F.

Bibl: R.D. Laing, *The Politics of the Family* (London and New York, 1971).

synergism. In BIOLOGY, the relationship between agents whereby their combined effect is greater than the sum of the effect of each one considered individually. Thus, considered as narcotics, barbituric acid derivatives and alcohol have a greater depressant effect than the sum of the two acting separately. The more general term SYNERGY can also bear this specific meaning.   P.M.

synergy. The additional benefit accruing to a number of SYSTEMS should they coalesce to form a larger system. This CONCEPT reflects the classical opinion that 'the whole is greater than the sum of the parts'. In practice, synergy may turn out to be negative, because the totality is ill-conceived or ineffectively organized. Synergy is formally studied as a property of systems by CYBERNETICS. In MANAGEMENT, synergy is the subject of measurement by OPERATIONAL RESEARCH, especially where business MERGERS are concerned; but the word is also frequently used in a much looser way in discussions of CORPORATE STRATEGY, simply to indicate general expectations of collaborative benefit. More generally still, the term is applied to the generation of unplanned SOCIAL BENEFITS among people who unconsciously cooperate in pursuit of their own interests and goals. The term derives from BIOLOGY, where it is an alternative term for SYNERGISM.   R.I.T.; S.BE.

synonymy, see under FREE VARIATION.

syntactics, see LOGICAL SYNTAX.

syntagmatic and **paradigmatic.** In LINGUISTICS, adjectives applied to two kinds of relationship into which all linguistic elements enter. Syntagmatic refers to the linear relationship operating at a given LEVEL between the elements in a sentence; paradigmatic refers to the relationship between an element at a given point within a sentence and an element with which, syntactically, it is interchangeable. For example, in the sentence *He is coming*, the relationship between *He, is, com-* and *-ing* is syntagmatic (at the level of MORPHOLOGY); the relationship between *He* and *She, is* and *will be*, etc. is paradigmatic.   D.C.

syntax. In LINGUISTICS, a traditional term for the study of the rules governing the way words are combined to form sentences in a language. An alternative definition (avoiding the concept of *word*) is the study of the interrelationships between elements of sentence structure, and of the rules governing the arrangement of sentences in sequences (see DISCOURSE). See also CONSTITUENT ANALYSIS; DEEP STRUCTURE AND SURFACE STRUCTURE; GRAMMAR.   D.C.

synthesis. The final stage, succeeding thesis and antithesis, in a DIALECTIC triad, a phase of the dialectic process. (See also DIALECTICAL MATERIALISM.) First some thought is affirmed; the *thesis*. On reflection this reveals itself as unsatisfactory, incomplete, or contradictory, and prompts the affirmation of its opposite: the *antithesis*. But further reflection shows that this too is inadequate and so it, in turn, is contradicted by the *synthesis*. This, however, does not, as in classical LOGIC, where double negation is identical with affirmation, simply reinstate the original thesis. The synthesis is held to embrace or reconcile the more rational and acceptable elements in the conflicting and now superseded thesis and antithesis from which it emerges in a 'higher unity'.   A.Q.

synthesizer. An electronic device for the production and control of ELECTRONIC MUSIC. Although this group of devices is extremely varied certain features are common among many of them. Firstly, the concept of modularity, where the individual units of the machine can be configured in various patterns to produce maximum flexibility of sound production; and secondly, the use of voltage or digital control of the individual units by other units. A typical synthesizer will use one or more oscillators or WHITE NOISE generators, controlled by a keyboard or other device, and feed the waveforms generated by them through filters (see ADDITIVE SYNTHESIS), envelope shapers (which control the dynamic shape of the sound), and amplifiers. Each of these devices will be under the control of other oscillators or performance controllers (footpedals, pitchwheels etc.). Early synthesizers (e.g. those developed by Robert Moog in the 1960s) were monophonic (i.e. capable of playing a single note at a time) and required MULTITRACK RECORDING to produce polyphonic music (e.g. Wendy Carlos, 'Switched on Bach'). During the 1970s the use of MICROPROCESSORS enabled the storing of the complex settings of the individual units and their configurations, enabling the instantaneous selection of pre-programmed sounds and facilitating the use of synthesizers in live music. Synthesizers are now normally polyphonic and frequently use SEQUENCERS to control them. Despite the suitability of synthesizers for experimentation, they have been used much more as substitutes for conventional instruments, especially in popular music (see POP).   B.CO.

Bibl: Deverahi, *The Complete Guide to Synthesizers* (New York, 1982).

synthetic, see under ANALYTIC.

synthetic chemistry. The laboratory or industrial preparation of chemical substances from simpler starting materials. Synthetic methods may be routine or directed to the preparation of new compounds.   B.F.

synthetic foods. Strictly, synthetic foods limited to certain VITAMINS and AMINO ACIDS, e.g. methionine, which can be synthesized on a commercial scale; in general usage (for which *unconventional foods* is perhaps a preferable term), foods derived from other than traditional sources of farm and fishery produce. PROTEIN foods which are essential for body growth have been a particular concern at a time of pressure on world food supplies. Unconventional sources include protein derived directly from leaves by mechanical and chemical processes (leaf protein), and from unicellular organisms grown on residues from the mineral oil industry, or on molasses or other CARBOHYDRATE materials. Conventional sources of protein such as soya beans, which in their normal form are not very palatable, may by suitable processing be converted to a form which tastes like meat and is acceptable as a substitute. Recently, BIOTECHNOLOGY has been utilized to produce synthetic foods.   K.E.H.

Bibl: N.W. Pirie, *Food Resources, Conventional and Novel* (Harmondsworth and Baltimore, rev. ed., 1976).

synthetism. One wing of the SYMBOLIST movement in painting, developed mainly by Gauguin and the young Émile Bernard, whose *Pots de grès et pommes* of 1887 was inscribed 'premier essai de synthétisme et de simplification'. With its use of clearly defined flat areas of colour (sometimes called *cloisonnisme* because of its dependence on *cloisons* or partitions), synthetism was quite different from the more atmospheric, SURREAL symbolism of Odion Redon and Gustave Moreau. Its adherents, who showed as a group at the Café Volpini in Paris in 1889, were drawn mainly from the PONT-AVEN school. J.W.

Bibl: H.R. Rookmaaker, *Synthetist Art Theories* (Amsterdam, 1959).

syphilis. A SEXUALLY TRANSMITTED DISEASE, caused by *Treponema pallidum*. After an incubation period of 9-90 days primary syphilis appears as a painless genital, anal or mouth ulcer. A few weeks later there is a generalized infection (secondary syphilis) with skin rashes, gland enlargement and other signs which run a fluctuating course for many months. Eventually, all symptoms and signs disappear, although the individual is still infected (latent syphilis). After 5-20 years, one third develop late syphilis, with major disease of the heart, nervous system and other areas, often with a fatal outcome.

Congenital syphilis affects babies who are infected from their mothers before birth. Syphilis was formerly common and, with good reason, dreaded. The use of arsenicals, introduced by Ehrlich, improved the prognosis, but penicillin proved to be a highly effective cure. Today, early syphillis is still common in some developing countries but uncommon elsewhere; in industrialized societies the majority of cases affect male HOMOSEXUALS. Late syphilis is now very rare.   J.D.O.

Bibl: Y.M. Felman (ed.), *Sexually Transmitted Diseases* (London, 1986).

system dynamics, see under SYSTEMS.

systematic theology, see DOGMATICS.

systematics, see under BIOSYSTEMATICS.

Système-Internationale-d'Unités, see SI UNITS.

systemic. Of or pertaining to a SYSTEM. In the SOCIAL SCIENCES, it is mainly used to qualify terms such as 'change', 'equilibrium', 'function' or 'contradiction' when they designate properties of social or political systems, as in various theoretical perspectives, e.g. GENERAL SYSTEMS THEORY (GST), PARSONIAN theory, MARXISM.
                                                     J.R.T.

systemic grammar. A theory of GRAMMAR which Halliday developed from his earlier SCALE-AND-CATEGORY GRAMMAR, the new name reflecting his view of language as an organization of *system networks* of contrasts.   D.C.

systems; systems approach; systems analysis.
   (1) A *system* is a group of related elements organized for a purpose. The nature of systems is studied by the science of CYBERNETICS and by GENERAL SYSTEMS THEORY (GST). A *systems approach* (or *systems analysis*, though this phrase also bears the narrower meaning defined in (2) below) is an approach to the study of physical and social systems which enables complex and dynamic situations to be understood in broad outline. It is a conceptual tool, the user of which may also receive scientific assistance from OPER-ATIONAL RESEARCH. The approach is valid whether the topic is a heating system, a postal system, a health or education system, a firm, an economy, or a government.

To identify a system it is necessary to distinguish its boundaries, to be aware of its purposes (whether these are a blueprint for its design or inferred from its behaviour), and to define the level of abstraction (see ABSTRACT) at which it is to be treated. Systems may turn out to contain recognizable *sub-systems*, sub-sub-systems, and so on. These arrangements are sometimes investigated as hierarchies; but because the arrangement often involves a nesting (in the manner of Chinese boxes) of systems within each other they may also be defined by RECURSION. One of the discoveries made by the systems approach is the extent to which attempts to improve the performance of a sub-system by its own criteria (*sub-optimization*) may act to the detriment of the total system and even to the defeat of its objectives.

In MANAGEMENT contexts, the systems approach concerns itself with growth and stability in the system under a range of possible futures, unpredictable perturbations, and alternative policies. The classic tool for studying these matters is a systems MODEL which is used for purposes of SIMULATION, and whose implications can be explored by means of a digital COMPUTER. *System dynamics* is a term coined by Jay Forrester for a style of model-building in which large structures are built which make little use of empirical evidence or previous knowledge of the subject. Forrester has shown how policies, decisions, STRUCTURE, and delayed responses are interrelated to influence growth and stability. First applied to industrial systems, his METHODOLOGY has subsequently been used to study urban and world ECOLOGICAL systems where the vision of an all-embracing model and its striking conclusions have gained a wide audience. The systems approach to a problem can alert scientists to interactions whose importance they have failed to recognize. However, systems analysis has also been applied to a number of disciplines where its contributions have yet to achieve significant influence.

See also MANAGEMENT INFORMATION

SYSTEM; METASYSTEM.

S.BE.; R.I.T.; J.A.M.; M.A.H.D.

(2) More narrowly, *systems analysis* is the first stage in presenting any large task to a computer (the other stages being PROGRAMMING and CODING). It is performed by a *systems analyst* and consists of analysing the whole task in its setting and deciding in outline how to arrange it for the computer; estimating how much work is involved and hence how powerful a computer will be needed; dividing the process into a number of relatively independent parts; and finally specifying each of these, together with their interconnections, in sufficient detail for a programmer to take over.

C.S.

Bibl: J.W. Forrester, *Industrial Dynamics* (London and Cambridge, Mass., 1961), *Urban Dynamics* (Cambridge, Mass., 1969), and World *Dynamics* (Cambridge, Mass., 1971); C.W. Churchman, *The Systems Approach* (New York, 1968); E. Laszlo, *The Systems View of the World* (New York, 1972); G.J. Klir (ed.), *Trends in General Systems Theory* (New York, 1972).

systems engineering, see CONTROL ENGINEERING; CYBERNETICS; SYSTEMS.

T

TA, see under TRANSACTIONAL ANALY-SIS.

table of mortality, see LIFE TABLE.

tableau-piège, see under COLLAGE.

taboo. A linguistic legacy to Europe from Polynesia, through Captain Cook. In its homelands the word seemed to mean both that which was holy and that which was prohibited. It is the latter sense upon which English has for the most part seized, and taboo (or tabu) is now, as noun, verb, and adjective, employed loosely to mean prohibition/prohibit/prohibited in the vast field of behaviour ranging from etiquette to RELIGION (but usually excluding law). In the SOCIAL SCIENCES, however, the term has taken on technical senses, some of which incorporate the apparent duality of its Polynesian origins. For many anthropologists, taboo means a RITUAL prohibition that may express either the sacredness (holiness) or uncleanness of what is set apart. The thing tabooed is in some fashion dangerous. Anthropologists utilizing Lévi-Strauss's structural method (see STRUCTURALISM) (e.g., Mary Douglas, *Purity and Danger,* 1966) have understood taboo as arising from the process of social classification. The duality is preserved in a different manner in FREUDIAN psychoanalytic theory (see PSYCHOANALYSIS), where taboo prevents people from doing what their unconscious desires impel them towards. INCEST and food taboos are among the commonest of those discussed in the literature. See also POLLUTION (2). M.F.;A.G.

Bibl: E. R. Leach, *Social Anthropology* (London, 1982).

tachisme, see under ACTION PAINTING.

tachyon. A hypothetical PARTICLE travelling faster than light. Because of the 'light barrier' of RELATIVITY theory, tachyons could not be produced by the ACCELER-ATION of ordinary particles. Tachyons would generate a special kind of electromagnetic RADIATION, but this has not been detected. M.V.B.

tacit knowledge. An idea formulated by Michael Polanyi (1891-1976) with wide-ranging implications in many fields of experience, though most commonly discussed in terms of its applicability to scientific knowledge. Polanyi established it as a fact of common PERCEPTION that we are typically aware of certain objects without our attention being fixed upon them. The former kind of perception ('tacit knowledge'), was not, he argued, an inferior or irrelevant dimension of CONSCIOUSNESS, interfering with deliberate attention. Rather it was integral to the entirety of our consciousness, forming the background grid which made focused perceptions possible, intelligible and fruitful. Polanyi made the comparison with certain acquired skills (e.g., manual dexterity) through which highly deliberate acts (e.g. composing on the piano) come within our grasp. Polanyi's insight has led others to build upon his work and stress how science itself is largely a 'craft skill', dependent (to a degree which major PHILOS-OPHIES OF SCIENCE scarcely recognize) upon know-how rather than explicit, formal methodological rules (see METH-ODOLOGY). R.P.

Bibl: M. Polanyi, *The Tacit Dimension* (London, 1966).

tagmemic grammar. A theory of GRAM-MAR developed by K.L. Pike in the early 1950s. The name reflects the use the theory makes of the CONCEPT of the *tagmeme,* a device for conveying simultaneously formal and functional information about a particular linguistic unit. Thus, in the sentence *The cat sat on the mat,* the formal information that *the cat* is a noun phrase and the functional information that it is the subject of the sentence are combined in a single tagmemic statement, written S: NP. Many of the principles underlying Pike's linguistic theory have since been applied to the analysis of non-linguistic phenomena (see also EMIC), of particular note being his *Language in Relation to a Unified Theory of Human Behaviour* (The Hague, 2nd ed., 1967). D.C.

take-off point. A phrase derived from W.W. Rostow's *Stages of Economic Growth* (1960). The essential idea is that there is a recognizable stage in a country's history, lasting for perhaps 20-30 years, during which the required conditions for sustained and fairly rapid growth are consolidated and beyond which such growth is more or less assured. The characteristic of this stage was defined as an increase in the proportion of NATIONAL INCOME that is saved from a low level to 10% or more. The idea has been seriously criticized by most development economists (see ECONOMIC DEVELOPMENT), but has become part of the language of economic development. I.M.D.L.; J.P.

take-overs, see under MERGERS.

tamizdat, see under SAMIZDAT.

Tantra. A discourse imparting doctrines in the tradition of Mahayana BUDDHISM, usually said to have been spoken by a mythical Buddha. Thousands of Tantras have been written from *c.* 500 A.D. onwards, and some have received a new attention as a result of the worldwide interest in Buddhism in the 19th and 20th centuries; most notably the *Tibetan Book of the Dead*, written probably in the 8th century to give guidance to dying persons. D.L.E.

Taoism. A RELIGION of the Chinese. Less official than CONFUCIANISM, it has been essentially a way (Chinese *Tao*) of life through virtue to prosperity, longevity, and immortality. Virtue has been seen as conformity to nature without and within man. This way has included both meditation in temples of great beauty and tranquillity, and a more popular traffic in charms and magical formulae, often linked with secret societies. Although the China Taoist Association was formed in 1957 with government permission, on the whole the COMMUNIST rulers of China since 1949 have suppressed Taoism. D.L.E.

Bibl: W. Chan, *Religious Trends in Modern China* (New York, 1953).

Tarski's theory of truth. The nature of TRUTH is a problem on which 20th-century philosophers, like those of previous ages, have not reached agreement. Certain philosophies (see PRAGMATISM) downgrade the idea of truth altogether; others have contended that truth is largely a formal property (e.g. the coherence of the components of a theory within a rational whole). Perhaps the most elementary and commonly persuasive notion of truth is that it lies in correspondence to the facts (a conception to the fore in the various forms of EMPIRICISM). In the 20th century, that view has been defended in the most subtle way by Alfred Tarski (1901-83), who pitched the discussion of truth on to a METALINGUISTIC plane, by stipulating rigid conditions under which 'truth language' would be applicable. Precisely, he argued that a statement such as 'snow is white' is true, if and only if, snow is indeed white. Such a formulation endowed the concept of truth with unambiguous linguistic meaning. Tarski's insight has often been said to provide support for philosophical REALISM. R.P.

Bibl: R. Harré, *Philosophies of Science* (Oxford, 1972).

taxation. The transfer of resources from private individuals, institutions, groups and firms to the government. Taxation can be on income, i.e. direct taxation; on wealth, i.e. capital taxation; or on transactions, i.e. indirect taxation. Governments levy taxes in order to cover the costs of providing PUBLIC GOODS and any losses of firms in the PUBLIC SECTOR, to redistribute income and wealth, to subsidize and encourage the consumption of particular goods and services (e.g. education), to control AGGREGATE DEMAND and to pursue various other aims. Taxation necessarily alters prices and incomes that would otherwise obtain in a FREE MARKET and is usually regarded as reducing ECONOMIC EFFICIENCY. The extent to which efficiency is reduced is disputed and of importance (see SUPPLY-SIDE ECONOMICS). A system of taxation should be designed so that while achieving the above aims, the chosen forms of taxation result in the minimum distortion of the economy and loss of economic efficiency (see POVERTY TRAP). A tax system is progressive/neutral/regressive, if the average rate of tax increases/stays the same/decreases as people get richer. In assessing the effects of increased public expenditure on the distribution of ECONOMIC WELFARE, the distribution of the benefits of the expenditure and the increased tax payments have to be considered. J.P.

Bibl: J.A. Kay and M.A. King, *The British Tax System* (Oxford, 3rd ed., 1983).

taxis, see under TROPISM.

taxonomic linguistics, see under LINGUISTICS.

taxonomy, see under BIOSYSTEMATICS.

TCA cycle, see KREBS CYCLE.

teaching machine. Any device which facilitates learning, from pebbles to film strip projectors. In current use the term refers usually to individually operated machines in which programmed material (see PACKAGES) can be exposed. The theory of INDIVIDUALIZED INSTRUCTION on which many such machines are based was realized in the 1950s and 1960s in programmes offering at first a linear sequence and later a branching programme which enabled better students to jump phases. See also PROGRAMMED INSTRUCTION.

W.A.C.S.

Bibl: J. Carmichael, *Educational Revolution* (London, 1969; New York, 1970).

team teaching. Teaching performed by a team of teachers responsible for a group or groups of pupils — either for all their activities (mainly in primary schools) or for certain subject-matters (mainly in secondary schools). A team may be *hierarchical* (with a leader bearing overall responsibility) or *collegial* (with members of equal STATUS deciding collectively how to share the workload). Team teaching is particularly appropriate in OPEN-PLAN SCHOOLS (to optimize use of space and avoid conflict between classes) and for curricula centred on PROJECT WORK (when teachers can take responsibility for groups of various sizes, enabling a wide range of instructional methods to be used). Some teachers feel that their creativity and spontaneity in dealing with pupils is restricted by the novel need to accept group decisions (and

in open-plan schools by the visual and acoustical proximity to colleagues).

E.L.-S.

Bibl: J.T. Shaplin and H.F. Olds (eds.), *Team Teaching* (New York, 1964).

technetronic society, see under POST-INDUSTRIAL SOCIETY.

technical progress. The processes by which scientific knowledge leads to the use of new production techniques and the introduction of new goods and services. Three separate processes can be identified in technical progress: invention, innovation and imitation. At any given moment of time, a society possesses a stock of scientific knowledge. This knowledge provides the base from which inventions can come. An invention is the discovery of a new production technique, good or service and is often distinct from the initial scientific discovery which ultimately leads to the invention. In most periods of history, the stock of scientific knowledge advances and, thus, the potential number of inventions increases. There are different views about the causes of inventions. These views are not necessarily contradictory and their validity may vary between different inventions. The act of invention may be a chance event and be characterized by many failed attempts; the success of an invention may be the result of the superior knowledge and abilities of the inventors; given the necessary scientific knowledge, an invention is inherently discoverable; inventions come from a sufficient and appropriate investment in scientific and inventive activities; and economic incentives lead to scientific discoveries and inventions. An innovation is the development of an invention so that it is actually used or produced in the economy. It has been suggested that inventions are often relatively inexpensive, though difficult, to discover, whilst the process of innovation is often relatively expensive. Finally, new production techniques and goods and services may be imitated by other firms. The two last stages of technical progress are important because they allow goods and services to be provided at a lower cost or they increase the range of goods and services on offer to consumers. One particular aspect of technical progress is *learning* *by doing.* Learning by doing is the accumulation of experience and innovative knowledge directly through work. This experience and knowledge is used to increase the overall productivity of the production process. Though conceptually and, in practice, difficult to measure, technical progress is generally thought to be an important factor in ECONOMIC GROWTH. See PATENT; RESEARCH AND DEVELOPMENT. J.P.

Bibl: P. Stoneman, *The Economics of Technological Change* (Oxford, 1983).

technocracy. Term coined in 1919 in California by an engineer, William Henry Smyth, for his proposed 'rule by technicians'. In 1933-4 it was taken over and popularized by Howard Scott, a former associate of Thorstein Veblen (whose book *The Engineers and the Price System*, 1921, was taken as a bible for the idea), and technocracy as a social movement had a brief vogue in the U.S.A. during the early depression years. During the 1960s the term gained wider currency in France, where it was identified with the theories of Saint-Simon (who predicted a society ruled by scientists and engineers) and used by writers such as Jean Meynaud to argue that 'real power' has shifted from the elected representatives to the technical experts and that there now 'begins a new type of government, neither DEMOCRACY nor BUREAUCRACY but a technocracy'. The power of the technocrats is identified with the rise of economic PLANNING, strategic thinking in defence matters, and the expansion of science and research. Most social analysts agree that in advanced industrial society the role of the expert has been enlarged but doubt that rule by technicians can supplant the political order.
D.B.

Bibl: W.H.G. Armytage, *The Rise of the Technocrats* (London, 1965); J. Meynaud, tr. P. Barnes, *Technocracy* (London, 1968; New York, 1969).

technological determinism. Although sometimes confused with HISTORICAL MATERIALISM, this is a simpler and cruder theory of social change. It asserts that most major changes in society are the product of changes in tools and techniques. Thus much of the FEUDAL organization of society is traced to changes in medieval warfare made possible by the invention of the stirrup; the invention of printing is held to be responsible for the Protestant Reformation; and the social changes brought about by INDUSTRIALIZATION are attributed to such inventions as the power loom and the steam engine. Today many who probably do not subscribe knowingly to technological determinism are looking to a future society, the 'information society', determined largely by the COMPUTER.

MARXISTS — and many others — criticize this view of change as naive. TECHNOLOGY is not neutral. Its development and applications are governed by social values and social interests — what Marxists call the 'social relations of production' (see MODE OF PRODUCTION). The applications of the computer, they say, are governed by the interest of the government in greater social control, and of the CAPITALISTS in greater profits. Nevertheless some form of technological determinism remains a popular philosophy. It seems to square very well with our everyday experience of an increasingly mechanized environment. K.K.

Bibl: L. White Jr, *Medieval Technology and Social Change* (Oxford, 1962); E.E. Morison, *Men, Machines and Modern Times* (Cambridge, Mass., 1966); L. Winner, *Autonomous Technology* (Cambridge, Mass., 1977).

technological forecasting. A range of techniques used, in formulating CORPORATE STRATEGY, to predict potential technological developments. The principal methods are intuitive ones based on individual expectations; the *Delphi technique* (developed by the Rand Corporation), in which experts work together in a laboratory situation to crystallize their reasoning and reach a consensus on likely developments; CORRELATION analysis; and imaginative statements (often called *scenarios*) of possible events and their likely outcomes.
R.I.T.

Bibl: J.R. Bright (ed.), *Technological Forecasting for Industry and Government* (Englewood Cliffs, N.J., 1968).

technological unemployment, see under UNEMPLOYMENT.

technology. The systematic study of techniques employed in industry, agriculture, etc. More generally, the term is used for any application of the discoveries of science, or the SCIENTIFIC METHOD, to the problems of man and his environment in peace and war. See also ENGINEERING, ENVIRONMENTAL CONTROL; METALLURGY.

M.V.B.

Bibl: J.D. Bernal, *Science in History*, 4 vols. (London, 3rd ed., 1969; Cambridge, Mass., 1971); A. Pacey, *The Culture of Technology* (Oxford, 1983).

technopolis. A term popularized in 1969 by Nigel Calder to describe a society which is moulded and continuously and drastically altered by scientific and technical innovation; scientific *policy* being either non-existent or concerned with such peripheral issues as efficiency per pound invested, or speed of results, rather than with ultimate direction or moral considerations.

P.S.L.

Bibl: N. Calder, *Technopolis* (London and New York, 1969).

tectonics. The study of the deformation of rocks, with the principal aim of establishing the extent and exact nature of the deformation and when it occurred. It may be possible to infer from the deformation the orientation of the stresses involved and the mechanism which produced them. Tectonics can be studied on all scales from microscopic distortions of single crystals to the displacement of whole continents (see PLATE TECTONICS).

J.L.M.L.

telecommunication. Communication over long distances, based on ELECTROMAGNETISM. In telephony and telegraphy signals are transmitted as electric impulses travelling along wires, while in radio and television the signals are transmitted through space as MODULATIONS of carrier waves of electromagnetic RADIATION. See also FIBRE OPTICS.

M.V.B.

teleological explanation, see under EXPLANATION.

teleology (or *consequentialism*). Literally, the study of ends, goals, or purposes; more specifically, the theory that events can only be explained, and that evaluation of

anything (objects, states of affairs, acts, agents) can only be justified, by consideration of the ends towards which they are directed. Teleologists contend that minds or living organisms can only be explained in a forward-looking way and that MECHANISTIC explanation in terms of efficient causes is inadequate. As an ethical doctrine (see ETHICS) teleology argues, in opposition to DEONTOLOGY, that rightness is not an intrinsic property of actions but is dependent on the goodness or badness of the consequences, whether actual, predictable, or expected, to which they give rise. There are, undoubtedly, teleological systems, i.e. complexes of events (e.g. a stock exchange or a cat stalking a bird) which take on a significant order only if seen as all directed towards some outlying purpose. The controversial issue is whether the teleology of the whole can be reduced (see REDUCTION) to the mechanically explicable behaviour of its parts (e.g. by taking the desires of the stockbrokers to buy and sell, or of the cat to kill the bird, as efficient causes). The invention of SERVO-MECHANISMS such as thermostats and self-correcting gun-aiming devices encourages the view that such reduction is possible in principle. Darwin's theory of NATURAL SELECTION supplied a mechanistic account of the EVOLUTIONARY process; the discovery of DNA (see NUCLEIC ACID) did much the same for the special properties of living matter. Kant reasonably described the argument from the evidences of design in the natural world to a supernatural designing intelligence as the teleological proof of God's existence.

A.Q.

telepathy, see under ESP.

Tel Quel. An influential French literary magazine, founded in 1960 by the novelist and critic Philippe Sollers (b. 1936). Its aims and objects are usefully stated in Sollers's *Logiques* (1968). Influences on the *Tel Quel* school include Bachelard, Ponge, Roussel, Barthes (see also SEMIOLOGY), and the quasi-Marxist EXISTENTIALISM of Sartre. The position of *Tel Quel* was originally aesthetic; but over its first decade this evolved into a complex ACTIVISM. Briefly, the *Tel Quel* school believes that certain writings (e.g. of de Sade, Lautréamont, Mallarmé, Artaud) could transform society for the better, but are ignored by society in various subtle ways. *Tel Quel* aims to restore to language its 'original revolutionary power', and proposes literature as the prime means of doing this because 'literature is a language made with language'.   M.S.-S.

temperature-humidity index (THI). An index of the effect on human comfort of temperature and humidity levels, 65 being the highest comfortable level.   C.E.D.

tension. In the NEW CRITICISM, a term defined by Allen Tate (who derives it from the logical terms *ex*tension and *in*tension — see CONNOTATION AND DENOTATION) as the sum total of meaning in a poem. The poem has a literal MEANING (extension) and a metaphorical one (intension); the simultaneity of these meanings results in tension. New Critics tend to judge poetry by its ability to achieve such tension.
                                                 M.S.-S.
Bibl: J.O.A. Tate, *Reason in Madness* (New York, 1941).

tensor. A generalization of the notion of VECTOR which can be used to represent RELATIONS between vectors. For example the elasticity tensor relates the deformation at each point of an elastic body to the applied stress. The *tensor calculus* was first developed in connection with differential GEOMETRY and was the fundamental tool used by Einstein in formulating the general theory of RELATIVITY.   R.G.

teratogen, see TERATOLOGY.

teratogenesis, see TERATOLOGY.

teratology. Term coined by Geoffrey St Hilaire in 1822 to describe the study of either cold- or warm-blooded abnormal animals. The word sprang into prominence and common usage, following the thalidomide disaster in 1962, to describe the study of environmental factors responsible for the birth of deformed humans, e.g. X-RADIATION, rubella and some drugs administered to the mother during pregnancy. Although it could be regarded as applicable to genetically-induced abnormalities it is not commonly used in this connexion. Deriving from teratology are

teratogen (a physical or chemical agent which produces abnormal young when the mother is exposed to its influence during pregnancy), and *teratogenesis* (the process by means of which teratogenic factors exert their deleterious effects). In current practice the word is usually confined to experimentation upon warm-blooded mammals such as rats, mice and rabbits and on rare occasions such as the Seveso tragedy to the epidemiological effects of a teratogen in the human. Most authorities stress the interplay of GENETIC and environmental factors in producing malformed mammalian young, including children.   D.H.M.W.
Bibl: D.H.M. Woollam, 'Basic Principles of Teratology' in R.R. Macdonald (ed.), *Scientific Basis of Obstetrics and Gynaecology* (Edinburgh and London, 3rd ed., 1985).

Terman-Merrill revision, see under MENTAL RETARDATION.

terminal. A device by which a human being can communicate directly with a COMPUTER. It consists typically of a typewriter-like keyboard and a VISUAL DISPLAY (or sometimes a printing device) controlled by the computer. Owing to the great disparity between the operating speeds of human beings and computers it is usual to attach several terminals (the figure may be as high as 500) to a single computer, which services them in rotation. Nowadays terminals contain MICROCOMPUTERS; sometimes these are PROGRAMMED to allow some processing of the information (such as simple editing) to be performed locally on the terminal itself, without interrupting the main *host* computer. Such devices are sometimes called *intelligent* terminals or *smart* terminals. The activities of *dumb* terminals, on the other hand, are confined to the input and display of information, and require the attention of the host at every keystroke and for every change on the screen. See also COMPUTING.   C.S.; J.E.S.

terms of trade. The quantities of goods and services (imports) that can be purchased from the proceeds of the sale of given quantities of goods and services (exports). An INDEX NUMBER measuring changes in the terms of trade is obtained by dividing an index number of prices of sales (exports) by one of prices of purchases (imports), a rise indicating an improvement. The concept may be applied to transactions within a country (e.g. between farmers and the rest of the economy), or between one type of product and another (e.g. between raw materials and manufactures), but is mostly applied to the imports and exports of a nation. Economists call these the *net barter terms of trade*, and have invented other concepts (e.g. 'gross barter', 'income', 'single', and 'double factorial' terms of trade) which have attracted less general interest.

M.FG.S.

Bibl: B. Sodersten, *International Economics* I (London, 1980).

terrestrial planets. The planets Earth, Mercury, Mars and Venus, grouped together because of their earthlike (terrestrial) appearance. They are also termed inner planets. They are solid, with rocky surfaces possessing thin gaseous atmospheres. The remaining OUTER PLANETS are mostly gaseous or liquid. Mars has been visited by the American Pioneer and Voyager Martian probes, Venus by the Soviet Venura probes. Mercury has been approached and filmed by the American Mariner 10 SPACE PROBE.   J.D.B.

territorial imperative. Phrase coined by the American scientific popularizer, Robert Ardrey, for the theory that man is a creature whose behaviour in relation to the ownership, protection, and expansion of the territory he regards as his or his group's exclusive preserve is analogous to the territorial behaviour of animals (see TERRITORY) and is acquired genetically in the same way. In accordance with the principles of territorial behaviour, mutual antagonism grows as natural hazards diminish.   D.C.W.

Bibl: R. Ardrey, *The Territorial Imperative* (New York, 1966; London, 1967).

territorial sea, see under LAW OF THE SEA.

territoriality. The process of attempting to affect, influence or control actions by delimiting and asserting control over TERRI-

TORY. Many studies emphasize territoriality as a fundamental human need based on identity, defence and stimulation, although spurious analogies are sometimes drawn between human needs and such animal behaviour as the need for an exclusive preserve for reproduction and security. It is therefore important to envisage human territoriality as conditioned primarily by cultural NORMS and values that vary in structure and function from society to society, and which also vary with the scale of social activity — from the territoriality inherent in the bubble of personal SPACE, through the territoriality which acts as a focus and symbol for group membership and identity (for example, urban gangs and their 'turfs'), to the territoriality underlying patterns of regional identification. While it has become common practice to envisage political SOVEREIGNTY as crucial to understanding the exercise of state POWER over territory, it is also important to acknowledge that the exercise of such power is invariably bound up with other aspects of territoriality, such as social consent and state LEGITIMACY.

GR.S.

Bibl: R.D. Sack, *Human Territoriality: Its Theory and History* (Cambridge, 1986).

territory.

(1) The portion of geographical SPACE under the jurisdiction of a recognized authority. Territorial claims have often been at the root of political tensions and conflicts; recently these claims have been related more to the resources available within the territory than to its function as shelter. Territorial SOVEREIGNTY extends over adjacent maritime and air spaces, and maritime powers are now widening the breadth of their TERRITORIAL SEAS and claiming control over the contiguous continental shelf.   J.G.

Bibl: R.Y. Jennings, *The Acquisition of Territory* (Manchester and New York, 1963); J. Gottmann, *The Significance of Territory* (Charlottesville, 1973).

(2) In ETHOLOGY, an area in which an organism or a group of individuals is dominant — e.g. the territory within which a male bird will allow no intrusion and towards which he acts in a way distinctly analogous to that of a human being

(in most societies) towards his private property, or the 'group territories' of lions, hyenas, and some other mammals and birds, which likewise evoke behaviour analogous to human behaviour (see DOMINANCE). This pattern of behaviour is known as *territoriality*. See also TERRITORIAL IMPERATIVE.   P.M.

Bibl: H. Kruuk, *The Spotted Hyena* (London and Chicago, 1972); G.B. Schaller, *The Serengeti Lion* (London and Chicago, 1972).

terrorism. The systematic use of coercive intimidation, usually to service political ends. It is used to create and exploit a climate of fear among a wider target group than the immediate victims of the violence, and to publicize a cause, as well as to coerce a target into acceding to the terrorists' aims. Terrorism may be used on its own or as part of a wider unconventional WAR. It can be employed by desperate and weak MINORITIES, by STATES as a tool of domestic and foreign policy, or by belligerents as an accompaniment in all types and stages of warfare. A common feature is that innocent civilians, sometimes foreigners who know nothing of the terrorists' political quarrel, are killed or injured. Typical methods of modern terrorism are explosive and incendiary bombings, shooting attacks and assassinations, hostage-taking and kidnapping, and hijacking. The possibility of terrorists using NUCLEAR, chemical, or bacteriological weapons cannot be discounted.

One basic distinction is between *state* and *factional* terror. The former has been vastly more lethal and has often been an antecedent to, and a contributory cause of, factional terrorism. Once regimes and factions decide that their ends justify any means or that their opponents' actions justify them in unrestrained retaliation, they tend to become locked in a spiral of terror and counter-terror. *Internal* terrorism is confined within a single state or region while *international* terrorism, in its most obvious manifestation, is an attack carried out across international frontiers or against a foreign target in the terrorists' state of origin. But in reality, most terrorism has international dimensions, as groups look abroad for support, weapons, and safe haven.

Terrorism is not a philosophy or a movement: it is a method. But even though we may be able to identify cases where terrorism has been used for causes most LIBERALS would regard as just, this does not mean that even in such cases the use of terrorism, which by definition threatens the most fundamental rights of innocent civilians, is morally justified. Paradoxically, despite the rapid growth in the incidence of modern terrorism, this method has been remarkably unsuccessful in gaining strategic objectives. The only clear cases are the expulsion of British and French colonial rule from Palestine, Cyprus, Aden, and Algeria. The continuing popularity of terrorism among NATIONALISTS and ideological and religious extremists must be explained by other factors: the craving for physical expression of hatred and revenge; terrorism's record of success in yielding tactical gains (e.g. massive publicity, release of prisoners and large ransom payments); and the fact that the method is relatively cheap, easy to organize, and carries minimal risk. Regimes of TOTALITARIANISM, such as NAZISM and STALINISM, routinely used mass terror to control and persecute whole populations, and the historical evidence shows that this is a tragically effective way of suppressing opposition and resistance. But when states use international terrorism they invariably seek to disguise their role, plausibly denying responsibility for specific crimes. Another major conducive factor in the growth of modern terrorism has been repeated weakness and APPEASEMENT in national and international reaction to terrorism, despite numerous anti-terrorist laws and conventions and much governmental rhetoric. Early writings on terrorism tended to treat it as a relatively minor threat to law and order and individual HUMAN RIGHTS. P. Wilkinson, in a series of studies, concluded that major outbreaks of terrorism, because of their capacity to affect public opinion and foreign policy and to trigger civil and international wars, ought to be recognized as a potential danger to the security and wellbeing of afflicted states and a possible threat to international peace.   P.W.

Bibl: P. Wilkinson, *Terrorism and the Liberal State* (London, 1986).

tertiary occupation, see under OCCUPA-TION.

tetrahedral theory. An extension of the CONTRACTION HYPOTHESIS to explain the distribution of the continents and oceans. If the earth was cooling and contracting, its shape would tend to become tetrahedral, since the tetrahedron is the regular figure with the smallest volume. Though the distribution of continents and oceans is roughly tetrahedral, with the oceans corresponding to the faces, the theory presents a picture which is inconsistent with ISOSTASY and it has therefore been abandoned. J.L.M.L.

Bibl: A. Holmes, *Principles of Physical Geology* (London and New York, 3rd ed., 1982).

tetranucleotide hypothesis. An influential conception in the emergence of modern BIOCHEMISTRY, the tetranucleotide hypothesis postulated that NUCLEIC ACIDS were made up of nucleotides (their basic building blocks) in proportions of equal mass. When first formulated, the theory argued that DNA consisted of just one each of the four nucleotides arranged in a chain. RNA was believed to be similarly composed. This notion was demonstrated to be unacceptable in the 1940s, when it was recognized that the structure of nucleic acids was far more complex. In the process, they ceased to be seen as nucleotides, and came to be reconceptualized as polynucleotides, comprising long chain MOLECULES with fixed sequences. The work of Chargaff and E. Vischer in particular demonstrated the different base proportions of DNA, posing in a particularly acute form the problem of its structure, which the work of Crick and Watson in the 1950s so spectacularly resolved. R.P.

Bibl: F.H. Portugal and J.S. Cohen, *A Century of DNA* (Cambridge, 1977).

text, theory of. Term used by the German critic Max Bense and others to convey the 'scientific' analysis of 'text' — chosen as a word free from the VALUE-JUDGEMENTS implicit in terms like 'literature' or 'poetry' — by largely quantitative methods such as STYLOMETRY. J.W.

text score. A musical score which, instead of conventional notation, uses words describing actions to be taken by the performers. Directions can range from specific physical actions to more meditative and intuitive instructions (e.g. Stockhausen's 'Aus den Sieben Tagen'). Text scores may also incorporate graphic and conventional MUSIC NOTATIONS. B.CO.

Bibl: R. Smith Brindle, *The New Music* (London, 1975).

textual criticism. The part of editing a literary work which deals with the establishment of the text. The need for textual criticism is occasioned by the fact that all texts of every kind tend to become *corrupt* (i.e. falsified) in the normal course of transmission. In many cases different witnesses offer variant readings at particular points, and often there are radically different versions of a work. It is now fairly generally agreed that the ideal of textual criticism is to present the text which the author intended.

Textual criticism was the principal form of literary study, by professionals and amateurs alike, from the time of classical antiquity until the 19th century. The main subjects were the New Testament and the Greek and Latin classical writers; the chief method was *emendation* of words or passages on aesthetic grounds, either by logic or by reference to the readings of other witnesses. The formalization of analysis (with the construction of *stemmata*, i.e. of family trees of witnesses) and the emergence of BIBLIOGRAPHY (as the detailed and systematic study of the printed book) at the end of the 19th century caused the practice of textual criticism to be confined to specialists, who have now brought editing to a laborious, sophisticated, and time-consuming level.

The textual critic needs a sound aesthetic (see AESTHETICS), a thorough knowledge of the text under consideration, and access to any authorial or other relevant statements about the text. The five major steps to textual criticism are *collecting* the *texts* (i.e. the various appearances of the *text*); *analysing* the differences between the texts; *selecting* the *copy-text* (i.e. the version regarded as most authoritative and therefore used as a basis); *perfecting* the copy-text (i.e. replacing passages known or thought to be corrupt by the introduction, from other sources, of readings known or thought to be authorial); and *explaining* and justifying the editor's procedures and decisions.

J.T.

Bibl: J. Thorpe, *Principles of Textual Criticism* (San Marino, 1972).

texture. In the NEW CRITICISM, the particular aspect of a poem as distinct from its abstract or universal aspect; just as the smooth or rough texture of a vase may be distinguished from its general design. John Crowe Ransom has elaborated this: the general design of a poem, its argument, is its STRUCTURE, while its texture consists of all its 'local' detail, its personal or unique qualities. In poetry, Ransom argues, texture clashes with and modifies structure. Compare TENSION.   M.S.-S.

Bibl: J.C. Ransom, *The World's Body* (London and New York, 1938).

TG, see under TRANSFORMATIONAL GRAMMAR.

Thatcherism. A term used mainly by media commentators and opponents to characterize the dominant political force in Britain since the election in 1979, and re-election in 1983 and 1987, of a Conservative government under the leadership of prime minister Margaret Thatcher. In so far as the term denotes a coherent set of values and policies, they may be said to derive in part from the theories of the New Right (see RIGHT). Thus Thatcherism has sought to substitute market forces for STATE action wherever possible (see PRIVATIZATION); to weaken the influence of TRADE UNIONS and reflect the trend towards CORPORATISM discernible in postwar Britain, and in its early years to use MONETARIST policies to control INFLATION. While reducing the area of state responsibility it has sought to raise the state's capacity to operate within its sphere: Thatcherism has combined an increase in the centralization of political authority with a more traditional CONSERVATIVE stress on law and order. It has drawn widespread criticism, including from within conservatism, as being negligent of the interests of the more disadvantaged groups and regions of the country,

and as inferring a mandate for radical policies from election victories won without popular majorities.   S.R.

Bibl: N. Bosanquet, *After the New Right* (London, 1983); H. Drucker *et al.*, *Developments in British Politics 2* (Basingstoke, 1986).

The Look. In film theory, this concept draws on both FREUDIAN and LACANIAN psychoanalysis to explain aspects of the relationship between film text and spectator (see CINEMATIC APPARATUS; SUBJECTIVITY IN CINEMA). Film theorists argue that looking in cinema involves not only voyeurism (in that the screen image, the object of the spectator's gaze, is distanced from him/her in such a way that a return of the look is impossible) but also NARCISSISM (in that the spectator recognizes and identifies with the human figure on the screen). The concept of The Look has been taken up by feminist film theory (see FEMINISM), in the argument that the female figure on the cinema screen is constructed pre-eminently as an object of looking, in a spectator-text relation which constructs a 'masculine' subject position from the spectator, regardless of his or her GENDER.

A.KU.

Bibl: A. Kuhn, *Women's Pictures: Feminism and Cinema* (London, 1982).

theatre anthropology, see under THIRD THEATRE.

theatre in the round. Any form of staging in which the acting area is surrounded on all sides by the audience, minimizing the scenic element and concentrating attention upon the figure of the actor. The use of this form is attested for some medieval and primitive drama; in the 20th century its attraction has lain in the sharp contrast it presents to 'picture-frame' NATURALISM (see OPEN STAGE). The first important central stage production of modern times was by Okhlopkov in Moscow (*The Mother*, 1933); the first permanent theatre in this form was the Penthouse Theater, University of Washington, Seattle (1940); the New Victoria Theatre, Stoke on Trent (1986), was Europe's first purpose-built theatre in the round. The form has been used for large-scale, circus-like productions with spectacular effects achieved by movement, costume, and mobile stage properties and units, and for small-cast plays where a sense of intimate involvement between actor and audience is required. Few directors, however, have been willing to confine their work exclusively to this form. M.A.

Bibl: S. Joseph, *Theatre in the Round* (London, 1967).

Theatre Laboratory. An itinerant and highly influential experimental Polish theatre company directed by Jerzy Grotowski (*b.* 1933). In Grotowski's theatre the actor became paramount, making use of all the physical and mental powers at his disposal; the emphasis was on austerity, poverty, and simplicity, in reaction against the 'wealth' of contemporary theatre; and the texts were mainly Grotowski's own radical adaptations of classic Polish works. The company was founded in 1959, gave its first performance outside Poland in 1966, and had a major influence on figures as diverse as the director Peter Brook and the choreographer Jerome Robbins. Also Grotowski's notion of a company as a monastic, self-contained troupe became gospel for many of the AVANT-GARDE, e.g. notably the LIVING THEATRE and Eugenio Barba's Odin Theatre (see THIRD THEATRE). After *Apocalypsis cum Figuris* (1969) no new theatre pieces were presented, and Grotowski concentrated upon research, teaching and theorizing, often obscurely, upon the nature of performance. The Laboratory Theatre was formally dissolved in 1984. M.BI.

Bibl: J. Grotowski, *Towards a Poor Theatre* (London, 1969; New York, 1970); J. Kumieya, *The Theatre of Grotowski* (London, 1985); Z. Osiński, *Grotowski and his Laboratory* (New York, 1986).

Théâtre Libre. An experimental Parisian theatre club founded in 1887 by André Antoine that had a profound influence on French play-writing, acting and design. It became a showplace for NATURALISTIC writers like Eugène Brieux dedicated to a theatre aimed at the cure of social evils; but it also staged controversial works by the great European dramatists such as Ibsen, Strindberg, Hauptmann, and Verga and the kind of *comédies rosses* ('cynical

comedies') popular in the closing years of the century. At the same time it helped to liberate French acting from sentimental rhetoric and scenic design from artificial prettiness. It also inspired the creation of similar theatres such as Otto Brahm's FREIE BÜHNE in Berlin and J.T. Grein's *Independent Theatre* in London. It closed in April 1897, largely for economic reasons, but its influence in Europe and beyond was incalculable. M.BI.

Bibl: O.G. Brockett and R.R. Findlay, *Century of Innovation* (Englewood Cliffs, N.J., 1973).

Théâtre National Populaire (TNP). A state-financed theatre, established in 1951 in the Palais de Chaillot, under the direction of Jean Vilar, with the express purpose of appealing to a wide popular audience and creating an atmosphere different from that of the commercial BOURGEOIS theatre. The TNP enjoyed a period of exceptional prestige when Gérard Philipe was its resident star, and it has done much to familiarize school-children and factory-workers with the drama, both French and foreign. In 1963 Vilar was succeeded as director by Georges Wilson, who carried on the same tradition of serious, eclectic theatre. J.G.W.

theatre of cruelty. A form of theatre which seeks to communicate to its audience a sense of pain, suffering, and the presence of evil, primarily through non-verbal means. The term was first used by the SURREALIST actor Antonin Artaud in his essay 'Le Théâtre de la cruauté' (1932). He developed his ideas further in a series of essays, letters, and manifestos published as *Le Théâtre et son double* (1938). Artaud rejected the Western tradition of theatre, whose emphasis upon REALISM and psychological character-study he considered trivial, and hoped to re-create theatre at the more universal level which he found in primitive RITUAL and oriental drama. Artaud's writing is visionary rather than practical, and no complete body of theory exists behind it. Outside France, where he had a strong influence upon the director Jean-Louis Barrault, Artaud was little known before the first English translation of his book in 1958. In the 1960s his ideas were widely discussed, and the concept of the theatre of cruelty was explored and developed, most notably in productions by Jerzy Grotowski (see THEATRE LABORATORY), Peter Brook, and the LIVING THEATRE. See also THEATRE OF THE ABSURD. M.A.

Bibl: A. Artaud, *The Theatre and its Double* (tr. M.C. Richards, New York, 1958; tr. V. Corti, London, 1970); M. Esslin, *Artaud* (London, 1976); R. Hayman, *Artaud and After* (Oxford, 1977).

theatre of panic. Term (*théâtre panique*) coined by the Spanish-born French dramatist, Fernando Arrabal, in 1962 to describe the kind of ceremonial theatre he favours. The reference is to the god Pan, a deity combining the attributes of rustic vitality, grotesque fun, and holy terror; and Arrabal's concept is a blend of tragedy and a Punch-and-Judy show, of bad taste and refinement, of sacrilege and the sacred. Heavily influenced by the theories of Antonin Artaud, Arrabal has put his ideas into practice in a number of ritualistic plays including *The Architect and the Emperor of Assyria* (1967) and *And They Handcuffed the Flowers* (1969). Similar ideas are apparent among French AVANT-GARDE companies, most notably Jerome Savory's rowdily picturesque Grand Magic Circus and latterly the Spanish group El Comediants. M.BI.

theatre of the absurd. Term coined in 1961 by the critic Martin Esslin to define a form of theatre which, rejecting NATURALISM as the basis for its presentation of character and action, uses a variety of dramatic techniques defying rational analysis and explanation to express, by implication rather than direct statement, the 'absurdity' of the human condition; Esslin adopts and expands the concept of the absurd employed by the EXISTENTIALIST Albert Camus in *Le Mythe de Sisyphe* (1942). The absurd is not so much a single, identifiable theatrical tradition as a common denominator to be found in the work of a number of 20th-century dramatists, who are individually indebted to a variety of independent traditions from DADA and SURREALISM to the routines of vaudeville and the circus. Some elements of the absurd may be traced back to Alfred Jarry's *Ubu Roi* (1896), and found in plays by

Cocteau and Ivan Goll written in the 1920s; but the term is usually associated with writers active after World War II, notably Samuel Beckett, Eugene Ionesco, N.F. Simpson, and Harold Pinter. In its rejection of rational, analytical processes, the genre has some affinities with THEATRE OF CRUELTY. M.A.

Bibl: M. Esslin, *The Theatre of the Absurd* (rev. ed., Harmondsworth, 1968; New York, 1969).

Theatre Workshop. A theatre company founded, with a policy of COMMITMENT to the LEFT, by Joan Littlewood and Ewan McColl in 1945, and housed after 1953 in the Theatre Royal, Stratford, East London. In the second half of the 1950s it presented work by new dramatists including Brendan Behan, Shelagh Delaney, and Frank Norman, all infused with a theatrical vigour that was indebted equally to the writers' WORKING-CLASS backgrounds and to Joan Littlewood's directorial style. In 1963 her production of *Oh What A Lovely War!* helped to inspire a distinctively English form of DOCUMENTARY theatre; beset by financial and other difficulties, Littlewood directed her last production in 1973. The title Theatre Workshop was abandoned in 1978. M.A.

Bibl: H. Goorney, *The Theatre Workshop Story* (London, 1981).

theism. Belief in at least one God (Greek *theos*) as the Creator of the universe and the Saviour and Ruler of human life, and as TRANSCENDENT because eternal and infinite (i.e. free from the limitations of time and space) as well as *immanent* (i.e. present and active in time and space). This belief produces the desire to understand any divine self-revelations and to enter, through prayer and corporate worship, into a humble relationship with God pictured as a person, specially as a Father, or with the gods. (DEISM, by contrast, denies the possibility of divine self-revelation.) *Polytheism* is the belief in many gods, and is generally regarded as more primitive than *monotheism*, the belief in One God who is in some sense 'Almighty' or sovereign. All this has been shaken by scientific EXPLANATIONS of previously mysterious phenomena and by the disintegration of the stable societies where RELIGION was at

855

home. Modern theologians have tried to reconcile the monotheism inherited from past ages of faith with the NATURAL SCIENCES' explanations of the EVOLUTIONARY emergence of matter, life, and man (see PROCESS THEOLOGY) and with the general process of MODERNIZATION. They have emphasized God's Being (more than mere existence) as the source, ground, and goal of all that exists or is possible, rather than God's miraculous interventions in the processes of nature. They have also stressed that much, if not all, talk of God (e.g. as being personal or 'above' us) is symbolic and may need a radical revision to be meaningful in our CULTURE. The most important Protestant theologian with such modern emphases was Paul Tillich (1886-1965, a German philosopher who acquired a wide influence in the U.S.A.).

For a sophisticated recent attempt to restate Christian belief while frankly abandoning the whole of theism, see DEATH OF GOD THEOLOGY. For its antecedents, see NON-THEISTIC RELIGION. For attempts to restate Christian theism, see DIALECTICAL THEOLOGY, EMPIRICAL THEOLOGY, and NEO-THOMISM. For the older identification of God with the universe, which still has some influence, see PANTHEISM. For the personal experience which is held to be a basis of theism, see MYSTICISM. Theism is professed by all Christians, Jews (see JUDAISM), and adherents of ISLAM, HINDUISM, and tribal religions. Many adherents of BUDDHISM also worship a divine Saviour. Under the pressure of SECULARIZATION, however, many nominal adherents of these religions live and think without much (if any) reference to theism. Their conception of religion is chiefly ethical (see ETHICS), and intellectually is marked by a cautious AGNOSTICISM. The more complete scepticism of ATHEISM rejects theism as an illusion and THEOLOGY as nonsense. On the whole, theism has declined as an intellectual force during the 20th century, together with the practices of prayer and corporate worship, although few people outside COMMUNIST countries admit to being convinced and consistent atheists.   D.L.E.

Bibl: K. Ward, *The Concept of God* (Oxford, 1974) and *The Living God*

(London, 1984); R.G. Swinburne, *Faith and Reason* (Oxford, 1984).

thematic analysis. A type of musical analysis proposed by Rudolph Réti and others which attempts to show an organic growth in musical works by the discovery of developments and transformations of small motivic cells (see also SCHENKER ANALYSIS).   B.CO.

Bibl: R. Réti, *Thematic Patterns in the Sonatas of Beethoven* (London, 1967).

thematic apperception test (TAT). A projective test (see PROJECTION; MENTAL TESTING) developed by Henry Murray, in which the subject is asked to describe what is happening in a series of standard pictures that are sufficiently vague to permit a variety of interpretations. Interpretations are assumed to reflect *themas* (i.e. themes) that play a major role in the subject's own life.   W.Z.

theodicy. In THEOLOGY, a theory that asserts God's justice (Greek *dike*) in creating the world. The need for such a theory is rendered acute by the problem of evil. There is evil in the world: either God could not prevent it (but he is by definition omnipotent), or he did not choose to do so (but he is by definition benevolent). The word was coined in 1710 by Leibniz, who argued that even if there were no specific evils in the created world it would still be imperfect, just because created and not the source of its own existence, as God, the most perfect being, is alleged to be. One attempted method of solving the problem of evil is to argue that evil is merely negative, an absence of good, and so not truly real. Another method, less elusive, is to attribute the world's defects to the free will with which God endowed the minds, human and possibly diabolic, which he created, a free spirit being more perfect, because more like God, than one that is not free.   A.Q.

Bibl: J.H. Hick, *Evil and the God of Love* (London and New York, 1966).

theology. The attempt to talk rationally about the divine (see THEISM). Every RELIGION produces some theology, but Christianity has been intellectually active to a unique, perhaps excessive, extent. The term is therefore mostly used in a Christian context. It may cover the historical study of Christian scripture, history, and thought on the largely tacit and unexamined assumption that these subjects are important because the Christian faith is correct; or it may refer to an explicit, systematic, and often-renewed attempt to work out doctrines in the light of this faith (see CRISIS THEOLOGY; DOGMATICS; EMPIRICAL THEOLOGY; PHILOSOPHICAL THEOLOGY). This acceptance of Christianity may be contrasted with the wider and more neutral approach of 'religious studies', which emphasize COMPARATIVE RELIGION.   D.L.E.

Bibl: P. Hodgson and R. King (eds.), *Christian Theology* (Philadelphia, 1982; London, 1983); A. Richardson and J. Bowden (eds.), *A New Dictionary of Christian Theology* (London and Philadelphia, 1983).

theology of hope. The discussion of the meaning of ESCHATOLOGY in Christian THEOLOGY produced, in reaction to Rudolf Bultmann's proposal to DEMYTHOLOGIZE the Biblical images, by interpreting them exclusively in personal terms as understood in CHRISTIAN EXISTENTIALISM, a proposal that God's control over nature and history should be reaffirmed. The promise of God's triumph was derived particularly from belief in the resurrection of Jesus from the dead in a glorified body. This new hopefulness was connected with a new mood of optimism in the 1960s. Jürgen Moltmann's *Theology of Hope* (in German, 1964) was an international influence among readers of theology although it was criticized as being insufficiently aware of the THIRD WORLD problems which preoccupied LIBERATION THEOLOGY. Later the general mood in Europe and the English-speaking world became less optimistic, and Third World Christians were tempted to despair, but there was no going back to existentialism's neglect of public affairs.   D.L.E.

Bibl: J. Moltmann, tr. J.W. Leitch, *Theology of Hope* (London and New York, 1967); R. Alves, *A Theology of Human Hope* (New York, 1969).

theoretical chemistry. An academic discipline in which theoretical PHYSICS is applied to chemical phenomena, such as BONDING, reaction rates (see CHEMICAL REACTION, CATALYSIS, COHESION etc.). Much effort is devoted to mathematical calculations of the properties of theoretical MODELS, using QUANTUM MECHANICS (hence the near-synonym *quantum chemistry*) and STATISTICAL MECHANICS.   B.F.

Bibl: P.W. Atkins, *Molecular Quantum Mechanics* (Oxford, 1970); R.P.H. Gasser, *Entropy and Energy Levels* (Oxford, 1974).

theory ladenness (of observation). Observation of the world and what happens in it, whether or not aided by instruments, is never free of the theories, beliefs, assumptions and expectations brought to the task by the observer himself. In philosophy this is put by saying that both the process of observation and the terms in which what is observed are described are 'theory-laden', that is, imbued with theoretical content by the observer. There is therefore no neutral or unalloyed access to a realm of pure 'facts', as had been hoped by philosophers in the tradition of EMPIRICISM, including some of the LOGICAL POSITIVISTS to whom the debate about theory-ladenness is chiefly owed.   A.C.G.

theory of everything, see under SUPERSTRINGS.

theory of three worlds. An expanded and updated version of Mao's 1964 concept of a 'Second Intermediate Zone', delivered by Deng Xiaoping to the 6th Special Session of the UNO General Assembly (10.4.74). The theory suggested that since the COLD WAR, there had been increasing collusion between the U.S. and the U.S.S.R. in their search for international HEGEMONY. As a response to the creation of this superpower bloc, the Chinese argued that the SOCIALIST camp was no longer in existence, and the COMMUNIST Party States of eastern Europe were now under IMPERIALIST domination. Similarly there had been a disintegration of the western bloc, which was now seeking greater unity in order to resist the expansion of U.S. hegemony. In essence, the superpowers made up the first world, the developing countries in Asia, Africa and Latin America the third, and the developed nations between the two made up the second world. The suggestion was that China, as a THIRD WORLD country, must increase its ties with other Third World nations to try and resist the superpowers' quest for world domination. S.B.

Bibl: J. Gittings, *The World and China* (London, 1974).

theosophy. A religious movement founded by Madame H.P. Blavatsky and Annie Besant in India towards the end of the 19th century and subsequently gaining adherents in many countries, specially in Germany, where in turn it gave rise to the ANTHROPOSOPHY taught by Rudolf Steiner. The terms come from the Greek, meaning respectively 'wisdom about God' and 'wisdom about Man'. D.L.E.

therapeutic community. Once the effectiveness of traditional therapies within the lunatic asylum or mental hospital was increasingly challenged from the 1920s, one alternative approach to be developed was the therapeutic community. This was a unit, generally within the hospital, involving up to around 100 patients, in which efforts were made to break down the traditional hierarchy of doctor/patient relations. Instead, both groups were urged to participate in creating a real 'community' environment, and patients were to 'become active participants in their own therapy'. Often this involved relatively democratic decision-making techniques on the ward, aimed at raising patients' levels of responsibility and group awareness. R.P.

therapeutic state. A notion advanced by the libertarian American psychiatrist, Thomas Szasz, to depict what he regards as an unholy alliance between public PSYCHIATRY and the powers of the central state. Just as the medieval church, with its inquisitorial powers, persecuted heretics in the service of social uniformity, so (argues Szasz) today's psychiatric profession polices DEVIANCY in the service of the central state. This occurs most nakedly in the abuses of Soviet psychiatry (BRAINWASHING), where departure from the party line is treated as a form of mental perversion; but the belief that those holding unorthodox views are in need of treat-

ment forms the rationale for a wide range of public medical interventions in Western societies too. Underpinning Szasz's argument is a radical scepticism about the very category of mental illness and a libertarian suspicion of professional power. More neutrally, the aspirations of any WELFARE STATE, aiming to rectify pre-existing deficiencies in health and opportunity, could be described as 'therapeutic'. R.P.

Bibl: Thomas Szasz, *The Therapeutic State* (New York, 1984).

Theravada, see under BUDDHISM.

theremin. An ELECTRONIC musical instrument invented *c.* 1924 by a Russian scientist of that name. Tone is generated by the proximity of the player's hand to a short antenna attached to two oscillators, one operating at a fixed frequency, the other at a variable frequency. The difference between the two frequencies causes a 'beat' effect which is the third 'AUDIO' FREQUENCY. The player controls pitch with one hand, volume with the other. A.H.

thermal neutron. A slow NEUTRON, whose KINETIC ENERGY is roughly equal to that of the random heat motion in the material through which it is passing. Thermal neutrons produce most of the FISSION reactions in a NUCLEAR REACTOR (see also MODERATOR). M.V.B.

thermal reactor, see under NUCLEAR REACTOR.

thermionics. The design of ELECTRONIC devices whose operation depends on the emission of ELECTRONS from the surface of a hot metal cathode (see ELECTRODE), e.g., the ELECTRON GUN in a CATHODE RAY TUBE, and the thermionic valve used in radio receivers and COMPUTERS before the advent of the TRANSISTOR. M.V.B.

thermistor. A substance whose resistance changes rapidly with temperature. This property enables thermistors to be used for making devices in control systems (see CONTROL ENGINEERING). The active element is a SEMICONDUCTOR such as a mixture of nickel and manganese oxides with finely divided copper. E.R.L.

thermochemistry. The part of THERMODY-NAMICS concerned with the accurate measurement of the heat given out or absorbed during CHEMICAL REACTIONS.
B.F.

thermodynamics. A branch of PHYSICS developed in the 19th century, dealing with heat and temperature. The subject is based on three laws:

(1) The *first law* connects thermodynamics with MECHANICS by the statement: 'Heat is a form of ENERGY.' This implies that no engine can produce work indefinitely without a permanent source of heat, so that 'perpetual motion machines' cannot be made.

(2) The famous *second law* expresses the irreversibility of processes: 'It is impossible to produce work by transferring heat from a cold body to a hot body in any self-sustaining process.' It is of course possible to use the reverse process — heat transfer from hot to cold — to produce work, and this is the basis of the internal combustion engine, the steam engine, and nuclear and conventional power stations. A mathematically equivalent form of the second law is: 'ENTROPY always increases in any closed system not in EQUILIBRIUM, and remains constant for a system which is in equilibrium.'

(3) The *third law* states: 'It is impossible to cool a system right down to the ABSOLUTE ZERO of temperature.'

In addition to their importance in the theory of heat engines and CRYOGENICS, these three laws provide relations between the thermal properties of materials (e.g. the amount of heat necessary to produce a given rise in temperature) and their mechanical properties (e.g. the pressure necessary to produce a given decrease in size). They involve no mention of the underlying atomic structure of matter; the more powerful methods of STATISTICAL MECHANICS enable the laws to be derived, and their significance understood, in terms of atomic motions.
M.V.B.

thermoluminescence. In ARCHAEOLOGY, a DATING technique based on the principle that, if a clay body is heated, ALPHA PARTICLES, trapped in the crystal LATTICE, will be released as light ENERGY which can be measured. The light is therefore propor-

tional to the number of trapped alpha particles which in turn are directly related to the degree of flawing of the lattice, the intensity of the RADIOACTIVE environment in which the object was buried, and the length of exposure. The first variable can be determined by re-exposing the sample to a source of known strength and measuring the light emitted on reheating; the second can be measured directly. It is thus possible to estimate the length of the exposure, which in terms of baked clay means the time between the last ancient firing (usually the date of manufacture) and the date of testing. The method has value as a means of absolute date assessment. It is also widely used to test the authenticity of artifacts out of CONTEXT.
B.C.

thermonuclear reaction. A CHAIN REACTION based on nuclear FUSION.
M.V.B.

thermonuclear war, see under WAR.

thermoplastic. A POLYMER (PLASTIC) which becomes soft and relatively fluid on heating but hardens on cooling. Such plastics, like polyvinylchloride, typically have long polymer chains with few chemical BONDS between the chains, and when hot are easily moulded, extruded, or rolled into sheets. Thermosetting plastics are originally semi-fluid polymers with quite short polymer chains which on heating react to give a rigid three-dimensional cross-linked network.
B.F.

thesis, see under SYNTHESIS.

THI, see under TEMPERATURE-HUMIDITY INDEX.

things-in-themselves, see NOUMENA.

third theatre. A term coined in 1976 by Eugenio Barba (b. 1936), to describe the nature and work of such groups as his own Odin Teatret (founded in Oslo in 1964), which exist on the margins of official culture, usually suffering from poverty, hardship and critical neglect and often living a nomadic or, as Barba puts it, 'migrant' existence. The allusion, which does not hold good in all particulars, is to the conditions experienced in the THIRD WORLD itself. Early in his career Barba formed an association with Grotowski, the influence of whose THEATRE LABORATORY can be seen in the long gestation period for Odin's theatre pieces accompanied by arduous physical and vocal training for the performers; and like Grotowski Barba has studied in great detail the performance techniques used in Oriental and other theatrical forms outside the realistic Western tradition. Equally important in Barba's thinking is a concern for the vanishing cultural traditions of non-industrial societies in Europe and the third world (he has worked extensively in South America and in southern Italy, where he was born), and he has developed the notion of *barter*, an exchanged demonstration of cultural skills in place of the conventional cash transaction which usually initiates or concludes a performance. Barba and his most sympathetic observer, the Italian scholar F. Taviani (b. 1946), have also speculated interestingly upon the sociology of the actor and his work within such a group. In 1979 Barba founded the International School of Theatre Anthropology (ISTA), a body whose sporadic conferences and training schools are devoted to 'a comparative study of acting techniques in an intercultural perspective'.   M.A.

Bibl: E. Barba, *Beyond the Floating Islands* (New York, 1986).

Third World. Collective term of French origin (*le Tiers-monde*), taken up by American writers, for those states not regarded or regarding themselves as members of either the developed CAPITALIST or the developed COMMUNIST 'worlds': they are thus classified by their state of economic development as 'underdeveloped', 'less developed', or 'developing' states (see UNDERDEVELOPMENT). The Third World includes most of the countries of Latin America and the recently independent states of Asia and Africa. Many of these share a colonial past and strong resentment against IMPERIALISM; they are poor and, thanks largely to the population explosion, are growing poorer by comparison with the industrialized nations; in foreign policy, following the Indian example, many of them have favoured NEUTRALITY. The Third World accounts for about one-third of the membership of UNO

and is strongly represented in UNCTAD.
                                    A.L.C.B.

thought police, see under ORWELLIAN.

three-age system. A simple technological MODEL used to order the past. It was introduced in Denmark in 1816-19 by C. Thomsen, who proposed that the prehistoric period (see PREHISTORY) could be divided into an Age of Stone, an Age of Bronze, and an Age of Iron. His theoretical scheme was soon shown by excavation to be largely valid. With numerous elaborations and subdivisions, including the subdivision of the Stone Age into *palaeolothic* ('Old Stone Age') and *neolithic* ('New Stone Age') periods by Sir John Lubbock in 1865, it was widely adopted in the Old World but the development of American and African ARCHAEOLOGY showed that it was not universally applicable. It is now regarded as of little further value, although its basic terminology is still used as a convenient shorthand.   B.C.

Bibl: G. Daniel, *The Three Ages* (Cambridge, 1943) and *The Origins and Growth of Archaeology* (Harmondsworth, 1967; New York, 1971).

three-body problem. A variety of questions arising from the fact that in the (Newtonian) theory of GRAVITATION one cannot solve completely the DIFFERENTIAL EQUATIONS which govern the motion of three or more bodies. One can compute approximate solutions, but these will only be valid for *limited* periods of time; they cannot tell one, for example, whether the earth and moon will *eventually* spiral away from the sun. Work on such qualitative problems was initiated by H. Poincaré (1854-1912) who developed and applied the methods of algebraic TOPOLOGY for this purpose.   R.G.

three worlds theory, see under THEORY OF THREE WORLDS.

threshold (or *limen*). In the measurement of sensation, the statistical point at which (1) two STIMULI resemble each other so closely as to be confusable (the *differential threshold*) or (2) a stimulus is so weak that its presence cannot be detected except by chance (the *absolute threshold*).   H.L.

throwback, see under ATAVISM.

thrust stage, see under OPEN STAGE.

thyristor. A SOLID-STATE DEVICE employing SEMICONDUCTORS and having some of the properties of an electrical switch, e.g. it can initiate a flow of current. However, it can only stop the flow if the voltage across the thyristor is reversed, and in this respect it behaves in much the same way as a gas-filled ELECTRONIC valve. The fact that thyristors have replaced such valves in virtually all applications is due to their advantages in size (a whole order of magnitude smaller than their valve counterparts), efficiency, robustness, and reliability, and to the fact that they require no separate heater circuit, as does the valve. The development of thyristors has extended the use of semiconductors into the 'power' field of electrical engineering in a similar way to that in which the TRANSISTOR has replaced the electronic valve. A single thyristor can regulate electric power supplies of the order of many kilowatts.

E.R.L.

Bibl: A.W.J. Griffin and R.S. Ramshaw, *The Thyristor and its Application* (London, 1965).

thyroid gland. An important endocrine gland (see ENDOCRINOLOGY) under the control of the PITUITARY and responsible for the control of basal metabolic rate. Anatomically the gland is a system of vesicles containing a secretory product of which a principal ingredient is thyroglobulin. Active thyroid hormones are thyroxin and triiodothyronine. Both contain iodine, and the working of the thyroid is dependent upon its being in adequate supply. Iodides are added to table salt in areas where iodine would otherwise be lacking.

P.M.

time and motion study, see under WORK STUDY.

time error. In PSYCHOPHYSICS, the tendency for the second of two stimuli — visual, auditory, or tactual — of equal magnitude to be judged as greater by virtue of the fact that the later is being judged against the earlier's diminished magnitude in immediate memory.

J.S.B.

time notation. A type of MUSICAL NOTATION pioneered by Earle Brown (also called *time-space notation*) where the durations of the notes are not indicated by conventional rhythmic symbols but by either the distance between the notes on the musical score or by the length of horizontal lines extending from them. This system is much less exact than conventional rhythmic notation and gives the performer more interpretational freedom (see INDETERMINACY).

B.CO.

Bibl: M. Nyman, *Experimental Music: Cage and Beyond* (London, 1974).

time series analysis, see under EXTRAPOLATION.

time-sharing, see under COMPUTING.

time-space notation, see under TIME NOTATION.

tissue. A system of CELLS which fulfils a definite PHYSIOLOGICAL or structural function — e.g. connective tissue, bone, cartilage, or nervous tissue.

P.M.

tissue culture. A system by which living CELLS in a normal or cancerous TISSUE can be cultivated and propagated for many generations of cell division outside the body in suitable nutrient media. Both connective tissue cells (fibroblasts) and epithelial cells have been cultivated in this way. It was at one time thought that tissue cultures lived indeterminately, and that a famous strain of fibroblasts derived from the heart of an embryonic chicken had been maintained for 10 or 20 years in the Rockefeller Institute. Newer evidence shows that this is not the case. Tissue cultures that remain DIPLOID in CHROMOSOME make-up have a determinate lifespan which varies in length in inverse proportion to the age of the organism from which the tissues were taken for cultivation. In the older forms of tissue culture the growth medium was a semi-solid one, being composed of a mixture of chicken's plasma (see SERUM) with a watery extract of chicken embryos which contains the full range of nutrient substances required for continued growth. Today, however, systems of fluid culture have become almost universally adopted. Long-cultivated tissues sometimes undergo a TRANSFORMATION associated with the acquirement of cancerous or malignant properties. Malignant strains have an indeterminate lifespan. Tissue cultures are widely used for the cultivation of viruses (see VIROLOGY) — e.g. polio virus — for the preparation of vaccines. P.M.

Titoism. A term invented to characterize the specific political evolution of Yugoslav domestic and foreign policies after Tito's break with Stalin in 1948; it has also been applied to the policies of other Communist parties displaying similar tendencies towards doctrinal REVISIONISM and national COMMUNISM. Internally, Titoism was marked by some attenuation of the Party's administrative (though not its political) role and of the power exercised by the political police. It permitted a far greater contact with other countries by liberalizing travel, allowing emigration, and developing the tourist industry. It reversed the harsh COLLECTIVIZATION drive in favour of individual small-scale farming. Its most novel policy, which it claims as its doctrinal trade-mark and the most distinctive characteristic of Yugoslav SOCIALISM, was that of introducing 'workers' self-government' through 'workers' councils', together with the industrial 'self-management' of enterprises in a *market socialism*. Political decentralization led to demands for autonomy in federal states on ethnic and economic grounds and this produced a certain reversal of Tito's policies, a clamp-down on 'anarcho-liberal' tendencies and on Croat and other local NATIONALISM.

Externally, Tito's foreign policy after 1948 became completely independent of the Soviet Union. It achieved this by taking advantage of the BALANCE OF POWER in Europe and by developing special relationships with the THIRD WORLD countries on the basis of NON-ALIGNMENT. The resumption of closer relations with the Soviet Union on the Party level did not impair Yugoslavia's jealously guarded independence, which was expressed not only in foreign policy, but also in cordial relations with those Communist parties (e.g. the Romanian, Italian and Spanish) which opposed the Soviet Union's attempts to re-establish its doctrinal and political leadership in the Communist movement, and to exclude China from it. L.L.

Bibl: M. Zaninovich, *The Development of Socialist Yugoslavia* (Baltimore, 1968); H.M. Christman (ed.), *The Essential Tito* (New York, 1970; Newton Abbot, 1971); D. Rusinow, *The Yugoslav Experiment, 1948-74* (London, 1977).

TM, see under TRANSCENDENTAL MEDITATION.

TNP, see THÉÂTRE NATIONAL POPULAIRE.

toasting, see under REGGAE.

TOE (theory of everything), see under SUPERSTRINGS.

tokomak. A very large piece of experimental equipment first developed in the U.S.S.R. which is used to study the conditions in which controlled nuclear FUSION might occur and the manner in which it could be exploited for power generation. Investigations are being undertaken on the behaviour of very dense currents of hydrogen IONS. Unfortunately such currents are usually unstable — they wobble and change shape and they can strike the walls of the confining chamber. A tokomak is an experimental chamber in which these instabilities are studied and removed. It consists basically of a large hollow ring inside which the ion currents circulate. Large coils around the ring produce a magnetic field which acts on the circulating ions in such a direction that their trajectory is stabilized. The very large ring at the JET laboratory, Culham, U.K. is a tokomak design. H.M.R.

tolerance. In IMMUNOLOGY, a state of specific non-reactivity towards a substance that would normally excite active IMMUNITY. The institution of specific tolerance is the goal to which all research in TISSUE and organ transplantation (see SURGERY) is directed. Many means of producing tolerance are in use, but its precise mechanism is not known. P.M.

tonality, see under ATONAL MUSIC.

tone-cluster (or *cluster*). A group of adjacent notes, usually played on a keyboard instrument, and not susceptible of conventional harmonic analysis. Tone-clusters may be played with the palm of the hand, the forearm, or a piece of wood or other material of a specified length. First appearing in the music of American AVANT-GARDE composers such as Charles Ives and Henry Cowell, they have now become a routine device and part of the normal vocabulary of music.   A.H.

tone-row, see under SERIAL MUSIC.

Tonton Macoute. In Haitian Creole literally: Uncle bagmen. A 10,000-strong para-military storm-troop organization, personally recruited from 1959 onwards by Jacques Duvalier, dictator of Haiti, to terrorize (see TERRORISM) political opponents and critics of the regime. Officially entitled *Volontaires de la Securité Nationale*, and untouched by any legal restraint, its members acquired a name for extortion, torture, and brutality. In the disorder which followed the fall from power of Duvalier's son Jean-Claude ('Baby-Doc') in 1986 the Macoutes became the target of much vengeful violence.   S.R.; D.C.W.
   Bibl: R.I. Rotberg, *Haiti: the Politics of Squalor* (Boston, 1971).

topic neutrality. The idea, introduced to PHILOSOPHY by Gilbert Ryle, that certain terms may be neutral with respect to a given context of DISCOURSE within which they occur. He defined the notion thus: expressions of, say, English are topic-neutral if a foreigner who understood *only* them when reading an English passage could not understand what the passage as a whole is about. It is suggested that the chief examples of topic-neutral words are the 'constants' of LOGIC, such as 'and', 'or', 'if', 'not'. Some philosophers argue that since these terms are fundamental to logic they should be regarded as neutral with respect to different ways of interpreting other logical terms. Ryle argued that any arbitrarily chosen topic-neutral words could serve as the constants of logic. The matter is controversial.   A.C.G.
   Bibl: G. Ryle, *Dilemmas* (London, 1954).

topodeme, see under DEME.

topological defect, see under STRINGS.

topological psychology. A form of PSYCHOLOGY associated with Kurt Lewin who, much influenced by GESTALT psychology, used topological GEOMETRY (i.e. non-metric spatial relations; see TOPOLOGY) to represent and theorize about the field of interacting psychological forces (the LIFE SPACE) within which a person lives and acts.   I.M.L.H.
   Bibl: K. Lewin, tr. F. and G.M. Heider, *Principles of Topological Psychology*, (London and New York, 1936).

topology. A branch of MATHEMATICS often picturesquely but inaccurately described as the study of those properties of figures in space which persist under all continuous deformations. Thus interlocking is a topological property of closed curves in 3 dimensions: one cannot separate two interlocked rubber bands without cutting one of them (a *dis*continuous deformation). But intuitively, as Kant emphasized, the above description is too narrow: intrinsically a (lined) left-hand glove does not differ from a right-hand one, but one cannot be continuously deformed into the other in 3 dimensions. Further, there is no reason to limit investigations to 3-dimensional space, or even to spaces which can be said to have a DIMENSION. All that is required of a general *topological space* is that there should be a notion of closeness (or *neighbourhood*) associated with it. Continuous FUNCTIONS, or *maps* from one space into another, are required to preserve the notion of closeness (see CONTINUITY); an invertible map is called a *homeomorphism*. Topology, then, is the study of those properties of topological spaces which are preserved by homeomorphisms. (And there *is* a homeomorphism of 3-dimensional space onto itself which turns a right-hand glove into a left-hand one.)
   General topology is concerned with the properties of 'figures' (which are often arbitrary collections of points) in general or only slightly specialized topological spaces. Among the CONCEPTS it studies are the notions of LIMIT and of *connectedness*.

Its theorems do not go deep, but they have a very wide range of application.

The most powerful and beautiful theorems of topology, however, concern more restricted 'figures' in spaces which are more specialized and which may carry additional structure. This makes it possible to represent the situation (in *combinatorial topology*) or to approximate to it (in *algebraic topology*) by a 'framework', or *complex* (e.g. a covering of a space by a network of triangles) to which numerical and algebraic methods can be applied. As in *analytic* GEOMETRY, feats of geometric insight can be replaced by more or less routine computations. (Perversely, *analytic topology* seeks to obtain results without resort to algebra.)

Homology theory is concerned with the notion of *boundary*; e.g. the boundary of a sphere in 3 dimensions is its 2-dimensional surface, which in turn has zero boundary. The formal properties of the boundary OPERATOR also recur in purely algebraic contexts; this is the prime ingredient of *homological* ALGEBRA. *Homotopy theory* is concerned with the properties of figures and of maps which persist under continuous deformation.

Various specific topological problems (e.g. the classification of the topological types of 2-dimensional surfaces) were solved in the 19th century. In the first half of this century the foundations of algebraic topology were developed. Many of the most powerful techniques and results belong to the last 25 years. But some classic problems (e.g. the classification of 3-dimensional manifolds) remain unsolved.

Apart from its intrinsic interest, topology is important because it can give significant qualitative results about continuous phenomena without requiring a knowledge of detail (see THREE-BODY PROBLEM). Applications to the theory of DIFFERENTIAL EQUATIONS have been particularly fruitful. Recently CATASTROPHE THEORY has used topology to classify the different ways in which a dynamical system can pass through a point of instability; qualitative applications have been made to ECONOMICS, SOCIOLOGY, and MORPHO-GENESIS.   R.G.

Bibl: R. Courant and H. Robbins, *What is Mathematics?* (London and New York,

1941); S. Barr, *Experiments in Topology* (New York, 1964; London, 1965).

torts. Wrongs done to others independent of any contractual relationship, for which the injured party may sue. Whereas the outcome of any action for breach of contract depends upon the terms of the contract concerned (see CONTRACT), tortious liabilities are of widely varying kinds. The commonest tort is negligence, the failure of a defendant to discharge an objectively tested duty of care towards others, albeit inadvertently, unintentionally or even unknowingly. Although the motive with which a tortious act is done is usually immaterial, so that a lawful act does not become unlawful merely because it is done with a bad motive, such as a wish to injure, there are some torts in which malice is an essential ingredient, e.g. fraud, malicious prosecution. Some torts may be directly intentional, e.g. assault, false imprisonment, while others may sometimes be voluntary and at other times involuntary, e.g. defamation, trespass to property, nuisance, interference with contractual relations or trade. The judicial remedy sought in civil proceedings for tort is normally damages, i.e. a sum of money to be paid by the defendant to the plaintiff to recompense him for his injury; but in some cases, e.g. nuisance to a neighbour, the court may grant an injunction ordering that the act complained about must cease.

                                                    D.C.M.Y.

Bibl: H. Street, *The Law of Torts* (London, 7th ed., 1983); J.G. Fleming, *An Introduction to the Law of Torts* (Oxford, 2nd ed., 1985).

total art. The creation of 'total environments' — walls, rooms, large spaces — usually involving various media, so as to disturb or in some way interest the spectator (or explorer). Examples are the houses, interiors, and accumulations (MERZ structures) built by Kurt Schwitters, and more recently the tableaux of Ed Kienholz. In its attempt to free the concept of art from its associations with collectors' pieces, and to break down the traditional barriers between 'art' and 'life', total art took inspiration from CONSTRUCTIVISM, SURREALISM, and DADA.   P.C.

Bibl: A. Henri, *Environments and Happenings* (London and New York, 1974).

total institution. A concept developed by the Chicago sociologist, Erving Goffman, to designate the special characteristics developed by institutions, such as mental hospitals and prisons, absolutely set apart from society at large, and with RITUALS which totally deny the individual, private existence of its occupants. Such institutions typically have a formal, official, society-oriented rationale (gaols are punitive, asylums are therapeutic). Goffman contended, however, that, by virtue of their isolation, they develop self-regulating systems and rationales of their own, essentially geared to their own internal self-perpetuation. Strategic adjustment among staff and patients alike through internal SUB-CULTURES subverts the explicit goals of the institution, produces a survivor mentality and creates institutional dependence. Goffman's work served as an important critique of classic institution-based reformist strategies. R.P.

Bibl: Erving Goffman, *Asylums* (Harmondsworth, 1968).

total serialization, see under SERIAL MUSIC.

total strategy. A term which denotes the principles and policies of the South African government in response to increasing opposition to APARTHEID since the mid-1970s. It attempts to reconstruct a stable base for the maintenance of white supremacy, if on changed terms. It includes the increasing militarization of the regime and centralization of political authority in the office of prime minister and the State Security Council; changes in policy towards the Southern African region, concessions to win support of the growing black PETIT BOURGEOISIE and divide opposition forces, and efforts to diffuse international condemnation of Apartheid.

S.R.

Bibl: R. Davies *et al.*, *The Struggle for South Africa*, 2 vols. (London, 1984).

total theatre. Theatre regarded as primarily a director's medium using the text as only a minor part of an overall theatrical experience of lights, music, movement of all sorts, sets, and costumes. The term was first used in the mid-1920s: an abortive *Totaltheater* planned by Walter Gropius for Erwin Piscator in Berlin; but the concept was first effectively executed by Jean-Louis Barrault in works like Claudel's *Christophe Colombe* (production of 1953) and Barrault's adaptation (with André Gide) of Kafka's *The Trial* (1947). Subsequently it was taken much further by other directors: especially the Italian, Luca Ronconi, in his travelling version of Ariosto's *Orlando Furioso* (1970), in which the peripatetic spectators were constantly engulfed by the action.

M.BI.

Bibl: E.T. Kirby (ed.), *Total Theater: A Critical Anthology* (New York, 1969).

total war, see LIMITED WAR.

totalitarianism. A theoretical view of NAZISM, FASCISM, and Soviet COMMUNISM which sees them as examples of a political system dominated by a single party and IDEOLOGY in which all political, economic, and social activities are absorbed and subsumed and all dissidence suppressed by police TERRORISM. Total monopoly of the ordinary flow of information and public argument is essential to such a system. This view was much current in the 1930s-1950s period among dissident MARXIST intellectual commentators on the *Gleichschaltung* (Nazification) of parties, TRADE UNIONS, universities, professional associations, etc. in Nazi Germany and on the degree of central control exercised by the STALINIST dictatorship in the U.S.S.R. It owes much to organic theories of the State. Later writers have tended to emphasize the degree to which rivalries for the leadership, factionalism, and the development, in industry, applied science, or the armed forces, of separate centres of POWER and influence and of hierarchies parallel to the party but essential to the State, preserve an element of PLURALÍSM and modify the earlier monolithic image of the totalitarian State. D.C.W.

Bibl: H. Arendt, *The Origins of Totalitarianism* (London, 2nd ed., 1961; New York, new ed., 1966); C.J. Friedrich *et al.*, *Totalitarianism in Perspective: Three Views* (London, 1969); L. Schapiro, *Totalitarianism* (London, 1972).

totemism. For long regarded as a large and heterogeneous set of religious practices in PRIMITIVE societies in which groups of people associated themselves, usually as DESCENT groups, with natural objects. In the early 1960s Claude Lévi-Strauss revived interest in the subject by radically changing our vision of it (*Le totémisme aujourd'hui*, 1962; Eng. trans., 1964). He argued that what had hitherto been treated under that head was a mode of thought and a classification of nature in relation to men. The argument sought to strip away both the religious and utilitarian elements that had accumulated in the theoretical writings since the last century. See also STRUCTURALISM.   M.F.

Bibl: J. Sturrock, *Structuralism* (London, 1986); S. J. Tambiah, *Culture, Thought and Social Action* (Harvard, 1985).

tower block, see POINT BLOCK.

town. A geographical term not easy to define. In Britain a clear-cut dichotomy between town and country, or rural and urban SETTLEMENT, does not exist at the present time either physically or socially. Instead there is an urban-rural continuum within which towns may be distinguished as foci where central services tend to concentrate. A.E. Smailes and F.H.W. Green have been responsible for investigating and identifying such foci of central services. In England, Scotland, and Wales they found that the best criterion for deciding what is or is not a town is afforded by the presence or absence of a bus station.   M.L.

townscape. The visual effect created by urban forms and usually considered analogous to the picturesque effects found in landscape. The idea stems from Camillo Sitte's *City Planning according to Artistic Principles* (Vienna, 1899), which was based largely on an analysis of the compositional elements of European urban squares. The term was given wide currency by the *Architectural Review* in the 1950s. Through the drawings of Gordon Cullen, it was directed towards an emphasis on ground surfaces, *street furniture* (lamp-posts, seats, bollards, etc.), and such qualities as spatial surprise and the visual effects of a mixture of urban activities.   M.BR.

Bibl: G. Cullen, *The Concise Townscape* (New York, 1971; London, 1972).

toxicology. The science of poisons — identification, mode of action, and antidotes. *Toxins* and *venoms* are poisons of biological origin. In general they are *antigens* and their remedies are *antibodies* (see IMMUNITY). Snake venoms are very often ENZYMES which have profound effects on blood-clotting processes, and for that reason may be used therapeutically, e.g. in haemophilia. The belief that very low doses of poisonous substances — e.g. strychnine — have a stimulatory and thus salutary effect is altogether without foundation. Toxins deprived of their poisonous but not their antigenic properties are described as *toxoids* — e.g. diphtheria or tetanus toxoid. Toxoids excite active immunity, and their use is greatly preferable to that of *antisera*, e.g. anti-tetanus SERUM. Vast numbers of industrial chemicals are now known to be poisonous substances: thus coal tar and its derivatives are CARCINOGENS, and organic solvents like carbon tetrachloride (used in the dry-cleaning industry) are known to cause grave liver damage.   P.M.

toxoids, see under PROPHYLAXIS.

trace element. Biologically important substances, also called *micronutrients*, and found, usually in minute amounts, in the soil and in food. Those needed for healthy plant growth are iron, molybdenum, boron, magnesium, copper, chlorine, and cobalt. For animals micronutrients include copper, iron, manganese, cobalt, zinc, molybdenum, iodine, and selenium. Certain animals and plants require specific elements which do not seem essential to most others, e.g. tunicates require vanadium, some plants need barium and strontium. Although needing only small amounts, living organisms concentrate trace elements in their TISSUES, sometimes having levels many thousand times higher than those found in soil or food. Trace elements are probably important as part of ENZYMES rather than as general tissue constituents. However, there is no rigid division in all animals between major nutrients and micronutrients.

Some soils are naturally deficient in trace elements (e.g. copper in South Australia), and until they are added farming is impossible. Micronutrients are also added to the diet of farm animals, particularly those reared intensively. But care must be taken to avoid overdosing, as trace elements may be very poisonous in excessive quantities. Thus copper in small amounts is needed by plants, but in higher concentrations is used as a fungicide and a weed-killer; and even man is harmed by water containing 10 parts per million.   K.M.

Bibl: G.W. Cooke, *The Control of Soil Fertility* (London, 1967).

trace theory. In GENERATIVE GRAMMAR since the late 1970s, an approach which provides a formal means of marking the place a grammatical constituent once held in the derivation of a sentence before the constituent was moved to another part of the sentence by a transformational rule. The position from which the constituent was moved is known as a 'trace'.   D.C.

Bibl: A. Radford, *Transformational Syntax* (Cambridge, 1981).

tracer. A distinguishable variant of some common ELEMENT which, being handled by the body in exactly the same way as its normal form, can be used as to follow the course of a metabolic reaction (see METABOLISM), in the body as a whole or in CELLS in a test-tube or other artificial environment. Tracer elements are distinguished from their normal counterparts by RADIOACTIVITY or by differences of mass. Tracer techniques represent the most important advance in biochemical METHODOLOGY in the present century, and it is no exaggeration to say that the whole of modern BIOCHEMISTRY and much of immunology (see IMMUNITY) is founded upon their use. An example in medicine is the use of radioactive iodine to examine the functions of the THYROID. Tracer technology is combined with microscopy in the technique known as *autoradiography*, in which a histological (see HISTOLOGY) section containing radioactive tracers is made, in effect, to take a photograph of itself by applying it to a photographic emulsion; see AUTORADIOGRAPH.   P.M.

trad. A conservative movement in JAZZ that swept America and Europe in the 1940s. Partisans of trad (short for 'traditional') declared, usually with great heat, that jazz was real only in its original state. The style of NEW ORLEANS alone was truly pure, though some CHICAGO players were acceptable. SWING, however, was decadent, and BEBOP a godless perversion. By the late 1940s trad bands were flourishing, attempting to keep the true flame alive, imitating the ancient classics with a zealot's passion. In the States the movement received a boost with the discovery of a living ancient, the trumpeter Bunk Johnson, who, given a new set of teeth and a horn, galvanized New Yorkers with his band of New Orleans veterans. To the supporters of bebop, however, trad was a travesty of the principle that jazz must always move forward, and they dismissed trad-lovers as 'mouldy figs'. But even today the music retains a broad appeal, frequently among people who would not otherwise consider themselves jazz fans, though it would not be unfair to say that what is referred to as 'trad' often lacks the real fundamentalist fervour and is inseparable from DIXIELAND.   GE.S.

trade or **business cycle.** Cyclical fluctuations in the level of economic activity, where activity is defined with reference to the degree of utilization of productive resources. There is more UNEMPLOYMENT and underemployment of labour and CAPITAL in the slump than in the boom of the cycle. In the context of ECONOMIC GROWTH, a cyclical recession (see DEPRESSION, sense 3) is usually reflected in a slowing down in the growth of NATIONAL INCOME, rather than an actual contraction. In the definition, it is usual to include only cycles lasting between one and twelve years. Historically, most cycles have been somewhere between three and twelve years in duration. The duration and severity of cycles has varied across time and between countries. The term is usually applied to fluctuations in economic growth that have some uniformity in the cyclical pattern, as distinct from more random changes in the economy. The most common explanation of trade cycles is one of instability. The booms of the cycle are cut off by shortages of FACTORS

OF PRODUCTION and by saving increasing as a proportion of income, as income rises, and, thus, AGGREGATE DEMAND failing to increase as quickly as output. These effects push the economy into recession. The economy recovers from this slump through the growth in consumption and government expenditure, and the level of certain forms of investment being relatively stable or increasing, in spite of income only growing slowly or even falling. This process leads to increases in the aggregate demand and brings a return to more rapid economic growth. Since World War II, deliberate government policies, usually related to BALANCE OF PAYMENTS considerations, have been prominent in causing or amplifying cycles in a number of countries, notably the U.K. (see STOP-GO). The terms the trade and business cycle are respectively British and American.   R.C.O.M.; R.H.; J.P.

Bibl: M.J. Artis, *The UK Economy* (London, 11th ed., 1986); D. Morris, *The Economic System in the UK* (Oxford, 3rd ed., 1985).

trade theory. The theory of comparative advantage is often used to explain and justify trade between countries. A country is said to have a comparative advantage/disadvantage in production of a good or service if the relative cost of production is low/high (see OPPORTUNITY COST). If resources in countries can be switched from areas of comparative disadvantage to areas of comparative advantage, the combined production of goods and services in all countries can be increased. Trade between countries allows consumers to benefit from the greater production. Specialization in production may be limited by the use of less productive inputs (e.g. land), diseconomies of scale, the difficulty of using resources that have been released from production in areas of comparative disadvantage and the costs of transport of goods and services to the final consumer. Alternatively, specialization may be encouraged by ECONOMIES OF SCALE. The importing of foreign goods and services increases competition. Foreign trade allows new TECHNOLOGY, ideas, attitudes and institutions to be acquired from abroad. The long term benefits and losses from trade depend on changes in relative

prices and demands for exports and imports, and economies of scale, EXTERNALITIES and technical progress in the production of exports and imports. See PROTECTIONISM, NEW INTERNATIONAL ECONOMIC ORDER and NEWLY INDUSTRIALIZING COUNTRIES.   J.P.

Bibl: R.E. Caves and R.W. Jones, *World Trade and Payments* (London, 4th ed., 1984).

trade unions. Trade unions are collections of workers who have freely combined in order to better represent their interests to their employers, or their interests as workers with other persons or bodies. Trade unions emerged from the INDUSTRIAL REVOLUTION in Europe in the late 18th and through the 19th centuries and were often based on existing professional guilds. The early unions were craft and locally based (viz. The Halifax Association of Carders and Tenters), with primarily Friendly Society functions. Only later did unions become industrially or generally based.

Trade unions rely on the collective strength and influence of their members (see COLLECTIVE BARGAINING). The International Labour Organization (see INTERNATIONAL TRADE UNIONS) guarantees workers the right to free trade unions in its Convention 87, adopted in 1948. Not every country has signed this convention.

Trade unions vary markedly in size, method of operation and scope. This latter varies from the company based Japanese union through the Italian general union to the large industrial West German or East European union. Political affiliations vary too. Although trade unions are thought to be on the SOCIALIST side of the political spectrum there are many CONSERVATIVE and CHRISTIAN DEMOCRAT unions around the world, especially in Europe and the less developed countries. In many countries, West Germany and Sweden especially but throughout most of western Europe, trade unions are regarded as one of the 'Social Partners' (see PARTICIPATION). In eastern Europe however unions are part of the formal political and social establishment. The growth of Poland's Solidarnosc through the early 1980s may be seen as a watershed in this respect (see SOLIDARITY). In general terms unions are tolerated as a necessary evil in democracies and incorporated or treated as actively hostile agents in less democratic societies. This is true of many developing countries in Asia, Latin America and Africa.

As the workforce and methods of work change, so the types of union and membership of unions change too. The major long-term changes affecting all trade unions in industrialized countries are: rising long-term UNEMPLOYMENT; increase in the number of women workers; increase in the number of part-time and temporary workers; the decline of the smoke-stack industries and the rise of the high technology industries; the increase in technically sophisticated jobs; the growth of the NEWLY INDUSTRIALIZED COUNTRIES and the increase in the use of new technologies. The tendency is for membership to diminish. This is true especially in the U.S., France and the U.K. B.D.S.

tradition-direction, see under OTHER-DIRECTION.

traditional grammar. A summarizing (and often pejorative) term in LINGUISTICS, referring to the set of opinions, facts, and principles which characterize grammatical analysis not carried out within the perspective of modern linguistics; e.g. the NORMATIVE emphasis of traditional grammar contrasts with the descriptive emphasis within linguistics. D.C.

trahison des clercs, see under INTELLECTUALS.

transactional analysis. In PSYCHO-THERAPY, a theoretical and practical approach developed by Eric Berne, and popularized in his book *Games People Play* (New York, 1964; London, 1966). Building on Freud's stress upon infantility and Adler's preoccupation with power strategies and LIFE STYLE, it postulates three positions from which people can communicate (child, adult, and parent) and six possible classes of transaction (e.g. work, pastimes, intimacy), of which games are most frequently the focus of transactional analysis. In a typical game, one player pretends to be having an adult-adult relationship with another, but is actually trying to manipulate the other into being a 'parent' to his 'child', and thereby to achieve a goal such as avoiding responsibility for his own actions. The analyst, usually working with a group (see GROUP THERAPY), exposes such games, and encourages more constructive ways of interacting. Transactional analysis (commonly shortened to TA) has become a major popularization of the concepts of unconscious PSYCHIATRY. R.P.;M.J.C.

transcendence. The state of being beyond the reach or apprehension of experience; its opposite is *immanence*. The THEIST's God, conceived as a creator external to the perceivable world he creates, is *transcendent*; whereas the PANTHEIST's God, who is identified with the perceivable world, or some part of it, is *immanent*. Kant held that the metaphysical (see METAPHYSICS) CONCEPT of the soul, as an unobservable SUBSTANCE underlying the particular mental states that are accessible to INTROSPECTION, is transcendent, as is the conception of nature as a unity or complete whole. There is an important distinction in the philosophy of Kant between the transcendent and the *transcendental*. The former is unknowable by our minds, dependent as they are on the senses for raw material (see SENSE-DATA). What is transcendental is the logical apparatus of concepts and principles, common to all rational minds, that organizes experience and is thus logically prior to it. The transcendental aspect of the mind's operations can be elicited by a critical philosophy that works out the PRESUPPOSITIONS of our knowledge. A.Q.

transcendental arguments. In PHILOSOPHY, an argument designed to show what must be the case if a certain region of thought or experience is to be possible. Although such arguments have been employed at least since Aristotle they are chiefly associated with Kant whose use of them is intended to establish that possession and application of certain concepts is indispensable to empirical experience. Since Kant, and particularly in recent philosophy, transcendental arguments have been used in various attempts to refute scepticism. If a sceptic argues that we are not justified in, say, believing that there is an external world, he might be refuted by a transcendental argument showing that such a belief is a necessary condition of our discourse and experience (our CONCEPTUAL SCHEME). A.C.G.

Bibl: R.C.S. Walker, *Kant* (London, 1978); B. Stroud, *The Significance of Philosophical Scepticism* (London, 1984).

transcendental meditation (TM). A technique, based on HINDU traditions, for relaxing and refreshing the mind and body through the silent repetition of a mantra. C.E.D.

transcription, see under NUCLEIC ACID.

transducer. A device for transforming one type of wave, motion, signal, excitation, or oscillation into another; the transformation is called *transduction*. For example, the crystal cartridge in a record-player is a transducer producing a varying electric signal from the oscillations of the stylus as it traverses the grooves of a gramophone record; a loudspeaker is a transducer producing sound waves from a varying electric signal; and a sense organ such as the eye is a transducer which converts information contained in light ENERGY into nervous impulses. M.V.B.; P.M.

transduction. (1) In PHYSICS, see under TRANSDUCER. (2) In BIOLOGY, see under TRANSFORMATION, sense 2(a).

transfer. In EDUCATIONAL PSYCHOLOGY, the improvement of one type of mental or motor activity by training in another, related one. Identical response elements may be transferred, when the new task has some of the same components as the old one; e.g. learning tennis after learning squash. Or rules may transfer, e.g. from one branch of MATHEMATICS to another. Or transfer may take place when the learning of a specific skill results in a nonspecific faculty being trained; e.g. the general logical discipline supposedly gained from chess-playing or learning Latin. Transfer may be positive (helpful) or negative (hindering). Negative transfer results either from *proactive interference* between moderately similar response patterns, each partially learned, where earlier learn-

ing of one affects later learning of another, or from *retroactive interference* with mastery of a previously learned skill by the learning of a new one. H.L.

transfer RNA, see under NUCLEIC ACID.

transference. For Freud, transference is a particular instance of the displacement of affect from one idea to another. The presence of the analyst as a person is one such displaced idea, which causes a resistance to the admission of the repressed wish which has been transferred to the person of the analyst. By virtue of the fact that the analyst has been invested with all the patient's desires, the patient is motivated to continue his analytical work: transference, for Freud, is both the greatest obstacle and the greatest assistance to the analytic cure. Transference is connected to a repetition of affects associated with UNCONSCIOUS ideas, and it is the task of the analyst to channel them towards associative verbalization; FREE ASSOCIATION produces a knowledge, an unconscious knowledge, of which the analyst is situated as the SUPPOSED SUBJECT.

The OBJECT RELATIONS school has used this therapeutic function of transference, to the point of making it the central point of reference in the interpretative work. Transference is encouraged in order to interpret the subject's relation to his whole or PART OBJECT. Analysts of this school, such as Michael Balint, centre their intervention on a dual relation, as it is understood to exist, between mother and infant. Jacques Lacan criticizes this 'two-bodies' psychology by posing a third term in the dual relation, the power of language, as the neutralizing factor which changes the previous one-to-one infantile relation to the world. For Lacan, transference is based on a radical demand for truth which, by never being satisfied by the analyst, opens up a desire for truth. The transference unfolds through a DIALECTIC. In the first moment, the analyst offers to listen to the analysand's radical demand; this offer creates a demand for truth, which is fundamentally a demand for absolute (transference) love — which the analyst cannot satisfy; in the third moment, this absolute demand, impossible to satisfy, becomes the evidence of the structure of human DESIRE.   B.BE.

transfinite, see under INFINITE.

transformation.
(1) In MATHEMATICS and PHYSICS the objects studied are often referred to by using *labels* (usually numerical). Examples: (*A*) the diagrams in a book are referred to by number: (*B*) the points in a plane are described by their COORDINATES; (*C*) VECTORS are described by their components. A systematic relabelling is called an *alias transformation* (or a *transformation of coordinates*). It can be specified by, and it is often identified with, a FUNCTION *f* given by (1) $a' = f(a)$, where a' is the new label of the object whose old label is a; *f* is a PERMUTATION of the labels. Note that in example (*B*) *f* consists of two real-valued functions, one for each coordinate. The result of successive transformations is obtained by composition: if $a'' = g(a')$, then $a'' = g(f(a)) = g.f(a)$. Equation (1) may be interpreted in another way: one regards a' as the (old) label of a different object, into which the object with label a has been sent by the transformation *f*; *f* is then called an *alibi transformation*. It represents a movement of the objects.

Any RELATION between, or function of, objects can be expressed in terms of their labels. In general this expression will change with relabelling. If it remains identically the same under a transformation *f*, or under all the transformations belonging to some set *S*, then the corresponding relation or function is said to be an *invariant* of *f* or *S*. If *f* is considered as an alibi transformation, then an invariant represents an unchanging feature of the situation; e.g. the distance between two points of a rigid body is invariant under any rotation of it. There are two classic problems: (1) given certain relations and functions to find the set (actually a GROUP) of all transformations (here called AUTOMORPHISMS) under which they are invariant; (2) given a group *G* of transformations, to find all (or, better, methods for constructing all) the invariants of *G*. Both problems are of great significance for physics. In the special theory of RELATIVITY it is postulated that light rays (as relations between points of SPACE-TIME)

are invariants; the corresponding group is the Lorentz transformations. Knowledge of the invariants of this group (and others) plays an essential role in the theory of the fundamental PARTICLES. See also PARITY.
                                                            R.G.
Bibl: J. Singh, *Mathematical Ideas* (London and New York, 1972).

(2) In BIOLOGY, (*a*) a change in the genetic make-up of a MICRO-ORGANISM, particularly a bacterium (see BACTERIOLOGY), brought about by a quasi-infective action of a NUCLEIC ACID. If the nucleic acid is introduced by a vector of some kind, e.g. a virus, the process is spoken of as *transduction*. (*b*) D'Arcy Thompson's 'method of transformations' was a scheme for showing up similarities and differences between outline drawings of related plants or animals by inscribing them within COORDINATE systems by which one can be shown to be a regular geometric transformation of the other. (*c*) A change that occurs in some CELLS under long-term TISSUE CULTURE as a consequence of which they change their appearance and habit of growth and acquire malignant properties.   P.M.

transformation-rules, see under AXIOMATICS.

transformational grammar (TG). Any GRAMMAR which operates using the notion of a *transformation*, a formal linguistic operation which alters ('rewrites') one sequence of grammatical symbols as another, according to certain conventions, e.g. 'transforming' active sentences into passive ones. This type of grammar was first discussed by Noam Chomsky (see CHOMSKYAN) in *Syntactic Structures* (1957) as an illustration of a powerful kind of GENERATIVE GRAMMAR. Several models of TG have since been developed, but the theoretical status of transformations has been questioned, and some contemporary approaches do without them (e.g. GENERALIZED PHRASE STRUCTURE GRAMMAR).
                                                            D.C.
Bibl: R. Huddleston, *An Introduction to English Transformational Syntax* (London, 1976).

transgenic animal. An animal that has developed from an *in vitro* fertilized egg (see INFERTILITY) that has had one or more extra GENES (transgenes) added to it. Since the gene is incorporated into the egg, it will be present in all TISSUES of the animal that develops, including the GONADS. Therefore, by inbreeding, the gene becomes a permanent part of the GENOME. Transgenic animals have become important in the study of DIFFERENTIATION and in DEVELOPMENTAL BIOLOGY. But they also have considerable agricultural potential. For example, animals provided with extra genes for growth HORMONE may grow more rapidly and yield more meat; and transgenic animals provided with a gene that has been manipulated so that it is active only in the mammary glands will excrete the product of the gene in their milk, from which it can readily be extracted. P.N.

transhumance. In GEOGRAPHY, regular seasonal cycles of livestock movement, e.g. the Turkana system of cattle movement between mountains and plains or the use of summer Alp pastures in central Europe. The basis of the movement is regular seasonal changes in pasture availability related to seasonal thermal and moisture cycles. Transhumance is more restricted in usage than pastoral NOMADISM, which describes irregular and nonseasonal herding movements. P.H.

transistor. A SOLID-STATE DEVICE (invented 1948), based on the action of junctions between SEMICONDUCTORS with different electrical characteristics, which can be used as an amplifier or RECTIFIER for electrical signals. Because of their small size, robustness, and safeness (since they operate at low voltages) transistors have virtually superseded THERMIONIC valves as the principal ELECTRONIC components in HI-FI, radio, television, and COMPUTERS. They have also rendered practicable medical and surgical apparatus which could not otherwise have existed. M.V.B.

transition element. Any ELEMENT with an unfilled inner ELECTRON SHELL. There are several groups of transition elements in the PERIODIC TABLE; elements within each group have closely similar physical and chemical properties. M.V.B.

transitional object. A term coined by the British psychoanalyst D.W. Winnicott, it refers to those objects, such as a teddy bear, a blanket, or any soft or hard toy which some children take to bed in the transition from waking to sleep, and to which the child forms a special attachment. Only by holding it and possessing it is the child helped to withstand frustration, deprivation, and changing situations. It designates the intermediate area of experience between the baby's fist-in-mouth and the teddy bear, that is, between subjective inner reality and shared external life, between me and not-me, and ultimately between oral eroticism and true OBJECT RELATIONS (see DEVELOPMENTAL THEORY). Its function is fundamental as regards the capacity to symbolize, as it constitutes a resting place in the effort to keep internal and external realities separated and yet inter-related. Although it has no symbolical value as such, it allows primary creative activity as the baby apprehends the object as its own creation in the wake of the primary illusion that the mother's breast was part of the infant. It is this illusion — that what the infant creates really exists — that allows for its growing ability to recognize and accept reality. Nevertheless, this illusory experience is retained throughout life in the experiencing that belongs to the arts, religion, and creative or scientific work. On the other hand, if the subject does not develop to a further stage of object relations, its pathological fixation can lead to fetishism in adult sexual life, or other symptoms such as addiction or stealing. B.BE.

translation, see under NUCLEIC ACID.

translocation. In GENETICS, a MUTATIONAL event by which part of one CHROMOSOME becomes attached to or intercalated into another chromosome. Translocations almost invariably have important genetic effects. P.M.

transmutation of elements, see under NUCLEAR REACTION.

transnational company, see under MULTINATIONAL COMPANY.

transnational relations; transnational society. Terms coined by Raymond Aron (*Paix et guerre entre les nations*, Paris, 1962) to describe the variety of relationships, activities, and organizations which operate across national frontiers and which include, for example, the Roman Catholic Church; MULTINATIONAL COMPANIES; TRADE UNIONS; professional, scientific, and sporting organizations; REVOLUTIONARY movements. Aron suggested that when such activities flourished, as in Europe before 1914, the freedom of exchange, of movement, and of COMMUNICATION, the strength of common beliefs, and the number of non-national organizations created a transnational society. He contrasted this with the period 1946-53 when the COLD WAR was at its height and communication between Western and Soviet Europe reduced to a minimum and conducted solely through governmental channels.   A.L.C.B.

Bibl: R.O. Keohane and J.S. Nye (eds.), *Transnational Relations and World Politics* (Cambridge, Mass., 1972); *International Affairs*, July 1976 issue.

transplants, see under SURGERY.

transport planning. The organization of movement systems, both public and private, within an urban or regional area, in order to relate the range of urban activities. Too often it has been restricted to *traffic* planning, i.e. to facilitating the movement of cars in towns, by means of road construction or management. Construction has included such systems as *ringways*, i.e. circular or tangential roads intended to deflect traffic from inner urban areas; the separation of intersecting roads by means of *fly-overs* or *underpasses*; and the linking of two major multilane roads by means of a *clover-leaf* intersection. Management methods include the designation of certain existing roads as *clearways* or *throughways* on which parking is prohibited at all times or during critical periods; one-way systems; and parking restrictions. The relation between traffic planning and general urban planning, and especially the notion of differentiating between different types of vehicular movement in order to create *environmental areas* (zones with no extraneous traffic), has been studied and is having some effect on practice. It has also been recognized that the preservation or revival of public transport is essential to the survival of cities. See also PEDESTRIAN SEGREGATION; RADBURN LAYOUT.   M.BR.

Bibl: R.B. Mitchell and C. Rapkin, *Urban Traffic* (London and New York, 1954); *Traffic in Towns:* Reports of the Steering Group and Working Group of the Ministry of Transport (London, 1963).

transposable element. A piece of DNA (seldom a GENE, but when so can be called a *jumping gene*) that can move from place to place in the GENOME. Most transposable elements move very infrequently and into a site that is chosen at random. The result may be harmful, beneficial or neutral and will be appropriately selected for or against, making an important contribution to the process of EVOLUTION. Often, instead of a simple move from one place to another, the original transposable element remains in place and it is a copy that is moved elsewhere. SELFISH DNA (see also NUCLEIC ACID) comprises transposable elements that have been copied and spread throughout the genome with little or no harmful effect.   P.N.

Bibl: B. Alberts, *Molecular Biology of the Cell* (New York, 1983); Benjamin Lewin, *Genes II* (Bristol, 1985).

transputer. A name for a particular MICROCOMPUTER in which the entire machine (PROCESSOR, STORE and INPUT/OUTPUT circuitry) is implemented on a single INTEGRATED CIRCUIT. It is thus simple to connect large numbers of these machines together for applications involving DISTRIBUTED COMPUTING. It is a play on the word *transput*, used by the HIGH-LEVEL PROGRAMING LANGUAGE Algol 68 to refer to input/output.   J.E.S.

transuranic element. Any artificially produced ELEMENT whose ATOMIC NUMBER exceeds 92. The atomic NUCLEUS of these elements is unstable and undergoes RADIOACTIVE decay or FISSION. About a dozen transuranic elements have been produced (usually in very small quantities) in NUCLEAR REACTORS.   M.V.B.

transverse stage, see under OPEN STAGE.

transvestism. The projection of an image and the wearing of clothes usually associated with the opposite sex. The practice is immemorial and, notwithstanding such conventions as the male portrayal of female roles on the Elizabethan stage, usually sexual in its implications. These may range from the overt expression of HOMOSEXUALITY to the widespread latent bisexuality implied by 'unisex' fashion in the late 1960s, as exemplified by such ROCK artists as David Bowie. A more recent element, reflected by the pop star Boy George, is the use of transvestism to deny the significance of GENDER ('gender bender'). Transvestism has been popularly accepted as an entertainment form ranging from 'drag' acts in British public houses to Andy Warhol's New York coterie.   P.S.L.
    Bibl: P Ackroyd, *Dressing Up: Transvestism and Drag, the History of an Obsession* (London, 1979).

trauma (Greek word for 'wound'). A physical injury or emotional shock such as may lead to TRAUMATIC NEUROSIS. In early FREUDIAN terminology the trauma is usually emotional (e.g. BIRTH TRAUMA) and can be specifically sexual (e.g. seduction by a parent). The trauma is supposed to break through the individual's defences, and in the absence of normal ABREACTION to cause a *foreign-body reaction* — the mental equivalent of the process whereby the TISSUES of the body wall off a foreign body lodged in them. Subsequent emotional arousal may reawaken early traumatic experience, resulting in an attack on DEFENCE MECHANISMS from inside and outside simultaneously. In Freud's later writings the concept of trauma assumes much less importance.   M.J.C.

traumatic neurosis. A NEUROSIS precipitated by extreme shock or TRAUMA, which upsets the previous stability of the person, and leads him (typically) to exhibit uncontrollable EMOTION, or to experience disturbances of sleep with ANXIETY dreams in which the trauma is relived. The precipitating trauma may be primarily emotional (e.g. seduction in childhood or terrifying experiences in battle) or purely physical

(e.g. severe concussion leading to the post-concussional SYNDROME, in which neurotic complaints such as blurred vision or lack of concentration are experienced).
                            B.A.F.; M.J.C.

traumatology. The term is used to describe the study of all aspects of injury to the soft TISSUES, bones and joints, however caused. When referring to soft tissues this means injury to such structures as muscle, ligaments and tendons. The subject includes the mechanism of injury, its effects (PHYSIOLOGICAL and PATHOLOGICAL), the healing process and diagnosis and treatment.   N.H.H.

Treasury, the. The government department which, in both the U.S.A. and Britain, by its influence over FISCAL POLICY and MONETARY POLICY, has a major role in formulating and executing government economic policy as a whole. The British Treasury's duties include not only the preparation of the budget and the coordination of overall economic policy but also, by tradition, a high degree of control over the expenditure of all government departments. The U.S. Treasury has two primary responsibilities: (1) to act as chief fiscal adviser to the President (supported by the Council of Economic Advisers and the Office of Management and Budget); (2) collects taxes, issues notes and coins and supervises the financial system.
                            D.E.; J.P.

tree diagram. A two-dimensional diagram used in GENERATIVE GRAMMAR as a convenient means of displaying the hierarchical structure of a sentence as generated by a set of grammatical rules.   D.C.
    Bibl: R. Huddleston, *An Introduction to English Transformational Syntax* (London, 1976).

tremendismo. A Spanish word not yet naturalized as 'tremendism'. The word *tremendista* was first applied to Camilo José Cela's novel *La Familia de Pascual Duarte (The Family of Pascal Duarte*, 1942) because the reader's shock and horror at what is revealed can only be described as 'tremendous'. Cela's Spanish precursors were 'Parmeno' and Emilio Carrere; but fundamentally *tremendismo* is a late, intensive, specifically Spanish development of NATURALISM arising from the horrors of the Civil War, the victory of the RIGHT, and Spain's consequent social backwardness. The savage vein, if not the term itself, continues in Spanish fiction and has been used to describe some Latin American novels of social protest. M.S.-S.

tribe. In ANTHROPOLOGY, a term too vaguely used for political entities, territorially defined, of differing scale. It is applied sometimes to (relatively) independent political entities, in which case it becomes analogous to 'nation' in more complex societies (though a tribe is not necessarily centralized and hierarchical in its organization); sometimes to divisions of such larger entities. A tribe is usually assumed to be culturally and linguistically homogeneous. The term *tribalism* has been applied to expressions and organizations founded upon a common ethnic identity in the cities of the underdeveloped world (e.g., P. Mayer, *Townsmen or Tribesmen*, 1961). Tribe/tribal/tribalism have been used as labels by anthropologists to designate groups regarded as premodern, non-literate or PRIMITIVE. Apart from the association of tribe with evolutionary ideas, it has very limited empirical value. The use of the concept of tribe by anthropologists represents the imposition of a non-indigenous concept and one which renders static a complex and fluid ethnographic reality. M.F.;A.G.
Bibl: M. Bloch, *Marxism and Anthropology* (Cambridge, 1983); R. G. Abrahams, *The Nyamwezi Today* (Cambridge, 1981).

tribology. The science and design of interacting surfaces in relative motion, including the study of such topics as friction and wear and the study and manufacture of bearing metals and lubricants. E.R.L.

tricarboxylic acid cycle, see KREBS CYCLE.

Trident. The successor to the Poseidon submarine MISSILE in the U.S., and the earlier Polaris system in the United Kingdom. Although superficially a replacement Submarine Launched Ballistic Missile (SLBM), it in fact greatly extends the destructive power of the submarine. Each missile will carry multiple warheads, highly accurate and with the capacity to manoeuvre in the atmosphere. It gives the submarine systems a range of about 6,000 miles, putting them on a par with many land-based systems. Consequently, it will have a powerful effect on the strategic balance, once the missile is in service during the 1990s. A.J.M.W.

Triennale, see under BIENNALE.

tropical diseases. Diseases such as the common cold are endemic world-wide but are not considered tropical *per se*. Diseases which are primarily acquired between the Tropic of Cancer on the 23°30′ N. parallel and the Tropic of Capricorn on the 23°30′ S. parallel are considered tropical. Diseases spread by contaminated food, drink and poor hygiene are the commonest tropical diseases. Parasites, bacteria (see BACTERIOLOGY) and viruses (see VIROLOGY) invade the body and cause diarrhoea, cramps, dehydration and, rarely, death. The body may develop some IMMUNITY after exposure, but typhoid, dysentery, worm infestations and food poisoning all need treatment. Apart from the diarrhoeal diseases, insect-borne diseases are the most common tropical infections. Malaria, yellow fever, typhus, filariasis, leishmaniasis and sleeping sickness are all transmitted by the bites of various insects such as mosquitoes, sandflies, tsetse flies and blackflies. PROPHYLAXIS against malaria is vital in most areas of Africa, Asia and Latin America and yellow fever vaccination is mandatory for travel in Africa. The use of insect repellent, insecticide, bed nets, screens and sensible clothing can all dramatically reduce the number of insect bites and, hence, the incidence of disease. A.P.H.

tropism.
(1) In BIOLOGY, an involuntary directional movement determined by the pattern of incidence of an external STIMULUS. For most ordinary purposes tropism and *taxis* can be regarded as synonymous. Orientations towards light, gravity, and sources of chemical stimuli are known as *photo-, geo-* and *chemo-taxis* or *-tropism* respectively. In 1975 MAGNETOTAXIC bac-

teria were discovered, and there is some evidence that other SPECIES, including pigeons and bees, can sense the Earth's magnetic field. Experiments on human sensitivity to MAGNETISM are inconclusive.

P.M.; M.R.

(2) In literary criticism, the word has been popularized by the French novelist Nathalie Sarraute (see NEW NOVEL), who sees mental life as being made up of myriads of infinitesimal responses to stimuli. The problem of REALISM is to translate these movements into words before they have been falsified by the grid of conventional language embodying ossified attitudes and beliefs.

J.G.W.

troposphere. In METEOROLOGY, the lowest layer of the earth's atmosphere. The thickness of the troposphere varies from about 7 or 8 km near the poles to about 16 km at the equator. It contains about three quarters of the mass of the atmosphere, and about 90% of its water vapour, so that almost all 'weather activity' directly relevant to man occurs in the lower layers of the troposphere. The upper boundary of the troposphere is termed the *tropopause*. See also STRATOSPHERE.

P.H.

Trotskyism. The version of MARXISM associated with the ideas of Leon Trotsky (1879-1940). The basis of Trotskyism is the concept of PERMANENT REVOLUTION, first formulated in 1906, according to which the uneven development of different countries meant that it was possible to envisage a direct transition to SOCIALISM in Russia provided there was also a rapid progress from the national to the international phase of socialist REVOLUTION. Banished from the Soviet Union, Trotskyism found its organizational expression in the Fourth INTERNATIONAL established in 1938 to oppose Stalin's COMINTERN. Although unable to develop into a mass movement and much plagued by sectarian in-fighting, Trotskyism has played a considerable role in the revival of socialist ideas since the 1960s. It combines an adherence to the original principles of BOLSHEVISM, a sharp rejection of any evolutionary, parliamentary road to socialism, a confidence in the revolutionary potential of the industrial proletariat, and a strong international dimension.

D.T.M.

Bibl: M. Lowy, *The Politics of Combined and Uneven Development* (London, 1981); E. Mandel, *Revolutionary Marxism Today* (London, 1979).

Truman Doctrine. An important declaration of U.S. foreign policy by President Truman in an address to Congress on 12 March 1947. At a time of growing tension between the Soviet Union and the Western world, Truman went on record as saying that 'it must be the policy of the U.S.A. to support free people who are resisting subjection by armed MINORITIES or outside pressures'. At the request of the President, Congress voted $400 million to help Greece and Turkey, and three months later the U.S. Secretary of State made the offer to Europe which became known as the MARSHALL PLAN. The Truman Doctrine is taken by historians to mark an important stage in the COLD WAR, a break with the U.S.A.'s traditional policy of no commitments in peace-time, and the first of many subsequent U.S. economic- and military-aid programmes.

A.L.C.B.

Bibl: J.M. Jones, *The Fifteen Weeks* (New York, 1955); J.L. Gaddis, *The United States and the Origins of the Cold War* (New York, 1972).

truth. (1) The property implicitly ascribed to a PROPOSITION by belief in or assertion of it; the property implicitly ascribed to a proposition by disbelief in or negation of it is *falsity*. There have been many theories of the nature of truth. The most common sees it as a *correspondence* between a proposition and the fact, situation, or state of affairs that verifies it (see VERIFICATION). To explain the MEANING of a sentence is to teach someone its truth-conditions, the circumstances under which it is correct to assert it; and, in the simplest cases, this is done by uttering it, in an exemplary way, in circumstances in which it is true. Thus, for someone to have learned the meaning of 'It is raining' is for him to have been trained to believe or be ready to assert it when it is, in fact, raining. The correspondence may, but need not, be regarded as some sort of natural *similarity* or *resemblance* between proposition and fact. (2) Some philosophers, holding that all awareness of facts is itself propositional, i.e. that it necessarily involves the assertion of some proposition, maintain that truth is a relation of *coherence* between propositions. (3) PRAGMA-TISTS define truth in terms of the *satisfactoriness of belief*, the empirically verifying fulfilment of expectations being only one form of this. (4) Occasionally truth has been taken to be a *quality* rather than a relation, a view which has some plausibility in connection with ANALYTIC propositions whose truth depends not on something external to them but on the meaning that is intrinsic to them.   A.Q.

truth-conditional semantics. An approach to SEMANTICS which maintains that meaning can be defined in terms of the conditions in the real world under which a sentence may be used to make a true statement. It can be distinguished from approaches which define meaning in terms of the conditions on the use of sentences in communication, such as in SPEECH ACT theory.   D.C.
   Bibl: F. Palmer, *Semantics* (Cambridge, 1981).

truth drug. A popular but misleading term for any chemical compound administered to an individual in order to obtain information which has been withheld, either consciously or not. In this sense the term was originally applied to scopolamine in 1932, but the evidence obtained since then argues against the validity of the original claims. In the diagnosis and treatment of some abnormal states, however, it may be useful to administer centrally-acting drugs which loosen the subject's inhibitions and so facilitate discussion. The term *narcoanalysis* is sometimes given to this procedure, for which the drugs most commonly used are the barbiturates and methedrine. There is no medico-legal justification for the use of such substances in judicial processes, since even if consent is given false statements can be made under their influence.   M.S.

truth-function. A compound PROPOSITION whose TRUTH or falsity is unequivocally determined by the truth or falsity of its components for all possible cases. Thus '*p* or *q*' is a truth-function of *p* and *q* since it is false if they are both false, but true if *p* is true or if *q* is true or if they both are. The

principle of EXTENSIONALITY states that *all* compound propositions are reducible (see REDUCTION) to truth-functions of their ultimate components. Some compound propositions, however, do not appear to be truth-functional at first glance: '*p* because *q*' cannot be true unless both *p* and *q* are true, but if they are it may be either true or false. See also PROPOSITIONAL CALCULUS.   A.Q.

truth-value. In standard or classical 'two-valued' LOGIC, TRUTH *or* falsity. Some logicians, however, have devised systems with more than two truth-values. INTU-ITIONISTS (sense 3) have contended that there is a third class of undecidable PROPO-SITIONS which are neither true nor false, and the formal properties of systems of logic with three or more truth-values have been investigated.   A.Q.

tumour virology, see under VIROLOGY.

Tupamaros. A band of Uruguayan urban GUERRILLAS, LEFT-wing REVOLUTION-ARIES, notorious for their practice of kidnapping prominent foreigners and holding them to ransom. Their name derives from that of the 18th-century Inca leader, Túpac Amarú. The Tupamaros achieved prominence in 1969 but by the end of 1974 had been crushed out of existence. Tactics similar to those employed by the Tupamaros, however, have been used by guerrilla groups in other Latin American countries, notably Argentina, where a large number of assassinations of political figures have been undertaken by RIGHT-wing as well as left-wing groups.   D.C.W.

turbine. An engine in which a fluid is forced past a series of vanes or blades that are mounted on a shaft and so shaped and positioned that the passage of fluid through the blades causes the shaft to rotate. Turbines are quick-starting, freer from vibration than reciprocating engines, and relatively light and compact — notably in the case of the *air turbine* used by dentists to propel dental drills at very high speeds. A *gas turbine* propels the gas through the blades by burning the gas, thus creating a pressure. Gas turbines are cheap to run on low-grade fuel, and are used to propel aircraft and high-powered railway locomotives. In the case of aircraft a propulsion jet is also incorporated, making a *turbo-jet* engine. The RAM-JET, although it has features in common with the turbo-jet, contains no turbine but operates more in the manner of an internal combustion engine, i.e. on a four-stroke cycle. *Steam turbines* are used extensively in power stations to drive alternators for the production of electric power.   E.R.L.

turbo-jet, see under TURBINE.

Turing machine. An ABSTRACT, mathematically defined 'machine' introduced by A.M. Turing in 1936 to make the idea of mechanical computability precise — by reducing it to the properties of a universal Turing machine. Turing machines form a very simple type of COMPUTER. In consequence of this simplicity, the resulting PROGRAMS are inordinately long. For this reason practical computers are not much like Turing machines. (See also RECURSIVE FUNCTION THEORY.)   C.S.

turn-round time, see under COMPUTING.

twelve-note music, see under SERIAL MUSIC.

twin paradox, see under CLOCK PARADOX.

two cultures, the. Term introduced in *The Two Cultures and the Scientific Revolution* (1959) by C.P. Snow (Lord Snow) in reviving an old controversy, that of science versus literature and/or religion. This was the Rede Lecture at Cambridge, and it was answered by F.R. Leavis (see LEAVISITE) in the Richmond Lecture at Downing College, Cambridge, in 1962. Snow diagnosed society's INTELLECTUALS as divided, unable to speak to each other, having no common language. Each group he called a 'CULTURE'; he maintained that scientists can't read and that 'humanists' can't understand even simple scientific CONCEPTS such as the second law of THERMODYNAMICS. Leavis's answer was perhaps no more ill-mannered and shot with sour irrelevancies than Snow's original lecture, brashly in favour of scientific culture in the interests of human survival, was ill-argued. The kernel of the dispute may be found, in a civilized form, in T.H. Huxley, *A Liberal Education and Where to Find It* (1868) and *Science and Culture* (1881), and in Matthew Arnold's answer, *Literature and Science* (1882). A.N. Whitehead's *Science and the Modern World* (1927) is a brilliant and reconciliatory essay by a truly distinguished mind.
M.S.-S.
Bibl: L. Trilling, *Beyond Culture* (New York, 1965; London, 1966).

two hemispheres, the. Studies of brain damage have suggested that the two halves (hemispheres) of the human brain may perform differing but complementary functions; and Roger Sperry has shown experimentally that, in cases where the hemispheres had been surgically separated, patients were being controlled by two distinct brains, neither of which 'knew' the recent experiences of the other half. Further investigation confirmed that the left hemisphere, which controls the right-hand side, is largely concerned with logical, sequential, and digital processes such as language, whereas the right hemisphere is much more concerned with spatial, musical, and pictorial functions. Non-human primates appear not to share this specialization of cerebral function, and it has been suggested that this development in human EVOLUTION was linked with tool use and the emergence of language. The educational and cultural implications of these findings are likely to be great. See also NEUROPSYCHOLOGY.
R.A.H.
Bibl: R.E. Ornstein, *The Psychology of Consciousness* (San Francisco, 1972; London, 1975); S.J. Dimond and J.G. Beaumont (eds.), *Hemisphere Function in the Human Brain* (London, 1974).

two-tone, see under REGGAE.

types, ideal, see IDEAL TYPES.

typological linguistics. An approach in LINGUISTICS which studies the structural similarities between languages, regardless of their history, as part of an attempt to establish a classification (or TYPOLOGY) of languages.   D.C.
Bibl: R.H. Robins, *General Linguistics: an Introductory Survey* (London, 1980).

typology. (1) Any system for classifying things, people, social groups, languages, etc., by types. Typology has long been a mainstay of ARCHAEOLOGY. The grouping of a series of artifacts according to type, and the arrangement of like types in the form of a type series illustrating change, have in the past been the major preoccupation of some archaeologists, and the basis for detailed chronologies. Many of these are of value, particularly those supported by independent chronological evidence. However, with the advent of absolute DATING methods, the need to construct elaborate typologies has decreased.　　B.C.

(2) In THEOLOGY and Christian art, the joining of ideas or images in the Old Testament with ideas or images in the New.

D.L.E.

U

UDA, see under ULSTER DEFENCE ASSOCIATION.

Ulster Defence Association (UDA). The largest of the Portestant 'paramilitary' groups in Northern Ireland, the UDA in 1971 took over and co-ordinated all the euphemistically named Protestant 'Defence Associations' which arose in response to the mainly Catholic CIVIL RIGHTS MOVEMENT. Organized on quasimilitary lines it has an estimated current membership of 10-12,000. Although many of its members have been convicted of murder, arson and other major crimes it has never been proscribed, and has on occasion organized mass demonstrations. Its most important involvement in non-TERRORIST politics occurred during the 'loyalist' STRIKE of May 1974, when with some intimidation but much genuine support it undermined the British government's attempt to establish new political arrangements in Ulster which did not discriminate against Catholics. It remains a powerful voice in Ulster politics.   M.W.
Bibl: P. O'Malley, *The Uncivil Wars* (Belfast and Boston, 1983).

Ulster Unionism. The descendant of the 19th-century tendency in Britain and Ireland which sought to maintain the political union of the two countries on the terms established by the Act of Union in 1800. Ulster Unionism itself dates from the mid-1880s when the receding prospects for maintaining the status quo caused many Unionists to redefine their goal to be the maintenance of constitutional and political links with Britain for the predominantly Protestant north of Ireland. The movement acquired firmer organizational form in 1904-05 with the foundation of the Ulster Unionist Council; it then became the core of the Unionist Party which dominated politics in Northern Ireland to the disadvantage of the Catholic population from partition in 1921 to the suspension of the province's Stormont-based Parliament in 1972 (see DIRECT RULE). Since 1971 the party has split into several distinct elements, of which the most significant are the Official Unionist Party and the Democratic Unionist Party. They are distinguished by the latter's more thoroughly intransigent approach to the maintenance of the Union, its more violent rhetoric and by its arguably more WORKING-CLASS base of support.   S.R.
Bibl: A.T.Q. Stewart, *The Narrow Ground: Aspects of Ulster 1609-1969* (London, 1977); P. O'Malley, *The Uncivil Wars* (Belfast and Boston, 1983).

Ulster Volunteer Force (UVF). Organized initially in 1912 by Sir Edward Carson to resist the granting of Irish Home Rule. Protestant extremists revived the title in 1966 for their organized efforts to counter the CIVIL RIGHTS MOVEMENT. Proscribed by the government of Northern Ireland in June of that year, it has remained illegal. Committed to a campaign of anti-Catholic violence, the UVF has claimed responsibility for hundreds of killings. Since 1980 its activities have been partly curtailed by the arrest and conviction of much of its leadership.   M.W.
Bibl: W.D. Flackes, *Northern Ireland: A Political Directory* (London, 1983); M. Farrell, *Northern Ireland: The Orange State* (London, 1980).

ultimate constituent (UC), see CONSTITUENT ANALYSIS.

ultracentrifuge, see under SEDIMENTATION.

ultraism. In general, extremism; specifically, a Spanish literary movement (*ultraismo*) that flourished around 1919-23 and is best characterized as Spanish EXPRESSIONISM. The chief theoretician and coiner of the term was Guillermo de Torre; other more important writers (Borges, Lorca, Cernuda, Salinas) were influenced by it. The ultraists' programme involved the purgation of all rhetorical, romantic, and anthropomorphic elements from poetic language. Partly SURREALIST, partly HERMETIC, ultraism reflected the peculiarly Spanish awareness of MODERNISM. Borges took ultraism back with him to Argentina, but soon abandoned it.
M.S.-S.

ultramontanism (from Latin *ultra montes*, 'beyond the mountains', i.e. the Alps viewed from France). The emphasizing of the doctrinal INFALLIBILITY and practical authority of the Pope, at the expense of the looser and more national organization of the CATHOLIC Church as advocated by the French 'Gallicans'. See also VATICAN COUNCIL II. D.L.E.

ultrasonics. The study of waves of the same physical nature as sound, i.e. longitudinal undulations of pressure and density, but whose frequency is so high that the waves are not heard by the human ear. Ultrasonic waves are usually generated by applying electrical oscillations to a quartz crystal TRANSDUCER, or by a MAGNETO-STRICTION oscillator. In the latter case a rod of FERROMAGNETIC material is alternately magnetized and demagnetized by means of a coil around it which carries alternating current. This current causes the rod to expand and contract at the same frequency as that of the current. The length of the rod is chosen to 'tune' at the frequency required to obtain increased amplitude of vibration. When one end of the rod is clamped, the ACOUSTIC waves are sent out from the opposite end.

Ultrasonic waves are used for nondestructive testing of metal castings which may contain cracks. Medical examination of unborn babies is carried out with *ultrasound*, and the short wavelength (centimetres or millimetres) enables fine detail to be detected. Very high intensity waves can, however, be destructive and are used for the scaling of boilers and in dentists' drills. In such circumstances the generator is placed near to the surface to be attacked. The action by which the sound waves rip off the surface layer is known as CAVITATION. High-ENERGY waves are being tested medically for brain surgery without opening the skull, for waves of given frequency can be made to produce cuts at a given depth of penetration in a given position. At lower intensities the waves can shake loose the MOLECULES of air nearest to a surface and not normally movable by CONVECTION. This effect is used to improve the heat transfer across a surface, as in boilers.

Many animals (e.g. dogs, bats, dolphins) and insects (mosquitoes, moths) are capable of hearing and in some cases emit-

ting ultrasound below about 100,000 Hz. They use it for sexual communication, 'seeing' in total darkness, and for the detection and evasion of enemies.

M.V.B.; E.R.L.

ultrasound, see under RADIOLOGY.

ultrastability. In CYBERNETICS, the capacity of a system in HOMOEOSTASIS to return to an equilibrial state after perturbation by unknown or unanalysed forces (against the intervention of which the system was not explicitly designed). S.BE.

ultra-violet. Electromagnetic RADIATION whose wavelengths are shorter than visible light but longer than X-RAYS. M.V.B.

ultra vires. Though of some importance in issues concerning capacity to CONTRACT, its main significance is as the primary ground upon which JUDICIAL REVIEW of administrative action is based, namely that the person or institution concerned acted outside his or its legal powers. Such powers are normally conferred by act of Parliament, or under the authority granted by statute. Determination whether a decision or action was *intra* (within) or *ultra* (beyond) the *vires* (powers) conferred is therefore largely a matter of statutory interpretation. Varieties of *ultra vires* activity are virtually unlimited, and may be either substantive or procedural. Thus, a power may have been exercised by the wrong institution, or by the right one but excessively, unreasonably, in bad faith, for an improper purpose, or against the wrong person. The institution exercising the power may have been improperly appointed or constituted. Some fact which is a condition precedent to the possession of the power may have been absent. Irrelevant considerations may have been taken into account. In some views an error of law by a deciding body renders the whole determination *ultra vires*. In any of these instances a decision by the court that the act was *ultra vires* means that it was void and of no effect. D.C.M.Y.

Bibl: D.C.M. Yardley, *Principles of Administrative Law* (London, 2nd ed., 1986); H.W.R. Wade, *Administrative Law* (Oxford and New York, 5th ed., 1982).

Umkhonto we Sizwe, see under AFRICAN NATIONAL CONGRESS.

uncertainty. In ECONOMICS, a decision or course of action is subject to uncertainty if the PROBABILITIES of the different possible outcomes are not known. Decision-making under pure uncertainty is difficult to analyse and, in this way, is to be distinguished from RISK. In practice, imprecise views or beliefs are usually held about the likelihoods of the different possible outcomes occurring.   J.P.
   Bibl: J.D. Hey, *Uncertainty in Economics* (Oxford, 1979).

uncertainty principle (or *indeterminacy principle*). A consequence of QUANTUM MECHANICS, discovered by Heisenberg in 1927, which states that it is impossible to measure the position and MOMENTUM of a PARTICLE simultaneously with more than strictly limited precision. In fact, the uncertainty in position, multiplied by the uncertainty in momentum, must always exceed PLANCK'S CONSTANT. This result arises from the WAVE-PARTICLE DUALITY: any attempt to fix the position of, say, a beam of ELECTRONS, by interposing a narrow slit in its path, will produce DIFFRACTION, i.e. a sideways spreading of the beam, which renders its direction, and hence its momentum, uncertain. The uncertainty principle is a special case of the COMPLEMENTARITY PRINCIPLE.   M.V.B.

unconscious. A familiar word with, in psychoanalytic theory, two meanings: (1) as an adjective applied to thoughts which cannot be brought to CONSCIOUSNESS by ordinary means, but only, if at all, by technical methods such as PSYCHO-THERAPY and PSYCHOANALYSIS (see also PRECONSCIOUS; REPRESSION); (2) as a noun in the expression 'the unconscious', i.e. the part of the mental system or MODEL which contains these unconscious thoughts. To be distinguished from SUBCONSCIOUS.
                                                         B.A.F.

uncrowning. According to the Russian critic Mikhail Bakhtin, the uncrowning of the mock-king is the central act of carnival and all carnivalesque festivals because it expresses what he called 'the joyful relativity of all structure and order' and the pathos of death and renewal (see CARNIVALIZATION and BAKHTINIAN).   P.B.

UNCTAD (United Nations Conference on Trade and Development). Set up by the General Assembly of the UNO in 1964 to provide a forum for the discussion of THIRD WORLD economic development, it has served to channel demands from the less developed countries (LDC) for a NEW INTERNATIONAL ECONOMIC ORDER (NIEO), officially launched by General Assembly resolution 3201 of 1974. Discussions have ranged from the promotion of LDC trade through a Generalized System of Preferences (GSP), freer transfer of TECHNOLOGY and the promotion of a manufacturing sector in LDCs. UNCTAD discussions tend to take place along 'group' lines with the 'Group of 77' representing the LDCs, Group 'B' the north and Group 'D' the SOCIALIST countries. The Group of 77 has been very critical in UNCTAD of the north's refusal to substantially accede to its demands and the use by the north of the GATT to restrict the growth of LDC products to northern markets, especially textiles. The UNCTAD has been criticized by the U.S. administration of indulging in a 'politicization' of the development debate.   A.W.
   Bibl: United Nations, *The History of UNCTAD, 1964-1984* (New York, 1985).

underdevelopment. The state of those countries which have successively and with increasing euphemism been termed backward, underdeveloped, less-developed (LDC), and developing (see also THIRD WORLD). The meaning of the terms development and underdevelopment are imprecise and, thus, there are sometimes differences in the classification of countries by these terms (see ECONOMIC DEVELOPMENT). Underdeveloped countries are usually taken as comprising the majority of independent countries in Central and South America, Africa, and Asia, the main exclusions being South Africa, Hong Kong, South Korea, Singapore, mainland China, and Taiwan. Turkey and the poorer countries of Southern Europe are sometimes included as underdeveloped. The original meaning, indicating that resources exist which have not been exploited, seems to have vanished. Although the word is now close in meaning to 'poverty', a few 'underdeveloped' countries, especially those with much oil and few people, are very rich in income per head. They may still be regarded as underdeveloped where the quality of INSTITUTIONS, the skills, educational attainments, and health of the people are well below those of countries of longerstanding wealth.   I.M.D.L.; J.P.

Bibl: M. P. Todaro, *Economic Development in the Third World* (London, 1985).

Underground. The name (recalling the resistance movements of World War II) under which in the mid 1960s an emergent movement of HIPPIES and kindred spirits expressed its corporate identity and sense of community in the face of opposition and even organized attack by the ESTABLISHMENT. The phenomenon first occurred in the U.S.A., but also emerged in other highly developed urban-industrial societies. Its LIFE STYLE, which was reminiscent of the BEATS, involved, typically, a tendency towards MYSTICISM, a taste for ROCK, the use of DRUGS, ideas of Universal Love expressed partly in terms of sexual PERMISSIVENESS, and a willingness to adopt communal forms of living without great regard for traditional standards. The movement, whose character is antitechnological, anti-materialist, experimental, and INDIVIDUALIST, and is therefore opposed to the tenets, customs, and values of MASS SOCIETY, has its own newspapers, films, plays, music, and art, and its own outlets for disseminating them — facts which lend some plausibility to the Underground's claim to be regarded as a *counter-culture* or an *alternative society*.

In order to survive and proselytize, the Underground required some relatively formal STRUCTURES, and these developed mainly through pressure from indigenous political elements; the earliest was the underground press, which described the new forms of life style, discussed the problems involved, and debated the strategies to be devised. Generally, however, the Alternative Society has limited its corporate activities to the establishment of selfhelp organizations which advise and assist DROP-OUTS, those in trouble over drugs, and those with medical, travel, or basic survival problems. Alternative living structures have emerged, such as COMMUNES, non-profit shops and entertainment facilities, and, for a brief period, alternative schools. For the majority of the population, however, a real alternative society in terms of parallel structures has yet to emerge.   P.S.L.

Bibl: R. Neville, *Play Power* (London and New York, 1970); T. Roszak, *The Making of a Counter-Culture* (Garden City, N.Y., 1969; London, 1970).

underidentification, see IDENTIFICATION.

underlying structure, see DEEP STRUCTURE.

unemployment. A member of the labour force is unemployed if he/she does not have a job. There are various different classifications of unemployment. Those persons not wishing to work at the going labour market wage rate are *voluntarily unemployed*. Those persons who are willing to work at the going wage rate but cannot find jobs are *involuntarily unemployed*. *Frictional unemployment* occurs as a result of a temporary disequilibrium in the labour market and the adjustment to EQUILIBRIUM not being immediate. Examples of such disequilibria are the entry of new workers into the labour force, the introduction of new production techniques, mismatches in the skills of the labour force and the demand for skilled labour, and changes in demand. If these disequilibria in the labour market persist for some time, the unemployment is referred to as *structural*. *Technological unemployment* in an industry occurs when the introduction of new TECHNOLOGY reduces the use of labour — the unemployment may be frictional or structural. FULL EMPLOYMENT occurs when the labour market is in equilibrium. In a dynamic economy (i.e. with people continuously entering and leaving the labour market) the equilibrium of the labour market necessarily has a certain amount of frictional unemployment, the level of which is termed the natural rate of unemployment. In theory and practice, it is often difficult to distinguish between the different types of unemployment.   J.P.

Bibl: J. Craven, *Introduction to Economics* (Oxford, 1984).

unified field theory. Early in his career Einstein enjoyed extraordinary success in revealing the links between fundamental phenomena of nature — above all, the relations between light, time and space — first in the special theory of RELATIVITY (1905) and then through the general theory of relativity (1916). This led him back to one of science's most fundamental ambitions, the attempt to demonstrate how all of nature's forces derive from one common unity and a single ultimate fundamental law of action. Einstein aspired to link electricity-magnetism, time and space, together with that force which had remained a mystery to Newton: GRAVITY. Einstein's own, largely solitary theorizings were matched by the attempts of others, including Theodor Kaluza, who postulated a five-dimensional GEOMETRY, in which gravity and ELECTROMAGNETISM determined the nature of time and space. Providing any kind of experimental corroboration for such hypotheses remained, however, a great stumbling-block. To the end of his life, Einstein sought the ultimate unified field theory, but it continues to elude science. See also GRAND UNIFICATION.   R.P.
Bibl: A. Einstein and L. Infeld, *The Evolution of Physics* (Cambridge, 1938).

unilateralism, see under MULTILATERALISM.

unilineal descent, see under BILATERAL/COGNATIC DESCENT.

Unitarian. A believer in God and in Jesus Christ's supreme goodness who rejects the doctrine of the Trinity, i.e. that God is 'Son' and 'Holy Spirit' as well as 'Father'. Unitarian congregations were first constituted in Europe in the 16th and 17th centuries, but have flourished chiefly in New England and elsewhere in the U.S.A. in the 19th and 20th centuries. Some Unitarians accept the authority of the Bible, but others are guided only by reason and conscience.   D.L.E.
Bibl: C.G. Bolam and H.L. Short, *The English Presbyterians, from Elizabethan*

Puritanism to Modern Unitarianism (London and Boston, 1968).

United Democratic Front (UDF). An umbrella organization in South Africa which emerged from the campaign by BLACKS and radical sympathizers against the ratification of the new constitution proposed in 1983, which maintained the political exclusion of blacks (see APARTHEID). The UDF endorses the 1955 Freedom Charter of the ANC and its allies which aims at the creation of a non-racial SOCIALIST state. Tactics include the mobilizing of black opposition to apartheid by a stress on local grievances (e.g. about the conditions of health services, housing, education etc. in the black townships), and the use of consumer boycotts. The UDF has been continually harassed by state authorities.   S.R.
Bibl: R. Osmond, *The Apartheid Handbook* (Harmondsworth and New York, 1986).

united front. An alliance between the COMMUNIST Party and other parties; distinguished from POPULAR FRONT by the fact that all parties in the former are regarded as WORKING-CLASS parties. In effect, the phrase is usually employed for cooperation between the Communist and SOCIAL DEMOCRATIC parties. In Communist tactical parlance a distinction is made between a 'United Front from above' (involving agreement between the two parties as such) and 'United Front from below' (implying united action by Communists and local Social Democratic members or branches against the Social Democratic leadership).   R.C.

United Nations Organization, see UNO.

Unity Theatre. A LEFT-wing, amateur theatre group established in London in 1935 with the object of presenting SOCIALIST and COMMUNIST plays and encouraging WORKING-CLASS dramatists. As well as presenting American, Russian, and British plays under the direction of André van Gyseghem, John Allen, Herbert Marshall, and others, it successfully pioneered the LIVING NEWSPAPER in England and produced a series of satirical pantomimes. Unity Theatre groups, most of them short-lived, were founded in a number of cities, and in 1946 it briefly established professional companies in London and Glasgow. M.A.

universal.

(1) In PHILOSOPHY, a term contrasted with *particular*: universals are abstract properties and RELATIONS, particulars the concrete things that exemplify them. Redness and fatherhood are universals; an individual tomato is a particular exemplifying the former, the pair of individuals composed of a man and his child are two particulars which, as a pair, exemplify the latter. Particulars are concrete in the sense that they are individuals or objects of reference with a position in time and also, ordinarily, in space. Universals are referred to by abstract nouns derived from verbs (e.g. 'suspicion'), from adjectives (e.g. 'roundness'), from prepositions (e.g. 'betweenness') and from common nouns (e.g. 'motherhood'). They either have no location in space and time or are indefinitely scattered throughout them (redness, one could say, is all over the place) and, if so, are frequently superimposed within them (a particular lemon, for example, has a multitude of properties at the same place at the same time). Particulars are ordinarily continuous in time and in space, and each excludes all other particulars, except its parts and the wholes it is a part of, from the spatio-temporal region it occupies. Logical, or Platonic, REALISM ascribes real existence to universals; NOMINALISM denies it to them. Those who deny that there is more to an individual thing than the set of its properties would seem committed to the view that particulars are reducible (see REDUCTION) to universals. A.Q.

(2) In LINGUISTICS, (*a*) a linguistic feature claimed as an obligatory characteristic of all languages; (*b*) a type of linguistic rule which is essential for the analysis of any language. Chomsky called the former *substantive* universals, the latter *formal* universals. The establishment of linguistic universals is of considerable contemporary interest, particularly in relation to the question of how children learn a language. See also INNATENESS HYPOTHESIS. D.C.

universalism, see under PATTERN VARIABLES.

universe of discourse. The field or range of entities to the members of which a particular discussion makes reference. Thus the universe of discourse of PHYSICS contains material bodies and physical forces; it does not contain mental images, political parties, or prime numbers. The notion of universe of discourse is convenient for the interpretation of statements about fictional or imaginary entities. 'There was no such person as Mr Pickwick' is true of the universe of discourse of actual men, but false of the universe of Dickensian characters. 'There was no such person as Mrs Pickwick' is true of both universes of discourse. A.Q.

University of the Air, see OPEN UNIVERSITY.

UNO (United Nations Organization). An international body established by charter on 26 June 1945 as world security organization with the following organs: Security Council, General Assembly, Secretariat-General, Economic and Social Council, Trusteeship Council, INTERNATIONAL COURT OF JUSTICE; to which various specialized agencies such as WHO, FAO, UNCTAD, etc. were added. Any of the five permanent members of the Security Council — Britain, China, France, the U.S.S.R., the U.S.A. — can veto proposals for action; hence, despite the obligation in the charter to maintain peace and security, the PEACE-KEEPING role passed in 1950 from the Security Council to the General Assembly. Intervention by arms against presumed aggression, as in KOREA in 1950-54, gave way to intervention, aimed merely at separating combatants, by military observers or U.N. emergency forces. From the mid 1950s onwards, with the creation of new states, the number of members grew very considerably, establishing a permanent majority of the new membership uncommitted either to Soviet or U.S. leadership, and absorbed after 1960 in activities critical of the residual colonial position of the leading European powers. The UNO has been criticized for not solving global problems but rather for discussing them endlessly in global conferences. The U.S. in particular has become increasingly critical of what it terms 'politicization' of the specialized agencies (the mixing of political with technical agenda items) and of profligate use of the budget by certain agencies. This has led to American and British withdrawal from UNESCO (1984-5) and a major financial crisis for the U.N. (1986-87).

D.C.W.;A.WI.

Bibl: H.G. Nicholas, *The U.N. as a Political Institution* (London and New York, 4th ed., 1971).

unsaturated. Term used from the early days of ORGANIC CHEMISTRY to signify a compound which can react (see CHEMICAL REACTION) by the addition of other chemical SPECIES. Unsaturated compounds contain at least one carbon ATOM with a double or triple BOND to its neighbour. Common examples include ethylene, acetylene, and allyl alcohol. Addition reactions to give SATURATED compounds usually occur rather readily, so that unsaturated compounds are important intermediates in the synthesis of organic compounds. POLYUNSATURATED FATS are thought to be the most healthy dietary form of fats (see DIET).   B.F.;P.N.

urban guerrilla, see under GUERRILLA.

urban history. The history of towns is a traditional branch of LOCAL HISTORY, but the term 'urban history' or 'the new urban history' came into use in the 1960s to refer to a new approach, practised most of all in the U.S.A. This new urban history is problem-oriented, concerned in particular with ECOLOGY, immigration, and SOCIAL MOBILITY. It draws heavily on urban SOCIOLOGY for its concepts and makes considerable use of quantitative methods.

P.B.

Bibl: H.J. Dyos (ed.), *The Study of Urban History* (London and New York, 1968); D. Fraser and A. Sutcliffe (eds.), *The Pursuit of Urban History* (London, 1983).

urban renewal. The rebuilding and/or rehabilitation of decaying urban areas through planning policies and, frequently, the provision of governmental and/or municipal finance. It tends to reduce the continually shrinking stock of inexpensive, and usually well-liked, buildings, and has often resulted in the displacement of the urban poor (a process sometimes known as *gentrification*) and of small but essential shops and workshops. Though often defended on the grounds that the needs of the motor car make such changes inevitable, heavy criticism, particularly in the U.S.A., has made urban renewal a highly suspect operation.   M.BR.

Bibl: J. Jacobs, *The Death and Life of Great American Cities* (New York, 1961; London, 1962).

urban revolution. Term used to describe the emergence of urban centres in the Middle East. The phrase was introduced into ARCHAEOLOGY by V.G. Childe as part of a broad scheme in which he suggested that man had passed through three great periods of change, the NEOLITHIC REVOLUTION, the urban revolution, and the INDUSTRIAL REVOLUTION. During the first he learned to produce food and acquired a static form of existence which paved the way for the second, the development of organized city life. Childe believed that cities developed rapidly in the valleys of the Tigris and Euphrates. Recent discoveries in Palestine and Turkey, however, have shown that the phenomenon was more widespread in time and space. The CONCEPT is now little used among archaeologists, although geographers still seem to find some value in it.   B.C.

Bibl: V.G. Childe, *New Light on the Most Ancient East* (London and New York, 1958) and *What Happened in History* (Harmondsworth and New York, 1942).

urban sprawl, see under SPRAWL.

urbanism. (1) An alternative term for URBANIZATION; (2) In America (and cf. French *urbanisme*), an alternative term for town-planning; (3) the urban character or typical condition of the town. The functions of the town should be largely divorced from the rural society surrounding it for this term to be applicable.   M.L.

urbanization. The process and effects of gathering people in cities and TOWNS. The concept covers urban expansion in area and population, the resulting changes in land use, ways of life, landscapes, geographical and occupational distribution of people, and their economic activities. The unprecedented scale and speed of urbanization in the 20th century — the majority of mankind will soon be living in urban places — has brought a host of urgent needs, from more housing to government reform and REGIONAL PLANNING, and has made it a major concern of our time. See also METROPOLIS; MEGALOPOLIS.　　　J.G.

Bibl: A. Toynbee, *Cities on the Move* (London and New York, 1970); C.A. Doxiadis, *Ecumenopolis* (in English; Athens, 1974).

urodynamics, see under UROLOGY.

urology. Branch of SURGERY dealing with the genito-urinary system. Concerned with diseases of the kidneys, ureter, bladder, urethra and male sexual organs, e.g. congenital disorders in the baby, renal infections of childhood and pregnancy, stone disease, CANCER of the testis, kidneys and bladder, prostatic enlargement, impotence and male INFERTILITY. In addition to listening to the patient and examination the urologist will require other investigations to get precision in diagnosis and treatment. The urine will be tested for infection and abnormal constituents, possibly including a CYTOLOGICAL search for cancer cells. Blood tests will measure kidney function and screen for stone disease and HORMONAL disorders. An X-RAY (urogram) using an injection of contrast which is concentrated by the kidneys will give a picture of the kidneys, ureter and bladder. Any abnormality of these organs may be further shown by *sonography* which provides a painless non-invasive image using *ultrasound.* Alternatively ISOTOPE studies may show abnormalities of function. Bladder function can be examined using *urodynamics* which often are combined with a video of voiding. Such visualization combined with pressure flow studies is helpful in patients with incontinence. Men with sexual problems may have the semen examined or erection studied by monitoring during sleep. The urologist has special expertise with *endoscopy* using an operating telescope to treat GENITO-URINARY disease. Nephroscopy through a small puncture in the loin examines the drainage system of the kidney, small stones can be removed. In cystoscopy the resectoscope is slid along the urethra from its natural external opening into the bladder which can be inspected, any stones or tumours removed; in men in whom the prostate gland has enlarged so as to block the outflow of urine, the prostate may be removed. The instrument may also be used to pass fine tubes up into the ureter (retrograde catheterization), but by using a longer telescope of about 1 metre the whole length of the ureter and renal pelvis may be seen. Any stones blocking the ureter may be removed and, if large, broken into small fragments by an ultrasonic probe passed up the ureteroscope. Any debris will be passed afterwards in the urine. Large stones in the kidney may not need a major cutting operation in the loin to remove them; if they cannot be removed endoscopically, external ultrasonic therapy can fragment the stone (extra-corporeal-shockwave therapy). The apparatus focuses a shock wave generated outside the body onto the exact site of the stone. The urologist may also do reconstructive surgery to deal with injury, narrowing (stricture) and deformities in the genito-urinary tract. Urology is an expanding speciality using precision and new technology such as FIBRE OPTICS, LASERS and MICROSURGERY to treat disease (see SURGERY).　　　R.M.J.

Bibl: H.N. Whitfield and W.F. Hendry (eds.), *Textbook of Genito-urinary Surgery* (Edinburgh and London, 1986).

user friendly. An adjective describing computer PROGRAMS that are easy to use. See MAN-MACHINE INTERFACE.　　　J.E.S.

utilitarianism. In ETHICS, the theory that takes the ultimate good to be the greatest happiness of the greatest number and defines the rightness of actions in terms of their contribution to the general happiness. It follows that no specific moral principle is absolutely certain and necessary, since the RELATION between actions and their happy or unhappy consequences varies with the circumstances. Sketched by earlier philosophers, notably David Hume (1711-76), utilitarianism was made fully explicit by Jeremy Bentham (1748-

1832) and, in a qualified way, by John Stuart Mill. It was widely rejected in their time for its unedifying HEDONISM (which was nevertheless altruistic). In this century it has been criticized for its commission of the supposed NATURALISTIC FALLACY. Its chief opponents are the kind of ethical INTUITIONISM that takes values to be quite distinct in nature from matters of empirical fact, and the DEONTOLOGY (often associated with that view) that holds certain kinds of conduct to be right or wrong intrinsically and quite independently of any consequences they may have.   A.Q.

Bibl: J.S. Mill, *Utilitarianism* (London, 1863); A. Quinton, *Utilitarian Ethics* (London, 1973).

utility theory. In ECONOMICS, an individual's consumption of goods and services satisfies human wants and, thus, yields utility. The degree to which goods and services satisfy wants is denoted by their utility. It is usually considered impossible to measure utility, but possible to produce a ranking, in order of preference, of different patterns of consumption. With certain assumptions of RATIONALITY, utility is considered as a measure of an individual's preferences for different patterns of consumption. Utility is a function of the goods and services consumed. Thus, to say that the set of goods and services A has more utility than the set B simply implies that A is preferred to B. The assumption that individuals make decisions upon consumption in accordance with their preferences is equivalent to assuming that individuals maximize their utility, i.e. they are rational. As the choice of consumption pattern is constrained by prices and income, a consumer will not purchase a further unit of a good unless it gives an addition to utility, which is termed the MARGINAL UTILITY, at least as great as that obtained by spending the same amount of money on some other good. Thus, the price of a good is related to the marginal utility of consumption. This proposition underlies the NEOCLASSICAL ECONOMIC THEORY of price and is used to justify the working of the PRICE MECHANISM. The concept of utility can be used to derive mathematical FUNCTIONS representing the demand for goods and ser-

vices. Such derivations ensure that the preferences underlying the demand functions are rational. These demand functions can be estimated by ECONOMETRIC methods. Utility theory is the basis of much of WELFARE ECONOMICS, consumer MICROECONOMICS and EXPECTED UTILITY THEORY.   D.E.; R.ST.; J.P.

Bibl: D. Begg *et al.*, *Economics* (London, 1984).

utopian ideal. An important strand in the development of planning and architecture based on the ideas of English, French, and American utopian reformers such as Robert Owen (1771-1858), Charles Fourier (1772-1837), and Etienne Cabet (1788-1858). Each of these tried to execute social experiments in which the physical disposition of buildings would correct the obvious evils of the industrial city and allow man to flourish fully as a rational and emotionally fulfilled being. Owen's cooperative at New Lanark in Scotland, Fourier's projected Phalanstery, and Cabet's Icarian settlements in the U.S.A. were all attempts to create an early form of SOCIALISM and give it visible expression. Each placed his ideal community in a rural setting but tried to provide it with urban facilities. This combination had a marked impact on the GARDEN CITY movement and, through its insistence on the relation of social wellbeing and buildings, on the whole modern movement in architecture.   M.BR.

Bibl: L. Benevolo, tr. J. Landry, *The Origins of Modern Town Planning* (London and Cambridge, Mass., 1967).

utopianism. A form of thinking invented by Sir Thomas More, in his *Utopia* (1516). Utopia is the perfect society that is nowhere — on earth, at least. In the two centuries after More, utopia functioned as a critical political and moral standard by which to judge the INSTITUTIONS and practices of European societies. In the 19th century, fired by the promise of the Industrial and French revolutions, men strove to realize utopia here on earth, sometimes in their own life time. Europe, and even more the new republic of America, was swept by a wave of secular MESSIANISM, of which SOCIALISM was the dominant expression. The socialist utopia took several forms. There were the practical utopian experiments, as in Robert Owen's New Lanark in Scotland and the Owenite New Harmony colony in Indiana. There were the fictional utopias such as Etienne Cabet's Icaria which were converted into actual utopian communities in the New World of America, itself regarded by many in a utopian light. And there were utopian social philosophies, such as those of Saint-Simon, Fourier, Comte, and Marx, which confidently looked forward to an end to scarcity and suffering in the impending scientific, socialist society. Even where, as in the United States, utopian communities such as the Shakers and Oneida still took their inspiration from Christian MILLENARIANISM, they tended to adopt the practices and outlook of modern socialism, becoming in the end practically indistinguishable from the secular utopian socialists.

Socialism is still the modern utopia, but far less clearly or confidently so. In the 20th century, assailed by the experience of two world wars, the Great Depression, German NAZISM, Russian STALINISM, and a glimpse of the destructive potential of the atomic bomb, utopia has been on the defensive — it has even been pronounced dead. In the first half of the century it was largely replaced by the ANTI-UTOPIA, a bleakly pessimistic rebuttal of the hope of utopia. But since the 1950s utopia has made a remarkable recovery, if not attaining the commanding position of the last century. The success of industrialism in raising standards of living world wide, coupled with the dazzling achievements of TECHNOLOGY — the moon landing, the MICROELECTRONIC revolution — has led to a new wave of technological utopianism that surpasses most SCIENCE FICTION. Optimistic philosophies couched in the terms of modern science, such as Pierre Teilhard de Chardin's *The Phenomenon of Man* (1959), have achieved great popularity. The 1950s and 1960s produced a stream of NEW LEFT utopias, blending Marx and Freud (see MARXISM; FREUDIAN) in a euphoric message of psychological and political liberation. These included Norman O. Brown's *Life Against Death* (1959), and Herbert Marcuse's *Eros and Civilization* (1955) and *An Essay on Liberation* (1969). In France, SITUATIONISM held the utopian banner aloft, especially in the events of MAY 1968. And there have also been many ecological utopias or 'ecotopias', giving a lead to the environmentalist movement of the 1970s and 1980s. Prominent among these have been Charles Reich's *The Greening of America* (1970), E.F. Schumacher's *Small is Beautiful* (1973), Ernest Callenbach's *Ecotopia* (1975) and Ursula Le Guin's *The Dispossessed* (1974). As the millennial year 2000 approaches, it is impossible to say whether hope or despair has the upper hand; but at the very least it is clear that utopia is far from dead. It may even be that, once invented, utopia becomes an existential necessity without which human social life could not be carried on. K.K.

Bibl: F.E. and F.P. Manuel, *Utopian Thought in the Western World* (Cambridge, Mass. and Oxford, 1979); K. Kumar, *Utopia and Anti-Utopia in Modern Times* (Oxford, 1987).

UVF, see ULSTER VOLUNTEER FORCE.

V

vaccine, see under PROPHYLAXIS.

vacuum strings, see under STRINGS.

valence (or *valency*).
(1) In CHEMISTRY, a NUMBER characteristic of a particular ELEMENT describing the number of BONDS that it makes with other ATOMS in a MOLECULE. Thus, in methane (CH_4) carbon forms four bonds with hydrogen, and is therefore four valent (or quadrivalent), while hydrogen is univalent. The same element may, however, have different valencies in different compounds — e.g. phosphorus trichloride (PCl_3) and phosphorus pentachloride (PCl_5). The explanation of valency in terms of the sharing of ELECTRONS between adjacent atoms (COVALENCY) is one of the major achievements of QUANTUM THEORY. B.F.
Bibl: C.A. Coulson, *Valence* (London and New York, 3rd ed., 1979).
(2) In LINGUISTICS (especially DEPENDENCY GRAMMAR) a term to refer to the number and type of bonds which syntactic elements may form with each other. A valency grammar presents a MODEL of a sentence containing a fundamental element (usually the verb) and a number of dependent elements (valents) whose number and type is determined by the valency attributed to the verb. For example, vanish is 'monovalent', as it can only take a subject, whereas scrutinize is 'bivalent', as it can take both a subject and an object. D.C.
Bibl: P. Matthews, *Syntax* (Cambridge, 1981)

validity. The characteristic of an INFERENCE whose conclusion must be true if its premises are (see SYLLOGISM). An inference can be valid and yet have a false conclusion, but only if not all of its premises are true. Equally, an inference can be invalid even though both its premises and its conclusions are true, for example, *some men are Catholics, some Catholics are pipe-smokers*, therefore *some men are pipe-smokers*. (The invalidity of the inference becomes clear if 'women' is substituted for 'pipe-smokers'.) A.Q.

value, theory of (or *utility theory of value*). There are two basic theories of value: the LABOUR THEORY OF VALUE and the UTILITY THEORY of value (although the phrase *theory of value* is often employed as a short way of indicating the *utility theory of value*). In the utility theory of value the relative value of a good is determined by the relative benefit derived from the consumption of an additional unit of the good. Thus, while water is essential to life, it is of little *value* as the benefit of drinking an additional gallon of water is small. If such a valuation of a good is greater than its cost of production, one may expect to find that in the future more resources are devoted to its production. The benefit of the consumption of each additional unit of the good tends to decline with increasing consumption of the good. Thus in the long run one may expect to find the valuation of a good equal to its cost of production. See NEOCLASSICAL ECONOMIC THEORY. J.P.
Bibl: M. Blaug, *Economic Theory in Retrospect* (Cambridge, 5th ed., 1985).

value analysis. The study of a manufactured product in order to identify opportunities for reducing the cost by improving style, shape, function, materials, or method of manufacture. R.I.T.
Bibl: L.D. Miles, *Techniques of Value Analysis and Engineering* (New York, 1961).

value-freedom (translation of the German *Wertfreiheit*). The exclusion of value-words and VALUE-JUDGEMENTS from the discussion of human and social affairs. Its adoption in the SOCIAL SCIENCES as a METHODOLOGICAL ideal (recommended by Max Weber) does not imply that the valuations of the men being studied cannot be discussed, or that the selection of the problem in hand for investigation does not reflect a value-judgement about its interestingness, or that logical evaluations about the strength of evidence and the VALIDITY of INFERENCES will not figure in it. What is excluded is the making by the social scientist of moral and political value-judgements about the people in his field of study. The aim is to minimize possibilities of disagreement by eliminating from scientific work controversial and disputable matter. It reflects a methodological value-judgement that to count as scientific a body of assertions must contain only what can be established objectively as true or reasonable by SCIENTIFIC METHODS. Though there is no inconsistency in that, it is an ideal that is hard to realize in practice. Synonyms for *value-free* are *value-neutral* and *ethically neutral*; its opposite is *value-loaded, evaluative*, or NORMATIVE.   A.Q.

value-judgement. An utterance which asserts or implies that some thing, person, or situation is good or bad, some action ought or ought not to be done. Value-judgements need not explicitly contain the pure value-words: good, bad, right, wrong, ought, and their obvious synonyms and cognates. 'That is stealing' is a value-judgement, since 'steal' means the same as 'take wrongly'. On the other hand, the presence of a pure value-word is not an infallible mark of a value-judgement. 'The train ought to have arrived by now', said at a distance from the station and in ignorance of the actual facts, is only vestigially evaluative, meaning simply that it is reasonable to believe that the train has arrived.   A.Q.

value of children. Phrase used to encapsulate a variety of COST-BENEFIT or SOCIAL-BENEFIT approaches to FERTILITY. The main areas of interest are the cost of rearing children as opposed to the income they can or will bring to the family; the emotional value of children; absolute and relative value of children, depending on the age structure of the population and the *dependency ratio* (the proportion of productive to non-productive members of the society); and, in one telling phrase about modern contracepting societies, fertility decisions regarding 'children as CONSUMER DURABLES'.   D.S.

Bibl: J.T. Fawcett, 'Value of children', *International Encyclopedia of Population* (New York, 1982), pp. 665-71.

value theory (in PHILOSOPHY), see AXIOLOGY.

Van Allen belts. Two groups of charged PARTICLES (discovered by the American physicist J.A. Van Allen in 1958) whose ORBITS lie just outside the earth. It is thought that the particles come from COSMIC RAYS and from the sun; their motion is influenced by the earth's MAGNETISM rather than by GRAVITATION.   M.V.B.

van de Graaf generator. A machine for producing the high voltages needed to accelerate SUBATOMIC PARTICLES (see ACCELERATOR). Electric charge is 'sprayed' onto a moving belt which transfers it to a large hollow metal sphere whose potential may eventually reach millions of volts.
                              M.V.B.

variable. A symbolic device essential in MATHEMATICS; the name, which is misleading, arose in connection with the CALCULUS. The fundamental use of variables is to express FUNCTIONS (e.g. $f(u,v) = u^2 + v^2 + 1$). The letters used for the ARGUMENT(s) of the function are the *independent* variables; if a letter is used to denote the value of the function it is called the *dependent* variable. Particular values of the function can be computed after assigning values to the variables which occur in its expression (its arguments). If an expression or statement depends on *all* the values of the function, as in '$\int f(x)dx$' or '$f(u,v)$ is positive for all u, v', then the (argument-denoting) variables are said to be *bound* and it makes no sense to substitute values for them. Otherwise they are *free*. Variables may be restricted by implicit or explicit hypotheses or conditions. If the problem is to find values for them which satisfy the conditions they are called *unknowns*. Symbols for constants (e.g. π) and for PARAMETERS can be thought of as variables which are restricted by more or less permanent hypotheses. When letters are used for purely manipulative purposes, without thought of assigning meaning to them, they are often called *indeterminates*.   R.G.

variable-metric methods, see under GRADIENT METHODS.

variable speed. Confusion arises from the different meanings of this term, notably as between engineers in Europe and their counterparts in America. In the latter the term applies to a motor whose speed varies as the result of an applied load — normally an undesirable property. In Britain it applies to a motor whose speed can be varied at will by the human operator — often a desirable property. Americans describe such a machine, more accurately, as an *adjustable* speed motor. E.R.L.

variable stars, see under PERIOD-LUMINOSITY RELATION.

variance. In STATISTICS, the variance of a DISTRIBUTION is a measure of how scattered it is — a measure of dispersion. The variance is the expected squared difference between the expected value of a RANDOM VARIABLE and its actual value — in mathematical terms it is $E((X - \bar{X})^2)$ where $\bar{X} = E(X)$ is the expected value of X. The variance is often denoted by σ^2, and its square root σ is called the *standard deviation*; it is a root mean square error. For the NORMAL DISTRIBUTION of mean 0 and variance 1 the probability of the interval $[-1.96, +1.96]$ is 0.95 — hence the rule of thumb that for a bell-shaped density function 95% of the probability lies within 2 standard deviations of the mean. R.SI.

variance, analysis of. In STATISTICS, a procedure for allocating the variability found in a population to different sources, as in attempting to determine crop yield as a function of fertilizer used, chemical composition of soil, amount of rainfall, etc. It requires a design for analysis that keeps the variables isolated. (Failure in this respect is known as *confounding* — as when a study of the effect of social CLASS on the rate of bodily growth ignores differences in the NUTRITION enjoyed by the different classes.) Its basic logic is the comparison of the total variability in a population with the variability contributed by each of the sources of variance studied, and its typical test for 'significance' of a source of variability is the ratio of the variance left after all known sources have been extracted. J.S.B.

variance-reduction methods, see under MONTE CARLO METHODS.

variation. In BIOLOGY, the process that leads to differentiation between the members of a single SPECIES. We may distinguish between (1) *heritable variation*, which is the consequence of GENETIC differences and may therefore be propagated to the next generation, and (2) *phenotypic variation*, the consequence of differences of ENVIRONMENT or upbringing. Phenotypic variation is not heritable and therefore makes no direct contribution to evolutionary change. See also POLYMORPHISM. P.M.

variety. In CYBERNETICS, the total number of possible states of a system, or of an element of a system. The *Law of Requisite Variety (Ashby's Law)* expresses the fact that 'only variety can absorb variety': a regulating system must be able to generate as many states as can the system regulated. S.BE.

Bibl: W.R. Ashby, *An Introduction to Cybernetics* (London and New York, 1956).

varve dating, see under DATING.

vasectomy. Division of the spermatic cords which convey spermatozoa from the testes to the urethra and thence to the exterior. When both cords are cut no sperm can pass and the man is thus rendered sterile. The operation is almost invariably successful, although sterility is not normally achieved for several weeks or even months until all living spermatozoa are finally lost; most doctors recommend the continued use of contraceptives (see CONTRACEPTION) until two semen specimens have been shown to contain no spermatozoa. Vasectomy can sometimes be reversed by reconnecting the cut ends of the cord, but is best confined to men who want to be made permanently sterile. D.A.P.

Vatican Council II. The ECUMENICAL Council (1962-4) opened by Pope John XXIII to renew Roman CATHOLICISM. Whereas the First Vatican Council (1869-70) had seen the triumph of ULTRAMONTANISM, this Council did much to authorize a more BIBLICAL THEOLOGY and the aspirations of the AGGIORNAMENTO. D.L.E.

Bibl: W.M. Abbott (ed.), *The Documents of Vatican II* (London and New York, 1966).

Vcheka, see under KGB.

VDU, see VISUAL DISPLAY UNIT.

vector. Many notions in GEOMETRY and PHYSICS (e.g. the instantaneous velocity of a PARTICLE, a force, a rotation of a body about a fixed point) are completely specified by giving a definite direction together with a (positive) numerical magnitude. Any such vector x can be represented geometrically by a line OP from O to P with the appropriate direction and with the distance OP equal to the magnitude of x. If QR is equal and parallel to OP, then QR represents the same vector. The components of the vector with respect to a given system of rectilinear axes Ox, Oy, Oz are then just the COORDINATES (x, y, z) of P. (1) The *sum* $x + x'$ of two vectors is defined as the vector whose components are $(x + x', y + y', z + z')$, or equivalently as the vector represented by the diagonal of the parallelogram with sides OP, OP'. (2) If a is a number (in this context also called a *scalar*) then the vector ax is defined as having components (ax, ay, az). The use of these (and certain other) notations allows geometric and physical facts to be described more succinctly and transparently than does the exclusive use of components. In studying continuous phenomena one is often concerned with a *vector field*, i.e. a FUNCTION which assigns a vector (as value) to each point of a region of space.

From a more abstract point of view, the above definitions, in particular (1) and (2), do not depend on there being precisely 3 components. A *vector space* (over the real numbers) is a MATHEMATICAL STRUCTURE for which the operations (1) and (2), obeying certain natural AXIOMS, are defined. Vector spaces are closely connected with the notion of LINEARITY and have application wherever that notion occurs.　R.G.

Bibl: J. Singh, *Mathematical Ideas* (London and New York, 1972).

vectors of disease. A vector is an insect or other organism that transmits a pathogenic fungus, virus (see VIROLOGY), bacterium (see BACTERIOLOGY), etc. to a human being. The vector is usually immune to the pathogen (an agent that can cause disease). One of the best examples is the anopheles mosquito. The mosquito bites an infected animal or human and ingests the malaria parasite which reproduces within the insect. It then injects the parasites into another human through its saliva causing malaria. Occasionally, human beings act as vectors of disease. Some people acquire organisms of diseases such as typhoid or salmonella but do not show any symptoms of the disease. However, they often pass the organism on to others, occasionally causing epidemics. Food handlers, for instance, have been pinpointed as the sources of outbreaks of salmonella and other food poisonings.　A.P.H.

Vedanta. A system of beliefs developed by many Indian thinkers (most notably Samkara in the 8th century A.D.) and based on four of the ancient scriptures of HINDUISM, all having the Sanskrit *veda*, knowledge, in their titles. The emphasis is on the unity of the ultimate *Brahman*, and on the unreality of the world in comparison.　D.L.E.

Bibl: C. Isherwood (ed.), *Vedanta for the Western World* (Hollywood, 1945; London, 1948).

vegans, see under DIET.

vegetarianism, see under DIET.

venereal disease, see under SEXUALLY TRANSMITTED DISEASE.

venereology, see under GENITO-URINARY MEDICINE.

venereophobia. A morbid fear of SEXUALLY TRANSMITTED DISEASE. This must be distinguished from a natural anxiety about the possibility of infection which anyone might feel, which is relieved by medical advice and reassurance. It is characteristic of venereophobia that the individual is convinced that a serious infection is present, and remains convinced of this despite repeatedly negative medical examination and laboratory tests. In the past, the fear was often of SYPHILIS but today it is usually of genital HERPES or AIDS. Venereophobia is difficult to treat. It may be a sign of an obsessional neurosis, DE-PRESSION or even of a paranoid PSYCHOSIS, and skilled psychiatric help is often needed. J.D.O.

verification. The establishment of a belief or PROPOSITION as true. The chief philosophical employment of the notion is in the verification principle of the LOGICAL POSITIVISTS which requires a proposition, if it is to be significant, to be verifiable by sense-experience (see SENSE-DATUM), or by attention to the MEANING of the words that express it, or, indirectly, by INFERENCE from propositions that are directly verifiable in either of these two ways, i.e. by INDUCTION or DEMONSTRATION. Formulation of the principle gave much difficulty. Whose experience is relevant? If, as seems reasonable, it is that of the speaker, are propositions about the past or other minds therefore meaningless? Must meaningful propositions be conclusively verifiable? Can the verification principle itself be verified? See also POPPERIAN. A.Q.

verism. In art and literature, an alternative name for NATURALISM (senses 4, 5). In its Italian form, *verismo*, the term was applied particularly to the violent, melodramatic operas, around 1900, of Puccini, Mascagni, and others. But the tendency began earlier in literature: in Edmondo De Amicis, and then — more certainly and deliberately — in Luigi Capuana and, particularly, in Giovanni Verga. The emphasis was ostensibly on truth-at-all-costs; but really on low life, gloom, dirt, poverty, violence, despair. The roots of verism are, for perhaps obvious reasons, Sicilian. M.S.-S.

vernacular. In architecture, adjective applied to an indigenous style of building that is largely untutored, but thought to be of considerable virtue and to some extent associated with a golden past. It is the architecture of the Cotswold village or the Mediterranean hillside town or the adobe settlement of the American Indian. Modern architects have often claimed as one of their aims the establishment of a new vernacular. M.BR.

Bibl: B. Rudofsky, *Architecture without Architects* (New York, 1964).

vers libre, see under FREE VERSE.

Verstehen. Term used in Germany from the late 19th century to denote understanding from within, by means of EMPATHY, intuition, or imagination, as opposed to knowledge from without, by means of observation or calculation. The term was employed in particular by the sociologist Max Weber and by philosophers of the NEO-KANTIAN school such as Dilthey and Rickert. *Verstehen* was thought by some to be characteristic of the SOCIAL SCIENCES as opposed to the NATURAL SCIENCES; by others, to be characteristic of history and literature, as opposed to the social sciences. Today, the value of *Verstehen* is debated mostly by sociologists. See also HERMENEUTICS; HISTORICISM. P.B.
Bibl: W. Outhwaite, *Understanding Social Life* (London, 1975).

vertical and lateral thinking. Terms coined by Edward de Bono for two contrasted but complementary modes of thinking. In PROBLEM-SOLVING, vertical thinking elaborates methods for overcoming obstacles in the chosen line of approach, while lateral thinking tries to bypass them by switching to a radically different approach involving a distinct reformulation of the problem. The two modes of thinking are characteristic of, respectively, CONVERGERS AND DIVERGERS. I.M.L.H.
Bibl: E. de Bono, *Lateral Thinking* (London and New York, 1970).

vertical integration. Control by one management of two or more steps in the process of production and distribution of a product, as when a book publisher acquires a printing press or a bookshop, or a firm which slaughters and packs broiler chickens for distribution obtains management control of the production process on farms through agreements with farmers. K.E.H.

vestigial organ. An organ which has been superseded or has become functionally redundant in the course of EVOLUTION. Such an organ often dwindles in size and loses its distinctive characteristics. The human vermiform appendix is a classical example — but possibly an erroneous one, because immunology (see IMMUNITY) warns us that such an important lymphoid organ should not too easily be dismissed as functionless. A better example is the pineal organ in the brain, the evolutionary remnant of what was at one time a functional median dorsal eye — a function still possessed by the pineal of the lampreys.

P.M.

Vichy. An inland spa in southern France, the seat of government of the capitulationist French regime headed by Marshal Pétain in July 1940, following France's defeat by the Germans. From 1940 to 1942 Pétain's government (the leading figure in which was Pierre Laval) administered the southern, unoccupied half of France, and Vichy, an AUTHORITARIAN regime with support from French FASCIST organizations, became a byword for military defeatism and the willingness of the wealthy to accept national defeat and humiliation rather than REVOLUTION. After the occupation of the whole of France by the Germans (November 1942), Vichy became openly collaborationist and its leaders were tried and convicted of treason after the defeat of Germany.   A.L.C.B.

Bibl: R. Aron, tr. H. Hare, *The Vichy Regime, 1940-1944* (London and New York, 1958); R.O. Paxton, *Vichy France* (New York, 1972; London, 1973).

videofrequency. A vibration frequency in the RADIO FREQUENCY region used to transmit television pictures.   M.V.B.

videotape. A kind of MAGNETIC TAPE used to store information which can be reconstructed into pictures; television programmes are stored on videotape. M.V.B.

Vienna Circle (*Wiener Kreis*). A group of philosophers, mathematicians, and scientists who came together under the leadership of Moritz Schlick in the late 1920s to inaugurate the school of LOGICAL POSITIVISM. Leading members were Rudolf Carnap, Friedrich Waismann, Otto Neurath, Herbert Feigl, Hans Hahn, Philipp Frank, Karl Menger, and Kurt Gödel. It was associated with a like-minded group in Berlin, led by Hans Reichenbach, and the two groups jointly published the journal *Erkenntnis*. Schlick's death in 1936 and Hitler's occupation of Austria in 1938 brought the Vienna Circle to an end as an organized group, but its ideas were developed, under the name of LOGICAL EMPIRICISM, by various members who emigrated to the U.S.A. and elsewhere.   A.Q.

Bibl: V. Kraft, *The Vienna Circle* (New York, 1969).

Vietcong. A blanket term coined by the government of South VIETNAM to refer to anti-government forces in order to give the impression that all rebels were COMMUNISTS. The successors of the pre-1954 VIETMINH guerrillas, the 'National Liberation Front' was initially an alliance of all opposition forces. From 1958 onwards, however, they became increasingly dependent on support and aid from North Vietnam. Communist cadres increased their influence, and by 1965, the Vietcong was wholly dependent on North Vietnam for any chance of gaining control in the south.

D.C.W.;S.B.

Bibl: D. Pike, *Viet Cong* (London and Cambridge, Mass., 1967).

Vietminh. Abbreviation of the VIETNAM *Duc Lap Dong Minh* (Vietnamese Independence League), founded in China in 1941. It was initially an alliance of COMMUNISTS and NATIONALISTS assisted and aided by the U.S. in the struggle against Japan, but after the Japanese surrender in 1945, it developed into a front organization for the Communist Party of Indo-China (founded by Ho Chi Minh in 1921). It was the Vietminh and Ho Chi Minh who emerged in control of North Vietnam after the defeat of the French in the first Vietnamese War, 1945-54.   D.C.W.;S.B.

Bibl: T.L. Hodgkin, *Vietnam: The Revolutionary Path* (New York, 1981).

Vietnam. A country of South-East Asia under increasingly unstable French colonial rule until 1954, then partitioned, and from 1960 to 1975 the scene of a civil war between the COMMUNIST government of North Vietnam (capital Hanoi) and the U.S. client government of South Vietnam (capital Saigon). The war expanded as American military involvement increased from 1964. It was maintained in the face of mounting criticism within the U.S. and throughout the world, and of fading chances of a resolution satisfactory to the U.S., until the cease-fire agreement of January 23 1973 ended active American military participation. The cease-fire was quickly broken; the U.S. continued to support the South's forces until February 1975; the fall of the Southern regime quickly followed US withdrawal of aid. American methods and ultimate failure to secure its objectives did much to damage the country's morale and prestige, and contributed to the fall of non-Communist governments in Laos and Cambodia. 'Vietnam' has become a byword for wars in which major powers invest massive resources in local conflicts on dubious moral and strategic grounds.   S.R.

Bibl: G. Herring, *America's Longest War: The United States and Vietnam 1950-75* (New York, 1979).

Village, the, see GREENWICH VILLAGE.

Vingt, les. Brussels artists' exhibiting society founded by Octave Maus, internationally significant for its support of the SYMBOLISTS and NEO-IMPRESSIONISTS. Among the artists featured in its first Salon (1884) were Renoir, Monet, Whistler, and the Belgians James Ensor and Théo van Rysselberghe.   J.W.

virology. The science that deals with the structure, properties and behaviour of the sub-microscopic infective particles known as viruses, especially as agents of disease. Viruses were at one time thought to be rudimentary living organisms, as if they were sub-microscopic bacteria using the CELL sap as a culture medium such as that in which bacteria grow (see BACTERIOLOGY). This description is now known to be misleading. Viruses do not grow in the conventional sense, and are not self-reproducing: they subvert the synthetic machinery of the cells which they infect in such a way as to produce more copies of themselves, and have no existence apart from the cells they infect. Thus viruses cannot like bacteria be cultivated in fairly simple media outside the body, but must be propagated either in TISSUE CULTURES or in embryonated hens' eggs (the discovery of Sir Macfarlane Burnet). All viruses contain NUCLEIC ACID (DNA or RNA). It is this that transforms the METABOLISM of the affected cell to make it produce more virus copies, usually at the cell's expense. Viruses that produce visible changes in the cells they infect are referred to as *cytopathogenic*. It is conceivable, though, that many other viruses exist which are not recognizable as viruses because they produce no such effects. Thanks to ELECTRON MICROSCOPY and orthodox chemical analysis the structure and composition of several viruses are now well known (e.g. human adenovirus 12 and tobacco mosaic virus). Viruses have a core of nucleic acid and an outer shell of PROTEINS. Because of their small size (of the order of millimicrons) they pass through filters fine enough to retain bacteria, and heat is the only reliable method of destroying them.

Diseases caused by viruses include smallpox (variola), cowpox (vaccinia), poliomyelitis, common colds (for which one or more of upwards of forty 'rhinoviruses' may be responsible), influenza, and some forms of hepatitis. In addition viruses are now known to cause certain human leukaemias and are implicated in other human tumours, particularly tumours of the cervix, liver and lymph glands; the science of *tumour virology* has been developed with the aid of viruses that cause malignant growths of many kinds in experimental animals. ANTIBIOTICS do not act upon viruses, but a naturally occurring agent, INTERFERON, may protect uninfected cells against infection by virus. Recovery or protection from a viral infection depends upon the action of antibodies (see IMMUNITY), and this also makes the basis of preventive methods.

Poliomyelitis vaccines are of two main kinds: (1) Salk vaccine (1954), an inactivated virus administered by injection, the preparation of which was made possible by the discovery of J.F. Enders and his colleagues that polio virus can be propagated in tissue cultures; and (2) an attenuated virus strain (1955), particularly associated with the names of H. Koprowski and A. Sabin, that can be taken by mouth. The result of these public-health procedures is that poliomyelitis like smallpox is a disappearing disease, and the

GENETIC information coded in the respective virus nucleic acids will be lost.

P.M.;P.N.

virtual memory. In COMPUTING, a technique whereby an OPERATING SYSTEM can relieve the user of the chore of managing the different kinds of STORE available. The user can work as though he had a much larger main store than is actually present; the operating system decides, using a HEURISTIC, which part of this is to be in the actual main store at any time while the remainder is kept on a backing store, parts of it being exchanged with information in the main store when the user requires them. The success in any particular application depends on how well the heuristic deals with the actual pattern of usage of store.

J.E.S.

virtual particles. PARTICLE which exists for a very short period of time and with an energy such that it is unobservable according to Heisenberg's UNCERTAINTY PRINCIPLE (that is, the act of directly observing such a particle would cause too large a perturbation to its lifetime and ENERGY). This brief existence is maintained in order to allow there to exist an interaction between two other particles. Individual virtual particles are unobservable although their collective effects upon ATOMIC ENERGY levels have been successfully predicted and observed to occur (see under LAMB SHIFT). Virtual particles can be transformed into individually observable (or real) particles by applying an external electric field across a vacuum. The resulting production of particles is called the *Schwinger process*. The existence of virtual particles can be exhibited by placing two parallel plates in a vacuum. Only virtual particles with a quantum wavelength which will fit exactly between the two plates will be present between the plates while all virtual particle wavelengths will be present outside. The greater pressure of the outside of the plates causes them to get closer. This is called the *Casimir effect*. GRAND UNIFIED THEORIES of ELEMENTARY PARTICLE physics are possible because the effective strengths of the different fundamental forces of nature change with the temperature of the environment in which they are measured.

The changes in effective strengths are created by the appearance and effects of virtual particles. These changes are found to be such that the STRONG, electromagnetic and WEAK INTERACTIONS will have the same strength at some very high temperature.

J.D.B.

Bibl: R. Feynman, *QED* (New York, 1986).

viscerotonia, see under PERSONALITY TYPES.

visual acuity. Provides a measure of the visual resolving power of the eye, or rather the macular region of the retina of the eye, which may be recorded either when working unaided or with the help of a correcting ophthalmic lens (see OPHTHALMOLOGY). The measurement of acuity is expressed as a function of both the size and the distance away of the object seen. In the U.K. the usual convention is to use test letters on the Snellen chart which determines the size of the letters to be read and under this convention the patient is placed at a distance of six metres from the Snellen chart. The acuity achieved is expressed in the clinical notes as a fraction, the numerator of which is determined by the distance at which the test was carried out, usually by convention six metres. Measured by these means normal visual acuity is expressed as 6/6. Using the same principle, but adopting slightly different conventions, the 6/6 vision in the U.S.A. is noted as 20/20 vision.

J.WI.

visual cliff. A device for testing young animals' PERCEPTION of depth. It consists of two identically patterned horizontal surfaces, one well below the other, the upper being extended over the lower by means of a sheet of transparent glass. An animal unwilling to move off the upper surface onto the transparent glass that projects over the lower surface is said to possess *depth perception*. Many SPECIES have been found to possess it at birth.

J.S.B.

visual display unit (VDU). A device by which the output of a COMPUTER is represented as a visual image on the screen of a CATHODE RAY TUBE. It normally contains a character generator, and so can be used as part of a TERMINAL to display text and, if it has a graphics capability, diagrams. It has the advantages of being rapid and silent, but cannot produce hard copy easily. With the aid of a device known as a LIGHT PEN it can also form part of an input device. See also COMPUTER-AIDED DESIGN; INPUT/OUTPUT. C.S.

vital registration, see under CENSUS.

vitalism. A miscellany of beliefs united by the contention that living processes are not to be explained in terms of the material composition and physico-chemical performances of living bodies. Woodger distinguishes several varieties of vitalism, one of which is *dogmatic vitalism*, such as we find in the writings of Hans Driesch (1867-1941) and Henri Bergson (1859-1941), according to which living things are animated by a vital principle such as an ENTELECHY (Driesch's term) or an *élan vital* or *life force* (Bergson's, popularized in England by G.B. Shaw). Dogmatic vitalism is contrasted with MECHANISM, the system of beliefs or lack of beliefs to which modern BIOLOGY and medicine owe all their great triumphs, and which consists, methodologically, of behaving *as if* all vital activities could be adequately explained in terms of material composition and physico-chemical performance. P.M.

vitamins. Originally defined as organic substances which cannot be synthesized in the body and must therefore be provided in small amounts ready-made in the DIET. There are, however, two exceptions to this definition, vitamin D can be made in the skin under the influence of sunlight, and niacin can be made from dietary tryptophan (found in all PROTEINS). Since most vitamins can exist in more than one chemical form (e.g. vitamin A is found preformed as retinol and in plant food as carotene; vitamin B6 exists in three forms) it is current practice to refer to each by its chemical name, e.g. pyridoxine, pyridoxamine or pyridoxol and to use the term vitamin, in this instance vitamin B6, as a generic descriptor. A severe deficiency of any vitamin gives rise to specific symptoms (vitamin C deficiency — scurvy; vitamin D deficiency — rickets). A.E.B.

Bibl: B.M. Barker and D.A. Bender, *Vitamins in Medicine* (London, 1982).

voiceprint. A visual representation of certain ACOUSTIC characteristics of the human voice, which it is claimed will uniquely identify an individual. The claims have been strongly attacked, particularly when voiceprinting was used as evidence in American courts of law in the mid 1960s, and there is as yet no general agreement as to its reliability. D.C.

voids. Large regions of intergalactic space found to contain no visible galaxies (see under GALAXY CLUSTERS and DARK MATTER). The largest is the Bootes void. These regions may contain large quantities of faint stars or dark matter. J.D.B.

volcanology. The study of volcanoes, their life-history, and their lava, gas, and fragmentary constituents. Volcanology is concerned with the study of all volcanoes, active, dormant and extinct, and their distribution in space and time. The monitoring of active volcanoes is an important social aspect of the subject but one in which long-term predictions of eruptions, though demanded, cannot be produced with any degree of certainty. J.L.M.L.

volition. An act of will or decision, conceived as a mental event immediately antecedent to voluntary bodily movement or action proper, as contrasted with purely reflex or automatic behaviour. Ryle, wishing to deny the existence of inner mental states in the interests of his version of BEHAVIOURISM, declared the concept of volition to be empty or mythical. Certainly not all voluntary action seems to be preceded by introspectible mental preliminaries (see INTROSPECTION), but some does. Against the view that the occurrence of volition is a CRITERION of freedom and responsibility in action Ryle argued that volitions are themselves represented as a species of, admittedly inward, actions about which the question of intention or voluntariness can again be raised, thus generating an infinite regress. A.Q.

Bibl: A.J. Kenny, *Action, Emotion and Will* (London and New York, 1963).

Volksbühne (The People's Stage). A German theatre association founded by Bruno Wille in 1890, which remains the most successful and longest-lived product of the European 'people's theatre' movement around that time. Starting with no theatre of its own, it split on the issue of alignment with the SOCIALIST Party, then reunited 70,000 strong to open its own Berlin theatre in 1914. Here Erwin Piscator (1893-1966), a pioneer of the EPIC and DOCUMENTARY theatres, became the chief director in 1924, leaving in 1927 to set up his own company with the support of the COMMUNIST section of the membership. Subsequent directors before the NAZI takeover included Karl Heinz Martin and Heinz Hilpert. Suppressed under the Nazis, it was reactivated after World War II but soon fell into two halves, one in East Berlin, the other in West. In 1962 the latter was again taken over by Piscator, who introduced the new documentary dramas of Rolf Hochhuth, Peter Weiss, and Heinar Kipphardt. Its new West Berlin theatre was opened in 1963.   J.W.

Bibl: H.F. Garten, *Modern German Drama* (New York, 1962; London, 2nd ed., 1964).

voluntarism.
(1) Any theory that emphasizes the role of the will in mental life, especially thinking and the pursuit of knowledge, or, again, in decisions about conduct. PRAGMATISM is voluntaristic in its conception of knowledge as subservient to action and of our CONCEPTS or beliefs as instruments devised by us for the satisfaction of our desires. The philosophy of Schopenhauer is a highly generalized form of voluntarism, in which ultimate reality is taken to be of the nature of will.   A.Q.

(2) In historical, political, and social theories about the behaviour of man voluntarism emphasizes the individual choice in decision-making, which it considers as not entirely determined by external conditions. It stands in contrast to the deterministic (see DETERMINISM) MODEL of human behaviour which excludes will and voluntary action as causative factors in individual experience and in society. In politics 'voluntarist' has usually been applied abusively to leaders who overestimate the ability of determined men to conquer circumstances. LENINISM is perhaps the best known example of a voluntarist political theory and practice, emphasizing the almost limitless possibilities open to a determined leader backed by a devoted party.   L.L.;A.R.

von Baer's principle, see under EMBRYOLOGY.

von Neumann computer. The most common form of COMPUTER design, with a PROCESSOR attached to a main STORE, together with various INPUT/OUTPUT arrangements. What limits its speed is that all the instructions and data must travel along the path from store to processor, creating the so-called *von Neumann bottleneck*, while at any time almost all the store and, indeed, much of the processor is idle. In FIFTH-GENERATION COMPUTERS new forms of COMPUTER ARCHITECTURE are being tried to overcome this problem.   J.E.S.

Vorticism. One of the very few English modern-form movements in the arts, and the one most contemporary with international developments in all the visual arts. Related to CUBISM and FUTURISM in painting, and partly emerging from IMAGISM in literature, it was a unique compound of new theories of energy and form, rare in England, in that it brought painters (e.g. William Roberts) and writers (especially Ezra Pound) together in the 'Great English Vortex'. Wyndham Lewis, its prime founder, was both: he saw the movement visually as 'a mental emotive impulse ... let loose on a lot of blocks and lines', verbally as a hard, unromantic, external presentation of kinetic forces. Pound, in parallel, dropped the neo-SYMBOLIST bias of Imagism, with which he was disillusioned, and emphasized the hard energy-centre in poetry. The movement, anti-representational, brutalist, an 'arrangement of surfaces', came out of the *Rebel Art Centre*, founded by Lewis, Edward Wadsworth, Christopher Nevinson, and others in 1913; associated painters and sculptors included Bomberg, Gaudier-Brzeska, and Epstein. A Vorticist exhibition was held at the Doré Gallery in March 1915; the main document of the movement was the visual-verbal manifesto-magazine BLAST. M.S.BR.

Bibl: R.G. Cork, *Vorticism and Abstract Art in the First Machine Age* (vol. 1, London, 1976).

voucher system. Begun in Alum Rock, California in the late 1960s, this allows parents a much wider choice of school for their children. Parents are given a voucher equivalent to the amount spent by the STATE on a school place. They may then take that voucher and their child to any school — public (i.e. state-maintained) or private. If the fees at a private school are higher than the value of the voucher, the parent pays the difference. Schools vied with each other for clients and many less popular schools were obliged to improve their standards or go under. The system was to be introduced in Britain and had the support of at least one Conservative education minister, but pilot attempts never got off the ground and it was eventually abandoned. J.I.

vraisemblance. A concept important in early STRUCTURALIST criticism and celebrated in a special number of the journal *Communications* in 1968. It is by *vraisemblance,* which might be loosely translated as 'fittingness', that a literary work is recognized, or recognizable, as inhering 'naturally' in a certain type of DISCOURSE, whose conventions are known in advance. The degrees of conformity or fittingness required for a work to be 'naturally' part of a certain kind of literary discourse vary from having to meet the basic demands of COMMON SENSE, through various culturally received conventions of likelihood, obviousness, relevance, pertinence, conformity etc., up through the conventions of given literary genres themselves, up to and including outright parody, where all claims for first-order fittingness are abandoned. *Vraisemblance* is related to the inescapability of what Julia Kristeva calls INTERTEXTUALITY and also to the doctrine of ÉCRITURE as propounded in 1953 by Roland Barthes. R.PO.

Bibl: J. Culler, *Structuralist Poetics* (London, 1975).

W

wage restraint, see under INCOMES POLICY.

Wageningen school, see under AGRARIAN HISTORY.

wages policy, see INCOMES POLICY.

Wall Street. The name given to the lower end of Manhattan Island, New York, where the world's most important financial centre — comprising banks, trust companies, insurance companies, exchanges, etc. — is situated, and which also houses the headquarters of most of America's largest business corporations. As a popular term Wall Street, or 'the Street', has become increasingly synonymous with the interests of American CAPITALISM and embraces businesses far removed physically from the area to which it properly refers.   D.E.

Wall, the, see BERLIN WALL.

Walras' Law. In ECONOMICS, this law states that the sum of the demand minus the supply of each good and service multiplied by its price must be equal to zero. This law should be true whether or not the economy is in EQUILIBRIUM. The proof of this law lies in the decision to supply a good or service implying a decision to consume a good or service of equal value. For a barter economy, this law is true by definition. However, when the KEYNESIAN distinction is made between notional and effective demand, it is clear that, for the former type of demand, the law is not true.
J.P.
Bibl: R. Levacic and A. Rebmann, *Macroeconomics* (London, 2nd ed., 1982).

Wankel engine (or *epitrochoidal engine*). A rotary internal combustion engine with no reciprocating parts. The rotating part is shaped like an equilateral triangle with slightly curved convex sides. The casting in which it rotates is so shaped that, when the rotor revolves eccentrically through the use of an epicyclic gear, the 3 spaces between the sides of the 'triangle' and the walls of the casing each go through the sequence: intake, compression, power stroke, exhaust, as is usual in conventional internal combustion engines. The tips of the triangular rotor make seals with the casing to separate the 3 chambers and enable the action to take place.   E.R.L.

war (or *warfare*). Developments in technological means of destruction in political organization, in the international system, and in analysis of the subject have led to the classification of different kinds of war. Thus *catalytic war* is conflict between two states brought about by the deliberate actions of a third. COLD WAR is a state of international conflict wherein all measures short of organized military violence are used to achieve national objectives. *Conventional war* is armed conflict between states in which NUCLEAR WEAPONS are not used; *nuclear war* (under which is subsumed *thermonuclear war*) is conflict in which they are. *Chemical warfare* involves the use of incendiary, asphyxiating, or otherwise noxious chemicals, *biological warfare* the use of living organisms such as disease germs; the two are often bracketed together as 'CBW' (chemical and biological weapons), although the employment or intended employment of (particularly) the biological component is more often asserted than proved. GUERRILLA war or *insurgency* is conflict conducted by irregular forces within a state and aimed at alienating the mass of the population from the authority of the established government with a view to its final overthrow. LIMITED WAR is military conflict limited either by terrain, the weapons used, or the objectives pursued. *Prolonged* or *protracted wars* extend over one or more decades. A recent example was the VIETNAM War. Success in these conflicts requires considerable social discipline and control. *Psychological warfare* involves the use of propaganda (by radio, agents, etc.) to weaken the morale of an adversary population or army, and to discredit the motives and diminish the authority of an adversary government.
A.F.B.; A.J.M.W.
Bibl: A.F. Buchan, *War in Modern So-*

901

ciety (London, 1968); W.H. McNeill, *The Pursuit of Power: Technology, Armed Force and Society Since AD 1000* (Chicago, 1982; Oxford, 1983).

war crimes. (1) Acts of provoking WAR which are crimes according to the *jus contra bellum*, the law against war; and (2) violations of the laws and customs of war and of the laws of humanity, the *jus in bello*. Trials for war crimes are, however, a feature almost entirely confined to the 20th century, apart from those which represent the exercise of martial law by a military authority against civilians. International tribunals for the trial of alleged war criminals were proposed after 1918 but came to nothing. After 1945 international tribunals sat in Nuremberg (see NUREMBERG TRIALS) and Tokyo. The victorious powers claimed the right to speak and act for the international community in judging the leaders of the defeated states on charges of both kinds. Their legal justification remains a subject of controversy. The Nuremberg and Tokyo verdicts, however, were reflected in a revision of manuals of military law even by the victorious powers.   D.C.W.

warfare, see WAR.

Warnock Report. Dame Mary Warnock was chairman of the Committee of Inquiry into Human Fertilization and Embryology, which was set up in July 1982 and which reported in June 1984. The committee took evidence from a wide range of interested parties, and reached a consensus view on most topics. A review of services for infertile couples was recommended, and the need for guidance as to what facilities should be available within the NHS. Both ARTIFICIAL INSEMINATION by donor (AID) and in vitro fertilization (IVF) should be legal, but should only be available at centres licensed by a new statutory body. They should be available for the prevention of inherited disease as well as the treatment of INFERTILITY. The law required changes to allow a child conceived in such a fashion to be the legitimate child of the woman who gave birth to him/her, with her husband as the registered father. In the event of the father's death preceding his child's birth,

such a child would be excluded from succession and inheritance unless *in utero* before the death. The donor of semen or egg should have neither rights nor duties towards their biological progeny, and their anonymity must be complete except where a friend or family member is involved. Donors must be examined medically, and be free of inherited and infectious disease as far as can be determined; a central register should be kept to prevent more than 10 children being sired by one man, and donors should not stand to make pecuniary gain. Selection of donors on all but a few characteristics (ethnic origin, health) should be avoided. The recommendations concerning surrogacy and embryo research were more controversial, and unanimity was not achieved. Surrogacy, with one woman carrying a fetus for another unable to do so, should not be illegal per se. Surrogacy agreements, however, should be illegal contracts, and surrogacy agencies should be banned — whether commercial or charitable. It should be illegal for professionals to promote private surrogacy arrangements in any way. The human embryo (fertilized egg) should be protected in law, and may not be allowed to develop beyond the 14-day stage in the laboratory: it may be used for research until then.   A.CL.

wart viruses. A large group of DNA viruses which cause warts and associated diseases in humans and animals. There are many types of human papillomavirus (HPV). Some (HPV 1, 2 and 4) cause common skin warts; others (HPV 6 and HPV 11) cause genital warts, a common SEXUALLY TRANSMITTED DISEASE. HPV 16 and HPV 18, however, are associated with premalignant and malignant disease of the vulva, cervix and penis. It has been known for a long time that cervical cancer is connected with an early age of first intercourse and multiple sex partners. It is possible that the sexual transmission of HPV 16 or HPV 18 may play a part in the development of genital percancer and CANCER. Probably these viruses do not act alone; other factors such as infection by other microbes, defective IMMUNITY and cigarette smoking are involved.   J.D.O.

Bibl: J.D. Oriel and J.R.W. Harris

(eds.), *Recent Advances in Sexually Transmitted Diseases 3* (London, 1986).

Washington Square Players, see under OFF-BROADWAY.

Watergate. The name is taken from an apartment-hotel-office complex in Washington D.C., in which the Democratic Party's National Committee kept its headquarters for the 1972 presidential election. It refers to the scandal whose roots lay in the burglary on 17 June 1972 by employees of the rival Campaign to Reelect the President, who seemed intent on placing electronic surveillance devices in the headquarters. The whole sequence of events known collectively as Watergate took over two years to unravel (if indeed the whole story can be said to have emerged). It was discovered that some of President Nixon's White House associates had planned the break-in; that they and others had conspired to cover it up, and that the president himself was drawn into the conspiracy. To the last he attempted to disguise his role, giving way only when the Supreme Court compelled him to relinquish tapes revealing his complicity. He finally resigned on August 9, almost devoid of political support and under the threat of impeachment by Congress. The episode also saw the conviction on a rich variety of charges of some 20 members of his circle, including his former Attorney-General and White House Chief of Staff. Its ramifications raised serious questions about the administration's disregard for law and ETHICS, about Nixon's moral and political judgement, and about the adequacy of safeguards against such events. Although Watergate produced a brief sense of crisis, it came to be often regarded in sanguine terms as proof of the political system's self-correcting capacity and as an end to the IMPERIAL PRESIDENCY.   S.R.

Bibl: T. White, *Breach of Faith* (New York, 1975).

wave function. The mathematical representation of the strength of the waves associated with matter according to the WAVE-PARTICLE DUALITY. Each state in QUANTUM MECHANICS is fully described by a wave function which varies from point to

point in space. The intensity of this wave at a given point gives the probability that a particle will be found there. For example, the wave function of an ELECTRON in an ENERGY LEVEL of an ATOM is characterized by oscillations in the region where an ORBIT of the same ENERGY would exist if the electron obeyed NEWTONIAN MECHANICS; outside this region, the wave function falls smoothly to zero, so that there is a high probability that the electron will be found somewhere near its Newtonian orbit.   M.V.B.

wave guide. A metal tube used to transmit MICROWAVES for use in RADAR; the ELECTROMAGNETIC equivalent of the old-fashioned 'speaking tube' for sound waves.   M.V.B.

wave mechanics, see QUANTUM MECHANICS.

wave-particle duality. The manifestation in matter (which usually behaves as if made of PARTICLES) of interference and DIFFRACTION behaviour characteristic of wave motion, and the manifestation in light (which usually behaves as waves of electromagnetic RADIATION) of collision, absorption, and emission in the form of discrete ENERGY packets resembling particles. This duality provides the experimental foundation of QUANTUM MECHANICS (see ELECTRON DIFFRACTION) and is an instance of the COMPLEMENTARITY PRINCIPLE.

The quantity that undulates in 'matter waves' is the probability of finding a particle (see WAVE FUNCTION), so that their physical nature is completely different from other wave motions (e.g. light or sound), although their mathematical form is similar. Likewise, PHOTONS, or 'particles' of light, have a REST MASS of zero, and so differ physically from particles of matter.   M.V.B.

weak anthropic principle, see under ANTHROPIC PRINCIPLE.

weak interaction. The force which causes the unstable ELEMENTARY PARTICLES (e.g. NEUTRONS) to decay. PARITY is not conserved during weak interactions, which are about a million million times weaker than the STRONG INTERACTIONS that bind NUCLEONS together. M.V.B.

Weathermen. A radical faction of the American NEW LEFT which issued from the SDS in Spring 1969. Its name derived from a manifesto whose title echoed singer Bob Dylan's observation that 'You don't need a weatherman to know which way the wind blows.' The Weathermen flirted unsuccessfully with the notion of alliance with the BLACK PANTHERS and, yet more improbably, with thoughts of stimulating a revolutionary movement of WORKING-CLASS youth. They were then left as a small, intense, self-elected revolutionary ELITE employing tactics of sabotage and bombing, mainly of public buildings. The movement faded during the early 1970s, suffering from government counter-measures and its own isolation. S.R.

Bibl: A. Matusow, *The Unraveling of America* (New York, 1984).

weights and **weighting,** see under INDEX NUMBER; MEAN.

Weimar Republic. The first German parliamentary democratic republic established on the abdication of Kaiser Wilhelm II on 9 November 1918, the constitution of which (promulgated 11 August 1919) was drawn up at Weimar, the Thuringian city associated with the memory of Goethe. Burdened by the resentments of the supporters of monarchism and by all the other resentments directed from the RIGHT against the terms of the Treaty of Versailles, challenged by a series of unsuccessful revolutionary outbursts on the LEFT, and under great external pressure from France, the Republic never captured the loyalties of a sufficient proportion of the German people. Its parliamentary government collapsed in 1930, after the onset of the world economic crisis, to be followed by a series of minority governments, acting under the reserve powers of the Presidency, until on 30 January 1933 Adolf Hitler, leader of the NAZI party, was established as Chancellor. The record of the Weimar Republic was taken by many as fundamental evidence of the German lack of capacity for DEMOCRACY or a democratic tradition, a view now increasingly difficult to maintain. In contrast to

its political vicissitudes, the period of the Weimar Republic was marked by a remarkable flowering of the experimental attitude in the arts, a view which has been confirmed in retrospect. D.C.W.

Bibl: P. Gay, *Weimar Culture* (New York, 1968; London, 1969); W. Laqueur, *Weimar* (London, 1974; New York, 1975).

welfare. The word 'welfare' in welfare legislation or the WELFARE STATE refers generally to government support for the poor, and particularly to the free or subsidized supply of certain goods or services, e.g. health and education. I.M.D.L.

welfare economics. The study of the desirability of different possible patterns of production and the distribution of the resulting output. This requires some measure, and, thus, implicit VALUE-JUDGEMENT of the welfare of each individual. This is normally taken as the UTILITY derived from the individual's consumption of goods and services. This view has been criticized because society often decides that people are not always the best judges of what is in their own best interests, e.g. compulsory education and government's provision of goods and services in kind rather than income to purchase them. With a measure of individual welfare, it is possible to use the concept of PARETO OPTIMUM (see ECONOMIC EFFICIENCY), beyond which it is impossible to construct a change that makes one or more persons better off, without making one or more persons worse off. As the Pareto Principle cannot distinguish between different Pareto Optima, it is necessary to use a value-judgement in comparing different Pareto Optima. It is very difficult to construct such a SOCIAL WELFARE function or see where it is going to come from (see IMPOSSIBILITY THEOREM). However, a social welfare function is implicit in most decisions that the government makes, though it is rarely explicitly specified. Welfare economics has not progressed very far from this nihilistic conclusion. However, welfare economics includes the study of the useful and important concepts of EXTERNALITIES, PUBLIC GOODS and MARGINAL-COST PRICING and encompasses all policy orientated ECONOMICS. It makes up a large part of economics and criticisms of its usefulness reflect the difficulty of making statements about the desirability of different social states, rather than any failing on the part of economists.   A.K.S.; J.P.

Bibl: J. Bonner, *Politics, Economics and Welfare* (Brighton, 1986).

welfare state. A political system assuming State responsibility for the protection and promotion of the social security and welfare of its citizens by universal medical care, insurance against sickness and unemployment, old age pensions, family allowances, public housing, etc., on a 'cradle to grave' basis. Social insurance was introduced in Germany in the 1880s and in Britain before 1914, but a comprehensive scheme (and the term 'welfare state') was first adopted by the British Labour Government of 1945-50. Similar provision is made by the State in many other countries, e.g. in Western Europe, Scandinavia, New Zealand. In recent years the welfare state has been criticized, particularly by the New RIGHT, as destroying the self-reliance of its beneficiaries, and in many countries has met difficulties caused by economic recession which undermines its fiscal base.   D.C.W.;S.R.

Bibl: R.M. Titmus, *Essays on 'The Welfare State'* (London, 1958); I. Gough, *The Political Economy of the Welfare State* (London, 1979).

Wellsian. Characteristic or reminiscent of the writings of H.G. Wells (1866-1946). The label is applied more to his numerous works of SCIENCE FICTION than to the comedies of, particularly, the shabby-genteel world (e.g. *Kipps, Tono-Bungay, The History of Mr Polly*) which are likely to prove his most enduring work.   O.S.

Weltanschauung (German for 'world-outlook'). General conception of the nature of the world, particularly as containing or implying a system of value-principles. Any total philosophical system may be so styled which derives practical consequences from its theoretical component. It is common for important but comparatively local scientific discoveries or conjectures to be generalized into total

systems of this kind, for example, those of Newton, Darwin, Marx, and Freud. A.Q.

Weltschmerz. German word ('world-pain') for a feeling of the overwhelming oppressiveness of existence that may colour an individual's entire WELTANSCHAU-UNG.   W.Z.

Werkbund. The *Deutscher Werkbund* was founded in 1907 by the architect and then Superintendent of the Prussian Board of Trade for Schools of Arts and Crafts, Hermann Muthesius, who had been influenced by William Morris and the ARTS AND CRAFTS MOVEMENT. The *Werkbund* attempted to harness the artist to machine production in order to ensure a place for Germany in the growing industrial export market. Its stated aim was to achieve quality through 'not only excellent durable work and the use of flawless, genuine materials, but also the attainment of an organic whole rendered functional, noble and, if you will, artistic by such means'. The idea had considerable diffusion: an Austrian *Werkbund* was started in 1910, a Swiss in 1913; the Design and Industries Association was founded in England in 1915 and a similar Swedish institution by 1917. An important *Werkbund* Exhibition was held at Cologne in 1914 at which Walter Gropius and Adolf Meyer designed a model factory. In 1919 Gropius went to head the BAUHAUS, which continued the ideals shaped by Muthesius.

M.BR.

Bibl: N. Pevsner, *Pioneers of Modern Design* (London and New York, rev. ed., 1960).

Wertfreiheit, see VALUE-FREEDOM.

western. A perennially popular genre in the American cinema since 1903, when *The Great Train Robbery* charted its main ingredients: the masked raiders, the hold-up, the chase, the gunfight. Its most frequently recurring theme is reflected in the equally perennial childhood game of cowboys and Indians. At its best, the western has an epic sweep and excitement matched by no other genre, and its greatest practitioner, John Ford, painted through his films an astonishingly detailed canvas portraying America's pioneer past. In the

1960s the genre suffered a surprising transplant to Italy, resulting in a sudden surge of 'spaghetti westerns'.   T.C.C.M.

Bibl: P. French, *Westerns* (London, 1973).

Whig interpretation of history. Defined by Herbert Butterfield, who coined this somewhat ETHNOCENTRIC term in 1931, as the tendency of historians to see the past as the story of the conflict between PROGRESSIVES and REACTIONARIES, in which the progressives, or Whigs, win and so bring about the modern world. He suggested that this was to overestimate the likenesses between present and past and to assume, fallaciously, that men always intend the consequences of their actions, whereas no one in the past actually willed the present.   P.B.

Bibl: H. Butterfield, *The Whig Interpretation of History* (London, 1931; New York, 1951).

white-collar crime. Coined by the American CRIMINOLOGIST Edward Sutherland in 1945, the term refers to crimes committed by businessmen and business corporations in the course of what they consider to be 'legitimate' business activities. These include false ADVERTISING, copyright infringement, unfair competition, bribery, fraud, tax evasion, unfair labour practices, and unhealthy or unsafe work environments. The term has been widened to include crimes committed by white-collar employees against their employers, such as pilfering company property and fiddling expenses. A more radical attempt to extend the concept even further, to include crimes of STATES and governments, has so far met with limited success, despite the examples of the NUREMBERG TRIALS of NAZI leaders, and the WATERGATE affair in America.

An outstanding feature of white-collar crime is that it is not popularly perceived as crime, at least not as serious crime. White-collar crime typically does not fit the stereotype of the individual criminal, assaulting or robbing another individual. It is often crime against institutions, not particular individuals. Its effects are frequently diffuse and long-term, making it difficult to be precise about attributing responsibility, and to lay charges against specific individuals. As a consequence judges and juries, fairly reflecting public opinion, tend to be lenient about such crimes. All these features are well illustrated in two famous cases: that of the Ford Motor Company and their Pinto car, whose propensity to explode in rear-end collisions was known to Ford executives; and that of the Distillers Company and their drug thalidomide, which given to pregnant mothers was responsible for congenital deformities in their babies.   K.K.

Bibl: E.H. Sutherland, *Principles of Criminology* (Philadelphia, 1955); S. Box, *Power, Crime, and Mystification* (London, 1984).

white dwarfs. A peculiar type of star came to be identified in the 1920s, typified by a combination of high temperature and low luminosity. This mixture of attributes seemed to suggest that such stars (termed 'white dwarfs') were extremely small, generally no bigger than the Earth. It seemed probable therefore that they were possessed of extremely high densities. This characterization of these problem stars was given theoretical credibility by the work of A.S. Eddington (1882-1944) and R.H. Fowler (1889-1944). Fowler's great breakthrough lay in applying to white dwarfs the QUANTUM STATISTICAL mechanics which had emerged from the conceptualizations of Pauli, Fermi and Dirac. (Thus the new PHYSICS came to the aid of ASTRONOMY, and astronomy provided an important application of QUANTUM MECHANICS.) Being typified by high density and small size, white dwarfs became an obvious focus of attention for those concerned with the implications of the general theory of RELATIVITY, in particular the phenomenon of the reduction in the frequency of light being emitted from an extremely dense GRAVITATIONAL field. This presumed effect was indeed verified (by Walter Adams in 1924), thus adding a confirmation of Einstein's general theory.   R.P.

Bibl: R.W. Smith, *The Expanding Universe* (Cambridge, 1982).

white noise, see under NOISE.

WHO (World Health Organization). A specialized agency of UNO, whose forerunners were the International Office of Public Health set up in Paris in 1909 and the Health Office of the LEAGUE OF NATIONS (1923). Its activities include the encouragement of research, the control of epidemic and endemic diseases (e.g. malaria), and aid to strengthen the national programmes of member states in the field of public health. Its headquarters are in Geneva. D.C.W.

whole food, see under MACROBIOTICS.

whole-tone scale. A musical scale in which the 12 semitones of the octave are divided into two sets of 6 equal tones, thus producing, e.g., the scale A, B, C sharp, D sharp, F, G, A. It appears a number of times in compositions by Liszt; but it was Debussy who exploited it to the full. Music based on the whole-tone scale gives a curiously nebulous effect, seeming to lack the positive character given by normal tonality (see under ATONAL MUSIC). This is partly because there are only two possible 'scales', each employing 6 of the 12 semitones. The equality of interval precludes the possibility of any other PERMUTATION, nor does any note in the 'scale' give the feeling of being a root or 'tonic'. A.H.

Whorfian. In LINGUISTICS, characteristic of, or a follower of, the views of Benjamin Lee Whorf (1897-1941), particularly the 'Sapir-Whorf hypothesis' (also propounded by Edward Sapir) that our conceptual categorization of the world is partly determined by the structure of our native language. The strong form of this hypothesis, that our conceptualization is largely or wholly determined in this way, has been rejected by most linguists. D.C.
Bibl: B.L. Whorf, ed. J.B. Carroll, *Language, Thought and Reality: Selected Writings* (London and New York, 1956).

Wiener-Gruppe (Vienna Group, not to be confused with the VIENNA CIRCLE). Five young writer-performers who collaborated in that city between 1952 and about 1960 in occasional readings, cabaret sketches, and early HAPPENINGS, often in a spirit akin to that of DADAISM. They were Hans Carl Artmann, writer and linguist, Friedrich Achleitner, originally an archi-

tect, the CONCRETE POET Gerhard Ruhm, the JAZZ musician Oswald Wiener, and the short-lived experimental prose writer Konrad Bayer. J.W.

Wiener Kreis, see VIENNA CIRCLE.

Wiener Werkstätte (Vienna Workshops). A manufacturing association of Austrian craftsmen and designers formed in 1903 by the architect Josef Hoffman and colleagues from the KUNSTGEWERBESCHULE and the Vienna SEZESSION. Notable for its fine modern furniture, jewellery, and cutlery. J.W.

WIMPS, see under DARK MATTER.

Winchester disc. A compact design of DISC STORE which (because it is well sealed) is relatively insensitive to its environment, commonly used with MICROCOMPUTERS. J.E.S.

wino, see under SUPERSYMMETRY.

winter of discontent. A tiresome cliché, maladapted from Shakespeare's *Richard III*, referring to the winter of 1978-9 in the United Kingdom. This period saw the final breakdown of the SOCIAL CONTRACT between TRADE UNIONS and the Labour government, as it attempted a fourth round of controlled pay increases. Numerous STRIKES, particularly among PUBLIC SECTOR workers, fuelled anti-union and anti-government sentiment which contributed to the election of a radical CONSERVATIVE government in 1979 (see THATCHERISM). S.R.
Bibl: C. Crouch, *The Politics of Industrial Relations* (London, 1982).

wish-fulfilment. FREUDIAN term for seemingly fortuitous actions, misperceptions, fantasies, and dreams that represent fulfilments of a conscious or UNCONSCIOUS wish. Freud claimed that such wish-fulfilment constituted the essence of dreams. I.M.L.H.

witchcraft. In ANTHROPOLOGY, a term usually restricted to mean causing harm to other people and their possessions by the involuntary exercise of extraordinary, mystical powers, and distinguished from

SORCERY, which is the intentional practice of rites for this purpose. Unlike sorcery, witchcraft can be known only after its alleged occurrence and by its alleged results. What anthropologists study, therefore, is *accusation* of witchcraft. These accusations are often closely examined in relation to the structure of the society (e.g. to see whether there is a tendency for particular classes of person to be accused, such as women married into patrilineally constituted domestic groups); and ideas of witchcraft are studied in relation to the total system of ideas about moral responsibility, right conduct, and causation. There has been increasing contact between anthropologists and historians in the study of witchcraft. The problems of interpretation raise serious questions concerning rationality, cultural RELATIVISM and ETHNOCENTRISM. M.F.;A.G.

Bibl: J. Favret-Saada, *Deadly Words: Witchcraft in the Bocage* (Cambridge, 1980); C. Larner, *Witchcraft and Religion* (Oxford, 1984).

Wobblies, the (American Industrial Workers of the World), see under SYNDICALISM.

women's liberation, see under FEMINISM.

word. In COMPUTING, the unit of information which is dealt with by the HARDWARE one at a time. Its size (known as the word-length) varies with the COMPUTER, common values being 1, 2 3, 4, 6 and 18 BITS. C.S.; J.E.S.

word class. In LINGUISTICS, a class of words which are similar in their formal behaviour (e.g. noun, adjective). Such CLASSIFICATIONS are made to facilitate the economic statement of grammatical rules, and many different detailed systems have been proposed, the most familiar being the system of *parts of speech*, which uses notional as well as formal criteria (see FORM). Various general classifications have also been used, e.g. the dichotomy between *form* (or *function*, or *grammatical*) *words*, whose primary role is to indicate grammatical relationships, and *content* (or *lexical*) *words*, whose primary role is to provide referential meaning (see REFERENCE); or the distinction between *open classes* of words (i.e. classes whose membership is capable of indefinite extension, e.g. nouns) and *closed classes* (or *systems*) of words (classes containing a small, fixed number of words, e.g. conjunctions). A classification of linguistic forms not restricted to the notion of words is a *form* class. D.C.

word processor. A MICROCOMPUTER dedicated to the handling of text, and hence allowing the AUTOMATION of many clerical procedures. J.E.S.

Work Projects Administration, see WPA.

work station. A MICROCOMPUTER which can either be used on its own or to communicate with a larger post COMPUTER. It can be thought of as a form of 'intelligent TERMINAL' sufficiently powerful to run PROGRAMS prepared by its user. J.E.S.

work study. A set of MANAGEMENT techniques, covering *method study* and *work measurement*, which are used to ensure efficient employment of people and other resources in carrying out specific tasks. Method study involves the systematic examination of ways of doing work and making improvements. Work measurement establishes the time needed for a qualified worker to carry out a specified job to a defined standard of performance. The older phrase *time and motion study* is seldom used professionally. R.I.T.

Bibl: International Labour Office, Geneva, *Introduction to Work Study* (Geneva, rev. ed., 1969).

work to rule. A form of strike without withdrawal of labour, in which OUTPUT is reduced by the workers taking the time needed to comply to the fullest extent with requirements of working rules drawn up by MANAGEMENT — for example, the rule that a driver shall satisfy himself that his vehicle is in serviceable condition before he takes it out. Those working to rule are able to place pressure on management, and intensify it at will without losing the pay due for hours worked. The employer has no remedy short of locking the workers out. E.H.P.B.

working class. Often used as a homely synonym for the more specialized Marxist concept of the PROLETARIAT, 'the working class' is both more and less than that. It is less in that it does not, unlike the Marxist concept, look forward to a future society conquered by, and remade in the image of, the working class. It is more in that it includes a range of values and cultural traits that go beyond the narrowly political role assigned to it by MARXISM. Working-class culture is largely defensive and CONSERVATIVE. It was shaped by the struggle for survival in the cities of the INDUSTRIAL REVOLUTION. In the course of this it elaborated the values of mutual aid, co-operation, and community. Working-class communities became largely self-reliant and inward looking, distrustful of MIDDLE-CLASS philanthropists and middle-class politicians, especially of the radical kind. In Germany, France, and Italy, though not in Britain and the U.S., workers supported SOCIALIST parties but mainly as agencies of social betterment, not as the spearhead of socialist REVOLUTION. The working class has remained cautious and pragmatic, willing to exert its industrial and political muscle only where gains are evident and immediate. It has in this sense developed only what Lenin called a 'TRADE UNION consciousness', and not the radical consciousness expected of it by Marx. While combative in the industrial sphere, it has found no difficulty in reconciling this toughness with a high degree of patriotism and NATIONALISM.

The traditional homogeneity of working-class communities has, since World War II, been declining. Urban redevelopment has broken up the old tightly-knit communities of the inner cities. Changes in work, especially with the introduction of new TECHNOLOGY, have produced a new skill hierarchy, cutting off a new skilled working class in the new industries from the unskilled and semi-skilled workers in the old declining 'smokestack' industries of the early Industrial Revolution. Much has been made by certain Marxists of the political potential of this 'new working class' of skilled technicians. They are seen as a better educated and more socially confident group who are likely to develop a more sophisticated and more radical CLASS consciousness than the old working class. In practice, as with the

new middle class, the new working class has been ambiguous in its CULTURE and politics. It has borrowed from the old working class a pragmatic outlook, and seems prepared to engage in hard bargaining for the best deal it can get from both state and industry, whatever the ideological outlook of their managers (see IDEOLOGY). K.K.

Bibl: K. Roberts, *The Working Class* (London, 1978); J. Clarke, C. Critcher, R. Johnson (eds.), *Working Class Culture* (London, 1979).

working-class conservatism. LEFT-wing thinkers have been puzzled and frustrated by what seems to them an anomaly. A substantial minority — between one-third and two-fifths — of the manual working class in western democracies has consistently supported CONSERVATIVE parties, instead of the labour or SOCIALIST parties which are the presumed 'carriers' of their CLASS interest. Early attempts at explanation, drawing on Walter Bagehot and Friedrich Engels, postulated a class of 'deferential workers' who accepted the old status hierarchy and clung to the view that the conservatives, as the party of the old ruling class, were the 'natural' leaders of society. Later theories have rested more on EMBOURGEOISEMENT and the idea of a DOMINANT IDEOLOGY. The problem has been complicated by the general decline of class-based voting in western societies in recent decades. Working-class conservatives are now really no more anomalous than MIDDLE-CLASS socialists; it may indeed be the working-class labour voter that is the fast vanishing species. Voting and party preference show a volatility and instability that is fair reflection of the more instrumental and calculating mood among voters of all classes of society. K.K.

Bibl: R.T. McKenzie and A. Silver, *Angels in Marble* (London, 1968); A. Heath *et al.*, *How Britain Votes* (Oxford, 1985).

working store, see under STORE.

World Bank, see under BRETTON WOODS.

World Community of al-Islam in the West, see under NATION OF ISLAM.

world-line. The notion of world-line arises from Minkowski's conception of SPACE-TIME, itself a reinterpretation of Einstein's special RELATIVITY. Within the unification of space and time implied by Minkowski's concept, world-line is the trajectory plotted by the history of a material point. It is the dimension of temporality; or, put in other terms, the distance between two events differentiated on the world-line is a measure of time. In Minkowski's formulation, the interval along the world-line measures its own proper time. Regarded, thus, in relation to the world-line, clocks can be said to be unaffected by relative motion.   R.P.

Bibl: C. Weiner (ed.), *History of Twentieth Century Physics* (New York, 1977).

world society theory. Conceives of the world as a society of individuals and communities rather than as a patchwork of competing nation-states. This idea has a long history and was reflected, for example, in medieval aspirations for the unity of Christendom, and later in Kant's idealistic proposals for securing perpetual peace. In addition to UTOPIAN schemes to transcend the nation-state, in the 1970s a group of mainly American scholars began to develop world society models and theories as a means of overcoming what they perceived as the serious limitations of the traditional state-centric approach. Theorists such as R. Keohane and J.S. Nye (1971) emphasized what they termed 'the characteristics of complexity and INTER-DEPENDENCE' such as 'multiple channels' linking societies, especially transnational connections. They challenged the assumption that states act as coherent units. One British contributor to this school is J.W. Burton (see COBWEB MODEL). Rather than accord primacy to diplomatic-strategic issues, contemporary world society theorists seek to give equal attention to 'new' global issues such as energy, resources, environment, and the use of the oceans. It is when they address such issues that they tend to smuggle in the NORMATIVE assumption that man's wants must be modified so that they can be more effectively matched with available resources. They have also been criticized for wishful thinking in assuming that the fragmentation of the world into nation-states is already being transcended and that the emergence of a uniform global society and culture would be a desirable development.   P.W.

Bibl: M. Smith, R. Little and M. Shackleton (eds.), *Perspectives on World Politics* (London, 1981).

world-view, see under WELTANSCHAUUNG.

Worpswede. North German village near Bremen, centre of an artists' colony (*c.* 1890-1914) whose outstanding figure was the short-lived Paula Modersohn-Becker (*d.* 1907), a forerunner of EXPRESSIONISM. Other members included Fritz Mackensen, Otto Modersohn, Heinrich Vogeler, and Hans am Ende. An account of the colony was given by Rilke in his *Worpswede* (1902).   J.W.

WPA (Work Projects Administration; later Work Progress Administration). A NEW DEAL organization, set up by President Roosevelt in 1935, with an initial appropriation of $4,880 million, to counter some of the effects of the post-1929 DEPRESSION. WPA, which included the Federal Arts, Theater, and Writers Projects (and, until 1939, the National Youth Administration), was killed by Congress long before its official death in 1943. The *Federal Arts Project* was mainly concerned with the rebuilding, redesigning, and mural decoration of public offices. The *Federal Theater Project* was the most remarkable in its results, since it implemented its intention to give dramatists and actors a livelihood without inhibiting their creative freedom. The guiding spirit and director was Hallie Flanagan, who inaugurated an experimental LIVING NEWSPAPER (which was edited by Arthur Arent, and from which emerged Joseph Losey and others), put on DOCUMENTARY and original plays, and staged important revivals. The Theater Project was effectually shut down in 1939, soon after Christopher Marlowe, author of one of these revived plays, had been indicted as a COMMUNIST. The *Federal Writers Project* was run by Henry G. Alsberg. Its most notable achievement was the production of the American Guide Series, a state-by-state portrait of the American people (which in the main they resented).   M.S.-S.

Bibl: H.F. Flanagan, *Arena* (New York, 1940); E.M. Gagey, *Revolution in American Drama* (New York, 1947).

X

X chromosomes, see under SEX CHROMO-
SOMES.

X-efficiency, see under ECONOMIC EF-
FICIENCY.

xenophobia. The condition of disliking individuals or groups thought of as foreign.
The 'groups' may range in size from an
entire continent (as with anti-American or
anti-European feeling) to a neighbouring
family of IMMIGRANTS (or even of migrants from another part of the country if
regarded as intrusive); and the dislike can
range in intensity from a normally controlled awareness of preferences to an abnormal state of pathological fear and ANX-
IETY. It commonly takes an ethnic form
(see RACE; ANTISEMITISM), and in its most
extreme and widespread forms of expression may reflect the paranoid, psychotic state (see PARANOIA; PSYCHOSIS) of
those in power, as it did with Hitler and
Stalin.   M.BE.

xerography. A photographic copying process for documents and line drawings with
a high degree of contrast. An image of the
original document is focused onto a type
of photoelectric surface which converts
light into electric charge. This ELECTRO-
STATIC image attracts charged ink powder,
which is in turn attracted to charged
paper; here it forms a visible image — the
copy — which is permanently fixed by
heating.   M.V.B.

X-ray astronomy. That branch of ASTRON-
OMY devoted to the study of celestial
bodies beyond our SOLAR SYSTEM which
emit X-RAYS. X-RADIATION is ELECTRO-
MAGNETIC radiation with wavelength in
the 0.0025 to 12 nm range and so with
ENERGY between 0.1 to 500 kv. Low energy X-rays are called soft X-rays; high
energy X-rays are called hard X-rays.
They are produced in the universe
wherever fast-moving ELECTRONS collide
with matter or move in magnetic fields.
This radiation band does not penetrate the
Earth's lower atmosphere and hence observations of astronomical X-ray sources
are made using balloons, ROCKETS and

SATELLITES. The first X-ray source to be
found (Scorpius X-1) was detected with a
rocket-borne detector in 1962. The first
X-ray observing satellite, Uhuru
(=Swahili for 'Freedom') was launched in
December 1970. Subsequent launches
have made surveys of the sky over X-ray
wavelengths and found X-ray emitting binary pairs of stars to be the most common
source of X-rays in our GALAXY. The
X-ray source Cygnus X-1 is almost certainly a BLACK HOLE accreting material
from a companion star. The infalling
material emits X-rays (see ACCRETION).
Hot intergalactic gas in rich clusters of
galaxies (see GALAXY CLUSTERS) emits X-
rays. There exists a diffuse low-intensity
background of X-rays in the universe,
which is believed to be caused by the
integrated emission from distant QUASARS
and other galaxies. In 1975 bursts of X-
rays were discovered from sources within
our galaxy. It is believed that they originate from sporadic accretion of material
on to condensed WHITE DWARFS and neutron stars (see PULSAR).   J.D.B.
  Bibl: N. Henbest and M. Martin, *The
New Astronomy* (Cambridge, 1983).

X-ray diffraction. The DIFFRACTION of
X-RAYS by the ATOMS in a crystal LATTICE,
which occurs because the wavelength of
the X-rays is comparable with the intera-
tomic spacing. X-ray diffraction is a principal tool in CRYSTALLOGRAPHY and BIO-
CHEMISTRY, where it has made possible the
structural analysis of DNA (see NUCLEIC
ACID) and other MACROMOLECULES associated with life.   M.V.B.

X-ray laser, see under STRATEGIC DE-
FENCE INITIATIVE.

X-rays. Electromagnetic RADIATION (discovered by Röntgen in 1895) whose wavelength is about 1,000 times smaller than
that of visible light, and which is emitted
during transitions of the innermost ELEC-
TRONS in an ATOM between low-lying EN-
ERGY LEVELS. X-rays are produced by
bombarding a metal target with fast electrons from an ELECTRON GUN. The medical usefulness of X-rays in forming

912

shadow images of bones arises because of the absorption of X-rays in a material increases rapidly with its density and ATOMIC NUMBER, and because X-rays can form an image on an ordinary photographic plate. See also X-RAY DIFFRACTION.

M.V.B.

Y

Y chromosomes, see under SEX CHROMO-SOMES.

Yale School. A group of literary critics influenced by Freud and the DECONSTRUC-TION of Derrida. During the 1970s it comprised Harold Bloom, Paul de Man, Geoffrey Hartman, J. Hillis Miller and Jacques Derrida. Since the death of Paul de Man and the removal of J. Hillis Miller and Derrida to California, the 'school' no longer exists. In its heyday it operated under the dual aegis of Paul de Man's *Blindness and Insight* (1971) and Harold Bloom's *The Anxiety of Influence* (1973). Paul de Man, following Derrida, regarded the literary text as a set of opposed possibilities which eventually led to an *aporia*, that is, when the text enforces a decision between two opposed readings and actually, for internal textual reasons, prohibits the choosing of either of these. This approach is given classical expression in *Allegories of Reading* (1979). Harold Bloom, choosing to regard the writing of poetry not so much as willing submission to the influence of a great 'precursor' as having to face the anguish and guilt of trying to 'replace' him (as a son attempts to 'replace' his father), introduced a heavily FREUDIAN element into a theory of the text that already emphasized READER-RESPONSE to a very high degree. Bloom's theory of the 'anxiety of influence', an anxiety which leads the poet to try and escape the implication of his own work through six rhetorical 'defence mechanisms' had a galvanizing effect upon literary theory generally. From 1973 literary critics were not able to avoid the implications of rhetorical-deconstructive and of Freudian-rhetorical theorizing. J. Hillis Miller emphasized the rhetorical and formally LINGUISTIC, non-referential nature of poetry, and Geoffrey Hartman acted as mediator for the theories of Derrida, while eventually adding a decided theological disclaimer of his own, *Saving the Text* (1981). Meanwhile, Derrida himself moved beyond his own contributions to the Yale School towards a new theory which re-investigated the PHENOM-ENOLOGY of the text, and started with a study of *Midrash* contributed to Harman and Budick's *Midrash and Literature* (1986). R.PO.

Bibl: J. Arac *et al.* (eds.), *The Yale Critics: Deconstruction in America* (Minnesota, 1983).

Yalta. A town in the Crimea, the scene (4-11 February 1945) of the second wartime SUMMIT conference between Churchill, Roosevelt, and Stalin. Even more than at Teheran the conference was marked by President Roosevelt's determination to subordinate every other consideration to winning Soviet good will and, a new development, to securing early Soviet participation in the war against Japan. Britain, much more concerned than the U.S.A. with the post-war settlement in Europe, secured a postponement (in practice, abandonment) of plans to dismember Germany, and a vote for France in the occupation and control of Germany. On all other issues, notably the post-war frontiers of Poland, the Soviet view was accepted. In the 1950s, Yalta became a point of attack for American RIGHT-wing critics of Roosevelt, who accused him of betraying America's long-term interests to the enemy of American DEMOCRACY. D.C.W.

Bibl: H. Freis, *Churchill, Roosevelt, Stalin* (London and Princeton, 1957); R. Hathaway, *Ambiguous Partnership: Britain and America 1944-47* (New York, 1981).

yang, see under MACROBIOTICS.

Yezhovshchina ('the Yezhov time'). The period of the most intense terror in Russia under Stalin, namely from September 1936 to December 1938, when Nikolai Yezhov (1894-1940) was People's Commissar for Internal Affairs, i.e. head of the secret police. It included the second and third great MOSCOW TRIALS, and the trial and execution of Marshal Tukhachevsky and other leading officers in June 1937. Soviet estimates published later imply that during this period at least seven million people were arrested, 90% of whom — including half the Party membership, three-quarters of the Central Committee, about half of the corps of officers, and several hundred writers, artists, and scientists — perished in FORCED LABOUR camps or by execution. After Yezhov's dismissal, he was himself shot. He was succeeded by Lavrenty Beria. R.C.

Bibl: R. Conquest, *The Great Terror* (London and New York, rev. ed., 1971).

yin, see under MACROBIOTICS.

yoga. The spiritual discipline of the higher forms of HINDUISM, including a carefully planned course of fasting with physical and mental exercises in order to concentrate the mind. In its narrower sense the term refers to a Hindu movement which produced the *Yoga Sutras*, scriptures describing union (Sanskrit *yoga*) with the supreme spirit after much self-sacrifice. As used in the West, the phrase may refer more loosely to exercises for mental and physical fitness, adapted from Indian sources. D.L.E.

Yom Kippur War, see under MIDDLE EAST WARS.

youth culture. A loosely-used label which in the 1960s and 1970s was often mistakenly employed as a synonym for *counter-culture* or *alternative society* (for both, see UNDERGROUND). The phenomenon is perhaps better seen as a sub-cultural form, though SUB-CULTURES necessarily challenge some aspects of HEGEMONY. In most advanced INDUSTRIAL SOCIETIES, and more frequently from a diffuse youthful energy than from conscious hostility to accepted adult values, adolescent and young adult communities have developed their own transient NORMS, values and LIFE STYLES symbolized by specific modes of dress, language, music and consumption patterns. A singularly important element of youth culture is style which is used both to express and resolve the structural and experiential contradictions of youth. It is nevertheless important to stress that not all young people subscribe to the culture named after them, that the age limits of its adherents have never been adequately defined, and that the common ingredient of many facets of youth culture is as a market for specific CONSUMER DURABLES (see CONSUMER SOCIETY; ADMASS; CONSPICUOUS CONSUMPTION). P.S.L.

Youth Training Scheme (YTS), see under MANPOWER SERVICES COMMISSION.

yuppie. Collective noun and acronym formed from an expanding group of Young Urban Professionals who began to come to prominence in the U.S. during the 1970s (as the post-war baby boom generation entered the career-oriented, child-rearing and home-buying phase of their lives). They now form a well-defined market for the purveyors of material and MEDIA artefacts, estate agents, high-status clothing and leisure services. Yuppies are career-oriented, upwardly mobile adults generally in the earlier stages of their working lives, living a consumption-oriented LIFE STYLE (see CONSPICUOUS CONSUMPTION). Well educated, MIDDLE CLASS and affluent, they appear thus far to be conventional in their ambitions. They represent a reaction to the earlier generation of professional cadres formed in the 1960s, whose LIBERALISM and often ambivalent relationship to work and the material benefits it bestows are seen as 'soft'. P.S.L.

Z

Zaum. The Russian word for trans-sense (transrational) language — the arbitrary combination of sounds, or the play with the MORPHOLOGICAL components of a familiar word practised by Russian FUTURIST poets, notably Kruchenykh and Khlebnikov. *Zaum* stemmed from the Futurists' belief that the word, as the material of poetry, should be emancipated from its 'traditional subservience to meaning' and become a self-sufficient entity, interesting for its outward form, i.e. its graphic and phonic characteristics. It led to the creation of poetic neologisms, or completely non-referential words. M.E.

Zeitgeist. German word meaning literally 'the Spirit of the Time (or Age)'. It is associated with attempts to epitomize the mode of thought or feeling deemed fundamentally characteristic of a particular period, e.g. to interpret the 19th century as an age of '*heroic materialism*' (Kenneth Clark). The term was first regularly employed by the German Romantics (see ROMANTICISM). Tempted always to reduce the past to essences, they often treated the *Zeitgeist* less as a conceptual instrument than as a grandiose historical character in its own right. Most historians handle the term with caution on the grounds that the characteristics of any historical period are more complex than a formulation of a *Zeitgeist* can suggest. See also CULTURAL HISTORY. M.D.B.

Bibl: G.W.F. Hegel, tr. H.B. Nisbet, *Lectures on the Philosophy of World History* (Cambridge, 1975).

Zen. The Japanese version of the Ch'an sect of BUDDHISM in China, noted for its simple austerity, its MYSTICISM leading to personal tranquillity, and its encouragement of education and art. Some of its scriptures and paintings have become widely known and admired in the West; and Aldous Huxley and others in California led something of a cult of Zen, which in the 1960s began appealing to students as a way of having religious experience without DOGMAS or religious INSTITUTIONS. The trouble is, however, that the reality experienced after ecstasy (*satori*) is hard to describe, and the approach to it hard to reconcile with reason. Many of the statements encouraged by the masters of Zen seem deliberately nonsensical — e.g. the idea of a single hand clapping — although they are intended to open the doors of PERCEPTION into a world of wonder. D.L.E.

Bibl: A. Watts, *The Way of Zen* (London and New York, 1957); D.T. Suzuki, *Manual of Zen Buddhism* (London, 1974).

Zero, Gruppe, see under KINETIC ART.

zero option, see under NUCLEAR WEAPONS, LIMITATION AND CONTROL.

zero point energy. The ENERGY of the motion remaining in a body at ABSOLUTE ZERO of temperature. The body is then in its *ground state* (see ENERGY LEVEL), which according to the UNCERTAINTY PRINCIPLE of QUANTUM MECHANICS cannot correspond to the complete absence of motion. M.V.B.

zero population growth (ZPG). A population where the number of births plus immigrants equals the number of deaths plus emigrants. Unlike a stationary STABLE POPULATION, this is a real phenomenon, one which has been almost achieved by many modern developed nations (and by some historical populations), and is often advanced as a solution to current world economic problems. D.S.

Bibl: R.L. Clark and J.J. Spengler, *The Economics of Individual and Population Ageing* (Cambridge and New York, 1980); J. Simon, *The Ultimate Resource* (Princeton, 1981).

zero-sum game, see under GAME THEORY.

Zhdanovshchina ('the Zhdanov time'). The period 1946-8, in which heavy Party pressure was brought to bear in the Soviet cultural field, under the aegis of Andrei Zhdanov, Secretary of the Central Committee in charge of IDEOLOGY. It was marked by attacks on many leading Soviet writers, notably Mikhail Zoshchenko, Anna Akhmatova, and Boris Pasternak.

R.C.

Bibl: H. Swayze, *Political Control of Literature in the USSR, 1946-1959* (Cambridge, Mass., 1962).

zino, see under SUPERSYMMETRY.

Zionism. The Jewish national movement to re-establish the Jewish nation in Palestine. Zionism was a SECULARIST and NATIONALISTIC transformation of an aspiration basic to orthodox JUDAISM, in reaction to the Czarist persecution of Russian and Polish Jewry and to other outbursts of ANTISEMITISM, e.g. during the DREYFUS CASE. Theodor Herzl, the founder of modern Zionism (who reported the Dreyfus trials for an Austrian paper), argued in his book, *Der Judenstaat,* that the only alternative to continued persecution was to found a Jewish state, and in 1897 he called the first World Zionist Congress in Basle. It was Chaim Weizmann (1874-1952) who insisted that a Jewish nation could only be re-created in Palestine, a course which became practicable with the BALFOUR DECLARATION of 1917. Since the foundation of the state of Israel in 1948, the term Zionism has a mainly historical meaning. It is still used, however, to describe (1) the organized sympathies and support of Jews in the West, especially in the U.S., for Israel; (2) the efforts by Soviet Jewry to emigrate to Israel; (3) the continuing promise by Israel to offer a national home to any Jew in the world who seeks it.

A.L.C.B.

Bibl: (1) For the early history, see two volumes by David Vital: *The Origins of Zionism* and *Zionism, the Formative Years* (Oxford, 1975 and 1982); (2) for a general account, W. Laqueur, *History of Zionism* (London, 1972).

zoo hypothesis, see under SEARCH FOR EXTRATERRESTRIAL INTELLIGENCE.

zoogeography. The branch of BIOGEOGRAPHY which studies the geographical distribution of animals. In any REGION this is determined by the nature of the vegetation on which the herbivorous animals (the vast majority) depend. Thus forest-inhabiting animals only occur after trees have grown up. On the world scale, climate and EVOLUTION are important. Many species are *stenothermous,* i.e. they exist only over a narrow range of temperature. Isolated areas, e.g. Australia, have seen the evolution and establishment of SPECIES (e.g. kangaroos and other large marsupials) which have been protected from competition with the 'higher' forms dominant elsewhere.

K.M.

Bibl: P.J. Darlington, *Zoogeography* (New York, 1957).

zoology. The science that deals with the classification (see BIOSYSTEMATICS), structure, and functions of animals, including by convention those CHLOROPHYLL-containing PROTOZOA which could equally well be classified as plants. The old-fashioned distinction between vertebrates and invertebrates is not taxonomically useful and makes no kind of sense in terms of PHYLOGENY. There is a tendency nowadays therefore to distinguish two main lines of descent among animals:

(1) a *chordate* line of descent including the chordates themselves (animals distinguished by the possession at some stage of their life history of a notochord, and a central NERVOUS SYSTEM in the form of a median dorsal hollow nerve tube), and certain other PHYLA related to the chordates by fundamental similarities of early development; these include those phyla of which typical members are sea-urchins, sea-cucumbers, and starfish (echinodermata), together with sea-squirts (tunicata), all forming together the chordate line of descent; and

(2) a miscellany of *non-chordate* phyla including the worms strictly so-called (annelida) and — wrongly so-called — the flatworms (platyhelminthes) and roundworms (nematodes) and one or two other groups of lesser importance.

P.M.

zoosemiotics, see under SEMIOTICS.

zygote. The single CELL that is the product of the fusion between an egg cell and a spermatozoon from which all vertebrate development proceeds. As a result of this fusion, a zygote contains the normal double complement (DIPLOID number) of CHROMOSOMES.

P.M.